ROUTLEDGE HANDBOOK OF STRENGTH AND CONDITIONING

Drawing on the latest scientific research, this handbook introduces the essentials of sport-specific strength and conditioning programme design for over 30 different sports. Enhanced by extensive illustrations and contributions from more than 70 world-leading experts, its chapters present evidence-based best practice for sports including football, rugby, tennis, hockey, basketball, rowing, boxing, golf, swimming, cycling and weightlifting, as well as a variety of wheelchair sports.

Every chapter introduces the fundamental requirements of a particular sport – such as the physiological and biomechanical demands on the athlete – and describes a sport-specific fitness testing battery and exercise programme. Additional chapters cover the adaptation of programme design for special populations, including female athletes, young athletes and athletes with a disability. Drawing on the experiences of Olympic and Paralympic coaches and trainers, it offers original insights and practical advice from practitioners working at the highest level.

Innovative, comprehensive and truly international in scope, the *Routledge Handbook of Strength and Conditioning* is vital reading for all strength and conditioning students and an invaluable reference for strength and conditioning coaches and trainers.

Anthony Turner is the Director of Postgraduate Programmes at the London Sport Institute, Middlesex University, UK, where he is also the Programme Leader for the MSc in Strength and Conditioning. Anthony consults with the British Military and several sports teams and athletes. He was also the Head of Physical Preparation for British Fencing between the London and Rio Olympics. Anthony is accredited (with distinction) with the National Strength and Conditioning Association and the UK Strength and Conditioning Association (UKSCA), and was awarded the 2015 UKSCA coach of the year for education and research. Anthony has published over 80 peer reviewed journal articles, is an Associate Editor for the *Strength and Conditioning Journal*, and completed his PhD examining physical preparation in Olympic Fencing.

ROUTLEDGE HANDBOOK OF STRENGTH AND CONDITIONING

Sport-specific Programming for High Performance

Edited by Anthony Turner

First published 2018
by Routledge

2 Park Square, Milton Park, Abingdon, Oxfordshire OX14 4RN
52 Vanderbilt Avenue, New York, NY 10017

Routledge is an imprint of the Taylor & Francis Group, an informa business

First issued in paperback 2020

Copyright © 2018 selection and editorial matter, Anthony Turner; individual chapters, the contributors

The right of Anthony Turner to be identified as the author of the editorial material, and of the authors for their individual chapters, has been asserted in accordance with sections 77 and 78 of the Copyright, Designs and Patents Act 1988.

All rights reserved. No part of this book may be reprinted or reproduced or utilised in any form or by any electronic, mechanical, or other means, now known or hereafter invented, including photocopying and recording, or in any information storage or retrieval system, without permission in writing from the publishers.

Notice:
Product or corporate names may be trademarks or registered trademarks, and are used only for identification and explanation without intent to infringe.

British Library Cataloguing-in-Publication Data
A catalogue record for this book is available from the British Library

Library of Congress Cataloging-in-Publication Data
Names: Turner, Anthony, editor.
Title: Routledge handbook of strength and conditioning : sport-specific programming for high performance / edited by Anthony Turner.
Other titles: Handbook of strength and conditioning
Description: Abingdon, Oxon ; New York, NY : Routledge, 2018. | Series: Routledge international handbooks | Includes bibliographical references and index.
Identifiers: LCCN 2017040329 | ISBN 9781138687240 (hardback) | ISBN 9781315542393 (ebook)
Subjects: LCSH: Physical education and training—Handbooks, manuals, etc. | Athletes—Training of—Handbooks, manuals, etc. | Weight training—Handbooks, manuals, etc. | Muscle strength—Handbooks, manuals, etc.
Classification: LCC GV711.5 .R69 2018 | DDC 613.7—dc23
LC record available at https://lccn.loc.gov/2017040329

ISBN: 978-1-138-68724-0 (hbk)
ISBN: 978-0-367-49904-4 (pbk)

Typeset in Bembo
by Apex CoVantage, LLC

CONTENTS

List of contributors   ix

SECTION 1
How to use this book   **1**

1 Introduction   3
  Anthony Turner

SECTION 2
Working with special populations   **5**

2 Applying strength and conditioning practices to female athletes   7
  Paul J. Read, Alicia Montalvo, Rich Blagrove, Rich Burden, Greg Myer and Rhodri S. Lloyd

3 Applying strength and conditioning practices to young athletes   23
  Rhodri S. Lloyd, John M. Radnor, Sylvia Moeskops, Robert W. Meyers, Paul J. Read and Jon L. Oliver

4 Applying strength and conditioning practices to athletes with a disability   38
  Tom Paulson and Vicky Goosey-Tolfrey

SECTION 3
Team sports   **49**

5 Soccer   51
  Perry Stewart and Matthew Springham

6	Rugby union *Craig Twist*	72
7	Rugby 7's *Dan Howells*	84
8	American football *Nick Winkelman*	102
9	Aussie rules football *Ian McKeown*	126
10	Field hockey *Ben Rosenblatt and Andy Hudson*	143
11	Ice hockey *Steve Nightingale and Adam Douglas*	157
12	Basketball *Rob Harley, Stuart Mills and Alex Bliss*	178
13	Cricket *Phil Scott and Ross Herridge*	194
14	Rowing *Alex Wolf*	218
15	Netball *Chris McLeod and Katie James*	233
16	Volleyball *Jeremy Sheppard, Paula Charlton, David Watts and Tim Pelot*	259
17	Handball *Marco Cardinale*	280
18	Wheelchair rugby *Ed Baker*	311

SECTION 4
Individual sports — **331**

19	MMA *Lachlan James, Brett Bartholomew, G. Gregory Haff and Vincent Kelly*	333

Contents

20	Karate *James Coy, Jon Cree and Anthony Turner*	359
21	Taekwondo *Rhys Ingram, Ailish McLaughlin and Yana Radcliffe*	371
22	Boxing *Alan Ruddock, Daniel Wilson and David Hembrough*	384
23	Fencing *Anthony Turner, Dai Fulcher, Sophie Weaver and Geoff Marshall*	400
24	Wheelchair fencing *Alex Villiere, Michael Edwards, Baldip Sahota and Anthony Turner*	413
25	Tennis *Emily Fanning and Floris Pietzsch*	433
26	Golf *Paul J. Read, Justin Buckthorp, Zachariah I. Gould and Rhodri S. Lloyd*	451
27	Sprint running *Jon Goodwin, Jonas Tawiah-Dodoo, Ruth Waghorn and James Wild*	473
28	Sprint cycling *Lynne Munroe and G. Gregory Haff*	506
29	Triathlon *Ian Pyper, Emma Deakin and Andrew Shaw*	526
30	Swimming *Chris Bishop*	540
31	Rock climbing *Noel Carroll*	553
32	Alpine skiing *Pete McKnight*	568
33	Freestyle snowsport *John Noonan*	583
34	Bodybuilding *Paul Comfort*	597

35	Powerlifting *Sean Maloney*	612
36	Weightlifting *Shyam Chavda and Greg Everett*	630

Index   *657*

CONTRIBUTORS

Ed Baker, formerly English Institute of Sport Lead Strength and Conditioning Coach for GB Wheelchair Rugby Team, UK and now Manager and Lead Neurorehabilitation Trainer, Neurokinex, UK.

Brett Bartholomew, Strength and Conditioning Coach, author, consultant and founder of The Bridge: Human Performance, USA.

Chris Bishop, Senior Lecturer in Strength and Conditioning at the London Sport Institute, Middlesex University where he is also the Programme Leader for the MSc in Strength and Conditioning. Chris is also a board director for the UK Strength and Conditioning Association.

Rich Blagrove, School of Health Sciences, Birmingham City University, Birmingham, UK.

Alex Bliss, Lecturer in Strength and Conditioning Science, St Mary's University, Twickenham, UK.

Justin Buckthorp, performance consultant for European Ryder Cup team and consultant to the European Tour Medical Team and European Tour Performance Institute.

Rich Burden, School of Sport, Health and Applied Sciences, St Marys University, London, UK.

Marco Cardinale, Head of Sport Physiology, Aspire Academy, Doha, Qatar; University College London, UK, and University of St. Mark & St. John, Plymouth, UK.

Noel Carroll, Academy Strength and Conditioning Coach, Arsenal FC, UK.

Paula Charlton, Senior Sports Physiotherapist and Strength and Conditioning Coach, Australian Institute of Sport, Australia.

Shyam Chavda, Technical Tutor in Sport Science, Middlesex University and Weightlifting Coach at British Weightlifting, UK.

Contributors

Paul Comfort, Programme Leader for the MSc in Strength and Conditioning, University of Salford, UK.

James Coy, Strength and Conditioning Coach.

Jon Cree, Strength and Conditioning Coach and Senior Lecturer, Middlesex University, UK.

Emma Deakin, Lead Physiotherapist, British Triathlon, English Institute of Sport, UK.

Adam Douglas, Manager of Sports Performance and IST Lead – Strength and Conditioning with Hockey Canada, and Head Strength Coach, York University, Canada.

Michael Edwards, Strength and Conditioning Coach and Lecturer, Middlesex University, UK.

Greg Everett, former Olympic weightlifter, weightlifting coach and author of several textbooks.

Emily Fanning, Head of Sport Science for Tennis, New Zealand.

Dai Fulcher, previously lead performance analyst, British Fencing UK. Now Data Analyst, Nike, UK.

Jon Goodwin, Programme Director, MSc Strength and Conditioning, St Mary's University, UK.

Zachariah I. Gould, Youth Physical Development Centre, Cardiff School of Sport, Cardiff Metropolitan University, UK and Golf Union Wales, Newport, Wales, UK.

G. Gregory Haff, Senior Lecturer and Course Coordinator for Strength and Conditioning at Edith Cowan University, Australia.

Rob Harley, Principle Lecturer, Sport and Exercise Science, University of Brighton, UK.

David Hembrough, Strength and Conditioning Coach at Sheffield Hallam University, working with professional and amateur boxers, UK.

Ross Herridge, Nottinghamshire County Cricket Club Strength and Conditioning Coach, UK.

Dan Howells, Head of Strength and Conditioning, England 7's, UK.

Andy Hudson, Head of Physical Preparation – England & GB Hockey, English Institute of Sport, UK.

Rhys Ingram, Strength and Conditioning Coach, GB Taekwondo, English Institute of Sport, UK.

Katie James, Strength and Conditioning Lead, England Women's 7s, English Institute of Sport, UK.

Lachlan James, Lecturer and Researcher in Sport Science, Federation University, Australia.

Vincent Kelly, Performance Science Consultant at Brisbane Broncos Rugby League Football Club and Lecturer in Sport and Exercise Science at the University of Queensland, Australia.

Contributors

Rhodri S. Lloyd, Senior Lecturer in Strength and Conditioning, Youth Physical Development Centre, Cardiff School of Sport and Health Sciences, Cardiff Metropolitan University, UK.

Sean Maloney, Strength and Conditioning Coach and Lecturer. Powerlifter and Powerlifting Coach.

Geoff Marshall, previously Lead Strength and Conditioning Coach, GB Fencing, UK. Now Head of Strength and Conditioning, Sevenoaks School, UK.

Ian McKeown, Head of High Performance at Port Adelaide FC, Australia.

Pete McKnight, Coaching & Sports Science Director, Hintsa Performance, Switzerland.

Ailish McLaughlin, PhD candidate in Exercise Physiology, English Institute of Sport, Liverpool John Moores University, and GB Taekwondo, UK.

Chris McLeod, Strength and Conditioning Technical Lead, English Institute of Sport, UK.

Robert W. Meyers, Principal Lecturer in Strength and Conditioning, Youth Physical Development Centre, Cardiff School of Sport and Health Sciences, Cardiff Metropolitan University, UK.

Stuart Mills, Principal Lecturer, Sport and Exercise Science, University of Brighton, UK.

Sylvia Moeskops, Technician-Demonstrator in Strength and Conditioning, Youth Physical Development Centre, Cardiff School of Sport and Health Sciences, Cardiff Metropolitan University, UK.

Alicia Montalvo, Florida International University, Miami, Florida, USA.

Lynne Munroe, PhD candidate in Sprint Cycling, Edith Cowan University, Australia.

Greg Myer, Division of Sports Medicine, Cincinnati Children's Hospital, Cincinnati, Ohio, USA.

Steve Nightingale, Strength and Conditioning Coach, Chinese Olympic Committee, China.

John Noonan, Head of Strength and Conditioning, Everton FC Academy.

Jon L. Oliver, Reader in Applied Paediatric Exercise Science, Cardiff School of Sport and Health Sciences, Cardiff Metropolitan University, UK.

Tom Paulson, Head of Paralympic Performance Support, English Institute of Sport, UK.

Tim Pelot, USA Volleyball, USA Committee, USA.

Floris Pietzsch, Senior Lecturer at Brighton University, UK.

Ian Pyper, Head of Physical Preparation, British Triathlon, English Institute of Sport, UK.

Yana Radcliffe, Performance Analyst, English Institute of Sport and GB Taekwondo, UK.

John M. Radnor, Lecturer in Strength and Conditioning, Youth Physical Development Centre, Cardiff School of Sport and Health Sciences, Cardiff Metropolitan University, UK.

Contributors

Paul J. Read, Athlete Health and Performance Research Centre, Aspetar Orthopaedic and Sports Medicine, Doha, Qatar.

Ben Rosenblatt, Lead Men's Physical Performance Coach, Football Association.

Alan Ruddock, Physiologist, working with professional and amateur boxers at Sheffield Hallam University, UK.

Baldip Sahota, British Wheelchair Fencing Coach, UK.

Phil Scott, England Cricket Team Strength and Conditioning Coach, UK.

Andrew Shaw, Lead Physiologist, British Triathlon, English Institute of Sport, UK.

Jeremy Sheppard, Director of Performance, Canadian Sport Institute Pacific, Canada.

Matthew Springham, Senior Lecturer in Strength and Conditioning Science, St Mary's University, Twickenham, UK.

Perry Stewart, Lead Academy Strength and Conditioning Coach (U9-16) at Arsenal Football Club, UK.

Jonas Tawiah-Dodoo, Director of Performance, Speedworks Training, consultants to professional Football and Rugby teams and international athletes.

Vicky Goosey-Tolfrey, Professor in Applied Disability Sport and Director of the Peter Harrison Centre for Disability Sport, Loughborough University, UK.

Anthony Turner, Director of Postgraduate Programmes, London Sport Institute, Middlesex University, UK.

Craig Twist, Professor of Applied Sports Physiology, University of Chester, UK.

Alex Villiere, Strength and Conditioning Coach, British Wheelchair Fencing, UK.

Ruth Waghorn, Speedworks and British Sailing, UK.

David Watts, Strength and Conditioning Coach, Queensland Academy of Sport, Australia.

Sophie Weaver, previously Lead Physiotherapist, British Fencing, UK. Now Lead Physiotherapist, GB Hockey, UK.

James Wild, Technical Lead for Performance, Surrey Sports Park, and speed consultant to Harlequins Rugby Club, UK.

Danny Wilson, Strength and Conditioning Coach, working with professional and amateur boxers at Sheffield Hallam University, UK.

Nick Winkelman, Head of Athletic Performance and Science, Irish Rugby, Ireland.

Alex Wolf, Learning Projects Lead, English Institute of Sport, UK.

SECTION 1

How to use this book

1
INTRODUCTION

Anthony Turner

As strength and conditioning coaches, it is very likely that we will work with a multitude of athletes across a variety of sports throughout our career. We are likely to work with males and females as they progress from childhood, through adolescence and into adulthood. Equally, with the ever-increasing popularity of the Paralympic and Invictus Games, we are likely to work with athletes who have a disability, again across numerous sports, and with each athlete presenting a different type of disability. As coaches, then, we need to be prepared and, before we even start working with them, understand the demands of each type of athlete and those of the sport they wish to excel in; that's where this book comes in. Herein you will find details pertaining to the strength and conditioning programming of over 30 sports, with the preceding chapters explaining how these can be adapted to suit your particular population (i.e., young, female or disability athletes). Each chapter is authored by experts in the field; this book as a whole has been written by over 70 experts from across the globe. They are all at the forefront of practice within high performance sport, each having accrued many years applying and refining their trade. This has enabled them to provide a first hand account of what actually happens when working as a practitioner, and thus combine evidence from the archives of research with their invaluable anecdotal evidence and wisdom. The freedom when constructing each chapter also allows them to elaborate on their coaching philosophy and make programming suggestions based on their objective assessment of the types of athletes, coaches and training environments that best describe each sport. Sometimes their experience and reflections contradict what is reported in the research or what would have been hypothesized. The reader should enjoy the challenges of these contradictions, recognizing the uniqueness of each coach, athlete, and training environment. With this in mind, it is prudent to read several chapters of a similar sporting context. This way you will get a variety of ideas for exercise selection around strength, power and conditioning, as well as methods around their programming and monitoring.

Chapter layout

Each of the sport-specific programming chapters has been written with a similar structure. This provides continuity for readers and better enables the navigation of each chapter, knowing what to expect from each. The layout of each chapter, along with a brief description of what to expect from each section, is provided below.

Introduction to the sport

This section lists general information, including the sport's global appeal and how sport science and strength and conditioning have been incorporated. It may also list significant rulings, including recent changes, which affect programming, for example.

Athletic demands

This section provides the reader with a needs analysis. It describes the biomechanical and physiological demands of the sport. It may detail, for example, intensity and metabolic demand, movement mechanics and requirements for speed and strength. It also lists statistics such as distance covered, number of sprints and changes in direction.

Injury prevalence

Common injuries and their prevalence will be addressed here. This will be used with the above information to design the training programme, ensuring exercise selection and testing is also geared towards athlete resilience and robustness.

Fitness testing battery

Based on the needs analysis above, including the injury prevalence section, a testing battery will be suggested. This is designed in order to assess the athlete's strengths and weakness against the relevant sport specific criteria (athletic demands and injury prevention and screening).

Programming

This will relate to all the information provided above. Types of periodization may also be discussed (e.g., in season *vs.* off season) and of course the use and rotation of various exercises. An exercise programme will normally be provided, which the reader can immediately implement.

Conclusion

The section brings it all together, with the authors providing their closing remarks, summing up the needs of the athlete and any pertinent reflections they have with regard to working in the sport.

References

These can be used as a list of further reading. References contain research articles, which examine in detail a specific component of that particular sport.

In closing, I hope you find this book a useful resource and, like I did while reviewing each chapter, learn a tremendous amount to enhance your strength and conditioning knowledge and practice, and challenge your current methodologies and ideologies.

SECTION 2

Working with special populations

2
APPLYING STRENGTH AND CONDITIONING PRACTICES TO FEMALE ATHLETES

*Paul J. Read, Alicia Montalvo, Rich Blagrove, Rich Burden,
Greg Myer and Rhodri S. Lloyd*

Introduction

In the past, some women may not have engaged in activities such as resistance training due to misconceptions and myths centred around unwanted changes in body composition and avoidance of activities that involve high intensity or external loadings (Ebben and Jenson, 1998). A cumulative body of evidence is now available to indicate that females who participate in well-designed athletic development programmes are capable of tolerating and adapting to the stresses imposed and often experience a range of health benefits (NSCA, 1989; Kraemer et al., 2001). Improvements in strength (Kraemer et al., 2001 Myer et al., 2005), sprint speed (Myer et al., 2005), jump performance (Myer et al., 2005) and sport specific measures have been shown following training programmes that include resistance training, plyometrics and dynamic balance exercises. In addition, beneficial changes to landing mechanics and known injury risk factors are possible (Myer et al., 2005), with knee injury incidence in female athletes 3.6 times lower in trained versus un-trained participants (Hewett et al., 1999).

As well as the positive effects on performance outcomes, numerous health benefits have been demonstrated following resistance training. These include enhanced bone modelling, stronger connective tissues, heightened joint stability and increases in lean body mass with concomitant reductions in fat mass. While the cumulative body of evidence suggests employing athletic development programmes with female athletes is beneficial, practitioners should be cognizant of specific sex-related differences in physical characteristics, body composition, biomechanics and training responsiveness. A deeper understanding of these factors will ensure that best practice is implemented and performance is enhanced when designing and evaluating training interventions. The aim of this chapter is to discuss key differences in strength and power development, physiological function and biomechanics in order to provide a clear practical application of how to effectively design, implement and monitor strength and conditioning provision for females.

Muscle mass, strength and power – natural development and trainability

Muscle mass

Peak muscle mass generally occurs earlier in females than males (16–20 vs. 18–25 years of age respectively) (Malina et al., 2004). Sex comparisons also show differences in hormone concentrations during puberty. Boys experience rapid increases in testosterone, growth hormone and insulin-like growth factor that lead to greater muscle mass. Conversely, heightened estrogen concentrations in females result in hip widening, breast development, greater body fat and, overall, relatively smaller increases in muscle mass than males. Total muscle mass is also commonly lower in females due to testosterone concentrations that are 10 times reduced when compared to their male counterparts.

Although estrogen also stimulates bone growth, boys have a longer growth period and commence puberty at a later stage, and therefore adult men tend to achieve greater overall stature than adult women. On average, adult women tend to have more body fat, less muscle and lower bone mineral density (BMD) than adult males (Johnston and Malina, 1966; Parker et al., 1990; Round et al., 1999; Malina et al., 2004). Furthermore, women tend to be lighter in total body weight than men and, although some female athletes may have lower fat percentages than untrained men, extremely low fat percentages in women may be associated with adverse health consequences (Otis et al., 1997; West, 1998).

Strength development

Peak strength levels in untrained females are typically attained by age 20 (Boden et al., 2000). There are minimal differences in strength between sexes during preadolescence, with youth females typically experiencing peak gains in strength after peak height velocity (PHV) (defined as the maximal accelerated growth spurt) (Malina et al., 2004). Following PHV, strength levels in boys further accelerate as characterised by a neuromuscular spurt which is likely due to hormonal changes. Conversely, for young females, a plateau in strength is expected during adolescence, and this has implications for both sports performance and injury risk. Girls experience increases in skeletal growth and gains in fat mass with less concomitant increases in skeletal tissue, muscle mass and strength (Malina et al., 2004). These changes result in a higher centre of mass, making dynamic stabilisation more challenging (Hewett et al., 2004), which highlights the importance of female athletes engaging in a supervised, developmentally appropriate, and technique driven strength and conditioning programme. It is possible to induce a neuromuscular spurt in females with the inclusion of resistance training and plyometric exercises that target deficits in neuromuscular control (Hewett et al., 1996). While strength and conditioning provision is recommended for youth of all ages, targeted neuromuscular training at or near the onset of puberty may further heighten improvements in strength, power and motor control (Myer et al., 2011b).

Adaptations to strength training

In terms of absolute strength, women typically display about two-thirds the strength of men (Lauback, 1976). Absolute lower body strength is generally closer to male values in comparison to the absolute values for the upper body. Sex-related differences in body composition, anthropometric characteristics and fat-free mass distribution (women tend to have less muscle mass above the waist) are largely attributable, and are apparent in recreationally trained individuals as well as highly trained athletes (Bishop et al., 1987).

Sex-related differences in relative muscular strength are greatly reduced. Relative to body weight, the lower body strength expressed by women is similar to that of men, although upper body strength is still considerably less. When comparisons are made relative to fat-free mass, differences in strength between men and women tend to disappear (105). There is also some data that indicate eccentric strength is more comparable between men and women than concentric strength when analysed relative to fat-free mass (Colliander and Tesch, 1989; Shephard, 2000). Furthermore, when strength is expressed relative to muscle cross-sectional area, no significant difference exists between sexes; suggesting that muscle quality (peak force per cross-sectional area) is not sex-specific (Miller et al., 1992; Castro et al., 1995). While the muscle fibers in men and women are also similar in fiber type distribution and histochemical characteristics, men tend to have a larger muscle fiber cross-sectional area than women (Miller et al., 1992). Notwithstanding the importance of these observations, strength and conditioning professionals need to remember that there is a wide range of strength abilities and that in some cases differences between two women may in fact be greater than differences between a man and a woman.

Adaptations to power training

Sex-related differences in power output are similar to those for muscular strength. In competitive weightlifters, power output relative to total body weight during snatch and clean pulling movements has been equated to approximately 63% of men's (Garhammer, 1991). Maximal vertical jump and standing long jump scores also tend to be lower in women than in men (Davies et al., 1988; Mayhew and Salm, 1990), although when expressed relative to fat-free mass, sex differences tend to reduce. Thus, it appears that differences in fat-free mass are not entirely responsible for the disparities in power output. Sex-related differences in rate of force development (Quatman et al., 2006; Quatman-Yates et al., 2013) and muscle activation strategies (Padua et al., 2005) could also be contributing factors (Ryushi et al., 1988).

Trainability of the female athlete

In spite of the aforementioned sex-related differences, baseline responses to resistance exercise occur in a similar manner. While men typically display heightened gains in absolute strength, relative increases are often the same or greater in women (Myer et al., 2005). This may reflect that baseline neuromuscular levels are lower on average in females (Myer et al., 2005). However, even though nervous system adaptations clearly contribute to the development of strength, the influence of muscle hypertrophy in women should not be overlooked. Specifically, through measurement of muscle cross-sectional area, relative short-term gains (up to 16 weeks) in muscle hypertrophy have been shown to be similar between sexes (Cureton et al., 1988; Häkkinen et al., 1992). Furthermore, it should be acknowledged that testosterone concentrations in women vary with training, and women with relatively high levels of testosterone may have more potential for an increase in muscle size and strength (Cumming et al., 1987; Häkkinen et al., 1990). In addition, exercise selection will alter the degree and rate of hypertrophy, with multi-joint movements, such as the squat, deadlift and Olympic weightlifting variations requiring a relatively longer neural adaptation period than those prescribed for single joint actions (Chilibeck et al., 1998). A genetic disposition to develop a large muscle mass may also be a contributing factor (Stewart and Rittweger, 2006) and should be considered in sports that are dependent on weight class.

Resistance training prescription for females

It is a misperception that women will lose flexibility or develop unwanted muscle bulk if they resistance train with weights. Due to the fact that there are no differences in the physiological characteristics of muscle between men and women, and because the movements and muscle groups involved in a particular sport or physical activity are consistent across genders, resistance training programs should be designed for the same purpose, regardless of the sex. The absolute resistance used for a given exercise is the only major alteration in the training prescription between sexes. It is particularly important for young female athletes to perform some type of resistance exercise regularly to approach their genetic potential in musculoskeletal strength and power during adulthood. Furthermore, emphasising development of the upper body is a fundamental training target for female athletes who participate in sports that require upper body strength and power. Inclusion of additional upper body exercises or sets is beneficial for women and may assist in the execution of key multi-joint exercises used to enhance sports performance.

Female athlete health and well-being

Bone mineral accrual

Resistance training and weight-bearing exercise has been shown to have a positive impact on bone health and enhance bone mineral density (BMD) in children and adolescents (Morris et al., 1997; Nichols et al., 2001; McKay et al., 2005). Data indicate that young athletes (age 12–16 years) involved in high impact sports possess higher BMD compared to participants from low impact sports and non-athletes of the same age (Nichols et al., 2006; Ackerman and Misra, 2011). Furthermore, elite adolescent weightlifters who regularly perform multi-joint resistance exercises at high loads display levels of BMD far superior to those of age-matched controls (Virvidakis et al., 1990; Conroy et al., 1993). This has implications for young girls and female athletes who are at an increased risk for developing osteoporosis later in life, characterised by low bone mass and an increased susceptibility to skeletal fractures.

Skeletal adaptation to stress is slow; thus, the pre-pubertal and pubertal years represent a sensitive period to promote accelerated gains in bone mass (Baxter-Jones et al., 2011). In late adolescence, approximately 90% of bone mass has been accrued (Hind and Burrows, 2007). Worryingly, adolescent female athletes who fail to maximise bone mass accrual during their developmental years are unlikely to compensate as they mature and enter adulthood (Drinkwater et al., 1990; Barrack et al., 2011). A permanently lower BMD compared to their genetic potential increases the risk of osteoporosis and sustaining fractures from falls in later life. It is therefore essential that appropriate exercise interventions are adopted and eating habits are closely monitored during these crucial years to maximise bone development. However, when volumes of repetitive loading and/or intensities of loading are excessive, the bone remodelling process cannot keep pace, eventually resulting in stress fractures. Stress fractures are most common in sports which demand repetitive forceful impacts, such as long distance running (Arendt et al., 2003). Early sport-specialisation, changes in running surface and rapid increases in training frequency, duration and intensity are all extrinsic factors associated with stress fractures in distance runners (Harrast and Colonno, 2010). Thus, appropriate periodisation and monitoring should be implemented routinely to reduce injury risk. The negative effects of intensive training routines are compounded by inadequate energy availability caused by a poor diet, excessive caloric expenditure or a combination of both (Christo et al., 2008). Menstrual cycle abnormalities are also a major risk factor for low BMD in adolescent athletes. Amenorrheic athletes typically have a 10% lower BMD compared to eumenorrheic athletes and are at greater risk of developing stress fractures (Thein-Nissenbaum et al., 2012). However, gymnasts have been shown to possess high BMD despite a high prevalence of menstrual dysfunction (Robinson et al., 1995; Malina et al., 2013); therefore, physical activity and energy availability appear to exert independent effects on bone status.

The female athlete triad

Intensive training and/or sub-optimal dietary intake during adolescence is likely to negate many of the benefits associated with sports participation, and instead cause a number of potentially serious health issues, including the female athlete triad, overuse injury and burnout (Brenner, 2007; DiFiori et al., 2014). The female athlete triad describes three inter-related components of health: energy availability, menstrual cycle function and bone mineral density (BMD) status, which each exist on a continuum from optimal health to disease. When intensive training regimens are combined with insufficient energy intake and recovery to support the exercise being undertaken, young female athletes are at risk of developing one, two or all three components of the female athlete triad (Winsley and Matos, 2011). A summary of the main warning signs for various stages of each continuum and risk factors associated with the triad is shown in Figure 2.1.

Insufficient energy intake to support the demands of the athlete's lifestyle is the primary driver of the triad, as a negative energy balance disturbs the metabolic and hormonal regulation of menstrual function, and compromises maintenance and development of bone (Hoch et al., 2009). It has been suggested that the triad should be viewed more as a syndrome resulting from energy deficiency, which leads to a host of physiological complications, including menstrual dysfunction, poor bone health, weak immunity and mental health issues (Nattiv et al., 2007).

Early sport-specialisation has also been identified as an independent risk factor for the female athlete triad (Winsley and Matos, 2011). The level of risk is further magnified in female athletes

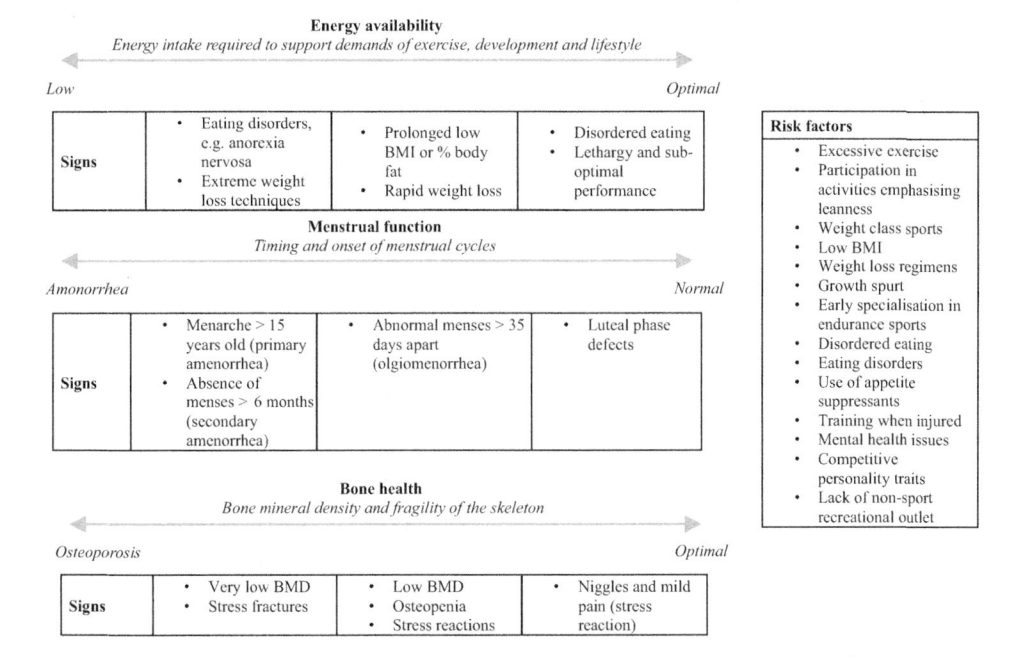

Figure 2.1 The female athlete triad. Signs, symptoms and risk factors

Table 2.1 Strategies to aid in the avoidance of the female athlete triad

Strategy	Person(s) responsible
Provide education and guidance to young female athletes and their parents	Sports coach and strength and conditioning (S&C) staff
Regular screening for components of the triad should be carried out by a qualified professional	Medical personnel and appropriately qualified sports science/S&C staff
Ensure optimal energy intake is the cornerstone of prevention methods	Athlete, coaches, parents
Coaches/parents should be vigilant to patterns of disordered eating	Coaches, parents
The oral contraceptive pill should be avoided as a firstline of treatment for menstrual dysfunction	Athlete, parents, appropriate qualified medical practitioners

who specialise in disciplines that demand high levels of leanness and endurance (such as gymnastics, dance, long distance running and figure skating), indicating that these athletes are particularly vulnerable (Winsley and Matos, 2011). The current consensus is that the occurrence of the triad is lower in adolescents versus adult and collegiate level athletes (Winsley and Matos, 2011). Nevertheless, adolescence is a critical period for accruing bone mass and there are long-term risks associated with triad disorders at a young age; thus, it is recommended that clear education and guidance is provided to athletes, coaches and parents, particularly in sports where there is the potential for higher risk (see Table 2.1).

Contemporary considerations for female athlete health

When working with female athletes, it is a prudent strategy for S&C coaches to work as part of a multi-disciplinary team or align themselves with health care professionals who are able to monitor and recognise signs and symptoms that are indicative of reduced health and well-being. This is especially important because of the potential health implications but also because of the resulting negative effects on performance. Whilst this can also be true for male athletes, sex-specific factors that are pertinent for females include menstrual cycle irregularities and dysfunction, menorrhagia (heavy menstrual bleeding) and iron status. These aspects will be described briefly here, and while application of monitoring tools and intervention may be outside the scope of the S&C coach, a greater awareness of these issues will allow practitioners to better understand their effects on health and performance and refer to appropriately qualified individuals, such as doctors and registered dietitians.

Menstrual cycle

Despite the physiology of the menstrual cycle being well understood, its relation to exercise is less well described (Bruinvels et al., 2016). The complexities of the menstrual cycle are thought to be the most significant barrier. Reproduction is the primary role for the ovarian hormones estrogen and progesterone, but they are also hypothesised to influence other physiological systems, and therefore exercise performance, by potentially altering substrate metabolism, thermoregulation, cognition, mood, and cardiovascular and respiratory function (Oosthuyse and Bosch, 2010). Unfortunately, research in these areas is sparse, and limited by targeting the participation of women in the early follicular phase of the menstrual cycle where estrogen and progesterone are at their lowest or when women are taking the oral contraceptive pill, which largely ignores the impact that fluctuations in the levels of estrogen and progesterone during each cycle may have.

Physical exercise is beneficial for female reproductive function and can improve menstrual cyclicity, ovulation and fertility (Reed et al., 2011). Equally, menstrual function is highly sensitive to physiological stress; therefore, female athletes engaged in intensive physical training programmes are susceptible to developing menstrual cycle dysfunctions. High amounts of stress cause a negative energy balance, first affecting the female reproductive system as it is non-vital for survival (Horn et al., 2014). Energy deficiency results in a hypometabolic state causing a reduction in estrogen, which reduces pulsatility of the gonadotropin-releasing hormone. The effect is manifested as amenorrhea (the absence of menses) or oligomenorrhea (menstrual cycles that occur > 35 days apart). There is a high prevalence of menstrual dysfunctions during adolescence, particularly in athletes involved in intensive sports training (Williams et al., 2001). Amenorrhea has been reported in 24% of female high school athletes from eight different sports (Rauh et al., 2010). Oligomenorrhea is also common (5–18% of adolescent athletes), but is difficult to diagnose in adolescents, as eumenorrhea is typically not established until early adulthood (Hoch et al., 2009).

Typically, adolescent athletes who present with amenorrhea possess significantly lower BMD compared to eumenorrheic (those displaying normal menstruation) young athletes and non-athletic controls (Barrack et al., 2008). Athletes with menstrual cycle abnormalities are also more likely to sustain a musculoskeletal injury compared to eumenorrheic adolescents (Thein-Nissenbaum et al., 2012). Although the association between menstrual disturbances and injury is not causative, a low energy state alters the profile of thyroid and stress hormones, which directly affects bone metabolism and the health of muscle and connective tissue (Christo et al., 2008). The impact of menstrual dysfunction upon performance is less certain; however, performance impairment has been shown in swimmers displaying ovarian suppression (Vanheest et al., 2014).

The use of the oral contraceptive (estrogen) pill (OCP) has been suggested for treatment of menstrual dysfunction in young women; however, its use remains questionable in young athletic females and, importantly, S&C coaches should not be involved in the decision of whether to take the pill or not. The effects of the OCP on BMD have provided conflicting results (Golden et al., 2002; Cobb et al., 2007; Mountjoy et al., 2014). Although monthly menstrual cycles appear to return with the administration of the OCP, this provides a false sense of normality for athletes who fail to address low energy availability. The OCP provides an artificial hormonal environment that supresses markers of bone formation and absorption, and thus may actually be harmful to overall bone health (Cobb et al., 2007).

Menstrual cycle irregularities

The average menstrual cycle for an adult female lasts for approximately 28 days and is characterised by a cyclical fluctuation in levels of the ovarian hormones estrogen and progesterone. The menstrual cycle can typically be divided into three phases: menstrual phase (Day 1–5), follicular phase (Day 6–14) and luteal phase (Day 15–28). A typical menstrual cycle is described in Figure 2.2. Research on menstrual cycle irregularities has traditionally focused on the female athlete triad (Nattiv et al., 2007) and the relative energy deficiency in sport (RED-S) syndrome (Mountjoy et al., 2014). The triad is presented as three interrelated components: energy availability, menstrual function and bone health, whereas RED-S was proposed as a broader and more comprehensive term for the triad (Mountjoy et al., 2014). RED-S is based on the understanding that the clinical manifestation is not a triad of energy availability, menstrual function and bone

Table 2.2 Four-part diagnostic criteria to determine the presence of heavy menstrual bleeding

Have you experienced any of the following during your period?
Flooding through to clothes or bedding
Need of frequent changes of sanitary towels or tampons (meaning changes every 2 hours or less or 12 sanitary items per period)
Need of double sanitary protection (tampons and towels)
Pass large blood clots

health but a syndrome that begins with relative energy deficiency and results in a multitude of physiological impairments in a number of areas, including metabolic rate, menstrual function, bone health, immunity, protein synthesis and cardiovascular and psychological health (Mountjoy et al., 2014).

Menorrhagia (heavy menstrual bleeding)

Amenorrhea, oligomenorrhea and dysmenorrhea (painful menstruation) have been the primary focus of the existing research; however, menstrual blood loss and the potential link to iron deficiency anaemia (IDA) has often been overlooked. Menorrhagia or heavy menstrual bleeding (HMB) is a highly prevalent condition with a quarter (27.2%) of 4,506 women surveyed from a general population across five European countries diagnosed with HMB (Fraser et al., 2015). Interestingly, the incidence of HMB appears to be greater in exercising populations compared to the general population. Fraser et al. (2015) showed that 35% of recreational runners and 37% of elite athletes surveyed reported experiencing HMB (Bruinvels et al., 2016). HMB can have a considerable negative impact on women's quality of life, time off from work or sport, energy levels and mood state and is strongly implicated in the incidence of iron deficiency amongst menstruating females. Four-part diagnostic criteria to determine the presence of heavy menstrual bleeding is described in Table 2.2 (Fraser et al., 2015).

The current evidence indicates that intensive physical training per se is unlikely to be a causative factor for menstrual irregularities in young females (Maïmoun et al., 2013). However, some young females might find themselves unintentionally in a chronic hypometabolic state due to the energy expenditure of exercise, combined with pressures to attain a lean physique for their sport. Heavy menstrual bleeding is also experienced by many exercising women and is associated with a higher incidence of iron deficiency anaemia. Coaches, athletes and the exercising public should be educated in the diagnosis and management of menstrual cycle irregularities, particularly heavy menstrual bleeding. It is recommended that women who experience heavy menstrual bleeding are tested by appropriately qualified individuals for iron deficiency anaemia.

Iron status

Maintaining an adequate iron status is vitally important as iron is an essential mineral required for oxidative energy metabolism and is a key component of haemoglobin and myoglobin, as well as cytochromes that are involved in electron transport. Although all cells need a small amount of iron, erythroid precursors require a substantial amount in order to produce haemoglobin. Common occurrences that contribute to iron loss include inadequate dietary intake, absorption in the intestines and blood loss. Inevitably there is a link between HMB and iron deficiency. A recent survey found that 22% of 271 exercising females experienced HMB and that these women had a lower haemoglobin concentration ([Hb]; 12.4 ± 1.7g/dL vs. 12.9 ± 1.2g/dL p<0.05), a lower mean ferritin (25.5 ± 25.4ug/L vs. 45.1 ± 41.8ug/L, p<0.05) and were more likely to have IDA than those women without HMB (Bruinvels et al., 2016). If a low iron status leads to anaemia the result will be a reduction in aerobic power. However, the diagnosis of IDA and subsequent treatment, using either oral supplements or intravenous injection, is relatively straight forward. A challenge that commonly occurs, particularly amongst female athletes, is when a low iron status is observed in the absence of anaemia and the meaning of such a condition is less clear.

Iron treatment in the form of either oral supplementation or intravenous injection are effective for increasing serum ferritin (sFer) (Burden et al., 2015) but rarely does it result in improvement in aerobic power and endurance performance. A recent randomised controlled trial that involved treating iron deficient elite endurance runners with either a 500mg intravenous iron treatment or a placebo injection resulted in an increase in sFer in the iron group yet no between-group differences in indices of red cell number, structure or function, total haemoglobin mass (tHb-mass) or surrogate measures of endurance performance including $\dot{V}O_{2max}$, running economy or time to exhaustion (Burden et al., 2015). Despite the athletes being considered 'iron deficient' via a diagnosis using traditional sFer reference ranges, the intravenous iron treatment showed no significant effect, suggesting that this relatively low level of sFer represented normal iron metabolism for this population. It is necessary to note that traditional reference ranges for markers of iron status, such as sFer, have been established from clinical or normal populations, which don't apply to athletes, particularly at the elite level, so caution should be taken when using them to interpret data for the purpose of determining iron deficiency in athletes.

While outside the scope of practice for S&C coaches and more closely linked to the role of registered dietitians within a multi-disciplinary team, intervening with oral supplements or intravenous treatments may also cause gastrointestinal side effects and potentially reduce the ability to absorb iron from the diet. It is important to consider the side effects that may result from supplementation and the implications for iron metabolism of unnecessary treatment. Individuals taking oral iron supplements may experience side effects, including abdominal pain, constipation, as well as the problem of compliance to treatment protocols. Although iron treatments are readily available and relatively safe, there is no universal dosing protocol and the implications of unnecessary treatment on iron metabolism need to be considered. The hours immediately after training or competition also represent a key time for nutritional strategies that aim to maximise recovery and adaptive processes, yet this may not be a suitable time to consume iron rich foods. It is plausible that an inability to fully absorb dietary iron following exercise may be a contributing factor to the high incidence of low iron status amongst endurance athletes. For these athletes who are considered iron deficient but not anaemic, a review of nutritional behaviours should be the first intervention.

Injury considerations for female athletes

Anterior cruciate ligament (ACL) injury in females

It is important for practitioners to be aware of the high incidence of knee injuries in female athletes, particularly in sports such as soccer and basketball (Alentorn-Geli et al., 2009). The increasing number of knee injuries may be reflective of heightened participation by women in organised sport, although other causative factors have been proposed and will form the basis of the discussion in this section. Identification of risk factors and prevention of anterior cruciate ligament (ACL) ruptures are of particular importance because of their traumatic nature and the potential for negative long term health outcomes. Female athletes are around six times more likely to sustain an ACL injury than males (Mihata et al., 2006; Joseph et al., 2013); thus, targeted strategies are required for this 'at risk' population.

Anatomical and hormonal factors may in part be responsible for the heightened risk in females – specifically, joint laxity, limb alignment, inter-condylar notch dimensions, ligament size and hormonal changes (Arendt and Dick, 1995; Moeller and Lamb, 1997; Wojtys et al., 1998; Hewett, 2000). However, alterations in neuromuscular function which lead to abnormal biomechanics (increased dynamic knee valgus upon contact with the ground) have also been proposed (Myer et al., 2013). Importantly, these deficits are modifiable and should be a primary target for strength and conditioning coaches in their attempts to reduce injury risk and enhance performance. Since most ACL injuries in female athletes occur from noncontact mechanisms (e.g., deceleration, lateral pivoting or landing [Boden et al., 2000]), regular participation in training programmes that are inclusive of resistance training, plyometrics, and agility and balance training and designed to enhance the strength of supporting structures and increase neuromuscular control of the knee joint are recommended to reduce the risk of sport-related injuries (Emery, 2005; Hewett et al., 2005). These programmes should commence prior to puberty in order to optimise training adaptations due to the neural plasticity associated with this phase of development (Myer et al., 2013) and be continued as the athlete progresses through adolescence and into adulthood.

Biomechanical considerations associated with injury in female athletes

Sex-dependent neuromuscular deficits have been indicated in female athletes, including: quadriceps activation (quadriceps dominance), frontal plane knee control strategies (ligament dominance), limb asymmetry (limb dominance) and core dysfunction (trunk dominance) (Hewett et al., 2010). These risk factors are associated with an inability to effectively dissipate ground reaction forces (GRFs) and control the location of their bodies' center of mass (COM) (Hewett et al., 2010). In addition to sex, age and stage of maturation are also important factors to consider. Younger athletes, and specifically those who have not yet experienced puberty, are smaller in size, and the changes that occur during puberty, such as the change in the location of the centre of mass, typically alter biomechanics and increase joint torques (Hewett et al., 2004).

Quadriceps dominance refers to an intra-limb imbalance in recruitment, coordination and strength between the knee extensors (quadriceps) and flexors (hamstrings) (Myer et al., 2004). Female athletes exhibit increased quadriceps and decreased hamstring recruitment compared to male athletes (Hewett et al., 1996), resulting in less knee flexion on ground contact, a greater reliance on the quadriceps to maintain stability and decreased ability of the flexors to limit knee extension during sport movements that require rapid decelerations. The quadriceps act to pull the tibia anteriorly relative to the femur with the ACL acting as restraint to resist this anterior translation; thus, female athletes who exhibit reduced activation of the flexors relative to the extensors will land with their knee in an extended position and are at a greater risk of ligament rupture. Therefore, practitioners should devise appropriate injury prevention strategies that target deficits in posterior chain strength. In collegiate female athletes a 6-week programme of emphasised hamstring resistance training significantly increased the functional hamstring: quadriceps (H:Q) ratio to acceptable levels (>1.0) for the reduction of ACL injuries (Holcomb et al., 2007). Significant improvements in hamstring peak torque and H:Q ratio have also been observed following 7 weeks of neuromuscular training that included both dynamic balance and plyometric exercises.

Reduced frontal plane control (or ligament dominance) results in an increase in dynamic knee valgus, a high-risk movement for ACL injury (Hewett et al., 2002). A contributing factor to this aberrant movement pattern in females is a relative decrease in musculoskeletal stiffness compared to males as they reach puberty (Granata et al., 2002). Inadequate musculoskeletal stiffness leads to the increased reliance on the joint and ligaments to achieve stability (Granata et al., 2002). During the prepubescent period, similar valgus alignment has been reported between boys and girls (Ford et al., 2010) and injury rates are lower at these younger ages (Bloemers et al., 2012; Van der Sluis et al., 2015). This is likely due to inferior body mass, shorter lever lengths, and lower expressions of muscular power and subsequent GRFs which are not of sufficient magnitudes to pose a discernable threat of injury (Fort-Vanmeerhaeghe et al., 2016).

Athletes who display ligament dominance have an increased reliance on passive restraints (ligaments and bones) relative to active restraints (muscles) to regain or maintain joint stability during sporting tasks. As a result, GRFs are absorbed to a greater extent through ligaments and joints instead of the quadriceps and posterior chain musculature, including the hamstrings, gluteals, gastrocnemius, and soleus, which may exceed their tensile strength limit (Hewett et al., 2010). Sporting movements such as cutting and landing require rapid execution, and high forces are experienced in short time periods, which are sufficient to cause ligament rupture (Hewett et al., 2010). Moreover, Krosshaug et al. (2007) using in-vivo video analysis reported that the timing of non-contact ACL injury ranged between 17–50 milliseconds following initial ground contact, emphasising the need for effective neuromuscular feed-forward activation. Thus, strength and conditioning coaches should be cognizant of the risks of knee positions indicative of reduced frontal plane control (valgus alignment) on ground contact due to their association with injury and increased load on the MCL and ACL in this position. Effective screening and intervention programmes should also be employed that target neuromuscular feedforward activity through the use of plyometrics as means of reducing potential risk (Chimera et al., 2004).

Leg dominance refers to inter-limb asymmetry with regard to strength, flexibility, coordination and control (Myer et al., 2004). The preferred or dominant limb is at heightened risk of injury due to a greater magnitude of the GRFs generated having to be absorbed by that limb (Myer et al., 2004), which may exceed the force absorption capacity of the soft tissue structures. In addition, continued asymmetrical loading will increase the risk of overuse injury. While both male and female athletes will have preferred limbs and may demonstrate asymmetry, limb dominance coupled with the other sex-specific risk factors described here can result in forces that are too great for joints and ligaments to withstand. For example, if a female athlete lands in a position of dynamic knee valgus, and her knee is in an extended position with heightened GRFs on that limb due to asymmetry, the likelihood of injury will clearly increase. Thus, training programmes that target the development of strength and landing mechanics using both bi-lateral and uni-lateral exercises is recommended.

Trunk dominance has been defined as an imbalance between the inertial demands of the trunk and the ability to resist perturbations to the centre of mass of the body (Myer et al., 2011a). The inability to dissipate force effectively results in excessive trunk motion primarily in the frontal plane, subsequently increasing knee joint torques (Zazulak et al., 2007). Rapid growth which occurs as a result of the pubertal growth spurt causes an increase in body mass and lever lengths, which cause a change in the location of the COM without concomitant and proportional change in strength for females due to the absence of a neuromuscular sport (Hewett et al., 2010). While male athletes also experience changes during puberty, they have a subsequent increase in lean muscle mass and strength that allows them to better manage their increased body size during sporting actions (Hewett et al., 2010). Though these changes begin in puberty, they persist as the athlete ages, as evident by deficits in trunk control of collegiate female athletes who subsequently went on to experience an ACL injury (Zazulak et al., 2007). Also, recent data have shown that

Paul J. Read et al.

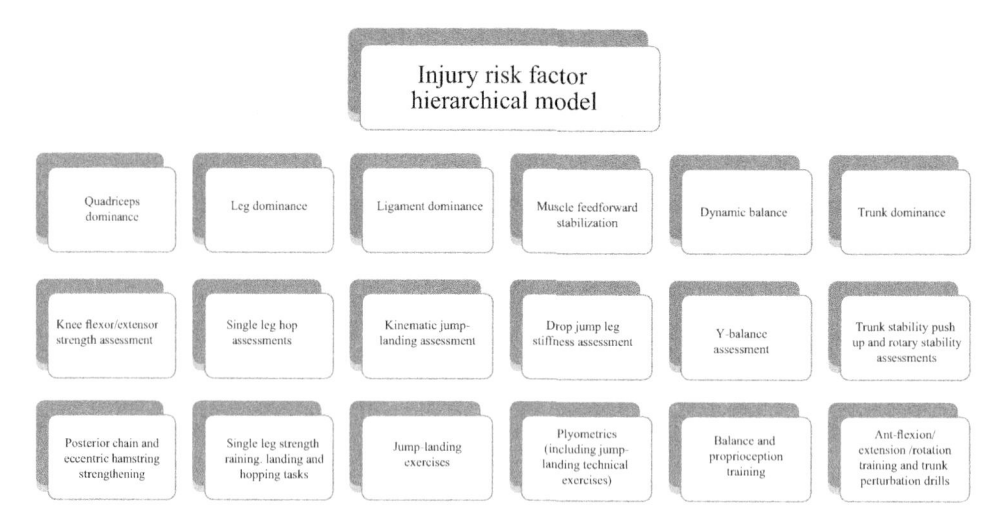

Figure 2.2 Injury risk factor hierarchical model. Reprinted with permission from Read et al. (2016). Neuromuscular Risk Factors for Knee and Ankle Ligament Injuries in Male Youth Soccer Players. *Sports Med.* DOI 10.1007/s40279–016–0479-z

The top tier of the model includes identification of the associated neuromuscular risk factors for ACL ligament injuries. Practitioners are then required to select appropriate assessments that are able to detect functional deficits assisting in the early identification of players at high risk (tier 2 of the model). The final step involves the selection of appropriate exercises that target each of the respective neuromuscular risk factors. It is proposed that following an appropriate training intervention, test performance will improve and subsequent neuromuscular deficits can be reduced, lowering injury risk.

the combination of valgus and ipsilateral trunk motion during a single leg drop vertical jump was more clearly associated with heightened injury risk in female team sport athletes than that of knee valgus alone (Dingenen et al., 2015).

Following the identification of prevalent injury risk factors, a systematic model has been proposed to screen athletes and subsequently develop individualised training programmes to reduce their relative risk (Figure 2.2). (Read et al., 2016). Using this system, each risk factor is linked to a neuromuscular screening assessment and target exercises are then selected to improve relevant neuromuscular control deficits. It is proposed that following an appropriate training intervention, neuromuscular deficits can be reduced, ultimately lowering injury risk (Read et al., 2016). In selecting exercises to reduce injury risk, strength and conditioning coaches are advised to consider integrated activities that develop fundamental movement skills to enhance skill related fitness and reduce the risk of sports related injury, such as resistance training, plyometrics and perturbation drills (Myer et al., 2005; Faigenbaum et al., 2011). This should be incorporated alongside the technical skill training of the sport to form an integral part of the athlete's periodised training programme.

Summary

Research shows that training modalities such as resistance exercise, plyometrics and balance training can be a safe and effective method of conditioning for males and females of all ages and abilities. The potential benefits are multifactorial, including positive effects on a variety of physical performance variables (e.g. strength and power), health markers (e.g. body composition and cardiac function) and psychosocial development (e.g. self-image and confidence). Moreover, regular participation in well-designed and targeted athletic development programmes can reduce the risk of sport-related and physical activity–related injuries. Sex-specific factors, including menstrual cycle irregularities and dysfunction, menorrhagia and iron status, should also be monitored in conjunction with appropriately qualified and medically trained professionals because of their known effects on female athlete health and performance.

References

Ackerman, KE, and Misra, M. Bone health in adolescent athletes with a focus on the female athlete triad. *Phys Sportsmed* 39: 131–141, 2011.

Alentorn-Geli, E, Myer, GD, Silvers, HJ, Samitier, G, Romero, D, Lazaro-Haro, C, and Cugat, R. Prevention of non-contact anterior cruciate ligament injuries in soccer players. Part 1: Mechanisms of injury and underlying risk factors. *Knee Surg Sports Traumatol Arthrosc* 17: 705–729, 2009.

Arendt, E, Agel, J, Heikes, C, and Griffiths, H. Stress injuries to bone in college athletes: A retrospective review of experience at a single institution. *Am J Sports Med* 31: 959–968, 2003.

Arendt, E, and Dick, R. Knee injury patterns among men and women in collegiate basketball and soccer: NCAA data and review of literature. *Am J Sports Med* 23: 694–701, 1995.

Barrack, MT, Rauh, MJ, and Nichols, JF. Prevalence of and traits associated with low BMD among female adolescent runners. *Med Sci Sports Exerc* 40: 2015–2021, 2008.

Barrack, MT, van Loan, MD, Rauh, MJ, and Nichols, JF. Body mass, training, menses, and bone in adolescent runners: A three-year follow-up. *Med Sci Sports Exerc* 43: 959–966, 2011.

Baxter-Jones, AD, Faulkner, RA, Forwood, MR, Mirwald, RL, and Bailey, DA. Bone mineral accrual from 8 to 30 years of age: An estimation of peak bone mass. *J Bone Miner Res* 26: 1729–1739, 2011.

Bishop, P, Cureton, K, and Collins, M. Sex difference in muscular strength in equally-trained men and women. *Ergonomics* 30: 675–687, 1987.

Bloemers, F, Collard, D, Paw, MCA, Van Mechelen, W, Twisk, J, and Verhagen, E. Physical inactivity is a risk factor for physical activity-related injuries in children. *Br J Sports Med* 46(9): 669–674, 2012.

Boden, BP, Dean, GS, Feagin JA, and Garrett, WE. Mechanisms of anterior cruciate ligament injury. *Orthopedics* 23: 573–578, 2000.

Brenner, JS. Overuse injuries, overtraining, and burnout in child and adolescent athletes. *Pediatrics* 119: 1242–1245, 2007.

Bruinvels, G, Burden, R, Brown, N, Richards, T, and Pedlar, C. The prevalence and impact of heavy menstrual bleeding (menorrhagia) in elite and non-elite athletes. *PloS one* 11(2): e0149881, 2016.

Burden, RJ, Morton, K, Richards, T, Whyte, GP, and Pedlar, CR. Is iron treatment beneficial in iron-deficient but non-anaemic (IDNA) endurance athletes? A systematic review and meta-analysis. *Br J Sports Med* 49(21): 1389–1397, 2015.

Castro, M, McCann, D, Shaffrath, J, and Adams, W. Peak torque per unit cross-sectional area differs between strength-training and untrained adults. *Med Sci Sports Exerc* 27: 397–403, 1995.

Chilibeck, P, Calder, A, Sale, D, and Webber, C. A comparison of strength and muscle mass increases during resistance training in young women. *Eur J Appl Physiol* 77: 170–175, 1998.

Chimera, NJ, Swanik, KA, Buz Swanik, C, and Straub, SJ. Effects of plyometric training on muscle-activation strategies and performance in female athletes. *J Athletic Train* 39: 24–31, 2004.

Christo, K, Prabhakaran, R, Lamperllo, B, Cord, J, Miller, KK, Goldstein, MA, Gupta, N, Herzog, DB, Klibanski, A, and Misra, M. Bone metabolism in adolescent athletes with amenorrhea, athletes with eumenorrhea, and control subjects. *Pediatrics* 121: 1127–1136, 2008.

Cobb, KL, Bachrach, LK, Sowers, M, Nieves, J, Greendale, GA, Kent, KK, Brown, BW Jr, Pettit, K, Harper, DM, and Kelsey, JL. The effect of oral contraceptives on bone mass and stress fractures in female runners. *Med Sci Sports Exerc* 239: 1464–1473, 2007.

Colliander, E, and Tesch, P. Bilateral eccentric and concentric torque of quadriceps and hamstrings in females and males. *Eur J Appl Physiol* 59: 227–232, 1989.

Conroy, B, Kraemer, W, Maresh, C, Fleck, S, Stone, M, Fry, A, Miller, P, and Dalsky, G. Bone mineral density in elite junior Olympic weightlifters. *Med Sci Sports Exerc* 25: 1103–1109, 1993.

Cumming, D, Wall, S, Galbraith, M, and Belcastro, A. Reproductive hormone responses to resistance exercise. *Med Sci Sports Exerc* 19: 234–238, 1987.

Cureton, K, Collins, M, Hill, D, and McElhannon, F. Muscle hypertrophy in men and women. *Med Sci Sports Exerc* 20: 338–344, 1988.

Davies, B, Greenwood, E, and Jones, S. Gender differences in the relationship of performance in the handgrip and standing long jump tests to lean limb volume in young athletes. *Eur J Appl Physiol* 58: 315–320, 1988.

DiFiori, JP, Benjamin, HJ, Brenner, JS, Gregory, A, Jayanthi, N, Landry, GL, and Luke, A. Overuse injuries and burnout in youth sports: a position statement from the American Medical Society for Sports Medicine. *Br J Sports Med* 48: 287–288, 2014.

Dingenen, B, Malfait, B, Nijs, S, Peers, KH, Vereecken, S, Verschueren, SM, and Staes, FF. Can two-dimensional video analysis during single-leg drop vertical jumps help identify non-contact knee injury risk? A one-year prospective study. *Clinical Biomechanics* 30(8): 781–787, 2015.

Drinkwater, BL, Bruemner, B, and Chesnut, CH III. Menstrual history as a determinant of current bone density in young athletes. *J Am Med Ass* 263: 545–548, 1990.

Ebben, WP, and Jensen, RL. Strength training for women: Debunking myths that block opportunity. *The Physician and Sportsmedicine* 26(5): 86–97, 1998.

Emery, C. Injury prevention and future research. *Med Sci Sports Exerc* 48: 179–200, 2005.

Faigenbaum, AD, Farrell, A, Fabiano, M, Radler, T, Naclerio, F, Ratamess, NA, Kang, J, and Myer, GD. Effects of integrative neuromuscular training on fitness performance in children. *Pediatr Exerc Sci* 23: 573–584, 2011.

Ford, KR, Shapiro, R, Myer, GD, Van Den Bogert, AJ, and Hewett, TE. Longitudinal sex differences during landing in knee abduction in young athletes. *Med Sci Sports Exerc* 42: 1923–1931, 2010.

Fort-Vanmeerhaeghe, A, Romero-Rodriguez, D, Montalvo, AM, Kiefer, AW, Lloyd, RS, and Myer, GD. Integrative neuromuscular training and injury prevention in youth athletes. Part I: Identifying risk factors. *Strength Cond J* 38(3): 36–48, 2016.

Fraser, IS, Mansour, D, Breymann, C, Hoffman, C, Mezzacasa, A, and Petraglia, F. Prevalence of heavy menstrual bleeding and experiences of affected women in a European patient survey. *International Journal of Gynecology & Obstetrics* 128: 196–200, 2015. doi:10.1016/j.ijgo.2014.09.027.

Garhammer, J. A comparison of maximal power outputs between elite male and female weightlifters in competition. *Int J Sport Biomech* 7: 3–11, 1991.

Golden, NH, Lanzkowsky, L, Schebendach, J, Palestro, CJ, Jacobson, MS, and Shenker, IR. The effect of estrogen-progestin treatment on bone mineral density in anorexia nervosa. *J Pediatr Adolesc Gynecol* 15: 135–143, 2002.

Granata, K, Padua, DA, and Wilson, S. Gender differences in active musculoskeletal stiffness. Part II. Quantification of leg stiffness during functional hopping tasks. *J Electromyogr Kinesiol* 12(2): 127–135, 2002.

Granata, KP, Wilson, SE, and Padua, DA. Gender differences in active musculoskeletal stiffness. Part I.: Quantification in controlled measurements of knee joint dynamics. *J Electromyogr Kinesiol*, 12(2): 119–126, 2002.

Häkkinen, K, Pakarinen, A, and Kallinen, M. Neuromuscular adaptations and serum hormones in women during short-term intensive strength training. *Eur J Appl Physiol* 64: 106–111, 1992.

Häkkinen, K, Pakarinen, A, Kyrolainen, H, Cheng, S, Kim, D, and Komi, P. Neuromuscular adaptations and serum hormones in females during prolonged power training. *Int J Sports Med* 11: 91–98, 1990.

Harrast, MA, and Colonno, D. Stress fractures in runners. *Clin Sports Med* 29: 399–416, 2010.

Hewett, TE. Neuromuscular and hormonal factors associated with knee injuries in female athletes: Strategies for intervention. *Sports Med* 29: 313–327, 2000.

Hewett, TE, Ford, KR, Hoogenboom, B, and Myer, G. Understanding and preventing acl injuries: current biomechanical and epidemiologic considerations-update 2010. *NAJSPT* 5(4): 234–251, 2010.

Hewitt, TE, Lindenfeild, TN, Riccobene, JV, and Noyes, FR. The effects of neuromuscular training on the incidence of knee injury in female athletes. *Am. J. Sports Med* 27: 699–704, 1999.

Hewett, TE, Myer, GD, and Ford, KR. Decrease in neuromuscular control about the knee with maturation in female athletes. *J Bone Joint Surg Am* 86(8): 1601–1608, 2004.

Hewett, TE, Myer, GD, and Ford, KR. Reducing knee and anterior cruciate ligament injuries among female athletes. *J Knee Surg* 18: 82–88, 2005.

Hewett, TE, Paterno, MV, and Myer, GD. Strategies for enhancing proprioception and neuromuscular control of the knee. *Clin Orthop Relat Res* 402: 76–94, 2002.

Hewett, TE, Stroupe, AL, Nance, TA, and Noyes, FR. Plyometric training in female athletes decreased impact forces and increased hamstring torques. *Am J Sports Med* 24: 765–773, 1996.

Hind, K, and Burrows, M. Weight-bearing exercise and bone mineral accrual in children and adolescents: A review of controlled trials. *Bone* 40: 14–27, 2007.

Hoch, AZ, Pajewski, NM, Moraski, L, Carrera, GF, Wilson, CR, Hoffmann, RG, Schimke, JE, and Gutterman, DD. Prevalence of the female athlete triad in high school athletes and sedentary students. *Clin J Sports Med* 19: 421–428, 2009.

Holcomb, WR, Rublet, MD, Lee, HJ, et al. Effect of hamstring-emphasized resistance training on hamstring: quadriceps strength ratios. *J Strength Cond Res* 21: 41–47, 2007.

Horn, E, Gergen, N, and McGarry, KA. The female athlete triad. *The Rhode Is Med J* 97(11): 18–21, 2014.

Johnston, FE, and Malina, RM. Age changes in the composition of the upper arm in Philadelphia children. *Hum Biol* 38: 1–21, 1966.

Joseph, AM, Collins, CL, Henke, NM, Yard, EE, Fields, SK, and Comstock, DA. A multisport epidemiological comparison of anterior cruciate ligament injuries in high school athletes. *J Athl Train* 48: 810–817, 2013.

Kraemer, W, Mazzetti, S, Nindl, B, Gotshalk, L, Bush, J, Marx, J, Dohi, K, Gomez, A, Miles, M, Fleck, S, Newton, R, and Häkkinen, K. Effect of resistance training on women's strength/power and occupational performances. *Med Sci Sports Exerc* 33: 1011–1025, 2001.

Krosshaug, T, Nakamae, A, Boden, BP, et al. Mechanisms of anterior cruciate ligament injury in basketball: Video analysis of 39 cases. *AM J Sports Med* 35: 359–367, 2007.

Lauback, L. Comparative muscle strength of men and women: A review of the literature. *Aviat Space Environ Med* 47: 534–542, 1976.

Maïmoun, L, Coste, O, Philibert, P, Briot, K, Mura, T, Galtier, F, Mariano-Goulart, D, Paris, F, and Sultan, C. Peripubertal female athletes in high-impact sports show improved bone mass acquisition and bone geometry. *Metabolism* 62: 1088–1098, 2013.

Malina, RM, Baxter-Jones, AD, Armstrong, N, Beunen, GP, Caine, D, Daly, RM, Lewis, RD, Rogol, AD, and Russell, K. Role of intensive training in the growth and maturation of artistic gymnasts. *Sports Med* 43: 783–802, 2013.

Malina, RM, Bouchard, C, and Bar-Or, O. *Growth, maturation, and physical activity* (2nd edn). Champaign, IL: Human Kinetics, 2004.

Mayhew, J, and Salm, P. Gender differences in anaerobic power tests. *Eur J Appl Physiol* 60: 133–138, 1990.

McKay, H, MacLean, L, Petit, M, MacKelvie-O'Brien, K, Janssen, P, Beck, T, and Khan, K. "Bounce at the Bell": A novel program of short bursts of exercise improves proximal femur bone mass in early pubertal children. *Br J Sports Med* 39: 521–526, 2005.

Mihata, LC, Beutler, AI, and Boden, BP. Comparing the incidence of anterior cruciate ligament injury in collegiate lacrosse, soccer, and basketball players: Implications for anterior cruciate ligament mechanism and prevention. *Am J Sports Med* 34: 899–904, 2006.

Miller, A., MacDougall, J, Tarnopolsky, M, and Sale, D. Gender differences in strength and muscle fiber characteristics. *Eur J Appl Physiol* 66: 254–262, 1992.

Moeller, J, and Lamb, M. Anterior cruciate ligament injuries in female athletes. *Phys Sportsmed* 25: 31–48, 1997.

Morris, F, Naughton, G, Gibbs, J, Carlson, J, and Wark, J. Prospective ten-month exercise intervention in premenarcheal girls: Positive effects on bone and lean mass. *J Bone Min Res* 12: 1453–1462, 1997.

Mountjoy, M, Sundgot-Borgen, J, Burke, L, Carter, S, Constantini, N, Lebrun, C, Meyer, N, Sherman, R, Steffen, K, Budgett, R, and Ljungqvist, A. The IOC consensus statement: beyond the Female Athlete Triad – Relative Energy Deficiency in Sport (RED-S). *Br J Sports Med* 48: 491–497, 2014.

Myer, GD, Brent, JL, Ford, KR, and Hewett, TE. Real-time assessment and neuromuscular training feedback techniques to prevent ACL injury in female athletes. *Strength Cond J* 33: 21–35, 2011a.

Myer, GD, Ford, FR, Best, TM, Bergeron, MF, and Hewett, TE. When to initiate neuromuscular training to reduce sport related injuries and enhance health and youth. *Curr Sports Med Rep* 10: 157–166, 2011b.

Myer, GD, Ford, KR, and Hewett, TE. Rationale and clinical techniques for anterior cruciate ligament injury prevention among female athletes. *J Athl Train* 39(4): 352, 2004.

Myer, GD, Ford, KR, Palumbo, OP, and Hewett, TE. Neuromuscular training improves performance and lower extremity biomechanics in female athletes. *J Strength Cond Res* 19: 51–60, 2005.

Myer, GD, Sugimoto, D, Thomas, S, and Hewett, TE. The influence of age on the effectiveness of neuromuscular training to reduce anterior cruciate ligament injury in female athletes: A meta-analysis. *Am J Sports Med* 41: 203–215, 2013.

National Strength and Conditioning Association. Strength training for female athletes. *NSCA J* 11: 43–55, 29–36, 1989.

Nattiv, A, Loucks, AB, Manore, MM, Sanborn, CF, Sundgot-Borgen, J, Warren, MP, and American College of Sports Medicine. American College of Sports Medicine position stand: The female triad. *Med Sci Sports Ex* 39: 1867–1882, 2007.

Nichols, D, Sanborn, C, and Love, A. Resistance training and bone mineral density in adolescent females. *J Pediatr* 139: 494–500, 2001.

Nichols, JF, Rauh, MJ, Lawson, MJ, Ji, M, and Barkai, HS. Prevalence of the female athlete triad syndrome among high school athletes. *Arch Paed Adoles Med* 160: 137–142, 2006.

Oosthuyse, T, and Bosch, AN. The effect of the menstrual cycle on exercise metabolism. *Sports medicine* 40(3): 207–227, 2010.

Otis, C, Drinkwater, B, and Johnson, M. American College of Sports Medicine: Position stand: The female athlete triad. *Med Sci Sports Exerc* 29: i–ix, 1997.

Padua, DA, Carcia, CR, Arnold, BL, and Granata KP. Sex differences in leg stiffness and stiffness recruitment strategy during two-legged hopping. *J Mot Behav* 37: 111–125, 2005.

Parker, DF, Round, JM, Sacco, P, and Jones, DA. A cross-sectional survey of upper and lower limb strength in boys and girls during childhood and adolescence. *Ann Hum Biol* 17: 199–211, 1990.

Quatman, CE, Ford, KR, Myer, GD, and Hewett, TE. Maturation leads to gender differences in landing force and vertical jump performance. *Am J Sports Med* 34: 806–813, 2006.

Quatman-Yates, CC, Myer, GD, Ford, KR, and Hewett, TE. A longitudinal evaluation of maturational effects on lower extremity strength in female adolescent athletes. *Pediatr Phys Ther* 25: 271–276, 2013.

Rauh, MJ, Nichols, JF, and Barrack, MT. Relationships among injury and disordered eating, menstrual dysfunction, and low bone mineral density in high school athletes: A prospective study. *J Athl Train* 45: 243–252, 2010.

Read, PJ, Oliver, JL, De Ste Croix, MBA, Myer, GD, and Lloyd, RS. Neuromuscular risk factors for knee and ankle injuries in male youth soccer players. *Sports Med* 46: 1059–1066, 2016. doi: 10.1007/s40279-016-0479.

Read, PJ, Oliver, JL, De Ste Croix, MBA, Myer, GD, and Lloyd, RS. The scientific foundations and associated injury risks of early soccer specialisation, *J Sports Sci*, 34: 2295–2302, 2016.

Reed, JL, Bowell, JL, Hill, BR, Williams, BA, De Souza, MJ, and Williams, NI. Exercising women with menstrual disturbances consume low energy dense foods and beverages. *Appl Physiol Nutr Metab* 36: 382–394, 2011.

Robinson, TL, Snow-Harter, C, Taaffe, DR, Gillis, D, Shaw, J, and Marcus, R. Gymnasts exhibit higher bone mass than runners despite similar prevalence of amenorrhea and oligomenorrhea. *J Bone Miner Res* 10: 26–35, 1995.

Round, JM, Jones, DA, Honour, JW, and Nevill, AM. Hormonal factors in the development of differences in strength between boys and girls during adolescence: A longitudinal study. *Ann Hum Biol* 26: 49–62, 1999.

Ryushi, T, Häkkinen, K, Kauhanen, H, and Komi, P. Muscle fiber characteristics, muscle cross sectional area and force production in strength athletes, physically active males and females. *Scand J Sports Sci* 10: 7–15, 1988.

Shephard, R. Exercise and training in women, part 1: Influence of gender on exercise and training response. *Can J Appl Physiol* 25: 19–34, 2000.

Stewart, CHE, and Rittweger, J. Adaptive processes in skeletal muscle: Molecular and genetic influences. *J Musculoskeltal Neruonal Interact* 6: 73–86, 2006.

Thein-Nissenbaum, JM, Rauh, MJ, Carr, E, Loud, KJ, and McGuine, TA. Menstrual irregularity and musculoskeletal injury in female high school athletes. *J Athl Train* 47: 74–82, 2012.

Van der Sluis, A, Elferink-Gemser, M, Brink, M, and Visscher, C. Importance of peak height velocity timing in terms of injuries in talented soccer players. *Int J Sports Med* 36(4): 327–332, 2015.

Vanheest, JL, Rodgers, CD, Mahoney, CE, and De Souza, MJ. Ovarian suppression impairs sport performance in junior elite female swimmers. *Med Sci Sports Ex* 46: 156–166, 2014.

Virvidakis, K, Georgiu, E, Korkotsidis, A, Ntalles, K, and Proukakis, C. Bone mineral content of junior competitive weightlifters. *Int J Sports Med* 11: 244–246, 1990.

West, R. The female athlete: The triad of disordered eating, amenorrhoea and osteoporosis. *Sports Med* 26: 63–71, 1998.

Williams, NI, Helmreich, DL, Parfitt, DB, Caston-Balderrama, A, and Cameron, JL. Evidence for a causal role of low energy availability in the induction of menstrual cycle disturbances during strenuous exercise training. *J Clin Endocrinol Metab* 86: 5184–5193, 2001.

Winsley, R, and Matos, N. Overtraining and elite young athletes. In: *The Elite Young Athlete*. Armstrong N, and McManus, AM (eds). Vol. 56, Med Sport Sci. Basel: Karger, 2011, pp. 97–105.

Wojtys, E, Huston, L, Lindenfeld, T, Hewett, T, and Greenfield, M. Association between the menstrual cycle and anterior cruciate injuries in female athletes. *Am J Sports Med* 26: 614–619, 1998.

Zazulak, BT, Hewett, TE, Reeves, NP, Goldberg, B, and Cholewicki, J. The effects of core proprioception on knee injury a prospective biomechanical-epidemiological study. *Am J Sports Med* 35(3): 368–373, 2007.

3
APPLYING STRENGTH AND CONDITIONING PRACTICES TO YOUNG ATHLETES

Rhodri S. Lloyd, John M. Radnor, Sylvia Moeskops, Robert W. Meyers, Paul J. Read and Jon L. Oliver

Introduction

Ever since Sid Robinson conducted the first experiment examining the response of children to exercise (Robinson, 1938), the field of paediatric exercise science has continued to advance our understanding of the way in which children respond to training. Now, nearly 80 years since Robinson's seminal work, the current evidence base shows that children differ to adults in terms of their acute cardiorespiratory response to exercise (Armstrong et al., 2015), metabolic and hormonal responses during exercise (Boisseau and Delamarche, 2000), ability to voluntarily activate muscle (Dotan et al., 2012), and the way in which they recover from high-intensity exercise (Falk and Dotan, 2006). Due to these physiological differences, adult-based training programmes should not be superimposed on young athletes, but rather training prescription should be commensurate with a child's levels of technical competency, training age, psychosocial maturity and stage of maturation.

The influence of growth and maturation

While notable differences in anatomy and physiology exist between children and adults, there are also clear differentiations between children and adolescents, which are mediated by growth and maturation. For example, force-producing capacities are lower in children when compared to adolescents or adults, partly as a result of the structure (O'Brien et al., 2010), size (Dotan et al., 2012), activation patterns (Dotan et al., 2013), and function (Waugh et al., 2013) of a child's muscle. Due to these inherent differences, children will typically be less effective at producing and attenuating forces, which may make them more susceptible to reductions in absolute physical performance. From a metabolic standpoint, research shows that children's metabolic profile favours oxidative metabolism (Ratel et al., 2006a), while recovery rates in youth (especially from high intensity exercise) are shorter than adults (Ratel et al., 2006b, Tibana et al., 2012). The greater fatigue resistance seen in children is typically due to a range of factors during exercise (e.g. smaller muscle mass, higher content of type I fibres, greater muscle oxidative activity, increased fat oxidation and lower impairment in neuromuscular activation and force output) and during recovery (e.g. faster PCr resynthesis, faster clearance of accumulated H+, faster regulation of acid-base balance, and faster return of cardiorespiratory parameters to baseline levels) (Ratel et al., 2006a). These two examples demonstrate potential age- or maturity-related effects on differential physiology between youth and adults, and underlines how such differences will likely impact upon training prescription. It should also be noted that as per adults, young athletes require the correct balance between training dosage in order to prepare them for the demands of sport, but also sufficient time for rest and recovery. However, what is unique to child and adolescent populations is that they will also require time outside of training to allow for natural growth processes to occur.

Throughout childhood and adolescence, all systems within the body (e.g. nervous, muscular, skeletal, endocrine) will develop independently and in a non-linear manner. *Biological maturation* is the process of progressing toward a mature state, and varies in magnitude (extent of change), timing (onset of change) and tempo (rate of change) between different systems in the body (Beunen and Malina, 2008) and between individuals (Lloyd et al., 2014c). Dependent on these variables, youth can be classified as biologically "ahead of" (early maturer), "on time" with (average maturer), or "behind" (late maturer) their chronological age (Malina et al., 2004). This inter-individual difference in biological maturation is evident when comparing a squad of young athletes of the same chronological age who may differ markedly in terms of maturation (Malina et al., 2012, Malina et al., 2015). Research shows that both physical and psychosocial development of children can be influenced by an individual's level of maturity (Lloyd et al., 2016a). For example, boys who experience maturation at an earlier stage than their peers will invariably be taller and heavier from late childhood and undergo a more intense adolescent growth spurt leading to large gains in muscle size and lean mass, and greater gains in force producing capacity. However, any discrepancies in stature between early, average and late maturers are almost nullified by the time they reach adulthood. Research has also shown that early maturing boys report more positive perceptions of their physical self (i.e. strength and power, physical fitness, physical appearance and sport competence) and possess higher levels of self-esteem compared to their peers (Cumming et al., 2012). Due to these preferential factors, it is unsurprising to observe earlier maturing youth choosing, and being selected for, those sports where greater size, strength and power are desirable attributes, such as in tennis (Myburgh et al., 2016), soccer (Malina et al., 2000), or basketball (Torres-Unda et al., 2013).

While certain aspects of growth and maturation are of benefit to performance and sporting success, rapid changes in the magnitude and rate of growth associated with the adolescent growth spurt have been shown to disrupt motor coordination (Philippaerts et al., 2006) and increase the relative risk of overuse and growth-related injury (Kemper et al., 2015, van der Sluis et al., 2014). During the growth spurt, youth are forced to move with increased mass and height of the centre of mass, without concomitant increases in neuromuscular adaptations, which lag behind in the maturational process. Additionally, from a psychosocial perspective, the way in which children are affected from maturing ahead of, or behind, their peers of the same chronological age remain unclear. Cumulatively, existing scientific evidence points to fact that the physical, physiological and psychosocial differences associated with childhood and adolescence makes the art of designing training programmes for youth an interesting and challenging process.

Developing movement skill competency

Determinants of movement skills

Fundamental movement skills (FMS) encompass locomotion, stabilisation and manipulation skills, which serve as building blocks for more complex movements commonly witnessed in sporting situations (Gallahue et al., 2012). Evidence suggests that developing a high level of movement

Table 3.1 Examples of different constraints on motor skill performance and development

Constraint	Variable	Example in practice
Individual		
Structural	Height, weight	Tall *versus* short adolescent male performing a bodyweight squat
Functional	Motivation, fear	Confident *versus* apprehensive child performing a jump from box
Task	Rules	Hopping on one leg *versus* hopping on either leg in relay races
	Degree of challenge	Throwing a ball for distance *versus* throwing at a target
	Type of equipment	Using a youth training barbell *versus* a full-size Olympic barbell
Environmental	Flooring	Horizontal jump on a concrete floor *versus* gymnastics matting
	Lighting	Practice in daytime *versus* floodlit evening training

skill competency in youth increases the likelihood of long-term participation in physical activity (Lloyd et al., 2014a). As a result, physically literate children may experience various health- and fitness-related benefits (Lubans et al., 2010), engage in higher amounts of physical activity (Barnett et al., 2009) and potentially reduce injury risk (Larsen et al., 2016) in comparison to their physically illiterate counterparts (Faigenbaum et al., 2016, Hardy et al., 2012). The development of FMS during childhood and adolescence occurs as a result of the interaction between individual, task and environmental constraints (Gallahue et al., 2012), and it is ultimately this interaction of constraints which leads to within- and between-individual variations in rates and magnitudes of motor skill development. Details of the different types of constraints and examples of how they can be manipulated by the strength and conditioning coach are presented in Table 3.1.

Movement competency is a multidimensional concept (Rudd et al., 2016) combining cognitive processing abilities with coordination and adequate amounts of relative strength (Lloyd et al., 2015). Although correct execution of fundamental motor skills requires coordinated sequencing of multimuscle, multijoint, multiplanar movements, there will always be a requirement for complementary force production and force attenuation. Neuromuscular coordination and force production are governed by neural activation and control, and thus it is optimal to target the development of motor skills and muscular strength at a time when the corticospinal tissue in children is highly "plastic" (Myer et al., 2013). Furthermore, the primacy of strength in the acquisition of all other fitness components (Behringer et al., 2011) warrants its inclusion as a training priority during all stages of any young athlete's development (Lloyd and Oliver, 2012, Lloyd et al., 2016a). Practitioners should not view coordination and muscular strength as separate entities but rather synergistic components of motor skill performance (Cattuzzo et al., 2014) that should be developed concurrently during early childhood.

Trainability of movement skills

Owing to the movement patterns and biomechanical similarities of FMS with sports-specific skills and daily living tasks (Tompsett et al., 2014), the trainability of movement competency in youth can be viewed as an essential component of training for lifelong physical development. Childhood appears to be the optimal time to develop motor skill competency, as neuromuscular maturation is heightened, due to greater levels of neural plasticity (Casey et al., 2005). However, irrespective of the accelerated maturation of the central nervous system, children will not naturally develop FMS without the opportunity to regularly practice these skills (Hardy et al., 2012). Research has demonstrated that with appropriately designed training programmes, inclusive of motor skill and strength development stimuli, children and adolescents can make worthwhile adaptations in motor skills (Faigenbaum et al., 2011). Previous meta-analytical data has shown that pre- and early-pubertal youth can achieve approximately 50% greater training-induced gains in motor skills following resistance training interventions compared to adolescents (Behringer et al., 2011). This suggests that motor skills are most trainable during early childhood, advocating the pre-pubertal years as the optimal time to begin fundamental motor skill training.

Prior to the onset of puberty, the training focus should centre around fundamental movement skills, followed by sports-specific skills during later developmental stages (Lloyd and Oliver, 2012). In addition to the development of FMS, strength and conditioning coaches should also look to develop a breadth of athletic motor skill competencies (AMSC), which incorporate upper body pushing/pulling and lower body bilateral/unilateral lower body movements, plyometric abilities, and trunk conditioning activities (Lloyd and Oliver, 2014). Figure 3.1 provides an overview of the AMSC. The use of educational gymnastics to teach movement concepts may offer a different and enjoyable addition to young athletes' programmes (Baumgarten and Pagnano-Richardson, 2010). Simple bodyweight management tasks involving gymnastic shapes, positions and partner balances can serve as a viable means of promoting multiple fitness components. This holistic approach to the physical training of youth aims to facilitate performance and increase young athletes' preparedness for the future demands of competitive sport.

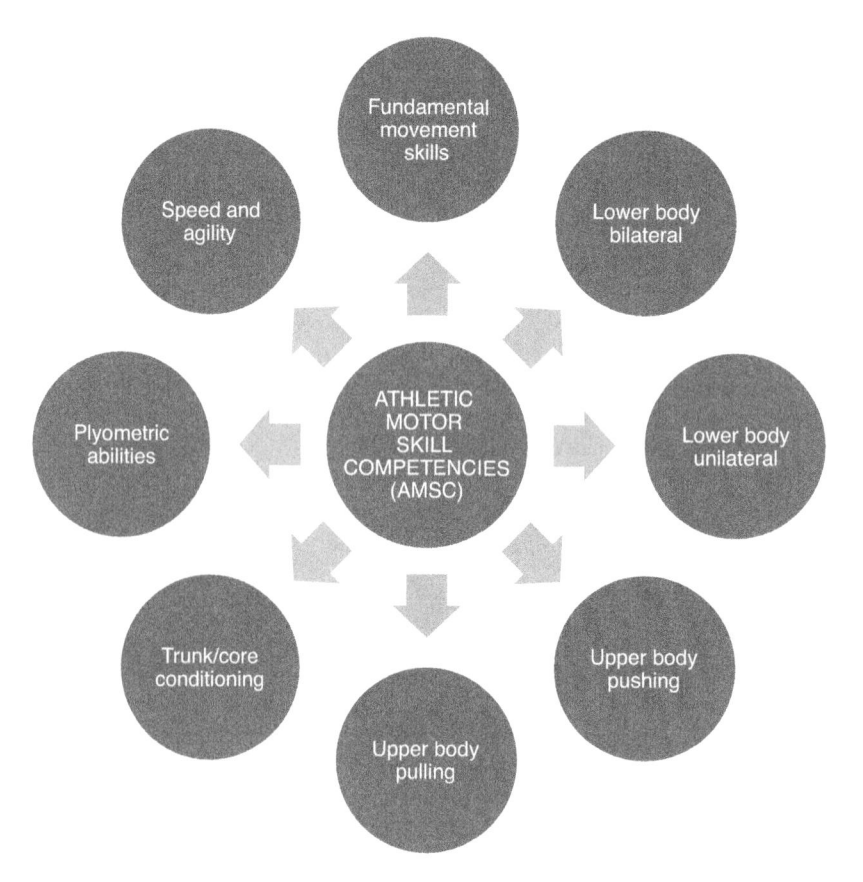

Figure 3.1 Athletic motor skill competencies (adapted from Lloyd and Oliver, 2014)

The development of broad ranging FMS is also of particular concern for those involved in early specialisation sports (Myer et al., 2015). Research has shown that these young athletes are potentially at a greater risk of injury due to muscular imbalances resulting from highly repetitive sports-specific training (Myer et al., 2015). Practitioners should attempt to address movement skill deficiencies and/or muscle strength imbalances in these athletes through the development of gross athleticism that has relevance to sports performance, instead of simply attempting to load movement patterns that closely mirror those seen in the sport. Another challenging scenario for strength and conditioning coaches is determining when adolescent athletes who have not previously participated in formalised strength and conditioning should enter their programme. In such a scenario, professionals working with paediatric populations should initially attempt to develop a breadth and depth of FMS and AMSC before progressing them to more advanced modes of training.

Developing strength and power

Determinants of strength and power

Muscle strength and power increase as children transition towards adulthood, often coinciding with changes in body weight and lean body mass (Malina et al., 2004). Considering that muscle cross-sectional area is a major predictor of force production in children (Tonson et al., 2008), a factor that results in the improved capacity to produce force during maturation may be an increase in muscle size (O'Brien et al., 2010). However, when normalised to muscle cross-sectional area (mCSA), adults still produce greater force than children (Falk et al., 2009). Therefore, it can be assumed that additional factors will influence force production as a result of growth and maturation. From a structural perspective, fascicle length increases from childhood through to adolescence (Kubo et al., 2014), which improves force production at higher shortening speeds and over larger length ranges, due to a greater number of sarcomeres in-series (Blazevich, 2006). Similarly, muscle fibre pennation angle increases throughout maturation (Binzoni et al., 2001), which results in a greater physiological mCSA and an increased number of muscle fascicles attaching to the aponeurosis or tendon, both of which increase force producing capacity.

Force production in children and adolescents is also influenced by maturation of the central nervous system, with specific adaptations including improvements in motor unit recruitment (Granacher et al., 2011), firing frequency and neural myelination (Kraemer et al., 1989, Ramsay et al., 1990). As children transition into adolescence, they will naturally improve their ability to recruit their high-threshold type II motor units, thereby enhancing their ability to produce both the magnitude of force output and rate at which the force is developed (Dotan et al., 2013). Other neural adaptations that manifest throughout childhood and adolescence impacting on strength and power production include increased muscle preactivation (Lloyd et al., 2012), decreased co-contraction (Croce et al., 2004), and reductions in electromechanical delay (Waugh et al., 2013). Combined, these structural and neural variables will influence the way in which young athletes can express strength and power during sports, and coaches should be aware of these developmental changes in order to be confident that those adaptations witnessed following a training intervention are not simply reflective of natural development mediated by growth and maturation.

Trainability of strength and power

It is now acknowledged by leading authorities that well-supervised resistance training is a safe and effective training mode for children and adolescents (Lloyd et al., 2014b). Significant improvements in the strength and power of youth have been reported following exposure to a variety of training protocols, including manual resistance, machine weights, plyometric training, medicine balls and elastic bands (Lloyd et al., 2014b). Research also shows that resistance training in children and adolescents can lead to significant improvements in strength beyond that produced by natural development (Lloyd et al., 2014b); however, the response to strength training may be influenced by maturation, with circa- and post-pubertal children displaying almost twice the gains in strength compared to pre-pubertal children (Behringer et al., 2010).

Meta-analytical data including 42 studies has shown that average resistance training prescription for youth is typically prescribed using 2–3 sets, 8–15 repetitions, and loads of 60–80% 1RM, with training periods lasting approximately 10 weeks (Behringer et al., 2010). However, a more recent meta-analysis that examined resistance training specifically in young athletes attempted to examine the optimal dose-response for youth. The research showed that the most effective training prescription for strength gains required longer periods of training (>23 weeks), the use of heavier loads (80–89% of 1 repetition maximum) and greater training volumes (5 sets of 6–8 repetitions) (Lesinski et al., 2016). Cumulatively, it would appear that as a child becomes more experienced and acquires higher levels of athleticism, resistance training prescription would need to change, especially in terms of the volume and intensity of training.

Recent data indicate that children and adolescents may respond differently to specific types of resistance training (Lloyd et al., 2016b, Radnor et al., 2017). Lloyd et al. (2016) showed that in response to a short-term training intervention, plyometric training elicited the greatest gains in markers of sprint and jump performance in children who were pre-peak height velocity, whereas combined strength and plyometric training was the most effective in eliciting change in the same variables for boys who were post-peak height velocity. On an individual response basis, Radnor et al. (2017) showed that irrespective of maturation, combined strength and plyometric training may serve as the most potent training stimulus for individuals to make short-term improvements in jump and sprint performance (Radnor et al., 2017). Considering that pre-pubertal children experience a natural increase in neural coordination and central nervous system maturation during childhood, the high neural demand during plyometric training may provide an augmented training response, recently termed "synergistic adaptation" (Lloyd et al., 2016b). Similarly, as post-pubertal children experience increases in testosterone and natural morphological changes that facilitate force generation, the combination of plyometric and strength training may result in a heightened maturity-related training stimulus (Lloyd et al., 2016b).

While most children will make positive adaptations from resistance training, there will be large individual variability in the response to resistance training due to the timing and tempo of maturation. Thus, practitioners should routinely change the primary training mode to facilitate long-term adaptation, and prescribe periodised and developmentally appropriate training programmes.

Developing speed

Determinants of speed

Sprint speed is suggested to develop in a non-linear fashion throughout childhood and adolescence (Malina et al., 2004), with spurts identified during both pre-adolescence and adolescence (Meyers et al., 2015a, Viru et al., 1999). Longitudinal data from boys suggest that peak improvements in sprint speed occur around the period of peak height velocity (Philippaerts et al., 2006). Furthermore, data collected over a two-year period suggest that 13–15 year old boys (circa-pubertal) elicit up to twice the improvement in sprint speed compared to 15–17 year olds (post-pubertal) (Hirose and Seki, 2015). Such observations further reinforce the non-linear nature of speed development in youth and the potential influence of maturational processes.

Speed is the product of step length and step frequency (Hunter et al., 2004), and in youth it has been suggested that step frequency is largely stable, with increases in sprint speed proportional to increases in step length and leg length (Schepens et al., 1998). However, more recent research has shown that step frequency may decrease during the pre-pubertal period, offsetting the increases in step length observed during this period, resulting in no increases in sprint performance (Meyers et al., 2015a). Once step frequency stabilised around peak height velocity, increases in speed became apparent (Meyers et al., 2015a). Multiple regression analysis has also indicated that maximal sprint performance in pre-pubertal boys may be more step frequency reliant (58% explained variance) whilst post-pubertal boys are marginally more reliant on step length (54% explained variance) (Meyers et al., 2015b), further highlighting the influence of maturation upon sprint performance in youth.

The role of strength and power as determinants of sprint performance in youth has been consistently supported in the literature (Lloyd et al., 2016b, Meylan et al., 2014a, Rumpf et al., 2012, Rumpf et al., 2015b). Rumpf et al. (2015b) reported that combined horizontal force and power accounted for 98–99% of the explained variance in sprint performance of boys classified as pre- and post-peak height velocity. Recent longitudinal data has also indicated that measures of relative force production alongside relative lower limb stiffness are also important determinants of maximal sprint performance for boys who are pre-pubertal and those experiencing peak height velocity, collectively accounting for 78–98% of the explained variance (Meyers et al., 2016).

Trainability of speed

The literature relating to the most effective training methods to enhance sprint performance in youth is sparse; however, a systematic review on youth sprint training (Rumpf et al., 2012) and a recent resistance training study (Lloyd et al., 2016b) have highlighted that plyometric training may be the most effective method to enhance sprint performance in pre-pubertal male youth, whilst a combined approach may be most beneficial for those post peak height velocity. Furthermore, a recent training study utilising sled-towing reported no significant changes in sprint performance for pre-pubertal male youth, yet significant increases for a combined circa/post-pubertal group in sprint speed, step length and step frequency as well as horizontal force, power and lower limb stiffness elicited during the sprint (Rumpf et al., 2015a). Such observations may question the role of resisted methods of training for sprint performance in youth; however, it is important to note that improvements in sprint performance in pre-pubertal samples have been reported following resistance training (~2.1%), despite the magnitude of these changes being reduced compared to circa- (~3.6%) and post-pubertal (~3.1%) groups (Meylan et al., 2014b). It is also important to note that there is a dearth of data pertaining to the effect of free sprinting upon sprint performance in youth, despite this mode of training having the highest potential for transfer to increased sprint performance over a range of distances in adults (Rumpf et al., 2016). These data reinforce that practitioners seeking to develop speed in children and adolescents should provide a varied training programme encompassing a variety of training stimuli, whilst being mindful of the favourable synergistic changes that may occur as a result of mapping the training stimuli with naturally occurring adaptations (Faigenbaum et al., 2016, Lloyd et al., 2016b).

Developing endurance

Determinants of endurance

Endurance is synonymous with the aerobic system and the ability to maintain lower intensity exercise over a long duration. However, the aerobic system also enables recovery to take place following bouts of high-intensity exercise. Endurance is determined by three physiological factors: peak oxygen uptake ($\dot{V}O_{2peak}$), the anaerobic threshold and economy. Peak oxygen uptake is the primary determinant of endurance exercise and is the product of cardiac output and the ability of the muscle to extract and utilise oxygen. Absolute values of $\dot{V}O_{2peak}$ increase by 150% in boys and 80% in girls between the ages of 8 and 16 years old (Armstrong and Welsman, 1994). These large gains are driven by growth in body size, heart size and blood volume increasing cardiac output. When compared to girls, boys experience greater gains in size during adolescence and also benefit from greater increases in red blood cells and haemoglobin, further enhancing oxygen transport capacity (Malina et al., 2004). Conversely, girls also have to contend with increased fat mass during adolescence and this will negatively affect events where body mass has to be moved.

In terms of muscle metabolism immature children have lower levels of glycolytic activity and are more reliant on aerobic energy compared to more mature children and adults. This means immature children produce less lactic acid, suffer less fatigue during exercise, can recover more quickly and can maintain exercise at a higher relative physiological intensity. Previous research has reported that the anaerobic threshold occurred at 71% of $\dot{V}O_{2peak}$ in 5–6 year old boys, reducing to 61% of $\dot{V}O_{2peak}$ in 15–16 year adolescent boys and with a similar trend observed in girls (Reybrouck et al., 1985). Running economy improves steadily with age in children and adolescents, with the oxygen cost of running at a set speed reducing by almost 20% from 5 to 18 years old in boys and girls (Mahon, 2008). Changes in body size, increases in strength, improvements in technique and reduced co-contraction may all help explain improvements in economy (Bar-Or and Rowland, 2004). The accumulation of the above physiological changes means that endurance performance improves markedly due to maturation, with one mile run times decreasing by ~20% in boys and ~6% in girls between the ages of 9 and 17 years old (Catley and Tomkinson, 2013).

Trainability of endurance

The "trigger hypothesis" suggested that children will not be responsive to training prior to the onset of puberty and the accompanying increases in circulating androgenic hormones (Katch, 1983). However, a series of review articles and expert statements examining a large body of evidence have all concluded that children and adolescents are responsive to aerobic training throughout maturation (Armstrong and Barker, 2011, Baxter-Jones and Maffulli, 2003, Baquet et al., 2003, Harrison et al., 2015, McNarry et al., 2014). Most of the evidence has focused on the trainability of $\dot{V}O_{2peak}$, with research suggesting that short-term training interventions typically improve $\dot{V}O_{2peak}$ by ~5–8% in both boys and girls (Armstrong and Barker, 2011, Baquet et al., 2003).

Table 3.2 provides guidelines to consider when designing an aerobic training program for youth. The most important factor is to ensure the intensity of exercise is sufficiently high. In team sports, small-sided games can provide a fun and stimulating challenge while providing a high exercise intensity that will stimulate improvements in endurance (Harrison et al., 2015), with less technically demanding games allowing children to maintain a higher work intensity (Harrison et al., 2014). Interval training has also been shown to be successful at increasing the anaerobic threshold of youth (Mahon and Vaccaro, 1989, McManus et al., 2005). It has been

Table 3.2 Factors to be considered when designing training programmes to maximise the improvement in the $\dot{V}O_{2peak}$ of youth (Armstrong and Barker, 2011; Baquet et al., 2003; Harrison et al., 2015; McNarry et al., 2014)

Genetics	Responsiveness to training will be influenced by genetics
Maturity	There is no need to align training to specific periods of maturation
Baseline fitness	Expect those with lower initial fitness to respond more to training
Type of exercise	Continuous and interval training can both be successful, but the latter is likely to provide better results
Frequency	Three sessions per week
Session duration	30–60 min
Intensity	Intensity is crucial, 85% HRmax to all-out exercise

stated that improvements are dependent on exercise being completed at a high intensity (Armstrong and Barker, 2011) and it is likely that the anaerobic threshold is more sensitive to training than $\dot{V}O_{2peak}$ in children and adolescents (Mahon, 2008). The benefits of endurance training to improve economy in youth are equivocal. It may be that long-term endurance training is needed to improve economy, or that other forms of training (such as strength and plyometric training) are more effective for improving economy, but more research is needed to confirm this.

Programming for athletic development

While practitioners will intuitively adopt their preferred philosophy of periodisation, it is generally accepted that in order to elicit the greatest adaptive response, systematic planning of sequential blocks of training is more effective than random and unplanned training. Recent literature has advocated that the training of young athletes should be viewed as a long-term process, to avoid coaches, parents, or the athletes themselves seeking short-term gains at the expense of the overall health and well-being of the child (Lloyd et al., 2015). While all youth can make worthwhile gains in physical performance in response to structured strength and conditioning programmes, coaches should never increase the intensity, volume or frequency of training at the expense of technical competency or the degree of enjoyment of the child.

Existing periodisation literature for training youth remains relatively short-term in nature. Behringer et al. (2010) published a meta-analysis examining the effectiveness of resistance training in children, and showed that the mean intervention period across the 42 included studies was just 9.9 ± 3.7 weeks. However, while the evidence base of long-term, periodised training interventions in young athletes remains somewhat sparse, more recent research (albeit lacking in specific training details) has shown the beneficial effects in young athletes of 2-year periodised training programmes on measures of strength (Keiner et al., 2013), power (Sander et al., 2013), and change-of-direction-speed (Keiner et al., 2014). Of note, Keiner et al. (2013) showed the potential trainability of strength in young athletes, with trained 16–19 year old soccer players expressing relative strength levels of 2.0×body weight in the squat exercise.

When looking to periodise training programmes, coaches will invariably separate the annual training plan into a combination of different periods, namely the: i) preparation period, ii) competition period and iii) transition period (Haff, 2013). The purpose of the preparation period is to suitably prepare the athlete for the demands of the next block of training (e.g. competition

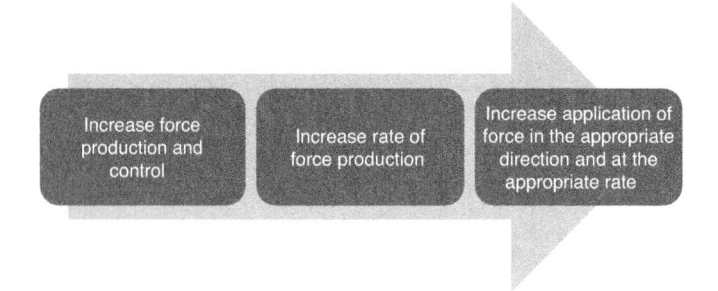

Figure 3.2 Systematic progression of force production

period) and is traditionally sub-divided into the general preparation phase (GPP) and the specific preparation phase (SPP). Classic periodisation literature suggests that the GPP should focus on using a variety of training means to develop the foundations of the athlete's training base across a range of fitness components and movement skills (Issurin, 2009). Conversely, the SPP takes on a more sport-specific training emphasis, ultimately trying to capitalise on the adaptations realised within the GPP (Bompa and Haff, 2009). Given the current prevalence of physical inactivity in youth (Tremblay et al., 2014) and that it is not uncommon for young athletes who are entering sporting pathways to show a lack of proficiency in key athletic movement patterns (Parsonage et al., 2014, Woods et al., 2016), coaches should devote more time to the GPP as opposed to advancing young athletes to the SPP before they are physically prepared to tolerate more sport-specific training. Within the GPP, coaches should seek to develop a breadth and depth of athletic motor skill competencies in their young athletes, aiming to develop both the quality of movement and the ability to produce and attenuate force. This approach is much like building a house, whereby the bricks need to be positioned carefully in straight lines (movement quality), but concrete (muscle strength) is required to make the house robust. Figure 3.2 provides an overview of how strength and conditioning coaches can approach the development of force producing capabilities in young athletes. Specifically, initial focus should be on enhancing the athlete's ability to produce force with control, following which emphasis can then be placed on increasing the rate of force production as most sports or recreational activities require rapid expressions of force. Finally, the application of force in the required direction and at the appropriate rates relevant for sports can then be targeted to optimise the transfer of training effect. As a caveat, coaches should remember that strength is the foundation for explosive movement (Cormie et al., 2011); thus, practitioners are advised to strategically develop this physical quality with their athletes prior to seeking more sports specific adaptations.

Novice athletes should remain in the GPP for a large proportion of the year (Haff, 2013), even if this includes portions of the competitive period, as they will likely continue to show physical adaptations simply from improving base levels of athleticism. However, for those athletes who have been integrated within a long-term athletic development pathway for a greater period of time, the coach will invariably need to be more systematic and intricate with their programming. For athletes that have accumulated more training experience, it is reasonable to expect more time being devoted to the SPP as they seek to build on their already developed athletic qualities. Recent evidence, albeit with small sample sizes, shows diminishing increases in strength and power as training experience increases, and that worthwhile changes in both qualities may take longer in those athletes who are closer to their ceiling potential (Baker, 2013). Therefore, more sophisticated arrangements of mesocycles (typically blocks of 4–6 weeks) and more targeted microcycle design (typically 7 days) will likely become necessary as the young athlete progresses along their sporting pathway.

Irrespective of training history, a young athlete needs to be afforded transition periods to enable recovery and regeneration from the multiple demands of training, competing and other stressors (e.g. school or social demands). However, unique to youth populations is that these periods of active recovery are necessary to facilitate growth-related processes to occur (Lloyd et al., 2016a). These phases are also important to safeguard against the negative effects of accumulated fatigue and potential risks of overuse injury. An example of this is apparent in recent recommendations whereby young baseball pitchers are encouraged to pitch for no more than 8 months within a 12-month time frame to reduce the risk of overuse injury in the shoulder (Rice et al., 2012). Abiding by the use of transition periods can be a challenging process for young athletes, as many will be involved in multiple sports during their childhood and adolescent years. For these multisport athletes, sporting seasons can trail one another or even overlap (e.g. winter and summer sports), resulting in youth not having a clear break in competition throughout the year. This underlines the need for a holistic and well-rounded approach to developing young athletes, where communication is a priority between those individuals involved in their development, such as parents, sports coaches, strength and conditioning coaches, and medical personnel.

Summary

It is clear that the most effective way to develop young athletes is for coaches to possess excellent levels of pedagogical and coaching skill, in addition to a sound underpinning knowledge of paediatric exercise science. Children and adolescents are unique populations that require developmentally appropriate training prescription to foster the long-term development of athleticism. While Olympic medals and World Championships are not won during the developing years, strength and conditioning coaches have a vital role to play in laying the foundations that will serve young athletes for a lifetime of successful sports participation.

References

Armstrong, N. and Barker, A. R. 2011. Endurance training and elite young athletes. *Med Sports Sci*, 56, 59–83.
Armstrong, N. and Welsman, J. R. 1994. Assessment and interpretation of aerobic fitness in children and adolescents. *Exerc Sport Sci Rev*, 22, 435–76.
Armstrong, N., Barker, A. R. and McManus, A. M. 2015. Muscle metabolism changes with age and maturation: How do they relate to youth sport performance? *Br J Sports Med*, 49, 860–4.
Baker, D. G. 2013. 10-year changes in upper body strength and power in elite professional rugby league players – The effect of training age, stage, and content. *J Strength Cond Res*, 27, 285–92.
Baquet, G., Van Praagh, E. and Berthoin, S. 2003. Endurance training and aerobic fitness in young people. *Sports Med*, 33, 1127–43.
Barnett, L. M., Van Beurden, E., Morgan, P. J., Brooks, L. O. and Beard, J. R. 2009. Childhood motor skill proficiency as a predictor of adolescent physical activity. *J Adolesc Health*, 44, 252–9.
Bar-Or, O. and Rowland, T. W. 2004. *Pediatric Exercise Medicine: From Physiological Principles to Health Care Application*. Champaign, IL: Human Kinetics.
Baumgarten, S. and Pagnano-Richardson, K. 2010. Educational gymnastics: Enhancing children's physical literacy. *J Phys Educ Recreat Dance*, 81, 18–25.
Baxter-Jones, A. D. and Maffulli, N. 2003. Endurance in young athletes: It can be trained. *Br J Sports Med*, 37, 96–7.
Behringer, M., Vom Heede, A., Matthews, M. and Mester, J. 2011. Effects of strength training on motor performance skills in children and adolescents: A meta-analysis. *Pediatr Exerc Sci*, 23, 186–206.

Behringer, M., Vom Heede, A., Yue, Z. and Mester, J. 2010. Effects of resistance training in children and adolescents: A meta-analysis. *Pediatrics*, 126, e1199–210.

Beunen, G. P. and Malina, R. M. 2008. Growth and biological maturation: Relevance to athletic performance. *In:* Hebestreit, H. and Bar-Or, O. (eds.) *The Young Athlete*. Oxford: Blackwell Publishing.

Binzoni, T., Bianchi, S., Hanquinet, S., Kaelin, A., Sayegh, Y., Dumont, M. and Jequier, S. 2001. Human gastrocnemius medialis pennation angle as a function of age: From newborn to the elderly. *J Physiol Anthropol Appl Human Sci*, 20, 293–8.

Blazevich, A. J. 2006. Effects of physical training and detraining, immobilisation, growth and aging on human fascicle geometry. *Sports Med*, 36, 1003–17.

Boisseau, N. and Delamarche, P. 2000. Metabolic and hormonal responses to exercise in children and adolescents. *Sports Med*, 30, 405–22.

Bompa, T. O. and Haff, G. G. 2009. *Periodization: Theory and Methodology of Training*. Champaign, IL: Human Kinetics.

Casey, B. J., Tottenham, N., Liston, C. and Durston, S. 2005. Imaging the developing brain: What have we learned about cognitive development? *Trends Cogn Sci*, 9, 104–10.

Catley, M. J. and Tomkinson, G. R. 2013. Normative health-related fitness values for children: Analysis of 85347 test results on 9–17-year-old Australians since 1985. *Br J Sports Med*, 47, 98–108.

Cattuzzo, M. T., Dos Santos Henrique, R., Re, A. H., De Oliveira, I. S., Melo, B. M., De Sousa Moura, M., De Araujo, R. C. and Stodden, D. 2014. Motor competence and health related physical fitness in youth: A systematic review. *J Sci Med Sport*, 19.

Cormie, P., McGuigan, M. R. and Newton, R. U. 2011. Developing maximal neuromuscular power: Part 1 – Biological basis of maximal power production. *Sports Med*, 41, 17–38.

Croce, R. V., Russell, P. J., Swartz, E. E. and Decoster, L. C. 2004. Knee muscular response strategies differ by developmental level but not gender during jump landing. *Electromyogr Clin Neurophysiol*, 44, 339–48.

Cumming, S. P., Sherar, L. B., Pindus, D. M., Coelho-e-Silva, M. J., Malina, R. M. and Jardine, P. R. 2012. A biocultural model of maturity-associated variance in adolescent physical activity. *Int Rev Sport Exerc Psychol*, 5, 23–43.

Dotan, R., Mitchell, C., Cohen, R., Gabriel, D., Klentrou, P. and Falk, B. 2013. Child-adult differences in the kinetics of torque development. *J Sports Sci*, 31, 945–53.

Dotan, R., Mitchell, C., Cohen, R., Klentrou, P., Gabriel, D. and Falk, B. 2012. Child-adult differences in muscle activation – A review. *Pediatr Exerc Sci*, 24, 2–21.

Faigenbaum, A. D., Farrell, A., Fabiano, M., Radler, T., Naclerio, F., Ratamess, N. A., Kang, J. and Myer, G. D. 2011. Effects of integrative neuromuscular training on fitness performance in children. *Pediatr Exerc Sci*, 23, 573–84.

Faigenbaum, A. D., Lloyd, R. S., MacDonald, J. and Myer, G. D. 2016. Citius, Altius, Fortius: Beneficial effects of resistance training for young athletes: Narrative review. *Br J Sports Med*, 50, 3–7.

Falk, B. and Dotan, R. 2006. Child-adult differences in the recovery from high-intensity exercise. *Exerc Sport Sci Rev*, 34, 107–12.

Falk, B., Usselman, C., Dotan, R., Brunton, L., Klentrou, P., Shaw, J. and Gabriel, D. 2009. Child-adult differences in muscle strength and activation pattern during isometric elbow flexion and extension. *Appl Physiol Nutr Metab*, 34, 609–15.

Gallahue, D. L., Ozmun, J. C. and Goodway, J. D. 2012. *Understanding Motor Development*. New York: McGraw-Hill.

Granacher, U., Goesele, A., Roggo, K., Wischer, T., Fischer, S., Zuerny, C., Gollhofer, A. and Kriemler, S. 2011. Effects and mechanisms of strength training in children. *Int J Sports Med*, 32, 357–64.

Haff, G. G. 2013. Periodization strategies for youth development. *In:* Lloyd, R. S. and Oliver, J. L. (eds.) *Strength and Conditioning for Young Athletes: Science and Application*. Oxford, UK: Routledge.

Hardy, L. L., Reinten-Reynolds, T., Espinel, P., Zask, A. and Okely, A. D. 2012. Prevalence and correlates of low fundamental movement skill competency in children. *Pediatrics*, 130, e390–8.

Harrison, C. B., Gill, N. D., Kinugasa, T. and Kilding, A. E. 2015. Development of aerobic fitness in young team sport athletes. *Sports Med*, 45, 969–83.

Harrison, C. B., Kilding, A. E., Gill, N. D. and Kinugasa, T. 2014. Small-sided games for young athletes: Is game specificity influential? *J Sports Sci*, 32, 336–44.

Hirose, N. and Seki, T. 2015. Two-year changes in anthropometric and motor ability values as talent identification indexes in youth soccer players. *J Sci Med Sport*, 19, 158–162.

Hunter, J. P., Marshall, R. N. and McNair, P. J. 2004. Interaction of step length and step rate during sprint running. *Med Sci Sports Exerc*, 36, 261–71.

Issurin, V. B. 2009. Generalized training effects induced by athletic preparation. A review. *J Sports Med Phys Fitness*, 49, 333–45.

Katch, V. L. 1983. Physical conditioning of children. *J Adolesc Health Care*, 3, 241–6.

Keiner, M., Sander, A., Wirth, K., Caruso, O., Immesberger, P. and Zawieja, M. 2013. Strength performance in youth: Trainability of adolescents and children in the back and front squats. *J Strength Cond Res*, 27, 357–62.

Keiner, M., Sander, A., Wirth, K. and Schmidtbleicher, D. 2014. Long-term strength training effects on change-of-direction sprint performance. *J Strength Cond Res*, 28, 223–31.

Kemper, G. L., Van der Sluis, A., Brink, M. S., Visscher, C., Frencken, W. G. and Elferink-Gemser, M. T. 2015. Anthropometric injury risk factors in elite-standard youth soccer. *Int J Sports Med*, 36, 1112–7.

Kraemer, W. J., Fry, A. C., Frykman, P. N., Conroy, B. and Hoffman, J. 1989. Resistance training and youth. *Pediatric Exercise Science*, 1, 336–50.

Kubo, K., Teshima, T., Ikebukuro, T., Hirose, N. and Tsunoda, N. 2014. Tendon properties and muscle architecture for knee extensors and plantar flexors in boys and men. *Clin Biomech (Bristol, Avon)*, 29, 506–11.

Larsen, L. R., Kristensen, P. L., Junge, T., Moller, S. F., Juul-Kristensen, B. and Wedderkopp, N. 2016. Motor performance as risk factor for lower extremity injuries in children. *Med Sci Sports Exerc*, 48, 1136–43.

Lesinski, M., Prieske, O. and Granacher, U. 2016. Effects and dose-response relationships of resistance training on physical performance in youth athletes: A systematic review and meta-analysis. *Br J Sports Med*, 50: 781–795.

Lloyd, M., Saunders, T. J., Bremer, E. and Tremblay, M. S. 2014a. Long-term importance of fundamental motor skills: A 20-year follow-up study. *Adapt Phys Activ Q*, 31, 67–78.

Lloyd, R. S., Cronin, J. B., Faigenbaum, A. D., Haff, G. G., Howard, R., Kraemer, W. J., Micheli, L. J., Myer, G. D. and Oliver, J. L. 2016a. National strength and conditioning association position statement on long-term athletic development. *J Strength Cond Res*, 30, 1491–509.

Lloyd, R. S., Faigenbaum, A. D., Stone, M. H., Oliver, J. L., Jeffreys, I., Moody, J. A., Brewer, C., Pierce, K. C., McCambridge, T. M., Howard, R., Herrington, L., Hainline, B., Micheli, L. J., Jaques, R., Kraemer, W. J., McBride, M. G., Best, T. M., Chu, D. A., Alvar, B. A. and Myer, G. D. 2014b. Position statement on youth resistance training: The 2014 International Consensus. *Br J Sports Med*, 48, 498–505.

Lloyd, R. S. and Oliver, J. L. 2012. The youth physical development model: A new approach to long-term athletic development. *Strength Cond J*, 34, 61–72.

Lloyd, R. S. and Oliver, J. L. 2014. The developing athlete. *In:* Joyce, D. and Lewindon, D. (eds.) *High Performance Sports Conditioning*. Champaign, IL: Human Kinetics.

Lloyd, R. S., Oliver, J. L., Faigenbaum, A. D., Howard, R., De Ste Croix, M. B., Williams, C. A., Best, T. M., Alvar, B. A., Micheli, L. J., Thomas, D. P., Hatfield, D. L., Cronin, J. B. and Myer, G. D. 2015. Long-term athletic development – part 1: A pathway for all youth. *J Strength Cond Res*, 29, 1439–50.

Lloyd, R. S., Oliver, J. L., Faigenbaum, A. D., Myer, G. D. and De Ste Croix, M. B. 2014c. Chronological age vs. biological maturation: Implications for exercise programming in youth. *J Strength Cond Res*, 28, 1454–64.

Lloyd, R. S., Oliver, J. L., Hughes, M. G. and Williams, C. A. 2012. Age-related differences in the neural regulation of stretch-shortening cycle activities in male youths during maximal and sub-maximal hopping. *J Electromyogr Kinesiol*, 22, 37–43.

Lloyd, R. S., Radnor, J. M., De Ste Croix, M. B., Cronin, J. B. and Oliver, J. L. 2016b. Changes in sprint and jump performances after traditional, plyometric, and combined resistance training in male youth pre- and post-peak height velocity. *J Strength Cond Res*, 30, 1239–47.

Lubans, D. R., Morgan, P. J., Cliff, D. P., Barnett, L. M. and Okely, A. D. 2010. Fundamental movement skills in children and adolescents: Review of associated health benefits. *Sports Med*, 40, 1019–35.

Mahon, A. D. 2008. Aerobic training. *In:* Armstrong, N. and Van Mechelen, W. (eds.) *Paediatric Exercise Science and Medicine*. Oxford, UK: Oxford University Press.

Mahon, A. D. and Vaccaro, P. 1989. Ventilatory threshold and VO2max changes in children following endurance training. *Med Sci Sports Exerc*, 21, 425–31.

Malina, R. M., Bouchard, C. and Bar-Or, O. 2004. *Growth, Maturation and Physical Activity*. Champaign, IL: Human Kinetics.

Malina, R. M., Coelho, E. S. M. J., Figueiredo, A. J., Carling, C. and Beunen, G. P. 2012. Interrelationships among invasive and non-invasive indicators of biological maturation in adolescent male soccer players. *J Sports Sci*, 30, 1705–17.

Malina, R. M., Eisenmann, J. C., Cumming, S. P., Ribeiro, B. and Aroso, J. 2004. Maturity-associated variation in the growth and functional capacities of youth football (soccer) players 13–15 years. *Eur J Appl Physiol*, 91, 555–62.

Malina, R. M., Pena Reyes, M. E., Eisenmann, J. C., Horta, L., Rodrigues, J. and Miller, R. 2000. Height, mass and skeletal maturity of elite Portuguese soccer players aged 11–16 years. *J Sports Sci*, 18, 685–93.

Malina, R. M., Rogol, A. D., Cumming, S. P., Coelho, E. S. M. J. and Figueiredo, A. J. 2015. Biological maturation of youth athletes: Assessment and implications. *Br J Sports Med*, 49, 852–9.

McManus, A. M., Cheng, C. H., Leung, M. P., Yung, T. C. and MacFarlane, D. J. 2005. Improving aerobic power in primary school boys: A comparison of continuous and interval training. *Int J Sports Med*, 26, 781–6.

McNarry, M., Barker, A. R., Lloyd, R. S., Buchheit, M., Williams, C. A. and Oliver, J. L. 2014. The BASES expert statement on trainability during childhood and adolescence. *The Sport Exerc Scientist*, 41, 22–3.

Meyers, R. W., Oliver, J., Hughes, M., Cronin, J. B. and Lloyd, R. S. 2015a. Maximal sprint speed in boys of increasing maturity. *Pediatr Exerc Sci*, 27, 85–94.

Meyers, R. W., Oliver, J. L., Hughes, M. G., Lloyd, R. S. and Cronin, J. B. 2015b. The influence of age, maturity and body size on the spatiotemporal determinants of maximal sprint speed in boys. *J Strength Cond Res*, 31(4), 1009–1016.

Meyers, R. W., Oliver, J. L., Hughes, M. G., Lloyd, R. S. and Cronin, J. B. 2016. The influenece of maturation on sprint performance in boys over a 21-month period. *Med Sci Sports Exerc*, 48(12), 2555–2562.

Meylan, C. M., Cronin, J. B., Oliver, J. L., Hopkins, W. G. and Contreras, B. 2014b. The effect of maturation on adaptations to strength training and detraining in 11–15-year-olds. *Scand J Med Sci Sports*, 24, e156–64.

Meylan, C. M., Cronin, J., Oliver, J. L., Hopkins, W. G. and Pinder, S. 2014a. Contribution of vertical strength and power to sprint performance in young male athletes. *Int J Sports Med*, 35(09), 749–754.

Myburgh, G. K., Cumming, S. P., Coelho, E. S. M., Cooke, K. and Malina, R. M. 2016. Growth and maturity status of elite British junior tennis players. *J Sports Sci*, 34(20), 1–8.

Myer, G. D., Jayanthi, N., Difiori, J. P., Faigenbaum, A. D., Kiefer, A. W., Logerstedt, D. and Micheli, L. J. 2015. Sport specialization, part I: Does early sports specialization increase negative outcomes and reduce the opportunity for success in young athletes? *Sports Health*, 7, 437–42.

Myer, G. D., Kushner, A. M., Faigenbaum, A. D., Kiefer, A., Kashikar-Zuck, S. and Clark, J. F. 2013. Training the developing brain, part I: Cognitive developmental considerations for training youth. *Curr Sports Med Rep*, 12, 304–10.

O'Brien, T. D., Reeves, N. D., Baltzopoulos, V., Jones, D. A. and Maganaris, C. N. 2010. Muscle-tendon structure and dimensions in adults and children. *J Anat*, 216, 631–42.

Parsonage, J. R., Williams, R. S., Rainer, P., McKeown, I. and Williams, M. D. 2014. Assessment of conditioning-specific movement tasks and physical fitness measures in talent identified under 16-year-old rugby union players. *J Strength Cond Res*, 28, 1497–506.

Philippaerts, R. M., Vaeyens, R., Janssens, M., Van Renterghem, B., Matthys, D., Craen, R., Bourgois, J., Vrijens, J., Beunen, G. and Malina, R. M. 2006. The relationship between peak height velocity and physical performance in youth soccer players. *J Sports Sci*, 24, 221–30.

Radnor, J. M., Lloyd, R. S. and Oliver, J. L. 2017. Individual response to different forms of resistance training in school-aged boys. *J Strength Cond Res*, 31(3), 787–797.

Ramsay, J. A., Blimkie, C. J., Smith, K., Garner, S., MacDougall, J. D. and Sale, D. G. 1990. Strength training effects in prepubescent boys. *Med Sci Sports Exerc*, 22, 605–14.

Ratel, S., Duche, P. and Williams, C. A. 2006a. Muscle fatigue during high-intensity exercise in children. *Sports Med*, 36, 1031–65.

Ratel, S., Williams, C. A., Oliver, J. and Armstrong, N. 2006b. Effects of age and recovery duration on performance during multiple treadmill sprints. *Int J Sports Med*, 27, 1–8.

Reybrouck, T., Weymans, M., Stijns, H., Knops, J. and Van Der Hauwaert, L. 1985. Ventilatory anaerobic threshold in healthy children. Age and sex differences. *Eur J Appl Physiol Occup Physiol*, 54, 278–84.

Rice, S. G., Congeni, J. A., Council on Sports, M. and Fitness. 2012. Baseball and softball. *Pediatrics*, 129, e842–56.

Robinson, S. 1938. Experimental studies of physical fitness in relation to age. *Arbeitsphysiologie*, 10, 251–323.

Rudd, J., Butson, M. L., Barnett, L., Farrow, D., Berry, J., Borkoles, E. and Polman, R. 2016. A holistic measurement model of movement competency in children. *J Sports Sci*, 34, 477–85.

Rumpf, M. C., Cronin, J. B., Mohamad, I. N., Mohamad, S., Oliver, J. L. and Hughes, M. G. 2015a. The effect of resisted sprint training on maximum sprint kinetics and kinematics in youth. *Eur J Sport Sci*, 15, 374–81.

Rumpf, M. C., Cronin, J. B., Oliver, J. and Hughes, M. 2015b. Kinematics and kinetics of maximum running speed in youth across maturity. *Pediatr Exerc Sci*, 27, 277–84.

Rumpf, M. C., Cronin, J. B., Pinder, S. D., Oliver, J. and Hughes, M. 2012. Effect of different training methods on running sprint times in male youth. *Pediatr Exerc Sci*, 24, 170–86.

Rumpf, M. C., Lockie, R. G., Cronin, J. B. and Jalilvand, F. 2016. Effect of different sprint training methods on sprint performance over various distances: A brief review. *J Strength Cond Res*, 30, 1767–85.

Sander, A., Keiner, M., Wirth, K. and Schmidtbleicher, D. 2013. Influence of a 2-year strength training programme on power performance in elite youth soccer players. *Eur J Sport Sci*, 13, 445–51.

Schepens, B., Willems, P. A. and Cavagna, G. A. 1998. The mechanics of running in children. *J Physiol*, 509 (Pt 3), 927–40.

Tibana, R. A., Prestes, J., Nascimento Dda, C., Martins, O. V., De Santana, F. S. and Balsamo, S. 2012. Higher muscle performance in adolescents compared with adults after a resistance training session with different rest intervals. *J Strength Cond Res*, 26, 1027–32.

Tompsett, C., Burkett, B. and McKean, M. R. 2014. Development of physical literacy and movement competency. *J Fitness Res*, 2, 53–74.

Tonson, A., Ratel, S., Le Fur, Y., Cozzone, P. and Bendahan, D. 2008. Effect of maturation on the relationship between muscle size and force production. *Med Sci Sports Exerc*, 40, 918–25.

Torres-Unda, J., Zarrazquin, I., Gil, J., Ruiz, F., Irazusta, A., Kortajarena, M., Seco, J. and Irazusta, J. 2013. Anthropometric, physiological and maturational characteristics in selected elite and non-elite male adolescent basketball players. *J Sports Sci*, 31, 196–203.

Tremblay, M. S., Gray, C. E., Akinroye, K., Harrington, D. M., Katzmarzyk, P. T., Lambert, E. V., Liukkonen, J., Maddison, R., Ocansey, R. T., Onywera, V. O., Prista, A., Reilly, J. J., Rodriguez Martinez, M. P., Sarmiento Duenas, O. L., Standage, M. and Tomkinson, G. 2014. Physical activity of children: A global matrix of grades comparing 15 countries. *J Phys Act Health*, 11 (Suppl 1), S113–25.

Van Der Sluis, A., Elferink-Gemser, M. T., Coelho-e-Silva, M. J., Nijboer, J. A., Brink, M. S. and Visscher, C. 2014. Sport injuries aligned to peak height velocity in talented pubertal soccer players. *Int J Sports Med*, 35, 351–5.

Viru, A., Loko, J., Harro, M., Volver, A., Laaneot, L. and Viru, M. 1999. Critical periods in the development of performance capacity during childhood and adolescence. *European Journal of Physical Education*, 4, 75–119.

Waugh, C. M., Korff, T., Fath, F. and Blazevich, A. J. 2013. Rapid force production in children and adults: Mechanical and neural contributions. *Med Sci Sports Exerc*, 45, 762–71.

Woods, C. T., McKeown, I., Haff, G. G. and Robertson, S. 2016. Comparison of athletic movement between elite junior and senior Australian football players. *J Sports Sci*, 34, 1260–5.

# 4

APPLYING STRENGTH AND CONDITIONING PRACTICES TO ATHLETES WITH A DISABILITY

Tom Paulson and Vicky Goosey-Tolfrey

Introduction

At the Rio 2016 Paralympic Games, over 4000 athletes from 176 countries competed for 528 medals in one of the world's largest sporting events. The rapid expansion in public interest and participation in disability sport over recent decades has been matched by a continued advancement in the standard of elite competition. The latter has been driven by an evolution in technical aids and equipment as can be seen by the images of Esther Vergeer's bespoke wheelchair tennis sports chair at the 2008 and 2012 Paralympic Games (Figure 4.1a and Figure 4.1b). Bespoke prosthetics are also now evident (Burkett 2010) and an increasingly specialised approach to sports science and sports medicine support is now being adopted by most countries (Diaper and Goosey-Tolfrey 2009; Webborn and Van de Vliet 2012). However, despite the growing interest in Paralympic sport (Summer and Winter) and wider adapted sports for individuals with a disability (e.g. cricket), the evidence base for supporting elite performance remains in its infancy. A lack of resource as well as small, heterogeneous pools of high performance athletes inhibits the publication of scientific data collected by high performance practitioners. Comprehensive restrictions on data sharing within high performance systems also limit the availability of information detailing physiological capacities and the physical preparation of elite performers. Subsequently, current practice is often adapted based on guidelines and experience supporting able-bodied (AB) athletes, with a heavy reliance on anecdotal evidence and practitioner experience (Graham-Paulson et al. 2015). Physical programming for athletes with a disability therefore relies on a creative delivery approach based on underpinning principles of physical development alongside a community of shared knowledge to inform sport and impairment-specific best practice.

Many principles in training prescription and performance monitoring are directly transferable between AB and disability sport, including the periodisation of training load (volume, intensity and modality) and the focus on developing sport-specific physical competencies. Paralympic practitioners are also faced with the challenge of identifying and implementing reliable protocols that detect small but meaningful changes in classification-specific performance outcomes (Goosey-Tolfrey and Leicht 2013; Paulson and Goosey-Tolfrey 2016). However, an athlete's impairment profile and anthropometrics have a large influence on what physical capacities and attributes may be trainable in a sport-specific context. For example, an athlete with a neurological impairment (e.g. cerebral palsy) may have altered voluntary muscle recruitment patterns

(a)

(b)

Figure 4.1a and b   Innovations in wheelchair design (credit John Lenton)

and a lower trainability of absolute strength and power than AB athletes. Yet, targeted functional movement training may increase co-ordination and movement efficiency, resulting in increased performance (Boyd and Goosey-Tolfrey 2012).

Consideration for the interface between athlete and equipment is also imperative when supporting an athlete with a disability. Wheelchair-based performance requires the seamless integration of both the athlete and their equipment into one functioning unit, known as the 'wheelchair-user interface'. The efficiency with which an athlete can apply force through the interface is a key determinant of the energetic demands of any movement and the subsequent performance outcome (e.g. acceleration, change of direction). Elsewhere, the volume of loading applied through a lower limb prosthetic may need to be periodised so to manage skin robustness and viability. Improving physical function without understanding and optimising the athlete's interface with their equipment (e.g. influence of prosthetic on gait and muscle recruitment, type of glove used) (Mason et al. 2013) may not necessarily improve performance outcomes.

The heterogeneity in impairment groups eligible for classification in the same sporting discipline presents a unique challenge for coaches and practitioners when considering 'benchmarks' of physical performance (e.g. tetraplegia vs. cerebral palsy). As well as enhancing physical capacities, strength and conditioning-based interventions must also focus on maintaining athlete robustness and training availability whilst considering environmental influences on health and performance. The following chapter will highlight considerations for the programming of interventions specific to the maintenance and enhancement of performance in athletes with a physical impairment. Where available, attention will be given to scientific literature that supports current practice. Unfortunately it is beyond the scope of this chapter to provide a comprehensive overview of considerations for supporting athletes with an intellectual, visual or hearing impairment. The basic principles of training programming and the expected adaptational responses to a training stimulus in these impairment groups remain largely consistent with AB practice. However, the communication of training requirements to athletes, the training environment in which an athlete is asked to operate and the supervision of individual sessions requires consideration on an athlete-to-athlete basis. More detailed information on supporting these athletes can be found elsewhere (Winnick and Porretta 2016).

Specifically, this chapter will provide an introduction to: i) impairment-specific considerations for working with athletes with a spinal cord injury, limb deficiency or cerebral palsy, including targeted interventions for maintaining athlete health and robustness; ii) sport-specific techniques and technologies available for profiling and monitoring physical performance; and iii) practical applications to effectively support athletes with a physical impairment as part of a multi-disciplinary team in high performance environments.

Impairment specific considerations

Athletes with a spinal cord injury (SCI)

Physical capacity has previously been described as the ability of the musculoskeletal, neurological, cardiovascular and respiratory systems to perform a level of physical work (Haisma et al. 2006). Spinal cord injury (SCI) is the most widely researched impairment group, with aerobic (peak oxygen uptake ($\dot{V}O_{2peak}$) and peak aerobic power), anaerobic (peak power) and strength-related capacities all inversely related to lesion level and injury completeness (Haisma et al. 2006). Functional impairment may be the result of traumatic injury, congenital disorder (spina bifida) or illness/infection (post-polio). Athletes are eligible to participate in a range of sports without a wheelchair (e.g. swimming, powerlifting, canoeing and rowing) and the wheelchair court sports (rugby, tennis and basketball), athletics (wheelchair racing and throwing events), handcycling and other skill-based sports (e.g. table tennis, archery, shooting, fencing, curling and skiing).

Due to the aforementioned lesion-level dependent impairment in cardiovascular function and muscle innervation (respiratory and skeletal), a number of targeted interventions to support the optimisation of physical capacity have been proposed in this population group. The redistribution of blood, both at rest and during exercise, in individuals with an SCI is impaired due to the lack of sympathetic vasoconstriction in inactive tissue below the lesion level (Theisen 2012). In athletes with paraplegia (thoracic-lumbar level), cardiac output ($\dot{Q}$) is maintained by elevations in resting and submaximal HR. In athletes with complete tetraplegia (cervical level), the redistribution of blood and ability to elevate $\dot{Q}$ is further limited due to the loss of autonomic control of vessels in the abdominal bed and cardiac tissue. A SCI above T5 results in the loss of sympathetic outflow to the heart, and maximal heart rates (HRpeak) of 100–140 b·min^{-1} are achieved primarily by the withdrawal of parasympathetic tone. Physiological interventions aimed at augmenting cardiorespiratory function and subsequent aerobic capacities in athletes with tetraplegia include the use of compression socks (Vaile et al. 2016) and abdominal binders (West et al. 2014) during acute training. Both may act to enhance venous return and consequently improve ventricular filling pressure, stroke volume and cardiac performance in those with compromised vascular function. Implementation of these compensatory aids during training may provide a tool for augmenting cardiovascular adaptation. Recently, the partial preservation of descending sympathetic control was found to be strongly correlated with indices of exercise performance, including 4-min push distance in wheelchair rugby (WR) athletes (West et al. 2014). These findings occurred in athletes with neurologically motor and sensory complete spinal lesions, suggesting 'autonomic completeness' is an important factor in determining both aerobic and anaerobic capacities.

The lesion-level dependent loss of upper limb (<C7–8), respiratory and trunk (<T12) and lower limb (L<) function also determines the remaining functional muscle groups available to contribute to physical work output. Where muscle innervation remains intact, functional movements and strength characteristics can be trained to the same extent as in AB athletes (see Wheelchair Rugby chapter and upper limb sports). Technical aids and adaptive equipment can be implemented to support exercise participation and compensatory muscle activation may replace the loss of functional agonist or antagonist action during some movements (Figure 4.2). In some cases asymmetry in remaining upper-limb or trunk function may influence bilateral force production and co-ordination and therefore should be assessed during initial functional movement screenings. For an overview of scientific literature outlining strength training programmes in athletes with an SCI, see Paulson and Goosey-Tolfrey (2016). The atrophy of lower limb muscle mass following an SCI (and trunk in cervical level injuries) results in higher fat mass and lower mass compared to age-matched AB groups. Subsequently, body composition equations adapted from AB equations are not suitable for use in SCI populations, and monitoring should focus on skinfold thickness, girths or lean mass of the upper limb only (Willems et al. 2015).

With respect to training respiratory muscle strength, previously only positive indicators of quality of life (i.e. reduced scores of breathlessness) were found following six weeks of inspiratory muscle training (IMT) in trained wheelchair basketball (WB) players of mixed physical disabilities (Goosey-Tolfrey et al. 2010). Elsewhere, more encouraging improvements have been reported by West and co-workers (2014) who examined a more homogeneous group of athletes (i.e. highly trained WR players with tetraplegia) and found a 15% increase in PO$_{peak}$ following a 6-week period of IMT training. Accordingly, IMT may provide a useful adjunct to strength training in this population, but current literature is inconclusive.

Figure 4.2 Active hands™ to provide grip function in the gym (credit Rav Bhurji)

Due to the relatively high mobility but low stability of the shoulder girdle, the repetitive loads experienced during manual wheelchair propulsion (daily ambulation and sports performance) and transfers provide a risk factor for chronic over-use injuries in manual wheelchair users (Webborn and Van de Vliet 2012). Impingement risk and rotator cuff pathologies are further increased by the forces experienced at extreme joint ranges during the wheelchair court sports (e.g. reaching overhead and passing) and field events (e.g. discus or javelin throws). Interventions should first ensure the robustness of an athlete's shoulder by re-enforcing positive functional movement patterns and symmetry in scapula kinematics through strength (e.g. elastic bands) and coordination (e.g. visual stimuli) exercises (Bergamini et al. 2015). Athletes should also be encouraged to perform regular maintenance (e.g. maintaining tyre pressure, cleaning castors and bearings) on their daily use wheelchairs to reduce rolling resistance and subsequent propulsive forces during everyday mobility. Where possible training programmes should consider the athlete's daily ambulation requirements to prevent overload of the muscle groups surrounding the shoulder girdle and optimise load prescription.

From an athlete health perspective the loss of autonomic function following high thoracic and cervical level injury also presents two distinct challenges – namely, *autonomic dysreflexia* and *impaired thermoregulation*. Autonomic dysreflexia is a potentially life-threatening bout of uncontrolled hypertension resulting from severe vasoconstriction and cardiac stimulation in response to a painful/noxious stimulus below the lesion level (Webborn and Van de Vliet 2012). The voluntary inducement of autonomic dysreflexia to enhance performance, known as 'boosting', is regarded as violation of anti-doping regulations (Webborn and Van de Vliet 2012). Reduced sympathetic input to the thermoregulatory centre also presents a loss of sweating capacity and loss of vasomotor control for redistribution of blood below the level of the spinal lesion. The scientific literature is well versed regarding the problems of exercise in the heat, the effects of dehydration and the benefits of acclimatisation for the AB athlete. However, there are a number of considerations for athletes with disabilities exercising in the heat where thermo-regulatory impairment increases the risk from heat-related illness (Griggs et al. 2015; Webborn et al. 2010). In brief, key findings suggest that i) wearing an ice vest prior to intermittent sprint exercise both reduces thermal strain and enhances performance and ii) hand cooling is effective as a cooling aid (Griggs et al. 2015). The practicality of cooling must be considered as wheelchair athletes would not wish to experience feelings of numbness of the hands when hand dexterity in court sports is of paramount importance. Prior heat acclimation protocols may provide one method of improving thermoregulatory stability and reducing heat stress when competing in challenging environments for prolonged periods (Castle et al. 2013) (e.g. tennis competition).

Limb deficiency

Limb deficiency is an impairment group constituting athletes with an absence of bones or joints as a resulting from congenital limb deficiency (e.g. dysmelia) or amputation following traumatic injury or vascular or bone pathologies. In contrast to athletes with an SCI, those with lower and/or upper limb deficiency may remain neurologically and physiologically homogenous with AB athletes. Cardiovascular responses are similar to those observed in AB athletes and metabolic adaptation to training will be maintained in the unaffected tissues. Interestingly, the reduction in total body mass but high work potential of remaining muscle groups can often reduce the clearance potential of blood lactate (e.g. during upper body exercise in individuals with double lower limb amputations). This reduced clearance potential can result in elevated blood lactate concentrations at a given exercise intensity compared to an AB athlete and is important to consider when longitudinally profiling an athlete physiological capacity. Nutritional strategies to support the buffering of hydrogen ions may support performance, but should be promoted alongside athlete education of supplement properties and possible side-effects (Graham-Paulson et al. 2015).

Primary areas for intervention following lower limb amputation or limb loss are i) reduced proprioception and a subsequent influence on co-ordination of movement patterns and control and ii) reduced force generating capacity due to loss of muscle mass in the affected limb. Importantly, removal of the femoral ends of major lower limb muscle groups during surgical processes associated with above and through knee amputations can result in alterations in agonist and antagonist actions and altered gait (Cardinale and Romer 2011). For a further review of biomechanical aspects of performance in athletes with an amputation, see Bragaru et al. (2011). Bespoke strength programmes to reduce inter-limb asymmetries, particularly around the hip, and develop neuromuscular control of affected muscles can help prevent injuries related to muscle imbalance. This includes targeted strengthening of the trunk and hip flexors/extensors to improve functional movement performance (Nolan 2012). Traditional strength and aerobic based training, including Olympic lifts, are achieved with limb deficient athletes via bespoke prosthetic adaptations, but attention should be given to loading of the Residual limb and prosthetic (Bragaru et al. 2012). The aforementioned alteration in muscle activation patterns may also alter lifting biomechanics and kinetic chain activity during strength/power and aerobic-based training and should be regularly monitored (Cardinale and Romer 2011). Even for sports involving wheelchair propulsion, training of the hip flexors/extensors via gluteal activation is important for enabling rotational movements performed in a seated position. The preservation and enhancement of trunk function provides stability and contributes to the generation of momentum when performing high intensity activities, including accelerations or rotations (Vanlandewijck et al. 2011).

Residual limb care is a vitally important aspect of maintaining robustness and training availability in athletes with an amputation and requires a multi-disciplinary approach to

Figure 4.3 Amputee paratriathlete Andy Lewis (credit British Triathlon)

management, with the athlete involved throughout. This is especially important for lower limb amputations where daily use and sporting prosthetics may be interchanged regularly and high levels of moisture and friction may reduce tissue viability (Figure 4.3). Awareness and regular monitoring of Residual limb condition as well as the preparation of alternative training strategies during high loading periods when tissue health may deteriorate can reduce days lost to training. Individual travel strategies should also be considered for long-haul travel where Residual limb volumes are known to change due to the accumulation of fluid if the prostheses are removed in flight. Alternatively, where the prostheses remains in place for a long duration, skin may become irritated, which in turn could influence training quality and injury risk pre-competition.

Cerebral palsy

Athletes with cerebral palsy (CP) or central neurologic injury, such as stroke, have a variety of impairment in sensation, motor control and communication ranging from mild to severe (Webborn and Van de Vliet 2012). Despite being one of the largest represented impairment groups at the summer Paralympic games, there is a dearth of scientific literature supporting practice with neurological impairments. What research exists (mainly paediatric exercise science) supports value of strength and aerobic capacity in adolescents with CP and relationships with functional performance in daily life (Lennon et al. 2015).

Before working with an athlete it is important to understand the level of functional impairment; only one limb affected (monoplegia), function influenced in lower limbs more than upper limbs and potential asymmetries (diplegia), one-side upper and lower limb (and trunk) influenced (hemiplegia) or all 4 limbs (quadriplegia). From a motor control perspective, athletes typically present an increased muscle tension and inability to stretch (Hypertonia), lack of co-ordination of muscle movements (Ataxia), un-balanced involuntary movements (Athetosis) or a combination, leading to reduced muscle power and functional performance (Lennon et al. 2015). Without due consideration to the athlete's impairment, the risk of overtraining, injury and heightened states of spasticity and muscle imbalance is significantly increased.

Excessive activation of primary antagonists during voluntary contractions is known to influence joint-movement and loading patterns during functional movements in athletes with CP (Cardinale and Romer 2011). Passive stretching is recommended to provide proprioceptive training of joint movement and increase joint range of motion (Boyd and Goosey-Tolfrey 2012). Further, the lack of neurological drive of voluntary contractions during training may not produce forces great enough to induce hypertrophy, with absolute forces lower in CP than AB athletes (Runciman et al. 2016). However, reinforcing primary movement patterns can enhance movement efficiency and co-ordination. Runciman et al. (2016) also observed similar fatigue profiles during maximal sprint cycling (30 sec wingate) in 5 elite athletes with CP age and performance-matched AB controls. This similarity in fatigue profiles may indicate that elite athletes with CP may have a different exercise response to less-trained counterparts as a result of high-level training over many years (Runciman et al. 2016). Elsewhere pacing strategies during interval-based exercise (repeated shuttle runs) have been shown to be different in CP versus AB athletes (Runciman et al. 2014). Conservative pacing strategies were employed to prevent premature fatigue suggesting a perceived inability to self-regulate efforts due to deficits in neurological function (Runciman et al. 2014). The potential early onset of fatigue needs to be carefully considered with programming training, either by increasing rest periods between sets/activities and/or support staff monitoring training intensity (Boyd and Goosey-Tolfrey 2012). The inhibited lactate release from spastic muscle and aforementioned motor impairments may influence the reliability of protocols for assessing aerobic and anaerobic capacity, yet specific evidence is limited (Lennon et al. 2015).

Sport-specific considerations

After appreciating the physiological, neurological and athlete health considerations between Olympic and Paralympic athletes, it is clear that the knowledge gleaned from AB literature may not always be directly applicable. Despite these impairment-specific characteristics, there are many similarities in how the sports are managed in the UK with the provision of sport science and the role of research and innovations to enhance performance. In the linear sports (e.g., handcycling vs. cycling, wheelchair racing vs. running), the physiological underpinnings of performance and profiling methods are often analogous. Yet consideration must be given to sport-specific functional movement requirements and potential influence of reduced cross sectional area of the upper limb on VO_2 kinetics and force generation potential. It is clear that technology has contributed to the enhanced sporting performances in these sports (e.g. carbon-fibre technologies), yet technology alone will not produce world class performance.

The wheelchair sports currently receiving the most attention in the scientific literature are the 'court sports' (i.e. basketball, rugby and tennis). A wider discussion on the functional classifications systems within each sport is beyond the scope of this review and is provided elsewhere (Tweedy and Diaper 2010). Importantly the aforementioned sports present similarities in terms of the intermittent movement dynamics of on-court performance and the need to optimise the interface between an individual athlete and their equipment. In contrast to the linear sports described previously, no single physiological parameter determines performance outcome in court-based sports. In competitive WT match-play, Sindall et al. (2013) observed higher average speeds and greater distances covered in high versus low ranking players. In addition, high ranked players also covered more distance at higher average HR than their opponents (Sindall et al. 2013). High ranking WR teams have been found to spend a greater time within high (>81–95%

peak speed) (2.9 ± 1.6%) and very high (>95% peak speed) (0.7 ± 0.8%) speed zones compared to low (1.5 ± 1.1% and 0 ± 0.4%) and mid-ranked teams (2.0 ± 1.3% and 0.3 ± 0.5%) across all classifications (Rhodes et al. 2015). Higher ranking teams also performed high intensity activities for greater distances and for a longer duration (Rhodes et al. 2015), although opposition characteristics, including style of play and ranking, clearly influence indices of game intensity. As well as linear performance parameters, WB players who represent national teams performed more frequent (+7%) and longer duration (+0.2 s) rotational activities and fewer braking activities compared to club level counterparts during simulated match-play (de Witte et al. 2016). Consequently, techniques for enhancing linear and rotational performance are important to prescribe training intensities to match or exceed the demands of the competition environment.

The indoor tracking system (ITS), as used by Rhodes et al. (2015), has been proved to be a valid and reliable tool for the assessment of distance/speed during a range of tasks specific to the wheelchair court sports (Rhodes et al. 2014). Importantly, the ITS has shown good reliability reliable even at maximal speeds (>4 m·s^{-1}), where random errors of <0.10 m·s^{-1}, with <2% CV were observed ((Rhodes et al. 2014). Subsequently, the ITS has been employed to profile the demands of competition and manipulation game simulation drills to enhance the intensity of on-court training.

Practical applications

The present chapter has outlined practical considerations and scientific literature regarding impairment and sport-specific training programming and profiling. The growing range of eligible impairments competing within disability sport and the fully individualised approach required to support high performance athletes means specialised training information is beyond the scope of this chapter. However, a number of key generic principles exist which provide the foundation upon which bespoke strength and conditioning programmes can be implemented:

- An understanding of the individual athlete's physical impairment profile, including a full medical diagnosis, screening of current functional movement pattern and previous illness/injury history is vital when beginning to support an athlete.
- Awareness of the potential physiological and neurological limitations to an athlete's physical capacity and competition performance helps target sport-specific interventions.
- Practitioners should also be fully aware of the athlete-equipment interface and the importance of optimising this relationship to support performance.
- A multi-disciplinary approach to the preparation and assessment of interventions aimed at enhancing physical performance is essential. Interventions may increase one element of performance (linear speed) but be detrimental to other parameters of athlete health or performance.

The following section is an example of how the above information can be used to create a practical checklist of considerations for delivering physical conditioning programmes for persons with a *spinal cord injury*:

1 Do you know the level and completeness of the spinal cord injury?
2 How much balance, trunk stability and muscle tone does the athlete have?
3 What is the functional range of movement of the shoulder girdle?
4 What event does the athlete compete in? Does the sport require rotational/non-linear movements?

5   Are adaptive training aids (e.g. active hands, abdominal binder) needed to enhance the training capabilities?
6   To preserve hand function, be careful that the athlete does not hyperextend the wrist with adaptive wrist cuffs.
7   Check for a history of orthostatic hypotension and/or autonomic dysreflexia in athletes with a lesion level above T6.

References

Bergamini E, Morelli F, Marchetti F, Vannozzi G, Polidori L, Paradisi F et al. Wheelchair propulsion biomechanics in junior basketball players: a method for the evaluation of the efficacy of a specific training program. *Biomed Res Int*. 2015; doi:10.1155/2015/275965.

Boyd C, Goosey-Tolfrey VL. Different populations: disabled players. In Williams M (ed), *The Science of Soccer* (Third Edition). London: Taylor & Francis. 2012; 259–270.

Bragaru M, Dekker R, Geertzen JHB. Sport prostheses and prosthetic adaptations for the upper and lower limb amputees: an overview of peer reviewed literature. *Prosthet Orthot Int*. 2012; 36(3): 290–296.

Bragaru M, Dekker R, Geertzen JHB, Dijkstra PU. Amputees and sports: a systematic review. *Sports Med*. 2011; 41(9): 721–740.

Burkett B. Technology in Paralympic sport: performance enhancement or essential for performance. *Br J Sports Med*. 2010; 44: 215–220.

Cardinale M, Romer L. Strength training. In Vanlandewijck YC, Thompson WR (eds), *The Paralympic Athlete: Handbook of Sports Medicine and Science*. London: Wiley. 2011; 156–171.

Castle PC, Kularatne PB, Brewer J, Mauger AR, Austen RA, Tuttle JA et al. Partial heat acclimation of athletes with spinal cord lesion. *Eur J Appl Physiol*. 2013; 113: 109–115.

de Witte AMH, Hoozemans MJM, Berger MAM, woude van der LHV, Veeger HEJ. Do field position and playing standard influence athlete performance in wheelchair basketball? *J Sports Sci*. 2016; 34(9): 811–820.

Diaper N, Goosey-Tolfrey VL. A physiological case study of a Paralympic wheelchair tennis player: Reflective practise. *J Sport Sci Med*. 2009; 8: 300–307.

Goosey-Tolfrey VL, Foden E, Perret C, Degens H. Effects of inspiratory muscle training on respiratory function and repetitive sprint performance in wheelchair basketball players. *Br J Sports Med*. 2010; 44: 665–668.

Goosey-Tolfrey VL, Leicht C. Field based testing of wheelchair athletes. *Sports Med*. 2013; 43(2): 77–91.

Graham-Paulson TS, Perret C, Smith B, Crosland J, Goosey-Tolfrey VL. Nutritional supplement habits of athletes with an impairment and their sources of information. *Int J Sport Nut Exerc Met*. 2015; 25(4): 387–395.

Griggs KE, Price MJ, Goosey-Tolfrey VL. Cooling athletes with a spinal cord injury. *Sports Med*. 2015; 45(1): 9–21.

Haisma JA, Woude van der LHV, Stam HJ, Bergen MP, Sluis TAR, Bussman JBJ. Physical capacity in wheelchair-dependent persons with a spinal cord injury: A critical review of the literature. *Spinal Cord*. 2006; 44: 642–652.

Lennon N, Thorpe, D, Balemans, AC, Fragala-Pinkham, M, O'Neil, M, Bjornson, K, … Dallmeijer, AJ. The clinimetric properties of aerobic and anaerobic fitness measures in adults with cerebral palsy: A systematic review of the literature. *Research in Developmental Disabilities* 2015; 45: 316–328.

Mason BS, Woude van der LHV, Goosey-Tolfrey VL. The ergonomics of wheelchair configuration for optimal performance in the wheelchair court sports. *Sports Med*. 2013; 43(1): 23–38.

Nolan L. A training programme to improve hip strength in persons with lower limb amputation. *J Rehab Med*. 2012; 8: 241–248.

Paulson T, Goosey-Tolfrey VL. Current perspectives on profiling and enhancing wheelchair court-sport performance. *Int J Sport Phsyiol Perf*. 2016; 12(3): 275–286.

Rhodes J, Mason BS, Malone LA, Goosey-Tolfrey VL. Effect of team rank and player classification on activity profiles of elite wheelchair rugby players. *J Sports Sci*. 2015; 33(19): 2070–2078.

Rhodes J, Mason B, Perrat B, Smith M, Goosey-Tolfrey V. The validity and reliability of a novel indoor player tracking system for use within wheelchair court sports. *J Sports Sci*. 2014; 32(17): 1639–1647.

Runciman P, Derman WE, Tucker R, Ferreira S. A descriptive comparison of sprint cycling performance and neuromuscular characteristics in able-bodied athletes and paralympic athletes with cerebral palsy. *Am J Phys Med Rehab.* 2014; 94(1): 28–37.

Runciman P, Tucker R, Ferreira S, Derman WE. Paralympic athletes with cerebral palsy display altered pacing strategies in distance-deceived shuttle running trials. *Scand J Med Sci Sports.* 2016; 26(10): 1239–1248.

Sindall P, Lenton JP, Tolfrey K, Cooper RA, Oyster M, Goosey-Tolfrey VL. Wheelchair tennis match-play demands: Effect of player rank and result. *J Sports Sci.* 2013; 8(1): 28–37.

Theisen D. Cardiovascular determinants of exercise capacity in the Paralympic athlete with spinal cord injury. *Exp Physiol.* 2012; 97(3): 319–324.

Tweedy S, Diaper N. Introduction to wheelchair sport. In: Goosey-Tolfrey VL (ed), *Wheelchair Sport* (First Edition). Champaign, IL: Hum Kin. 2010; 3–27.

Vaile J, Stefanovic B, Askew CD. Effect of lower limb compression on blood flow and performance in elite wheelchair rugby athletes. *J Spinal Cord Med.* 2016; 39(2): 206–211.

Vanlandewijck YC, Verellen J, Tweedy S. Towards an evidence-based classification in wheelchair sports: impact of seating position on wheelchair acceleration. *J Sports Sci.* 2011; 29(10): 1089–1096.

Webborn N, Price MJ, Castle PC, Goosey-Tolfrey VL. Cooling strategies improve intermittent sprint performance in the heat of athletes with tetraplegia. *Br J Sports Med.* 2010; 44(6): 455–460.

Webborn N, Van de Vliet P. Paralympic medicine. *Lancet.* 2012; 379: 65–71.

West C, Campbell IG, Mason B, Goosey-Tolfrey VL, Romer LM. Effect of an abdominal binder on measures of field-based fitness in Paralympic wheelchair rugby players. *Aus J Sci Med Sport.* 2014; 4: 351–355.

Willems A, Paulson TAW, Keil M, Brooke-Wavell K, Goosey-Tolfrey VL. Dual-energy X-ray absorptiometry, skinfold thickness and waist circumference for assessing body composition in ambulant and non-ambulant wheelchair games players. *Front Exerc Physiol.* 2015 Nov 27; 6: 356. doi: 10.3389/fphys.2015.00356. eCollection 2015.

Winnick J, Porretta D. *Adapted Physical Education and Sport* (Volume VI). Dubuque, Iowa: Human Kinetics. 2016; 648 pages. ISBN-13: 9781492511533.

SECTION 3

Team sports

5
SOCCER

Perry Stewart and Matthew Springham

Introduction

Soccer is the world's most popular sport, with the Federation of the International Football Association (FIFA) estimating that more than 270 million people are actively involved in the sport worldwide. Like many sports, successful performance requires a multitude of interconnecting factors, such as technical, tactical, psychological and physical proficiency. Although the application of sport science in soccer is relatively new, it is accepted that the application of sport science can assist in enhancing performance and reducing the risk of injury. With the ever-increasing financial incentives (professional contracts, sponsorships, TV rights) within the professional world, it is perhaps unsurprising that the demand for scientific support services such as strength & conditioning (S&C) has increased.

In elite performance environments it is essential to understand the athletic demands of the sport. Such information enables the S&C coach to optimise the training and recovery process to ensure the player is physically prepared for the rigors of competition. Advancements in sport science technology has enabled scientists and practitioners to quantify the physical demands of soccer through such means as time motion analysis (semi-automated video analysis systems & global positioning system (GPS)), heart rate (HR) monitoring, biological markers (typically blood and salivary analysis) and perceived exertion (sRPE). Such information allows the S&C coach to select relevant fitness tests and appropriately plan and periodise programmes to optimise performance and reduce the risk of injury. The aim of this chapter is to review the athletic demands and injury prevalence, identify appropriate fitness tests, and provide practical guidance in programming.

Match demands

Soccer is an intermittent sport where brief bouts of high intensity actions alternate with longer periods of low intensity activity (Rampinini et al., 2007). Regardless of the method used to quantify player activity, it is accepted that players typically cover between 9–14 km of total distance during an elite match, with 1–3 km constituting high intensity distance (Bangsbo et al., 1991; Mohr et al., 2003; Bradley et al., 2009). Bradley et al. (2009) reported that during a typical English Premier League match, players stand for 5.6% of total time, walk (0.7–7.1km.h) for 60%, jog (7.2–14.3km.h) 26%, and perform running (14.4–19.7km.h), high speed running (19.8–25.1km.h) and sprinting (>25.1km.h) for 6%, 2% and 1% respectively. Low intensity activity represents 85% of total time, with high intensity runs representing 9% (remaining time spent stood still). On average sprint bouts occur every 90–120 seconds, each lasting 2–4 seconds with approximately 96% of sprints being less than 30m (Bangsbo et al., 1991; Reilly and Thomas, 1976). Elite soccer players perform 150–250 brief, intense actions during a game and make 1,200–1,400 changes of direction (Mohr et al., 2003; Bangsbo, 1992). The majority of these efforts are short duration, high intensity movements, and even at low absolute velocities can elicit a high metabolic and mechanical demand. Interestingly Faude et al. (2012) reported that 45% of German national league goals were scored by players performing straight sprints, 16% following jumps, and 6% following rotational and change of directional sprints. Similarly, the assisting player performed straight sprints prior to a goal being scored, followed by rotations, jumps and change of directional sprints (Faude et al., 2012). This highlights the importance of speed and other explosive qualities in determining the outcome of the game. In summary, speed, agility and power are critical physical qualities within elite soccer.

Reporting mean values to quantify match demands undoubtedly underrepresent the most intense periods during match play. Mean metabolic responses to match play have been reported as 70% of maximal oxygen uptake and 4–6mmol/L of blood lactate concentrations (Mohr et al., 2005). However, heart rate can exceed 95% of its maximum, and peak blood lactate concentrations can reach 8–14mmol/L (Ali and Farrally, 1991; Bradley et al., 2009; Mohr et al., 2003) during the most intense periods of a match. Similarly, Di Mascio and Bradley (2013) found that high speed running performance of English Premier League players markedly vary during intense periods compared to the match average and that high speed running is dependent on positional role. From this it can be determined that elite modern soccer players require high aerobic and anaerobic capabilities to prepare them for multiple high intensity bouts of activity during competition.

Positional variations

Further to understanding the physical demands of the average player, the S&C coach must consider the significant positional variations in activity profiles (Table 5.1). Typically, the five positional categories are described as central defenders, full-backs, central midfielders, wide midfielders and attackers. Within the English premiership, wide and central midfielders cover greater total distance compared with central defenders, full-backs and attackers (Bradley et al., 2009). Also, wide midfielders cover greater distance in high intensity running compared with all other positions (Bradley et al., 2009). Full-backs and wide midfielders cover greater distance at higher speeds when compared to central and attacking positions (Bradley et al., 2009). Data from the Spanish premier division (La Liga) reported similar findings using GPS (as opposed to multi-camera computerised tracking system), but in addition reported that although central defenders covered lower total distance and least amount of running at high intensity, they do perform a greater number of accelerations than any other position (Mallo et al., 2015). From this research

Table 5.1 Distances covered in different speed zones during English Premier League matches according to playing position

	Central defenders	Full backs	Central midfielders	Wide midfielders	Attackers
Total distance (m)	9885±555	10710±589	11450±608	11535±933	10314±1175
High intensity running (m)	1834±256	2605±387	2825±473	3138±565	2341±575
Very high intensity running (m)	603±132	984±195	927±245	1214±251	955±239
Sprinting (m)	152±50	287±98	204±89	346±115	264±87

it is evident that specific work:rest ratios exist between positions; 1:4 for central defenders and 1:2 for all other positional roles. Such research provides valuable information for the S&C coach who can develop position-specific testing protocols and conditioning drills.

Standard of competition

With running performance proving such an important factor in soccer, it could be assumed that those playing at higher levels of competition exhibit increased physical capacity. Mohr et al. (2003) found this to be true when comparing elite players from an elite Italian team competing in the UEAFA Champions League and players from a top Danish team. The results showed that the higher performing players completed greater high speed running (28%) and sprinting (58%) compared with their Danish counterparts. Similarly, Ingebrigsten et al. (2013) reported that within the Danish league, top ranking teams performed greater high intensity running (31–38%) when compared to middle and bottom ranking clubs in the same league. However, Bradley et al. (2013) contests the assumption that 'top class' teams cover greater distances at higher speeds. After extensive analysis of English players competing in the Premier League, Championship and League 1, it was reported that Premier League players covered the least amount of high intensity running compared with the lower levels of competition. However, Premiership players completed a greater number of successful passes, forward passes, balls received, and touches per possession compared with their Championship and League 1 counterparts. League 1 players covered the greatest high intensity running distance when compared to Premier League and Championship players. Interestingly the players within League 1 and Championship performed more headers and interceptions than those playing within the Premiership. These observations imply that technical ability and tactical preferences impact the amount and type of running performed.

Age variations

For those working with youth athletes it is pertinent to understand the physical demands within elite youth soccer. From the work of Goto et al. (2015a,b), it can be concluded that total match running distance and high-speed running distance increases with age as demonstrated in Table 5.2. Interestingly running performance has also shown the potential to distinguish between

Table 5.2 Distance covered in each speed zone (m.h^{-1}) for U9–U16 age groups from English Premier League Academy. Speed zones were determined by mean squad speed scores

	Standing & walking (m)	Jogging (m)	Low speed running (m)	Moderate speed running (m)	High speed running (m)
U9★	966±89	1560±207	1189±239	462±109	166±52
U10★	865±131	1594±229	927±208	485±139	186±60
U11★★	994±93	1665±191	1609±240	887±129	493±138
U12★★	1084±93	1924±185	1501±162	888±157	493±216
U13★★	1006±242	1974±196	1726±218	893±286	504±203
U14★★	1109±95	1853±136	1831±319	926±159	554±140
U15★★	1035±77	2114±128	1964±251	1056±164	537±138
U16★★	1047±142	2115±155	1886±284	977±214	503±122

★Adapted from Goto et al. (2015a)
★★Adapted from Goto et al. (2015b)

Table 5.3 Performance and technical differences between male and female soccer players competing in UEFA Champions League

	Male	*Female*
Total distance (m)	11,142	10,754
High intensity running distance (m) (>15km.h)	2,140	1,649
Successful passes (%)	79.4	71.5
Total balls lost	12.6	17.4
Time in possession (s)	69.6	66.5

Adapted from Bradley et al. (2013)

retained and released groups in some age groups in an English Premier League Academy (Goto et al., 2015a,b).

Gender variations

Female soccer players demonstrate lower levels of physical capacities across both aerobic and anaerobic fitness tests (Mujika et al., 2009) and therefore perhaps unsurprisingly demonstrate inferior physical workloads during matches when compared to their male counterparts. Bradley et al. (2013) reported that male soccer players covered 2.5% more total distance and 30–35% more high intensity running when compared to females of a similar competitive standard (UEFA Champions League) (Table 5.3).

Implications of fatigue

An evident consequence of competition is the impact of fatigue on physical performance. Research demonstrates that there is a significant decline in running performance between 1st and 2nd half (Mohr et al., 2003; Bradley et al., 2009, Bradley et al., 2010). Vigne et al. (2010), reported that players covered significantly less distance across all speed categories, most notably distances covered at very high intensity. The work-to-rest profile also changed from 1st to 2nd half, with a greater number of recovery bouts of >120 s significantly increasing. Bradley and Noakes (2013) found that players covering greatest total distances in the 1st half demonstrated a 12% reduction in high intensity running, whilst players covering moderate and low distances in the first half reported no changes. It is also evident that temporary fatigue during a match exists, with Mohr et al. (2003) reporting that the amount of high intensity running in the 5 min period immediately after the most intense 5 min was less than the average of the entire game. In addition to the reduced physical performance throughout a soccer match, match induced fatigue could also reduce technical capabilities, both of which are considered contributors to match outcome.

Situational and tactical factors

The roles of situational variables that influence physical performance in soccer have been summarised by Lago-Peñas (2012):

- *Match Status* – players perform significantly less high intensity activity when winning than when losing or drawing.

- *Quality of Opposition* – total distance and high intensity running is higher against 'better' opposition than against 'weaker' opponents.
- *Match Location* – home teams cover greater distances compared with away teams.

It is worth noting that tactical factors such as playing formation (4–4–2, 4–3–3 and 4–5–1) does not influence the overall activity profile of players, with the exception of attackers in a 4–3–3 formation, who perform 30% more high intensity running than attackers in 4–4–2 or 4–5–1 formations (Bradley et al., 2011).

Injury prevalence

Similar to all contact sports, injuries within soccer are inevitable. It has been reported that the risk of injury to professional soccer players is approximately 1000 times higher than the risk within industrial occupations (Hawkins and Fuller, 1999). Ekstrand et al. (2009, 2011) concluded that within European professional men's soccer, a player sustains on average 2 injuries per season, missing on average 37 days per season. Therefore a team with 25 squad members can expect 50 injuries per season, with each player being unavailable for 12% of the season (Ekstrand et al., 2011).

Injuries that render a player unavailable within professional soccer have significant consequences for both the individual and club. It is not uncommon for a player's monetary value and salability to decrease as a result of a distinctive injury history. In addition to impacting the player, their reduced market value impacts the club's ability to maximise the return of investment. It is also reported that 47% of players are forced to retire from professional soccer due to acute or chronic injury, and in many cases injury cuts a player's career shorter than anticipated (Fuller et al., 2012). With reduced player availability, a manager is unable to field the best players; team performance will typically suffer and consequently affect team positioning/status. Arnason et al. (2004a) reported a significant relationship between the total number of days lost to injury and overall team performance (league status). The authors logically speculated that injuries to key players would detract from team success.

Although there remains no consensus regarding the medical definition of an injury, categorisations can be identified as contact (traumatic injury resulting from contact), acute non-contact (musculoskeletal damage following non-contact activities such as running, turning, jumping and shooting) and chronic non-contact/overuse (continued or repetitive actions/loading in excess of the player's physical tolerance). Interestingly, the incidence of injuries during matches is on average 4–6 times higher than those sustained during training (Hawkins and Fuller, 1999; Junge and Dvorak, 2004). More injuries occur during the last 15 min period of each half (Hawkins and Fuller, 1999; Junge and Dvorak, 2004), implying that fatigue also plays an important role in players sustaining match related injuries. Tackling (4–40%) and being tackled (15–23%) are the most common mechanisms of contact injury (Wong and Hong, 2005). Injuries resulting from contact are significantly higher in matches when compared to training (Ekstrand et al., 2011). It is presumed that during matches the intensity and speed of play encourages more body contact (such as, blocking, tackling, collisions) between opposing teams, thus explaining the increased risk of injury.

Non-contact injuries are reportedly more prevalent than contact injuries (Hawkins and Fuller, 1999; Hawkins et al., 2001), with the magnitude of these injuries representing between 26%–59% of all injuries (Junge and Dvorak, 2004). The most common mechanisms of non-contact injuries include running (19%), turning (8%), shooting (4%) and landing (4%) (Hawkins et al., 2001). Nielsen and Yde (1989) found that of all lower extremity injuries, 34% could be classified as overuse. Reoccurring injuries (i.e. that of the same type and location) reportedly account for 20–27% of all injuries (Junge and Dvorak, 2004), perhaps indicating inadequate rehabilitation and/or insufficient recovery time being applied. Acute and chronic non-contact injuries, including those of a reoccurring nature, have the greatest potential to be avoided with appropriate management.

Injury incidence appears to increase as the level of competition progresses and as youth players mature with age (until 17–18 years old when injury incidence is similar to adult population) (Junge and Dvorak, 2004). There is evidence to suggest a difference in injury rates between sexes, with females reporting higher incidence of injury overall and greater amounts during training (Wong and Hong, 2005). Peterson et al. (2000) reported that female players with lower skill levels experience twice as many injuries compared with higher skilled players. Despite the S&C coach being unable to prevent the occurrence of injuries, there seems to be a prudent opportunity to reduce the risk of non-contact and overuse injuries through appropriate planning of training/competition and physical preparation.

Anatomical location, nature and severity

Between 61% and 90% of all injuries occur in the lower extremities (hip, groin, upper leg, knee, lower leg, ankle and foot), with goalkeepers experiencing more head, face, neck and upper extremity injuries (Dvorak and Junge, 2000). The most injured anatomical regions are ankle, knee, upper leg, groin and hip. However, the most commonly injured sites for male soccer players were ankle (20%), upper leg (17%) and knee (15%), with those for female players being knee (24%), ankle (21%) and upper leg (16%) (Junge and Dvorak, 2004.

Strain, sprain and contusions are the most common types of injury sustained in soccer, representing 41%, 20% and 20% of all injuries respectively (Hawkins and Fuller, 1999; Wong and Hong, 2005). A total of 81% of all upper leg injuries were muscular strains, with significantly more (64%) injuries sustained to the posterior thigh (hamstring) compared with anterior (quadriceps). This may suggest that not enough attention has been paid to preparing the hamstring group. 76% of all ankle injuries and 45% of all knee injuries are classified as ligamentous sprains (Hawkins and Fuller, 1999).

Following a review of the literature, Wong and Hong (2005), state that the majority of all injuries, regardless of age (adolescent, professional and senior), were of minor severity (<7 days), followed by moderate (8–29 days) and lastly major (>30 days).

Risk factors

Although there is no prevailing method to predict where, when or how an injury will occur, Bahr and Krosshaug (2005) state that it is the presence of both intrinsic and extrinsic risk factors that render a player susceptible to injury:

Intrinsic

- Age
- Sex
- Body composition
- Previous injury
- Physical fitness

- Anatomy
- Skill level
- Psychological factors

Extrinsic

- Environment
- Surface
- Sports equipment
- Human factors (referee, opponents, rules)

The interaction between these risk factors during an inciting incident (such as playing situation, player behavior, biomechanical, training/competition program) result in a player sustaining an injury. Therefore, to reduce the risk of injury, the S&C coach can:

- Monitor workloads
- Manage fatigue
- Apply adequate rehabilitation with sufficient recovery time for players returning from injury
- Deliver appropriate warm up and cool down
- Insist protective equipment (shin pads) are worn
- Encourage adherence to rules

Fitness testing

Successful match play requires players to demonstrate proficiency in numerous physical qualities, including aerobic and anaerobic capacity, strength, power, speed, and agility (Reilly and Doran, 2003). Assessing physical abilities of players and squads elicits critical information that can be used for talent identification, optimizing training prescription and providing objective markers for players returning from injury. However, it must be understood that although fitness tests isolate and evaluate specific physical abilities, it can not be used as a direct reflection of a player's overall ability due to the detachment from technical, tactical psychological and social capabilities.

Before selecting testing protocols, the S&C coach should consider the validity, reproducibility and sensitivity to change in performance. Also, as stated previously the physical demands vary according to age, gender, level of competition, position and playing style, which may influence test selection. Despite increased reliability associated with laboratory tests it is logistically very difficult to get an athlete or a team of athletes to a testing laboratory. Laboratory tests are often very expensive and time consuming, thus making them inaccessible for regular use even for clubs with sound financial backing. These inhibitory factors have lead to the use of valid and reliable field tests. Field based tests are a popular and more accessible form of assessing players physical characteristics due to simplicity, time efficiency, and minimal equipment required. It is important to organise testing at a time that has minimal disruption to the training week, but also allows the players to test in optimal conditions (i.e. not directly after a training session or match). Typically testing sessions are first administered when players return after the off season and the same battery of tests are systematically re-administered at the end of preseason, midseason and end of season to assess progress and make programme alterations. Sequencing of tests is important, and Harman (2008) recommends resting and non-fatiguing tests first (e.g. body composition, flexibility and jump tests), followed by tests for power, strength and agility, then sprints, and finishing with anaerobic and aerobic capacity. Finally, the S&C coach should aim to test within a standardised environment for example for best practice the below considerations should be applied with consistency (adapted from Van Winckel et al., 2014):

- Time of day
- Duration since last training session/match
- Equipment used
- Surface (an indoor surface is preferable for consistency)
- Personnel
- Standardised warm up preceding testing
- Temperature and humidity
- Nutrition
- Medication
- Players motivation
- Encouragement

Once testing has been completed, analysis, interpretation and communication of results is key to informing relevant stakeholders (players, coaches, support staff). Analysis of smallest worthwhile change and the use of individual coefficients of variation (Turner et al., 2016) are recommended statistical methods to observe meaningful changes within player scores. Z-score analysis is recommended for between player comparisons.

The following is a non-exhaustive list of tests that should be considered when fitness testing soccer players.

Anthropometry

Test: Height, Weight, Body composition (fat mass, fat free mass)

Rationale: Reduced body fat percentage is associated with enhanced physical performances (Ostojic, 2003).

Method: For the most comprehensive and reliable results, laboratory based protocols such as dual-energy x-ray absorptiometry (DEXA) and hydrostatic weighing are preferable. However, these methods can prove both financially costly and time consuming. The most commonly used field based test to determine body composition is skinfold assessment. It is recommended by the International Society for the Advancement of Kinanthropometry (ISAK) that an 8 site protocol (triceps, biceps, subscapular, iliac crest, supraspinale, abdominal, quadriceps, & medial calf) be used.

Power

Test: Vertical Jumps

Rationale: During a match soccer players complete frequent explosive movements such as kicking, sprinting, jumping, changing direction and tackling. Vertical jump height has been significantly related to short sprint performance and overall team success (Arnason et al., 2004b) in soccer.

Method:

Squat jump (SJ) – is a concentric only movement that has been associated with muscular strength.

Counter movement jump (CMJ) – is considered a slow SSC movement that involves both eccentric and concentric muscle actions. It has been associated with sprint performance and strength (Wisloff, 2004).

Continuous in-place jumps (either straight legged (CJS) or bent leg (CJB)) – are considered faster SSC movements that provide information on an athlete's ability to utilise elastic energy.

Strength

Test: Commonly accepted strength tests have included maximum muscular strength assessed via 1, 3 or 5 repetition maximum (typically in a squat or ½ squat movement), isometric mid thigh pull (IMTP) to assess force-time characteristics and isokinetic dynamometry (typically used to assess knee extensor/flexor strength). All methods have previously been shown to be valid and reliable; however, to test using isometric and isokinetic methods requires specialist and expensive equipment reducing its feasibility.

Rationale: Maximal strength can determine sprint performance, jump height and team performance in elite level soccer (Wisløff et al., 1998; Wisløff et al., 2004).

Method: If a player exhibits safe squatting technique and has an acceptable training age, it is recommended that he/she perform a 1, 3 or 5 repetition maximum squat. A detailed description of this protocol is described by the NSCA (Harman, 2008). If a player does not demonstrate the appropriate pre-requisite technique and training, age strength may be inferred via the squat jump (Turner et al., 2011).

Agility

Test: Change of direction speed (CODS) test

Rationale: Players make 1,200–1,400 changes of direction during a match (Bangsbo, 1992). Mirkov et al. (2008) reported that one of the most prominent indicators of overall soccer performance may be agility testing.

Method: Although it is generally accepted that agility is a rapid whole body movement with change of velocity or direction in response to a stimulus (Sheppard and Young, 2006), no soccer-specific test has been developed to capture this quality. Therefore, CODS tests are the most reliable way of determining a player's ability to change direction despite the closed environment in which they are performed. Although Stewart et al. (2014) found that six CODS tests were significantly correlated, it may still be beneficial to employ a test that most closely replicates the movement patterns within soccer. Therefore, it is recommended that either the pro-agility (5–10–5) or 505 tests be administered. In addition to recording the time it takes to complete the test, it may be valuable to calculate the COD deficit (for 505 test; Nimphius et al., 2013) and attain video footage to assess the biomechanical efficiency of the movement.

Speed

Test: Linear speed tests
Rationale: On average, sprint bouts occur every 90–120 seconds, each lasting 2–4 seconds,

with approximately 96% of sprints being less than 30m (Bangsbo et al., 1991; Reilly and Thomas, 1976). It should be noted that acceleration, maximum speed and agility are specific qualities that are not interchangeable (Little and Williams, 2005) and should therefore be tested separately.

Method: Using photo electric timing gates to enhance reliability, players should complete 0–10m as a measure of acceleration and 0–30m as a measure of maximal speed.

Endurance

Test: Yo-Yo Intermittent Recovery Tests (IR), Level 1 & 2.

Rationale: A key component in competitive soccer is the ability to perform intermittent, high intensity exercise for prolonged periods of time. The Yo-Yo IR tests have been significantly related to high intensity activity, high intensity running and total distance covered in match play (Castagna et al., 2009; Bradley et al., 2010).

Method: The Yo-Yo IR Level 1 focuses on the capacity to perform intermittent exercise and is recommended for younger players or those with lower training ages, whilst the IR Level 2 test determines an individuals ability to recover from repeated exercise with a high contribution being demanded from the anaerobic energy system.

It is prudent to mention that the inclusion of a movement screen within a testing battery is recommended for identifying movement dysfunctions. However, the authors believe it is beyond the scope of this chapter to accurately discuss and suggest a specific screening protocol. Other fitness tests, different to the aforementioned, such as repeated sprint ability (RSA) and maximal aerobic speed (MAS) tests, may also be considered by the S&C coach to provide additional and valuable information to guide training prescription.

Programming

Programming is often based on practitioner experience and anecdotal evidence (Plisk and Stone, 2003) as much as it is based on empirical scientific principles. Therefore, a single 'correct' S&C strategy for soccer is unlikely to exist. However, this section offers some critically appraised and evidence led interventions to help improve the physical performance of elite soccer players. For the purpose of this section the term 'strength training' encompasses the relevant sub-qualities of strength that are likely to form a part of the training process (i.e. strength endurance, hypertrophy, maximal strength, strength-speed, speed-strength and power). Similarly, 'conditioning' encompasses the sub-qualities of fitness training pertinent to the physical development of elite soccer players (i.e. aerobic and anaerobic capacity, acceleration, maximal speed, deceleration, change of direction and agility).

Before writing a programme the S&C coach must comprehend the context in which to plan (e.g. male or female players? youth or adult? elite or non-elite playing standard? injury history? training age? playing experience? fitness capabilities? load management requirements?). In addition, the position-specific demands of match play and tactical philosophy must also be considered. Once you have understood the aforementioned, it is critical to identify the fixture distribution and density, which varies greatly between leagues and teams. For example, excluding domestic and European cup competition fixtures, English Premier League (EPL) teams played 38 games in ~41 weeks during the 2015–2016 season, playing twice in one week on ~4 occasions. Conversely, Football League Championship (FLC) teams played 46 games in ~40 weeks, playing twice in one week on ~11 occasions. Mean weekly fixture density for the EPL and FLC during this season equated to 0.93 and 1.15. Accordingly, a team-specific season plan (often referred to as a macrocycle) that considers the undulating training stress and recovery requirements of individual players in the context of the acute and longitudinal fixture demands is warranted.

Traditional or linear periodised training models are recommended for athletes who are required to peak for a single or acute phase of competition. Conversely, non-traditional or non-linear periodised training models are recommended for athletes who are required to peak frequently (once or twice a week) for a sustained period of time (Turner, 2011). The soccer season can be divided into 3 phases: preseason training (~6 weeks), the competitive season (~35–40 weeks) and the closed season (~4–6 weeks). Soccer players are required to peak towards the end of preseason training and maintain performance for the duration of the competitive season. Accordingly, a linearly periodised model is recommended during the preseason phase, and a non-linear model is recommended during the competitive season. A non-linear form of periodisation is more viable to team sports during the in-season as it involves changes in bio-motor emphasis and volume loads on either a session-to-session or weekly basis. One of the merits of this system is suggested to be the ease with which sessions can be quickly tailored and administered to the intense and variable competition schedule.

Successfully planning an S&C programme for soccer is multifaceted and complex, and requires the application of concurrent training (simultaneously developing different physical qualities) throughout the season. Concurrent strength and endurance training produces an interference effect that compromises strength adaptation. A number of strategies have been proposed to minimise this interference effect that should be incorporated into training planning where possible: 1) use high intensity interval formats to stimulate endurance adaptation, 2) train strength after endurance when both are trained on the same day, 3) avoid strength training after exhaustive endurance sessions for ~24 hours, 4) schedule a recovery meal between sessions on these days and 5) avoid unnecessary volume in strength sessions (Blagrove, 2014).

PRESEASON TRAINING

Strength

The aim of preseason training is to prepare players for the aforementioned demands of competitive soccer match play. The use of two blocks of training using a 2:1 weekly loading paradigm has been recommended for use in soccer (Burgess, 2014). Block 1 should be considered as general preparation training (GPT) and block 2 as sport specific training (SST). GPT should increase aerobic and anaerobic capacity and neuromuscular function and capacity whilst the SST should develop sport-specific physical qualities.

A primary objective of a preseason strength programme is to enhance the body's ability to tolerate load and improve working capacity. Though optimal practice might be to complete a strength programme two to three times a week, this is currently not typical practice in most professional environments. Opportunities for strength training during this period reduce towards the end of preseason training when players are required to play in friendly fixtures once or twice a week and the relative importance of 'freshness' and recovery increases. Accordingly, achieving significant strength adaptation in the preseason period is challenging owing to the low frequency of stimulus delivery possible.

This scenario has led to the development of an 'alternate strength model for preseason preparation' (Burgess, 2014), in which general preparation training is prescribed in preseason and progresses to SST once the competitive season starts. There are many merits of this model for teams who start the competitive season with a low fixture density, but this model may have less relevance for teams that start the season with a high fixture density. In these scenarios the capacity to complete comprehensive strength development sessions is limited, giving rise to the need to complete SST during preseason.

The strength programme should take into consideration the injury history, training age, movement competency and individual training needs of the player. Typically, the emphasis in the GPT phase is strength and this progresses to a speed-strength and speed focus in the SST phase. To promote dynamic correspondence, exercise selection should be based on kinetic and kinematic specificity (Gamble, 2009). Accordingly, programming should utilise dynamic, closed chain, triple flexion-extension movement patterns of the ankle, knee and hip. During the GPT phase programming should focus on force development through larger joint range with a higher load–lower velocity theme, predominantly using bi-lateral exercises. This will promote anatomical adaptation and improve a player's working capacity. During the SST phase programming should focus on rate of force development through the joint ranges of soccer movement patterns; with

GPT phase strength programme		
Warm up	**Exercise**	**Organisation**
Myofascial:	Self-directed foam roll	5 minutes
Mobility:	Laying thoracic spine open	2X6 L/R
	Static stretching	2–3 minutes
	Active hip mobility hurdle complex	2–3 minutes
Activation:	Clams	2X12 L/R
	lateral, diagonal, forward, backward mini band walks	2X10 meters
	Kettle bell goblet squat	2X8
Strength programme	**Exercise**	**Organisation**
1a	Front squat	3X8
1b	Bi lateral box jump to 1 leg land to 'A' stance	3X4 alt L/R landing
2	Romanian deadlift	3X8
3a	Bulgarian split squat	3X8
3b	1 leg isometric hamstring bridge (extended knee)	20 sec hold. 3X L/R
4a	Pull up	3X8
4b	½ kneeling, single arm dumbbell shoulder press	3X8 L/R

Figure 5.1 Example strength programme during the GPT phase

SST phase strength programme		
Warm up	**Exercise**	**Organisation**
Myofascial:	Self-directed foam roll	5 minutes
Mobility:	Laying thoracic spine open	2X6 L/R
	Static stretching	2–3 minutes
	Active hurdle hip mobility complex	2–3 minutes
Activation:	Single leg glute bridge	2X10
	lateral, diagonal, forward, backward band walks	2X10 meters
	Isometric single leg ½ squat on airex pad	2X30s L/R
Strength programme	**Exercise**	**Organisation**
1a	Back squat	3X4 (>1.8m/s)
1b	Alternate leg lateral bound	3X3 L/R
2a	Keiser resisted lunge to box step 'A-stance'	3X4 L/R
2b	Single leg box jump - same leg landing	3X4 L/R
3	Glute ham bench 1 leg isometric hip extension (Olympic bar)	30 sec hold. 3X L/R
4a	Single arm dumbbell push press	3X6 L/R
4b	Single arm dumbbell row	3X6 L/R

Figure 5.2 Example strength programme during the SST phase

a lower load–higher velocity theme, predominantly using unilateral exercises. Example strength programmes are offered in Figures 5.1 and 5.2. Alongside any strength programme a player should have a corrective programme that focuses less on external load and is progressed through complexity of movement. Such programmes are designed to address individual player's postural or movement dysfunctions and typically include self-myofascial release (SMR), mobility, muscle activation, stability training (typically focused at the hip, trunk and thoracic regions) and movement patterning (to correct any kinematic and kinetic dysfunctions).

Conditioning

The objective of a preseason conditioning programme is to develop aerobic and anaerobic capacity using methods that stimulate the metabolic, kinetic and kinematic demands of soccer match play. Accordingly, emphasis should be placed on improving the ability to perform isolated and repeated bouts of high intensity activity. Varying formats of high intensity interval (HIIT) training should be used alongside repeated sprint and speed training to improve aerobic and anaerobic function (Buchheit and Laursen, 2013a,b). Conditioning should progress from an extensive to intensive aerobic development focus in the GPT phase and from a speed to a repeated sprint ability (RSA) development focus in the SST phase.

The use of conditioned soccer practices can be a time efficient way of achieving multiple (physical, technical and tactical) outcomes from training. This is particularly advantageous during preseason when holistic player development is required in a relatively short period of time. Table 5.4 demonstrates how manipulating soccer practice conditions can impact the physical outcomes achieved. Running sessions not only facilitate physical development but allow the strength and conditioning coach to deliver highly controlled metabolic or movement skill sessions.

Despite the obvious merits of conditioned soccer practices, GPS and heart rate (HR) telemetry data demonstrates that some players receive an insufficient physical stimulus from soccer training alone. This is particularly true for defensive and technically advanced players during small sided game (SSG) and directional possession practices. Accordingly, a mixed approach to conditioning is recommended to ensure that each player receives the correct series of physical stimuli. Detailed analysis of GPS and HR data will allow the strength and conditioning coach to identify if the physical objectives are achieved in sessions. If this is not the case, supplementary conditioning sessions should be considered. A sensitive, longitudinal physiological monitoring system should be implemented to identify if players are coping with the imposed training demands. This information should be fed back to players and coaches and used to inform future training planning. Example sessions across the preseason phase are offered in Figures 5.3, 5.4 and 5.5 below. These figures demonstrate how training themes might be progressed during preseason training.

Table 5.4 Soccer practice structure and physical outcomes

Practice size	Large	Medium	Small
Number of players	~9V9–11V11	~5V5–8V8	~3V3–4V4
Approximate pitch dimension (m)	~60–80X~60+	~30–40X~40–60	~15–20X~20–30
Timings and organisation	**Extensive**	**Moderate**	**Intensive**
Time (mins)	~8+	~4–6	~2–4
Repetitions	~2–4	~4–6	~8–12+
Physical outcomes	↑ sprint distance	↑ accelerations and decelerations	↑ accelerations and decelerations
	↑ high speed running	↑ high speed running	↑ change of direction
	Aerobic	Aerobic and anaerobic	Anaerobic

			Football session: extensive endurance focus			
	Warm up	Athletic development	Practice 1	Practice 2	Practice 3	Conditioning
Focus	Movement preparation	Eccentric control and low level linear plyometrics	Technical skills	Possession: 8V8	Possession: 8V8 end zone game	Aerobic capacity
Timings	~10 minutes	~10 minutes	2X3 minutes	2X6 minutes. (1:0.25)	2X6 minutes. (1:0.25)	30 second run, 30 second rest X12
Notes			Low to moderate running speeds	Extensive and expansive. Non-directional	Extensive and expansive. Directional	Controlled 120% maximal aerobic speed. Linear

Figure 5.3 Example training session from early-preseason

	Warm up		Football session: intensive endurance focus			
	Warm up	Athletic development	Practice 1	Practice 2	Practice 3	Conditioning
Focus	Movement preparation	Acceleration mechanics. Moderate level multi directional plyometrics	Passing practice	Possession: 4V4	Game: 4V4	Repeated high intensity efforts (30 meter sprints)
Timings	~10 minutes	~10 minutes	2X3 minutes	4X4 minutes. (1:0.5)	2X4 minutes. (1:0.5)	25 second passive recovery between efforts X10
Notes			High running speeds. Multiple changes of direction	Intensive. Non-directional	Intensive. Directional	Linear

Figure 5.4 Example training session from mid-preseason

	Warm up			Football session: repeated high intensity efforts focus		
	Warm up	Athletic development	Conditioning	Practice 1	Practice 2	Practice 3
Focus	Movement preparation	Resisted sprint mechanics	Maximal 20m sprint within technical passing practice	High intensity opposed finishing practice	Overload possession: 6V6V6	High intensity attack versus defence wave game
Timings	~10 minutes	~15 minutes	~10 repetitions. (1:5+)	3X3 minutes	9X3 minutes. (1:2)	~10X ~20 second repetitions. (~1:3 to 1:5)
Notes		8X~10m efforts. (1:5+)	Maximal acceleration and deceleration components		Alternate overload team each repetition	Long sprint distance (~25m) component in each repetition

Figure 5.5 Example training session from the SST phase of preseason training

Competitive season training

The objective of strength and conditioning programming in the competitive season is to maximise player physical performance potential in games. This process can be complicated by the idiosyncrasies of the professional soccer training environment. For example, players rotate between starting, substitute and non-squad roles owing to injury or tactical reasons and therefore have varying technical, tactical and physical development training needs. Furthermore, some players might require modified training for injury management purposes or be required to participate in national team activities across the season. Owing to these factors players accumulate different volumes of training and match play load and varying levels of acute and chronic fatigue across the season. Accordingly, the training system employed needs to be malleable enough to accommodate for individual player training stress and recovery requirements.

A number of training models have been proposed to optimally prepare teams for match play in one and two game weeks (Delgado-Bordonau and Mendez-Villanueva, 2012). Two popular models, both named loosely after their country of origin, are highlighted in Tables 5.5 and 5.6 below.

Though these models might serve as useful templates, a 'one size fits all' approach to team preparation should be used with caution owing to differences in fixture distribution and density between leagues and teams.

Table 5.5 Distribution of training load in two popular soccer training models: one game weeks

Training day	English/'classical' model	Portuguese model
MD	Game	Game
MD+1	Off	Off
MD+2	Low	Active recovery
MD-4	High	High/intensive ('strength')
MD-3	Off	Moderate/extensive ('endurance')
MD-2	Moderate	Moderate ('speed')
MD-1	Low	Low-moderate ('activation')
MD	Game	Game

Table 5.6 Distribution of training load in two popular soccer training models: two game weeks

Training day	English/'classical' model	Portuguese model
MD	Game	Game
MD+1	Active recovery	Active recovery
MD-1	Low	Low-moderate ('activation')
MD	Game	Game
MD+1	Active recovery or off	Active recovery
MD-2	Moderate	Moderate ('speed')
MD-1	Low	Low-moderate ('activation')
MD	Game	Game

Competition phase strength programme		
Warm up	Exercise	Organisation
Myofascial:	Self-directed foam roll	5 minutes
Mobility:	Static stretching	2–3 minutes
	Active hurdle hip mobility complex	2–3 minutes
Activation:	Glute bridge march	2X8 L/R
	Overhead lunge (sagittal and lateral)	2X6 L/R
	Single leg ½ squat on airex pad	2X8 L/R
Strength programme	**Exercise**	**Organisation**
1a	Trap bar deadlift	3X6
1b	Single leg box jump - same leg landing	3X4 L/R
2a	Bulgarian split squat with lateral RNT	3X6
2b	Glute ham bench single leg isometric hip extension (Olympic bar)	30 sec pulse. 3X L/R
3a	Split stance, single arm Keiser/cable row	3X8 L/R
3b	Split stance, single arm Keiser/cable press	3X8 L/R

Figure 5.6 Example strength programme during the competitive season phase

Fixture density should dictate the frequency and content of strength sessions during the competitive season. Strength and corrective programmes can each be completed once during single-game weeks, most suitably on match day (MD) -4 and MD-2 depending on the microcycle structure employed. To prevent de-training of strength sub-qualities, strength programming must stimulate multiple areas of the force-velocity curve. Exercise selection and programming should be regularly reviewed and progressed in line with adaptation and movement competency to avoid monotony. During two game weeks it is likely that only one remedial session can be completed, most suitably on MD-2. Supplementary strength sessions should be scheduled for players with lower match play exposure. Figure 5.6 shows an example competitive phase strength session.

Conditioning adaptations achieved during preseason are largely maintained through soccer training and match play during the competitive season. To avoid de-training, training and match play load, performance testing and physiological monitoring data should be used to guide the training decision making process. Supplementary conditioning sessions should be considered for players who are at risk of de-training, as might be the case with substitutes, non-squad players and players who play in less physically demanding positions. Specific conditioning sessions should be implemented. Examples of how conditioning activities might be distributed across single and double game weeks in a team adopting an 'English'/'Classical' microcycle structure are highlighted in Figure 5.7, below.

Closed season training

The closed season should include a period of recovery (~2 weeks) and a transition training phase (~2–4 weeks). Periods of absolute (~1 week) and light active (~1 week) recovery should be planned to dissipate any neuromuscular and/or psychological fatigue. The transition phase should decrease the extent of detraining experienced across the closed season and enable players to better tolerate the intensity of preseason training (Silva et al., 2016). The transition programme is also likely to attenuate a 'spike' in acute vs chronic workload experienced at the onset of preseason training (Gabbett et al., 2016). This, in turn, may reduce risk of injury.

It is critical that the 'minimal effective dose' is prescribed in order to promote player compliance (Silva et al., 2016). Strength programming during this phase should focus on improving movement competency and addressing specific dysfunctions. It provides an opportunity to focus

One game microcycle

	Athletic development	Football training	Conditioning	Strength
MD	Game		Substitutes and non squad: HIT.	Non-squad: strength programme
MD+1			Recovery day	
MD+2	n/a	Moderate volume/intensity	Substitutes and non squad: profile specific conditioning	n/a
MD-4	Speed: acceleration skills / max speed	High volume/intensity	n/a	Strength programme
MD-3			Recovery day	
MD-2	Speed: change of direction skills	Low volume/high intensity	n/a	Remedial programme
MD-1	Reactive change of direction	Very low volume/high intensity	n/a	n/a
MD	Game		Substitutes and non squad: HIT.	Non-squad: strength programme

Two game microcycle

	Athletic development	Football training	Conditioning	Strength
MD	Game		Substitutes and non squad: HIT.	Non-squad: strength programme
MD+1	*Speed: acceleration skills**	*Moderate volume/high intensity**	n/a	n/a
MD-1	Reactive change of direction	Very low volume/intensity	n/a	n/a
MD	Game		Substitutes and non squad: HIT.	Non-squad: strength programme
MD+1			Recovery day	
MD-2	n/a	Low volume/ intensity	n/a	All players: remedial programme
MD-1	Reactive change of direction	Very low volume/moderate intensity	n/a	n/a
MD	Game		Substitutes and non squad: HIT.	Non-squad: strength programme

*Session only applicable to players who did not play in the preceding game. Players that played in the preceding game complete an active recovery session.

Figure 5.7 Distribution of strength and conditioning activities during single and double game weeks in a team adopting an 'English'/'Classical' microcycle structure

Training day	Accelerations	High speed running	Conditioning
1	n/a	4X20 meter 80% efforts (1:5)	4X30 second linear run: 60 second rest.100% maximal aerobic speed (X2). 2 minutes recovery between sets.
2	Recovery day		
3	n/a	6X30 meter 80% efforts (1:5)	4X30 second linear run: 60 second rest.120% maximal aerobic speed (X2). 2 minutes recovery between sets.
4	Recovery day		
5	n/a	6X40 meter 80% efforts (1:5)	4X30 second linear run: 45 second rest.100% maximal aerobic speed (X2). 2 minutes recovery between sets.
6	Recovery day		
7	4X5 meter maximal efforts	8X40 meter 80% efforts (1:5)	4X30 second linear un: 45 second rest.120% maximal aerobic speed (X2). 2 minutes recovery between sets.
8	Recovery day		
9	6X5 meter maximal efforts	8X50 meter 90% efforts (1:5)	4X30 second linear run: 30 second rest.100% maximal aerobic speed (X2). 2 minutes recovery between sets.
10	Recovery day		
11	4X10 meter maximal efforts	8X50 meter 90% efforts (1:5)	4X30 second linear run: 30 second rest.120% maximal aerobic speed (X2). 2 minutes recovery between sets.
12	Recovery day		
13	6X10 meter maximal efforts	8X50 meter 90% efforts (1:5)	4X30 second linear run: 30 second rest.120% maximal aerobic speed (X3). 2 minutes recovery between sets.
14	Recovery day		

Figure 5.8 Example conditioning programme during the transition phase

on a whole body approach within a high volume, low load theme. Metabolic conditioning should be programmed to stimulate aerobic and anaerobic metabolism and progressively expose players to increasing acceleration, sprint and high speed running distances.

Conclusion

Soccer is an intermittent sport that relies on the capacity to perform isolated and repeated bouts of high intensity activity. The demands of match play and training vary considerably at both inter- and intra- team levels and are influenced greatly by contextual (e.g. age, gender and competition level) and situational factors (e.g. match status, opposition, match location and tactics). Positional variation is typically explained by the different tactical responsibilities of each position, whereas variation between teams is largely explained by variation in the training and playing philosophies employed by coaches. Although soccer is a team sport, it is essential for the S&C coach to consider factors such as biological age (in youth populations), training age, injury history, movement competency and physiological profile of the individual player before prescribing a training programme.

Injuries are inevitable in soccer and can be detrimental to both the individual player (short and long term) and team. Non-contact injuries are more prevalent than contact injuries and typically occur during running, turning, shooting and landing. Although the S&C coach is unable to prevent the occurrence of injuries, it seems prudent to appropriately plan corrective and strength programmes to combat the common injuries experienced within soccer (which can be specific to the population i.e. age, gender and competition level).

Regular fitness testing provides critical information that can be used to optimise periodisation and training prescription. It is suggested that anthropometry, power, strength, change of direction speed, linear speed and endurance should be tested. The selected tests should demonstrate adequate validity, reproducibility and sensitivity to change in performance. The results should be appropriately analyzed and interpreted before being effectively communicated to the player, coach and other stake holders.

Successfully planning an S&C programme for soccer is multifaceted and complex, which is confounded by the fact that concurrent strength and endurance training is implemented throughout the year. Although training emphasis (both on and off the pitch) will change throughout the season, it is accepted that well-developed aerobic and anaerobic energy systems support the capacity to repeatedly perform high intensity efforts during match play and subsequently help to protect players against sustaining 'preventable' injuries. Energy system development should principally be accomplished using high intensity interval training techniques through the careful manipulation of soccer training practices and highly controlled running sessions. Gym based sessions should be scheduled after conditioning sessions with the emphasis on individual development of strength, power and speed.

References

Ali, A. and Farrally, M. 1991. Recording soccer players' heart rates during matches. *Journal of Sports Sciences*, 9(2), pp. 183–189.

Arnason, A., Sigurdsson, S.B., Gudmundsson, A., Holme, I., Engebretsen, L. and Bahr, R. 2004a. Physical fitness, injuries, and team performance in soccer. *Medicine & Science in Sports & Exercise*, 36, pp. 278–285.

Arnason, A., Sigurdsson, S.B., Gudmundsson, A., Holme, I., Engebretsen, L. and Bahr, R. 2004b. Risk factors for injuries in football. *The American Journal of Sports Medicine*, 32(suppl 1), pp. 5S–16S.

Bahr, R. and Krosshaug, T. 2005. Understanding injury mechanisms: a key component of preventing injuries in sport. *British Journal of Sports Medicine*, 39(6), pp. 324–329.

Bangsbo, J. 1992. Time and motion characteristics of competitive soccer. *Science and Football*, 6, pp. 34–42.

Bangsbo, J., Nørregaard, L. and Thorsoe, F. 1991. Activity profile of competition soccer. *Canadian Journal of Sport Sciences = Journal canadien des sciences du sport*, 16(2), pp. 110–116.

Blagrove, R. 2014. Minimising the interference effect during programmes of concurrent strength and endurance training. Part 2: programming recommendations. *Professional Strength and Conditioning*, 32, pp. 13–20.

Bradley, P.S., Carling, C., Archer, D., Roberts, J., Dodds, A., Di Mascio, M., Paul, D., Gomez Diaz, A., Peart, D. and Krustrup, P. 2011. The effect of playing formation on high-intensity running and technical profiles in English FA Premier League soccer matches. *Journal of Sports Sciences*, 29(8), pp. 821–830.

Bradley, P.S., Carling, C., Diaz, A.G., Hood, P., Barnes, C., Ade, J., Boddy, M., Krustrup, P. and Mohr, M. 2013. Match performance and physical capacity of players in the top three competitive standards of English professional soccer. *Human Movement Science*, 32(4), pp. 808–821.

Bradley, P.S., Di Mascio, M., Peart, D., Olsen, P. and Sheldon, B. 2010. High-intensity activity profiles of elite soccer players at different performance levels. *The Journal of Strength & Conditioning Research*, 24(9), pp. 2343–2351.

Bradley, P.S. and Noakes, T.D. 2013. Match running performance fluctuations in elite soccer: indicative of fatigue, pacing or situational influences? *Journal of Sports Sciences*, 31(15), pp. 1627–1638.

Bradley, P.S., Sheldon, W., Wooster, B., Olsen, P., Boanas, P. and Krustrup, P. 2009. High-intensity running in English FA Premier League soccer matches. *Journal of Sports Sciences*, 27(2), pp. 159–168.

Burgess, D. 2014. Optimising preseason training in team sports. In: D. Joyce and D. Lewindon, eds., *High Performance Training for Sports*, 1st ed. Champaign, IL: Human Kinetics, pp. 277–291.

Castagna, C., Impellizzeri, F., Cecchini, E., Rampinini, E. and Alvarez, J.C.B. 2009. Effects of intermittent-endurance fitness on match performance in young male soccer players. *The Journal of Strength & Conditioning Research*, 23(7), pp. 1954–1959.

Delgado-Bordonau, J. and Mendez-Villanueva, A. 2012. Tactical periodization: Mourinho's best kept secret? *Soccer Journal*, 57, pp. 29–34.

Di Mascio, M. and Bradley, P.S. 2013. Evaluation of the most intense high-intensity running period in English FA premier league soccer matches. *The Journal of Strength & Conditioning Research*, 27(4), pp. 909–915.

Ekstrand, J., Hägglund, M. and Waldén, M. 2011. Epidemiology of muscle injuries in professional football (soccer). *The American Journal of Sports Medicine*, 39(6), pp. 1226–1232.

Faude, O., Koch, T. and Meyer, T. 2012. Straight sprinting is the most frequent action in goal situations in professional football. *Journal of Sports Sciences*, 30(7), pp. 625–631.

Fuller, C.W., Junge, A. and Dvorak, J. 2012. Risk management: FIFA's approach for protecting the health of football players. *British Journal of Sports Medicine*, 46(1), pp. 11–17.

Gabbett, T.J., Hulin, B.T., Blanch, P. and Whiteley, R. 2016. High training workloads alone do not cause sports injuries: how you get there is the real issue. *British Journal of Sports Medicine*, 50(8), pp. 444–445.

Gamble, P. ed. 2009. *Strength and Conditioning for Team Sports: Sport Specific Physical Preparation for High Performance*, 1st ed. London: Routledge, pp. 1–10.

Goto, H., Morris, J.G. and Nevill, M.E. 2015a. Match analysis of U9 and U10 English Premier League Academy soccer players using a global positioning system: relevance for talent identification and development. *The Journal of Strength & Conditioning Research*, 29(4), pp. 954–963.

Goto, H., Morris, J.G. and Nevill, M.E. 2015b. Motion analysis of U11 to U16 elite English Premier League Academy players. *Journal of Sports Sciences*, 33(12), pp. 1248–1258.

Harman, E. 2008. Principles of test selection and administration. In: T.R. Baechle and R.W. Earle, eds., *Essentials of Strength Training and Conditioning*, 3rd ed. Champaign, IL: Human Kinetics, pp. 238–246.

Hawkins, R.D. and Fuller, C.W. 1999. A prospective epidemiological study of injuries in four English professional football clubs. *British Journal of Sports Medicine*, 33(3), pp. 196–203.

Hawkins, R.D., Hulse, M.A., Wilkinson, C., Hodson, A. and Gibson, M. 2001. The association football medical research programme: an audit of injuries in professional football. *British Journal of Sports Medicine*, 35(1), pp. 43–47.

Ingebrigtsen, J., Shalfawi, S.A., Tonnessen, E., Krustrup, P. and Holtermann, A. 2013. Performance effects of 6 weeks of aerobic production training in junior elite soccer players. *The Journal of Strength & Conditioning Research*, 27(7), pp. 1861–1867.

Junge, A. and Dvorak, J. 2004. Soccer injuries. *Sports Medicine*, 34(13), pp. 929–938.

Lago-Peñas, C. 2012. The role of situational variables in analysing physical performance in soccer. *Journal of Human Kinetics*, 35(1), pp. 89–95.

Little, T. and Williams, A.G. 2005. Specificity of acceleration, maximum speed, and agility in professional soccer players. *The Journal of Strength & Conditioning Research*, 19(1), pp. 76–78.

Mallo, J., Mena, E., Nevado, F. and Paredes, V. 2015. Physical demands of top-class soccer friendly matches in relation to a playing position using global positioning system technology. *Journal of Human Kinetics*, 47(1), pp. 179–188.

Mirkov, D., Nedeljkovic, A., Kukolj, M., Ugarkovic, D. and Jaric, S. 2008. Evaluation of the reliability of soccer-specific field tests. *The Journal of Strength & Conditioning Research*, 22(4), pp. 1046–1050.

Mohr, M., Krustrup, P. and Bangsbo, J. 2003. Match performance of high-standard soccer players with special reference to development of fatigue. *Journal of Sports Sciences*, 21(7), pp. 519–528.

Mohr, M., Krustrup, P. and Bangsbo, J. 2005. Fatigue in soccer: a brief review. *Journal of Sports Sciences*, 23(6), pp. 593–599.

Mujika, I., Santisteban, J., Impellizzeri, F.M. and Castagna, C. 2009. Fitness determinants of success in men's and women's football. *Journal of Sports Sciences*, 27(2), pp. 107–114.

Nielsen, A.B. and Yde, J. 1989. Epidemiology and traumatology of injuries in soccer. *The American Journal of Sports Medicine*, 17(6), pp. 803–807.

Nimphius, S., Geib, G., Spiteri, T. and Carlisle, D. 2013. Change of direction deficit measurement in division I american football players. *Journal of Australian Strength and Conditioning*, 21(S2), pp. 115–117.

Ostojic, S.M. 2003. Seasonal alterations in body composition and sprint performance of elite soccer players. *Journal of Exercise Physiology*, 6(3), pp. 11–14.

Peterson, L., Junge, A., Chomiak, J., Graf-Baumann, T. and Dvorak, J. 2000. Incidence of football injuries and complaints in different age groups and skill-level groups. *The American Journal of Sports Medicine*, *28*(suppl 5), pp. 51–57.

Plisk, S. and Stone, M. 2003. Periodization strategies. *Strength and Conditioning Journal*, 25, pp. 19–37.

Rampinini, E., Coutts, A.J., Castagna, C., Sassi, R. and Impellizzeri, F.M. 2007. Variation in top level soccer match performance. *International Journal of Sports Medicine*, *28*(12), pp. 1018–1024.

Reilly, T. and Doran, D. 2003. Fitness assessment. *Science and Soccer*, 2, pp. 21–46.

Reilly, T. and Thomas, V. 1976. A motion analysis of work-rate in different positional roles in professional football match-play. *Journal of Human Movement Studies*, *2*(2), pp. 87–97.

Sheppard, J.M. and Young, W.B. 2006. Agility literature review: Classifications, training and testing. *Journal of Sports Sciences*, *24*(9), pp. 919–932.

Silva, J., Brito, J., Akenhead, R. and Nassis, G. 2016. The transition period in soccer: A window of opportunity. *Sports Medicine*, 46, pp. 305–313.

Stewart, P.F., Turner, A.N. and Miller, S.C. 2014. Reliability, factorial validity, and interrelationships of five commonly used change of direction speed tests. *Scandinavian Journal of Medicine & Science in Sports*, *24*(3), pp. 500–506.

Turner, A. (2011). The science and practice of periodization. *Strength and Conditioning Journal*, *33*, pp. 34–46.

Turner, A., Bishop, C., Springham, M. and Stewart, P. 2016. Identifying readiness to train: when to push and when to pull. *Professional Strength and Conditioning*, *42*, p. 19.

Turner, A., Walker, S., Stembridge, M., Coneyworth, P., Reed, G., Birdsey, L., Barter, P. and Moody, J., 2011. A testing battery for the assessment of fitness in soccer players. *Strength & Conditioning Journal*, *33*(5), pp. 29–39.

Van Winckel, J., McMillian, K., Meert, J.P., Berckmans, B. and Helsen, W. 2014. Fitness testing. In: J. Van Winckel, W. Helsen, K. McMillian, D. Tenney, J.P. Meert and P. Bradley, eds., *Fitness in Soccer: The Science and Practical Application in Soccer.* Manipal Technologies Ltd., India: Moveo Ergo Sum/Klein-Glemen, pp. 123–148.

Vigne, G., Gaudino, C., Rogowski, I., Alloatti, G. and Hautier, C. 2010. Activity profile in elite Italian soccer team. *International Journal of Sports Medicine*, *31*(05), pp. 304–310.

Wisløff, U., Castagna, C., Helgerud, J., Jones, R. and Hoff, J. 2004. Strong correlation of maximal squat strength with sprint performance and vertical jump height in elite soccer players. *British Journal of Sports Medicine*, *38*(3), pp. 285–288.

Wisløff, U., Helgerud, J. and Hoff, J. 1998. Strength and endurance of elite soccer players. *Medicine and Science in Sports and Exercise*, *30*, pp. 462–467.

Wong, P. and Hong, Y. 2005. Soccer injury in the lower extremities. *British Journal of Sports Medicine*, *39*(8), pp. 473–482.

6
RUGBY UNION

Craig Twist

Introduction to the sport

Rugby union is a worldwide game played by ~5 million male and female players as professionals, amateurs and in schools. Governed globally by World Rugby, member unions are grouped into six tiers based on playing strength and potential. International competition for males and females includes the World Cup held every four years, contested between Tier 1 and Tier 2 nations. Age-grade equivalents include the annual World Rugby Under-20 Championship and the World Rugby Under-20 Trophy. The Northern and Southern Hemispheres also hold annual Tier 1 international competitions for both sexes and age grades, these being Six Nations (England, Ireland, Scotland, Wales, France and Italy) and The Rugby Championship (Australia, New Zealand, South Africa and Argentina), respectively. The male professional club game has high profile competitions, for example the Premiership (UK), Pro-12 (Ireland, Scotland and Wales) and Super 14 (Australia, New Zealand and South Africa). Rugby sevens has also popularised, most likely because of tournaments such as HSBC Sevens, Women's Sevens and its introduction to the 2016 Olympic Games. Other modified versions of the game, such as touch, tag and wheelchair rugby are also popular but are beyond the scope of this chapter.

Athletic demands

Match characteristics of 15-a-side rugby match play

The 15-a-side game of rugby union is an 80-minute intermittent sport predominated by low-intensity activity (e.g. standing, walking, and jogging) punctuated by brief periods of high-intensity effort (e.g. striding, sprinting, tackling, scrummaging, rucking, mauling, lifting), and is summarised in Table 6.1. Involvement in specified movements and activities are influenced by several factors, including playing position (i.e. forwards (prop, hooker, lock, flanker) cf. backs (scrum-half, fly-half, centre, wing and fullback), playing standard (international cf. club) and the specific role imposed on the player by a coach (Quarrie et al., 2013; Cahill et al., 2013). Numerous contextual factors will also influence a player's movement characteristics, such as players' physical qualities (see below), phase of the season, recovery between matches, opposition and match outcome (Kempton and Coutts, 2016). Backs typically cover greater total distance

Table 6.1 Summary of movement and activity characteristics by position during 15-a-side rugby match play

	Front-row	Back-row	Inside backs	Outside backs
Total distance (m)	4500–5500	5000–5500	5500–7000	4500–6000
Relative distance (m/min)	64	65	72	68
High-intensity running (m)[a]	400–600	500–900	600–1000	600–1000
Low intensity activity (m)[b]	4000–5000	4500–4800	5000–6000	4000–5000
Sprints <20 m (no.)[c]	20–30	25–35	35–45	20–40
Sprints >20 m (no.)[c]	5–10	8–12	10–15	10–15
Collisions (no.)[d]	10–20	15–25	10–15	8–12
Static exertions (no.)	90–95	85–90	28–32	15–20
Work-to-rest ratio[e]	1:4–1:7	1:4–1:6	1:5–1:21	1:6–1:23

[a] High-intensity running: >5.1 m/s;
[b] Low-intensity activity: <5 m/s;
[c] Sprints ≥6 m/s;
[d] Collisions: making or being tackled;
[e] Work-to-rest ratio: duration of each interval of high-intensity of work divided by the duration of the following rest interval (Austin et al., 2011); Movement data are based on mean ± SD values taken from time motion data on professional rugby union (Austin et al., 2011; Cahill et al., 2013)

during match play compared to forwards, comprising more low-intensity activity and high-intensity running (Quarrie et al., 2013; Cahill et al., 2013; Austin et al., 2011). These differences are explained by more field space and specific offensive and defensive responsibilities of backs. Of the back positions, the scrum-half occupies a unique role that requires a higher number of involvements with the ball and more time in moderate to high speed (20–90% maximum) running than other positions (Quarrie et al., 2013; Cahill et al., 2013). While forwards are involved in less overall and high-intensity running, they perform more high intensity activity (~9 min per match) compared to backs (~3 min per match) due to a greater involvement in static exertions and physical collisions (i.e. rucks, mauls, scrums, tackles (Austin et al., 2011; Quarrie et al., 2013)). Unfortunately, no studies to date have reported the movement or physiological characteristics of female 15-a-side rugby match play.

Match characteristics and physical qualities of rugby sevens players

Rugby sevens is played as 2 × 7 min halves (2 × 10 min in cup finals) with a 2-minute half time, contested by seven players (three forwards and four backs) using the same rules and same size playing area as the 15-a-side version. The game is typically played as a two to three day tournament comprising two to three matches per day. In male and female players overall distance covered (~1500 m) in a match is lower than 15-a-side because of the shorter playing time. However, relative distance (86–130 m/min; Higham et al., 2012; Ross et al., 2015b) is higher due to reduced player numbers, allowing more open spaces and increased movement (Table 6.2). Players of both sexes demonstrate mean heart rates of ~80–90% maximum during a match that suggests a high physiological load (Portillo et al., 2014). While only small differences are observed in total distance, high- and low-intensity activities between positions during international match play, backs perform more high speed movements of longer distances and involvements with the ball and forwards are involved in more contacts (Ross et al., 2015b). Reductions in high intensity

Table 6.2 Summary of movement and activity characteristics during men's and women's rugby sevens match play

	Men		Women
	Forwards	Backs	All players
Total distance (m)	1400–1700	1400–1700	1300–1500
Relative distance (m/min)	100–120	100–120	95–105
High-intensity running (m)[a]	100–300	300–500	120–220
Sprints (no.)[b]	2–9	3–12	4–10
Collisions (no.)	5–10	2–6	–
Work-to-rest ratio[c]	1:0.5	1:0.5	1:0.3

[a] High-intensity running: >5 m/s;
[b] Sprints: ≥6 m/s;
[c] Work-to-rest ratio: duration of each interval of high-intensity of work divided by the duration of the following rest interval (Austin et al., 2011); Movement data are based on mean ± SD values taken from time motion data on rugby sevens (Higham et al., 2012; Portillo et al., 2014; Ross et al., 2015b)

running in the second half of matches suggest that players demonstrate fatigue within a single match (Higham et al., 2013; Ross et al., 2015b). However, players seem to be capable of maintaining running demands across a multi-day tournament (Higham et al., 2012; Ross et al., 2015b). There are often short periods of time (~5–7 days) between tournaments that involve flights across multiple time zones, which means that players can sometimes play with symptoms of travel-related fatigue (West et al., 2014).

Influence of physical qualities on rugby match play and injury

Clear differences exist in the physical qualities between positions and playing standards in 15-a-side rugby (Argus et al., 2012a; Smart et al., 2013; Barr et al., 2014; McMaster et al., 2016). These differences are explained by the specific roles performed by various positions (Smart et al., 2014; McMaster et al., 2016) and a higher training load in professional compared to amateur players (Smart et al., 2013). As playing standard increases, players are heavier with greater lean mass and lower body fat (Smart et al., 2013), have greater sprint speed (Smart et al., 2013) and sprint momentum (i.e. sprint speed × body mass; Barr et al., 2014), possess higher maximal strength and power (Argus et al., 2012a; Smart et al., 2013), and a better repeated sprint ability (Smart et al., 2013). Regardless of playing standard, forwards are typically taller, heavier, possess higher percent body fat, greater absolute strength and power, slower sprint speeds and lower aerobic capacities compared to backs (Smart et al., 2013; Smart et al., 2014; McMaster et al., 2016; Swaby et al., 2016).

Physical qualities are also known to positively influence match performance in rugby players (Smart et al., 2014; Swaby et al., 2016). For example, players with a higher intermittent running capacity cover more total distance during matches (Swaby et al., 2016). Similarly, sprint times are negatively correlated with line breaks, distance covered and tries scored (Smart et al., 2014). While their presence indicates some relevance, these associations are generally low to moderate in magnitude and suggest that a large proportion of the variability in match performance is not determined entirely by players' physical qualities (Smart et al., 2014). Greater homogeneity in the physical qualities of elite players is likely to explain the low to moderate correlations and means factors such as experience, tactical awareness, skill and mental attributes become more important to success as playing standard improves (Smart et al., 2014).

In rugby sevens, physical qualities differentiate between playing performance and standard in both male (Higham et al., 2013; Ross et al., 2015a) and female players (Goodale et al., 2016). Higher standard players are characterised as possessing superior repeated sprint ability, sprint performance, lower limb power and aerobic capacity than lower standard players (Ross et al., 2015a) and than 15-a-side players (Higham et al., 2013). Differences in physical qualities between rugby sevens forwards and backs are small (Ross et al., 2015a), which likely reflects the coaches' preference for selecting highly mobile and dynamic forwards (i.e. back row) to meet the high intensity characteristics of this form of rugby. Improved physical qualities might also enable players to resist fatigue both within (first vs. second half) and between multiple matches during tournaments that contributes to optimised performance and reduced injury incidence (Fuller et al., 2016). Accordingly, rugby sevens players require well-developed physical qualities superior to those of 15-a-side players that enable them to perform the high intensity movement characteristics and tolerate these during tournament schedules.

Improved aerobic fitness and higher body mass in collision sport athletes is associated with a lower risk of injury, reduced injury severity and the ability to tolerate increases in training load (Gabbett and Domrow, 2007). Conversely, Quarrie and colleagues reported that the superior physical qualities did not necessarily minimise injury incidence in high standard rugby players (Quarrie et al., 2001). The authors posited that while soft tissue injuries might be protected against, injuries sustained through blunt force trauma (i.e. collisions) are less likely to be influenced by an individual's physical qualities. This notwithstanding, improved physical qualities are likely to improve a player's resilience to training and match loads (Gabbett, 2016) and ensure they are capable of maintaining appropriate technique during collisions (Gabbett, 2008).

Injury prevalence

The physical demands of rugby described earlier in this chapter mean players are regularly exposed to injury risk during training and playing (Williams et al., 2013; Fuller et al., 2016), the occurrence of which compromises a player's ability to train and compete and can negatively impact on team success (Williams et al., 2016). Accordingly, coaches and players should seek to understand the incidence, types and mechanisms of injury that allow appropriate training and education to minimise such risks.

A recent meta-analysis reported injury incidence as 81 injuries per 1000 player hours for male professional rugby players (Williams et al., 2013). These values are lower than those reported in men's community (14 to 52 injuries per 1000 player hours; Schneiders et al., 2009), youth (16–49 injuries per 1000 player hours; Kerr et al., 2008) and women players (16–38 injuries per 1000 player hours; Kerr et al., 2008; Schick et al., 2008), but ~25% lower than values reported in elite rugby sevens (108 injuries per 1000 player match hours; Fuller et al., 2016). Contrasts in injury incidence likely reflect the differences in match and training characteristics between standards and variants of the game. The mean time lost from match play and training because of injury (i.e. injury severity) is reported as 20 days in professional male players (Williams et al., 2013), but increases dramatically for community players (~8 weeks, Roberts et al., 2013), rugby sevens (44 days, Fuller et al., 2016) and women (55 days, Taylor et al., 2011). These contrasts perhaps reflect differences in the standard of medical care afforded to professional and amateur players, the emphasis on player availability at the elite standard and, in the case of rugby sevens, the rigours of tournament match play. Care should also be taken when interpreting mean injury severity data, as values are inflated by more serious injuries that cause extended periods of recovery.

Collisions are responsible for the majority of match-related injuries across all standards of the game, with a higher percentage (~80%) in male professional (Williams et al., 2013) and community players (Roberts et al., 2013) than youth (~50–60%) and women players (~40–70%; Schick et al., 2008; Taylor et al., 2011). The effect of player role in the collision on injury risk is not clear, with some studies reporting a higher risk for the offensive player, i.e. being tackled (Kerr et al., 2008; Roberts et al., 2013; Williams et al., 2013), and others suggesting the defensive player, i.e. the tackler (Schneiders et al., 2009). Of the total number of injuries sustained, most (~35–70%) are reported in the lower limb compared to upper limb (~17–25%), head/neck (~10–34%) and trunk (~7–12%) (Schick et al., 2008; Taylor et al., 2011; Williams et al., 2013; Roberts et al., 2013; Fuller et al., 2016). These comprise mostly muscle/tendon and joint and ligament-type injuries, albeit fractures and bone injuries present the longest time loss to training and match play (Williams et al., 2013; Roberts et al., 2013; Taylor et al., 2011). While most injuries are sustained in the third quartile of a match (119 per 1000 hours), high values are also reported for the second (112 per 1000 hours) and final quartiles (108 per 1000 hours) (Williams et al., 2013). A higher incidence of injuries in the second half of rugby sevens matches and as tournaments progress suggests player fatigue plays a key role (Fuller et al., 2016). Collectively, these data indicate that training should prepare players for the physical and technical rigours associated with tackling and high intensity running, and be capable of maintaining these actions under fatigue. Increased injury incidence immediately after a half-time break also suggests that coaches should consider the activities used during this period to optimise muscle and cognitive function (Russell et al., 2015).

While excessive training loads are associated with increased injury risk, those players exposed to insufficient training stimuli are also likely to be vulnerable (Cross et al., 2015; Gabbett, 2016). An 'optimal' training dose is therefore required to ensure players are physically robust enough to deal with the rigours of training and match play, but that does not evoke excessive fatigue to increase injury susceptibility (Cross et al., 2015; Gabbett, 2016). Players should be exposed to a physically demanding but appropriate training dose that is administered in a progressive manner (Gabbett, 2016). The use of careful monitoring will enable practitioners to understand the response to training and avoid unnecessary 'spikes' in an individual's training load that might expose them to an increased injury risk.

Fitness testing for rugby

Profiling of physical qualities in rugby players enables a coach to evaluate the effectiveness of a training intervention (Argus et al., 2012b; Austin et al., 2013), assess a player's readiness to compete (Goodale et al., 2016; Swaby et al., 2016), and discriminate between playing standard (Argus et al., 2012a; Smart et al., 2013; Ross et al., 2015a). The physical qualities of interest in rugby players might be classified broadly as: body composition, maximal upper and lower body strength, upper and lower body power output, acceleration (including sprint momentum), maximal running speed and intermittent running capacity. Several tests exist for each of these qualities, with the most appropriate and commonly used presented in Table 6.3. Despite the potential of a standardised battery of tests to provide comparative data between groups and positions, this approach is unlikely to be adopted given that test choice is typically defined by the club's strength and conditioning staff based on personal preference and experience. Regardless of the tests selected, strength and conditioning coaches should consider the following principles to establish the integrity of any test:

1   **Specificity** – Practitioners should first establish the physical qualities pertinent to the individual and team based on standard of play, positional requirements, injury prevention and tactical requirements by the coach.

Table 6.3 Recommended tests for assessing the physical qualities of rugby players

Physical quality	Proposed measurements	Relevance to performance	Limitations	Suggested reading
Anthropometry	i. Body mass (kg) ii. Stature (kg) iii. Sum of seven skinfolds (mm) iv. Lean mass index (body mass/sum skinfolds$^{0.14}$)	Higher standard players are typically taller, heavier and leaner than lower standard players.	No direct measure of body composition (i.e. lean and fat mass). Skilled practitioner is required to enable accurate and reliable measures.	Higham et al. (2013) Smart et al. (2013)
Lower and upper body maximum strength	i. 3–5 RM isoinertial back squat ii. 1–3 RM isoinertial bench press	Diagnostic tests representing maximal force production that reflects the functional strength of the rugby player and influence power and ballistic capabilities. Can also be used for prescription of training load.	Athletes often require lifting experience and skill to execute tests effectively and without increased risk of injury.	Argus et al. (2012b)
Lower and upper body muscle power	i. Power-load profile (0–80% 1RM) for bench throw and jump squat	The ability to generate high power outputs against heavier loads is characteristic of higher standard rugby players. Measures can be used for prescription of training load.	Procedures require use of specialist equipment (e.g. rotary encoder) and can be time consuming when dealing with large squads.	Argus et al. (2012b) McMaster et al. (2016)
Sprint speed and sprint momentum ($kg \cdot m^{-1} \cdot s^{-1}$)	i. 5–20 m sprints (all positions) with and without ball ii. 30–80 m sprints (backs only)	Sprint capability is related to key match performance indicators. Momentum enables understanding of the interaction between a player's body mass and sprint speed.	More work needed to understand exactly how sprint momentum influences performance.	Higham et al. (2013) Smart et al. (2013) Barr et al. (2014)
Repeated high intensity effort (RHIE) ability	i. RHIE position-specific test for forwards and backs	RHIE ability differentiates between playing standards. Allows coaches to understand how players tolerate intense periods of activity, i.e. worse-case scenario.	A player's tackle quality can influence the value of the test.	Austin et al. (2013)
Intermittent endurance capacity	ii. Yo-yo intermittent recovery test level 1	Relates to match running characteristics, recovery and reduced injury risk. Data can also be used to understand adaptation to training.	Focuses solely on running capability with no consideration of collisions.	Austin et al. (2013) Higham et al. (2013)

2 **Sensitivity** – Tests of physical qualities should be capable of: i) detecting individual physiological and performance adaptations to the training stimuli applied; ii) differentiating between standards of play (e.g. elite, sub-elite, sex, age).
3 **Reliability** – Practitioners should be aware of the typical variation, or 'noise', within a test before its selection for use with the players. Indeed, the simple observation of a change in any measure should be interpreted with caution if its reliability is poor. Therefore, the first stage of detecting a meaningful change in a player's physical qualities should be to establish the inter-day reliability of the measure (CV) for each individual by simply taking repeated measures in similar conditions (i.e. non-fatigued, same time of day, controlled diet etc.), and calculating the (SD/mean) ×100. Based on modified standardised effects, this can be multiplied by factors of 0.3, 0.9 and 1.6 to determine what would be a small, moderate and large change in the measure, respectively (Hopkins et al., 2009). In this way, the reliability of the measure is accounted for when detecting a meaningful change, and the magnitude of that change can be determined.
4 **Practicality** – Testing practices should allow the measurement of large numbers of players at one time with minimal disruption to the training schedule. Data generated should be easy to disseminate and interpret by the coach, medical team and player. The information provided should be meaningful to inform the relevant aspects of the training programme and player performance.
5 **Frequency** – Once a battery of tests is decided, these should be scheduled at appropriate time points throughout the season to enable evaluation of the training programme (i.e. before and after specified training blocks) and player performance capabilities.

Programming

Rugby requires the individual (player) and collective (team) development and maintenance of multiple physical, technical and tactical qualities across the transition (off season), preparation (pre season) and competition (in season) macrocycles. Programming is further challenged by increased frequency of match play during the competition phase, match difficulty, team performance, player availability (i.e. international duty, injury), and travel requirements.

Off season

This phase prepares players for the forthcoming pre season using low-moderate intensity training to prevent substantial detraining and reduce injury risk (Gabbett and Domrow, 2007). In addition, some players will undergo surgery to correct injuries that require a period of rehabilitation. Accordingly, players returning to training should do so using carefully prescribed training loads that ensure they are able to return safely to full training (Gabbett, 2016).

Resistance training should emphasise unilateral exercise (e.g. single-leg squats; dumbbell press) to address any potential bilateral asymmetries and anterior to posterior strength imbalances (e.g. shoulder internal vs. external rotators). Allocation of equal time to upper body 'pushing' and 'pulling' strength, as well as isometric strength of the trunk and abdominal muscle should also be addressed over the off season. Two sessions per week using training loads of ~70% one repetition maximum (1RM) with 2–3 sets of 10–12 repetitions should be used.

Player conditioning during the off season should preserve aerobic capacity to minimise injury risk during the subsequent general preparatory mesocycle (Gabbett and Domrow, 2007) and prevent increases in body fat. Low impact activities (e.g. cycling or rowing) performed twice per week for 40–60 minutes at 70–80% maximum heart rate should be accompanied by a more specific interval running session. The latter should last approximately 20–30 minutes (including a warm-up and stretching), using short (~30–60 s) intervals at or just below maximal aerobic speed with a 1:1 work to rest ratio.

Pre season

The rugby pre season is typically 10–14 weeks in duration and is divided into mesocycles of general preparation (3–4 weeks), specific preparation (6–8 weeks) and pre-competition (2–3 weeks). However, the length of each mesocycle will vary in the case of players who have undergone rehabilitation form surgery during the off season or those with international commitments.

General preparation phase

Improvements in maximal strength in elite rugby players are highly related to increased lean mass (Appleby et al., 2012). Accordingly, resistance training during the general preparation phase can be used develop muscle hypertrophy, particularly in those players with poorer maximal strength and low total body mass. This should be conducted as part of a long-term training strategy over several seasons that encourages realistic increases in lean mass (6–13% in trained rugby players; Appleby et al., 2012) appropriate to the individual's needs and maturational status (Argus et al., 2012a). Compound multi-joint exercises that employ large muscle groups (e.g. deadlifts, squats, bench press and chin-ups) should be used ~4 sessions per week, with training intensities of 75–85% 1RM varied throughout the mesocycle in a non-linear fashion to elicit a hypertrophic response (Wernbom et al., 2007). Olympic lifts can also be introduced for novice lifters or revisited to refine players' technique so that these exercises can be used safely and effectively in subsequent phases of the programme.

Given the importance to match running capability (Swaby et al., 2016) and reduced injury risk (Gabbett and Domrow, 2007), two sessions per week during the pre season phase should be dedicated to improving aerobic power. Shorter intervals (15–30 s) at running speeds corresponding to >100% of the individual's maximal aerobic speed with a 1:1 work-to-rest ratio have been recommend for rugby union players (Swaby et al., 2016). Individualised running speeds should be prescribed based on maximal running speed derived from physical profiling. Adopting this mode of training will also minimise any potential interference effects and ensure the appropriate adaptations of both resistance and endurance training are met (Wilson et al., 2012). Position-specific skills training that will provide a conditioning stimulus will also be employed during this phase. Preconditioning practices can address movement mechanics and mobility, as well as re-introduce low intensity plyometric and change of direction drills.

Specific preparation phase

Resistance training should address the development of muscle power, particularly against heavy loads, given it discriminates between higher and lower standard players (Argus et al., 2012a). Individual player load-velocity relationships should be profiled to identify individual characteristics and inform training prescription. For example, players who are force dependent might benefit from a greater focus on velocity-oriented resistance training, while velocity-dependent players might address maximal strength development. This notwithstanding, continued development of maximal strength using compound lifts (e.g. back squat, bench press) is important for power development and should be addressed using weekly undulating periodisation to vary training loads based around 3–5 sets of 4–10 repetitions with loads 80–90% 1RM (McMaster et al.,

2013). These should be accompanied with 3–5 sets of loaded ballistic exercises (e.g. jump squats, bench throws), ideally with loads corresponding to the individual's optimal load for power output (20–60% 1RM, Argus et al., 2012a; McMaster et al., 2013). The programme might also utilise Olympic lifts (or derivatives, dependent on player skill) to enhance the movement specific rate of force development and optimise power output against heavier loads (McMaster et al., 2013).

During specific preparation, conditioning should replicate the running and collision-oriented (i.e. tackles, grappling, wrestling) activities that a player performs during competitive matches. Indeed, training practices should be based upon data generated from time motion analysis and relate to the specific demands of the individual (see Tables 6.1 and 6.2). While understanding the mean distances and activities performed by a player provide a basis on which to design training practices, coaches should acknowledge that these fail to account for the most intense passages of play that an individual and team might experience. Without exposure to these intense periods of activity as part of their conditioning, players might be vulnerable to fatigue that leads to them making errors during intensified periods of match play or to an increased risk of injury (Austin et al., 2011; Gabbett, 2016). Accordingly, conditioning coaches should understand what a *'worst-case scenario'* comprises in terms of running, collision-based activity and skill, and ensure players are exposed to these in an appropriate manner within this phase of the training programme. The use of game-specific intervals and small-sided games provide appropriate modes of exposing players to the necessary training dose.

Pre-competition phase

During the pre-competition period, training will be dictated by the number of friendly fixtures, days between each and the shift in training emphasis towards tactical awareness. The specific preparation mesocycle is likely to comprise 2–3 seven-day microcycles based on the turnaround between matches. With the introduction of fixtures and short turnarounds, the strength and conditioning coach will focus more on player recovery and establishing a training routine mimicking that for the season ahead.

In season

In season comprises early, mid, late and peaking (i.e. play-offs and finals) mesocycles. During this phase coaches must carefully titrate the training loads and recovery to ensure that players are capable of meeting the weekly demands of match play. Therefore, high load-volume training sessions should be conducted in the middle of the week and training load-volumes tapered towards the end of the week to avoid residual fatigue ahead of the next match.

Given that the competitive rugby season can be ~30 weeks duration, strategies to maintain maximal strength and power in season are important. Two sessions per week seem sufficient to maintain maximal neuromuscular performance (Baker, 2001; Argus et al., 2012b; McMaster et al., 2013) alongside match, training and recovery requirements. Using 3–4 week cycles with linear weekly increases in intensity (%1RM), resistance training early in the week should emphasise maximal strength with a second session 2–3 days later focusing on power development (Baker, 2001; Argus et al., 2012b). Maximal strength sessions should employ 4–6 compound exercises per session (e.g. back squat, deadlift, loaded prowler pushes, bench press, loaded chins), using 3–4 sets of 2–6 repetitions and loads ranging from 80–100% 1RM. Power sessions should use 3–4 sets of 2–6 repetitions at 40–60% 1RM with 4–6 appropriate training approaches (e.g. loaded squat jumps, plyometrics, Olympic lifts, loaded sled sprints).

While approaches to in season rugby conditioning are scarce in the literature, in the author's experience coaches should endeavour to include some conditioning that maintains physiological capacity across this period. With matches and recovery taking priority, conditioning practices should be scheduled alongside resistance, technical and tactical training such that interference effects (Wilson et al., 2012) and residual fatigue are avoided. Coaches might think carefully about the integration of small-sided games to simultaneously address appropriate skills, movement characteristics and internal responses (Halouni et al., 2014). Volume should be low in magnitude (1–2 sessions per week, 20–30 min) but maintain internal and external loads that replicate or, where appropriate, are above those encountered during match play. For players identified with poor physical capacities or who are not regularly selected for matches, additional conditioning might be necessary to avoid detraining and the increased risk of injury.

Conclusion

Rugby union is an intermittent collision sport, the characteristics of which are dependent on, amongst other contextual factors, the game format (15-a-side cf. 7-a-side), playing standard, player position and individual physical qualities. The characteristics of rugby match play and training mean that players are exposed to an increased risk of injury, for which incidence and severity are again dependent on format, standard and demands imposed on the individual. While collisions account for the majority of match-related injuries, players exposed to insufficient or excessive training doses also present an increased risk of injury. The strength and conditioning coach therefore holds a fundamental role in designing appropriate training programmes that ensure the rugby player is capable of meeting the demands of match play and that their risk of injury is minimised. These requirements should be met using an appropriately periodised and carefully evaluated training programme that comprises off season, pre season and in season macrocyles. However, practitioners should be capable of adapting the training content to respond to the individual, team and coach's performance needs.

References

Appleby, B., Newton, R.U. and Cormie, P. (2012) Changes in strength over a 2-year period in professional rugby union players. *Journal of Strength and Conditioning Research*, 26, pp. 2538–2546.

Argus, C.K., Gill, N.D. and Keogh, J.W. (2012a) Characterization of the differences in strength and power between different levels of competition in rugby union athletes. *Journal of Strength and Conditioning Research*, 26, pp. 2698–2704.

Argus, C.K., Gill, N.D., Keogh, J.W., McGuigan, M.R. and Hopkins, W.G. (2012b) Effects of two contrast training programmes on jump performance in rugby union players during a competition phase. *International Journal of Sports Physiology and Performance*, 7, pp. 68–75.

Austin, D., Gabbett, T. and Jenkins, D. (2011) Repeated high-intensity exercise in professional rugby union. *Journal of Sports Sciences*, 29, pp. 1105–1112.

Austin, D.J., Gabbett, T.J. and Jenkins, D. (2013) Reliability and sensitivity of a repeated high intensity exercise performance test for rugby league and rugby union. *Journal of Strength and Conditioning Research*, 27, pp. 1128–1135.

Baker, D. (2001) The effects of an in-season of concurrent training on the maintenance of maximal strength and power in professional and college-aged rugby league football players. *Journal of Strength and Conditioning Research*, 15, pp. 172–177.

Barr, M.J., Sheppard, J.M., Gabbett, T.J. and Newton, R.U. (2014) Long-term training-induced changes in sprinting speed and sprint momentum in elite rugby union players. *Journal of Strength and Conditioning Research*, 28, pp. 2724–2731.

Cahill, N., Lamb, K.L., Worsfold, P., Headey, R. and Murray, S. (2013) The movement characteristics of English Premiership rugby union players. *Journal of Sports Sciences*, 31, pp. 229–237.

Cross, M.J., Williams, S., Trewartha, G., Kemp, S.P.T. and Stokes, K.A. (2015) The influence of in-season training loads on injury risk in professional rugby union. *International Journal of Sports Physiology and Performance*, 11, pp. 350–355.

Fuller, C., Taylor, A.E. and Raftery, M. (2016) Should player fatigue be the focus of injury prevention strategies for international rugby sevens tournaments? *British Journal of Sports Medicine*, 50, pp. 682–687.

Gabbett, T.J. (2008) Influence of fatigue on tackling technique in rugby league players. *Journal of Strength and Conditioning Research*, 22, pp. 625–632.

Gabbett, T.J. (2016) The training-injury prevention paradox: should athletes be training smarter *and* harder? *British Journal of Sports Medicine*, 50, pp. 273–280.

Gabbett, T.J. and Domrow N. (2007) Relationships between training load, injury, and fitness in sub-elite collision sport athletes. *Journal of Sports Science*, 25, pp. 1507–1519.

Goodale, T.L., Gabbett, T.J., Stellingwerff, T., Tsai, M.C. and Sheppard, J.M. (2016) Relationship between physical qualities and minutes played in international women's rugby sevens. *International Journal of Sports Physiology and Performance*, 11, pp. 489–494.

Halouni, J., Chtourou, H., Gabbett, T., Chaouachi, A. and Chamari, K. (2014) Small-sided games in team sports training: a brief review. *Journal of Strength and Conditioning Research*, 28, pp. 3594–3618.

Higham, D.G., Pyne, D.B., Anson, J.M. and Eddy A. (2012) Movement patterns in rugby sevens: effects of tournament level, fatigue and substitute players. *Journal of Science and Medicine in Sport*, 15, pp. 277–282.

Higham, D.G., Pyne, D.B., Anson, J.M. and Eddy, A. (2013) Physiological, anthropometric, and performance characteristics of rugby sevens players. *International Journal of Sports Physiology and Performance*, 8, pp. 19–27.

Hopkins, W.G., Marshall, S.W., Batterham, A.M. and Hanin, J. (2009) Progressive statistics for studies in sports medicine and exercise science. *Medicine and Science in Sports and Exercise*, 41, pp. 3–12.

Kempton, T. and Coutts, A.J. (2016) Factors affecting exercise intensity in professional rugby league match-play. *Journal of Science and Medicine in Sport*, 19, pp. 504–508.

Kerr, H., Curtis, C., Micheli, L., Kocher, M.S., Zuakowski, D., Kemp, S.P. and Brooks, J.H. (2008) Collegiate rugby union injury patterns in New England: a prospective cohort study. *British Journal of Sports Medicine*, 42, pp. 595–603.

McMaster, D.T., Gill, N., Cronin, J. and McGuigan, M. (2013) The development, retention and decay rates of strength and power in elite rugby union, rugby league and American football. *Sports Medicine*, 43(5), pp. 367–384.

McMaster, D.T., Gill, N.D., Cronin, J.B. and McGuigan, M.R. (2016) Force-velocity-power assessment in semiprofessional rugby union players. *Journal of Strength and Conditioning Research*, 30, pp. 1118–1126.

Portillo, J., Gonzalez-Rave, J.M., Juarez, D., Garcia, J.M., Suarez-Arrones, L. and Newton, R.U. (2014) Comparison of running characteristics and heart rate response of international and national female rugby sevens players during competitive matches. *Journal of Strength and Conditioning Research*, 28, pp. 2281–2289.

Quarrie, K., Alsop, J., Waller, A., Bird, Y.N., Marshall, S.W. and Chalmers, D.J. (2001) The New Zealand rugby injury and performance project. VI. A prospective cohort study of risk factors for injury in rugby union football. *British Journal of Sports Medicine*, 35, pp. 157–166.

Quarrie, K.L., Hopkins, W.G., Anthony, M.J. and Gill, N.D. (2013) Positional demands of international rugby union: evaluation of player actions and movements. *Journal of Sports Science and Medicine*, 16, pp. 353–359.

Roberts, S.P., Stokes, K.A. and Trewartha, G. (2013) Epidemiology of time-loss injuries in English Community level Rugby Union. *British Medical Journal*, 15, e003998.

Ross, A., Gill, N.D. and Cronin, J.B. (2015a) Comparison of the anthropometric and physical characteristics of international and provincial rugby sevens players. *International Journal of Sports Physiology and Performance*, 10, pp. 780–785.

Ross, A., Gill, N.D. and Cronin, J.B. (2015b) The match demands of international rugby sevens. *Journal of Sports Sciences*, 33, pp. 1035–1041.

Russell, M., West, D.J., Harper, L.D., Cook, C.J. and Kilduff, L.P. (2015) Half-time strategies to enhance second-half performance in team-sports players: a review and recommendations. *Sports Medicine*, 45, pp. 353–364.

Schick, D.M., Molloy, M.G. and Wiley, J.P. (2008) Injuries during the 2006 Women's Rugby World Cup. *British Journal of Sports Medicine*, 42, pp. 447–451.

Schneiders, A.G., Takemura, M. and Wassinger, C.A. (2009) A prospective epidemiological study of injuries to New Zealand premier club rugby union players. *Physical Therapy in Sport*, 10, pp. 85–90.

Smart, D., Hopkins, W.G., Quarrie, K.L. and Gill, N. (2014) The relationship between physical fitness and game behaviours in rugby union players. *European Journal of Sports Science*, 14, pp. S8–S17.

Smart, D.J., Hopkins, W.G. and Gill, N.D. (2013) Differences and changes in the physical characterictics of professional and amateur rugby union players. *Journal of Strength and Conditioning Research*, 27, pp. 3033–3044.

Swaby, R., Jones, P.A. and Comfort, P. (2016) Relationship between maximum aerobic speed performance and distance covered in rugby union games. *Journal of Strength and Conditioning Research*, 30(10), pp. 2788–2793. doi:10.1519/JSC.0000000000001375

Taylor, A.E., Fuller, C.W. and Molloy, M.G. (2011) Injury surveillance during the 2010 IRB Women's Rugby World Cup. *British Journal of Sports Medicine*, 45, pp. 1243–1245.

Wernbom, M., Augustsson, J. and Thomeé, R. (2007) The influence of frequency, intensity, volume and mode of strength training on whole muscle cross-sectional area in humans. *Sports Medicine*, 37, pp. 225–263.

West, D.J., Cook, C.J., Stokes, K.A., Atkinson, P., Drawer, S., Bracken, R.M. and Kilduff, L.P. (2014) Profiling the time-course changes in neuromuscular function and muscle damage over two consecutive tournament stages in elite rugby sevens players. *Journal of Science and Medicine in Sport*, 17, pp. 688–692.

Williams, S., Trewartha, G., Kemp, S., Brooks, J.H., Fuller, C.W., Taylor, A.E., Cross, M.J. and Stokes, K.A. (2016) Time loss injuries compromise team success in elite Rugby Union: a 7-year prospective study. *British Journal of Sports Medicine*, 50, pp. 651–656.

Williams, S., Trewartha, G., Kemp, S. and Stokes, K. (2013) A meta-analysis of injuries in senior men's professional rugby union. *Sports Medicine*, 43, pp. 1043–55.

Wilson, J.M., Marin, P.J., Rhea, M.R., Wilson, S.M., Loenneke, J.P. and Anderson, J.C. (2012) Concurrent training: a meta-analysis examining interference of aerobic and resistance exercise. *Journal of Strength and Conditioning Research*, 26, pp. 2293–2307.

7
RUGBY 7'S

Dan Howells

Introduction

Rugby sevens differs markedly with respect to the physical demands of the 15-a-side format (Higham et al., 2013) and is described as an intermittent contact sport (Ross et al., 2014). It is played on a field with the same dimension constraints as the 15-a-side game. Seven players per team take the field for competition, with 5 rolling substitutions available within a game from the 5 available substitutes. The game involves two 7 minute halves, interspersed by a 2 minute half time interval. It is often played in a tournament style consisting of a pool stage and an elimination stage, with teams contesting 5–6 games over the course of 2–3 days, which is in stark contrast to the 15-a-side game that contests only 1 match per day and rarely on consecutive days (Ross et al., 2014).

Within the elite area of rugby sevens, the World Series comprises 10 competitions for Men's and 6 for the Women's, dispersed across the year between early December and mid May. Each competition is played in a major city worldwide, and therefore involves extreme travel, which must be factored into a team's physical preparation plan by practitioners. Competitions are often paired and performed on back to back weekends, which can result in players competing again in as little as 6 days after a tournament ends, with long haul travel often involved. Such aspects as regular travel fatigue and jet lag are unique and diverse factors that must be considered alongside the many common aspects of physical preparation that are considered as a mainstay of strength and conditioning practice.

Physical demands

Understanding the physical demands of the sport is pivotal for effective planning and programming, in order to maximise athletic performance and on field transfer to competition. Understanding the game-specific activities performed by players during sevens competition allows a strength and conditioning coach to quantify the external load endured and the frequency upon which specific tasks are performed (Ross et al., 2014). Training programmes should be planned in order to cope with these demands during performance, by following clear philosophies and/or periodisation models, with the primary outcome being either direct or indirect on field performance enhancement.

Comparison to the 15-a-side version of the game gives a strong understanding of the increased intensity demands placed on the body during sevens competition. In the extreme case, international rugby sevens players have been shown to have to cover the ground at a rate of 120m.min^{-1}, which is a 69% greater relative distance compared with professional rugby union backs (mean 71m.min^{-1}) and loose forwards (mean 65m.min^{-1}) within the 15's game (Higham et al., 2012; Ross et al., 2014). It has been demonstrated that international sevens demands can range between 96–120m.min^{-1} (Higham et al., 2012; Murray and Varley, 2015), whereas domestic level intensity appears to be lower at 98–108m.min^{-1} (Suarez-Arrones et al., 2012; Suarez-Arrones et al., 2016). This disparity can be attributed to a higher ball in play duration evident in the international game, which has been demonstrated to be approximately 13% longer (Ross et al., 2014).

Understanding the types of movement demand contributing to on field performance has important implications for a player's athletic development programme. Coaches should look to prepare players to be able to withstand the stresses associated with these game demands. High speed running has been observed to contribute to as much as 21% of total running load in international competition (Ross et al., 2015). When compared to elite 15's players, elite rugby sevens players cover approximately 45% greater total distance per min with a higher proportion of that distance at high velocity (~135% greater distance covered per min at speeds in excess of >5m.s^{-1}) (Higham et al., 2012). Positional differences (backs and forwards) have been researched with little or trivial differences between positions for high speed running and total distance. This would make planning for the strength and conditioning coach somewhat easier with respect to running demands, based on the notion that backs and forwards are more interchangeable in rugby sevens, and game style is associated with player roles as opposed to player positions (heavier backs often play in the forwards, for example).

Below demonstrates the typical game demands for a group of sevens players across a 6 game completion weekend. Note the differences between the variables especially game 4 and 5 that reflect a intensity of less than 100m.min^{-1}, yet have the highest requirement of high speed running exposure (23% of total work) compared to the other games. Game 6 was a 10 minute each way final, demonstrating further increases in volume of work players can be exposed to when they are potentially at their most fatigued state.

Table 7.1 GPS data from a World Series event demonstrating how demands vary between games. Data represents a full Match (14 minutes) of rugby sevens exposure

Game	Average of distance (metres)	Average intensity (metres per minute)	Average distance of high speed metres >5m.s (metres)	Average of high speed metres as % of total distance	Average sprint speed >7m.s (metres)	Average number of accelerations >3.0m.s.s	Average number of decelerations (− m.s.s)	Average number of sprints
1	1718	100	302	17%	62	13.4	15.4	14.6
2	1712	94	334	19%	100	16.5	18.4	15.6
3	1644	112	302	18%	34	14.0	24.6	17.2
4	1520	98	346	23%	82	13.4	15.8	16.0
5	1634	88	364	23%	96	13.8	19.6	16.0
6	2156	91	382	18%	82	16.3	21.4	20.2

Metabolic demands

In addition to external load, internal load is an important consideration. Internal load is the cost that external load imposes upon the body, and includes rugby specific contact components of the game. Observing heart rate during a game as a marker of internal load and metabolic intensity, studies have shown average intensities of 86–88% of maximum heart rate, with peak heart rates reaching 92–94% of maximum (Granatelli et al., 2014). Blood lactate (BLa) concentrations give a simple understanding of glycolytic contributions, with BLa shown to be 8.7+1.7 and 11.2+1.4mmol/L at the end of 1st and 2nd halves respectively (Granatelli et al., 2014).

These observations clearly demonstrate the extremely demanding and glycolytic nature of the sport, and the importance of the ability to recover efficiently between bouts of intense repeated actions within the game. Rugby sevens is clearly a mixed energy system sport, played at high relative speeds; therefore, it is vital that players have a strong aerobic base in order to resist fatigue and express the high velocity movements and collisions required in the game. That is not to say that maximising aerobic potential should come at the expense of those physical qualities that may make a player unique (strength, power, speed). Moreover, it demonstrates that there will always be a delicate balance in terms of energy system development and that not all training stimuli will benefit players in the same way. For example, a player who typically tends to find themselves on the outside of the field as a winger is likely to be required to perform repeated single sprint activities, with very low intensity recovery efforts between (typically) 20s and 60s in duration. A volume of aerobic work may benefit them in their recovery ability between bouts, but, in contrast, should this aerobic training volume be too high, it may dampen their ability to express maximum acceleration and velocity within their efforts. It is the role of the strength and conditioning coach to decide, alongside technical coaches, where a player's individual physical plans should be directed, so to match the technical and tactical requirements of that player in the overall team's composition. Simply striving for every player to be "fitter, faster, stronger" is naïve in terms of physical development and often results in generic programmes for a team of very individual athletes. Improving one variable can often come at the cost of another, and therefore understanding interplay between concurrent stimuli alongside the lasting effects of adaptations and training residuals is crucial within a strength and conditioning plan for team sports such as rugby sevens.

Devil in the detail – taking a deeper look at physical demands of the game: work:rest (W:R)

The relationship between work and rest within rugby sevens has been described as a ratio of 1:0.5 W:R (Suarez-Arrones et al., 2012). A simple ratio, however, tells us nothing as practitioners about duration of work and rest. Understanding the level of competition and the effects this has on work demands is key. International matches have ~13% longer total ball-in-play duration and ~15% greater average ball in play cycle (Ross et al., 2014). Ball in play cycle best describes the duration from the start of a play to the end of it, with cessation evident either through a knock on, try, penalty, or ball in touch, as examples. What is worthy of note, however, is that there are no observed differences between standards of play and the duration of an average recovery (ball out of play) cycle length (Ross et al., 2014). This means that as the standard of play increases, so too does work duration, influencing the ratio and therefore the demands of the game. Longer ball in play (or "work") passages occur in the game at the elite level also, with international matches displaying ~11% greater proportion of long work passages (>45s) and ~7% greater very long (>60s) work passages (Ross et al., 2015).

"Worst case" versus "average" scenarios

Research tends to produce mean or average data, and therefore it is imperative for practitioners to perform their own analysis of the maximum outputs required by their players, both based on evolution of the game itself, and the ever changing nature of sport. This, in conjunction with a clear understanding of the demand of the game style that a coach would like to play, is of great importance. Resolving to match the average demands within training means that a high proportion of the time players may fall short in matching the worst case/maximum game demands placed upon them in competition. With fatigue comes decreased performance and skill execution alongside potential increases in injury risk. All of these outcomes result in a reduced likelihood of success.

To use a case study example, it was recognised that average work periods (ball in play) were shown to increase by 8s, and average rest periods extended by 9s in length, over 2 consecutive seasons. Reminding ourselves that the "average" work duration is 25–35s in length from this example, when looking at the *longest* ball in play cycle time (*worst case scenario*), this increased from 108s to 138s in length! As per research between elite and non-elite teams, recovery periods remained consistent. In such a scenario, this dramatically increases a work:rest ratio to 3.3:1! Around 12–18 passages of work occur in each game, and although a single game is unlikely to have multiple passages of worst case scenarios, being successful when you are exposed to these demands as a team could mean the difference between success and failure in match outcome. Interestingly, the same data demonstrated that the higher the number of tries scored, the more total rest there was within the duration of the game. This demonstrates the importance of being clinical in skill execution, as scoring more tries can be conserving of fatigue, which is vital when considering competitions consist of up to 6 games over 2–3 days.

Understanding game demands with increasing levels of specificity is key. By using GPS technology as a simple means of assessing game demands, each level of analysis can give a deeper understanding of how total work (distance) is expressed. Distance and/or work rate (metres per minute) may never change, but the path of how that metric was attained will vary greatly, player to player and game to game. For example, 1500m of total distance could be achieved by both player A and player B in the same game, but the percentage of that work spent working at above sprint speed thresholds could vary greatly between players. This would result in a need for different management for each player in preparation periods and potentially load management during competition time also. Figure 7.1 highlights various levels of interpretation and its contribution to a single variable representing total work.

When looking towards more specific actions that contribute to game workload as previously mentioned, we could look to interpret high speed running (>5m.s^{-1}), very high speed running (>7m.s^{-1}), in addition to accelerations and decelerations as an indication of total change of direction demand. This is before considering rugby specific activities such as a carry, clear out, tackle, jump, lift, scrum, kick and pass. Although these latter sports specific movements are largely

Table 7.2 Typical average ball in play duration and rest durations on the world series across two consecutive seasons, compared to worst case scenarios and longest passage durations

Season	Average work duration (secs)	Average rest duration (secs)	Work:Rest ratio (W:R)	Worst case (longest) passage duration (secs)
A	25	32	1:1.3	108
B	33	41	1:1.3	138

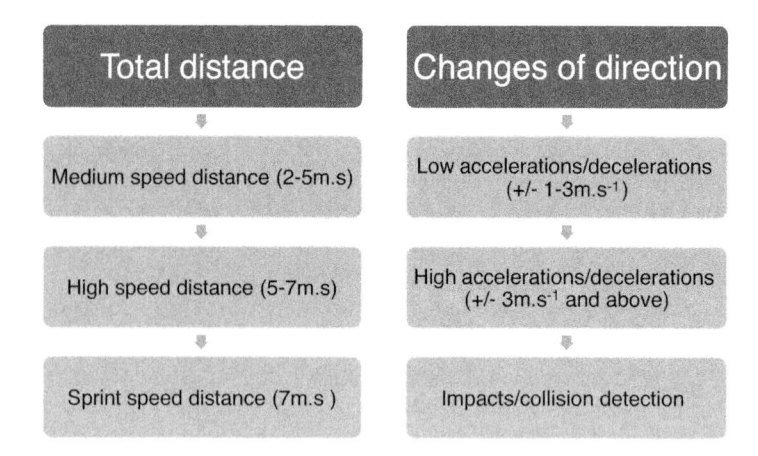

Figure 7.1 A visual example of how simple GPS metrics (total distance and changes of direction) can be analysed at subsequent levels for use in monitoring or characterising game demands in rugby sevens

technical in nature, the intensity and frequency of these will, of course, contribute to total workload and game demands, and must be understood as part of the whole picture regarding physical preparation for rugby sevens.

Epidemiology

It is essential to take note of the epidemiology associated within rugby sevens. A strong strength and conditioning practitioner should base their injury prevention, robustness or anti fragile philosophies and prescriptions on evidence based information pertaining to the frequency and severity of injury risk within a sport. Player availability for the main modality of training (rugby training itself) should be of the upmost importance to a practitioner, in order to maximise on field impact for the technical coaches.

Given the contact nature of the game, it has been suggested that match related injuries between the 15-a-side game and sevens are similar. It is well known that rugby union results in both contact and non contact (musculoskeletal) injuries, but the severity of these injuries in rugby sevens appears to outweigh that of the 15-a-side game.

Recent research by World Rugby investigating rugby sevens highlighted the frequency of injury rate from within international matches on the HSBC World Sevens Series: 108.7 injuries per 1000hrs of match exposure (Fuller and Taylor, 2016). In the 15-a-side version of the game, a study of the 2015 World Cup analysis of injury incidence was represented as 90.1 injuries per 1000hrs match exposure (Fuller et al., 2017a). When comparing the World Series (7's) over 8 seasons with the 2015 World Cup (15's), it appears there is consistency in the incidence being more prevalent for backs (118.2 in 7's and 100.4 in 15's respectively) than for forwards (95.7 versus 81.1 respectively). An additional difference between variations of the game is observed in severity – that is, days lost on average through injury. In the 15-a-side game, the mean severity is expressed as 30.4 days lost from match injuries, and 14.4 from training injuries (Fuller et al., 2017a), whereas the game of sevens is considerably higher at 44.2 days when looking at trends over the 2008–2016 seasons for match injuries sustained (Fuller and Taylor, 2016). Injury risk reduction therefore forms a pivotal component of training within the strength and conditioning and medical teams' philosophy around building the robust athlete for rugby sevens.

Table 7.3 The most common injuries sustained by backs and forwards in rugby sevens. Data taken from 2008–2016 seasons

Backs		Forwards	
Injury	%	Injury	%
Hamstring muscle strain	12.6	Concussion	12.8
Concussion	11.1	Knee MCL sprain	5.9
Lateral ankle ligament sprain	6.3	Lateral ankle ligament sprain	5.3
Knee MCL sprain	6.1	Quadriceps haematoma	5.0
Tibiofibular syndesmosis injury	4.4	Hamstring muscle strain	4.0

Table 7.4 Highest time loss injuries (burden) sustained by backs and forwards in rugby sevens. Data taken from 2008–2016 seasons

Backs		Forwards	
Injury	Injury burden, %	Injury	Injury burden, %
Anterior cruciate ligament	12.2	Anterior cruciate ligament	11.0
Hamstring muscle strain	10.4	Shoulder dislocatn/instability	7.8
Knee MCL sprain	7.5	Tibia/fibula fractures	6.2
Shoulder dislocation/instability	6.7	Knee MCL sprain	6.0
Syndesmosis injury	6.4	Concussion	5.8

It is clear that in terms of potential preventable injuries, hamstring strains, knee MCL strains, and ankle ligament sprains form a high proportion of reported injuries in rugby sevens. This again should contribute to the knowledge of the strength and conditioning practitioner, and he/she should respect this information within planning an overall season and individual microcycles. The nature of these injuries, often referred to as "preventable" injuries, versus the vastly uncontrollable nature of "contact" injuries suggests just that, and training correctly could positively reduce risk or these occurring. Therefore, every measure should be taken to minimise risk of such injuries occurring. In addition to understanding what types of injuries occur within the game, understanding those injuries with highest time loss implications for training is also important, as illustrated in Table 7.4.

The two most common mechanisms of injury for backs are being tackled (33.1%) and running (22.5%) whereas for forwards being tackled (30.9%) and the act of tackling itself (25.9%) appear the most common causes of injury (Fuller and Taylor, 2016). All of these mechanisms are obviously amplified when these actions are performed at higher speeds. There is no conclusive reason for the severity of injuries being greater in the game of sevens. One study looked at the timing of injuries and suggested a fatigue element that contributes to injury within the format of rugby sevens competitions. The authors observed that the likelihood of injury was not only increased in the second half versus first half of competition, but that injury risk was evidently higher in game 3 versus game 1 of each day, and the risk increased further between day 2 versus day 1 of competition (Fuller et al., 2017b). This highlights the importance of enhancing players' ability to resist fatigue as part of the physical preparation plans of a coach.

With fewer people on the field of play and the same pitch dimensions, the likelihood of being involved in a high frequency of varied actions obviously increases. The number of collision based

Table 7.5 Mechanisms of injury sustained by backs and forwards in rugby sevens. Data taken from 2008–2016 seasons

Series/cause of onset	% (95% confidence interval)		
	Backs	Forwards	ALL players
All series (2008/09–2015/16)			
Collision	12.2 (9.3–15.0)	12.6 (9.0–16.3)	12.3 (10.1–14.6)
Kicking	0.8 (0–1.5)	0.0 (–)	0.5 (0–1.0)
Lineout	0.0 (–)	2.2 (0.6–3.8)	0.8 (0.2–1.5)
Maul	0.4 (0–0.9)	0.3 (0–0.9)	0.4 (0–0.8)
Ruck	6.1 (4.0–8.2)	12.0 (8.4–15.6)	8.3 (6.5–10.2)
Running	22.5 (18.9–26.2)	9.5 (6.2–12.7)	17.5 (14.9–20.1)
Scrum	0.0 (–)	1.6 (0.2–2.9)	0.6 (0.1–1.1)
Tackled	33.1 (29.1–37.2)	30.9 (25.8–36.0)	32.3 (29.1–35.5)
Tackling	21.4 (17.8–24.9)	25.9 (21.0–30.7)	23.1 (20.2–26.0)
Other	3.5 (1.9–5.1)	5.0 (2.6–7.5)	4.1 (2.8–5.5)

activities made cumulatively across a whole competition (6 games) is obviously high for those players with high percentages of game involvement. As discussed, evidence suggests the pace of rugby sevens to be faster than in 15's with greater average speeds and vastly higher percentages of high speed running relative to the total workload. This is likely to contribute to heightened aspects of fatigue, with resultant increased risk for muscular injury, in addition to higher speed collisions for contact related injuries. When coupled with an increased frequency of collision based activities in the game of rugby sevens, the importance of injury prevention and player availability for matches becomes an obvious contributor to on field outcomes.

This demonstrates to the strength and conditioning coach that there are significant focal points in terms of player robustness that should be of primary focus in a sevens specific programme. In addition to frequency, location and type of injury, identifying that the risk of injuries is significantly more likely in the second half versus first half of a game (Fuller et al., 2017b) should highlight the importance of building a robust athlete to play the game of sevens. Whether that be shoulder health and function or posterior chain strength development methods need to be employed to maximise player resilience and reduce injury risk. Maximising player availability for training and matches must be a high priority outcome for the strength and conditioning coach.

"Physical assessments" as opposed to "fitness testing"

The word "test" defines that success or failure may ensue from the results collected. In terms of athletic development, utilising the term "assessment" can help the practitioner and the athlete realise that these results should be collected as part of a journey of athletic development, and serve a purpose to assess the current status or physical stage of development of the athlete. Approaching such assessments in this way, and integrating them as part of a planned season, can mean that there will be less negative impact from unanticipated results, and constructive outcomes can be generated between athlete, strength and conditioning coach and technical coaches with respect to the direction of future programming. The most important principle when choosing what assessments are suitable is that the assessment **must directly inform decisions regarding programming.**

In terms of fitness or "physical assessments", it is important to choose assessments that link the direct philosophy of the strength and conditioning coach in terms of what he/she values as influential for performance transfer. As a minimum, it should be expected that primary assessments result in some form of strength, power, speed and fitness being assessed. These primary assessments should give relatively instant feedback as to the capabilities of a player, and the coach should be able to inform their decisions about programming from them. The strength and conditioning coach can then delve in to deeper detail using secondary assessments. These should be used to identify more specific problems or limitations to performance within a player's physical profile, which in turn provides the practitioner with an opportunity to create innovative solutions to problems. For example, a simple primary speed test will create an outcome result – the time in which it takes to go from standing to 20m, for example. Alongside high speed camera technology (secondary assessment), it may be subjectively deemed that a player is not reaching triple extension in the early acceleration phase during playback, and that this may be a limitation to the outcome result (time). Further investigation towards this limitation in movement may then demonstrate that the player is deemed strong enough (from a primary test, such as a squat or isometric mid thigh pull) to be able to produce triple extension but is failing to do so when exposed to small time frames within which to produce high ground reaction forces. On further analysis, the player may appear to have excessive ankle dorsi-flexion and a poor single leg RSI score that appears to prevent him from producing force at a stiff ankle shank. Building this type of picture by layering primary and secondary assessments helps the practitioner understand the specific limitations to physical outputs and promotes a solutions based approach to performance enhancement and long term athletic development.

Tables 7.6 and 7.7 highlight typical primary and secondary assessments alongside low cost alternatives that would help to evaluate these typical physical variables. Where there are suggested

Table 7.6 Examples of primary fitness assessments used to evaluate physical profiles of rugby sevens players

PRIMARY physical qualities	Assessment	Pros	Cons	Elite score	Alternative assessment (elite score)
Aerobic–anaerobic fitness	YoYo IR1	Assess large groups Portable Can derive MAS from end level	High volume of load and accelerations and decelerations Fatigue inducing	L20+	MAS time trial e.g., 1200m (<4:00min = 5m.s)
Acceleration speed	0–30m sprint (From 30cm start, split stance, static start)	Portable No habituation required	Time consuming Timing gates required	<3.9s	n/a
Maximum velocity	Flying 10m Sprint	Portable No habituation required	Time consuming Timing gates required	<1.0s	n/a
Strength	Isometric mid thigh pull 3RM bench 3RM pull up	All players can perform irrespective of lower limb modifications Easy to perform Easy to perform	Neurally fatiguing Specialist equipment required Neurally fatiguing Neurally fatiguing	>5.0x BW (inclusive of system mass)	3RM squat
Power	60kg Jump squat	Portable transducers available	Assumptions made in	>75w.kg	Standing broad jump (>2.80m)

Table 7.7 Examples of secondary fitness assessments used to evaluate physical profiles of rugby sevens players

SECONDARY physical qualities	Assessment	Pros	Cons	Elite score	Alternative assessment (elite score)
Reactive Strength **Knee/ankle Ankle**	Drop jump SL drop jumps	Very specific assessment of SSC ability Very specific assessment of SSC ability	Specialist equipment required High stress for tendons High skill and coordination requirement	RSI >3.0 SL RSI >2.0	3x bunny bound for distance 3x SL hop for distance
Unilateral strength Single leg calf strength Single leg strength	SL peak plantar Isometric force Single leg squat (140deg knee)	Quick and simple to evaluate Provides asymmetries Quick and simple to evaluate Provides asymmetries	Specialist equipment required Neurally fatiguing Specialist equipment required Neurally fatiguing	$3.0 \times BW$ $4.0 \times BW$	Calf capacity test – SL calf raise reps to failure off 20cm box, knee fully extended (>30reps) Single Leg/Pistol Squat Capacity Test
Hamstring strength	NordBord	Quick and simple to utilise	Neurally fatiguing	Minimum threshold $4.0 \times BW$	Hamstring capacity Test – hip bridge reps to failure off 40cm box with knee at 140deg (elite score >40 e/s)

minimum standards for these assessments, this must be interpreted with caution, and it is always advisable to create an assessment of the standards required for the sport in question.

In a high performance environment, it wouldn't be uncommon to have a range of primary assessments that are performed by all players at specific points in the season, with an accompanying "toolbox" of secondary assessments that become utilised in a player or situation specific manner. These secondary assessments can also be perceived as monitoring tools, and could be utilised more frequently. For example, using the same example of a single leg drop jump RSI, this could be utilised as an in session training tool to monitor athletic progress, as it will be time efficient and provides instant feedback to the player. Alternatively, weekly secondary assessments often prove useful within late stage rehab to help practitioners understand where a player sits with respect to a perceived return to training. A simple "reps to failure" calf capacity test can very simply help inform a practitioner of a players readiness to tolerate specific running loads in late stage rehab after a significant calf injury, and it is both simple and time efficient in nature.

It is important that the practitioner truly understands the impact of performing such assessments on future training sessions also. For example, performing maximally fatiguing repeat sprints, or a bleep test to exhaustion, immediately prior to a full training session would not be wise with respect to musculoskeletal injury risk. Therefore, careful planning to ensure the assessment does not impact on the quality of technical work desired by rugby coaches is key. The coach should always consider the benefits and limitations of any test by weighing up the impact of these on the immediate training session(s) following an assessment.

Programming

As described in the introduction, competition for rugby sevens generally occurs in blocks of 2 consecutive weekends, including extensive long haul travel, interspersed by 3–6 weeks. The season start often occurs after a significant pre season period that can be 12–16 weeks in length. It is important therefore to plan blocks of training to offer clear direction to the players and coaches. The yearly plan for rugby sevens does not follow a typical team sport in season pattern consisting of matches week in week out. Rugby sevens tends to mimic more closely sports that have significant preparation periods prior to competition, such as track and field. These sports benefit from clear opportunities to promote repeated bouts of stress and adaptation across preparation cycles, whilst focusing more on longer and more advantageous tapering periods into competitions set weeks/months apart.

Continued physical development should be the priority for every player throughout the season, and for young players with low training ages, this focus throughout the year is highly achievable. However, those mature players with high outputs (strength, power, speed, and endurance qualities) may be more susceptible to fatigue, and more specific tapering methods are likely required in order to create full adaptation and realisation of the programme goals. Reliable and simple monitoring tools should help inform these processes.

In team sports per se, the concurrent training conundrum needs to be addressed within a strength and conditioning coaches philosophy. As per the needs analysis, it is evident that work rates are high, and body mass of players are lower than in the 15-a-side game. This demonstrates the obvious requirement for speed and fitness to be at the forefront of a rugby sevens programme. Common sense within programming must therefore prevail when planning a typical week. Where speed is important, freshness is key to ensuring this quality can be improved systematically. On such a day, on field rugby work may have to be a secondary focus for that day of training. In contrast, focused rugby training days may consist of significant high intensity work, and as such may become a priority session, with an upper body weights session in the afternoon becoming secondary in nature. Providing as many players for rugby training as possible should always be an aspect a strength and conditioning coach is measured on in terms of effective outcomes, and simple common sense planning of a weekly structure is one simple way to help maximise this.

Some key aspects upon which a training programme for rugby sevens are considered below:

- **Rugby training should always be prioritised as the specific form of training in a well planned programme** – *therefore, all decisions around training management should revert to this goal.*
- **Clear measureables for training intensity/volume should be determined and reflected in a planned week** – *it is vital all staff (and athletes) appreciate this classification and language. It should remain simple, quick to associate with, along the lines of "high, medium, low" intensity days, and/or session RPE.*
- **Daily opportunities for mobility or "prep to train" should be factored in to a schedule** – *this is often an overlooked aspect but with training stress and cumulative fatigue occurring throughout a week, opportunities to regain muscle length and joint ROM will minimise injury whilst also promote active recovery and blood flow.*

- **Speed work should follow days off or very low activity days.**
- **Rugby sevens players with high running outputs will often struggle to perform for 3 consecutive days of training within a week with meaningful outputs (technically and physically)** – *it would be counterproductive to plan for 3 consecutive days of demanding work unless significant periods of recovery are factored into these periods within a week or significantly low stress/technical days are included.*
- **On days where rugby is performed both morning and afternoon, consideration to total workload needs careful planning to ensure spikes in load for individual players do not occur.*
- **Daily monitoring should be performed to help inform decisions about training management** – *this data doesn't need to be complex, but it should be consistent and managed in a way that provides information to all coaches for them to make informed decisions about player and squad management.*
- **A solutions based approach should always be the focal point of maximising the training week** – *where players may require modifications, creativity should be sought in order to create the same desired stimulus in a varied manner. A tendency in team sports who have to play weekly is to "off load" individuals in order to maximise preparation for game day based on various symptoms. If this happens weekly, it results in a spiral effect of deconditioning that neglects to deal with the actual cause of the issues, which are usually independent of the symptoms presented.*
- **Alternative aspects of stress should always be considered in populating a training week** – *meetings, reviews, contract discussions, exams and training reviews are all examples of elements within a professional athlete's working week that can often add to the overall stress of a training day/week/cycle and should also be periodised in nature to maximise a player's performance on field.*
- **Competition weeks should include a vast increase in recovery opportunities to maximise the taper (volume reduction), with intensity being retained in only key periods of training throughout the week** – *whereby international teams are involved in long haul travel, the management of a taper is key to maximising adaptations pre competition and creating freshness and readiness to compete.*
- **The training week/plan should be only a blueprint for what is ideal in the strength and conditioning coach's mind and he/she should have the experience and expertise to "push or pull" an individual's training week in terms of stress, based on their needs** – *a key example of this in rugby sevens is after long haul travel and within the taper, when some individuals take longer to acclimate to new time zones, and training adaptations may be required for them as individuals. In contrast, a player who is has recently returned from injury may need more conditioning than a pre competition rugby session can provide, with extra conditioning and/or strength stimuli needing to be factored into their schedule.*

Table 7.8 shows examples of typical weekly structures that may be used in a) a preparation block and b) an in competition period. The first example reflects the previously detailed principles of programming.

To best reflect how various training components are managed within rugby sevens, it would be sensible to take an approach whereby each component of fitness is described independently in terms of key areas for consideration in their programming, with examples of session detail included within each.

Table 7.8 A typical weekly structure when planning a preparation block for rugby sevens players

Monday (medium)	Tuesday (hard)	Wednesday (low)	Thursday (very hard)	Friday (low-med)	Saturday (low)	Sunday (rest)
Monitoring	Monitoring	Monitoring @ home	Monitoring	Monitoring	Monitoring @ home	Monitoring @ home
Physical prep (mobility/activations)	Physical prep (mobility/activations)	Soft tissue active recovery pool sessions low level aerobic work	Physical prep (mobility/activations)	Physical prep (mobility/activations)	active recovery top ups or additional training components	rest
MORNING TRAINING						
AM speed (acceleration bias)	**AM rugby** – hard		**AM speed** (velocity bias)	**AM rugby** – low/medium (additional conditioning as required)		
AM gym (lower strength bias)	Rest		**AM gym** (whole body bias)			
AFTERNOON TRAINING						
PM rugby – medium	**PM gym** (upper bias + posterior chain)		**PM rugby** – medium	**PM gym** (circuits/extras)		

Table 7.9 In contrast to the preparation block, a typical weekly structure leading into a competition weekend for rugby sevens players

Monday (medium)	Tuesday (hard)	Wednesday (low)	Thursday (very hard)	Friday (low-med)	Saturday (competition)	Sunday (competition)
Monitoring	Monitoring	Remote monitoring	Monitoring	Monitoring	Monitoring	Monitoring
Physical prep (mobility/activations)	Physical prep (mobility/activations)	Physical prep (mobility/activations)		Physical prep (mobility/activations)		
MORNING TRAINING						
AM gym (whole body strength & power)	**AM rugby** – medium (including speed/agility work)	**AM gym** (whole body power biased)	Rest day & soft tissue work	**AM rugby** – low volume, medium intensity	Activation session (3hrs pre 1st game)	Activation session (3hrs pre 1st game)
AFTERNOON TRAINING						
PM recovery session – optional/own time	**PM recovery session** – optional/own time	**PM rugby** – high intensity and low volume *Non negotiable recovery* – hydrotherapy and cryotherapy		*Non negotiable recovery* – individual athlete choices	Match routines and recovery	Match routines and recovery

Speed and agility

The inclusion of speed and agility training is obvious for rugby sevens. With so many high speed efforts and sprint activities within the game, the requirement of speed training is simply a non negotiable training stimulus. As a result of these game demands, it is a vital stimulus for injury prevention first and foremost, and may be included as part of a programme merely on that reason alone.

Agility, or change of direction work, is an integral part of preparation for rugby sevens. A player who has the potential to produce high maximal sprinting velocities, but fails to do so due to their inability to break the organised defence with footwork to create space, is a wasted resource. Much like most skilled movements, practice and repetition is key, and creating constraints in drill type activities whereby players can seek the opportunity to learn from different responses is important. Providing the player with the required skillset and opportunity to choose the right movement strategy for a change of direction, at the right time and based on the environment they see in front of them is fundamental to creating a player who can beat opposing players.

Some key considerations for speed/agility development

- **Focusing on separate aspects of acceleration and max velocity work is preferred** – *this allows the player to truly focus on the key attractors and technical models required for each component of speed.*
- **Each should be practiced in as fresh a state as possible** – *this will help minimise cumulative fatigue affecting the outcomes of sessions and maximise opportunity to train with maximum intent of speed of movement.*
- **Thorough warm ups (≥ 15 mins) should include drills that complement direct transfer to the session focus** – *a selection of drills that reflect acceleration or max velocity positions, demands, and co-ordination demands.*
- **Consolidate a technical model for acceleration, but vary the constraints** – *acceleration rarely occurs in sevens from a typical static start; therefore, transitional movements into maximum acceleration patterns should also be mastered.*
- **Speed can transfer from the gym also** – *gym sessions during late stage development / late pre season should involve "special" exercises that aim to transfer to speed development, especially whereby volume of speed work may need to be reduced in nature to facilitate more rugby placed work.*
- **Jumps and plyometrics form an integral component for speed development** – *horizontal jumps such as prowler bounds are an effective means for explosive acceleration development. Athletes should progress from extensive to intensive jump/plyometric work to ensure tolerance and capacity to repeated jumping and landing are developed prior to intensive activities.*
- **Variable resistance methods (pulleys, sleds, prowlers) should be utilised** – *these are extremely useful for an athlete to learn how to apply force in different ways, and learn how they express their own speed and could be chosen as a modality based on time of year (overload versus taper) or for level of competency.*
- **Utilise game specific agility practices within rugby where possible** – *these include 20-minute allocation of training as part of a rugby session, with ball in hand. Utilising players as defenders helps the attacking player learn how to decide on the strategy they wish to use based on the shapes and movement speed that the defender expresses, as opposed to running through pre determined agility drills. It is important to develop the underpinning change of direction skills that you wish to use as a coach first and foremost, but often constraints led approaches to agility development lend best for learning in more experienced athlete. Players are competitive, so constraining the way a defender must present themselves (over chasing the attacker, for example) will often lead to better attacking outcomes from the opposing player and greater learning outcomes.*

Strength and power

Strong athletes are often considered robust athletes. Therefore the focus on getting strong and staying strong should always be a primary aim of physical development for rugby sevens. Once certain levels of strength are attained, the residual effects of this quality are longer lasting in nature. As a player develops these realms of strength, more variable stimuli such as power development can come to the forefront of a programme for an athlete. The same is less evident for younger athletes, and it may be considered that their work continues with key strength lifts forming the majority of their programme, irrespective of time of year, until adequate levels of strength are achieved.

The staple for any strength development programme must include the go to exercises that recruit large muscle groups and large motor pools for neural adaptation. That said, decisions on programming must be player centred and not ego driven. Every coach desires to see their athletes squat, but if a player has hip impingements and squatting aggravates this issue, it is common sense to find a sensible plan B that still creates the **original desired adaption of** neural adaptation that was originally programmed for. Often, such modifications see an unloading of a joint, but also the unloading of the original desired stimulus, and thus it is crucial that the modified exercise option still looks to develop the player in the desired manner.

Below highlights a typical block approach to strength development whereby intensity is increasing across a 4 week block. By refraining from rigid week to week progressions, and creating classifications for weeks such as medium, high, very high and de-load weeks, the player can appreciate where they are required to push hardest. Coaches in rugby sevens must be adaptable in their approach as week to week games do not occur. It is not uncommon to plan a block and have a player pick up a lower limb contact incident that then requires training modification in the gym as early as week 1. By using an intensity classification, these weeks can easily be alternated with each other. As an example, if modification is required in week 1, this then simply becomes the deloaded week, with weeks 2–4 being progressive in intensity. If it occurs in week 2, then weeks 3 and 4 become intensified by comparison. With a team sport that often has 20+ squad members, such adaptability and simplicity provides for successful training outcomes.

Some coaches plan segmental programmes, i.e. upper body days and lower body days. Others perform conjugate approaches. This is at the coaches' discretion and many of these methods serve certain times of the sevens season better than others. What is worth considering is that the key is to be prepared for real world modifications by ensuring your weekly programme consists of the stimulus (not the exercise) you require by the end of that given week. In rugby sevens, in a non-competition week, it is easy to achieve 4 lifting sessions weekly in pre season. This doesn't mean all sessions need to be focused on lifting. Focusing on 3 sessions in a given week allow for a player to "catch up" should modifications have occurred earlier in a week. The below table

Table 7.10 Typical block approach to strength training development within rugby sevens

Week	Intensity	Sets × Reps
Week 1	Medium	4 × 5
Week 2	Hard	4 × 4
Week 3	De-load	2–3 × 2–3 (same intensity as week 2)
Week 4	Very hard	5 × 2

shows how you could split your strength work within a block over 3 sessions. Pay attention to the detail that each session is merely biased towards lower, upper and whole body focuses. This means each session will have an aspect of another body part within it. This allows for the player to, if they miss 1 session in a week, still achieve considerable volume for both upper and lower body segments, and hopefully achieve a minimum effective dose for maintenance of physical qualities in the least.

Power development should be secondary in nature with respect to first prioritising strength development of the developing rugby sevens athlete. For mature rugby sevens athletes, power training plays a pivotal part in development and can factor in earlier within the pre season and as early as week 1. The importance of high levels of strength being required to underpin power development adds weight to this philosophy. There are many ways to develop power, whether that be Olympic lifts, jumps, or throws. What should be adhered to is that power programmes continue to maintain strength qualities with minimum effective dosages, and that the methods chosen are suitable for the athlete in question. There is unquestionable evidence that all the mentioned methods can improve power, but each must be chosen based on context and not coaching ego once more. Olympic lifting can provide a desired stimulus, but if "learnt" or performed

Table 7.11 Example programme during a strength development block, illustrating a bias approach to planning session content

Session 1		Session 2		Session 3	
Lower body bias		*Upper body bias*		*Whole body bias*	
A1 Back squat	4 × 5	A1 bench press	4 × 5	A1 BB step ups	4 × 5e/s
		A2 pull ups	4 × 5		
B1 SL hip thruster	4 × 8e/s	B1 RDL	4 × 5	B1 BB push press	4 × 5
B2 OH push ancillary	3 × 10–12			B2 ancillary chest	3 × 10–12
C1 lateral slideboard	4 × 8e/s	C1 DB seated shoulder press	4 × 5	C1 ancillary LB (e.g., goblet squat)	3 × 10
C2 DB walking lunges	3 × 8e/s	C2 ancillary row	3 × 10–12	C2 ancillary row	3 × 10–12

Table 7.12 Example of programmes from within a power development block, typically used leading up to competition

Session 1		Session 2	
Strength–speed bias		*Speed–strength bias*	
A1 power clean	4 × 2–3	A1 jump squat (high velocity)	4 × 4
A2 individual injury prevention	as per req	A2 box jump	4 × 2
B1 banded bench press	3 × 4	B1 hurdle bounds	3 × 5
B2 pull ups	3 × 3	B2 DB SA rows	3 × 5e/s
B3 MB slams	3 × 5		
C1 SL step up	3 × 4e/s	C1 DB chest press	3 × 5
C2 push press	3 × 4	C1 plyo activity:	3 × 5–6 contacts
C3 isometric hamstring bridge	3 × (2 × 10s)e/s	*E.g. hurdle bounds*	
		E.g. alternating bounds	

with poor technical proficiency, then these will not provide the necessary stimulus for power development. If poor form occurs, would a simple exercise selection such as jump squats be more effective to achieve maximum power output by comparison? These choices are down to the art of coaching, irrespective of sport. As we move towards a taper close to competition, power work should predominate the volume of work in the gym, with high speed focuses within movements/exercises selected, and minimum effective dose strength stimuli programmed. Preservation of readiness and freshness to compete predominate over chasing physical adaptations and gains so close to competition in a technical team sport.

Metabolic qualities/fitness

Rugby sevens no doubt requires exceptional levels of fitness. The most vital component is the development of a large aerobic base that can provide the basis from which a player can express all of their other physical qualities. Speed, power, strength and anaerobic qualities will all dissipate during times of duress when there is insufficient recovery time. The aerobic base helps minimise these required recovery times and can add weight to the repeatability of a given physical quality. Aerobic development should form a large basis of work in the off season and early pre season periods in order to prep for late pre season work that can be more intensive in nature. This can stem from many modalities, both on feet and off feet in nature. A logical progression throughout

Table 7.13 Examples of varied methods of metabolic conditioning

BLOCK	AIMS	Modalities	Frequency	Examples
A	Build aerobic base	Extensive intervals	3–5 × week	30–60s Tempo runs 8–12min work time W:R 2:1 E.g. 2 × (5 × 60s runs):60s low intensity rest btw reps 2min btw sets
B	Develop anaerobic capacity Increase tolerance to fatigue (resistance)	Intensive intervals	2–3 × week based on individual needs (high and low fitness groups)	10–30s MAS efforts 105–135% MAS 8–16min work time W:R 1:1 E.g. 3 × (6 × 20s on:20s off) @ 115–120% MAS 2min rest btw sets
C	Develop mixed energy system interactions	Gameplay	1–2 × week (volume and intensity specific to the time of year e.g. pre comp versus pre season) Aim to accumulate 12–25min game time	**Pre season:** 3–5 × 4–5min games (12–25mins) 7v7 Gameplay "continuous/extensive" **Pre competition:** 6–8 × 2–3min games (12–24min) 7v7 Gameplay 1 restart per minute from set piece/kick offs "interval/intensive" 30s max rest btw within game restarts

the pre season is to progress from extensive aerobic work to intensive anaerobic work, whilst looking to match and exceed worst case scenarios that players are pre disposed to during gameplay rugby training activity. During the competitive in season period, much of the intensity derived work should come from gameplay in order to get much of the adaptation from rugby and limit the amount of on feet additional stress. This is especially important in season when there is likely a reduction in overall training volume, as a result of readiness to perform and competition performance itself becoming priority.

Below demonstrates three blocks of typical metabolic focused work that could form part of the sevens physical preparation plan, additional to rugby itself. Block A can be considered early pre season, Block B late pre season, and Block C between competitions and in season. *(Note that work time describes the sum of meaningful work intervals, excluding including any rest between reps or sets.)*

Tapering

The taper period can be more systematic and effective within sevens compared to the 15-a-side game. In 15-a-side rugby union, tapering often expresses itself within each part of a microcycle or week of training between consecutive games. Early parts of the week are used for loading with latter days in the week tapered in preparation for a match. The clear distinct phases on the world series for sevens mean that cycles of training for adaptation, followed by a taper and competition, can reoccur 4–5 × within the season. The taper should occur around 10 days out from competition and should accommodate for such considerations as long haul travel, the effects of jet lag and overcoming travel fatigue and immune suppression, alongside time zone differences at the destination city.

This taper should focus primarily on reductions in volume of work with intensity of work maintained throughout. The taper should be assessed using monitoring methods in order to adjust loading and recovery strategies as required. Day to day monitoring is fundamental to evaluate the adaptations to a taper. Some key areas to consider for a taper period are outlined below:

- **The subsequent day to tapering should be the last heavy focus for both on feet stress and neural stress from strength training.**
- **Training volumes should be reduced thereafter to facilitate the taper** – *for on field work, this could be time related in terms of session duration, or volume related in terms of distance covered in training. It's preferable that both occur at the same time.*
- **Intensity for segments of training should stay high, at a rate matching worst case scenarios** – *rest period between these passages of play/drills/games should be extended to ensure quality is retained, and cumulative fatigue is minimised. A minimum effective dose for this intensity related work should be determined to maximise the taper period.*
- **Training needs to be factored in specifically with respect to long haul travel** – *low complexity sessions should be completed in the first 24hrs after arrival, with level of intensity, skilled movement demand and speed of movements increasing slowly over the next 2–3 days. Strict conversations between the strength and conditioning and technical coaches, are key to ensure preparation is detailed out with respect to the time travelled and the jet lag factor associated with travel. A high degree of variation in training should be planned for and acted upon daily, as some players will respond better than others to the taper and the long haul travel.*

References

Fuller, C.W. and Taylor, A. (2016). *World Rugby Surveillance Studies – Sevens World Series – Men*. Available at http://fpr.pt/wp-content/uploads/2017/03/WR_Sevens_Men_2016_Review.pdf

Fuller, C.W., Taylor, A., Kemp, S.P.T. and Raftery, M. (2017a). Rugby World Cup 2015: World Rugby Injury Surveillance Study. *British Journal of Sports Medicine*, 51, 51–57.

Fuller, C.W., Taylor, A. and Raftery, M. (2017b). 2016 Rio Olympics: An Epidemiological Study of the Men's and Women's Rugby-7s Tournaments. *British Journal of Sports Medicine*, 1, 1–8.

Granatelli, G., Gabbett, T.J., Briotti, G., Padulo, J., Buglione, A., D'Ottavio, S. and Ruscello, B.M. (2014). Match Analysis and Temporal Patterns of Fatigue in Rugby Sevens. *The Journal of Strength & Conditioning Research*, 28(3), 728–734.

Higham, D.G., Pyne, D.B., Anson, J.M. and Eddy, A. (2012). Movement Patterns in Rugby Sevens: Effects of Tournament Level, Fatigue and Substitute Players. *Journal of Science and Medicine in Sport*, 15(3), 277–282.

Higham, D.G., Pyne, D.B., Anson, J.M., Hopkins, W.G. and Eddy, A. (2013). Comparison of Activity Profiles and Physiological Demands Between International Rugby Sevens Matches and Training. *The Journal of Strength & Conditioning Research*, 30(5), 1287–1294.

Murray, A. and Varley, M.C. (2015). Effect of Profile of International Rugby Sevens: Effect of Score Line, Opponent, and Substitutes. *International Journal of Sports Physiology and Performance*, 10, 791–801.

Ross, A., Gill, N.D. and Cronin, J.B. (2014). Match Analysis and Player Characteristics in Rugby Sevens. *Sports Medicine*, 44(3), 357–367.

Ross, A., Gill, N.D. and Cronin, J.B. (2015). A Comparison of the Match Demands of International and Provincial Rugby Sevens. *International Journal of Sports Physiology and Performance*, 10(6), 786–790.

Suarez-Arrones, L.J., Nunez, F.J., Portillo, J. and Mendez-Villanueva, A. (2012). Running Demands and Heart Rate Responses in Men Rugby Sevens. *The Journal of Strength & Conditioning Research*, 26(11), 3155–3159.

Suarez-Arrones, L.J, Nunez, F.J., Saez de Villareal, E., Galvez, J., Suarez-Sanchez, G. and Munguia-Izquierdo, D. (2016). Repeated-High-Intensity-Running Activity and Internal Training Load of Elite Rugby Sevens Players During International Matches: A Comparison Between Halves. *International Journal of Sports Physiology and Performance*, 11, 495–499.

8
AMERICAN FOOTBALL

Nick Winkelman

Introduction

American football (AF) is the most watched professional sport in the United States of America (Hoffman, 2008), with an average of 25 million fans tuning in every Sunday and Monday night to watch their favorite professional team compete (Chase, 2015). Considering the popularity of the sport, it is not surprising that over 1 million high school students participate in AF every year, with 73,000 going on to play competitive football in college (NCAA, 2016). However, the opportunity to play professional football, while the dream for so many young men, is only realized by a small number of athletes, with only 253 players drafted into the National Football League (NFL) each year. This means that only 1.6% of eligible collegiate players ever get into the NFL (.02% of high school players).

As difficult as it is to make it into the NFL, it is equally hard to stay on an active 53-man roster. While there are 1696 active players across the 32 NFL teams, the average career length is 2.66 years, which is down from an average of 4.99 years in 2000 (Arthur, 2016). Thus, players at all levels need to be disciplined in their technical, tactical, physical, and psychological preparation if they want to optimize on-field performance and career longevity.

The game itself is characterized by four 15-minute quarters in college and NFL and 12-minute quarters in high school, with half-time varying between 12 and 20 minutes, depending on level of play. The game is played with 11 players on offense and defense on a field 360 feet in length by 160 feet in width. The average high school team will play 8 to 10 games in a season, not including playoff games, while a typical college season consists of 10 to 13 games plus a bowl game if the team qualifies. NFL teams will play 4 pre-season games and 16 in-season games over the course of a 17-week season (i.e., one bye week). The top 12 teams will advance to the playoffs during January, with the top two teams competing in the Super Bowl the first weekend in February.

To understand how to prepare an athlete for the demands of AF, it is important to analyze the following playing requirements: positional analysis (distance/intensity), game analysis (work to rest), and, strength and speed quality analysis. Subsequent sections will focus on current strength and conditioning practices and considerations for optimizing transfer of training and mitigating detraining. The final section will focus on general and specific training strategies with an emphasis on strength, power, and speed. For the purpose of this chapter, playing requirements and associated training recommendations will specifically focus on the collegiate and professional player.

Playing requirements

Positional analysis

Each team will have a defense and an offense prepared to step on the field, with each position requiring a distinct set of technical, tactical, physiological, and biomechanical qualities. Research has shown that the average distance covered at various velocities and the number of accelerations and decelerations performed during a match vary greatly across offensive and defensive positions (Wellman, Coad, Goulet, and McLellan, 2016).

On offense (Wellman et al., 2016), the total distance covered by a wide receiver (5,530.6 ± 996.5m) is significantly farther than the distances achieved by running backs (3,140.6 ± 685.6m), quarterbacks (3,751.9 ± 801.9), tight ends (3,574.2 ± 882.2m), and offense linemen (3,652.4 ± 603.0m). Similarly, the high intensity sprint distance (16.1–23 km·h^{-1}) and maximal effort sprint distance (>23 km·h^{-1}) covered by a wide receiver (655.2 ± 196.3m; 315.8 ± 163.2m) is also significantly farther than the distances achieved by running backs (303.1 ± 118.7m; 101.2 ± 71.7m), quarterbacks (138.1 ± 65.1m; 76.9 ± 46.0m), tight ends (336.6 ± 137.8m; 40.3m ± 47.4m), and linemen (131.1 ± 65.7m; 9.3 ± 11.3m). Finally, the number of maximal effort sprints and the number of high intensity accelerations and decelerations (2.6–3.5 m·s^{-2}) completed by a wide receiver (12.7 ± 5.7; 38.2 ± 13.1; 18.5 ± 13.1) is also higher than the number achieved by running backs (4.6 ± 3.1; 18.7 ± 7.7; 7.9 ± 7.7), quarterbacks (2.8 ± 1.9; 21.0 ± 7.8; 9.7 ± 7.8), tight ends (1.5 ± 1.6; 21.4 ± 14.3; 9.3 ± 14.3), and linemen (0.3 ± 0.5; 16.5 ± 5.9; 8.3 ± 5.9).

On defense (Wellman et al., 2016), the total distance covered by defensive backs (4,696.2 ± 1,114.8m) and linebackers (4,145.4 ± 980.3) is significantly farther than the distances achieved by defensive ends (3,276.6 ± 815.2) and defensive tackles (3,013 ± 650.9m). Similarly, the high intensity sprint distance (16.1–23 km·h^{-1}) and maximal effort sprint distance (>23 km·h^{-1}) covered by defensive backs (513.8 ± 155.5m; 247.0 ± 113.1m) and linebackers (435.0 ± 165.0) is also significantly farther than the distances achieved by defensive ends (226.0 ± 96.1; 29.2 ± 24.1) and defensive tackles (158.6 ± 62.0m; 7.7 ± 10.9m). Finally, the number of maximal effort sprints and the number of high intensity accelerations and decelerations (2.6–3.5 m·s^{-2}) completed by a defensive back (10.6 ± 4.3; 32.2 ± 11.4; 19.4 ± 11.4) is higher than the number achieved by linebackers (8.0 ± 4.1; 26.4 ± 11.0; 14.3 ± 11.0), defensive ends (1.4 ± 1.4; 20.0 ± 6.8; 10.6 ± 6.8), and defensive tackles (0.4 ± 0.6; 15.4 ± 5.7; 7.9 ± 5.7).

In a practical context, by understanding the metabolic and mechanical demands imposed on the player, coaches can strategically derive practice sessions that emulate game demands. Moreover, this information plays an important role in managing player workload, as one would not expect a lineman, for example, to achieve the same amount of high speed sprinting distance in practice as a wide receiver, tight end, or running back. However, based on game demands, it makes sense to derive a similar conditioning drill for offensive lineman and defense tackles, as their game demands are comparable. Thus, absolute and relative assessments of playing demands are vital for conditioning players in the context of the game and deploying position specific programming.

Game analysis (W:R)

Competition workload modeling (Plisk and Gambetta, 1997) has been suggested as a method of designing position-specific and game-specific conditioning. To do this it is important to have a detailed understanding of the work to rest ratios (W:R), average number of plays per series, rest between series, and total number of series per game (Rhea, Hunter, and Hunter, 2006). It has been reported that an NFL team may execute 12–13 offensive series a game with an average of 5.3 to 5.6 plays per series (Hoffman, 2008; Plisk and Gambetta, 1997). Additionally, data on rest between offensive series in college football games has been shown to range from 10:53 ± 3.20 minutes for running dominant teams to 12:15 ± 5:13 minutes for passing dominant teams (Iosia and Bishop, 2008).

In a detailed analysis of football competition modeling, Rhea et al. (2006) found that the average W:R for a play in collegiate and NFL football games were 5.60:33.98s (1:6.07) and 5.70:35.24s (1:6.02), respectively. In the same study, the authors found that the average work time for run plays was 5.16 ± 1.48s and pass plays was 5.87 ± 1.54s in NFL football games. Note that these W:R ratios represented play with no additional stoppage, where stoppage represents additional rest due to timeouts, penalties, injuries, end of quarter/half, first-down measurements, or commercial timeouts (Iosia and Bishop, 2008; Rhea et al., 2006). Similarly, Iosia and Bishop (2008) analyzed film from 6 NCAA Division I college football teams based on style of play. Within each style of play they developed W:R ratios for stoppage, no stoppage, and short rest or worst case scenarios (WCS). The W:R ratios for passing teams were 5.41:45.92s (1:8), 5.41:38.08s (1:7), and 5.41:16.59s (1:3), respectively. The W:R ratios for running teams were 4.84:46.93s (1:10), 4.84:35.06s (1:7), and 4.84:16.59s (1:3), respectively. Based off of the identified W:R ratios, Iosia and Bishop (2008) recommend the following three-component conditioning model: Worst Case Scenario (Ratio 1:3), Skill Endurance (Ratio 1:7), and Skill Development (Ratio 1:10). This conditioning model provides an evidence-based framework for designing game-specific drills that place the necessary metabolic and mechanical demands on the player to ensure the development of the relevant energy systems within the context of a tactically appropriate work to rest interval.

While the last two sections inform how a sport coach can effectively design football practice, they also provide the strength and conditioning professional with the insights required to formulate highly transferable position-specific and game-specific drills for players. Moreover, in the context of rehabilitation, therapy professionals can use this information to derive specific return to running and return to play plans that ensure the program of work is moving towards the distances and intensities required within the game and across positional groups.

Strength and speed quality analysis

Strength, power, and speed are important athletic qualities for all AF players. The physicality and ever increasing speed of the game requires a caliber of player who has the prerequisite strength to be effective in both contact and evasion. What's more, the expression of maximal strength and power are commonly associated with measures of linear and multidirectional speed (Davis, Barnette, Kiger, Mirasola, and Young, 2004; Spiteri et al., 2014), highlighting why it is important for skill players (SP), big skill players (BSP), and linemen (LM) to be able to maximally and rapidly express force as the game demands (see Table 8.1 for position categories).

While coaches would be ill-advised to apply an overly generic approach to strength and power development across all positions, the evidence does suggest that there are minimal standards that separate players in different divisions of collegiate football and draftees entering the NFL. For example, the early work of Fry and Kraemer (1991) showed that players in first division college

Table 8.1 American football position categories

Position category	Offense	Defense
Skill players (SP)	• Wide receivers (WR) • Running backs (RB) • Quarterbacks (QB)	• Cornerbacks (CB) • Strong safety (SS) • Free safety (FS)
Big skill players (BSP)	• Fullbacks (FB) • Tight ends (TE)	• Linebackers (LB) • Defensive ends (DE)
Lineman (LM)	• Center (C) • Offensive guard (OG) • Offensive tackle (OT)	• Defensive tackle (DT) • Nose guard (NG)

Table 8.2 Difference between drafted and non-drafted players at NFL combine

Position	Skill players	Big skill players	Linemen
Significant difference	• 40yd dash • Vertical jump • Pro-agility drill • 3-cone (L-drill)	• 40yd dash • 3-cone (L-drill)	• 40yd dash • 3-cone (L-drill) • 225 bench test
Non-significant difference	• 225 bench test • Broad jump • Height/body mass	• 225 bench test • Pro-agility drill • Vertical/broad jump • Height/body mass	• Pro-agility drill • Vertical/broad jump • Height/body mass

programs (i.e., Division I) were stronger (Bench Press and Squat), more powerful (Power Clean and Vertical Jump), and faster (40-yard sprint) than third division players (i.e., Division III). In support of these findings, Garstecki, Latin, and Cuppett (2004) showed that Division I players outperform Division II players on the same measures of strength, power, and speed. Thus, while a certain level of strength, power, and speed does not ensure entry into a Division I program, it would appear that the developed or innate ability to express these qualities becomes increasingly important as the level of play rises.

From an NFL combine perspective, Sierer, Battaglini, Mihalik, Shields, and Tomasini (2008) found that performance on multiple tests were associated with draft status. As can be seen in Table 8.2, the athletic quality standards that separate drafted and non-drafted players are slightly different for each positional category. Collectively, drafted players are consistently faster and more agile than non-drafted players, with drafted LM outperforming non-drafted LM in the 225 bench press test, and drafted SP outperforming non-drafted SP in the vertical jump. What's more, McGee and Burkett (2003) observed that high draftees (Rounds 1–2) performed significantly better on the broad jump, vertical jump, and 3-cone agility drill compared to low draftees (Rounds 6–7), providing further support for the importance of power and agility. Interestingly, McGee and Burkett (2003) also examined if the NFL Combine tests were better at predicting the draft status of certain positions over others. The regression equations across positions showed that wide receivers ($r^2 = 1.0$), running backs ($r^2 = 1.0$), and defensive backs ($r^2 = 1.0$) had the strongest associations between combine performance and draft status, with quarterbacks ($r^2 = 0.841$), offensive linemen ($r^2 = 0.698$), defensive linemen ($r^2 = 0.592$), and linebackers ($r^2 = 0.223$) showing weaker associations. The results of this regression analysis highlight that the athletic qualities measured at the NFL Combine are likely biased towards the SP, suggesting that teams assessing quarterbacks, linemen, and linebackers base their draft decisions on additional athletic qualities not directly assessed at the NFL Combine. This finding is not surprising considering the importance of speed, power, and agility to SP, and the fact that the maximal and explosive strength requirements associated with BSP and LM are not directly assessed at the NFL Combine. Thus, it is important to consider the differences in strength quality needs across positional groups and how these should be practically addressed.

To understand the strength quality needs of each position, it is helpful to examine positional norms at the NFL Combine. Specifically, Robbins (2011) examined the NFL Combine performance of all players drafted between 2005 and 2009. The results showed that cornerbacks, safeties, and wide receivers are the fastest players over 10-yards and 20-yards, while cornerbacks and wide receivers are the fastest over 40-yards. Conversely, offensive linemen are the slowest over 10-yards, 20-yards, and 40-yards. Further, defensive backs produce the largest vertical jump heights, while defensive backs and wide receivers produce the largest horizontal jump distances. Once again, offensive linemen have the lowest performance on both the vertical and horizontal jump tests. Interestingly, offensive and defensive linemen are the slowest on the pro-agility and 3-cone drill; however, there are no significant difference between any other positions. Thus, the agility tests at the NFL Combine provide the least discriminative value for judging positional differences at the elite – drafted – level. Finally, defensive tackles, offensive guards, and centers perform the best on the 225 bench press test, while defensive backs perform the worst.

The preceding evidence provides a clear picture of the shared and differential needs of each playing position. Specifically, SP require a strength profile that directly supports the expression of speed, power, and agility. Known correlations between strength and the discussed performance outcomes suggest that SP should focus on maximizing relative strength, explosive strength, and reactive strength (Bompa and Carrera, 2005; Stone, Stone, and Sands, 2007a). Conversely, while the expression of speed, power, and agility discriminate between draft status in LM (Sierer et al., 2008), relative to their skilled counterparts, LM require higher absolute levels of maximal strength, starting strength, and explosive strength (Bompa and Carrera, 2005; Stone et al., 2007a). BSP, on the other hand, will fall somewhere in between the strength quality needs of LM and SP based on their diverse positional demands and the tactics deployed by their team. See Table 8.3 for strength quality definitions (Poliquin and Patterson, 1989; Stone, Stone, and Sands, 2007b).

Table 8.3 Strength qualities defined

Maximal strength	Peak force the neuromuscular system is capable of producing during a single repetition irrespective of time.
Relative strength	Peak force the neuromuscular system is capable of producing during a single repetition irrespective of time, per kilogram of body weight.
Maximal power	Peak wattage (force × velocity) the neuromuscular system is capable of producing at a given load.
Speed-strength	Highest rate of force development the neuromuscular system is capable of producing at a given load.
Starting strength	Maximal rise in force the neuromuscular system is capable of producing during the start of a movement (40–50ms).
Explosive strength	The ability of neuromuscular system to generate maximal rise in force once movement has started (100+ms).
Reactive strength	The ability of the neuromuscular system to maximize the use of the stretch shortening cycle during short ground contacts (<250ms) and often under high ground reaction forces.

When evaluated in the context of the game, the findings and recommendations noted above make sense. Specifically, LM have the largest body masses, highest combative demands, and lowest running demands. Moreover, a key technical requirement of the position is to explode from a static position, control the space between them and an opponent, and drive block or shed an opponent weighing an average of 133.4 ± 5kgs (Kraemer et al., 2005). Thus, starting and explosive strength are vital for controlling space and minimizing the force generating time an opponent has, while maximal strength is critical to dominate the actual contact, as LM are managing their body weight in addition to that of the players across from them. In contrast, SP have the smallest body masses, lowest combative demands, and highest running demands. From a technical perspective, SP are required to control a significantly larger area between them and their opponent compared to LM. What's more, offensive SP must engage in evasive decision making while defensive SP engage in attacking oriented decision making. Thus, the relative strength needs of SP is a reflection of their need to manage their own body mass in space. Further, a SP's ability to express explosive strength and reactive strength becomes essential when it comes to controlling or evading collisions. Again, BSP must manage a game profile that falls between that of LM and SP.

Current impact of athletic performance

Prior to discussing strategies for optimizing the athletic development of AF players, it is important to consider the historical influence strength and conditioning programs have had on the player attributes discussed above. A considerable amount of research has evaluated the differential impact of various periodization and programming strategies (e.g., Hoffman et al., 2009) and the implications of various training methods (e.g., Hoffman, Cooper, Wendell, and Kang, 2004); however, this section will examine the effect of longitudinal programs on strength, power, speed, and agility development. Specifically, of practical interest to strength and conditioning coaches, especially those working with athletes over four year cycles (i.e., high school and college), are the changes to key performance attributes that can be expected over a multi-year time period (see Table 8.4).

Stodden and Galitski (2010) examined the performance changes of 84 athletes on a Division I team over the course of four years. The results showed varying degrees of improvement for the vertical jump, pro-agility drill, and 40-yard dash across SP, BSP, and LM. Generally speaking, there were small improvements in the vertical jump and the pro-agility; however, these improvements were only observed during the first two years. The only exception is the improvement in pro-agility performance for linemen during their fourth year. What's more, examining the positions collectively, there were very small changes in the 40-yard dash time during year one with no further improvements observed during the subsequent years.

Hoffman, Ratamess, and Kang (2011) followed 289 Division III players over the course of their four to five years on the team. Both backs and linemen made large improvements in their maximal upper body and lower body strength, with these changes being spread across the four-year cycle. Conversely, improvements in the vertical jump were smaller in comparison and were only realized in the final year of assessment. Smaller still, were the improvements in the pro-agility and the 40-yard dash, which were only observed in years three or four, if at all.

Jacobson, Conchola, Glass, and Thompson (2013) followed 92 Division I players over the course of their four years on the team. Similar to Hoffman et al. (2011), the results showed that players made large improvements in maximal upper body and lower body strength, followed by significantly smaller changes to vertical jump performance and 40-yard dash times. Moreover, most of these improvements were observed in the first year, suggesting that there is either a ceiling

Table 8.4 Longitudinal changes to athletic performance qualities

	SP (QB, RB, WR, DB)				BSP (TE, LB)				LM (OL, DL)			
	BP	SQT	CMJ	PA	40	BP	SQT	CMJ	PA	40	BP	SQT	CMJ	PA	40
Secora, Latin, Berg, and Noble (2004) Division 1 Δ 1987–2000	13%	8%	10%	–	–1%	5%	8%	9%	–	–1%	3%	4%	6%	–	0%

	SP (RB, WR, DB)				BSP (QB, TE, LB)				LM (OL, DL)			
	BP	SQT	CMJ	PA	40	BP	SQT	CMJ	PA	40	BP	SQT	CMJ	PA	40
Stodden and Galitski (2010) Division 1A Δ Yr1 – Yr4	–	–	–1%	–8%	–2%	–	–	13%	–13%	–2%	–	–	6%	–7%	–2%

	BACKS (QB, RB, WR, DB)								LM (OL, DL, TE, LB)			
	BP	SQT	CMJ	PA	40						BP	SQT	CMJ	PA	40
Hoffman et al. (2011) Division 3 Δ Yr1 – Yr4	12%	16%	7%	–4%	–2%						23%	26%	9%	–1%	–2%

	SP (WR, DB)								LM (OL, DL)			
	BP	SQT	CMJ	PA	40						BP	SQT	CMJ	PA	40
Jacobson et al. (2013) Division 1 Δ Yr1 – Yr4	34%	32%	8%	–	–2%						18%	27%	2%	–	–3%

effect on these qualities or a varied training approach may be required to stimulate further gains in the subsequent years.

When examined collectively, there are inherent strengths and weaknesses in the representative programs described above. First, it is evident that players have gotten stronger over the years (Secora et al., 2004) and that programs are very effective at systematically improving maximal upper body and lower body strength (Hoffman et al., 2011; Jacobson et al., 2013); however, it is equally evident that existing programs are ineffective at improving speed and agility, and to a lesser degree, vertical jumping ability. In attempting to explain these latter observations, Hoffman et al. (2011, p. 2356) note "that VJ, speed, and agility are fitness components that are more difficult to improve during an athletes' career." They go on to support their conclusion by stating "that these performance variables are a function of the genetic factors that impact the athletic potential of all athletes." Furthermore, in interpreting their findings, Jacobson et al. (2013, p. 2353) "suggest that speed cannot be significantly improved in elite athletes over 4 years of training," and note that "it is generally agreed on that athletes who excel in speed possess higher proportions of the type of muscle fibers that lend themselves to the activity" (p. 2352). Thus, the question that needs to be asked in relation to speed and agility development is one of nature versus nurture.

The nature argument, which is the stance taken by the preceding authors, would suggest that we should recruit and draft for speed. This was the infamous stance taken by Al Davis (1929–2011), owner of the Oakland Raiders, and echoed when Hue Jackson, the head coach of the Oakland Raiders during the 2011 draft, said "we don't run from speed, we run to speed, especially [when a guy] can play." Conversely, a nurture argument would recognize that while each person has a different genetic potential, there is still an opportunity for relative improvement based on the person's proximity to their *performance ceiling*. Likely, the answer falls somewhere between these two arguments, with the former imposing limitations on the latter. However, with the general importance of speed and agility to all positional categories (McGee and Burkett, 2003; Robbins, 2011), it would be unwise to take the stance reflected in Hoffman et al. (2011) and Jacobson et al. (2013) concluding remarks, as this would lead coaches to believe that time would be better spent developing a more trainable set of athletic qualities (e.g., maximal strength). To the contrary, the evidence for the trainability of speed is robust (for review, see Rumpf, Lockie, Cronin, and Jalilvand, 2016), with emerging evidence suggesting that the improvement in movement quality, as expressed in a speed, agility, and jumping context, is critical for injury prevention and overall physiological efficiency (Frank, 2016). Thus, it is important to consider the interplay between strength, power, and speed, and the relative importance of training age in mediating the transfer of training between these key athletic qualities.

Transfer of training

To optimize on-field performance, it is important to consider how general and specific methods of training differentially influence the expression of the athletic qualities discussed above. While maximal strength, which is commonly developed using general methods, is a highly trainable quality and correlated with speed (Young, McLean, and Ardagna, 1995), agility (Spiteri, Cochrane, Hart, Haff, and Nimphius, 2013), and power (Hori et al., 2008), it is important to consider that correlation does not necessarily imply causation. Thus, it is paramount for strength and conditioning coaches to consider how to balance general and specific training in an effort to optimize transfer of training to the attributes required for on-field success.

Zatsiorsky and Kraemer (2006) have proposed a method for assessing transfer of training, which can be "conceptually expressed as gain in performance/gain in trained exercise" (Young,

2006, p. 74). For example, the following formula can be used to calculate the transfer of training between an improvement in maximal lower body strength and an improvement in sprint performance.

$$\text{Transfer of training effect} = \frac{\text{Effect size of change in sprint performance}}{\text{Effect size of change in maximal lower body strength}}$$

To illustrate how to use the formula, we can use data from the Jacobson et al. (2013). As noted in the preceding section, SP improved their lower body squat strength by 32% over four years, which is equivalent to a very large effect size ($d = 2.27$), and reduced their 40-yard dash sprint times by 2% over four years, which is equivalent to a medium effect size ($d = 0.615$). The calculated transfer of training would be considered small to medium ($d = 0.27$). Conversely, the same improvement in lower body strength had a far greater effect ($d = 0.50$) on vertical jump performance (See http://rpsychologist.com/d3/cohend/ for a simple way to interpret and apply effect sizes). Thus, the level of transfer from a general activity (e.g., squatting) to a specific activity (e.g., sprinting or jumping) is likely a function of the common neuromuscular demands native to each task (Baker, 1996; Wilson, Murphy, and Walshe, 1996). That is, the movement specificity of the general activity mediates the magnitude of transfer to the specific activity. For example, quarter squats have been shown to elicit greater improvements in sprint performance than full squats alone (Rhea et al., 2016).

To further evaluate the impact of general and specific methods on transfer of training, it is helpful to re-examine the results and associated program used by Hoffman et al. (2011), which is described in Hoffman et al. (2004). Recall that the author's state that the trainability of speed and agility is limited due to genetic factors. However, to qualify the genetic predisposition argument, it is instructive to examine another interpretation of their findings. Specifically, it is plausible that the negligible changes to speed and agility were due to limited exposure to specific speed and agility work. Specifically, Hoffman et al. (2004) note that while the off-season strength program was spread over three, five-week phases, speed and agility training did not begin until the last five-week phase at a frequency of two days per week. Examining the program, there were only two repetitions of sprinting over 30-meters per session, which were preceded by eleven different technique drills. Therefore, these players completed a total of sixteen effortful sprints in a speed development context over the course of the 15-week program. When benchmarked against recent recommendations for improving speed (Petrakos, Morin, and Egan, 2016; Rumpf et al., 2016), it is not surprising that the players involved in this program only improved their 40-yard dash times by 2%.

Contrary to the findings reported by Hoffman et al. (2011) and Jacobson et al. (2013), reviews by Seitz, Reyes, Tran, de Villarreal, and Haff (2014) and Rumpf et al. (2016) present a more promising view of the trainability of speed. For example, Seitz et al. (2014) reviewed the transfer effect of lower body strength development to linear speed (see Table 8.5). The results showed that the average decrease in sprint times across a range of sprint distances up to 40-meters were −3.11 ± 2.27% for the experimental groups and −0.05 ± 2.13% for the control groups. Further examination revealed a number mediating factors. First, while not statistically significant, a practically significant finding showed that experimental conditions using medium training loads (60–84.9% of 1RM) or a combination of heavy (>85% of 1RM) and very light loads (<40% of 1RM) produced the largest transfer effects to sprint performance (−3.26 ± 2.10%; −2.78 ± 2.03%). Similarly, strength training only (i.e., back squat) and combined strength and plyometric training (i.e., back squat + loaded CMJ/JS + plyometrics) produced the largest transfer effects to sprint performance (−3.33 ± 2.33%; −3.20 ± 1.77%). Further, experimental conditions using

Table 8.5 Summary of results reported by Seitz et al. (2014)

Variable category	Variable	No. participants	% Change ± SD	Effect size ± SD
Group	Experimental	52	−3.11 ± 2.27	−0.87 ± 0.81
	control	33	−0.05 ± 2.13	0.02 ± 0.52
Type of exercise	Back squat	36	−3.33 ± 2.33	−0.81 ± 0.49
	Back squat + loaded JS/CMJ + plyometric	13	−3.20 ± 1.77	−1.20 ± 1.34
	Loaded JS/CMJ	3	−0.02 ± 1.26	−0.29 ± 0.25
Load intensity	High (>85% of 1RM)	3	−5.02 ± 4.60	−0.52 ± 0.23
	Medium (60–84.9% of 1RM)	34	−3.26 ± 2.10	−0.97 ± 0.92
	Light (40–59.9% of 1RM)	3	−0.82 ± 0.60	−0.16 ± 0.15
	Heavy + very light (<40% of 1RM)	12	−2.78 ± 2.03	−0.82 ± 0.55
Sprint test	<20 meters	27	−3.60 ± 2.35	−0.99 ± 1.01
	20–40 meters	25	−2.58 ± 2.09	−0.73 ± 0.52

more than two lower body lifts per week resulted in significantly lower transfer effects than those lifting one to two times per week. Finally, experimental conditions using shorter inter-set rest periods (e.g., 60–90 seconds) resulted in significantly lower transfer effects than those using longer rest periods (e.g., 2–3 minutes). In sum, programs using multiple training methods and medium training loads (i.e., medium only or high load/very light load) with long inter-set rest periods (i.e., 2–3 minutes), spread out over one to two lower body sessions per week, will support the largest transfer between strength and speed. However, the fatigue or "overwork" induced by maintaining a high average training intensity or programming more than two lower body sessions per week may thwart the development of sprint speed. With this in mind, if a coach feels that a high training intensity or lower body training frequency is necessary, then it would be advisable not to stress the concurrent development of speed within this phase of training.

Building on the findings of Seitz et al. (2014) and Rumpf et al. (2016) reviewed the influence of general training (i.e., strength, power, or plyometrics), sprint specific training, and combined training methods on speed development (see Table 8.6). The results showed that relative to general training and combined training methods, sprint specific methods produced the largest reduction in sprint times across 0–10 meters (−1.82 ± 4.21%, −2.81 ± 3.07%, −4.10 ± 2.15%), 0–20 meters (−1.57 ± 3.52%, −2.61 ± 3.35%, −3.77 ± 2.37%), 0–30 meters (−1.44 ± 3.14%, −2.02 ± 2.89%, −3.63 ± 2.37%), and 31+ meters (−1.65 ± 1.42%, −1.39 ± 0.64%, −2.11 ± 1.47%). Thus, while strength training, especially when combined with plyometric training, has a positive impact on the expression of speed, it would appear that the law of specificity is upheld, with sprint training having the largest transfer to changes in sprint performance.

Considering that both Seitz et al. (2014) and Rumpf et al. (2016) reviewed research using participants of various experience levels, it is important to consider the role of training age on the application of methods that are general, specific, or combined. In the now highly cited paper by Cormie, McGuigan, and Newton (2010), the authors evaluate the differential impact of maximal strength versus ballistic power based training on a diversity of athletic qualities in a group of relatively weak men (i.e., low training age). Using the zones described by Seitz et al. (2014), the maximal strength group (ST) used medium to heavy loads during the back squat and the ballistic power group (PT) used very light loads in combination with jump squats. The results showed that both groups expressed similar improvements in peak power during vertical

Table 8.6 Summary of results reported by Rumpf et al. (2016)

Distance (M)	Training type	No. studies	No. participants	Sessions per week	Number of weeks	% Change ± SD	Effect size ± SD
0–10	Specific: free sprinting	6	55	2–3	6–8	−3.51 ± 2.91	−0.92 ± 1.17
	Specific: resisted sprinting	7	71	2–3	6–8	−4.60 ± 1.26	−1.28 ± 1.05
	Non-specific: plyometric training	7	148	2–4	5–15	−2.39 ± 4.84	−0.35 ± 0.74
	Non-specific: power training	6	127	2–4	5–10	−1.23 ± 3.52	−0.01 ± 1.28
	Non-specific: strength training	9	135	2–3	3–10	−1.00 ± 3.91	−0.33 ± 0.95
	Combined: specific & non-specific	–	–	–	–	−2.81 ± 3.07	−0.59 ± 0.46
0–20	Specific: free sprinting	5	76	2–3	6–8	−3.28 ± 3.04	−0.71 ± 1.13
	Specific: resisted sprinting	3	82	2–3	6–8	−4.27 ± 1.49	−1.49 ± 1.14
	Non-specific: plyometric training	8	240	2–4	5–15	−1.76 ± 4.12	−0.28 ± 0.70
	Non-specific: power training	8	198	2–4	5–10	−1.40 ± 2.99	−0.12 ± 1.07
	Non-specific: strength training	11	219	2–3	3–10	−0.98 ± 3.41	−0.23 ± 0.84
	Combined: specific & non-specific	–	–	–	–	−2.61 ± 3.35	−0.56 ± 2.61
0–30	Specific: free sprinting	6	88	2–3	6–8	−3.06 ± 2.92	−0.71 ± 1.06
	Non-specific: plyometric training	9	284	2–4	5–15	−1.53 ± 3.83	−0.24 ± 0.65
	Non-specific: power training	10	321	2–4	5–10	−1.47 ± 2.75	−0.20 ± 0.93
	Non-specific: strength training	14	320	2–3	3–10	−0.93 ± 3.05	−0.23 ± 0.75
	Combined: specific & non-specific	–	–	–	–	−2.02 ± 2.89	−0.42 ± 0.52
31+	Specific: free sprinting	4	34	2–3	6–8	−2.21 ± 1.68	−1.32 ± 1.20
	Non-specific: plyometric training	2	27	2–4	5–15	−0.96 ± 1.16	−0.29 ± 0.37
	Non-specific: power training	3	47	2–4	5–10	−1.27 ± 1.75	−0.33 ± 0.35
	Non-specific: strength training	5	63	2–3	3–10	−2.20 ± 0.45	−0.55 ± 0.25
	Combined: specific & non-specific	–	–	–	–	−1.39 ± 0.64	−0.45 ± 0.33

jumping (ST = 17.7 ± 9.3%; PT = 17.6 ± 4.5%) and changes to 40-meter sprint times (ST = 2.2 ± 1.9%; PT = 3.6 ± 2.3%); however, the strength training group made significantly larger gains in maximal squat strength than the power training group (ST = 31.2 ± 11.3%; PT = 4.5 ± 7.1%). The authors provide the following concluding remarks about the differential application of strength versus power training in relatively weak individuals (Cormie et al., 2010, p. 1597):

> The ability of heavy strength training to render similar short-term improvements in athletic performance as ballistic power training, coupled with the potential long-term benefits of improved maximal strength, makes heavy strength training a more effective training modality for relatively weak individuals (i.e., previously untrained individuals). Thus, an individual does not necessarily need to place a focus on ballistic power training until a solid foundation of strength is obtained (i.e., squat 1RM/BM ratio ³ 1.60).

This provides strong evidence that strength and conditioning coaches, particularly those working with high school athletes or college athletes with a low training age, would be advised to prioritize strength development, as the transfer to the specific activities relevant to AF would be quite high. What's more, while not statistically significant, the results did show that ballistic power training was more effective for improving sprint times. Thus, the inclusion of specific power and speed training is still warranted. Coaches are encouraged to focus on developing 'movement literacy' early on and progress towards performance.

In a now classic study by Baker (2001), the author examines the load that maximizes upper body power output in groups of professional rugby league players (PRO) and collegiate rugby league players (COL). The results showed that compared to the college players, the professionals were significantly stronger (PRO = 134.8 ± 15.2kg; COL = 111.0 ± 15.3kg) and consequently produced maximal power using significantly higher loads (PRO = 69.1 ± 7.5kg; COL = 60.7 ± 9.6kg), which is not surprising. However, the percent of maximum strength that maximized power was significantly lower in the professionals compared to the college players (PRO = 51.1 ± 5.3%; COL = 54.9 ± 5.6%). What's more, when each group was further broken into the strong (S) and less strong (LS) players, the trend remained, with the stronger professional's players using a lower percentage of their maximal strength to produce maximal power than the weaker players (S = 46.9 ± 6%; LS = 54.1 ± 2.9%). The same pattern existed in the collegiate players (S = 51.5%; LS = 58.4%). Baker (2001, p. 34) summarizes his findings as follows:

> As players become stronger they have probably adopted the strategy of increasing power initially by increasing the absolute load while maintaining movement speed. However, once a base level of maximal strength has been attained and further large gains in strength are less likely to occur, it may be difficult to increase power by increasing the Pmax load; rather, power is increased by increasing the speed at which each load is lifted.

When the results of Baker (2001) are considered with the findings of Cormie et al. (2010), a clear picture of how to manage general versus specific training starts to emerge. Specifically, players with a low training age will reap general (i.e., strength) and specific (i.e., speed and power) adaptations from using general training methods. However, as a player becomes stronger, the association between improvements in strength and power change, requiring a coach to prioritize the prescription specific power and speed training if the goal is to make further improvements to power and speed. Interestingly, Baker (1996, p. 134) had already made this observation, suggesting

Table 8.7 Baker (1996) recommendations for applying general and specific training methods

"1. The vertical jump of beginners can be increased with general strength training exercises such as squats. Elite strength athletes may not record VJ improvements if they only perform general strength exercises such as squats and very heavy weightlifting exercises."

"2. Combined methods of strength training seem to offer the greatest (i.e. General – Squats; Specific – Loaded/Unloaded Jumps) training stimulus by training the contractile and neural/elastic components, perhaps relatively independently."

"3. If not implementing a combined approach, the single best method appears to be special strength jump squats, ideally with a load that approximates maximal power load."

that "training age may dictate to what degree an exercise (i.e., general vs. specific) is appropriate." His recommendations for improving jump performance, which could easily be applied to other speed, agility, and power qualities, are summarized in Table 8.7.

Training residuals

Another consideration for strength and conditioning coaches is the differential application of general and specific training throughout the season. That is, the transition from off-season preparation to in-season execution will result in coaches strategically lowering training frequency and volume, while maintaining training intensity. This overall reduction in training exposure requires coaches to prioritize certain athletic qualities, while de-emphasizing others. To effectively make this decision, coaches need to clearly identify what qualities are maintained by playing the sport and what qualities need off-field training exposure (e.g., maximal strength). This latter need requires coaches to select the key qualities they will devote training time to at the possible expense of others. Conceptually, to effectively prioritize off-field training during the in-season, coaches should understand the decay rates and associated residual training effect associated with a given athletic quality. That is, the length of time improvements in a given athletic quality can be maintained following the cessation of the training stimulus that gave rise to the adaptation (Issurin, 2013).

McMaster, Gill, Cronin, and McGuigan (2013) examined the decay rates of strength and power across a variety of contact team sports, including AF. The results showed that coaches can expect a 14.5 ± 14.3% reduction in maximal strength after training has ceased for 7.2 ± 5.8 weeks. However, over shorter durations of detraining (2–3 weeks), athletes will experience significantly smaller changes to upper and lower body strength (1.2% decrease). In contrast to strength, power (measured by vertical jump height) decreases to a far lesser degree (–0.4 ± 3.2%) over a similar detraining time period (7.6 ± 5.1 weeks). However, this may be mediated by the nature of the sport. For example, Babault, Cometti, Bernardin, Pousson, and Chatard (2007) found that elite rugby union players can maintain vertical jump performance over 6–12 weeks with five rugby practices per week and no strength or power training; however, Schneider, Arnold, Martin, Bell, and Crocker (1998) found that Canadian football players experienced a 2.9% to 4.8% reduction in vertical jump performance across a 16-week season. Thus, the nature of the practice stimulus has a direct impact on the level of programming required to maintain a given athletic quality.

Issurin (2010) provides considerations around factors that can influence decay rates and training residuals. First, the longer the training duration before cessation of training, the longer the resultant training residual. Second, athletes with higher training ages will have longer training residuals than individuals with a shorter training age. To illustrate these two points, consider how this could inform programming for a freshman on a college team versus a senior on that same team. The freshman, who is possibly playing less than the senior, would likely need a larger in-season stimulus to maintain or develop strength and power. Conversely, the senior, who has three more years of training, may require less overall strength and power work, affording them the opportunity to focus on different athletic qualities (e.g., speed and power). Third, as noted above, the characteristics and type of physical loads imposed on the body as a result of playing the sport have a direct impact on the athletic qualities that require exposure off the playing field. Finally, athletic qualities associated with morphological changes (e.g., aerobic capacity and maximal strength) will have longer training residuals than those associated with enzymatic (e.g., anaerobic capacity) or neurological changes (e.g., maximal velocity) (Issurin and Yessis, 2008a, 2008b; Issurin, 2010).

In sum, the use of general and specific training methods is mediated by the relative training age of the player and the seasonal time period. There is no one way to optimize the development of the key athletic qualities underpinning AF performance; however, the principles discussed in the preceding sections provide coaches with a framework that can inform the prescription of individualized player programs. The subsequent sections will discuss general and specific training methodology that can be used in concert with the mediating factors discussed above.

Program design considerations

The needs analysis described in the previous sections provides strength and conditioning coaches with an understanding of the technical and tactical nature of the game and the underpinning physical requirements. What's more, the discussion around current practices, transfer of training, and training residuals highlighted important opportunities to progress beyond the strength focused program to a holistic approach that equally weights the importance of strength and speed based on training age and time of year. Thus, this section seeks to build on the current practices noted above, and provide practical examples to support the training age appropriate transfer of training.

Before describing the relevant methods associated with the physical development of the AF player, it is important to briefly discuss the framework that will be used to categorize and label each method on a progressive scale from general to specific. Table 8.8 provides a breakdown of the 5 factors that will be used to grade the specificity of a method relative the athletic quality it is meant to influence. While these are not the only factors that can be used to qualify a method as general or specific, the 5 factors do provide coaches with a heuristic or mental model to quickly assess the relative specificity of a given training method. Specifically, methods that only account for 1 or 2 factors can be considered general, while methods that account for 4 or 5 factors can be considered specific.

To illustrate how to use Table 8.8, consider a coach who would like to identify the best methods for improving their players' sprint speed on the field. If the coach in question is working with a player with a low training age, then they may elect to focus on the development of maximal

Table 8.8 Framework for qualifying the general versus specific nature of a training method

Kinetic factors	Factor 1	Magnitude of force	Low ↔ high
	Factor 2	Rate of force development	Slow ↔ fast
	Factor 3	Direction of force	Vertical ↔ horizontal
Kinematic factors	Factor 4	Range of motion	Partial ↔ full
	Factor 5	Coordination	Non-specific ↔ specific

strength in the back squat, as the coach knows that this will have a large impact on strength and transfer to sprinting (Cormie et al., 2010). Based on the framework, this would be considered a general method, as the development of maximal strength in the back squat only accounts for 1 or 2 of the 5 factors. Specifically, maximal lower body strength accounts for Factor 1, as the high magnitude of force will support the development of the force requirements during linear sprinting. Factor 4 may also be accounted for based on the range of motion of the movement (e.g., quarter-squat vs. full-squat). However, Factor 2 is not achieved as the load will be too heavy to permit a similar rate of force development, Factor 3 is not achieved as the direction of force is purely vertical opposed to vertical and horizontal, and Factor 5 is not achieved as the back squat does not significantly overlap with the coordination profile used during sprint.

Conversely, if the coach is training a player with a high training age, then they may elect to focus on the direct development of speed through the use of waist loaded sled sprints (Kawamori, Newton, Hori, and Nosaka, 2014). In this case, the sled sprints would be considered specific to sprinting, as the magnitude of force is at or above the force required during a free sprint (Factor 1); the intended rate of force development would be similar to a free sprint, with the actual rate of force development mediated by the sled load (Factor 2); the direction of force is similar to a free sprint (i.e., horizontal), with the nature of sled sprints allowing for an increase in horizontally directed force as the sled load increases (Factor 3); the range of motion would be very similar, with an increase in load likely resulting in decreased range of motion in favor of a shorter stride length (Factor 4); and the coordination profile would be very similar with light weights (e.g., <10% of body weight), while heavier loads would change the nature of the player's normal sprint coordination in favor of a coordination profile suited to deal with the sled load (e.g., increased body angle, increased horizontally direct force, and shorter stride length) (Factor 5).

The example above highlights a number of important considerations when it comes to programming for AF – or any sport, for that matter. First, general and specific methods are relative concepts. That is, squatting is specific to squatting but would be considered general to the development of sprint speed. Thus, the grading of a given method must occur in the context of the outcome athletic quality it is meant to improve. What's more, as the example above showed, the training age of the player as well as the time within the season will influence the differential application of a given general or specific training method. To further apply this concept to the collegiate and professional player, general and specific training methods will be discussed relative to their specific impact on strength, power, speed, and agility.

General methods

As discussed in the strength and speed quality analysis section, all playing positions require a strong base of strength and power. These qualities are vital for players during contact, but also underpin more specific strength qualities (i.e., starting strength, explosive strength, and reactive strength). What's more, the expression of speed and agility in the various contexts of the game that demand the ability to attack, defend, and control space requires the player to have a blend of these strength qualities. Thus, the following sections will discuss a cross-section of methods known to improve the general ability to express strength and power.

Maximal strength development

The strength and conditioning literature is chock-full of varying recommendations for improving maximal strength and relative strength. Most recently, McMaster et al. (2013) systematically reviewed 27 studies that examined the longitudinal effects of training on maximal strength development. The authors contextualized their results in terms of intensity relative volume (IRV = sets × repetitions × intensity) and weekly training frequency. Aligned with current recommendations for improving maximal strength (Haff and Triplett, 2015; Stone et al., 2007b), the core finding showed that IRVs ranging from 11 to 20 units (3.4 ± 1.2 sets of 6.5 ± 3.3 reps at 77 ± 7%) per major movement (i.e., bench press and squat) produced the largest sessional increases in strength (0.55% per training session). What's more, training frequencies per muscle group of two, three, and four times per week elicited average weekly improvements of 0.9%, 1.8%, and 1.3%, respectively. It should be noted that at these frequencies, lower body strength increased at a rate 1.7x faster than upper body strength. Thus, for the same prescribed IRVs, the lower body is more responsive to strength development, highlighting that the upper body may need more IRV units to achieve comparable changes to strength. Interestingly, Charles Poliquin advocated that the upper body required greater IRVs than the lower body to generate comparable changes in strength and hypertrophy (Poliquin, 2004). Finally, McMaster et al. (2013) projected that training programs using the above guidelines can expect percent improvements of 0.42%, 2.1%, 4.2%, and 8.4% across 1, 5, 10, and 20 sessions, respectively.

In addition to optimizing IRVs and training frequency, strength and conditioning coaches should give consideration to the specificity of the movement range of motion (i.e., Factor 4). Specifically, Rhea et al. (2016) had 28 collegiate athletes with >2 years of continuous strength training experience (>1.5x body weight back squat) complete a 16-week strength training program (two lower body sessions per week) using either a quarter-squat (knee angle 55–65º), half-squat (knee angle 85–95º), or full-squat (knee angle >110º). The quarter-squat group achieved improvements of 12%, 6%, and 2% for the quarter-squat, half-squat, and full-squat, respectively. The half-squat group achieved improvements of 7%, 14%, and 0% for the quarter-squat, half-squat, and full-squat, respectively. The full-squat group achieved improvements of 0%, 5%, and 17% for the quarter-squat, half-squat, and full-squat, respectively. Thus, the law of specificity holds true for the range of motion trained. However, the interesting finding was the transfer of training that occurred between the type of squat and vertical jump and 40-yard dash performance. The results showed that compared to the full-squat and half-squat, the quarter-squat elicited a greater transfer to both the vertical jump (FS = 1%; HS = 7%; QS = 15%) and the 40-yard dash (FS = 0%; HS = 1%; QS = 2%).

In sum, using lower body maximal strength as an example, it is evident that squatting is more specific to jumping (i.e., Factor 1 and Factor 3) than it is to sprinting (Factor 1); however, in both cases, the level of transfer is mediated by the specificity of the range of motion (i.e., Factor 4). This is not to say that strength and conditioning coaches should not prescribe full range of motion squats, quite the contrary; however, as a player becomes stronger, it can be recommended that a certain percent of the total training volume should be dedicated to squatting at a depth that will have greater transfer to the movements that are relevant to the player's success on the field (i.e., jumping and sprinting). Moreover, these principles can and should be applied to any general movement meant to support the development of maximal strength.

Maximal power development

Similar to maximal strength, the development of maximal power has become a well-studied topic within the strength and conditioning community. Despite its ubiquity, there is still a wide range of opinions on how to specifically develop it. Combing the results of McMaster et al. (2013) and Soriano, Jiménez-Reyes, Rhea, and Marín (2015) provides a clear view of how to develop maximal power. Specifically, for the heavier loads that are needed to elicit maximal power during Olympic lifting (i.e., Hang Clean and Power Clean), the IRVs should be between 9 and 27 units

(3.8 ± 0.8 sets of 6.4 ± 2.0 reps at ≥70%) for each major lift. For the moderate loads that are needed to elicit maximal power during squatting and bench press throws, the IRVs should be between 7 and 17 units (3.8 ± 0.8 sets of 6.4 ± 2.0 reps at >30% to <70%). Finally, for the light loads that are needed to elicit maximal power during the jump squat, the IRVs should be between 4 and 12 units (3.8 ± 0.8 sets of 6.4 ± 2.0 reps at <30%).

The inclusion of contrast or complex training (alternating between heavy and light loads) can be used to optimize the expression of power within the targeted light lift (e.g., jump squat) (Baker, 2003), while also improving the resultant transfer to sprint speed (Rumpf et al., 2016; Seitz et al., 2014). Baker (2003) recommends using moderate loads (65% of 1RM) to potentiate the expression of power in light loaded movements (<30% of 1RM), with three minutes of rest between the sets. What's more, recent evidence from Scott, Ditroilo, and Marshall (2016) suggest that when using heavy loads (93% of 1RM) before a countermovement jump, the use of a hexagonal bar deadlift elicits greater power and performance than a back squat. Once again, it is evident that the optimization of acute and chronic transfer requires that both kinetic factors and kinematic factors are considered during the exercise selection process.

Cluster methods

Originally advocated by Charles Poliquin and Christian Thibaudeau (Bain, 2012), cluster sets (CS) have been proposed as a general training method that can be used to enhance the expression of strength and power beyond traditional set (TS) structures (Haff et al., 2008). Specifically, CS are characterized by using inter-repetition rest periods ranging from 10–30s, which provides more total rest than performing repetitions in the continuous manner common to TS. CS have also been extended to variations in intra-set rest periods, where shorter-rest periods are injected between smaller clusters of repetitions (e.g., 6 sets of 3 reps with 60s between sets versus 3 sets of 6 reps with 120s between sets). The objective of manipulating inter-repetition and intra-set rest periods is to improve the expression of force and velocity that can be achieved during any one repetition by mitigating the accumulative effects of fatigue. That is, velocity and the expression of power can be maintained to a far greater degree using CS compared to TS (Tufano et al., 2016). What's more, due to the rest between repetitions, CS allow for a greater density of work to be achieved at a given percentage of maximum (Tufano, Brown, and Haff, 2017). Thus, CS not only support the acute maintenance of power, but also support the long-term generation of strength and hypertrophy due to the increased volume load and total work that can be achieved in a single session.

A word of caution: while the benefits of CS compared to TS are undeniable, this method is very advanced and should primarily be used with players of a high training age. Practically speaking, even when working with players with a high training age, this method should not be used more than two times per week for upper body lifts and one time per week for lower body lifts. What's more, while this method can be used with great success during the in-season, it is not recommended that this method be introduced for the first time during the in-season.

Accommodation methods

Similar to clusters, accommodation or variable resistance training can be used to enhance force and power production beyond that of mass-only barbell work. By using chains or elastic bands that are anchored to a barbell, the athlete is able to "optimally load muscles throughout the range of motion by using the mechanical advantage of muscles" (Wallace, Winchester, and McGuigan, 2006, p. 268). That is, the band or chain unloads (due to band slack and the chain resting on the ground) during the downward (eccentric) portion of the motion where the muscle is at a mechanical disadvantage (lengthened) and then reloads (due to band stretch and the chain coming off the ground) during the upward (concentric) portion of the motion where the muscle is at a mechanical advantage (shortened). It is this latter function of accommodation training that makes it unique and beneficial for strength, power, and speed athletes. Specifically, when coaches load barbell movements (i.e., bench press and back squat) using the recommendations for optimizing power (i.e., >30% to <70%), it is often the case that the athlete will have to decelerate the bar for upwards of 40% of the terminal portion of the movement (Newton, Kraemer, Häkkinen, Humphries, and Murphy, 1996). In contrast to mass only, accommodation training allows the bar to be accelerated through the entire range of motion, which is functionally relevant to the way force is expressed in AF (e.g., finishing a tackle).

The ability to accelerate the bar through the complete range of motion provides a number of benefits that can be leveraged to complement the traditional slow/heavy lifts. Specifically, Wallace et al. (2006) showed that when 20% and 35% of a total bar weight of 85% of a 1RM was provided by elastic band resistance, participants were able to generate 16% and 21% more force than in the mass only condition. Additionally, when 20% of the total bar weight was elastic band, the participants generated 24% more power than the mass only condition. These results, in addition to more recent findings (Paditsaeree, Intiraporn, and Lawsirirat, 2016; Rhea, Kenn, and Dermody, 2009), support the use of accommodation training for increasing force and power production. While the percent of load accounted for by chain or elastic band resistance may vary based on goals (i.e., less accommodated resistance for strength and more accommodated resistance for speed), a general recommendation is to stay between 10% and 30% of total load.

In sum, the general methods described in this section provide a range of training solutions for the development of strength and power. The selection of a given method should be based on training age, seasonal time point, and desired level of transfer to an outcome athletic quality. In many instances, as noted by Coach Darryl Eto, "the best method is the one the player has not adapted to yet." Thus, as suggested by Christian Thibaudeau, while the primary movements may stay relatively constant in the program (i.e., bench press, squatting, deadlifting, Olympic lifting, etc.), it is advisable to strategically look at the loading methods deployed (i.e., traditional sets, cluster sets, accommodation training, etc.) and the way with which the movement is performed (i.e., partial vs. full range of motion, hexagonal bar vs. straight bar, etc.). The following section will now discuss specific methods for the development of power, speed, and agility.

Specific methods

Plyometrics

As previously discussed, the inclusion of plyometric training can improve the transferability between strength, power, and speed. For this reason, it is important that coaches have an understanding of how to integrate plyometrics into a player's program. While there are many papers on the subject, two meta-analytical studies by de Villarreal, Kellis, Kraemer, and Izquierdo (2009); de Villarreal, Requena, and Cronin (2012) provide a relevant summary of how best to program the integration of plyometrics.

In their first review on the topic, de Villarreal et al. (2009) examined fifty-six studies in an effort to extrapolate how to optimize the programming of plyometrics. Using vertical jump improvements as the outcome variable, the results showed that programming two sessions per week over a 10-week period, with an average of 50 jumps per session, resulted in the largest improvements in vertical jump performance. What's more, the evidence also suggests that a combination of plyometric methods (i.e., squat jump, countermovement jump, and drop jump) is preferred rather than prioritizing one type over the other.

In a follow-up review, de Villarreal et al. (2012) evaluated 26 studies on the influence of plyometric training on sprint performance. The results showed that the impact of plyometrics on sprint performance is maximized when programs last 6 to 8 weeks, with 3 to 4 sessions per week, and >80 contacts per session. Note that it would be unwise to program 80 plyometrics contacts per session without balancing this contact recommendation against the contacts naturally occurring during AF practice and speed sessions. Many of these studies are not dealing with players in a full-time sport with a need to win on the weekend, thus a progressive approach that minimizes rapid spikes in volume of contacts would be recommended.

From a practical standpoint, de Villarreal et al. (2012, p. 582) make the following statement about how to optimize the transfer between plyometrics and sprinting:

> A combination of plyometric exercises (i.e., SJ + DJ, bounding + CMJ) resulted in better training effects (ESs = 0.76) compared with the use of a single type of exercise (DJ) (ESs = 0.27). The higher improvements in sprint performance may be because of a training specificity. It is possible that a training program incorporating more horizontal acceleration (e.g., bounding and form running) may improve sprint times.

This statement is supported by the findings of Fairchild, Amonette, and Spiering (2011) who showed that the broad jump was the single best performance correlate to 10-yard sprint times ($r = -0.73$), 20-yard sprint times ($r = -0.80$), 40-yard sprint times ($r = -0.69$), and the 3-cone agility drill ($r = -0.63$) at the NFL Combine. What's more, evidence continues to point towards horizontally focused plyometrics transferring to horizontally demanding tasks (i.e., acceleration and agility) (Holm, Stålbom, Keogh, and Cronin, 2008; McCurdy et al., 2010), while vertically focused plyometrics transfer to vertically demanding tasks (i.e., max velocity sprinting and vertical jumping) (Kale, Asçi, Bayrak, and Açikada, 2009).

Sprinting

As noted earlier, one of the best ways to get faster is to simply run fast (Rumpf et al., 2016). That is, a coach seeking to improve the speed of their players should look to strategically develop this quality in the off-season and maintain it throughout the in-season. From a methodology standpoint, research supports the use of free sprinting and resisted sprinting to develop speed over various distances (Petrakos et al., 2016).

Kawamori et al. (2014) produced one of the first studies to evaluate loading parameters during resisted sprinting. The results showed that after training 2 times a week for 8 weeks, the group using the lighter loads (10% reduction in sprint velocity) improved their 10-meter time by 3.0 ± 3.5%, while the group using heavier loads (30% reduction in sprint velocity) improved their 5-meter and 10-meter times by 5.7 ± 5.7% and 5.0 ± 3.5%, respectively. While the difference between groups didn't reach statistical significance, it is evident that heavier sled sprints may impart greater value, especially over 5 and 10 meters. Research has since shown that heavier sled loads are valuable for improving sprint speed over 10 and 20 meters (Morin et al., 2016), with recommendations suggesting that loads as high as 69 to 96% body mass are required to maximize power output during sled sprinting (Cross, Brughelli, Samozino, Brown, and Morin, 2017). What's more, Seitz, Mina, and Haff (2017) showed that rugby league players improved their 20-meter sprint times by –0.95 ± 2.0%, –1.80 ± 1.43%, and –1.54 ± 1.54% at 4-minutes, 8-minutes, and 12-minutes following a potentiating sled push at 75% of their body weight. Thus, both heavy sled pushes and pulls have been shown to have acute and chronic benefits to sprint performance over 20-meters.

In summarizing the extent of the current literature on resisted sprinting, Petrakos et al. (2016) provides the following three recommendations: (1) resisted sled sprinting (12–43% of body mass) is effective for improving of sprint performance in trained individuals, with lighter loads providing a stimulus comparable to un-resisted sprinting; (2) combining resisted sprinting with un-resisted sprinting or plyometric training may provide benefits to sprint acceleration beyond that of un-resisted sprinting alone; and (3) sprint adaptations may be velocity specific with heavy sled loads (>20%BM) transferring to initial acceleration, and light sled loads (<10%BM) improving the maximal velocity phase of sprinting.

As clearly identified by Rumpf et al. (2016), un-resisted and resisted sprinting should both be included in a comprehensive approach to developing speed. What's more, referencing the research cited in the transfer of training section, it would be prudent for coaches to progressively increase the amount of time spent on resisted and un-resisted sprinting as the training age and strength of the player increases. From an applied standpoint, the following can be used as general guidelines for programming sprint training: (1) to improve acceleration over 0–20 yards, players should perform 6–12 full speed efforts over 15–20 yards over the course of 1–2 training sessions per week lasting no longer than 45 minutes; and (2) to improve maximal velocity over 20 yards, players should perform 3–6 full speed efforts over 20–50 yards over the course of 1–2 training sessions per week lasting no longer than 45 minutes. Note that technical drills and sub-maximal sprint efforts would be included within the 45 minutes to augment the development of coordinative capacities specific to acceleration (0–20 yards) and maximal velocity sprinting (>20 yards).

Agility

Agility plays a very important role on both the defensive and offensive sides of the ball. To be effective a player must be able to evade or engage their opponent while controlling the space around them. In excelling within this skill set, players need to be effective at making high-speed decisions while accelerating, decelerating, and changing direction in a time and space constrained environment. While the sport provides the most potent environment for developing agility in the relevant context, it does so in an inconsistent and unpredictable manner. That is, the movements a player uses on the field (e.g., change of direction) are a consequence of the outcomes they are trying to achieve (e.g., feign a defender). Thus, as outcomes change within and across series of play, so do the required movement solutions. For this reason, strength and conditioning coaches are advised to include agility methods to ensure that all necessary movement patterns and movement sequences are developed in a manner that will transfer to the field.

Despite the importance of agility, the evidence for the trainability and the transfer of training from general methods is quite limited (Brughelli, Cronin, Levin, and Chaouachi, 2008). However, understanding the differential elements of agility goes a long way towards informing a programming model that reflects the demands of the game. Specifically, Sheppard and Young (2006), highlighting the importance of context and decision making in sport, have proposed that agility be re-contextualized as reactive agility (i.e., open skills) and non-reactive agility or change of direction (COD) (i.e., closed drills). Specifically, reactive agility is a rapid whole-body movement with change of velocity or direction in response to a stimulus, while non-reactive agility is a rapid whole-body movement with change of velocity or direction that is pre-determined. While both forms of agility develop the physical qualities associated with agility, the former does so in the context of a sport relevant decision. It is this decision making aspect of agility that has been shown to discriminate between professional and amateur players across various team sports

(Gabbett, Kelly, and Sheppard, 2008; Sheppard, Young, Doyle, Sheppard, and Newton, 2006). Therefore, a comprehensive agility program should seek to develop the movement patterns (e.g., COD, shuffle, backpedal, crossover, etc.) and movement sequences (e.g., cut to crossover to acceleration) through non-reactive means, while also applying these movement skills within a reactive agility context (e.g., mirror drills or isolated game specific scenarios). The integration of reactive and non-reactive agility supports the development of good decision making on the back of effective and efficient movement capacity.

Concluding remarks

The AF player requires a robust physical profile to thrive in the high-speed chaos that is "America's Game." However, within this chaos lies the formidable challenge of developing players for the unique physical demands native to each position. To do this the strength and conditioning coach must have a detailed appreciation of the game and positional demands and be armed with an understanding of the general and specific training methods that can be used to develop players across a season and throughout their career. As discussed in the preceding sections, to effectively develop players and deploy the right training methods, it is paramount that strength and conditioning coaches understand how training age influences transfer of training and training residuals. Equipped with this information, coaches will be able to develop individualized player plans that ensure everyone who steps on the field is "fit for purpose" and physically empowered to excel every time they play this great game.

References

Arthur, R. (2016). *The Shrinking Shelf Life of NFL Players*. Retrieved from www.wsj.com/articles/the-shrinking-shelf-life-of-nfl-players-1456694959

Babault, N., Cometti, G., Bernardin, M., Pousson, M., and Chatard, J.-C. (2007). Effects of electromyostimulation training on muscle strength and power of elite rugby players. *The Journal of Strength & Conditioning Research*, 21(2), 431–437.

Bain, J. (2012). *Cluster Training*. Retrieved from www.elitefts.com/education/training/cluster-training/

Baker, D. (1996). Improving vertical jump performance through general, special, and specific strength training: A brief review. *The Journal of Strength & Conditioning Research*, 10(2), 131–136.

Baker, D. (2001). Comparison of upper-body strength and power between professional and college-aged rugby league players. *The Journal of Strength & Conditioning Research*, 15(1), 30–35.

Baker, D. (2003). Acute effect of alternating heavy and light resistances on power output during upper-body complex power training. *The Journal of Strength & Conditioning Research*, 17(3), 493–497.

Bompa, T.O., and Carrera, M.C. (2005). The yearly training plan. In *Periodization Training for Sports* (pp. 107–148). Champaign, IL: Human Kinetics.

Brughelli, M., Cronin, J., Levin, G., and Chaouachi, A. (2008). Understanding change of direction ability in sport: A review of resistance training studies. *Sports Medicine*, 38(12), 1045–1063.

Chase, C. (2015). The NFL is insanely popular on TV, in 17 highly-rated facts. *USA Today*. Retrieved from http://ftw.usatoday.com/2015/11/nfl-tv-ratings-rankings-no-1-show-snf-mnf-local-markets

Cormie, P., McGuigan, M.R., and Newton, R.U. (2010). Adaptations in athletic performance after ballistic power versus strength training. *Medicine & Science in Sports & Exercise*, 42(8), 1582–1598.

Cross, M.R., Brughelli, M., Samozino, P., Brown, S.R., and Morin, J.-B. (2017). Optimal loading for maximising power during sled-resisted sprinting. *International Journal of Sports Physiology and Performance*, 1–25.

Davis, D.S., Barnette, B.J., Kiger, J.T., Mirasola, J.J., and Young, S.M. (2004). Physical characteristics that predict functional performance in Division I college football players. *The Journal of Strength & Conditioning Research*, 18(1), 115–120.

de Villarreal, E.S., Kellis, E., Kraemer, W.J., and Izquierdo, M. (2009). Determining variables of plyometric training for improving vertical jump height performance: A meta-analysis. *The Journal of Strength & Conditioning Research*, 23(2), 495–506.

de Villarreal, E.S., Requena, B., and Cronin, J.B. (2012). The effects of plyometric training on sprint performance: A meta-analysis. *The Journal of Strength & Conditioning Research*, 26(2), 575–584.
Fairchild, B., Amonette, W., and Spiering, B. (2011). Prediction models of speed and agility in NFL combine attendees. *The Journal of Strength & Conditioning Research*, 25, S96.
Frank, B. (2016). *The Influence of Movement Profile on The Female Athlete's Biomechanical Resilience & Training Load Response to Controlled Exercise Exposure.* (PhD), The University of North Carolina, Chapel Hill, NC.
Fry, A.C., and Kraemer, W.J. (1991). Physical performance characteristics of American collegiate football players. *The Journal of Strength & Conditioning Research*, 5(3), 126–138.
Gabbett, T.J., Kelly, J.N., and Sheppard, J.M. (2008). Speed, change of direction speed, and reactive agility of rugby league players. *The Journal of Strength & Conditioning Research*, 22(1), 174–181.
Garstecki, M.A., Latin, R.W., and Cuppett, M.M. (2004). Comparison of selected physical fitness and performance variables between NCAA Division I and II football players. *The Journal of Strength & Conditioning Research*, 18(2), 292–297.
Haff, G.G., Hobbs, R.T., Haff, E.E., Sands, W.A., Pierce, K.C., and Stone, M.H. (2008). Cluster training: A novel method for introducing training program variation. *Strength & Conditioning Journal*, 30(1), 67–76.
Haff, G.G., and Triplett, N.T. (2015). *Essentials of Strength Training and Conditioning*, 4th Edition. Illinois, USA: Human Kinetics.
Hoffman, J.R. (2008). The applied physiology of American football. *International Journal of Sports Physiology and Performance*, 3(3), 387–392.
Hoffman, J.R., Cooper, J., Wendell, M., and Kang, J. (2004). Comparison of Olympic vs. traditional power lifting training programs in football players. *The Journal of Strength & Conditioning Research*, 18(1), 129–135.
Hoffman, J.R., Ratamess, N.A., and Kang, J. (2011). Performance changes during a college playing career in NCAA division III football athletes. *The Journal of Strength & Conditioning Research*, 25(9), 2351–2357.
Hoffman, J.R., Ratamess, N.A., Klatt, M., Faigenbaum, A.D., Ross, R.E., Tranchina, N.M., . . . Kraemer, W.J. (2009). Comparison between different off-season resistance training programs in Division III American college football players. *The Journal of Strength & Conditioning Research*, 23(1), 11–19.
Holm, D.J., Stålbom, M., Keogh, J.W., and Cronin, J. (2008). Relationship between the kinetics and kinematics of a unilateral horizontal drop jump to sprint performance. *The Journal of Strength & Conditioning Research*, 22(5), 1589–1596.
Hori, N., Newton, R.U., Andrews, W.A., Kawamori, N., McGuigan, M.R., and Nosaka, K. (2008). Does performance of hang power clean differentiate performance of jumping, sprinting, and changing of direction? *The Journal of Strength & Conditioning Research*, 22(2), 412–418.
Iosia, M.F., and Bishop, P.A. (2008). Analysis of exercise-to-rest ratios during division IA televised football competition. *The Journal of Strength & Conditioning Research*, 22(2), 332–340.
Issurin, V.B. (2010). New horizons for the methodology and physiology of training periodization. *Sports Medicine*, 40(3), 189–206.
Issurin, V.B. (2013). Training transfer: Scientific background and insights for practical application. *Sports Medicine*, 43(8), 675–694.
Issurin, V.B., and Yessis, M. (2008a). *Block Periodization: Breakthrough in Sports Training* (Vol. 1). MI: Ultimate Athlete Concepts.
Issurin, V.B., and Yessis, M. (2008b). *Principles and Basics of Advanced Athletic Training*. Ultimate Athlete Concepts.
Jacobson, B.H., Conchola, E.G., Glass, R.G., and Thompson, B.J. (2013). Longitudinal morphological and performance profiles for American, NCAA Division I football players. *The Journal of Strength & Conditioning Research*, 27(9), 2347–2354.
Kale, M., Asçi, A., Bayrak, C., and Açikada, C. (2009). Relationships among jumping performances and sprint parameters during maximum speed phase in sprinters. *The Journal of Strength & Conditioning Research*, 23(8), 2272–2279.
Kawamori, N., Newton, R.U., Hori, N., and Nosaka, K. (2014). Effects of weighted sled towing with heavy versus light load on sprint acceleration ability. *The Journal of Strength & Conditioning Research*, 28(10), 2738–2745.
Kraemer, W.J., Torine, J.C., Silvestre, R., French, D.N., Ratamess, N.A., Spiering, B.A., . . . Volek, J.S. (2005). Body size and composition of National Football League players. *The Journal of Strength & Conditioning Research*, 19(3), 485–489.

McCurdy, K.W., Walker, J.L., Langford, G.A., Kutz, M.R., Guerrero, J.M., and McMillan, J. (2010). The relationship between kinematic determinants of jump and sprint performance in division I women soccer players. *The Journal of Strength & Conditioning Research*, 24(12), 3200–3208.

McGee, K.J., and Burkett, L.N. (2003). The National Football League combine: A reliable predictor of draft status? *The Journal of Strength & Conditioning Research*, 17(1), 6–11.

McMaster, D.T., Gill, N., Cronin, J., and McGuigan, M. (2013). The development, retention and decay rates of strength and power in elite rugby union, rugby league and American football: A systematic review. *Sports Medicine*, 43(5), 367–384.

Morin, J.-B., Petrakos, G., Jimenez-Reyes, P., Brown, S.R., Samozino, P., and Cross, M.R. (2016). Very-heavy sled training for improving horizontal force output in soccer players. *International Journal of Sports Physiology and Performance*, 12, 1–13.

NCAA. (2016, August 25). *Estimated Probability of Competing in College Athletics*. Retrieved 11/19/2016, from www.ncaa.org/about/resources/research/estimated-probability-competing-college-athletics

Newton, R.U., Kraemer, W.J., Häkkinen, K., Humphries, B.J., and Murphy, A.J. (1996). Kinematics, kinetics, and muscle activation during explosive upper body movements. *Journal of Applied Biomechanics*, 12(1), 31–43.

Paditsaeree, K., Intiraporn, C., and Lawsirirat, C. (2016). Comparison between the effects of combining elastic and free-weight resistance and free-weight resistance on force and power production. *The Journal of Strength & Conditioning Research*, 30(10), 2713–2722.

Petrakos, G., Morin, J.-B., and Egan, B. (2016). Resisted sled sprint training to improve sprint performance: A systematic review. *Sports Medicine*, 46(3), 381–400.

Plisk, S.S., and Gambetta, V. (1997). Tactical metabolic training: Part 1. *Strength & Conditioning Journal*, 19(2), 44–53.

Poliquin, C. (2004). *The Poliquin International Certification Program: Theory Manual 1*. East Greenwhich, RI: Poliquin Performance Center.

Poliquin, C., and Patterson, P. (1989). Terminology: Classification of strength qualities. *Strength & Conditioning Journal*, 11(6), 48–52.

Rhea, M.R., Hunter, R.L., and Hunter, T.J. (2006). Competition modeling of American football: Observational data and implications for high school, collegiate, and professional player conditioning. *The Journal of Strength & Conditioning Research*, 20(1), 58–61.

Rhea, M.R., Kenn, J.G., and Dermody, B.M. (2009). Alterations in speed of squat movement and the use of accommodated resistance among college athletes training for power. *The Journal of Strength & Conditioning Research*, 23(9), 2645–2650.

Rhea, M.R., Kenn, J.G., Peterson, M.D., Massey, D., Simão, R., Marin, P.J., . . . Krein, D. (2016). Joint-angle specific strength adaptations influence improvements in power in highly trained athletes. *Human Movement*, 17(1), 43–49.

Robbins, D.W. (2011). Positional physical characteristics of players drafted into the National Football League. *The Journal of Strength & Conditioning Research*, 25(10), 2661–2667.

Rumpf, M.C., Lockie, R.G., Cronin, J.B., and Jalilvand, F. (2016). Effect of different sprint training methods on sprint performance over various distances: A brief review. *The Journal of Strength & Conditioning Research*, 30(6), 1767–1785.

Schneider, V., Arnold, B., Martin, K., Bell, D., and Crocker, P. (1998). Detraining effects in college football players during the competitive season. *The Journal of Strength & Conditioning Research*, 12(1), 42–45.

Scott, D.J., Ditroilo, M., and Marshall, P. (2016). Complex training: The effect of exercise selection and training status on post-activation potentiation in rugby league players. *The Journal of Strength & Conditioning Research*, 28(3), 706–715.

Secora, C.A., Latin, R.W., Berg, K.E., and Noble, J.M. (2004). Comparison of physical and performance characteristics of NCAA Division I football players: 1987 and 2000. *The Journal of Strength & Conditioning Research*, 18(2), 286–291.

Seitz, L.B., Mina, M.A., and Haff, G.G. (2017). A sled push stimulus potentiates subsequent 20-m sprint performance. *Journal of Science and Medicine in Sport*, 20(8), 781–785.

Seitz, L.B., Reyes, A., Tran, T.T., de Villarreal, E.S., and Haff, G.G. (2014). Increases in lower-body strength transfer positively to sprint performance: A systematic review with meta-analysis. *Sports Medicine*, 44(12), 1693–1702.

Sheppard, J.M., Young, W.B., Doyle, T., Sheppard, T., and Newton, R.U. (2006). An evaluation of a new test of reactive agility and its relationship to sprint speed and change of direction speed. *Journal of Science and Medicine in Sport*, 9(4), 342–349.

Sheppard, J.M., and Young, W.B. (2006). Agility literature review: Classifications, training and testing. *Journal of Sports Sciences*, 24(9), 919–932.

Sierer, S.P., Battaglini, C.L., Mihalik, J.P., Shields, E.W., and Tomasini, N.T. (2008). The National Football League combine: Performance differences between drafted and nondrafted players entering the 2004 and 2005 drafts. *The Journal of Strength & Conditioning Research*, 22(1), 6–12.

Soriano, M.A., Jiménez-Reyes, P., Rhea, M.R., and Marín, P.J. (2015). The optimal load for maximal power production during lower-body resistance exercises: A meta-analysis. *Sports Medicine*, 45(8), 1191–1205.

Spiteri, T., Cochrane, J.L., Hart, N.H., Haff, G.G., and Nimphius, S. (2013). Effect of strength on plant foot kinetics and kinematics during a change of direction task. *European Journal of Sport Science*, 13(6), 646–652.

Spiteri, T., Nimphius, S., Hart, N.H., Specos, C., Sheppard, J.M., and Newton, R.U. (2014). Contribution of strength characteristics to change of direction and agility performance in female basketball athletes. *The Journal of Strength & Conditioning Research*, 28(9), 2415–2423.

Stodden, D.F., and Galitski, H.M. (2010). Longitudinal effects of a collegiate strength and conditioning program in American football. *The Journal of Strength & Conditioning Research*, 24(9), 2300–2308.

Stone, M.H., Stone, M., and Sands, W.A. (2007a). Developing resistance training programs. In *Principles and Practice of Resistance Training* (pp. 287–294). Champaign, IL: Human Kinetics.

Stone, M.H., Stone, M., and Sands, W.A. (2007b). *Principles and Practice of Resistance Training*. Illinois, USA: Human Kinetics.

Tufano, J.J., Brown, L.E., and Haff, G.G. (2017). Theoretical and practical aspects of different cluster set structures: A systematic review. *The Journal of Strength & Conditioning Research*, 31(3), 848–867.

Tufano, J.J., Conlon, J.A., Nimphius, S., Brown, L.E., Seitz, L.B., Williamson, B.D., and Haff, G.G. (2016). Maintenance of velocity and power with cluster sets during high-volume back squats. *International Journal of Sports Physiology and Performance*, 11(7), 885–892.

Wallace, B.J., Winchester, J.B., and McGuigan, M.R. (2006). Effects of elastic bands on force and power characteristics during the back squat exercise. *The Journal of Strength & Conditioning Research*, 20(2), 268–272.

Wellman, A.D., Coad, S.C., Goulet, G.C., and McLellan, C.P. (2016). Quantification of competitive game demands of NCAA Division I college football players using global positioning systems. *The Journal of Strength & Conditioning Research*, 30(1), 11–19.

Wilson, G.J., Murphy, A.J., and Walshe, A. (1996). The specificity of strength training: The effect of posture. *European Journal of Applied Physiology and Occupational Physiology*, 73(3–4), 346–352.

Young, W.B. (2006). Transfer of strength and power training to sports performance. *International Journal of Sports Physiology and Performance*, 1(2), 74–83.

Young, W.B., McLean, B., and Ardagna, J. (1995). Relationship between strength qualities and sprinting performance. *The Journal of Sports Medicine and Physical Fitness*, 35(1), 13–19.

Zatsiorsky, V.M., and Kraemer, W.J. (2006). *Science and Practice of Strength Training*. Champaign, IL: Human Kinetics.

9
AUSSIE RULES FOOTBALL

Ian McKeown

Introduction

Australian Football (AF) is currently played in over 30 structured leagues throughout 30 countries worldwide. The premier competition, the Australian Football League (AFL), is played in all seven of Australia's states and territories and is currently the most popular football code in Australia. Undoubtedly, its strongest following is in the southern state of Victoria, where it originated in 1858. Australian Football is a contact, invasion game that generally involves fewer collisions and tackling than rugby union and rugby league. The objective and game structure of AF are similar to those of football (soccer); it has been described as a running game combining athleticism with speed and requiring skillful foot and hand passing. In modern AF two teams contest play over four 20- to 30-minute periods with the objective of scoring more points than the opposition to win. Each quarter can include about 10 extra minutes of stoppage time, which brings the total time of a game to approximately 120 minutes (Gray and Jenkins, 2010).

A team is composed of 22 players, with 18 players allowed on the field at any one time. The remaining four players make up the interchange bench and these players can be rotated onto the field, as the coach deems necessary. In the AFL from 2016 an interchange cap of 90 has been set in place. This rule has progressively changed in recent years from 120 in 2015, and prior to that rotations were unlimited.

Eighteen professional senior sides compete against each other in the AFL and, similar to other football codes, game demands at the elite level in the AFL have changed considerably in recent years. Rule changes in recent years have increased the flow and speed of the game; there has been a reduction in the time taken for umpires to restart play, and for players to kick-in or take a set shot at goal.

The nature of the sport as an ultimate balance between extremes of endurance capacity, strength, and combative skills alongside the resources that have been able to be appropriated in this area in recent years has lead to AFL clubs being renowned worldwide as pioneers for best practice player preparation and management.

Athletic demands

The movement patterns of AFL football can be described as highly intermittent with repeated bouts of shorter lower-intensity walking and jogging (Wisbey et al., 2010). Rotations have lead to a change in this output each year with the most recent year producing longer bouts on field.

Anecdotally this has lead to a decrease in the amount of top-end speed efforts; however, work rate and peak speeds are still reached despite longer bouts with no rest. Australian Football players require well-developed physical capacities to cope with the demands of competition. Recent match analysis shows that at the professional level, AF players travel approximately 11–13 km during matches at an average speed of 108–128 m.min^{-1} and peak speeds in excess of 9 m.s^{-1} (Bilsborough et al., 2015). The technical demands require that many physically challenging skills be completed, including kicking, jumping, tackling, jostling, and colliding with opponents. Additionally, although the number of tackles in each match in elite AF is considerably less than other contact team sports, such as rugby union and rugby league, many of these (approx. 38%) are completed at high speeds (>14.4 km.h^{-1}), further demonstrating the intense nature of AF (Bilsborough et al., 2015).

Australian Football is often considered the ultimate mixture of athleticism with competing demands resulting in well-rounded players who, in general, need to compete with the physicality of a tackling and contact sport, but also be able to cope with total volume of running and the intensity of that running, which is considered exceptional when compared to other team sports.

Injury prevalence

There is, not surprisingly, some attrition when training and competing in a sport with the physical demands of AF. The typical running-based injuries of hamstring, groin, and calf strains are coupled with the contact injuries of knee ACL, shoulder and ankle sprains, and concussion (Table 9.1). The incidence of certain injuries and injury types may have fluctuated slightly over the years, but overall a constant injury incidence in AFL is reported (Orchard et al., 2014). Rule changes around tackling and body contact have addressed elements of the sport to aid in reducing the risk of concussion, for example. Other changes or interpretations of the rules have lead to an increase in intensity of running, which would logically increase some of the injuries related to change of direction and high-speed running. This risk, however, has been mitigated by the improvement in understanding and treatment of such injuries and the increase in physical

Table 9.1 Injury incidence in AFL (new injuries per club per season) – modified from Orchard et al. (2014) and Orchard (2015)

Injury type	2002–4	2005–7	2008–10	2011–13	2014
Concussion	0.4	0.4	0.5	1.0	1.3
Shoulder sprains and dislocations	1.1	1.3	1.6	1.4	1.2
Forearm/wrist/hand fractures	1.0	1.1	1.2	1.1	1.1
Lumbar and thoracic spine injuries	1.1	1.6	1.5	1.6	1.7
Groin strains/osteitis pubis	3.3	3.4	3.6	2.7	2.6
Hamstring strains	5.5	6.1	6.5	5.3	5.2
Quadriceps strains	1.8	1.8	1.9	1.6	1.1
Knee ACL	0.6	0.7	0.7	0.9	0.7
Knee MCL	0.9	1.0	0.9	0.8	0.7
Ankle joint sprains, including syndesmosis sprains	2.5	2.3	2.8	3.1	3.1
Calf strains	1.5	1.6	1.7	3.0	2.6
Medical illnesses	2.2	1.6	2.4	2.1	2.4
New injuries/club/season	34.4	34.6	37.8	39.3	36.1

preparation science underpinning strength and conditioning practices at the same time (this is discussed later). The AFL support a league-wide injury audit each year (Table 9.1), which provides a transparent analysis of the frequency patterns emerging allowing public access and wide spread discussion around the injuries sustained, leading to rule changes with a primary goal of improving player safety (Orchard et al., 2013).

Fitness testing

The national combine presents a battery of tests that are used to talent identify junior players as part of the draft system into the AFL. These include anthropometric (height, weight) and physical performance tests: standing vertical jump (bilateral and unilateral), AFL agility test, 20m sprint, and 20m multi-stage fitness test. Logistic regression models of these tests and players drafted into the AFL showed the multistage fitness test, height and 20m sprint time as the most important attributes for predicting draft success (Woods et al., 2015). These results reflect the athletic demands of the sport, where speed and endurance are vital for success, along with being taller and jumping higher for contested aerial skills, again vital in a collision based sport. Fitness testing alone will not discriminate between levels of performers, however. Assessment of cognitive recognition and play identification must be included as part of the talent identification process (Robertson et al., 2015). The use of decision making and position-specific context to performance test should be striven to be included. This is not always within the remit of the strength and conditioning (S&C) coach, but the point should still be considered when interpreting results of testing sessions.

Apart from its use in combine situations, fitness testing should be embedded into the program as much as possible, to allow continual monitoring and assessment of performance changes without the need to disrupt the program. Sub-maximal tests of fitness, as discussed shortly, may be of use in this environment from a conditioning point of view.

Strength and power measures such as jump performance and maximal strength tests should also be incorporated into the program. Traditional strength measures of upper body (bench press and bench pull) and lower body (back squat and deadlift) maximal strength are easily administered tests. The use of velocity-based methods can infer maximal strength and power performance changes with sub-maximal loads, too (Cormie et al., 2011). Aside from performance testing, jump data is also frequently assessed as a measure of neuromuscular fatigue. This has been utilized throughout the AFL, based on the seminal work of Cormack et al. (2008). Being able to inform the coaches of the fatigue-state of each player alongside measures of wellness can improve the prescription or management of training load of each player for the upcoming week. For example, being able to frequently assess this variability in performance can ensure you are able to determine when fatigue is an issue and performance is below typical scores and put in place appropriate measures.

The relatively high incidence of hamstring injuries in the AFL (see Table 9.1) has made them an ideal cohort for injury prediction analysis. Recent work of Opar et al. (2014) has shown that eccentric hamstring strength in excess of 280N during a Nordic hamstring curl will reduce injury risk by over 4 times. Age and previous injury history are two non-modifiable risk factors here, highlighting the need for strength training to improve eccentric hamstring strength as part of an athletic development program.

Programming

The level of influence the strength and conditioning coach can have in the AFL setting is quite extensive. This expanse of influence means that the S&C coach cannot think in isolation regarding the elements of the program but has the chance to influence and drive their concepts and coaching themes throughout the program, creating sessions that are complementary to each other. This can provide better context to the sessions or particular drill/exercise, which will create more buy-in and transfer to performance.

Of course, this is how the S&C coach should work anyway, whether in isolation or as part of a performance team, where you can rely on the sports science and sports medicine professionals to coordinate their input into the program towards a global set of principles. This involves excellent working relationships with strong communication, mutual professional respect, humility and good leadership.

Although the organization and planning of the program are priority skills in S&C, the ability to utilize these skills and deliver to the athlete an optimal program that they buy in to and achieve a transfer to their training and performance are critical. It is often said that the best program, poorly coached, is far worse than a bad program, well coached. With this in mind, I implore you to understand the underpinning concepts of programming and technical coaching and to continually evolve these skills but never lose sight that the key goals of the program are to connect with the athlete and best prepare them within the unique constraints of your environment.

Being able to consider the current environment and relationships will influence your programming and coaching practices. For example, being able to work closely and collaborate with the physiotherapist can create a stronger injury prevention element of the program. If, however, this relationship is flawed, how the program is delivered may be negatively influenced. Having strong working relationships across all professionals is essential in order to pull upon different areas of expertise for the purpose of delivering the best program possible.

The ability to understand the underpinning best-practice theory behind the organization of training and being able to adapt and apply to your particular situation is the best way to address the periodization framework of the program. Being pragmatic of the demands of the sport and how to best fit everything in to a logical systematic progression can only be achieved with in-depth understanding of the concepts behind periodization.

Periodization

Within team sports, it is much more effective to disregard (but respect) the classical block and linear periodization models in favor of a more fluid and conjugated model. This is due to the continual battle between physical performance qualities coupled with the need to train and compete at a high level across long seasons. A simplistic model may be applicable in youth sports or beginners, however, and must not be simply discounted. Undulating the priority and intensity of sessions throughout the micro- and mesocycles will enable all qualities to be at suitable level across a longer time frame, rather than having one quality peak relative to another for shorter periods. This is typically considered the difference between block or linear periodization and conjugated or missed methods models. As players are typically required to perform at their best each weekend as well as train adequately throughout the week, it is preferential to use a mixed methods-type of concept as a framework for programming. As such, the periodization or organization of the training, particularly in-season, is governed by the fixture schedule. Having shorter or longer breaks will determine the in-week training and therefore confine the training load to what can be appropriately completed. When planning the total training load and the distribution of strength versus conditioning load, it is important to fluctuate the intensity and volume of the loading. It is equally important to ensure that these fluctuations are sustainable by keeping the peaks and troughs within reasonable magnitudes. Using rolling averages of 7-day and 28-days can illustrate the acute load and chronic loads that are prescribed using various training metrics. By ensuring appropriate training loads, the S&C can continue to develop fitness and combat injury risk through training increases that are acutely too high or chronically too low (Gabbett, 2016; Gabbett et al., 2016).

Preseason programming

Preseason in AFL is one of the longest in professional sports (14–16 weeks) and is the optimal opportunity to improve upon the physical characteristics of each player. As there are no fixtures to contend with, a more traditional periodization model can be adopted where certain physical qualities may be more of a focus than others in a linear process. In ARF these are typically general fitness, leading to specific fitness and game simulation, and general preparation strength followed by maximal strength and power development. For the large part, this is still within the confines of a mixed or conjugated model. The planning of the preseason can only be initiated after a thorough needs analysis that includes the style of play and the physical demands expected for the following season in collaboration with other coaches and support staff. The progression of the qualities required for this plan is then typically based upon the preference of the head of S&C and their biases. There will always be the issue of interference with concurrent training where the effects of maximal strength training, for example, will be hindered by the inclusion of running and games-based training into the program (McGuigan et al., 2009). This is the same in all team sports and it is the strength and conditioning coach's responsibility to consider this and manage the training load and the performance expectations around this period. In order to combat the conflicting physical performance qualities both from within a strength point of view, and from within conditioning point of view, and then overall; a conjugated or mixed method has to be employed by training each strength quality within a week but with different levels of concentration. Within preseason, each day and each week will have an overall theme; however, within each module or session, there may be different sub-qualities that are touched upon. The competing demands placed on the players make it imperative to plan and organize well but also to monitor wellness and fatigue as a result of the training through whatever methods you so chose. This is largely decided upon due to human resources available and the cost of each method employed (Table 9.2).

Table 9.2 Preseason weekly schedule

	Day 1	Day 2	Day 3	Day 4	Day 5	Day 6	Day 7
AM	Field training	Strength training – upper body volume	Field training	Day off – recovery/regeneration	Field training	Running only	Day off – recovery/regeneration
PM	Strength training – lower body explosive strength/upper body max strength		Strength training – lower body control and skill development/upper body explosive strength		Strength training – lower body max strength/upper body control and skill development	Strength training – optional upper body upper body hypertrophy	

As shown in Table 9.2, an optimal framework of weekly periodization may incorporate variations of loading through lower and upper body with variable strength sub-qualities being the focus at any one time. This is a better way to describe the split in training rather than upper body day versus lower body day, as the terminology is more accurate. Ambiguous, general descriptions of themes are inappropriate in a complex system of sports performance training.

Typically in preseason there is time to afford 4-week training programs with step progressions in loads. There is no doubt however that a lot has to still be fitted into this period. A concept that can help manage the loading, considering there is usually only time for 2 or 3 cycles in preseason, is to use the 4th week of the program, typically a de-load week, to introduce the new program rather than complete the de-load week of the previous program. This can enable a more aggressive loading come the first week of the planned next program, enabling an accommodating period to the new program, and increasing the variation within the program. As team sports require a multitude of movements and planes to be trained, it is often not the strength capacity that is the limiting factor but range and depth of exposure to variety that is challenged. This concept of using the 4th week as an introduction week to the new program can help manage this.

In-season programming

In-season planning and organization of training load is largely dictated by the fixture list and mandatory days off in the AFL. Depending on the break between games there can be more or less opportunity to train during the week. The load prescribed will often be changed according to the prior games' intensity and volume along with the subsequent fixture as this will have more of an effect on the recovery or readiness status of the players. The variability in post-game training load should be individualized to each player. The first few days post-game should be focused on recovery and resetting the body for the next week and preparing for the next game. As AF is typically played on the weekend, unlike other sports like soccer, training in-week can be much more intense. This goes for on field and off-field sessions where the middle of the week will include a spike in training load with main strength sessions and on-field sessions on the same day. Table 9.3 depicts a typical week, including all sessions that could be placed into the program. As you can see there is a peak in the load of the game and also one further peak mid-week. Throughout the in-season period it is advised to continue with the mindset of further development across all physical qualities rather than maintenance. Maintenance in-season should not be the goal; continual development should be. Games will increase match-fitness in the players naturally as the season progresses; strength and the sub-qualities thereof must also be continually touched on in order to promote this continual development (McMaster et al., 2013). A variety of training methods will need to be incorporated in order to cope with the modifications required due to soreness and fatigue from games and training. The nature of contact sports will mean that

Table 9.3 Typical weekly schedule 7-day break between games

	Day 1	Day 2	Day 3	Day 4	Day 5	Day 6	Day 7
AM	Rest and recovery	Mobility and light strength session	Day off	Main field training	Strength training	Easy field session	Game day
PM	Rest and recovery	Easy run		Main strength session	Rest	Rest	

certain players will come off games with injuries that will limit them during the week but still play full games at the weekend. Due to this, rather than omitting certain exercises completely that are in place for a specific loading stimulus, the strength and conditioning coach must be able to substitute the exercise while limiting any moderating effects of this change. First intimately understanding and planning the stimulus, whilst having a bank of alternatives that satisfy the sub-quality sought, best achieves this. A hierarchy of loading parameters will make this process more readily available for the coach.

Conditioning programming

In order to achieve the tactical and technical demands of play, players are required to cover work loads of between 108 and 128 m.min^{-1} with intermittent bursts of speed, change of direction, accelerations, jumping, and colliding along with ball skills of kicking and handballing. To achieve the level of conditioning required, training should ideally incorporate as much team play or context-specific work wherever possible. There are constraints of technical and physical ability to consider here. The drills may break down due to technical proficiency rather than physical ability; secondly, the specificity of the drills may unduly overload the body before a pre-requisite fitness or resilience has been achieved, leaving players at risk of injury. To combat this deficiency, the conditioning of each player may be bolstered with alternative conditioning stimulus that may be off-feet or non-weight bearing in order to gain adaptation to specific energy systems without the structural demands placed on the body in running and game-play situations, in particular. The overload in game specific play assumes a level of competence and resilience to be able to cope with this structurally. This advanced training methodology may not be appropriate for developing players; in this case, training drills must be carefully monitored and managed, the delicate balance between technical and tactical improvement must be sought without excessive load risk for the players. The main aim of every strength and conditioning program must be to have healthy players on the field at all times. Oftentimes this goal and the intricate balance with the sports coach's goals is forgotten.

Although alternative conditioning is a viable and a constructive addition to the overall training program, coaches must consider that adaptation to running loads is required and players should be encouraged wherever possible to do as much of their conditioning on-feet as possible. This will aid in the adaptation of the lower limb structures to the intensity and volume required. If they are constantly off-feet or doing alternative conditioning they will improve their energy system capacities; however, these will not be specific to the game and therefore not transfer to on-field performance. It is imperative in this situation to ensure training load and structural load is considered. Placing these demands on players, especially younger players, will bring about inherent injury risk if load is not managed well.

Strength programming

Strength alongside running ability is a cornerstone of athletic development in AF. There is no doubting there is a large component of strength required to meet the demands of training and competition. How the strength sub-qualities are developed and organized is the true skill of strength and conditioning coaching, especially with such a plethora of competing demands at one time.

Strength training should be underpinned with resilient movement ability of the foundational patterns required in the sport. In this case, single leg control, hip stability, integration of trunk and upper body pulling and pushing, rotation and grappling skills should underpin all exercise selection. These qualities can be exposed and tested under compound movements of lunging, squatting, pulling and pushing – not only under progressive loads lifted but through variation and complexity of movement.

A strong foundation of movement ability should be the goal of coaches working with a senior playing group, while also increasing these foundations of movement ability, a concurrent increase in strength and power performance is required. The increase in complexity through load and variation of these foundation movements will develop players that are more resilient to the physical outputs they are required to have to meet the technical and tactical demands placed on them by their coaches.

An important consideration of strength programming in AF is the strong influence body composition has on playing performance. Improvements in strength can lead to increases in total body mass, even if this is lean tissue mass, this extra mass may have detrimental effects on running ability which is crucial considering the distances each player must cover. Therefore when programming strength training sessions it is imperative to consider the volume of training and the possible hypertrophic effects this training may have. Collaboration here with nutrition specialists will help with this training quandary. This is particularly important in early years within a senior program as an increase in training load multiplied by an inordinate increase in body mass can lead to an increase in stress-related injury risk. By training well in a balanced program, first-year players (post-draft year) can still expect to gain 4–5 kg of mass without traditional high-volume training programs. This is a realistic increase in mass that, coupled with the increase in training load, should be manageable for all players.

In the team sport environment the strength-training component of the program can also be seen as an opportunity to place context to other exercises and drills present within the program. By having influence on the entire physical preparation of the players, common themes and coaching cues should be seen throughout the program where exercises placed in the strength program can have mutually complementary effect on drills and exercises and even performance on field. Examples are best illustrated where the drill can be broken down from a conditioning or speed drill and coached intensively and precisely in the gym setting where there is potentially more time and the environment is less chaotic, allowing the player to practice deeply the areas of dysfunction to their technique. An example would be to include running drills that may be required within on-field warms ups within the strength session, possibly as a substitute for contrast exercises post heavy lifts. This affords more time to coach the movements and allow the players to practice in different environments.

This point also carries further weight where each and every strength training exercise prescribed by the strength and conditioning coach must have relevance beyond the simple need to get stronger or bigger. Each exercise should have a rationale specific to each player that satisfies some element of them becoming a better player. These points should be communicated to the players in the coaching environment, creating a squad of players who understand intimately what they are doing and why they are doing each exercise, creating more accountability to their performance but also creating greater or deeper contextual relevance, which is seen to enhance transfer to performance on field. An example could be the use of single arm dumbbell bench press. Not only is it used as a variation for pressing strength, but the resistance of the trunk against rotation to that loaded side plus shoulder integrity create an exercise that is important for developing anti-rotation strength and coordinating hip and trunk stability with upper body strength, useful in acceleration and running mechanics and tackling/contact situations.

Special exercises for Australian Football

There are a multitude of training methods available to the strength and conditioning coach. There are no incorrect or wrong methods, only methods and techniques that may be more suitable at one particular time with a particular set of players or athletes. A successful strength program should complement the overall goals of the training program both from a physical performance and technical/tactical point of view. The methods employed should be based upon a strong and unequivocal foundation of fundamental movement abilities. In youth and inexperienced training groups, the majority of the program should be focused on improving these fundamental abilities. As players progress through the youth ranks and into senior football, ideally their movement ability has preceded the intensities and qualities required, enabling them to withstand the rigors of training and competition at their new level. Only once players have a strong and well-rounded movement vocabulary will special exercises then be introduced. The following are examples of exercises employed at appropriate times for each player that aid in improving and protecting them from the demands of AF.

Strength/power

Building upon the basic and fundamental strength lifts of squatting, hinging, pushing and pulling are the more body position-specific movements for generating maximal force and power. There are many avenues to train power and force development. Olympic lifting and the derivatives thereof are always popular; however, there are alternatives that may be better suited to your particular group. Jumping under load is a popular method with simple measuring devices providing feedback to the velocity of the lift in question and an ideal motivational and monitoring tool. Bench press throws (Figure 9.1) and medicine ball throws (Figure 9.2) provide upper body alternatives where measuring height or distance is a simple but effect method for providing performance feedback.

(a) (b)

Figure 9.1a and b Bench press throw

Figure 9.2a and b Single arm medicine ball shot put – split position

Running performance

Transfer of strength qualities to running performance, whether through more force translation into the ground or via better running mechanics, is a topical goal of the performance enhancement element of any strength and conditioning program. Transfer of skills using resistance-training methods as the stimulus can provide greater motor control challenges and opportunities, and therefore a theoretical environment of optimal skill transfer (Bosch and Klomp, 2005). Alongside performance enhancement, running with improved skill can also alleviate poor joint positions that, when placed under fatigue or extreme loads, can lead to injury. A power step up as shown in Figure 9.3 challenges lower limb stiffness and aggressive transfer of limbs, which can be used to reinforce body positions and force application required during sprinting.

When considering special exercises like these examples, a coach must have first developed a technical model of running, for example, and a pathway that works towards it with simple progressions that provide context to drills and exercises used in other areas of the program. Understanding what is good running mechanics and what are the key performance indicators and impediments to achieving this for each athlete or player will dictate what you prescribe and how you coach each individual.

Injury prevention

Injury prevention should not revolve around certain exercises but should consider the entire system as an injury prevention method. Good training prescription should unequivocally consider injury prevention alongside performance enhancement; as mentioned previously,

Figure 9.3a Power step up
(Start position in traditional "A" drill stance)

Figure 9.3b
(Transfer limb with mid-foot strike and stiff lower limb)

Figure 9.3c
(Secondary limb transfer onto 30cm box, finishing in "A" position)

the main aim of the strength and conditioning program should be to have a healthy players on the field at all times. Although risk factors have been identified in the literature, the overarching risk factor is previous history of that injury; this further emphasizes the crucial role of having a S&C program from the formative years in sport that can mitigate as many areas of risk as possible through systematic, logical progressions of programs while also improving athletic performance. The ability to move, run, jump and land well, coupled with being strong enough and fit enough with appropriate progressions in loads, will supersede any individual exercises to be prescribed. Traditional strength exercises exposing hamstring strength such as Nordic hamstring curls, Romanian deadlifts and all the derivatives thereof should be considered. That being said, alongside a well-rounded strength program there are structural challenges that may add some specificity to the provocative movements that are seen in AF. One such movement is the aggressive stretch of the posterior chain (including neural components) typically seen when over-striding, stumbling after a push in the back, or attempting to pick up a ground ball. Considering the frequency of hamstring injuries in AF there, should be attention paid to common injuries. The water skier with cable as shown in Figure 9.4 provides some familiarity to this movement; creating control in such provocative and dangerous hip and trunk positions can aid in injury prevention. This movement can be progressed via increasing loads on the cable or by introducing perturbations by hitting the cable with a stick.

(a) (b)

Figure 9.4a and b Water skier

Ian McKeown

Trunk integration

Core exercises should be seen as an integral part of the program. Better referred to as trunk integration exercises, the exercises should incorporate challenges of the hip and pelvis to interact with the spine and rest of the body in an optimal pattern, under load, speed, and complexity. Essentially, every exercise used in a program should consider trunk integration. Trunk integration is important for spinal health from a low-level control point of view. Due to the multi-planar, multi-dimensional nature of Australian Football, players have to be able to tolerate large rotation and torsional forces across the body made during contact, kicking, and tackling, for example. Fighting against/with rotation and/or flexion/extension in exercises will supplement the program together with the fundamentals of core control. Figures 9.5, 9.6 and 9.7 illustrate unilateral, anti-rotation in multiple planes of movement, all incorporating total body control with contribution from both upper and lower body together with core control.

Warm ups

A critical element of the strength and conditioning coach's role should be to coach the warm up for each session. The warm up should be seen as a great opportunity to reinforce the coaching cues from other sessions and to further develop athleticism in each player and should therefore be planned and periodized accordingly. The warm up should prepare the players for the upcoming session; however, the opportunities to underline strong movement ability and mindful execution is often waylaid by the apparent need to get into the main elements of the session as soon as possible. A well thought out and coached warm up can add a lot of value to the overall program. The following are basic examples of what should be included in a typical warm up for sessions.

(a)   (b)

Figure 9.5a and b Single arm dumbbell press

(a)

(b) (c)

Figure 9.6a–c Pallof press and lift

(a)   (b)

Figure 9.7a and b   Single arm/single leg cable row

Table 9.4 Example of Warm Ups Examples in Table 9.3 are given to illustrate the progressive increase in intensity towards the start of the session. The on-field warm up should be considered more of a speed development session; other warm ups through the week can emphasize the technical development of change of direction skill

Strength session	*On field*
Lateral band walk × 10 steps each way	Side shuffle (switch each 4 steps) 2 × 20m
Single leg RDL × 6 each leg	Carioca 2 × 20m
Push up with rotation × 5 each way	Walking lunge with hip lift 2 × 10m
Spiderman walk × 12 steps	Leg swings × 10 each way
Diagonal bound and stick × 3 each way	A skip 2 × 20m
★Do as a circuit × 2	Dribble – small 2 × 20m
	Dribble – medium 2 × 20m
	Zig zag or swerve runs 2 × 30m
	Build ups with dribble start 2 × 50m
	Acceleration starts 3 × 10m

★Set up with lanes of markers at 0m, 10m, 20m, 30m, and 50m
★★Set up with coaches at the end of each lane of cones to introduce football at end of each effort

Youth development

For the junior player emphasis must be placed on obtaining a well-rounded exposure to multiple sports and environments alongside a wide range of training modalities. Long-term player development models should be closely based on the recommendations of such conceptual models as

LTAD (Balyi) or more recently the Youth Physical Development (Balyi and Hamilton, 2005; Lloyd and Oliver, 2012).

The balance with these age group players is to prepare each player adequately for the immediate challenges they face on the field but also consider the long-term well being of the player. Attempt to develop an athletic player with a multitude of physical characteristics suited to the game but also realize the player is still developing and should not be seen as a finished article but given the best chance to train for a long time and play throughout a senior playing career.

Conclusion

Australian Football requires a complex interaction of competing demands that are at the extreme end of each performance spectrum. Players must be capable of running extensive distances at high speed and with great agility but also be able to withstand and impart punishing forces for contact situations. A program must be able to balance these competing demands, minimizing the interference effect of concurrent training, through developing a systematic program of load progressions underpinned by movement ability that provides the basis for the advanced training methods and game-specific drills utilized for increasing physical capacity to play the sport at the highest level. The priority of such a program is to ensure a healthy playing squad who and train and compete when required; only then can performance improvements for physical characteristics be considered.

References

Balyi, I. and Hamilton, A. 2005. Long-term Athlete Development: Trainability in Childhood and Adolescence. *Coaching Update*, 20, 10–13.

Bilsborough, J. C., Greenway, K. G., Opar, D. A., Livingstone, S. G., Cordy, J. T., Bird, S. R. and Coutts, A. J. 2015. Comparison of Anthropometry, Upper-body Strength, and Lower-Body Power Characteristics in Different Levels of Australian Football Players. *The Journal of Strength & Conditioning Research*, 29, 826–834.

Bosch, F. and Klomp, R. 2005. *Running: Biomechanics and Exercise Physiology in Practice*. London, UK: Elsevier Churchill Livingstone.

Cormack, S. J., Newton, R. U., McGuigan, M. R. and Cormie, P. 2008. Neuromuscular and Endocrine Responses of Elite Players During an Australian Rules Football Season. *International Journal of Sports Physiology and Performance*, 3, 439–453.

Cormie, P., McGuigan, M. R. and Newton, R. U. 2011. Developing Maximal Neuromuscular Power: Part 2 – Training Considerations for Improving Maximal Power Production. *Sports Medicine*, 41, 125–146.

Gabbett, T. J. 2016. The Training-injury Prevention Paradox: Should Athletes Be Training Smarter and Harder? *British Journal of Sports Medicine*. doi:10.1136/bjsports-2015-095788.

Gabbett, T. J., Hulin, B. T., Blanch, P. and Whiteley, R. 2016. High Training Workloads Alone Do Not Cause Sports Injuries: How You Get There Is the Real Issue. *British Journal of Sports Medicine*. doi:10.1136/bjsports-2015-095567.

Gray, M. A. J. and Jenkins, D. G. 2010. Match Analysis and the Physiological Demands of Australian Football. *Sports Medicine*, 40, 347–360.

Lloyd, R. S. and Oliver, J. L. 2012. The Youth Physical Development Model: A New Approach to Long-Term Athletic Development. *Strength & Conditioning Journal*, 34, 61–72.

McGuigan, M. R., Cormack, S. and Newton, R. U. 2009. Long-term Power Performance of Elite Australian Rules Football Players. *Journal of Strength and Conditioning Research*, 23, 26–32.

McMaster, D., Gill, N., Cronin, J. and McGuigan, M. 2013. The Development, Retention and Decay Rates of Strength and Power in Elite Rugby Union, Rugby League and American Football. *Sports Medicine*, 43(5), 367–384.

Opar, D. A., Williams, M., Timmins, R., Hickey, J., Duhig, S. and Shield, A. 2014. Eccentric Hamstring Strength and Hamstring Injury Risk in Australian Footballers. *Medicine & Science in Sports & Exercise*, 46.

Orchard, J. W. 2015. Men at higher risk of groin injuries in elite team sports: a systematic review. *British Journal of Sports Medicine*, 49(12), 798–802.

Orchard, J., Seward, H. and Orchard, J. 2014. *AFL Injury Report: 2014 Season*. Available: www.afl.com.au/staticfile/AFL Tenant/AFL/Files/2014-AFL-Injury-Report.pdf [Accessed April 2016].

Orchard, J. W., Seward, H. and Orchard, J. J. 2013. Results of 2 Decades of Injury Surveillance and Public Release of Data in the Australian Football League. *The American Journal of Sports Medicine*, 41(4), 734–741. doi:10.1177/0363546513476270.

Robertson, S., Woods, C. and Gastin, P. 2015. Predicting Higher Selection in Elite Junior Australian Rules Football: The Influence of Physical Performance and Anthropometric Attributes. *Journal of Science and Medicine in Sport*, 18, 601–606.

Wisbey, B., Montgomery, P. G., Pyne, D. B. and Rattray, B. 2010. Quantifying Movement Demands of AFL Football Using GPS Tracking. *Journal of Science and Medicine in Sport*, 13, 531–536.

Woods, C. T., Raynor, A. J., Bruce, L., McDonald, Z. and Collier, N. 2015. Predicting Playing Status in Junior Australian Football Using Physical and Anthropometric Parameters. *Journal of Science and Medicine in Sport*, 18, 225–229.

10
FIELD HOCKEY

Ben Rosenblatt and Andy Hudson

Introduction to the sport

Hockey can be described as a high intensity, repeat sprint sport that also requires a high level of aerobic capacity (Spencer et al., 2004). Hockey at the elite end of the spectrum requires players to maintain work quality through the course of a tournament (Jennings, 2011; Spencer et al., 2005), which may be as many as eight matches in 13 days. As a consequence there are different physical challenges placed on these players, coupled with the fact that in many instances the tournaments are held in hot and humid climatic conditions.

The non-elite player may more often experience one match per week and inevitably in an environment they are chronically acclimatised to. As a consequence there are different demands placed on these different player groups. The elite player may need to develop a high tolerance to lots of training as a vehicle for developing 'tournament durability'. The club player may need to focus on the physical challenges of the 'one off' game.

Both international and domestic matches are 11v11 and involve rolling substitutions. Whilst domestic teams compete over two halves of 35 minutes (separated by a 10 minute break), international teams compete over four quarters of 15 minutes (separated by two 2 minute quarter time breaks and a 10 minute half time break). Teams are made up of 16 players who must remain the same across the course of an international tournament.

In the UK, domestic teams typically train two nights per week and usually undertake strength and conditioning sessions two to three times per week. International teams typically run a centralised training programme in which the athletes are expected to train five to six times per week, train and play for their club once per week and undertake three to four strength and conditioning sessions per week.

Athletic demands and fitness testing battery

Due to ball speeds associated with passing in hockey, there is a large requirement on the attacking players to press high up the pitch and there is high opportunity for transition. This results in a very high repeated sprint demand on attacking players who require more frequent rotations than defending players. In a typical match, defending players are likely to play for 40–60 minutes, whilst attacking players are more likely to play for 30–45 minutes. They typically cover a similar distance of 6500–7000m, resulting in a higher density of efforts for the attacking players compared to the defending players (unpublished GB Hockey data). During particularly intense periods of play, there may be an expectation for an attacking player to cover up to 350m of running in a minute (unpublished GB Hockey data). As a consequence, not only is there a physical requirement to sprint fast, but also be able to repeat those sprints across the spell you are on the pitch for and sustain them throughout a match (and if you are an international player, across the course of a tournament).

Table 10.1 The unique, key movement patterns of hockey

Ball carry 1 – side on view

Pass – slap

Pass – forehand hit

Pass – reverse hit

Squatting block

Reverse stick block

Open stick block

Corner injector

Corner trapper

Corner flicker

Goalkeeper, post man and number 1 runner

Table 10.2 The physical demands, requirements, assessments and benchmarks associated with physical capability to compete at international hockey

Physical demand	Physical requirement	Physical assessment	International benchmark
Training durability	Lateral trunk endurance	Lateral trunk hold	2 minutes
	Hip extensor endurance	Supine hip extension hold	2 minutes
	Plantar-flexion endurance	Heel raise	35 reps
Tournament durability	Lower limb strength	Back squat	1.7 × BW (female)
			2.0 × BW (male)
	Aerobic fitness	30:15 intermittent fitness test	20.5 (female)
			21.5 (male)
Repeated high intensity efforts	Acceleration	5m sprint	<1.0s (female)
			<0.9s (male)
	Max speed	40m sprint	
	Agility	20m shuttle	<7.0s (female)
			<6.8s (male)
	Repeated sprint ability	8 × 20m shuttle every 30s	<7.4s (female)
			<7.0s (male)

Compared to other team sports, the most obviously unique aspect of hockey is the requirement to use a stick to hit a ball on the floor. This requires the athlete to lower their centre of mass closer to the floor when dribbling, passing, shooting and tackling. There are a series of key positions which an outfield player will have to adopt within a match. These become more or less important given the frequency with which they occur or with the level of influence they exact on the outcome of the match. This places obvious unique physical demand on the hockey player compared to the more generic aspects of repeated high intensity sprint and change of direction efforts required from most team sports. From a biomechanical perspective, lowering the centre of mass closer to the floor (whilst maintaining it over of the base of support to retain balance) requires large hip flexion and abduction range of motion and large knee and hip extensor strength to appropriately control the descent at high speeds. Additionally, large trunk strength (particularly in the frontal and transverse planes) is critical to retaining balance whilst lowering the centre of mass to manipulate the ball.

For international teams, the ability to remain injury free and not fatigue across the course of a dense tournament schedule is particularly important for success (tournament durability). As a consequence, athletes must have the physical capability to endure high volumes of intense hockey training to prepare them for the rigours of international competition (training durability). To lower the physical cost of the high volumes of intense running and changes of direction, appropriate levels of aerobic fitness, lower limb strength and trunk, adductor, plantar-flexion, and hip extensor endurance require development. This can be summarised in Table 10.2.

Injury prevalence

Common injuries in hockey are those which are prevalent in most multi-directional, repeated high intensity effort, team sport games. Due to frequent and demanding changes of direction, athletes can suffer ankle inversion/eversion injuries, they can develop hip adduction and flexion overload issues and knee abduction injuries. Due to the frequent high speed running and decelerations, hockey players can also suffer from Achilles, patella and high hamstring tendinopathies as well as hamstring and calf strains. The frequent and repetitive time spent in hockey specific positions also means that hip adduction and flexion overload issues are common as well as generic lower back pain. Based on the training and tournament durability demands of playing hockey, effective risk diagnostics is essential to appropriate strength and conditioning prescription in order to reduce vulnerability to injury.

Programming

Based on the athletic needs section, this section has been split into three phases: training durability, tournament durability and repeated high intensity efforts.

Training durability

The development and maintenance of hip and thoracic range of motion is critical to be able to tolerate the high volumes of repetitive hockey specific activities required for technical development. The following activities can be used frequently as a warm up to prepare the athlete for the training demands and generate long term development (see Table 10.3).

Table 10.3 Activities to develop hip and thoracic range of motion as part of a warm up

Activity	Key points & prescription	Key technical stages
Down face dog to lunge rotate	• Spinal mobility • Hip range with trunk rotation • 2 × 8 reps of sequence	

Activity	Key points & prescription	Key technical stages
Warrior poses	• Spinal mobility • Hip range with side flexion • 2 × 8 reps of sequence	
Spider crawls	• Hip mobility • Control forward flexion • 3 × 10 metres crawl	
Lunge & rotate	• Hip mobility • With trunk rotation • 3 × 10 metre sequence	

(Continued)

Table 10.3 (Continued)

Activity	Key points & prescription	Key technical stages  
Duck walks	• Stay low conditioning • 3 × 20 metres	 

Activity	Key points & prescription	Key technical stages
Off set lunge & sweep	- In place or series - Hip & trunk mobility - 3 × 8	  
Hurdle side over & under	- Get low conditioning - Hip range with trunk stability - 2–8 × 20 seconds work to rest	 

(*Continued*)

Table 10.3 (Continued)

Activity	Key points & prescription	Key technical stages 
Stick forward under	• Stay low ability • Hip range with trunk stability • 3 × 8 reps	 
Squat & transfer	• Stay low conditioning • 2–8 × 20 seconds work to rest	

Field hockey

Activity	Key points & prescription	Key technical stages
Rapid hurdle rotations	• Hip conditioning • Internal & external • 2–8 × 20 seconds work to rest	

Table 10.4 Examples of circuits to develop strength endurance of key anatomical structures for hockey

	Bridge circuit	*Squat & lunge circuit*	*Trunk circuit*
1	Double leg bridge hold (short)	Sumo squat	Pot stir left
2	Left leg bridge hold (short)	Sumo hold	Pot stir right
3	Right leg bridge hold (short)	Right reaching lunge	Left side plank pull
4	Double leg bridge hold (long)	Left reaching lunge	Left side plank pull
5	Left leg bridge hold (short)	Right side lunge	Kneeling pallof left
6	Right leg bridge hold (short)	Left side lunge	Kneeling pallof right
7	Bridge walk outs	Right reverse lunge with twist	Kneeling Saxon left
8	Bridge marching (long)	Left reverse lunge with twist	Kneeling Saxon right
9	Left leg bridge hold (long)	Sumo squat	Kneeling rotation left
10	Right leg bridge hold (long)	Sumo hold	Kneeling rotation right

The development of adductor, trunk, plantar-flexion and hip extension strength and endurance is also critical to preparing the hockey players for high volumes of hockey training. This can be effectively delivered through capacity building circuits two to three times per week. As with all activities, training prescription must adhere to the principles of progressive overload and recovery to facilitate adaptive responses (Table 10.4).

Table 10.5 6 week progression of circuits to improve hockey training durability

Week	Frequency	Sets	Time per exercise
1	2	1	20s
2	2	1	30s
3	2	2	30s
4	3	1	30s
5	3	2	30s
6	3	2	35s

Table 10.6 A theoretical 6 week model of developing tolerance to high training volumes and aerobic fitness based on training three times per week (based on training three times per week and lifting twice per week)

Week	Total minutes of 11v11 training per week	Total minutes of running conditioning per week	Strength training volume and intensity
1	80	60	3 × 10 @ 60%1RM
2	100	50	3 × 8 @ 70%1RM
3	120	40	4 × 6 @ 70%1RM
4	100	20	4 × 4 @ 80%1RM
5	160	0	4 × 2 @ 90%1RM
6	200	0	3 × 2 @ 90%1RM

Tournament durability

As discussed earlier, high chronic training loads, lower limb strength and aerobic endurance are critical to tournament durability for hockey players. In this section, some of the strategies used to develop these aspects of physicality have been discussed.

Recent research has shown that high chronic sport specific training loads build athlete durability but should be built up over long periods of time (Gabbett, 2016). Strength and conditioning can be viewed as supplementary training and used to prepare athletes for higher training loads.

For example, during a 6 week preparation phase, supplementary running conditioning could be used to improve the team's aerobic fitness and the volume and density of hockey training could be reduced. In a linear manner, the volume of running conditioning could be reduced and the volume and density of hockey training increased in order to both increase aerobic fitness and the player's capability to tolerate high training loads (Table 10.6). Similarly, a large volume of strength training can be used early in the cycle to prepare the athletes for the higher volume of mechanical strain experienced during higher volumes of hockey training.

Tournament preparation

Tournaments require the athletes to be durable and repeat frequent and effective repeated sprints. Described below is a strategy used to prepare the GB Men's Hockey team for the London 2012 Olympic Games.

Phase 1

October

Week 40 – 17/10/2011

Component	Monday	Tuesday	Wednesday	Thursday	Friday	Saturday	Sunday	
Rehab/ physical 1	Speed	Speed	Gym		Speed			Soft tissue conditioning+ work capacity+ Euro hockey (Fri-Sun) for selected players
Physical development	Gym	Conditioning	Robustness		Conditioning			
Hockey training		GB - 2 x 2 hour pitch		GB - 2 x 2 hour pitch	GB - 2 x 2 hour pitch		PNL	

Week 39 – 24/10/2011

Component	Monday	Tuesday	Wednesday	Thursday	Friday	Saturday	Sunday	
Rehab/ physical 1	Active recovery	Jump & force tests	Active recovery	Fitness testing	Low impact conditioning			S&C test week-no GB hockey - total training volume de load
Physical development		Muscle conditioning tests						
Hockey training						PNL		

Figure 10.1 Competition countdown: Weeks 40 and 39 – extracted from the main planner

In Figure 10.1 (Week 40) it can be seen that in addition to the two pitch sessions in the early part of the week there has also been a 'conditioning' session prescribed. But as has already been highlighted, this will mean different things to different players.

What you can see below in Figure 10.2 is some prescription targeted around developing maximal aerobic speed as determined by the 30:15 Intermittent Fitness Test (Buchheit, 2008). By working at MAS for the longer interval session the prescription targets the needs of the midfield players. In this phase the shorter interval session meets the requirements of the Forwards (indicated as Session 1).

Figure 10.3 is a 7 week extract (October into November) from a 12 month long-term planner. This period is after a major competition held in the July and after a prescribed rest and active recovery period. The players have also had an appropriately prescribed transition to full training.

This planner is for players who are a mature group of Internationals 12 months out from an Olympic Games, but the key principles are as relevant for the club player: get them running quickly (with game specific movement skills) as soon as possible and develop the ability to endure that intensity for as long as possible. In order to do this, it's necessary to ensure they are safe to run fast, hence the priority of developing general and specific strength and muscular conditioning qualities. (It's important to note that targeting the physical quality is the basis for prescription, this is indicated by the 'Key Focus' areas. The macro does also provide examples of appropriate exercises that will allow these qualities to be developed).

At international level a decision has to be made about which tournament out of the 2 or 3 that may be played in the year is most important. When that's decided then some of the training that is prescribed around the tournaments of lesser importance may contradict a good performance at them. This is the case in Figures 10.1 and 10.2 where the priority is developing work capacity for future training, even though there is a competition in November.

General prep (London - week 40)		
Week commencing		17/10/2011
		Session
Distance (m = metres): Sh = shuttle: Str = straight	1	2
		Percentage of MAS
	105%	85%

MAS km/h	MAS m/s	Sh (m)	Str (m)
23	6.4	30.35	162.92
22.5	6.3	29.69	159.38
22	6.1	29.03	155.83
21.5	6.0	28.37	152.29
21	5.8	27.71	148.75
20.5	5.7	27.05	145.21
20	5.6	26.39	141.67
19.5	5.4	25.73	138.13
19	5.3	25.07	134.58
Work:rest ratio (seconds)		10:10	30:15
Reps		10	8
Sets		3	3
Rest between sets		3mins	3mins
Session duration		16mins	24mins
Notes:		Pre hockey	Post hockey

Figure 10.2 Conditioning prescription for maximal aerobic speed (Week 40 – from Olympic Games)

At domestic level there may not be the opportunity to develop certain physical characteristics so intensively. That does not mean they shouldn't be developed, but the expectation should be that they need a longer period of development.

Conclusion

Hockey requires multiple repeated sprints and changes of direction just as most team sports do. There are multiple unique movement patterns and running demands that take place as a consequence of the demand of hitting a ball and rolling substitutions. Additionally, the dense tournament structure at international level requires athletes to perform repeated high intensity efforts day after day. To prepare athletes for these unique demands, they must have the capacity to train frequently and with sufficient intensity to get better at the game. They must have the strength and the fitness to recover from matches and the periodisation and prioritisation of training must be effective to allow the players to allow the players to effectively execute the complex skills and decisions across the entirety of a tournament.

YEAR	Physical preparation planner						
MONTH	October					November	
MONDAYS	3	10	17	24	31	7	14
WEEK NO	42	41	40	39	38	37	36
Competition							Match
National training							
League & European comp	& Euro		& Euro				
Testing				Test week		Strength Monitoring	
Training phase	Speed / strength & muscle conditioning						COMP
Intensity							
Volume							
Overview		Quick return to high intensity speed work & development of basic strength + Individually prescribed conditioning			Game specific conditioning work		Maintain good recovery strategies along with injury
Strength/ power							
* Key focus	Development of baseline global strength - Re-establish technique of Olympic lifts						
* Key activities	Clean, squat/ clean pull, front squat + development lifters = jump & shrug/ deadlift						
* Frequency	2	2	2	1	2	2	
Muscular condition & robustness							
* Key focus	Whole body off feet conditioning + Key focus on high volume muscle conditioning + Hip & groin/ Adductor and hamstring						Non selected player group to continue under supervision- sessions based on game specific needs to replicate the tournament + Players will continue to develop individual weaknesses.
* Key activities	High volume/ low force SL exercises progressing to high force eccentric load - GB leg extensions, SL assisted eccentric, Nordic curls & Bosch hamstrings.						
* Frequency	3	3	3	1	3	3	
Flexibility / prehab & trunk							
* Key focus	Specific isolated ROM around anterior hip + Individually targeted prehab + High volume trunk to high force trunk by week '41' + Foot conditioning						
* Key activities	BPC targets for 'Trunk' + Bridging positions to Hanging raises & Hanging wipers + Reformer work + Shoe off work						
* Frequency	6	6	6	6	6	6	
Speed/ game speed							
* Key focus	Review & development of speed technique + Return to high intensity running asap				Repeat game specific sprint work		
* Key activities	Acceleration/ Deceleration drills in gym session + High speed running during pitch session - Pop ups + Pop & Bleed + Scooter + Stick runs						
* Frequency	2	2	3	1	3	2	
Physical conditioning							
* Key focus	Development of MAS				Special Endurance & MAS		
* Key activities	10:10 + 30: 15 + Speed endurance ----- Game RSA						
* Frequency	2	2	2	1	3	2	

Figure 10.3 Extracted from a long term macro planner

References

Buchheit, M. (2008). The 30–15 intermittent fitness test: Accuracy for individualizing interval training of young intermittent sport players. *JSCR* 22(2): 365–374.

Gabbett, T. J. (2016). The training-injury prevention paradox: Should athletes be training smarter and harder? *British Journal of Sports Medicine*, bjsports-2015 50: 273–280.

Spencer, M., Lawrence, S., Rechichi, C., Bishop, D., Dawson, B. and Goodman, C. (2004). Time-motion analysis of elite field hockey, with special reference to repeated-sprint activity. *JSS* 22(9): 843–850.

Spencer, M., Rechichi, C., Lawrence, S., Dawson, B., Bishop, D. and Goodman, C. (2005). Time-motion analysis of elite field hockey during several games in succession: A tournament scenario. *Journal of Science and Medicine in Sport* 8: 382–391.

11
ICE HOCKEY

Steve Nightingale and Adam Douglas

Introduction

Ice hockey is a sport with worldwide appeal. According to the sport's national governing body, the International Ice Hockey Federation (IIHF), organised ice hockey exists in 74 member associations across the world, from the traditional powerhouses of Canada and the USA to Australia, China, Mexico, and Great Britain (IIHF, 2016). In addition to adult men's leagues, there are a range of female only leagues and age banded leagues for children. In total, the IIHF's most recent player survey recorded over 1.8 million registered players worldwide (IIHF, 2016).

As is the way in any professional sport, hockey organisations will look to employ a variety of methods to improve and succeed. Performance analytics, nutrition, psychology and sports science are all incorporated to various degrees, depending on the organisation. Ice hockey is a fast paced, physically demanding, full contact sport. The provision of strength and conditioning to ensure players' readiness to undertake such stress varies widely, depending on the leagues and organisations.

Athletic demands

Ice hockey is an intermittent team sport characterised by high intensity, short duration bursts of maximal power, whilst also requiring players to have well rounded physical capabilities, including speed, strength and endurance, alongside the ability to execute a variety of skilled manoeuvres. A typical game lasts for 60 minutes, and apart from the goalkeeper, players take it in turns to perform on the ice. These shifts vary due to a number of factors, but they generally last between 30 and 90 seconds, are interspersed with between 2 and 5 minutes of recovery, and number around 15 to 20 each game. Within the shifts themselves, work is not completed at a constant speed or intensity. Players are afforded brief recovery periods during whistle stops for infractions, and when performing at low or moderate intensities, such as gliding or standing still.

It is widely regarded that anaerobic glycolysis provides the body with energy for high intensity efforts lasting ~15 seconds to 2 minutes, and therefore this has led to the notion that this is the primary energy system responsible for fuelling hockey performance. Many attempts to quantify the energy demands of the sport have been made, with some research suggesting that over two-thirds of energy demand is met through the anaerobic glycolytic system (Green and

Houston, 1974). Most of these attempts have used the time-motion analysis (TMA) technique, which involves setting up video recording equipment, monitoring players' movements and categorising them according to their intensity. The TMA method has been widely used across many team sports, but is often criticised when applied to sports where player movements are extremely explosive and short in duration, and therefore difficult to record accurately. Consequently, more individual, on-player methods have been used during practices and games to determine more accurate estimates of exercise intensity, including recording heart rate, training impulse and blood lactate concentrations.

The point at which an athlete moves from aerobic metabolism to the anaerobic glycolysis system can be marked as the lactate threshold, defined as "the point in time during exercise of increasing intensity when the rate of lactate production exceeds the rate of lactate clearance" (Kenney et al., 2015). However, measuring and recording blood lactate can be challenging from a practical standpoint. Previous studies have involved taking samples several minutes after the final moments of play (Green and Houston, 1974) and within 2 minutes of the completion of each shift of a game (Noonan, 2010), with both reporting large variations (1.2 to 8.9mmol.L^{-1} and 4.4 to 13.7mmol.L^{-1} respectively).

The heart rate based 'training impulse' (TRIMP) method has also been used to determine playing intensity. Data presented by Snyder et al. (2010) and Myatt et al. (2010) show around 20% of game time is spent at TRIMP level 5 (high intensity).

As mentioned, a hockey shift is intermittent in nature and rarely exceeds 90 seconds. Therefore, it can be estimated that a shift will consist of around 18 seconds of high intensity work. Although shift work:rest ratios vary between position and game-play situation (i.e. power plays and penalty kills), Jackson et al. (2016) reported a mean "even strength" work:rest ratio of 1:1.6 for all players (excluding goalkeepers). It is therefore logical to suggest that these 18 seconds will be an accumulation of short duration efforts (Stanula et al., 2014). It is prudent to suggest that high intensity energy demand of this duration is more likely to be predominantly met through the alactic (ATP-PC) system (Glaister, 2005), supported by a robust aerobic system. Increased oxygen availability has been shown to correlate with improved PCr recovery kinematics, resulting in a higher PCr availability at the onset of high intensity work, reducing the demand on the anaerobic glycolytic system to maintain the required rate of ATP turnover (Glaister, 2005). A high aerobic capacity has been reported in hockey players across levels of performance (see Table 11.1). This has led the authors to describe hockey as an 'alactic-aerobic' sport.

Table 11.1 Maximal oxygen uptake of players

Study	Gender	Level	VO_2 *(ml.min^{-1})*
Burr et al. (2008)	Male	NHL	57.4
Durocher et al. (2010)	Male	NCAA (I and III)	46.9
Green et al. (2006)	Male	NCAA I	59
Montgomery (2006)	Male	NHL	59
Peyer et al. (2011)	Male	NCAA I	57.8
Vescovi et al. (2006)	Male	NHL draft	58.4
Ransdell et al. (2013)	Female	International	48.6
Carey et al. (2007)	Female	NCAA III	50.3
Geithner et al. (2006)	Female	Canadian University	44.6

The biomechanics of ice skating and characteristics of game play have been covered in detail (Manners, 2004; Jackson et al., 2016; Buckeridge et al., 2015; Upjohn et al., 2008). Hockey S&C coaches should consider the specific elements of skating when designing a program, due to differences between skating and normal running technique placing greater demand on the abductors and adductors. Forward skating requires movement in the posterolateral plane, using the hip extensors and abductors. As the weight is shifted to the glide leg, hip and knee flexors and extensors co-contract to maintain stability and balance. In the crossover step, the adductors are activated to push against the outside edge of the skate and propel the body sideways. Effective use of the adductors is also key in the return phase of the stride to pull the push off leg back under the body in preparation for the next stride. Although skating or gliding forwards is the most common skating action during a game, backward skating also occurs, with Jackson and colleagues (2016) suggesting defenders are required to skate backward more frequently than forwards (~20% and ~8%, respectively). This may present challenges to the strength coach used to working only with forward motion. According to Manners (2004), the backward push off stride requires a combination of hip extension, adduction, and external rotation, along with knee extension while the glide leg also requires the co-contraction of hip and knee flexors and extensors to maintain balance. Consideration of these movements when executing program design is important, to ensure training is following the specific adaptation to imposed demands principle.

Injury prevalence

As hockey is played as a contact sport, injuries are commonplace. The risk of an injury (IR) occurring can be defined as the number of injuries reported divided by the total player-time at risk, and is reported as Athlete Exposures (AE) (Knowles et al., 2006). Reported injury rates for hockey vary depending on study methodology, and are summarised in Table 11.2, alongside injury rates of similar sports. Due to regulations in the female game making body and board checking illegal, incidences of contact are reduced, but not eliminated. In addition, male players are generally taller and heavier than their female counterparts and the male game is played at a greater speed.

Table 11.2 Injury rates

Sport	Gender	Level	IR (/1000 AE)	Reference
Ice hockey	Male	NHL	15.6	(McKay et al., 2014)
Ice hockey	Male	WC/WOG*	14.2	(Tuominen et al., 2015)
Ice hockey	Male	NCAA	13.8	(Flik et al., 2005)
Ice hockey	Male	NCAA	16.3	(Agel et al., 2007)
Ice hockey	Male	Elite	15.9	(McColloch and Bach, 2007)
Field hockey	Male	Elite	11.1	(McColloch and Bach, 2007)
Lacrosse	Male	Elite	11.5	(McColloch and Bach, 2007)
Soccer	Male	Elite	18.8	(McColloch and Bach, 2007)
American football	Male	Elite	33.0	(McColloch and Bach, 2007)
Ice hockey	Female	NCAA	12.1	(Agel and Harvey, 2010)
Ice hockey	Female	CWUAA**	7.8	(Schick and Meeuwisse, 2003)

* World Championships/Winter Olympic Games
** Canadian West Universities Athletic Association

Table 11.3 Injury prevalence in games and practice

Games			Gender	Reference
Most common	Head (20.1), thigh (11.6) and knee (9.2)		Male	(McKay et al., 2014)
	Concussion (22.9%)		Male	(Flik et al., 2005)
	Knee internal derangements (e.g. cruciate ligament injury) (13.5%), concussions (9.0%) and shoulder ligament trauma (8.9%)		Male	(Agel et al., 2007)
	Musculoskeletal injuries (strains, sprains and contusions) and concussions		Female	(MacCormick et al., 2014)
Mechanism	Player-to-player contact (47.7%), other contact (i.e. player-to-boards) (21.6%)		Male	(Agel et al., 2007)
	Player-to-player contact (32.8%), other contact (i.e. player-to-boards) (18.6%)		Male	(Flik et al., 2005)
Practice				
Most common	Pelvis/hip (13.1%), knee internal derangement (10.1%), ankle (5.5%)		Male	(Agel et al., 2007)
Mechanism	Other contact (33.0%), player-to-player contact (32.0)		Male	(Agel et al., 2007)

Regardless of gender, the leading cause of in-game injuries is player-to-player contact, followed by 'other types of collisions' (i.e. player-to-boards) (Agel and Harvey, 2010; Flik et al., 2005; MacCormick et al., 2014). See Table 11.3 for a summary of common causes and locations of injuries for both practices and games.

Brainard et al. (2012) found that collegiate female hockey players reported higher incidence rates of concussions when compared to males, despite males being subjected to more frequent and more violent impacts. Whilst the reasons for this remain unanswered, it may be related to the larger muscle mass of male players being able to withstand impact forces more successfully.

Tyler et al. (2001) investigated the influence of hip adductor and abductor strength on groin injuries and found that athletes who suffered in-season groin injuries had an 18% lower hip adduction strength than athletes who did not suffer this type of injury. In addition, the players who suffered an in-season groin injury had an adduction strength of 78% of abduction strength, whereas players who were not injured had an adduction strength of 95% of abduction strength. The study concluded that an adductor to abductor strength ratio of less than 1:1.25 was a significant factor in increasing the occurrence of injury.

Fitness testing battery

As with many sports, the tests used within hockey vary from team to team and coach to coach. The availability of resources, including equipment, money, staff and knowledge, all play a part in the testing battery a team will be able to undertake. Whichever tests are selected, two factors require consideration. Firstly, it is important to ensure that they cover the following qualities: aerobic capacity, anaerobic capacity, upper and lower body strength, lower body power and speed/acceleration. Secondly, the tests should be chosen on their reliability and consistent availability of equipment. It is important to keep the testing battery the same as much as possible over time, to ensure worthwhile comparisons can be made and the data used for long term athletic development.

Table 11.4 Selection of fitness tests

Fitness component	Recommended tests	Modality	Intraclass R	Reference
Aerobic capacity	YoYo intermittent test	Off-ice	0.95	(Thomas et al., 2006)
	30–15 IIT	On-ice	0.96	(Buchheit et al., 2011)
Anaerobic capacity	Wingate 30-second test	Off-ice	0.98	(Jaafar et al., 2014)
	RAST	Off-ice	0.97	(Zagatto et al., 2009)
Upper body strength	1RM bench press	Off-ice	0.97	(Gutowski and Rosene, 2011)
	Grip dynamometer	Off-ice	0.98	(Allen and Barnett, 2011)
Lower body strength	1RM back squat	Off-ice	0.92	(McBride et al., 2002)
	High thigh clean pull	Off-ice	0.97	(Kawamori et al., 2006)
Lower body power	Vertical CMJ	Off-ice	0.99	(Burr et al., 2007)
	Horizontal broad jump	Off-ice	0.95	(Maulder and Cronin, 2005)
Acceleration/speed	~5m/~20m sprint	On-ice	0.80/0.76	(Bracko, 2001)
		Off-ice	0.89	(Triplett, 2012)

Support can be found in research for the value of both on-ice and off-ice testing; therefore, it ultimately should fall to the strength and conditioning coach to decide, basing their opinion on what they intend to use the testing for and the resources available to them. It is our aim in this section to present a range of tests suitable for each component (Table 11.4), which will allow coaches to design a testing battery appropriate to their individual circumstances.

- **Testing aerobic capacity** – Methods of measuring maximum VO_2 can be conducted directly using gas analysis equipment; however, this presents several problems. Equipment can be expensive and require experienced technicians to collect the data correctly. As athletes are tested individually, this can also be a time-consuming practice. Field tests can be used to indirectly predict maximum VO_2 values from normative data, which may be more efficient in a team environment. The multi-stage fitness test (beep test) has been traditionally used; however, it is generally accepted that intermittent test protocols, such as YoYo test and the 30–15 Intermittent Ice Test, are more valid, whilst maintaining high levels of reliability (Buchheit et al., 2011; Thomas et al., 2006).
- **Testing anaerobic capacity** – The 30-sec Wingate test is a popular method to determine maximal power, relative power, and total work and fatigue levels. Although this test does require relatively expensive equipment, it is short in duration and highly reliable. A field based test which could be used to determine anaerobic capacity is a repeated sprint ability (RSA) test. However, there is a wide range of protocols and at present, there is no 'gold standard' protocol identified for hockey. One protocol, the Running Anaerobic Sprint Test (RAST), described by Zagatto and colleagues (2009), has shown strong test-retest reliability and high correlation to Wingate test results.
- **Testing upper and lower body strength** – Strength testing can be performed using a variety of methods, all of which have advantages and limitations. Regarding upper body strength, both 1 repetition maximum bench press and hand grip dynamometer tests have been positively linked to measures of success in hockey in regards to shot speed (Wu et al., 2003), and season +/− outcome (Peyer et al., 2011). Whilst both tests are deemed to be highly reliable, the validity of grip dynamometry has been questioned, whereas 1RM bench press testing has been deemed to be a valid measure for team contact sports

requiring upper body strength (National Strength and Conditioning Association, 2012). In terms of lower body strength, isometric mid-thigh pull tests have been increasingly used to determine strength, power, and rate of force development (RFD). However, this type of testing requires force plates, and testing is time consuming. 1RM back squat testing is a tried and tested method, which is highly reliable.

Testing lower body power – The strength and conditioning coach should consider both vertical and horizontal movements, which are traditionally performing using counter movement jumps (CMJs). Vertical CMJs can be measured using a basic method of marking standing reach height on a wall and marking peak jump height, measuring the distance. However, this method lacks reliability as it is hard for athletes to consistently mark the wall at the top of their jump. The use of specific equipment can be used to improve the reliability and accuracy of this test. The Vertec, a popular device where athletes push protruding moveable vanes away from the central post of the equipment, is a relatively cheap piece of equipment which has been proven to be highly reliable (Burr et al., 2007). Electronic measures, such as the Just Jump testing mat and the Fusion Smartspeed system, offer other alternatives to testing, and ultimately the equipment used will depend on the specific budget of the organisation undertaking the testing. Horizontal jump testing, in the format of broad jumps, have been shown in research to have links to on-ice skating performance. Providing the same protocols are followed, these methods are reliable, cheap, and efficient ways of determining lower body power output in large teams.

Testing speed/acceleration – Despite off-ice testing protocols coming under criticism for not matching the biomechanical movements of on-ice tests, off-ice sprints have consistently demonstrated a strong relationship with on-ice versions. Forty-yard sprints have been commonly used, although given the movement analysis discussed above, this distance seems unlikely to be relevant to hockey. Shorter (5m to 20m) distances appear to be more relevant to the sport.

Programming

When organising training prescription for a hockey athlete, a strength and conditioning professional needs to have an understanding of the yearly plan based on the competition season and subsequent offseason. This can vary depending on the age and level of the athlete. For example, in North American professional hockey, the pre-season training period is approximately 2 weeks long in September; the in-season period runs from October through April or May/June, depending on how the team performs in the play-offs. In international competition, the World Championships fall towards the end of the season, typically March and April, with training camps run by the various countries occurring periodically throughout the year. Based off the schedule of the athlete and team, the first step to planning a successful season of training is to create a detailed yearly training plan (YTP).

The YTP can be a powerful tool to assist in the design and direction of the strength and conditioning program. When creating a YTP, it is best to work backwards from major competitions. Include all main camps and competitions, including any testing sessions to provide an overview of the year. From there, fill out the YTP to include all macrocycles, mesocycles, and/or microcycles, as well as the on-ice volume from games and practices.

Figure 11.1 provides an example of an YTP for an International hockey athlete. This athlete needs to peak for the World Championships at the beginning of April. The YTP allows the

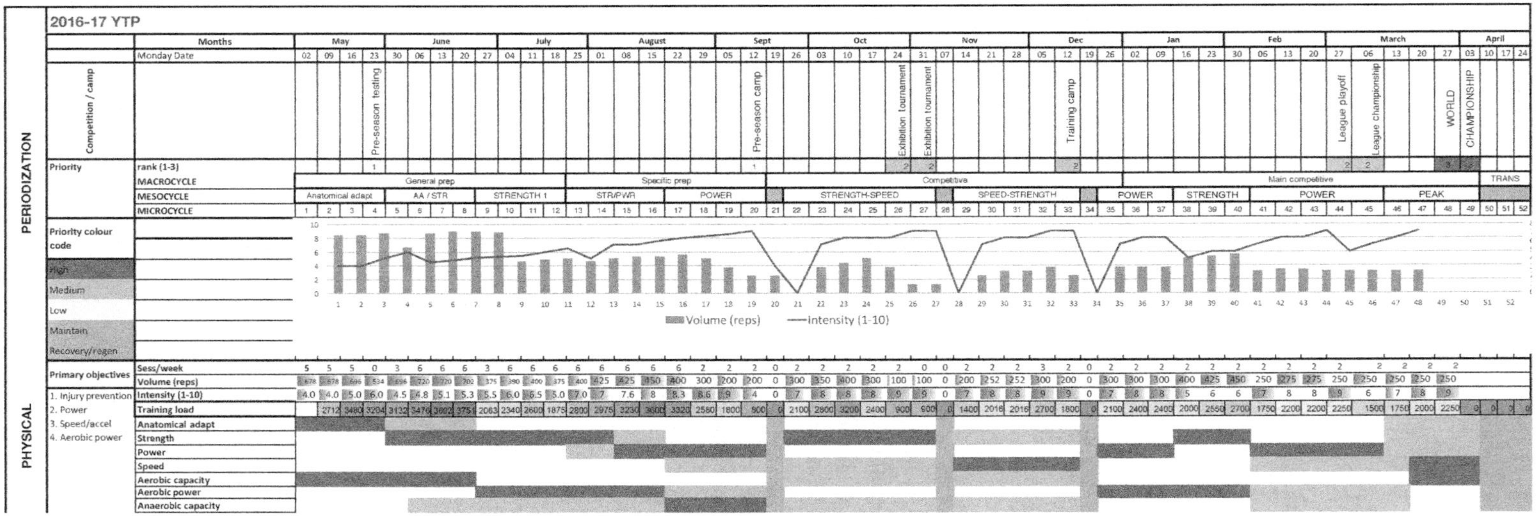

Figure 11.1 YTP

strength and conditioning coach to understand volume and intensity to allow the athlete to train hard, while not detracting from their in-season on-ice abilities.

In-season training

During the season, the focus is on-ice performance. Off-ice strength and conditioning needs to assist and support the on-ice product. It is possible to train athletic qualities important for hockey players (speed, strength, power, agility); however, this needs to be done with a systematic method.

Using the YTP in Figure 11.1, there are four in-season phases, with the focus changing every 4–6 weeks. One strategy to in-season training is to program longer mesocycles to minimise the potential of delayed onset muscle soreness that can be associated with the changing of exercises or intensities. The selection of in-season exercises should be driven by an athlete's experience and training age. Choose exercises that the athletes are familiar with and can complete successfully, while maintaining the proper training effect or desired outcome needed.

Off-season training

Off-season training allows the strength coach to program and prepare their athletes to improve their areas of weakness, while readying them for the long season ahead. Athletes should use the initial part of the off-season to rehabilitate or heal from the previous season. Hockey is a fast and aggressive sport, so most athletes need time at the end of their season to rest and recover.

With no on-ice focus, the off-season can be more robust and complete as it relates to all of the elements that get built into the training program. This includes linear and lateral movement training, plyometric work, and conditioning sessions for the athlete. With the unique movement demands of the skating stride, it is important to program both linear and lateral movement patterns into off-ice work. Multi-directional movement exercises should be included in all elements of the off-season program, in the warm-up, in the gym, and during their conditioning.

Each of the subsequent sections of this chapter will further break down the elements that should be considered when programming for hockey players, both in-season and off-season. You will see how progressions and exercise selections are important to maximise the athleticism of your athlete, as well as how to best prepare them for the demands of the game.

Warm ups

The structure of the warm-up is important as it allows the strength coach to plan proper progressions for the session and it allows the athlete a familiar start to their training session or practice/game. The warm-up allows the coach to prescribe specific movement patterns or areas to focus on that the athlete is deficient in. Due to the nature of the sport, warm-ups should be lower body focussed, including multi-directional hip mobility, ankle mobility, and torso stability with a neutral hip position. Prior injury history can help dictate areas to focus on in the warm-up; typically hip/groin injuries or low back pain are common areas of concern for hockey athletes.

Each warm-up should progress through these different stages, taking between 20–25 minutes in length: General Aerobic/Continuous movement (5 minutes), Self-Myofascial Release (5 minutes), Mobility/Activation (3 minutes), Movement Preparation (10 minutes), and Neural Activation/Intensity (2 minutes) (see Tables 11.5 and 11.6).

Table 11.5 Warm up progressions

General aerobic/ continuous movement	• Low level activity • Increase core body temperature and prepare the body for the activity to follow • Exercises can include typical cardiovascular work such as jogging or riding an exercise bicycle • Coaches can also be creative and include multi-directional work in the form of multiple running drills (forwards, backwards, shuffling, skipping) or variations of games such as tag, handball, or soccer
Self-myofascial release	• SMR has been shown to improve athletic performance in the short term when combined with a dynamic warm-up (Peacock et al., 2014) • Benefits include improved flexibility and range of motion, improved muscle tone (Jay et al., 2014, Skarabot et al., 2015) and perceived soreness (MacDonald et al., 2014) • Spend 30–45 seconds in each muscle group for general preparation • Emphasis should be placed on major muscle groups or areas that are typically tight or sore such as the hips or groin area, using foam rollers, lacrosse balls, and/or massage sticks
Mobility/activation	• Promote proper ranges of motion • Bring attention to important muscle groups or areas of the body that will help the athlete have a positive outcome • Focus on improving ankle, hip, and thoracic spine mobility (Boyle, 2012) • Include multi-planar hip movementsActivation portion: • Involves bodyweight or light resistance exercises involving the gluteal muscles and/or abdominals to reduce injury and improve lower extremity control (Distefano et al., 2009)
Movement preparation	• Build intensity in a progressive fashion • Move from general movements (squatting, lunging, reaching) to specific movements (bounding, multi-directional sprinting) and from lower intensity to higher intensity work • Focus on linear movements, lateral movement patterns, or multi-directional patterns • Through the course of the off-season, these drills can be taught in a progressive fashion, from in-place, to marching, skipping, then full-speed
Neural activation/ intensity	• Most focused and highest intensity portion • Elicit a higher force output through post-activation potentiation • Move quickly for a short period of time (sprinting, jumping) or by explosive lifting with light loads • Plyometric drills are typically used to improve the neuromuscular system. It is important to remember that this is part of the warm-up and the athlete or coach should not be seeking a large training stimulus. The goal is to get the athlete moving fast and quick, followed by a period of rest

Table 11.6 Linear, lateral and multidirectional warm up

	Linear warm-up	Lateral focused	Multi-directional
General aerobic/ continuous movement (5 minutes)	Low level activity. Can be traditional bike/jogging or coaches can incorporate multiple movements (jog, skip, shuffle) or various games of tag		
Self-myofascial release (5 minutes)	Focus on major muscle groups or areas that are typically tight or sore. Spend 30–45 seconds in each muscle group		
Mobility/ activation (3 minutes)	Wall-based ankle mobility Sumo squat to stand Glute bridge	Pigeon glute stretch Kneeling adductor mobility Mini-band lateral step	Multi-directional lunge (forwards, backwards, lateral, diagonal) Mini-band forward and lateral walks
Movement preparation (10 minutes)	In-place elbow to instep with straight leg toe raise In-place single leg romanian deadlift with forward reach Hand walkout with push-up Walking knee hug Linear march Linear "A" skip Straight leg march Straight leg skip Backwards run	In-place split squat In-place lateral squat Walking leg cradle Walking crossover lunge Lateral march Lateral "A" skip Lateral shuffle High knee carioca Quick feet carioca Backpedal to shuffle	Walking lunge with rotation Hand walkout to push-up Bear Crawl (opposites) – forwards and backwards Backwards walking lunge Figure "8" shuffle Figure "8" carioca Shuffle to forward run Shuffle to backwards run Shuffle to carioca
Neural activation/ intensity (2 minutes)	In-place fast foot run (pitter patter)	Quick lateral line hops – continuous	5–10–5 cone agility

Difference between in-season and off-season warm-ups

There are important differences to consider when planning in-season versus off-season dynamic warm-ups. Typically, off-season warm-ups can be longer as the subsequent training session may not have a fixed start and finish time. During the season, strength coaches need to make sure that they provide adequate time for the athletes to dress in their hockey equipment before the on-ice session begins. Additionally, these warm-ups provide a daily opportunity to address potential weakness or movement deficiencies with the athletes, and it is also important to incorporate some element of reactionary stimulus.

For in-season warm-ups, the type of session can change the order or structure of the warm-up. For games, there is usually a period of time given to the athletes to have an "on-ice" warm-up, where they can skate and shoot at various intensities through team or coach selected drills. As such, this can change the neural activation/intensity drills selected, to include some high-speed, high-intensity footwork drills that include some reaction to visual or verbal stimulus to change direction or pattern. In practice sessions, the athletes need to be ready to perform from the start,

Table 11.7 Different game and practice examples of neural intensity drills

	Pre-practice	Pre-game examples
Neural intensity drills	Backpedal to forward acceleration Shuffle to acceleration Backpedal to forward sprint Shuffle to forward sprint Multiple vertical jump to forward sprint Partner mirror shuffle with break-off sprint 5–10–5 cone agility	3–4 sets of 5 seconds effort In-place quick feet run (pitter patter) In-place rapid jumps (attack the ground, only off ground 1 inch) In-place rapid jumps with hip twist Double leg lateral line hops – quick Single leg lateral line hops

Table 11.8 Typical off-season training session

Name	Description	Duration
Dynamic warm-up	Multi-directional movement with a progressive build in intensity	20–25 minutes
Power pairing	Daily pairing of upper body and lower body power exercise	5 minutes
Skating simulation	Movement-based drills to mimic on-ice skating patterns	10 minutes
Primary lifts	1–2 main exercises for the session	20 minutes
Assistance lifts	Lifts designed to support overall training goal	15 minutes

without always having a period of free time on the ice to warm-up. Therefore, a good strategy is to build in some multi-directional full stride sprinting within this portion of the pre-practice warm-up.

When building out the strength and conditioning plan for the athlete to start the off-season, the strength and conditioning coach should collect information from different sources that can help better individualise the training that is prescribed. This can include information derived from physical or physiological testing, physical screening/assessment from medical professionals, and on-ice feedback from coaches.

Early off-season programming should focus on quality movement execution and building strength. It is important to develop a strong foundation from which to build athleticism off. As the off-season progresses, the training can start to shift to more performance-based work, including power production, and higher level speed/agility work. The work shifts from more general preparation to specific preparation as the athlete gets further into the off-season and closer to the competition phase. A simple, structured daily training plan for a hockey athlete should consist of the sections shown in Table 11.8.

Power pairings

Hockey is a strength and power sport. Athletes can benefit from small exposures of power training every training session. Often, athletes need to be taught how to maximise the power produced by their hips and torso. By pairing a lower body bodyweight explosive exercise with an upper body medicine ball exercise, you can work on creating full body power. It is important to teach the athletes to move in all planes of movement – therefore the coach can use the drills in Table 11.9 as a logical sequencing of movement through the training phases.

Table 11.9 Training progressions

	PHASE ONE	PHASE TWO	PHASE THREE
POWER PAIRINGS	Box jump and stick	Lateral box jump and stick	Drop jump to box jump	Lateral hurdle jump and stick	Drop jump to vertical jump	Multiple lateral hurdle jumps – continuous
	Kneeling medicine ball shotput throw	Kneeling medicine ball side toss	Half kneeling medicine ball shotput throw	Half kneeling medicine ball side toss	Standing medicine ball shotput throw	Standing medicine ball side toss
SKATING SIMULATIONS	Heel to toe low sit	Knee to heel then heel to toe step	Single leg squat knee to heel touch	In-place side to side stride – low and continuous	Single leg 90 degree hop and stick	Single leg hop and stick over hurdle – same leg
	Side shuffle step	In and outs with athletic stance	Single leg lateral Cable squat to pull across body	Standing side cross-over push	In-place single leg stride (abduct and extend)	3 step side cross-over – low hip position
PRIMARY LIFTS	DB goblet squat	DB bench press	Front squat	Loaded jump squat	Hang clean	Loaded jump squat
	DB romanian deadlift	Chin-up	Barbell deadlift	Barbell bench press	Back squat	Bench press
			Barbell reverse lunge	Chin-up	Barbell romanian deadlift	Pull-ups
ACCESSORY LIFTS	DB rear foot Elevated split squat	Half kneeling DB shoulder press	DB lateral lunge	Standing single arm landmine press	Barbell rear foot elevated split squat	Split squat single arm landmine press
	TRX leg curl	DB supported bent over row	Barbell hip thrust	Single arm DB unsupported row	Single arm and leg DB romanian deadlift	Single arm and leg bent over row
	Landmine rotation	Half kneeling cable axe lift	Side plank with hip raise	Standing cable axe lift	Landmine rotation – explosive	Explosive cable axe lift

Skating simulations

The purpose of skating simulations is to mimic certain positions and postures that are critical to the skating stride. By working these drills in a controlled environment, the athlete can begin to feel more comfortable in positions with greater dorsi-flexion, improved upper body posture, and improved movement through the hip. An added benefit is that the athletes learn body control, with improved and hip and core stability; both important for efficient skating mechanics. Due to the low volume and low intensity of the drills, skating simulations are best prescribed on multiple days of the week to allow for high levels of exposure. They can be used as an extended warm-up on strength training days, as well as to reinforce proper positioning and movement skills on speed and agility training days.

Primary lifts and accessory lifts

Primary lifts are the main focus of the training session. These can be 1–2 exercises within that day. The focus should be strength and/or power exercises that provide the largest training stimulus. Accessory lifts can either complement the primary exercises or focus on another area of the body that needs to be addressed.

Difference between in-season and off-season strength training programs

The main difference when programming for in-season versus off-season strength training is the need to reduce volume while maintaining a high intensity. Exercise selection should be limited to exercises that do not cause soreness or overt fatigue. With shorter sessions, the strength coach should focus on the exact training quality they want to target (i.e. power) and focus the exercises around improving that quality, while eliminating the non-pertinent work.

Speed and agility/change of direction

Hockey is a multi-directional sport, and therefore players need to learn to move efficiently in multiple planes of movement. When planning off-ice speed and agility training for hockey athletes, it is important to select drills that force the athlete to move in many different directions and at high speed, whilst controlling their body.

A simple way to organise a speed and agility program is to section the sessions and drills into speed movement and multi-directional/change of direction drills. Much like work done in the gym, movement training needs to follow a progression-style fashion where current drills build on movements that the athlete has been exposed to in previous training phases.

Speed

Speed is a necessary quality for a hockey player to develop. While the mechanics of the hockey stride vary from sprinting, the ability to generate force is needed to propel the skater forward. Explosiveness is an important training quality that can be accomplished through off-ice speed work such as sprint mechanics and acceleration drills. Early off-season prescription might focus on mechanics and how to push power into the ground, with mid-to-late off-season speed training

Table 11.10 Movement training day example

	EXERCISE	SETS	REPS/TIME/DISTANCE
GENERAL MOVEMENT	10 minutes general movement – can be small area game, jog, bike, etc. – continuous movement	1	10 minutes
DYNAMIC MOVEMENT	Walking lunge w overhead reach	1	20m
	Inchworm	1	6
	Elbow to instep w straight leg toe raise	1	6 L/R
	1/4 squat to knee hug	1	20m
	1/4 squat to leg cradle	1	20m
	Linear skip	1	20m
	Lateral skip	1	20m
	High knee run	1	20m
	Backpedal to acceleration	1	20m
	Shuffle to acceleration	1	20m
	Carioca to acceleration	1	20m
NEURAL PREP	4 tuck jump to stagger stance landing – PAUSE – to 5m sprint	4	1 min rest
SPEED	1. 3-step bound (cover as much ground as possible)	3	*(rest 1 min b/w sets)*
	2. 3-step sprint	3	*(rest 90s b/w sets)*
	3. 10m sprint (think 3 steps STRONG to lengthen stride)	3	*(rest 2 mins b/w sets)*
SKATING SIMULATION	1. Low side step (ensure full extension)	3	10 L/R *(1 min rest)*
	2. 3-step cross-over	3	10 L/R *(1 min rest)*
	3. Low walk	3	50m *(1 min rest)*
AGILITY MOVEMENT	1. 20m sprint	3	*3 min rest b/w sets*
	2. 10m shuffle to 10m sprint	2 L and 2 R	*3 min rest b/w sets*
	3. 5m lateral shuffle to 10m FWD sprint	2 L and 2 R	*3 min rest b/w sets*

centered around resisted sprint training using sleds or towing harnesses. Sprint training is very taxing on the central nervous system; therefore, it is important to factor in longer rest-periods of the athlete during these sessions.

Agility/change of direction

Ice hockey athletes need to be able to change direction at high speeds. While most of the game is spent in a two-foot glide position (Bracko et al., 1998; Jackson et al., 2016), athletes move out of these positions to chase the puck, an opponent, or to gain or close space on the ice. The progression of agility and change of direction drills should move from non-reactive, closed skills to reactive-based, open skills where the athlete is forced to react to a visual or auditory situational stimuli. Coaching points for the progression of coaching speed and acceleration drills can be seen in Table 11.11, and drill examples are provided in Table 11.12.

Table 11.11 SAQ coaching points

Level	Coaching points
Level 1: posture and position	• Teach the athlete proper posture and positioning to change direction. • Drills are of a lower intensity and higher volume to help the athlete learn the proper positions needed to change direction.
Level 2: movement requiring various forms of locomotion/ coordination	• Builds off positions taught in the first progressions, now with gross movement in and out of those positions. • Combination of different movements allows the athlete to begin to understand how to better coordinate their body while moving quickly.
Level 3: agility patterns with 90 degrees or less with various forms of locomotion	• Controlled cutting and change of direction patterns. • Teach the athlete how to maintain speed through the change of direction.
Level 4: open agility patterns and reactionary work	• Various movements and cutting patterns. • Addition of reactive cutting increases the sport-specificity by mirroring or having to read and react to the movements of a training partner.

Table 11.12 SAQ progressions

	Drill examples
Level one – posture and position	Wall-based linear speed drills – single exchange, multiple exchange Line drills – single leg lateral push and return, single leg line hop and stick – land on same leg and/or opposite leg Rapid line drills – double leg over line and back, single leg over line and back
Level two – movement with various forms of locomotion/ coordination	Resisted linear speed – march to skip to sprint with elastic resistance Lateral to linear speed – crossover to sprint, shuffle step to sprint Speed/movement coordination – combine movement patterns at speed (shuffle to sprint, carioca to sprint)
Level three – agility patterns with 90 degree or less cuts	Cone drills with tight angle cuts – mix in forwards, backwards, lateral movements "W" cone drill – sprint forwards, backpedal back "L" cone drill – sprint forward, shuffle lateral
Level four – open agility patterns and reactionary work	Multiple cone drill options, add a reaction cut based off coach cue or partner movement 4 cone mirror touch – set up 2 stations facing each other, with 4 cones creating a box. Have 2 athletes start in the middle, facing each other with one designated the "leader". The leader will proceed to touch all 4 cones in a random order, the "follower" must mirror the same order of the cone touch at the same time

Table 11.13 Energy systems overview

Energy system	Description	Work:rest ratio	Example
Aerobic capacity	Can be used to promote recovery or build a base	1:0 or 1:1	10 × 100m tempo sprint at 65–75% maximum running speed
Aerobic power	Work performed at or near $\dot{V}O_{2max}$	1:2, work bouts should range from 2–12 minutes, with the goal of accumulating 12–15 minutes per session	5 × 2 min fast run with 4 minute walk/jog
Lactate capacity	Ability to withstand work done at or just below Lactate Threshold.	1:1 to 1:5, work to accumulate between 2–6 minutes of work per session	5 × 45 second sprint with 2 minute rest
Lactate power	Maximum work effort. All out intensity	1:5–1:10, work bouts 10–30 seconds in duration, working to accumulate 2–4 minutes per session	20 × 10 second lateral shuffle between 2 cones with 60 second rest

Energy system development/conditioning

When creating Energy System Development (ESD) programs for ice hockey players, the focus during the early off-season should be on developing the capacity of the aerobic system. This can be accomplished with various methods (running, biking) and changing the duration and pace of the work prescribed. Depending on the fitness and injury history, ice hockey players should be able to jog/sprint for most of their conditioning work. The athletes spend their competitive season indoors – as such, a simple change of environment to outside can have a positive effect on mood and compliance to the necessary work. Bike work can be prescribed to off-load the athlete or to change the stimulus – but it should not make up the bulk of the off-season conditioning basis. The energy systems important for hockey can be broken into four categories: aerobic capacity and power, and lactate capacity and power.

Difference between in-season and off-season energy systems development

During a season, the athlete is skating frequently. Thus, they are receiving a cardiovascular stimulus from their training. During games, on-ice mean heart rates have been measured at around 92% of maximum during a shift, and between 70–80% of maximum in-between shifts (Jackson et al., 2016). Realising that during a season the athletes will receive a lot of volume between 70–92% of maximum heartrate, it is best to prescribe work outside of these zones. Athletes should perform some aerobic capacity work, as well as some lactate power and alactic work, to complement the mainly anaerobic work that they will do in-season.

Goalie modifications/considerations

The goalie position is drastically different in both the energy demands as well as movement demands that the athletes are placed under. As such, their training needs to reflect these differences. For a summary of changes, refer to Table 11.15.

Table 11.14 Off-season ESD plan

WEEK	ESD 1	ESD 2	ESD 3	ESD 4
1	2 × (3 × 200m Sprint every 3 minutes) – 5 min rest between sets (limit the # of change of directions if possible)	20min Z1/Z2 Run		
2	2 × (4 × 200m Sprint every 3 minutes) – 5 min rest between sets (limit the # of change of directions if possible)	20min Z1/Z2 Run		
3	2 × (4 × 200m Sprint every 2 minutes) – 5 min rest between sets (limit the # of change of directions if possible)	20min Z1/Z2 Run	20min Z1/Z2 Run	
4	6 × 200m Sprint every 2 minutes (limit the # of change of directions if possible)	20min Z1/Z2 Run	20min Z1/Z2 Run	
5	7 × 200m Sprint every 2 minutes (limit the # of change of directions if possible)	Shuttle runs – 6 × 150m (25m cone) Rest until HR hits Z1 and repeat	25min Z1/Z2 Run	
6	8 × 200m Sprint every 2 minutes (limit the # of change of directions if possible)	Shuttle runs – 7 × 150m (25m cone) Rest until HR hits Z1 and repeat	25min Z1/Z2 Run	
7	8 × 200m Sprint every 2 minutes (limit the # of change of directions if possible)	Shuttle runs – 8 × 150m (25m cone) Rest until HR hits Z1 and repeat	25min Z1/Z2 Run	
8	8 × 200m Sprint every 2 minutes (limit the # change of directions if possible)	30min Z1/Z2 Run	Shuttle runs – 8 × 150m (25m cone) Rest until HR hits Z1 and repeat	30min Z1/Z2 Run

Table 11.15 Summary of modifications for goalies

Fitness component	Modification
Dynamic warm-up	With the stress put on the hips by the butterfly style of play, hip mobility needs to be addressed with a warm-up including drills that target: mobility/activation, dynamic movement, neural activation focusing on quick movements plus eye tracking, and explosive lateral movement work. The inclusion of a tennis ball or reaction ball in the neural activation portion can help to begin their focus on tracking objects, a crucial skill.
Skating simulations	Some of the skating simulation work for skaters can be applied to goalies as one of its main focuses is stability and mobility under control. Many of the single leg stance drills will be helpful for goalies to strengthen their balance. Goalie specific skating simulation movements focus on incorporating the initial positioning and working on the movement skill to improve the lateral push.

(Continued)

Table 11.15 (Continued)

Fitness component	Modification
Strength	Include a greater focus on building strength in the frontal plane, as well as strength and stability in both a tall kneeling and half kneeling position – for example, lateral lunges or lateral step-ups. Goalies need to be stable and strong in both tall kneeling (both knees down) and half kneeling positions; therefore, doing some pushing and pulling from these positions will challenge their ability to maintain proper body position.
Speed and agility	The initial focus of movement should come from the hip. The ability to fully abduct, internally rotate, and extend the hip is important for when the goalie has to push laterally from their butterfly position. All goalie movement drills build off the base of a good lateral push, while also incorporating some rotation to square up to the direction that they are facing.
	Start movements with a head-shoulder turn to square up off a pivot step. This prevents any lag of the upper body rotating to square up, which when on-ice can cause the goalie to cover less of the net when attempting to stop the puck. Butterfly-style goalies spend a lot of the game transitioning from a knees down position, to a half-kneeling push, to standing, and their ability to efficiently get up and into position is an important factor to stop the puck. A lot of their movement drills should start in a half-kneeling position, which simulates them pushing off their outside foot.
	Ensure some linear speed work is included. Sprint progressions will help strengthen the hip musculature and teach how to create hip flexion and extension. Short sprints/resisted sprints will benefit their ability to be powerful when pushing in the crease.
Energy systems development	To meet the demand of playing the whole game, a strong aerobic system is needed. Once the aerobic foundation is developed, much of the goalie conditioning should focus on anaerobic work, specifically lactate power work. Interval work using the work:rest intervals outlined in the Energy System Development section can be prescribed. These intervals can include multi-directional work, such as maximum speed lateral shuffles between two cones for a certain amount of time to better reflect the movements performed on the ice.

Table 11.16 Example of goalie warm up

	Warm up example 1	Warm up example 2
Mobility/ activation	Foam roll – adductors and hip focus Quadruped adductor rock back Quadruped opposite arm and leg extension	Quadruped fire hydrant Quadruped hip circles – forwards and backwards Mini band forward, backward, lateral step
Movement preparation	Reverse lunge with twist Handwalk with push up High knee run – asymmetrical every 3 steps Butt kick run – asymmetrical every 3 steps Lateral march Quick feet carioca	Banded side lying clam Quadruped forward, backward, lateral crawl 3-way lateral lunge (out, back, down, shuffle) Forward walking lunge with overhead reach Shuffle acceleration (slow to fast) 45 degree shuffle, forward and backwards
Neural preparation	Two foot lateral line hops – quick Two foot lateral line hops with tennis ball throw and catch Continuous lateral shuffle with tennis ball throw and catch	Single leg drop squat Single leg drop squat to single leg vertical jump Single leg drop squat to lateral bound with tennis ball catch
Explosive lateral movement	Shuffle from stomach start Shuffle from tall kneeling start Shuffle from half kneeling start	Continuous lateral bound Multi-cone shuffle (forward, backwards, sideways)

Table 11.17 Goalie skating simulations

	PHASE ONE	PHASE TWO	PHASE THREE
GOALIE OFF-ICE MOVEMENT SIMULATIONS	Half kneel to head-shoulder turn 90deg pivot Get-up on cue Half kneel to head-shoulder turn pivot to 3 step sprint Lateral shuffle step SLOW – push off back leg	3 Step shuffle to head-shoulder turn 45deg backwards lateral bound and stick 1/2 kneel to tennis ball drop and GO lateral start (head-shoulder turn)	Tennis ball throw and catch off wall with forward/backward movement continuous Tennis ball throw and catch off wall with lateral side step movement continuous

Conclusion

A well-developed strength and conditioning program for an ice hockey athlete needs to be multi-faceted to match the demands of the sport. Based off the time of the year, the athlete should be following a well-structured and balanced training plan that includes elements to improve aerobic and anaerobic fitness, upper and lower body strength, lower body power, and speed, agility and quickness. By following a well-structured and progressive strength and conditioning plan, ice hockey athletes will improve their physical fitness, in turn decreasing their risk of injury and increasing their ability to perform on the ice during competition.

References

Agel, J., Dompier, T., Dick, R. and Marshall, S., 2007. Descriptive Epidemiology of Collegiate Men's Ice Hockey Injuries: National Collegiate Athletic Association Injury Surveillance System, 1988–1989 Through 2003–2004. *Journal of Athletic Training*, 42(2), pp. 241–248.

Agel, J. and Harvey, E. J., 2010. A 7-year review of men's and women's ice hockey injuries in the NCAA. *Canadian Journal of Surgery*, 53(5), p. 319.

Allen, D. and Barnett, F., 2011. Reliability and Validity of an Electronic Dynamometer for Measuring Grip Strength. *International Journal of Therapy and Rehabilitation*, 18(5), pp. 258–265.

Boyle, M., 2012. *Advances in functional training: Training techniques for coaches, personal trainers and athletes.* s.l.: On Target Publications.

Bracko, M. R., 2001. On-Ice Performance Characteristics of Elite and Non-Elite Women's Ice Hockey Players. *Journal of Strength and Conditioning Research*, 15(1), pp. 42–47.

Bracko, M. R. et al., 1998. Performance Skating Characteristics of Professional Ice Hockey Forwards. *Research in Sports Medicine: An International Journal*, 8(3), pp. 251–263.

Brainard, L. et al., 2012. Gender Differences in Head Impacts Sustained by Collegiate Ice Hockey Players. *Medicine and Science in Sports and Exercise*, 44(2), pp. 297–304.

Buchheit, M., Lefebvre, B., Laursen, P. and Ahmaidi, S., 2011. Reliability, Usefulness, and Validity of the 30–15 Intermittent Ice Test in Young Elite Ice Hockey Players. *Journal of Strength and Conditioning Research*, 25, pp. 1457–1464.

Buckeridge, E. et al., 2015. An On-Ice Measurement Approach to Analyse the Biomechanics of Ice Hockey Skating. *PLoS ONE*, 10(5), p. e0127324.

Burr, J. et al., 2008. Relationship of Physical Fitness Test Results and Hockey Playing Potential in Elite-Level Ice Hockey Players. *Journal of Strength and Conditioning Research*, 22(5), pp. 1535–1543.

Burr, J., Jamnik, V., Dogra, S. and Gledhill, N., 2007. Evaluation of Jump Protocols to Assess Leg Power and Predict Hockey Playing Potential. *Journal of Strength and Conditioning*, 21(4), pp. 1139–1145.

Carey, D., Drake, M., Pliego, G. and Raymond, R., 2007. Do Hockey Players Need Aerobic Fitness? Relation Between VO2max and Fatigue During High-Intensity Intermittent Ice Skating. *Journal of Strength and Conditioning Research*, 21(3), pp. 963–966.

Distefano, L., Blackburn, J., Marshall, S. and Padua, D., 2009. Gluteal Muscle Activation During Common Therapeutic Exercises. *Journal of Orthopadic and Sports Physical Therapy*, 39(7), pp. 532–540.

Durocher, J., Guisfredi, A., Leetun, D. and Carter, J., 2010. Comparison of On-ice and Off-ice Graded Exercise Testing in Collegiate Hockey Players. *Applied Physiology, Nutrition and Metabolism*, 35, pp. 35–39.

Flik, K., Lyman, S. and Marx, R., 2005. American Collegiate Men's Ice Hockey: An Analysis of Injuries. *American Journal of Sports Medicine*, 33(2), pp. 183–187.

Geithner, C., Lee, A. and Bracko, M., 2006. Physical and Performance Differences Among Forwards, Defensemen, and Goalie in Elite Women's Ice Hockey. *Journal of Strength and Conditioning Research*, 20(3), pp. 500–505.

Glaister, M., 2005. Multiple Sprint Work. *Sports Medicine*, 35(9), pp. 757–777.

Green, H. and Houston, M., 1974. Effect of a Season of Ice Hockey on Energy Capacities and Associated Functions. *Medicine and Science in Sports*, 7(4), pp. 299–303.

Green, M., Pivarnik, J., Carrier, D. and Womack, C., 2006. Relationship Between Physiological Profiles and On-ice Performance of a National Collegiate Athletic Association Division I Hockey Team. *Journal of Strength and Conditioning Research*, 20(1), pp. 43–46.

Gutowski, A. E. and Rosene, J. M., 2011. Preseason performance testing battery for men's lacrosse. *Strength & Conditioning Journal*, 33(2), 16–22.

IIHF, 2016. *IIHF Member National Associations* [Online]. Available at: www.iihf.com/iihf-home/the-iihf/members/ [Accessed 23 April 2016].

Jaafar, H. et al., 2014. Effects of Load on Wingate-test Performances and Reliabilty. *Journal of Strength and Conditioning Research*, 28(12), pp. 3462–3468.

Jackson, J. et al., 2016. Movement Characteristics and Heart Rate Profiles Displayed by Female University Ice Hockey Players. *International Journal of Kinesiology and Sports Science*, 4(1), pp. 43–54.

Jay, K. et al., 2014. Specific and Cross Over Effects of Massage for Muscle Soreness: Randomized Controlled Trial. *International Journa of Sports Physical Therapy*, 9(1), pp. 82–91.

Kawamori, N., Rossi, S. J., Justice, B. D. and Haff, E. E., 2006. Peak Force and Rate of Force Development during Isometric and Dynamic Mid-Thigh Clean Pulls Performed at Various Intensities. *Journal of Strength and Conditioning Research*, 20(3), p. 483.

Kenney, L., Wilmore, J. and Costill, D., 2015. *Physiology of sport and exercise*. 5th ed. Champaign: Human Kinetics.

Knowles, S., Marshall, S. and Guskiewicz, K., 2006. Issues in Estimating Risks and Rates in Sports Injury Research. *Journal of Athletic Training*, 41(2), pp. 207–215.

MacCormick, L., Best, T. and Flanigan, D., 2014. Are There Differences in Ice Hockey Injuries Between Sexes? *The Orthapaedic Journal of Sports Medicine*, 2(1), pp. 1–7.

MacDonald, G., Button, D., Drinkwater, E. and Behm, D., 2014. Foam Rolling as a Recovery Tool After an Intense Bout of Physical Activity. *Medicine & Science in Sports and Exercise*, 46(1), pp. 131–142.

Manners, T., 2004. Sport-Specific Training for Ice Hockey. *Strength and Conditioning Journal*, 26(2), pp. 16–21.

Maulder, P. and Cronin, J., 2005. Horizontal and Vertical Jump Assessment: Reliability, Symmetry, Descriminative and Predictive Abilty. *Physical Therapy in Sport*, 6, pp. 74–82.

McBride, J. M., Triplett-McBride, T., Davie, A. and Newton, R. U., 2002. The Effect of Heavy-vs. Light-Load Jump Squats on the Development of Strength, Power, and Speed. *The Journal of Strength & Conditioning Research*, 16(1), 75–82.

McColloch, P. and Bach, B., 2007. Injuries in Men's Lacrosse. *Orthopedics*, 30(1), pp. 29–34.

McKay, C., Tufts, R., Shaffer, B. and Meeuwisse, W., 2014. The Epidemiology of Professional Ice Hockey Injuries: A Prospective Report of Six National Hockey League Seasons. *British Journal of Sports Medicine*, 48(1), pp. 57–62.

Montgomery, D., 2006. Physiological Profile of Professional Hockey Players – A Longitudinal Comparison. *Applied Physiology, Nutrition and Metabolism*, 31, pp. 181–185.

Myatt, C., Wilson, R., Malzahn, J. and Synder, A., 2010. Training Impulse (TRIMP) Values During One Week of Practices and Games at the End of an Elite Youth Ice Hockey Season. *Journal of Strength and Conditioning*, 24, p. 1.

National Strength and Conditioning Association, 2012. *NSCA's Guide to Tests and Assessments*. Illinois, USA: Human Kinetics.

Noonan, B., 2010. Intragame Blood-lactate Values During Ice Hockey and Their Relationship to Commonly Used Testing Protocols. *Journal of Strength and Conditioning Research*, 24(9), pp. 2290–2295.

Peacock, C. et al., 2014. An Acute Bout of Self-myofascial Release in the Form of Foam Rolling Improves Performance Testing. *International Journal of Exercise Science*, 7(3), p. 5.

Peyer, K., Pivarnik, J., Eisenmann, J. and Vorkapich, M., 2011. Physiological Characteristics of National Collegiate Athletic Association Division I Ice Hockey Players and Their Relation to Game Performance. *Journal of Strength and Conditioning Research*, 25(5), pp. 1183–1192.

Ransdell, L., Murray, T. and Gao, Y., 2013. Off-ice Fitness of Elite Female Ice Hockey Players by Team Success, Age, and Player Position. *Journal of Strength and Conditioning Research*, 27(4), pp. 875–884.

Schick, D. and Meeuwisse, W., 2003. Injury Rates and Profiles in Female Ice Hockey Players. *American Journal of Sports Medicine*, 31(1), pp. 47–52.

Skarabot, J., Beardsley, C. and Stirn, I., 2015. Comparing the Effects of Self-myofascia Release With Static Stretching on Ankle Range of Motion in Adolescent Athletes. *International Journal of Sports Physical Therapy*, 10(2), p. 203.

Snyder, A., Wilson, R. and Malzahn, J., 2010. Training Impulse (TRIMP) During Practice and Games for Elite Level Youth Ice Hockey Players. *Journal of Strength and Conditioning Research*, 24, p. 1.

Stanula, A. et al., 2014. The Role of Aerobic Capacity in High Intensity Intermittent Efforts in Ice Hockey. *Biology of Sport*, 31(3), pp. 193–199.

Thomas, A., Dawson, B. and Goodman, C., 2006. The Yo Yo Test: Reliability and Association With a 20-m Shuttle Run and VO2max. *International Journal of Sports Physiology and Performance*, 1, pp. 137–149.

Triplett, N., 2012. Speed and agility. In: T. Miller, ed. *NSCA's guide to tests and assessments*. Illinois, USA: Human Kinetics, pp. 253–274.

Tuominen, M. et al., 2015. Injuries in Men's International Ice Hockey: A 7-year Study of the International Ice Hockey Federation Adult World Championship Tournaments and Olympic Winter Games. *British Journal of Sports Medicine*, 49, pp. 30–36.

Tyler, T., Nicholas, S., Campbell, R. and McHugh, M., 2001. The Association of Hip Strength and Flexibility With the Incidence of Adductor Muscle Strains in Professional Ice Hockey Players. *American Journal of Sports Medicine*, 29(2), pp. 124–128.

Upjohn, T., Turcotte, R., Pearsall, D. and Loh, J., 2008. Three-dimensional Kinematics of the Lower Limbs During Forward Ice Skating. *Sports Biomechanics*, 7(2), pp. 206–221.

Vescovi, J., Murray, T., Fiala, K. and VanHeest, J., 2006. Off-Ice Performance and Draft Status of Elite Ice Hockey Players. *International Journal of Sports Physiology and Performance*, 1, pp. 207–221.

Wu, T. et al., 2003. The Performance of the Ice Hockey Slap and Wrist Shots: The Effects of Stick Construction and Player Skill. *Sports Enginerring*, 6(1), pp. 31–39.

Zagatto, A., Beck, W. and Goratto, C., 2009. Validity of the Running Anaerobic Sprint Test for Assessing Anaerobic Power and Predicting Short-Distance Performances. *Journal of Strength and Conditioning Research*, 23(6), pp. 1820–1827.

12
BASKETBALL

Rob Harley, Stuart Mills and Alex Bliss

Introduction to the sport

Basketball is a team sport played worldwide by both males and females and of players of all ages and is suggested to be one of the most popular sports in the world today (Hoffman, 2003). It is played between two teams with five players from each team on the court at any one time. The game allows for rolling substitutions and the number of substitutes varies, depending upon the code being played, between five, under International Basketball Federation (FIBA) rules, and eight, under National Basketball Association (NBA) rules. The full size court is 28m by 15m (FIBA) or 29m by 15m (NBA) and games are played in four quarters of 10 minutes (FIBA) or 12 minutes (NBA), with slight variations for American college games. Prior to the year 2000 teams had 30 seconds to make a shot and 10 seconds to cross the half way line. This was changed to 24 seconds to make a shot and 8 seconds to cross the half way line, and it would appear that this rule change, to make the game faster and more exciting for the spectators, has influenced the level of fatigue players are experiencing during a game. Research by McInnes et al. (1995) prior to the rule change reported that fatigue wasn't evident within basketball as there was no difference in the movement characteristics between the four quarters of play. Whereas Ben Abdelkrim et al. (2007, 2010a) has demonstrated players are negatively influenced by fatigue during the 2nd and 4th quarters of games, emphasising the importance of physical conditioning to reduce the early onset of fatigue and the negative effects this can have on physical ability and decision making. Although Hoffman (2003) stated that large differences in the way the game is played (i.e. slow offenses vs running fast breaks) will influence the physiological load placed upon the players, in order for coaches to be able to implement a variety of tactical strategies, players need to be prepared for the hardest physical scenario to make sure they are giving themselves the best opportunity to optimise their technical abilities. Therefore, the aim of this chapter is to evaluate published literature to establish the physiological/physical demands of the sport leading to the design of specific conditioning programmes in order to help reduce risk of injuries and optimise physical performance. This chapter is deliberately non prescriptive, as training prescription depends upon a variety of factors related to the individual players circumstances (e.g. training status, injury history, time available for training, the volume of squad training being performed, etc.). Coaches are advised to assess their client's readiness to train using functional movement and physical competency assessments described later in this chapter. Also, through the implementation of an appropriate battery of fitness tests, coaches can identify players' physiological strengths and weaknesses, develop individual training programmes and monitor the effectiveness of their interventions.

Athletic demands

An early study relating to the athletic demands of basketball was carried out by McInnes et al. (1995). They quantified the movement patterns using eight movement categories, heart rate (HR) responses and blood lactate concentrations of elite male basketball players in order to describe the physiological strain placed upon the players during match play. More recent studies (Ben Abdelkrim et al., 2007; Matthew and Delextrat, 2009; Ben Abdelkrim et al., 2010a; Scanlan et al., 2011) have replicated the research of McInnes et al. (1995), but with added movement categories (dribbling, upper body movement, and two states of static exertion: picks and positioning) as, according to Ben Abdelkrim et al. (2007), the physiological strain required to perform these type of movements has been under estimated. Scanlan et al. (2011) reported that elite players perform significantly more total match movements when compared with their sub-elite counter parts and Ben Abdelkrim et al. (2007) found that guards exhibit significantly higher movement frequencies than forwards and centres, indicating the importance the importance of conditioning required for elite performance, especially for the guards. Conditioning work should therefore involve activity in the nature of repeated bursts of high intensity, employing the movement patterns used in game situations and described in the movement category research. This conditioning can be achieved through off court specific conditioning training as well as on court conditioning work. Delextrat and Martinez (2014) have demonstrated that improvements in aerobic fitness can occur during the season with the addition of two extra conditioning sessions per week over a six week period in regional level under 17 players. Similar improvements in aerobic fitness occurred through both intervention strategies employed in their research; however, the players who performed the additional small sided games (2 vs 2 on a full length, half width, court) showed larger improvements in defensive agility, shooting skills and upper body power compared to those players who performed the high intensity running training (repeated bursts of 15 seconds of running at 95% of maximal running velocity followed by 15 seconds of jogging). Therefore task specific training is highly recommended, especially with junior players.

Playing time proportion of different intensities

Looking at the durations of the different movement categories can provide a greater understanding of the specific demands of basketball. Typically, movements have been split into low, medium, and high intensity activities. Live playing time for each movement level of intensity reported within scientific studies tends to be fairly consistent for elite male players across studies, with percentages of 51–53%, 24–31%, and 15–20% for low, medium, and high intensities respectively (Ben Abdelkrim et al., 2007; Ben Abdelkrim et al., 2010a; McInnes et al., 1995). Interestingly, it has been shown that the intensity during practice games is lower than during competition (Rodriguez-Alonso et al., 2003); therefore, one would expect the percentage of high intensity movement to be greater in competition games.

How frequently players engage in high intensity movements during a game has been shown to be influenced by player position, with centres (14.7%) spending significantly lower live time performing high intensity movements compared with guards (17.1%) and forwards (16.6%) (Ben Abdelkrim et al., 2007). How the level of competition affects the proportion of time at different intensities is less clear. Ben Abdelkrim et al. (2010a) reported that international level players (INP) spent significantly more live time in high intensity activities (high intensity shuffling, intense static actions and sprinting) than national level players (NLP). Surprisingly, INP also spent a greater amount of time standing still and walking (low intensity activity) compared to NLPs, perhaps reflecting a low level of conditioning. It was thought that increased periods of passive recovery may enhance repeated sprinting within basketball and therefore may have partially influenced the increased time performing high intensity movements. However, Scanlan et al. (2011) reported conflicting findings, with elite level players spending total longer durations performing jogging and running activities than sub-elite players. The total time spent standing/walking and sprinting appears to be greater for sub-elite players, suggesting that sub-elite players spend more time performing maximal intensity activity and therefore subsequently experience longer low intensity periods in order to recover. One explanation provided for the conflicting finding was that the two studies were investigating male players of different ages, with the mean (SD) age of players within the Scanlan et al. (2011) study being 10 years older at 28.3 (4.9) vs. 18.2 (0.5). The possible differences in skill level, match structure and decision-making ability were also proposed reasons for the conflicting findings relating to how the competition level affects time spent within different intensity activities.

The majority of studies have not measured the distance travelled during competition, as it has been felt that the high levels of game time spent shuffling (31%), where players cover little distance despite working at a high intensity, would underestimate the physiological demands of the game (McInnes et al., 1995). Ben Abdelkrim et al. (2010b) did report the distances covered during different movement activities and compared between the two halves. During the second half the distance covered by sprinting, striding and sideways running was reduced in comparison to the first half. Large variations were found in the distance covered when maximal and high speed running, as well as for sideways running, with both maximal and high speed running distance being significantly correlated with aerobic endurance performance (20 metre shuttle run test). This evidence helps build the case for a strong emphasis to be placed upon aerobic endurance training. Ben Abdelkrim et al. (2010b) also reports that the distance travelled in high intensity shuffling was associated with agility performance (Agility T-test) which helps build the case for the inclusion of agility tasks as part of a fitness assessment battery.

Heart rate response

Whether the percentage of live time engaged in high intensity activity is closer to 6% (Bishop and Wright, 2006) or within the region of 15–20% (Ben Abdelkrim et al., 2007; Ben Abdelkrim et al., 2010a; McInnes et al., 1995), both values do not appear to reflect the high heart rate (HR) responses recorded during basketball games. Mean match HR reported, expressed as a percentage of maximum HR, have all consistently been high, ranging from 88.0 to 94.6 percent of HRmax (Ben Abdelkrim et al., 2007; Ben Abdelkrim et al., 2010a; McInnes et al., 1995; Narazaki et al., 2009; Rodriguez-Alonso et al., 2003). The finding that there was no significant relationship between the percentage of live time spent in high intensity activity and the HR responses during competition (Ben Abdelkrim et al., 2007) suggests that other factors play a role in the observed high game HRs. Ben Abdelkrim et al. (2010a) comments that the higher than expected HR values reported for the relatively low percentage of total time engaged within high intensity activity could be a consequence of frequent changes in category of movement within basketball, which is associated with the need to overcome inertia, which requires a great deal of energy expenditure. The number of activity changes throughout a game should therefore also be taken into account when estimating exercise intensity. The involvement in intense static activities also appears to contribute to the high cardiovascular stress observed, with the upper body demands of shooting, passing and rebounding leading Ben Abdelkrim et al. (2010a) to emphasise the importance of strength training in an attempt to develop the ability of players to withstand the repeated physical challenges exerted by opponents.

It appears that the higher the standard of basketball the greater the mean HR, which would be expected considering that elite players perform significantly more total match movements when compared with their sub-elite counterparts (Scanlan et al., 2011). INPs spend significantly longer times with HRs greater than 95% of HRmax than NLPs do (17.8 vs. 15.2%). The amount of match time spent in the high intensity zone (between 85 and 95% of HRmax) is also significantly higher for INPs (59.1 vs. 54.4%) (Ben Abdelkrim et al., 2010a). For INPs 77% of live time was spent with a HR greater than 85% HRmax, which is similar to the value of 75% reported by McInnes et al. (1995) for elite male players, further illustrating the high cardiac stress encountered during competitive basketball and the need for appropriate conditioning work to prepare players to cope with these high cardiac demands.

Blood lactate

Blood lactate concentrations during match play have been reported with mean lactate levels ranging from 3.2 to 8.5 mmol/L (Ben Abdelkrim et al., 2007; Ben Abdelkrim et al., 2010a; McInnes et al., 1995; Narazaki et al., 2009; Rodriguez-Alonso et al., 2003), indicating that glycolysis makes an important contribution to energy production during basketball. The variability appears to be due to player position, with guards having higher lactate levels than centres (Ben Abdelkrim et al., 2007; Rodriguez-Alonso et al., 2003) as well as the level of competition, with more elevated levels in international players compared to national players (Ben Abdelkrim et al., 2007) again illustrating the higher game intensity of international vs national level play.

Fatigue

The extent to which fatigue occurs within the game has been examined. Prior to the significant rule change in 2000 that reduced total attack time from 30 to 24 seconds, and the reduction from 10 to 8 seconds to cross the half way line, it appeared fatigue wasn't evident as there was no difference in the movement characteristics between the four quarters of play (McInnes et al., 1995). Studies since the rule change have, however, found that first and third quarters of male games are played at higher exercise intensities, with a notable decrease in the amount of high intensity activity during the second and fourth quarters. Blood lactate concentrations at half time were also significantly greater than at full time (Ben Abdelkrim et al., 2007; Ben Abdelkrim et al., 2010a), perhaps indicating the inability of players to maintain a high work output.

Oxygen consumption

Narazaki et al. (2009) has reported positive correlation between player's $\dot{V}O_{2max}$ and $\dot{V}O_2$ during game play, and a strong negative correlation between $\dot{V}O_{2max}$ and percent of duration of walking and standing during play, suggests that enhancement of aerobic power is important within basketball. Ben Abdelkrim et al. (2007) and Ben Abdelkrim et al. (2010a) similarly reported positive relationships between the live time spent in high intensity activity and $\dot{V}O_{2max}$.

Tactical strategy and implications on athletic demands

The extent to which the tactical strategy employed during a game influences exercise intensity was investigated by Ben Abdelkrim et al. (2010a). They found that the exercise intensity during basketball was not affected by the defence strategy adopted, with similar percentages of time spent with HRs above 95 and 85% of HRmax, which were 16.9% and 72.7%, and 16.6% and 72.7% during man-to-man and zone marking defence games respectively. There were no mean or peak blood lactate concentration differences, and similar times were also spent in intense activities. There were differences in terms of time spent sprinting and high intensity shuffling with time spent sprinting being greater during man-to man games, and more high intensity shuffling during zone defence games.

Athletic demands summary and implications for training

It is evident that to optimise on court athletic performance a good level of aerobic conditioning is required in order maintain a high work output and to reduce the effects of fatigue. Castagna et al. (2010) emphasised the consequence of the changes in directional modes of activity on the physiological demands of the basketball play and therefore recommended nonorthodox directional modes be implemented during basketball specific training drills.

Injury prevalence

Although basketball is considered a non-contact sport, research indicates that there is a high injury incidence rate, with game-related injury rates per 1000 athlete exposures ranging from 7.7 (Agel et al., 2007) to 24.9 (Deitch et al., 2006), resulting in basketball having one of the highest frequencies of injuries amongst non-contact sports (Meeuwisse et al., 2003; Conn et al., 2003). Injuries within the sport, however, aren't restricted to games, although injuries within a game situation are almost two times higher than during practices (Agel et al., 2007). It appears that players may be more prone to injury earlier in the season with pre-season practice injury rates reported at almost three times higher than in-season practice. The injury rate in regular-season games was also 1.4 times higher than in post-season games (Agel et al., 2007; Dick et al., 2007). Agel et al. (2007), suggests deconditioning from the off-season and increased intensity of the preseason practices as players try to earn a starting position as possible factors for the increased injury risk, highlighting the importance of careful planning of preseason conditioning.

Comparisons between professional women's and men's basketball injuries indicate that the frequency of women's injuries is 1.6 times higher than for men (Zelisko et al., 1982), and with regard to game-related injury, the rate per 1000 athlete exposures is 1.3 times greater for women than men; however, gender did not significantly alter the nature, distribution and rate of most game-related injuries (Deitch et al., 2006). In agreement with other studies, (Agel et al., 2007; Dick et al., 2007), injury to the lower extremity was the most common game related injury, with Deitch et al. (2006) reporting the lower extremity accounting for 65% of men's injuries and 66% for women's injuries. The most common lower extremity game injuries are ankle ligaments, knee injuries (internal derangements and patellar conditions), and concussions, with upper leg muscle-tendon strains also common in practices. However, for severe injuries, i.e. injuries that resulted in at least ten consecutive days of restricted or total loss of participation, injury to the knee was the most common cause. Most game (52.3%) and practice (43.6%) injuries were the result of player contact, although the majority of the severe knee injuries were associated with noncontact (Agel et al., 2007; Dick et al., 2007; Starkey, 2000).

Within a 13-year review of Anterior Cruciate Ligament (ACL) injury in NCAA basketball and soccer, Agel et al. (2005), found specifically for basketball ACL injuries that the majority were noncontact with 75.7% for women and 70.1% for men. This frequency of noncontact versus contact ACL injuries was significantly different to soccer ACL injuries where the women and men noncontact percentages were less, at 58.3% and 49.6% respectively. The ACL injury rate, expressed as rate of injury per 1000 athlete-exposures, remained stable in collegiate basketball and soccer over the 13-year time span, and remained higher in both female (0.33) and male (0.11) soccer players than in female (0.29) and male (0.08) basketball players. As found with the overall injury rates within basketball, the ACL injury rate was significantly higher for women than men in both basketball and soccer. A systematic review by Stevenson et al. (2015) assessing the effectiveness of neuromuscular training in reducing the incidence of ACL injuries in female athletes suggested that plyometrics, which integrates strength, agility and balance training, is an important component of neuromuscular training programs as some studies involving plyometric training reduced ACL injury risk. The implications of these findings will be discussed in the prescription element of this chapter.

Meeuwisse et al. (2003), investigating injury rates over a two-year period within Canadian men's intercollegiate basketball, in agreement with later research (Agel et al., 2007; Dick et al., 2007; Deitch et al., 2006), found that the ankle had the overall highest injury rate, but for severe injuries, classified as injuries resulting in seven or more sessions missed, the knee had the highest injury rate. Meeuwisse et al. (2003), investigating in detail the mechanism of injury in order to determine rates and risks of injury in relation to player position and court zone, reported that the greatest number of injuries occurred in the key, which accounted for 44.7% of all injuries. This was thought to be as a result of the high amount of playing time spent in the key, and the increased player-to-player contact due to higher player concentration, as the majority of injuries were contact injuries, with player contact accounting for 79.8% of contact injuries. With regards to player position risk, centres had a significantly higher rate of injury compared with forwards and guards, with their rate of knee, ankle, and foot injury being 13, 4.5, and 10 times greater, respectively, than players in the forward position, who had the lowest injury rate. It was speculated that centres may have an increased injury risk due to their tending to move in the areas of highest player concentration and thus experiencing increased potential for contact; however, they concluded that further investigation was warranted into the reason why centres were so predisposed to injury. Although the overall injury rate within the Meeuwisse et al. (2003) study was 4.9 injuries per 1000 athlete exposures, lower in comparison to other studies (Agel et al., 2007; Cumps et al., 2007; Dick et al., 2007), the percentage of athletes injured over the two year study period was 44.7%. When this data is also considered alongside the 67.7% of participating players being affected by injuries within just one competitive season (Cumps et al., 2007), it does appear to support the conclusion by Cumps et al. (2007), that basketball should be designated as a high-risk sport. Implications for appropriate injury reduction strategies will be discussed in the programming section.

Fitness assessment

The assessment of fitness can be beneficial for a variety of reasons within a team sport setting. Fitness profiles can be used to identify physiological/physical strengths and weaknesses and help shape an individual's training programme. Performed on a regular basis, they can help assess the effectiveness of training interventions (Harley and Doust, 1997). As described in the athletic demands section, basketball requires players to possess high levels in a variety of components of fitness, as the game stresses both the aerobic and anaerobic energy production pathways and fatigue has been shown to influence the amount of high intensity activity being performed during the later stages of the quarter, irrespective of playing standard (Ben Abdelkrim et al., 2010a). The game involves numerous high intensity actions involving changes of direction, accelerations and decelerations, which require muscular strength, power and endurance. These physical attributes need to be combined with a good level of aerobic power because of the high cardiac stress required highlighted in the athletic demands section of this chapter.

It is therefore proposed that coaches should select and implement a fitness testing battery. The selection of tests in the battery will depend upon the facilities, time and resources available to the tester. Whichever tests are selected, it is important to select tests that have high ecological validity as well as good reliability. Simenz et al. (2005) surveyed the practices of NBA strength and conditioning (S & C) coaches. From the 20 out of 29 coaches who responded, they reported testing an average of 7.3 parameters of fitness using 7.8 specific tests, thereby reiterating the importance of employing a battery of fitness tests to assess a variety of components of fitness related to the physical demands of the basketball. The implementation strategy (frequency, number of tests, etc.) will depend upon the different circumstances of the team involved. Coaches are recommended to select one aerobic test and a variety of speed, power and agility assessments from Table 12.1, depending upon access to equipment and time availability.

Functional movement screening (FMS)

Simenz et al. (2005) reported that 15 out of the 20 coaches who responded to their practice review reported assessing flexibility using a variety of assessment techniques. Nine of those 15 reported using the sit and reach test and one reported using the Gray Cook method of functional movement screen (FMS) (Cook et al., 2006a, 2006b). The crude assessment of one aspect of flexibility (i.e. the sit and reach tests) has subsequently been superseded and coaches are referred to the procedures outlined by Cook et al. (2006a, 2006b). This screening battery allows coaches to assess proficiency in a variety of movement patterns using a 4-point scale (from 0 = "in pain" to 3 = "perfect movement pattern") with a perfect score on all seven assessments leading to a total score of 21. S & C coaches are referred to Cook et al. (2006a, 2006b) for grading system. The aim of the screen is to assess compensatory movements that may lead to increased injury risk to target specific interventions with appropriate corrective exercises. Scoring proficiency on the FMS has been linked with the ability to predict injury risk, with players scoring a total of 14 or less resulting in a 4-fold increase in lower extremity injury risk (Chorba et al., 2010). This study was performed on 38 NCAA division II female game players, including basketball, volleyball and soccer players who were tracked over the course of one season. Gulgin et al. (2014) found that the FMS scores were similar among raters of various levels of experience, although they reported that expert raters were more critical than novice raters in the interpretation of the scoring criteria. A meta-analysis of 7 papers on the inter-rater and intra-rater reliability of the FMS published by Cuchna et al. (2016) reported good inter-rater and intra-rater reliability with a summary ICC of 0.843 and 0.869 respectively. They concluded that the FMS is a reliable tool for clinical practice.

Physical competency assessment

Physical competency assessments are becoming more prevalent in the field of strength and condition. The ability to perform strength tasks with good form, without displaying compensatory movement patterns, muscle imbalances or muscle tightness is a prerequisite required before any

Table 12.1 Fitness tests

Component of fitness	Test name	Brief description of protocol	Strengths/weaknesses of the test	Reported data on validity/reliability	Normative data
Aerobic fitness	$\dot{V}O_{2max}$	Graded exercise test with oxygen uptake.	Expensive lab based assessment.	Gold standard assessment of aerobic power.	Ziv and Lydor (2009) reported values of 59 ml.kg^{-1}.min^{-1} for male and 51 ml.kg^{-1}.min^{-1} for female NCAA division I players. Narazaki et al. (2009) reported 57.5 (8.2) ml.kg^{-1}.min^{-1} for male and 50.3 (5.9) ml.kg^{-1}.min^{-1} for females NCAA division II players. Abdelkrim et al. (2010) reported junior male international players at 54.4 (1.9) ml.kg^{-1}.min^{-1} and the national level players at 51.6 (2.0) ml.kg^{-1}.min^{-1}.
	Predicted $\dot{V}O_{2max}$ using the MST	Incremental test performed over a 20 metre circuit.	Simple field test which involves running over a 20 metre track involving accelerations and decelerations.	Highly correlated with $\dot{V}O_{2max}$ (Ramsbottom et al., 1988).	
	MST performed dribbling a basketball	Incremental test performed over a 20 metre circuit.	Task specific as it includes dribbling the ball.	Highly correlated with the MST test (r=0.99). Test retest correlation of r=0.95 and a CV% 1.1% (Harley et al. in Winter, 2007).	Harley (1997) reported a predicted value of 53.6 (3.3) ml.kg^{-1}.min^{-1} for male University players. y=3.57 + 0.992x (x = predicted max with ball, y = predicted max without ball) (Harley, 1997).
	Yo-Yo IR1	Incremental running task involving accelerations and decelerations with short recovery periods.	Simple field test with task specificity.	Highly correlated with $\dot{V}O_{2max}$ (r=0.77, P<0.0001).	Castagna et al. (2008) reported the mean distance covered on the Yo-Yo IR1 by a group of junior basketball players to be 1678 (397) m.
	Intermittent shuttle run test (ISRT)	Field assessment of lactate threshold.	Field test involving multiple changes of direction but involves finger prick blood sampling.	Strong relationship with treadmill assessment method (r=0.82, p<0.001) (Castagna et al., 2010).	Castagna et al. (2010) reported the mean speed at ISRT-LT for a group of junior basketball players to be 10.1 (1.7) km.h^{-1}.
Anaerobic power	Adapted line drill	Simple field test.		CV = 1.3% (Harley et al. in Winter et al., 2007).	English national league players males 26.3 s and females 30.6 s.

(Continued)

Table 12.1 (Continued)

Component of fitness	Test name	Brief description of protocol	Strengths/weaknesses of the test	Reported data on validity/reliability	Normative data
Speed	20 metre sprint test		Simple field test but requires photo electric cells.	Test retest correlation of r=0.96 CV=1.6% (Harley et al. in Winter et al., 2007).	English national league players males 3.12 s and females 3.45 s.
Lateral quickness	Lateral movement test	36 metres of lateral movement with 6 changes of direction.	Simple field test	Test retest correlation of r=0.68 CV=2.8% (Harley et al. in Winter et al., 2007).	English national league players males 10.80 s and females 12.08 s.
	T test	Forward sprint (9.14 m) followed by a lateral shuffle with 2 changes of direction (36.56 m) followed by back peddling (9.14m).	Simple field test	Semnick (1990).	9.25 s for male Turkish First division players (Alemdaroğlu, 2012).
Leg power	Vertical jump test	Counter movement jump with arm swing (using a switch mat and timer method).	Simple field test	Test retest correlation of r=0.91 Cv=2.4% (Harley et al. in Winter et al., 2007).	English national league players, males 47 cm and females 33 cm.
Reactive strength	Reactive strength index (RSI) McClymont and Hore (2003).	RSI involves recording contact time following a depth jump and flight time. RSI can be calculated by dividing height jumped in mm by contact time in ms.	Simple field test	The CV% ranged from 2.1% to 3.1% for drop jump heights of 50cm and 20cm respectively (Markwick et al., 2015).	Range for RSI for elite basketball players is between 1.5 and 2.5 (Markwick et al., 2015).
Strength	For strength assessments coaches are directed towards physical competency assessments.				

athlete can be loaded to improve functional strength. Exercises, such as the squat, one legged squat, lunge, hop and hold, pull ups and push ups should be assessed in terms of movement proficiency (control, symmetry and range of motion during the movements through the required rep range) prior to loading the client. One repetition max testing can be used to assess strength; however, technique can influence performance and sometimes technique is compromised during the execution of testing. Physical competency assessment standards for elite and sub elite basketball players, however, has currently not been reported in the literature. Readers are directed to the physical competency section of the tennis chapter in this book, as the Lawn Tennis Association S & C department have developed a battery of physical competency assessments with full explanation of protocols and levels of competency. Future research needs to be conducted on elite and sub-elite basketball players to develop appropriate physical competency levels for basketball players of different genders, playing standards and age groups. As a guideline it is fairly common practice for trained basketball players to be able to perform a 1 repetition maximum back squat of one and a half times their body weight and 10 wide armed pronated grip pull ups with a resistance of 10% body weight using a weighted vest.

Training programme design

Successful performance in basketball requires the athlete to have effective physical conditioning that will allow them to repeatedly and consistently overcome the on court demands placed upon them. The detailed demands of the sport have been discussed earlier in this chapter. It is clear that basketball players are required to possess an effective aerobic and anaerobic energy production profile in order to maintain a high physical intensity and perform multiple short duration, high intensity actions (in a variety of planes of motion and with numerous changes of direction) throughout the duration of the match.

Periodisation

The complexity of providing programs for basketball players that achieve the aforementioned objectives often necessitates that whole training is compartmentalised (through periodisation) into smaller, focused training blocks or cycles (macrocycle, mesocycle, microcycle). Simenz et al. (2005) showed that 85% of NBA coaches implemented a periodised training model and that the type of periodisation used varied between coaches (Simenz et al., 2005). Periodisation training involves the manipulation of the two key training variables, volume and intensity. This manipulation alters the physiological stimulus provided to the body's systems in an effort to maximise the desired adaptations targeted through the particular training cycle (e.g. increased muscle size during a hypertrophy cycle). An overload phase, which provides a training stimulus, is typically followed by a period of reduced volume and intensity, which allows for recovery and subsequent adaptation to occur (Nunes et al., 2014).

If employing a block-periodised model, the S&C coach will prioritise anatomical adaptation and hypertrophy in pre-season. The anatomical adaptations and hypertrophy phases of training will strengthen the tendons, ligaments and joints and increase the muscle cross-sectional area, which lays the foundations for the other phases of training (Bompa and Buzzichelli, 2015) and the development of sport-specific physical qualities. Following a hypertrophy mesocycle, coaches may choose to prescribe training cycles that develop maximal strength before transferring into specific strength. This will typically occur as the season shifts from preparation to competition.

Programming

Although the terms periodisation and programming are often used interchangeably, they refer to different aspects of training design. Periodisation is the combination of programming and planning, whereas programming is the act of filling the structured plan with training modalities (Bompa and Buzzichelli, 2015). When programming for basketball, the S&C coach needs to focus on developing the specific physical qualities needed for successful performance, individualised to the athlete. The goal of the programme is to allow the athlete to reach peak performance at the time of major competitions or key matches (Bompa and Buzzichelli, 2015).

The explosive/reactive nature of the movements in basketball require concentric (generation of ground reaction force for jumping and running) and eccentric (force absorption on landing and during deceleration) strength. The movements above can be described as stretch shortening cycle activities and require the athlete to generate high rates of force development (Taylor, in Jeffreys and Moody, 2016) sometimes with minimal ground contact time. Greater muscular strength is associated with improved force-time characteristics (e.g. rate of force development, external mechanical power) general sport specific movement performance (e.g. jumping, change of direction) and a reduction in injury rates (Suchomel et al., 2016). Therefore, it appears crucial that the S&C programme for the basketball athlete incorporates exercise selections that promote improvements in muscular strength, particularly those that generate high rates of force development and improve stability. A recent meta-analysis concluded that Olympic lifting is an effective training modality for improving vertical jump performance (Hackett et al., 2016). It is important to note in this review article similar effects on vertical jump were observed for plyometric training. The amount of time the strength and conditioning coach has access to the players may influence the intervention given because of the technical nature of performing Olympic lifts and the time it takes to learn proficient technique.

Training prescription and exercise selection

The proportion of energy production from aerobic and anaerobic pathways is still under some debate; however, the importance of anaerobic fitness in order to perform short duration high intensity movements (sprints, jumps, changes of direction, blocking, etc.) is without question. The importance of players possessing a high level of aerobic fitness has been questioned by Taylor (2004), who advocates the implementation of a tactical metabolic training model where interval conditioning drills are based upon time-motion analysis data, which he suggests is predominately aimed at the improvement of anaerobic capacity. On the other hand, Ben Abdelkrim et al. (2009) and Ben Abdelkrim et al. (2010a) provide evidence to support the importance of players possessing a good level of aerobic conditioning. Increases in blood metabolites in the later parts of the games combined with a drop in high intensity activity in the 2nd and 4th quarters demonstrate an increasing aerobic contribution and increase in fatigue in the later stages of matches, leading Ben Abdelkrim et al. (2009, p. 772) to conclude that "maximal aerobic power training should form a significant part of any physical fitness program for competitive basketball players."

The authors of this chapter agree with both Taylor (2004) and Ben Abdelkrim et al. (2009) conclusions based upon their research findings but feel that Taylor (2004) is underestimating the aerobic contribution to energy production in his definition of his tactical metabolic training model. Therefore, an impactful training programme for basketball players needs to develop the physiological characteristics required to enable the athlete to achieve a consistent high work rate, reduce the effects of accumulative fatigue along with the increased ability to perform repeated short term anaerobic activities. Implementing interval training that mimics the demands of

Table 12.2 Example on court interval training principles

Work time (s)	Intensity (% of perceived maximum effort)	Distance and task	Work:rest ratio with active recovery
Short term (approximately 5 seconds)	95%	17 m with 2 changes of direction. Base line to free throw line back to back pedal to base line and sprint back to three throw line.	Approximately 1:10 Slow jog the rest of the length of the court and back
Short–medium term (approximately 7 to 10 seconds)	90%	28 m with 1 change of direction. Base line to half way line and back.	1:5 Slow jog two lengths of the court recovery
Medium term (10 to 15 seconds)	85%	39.6 m with 3 changes of direction. Base line to free throw line back pedal to base line sprint back to the half way line and back to base line.	1:5 Slow jog two lengths of the court recovery
Long term (25 to 30 seconds)	80%	84 m with 5 changes of direction. Base line to free throw and side step back to base line, run back to the half way line and run back to base line, run to far three throw line and back to base line.	1:3 Slow jog two lengths of the court recovery

the sport, which involves repeated high intensity short duration efforts with multiple changes of direction, including a variety of movement patterns, is recommended based on the training principles outlined in Table 12.2. As discussed previously improvements in aerobic performance along with improvements in technical ability can also be achieved through small sided games (Delextrat and Martinez, 2014). The key with interval training is to adjust the work intensity according to the duration of the interval to optimise physiological overload. The shorter the interval the higher the intensity at which the exercise can be performed and visa versa. If intervals are performed at too high an intensity for too long, metabolic waste products will accumulate and the player's ability to perform the next rep with the desired intensity will be compromised. This type of on court interval training should be performed during the pre-season and in season training phases.

When considering programming at the sessional level, exercises that require the athlete to generate high rates of force development and impulse production, through use of whole-body or multi-joint movements (e.g. squats and derivatives, Olympic lifts and derivatives, plyometrics) should be planned early in the session while players are fresh (Taylor, in Jeffreys and Moody, 2016) minimising the risk of fatigue negatively influencing the quality of the movements performed (Plisk, 2008). In a recent meta-analysis, it was shown that when selecting exercises that encourage high rates of force development, loads of greater than 70%1RM result in greater power production in power clean and hang power cleans, loads between 30 and 70%1RM provide an optimal for power production during squat exercises, and less than 30%1RM generates higher peak power production for jump squats (Soriano et al., 2015). Coaches are recommended to gain optimal power profiles for different exercises for each athlete using velocity based tools such as a GymAware or velocity band. An example specific strength, high-rate force development programme is provided in Table 12.3. It should be noted

Table 12.3 Session examples focusing on high rate of force development exercise. BB= barbell BM = body mass

Exercise	Sets	Reps	Load (kg)
Power clean	3	4	>70%1RM
Push jerk	3	4	>70%1RM
Weighted pull ups	3	4	>30 to <70%1RM
Squat	3	4	70%1RM
Power snatch	3	4	>70%1RM
BB countermovement jump	3	4	<30%1RM
Bench press	3	4	>70%1RM
Glute bridge	3	10	50–75%1RM
Broad jump	4	5	BM
Bounding	4	5	BM
Pogo jumps	4	5	BM
Jerk jumps	4	5	BM

that the exercises selected and the programme presented are a general guide; it will not be appropriate for all basketball athletes. If the S&C coach decides to implement the programme, they should do so after an appropriate warm up, and after considering a number of factors including (but not exclusive to) the athlete's movement competency, current level of strength, training background, injury history, training focus, stage of the annual periodised cycle, and upcoming competition/training schedule.

Plyometric training

As mentioned earlier in the chapter there is evidence to suggest that the implementation of plyometric type exercise into a player's training programme will not only enhance vertical jump ability (Hackett et al., 2016) but will also lead to reduced risk of ACL injury (Stevenson et al., 2015). Drills should include combinations of bounding, hopping and depth jump exercises that involve the stretch shortening cycle, performed in short bouts (between one and four maximal jumps) at maximal intensity activity with the aim of keeping the ground contact time as short as possible between foot contacts. The total ground contacts during any one plyometric session will vary depending upon a player's level of conditioning and could vary from between 30 (novice athlete) and 200 (trained athlete) foot contacts. For a more detailed discussion on plyometric training principles, practice and screening assessments, see Goodwin and Jeffreys in Jeffreys and Moody (2016).

Hydration effects on basketball performance

It has been demonstrated that dehydration can negatively influence attentional vigilance (Baker et al., 2007a) and basketball skilled performance (Baker et al., 2007b) and that players are poor at estimating sweat loss (Thigpen et al., 2014). Thigpen et al. (2014) also reported the NCAA division II players in their study reported to training in a state of hypohydration; therefore, S&C coaches should be vigilant in educating and monitoring hydration status during training and competition to help avoid the negative effects of hypohydration on performance.

Conclusion

The design of any individual physical training programme will depend upon a variety of factors including (but are not exclusive to) training status of the player, time and facilities available, the player's physical strengths and weaknesses, and the volume/intensity of training stimulus being implemented through on court sports specific training. Using the assessments and screening tools described earlier in the chapter, coaches can prioritise the areas in which players require improvement as part of their individual training programmes and monitor the effectiveness of their interventions. Strength and conditioning coaches working in basketball are encouraged to develop a philosophy of practice based upon the evidence provided and develop individual training programmes for their clients aimed at consolidating their strengths and addressing areas of weakness. Effective physical conditioning for basketball players is multifaceted and complex. From an energy systems perspective, basketball athletes are required to effectively develop both aerobic and anaerobic energy pathways to meet the demands of match play. From a muscular strength perspective, developing strong, robust players who express sound movement capabilities is desirable. Improving muscular strength (throughout the strength/speed continuum) can bring about desirable alterations to the physical qualities of the basketball player and helps to reduce the risk of lower limb injuries that were highlighted earlier in the chapter. The foundation of any strength programme is to develop the physical competency of the player by addressing any muscle imbalances, improving functional range of motion and improving sports specific movement force production. These improvements can help to influence in-game movements (jumping, landing, change of direction, etc.) and therefore the likelihood of successful performance and reduction in injury prevalence. Finally the aims of the strength and conditioning coach should be integrated with the aims of other members of the athlete support team (e.g. technical coaches, team managers, etc.) to help create a successful, well designed, and considered strength and conditioning support programme which needs to be communicated effectively to the athletes to aid compliance.

References

Abdelkrim, N. B., Castagna, C., Jabri, I., Battikh, T., El Fazaa, S. and El Ati, J. (2010) "Activity Profile and Physiological Requirements of Junior Elite Basketball Players in Relation to Aerobic-Anaerobic Fitness". *The Journal of Strength & Conditioning Research*. 24(9): 2330–2342.

Agel, J., Arendt, E.A. and Bershadsky, B. (2005) "Anterior Cruciate Ligament Injury in National Collegiate Athletic Association Basketball and Soccer: A 13-Year Review". *American Journal of Sports Medicine*. 33: 524–530.

Agel, J., Olson, D.E., Dick, R., Arendt, E.A., Marshall, S.W. and Sikka, R.S. (2007) "Descriptive Epidemiology of Collegiate Women's Basketball Injuries: National Collegiate Athletic Association Injury Surveillance System, 1988–1989 Through 2003–2004". *Journal of Athletic Training*. 42(2): 202–210.

Alemdaroğlu, U. (2012) "The Relationship Between Muscle Strength, Anaerobic Performance, Agility, Sprint Ability and Vertical Jump Performance in Professional Basketball Players". *Journal of Human Kinetics*. 31(1): 149–158.

Baker, L., Conroy, D. and Kenney, W. (2007a) "Dehydration Impairs Vigilance-related Attention in Male Basketball Players". *Medicine and Science in Sport and Exercise*. 39(6): 976–983.

Baker, L., Dougherty, K., Chow, M. and Kenney, W. (2007b) "Progressive Dehydration Causes a Progressive Decline in Basketball Skill Performance". *Medicine and Science in Sport and Exercise*. 39(7): 1114–1123.

Ben Abdelkrim, N., Castagna, C., El Fazaa, S. et al. (2010a) "The Effect of Players' Standard and Tactical Strategy on Game Demands in Men's Basketball". *The Journal of Strength & Conditioning Research*. 24(10): 2652–2662.

Ben Abdelkrim, N., Castagna, C., El Fazaa, S., Tabka, Z. and Ati, J.E. (2009) "Blood Metabolites During Basketball Competitions". *The Journal of Strength & Conditioning Research*. 23(3): 765–773.

Ben Abdelkrim, N., Castagna, C., Jabri, I. et al. (2010b) "Activity Profile and Physiological Requirements of Junior Elite Basketball Players in Relation to Aerobic-Anaerobic Fitness". *The Journal of Strength & Conditioning Research*. 24(9): 2330–2342.

Ben Abdelkrim, N., El Fazaa, S. and El Ati, J. (2007) "Time-Motion Analysis and Physiological Data of Elite Under 19-Year-Old Basketball Players During Competition". *British Journal of Sports Medicine*. 41(2): 69–75.

Bishop, D.C. and Wright, C. (2006) "A Time-motion Analysis of Professional Basketball to Determine the Relationship Between Three Activity Profiles: High, Medium and Low Intensity and the Length of the Time Spent on Court". *International Journal of Performance Analysis in Sport*. 6(1): 130–139.

Bompa, T. and Buzzichelli, C. (2015) *Periodization Training for Sports*, 3rd ed. Leeds, UK: Human Kinetics.

Castagna, C., Impellizzeri, F.M., Rampinini, E., D'Ottavio, S. and Manzi, V. (2008) "The Yo – Yo Intermittent Recovery Test in Basketball Players". *Journal of Science and Medicine in Sport*. 11(2): 202–208.

Castagna, C., Manzi, V., Impellizzeri, F., Chaouachi, A., Ben Abdelkrim, N. and Ditroilo, M. (2010) "Validity of an On-Court Lactate Threshold Test in Young Basketball Players". *The Journal of Strength & Conditioning Research*. 24(9): 2434–2439.

Chorba, R.S., Chorba, D.J., Bouillon, L.E., Overmyer, C.A. and Landis, J.A. (2010) "Use of a Functional Movement Screening Tool to Determine Injury Risk in Female Collegiate Athletes". *North American Journal of Sports Physical Therapy*. 5(2): 47–54.

Conn, J.M., Annest, J.L. and Gilchrist, J. (2003) "Sports and Recreation Related Injury Episodes in the US Population, 1997–99". *Injury Prevention*. 9: 117–123.

Cook, G., Burton, L. and Hoogenboom, B. (2006a) "Pre-participation Screening: The Use of Fundamental Movements as an Assessment of Function – Part 1". *North American Journal of Sports Physical Therapy*. 1(2): 62.

Cook, G., Burton, L. and Hoogenboom, B. (2006b) "Pre-participation Screening: The Use of Fundamental Movements as an Assessment of Function – Part 2". *North American Journal of Sports Physical Therapy*. 1(3): 132.

Cuchna, J.W., Hoch, M.C. and Hoch, J.M., (2016) "The Interrater and Intrarater Reliability of the Functional Movement Screen: A Systematic Review With Meta-analysis". *Physical Therapy in Sport*. 9: 57–65.

Cumps, E., Verhagen, E. and Meeusen, R. (2007) "Prospective Epidemiological Study of Basketball Injuries During One Competitive Season: Ankle Sprains and Overuse Knee Injuries". *Journal of Sports Science and Medicine*. 6: 204–211.

Deitch, J.R., Starkey, C., Walters, S.L. and Moseley, J.B. (2006) "Injury Risk in Professional Basketball Players: A Comparison of Women's National Basketball Association and National Basketball Association Athletes". *American Journal of Sports Medicine*. 34: 1077–1083.

Delextrat, A. and Martinez, A. (2014) "Small-Sided Game Training Improves Aerobic Capacity and Technical Skills in Basketball Players". *International Journal of Sports Medicine*. 35(5): 385–391.

Dick, R., Hertel, J., Agel, J., Grossman, J. and Marshall S.W. (2007) "Descriptive Epidemiology of Collegiate Men's Basketball Injuries: National Collegiate Athletic Association Injury Surveillance System, 1988–1989 Through 2003–2004". *Journal of Athletic Training*. 42: 194–201.

Goodwin, J. and Jeffreys, I. (2016) "Strength and Conditioning for Basketball". In Jeffreys, I., and Moody, J. (eds.), *Strength and Conditioning for Sports Performance*. Abingdon, UK: Routledge.

Gulgin, H. and Hoogenboom, B. (2014) "The Functional Movement Screening (FMS)™: An Inter-rater Reliability Study Between Raters of Varied Experience". *International Journal of Sports Physical Therapy*. 9(1): 14–20.

Hackett, D., Davies, T., Soomro, N. and Halaki, M. (2016) "Olympic Weightlifting Training Improves Vertical Jump Height in Sports People: A Systematic Review With Meta-analysis". *British Journal of Sports Medicine*. 50: 865–872.

Harley, R.A. (1997) *The Development, Evaluation and Implementation of Sports Specific Fitness Monitoring in Basketball*. Unpublished Master of Philosophy Thesis, University of Brighton.

Harley, R.A. and Doust, J.H. (1997) *Strength and Fitness Training for Basketball: A Sports Science Manual*. Leeds: National Coaching Foundation.

Harley, R.A., Doust, J. and Mills, S. (2007) "Chapter 30: Basketball". In Winter, E., Jones, A., Davidson, R., Bromley, P., and Mercer, T. (eds.), *Sport and Exercise Physiology Testing Guidelines*. London: Routledge.

Hartmann, H., Wirth, K., Keiner, M., Mickel, C., Sander, A. and Szilvas, E. (2015) "Short-term Periodization Models: Effects on Strength and Strength-speed Performance". *Sports Medicine*. 45(10): 1373–1386.

Hoffman, J.R. (2003) "Physiology of Basketball". In D.R. Mckeag (ed.), *Handbook of Sports Medicine and Science: Basketball*, pp. 12–25. London: Blackwell Science.

Markwick, W.J., Bird, S.P., Tufano, J.J., Seitz, L.B. and Haff, G.G. (2015) "The Intraday Reliability of the Reactive Strength Index Calculated From a Drop Jump in Professional Men's Basketball". *International Journal of Sports Physiology and Performance*. 10(4): 482.

Matthew, D. and Delextrat, A. (2009) "Heart Rate, Blood Lactate Concentration, and Time – Motion Analysis of Female Basketball Players During Competition". *Journal of Sports Sciences*. 27(8): 813–821.

McClymont, D. and Hore, A. (2003) "Use of the Reactive Strength Index RSI as a Plyometric Monitoring Tool". In *5th World Congress of Science in Football*, Lisbon.

McInnes, S.E., Carlson, J.S., Jones, C.J. and McKenna, M.J. (1995) "The Physiological Load Imposed on Basketball Players During Competition". *Journal of Sports Sciences*. 13(5): 387–397.

Meeuwisse, W.H., Sellmer, R. and Hagel, B.E. (2003) "Rates and Risks of Injury During Intercollegiate Basketball". *American Journal of Sports Medicine*. 31: 379–385.

Narazaki, K., Berg, K., Stergiou, N. and Chen, B. (2009) "Physiological Demands of Competitive Basketball". *Scandinavian Journal of Medicine & Science in Sports*. 19(3): 425–432.

Nunes, J.A., Moreira, A., Crewther, B.T. et al. (2014) "Monitoring Training Load, Recovery-Stress State, Immune-Endocrine Responses, and Physical Performance in Elite Female Basketball Players During a Periodized Training Program". *Journal of Strength and Conditioning Research*. 28: 2973–2980.

Plisk, S. (2008) "Speed, Agility, and Speed-Endurance Development". In Beachle, T.R. and Earle, R.W. (eds.), *Essentials of Strength Training and Conditioning*, 3rd ed., pp. 458–485. Champaigh, IL: Human Kinetics.

Ramsbottom, R., Brewer, J. and Williams, C. (1988) "A Progressive Shuttle Run Test to Estimate Maximal Oxygen Uptake". *British Journal of Sports Medicine*. 22(4): 141–144.

Rodriguez-Alonso, M., Fernandez-Garcia, B., Perez-Landaluce, J. et al. (2003) "Blood Lactate and Heart Rate During National and International Women's Basketball". *Journal of Sports Medicine and Physical Fitness*. 43(4): 432.

Scanlan, A., Dascombe, B. and Reaburn, P. (2011) "A Comparison of the Activity Demands of Elite and Sub-elite Australian Men's Basketball Competition". *Journal of Sports Sciences*. 29(11): 1153–1160.

Seminick, D. (1990) "The Line Drill Test". *National Strength and Conditioning Association Journal*. 12(2): 47–49.

Simenz, C.J., Dugan, C.A. and Ebben, W.P. (2005) "Strength and Conditioning Practices of National Association Basketball Association Strength and Conditioning Coaches". *Journal of Strength and Conditioning Research*. 19(3): 495–504.

Soriano, M.A., Jimenez-Reyes, P., Rhea, M.R. and Marin, P.J. (2015) "The Optimal Load for Maximal Power Production During Lower-Body Resistance Exercises: A Meta-Analysis". *Sports Medicine*. 45(8): 1191–1205.

Starkey, C. (2000) "Injuries and Illnesses in the National Basketball Association: A 10-year Perspective". *Journal of Athletic Training*. 35: 161–167.

Stevenson, J.H., Beattie, C.S., Schwartz, J.B. and Busconi, B.D. (2015) "Assessing the Effectiveness of Neuromuscular Training Programs in Reducing the Incidence of Anterior Cruciate Ligament Injuries in Female Athletes: A Systematic Review". *The American Journal of Sports Medicine*. 43(2): 482–490.

Suchomel, T.J., Nimphius, S. and Stone, M.H. (2016) "The Importance of Muscular Strength in Athletic Performance". *Sports Medicine*. 46(10): 1419–1449.

Taylor, J. (2004) "A Tactical Metabolic Training Model for Collegiate Basketball". *Strength and Conditioning Journal*. 26(5): 22–29.

Taylor, J.H. (2016) "Strength and Conditioning for Basketball". In Jeffreys, I., and Moody, J. (eds.), *Strength and Conditioning for Sports Performance*. Abingdon, UK: Routledge.

Thigpen, L.K., Green, J.M. and O'Neal, E.K. (2014) "Hydration Profile and Sweat Loss Perception of Male and Female Division II Basketball Players During Practice". *Journal of Strength and Conditioning Research*. 28(12): 3425–3431.

Winter, E.M., Bromley, P.D., Davidson, R.C., Jones, A.M. and Mercer, T.H. (2007) *Sport and Exercise Physiology Testing Guidelines: The British Association of Sport and Exercise Sciences Guide*, Vol. 1. London: Routledge.

Zelisko, J.A., Noble, H.B. and Porter, M. (1982) "A Comparison of Men's and Women's Professional Basketball Injuries". *American Journal of Sports Medicine*. 10: 297–299.

Ziv, G. and Lidor, R. (2009) "Physical Attributes, Physiological Characteristics, On-Court Performances and Nutritional Strategies of Female and Male Basketball Players". *Sports Medicine*. 39(7): 547–568.

13
CRICKET

Phil Scott and Ross Herridge

Introduction

Over the past two decades there has been a rise in popularity in cricket with over 100 nations recognized by the International Cricket Council (ICC) (Johnstone and Ford, 2010). The general aim of the game is for one batting team to try and score as many runs as they can against a team trying to restrict these runs by taking wickets through bowling and fielding.

Both domestic and international cricket involve three types of format: 20-over (T20), 50-over and multiple day. T20, the most intense format, will last around 3 hours where the maximum number of overs allowed to bat and bowl/field for each team is 20 overs, with each bowler allowed a maximum of 4 overs (Duffield *et al.*, 2009; Petersen *et al.*, 2010; McNamara *et al.*, 2013; Mukandi *et al.*, 2013). 50-over cricket, lasting 6–7 hours, follows the same concept except bowlers are allowed to bowl up to 10 overs each (Duffield *et al.*, 2009; Petersen *et al.*, 2010; McNamara *et al.*, 2013; Mukandi *et al.*, 2013). Multiple day cricket is played up to a maximum of 4 days at first-class domestic level and 5 days for international Test matches. For multiple day cricket there is simply a limit on how many times each team can bat and bowl/field for, which is twice, with no limits on overs bowled for bowlers and a minimum of 96 overs in a day's play which will last around 7–8 hour including breaks (Duffield *et al.*, 2009; Petersen *et al.*, 2010; McNamara *et al.*, 2013; Mukandi *et al.*, 2013).

Players have differing roles within the team including batsmen, bowlers, wicket-keepers and all-rounders (i.e. a specialist batter and bowler or wicket-keeper and batsman) with all players fielding at any one point during the match (McNamara *et al.*, 2013; Duffield *et al.*, 2009). With these different roles within the team and match formats, there are obviously varying physiological demands for each position. Understanding the physical demands of a sport is key for any conditioning coach when programming, yet research with elite cricket players is limited (Duffield and Drinkwater, 2008). Previous research in cricket has included biomechanical analysis (Welch *et al.*, 1995; Bartlett *et al.*, 1998; Hurrion *et al.*, 2000), injury surveillance (Elliot, 2000; Pyne *et al.*, 2006; Orchard *et al.*, 2015), time motion analysis (Duffield and Drinkwater, 2008; Rudkin, 2008; Petersen *et al.*, 2010; Petersen *et al.*, 2011), bowling workloads (Dennis *et al.*, 2003; Dennis *et al.*, 2005; McNamara *et al.*, 2013) and physiological responses (Christie *et al.*, 2008; Duffield *et al.*, 2009; Petersen *et al.*, 2011; McNamara *et al.*, 2013).

The physical demands for cricketers have risen dramatically over the past decade especially with the introduction of T20 cricket. It is common to see the fixture list for a first class player in England to include 100 days of play during the six month season, often playing 5 days out of 7 in a week, alongside travelling to different venues (Johnstone et al., 2014). Not only is the sheer volume of matches high, the fixtures may vary between multi-day matches and more intense T20 or one-day matches, although the English Cricket Board (ECB) are currently in the process of addressing this to help the game move forward.

This chapter aims to provide a needs analysis and strength and conditioning programme for cricket players, namely batsmen and bowlers. It will identify pertinent physiological demands, injury analysis, a traditional and alternative fitness testing battery, and a suggested program for a fast bowler and a batter.

The biomechanical and physiological demands of cricket

Cricket is a highly intermittent short sprint sport with a substantial base of low intensity activity that varies depending on the format. For example, the shorter formats (T20 and 50-over) are more intense per unit of time whilst multiday cricket have a greater total load (Petersen et al., 2010). Concentrating specifically on batting in the shorter formats of the game, scoring a 100 runs in 50-over cricket has been reported to have a high to low intensity activity (HiLiA) ratio of 1:47 (Duffield and Drinkwater, 2008) and 1:50 (Petersen et al., 2010), which is more than sufficient time to replenish the phosphocreatine stores, especially when the high intensity activities last on average 2.6 ± 1.1 seconds (striding) and 1.2 ± 0.9 seconds (sprinting) (Duffield and Drinkwater, 2008). Petersen et al. (2010) reported there to be a lower and therefore more intense HiLiA ratio in T20 of 1:38 with a mean heart rate of 149 ± 17 beats.min^{-1}. These ratios are reported to be carried out over a distance of 8.7 ± 0.6 km in a one-day innings (up to 4 hours) with 500m of sprinting (Petersen et al., 2010). In a full T20 innings of 80 minutes, a distance of 3.5 ± 0.2 km is covered with 175 ± 97 m of sprinting (5.01 m.s^{-1} or > 18kph), a mean heart rate of 144 ± 13 beat.min^{-1} and max heart rate of 181 ± 14 beat.min^{-1} (Petersen et al., 2010). The sprints that take place as a batsman are constantly between two sets of stumps 22 yards (20.1m) apart, highlighting the importance of change of direction and thus the ability to accelerate and decelerate to a high skill level. With the ability of the batsman to make use of the crease (where they must stand in order not to be 'run out') through running in their bat, this sprint distance can be taken down to 19.4 yards (17.7m). The batsman can reach speeds of up to 26–28 kph running between the wickets (personal unpublished data; Source: Catapult GPS). Note that this reports only one skill and that the batsman will then have to field for the duration of the opposing team's innings.

Similar themes exist in terms of intensity for non-bowling fielders, such as 1:43 and 1:62 HiLiA ratio for T20 and one-day respectively (Petersen et al., 2010). Specifically, the fast bowlers have less recovery time with 1:25 and 1:25 HiLiA ratio for T20 and one-day respectively (Petersen et al., 2010). In total, they will be covering 13.4 ± 0.7 km (316 ± 121m of sprinting) in one-day cricket and 5.5 ± 0.4 km (406 ± 230m of sprinting) in T20 cricket with a mean heart rate of 133 ± 12 beat.min^{-1} and maximum of 181 ± 10 beat.min^{-1} (Petersen et al., 2010). More recently, bowlers have been seen to cover up to 8 km during T20 match fielding sessions (personal unpublished data; Source: Catapult GPS). The higher number of sprinting metres in T20 compared to 50-over cricket, although over a lesser time, could be due to the high intensity nature of the format and the fielding that also has to be carried out after or during their bowling spells. Interestingly, Petersen et al. (2010) reported that only fast bowlers had more than one repeated sprint bout (a cluster of three or more sprints with less than 60 seconds recovery) with an average of 4.8 ± 1.4 sprints and 5.0 ± 1.4 sprint for T20 and one day matches respectively and these numbers generally matched the number of overs bowled. Petersen *et al.* (2010) also reported that efforts from fast bowlers > 12.5 kph only lasted an average of 2.7 seconds, which at sprinting speeds would translate to around 15–20 m of work, that being either a run up for a delivery or accelerating towards a ball in the field.

Since we know that higher levels of lower limb strength are associated with improved power output (Stone, 2003), sprint time (Comfort *et al.*, 2012; Hermassi *et al.*, 2011; McBride *et al.*, 2009), 180º change of direction time (Castillo-Rodriguez *et al.*, 2012) and throwing velocity (Chelly *et al.*, 2010; Hermassi *et al.*, 2011), then both batsmen and bowlers should seek improvements in strength and power qualities in order to impact on their physical performance on the field. Also it is known that upper body strength is positively correlated ($r = 0.63$) to maximum hitting distance in cricket batting (Taliep *et al.*, 2010) and ball release speed in fast bowling (Pyne *et al.*, 2006), whilst rotational torso strength (Szymanski *et al.*, 2007) and upper body strength, specifically the bench press (Miyaguchi *et al.*, 2012) is correlated ($r = 0.59$) to higher bat swing velocities.

Bowlers undergo a large amount of twisting, bending, rotation, flexion and extension over a short period of time (McGrath *et al.*, 1996). Biomechanical and kinematic determinants of fast bowling have been reported to be related to run up speed, upper trunk flexion from front-foot contact until ball release, shoulder angle at front-foot contact and knee angle of the front leg on release (Glazier *et al.*, 2000; Loram *et al.*, 2005; Portus *et al.*, 2007; Salter *et al.*, 2007; Worthington *et al.*, 2013). Fast bowlers have to endure high peak vertical ground reaction forces (vGRF) (3–12 times body weight) on front foot contact at the crease (Foster *et al.*, 1989; Elliott, 2000; Hurrion *et al.*, 2000; Phillips *et al.*, 2010) and therefore need to be strong enough to cope with this requirement that has to be repeated up to 24 times in a T20 match and 60 times in a 50-over match, along side all the other factors previously mentioned. There are two types of front foot contact at the crease when bowling, the heel-toe or the flat foot contact. In the flat foot contact, peak average vertical ground reaction force (vGRF) occurs 23 milliseconds (ms) after initial contact and the heel-toe technique occurs at 32 ms with an average vGRF of 5.3 body weight (Stuelcken *et al.*, 2007). Either way, this is a high amount of force to be absorbed and controlled in a short time frame, especially as coaches are looking for as little bend or as much stiffness in that front leg as possible on delivery. This enables maximum transfer of force and again highlights the need for high levels of strength and stiffness alongside speed and efficiency of the run up.

When striking the ball powerfully, a batsman requires a stable base from which power is delivered in a sequenced and coordinated fashion initiated at the hips, through the trunk and transferred through the arms to the bat (Shaffer *et al.*, 1993). The key movements when batting include a largely lateral lunge type movement towards the ball with a rotational component when striking (Garhammer, 1983). The torso/trunk strength is a key factor in the ability to powerfully strike a ball with improved rotational strength being shown to improve bat velocity, angular hip velocity and angular shoulder velocity (Szymanski *et al.*, 2007). The antagonistic muscles play a large role in delivering speed and accuracy of the striking of the ball allowing large deceleration forces to be used after high-speed contact (Stretch, 1993c; Wierzbicka and Wienger, 1996). As mentioned, batsmen are required to run between the wickets, indicating that change of direction ability, acceleration and deceleration play, arguably, more of a role for batsman than fast bowlers; although when required to bat the fast bowlers will still have to deliver these skills. Note that if the fast bowlers are in bat and required to run between the wickets, it generally means the situation of the game is near the end and runs at this time point are likely to be important and can be the difference between winning and losing; therefore, bowlers must also be able to deliver these change of direction based skills to a high level.

In conclusion, it is essential for cricket players to reach and maintain an adequate level of strength and power in order to optimize performance and reduce injury.

Injury prevalence

Although strictly a non-contact sport, cricket injuries can result in a number of ways, with impact injuries resulting from a direct blow from the ball, bat or unusually as a result of a collision between two players (Finch et al., 1999). Protective equipment and game rules have developed largely over the past decade with the aim to prevent these injuries. At the elite level, overuse injuries are more common, especially with the upsurge in volume of fixtures in first-class cricket (Orchard et al., 2005; Orchard et al., 2014). In terms of physical preparation, strength and conditioning training can facilitate a reduction in non-contact injuries.

Table 13.1 shows injury prevalence by player position in elite Australian cricket players; data was collected during the seasons of 2005–6 to 2013–14. This data indicates that consistently, for over more than a decade, fast bowlers are at higher risk of injury. These are supported by further longitudinal studies as shown in Table 13.2.

In an additional longitudinal study with elite Australian cricketers, it was reported that fast bowlers are 3 times more likely to be injured than other positions (Orchard et al., 2006). Injury sites reported are identified in Table 13.3 with the most common site for fast bowler injuries

Table 13.1 Injury prevalence by player position 2005–6 to 2013–14 of elite Australian cricket players

	Av 96–7 to 04–5	Av 05–6 to 13–14	2005–6	2006–7	2007–8	2008–9	2009–10	2010–11	2011–12	2012–13	2003–14
Batsman	4.4%	7.2%	6.4%	5.4%	7.0%	6.7%	7.3%	9.1%	9.2%	5.6%	7.8%
Keeper	2.0%	5.1%	3.0%	0.5%	1.7%	3.0%	9.0%	8.0%	13.6%	1.2%	3.2%
Pace bowler	15.2%	19.9%	14.4%	18.8%	18.8%	19.7%	21.0%	24.2%	25.0%	19.8%	16.9%
Spinner	4.1%	7.2%	8.5%	18.8%	9.9%	3.8%	3.5%	10.8%	10.4%	10.8%	4.7%

Table 13.2 Longitudinal studies monitoring injuries of elite cricketers by playing position

Author	Study	Comments	Batsmen	Wicket keeper	Pace bowler	Spin bowler	Fielding	Other
Orchard et al. (2002)	Injury prevalence to Australian crickets at first class level 1995–2001	Values are total number of incidences	56	4	126	60	281	
Stretch (2003)	Longitudinal study of the nature of injuries to South African cricketers	Values are percentages over a 3-season period	17.1	Included in fielding section	41.3	28.6		13
Orchard et al. (2005)	Injuries to male cricketers over a 10-year period	2004–2005 season. Values are a percentage of injury prevalence	9.5	3.2	9.5	4.2	Not reported	
Orchard et al. (2014	Injury report 2014 – cricket Australia	2013–14 season. Values are a percentage of injury prevalence	7.8	3.2	16.9	4.7	Not reported	

Table 13.3 Injury seasonal incidences by body area (injuries per squad, per season) of elite male Australian cricketers over a 10-year period

Region	1995–96	1996–97	1997–98	1998–99	1999–2000	2000–01	2001–02	2002–03	2003–04	2004–05
Head/facial	0.7	0.0	0.2	0.2	0.3	0.2	1.3	0.2	0.3	0.3
Neck	0.2	0.4	0.0	0.0	0.2	0.3	0.0	0.0	0.0	0.0
Shoulder	7.0	0.0	1.4	1.2	1.4	1.0	1.6	1.4	0.4	1.1
Arm/elbow	0.0	0.2	0.3	0.5	0.5	0.5	0.0	1.1	0.1	0.3
Wrist/hand	1.4	1.6	1.3	1.6	1.4	2.2	1.8	1.8	1.6	2.3
Trunk	0.7	1.4	1.1	2.1	1.0	2.2	2.3	0.5	1.6	1.4
Low back	1.6	1.6	1.1	2.0	1.6	1.9	1.6	3.4	2.7	1.4
Groin/thigh	3.4	2.7	5.2	5.2	2.4	4.5	3.6	4.2	5.9	3.3
Knee	0.5	2.0	1.3	2.3	2.2	2.4	2.0	1.0	0.8	0.9
Shin/foot/ankle	3.0	1.8	2.3	2.3	2.6	1.9	3.4	3.4	3.7	3.2
Illness	0.5	1.3	1.6	9.0	2.6	0.3	0.9	1.0	0.8	1.1
Total injures	12.6	13.0	15.8	18.4	16.2	17.5	18.3	17.8	18.1	15.1

being the hip area/lower back and adolescent bowlers being at higher risk of injury (Stretch, 2003); this is supported by Foster et al. (1989) and Elliott (2000). This is somewhat unsurprising due to the high impact nature of fast bowling (see biomechanical and physiological demands of cricket section) which is absorbed by soft tissues and the lower back (Foster et al., 1989; Elliott, 2000; Hurrion et al., 2000; Mukandi et al., 2013).

Another reason fast bowlers are at significantly higher risk of injury is the workload they have to endure during a match. Across all formats of the game, fast bowlers cover 20–80% greater distances, 2–7 times more high intensity distance with significantly less recovery time between bouts (Hulin et al., 2014). The fact that during the delivery stride bowlers have to absorb 3–12 times their body weight (Foster et al., 1989; Elliott, 2000; Hurrion et al., 2000; Phillips et al., 2010), with an action including lateral flexion/extension and rotation up to 150 times during a single day, may highlight a factor as to why stress fractures and hamstring/trunk soft tissue injuries are prevalent in fast bowlers (Foster et al., 1989; Elliott, 2000; Stretch, 2003; Orchard et al., 2002; Orchard et al., 2009; Orchard et al., 2014) as well as why they experience more biomechanical impact injuries such as ankle sprains or chronic shoulder issues.

It has been suggested that bowlers who bowl fewer than 40 deliveries per session (training or match) may be at an increased risk of injury, and should thus aim to bowl 123–188 balls per week; this suggests there is a minimum as well as maximum threshold for bowling workload that can predict injury (Dennis et al., 2003). Supporting this, Hulin et al. (2014) stated that bowlers with fewer than 2 days or more than 5 days between bowling sessions could be at higher risk of injury. Of note is the finding from Stretch (2003) that 45.3% of fast bowlers' injuries took place in the pre or early part of the season. The start of the cricket season signifies a large increase in volume load for a player compared to the off-season, with matches across different formats alongside training, which means overs bowled per week for a player will naturally spike. This information highlights the previous point that being appropriately conditioned and monitoring load is key for injury prevention. This information has implications for strength and conditioning coaches looking at workload monitoring of fast bowlers. Coaches should be aware of the physical demands of bowling and the risk of injury when under bowling as well as over bowling, along with the acute cumulative effect of bowling on chronic load and its risk of injury as stated above.

Other injuries that happen during fielding and batting typically occur to the lower limbs. The nature of cricket means that there are intermittent bursts in high intensity sprinting to stop a ball or to run a quick single when batting, mixed with long periods of standing in the field or jogging/walking. These intermittent high intensity efforts mean the muscles in the lower limbs are more susceptible to injury so appropriate conditioning of this region is vital alongside an approach to positively effect running mechanics (Small et al., 2009).

Fitness testing battery

In this section we will present first what is generally considered the standard, most used tests in professional cricket today (Table 13.4). Table 13.5 presents a list of exercises or tests that are also useful but used by various practitioners within the sport on a varying basis.

Fitness testing during the off-season gives players a focus point during a training block by setting them individual physical targets based around the results. Under guidelines set by the national governing body, the ECB, testing must take place at three time points during the season (start of the off-season, start of the playing season and end of season). Prescription of tests within the battery can also be limited as counties must administer certain tests as a monitoring tool for all county players set by the ECB, which may limit the opportunity of some tests (e.g. the Yo-Yo Intermittent Recovery Test must be administered, which limits the opportunity to complete the MAS 30–15 test due to fatiguing factors). However, beyond this coaches can choose what and when to test.

Testing can be used as a useful monitoring tool to judge the efficacy of the programs that coaches deliver. If players' results are not as expected after a training block, then it will allow coaches to reflect and address the player or programme delivery accordingly. Testing opportunities in-season are limited due to the fixture list, with this in mind useful monitoring tools can be used to track changes in physical performance. Jump tests are commonly used as well as maximal strength testing days if the schedule allows for this alongside the use of timing gates during speed sessions. As a general rule, strength maintenance is the main focus during the season whilst concentrating more on player's recovery and physical preparation for fixtures.

Table 13.4 Traditional fitness testing battery

Test	Description
Functional movement screen	Over head squat, single leg squat assessment for movement deficiencies (Dennis et al., 2008).
Skinfold assessment	Using the ISAK method, sum of 80 (Portus et al., 2000).
Counter movement jump	CMJ for the test of lower body power. Ideally the test would include peak power (Owen et al., 2013) although CMJ with jump height is often used.
5m, 10m, 20m, 40m sprint time	Both acceleration and top speed are tested covering all possibilities in the field.
Run 2 between the wickets	This is batsman specific, testing the ability to accelerate and decelerate whilst running between the wickets with a bat in hand.
3–5 RM strength	Testing for strength within the back squat, pull ups, bench press. With a county pre-season these tests can almost be accumulated through normal training sessions especially at the end of the preseason training block.
YOYO Intermittent Recovery Test	An aerobic inter-effort recovery capacity test that includes acceleration and deceleration.

Table 13.5 Alternative tests that can and have been used

Agility tests

Repeated run 2 – This is the same set up as the 'run 2' but the athlete competes six runs in a row starting every 30 seconds. From this a Phosphocreatine decrement percentage score can be obtained: ((first time–last time)/first time)*100.

505 agility – This test is used to measure the change of direction skill and shows a strong correlation ($r = 0.909$–0.934; $p \leq 0.01$) towards cricket specific sprint tests running between the wickets with a bat in hand (Foden *et al.*, 2015).

40m Repeated sprint test

This follows the same protocol as above; however, it excludes the timing of the acceleration and deceleration phase.

Variations of jump tests

These can include a bilateral or unilateral drop jumps aiming towards minimal contact time and maximal height, which will be reflected in the Reactive Strength Index (RSI) score (Flanagan and Comyns, 2008). Squat jump can be utilized alone or alongside the CMJ for an eccentric utilization ratio (EUR) (McGuigan *et al.*, 2006).

Variations of medball throw tests

Throws including a rotational element, from standing or kneeling, for batsman specific testing could be used as an 'on the road' marker within a training session.

Alternative aerobic testing

The 30–15 intermittent fitness test is an accurate method of measuring aerobic fitness whilst the athletes work at high intensities (Buchheit, 2008). A maximal aerobic speed test (MAS) (Leger *et al.*, 1988) originating from the University of Montreal Track Test can also be used and is easy to administer especially with known distances around a cricket pitch.

Within the international set up, the national side has a particularly heavy schedule. For example, the national team had a schedule that meant they were on the road for > 300 days in 2015 with a similar schedule in 2016 onwards. With this in mind, the traditional testing is harder to administer in terms of set times of the year, availability of facilities when abroad, and equipment due to the fact that there are limitations on the amount of kit that it is possible to carry around with the team. Therefore, other ways of monitoring the players have to be designed. The ideal situation for on the road testing is to take up as little training time as possible and therefore aiming to test as an add on to the warm up or within gym sessions is preferred. *Situation 1* – The players will warm up on the field every day finishing with some high intensity sprints of various distances, which is a perfect situation to tag on a timed sprint through the timing gates or utilizing the GPS monitoring to gain a top speed. *Situation 2* – A similar method can be used with the 'run 2' test where a fielding session can be used to challenge the players running between the wickets. Simply set up some timing gates or GPS feedback for the batsman and you have a competitive situation to test the players' skills under pressure. *Situation 3* – One other method used is a regression of training content – for example, in the traditional method one would test an athlete using a YOYO, 30–15 test or MAS test and then produce their cardiovascular (CV) training from that. Working in reverse, it is possible to track the players' levels. For example, if they can complete 18 reps of 85 m in 15 seconds with a rest period of 15 seconds, then you know that athlete would be able to achieve around level 20.1 (2400m) in the YOYO test. Therefore, instead of carrying out official testing at training you can complete a training session from which adaptations will occur as well as monitor their CV levels.

In conclusion, you will be challenged by the constraints of your environment and the athlete standing in front of you, so traditional tests that look simple on paper may not be simple to administer and a new method must be created. Building these into warm-ups can be a good way of accommodating a very busy schedule.

Programming

Programming will inevitably be dictated by the individual needs of each player's position, training age, injury history, movement limitations, aims and targets. However, detailed below is what could be considered a basic structure from which to start for both a bowler (Tables 13.7, 13.8, 13.9) and batter (Tables 13.10, 13.11, 13.12). We have left out the wicket keeper position for this chapter. You will notice that because of the standardized example program, we have gone on to detail other potential and specific exercises commonly used on batsman and bowlers (Table 13.13).

As previously mentioned, the challenges in cricket involve large amounts of travel to both foreign countries and other grounds around the UK, with some 2nd XI/'out' grounds not having facilities that would accommodate all these exercises. With this being the case, it is a great test of imagination to create a situation where the athletes can still gain the adaptations they need. For the occasions where there are simply no facilities, you would bring a bag of equipment that can be used, such as medicine balls, weights vest, resistance bands, hurdles, TRX, etc. You may find that days like this can involve a running conditioning, mobility, prehab work or trunk conditioning session, and if there are steps/walls/grassy banks around then you can complete a plyometric session. For example, in South Africa the sloped grassy banks and old school stands with large steps are present in most grounds and make for a perfect alternative. Sprint acceleration work can be carried out utilizing the gradient from the grassy bank while plyometric work up to a single step for box jumps, down from a step for drop jumps or using the whole stand for repeated jumps can be an effective alternative.

An observation when looking at periodization is the contrast in training opportunity between the off-season and in-season. There are in-season challenges for programming as already discussed; however, off-season opportunities are in stark contrast to this, allowing for more of a traditional approach to training. Table 13.6 shows a common approach to the winter training period for a first class cricketer with volume and intensity dovetailing one another leading into the season. Commonly, players are given 3–6 weeks off, post a grueling season as well as 2–3 weeks off over the Christmas period; this typically tends to be in line with the technical coaches' training and opportunity to rest whilst being four months away from the start of the next season. As March/April time approaches, training will tend to lean more towards an untraditional approach as the volume of technical training and match time rises. Although this is common, it is not a 'one size fits all approach'; with the length of off-season, training plans are very much individualized to each player and their positional demands.

In contrast to this, within the first class season and international fixtures there is a very different structure due to the sheer number of playing days. Traditional periodization goes somewhat out of the window. There is the question: 'how often should you do a strength session?' Or more appropriately 'how often *can* you do a strength session?'. The answer will be: 'it depends'. It will depend on the type of match phase you are in. For example, with a T20 block you may play every 3–4 days, where it is easier to carry out a strength session after 24–48 hours of recovery as a bowler, whereas a batsman, with a lower workload, may be able to complete the session sooner. In a multiple day or Test match where all players may have fielded for up to 100–120 overs (6–7 hours) as well as bowled up to 25 overs in a day, there may be the need for a recovery focus before they either go straight out to bat or prepare to bowl again in the second innings. In that case, you

Table 13.6 A common approach to periodization for a first class county off-season

Month	Oct	Nov			Dec				Jan				Feb				Mar				Start of season
Week	– – –	1	2	3	4	5	6	7	8	9	10	11	12	13	14	15	16	17	18	19	
Main focus	Rest	Anatomical adaptation			Rest				Strength/power				Power/speed				Speed				

Table 13.7 Bowler strength/power program

Bowler option 1 exercise	Sets	Reps
Glute thrust	3–5	10–15 + 10 sec isometric hold on last rep
SA row	3–5	8–10
Box jump/plyometric variation	3–5	6–8
*Specific mobility super set	3–5	–
Explosive landmine press/BB split jerk	3–5	5–8 each side
DB step up to box/lunge variation	3–5	4–6 each side
DL/SL RDL	3–5	5–8
Bowler pull-overs (Figure 13.2)	3–5	8–12

Bowler option 2 exercise	Sets	Reps
Hex bar DL/back squat	3–5	3–6
*Specific mobility super set	3–5	–
Pull ups (weighted)	3–5	3-max
Med ball slam variation	3–5	6
Hang power clean/reactive jump squats	3–5	3–6
supine row/prone pull	3–5	4-max
Nordics	3–5	3–8

SA = single arm; BB = barbell; DB = dumbell; DL = double leg; SL = single leg; RDL = Romanian deadlift; OH = over head

would miss a strength session during the game and complete one as soon as able after the game before the next match started.

The sheer volume of matches and short time frames between them requires a large focus on recovery. There are numerous methods of recovery available, but what seems to be the best approach is the idea that the player is content with their choices. Passive recovery methods such as massage, compression garments and naps; active methods such as hydrotherapy and mobility as well as nutrition all play a large part in the process. Teams will vary the type of approach, but it is not uncommon to see group active recovery sessions and then individuals, thereafter, making the choice as to what they would like to pursue.

One avenue explored in order to get your athletes able to complete a strength/power session whilst also optimizing performance for a match is priming. This is traditionally looked upon as a same day modality (Cook et al., 2013b; Ekstrand et al., 2013; Kilduff et al., 2013) where athletes would complete strength or sprint sessions 3–6 hours prior to competition to enhance performance, which would lend itself to the T20 competition particularly. This concept of priming also enables athletes who like their game day routine not to be disturbed to engage in a performance enhancing strategy as well as a beneficial strength session, which would also aid in the reduction of any strength loss by maintaining strength through one to two sessions a week in-season (Graves et al., 1988).

With reference to Table 13.7, the bowler's program, it has been set up to include a strength and power focus and would be carried out in the early January period of pre-season. Exercises can be carried out in supersets to increase training density and improve time efficiency. If athletes cannot carry out a particular exercise due to skill level or a mechanical restriction there are alternatives offered. For example, an alternative to the preferred barbell split jerk could be a single arm jammer (Figure 13.10). The bowler's program will have more of an emphasis on lateral flexion, both through range (medicine ball slams) (Figure 13.1) and also in terms of reactive stiffness (Explosive Pallof Press or OH stiff catch and slam).

(a)

(b)

(c)

Figure 13.1a–c

(a)

(b)

Figure 13.2a and b

Table 13.8 Bowler alternative exercises

Lower & trunk exercise	Lower strength	Lower power
KB overhead press to box step ups (Figure 13.3)	Unbalanced (via weighted band) Box step ups (Figure 13.9)	Jerk
OH medball hop into throw/slam (Figure 13.1)	–	SA jammer (Figure 13.10)
Farmer/OH/SA OH farmer walks	–	SL clean to box step (Figure 13.8) & SL drive to box with plate (Figure 13.12)
OH stiff catch and slam	–	Medball toss (Figure 13.5)
Turkish get ups	–	–

(a) (b)

Figure 13.3a and b

Table 13.9 Bowler trunk conditioning

Exercise	Reps	Sets	Rest
Landmines	6–8 each side	3–4	1 min between rounds
Side plank hip raises	15–20 each side		
Explosive pallof press	5–10 each side		
Med ball slams	6–10 each side		
Ab roll outs	5–10		
Cable twists	6–10 each side		

Table 13.10 Batter strength/power program

Batter option 1 exercise	Sets	Reps
Glute thrust	3–5	10–15 + 10 sec isometric hold on last rep
SA row	3–5	8–10
Box jump/plyometric variation	3–5	6–8
*Specific mobility super set	3–5	–
Reactive jump squats	3–5	6–8
DB step up to box/lunge variation	3–5	4–6 each side
Dl/SL RDL	3–5	5–8
Towel/fat grip pull ups	3–5	5–12

Batter option 2 exercise	Sets	Reps
Hex bar DL/back squat	3–5	3–6
*Specific mobility super set	3–5	–
Hang power clean/reactive jump squats	3–5	3–6
Supine row/prone pull	3–5	5–10
Higuchi isometric cable rotation (Figure 13.4)	3–5	2 × 5 sec hold each arm
Rotational med ball throw variation (Figure 13.7)	3–5	6 each side
Plate grabs	3–5	15–20 each side
Nordics	3–5	5–8

Table 13.11 Batter alternative exercises

Lower & trunk exercise	Lower strength	Lower power
Good morning with OH press (Figure 13.6)	Unbalanced (via weighted band) Box step ups (Figure 13.9)	Jerk
Goblet squat with OH press	–	SA jammer (Figure 13.10)
–	–	SL clean to box step (Figure 13.8)
–	–	Resisted lateral shuffle

(a) (b)

Figure 13.4a and b

(a) (b)

Figure 13.5a and b

(a)

(b)

Figure 13.6a and b

(a)

(b)

Figure 13.7a and b

(a)

(b)

Figure 13.8a and b

(a)

(b)

Figure 13.9a and b

Cricket

Figure 13.10a and b

Table 13.12 Batter trunk conditioning

Exercise	Reps	Sets	Rest
Landmines	6–8 each side	3–4	1 min between rounds
Explosive pallof press	5–10 each side		
Rotational med ball throws (Figure 13.7)	6–10 each side		
Good morning with OH press	10		
Ab roll outs	5–10		
Cable twists	6–10 each side		

The batsmen have a larger focus of rotational power development and grip strength exercises for striking the ball. There is a large demand in cricket of strength and power from a single leg base, be it bowling or batting, hence the single leg focus along side the traditional bilateral compound exercises. There is a larger emphasis for all players on the upper body pull to ensure stability around the shoulder joint with the high demand of throwing and bowling actions. With the occurrence of shoulder impingement issues within cricket a key exercise, whilst still being able to maintain upper body strength, is the floor press (Table 13.13) that restricts the depth of movement thus reducing the strain through the anterior shoulder.

Table 13.13 Any player alternative exercises

Lower & trunk	Lower strength	Lower power	Upper strength	Upper power	Trunk
Turkish get ups	Unbalanced (via weighted band) box step ups (Figure 13.9)	Jerk/rack jerks	Flat/incline bench press	Clap press ups	Pallof press variations
Goblet squat with OH press	Pause/tempo lifts/ Anderson squat	SA jammer (Figure 13.10)	Floor press	Lying/standing medball chest throws	GHR with medball trunk rotations/isometrics (figure 13.13)
Goblet squat holds	Bulgarian split squats	SL clean to box step (Figure 13.8)	Flat/incline DB bench press	—	Russian twists
Good mornings	Leg press/SL leg press	Resisted lateral shuffle	Bench press with chains	—	Walking hip locks
Walking lunge with banded weight on one side	Occlusion training	Drop jumps/SL drop jumps/ reactive to direction drop jumps	Wide/narrow pull ups	—	—
—	SA DB bent over row	Low squat acceleration drives/speed ¼squats	Chin ups	—	—
—	—	Clean high pulls	—	—	—
—	—	SL KB swings	—	—	—
—	—	High box acceleration drives (Figure 13.11)	—	—	—
—	—	DB snatch	—	—	—
—	—	sprint/resisted sprint accelerations	—	—	—

(a)

Figure 13.11a and b

(b)

(a)

Figure 13.12a and b

(b)

(a) (b)

Figure 13.13a and b

Note in Table 13.13 occlusion is training referenced as a lower body strength option. It is particularly useful in situations where players have an issue in heavy loading of their back or lower body. With this method you can utilize low load resistance exercise resulting in increased strength and even power gains (Cook *et al.*, 2013a) via the secretion of growth hormone through the accumulation of metabolites in the local area. This opens up an alternative method that can be used throughout the season especially when there is also limited muscle damage caused (Takarada *et al.*, 2000).

Conclusion

Cricket is a high skill sport that involves a large physical demand on players no matter what role you play, with bowlers at a higher risk than any other players due to the physical load and strain they experience. The testing of players will be largely dictated by your environment and situation as can be seen by the differences between the first class and international set ups. There is no one perfect testing protocol, as each team will demand various needs. Programming, as always, will be individualized to suit the time of year, phase of plan, playing schedule, training age, individual needs and restrictions of the player in question. Working closely with the science and medicine team to ensure the program includes an integrated injury prevention protocol is key.

It is the authors' belief that key moments in the game can be decided by a split second or distance and the athlete with a higher power output will be the difference if skill levels are equal. Whether it is bowling fast, power hitting, running between the wickets or stopping a boundary in the field, there is an explosive element to it. Power is underpinned by strength and improving these qualities will make a large impact on the player's ability to perform in game changing situations.

References

Bartlett, R. M., Storey, D., and Simmons, B. (1998). Measurement of upper extremity torque production and its relationship to throwing speed in the competitive athlete. *American Journal of Sports Medicine*, 17(1), pp. 89–96.

Buchheit, M. (2008). Field tests to monitor athletic performance throughout a team-sport season. *Science and Sports*, 23(1), pp. 29–31.

Castillo-Rodrıguez, A., Fernandez-Garcia, J. C., Chinchilla-Minguet, J. L., and Carnero, E. A. (2012). Relationship between muscular strength and sprints with changes of direction. *Journal of Strength and Conditioning Research*, 26(3), pp. 725–732.

Chelly, M. S., Hermassi, S., and Shephard, R. J. (2010). Relationships between power and strength of the upper and lower limb muscles and throwing velocity in male handball players. *Journal of Strength and Conditioning Research*, 24(6), pp. 1480–1487.

Christie, C. J., Todd, I. J., and King, G. A. (2008). Selected physiological responses during batting in a simulated cricket work bout: A pilot study. *Journal of Science and Medicine in Sport*, 11(6), pp. 581–584.

Comfort, P., Bullock, N., and Pearson, S. J. (2012). A comparison of maximal squat strength and 5-, 10-, and 20-metre sprint times, in athletes and recreationally trained men. *Journal of Strength and Conditioning Research*, 26(4), pp. 937–940.

Cook, C. J., Kilduff, L. P., and Beaven, M. (2013a). Improving strength and power in trained athletes with 3 weeks of occlusion training. *International Journal of Sports Physiology and Performance*, 9(1), pp. 166–172.

Cook, C. J., Kilduff, L. P., Crewther, B. T., Beaven, M., and West, D. J. (2013b). Morning based strength training improves afternoon physical performance in rugby union players. *Journal of Science and Medicine in Sport*, 17(3), pp. 317–321.

Dennis, R., Farhart, R., Goumas, C., and Orchard, J. (2003). Bowling workload and the risk of injury in elite cricket fast bowlers. *Journal of Science and Medicine in Sport*, 6(3), pp. 359–367.

Dennis, R., Finch, C., Elliott, B., and Farhart, P. (2008). The reliability of musculoskeletal screening tests used in cricket. *Physical Therapy in Sport*, 9(1), pp. 25–33.

Dennis, R. J., Finch, C. F., and Farhart, P. J. (2005). Is bowling workload a risk factor for injury to Australian junior cricket fast bowlers? *British Journal of Sports Medicine*, 39(11), pp. 843–46.

Duffield, R., Carney, M., and Karpinnen, S. (2009). Physiological responses and bowling performance during repeated spells of medium-fast bowling. *Journal of Sports Sciences*, 27(1), pp. 27–35.

Duffield, R., and Drinkwater, E. J. (2008). Time – motion analysis of test and one-day international cricket centuries. *Journal of Sports Sciences*, 26(5), pp. 457–464.

Ekstrand, L. G., Battaglini, C. L., McMurray, R. G., and Shields, E. W. (2013). Assessing explosive power production using the backward overhead shot throw and the effects of morning resistance exercise on afternoon performance. *Journal of Strength and Conditioning Research*, 27(1), pp. 101–106.

Elliott, B. (2000). Back injuries and the fast bowler in cricket. *Journal of Sports Science*, 18(12), pp. 983–991.

The English Cricket Board. (2013). *The LV= County Championship and Other First Class Matches*. Accepted as varied hereunder the laws of cricket, 2000, 5th edition. Available at: http://static.ecb.co.uk/files/3140-fc-domestic-lvcountychamp2013-p17-62-lr-12370-12370.pdf

Finch, C. F., Elliott, B. C., and McGrath, A. C. (1999). Measures to prevent cricket injuries. *Sports Medicine*, 28(4), pp. 263–272.

Flanagan, E., and Comyns, T. (2008). The use of contact time and the reactive strength index to optimise fast stretch-shortening cycle training. *Journal of Strength and Conditioning Research*, 30(5), pp. 33–38.

Foden, M., Astley, S., Comfort, P., McMahon, J. J., Matthews, M. J., and Jones, P. A. (2015). Relationships between speed, change of direction and jump performance with cricket specific speed tests in male academy cricketers. *Journal of Trainology*, 4(2), pp. 37–42.

Foster, D., John, D., Elliot, B., Ackland, T., and Fitch, K. (1989). Back injuries to fast bowlers in cricket: a prospective study. *British Journal of Sports Medicine*, 23(3), pp. 150–154.

Garhammer, J. (1983). A kinesiological analysis of hitting for baseball. *Strength and Conditioning Journal*, 5(2), pp. 7–7.

Glazier, P., Paradisis, G., and Cooper, S. (2000). Anthropometric and kinematic influences on release speed in men's fast-medium bowling. *Journal of Sports Sciences*, 18(12), pp. 1013–1021.

Graves, J. E., Pollock, M. L., Leggett, S. H., Braith, R. W., Carpenter, D. M., and Bishop, L. E. (1988). Effect of reduced training frequency on muscular strength. *International Journal of Sports Medicine*, 9(5), pp. 316–319.

Hermassi, S., Chelly, M. S., Tabka, Z., Shephard, R. J., and Chamari, K. (2011). Effects of 8-week in-season upper and lower limb heavy resistance training on the peak power, throwing velocity, and sprint performance of elite male handball players. *Journal of Strength Conditioning Research*, 25(9), pp. 2424–2433.

Hulin, B. T., Gabbett, T., Blanch, P., Chapman, P., Bailey, D., and Orchard, J. W. (2014). Spikes in acute workload are associated with increased injury risk in elite cricket fast bowlers. *British Journal of Sports Medicine*, 48(8), pp. 708–712.

Hurrion, P. D., Dyson, R., and Hale, T. (2000). Simultaneous measurement of back and front foot ground reaction forces during the same delivery stride of the fast-medium bowler. *Journal of Sports Sciences*, 18(12), pp. 993–997.

Johnstone, J. A., and Ford, P. A. (2010). Physiologic profile of professional cricketers. *Strength and Conditioning*, 24(11), pp. 2900–2907.

Johnstone, J. A., Mitchell, A. C. S., Hughes, G., Watson, T., Ford, P. A., and Garrett, A. T. (2014). The athletic profile of fast bowling in cricket: a review. *Journal of Strength and Conditioning Research*, 28(5), pp. 1465–1473.

Kilduff, L. P., Finn, C. V., Baker, J. S., Cook, C. J., and West D. J. (2013). Preconditioning strategies to enhance physical performance on the day of competition. *International Journal of Sports Physiology and Performance*, 8(6), pp. 677–681.

Leger, L. A., Mercier, D., Gadoury, C., & Lambert, J. (1988). The multistage 20 metre shuttle run test for aerobic fitness. *Journal of Sports Sciences*, 6(2), pp. 93–101.

Loram, L., McKinon, W., Wogmoor, S., Rogers, G., Nowark, I., and Harden, L. (2005). Determinants of ball release speed in schoolboy fast-medium bowlers in cricket. *Journal of Sports Medicine and Physical Fitness*, 44(4), pp. 483–490.

McBride, J., Blow, D., Kirby, T., Haines, T., Dayne, A., and Triplett, T. (2009). Relationship between maximal squat strength and five, ten and forty yard sprints. *Journal of Strength and Conditioning Research*, 23(6), pp. 1633–1636.

McGrath, A. C., & Finch, C. F. (1996). Bowling cricket injuries over: A review of the literature. Monash University Accident Research Centre.

McGuigan, M. R., Doyle, T. L., Newton, M., Edwards, D. J., Nimphius, S., and Newton, R. U. (2006). Eccentric utilization ratio: effect of sport and phase of training. *Journal of Strength and Conditioning Research*, 20(4), pp. 992–995.

McNamara, D., Gabbet, T., Naughton, G., Farhart, P., and Chapman, P. (2013). Training and competition workloads and fatigue responses of elite junior cricket players. *International Journal of Sports Physiology and Performance*, 8(5), pp. 517–526.

Miyaguchi, K., and Demura, S. (2012). Relationship between upper-body strength and bat swing speed in high school baseball players. *Journal of Strength and Conditioning Research*, 26(7), pp. 1786–1791.

Mukandi, I., Turner, A., Scott, P., and Johnstone, J. (2013). Strength and conditioning for fast bowlers. *Strength and Conditioning Journal*, 36(6), pp. 96–106.

Orchard, J. W., Blanch, P., Paoloni, J., Kountouris, A., Sims, K., Orchard, J. J., and Brukner, P. (2015). Cricket fast bowling workload patterns as risk factors for tendon, muscle, bone and joint injuries. *British Journal of Sports Medicine*, 49, pp. 1064–1068.

Orchard, J. W., James, T., Alcott, E., Carter, S., Farhart, P., and Newman, D. (2002). Injuries in Australian cricket at first class level 1995/1996 to 2000/2001. *British Journal of Sports Medicine*, 36(4), pp. 270–276.

Orchard, J. W., James, T., and Portus, M. R. (2006). Injuries to elite male cricketers in Australia over a 10-year period. *Journal of Science and Medicine in Sport*, 9(6), pp. 459–467.

Orchard, J. W., James, T., Portus, M., Kountouris, A., and Dennis, R. (2009). Fast bowlers in cricket demonstrate up to 3- to 4-week delay between high workloads and increased risk of injury. *The American Journal of Sports Medicine*, 37(6), pp. 1186–1192.

Orchard, J., Kountouris, A., Sims, K., Orchard, J., Beakley, D., and Brukner, P. (2014). *Injury Report 2014 – Cricket Australia*. Available at: www.johnorchard.com/resources/CA2014InjuryReportfinal.pdf

Orchard, J., Newman, D., Stretch, R., Frost, W., Mansingh, A., and Leipus, A. (2005). Consensus statement: methods for injury surveillance in international cricket. *Journal of Sports Science & Medicine in Sport*, 39(4), p. e22.

Owen, N. J., Watkins, J., Kilduff, L. P., Bevan, H. R., and Bennett, M. (2013). Development of a criterion method to determine peak mechanical power output in a countermovement jump. *Journal of Strength and Conditioning Research*, 28(6), pp. 1552–1558.

Petersen, C., Pyne, D., Dawson, B., Kellett, A., and Portus, M. (2010). Movement patterns in cricket vary by both position and game format. *Journal of Sports Sciences*, 28(1), pp. 45–52.

Petersen, C. J., Pyne, D. B., Portus, M. R., and Dawson, B. T. (2011). Comparison of player movement patterns between 1-day and test cricket. *Strength and Conditioning Journal*, 25(5), pp. 1368–1373.

Phillips, E., Portus, M., Davids, K., Brown, N., and Renshaw, I. (2010). *How Do Our 'Quicks' Generate Pace? A Cross Sectional Analysis of the Cricket Australia Pace Pathway*. Paper presented at the Conference of Science, Medicine & Coaching in Cricket, Gold Coast, Australia. Available at: www.clearinghouseforsport.gov.au/__data/assets/pdf_file/0005/376448/CA_conference_2010.pdf

Portus, M., Mason, B., Elliot, B., Pfitzner, M., and Done, R. (2007). Technique factors related to ball release speed and trunk injuries in high performance cricket fast bowlers. *Sports Biomechanics*, 3(2), pp. 263–283.

Portus, M., Sinclair, P., Burke, S., Moore, D., and Farhart, P. (2000). Cricket fast bowling performance and technique and the influence of selected physical factors during an 8- over spell. *Journal of Sports Sciences*, 18, pp. 999–1011.

Pyne, D., Duthie, G., Saunders, P., Petersen, C., and Protus, M. (2006). Anthropometric and strength correlates of fast bowling speed in junior and senior cricketers. *Journal of Strength and Conditioning Research*, 20(3), pp. 620–626.

Rudkin, S. T., and O'Donoghue, P. G. (2008). Time-motion analysis of first-class cricket fielding. *Journal of Science and Medicine in Sport*, 11(6), pp. 604–607.

Salter, C., Sinclair, P., and Portus, M. (2007). The associations between fast bowling technique and ball release speed: A pilot study of the within-bowler and between bowler approaches. *Journal of Sports Sciences*, 25(11), pp. 1279–1285.

Shaffer, B., Lobe, F. W., Pink, M., and Perry, J. (1993). Baseball batting: an electromyographic study. *Clinical Orthopedics and Related Research*, 292, pp. 285–298.

Small, K., McNaughton, L. R., Grieg, M., Lohkamp, M., and Lovell, R. (2009). Soccer fatigue, sprinting and hamstring risk. *International Journal of Sports Medicine*, 30, pp. 573–578.

Stone, M. H. (2003). Power and maximum strength relationships during performance of dynamic and static weighted jumps. *Journal of Strength and Conditioning Research*, 17(1), pp. 140–147.

Stretch, R. A. (1993). *A Biomechanical Analysis of Batting in Cricket*. Unpublished doctoral dissertation, University of Port Elizabeth, Port Elizabeth, South Africa.

Stretch, R. A. (2003). Cricket injuries: a longitudinal study of the nature of injuries to South African cricketers. *British Journal of Sports Medicine*, 37(3), pp. 250–253.

Stretch, R. A., Bartlett, R., and Davids, K., (2000). A review of batting in men's cricket. *Journal of Sports Sciences*, 18, pp. 931–949.

Stretch, R. A., and Orchard, J. J. (2003). Cricket injuries: a longitudinal study of the nature of injuries to South African cricketers. *British Journal of Sports Medicine*, 37(3), pp. 250–253.

Stuelcken, M., Pyne, D., and Sinclair, P. (2007). Anthropometric characteristics of elite cricket fast bowlers. *Journal of Sports Sciences*, 25(14), pp. 1587–1597.

Szymanski, D. J., McIntyre J. S., Szymanski, J. M., Bradford, T. J., Schade, R. L., Madsen, N. H., and Pascoe D. D. (2007). Effect of torso rotational strength on angular hip, angular shoulder, and linear bat velocities of high school baseball players. *Journal of Strength & Conditioning Research*, 21(4), pp. 1117–1125.

Takarada, Y., Takazawa, H., Sato, Y., Takebayashi, S., Tanaka, Y., and Ishii, N. (2000). Effects of resistance exercise combined with moderate vascular occlusion on muscular function in humans. *Journal of Applied Physiology*, 88(6), pp. 2097–2106.

Taliep, M. S., Prim, S. K., and Gray, J. (2010). Upper body muscle strength and batting performance in cricket batsmen. *Journal of Strength & Conditioning Research*, 24(12), pp. 3484–3487.

Welch, C. M., Banks, S. A., Cook, F. F., and Draovitch, P. (1995). Hitting a baseball: A biomechanical description. *Journal of Orthopedic and Sports Physical Therapy*, 22(5), pp. 193–201.

Wierzbicka, M. M., and Wienger, A. W. (1996). Accuracy of motor responses in subjects with and without control of antagonist muscle. *Journal of Neurophysiology*, 75(6), pp. 2533–2541.

Worthington, P., King, M., and Ranson, C. (2013). The Influence of cricket fast bowlers' front leg technique on peak ground reaction forces. *Journal of Sports Sciences*, 31(4), pp. 434–441.

14
ROWING

Alex Wolf

Introduction to the sport

Regatta rowing is completed over 2000m and requires a mixture of aerobic and anaerobic power throughout the race (Mäestu et al., 2005). Around 65–85% of the rowing performance is accounted for by aerobic fitness (Droghetti & Nilsen, 1991). The anaerobic energy contribution has been estimated to be 21–30% (Secher, 1975) with the first and last 250m having the greatest anaerobic contribution (Secher & Volianitis, 2007). Rowing has a very high physiological demand, which requires rowers to have a high degree of endurance and anaerobic power, while also possessing excellent technical efficiency (Mäestu et al., 2005; Nevill et al., 2011). A review of the Rio 2016 Olympic Games A Finals winning time show events can last from 05:29.63 (Men's coxed 8) to 07:21.54 (Women's Single Scull). These times are influenced by the crew number, competition classification (lightweigt or open weight), sweep rowing (one oar per rower) or sculling (two oars per rower) and gender (Ingham et al., 2002). There are other factors that also contribute to the performance such as wind speed and direction and water and air temperature to name a few, which all impact on the water and air resistance, which will in turn alter the degree of drag while racing (Ingham et al., 2002; Mäestu et al., 2005, Nevill et al., 2011).

Athletic demands

The mechanical demands of rowing have been investigated by Hartman et al. (1993) where rowers' peak forces within the first 10 strokes while on a rowing ergometer were estimated to be 1352 Newton's (N) for males and 1019 N for females. Male single scullers have also recorded 1000–1500 N within the first 10 seconds of racing (Steinacker, 1993). Strength training has been demonstrated to have the biggest impact on the start of the race (Lawton et al., 2011), where the largest forces have also been measured (Steinacker, 1993). This is most likely due to the need to accelerate the boat from a stationary position up to race speed (Lawton et al., 2011). Impressively, the rowers are able to maintain 65–70% of the force produced within the first 10 seconds for the remainder of the race (Steinacker, 1993). Rowers will on average take 220–250 strokes per race (Secher, 1993). With rowing economy being an important component of performance, there is evidence that stronger rowers have an increased economy when compared to weaker athletes (Bourdin et al., 2004).

Some research has shown that peak rowing ergometer power can account for as much as 92% of the 2000m ergometer performance (Bourdin et al., 2004). Ergometer power strokes (five maximum effort repetitions with a stationary flywheel), which are an assessment of peak power, have also been shown to predict rowing performance alongside several other aerobic performance metrics (Ingham et al., 2002). The power produced by a rower as measured at the oar has been recorded as high as 450–550 watts (Steinacker, 1993). The largest force seen during a rowing stroke is just after the catch during the initial drive phase (Schwanitz, 1991). This is achieved with a large leg drive (Schwanitz, 1991). The total contribution of power produced during a rowing stroke can be divided between the legs, trunk and arms (Klesnev, 1991). The legs contribute 46%, 31% from the trunk and 23% from the arms (Klesnev, 1991). The legs utilise 95% of their maximum capacity, the trunk 55% and the arms 75% (Klesnev, 1991). As much as 70% of the total muscle mass of a rower is used to accelerate the boat (Secher, 1975). Rowing is a whole coordinated movement with a need to link the leg drive through the trunk and apply to the oar handles through the arms (Lawton et al., 2011).

There is compelling evidence that rowers need the ability to repeatedly produce sustained periods of force development, but also force and power measurements have been demonstrated to be related to 2000m performances (Ingham et al., 2002; Steinacker, 1993). There is good evidence that maximum bench pull and leg press performance have been correlated to rowing performance (Izquierdo-Gabarren et al., 2010) and strength training can have a large impact on start performance (Lawton et al., 2011). With strength training being shown to aid start performance (Lawton et al., 2011), there is also the opportunity for it to help develop rowing economy (Bourdin et al., 2004). Stronger athletes can have a greater fatigue resistance and have better anaerobic capacities, and therefore be more economical (Stone et al., 2006) when compared to less strong athletes. These are desirable physical qualities for successful rowers as for the same given workload the metabolic demand will be less (Stone et al., 2006). It is clear that strength and power training can be performance enhancing for rowing and should be considered when planning the training of the rower.

Injury prevalence

As described above, rowing is a whole body movement, transferring load from the foot stretcher through the rower himself and onto the oar handle, resulting in propulsion of the boat. Because of this whole body action and the large demand placed upon the mid-section of the rower, the most common injuries suffered are across the chest wall, ribs and the spine, with the lumbar spine being mainly affected (Hickery et al., 1997). Females have a high incident of chest wall injuries while their male counterparts tend to suffer from a greater number of lumbar spine injuries (Hickery et al., 1997).

There is a large back extension movement during the drive phase (Secher, 1993) which contributes to around one third of the power produced by the rower during the rowing stroke (Klesnev, 1991). Recent evidence from a colleague, Erica Buckeridge, nicely demonstrated that incremental training intensities increases loads on the lower back of the 12 elite female rowers tested (Buckeridge et al., 2014). There has been some evidence that rowers who suffer from back pain have larger back muscles (McGregor et al., 2002); however, it is unknown if this is causative or as a result of back pain (Lee et al., 1999). Research on elite oarsmen, however, proposes that hypertrophy of the back may be a result of altered lumbopelvic rhythm due to back pain (Lee et al., 1999). Research from the same colleague identified a large variation in left-right foot force asymmetries across an elite cohort or female and lightweight male rowers (Buckeridge, 2016). These points are important considerations due to the adaptive response of the rower to the loading placed upon them during training and competition, but it is not entirely clear whether these adaptive responses are causative or as a result to the loading.

It would be prudent for rowers to spend time developing the necessary hip and leg physical qualities to help manage the imbalances with the intention to maintain this imbalance within a 'safe' bandwidth, as identified by the clinical and physical preparation team. This includes developing the high load strength qualities with appropriate movement mechanics. This would allow the rower to potentially load appropriately through the leg drive and off load the back as the prime force producer (McGregor et al., 2002). Developing the physical qualities across the trunk to sustain continual loading and at times very high load, is essential in managing the rower's back health. Using the exercise prescription tools in a recent article that was co-authored with Simon Spencer and Alison Rushton (Spencer et al., 2016) allows effective training programmes based on the intention and outcome of the preferred adaptive response. The blend of prescribing low and high intensity training, developing the trunk's capacity to tolerate repeated loading while developing motor control, has been hugely effective in managing the spinal health of all athletes I have worked with. While there is a potential injury risk across the low back and hip, there is good evidence that asymmetrical loading can result in a decrease in horizontal foot force that is necessary to effectively propel the boat and therefore have a significant performance impact too (Buckeridge, 2016).

High spinal flexion and compression forces are experienced during the rowing stroke with sweep rowers having the additional stress of high rotational forces (Adams & Dolan, 1995). Sweep rowers have demonstrated asymmetrical patterns between the left and right Erector Spinae muscles during extension (Parkin et al., 2001). This is significantly related to rowing side, which could be related to the incidence of back pain experienced by rowers (Parkin et al., 2001). There will always be asymmetries during sweep rowing, and they may actually be necessary for improved rowing performances. Again, managing the asymmetry may help protect the rower from back complaints. In conjunction with the clinical team, developing a training programme that helps to manage this risk is essential. Using the same exercise prescription tool described above will allow for a training programme to meet the individual needs of each rower (Spencer et al., 2016).

Posterior rotation of the pelvis, which allows the lumbar spine to flex (Gajdosik et al., 1992), is common across rowers. Having an increase in lumbar flexion is a risk factor for the onset of low back pain (Adams & Dolan, 1995). The length and stiffness of the hamstring complex is a major restriction in pelvic motion (Gajdosik et al., 1992). Regardless of the degree of posterior hip rotation a rower may experience, all rowers should maintain an adequate level of hamstring length to avoid the lumbar spine being pulled into an unwanted flexed position. Having a hamstring complex and posterior hip (Glut Max) with the capacity to resist the counter rotation forces placed upon the pelvis, especially during the catch and initial drive phase of the rowing strike, will also help to manage pelvic rotation. Traditionally, straight legged hamstring training such as Good Mornings or Romanian Deadlifts were thought to be effective in developing the higher force tolerance of the hamstring complex. However, rowing populations tend to bias the loading with their lumbar and thoracic musculature over their hamstring complex. This may be due to the mechanical (dis)advantage the spinal musculature has when there is a forward pitch of the spine as the rower rotates around the hip. Rowers also tend to have a stronger musculature around the lumbar and thoracic region due to the extension movement of the drive phase, which could bias the loading of the spinal musculature during these exercises (Secher, 1993). Knee dominant hamstring exercises have been found to be better in developing the high force qualities of the hamstring in relation to managing pelvic rotation. As rowers develop high force capabilities across the hamstring complex, straight legged exercises can be re-introduced.

The inclusion of posterior hip dominant exercises such as loaded hip bridges would also be recommended.

Rib cage compression is one mechanism of rib injury (Vinthers, 2008). Vinthers research shows a close timing of peak neuromuscular activity and peak handle force observed in conjunction with high isometric force of the thoracic muscles (Vinthers, 2008). During high force activities such as rowing, this places large forces across the rib cage. The bench pull is a very common exercise used by rowers to develop upper body pulling force. It is likely that the timing of peak neuromuscular activity and force production will occur at a similar time. When a rower is lying prone on the bench with the load pulling them into the bench, this is likely to further amplify the compression on the rib cage and therefore increase the risk of rib cage injury. While bench pull is a common exercise within the rowing programme and this author by no way suggests it should not be used, caution should be taken, especially with those recovering from rib and chest complaints. During high volume rowing training and/or upper body strength training, alternatives to bench pull should be considered to manage the risk. Alternative pulling exercises such as bentover row or seated row may help reduce the exposure of high load rib compression.

An additional note should be made on lightweights and a potential risk of rib injury. Lightweight rowers continually attempt to maintain a low body mass due to the weight restriction during competition. This can place physical additional demands on the rower. Calorie restriction can negatively affect bone mineral density due to decreases in testosterone levels (Talbott & Shapses, 1998). There is strong evidence that endurance athletes have already supressed testosterone levels (Hackney, 2001). These two points, alongside the risk factors of chest wall and rib health in rowing populations, put lightweight rowers at a potentially greater risk of injury (Vinthers et al., 2008). Careful monitoring of health and well-being of all rowers – but particularly lightweights – is important to manage this risk. It is, however, important to note that strength training has been shown to help with bone formation and is site specific (Vinthers et al., 2008). Using strength training to manage chest wall and rib health is an important part of training for lightweights rowers. Pullovers and overhead lifting are good exercises to locally load the chest wall and rib cage.

Fitness test battery

It is important to continually monitor the rowers' response to the training to ensure it meets the specific needs established within the programme. With regular monitoring, it is possible to manipulate the training programme based on the results and ensure the rower continues to make sufficient progress. Monitoring can be a standalone testing of key physical characteristics or can use the within-training metrics to track changes. Both have their advantages but equally their disadvantages, so consideration is needed in determining when to employ one over the other or, in some parts of the programme, use both. Timing and proximity to major competitions or training blocks, chronological age, training age and experience of training and testing, time and resources available are example considerations to make when determining how and what to monitor.

Heavy strength training

A comprehensive overview of the required strength needs for rowers has been established by McNeely et al. (2005) outlining the strength to bodyweight ratios required for key exercises. Table 14.1 and 14.2 outline the bodyweight factors for key exercises from U23's through to Olympic level athletes for men and women respectively.

Table 14.1 Strength to bodyweight factors for males

Exercise	U23	Club	National	Olympic
Squat	1.3	1.4	1.7	1.9
Deadlift	1.3	1.4	1.7	1.9
Bench pull	0.9	1.05	1.2	1.3

Source: Adapted from McNeely et al. (2005).

Table 14.2 Strength to bodyweight factors for females

Exercise	U23	Club	National	Olympic
Squat	1	1.25	1.4	1.6
Deadlift	1	1.25	1.4	1.6
Bench pull	0.8	0.95	1.1	1.2

Source: Adapted from McNeely et al. (2005).

Table 14.3 1RM prediction coefficients

Repetitions	Coefficient
1	1.00
2	1.04
3	1.09
4	1.13
5	1.18
6	1.22
7	1.25
8	1.29
9	1.33
10	1.36

Source: Adapted from Thompson and Wolf (2015).

These are useful guides to help with monitoring and programming by providing potential targets for rowers to attain. As mentioned in the previous paragraph, dedicated testing sessions can be utilised with the specific purpose of assessing this characteristic through repetition maximum (RM) testing. The alternative is to use training loads within a session and predict their RM (Thompson & Wolf, 2015). Table 14.3 below identifies coefficient factors that can be used to predict a 1RM based on the number of repetitions completed within a set. Simply identify the number of repetitions the rower lifted between 1 and 10 and then multiply the load lifted with the corresponding coefficient factor (Thompson & Wolf, 2015). For instance, a female rower who lifted 70kg for 4 repetitions while completing the bench pull would multiply 70kg by 1.13, the coefficient for 4 repetitions. This would predict the rowers 1RM to be 79kg. The limitation of this method and all other predictive equations is the gradual inaccuracy in predicting 1RM as the number of repetitions increase; there is a greater degree of accuracy with 5 repetitions or less (Thompson & Wolf, 2015). This needs to be taken into consideration when using this information for monitoring and writing training programmes. However, it is a good guide to get a general idea of what the rower's progress is.

Power assessment

Using rowing ergometers to measure mechanical power output is not only relatively simple but specific to the sport itself. Most rowing clubs have ergometers and they can easily be set up to complete short ergometer sprints. There are two methods in which to administer the sprints, again both with advantages and disadvantages. The first method is to complete a 250m sprint (Jefferys & Moody, 2016). Set the ergometer computer display to row 250m. It is ideal to set the drag factors at a specific load across the squads to ensure consistency with testing. Setting the drag factor to 130 for females and 135 for males on Concept II ergo's is common (Jefferys & Moody, 2016). The assessment is rate capped at 44–42 strokes per minute with rowers needing to complete a three quarter or greater slide through in the test (Jefferys & Moody, 2016). The goal is to complete the 250m as quick as possible. At the end of the test, take the average power of the test from the ergometer computer display. Table 14.4 gives ranges of the average power typical of rowing populations across males and females along with open weights and lightweights (Jefferys & Moody, 2016). The lower end of the range is where club and U23 rowers would be expected to perform. The advantage of this test is it requires a high degree of technical competency in the rowing stroke, which makes it very specific to the sport. However, the disadvantage is the high metabolic cost. It can take over 40–45 seconds to complete, which can impact other training within the session or day.

The second test is using shorter ergometer sprints such as a 7–10 power stroke protocol (Thompson & Wolf, 2015). Again it is important to measure watts rather than split time as this provides a greater degree of accuracy (Thompson & Wolf, 2015). Rowers can either start from a dead start or rolling start. However it is important to keep this consistent between tests. It is also important to be consistent with setting drag factors. The rower is required to row as hard as they can per stroke for the 7–10 strokes within the test. Once finished, review the ergometer computer display to determine the greatest average power achieved. The advantage of this test is the speed in which it takes to complete and the low metabolic cost associated with it. It can be completed within training sessions with ease. The disadvantage is that the degree of technical competency needed to complete this. Rowers often shorten their strokes to maximise the power output. Careful management of how the rowers perform this test is important to ensure reliability of testing.

It is important to note that rowers should complete a thorough warm up with several high intensity bursts on the ergometer. This type of ergometer training may not be regularly used so is important to prepare the rower for the higher intensity work to be completed (Jefferys and Moody, 2016). It is worth considering fixing the ergometer during the testing as the high

Table 14.4 Mean power goals for 250m ergometer sprint

Category	Average power (watts)
Open weight men	700–900
Open weight women	420–580
Lightweight men	550–750
Lightweight women	380–500

Source: Adapted from Jeffreys and Moody, 2016.

intensity work often moves the ergometer throughout the test (Jefferys and Moody, 2016). When rowers are competing against each other, the best results are often achieved (Jefferys and Moody, 2016).

How often to monitor

Ongoing monitoring of performance is essential to ensure rowers training remains on track. While standalone training can give accurate measures of where the rower's current standards are, they can be time consuming and physically cost the rower. This can have an impact on the rest of training process. While using within training session monitoring may not be as accurate as standalone testing, it will give you a good gauge on how the rower is performing and if any modifications can be made to keep them on track. For further information around the monitoring of rowing training, refer to Chapter 7 in *Training for the Complete Rower: A Guide to Improving Performance* (Thompson and Wolf, 2015), which gives a comprehensive overview of all land training.

Programming

The majority of the aerobic water and land based training is regularly prescribed by rowing coaches themselves. The ability for the strength and conditioning (S&C) coach to prescribe this type of training is limited. The majority of the time of the S&C coach is spent developing the force and power characteristics demonstrated to be impactful for rowing performance. With the rowing coach managing the majority of aerobic training, it is imperative the S&C coach has a firm grounding and understanding of the rowing coach's training programme and their philosophical approach to performance. This allows the S&C programme to be aligned to the overall outcome. If this is not achieved, it is possible the programme could be trying to develop competing physical characteristics or impact on important technical and tactical outcomes. Working with the rowing coach, discussions around how strength training outcomes can impact the anaerobic physical qualities, such as the start or bursts of speed during the 2000m race, can give clarity on where to spend time with training. Understanding the technical and tactical model will allow greater understanding of how force and power characteristics can support rowing economy. Lastly but equally important is the aligned approach to manage the risk of common injuries outlined in the injury prevalence section. S&C training can positively impact the performance threat management with allied disciplines such as physiotherapy and nutritional support. For those who deliver larger amounts of aerobic water and land training, Chapters 1 to 5 in *Training for the Complete Rower: A Guide to Improving Performance* (Thompson and Wolf, 2015) give a comprehensive overview on the considerations to take when organising this training.

Figure 14.1 provides an abbreviated example overview of the annual plan for a high performance club rower. This includes major calendar events such as trials, competitions and testing. The strength diagnostics and anthropometric testing has been placed specifically to measure the potential changes through the blocks of strength training. Primary training focuses are identified in dark grey while secondary focuses are in light grey. The training focuses are identified as outcomes rather than methodologies. This is expanded upon later within this chapter. However, for greater insight, please refer to *Spinal-Exercise Prescription in Sport: Classifying Physical Training and Rehabilitation by Intention and Outcome* (Spencer et al., 2016) and Chapter 6 in *Training for the Complete Rower: A Guide to Improving Your Performance* (Thompson and Wolf, 2015).

An example of a typical training week for a high performance rower during the winter and early spring can be found in Figure 14.2. Rowers will often train twice daily for six days a week and sometimes train every day during heavy training blocks. Strength training accounts for up to

Week	Month	Monday	Calendar	Phase	Conditioning	Technical	High force	RFD
1	Sept	12	Return to training	Gen conditioning	Primary focus	Primary focus		
2	Sept	19		Gen conditioning	Primary focus	Primary focus		
3	Sept	26		Gen conditioning	Primary focus	Primary focus		
4	October	3	Strength diagnostics & anthropometrics	Gen conditioning	Primary focus	Primary focus		
5	October	10		Gen conditioning	Primary focus	Primary focus		
6	October	17	British rowing championship	Strength 1	Primary focus	Primary focus		
7	October	24		Strength 1	Primary focus	Primary focus	Secondary focus	
8	October	31	GB rowing 1st assessment trials	Strength 1	Primary focus	Primary focus	Secondary focus	
9	November	7		Strength 1	Primary focus	Primary focus	Secondary focus	
10	November	14	Strength diagnostics & anthropometrics	Strength 1	Primary focus	Primary focus	Secondary focus	
11	November	21		Strength 1	Secondary focus		Primary focus	
12	November	28		Strength 1	Secondary focus		Primary focus	
13	December	5	British indoor rowing championship	Strength 1	Secondary focus		Primary focus	
14	December	12		Strength 1	Secondary focus		Primary focus	
15	December	19	GB rowing 2nd assessment trials	Strength 2	Secondary focus		Primary focus	
16	December	26		Strength 2	Secondary focus		Primary focus	
17	January	2		Strength 2	Secondary focus		Primary focus	
18	January	9	Banyoles, Spain - training camp	Strength 2	Secondary focus		Primary focus	
19	January	16	Banyoles, Spain - training camp	Strength 2	Secondary focus		Primary focus	Secondary focus
20	January	23	Strength diagnostics & anthropometrics	Strength 2	Secondary focus		Primary focus	Secondary focus
21	January	30		Strength 2	Secondary focus		Primary focus	
22	February	6	GB rowing 3rd assessment trials	Strength 2	Secondary focus		Primary focus	
23	February	13		Strength 3	Secondary focus		Primary focus	Secondary focus
24	February	20		Strength 3	Secondary focus		Primary focus	Secondary focus
25	February	27		Strength 3	Secondary focus		Primary focus	Secondary focus
26	March	6	Women's head of the river	Strength 3	Secondary focus		Primary focus	Secondary focus
27	March	13		Strength 3	Secondary focus		Primary focus	Secondary focus
28	March	20		Strength 3	Secondary focus		Primary focus	Secondary focus
29	March	27		Strength 3	Secondary focus		Primary focus	Secondary focus
30	April	3	Strength diagnostics & anthropometrics	Strength 3	Secondary focus		Primary focus	Secondary focus
31	April	10		Specific prep	Secondary focus			Primary focus
32	April	17		Specific prep	Secondary focus			Primary focus
33	April	24	British University & Colleges Sports regatta	Specific prep	Secondary focus			Primary focus
34	May	1		Specific prep	Secondary focus		Secondary focus	Primary focus
35	May	8		Specific prep	Secondary focus		Secondary focus	Primary focus
36	May	15	Banyoles, Spain - training camp	Specific prep	Secondary focus			Primary focus
37	May	22	Banyoles, Spain - training camp	Specific prep	Secondary focus			Primary focus
38	May	29	Metropolitan regatta	Competition	Secondary focus		Secondary focus	Primary focus
39	June	5		Competition	Secondary focus		Secondary focus	Primary focus
40	June	12		Competition	Secondary focus			Primary focus
41	June	19		Competition	Secondary focus			Primary focus
42	June	26	Henley royal regatta	Competition	Secondary focus			Primary focus

Key:
Primary focus
Secondary focus

Figure 14.1 An abbreviated example of an annual training plan for a high performance rower

	Monday	Tuesday	Wednesday	Thursday	Friday	Saturday	Sunday
Session 1	Off	12km ergo	16km rate 24	16km rate 24	12km ergo	20km rate 18/19	30 minute ergo rate 20
Session 2	Off	Strength training	12km ergo	Strength training	Off	12km inc. 2 x 4000m rate 22	Strength training

Figure 14.2 An example weekly training plan of a high performance rower during September to April

	Week 1		Week 2		Week 3		Week 4	
	Sets x reps	% 1RM	Sets x reps	% 1RM	Sets x reps	% 1RM	Sets x reps	% 1RM
Back squat	4 x 8	80%	4 x 6	85%	5 x 5	87%	4 x 3	93%
Leg press	4 x 8	80%	4 x 6	85%	5 x 5	87%	4 x 3	93%
Bench press	4 x 8	80%	4 x 6	85%	5 x 5	87%	4 x 3	93%
Bench pull	4 x 8	80%	4 x 6	85%	5 x 5	87%	4 x 3	93%

Figure 14.3 An example of a typical high force focused strength training programme

30% of the entire training week and fluctuates between 10–30% throughout the year. While success has been had with making significant gains with strength training performances with it being the first session in the day, the preference is to keep the session as the final session. Anecdotally, there seems to be greater success when strength training is performed as the last session of the day.

Figure 14.3 identifies the key focuses of strength training based on outcome of training. It is important to note strength training is a methodology and not an outcome. As demonstrated at the start of this chapter, force and power characteristics are related to performance and it is these that the S&C coach is trying to change. Therefore the outcome of strength training methods is to develop force and velocity characteristics. Getting stronger is a nice side effect! Table 14.5 identifies the framework of how strength training programmes can be tailored for each specific outcome required for a rower during the season. By following the framework and manipulating the programme, the ability to optimise training outcome is increased. In a concurrent training sport which is heavily biased to endurance based training, it is important to maximise every opportunity to develop the strength training associated outcomes. The table also identifies the types of testing that can be completed to determine the level of change within the associated training outcome. While some of these may be more direct measures of change (short ergometer sprints), others are not so direct. For instance increases in how much a rower can squat is exactly that, and not a direct measure of how much force the athlete can produce during concentric triple extension. While some assumptions can be linked to this, caution is needed as increases in squat performance do not always correlate to increased force expression.

Figures 14.3 and 14.4 are examples of typical high force and rate of force development programmes. The term 'power' is often used to describe explosive strength training methodologies. The power assessment outlined in the Fitness Testing Battery section of this chapter refers to the unit of measurement rather than how the assessment is completed. Figures 14.3 and 14.4

Table 14.5 Strength training based on outcome with the associated methodologies to develop them

OUTCOME	METHOD	LOAD	VELOCITY	FREQUENCY	SETS	REPS	TEMPO	TESTING
Maximal force Expression	Heavy strength Training	High	Mod-high	2 to 5 × Week	3 to 6 /exercise	1 to 5 6 to 10	Explosive to 202	1–3 rep max, isometric F_{max} & isokinetic T_{max}
Rate of force Development	Explosive strength Training	Low-mod	High	1 to 4 × Week	3 to 6 /exercise	1 to 8	Explosive	Short ergometer sprints, countermovement jump (Impulse characteristics & peak instantaneous power), isometric RFD & isokinetic RTD.
Muscle & tendon mass	Hypertrophy	Mod-high	Low-mod	3 to 6 × Week	4 to 8 /exercise	6 to 25 +	202 to 303	Skinfolds, girths, body mass, DEXA, MRI,
Tissue tolerance	Work capacity	Low-mod	Low-mod	3 to 6 × Week	1 to 10 /exercise	10 to 25 +	101 to 303	work capacity testing (i.e. prone extension or press ups to failure)

(a)

Exercise	Sets x reps	% 1RM
Box jumps	4 x 5	Body weight only
Power cleans	4 x 3	90-93%
Loaded jump squats	4 x 5	30-40%
Speed bench pull	4 x 5	30-40%

(b)

Exercise	Sets x reps	% 1RM
Power cleans	3 x 3	90-93%
Loaded jump squats	3 x 5	30-40%
Speed bench pull	3 x 5	30-40%
Back squats	4 x 5	87%
Bench pull	4 x 5	87%

Figure 14.4a and b An example of a typical rate of force focused strength training programme (4a) and integrated high force and rate of force focused strength training programme (4b)

are typical strength training programmes and may not necessarily differentiate from strength training programmes for any other athlete within another sport. There are no secret exercises within rowing or endurance based sports. The exercises are similar if not the same to most other programmes. The differentiation of all programmes refers back to outcome not methodology. The primary focus is to prescribe training based on the outcome of Figure 14.3 above.

The annual plan in Figure 14.1 highlights that conditioning is primary and secondary focus throughout the season. Conditioning refers to work capacity which can be described as the body's ability to produce or tolerate variable intensities and durations of work (Spencer et al., 2016). This contributes to the ability of a rower to perform more efficiently within the sport (Spencer et al., 2016). It is important to note work capacity is a training outcome and not a performance outcome (Spencer et al., 2016). It is the accumulation of training of many months which results in chronic local adaptation to muscle and tendon and increases metabolic biogenesis (Spencer et al., 2016). The athlete is able to increase the amount of work it can do during repeated efforts, increase the tolerance of local musculature to larger training volume and supports the performance of work at intensities and durations closer to that of competition (Spencer et al., 2016). Work capacity training can have a low biological cost which allows for this type of training to be completed on an almost daily basis (Spencer et al., 2016; Thompson & Wolf, 2015). This type of training is hugely valuable to prescribe around high injury risk sites such as the chest wall, lumbar spine and hips to help increase their tolerance to training and competition (Spencer et al., 2016; Thompson & Wolf, 2015). This type of training can be completed at the start of training sessions as part of the extended warm up of a strength training session. The exercises are often similar (but at different intensities) to those within the main body of the training programme. It can be focused around individual rowers' needs and requires very little equipment or space. The exercises are often completed under a slow tempo at low load, to ensure the muscle-tendon units

Exercise	Focus	Volume
Hip bridge (dumbbell on hips)	Hips	1 x 60 seconds
Dumbbell pullover	Chest wall	1 x 60 seconds
Single arm dumbbell press - left	Chest wall	1 x 60 seconds
Single arm dumbbell press - right	Chest wall	1 x 60 seconds
Dumbbell bentover row	Lumbar spine	1 x 60 seconds
Dumbbell stiff leg deadlift	Lumbar spine	1 x 60 seconds
Split squat - left	Hips	1 x 60 seconds
Split squat - right	Hips	1 x 60 seconds

Figure 14.5 An example of a typical conditioning session focusing on the lumbar, hip, spine and chest wall

are under constant load and there is no inertia assisting with the movement. This is to optimise the adaptation process. An example of a work capacity training programme can be found below in Figure 14.5 with specific focus around the lumbar spine, hips and chest wall.

Hypertrophy consideration

Rowing physical preparation is heavily aerobically biased with the majority of the training programmed dedicated to this (Droghetti & Nilsen, 1991). A small percentage of the training programme with be biased toward strength training (Lawton et al., 2011). It is not possible to organise training without concurrently developing aerobic fitness with force and power focused training (Lawton et al., 2011). Concurrent training has many advantages including developing multiple fitness qualities simultaneously. However, a disadvantage is the interference effect (Nader, 2006). While aerobic biased adaptations may not be affected (any in some cases improved) by the concurrent training of force and power, the opposite is not true (Nader, 2006). The adaptation of force and power characteristics are often blunted by the heavily biased aerobic training (Nader, 2006). While force and velocity characteristics are more easily managed, the development of muscle cross sectional area or muscle hypertrophy is much harder to develop.

There are times when a rower will need to increase muscle size post an injury or for a performance outcome such as increased force expression of leg and hip extension. The most successful changes that have been made is when the priority of training has been given to strength training and a reduction in aerobic biased training. For this to be possible, there has to be an agreed plan with the coach and athlete of the priority of increase muscle mass and for what purpose. Once this has been achieved, there is a need for a reduction of aerobic biased training and an increase in strength training. The only time significant muscle mass changes have occurred is when there has been an equally significant reduction in aerobic biased training. Unless this area is addressed, the interference affect is too large with muscle mass changes blunted. The winter is often the best time to complete this type of training with aerobic training at its lowest. It is also important to note that for even small changes in muscle mass, giving appropriate time in the training programme is essential. Often 10–16 weeks is normal to elicit the required changes while giving less time leads to disappointing results. Figure 14.6 gives an example of a typical hypertrophy

	Week 1		Week 2		Week 3		Week 4	
	Sets x reps	% 1RM	Sets x reps	% 1RM	Sets x reps	% 1RM	Sets x reps	% 1RM
Back squat	4 x 12	> 70%	4 x 15	> 65%	4 x 18	> 60%	4 x 15	> 67%
+ Single leg press ★	4 x 12	> 70%	4 x 15	> 65%	4 x 18	> 60%	4 x 15	> 67%
Leg press	4 x 12	> 70%	4 x 15	> 65%	4 x 18	> 60%	4 x 15	> 67%
+ Leg extension ★	4 x 12	> 70%	4 x 15	> 65%	4 x 18	> 60%	4 x 15	> 67%

Figure 14.6 Example lower body hypertrophy training programme using supersets
★ *Complete sets to failure to increase mechanical and metabolic stress*

programme using supersets to help increase the mechanical tension and metabolic stress required to induce muscle or tendon mass changes.

Training experience consideration

Analysis of Olympic, National and Club level open weight male rower's strength qualities demonstrated Olympic standard rowers were stronger than National level, who were in turn stronger than club level rowers (Secher 1975). Strength to bodyweight ratios were 2.30, 2.20 and 2.07 for Olympic, National and club ratios respectively (Secher 1975). A more recent study found female varsity rowers were shown to have a greater vertical jump than novice rowers, suggesting that force and power qualities develop as well as the expected aerobic qualities (Battista et al., 2007). This evidence along with personal experience supports the rationale for force and power qualities being developed simultaneously with aerobic qualities as rowers progress from being a novice to a high performing athlete.

Conclusion

The development of force and power characteristics is integral to the continued improvement of rowing performance. Due to the concurrent nature of the training year, it is important to organise the training programme to ensure the rowers benefit from optimal adaptations. While force and power characteristics alone will not make the boat go faster, there is no doubt that improvements in these areas specific to rowing will aid performance. However, developing these characteristics in isolation with little regard to the rest of the training process will limit performance. Understanding the coaches' philosophy of how they put together a medal winning performance is fundamental. This will allow the S&C coach to align their programme to overall performance plan. A colleague of mine, Professor Dave Collins, reminded me several years ago that the role of S&C is not to make strength and conditioning look good but to make performance good. Judging the success of a training programme solely on weight room performance is futile as this is ultimately not the event. It is important to track changes in weight room performance but when the programme is aligned to boat performance and how a rower achieves this, including the physical characteristics required (and how much), the entire training process is aligned regardless of who delivers it. Without alignment, we deliver in a silo approach with little regard to the rest of the training process. No matter how good the programme is or how well it is coached, without the full alignment to the coaches' philosophy of performance, it will always be limited. The greatest successes achieved and the most enjoyable and fulfilling times has been working within a sport (including rowing) where this has been the norm. It is easy to write a strength training programme, but to truly align the programme to performance – that is the exciting challenge that lies ahead.

References

Adams, M., & Dolan, P (1995) Recent advances in the lumbar spine mechanics and their clinical significance. *Clinical Biomechanics*. 10, 13–19.

Battista, R. A., Pivarnik, J. M., Dummer, G. M., Sauer, N., & Malina, R. M. (2007) Comparisons of physical characteristics and performances among female collegiate rowers. *Journal of Sports Sciences*. 25, 651–657.

Bourdin, M., Messonnier, L., Hager, J. P., & Lacour, J. R. (2004) Peak power output predicts rowing ergometer performance in elite male rowers. *International Journal of Sports Medicine*. 25, 368–373.

Buckeridge, E. (2016) Incremental training intensities increases loads on the lower back of elite female rowers. *Journal of Sports Sciences*. 34, 369–378.

Buckeridge, E. M., Bull, A. M., & McGregor, A. H. (2014) Foot force production and asymmetries in elite rowers. *Sports Biomechanics*. 13, 47–61.

Droghetti, P. K., & Nilsen, T. (1991) The total estimated metabolic cost of rowing. *FISA Coach*. 2, 1–4.

Gajdosik, R., Hatcher, C., & Whitesell, S. (1992) Influence of short hamstring muscles on the pelvis and lumbar spine in standing and during the toe touch test. *Clinical Biomechanics*. 7, 38–42.

Hackney, A. C. (2001) Endurance exercise training and reproductive dysfunction in men: alterations of the hypothalamic – pituitary-testicular axis. *Current Pharmaceutical Design*. 7, 261–273.

Hartman, U., Mader, A., Wasser, K., & Klauer, I. (1993) Peak force, velocity, and power during five and ten maximal rowing ergometer strokes by world class female and male rowers. *International Journal of Sports Medicine*. 14 (Suppl. 1), S42–S45.

Hickery, G. J., Fricker, P. A., & McDonald, W. A. (1997) Injuries to elite rowers over a 10-year period. *Medicine and Science in Sports & Exercise*. 29, 1567–1572.

Ingham, S. A., Whyte, G. P., Jones, K., & Nevill, A. M. (2002) Determinants of 2000m rowing ergometer performance in elite rowers. *European Journal of Applied physiology*. 88, 243–246.

Izquierdo-Gabarren, M., Txabarri-Exposito, R. G., Villarreal, E. S., & Izquierdo, M. (2010) Physiological factors to predict on traditional rowing performance. *European Journal of Applied Physiology*. 108, 83–92.

Jefferys, I., & Moody, J. (2016) *Strength and conditioning for sports performance*. London, UK: Routledge.

Klesnev, V. (1991) *Improvement of dynamical structure of the drive in rowing*. PhD Thesis, Saint-Petersburg Institute of Sport.

Lawton, T. W., Cronin, J. B., & McGuigan, M. R. (2011) Strength testing and training of rowers: a review. *British Journal of Sports Medicine*. 41, 413–432.

Lee, J. H., Hoshino, Y., Nakamura, K., Kariya, Y., Saita, K., & Ito, K. (1999) Trunk muscle weakness as a risk factor for low back pain. *Spine*. 24, 54–57.

Mäestu, J., Jürimäe, J., & Jürimäe, T. (2005) Monitoring of performance and training in rowing. *Sports Medicine*. 35, 597–617.

McGregor, A. H., Anderton, L., & Gedroyc, W. M. W. (2002) The trunk muscles of elite oarsmen. *British Journal of Sports Medicine*. 36, 214–217.

McNeely, E., Sandler, D., & Bamel, S. (2005) Strength and power goals for competitive rowers. *Strength and Conditioning Journal*. 27, 10–15.

Nader, G. (2006) Concurrent strength and endurance training: from molecules to man. *Medicine & Science in Sports & Exercise*. 38, 1965–1970.

Nevill, A. M., Allen, V. S., & Ingham, S. A. (2011) Modelling the determinate of 2000m rowing ergometer performance: a proportion, curvilinear allometric approach. *Scandinavian Journal of Medicine & Science in Sport*. 21, 73–78.

Parkin, S., Norwicky, A. L., Rutherford, O. M., & McGregor, A. H. (2001) Do oarsmen have asymmetries in the strength of their back and leg muscles? *Journal of Sports Science*. 19, 521–526.

Schwanitz, P. (1991) Applying biomechanics to improve rowing performance. *FISA Coach*. 2, 1–7.

Secher, N. H. (1975) Isometric rowing strength of experienced and inexperienced oarsmen. *Medicine & Science in Sport*. 7, 280–283.

Secher, N. H. (1993) Physiological and biomechanical aspects of rowing: implications for training. *Sports Medicine*. 15, 24–42.

Secher, N. H., & Volianitis, S. (2007) *Rowing*. Oxford, UK: Wiley-Blackwell.

Spencer, S., Wolf, A., & Rushton, A. (2016) Spinal-exercise prescription in sport: classifying physical training and rehabilitation by intention and outcome. *Journal of Athletic Training*. 51, 613–628.

Steinacker, J. M. (1993) Physiological aspects of training in rowing. *International Journal of Sports Medicine*. 14, 3–10.

Stone, M. H., Stone, M. E., Sands, W., Pierce, K. C., Newton, R. U., Haff, G. G., & Carlock, J. (2006) Maximum strength and strength training – a relationship to endurance? *Strength and Conditioning Journal*. 28, 44–53.

Talbott, S. M., & Shapses, S. A. (1998) Fasting and energy intake influence bone turnover in lightweight male rowers. *International Journal of Sports Nutrition*. 8, 377–387.

Thompson, P., & Wolf, A. (2015). *Training for the complete rower: A guide to improving your performance*. Wiltshire, UK: Crowood Press.

Vinthers, A. (2008) *Rib stress fractures in elite rowers*. Lund, Denmark: Lund University.

Vinthers, A., Kanstrup, I. L., Christiansen, E., Ekdal, C., & Aagaard, P. (2008) Testosterone and BMD in elite male lightweight rowers. *International Journal of Sports Medicine*. 29, 803–807.

15
NETBALL

Chris McLeod and Katie James

Introduction (including athletic demands)

Netball is played by women at the elite and professional level. It is currently the largest female participation sport within the UK with 140,000 playing on a weekly basis (England Netball, 2012). Netball is a 7-a-side court-based invasion game played for 60 minutes split into 15 minute quarters. As an intermittent sport, the game consists of rapid acceleration and decelerations with frequent changes in direction and jumping, bounding and leaping actions. Netball is unique among team sports due to the specificity of positions, their court limitations and the technical skill required to play the position in the area of the court each player is allowed to operate (Trisha, 2011). In addition, the small court size (30.5m × 15.25m) increases the explosive, repetitive and tactical nature of the sport. It is important to note some critical rules that affect the athletic demands. In netball, no rolling substitutions are permitted; therefore, unless injured, athletes must play for a minimum of 15 minutes at a time. In addition, all players must abide by the stepping rule, in which a player must release a ball they have received within two steps. This latter rule has implications for injury and performance which will be discussed in more depth later. The major competitions for the national teams are the Commonwealth Games and World Cup, which occur every 4 years. During these competitions, teams will normally play 8 games in 10 days. Netball players, therefore, require the ability to repeat athletic and tactical performances on consecutive days with minimal recovery.

Research on the physical demands of netball predicted players cover between 2000–8000m in a game (Davidson and Trewartha, 2008), with the range due to position specific restrictions. Furthermore, as would be expected, research and data collected suggests that as the level of competition increases, so does the distance each position on court covers. Data collected on the Australian National teams suggests a new movement pattern is adopted every 2.7–5s, depending on position (Fox et al., 2013), with players who are more active and with more access to space on the court recording the most frequent changes in activity.

Literature suggests that each position has a specialised activity pattern. Loughran and O'Donoghue (1999) attempted to classify common netball movements. They suggest high intensity activities include running, shuffling, sprinting and netball specific movements with and without the ball. All other activities are considered low intensity.

Table 15.1 Summary of research describing distance covered in a game (values are in meters)

Authors	Study design	GK	GD	WD	C	WA	GA	GS
Davidson and Trewartha (2008)	English super league English super league N=6 (x2/position) N=6 (x2/position) Individual tracking for 60 minute games 4 games included	4283 ± 261			7984 ± 767			4210 ± 477
O'Donoghue and Loughran (1998)	British University games N=28 (x4/position) Computerised time-motion analysis on one quarter	~500	~1000	~1000	~1500	~1150	~1150	~450

Goal keeper (GK), goal defence (GD), wing defence (WD), centre (C), wing attack (WA), goal attack (GA), goal shooter (GS)

Table 15.2 Summary of research describing time active in a game

Playing position	Restricted surface area of court (m²)	Mean percentage of time active in a game				
		Fox et al. (2013)	Williams and O'Donoghue (2005)	Steele and Chad (1991)	Davidson and Trewartha (2008)	Gasston and Simpson (2004)
GK/GS	155	54	47–51	19–26	22–26	
WA/WD	301	72–76	53–61	23–31		
GA/GD	310	75–76	40–47	23–30		47 (GA)
C	446	83	73	45	55	

Injury prevalence

Non-contact landing mechanisms have been highlighted as a cause of significant injury in netball and constitute a common factor in female athletes who sustain anterior cruciate ligament (ACL) injuries. Otago (2004) investigated modifying the footwork rule to include an extra step and examined the effects of this on peak vertical ground reaction force (VGRF) and peak braking forces. This study analysed five different landing techniques with two of the five including an extra step. No significant difference was found between the landings and therefore no recommendation was made to change the footwork rule despite higher than previously reported Peak VGRF values at 3.53–5.74 times body weight. Steele and Milburn (1988) reviewed selected anthropometric measures and their relationship to landing kinematics in 21 midcourt netball athletes. Significant correlations ($r = 0.629$) were found in athletes with higher body mass who demonstrated larger braking forces when landing on their non-dominant leg and a lack of ankle range of movement, resulting in higher VGRF production.

Landings within netball are frequent, of significant force in vertical and horizontal planes and dependent on tactical and technical factors (Otago, 2004). Athletes require versatile landing strategies that incorporate adequate range of movement in the lower extremity to dissipate energy through the kinetic chain (Myer et al., 2013). This is key in female athletes who demonstrate decreased hip and knee flexion during landing tasks, which creates increased ACL loading (Alentorn-Geli et al., 2009).

As netball requires athletes to land with both a bilateral and unilateral stance, symmetry between dominant and non-dominant leg should be addressed to ensure capacity to manage the GRF associated with landing activities.

The footwork rule, requiring deceleration within one and a half steps, requires significant work from the posterior chain muscles to achieve this. The hamstrings are considered to have a key role as ACL agonists. They resist sheer forces (Zebis et al., 2013) and reduce the resultant loads by acting as an antagonist to the quadriceps (Alentorn-Geli et al., 2009). Finally, as netball athletes completed on average one jump per minute of matchplay, resistance to neuromuscular fatigue is crucial in order to mitigate the adverse effects of a delayed coordinated neuromuscular response to unanticipated landings which could lead to an ACL injury (Myer et al., 2012). Anterior Cruciate Ligament injuries continue to be a major time-loss injury in elite female sports (Myer et al., 2012, 2013). The high injury rates seen in netball may be the result of a multiple internal and external risk factors these are outlined below:

Internal risk factors

Age (maturation, aging)

- Athletes start playing intensively during teenage years.
- Can continue to play until early 30s at international level.
- Predisposition to valgus knee position seen throughout adolescence and adulthood.

Sex

- Female, 3–5 times more likely to sustain ACL injury
- Health (e.g. history of previous injury, joint instability)
- High proportions of athletes have had previous injury
- 72% previously ankle sprain of which 93% defined as having chronic ankle instability (CAI) (Attenborough et al., 2016)

Physical fitness

Need physical qualities to cope with demands and tolerate:

- 3.53–5.74 × BW VGRF
- 1 jump per minute
- Majority of landings are single leg

Anatomy/biomechanics

- Increased laxity and greater AP translation in female athletes
- Females are quadriceps dominant or hamstring deficient in cutting and jump landings
- Females have earlier and longer quadriceps activation on foot contact

Skill level

- Requirement for unilateral and bilateral landings. Rapid changes of direction, including a vertical jump element, with one and a half step deceleration
- Psychological factors (e.g. competitiveness, motivation, perception of risk)
- Athletes aware of risk through seeing other athletes injure
- Continuous decision making required throughout game due to limited time available to retain the ball (3s)

Exposure to external risk factors

- Sports factors (e.g. coaching, rules, referees)
- Footwork rule requiring rapid deceleration
- Able to contest for ball but no contact – open to interpretation by umpires
- Protective equipment (e.g. helmet, shin guards)
- Some use of ankle braces or taping not standardised

Fitness testing battery

The information above gives a good overview of the demands of international netball. However, the importance of understanding this can only be seen through our ability to use this information to positively influence coaching decisions that add value to performance. From a decision making perspective, the following section will talk through a framework (Figure 15.1) that can be used to make performance programming, planning and testing decisions. It is important to

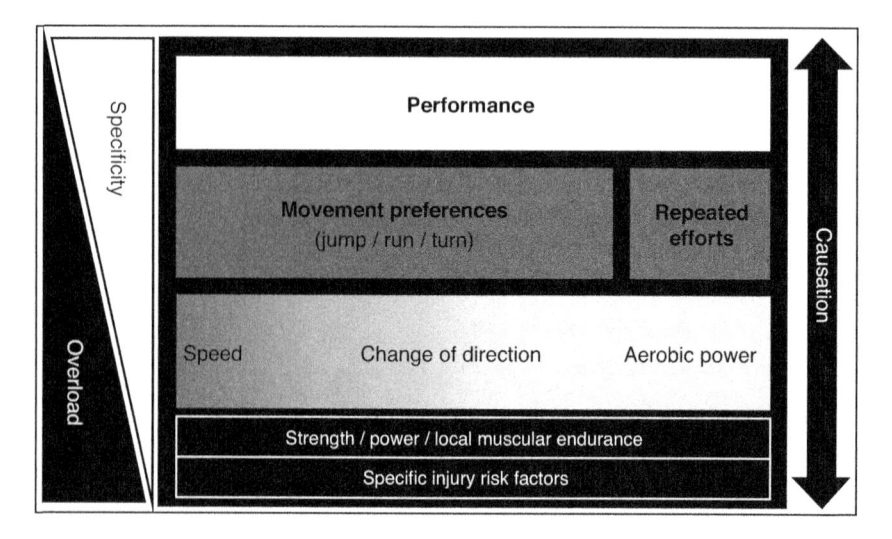

Figure 15.1 Performance framework underpinned by testing and monitoring

note that this is not a 'deterministic performance model' but a performance framework, which is used to:

1 Understand the performance needs of the sport, group, team and individual athlete (*reducing injury risk is seen as a key component in 'performance need'*).
2 Give increased understanding and insight into the athlete's strengths and key areas for development in the sport specific context.
3 Understand the athlete's physical profile to improve training direction.

The framework is not written to be restrictive but an adapting conceptual model that reflects the current thinking of the coaching and sports science team. It is recognised that this model is not perfect, but it is an attempt to shift from the historical ideal of preordained "best" training structures and towards a philosophy characterised by an adaptive readiness to respond to emerging "information" (Kiely, 2012).

Through the next section, the intention is to give a staged overview of the performance framework and discuss how this influences testing and monitoring. Specific examples of how this framework can be used in decision making for programming, planning and coaching, will also be discussed in a later section. It must be noted that this framework is primarily concerned with the physical development of the athlete.

Stage one: information gathering

The first stage of the framework is to gather information (coaches' opinion, qualitative and quantitative data trends and regular monitoring (Kiely, 2012)) to highlight key areas of strength and areas for development for each athlete. As can be seen from Figure 15.1, the higher up the framework you go, the more competition/match specific the information is, and the further down you go, the more reliable and repeatable the information (collected in testing) becomes. As a side note, there will always be outliers.

The framework adheres to some key principles:

1 Context of the framework is driven by netball performance (discussed in detail below).
2 The key elements are derived by a combination of expert opinion, context specific data and key research.
3 Upward and downward causation is present.
4 The further down the framework you go, the higher the chance for overload, while the further up, the greater the opportunity for specificity.

While all the above are important considerations, the third is important because the figure can be wrongly interpreted to imply that the factors at the bottom are developed to affect the layer above. While this may be the case, the reality is that the complex nature of sports performance means that adaptations in the top levels can positively affect those below. For example, an intense competition (performance) may positively impact change of direction and speed characteristics.

Stage two: testing and interpreting

The information gathered in stage one can be put into Figure 15.2. Explanations for the testing batteries used can be found in Table 15.3. This stage also requires some interpretation of data from testing.

[Framework diagram]

Performance
Coach philosophy / game + tournament demands / match data and video / coach + player feedback

Movement preferences: 10m speed / 15-0-5 / CMJ / step and jump / run and jump
Repeated efforts: Shuttle test

Speed: 10m / 20m speed
Change of direction: 15-05 (total / split / utilisation ratio)
Aerobic power: 30 – 15 (MAS)

Strength / power / local muscular endurance
MTIP / CMJ / drop jump / push up / trunk holds / supine pull / hamstring bridge / calf raise
Specific injury risk factors

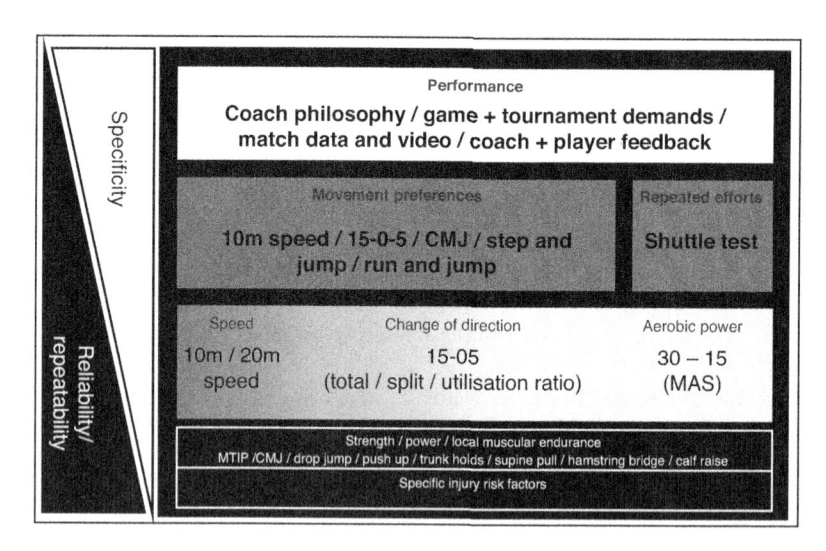

(Left axis: Specificity; Reliability/repeatability)

Figure 15.2 Performance framework underpinned by testing and monitoring (example)

Table 15.3 Testing batteries

Test(s)	Purpose	Variables used	Notes
10m speed	To measure acceleration ability	10m time (sec)	Timing gates at 10m, start 30cm behind line
15-0-5	To measure change of direction performance	Total time (sec) Turn time (sec) (Total time – first 10m and last 10m split) Utilisation ratio (Total time / 10m time) × 100)	Timing gates at 10m, start 30cm behind the line. First 10m split must be within 10% of acceleration time
Step and jump	To measure the ability to run and jump	Jump height (cm) Total height (cm)	Start 5m away and jump straight below vertex
CMJ	To measure leg extension power	PP/BW Jump Height (cm)	Hands on hips
Shuttle test	To measure the ability to repeat high intensity accelerations and change of direction	1st rep distance (m) 1 set total (m) 1 + 2 set total (m)	30 on, 25 off × 6 repeated shuttle (5m, 10m, 15m, 20m, 25m) two sets for mid court, 2 mins rest between
30-15	To measure maximal aerobic running speed	MAS – km/hr	
Mid thigh isometric pull (MTIP)	To measure the athletes ability to produce lower body force	Peak force (N) Peak force/BW (N/kg)	
Drop jump (DL/SL)	To measure the ability to generate reactive strength	Jump height (cm) Contact time (sec) RSI (flight time/contact time) Left to right symmetry	DL – from 40cm, SL from 20cm
Push up/trunk holds/supine pull/hamstring bridge/single leg calf raise	To measure endurance capacity in specific movements	Total reps	Note movement issues you may have observed. Ask the athlete what was the cause of the test ending

Netball

Figure 15.3 Scale to identify physical strengths and weaknesses of individual players

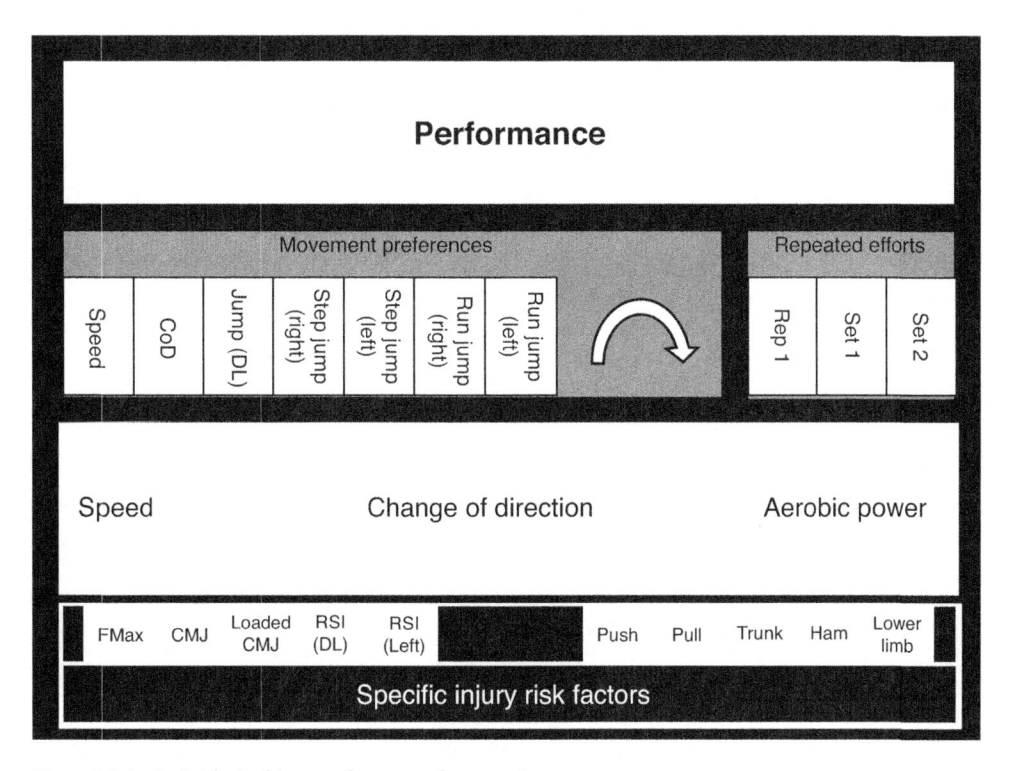

Figure 15.4 Individual athlete performance framework

To interpret the data and to set targets for individuals, each of the above tests can be placed on a 1–15 scale. This scale is based on current sport specific data as well as elite norms from other female strength/power sports. Whilst the specifics of this are outside the realms of this chapter, the scale below (Figure 15.3) shows how the 1 to 15 scale is defined. When players are scoring between 13–15, this can be seen as their '*super strength*'; below 6 / 7, it is thought to limit performance at the international level. The intention realistically is not to necessarily get all athletes to level 15 in all tests, but to remove rate limiters to performance, improve position specific factors and enhance athlete specific '*super strengths*'. The other major strength is that this is an easy way to create a common language between players, coaches and sport science staff around player profiles, individual athlete plans and team requirements.

Stage three: creating individual performance frameworks

The information that has been gathered and interpreted is then fed into a template (Figure 15.4) which produces an individual athlete performance framework.

Stage four: decision making

The next important element is how this information is used to make decisions. The following section will outline some of the theoretical underpinnings to each element of the performance framework.

Performance

The "performance" element is based on the coach's opinion, objective and subjective data and should contain the performance question(s) that you are trying to answer. These should begin with macro level questions, followed by meso and finally micro. This then forms a coherent performance plan. These questions will give direction to the training process to allow the creation of 'dynamic tension' between structural rigidity and responsive adaptability (Kiely, 2012). The structure is given by the clarity of performance questions and the performance framework, which allows flexibility in programming, planning and coaching. While the performance questions can range among the macro, meso and micro level, there is a set structure that allows the intervention to be impactful.

Structuring the performance question

The performance should be written in easily understood language to provide clear direction, but avoid being overly rigid in specifying how this should be delivered. There is a consistent structure to this, which is:

- How might ..... Who .... Do ...... What .... Impact

Example

How might the midcourt (*who*) increase (*do*) their ability to repeatedly change direction (*what*) so that they can turnover more balls (*impact*)?

(Modified from Isaksen et al., 2011)

Movement preference

The movement preferences are based on the underlying movements of sports performance. From a netball specific perspective, the possible combinations can be seen below in Figure 15.5.

The need to understand the movement preferences of athletes is important when considering the coaches' long-term philosophy, the opposition and the physical, technical and tactical requirements of each game. From a physical perspective it is important to understand what movements the athletes can perform and what are their 'preferred' movements. These preferences will be influenced by internal factors (e.g. limb length and sporting history) and external factors (e.g. sport specific context).

While there are some general physical qualities that underpin all of the tests, jumping, sprinting and change of direction abilities could represent separate and mainly independent motor abilities (Salaj and Markovic, 2011). There may also be variation in the magnitude of the limb to

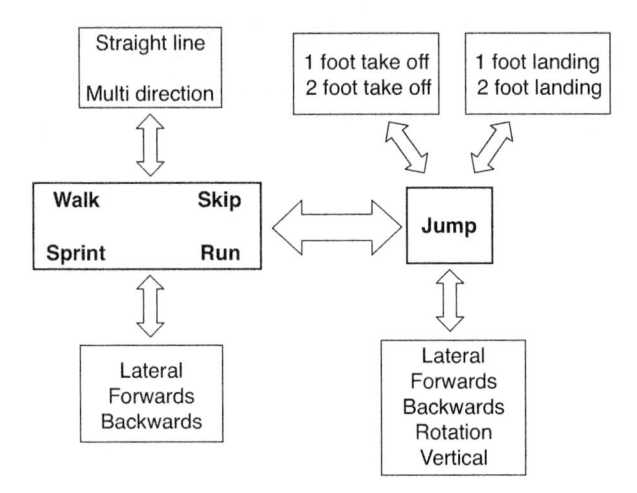

Figure 15.5 Netball specific movement patterns

limb asymmetry depending on the variable and direction used to quantify the asymmetry (Hewit et al., 2012). Because of this the range of tests give an excellent insight into the movement preferences of the athlete(s) related to the key movements involved in netball performance.

Repeated effort

While much has been written about repeated speed/effort training and its determinants, in a bid to further understand the physical effort it would take to win a World Championship a '*maximum effort*' game was recreated. The process for this was:

- Model '*what the players would need to do from a physical perspective to produce the game required to win the world championships?*' This was based on current AND previous coach information, international match statistics and expert coach opinion based on where the game may be heading in the future.
- How a game may look at its most physically demanding for each position was then calculated. This was then recreated using a specific bleep test where players ran and jumped on court using position specific routes and work rest intervals ($n = 16$ National squad players).
- Key tests (10m speed, CMJ, drop jump) were taken pre-test, at the end of each quarter and after the match (24 hours and 48 hours post-test).

The results showed that from a physical perspective the largest predictor of speed and power at the end of the simulation was speed and power at the start. This was consistent across all positions, with the correlation being greater for the end positions (r=.94) when compared to the mid court (r=.84). This would make sense due to both the higher amount of metres covered and change of directions performed. This increased reliance on endurance qualities may account for these lower correlations. The mid-court athletes with the lowest $\dot{V}O_{2max}$ (via bleep test) showed the biggest drop in speed/power measures. This was in line with work done by Bishop et al. (2003) who suggested that that if $\dot{V}O_{2max}$ is below 50–60ml/kg (11–13 on bleep test) it may still be a limiting factor in repeated speed ability.

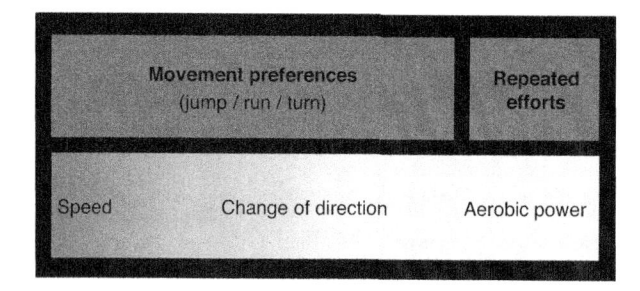

Figure 15.6 Repeated effort performance framework

This, together with current research, means that the philosophy around developing on court fitness is:

1   Physical on court performance is characterised by movement preferences and the ability to repeat high intensity movements
2   The ability to perform these are underpinned by change of direction, acceleration ability and jumping ability
3   The ability to repeat these are supported by an athlete's maximum aerobic speed

Again, this is not a one size fits all approach but gives a framework to make training decisions.

Strength/power/local muscular endurance

The final element is the strength/power and local muscular endurance characteristics of the athlete. The key here are that the tests used are repeatable and reliable and have face validity, and when decisions are made to develop specific qualities they are linked to performance parameters. The intention is that global measures (such as PP/BW, change of direction and 10m speed) give insight into '*what*' the athlete(s) can do and then other measures (such as flight time: contact time ratio, utilisation ratio and stride length, stride frequency) give insight into '*how*' they do it.

Programming

The penultimate section will now discuss how this framework is used to influence programming, planning and decision making. This will be done through three examples, showing a season planner, an individual athlete plan and then how the framework can be used on more acute performance questions.

Figure 15.7 below shows a sample season leading up to a major championships. The key principles of the planning are:

1   Performance priority driven
    Qualities are developed based on key performance questions linked to short and long term performance.
2   Criteria driven
    While there is distinct training blocks these are more fluid in nature based on the successes and gains made in the preceding block. For example, a critical amount of strength/power is needed before specific conditioning becomes relevant.
3   Individual athlete plans
    There is 'room' within the plans for individual athletes to develop qualities that are specific to them and their role within the team.

<table>
<tr><td></td><td>Wk 1</td><td>Wk 2</td><td>Wk 3</td><td>Wk 4</td><td>Wk 5</td><td>Wk 6</td><td>Wk 7</td><td>Wk 8</td><td>Wk 9</td><td>Wk 10</td><td>Wk 11</td><td>Wk 12</td><td>Wk 13</td><td>Wk 14</td><td>Wk 15</td><td>Wk 16</td><td>Wk 17</td><td>Wk 18</td><td>Wk 19</td><td>Wk 20</td><td>Wk 21</td><td>Wk 22</td><td>Wk 23</td><td>Wk 24</td><td>Wk 25</td><td>Wk 26</td><td>Wk 27</td><td>Wk 28</td><td>Wk 29</td><td>Wk 30</td><td>Wk 31</td><td>Wk 32</td><td>Wk 33</td><td>Wk 34</td><td>Wk 35</td></tr>
<tr><td></td><td></td><td>National selections</td><td colspan="2">World series</td><td colspan="5">Pre season</td><td colspan="3">Test matchs series</td><td colspan="10">National competition</td><td colspan="3">Mid season break</td><td colspan="5">National competition</td><td colspan="2">National finals</td><td colspan="2">Travel/comp prep</td><td>World championships</td></tr>
<tr><td colspan="36">1. Short to long</td></tr>
<tr><td>Movement skill(s)</td><td colspan="35">Athelete / group specific</td></tr>
<tr><td>Primary</td><td colspan="9">Strength</td><td colspan="3" rowspan="3">Competition</td><td colspan="10">Strength</td><td colspan="3">Spec power</td><td colspan="5">Specific conditioning</td><td colspan="2" rowspan="3">Competition</td><td colspan="3">Specific power</td></tr>
<tr><td>Secondary</td><td colspan="9">Conditioning (long intervals)</td><td colspan="10">Specific power (CoD / acceleration)</td><td colspan="3">Off feet cond</td><td colspan="5">Specific power (Cod / Acc)</td><td colspan="3">Specific cond</td></tr>
<tr><td>Supplementary</td><td colspan="9">Lower limb / trunk / hip LME</td><td colspan="10">Conditioning (short intervals)</td><td colspan="3">Drivers</td><td colspan="5">Strength</td><td colspan="3">Drivers</td></tr>
<tr><td colspan="36">2. Long to short</td></tr>
<tr><td>Movement skill(s)</td><td colspan="35">Athelete / group specific</td></tr>
<tr><td>Primary</td><td colspan="9">Strength</td><td colspan="3" rowspan="3">Competition</td><td colspan="10">Conditioning (short intervals)</td><td colspan="3">Spec power</td><td colspan="5">Specific conditioning</td><td colspan="2" rowspan="3">Competition</td><td colspan="3">Specific power</td></tr>
<tr><td>Secondary</td><td colspan="9">Conditioning (long intervals)</td><td colspan="10">Specific power (CoD / acceleration)</td><td colspan="3">Off feet cond</td><td colspan="5">Specific power (Cod / Acc)</td><td colspan="3">Specific cond</td></tr>
<tr><td>Supplementary</td><td colspan="9">Lower limb / trunk / hip LME</td><td colspan="10">Strength</td><td colspan="3">Drivers</td><td colspan="5">Strength</td><td colspan="3">Drivers</td></tr>
</table>

Figure 15.7 Individual athlete plan

Table 15.4 Definition of individual athlete planning terminology

Theme	Purpose
Movement skill(s)	To develop movement preferences in a way that has a meaningful transfer to sports performance/training
Strength	To develop the ability to produce maximal force in a way that has a meaningful transfer to sports performance/training
Local musular endurance (LME)	To develop the ability to repeatedly produce force in a specific muscle group in a way that has a meaningful transfer to sports performance/traning
Conditioning	To develop aerobic power in a way that positvely influences repeated speed ability
Specific conditioning	To develop repeated efforts in a way that positively influences on court performance
Specific power	To develop the ability to produce power in movements that are linked to sports performance
Competition	Optimise preparation and recovery in a way that positively effects competition performance
Drivers	To develop underlying issues/athlete specific known injury risk factors

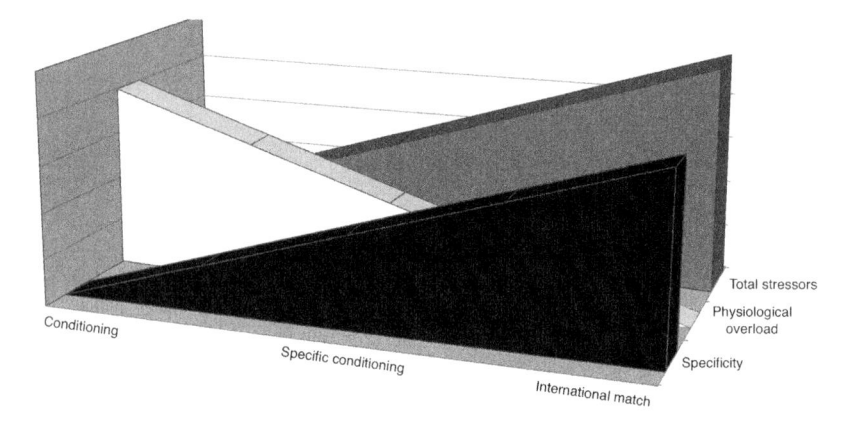

Figure 15.8 Individual athlete continuum

The purpose/explanation of each training phase labelled in Figure 15.7 can be seen below in Table 15.4.

As can be seen from Figure 15.7, there are two dominant planning schemes. They can be characterised as short-long or long-short. Based on the individual athlete profile the athletes will either develop:

1   Strength/power and then specific conditioning
2   Aerobic power and then specific conditioning

This approach should be consistent with the key principles discussed in the repeated speed section above. The use of specific power pre competition is important from a physical, psychological and team perspective. This would look more like the classic repeated speed work with short sprints interspersed with varying rest. While current research suggests that this may not be the 'optimal' approach to develop repeated speed/effort ability, it is enough to maintain qualities pre competition but more importantly can give psychological confidence in the player's ability to execute the game plan/strategy. This continuum is visualised below in Figure 15.8.

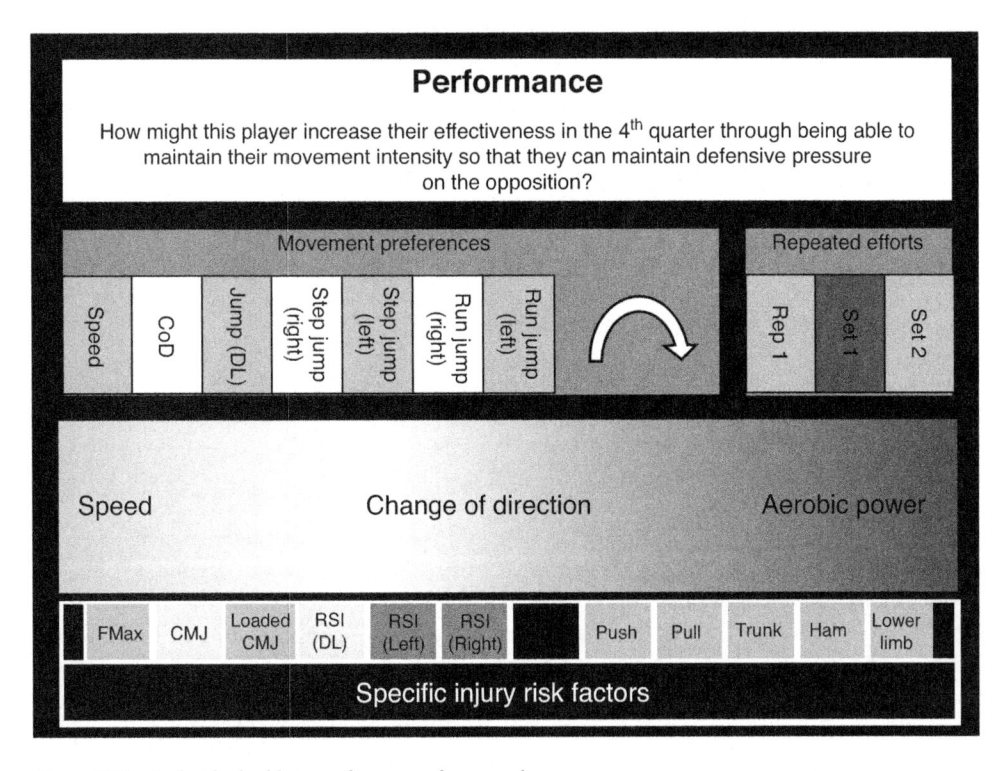

Figure 15.9 Individual athlete performance framework

ATHLETE PROFILE

As can be seen from the planning above (Figure 15.7), there are main headings for the training phases which allow individualisation in the specific areas. The following information aims to show the decision making around a specific athlete profile within the year plan above. Figure 15.9 shows a specific profile for an individual athlete with the colour scheme reflecting where each quality sits against the levels 1–15.

While the information above does not give us all of the answers, it does point us towards areas of development related to the performance question. The information shows that the key strengths of the athlete are:

- Speed
- Maximum Force (FMax)
- Loaded CMJ
- Lower muscular endurance

Those areas that are seen as rate limiters are:

- Repeated effort (Set 1)
- Aerobic power
- SL RSI
    - Change of direction is below required level

Given this information the key training priorities are:

1   **Change of direction (CoD) ability**

This is seen as priority due to the fact that it is difficult to repeat something that you have not got. Therefore, by raising the ability to change direction it gives a higher starting point and less cost for the same absolute intensity. Within this SL RSI should be focused on due to the relationships between this and the ability for an athlete to effectively decelerate (Netball national player data).

2   **Aerobic power (maximal aerobic speed (MAS))**

Programming for change of direction

What is important in the language used here is that we are developing change of direction speed and not agility. The key differentiation here is that agility involves perception action coupling with sport specific information while change of direction does not. This is not to say that agility is not important but the change of direction test may help us highlight where specific development areas are and CoD performance has been more strongly linked to physical qualities (Young et al., 2015). For example, if the coach reports an issue on court but CoD speed is good, then more work may need to go into developing perception–action coupling in sport specific situations. One of the reasons a 180° turn is used is that our research has shown that most of the variance within 45°, 90° and 125° turns can be explained by straight line speed and 180° turn performance. This allows us to use two tests to infer performance across CoD performance.

While the information in Figure 15.10 has been discussed early in this chapter, Figure 15.11 is concerned with a more qualitative description of performance. The key principles are:

1   The type of change of direction performed is determined by the pre velocity and the post velocity. For example, a swerve would have higher pre and post speeds than a 5–0–5 test.
2   In good change of direction performance, there are critical positions that the athlete has to be able to produce.
3   The further down the framework you go, the increased chance for overload, while the further up, the greater the opportunity for specificity.
4   The ability to create these positions is determined by the balance between the required change in momentum and the force potential of the individual.

The key positions are:

1   Penultimate step

The last step before the change of direction and is crucial to 'set up' effective change of direction. This is characterised by placing a foot in front of the CoM, contralateral upper body rotation towards stance leg, gap between knees and 'active' foot placement, which is often flat when the shin is perpendicular to the ground.

2   CoD step

The key change of direction step and is crucial to 'set up' the first acceleration step. This is characterised by upper body rotation towards direction of travel, minimal contralateral hip drop and a knee to knee gap in the frontal plane.

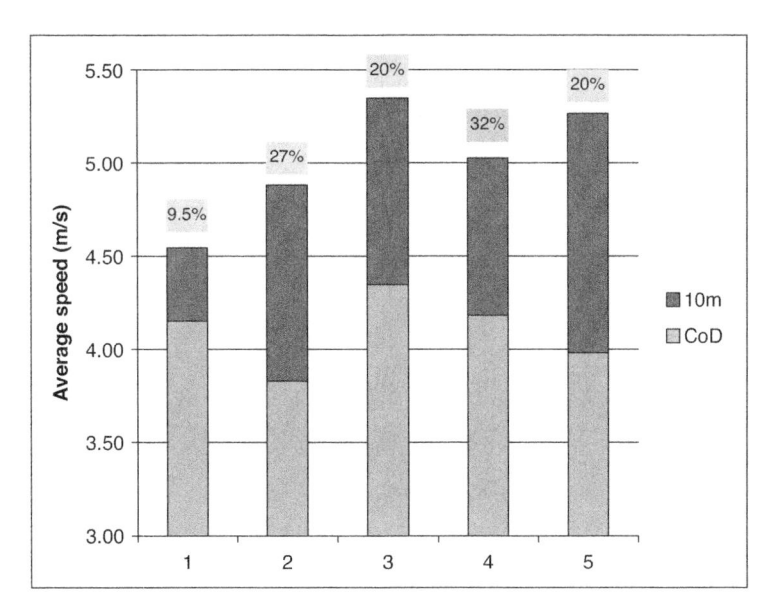

Figure 15.10 Player change of direction profiles (number above bar is utilisation ratio, (CoD time − 10m speed / 10m speed)).

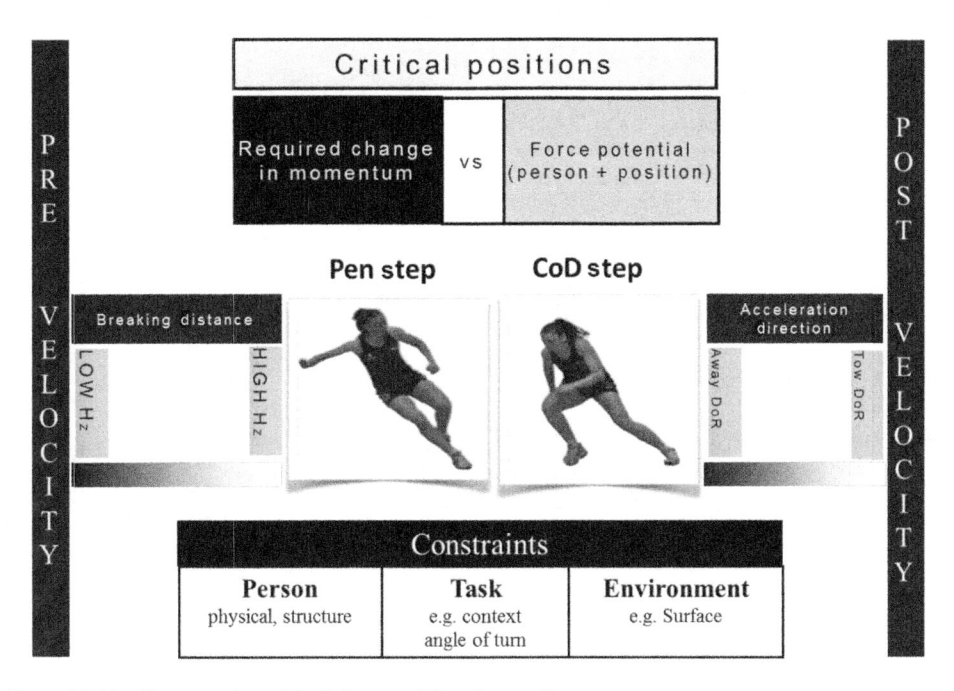

Figure 15.11 Conceptual model of change of direction performance

How the athlete gets in and out of the key positions is characterised by:

1   Deceleration distance

The distance between the first deceleration step and the change of direction step. This is further characterised by deceleration frequency which is the deceleration distance/number of steps. This is not right or wrong but can give insight into an athlete's movement preferences.

2   Acceleration direction

The direction of the first acceleration step. For most turns, the best performers get their first step towards the intended direction of travel.

The athlete in question is athlete 5 in Figure 15.10 and the key points of information are:

1   Good 10m speed but a large utilisation ratio (Figure 15.10).
2   From a qualitative viewpoint (Figure 15.11 as a framework): large, high frequency deceleration distance and a first step that is not towards the direction of travel.

Table 15.5 below shows the classes of exercises used and Table 15.6 shows the specific exercises used in this example with the intention of changing:

1   Leg extension strength via changes in CSA
2   SL Reactive strength index
3   First acceleration step in the direction of intended travel

Table 15.5 Change of direction – key principles and exercises

	Structure	*Local*	*Global*	*Specific*
Key principles	Adaptation is specific to desired outcome	Internally specific (MTU)	Outcome specificity	Specificity of: 1. Purpose 2. Physical 3. Technical/tactical 4. Psychological
Example outcome	Increased CSA	Improved pre activation	Improved 'closed' change of direction ability	Perception – action coupling
Example exercise(s)	Leg press/heavy calf raise	Kettlebell swing/ drop jump variations	Wall run(s)	Conditioning game(s)

Table 15.6 Change of direction – structural, local and global exercises

	Structure	*Local*	*Global*
Exercise(s)	Back squat/leg press	SL drop jump 1. Intensity focus = box height/contact time as variables) 2. Variation focus = contact time/surface type as variable)	Wall runs

Programming for aerobic power

The below is an example of how you might include some additional aerobic training into an athlete's schedule twice a week. This programme uses maximal aerobic speed (MAS) training and not skill-based games. The intensities are based from the scores of an intermittent MAS test e.g. 30–15 (velocity intermittent fitness test (VIFT)). There are two types of sessions, each are progressed throughout the week. In each progression (apart from the last session), no more than one variable is adjusted. This programme is an "off-season" programme for developing aerobic power and is an example of the long to short model periodisation already described, whereby aerobic power is developed before sport specific conditioning. This programme will develop the athlete's $\dot{V}O_{2max}$ and therefore, would reduce the drop off in sport specific speed and power performances during more specialised training and games.

Below is a table of variables, which can be used to manipulate MAS training sessions, in order to achieve a desired outcome. It is important to note that aerobic power can also be developed by small sided games but it is the thought in this style of periodisation, where skill might affect the development of aerobic power, that these should be incorporated later in the season.

Table 15.7 Example of maximal aerobic speed training programme

Week:	1		2		3		4		5	
Session:	1	2	1	2	1	2	1	2	1	2
Work:rest	30:30	15:15	30:30	15:15	30:30	15:15	30:30	15:15	30:30	15:15
Intensity	100%	105%	105%	108%	105%	110%	105%	110%	108%	115%
Shuttle Style	Straight Preferred	Long Shuttle	Straight Preferred	Long Shuttle	Straight Preferred	Long Shuttle	Straight Preferred	Long Shuttle	Straight Preferred	Long Shuttle
Reps	12	15	12	15	9	15	12	12	12	15
Sets	2	2	2	2	3	2	3	3	3	3
Rep rest intensity	Passive	25%	Passive	25%	Passive	25%	Passive	25%	Passive	25%
Set rest intensity	Passive	Passive	Passive	Passive	Passive	Passive	Passive	Passive	Passive	Passive
Rest between sets	3 minutes	3 minutes	3 minutes	3 minutes	3 minutes	3 minutes	3 minutes	3 minutes	3 minutes	3 minutes

Table 15.8 Variables of maximal aerobic speed programming

Work duration	The length of time an athlete is running for. The longer the duration, the more reliant on the aerobic metabolism. Shuttles can last from 6s to 3 minutes. For team sport athletes, a cap of 45s is suggested.
Work: rest ratio	This represents the difference between the work and rest durations. Typically aerobic ratios are 1–2:1.
	Ratio of 1:2–5 would typically develop high speed endurance. Ratio of 2:1–1:5 would have an anaerobic overload.
	Ratio of 1:2–1:10 would have a speed development focus.

(Continued)

Table 15.8 (Continued)

Intensity	This is typically derived from a maximal aerobic speed test such as the 30–15VIFT. Please note if you use an intermittent test, the final score achieved will be around 120% of that achieved on a continuous test. If using an intermittent test aerobic running intensities would range from 100–115%.
	Mean HR for aerobic training is typically around 80% of maximum. Although a range of 80–100% can be expected.
Changes of direction	The number of shuttles and changes of direction involved will increase/decrease the neuromuscular demand of the exercise.
Reps + sets	Reps and sets can be manipulated to affect volume and work and distance covered.
Rep rest intensity	This can be passive or active. Active rest will stop the body's buffering ability.
Set rest intensity	This can be passive or active. Active rest will stop the body's buffering ability.
Rest between sets	This can be manipulated depending on level of recovery you require prior to successive sets.
Surface	This can be manipulated if you require athletes to have good ankle stability and if athletes react to hard surfaces.
Type	Aerobic training can be made off-feet if you are managing athletes 'on-feet time'.

ACUTE PERFORMANCE QUESTIONS

The final programming section is concerned with acute performance questions. The case study here is based on the question:

> *"Can our current defenders take high turnover ball from the top 3 attackers in the world?"*

This creates an opportunity:

> *"How to get defenders to be able to take high ball from opposition attackers to decrease shooting opportunities and increase turnovers?"*

Before we can write a programme to influence this we must understand what the athletes need to be able to do. As can be seen in Figure 15.12, in order to take high ball from top attackers, defenders must be able to have a total jump and reach of 310 cm.

The movement preference information then gives us some insight into where the areas of development may be needed.

As can be seen in Figure 15.13, the only player who can currently achieve the height of 310cm is player 1 (only in the run and jump). This has large implications for the tactics/strategies available to the coach and the information highlights some key needs of the players. Figure 15.14

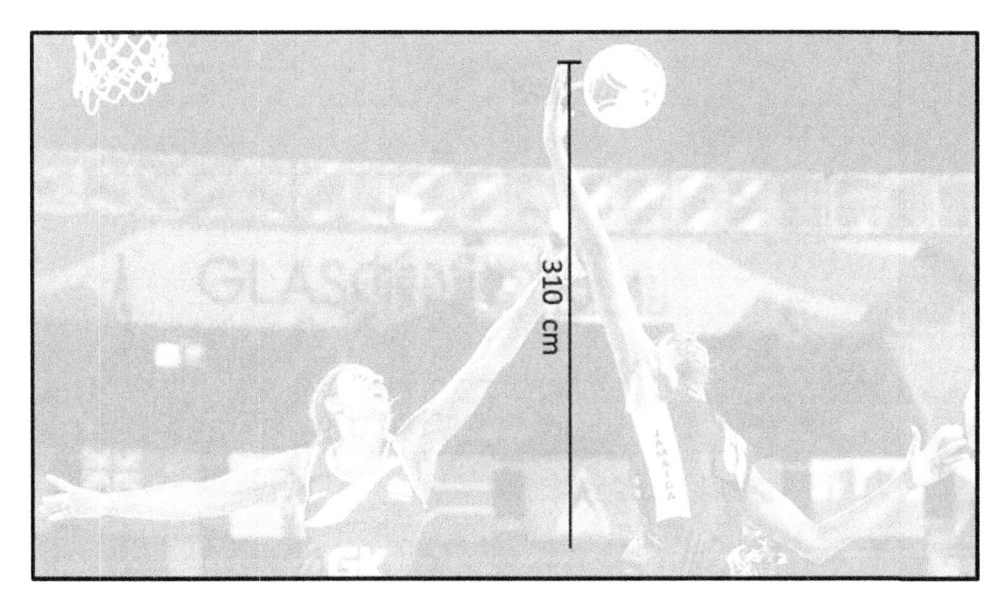

Figure 15.12 Performance question: maximal jump height of defenders **275cm** (Stand and reach) + **35cm** (jump height) = **310cm** (total height)

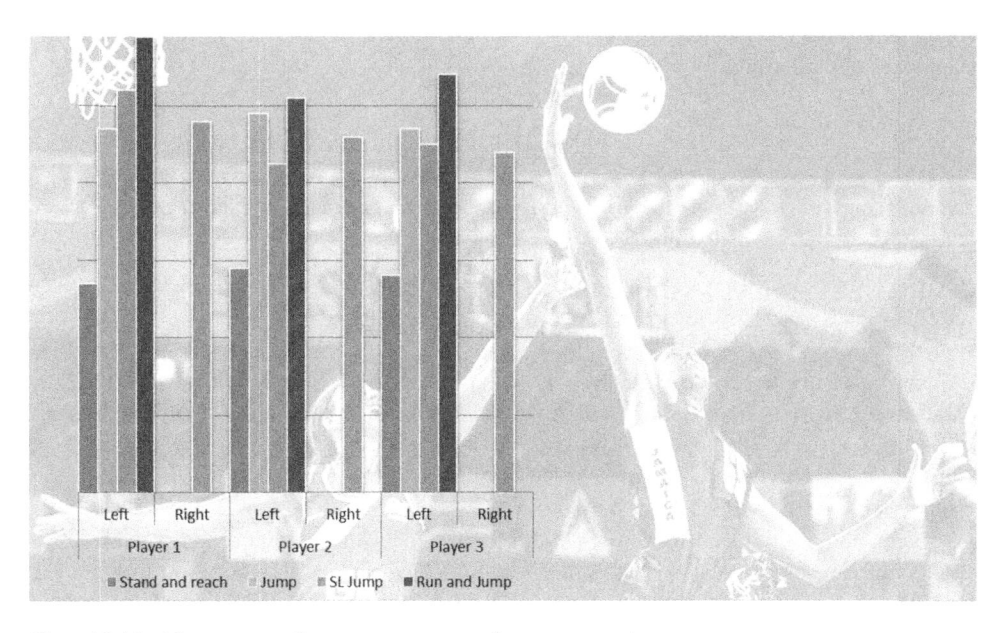

Figure 15.13 Movement preferences to answer performance question

	Player 1		Player 2		Player 3	
	Left	Right	Left	Right	Left	Right
Stand and reach (CM)	254		258		256	
Jump (CM)	294		298		294	
SL jump (CM)	304	296	285	292	290	288
Run and jump (CM)	318		302		308	
10m time						
CoD						
Utilisation ratio						
Turning	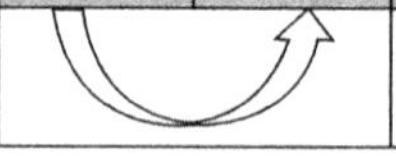 ↰		 ↱		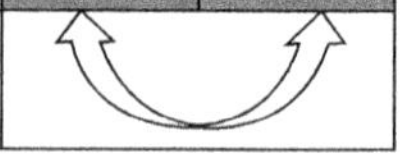 ↰	

Figure 15.14 Individual player movement preference

also include 10m time, change of direction time and their turning preference (way they prefer to turn). In summary, therefore:

Player 1

Can achieve the height with a run and jump and has good acceleration and change of direction ability (with a preference for anti-clockwise turning). Training may need to focus on double and single leg jumping ability.

Player 2

Cannot achieve the height on any jumps and has poor 10m and change of direction times (with a preference for clockwise turning).

Player 3

Cannot achieve the height on any jumps but has good 10m and change of direction ability.

The below is an example programme to develop jump, 10m and change of direction performance in player 2. Please note, these focus primarily on structural and local adaptations. Global and specific adaptations can be developed alongside on the court within netball and specific training sessions.

The intention if this information is simply to add value to the coach's decision making process and highlight key areas for development. It also means that training decisions can be more focused if the coach knows whether the athlete has the physical ability to perform the required match specific tasks. This was highlighted in a small study comparing the perception of a top international coach on how well the players could perform key movements and then the reality if the physical data out if context (>0.2 rank correlation).

Table 15.9 Example programme to improve jump performance

Jumping programme		
Hang clean	4 × 4	Structure
Back squat	5 × 4	Structure
Repetitive hurdle jumping (×5)	4 × 5	Local
Single leg drop jump	3 × 3	Local
Kettlebell swings	3 × 12	Local
Ankle drills	4 × 20m	Local

Table 15.10 Example programme to improve 10m performance

10m programme		
Hip thrust	5 × 4	Structure
Dead leg press	5 × 3	Structure
Broad jump	3 × 4(×1)	Local
Glute-ham raise	4 × 6	Structure
Romanian deadlift	4 × 5	Structure
Heavy acceleration walks	6 × 30m	Global

Table 15.11 Example programme to improve change of direction performance

Change of direction programme		
Deadlift	5 × 5	Structure
Bulgarian squat	4 × 6	Structure
Lateral single leg depth jump	3 × 3	Local
Weighted lateral slide board	4 × 10	Global
Single leg good morning	4 × 6	Structure
Nordic hamstring curl	4 × 5	Structure

Specific injury risk factors

As has been described above the process is first to understand the demands of the game, then the key principles and then how this impacts individual specific programming and planning interventions.

Programming to reduce injury risk

As can be seen from the information above, injury risk is highly complex and there are many interrelated factors. It is, therefore, not the intention of the authors to try and simplify this and give cookie cutter programmes and exercises but instead to give examples of the thinking behind exercise selection and injury risk in specific areas. To do this we have chosen to focus on the hip

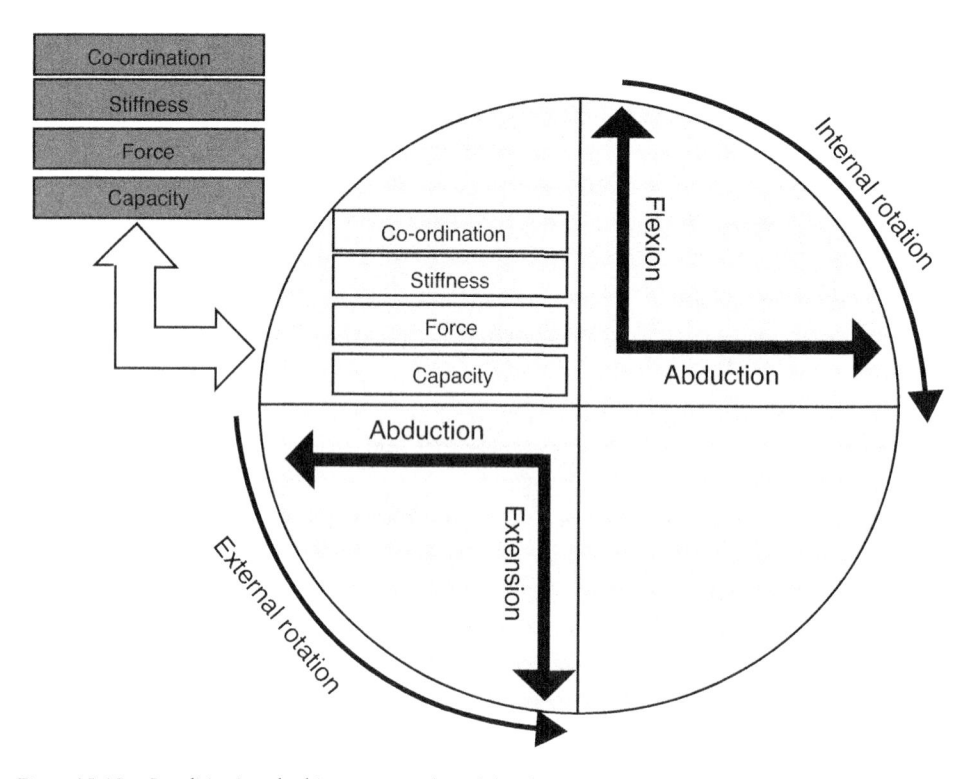

Figure 15.15 Conditioning the hip conceptual model – the 5D hip

and its relation to injury risk in netball. The following information will cover a philosophical model which is followed by some thoughts on how this affects exercise selection.

Conditioning the hip in netball

The model below is referred to as the 5D hip as it is concerned with making the hip function in 5 dimensions. The dimensions are:

Space (3 dimensions)
Context/Coordination
Time

Dimensions 1 to 3: space

The first three dimensions of conditioning the hip are forwards – backwards (flexion/extension), side to side (abduction/adduction) and rotation (internal and external). When discussing hip conditioning in recent times there is often a quick leap to posterior chain strength and glute activation and, while these elements are not by themselves wrong, if taken in isolation they can ignore and discount the complex nature of the hip.

Given the variety of roles muscles must perform dependent on the task, limb position and speed, there is a strong argument that we need to start discussing total hip conditioning before we begin to isolate. A full overview is outside the realms of this chapter, but some specific considerations are discussed below.

The 3D hip

The common hip strategies are around improving hip extension capability through specific training focusing on 'posterior chain strength' and improving hip abduction strength through specific focus on glute med coordination and/or strength. Sometimes the forgotten areas can be hip flexion and adductor strength.

Hip flexion

Research supports the importance of the hip flexors in hip extension torque (although carried out with elite sprinters) where a strong relationship was found between hip flexion and hip extension strength (Guskiewicz et al., 1993) and running speed. (Hoshikawa et al., 2006). All of this points to the importance of hip flexor strength in optimising hip function and specifically hip extensor power through effective energy transfer. The hip flexor is the only muscle that has the anatomical potential to contribute to stability and movement of the trunk, pelvis and legs (Torry et al., 2006). This cannot be ignored and is crucial for the hips' role in transferring energy/force through the body.

The final consideration is the relationship between hip flexion and pain/injury. While many studies have focused on transverse abdominus and multifidus cross section area and control when pain is present, a similar pattern is seen in the hip flexors with specific decreased cross sectional area seen in chronic pain.

Hip flexion is an important element in preparing the hip for the demands that are placed on it. Key considerations for coaches are:

- Hip extension power is closely related to and may be limited by hip flexor strength and cross sectional area.
- Well coordinated flexion of the opposite limb can enhance extension power through reflexes and through optimising length relationships of the hamstrings.
- Changes in coordination and cross sectional area within the hip flexors can occur with pain and/or injury in and around the hips.

Hip adduction

The adductor group is made up of four muscles (Longus, Magnus, Brevis and Gracilus). These muscles all adduct the hip but are also involved in hip flexion/extension and internal rotation depending on the position of the limbs. The crucial aspect of this is that without adductor strength, capacity and coordination, they are unable to assist in hip flexion, hip extension and rotational tasks. This means that issues may often appear at other sites such as Psoas, Biceps Femoris and Obliques, but this may be due to the fact that the adductor group is unable to assist with the movement tasks. The importance of the adductor group has been confirmed by Tyler et al. (2001), who showed that athletes who do not have a high add:abd strength ratio are more at risk to hip related injury. This once again highlights the important of 5D conditioning of the hip.

- When looking at the hip, it is crucial we consider its functional anatomy and implications for health and performance.
- As well as general strength/conditioning (to be discussed later), balance in the 3 dimensions is key to hip health, energy transfer and performance.

Dimension 4: context/coordination

Dimension 4 is referred to as context; it is concerned with how the individual coordinates what they have in specific contexts. On a local level, this is how the hip coordinates and then, on a global level, how it integrates this into the specific movement.

For something to be context/coordination specific, it must:

- Overload the amount and or rate of force.
- Specific rate and time of maximum force production (rate of force development).
- Specific type of muscular contraction.

(Variation on Dynamic Correspondence model, Siff and Verkhoshansky, 2009)

One of the areas that becomes clear when discussing jumping, running and throwing is the specific nature of the coordination within a sport specific task. This can be seen from an inter muscular coordination perspective, but also from an overload perspective. This is shown in work by Chumanov et al. (2007) which, through exploring muscle tendon interaction, reinforces how specific the muscle tendon loading is in high intensity tasks. This highlights an obvious, but often missed element of conditioning the hip: that for optimal conditioning and adaptation, there must be regular and consistent high intensity repetitions of the competition task. While we can develop physical capacity, the unique demands of the tasks mean that it needs to be done near to 100% maximum on a regular basis.

- Coordination can be specific on local level (hip) and global within the movement pattern.
- The specific nature of coordination means that the specific exercises that adhere to the three rules above must be incorporated consistently in the training programme to place the specific demands on the hip musculature.

Dimension 5: time

The fifth and final dimension is time. This is concerned with whether the hip can function and continue to function optimally over time. While coordination is important, the underlying physical qualities give the engine for this.

The physical qualities that underpin this are force, capacity and stiffness.

1   Force

Ability of the muscle to exert force in a specific movement.

2   Capacity

Ability to repeatedly exert force in a specific movement.

3   Stiffness

Ability of the muscle tendon unit to absorb force and rebound.

Table 15.12 Conditioning the hip – key principles and associated exercises

	Capacity	Force	Stiffness	Coordination
Sampe exercise	Adductor side bridge	Back squat	Kettle bell swing	Lateral drop jump
Key principles	High time under tension (TUT)	High load	Overload the amount and/or rate of force. Specific rate and time of maximum force production (rate of force development) and muscular contraction (see Earp et al., 2014 for insight into specifics).	
			Internally specific	Internally and externally specific

The purpose of the information above is to give a framework for conditioning the hip for health and performance in netball. Whilst specific outcomes may be dependent on the athlete, this gives us some general coaching principles:

- Training should develop high force, capacity and stiffness qualities of the hip extensors, flexors, abductors, adductors, internal and external rotators. The aim of this to create a balanced hip.
- Coordination can and should be developed around the hip, using specific exercises and regular exposure to the specific sporting movement.

While it is difficult to give specifics due to the unique nature of the individual plan, Table 15.5 describes the key principles of each category and associated example exercises.

Conclusion

This commentary on strength and conditioning has demonstrated the complexity that is evident in netball. What has been provided is a framework which can be used in the decision making process to develop programmes which take into account individual needs whilst respecting the philosophy of the coach. The authors would like to acknowledge that many of the concepts of our netball training philosophy have come from countless conversation with the netball coach, Lyn Gunson.

References

Alentorn-Geli E et al. Prevention of non-contact anterior cruciate ligament injuries in soccer players. Part 1: Mechanisms of injury and underlying risk factors. *Knee Surg Sports Traumatol Arthrosc.* 2009; 17(7): 705–729.

Attenborough, AS, Sinclair, PJ, Sharp, T, Greene, A, Stuelcken, M, Smith, RM, and Hiller, CE. A snapshot of chronic ankle instability in a cohort of netball players. *J Sci Med Sport.* 2016; 19(5): 379–383.

Bishop D, Lawrence S, and Spencer M. Predictors of repeated-sprint ability in elite female hockey players. *J Sci Med Sport.* 2003; 6(2): 199–209.

Chumanov ES, Heiderscheit BC, and Thelen DG. The effect of speed and influence of individual muscles on hamstring mechanics during the swing phase of sprinting. *J Biomech.* 2007; 40: 3555–3562.

Davidson A and Trewartha G. Understanding the physical demands of netball: A time-motion investigation. *Int J Perform Anal Sport.* 2008; 8: 1–17.

Earp JE, Newton RU, Cormie P, and Blazevich AJ. The influence of loading intensity on muscle-tendon unit behavior during maximal knee extensor stretch shortening cycle exercise. *Eur J Appl Physiol.* 2014; 114: 59–69.

Fox A et al. Activity profiles of the Australian female netball team players during international competition: Implications for training practice. *J Sports Sci.* 2013; 31(14): 1588–1595.

Gasston V and Simpson C. A netball specific fitness test. *Int J Perform Anal Sport.* 2004; 4: 82–96.

Guskiewicz, K, Lephart, S, and Burkholder, R. The relationship between sprint speed and hip flexion/extension strength in collegiate athletes. *Isokinetics and Exercise Science.* 1993; 3(2): 111–116.

Hewit JK, Cronin JB, and Hume PA. Asymmetry in multi-directional jumping tasks. *Phys Ther Sport.* 2012; 13: 238–242.

Hoshikawa, Y, Muramatsu, M, Iida, T, Uchiyama, A, Nakajima, Y, Kanehisa, H, and Fukunaga, T. Gender differences in yearly changes in the cross-sectional areas and dynamic torques of thigh muscles in high school volleyball players. *International Journal of Sport and Health Science.* 2006; 4, 29–35.

Isaksen SG, Dorval KB, and Treffinger DJ. *Creative Approaches to Problem Solving: A Framework for Innovation and Change* (3rd ed.). Thousand Oaks, CA: Sage, 2011.

Kiely J. Periodization paradigms in the 21st century: Evidence-led or tradition-driven? *Int J Sports Physiol Perform.* 2012; 7(3): 242–250.

Loughran BJ and O'Donoghue PG. Time-motion analysis of work-rate in club netball. *J Hum Mov Stud.* 1999; 36: 37–50.

Myer GD et al. An integrated approach to change the outcome part I: Neuromuscular screening methods to identify high ACL injury risk athletes. *J Strength Cond Res.* 2012; 26(8): 2265–2271.

Myer GD et al. Clinic-based algorithm to identify female athletes at risk for anterior cruciate ligament injury: letter to the editor. *Am J Sports Med.* 2013; 41(1): NP1–6.

O'Donoghue P and Loughran B. *Analysis of Distance Covered During Intervarsity Netball Competition.* Presented at Book of Abstracts, World Congress of Notational Analysis of Sport IV, 1998.

Otago L. Kinetic analysis of landings in netball: Is a footwork rule change required to decrease ACL injuries? *J Sci Med Sport.* 2004; 7: 85–95.

Salaj S and Markovic G. Specificity of jumping, sprinting, and quick change-of-direction motor abilities. *J Strength Cond Res.* 2011; 25: 1249–1255.

Siff M and Verkhoshansky Y (eds). *Supertraining* (6th ed.), 2009.

Steele JR and Chad KE. *An Analysis of the Movement Patterns of Netball Players During Match Play: Implications for Designing Training Programs.* National Sports Research Centre, 1991.

Steele JR and Milburn P. Ground reaction forces on landing in netball. *J Hum Mov Stud.* 1988; 13: 399–410.

Torry MR, Schenker ML, Martin HD, Hogoboom D, and Philippon MJ. Neuromuscular hip biomechanics and pathology in the athlete. *Clin Sports Med.* 2006; 25: 179–197, vii.

Trisha. 2011. *Physical Preparation for Netball – Part 1: Needs Analysis and Injury.* pp. 1–6.

Tyler TF, Nicholas SJ, Campbell RJ, and McHugh MP. The association of hip strength and flexibility with the incidence of adductor muscle strains in professional ice hockey players. *Am J Sports Med.* 2001 Mar–Apr; 29(2): 124–128.

Williams R and O'Donoghue P. Lower limb injury risk in netball: A time-motion analysis investigation. *Journal of Human Movement Studies* 2005; 49: 315–331.

Young WB, Dawson B, and Henry GJ. Agility and change-of-direction speed are independent skills: Implications for training for agility in invasion sports. *Int J Sports Sci Coach.* 2015; 10: 159–169.

Zebis MK et al. Kettlebell swing targets semitendinosus and supine leg curl targets biceps femoris: An EMG study with rehabilitation implications. *Br J Sports Med.* 2013; 47(18): 1192–1198.

16
VOLLEYBALL

Jeremy Sheppard, Paula Charlton, David Watts and Tim Pelot

Introduction to the sport

Volleyball is amongst the most popular team sports worldwide, with reported participation rates ranking only second to soccer (Reeser et al., 2006). The sport is enjoyed at all competitive levels (junior, amateur, professional and Olympic) and since the inclusion of volleyball at the 1964 summer Olympic games in Tokyo, its popularity has continued to increase. According to the Federation International De Volley-Ball (FIVB) founded in 1947, the sport currently has over 200 member countries and approximately 150 million players participating (Bahr and Bahr, 1997). The worldwide popularity of volleyball is perhaps due, in part, to the minimal equipment requirements (only a net and ball) and non-contact nature of the game whereby opposing players are separated across a net, which lends itself to participation across genders and a variety of ages. Teams consist of six players per side, one setter, two middle blockers, one pass hitter and an opposite, in addition to recent rule changes denoting the inclusion of a defensive, non-jumping specialist – the Libero. The volleyball court is divided into front and back sections by the attack line (or three-metre line), with the majority of jump/landing activity (spiking, blocking and setting) occurring by the three players in the front court. Each time service is won back from the opposition, the players must rotate once by one position clockwise. Game rules stipulate the ball to be in rebound only, contributing to ensuring the game is interesting and spectator friendly, as the ball is in constant motion.

Athletic demands

Volleyball is characterized by frequent short bouts of high-intensity exercise, followed by periods of low-intensity exercise and brief rest periods (Sheppard et al., 2009b). The high-intensity bouts of exercise with relatively short recovery periods, coupled with the total duration of the match (~60–90 minutes), suggests that volleyball players require well developed anaerobic alactic (ATP-CP) and anaerobic lactic (anaerobic glycolytic) energy systems, as well as reasonably well developed aerobic capabilities (Sheppard et al., 2008c). Collectively, volleyball players possess considerable speed and muscular power and the ability to perform these repeated maximal efforts with limited recovery for the duration of the match (Sheppard et al., 2007).

Based on testing results and observation of match conditions, considerable demands are placed on the neuromuscular system during the various sprints, dives, jumps and multi-directional court movements that occur repeatedly during competition (Sheppard et al., 2009b). Importantly, volleyball involves a great deal of defensive and offensive jumping activities, which primarily feature jumping to spike the ball (jumping to hit the ball over the net) and blocking (jumping to extend hands above the net to defend the angle of attack of the spike). Depending on position, jumping activity can involve 100–150 maximum effort jumps per match, whilst the setter will perform often 20 more additional jumps per set (~60–100 per match), generally at less than maximal intensity, in the act of setting the ball to an attacker on their team, a skill termed a *jump set* (Sheppard et al., 2009b). The greatest blocking demand is placed on the Middles in comparison with Setters and Outsides, with Setters and Outsides involved in a similar volume of blocking demands. In addition, Middles perform the most spike jumps, followed by Outsides then Setters. As such, the maximum effort jump and landing demands of Middles are greatest of all positions, which is particularly noteworthy when you consider that these athletes tend to be the tallest and heaviest position players on a volleyball team. However, this cannot be assumed to equate to the highest total physiologic stress because, on nearly all teams, the middle player is removed from the majority of back-court play by the defensive specialist libero position. This significantly reduces the total physiologic load of the middle player.

Our observations show that national team training can involve as many as 5000 jumps in a week (with 2000–3000 jumps/week common at national team level), of which half may be maximal effort jumps. These jumping activities can include both horizontal approach movements (spike jumps), as well as movements without an approach (jump setting, jousts, blocking). Considering the tactical nature of these jumping activities, and the frequency that they occur in a typical match, both counter-movement jump ability (i.e. jump and reach height) and approach jump ability (i.e. spike jump height) are considered critical performance indicators in elite volleyball (Sheppard et al., 2009a).

An analysis of volleyball's demands also has implications in regard to the very fast movement demands to get into position to perform attack and block jumps, change position to defend or vice-versa, or to chase down an errant ball not played well by a team-mate. For example, Middles not only perform block jumps in a middle-net position but must often move very rapidly to the left or right side to assist Outsides with blocking duties toward the sideline. Outsides must often move rapidly to the middle-net position to assist Middles with blocking tasks, and setters must often move into and out of their setting position (generally adjacent to the net) to perform blocks and sets at the net, passing and defending, dives, etc. Importantly, the libero position, as a back court only player, performs essentially *no* jumps, yet is required to move into and out of positions to pass the ball off of serve, and defend opposition attacks in the back court.

It is easy to recognize that volleyball's dynamic athletic demands primarily revolve around the jump and land stress that must be considered, but the strength and conditioning coach must also consider the rapid multi-directional movement demands that all positions require. Volleyball players are an exciting challenge for the strength and conditioning coach; they are the best vertical jumpers in the world, and (with the exception of the libero) they are generally very tall, they must be fast and athletic in multi-directional movement and able be to perform a myriad of skills such as diving to the ground to pass the ball, perform passing from the ground, and execute blocks and attacks in the air. And, of course, volleyball is a highly skilled sport, taking years of relatively high volume training to achieve mastery, further adding the challenge of developing athletic superiority, whilst aiming to avoid chronic injury and injury stress.

Injury prevalence

Volleyball is considered a relatively safe sport, with the rate of acute injuries across all levels of competition as low as five percent of that observed in professional soccer (Waldén et al., 2005). Acute injuries are more commonly sustained in competition with similar rates reported for world class, national division and national collegiate athletes of between three to 4.6 injuries per 1000 hours with somewhat lower rates reported during training (between one and four per 1000 hours) (Agel et al., 2007; Bahr and Bahr, 1997; Bere et al., 2015; Verhagen et al., 2004). Patterns of acute injuries are also fairly consistent across levels of competitions, with ankle sprains ranking the highest, accounting for nearly half of all volleyball related injuries (Verhagen et al., 2004), followed by knee, shoulder and lower back complaints (Bahr, 2009; Bere et al., 2015). Acute injuries sustained in competition are generally not severe with an average of up to two days of missed training and competition reported for world class athletes (Bere et al., 2015). However, ankle sprains also represent high severity of injury with an average of over four weeks of missed training and competition reported (Verhagen et al., 2004).

Whilst the rate of acute injuries in volleyball is relatively low, chronic overuse injuries are highly prevalent and are underrepresented in time-loss injury statistics where athletes continue to train despite experiencing pain and reduced function (Bahr, 2009). As volleyball is a sport characterized by repetitive maximal and sub-maximal jump and land efforts (Sheppard et al., 2009b), athletes experience high weekly jump counts during training and competition. Subsequently, there is a high demand on the rapid and repeated application of large amounts of force from the lower limb musculature and the prevalence of patellar tendinopathy has been reported to be as high as 45% (Lian et al., 2005). Despite representing only a small proportion of time lost from competition and training, patellar tendinopathy and other overuse injuries may have a substantial negative effect on an athletes career (Kettunen et al., 2002).

Risk factors for injury

Previous injury is the most considerable risk factor for sustaining an ankle sprain. Volleyball athletes with a recent history of ankle sprain are almost ten times more likely to re-injure (Bahr and Bahr, 1997). With respect to overuse injuries there is some evidence to suggest that the following may be risk factors for developing patellar tendinopathy: higher weight and body mass index, higher waist-to-hip ratio, leg-length difference, lower arch height of the foot, reduced quadriceps and hamstring flexibility, lower quadriceps strength and higher vertical jump performance (van der Worp et al., 2011). However, all nine of these risk factors can be related to loading of the patellar tendon in some way and increased training volume and match play exposure have also been linked with the development of patellar tendinopathy. A four-year longitudinal study of elite, adult volleyball athletes demonstrated significantly increased risk of injury for every additional hour of training and set of match-play performed per week (Visnes and Bahr, 2013). It is reasonable to assume that together with total training and competition exposure, vertical displacement may also be important with respect to increased injury risk, given that magnitudes of two to four times body weight may be experienced during landing (McNitt-Gray, 1993).

Injury prevention

Acute injury

The successful prevention of ankle sprains in volleyball athletes is well documented. A recent systematic review of multiple athletic populations (including volleyball athletes) has reported a reduction of ankle sprain by 69% with the use of ankle braces and 71% by the use of ankle tape among previously injured athletes (Dizon and Reyes, 2010). Additionally, a two-fold reduction in ankle sprains in volleyball athletes has been demonstrated following the introduction of an injury prevention program involving injury awareness education, technical training (with emphasis on take-off and landing technique for blocking and attacking) and a balance board training program for players with recurrent sprains (Bahr et al., 1997). Therefore, it is recommended that these strategies be prospectively introduced to all levels of volleyball participation where possible.

Overuse injury

Systematic approaches to jump load quantification and management in volleyball athletes may assist the prevention of load related, overuse injuries such as patellar tendinopathy. Traditionally, methods for counting jumps have been constrained to notational video analysis conducted retrospectively (Bahr and Bahr, 2014). This method is time-consuming, labour intensive and not feasible outside of the research setting. Recently, more novel and clinically feasible methods have emerged with the introduction of wearable technology, whereby jump count and height may be measured in real-time with accelerometers (Gageler et al., 2015; Jarning et al., 2015; Charlton et al., 2016). These devices along with careful monitoring may allow for safe workload prescriptions to be determined.

Injury rehabilitation

The rehabilitation of acute ankle sprains may benefit from an accelerated intervention incorporating early exercise therapy (Bleakley et al., 2010). Eccentric training protocols have been shown to be an effective method of rehabilitation for patellar tendinopathy; however, they can result in an increase in pain if applied in season. Both isometric and isotonic exercise programs have been shown to decrease patellar tendon pain and improvement in function without a modification of training and competition load (van Ark et al., 2015). It is therefore recommended that a program of isometric exercise be implemented for the treatment of patellar tendinopathy if the athlete is currently competing and a program incorporating eccentric exercises may be applied out of season.

Fitness testing battery

Medical assessment

As part of a comprehensive sport program, athletes should undertake a thorough evaluation of their injury history, and a general health screen, both of which should be conducted by the appropriate medical staff member (i.e. Sports Physician). This should be completed *at least* yearly and most certainly upon the intake of a new athlete into a program, prior to any participation.

In addition, and in part guided by the knowledge gained through evaluation of their previous injury history and the injuries most commonly occurring in volleyball, a para-medical physical therapy professional (e.g. physiotherapist, chiropractor, osteopath, athletic therapist) should complete a thorough orthopaedic assessment to elucidate improper motions or tissues of particular concern, the specific methodologies of which are detailed elsewhere (Joyce and Lewindon, 2016). It is also suggested that this assessment be performed in collaboration with the strength and conditioning coach, and if possible, the volleyball coach. This information can then be shared amongst the entire coaching and performance staff, in order to determine how best to individualize training loads and interventions to reduce the risk of injury, increase resiliency, and increase performance. The status of these considerations can then be re-evaluated throughout training and competition periods, and adjustments made accordingly.

Mobility and volleyball athletic competence test

In addition to the hands-on orthopaedic screen, some basic assessments of mobility and athletic competence, relevant to the demands of volleyball, should be assessed regularly so that program design can be tailored accordingly (e.g. weekly). Key priorities to consider are thoracic rotation, shoulder mobility, and ankle dorsi-flexion range. Although the strength and conditioning coach may favour additional or different tests at various testing occasions, weekly assessment of these motions are strongly recommended to ensure unrestricted movement. This is due to the particularly high volume of time spent overhead in training, dynamic rotational motions (spiking) and repeated landings. It is our experience that even short-term restrictions in thoracic, shoulder, and ankle mobility during periods of high volleyball training load results in motion compensation that lead to lost training time as a result of pain or injury.

As part of a long-term athlete development ethos, we believe in the importance of measuring general athletic competence, which is framed and interpreted not as sport-specific, but more so sport *relevant* for volleyball. Furthermore, if long-term athletic development is an aim, then assessing it is a priority to ensure accountability and targeted interventions to improve it.

Table 16.1 outlines an example athletic competency test that has been used in various contexts in Australian men's volleyball. Note that the training ages refer to entry into a specific high-performance volleyball specialization program that generally began at age 14. As such most athletes

Table 16.1 Athletic Competency Test for male athletes entering volleyball specialization

Playing level Typical age Specialization training age	Talent development 14–15 years old 0–1 years	State team 16–17 years old 2–3 years	Junior national team 18–19 years old 4–5 years	National team 20–22 years old over 6+ years
Movement category	Level 1	Level 2	Level 3	Level 4
Bi-lateral squat	Unloaded snatch squat	Snatch squat	Snatch squat	Snatch squat
	10 repetitions	5 repetitions, 25% body-weight	5 repetitions, 50% body-weight	3 repetitions, 75% body-weight
Single leg squat	SL box parallel box squat	SL squat	SL squat-10 kg plate hold	SL squat-10 kg plate OH
	5 repetitions	5 repetitions	5 repetitions	5 repetitions
Upper body pull	Pronated pull up	Pronated pull up	Pronated pull Up+10% BW	Pronated pull Up+20% BW
	5 repetitions	10 repetitions	10 repetitions	5 repetitions
Upper body push	Push up-5 kg plate	Push up-10 kg plate	Push up-15 kg plate	Push up-20 kg plate
	10 repetitions	10 repetitions	10 repetitions	10 repetitions
Ankle strength-end	SL calf raise	SL calf raise	SL calf raise	SL calf raise
	10 repetitions	15 repetitions	20 repetitions	25 repetitions
Torso stability end	Lateral bridge	SL calf raise	SL calf raise	SL calf raise
	60 seconds	90 seconds	120 seconds	120 seconds

*Tests are scored on a 3 point total scale based on number of repetitions performed correctly, and proportionate fractions thereof (1 point for ≤ 1/3 of reps or time; 2 points for ≤ 2/3 of reps or time). Single Leg (SL) squat and calf raise are scored separately for both legs, torso stability scored separately for each side, and not averaged.

entering this pathway had played on a school volleyball team for >3 years, and had also participated in other school sports and activities developing some form of basic physical literacy. These guidelines are context specific and often vary dependent on the individual. For example, a national team player may require assessment against expectations in level 1 and 2 despite their advanced competitive level, yet they may progress to level 4 expectations with appropriate attention in only a year. If applying these expectations to developmental players from the beginning of their volleyball journey, and sequentially developing greater athletic competency through increases in movement complexity (including volume and load), we have found that during physical maturation, these athletes remain robust and generally well prepared to tolerate the high volumes and intensities of the sport. Practitioners are encouraged to complement their testing batteries with their own bespoke movements and expectations that are context specific, and this example is provided only as a framework.

Strength and speed-strength assessment

With athletes who have well developed lifting competency, common lifting maximums in volleyball to assess maximum strength and speed-strength include 1 repetition maximum (1 RM) Snatch, Front Squat, and Pronated Pull Up and/or Clean/Hang Clean, Squat, and Neutral Grip Pull Up. In the competent population, these lifts are easy to assess as part of training programming (i.e. 'in session' assessment, using singles or 2–3 RM sets as appropriate). There is also the potential for these lifts to set minimum and 'benchmark' standards in the physically mature population, which has the additional benefit of promoting a competitive physical culture.

In addition, rep maximums may allow practitioners the ability to compare the performance of one lift to another. For example, at the start of the preparation period, if a volleyball player is able to Snatch 75 kg, but is only able to Squat 100 kg, then this could suggest that the player could benefit from placing more emphasis on developing a higher level of general strength.

For greater depth of analysis and interpretation, a position transducer or, ideally, a force platform can be used for additional assessments at separate testing occasions (Table 16.2). Depending on the time available, and the number of tests chosen, this type of assessment can integrate into

Table 16.2 Two testing suite options relevant for volleyball athletes using either a Linear Position Transducer or Force Platform and incorporating jump squats (JS) and or an isometric mid-thigh pull (IMTP)

Movement	Force platform testing protocol	Position transducer protocol
Iso-metric mid-thigh pull	Peak force (N) & peak force/body-mass	
Unloaded jump squat	Jump height (cm) & peak force	Jump height (cm)
Loaded jump squat 50% and 100% of body-mass		Jump height (cm)
considerations		Depth of CM of loaded JS must equate to that of the unloaded
Interpretation	Ratios of 'dynamic force' (JS peak force) compared to 'absolute force' (IMTP peak force) can be compared to reflect where speed-strength and maximum strength priorities may be, with a 'balanced' range ~65–75%	Ratios of 'strength-speed' (50 and 100% loaded JS) can be compared to 'speed-strength' (unloaded JS) to reflect where speed-strength and strength-speed/maximum strength priorities may be, with a 'balanced' range ~35% and 65% jump heights for 50% and 100% body-mass JS loads

Table 16.3 Use of countermovement vertical jump (CMVJ), depth jump (DJ) and spike jump (SPJ) for comparison, to determine the preparedness of different neuromuscular qualities in volleyball players

Jump type	Implications	Options
CMVJ	SSC inclusive jumping ability	Single arm or in block jump style with 2 hands
Depth jump (DJ)	High-stretch load tolerance jumping	Multiple height (20, 30, 40 cm) to determine appropriate training heights
Spike jump (SPJ)	Jump ability from run-up	Jump Height (cm)
Interpretations	CMVJ:DJ is used to determine whether the athlete has a high stretch load tolerance, with reference values where DJ height is ~10–20% higher than CMVJ.	
	CMVJ:SPJ is used to determine whether the athlete is able to adequately convert their horizontal run up into vertical impulse, with reference values where SPJ height is ~15–30% higher than CMVJ.	
	Multiple DJ heights (e.g. 20, 30, 40+ cm) are used to determine which height elicits an optimal SSC stimulation, and the height at which the stretch load elicits the first negative (lower than CMVJ) performance, representing the maximum trainable height.	

the assessment and monitoring program ranging from weekly (e.g. weekly jump squat test), monthly or quarterly (all tests). A detailed methodological explanation of various testing protocols is beyond the brevity required in this chapter, and so the reader is directed to more detailed manuscripts specific to the topic (Cardinale et al., 2011; Sheppard et al., 2008a; Tanner and Gore, 2013).

Vertical jumping assessment

Even if a practitioner has access to kinetic assessment, made possible by a force platform, we maintain that the vertical jump and reach assessments, performed on a standard paned jump and reach device, is an integral component of assessing volleyball athletes. The methodologies for these we've described in detail elsewhere (Sheppard et al., 2008b; Sheppard et al., 2008d). Although many different jump types can be performed and most have a reasonable rationale, we encourage the following; countermovement vertical jump (CMVJ), spike jump (SPJ), and depth jumps (DJ) (Table 16.3).

Conditioning assessment

Many volleyball programs have implemented various assessments of conditioning performance, using, for example, standard tests with cycling ergometers or the running based multi-stage 'beep' test. These tests offer reliable and standardized test methods that are valid to assess endurance, and there are numerous normative values that can be referred to. Our experience with these tests is that, though they may be valid in assessing an athlete's endurance, at the higher levels of volleyball, they are no longer able to differentiate between higher and lower performers. This leads to limitations in their discriminant validity in the context of elite volleyball (i.e. national team volleyball players who run to stage 13 on the beep test are no 'fitter' or resilient for volleyball than those that run to stage 12).

As a result of this consideration, current author Sheppard and colleagues developed and validated the Australian Institute of Sport Repeat Effort Test (AIS-RET) (Sheppard et al., 2007) based on detailed time and motion analysis of elite male volleyball competition. This volleyball specific test combines vertical jump assessments with specific court speed movement and blocking efficacy, all performed with short recovery, thus reflecting the conditioning demands of repeated high intensity rallies (Tanner and Gore, 2013). The test provides valuable information on the athlete's conditioning performance based on their average speed (4 ×multi-planar fast court movements), jump height (8 spike jumps total), and blocking accuracy throughout the test, in comparison to their best (first repetition) performance. This method has been used to assess improvements in athlete conditioning after targeted emphasis in order to benchmark players who are returning to national team duties from their professional clubs, and for evaluating return to competition fitness in the return to performance from injury.

It is acknowledged that the AIS-RET requires several practitioners to run the test, considerable athlete familiarization, and some advanced and even custom made equipment. As such, it is likely not suitable for all contexts. However, an individual practitioner with only a jump and reach device and timing method (timing lights or switch mat) could modify the test to simply measure jumps prior to and immediately after an up and back 9 m lateral shuffle along the front court, using a 15–20 second time period before repeating 4–6 times, allowing a total of 8–12 measured jumps and 4–6 speed shuffles. As with the AIS-RET, conditioning can be reflected by the average jump and time, compared to the first jump and time performed under non-fatigued conditions.

Programming

As detailed in the athletic demands section of this chapter the elite volleyball athlete is required to repeatedly produce high intensity efforts with a relatively small amount of rest between each effort. Primarily, these efforts are in the form of jumps, changes of direction and sport specific actions performed with a maximal expression of force. Therefore, when planning the physical preparation for volleyball athletes, these demands need to be addressed in order to adhere to the principle of specificity, while also being implemented within the context of the overall training plan for the athlete. As such the following section of this chapter aims to provide insight into how to physically prepare volleyball athletes to meet the extreme demands of the sport.

Strength and power for volleyball

Resistance training is a highly utilized method of physical training in volleyball and while there can be many reasons to support its application, the primary reasons are the development of muscular size and strength in order to produce the explosive movements demanded by the sport. This is primarily achieved through the use of heavy resistance training, weightlifting and the use of novel training methods such as complex training. Given the influence that heavy resistance training can have on enhancing the maximal concentric contraction occurring during explosive jumping and reducing the inhibition seen in eccentric contraction during landings, it appears that heavy resistance training is a vital mode of training for elite volleyball players. Examples of maximal strength programming can be seen in Table 16.4.

Once an appropriate level of maximal strength has been attained, the training focus can then be shifted to more power oriented exercises. As power output is dependent on both force and velocity, a commonly used method of training this quality is weightlifting. The snatch, the clean, the jerk and the many derivatives of these exercises require the athlete to not only produce a high level of force but to do so with a high velocity. While there is most certainly a requirement for technical proficiency in these movements to facilitate efficient transfer of enhanced physical capacity to jump

Table 16.4 Heavy resistance training session

Exercise	Set number	Reps	%1RM	Load (kg)
Back squat	1	3	85%	127.5
1RM = 150	2	3	88%	132
	3	3	90%	135
	4	3	93%	140
	5	3	93%	140
Bench press	1	5	87%	100
1RM = 115	2	4	91%	105
	3	3	93%	107
	4	2	95%	110
	5	2	95%	110

*Warm up sets not included

Table 16.5 Complex training example

Exercise	Set number	Reps	%1RM	Load (kg)
Back squat	1	3	85%	136
Jump squat	1	5	30%	47.5
Back squat	2	3	85%	136
Jump squat	2	5	30%	47.5
Back squat	3	3	85%	136
Jump squat	3	5	30%	47.5
Back squat	4	3	85%	136
Jump squat	4	5	30%	47.5
Back squat	5	3	85%	136
Jump squat	5	5	30%	47.5

*Back squat to be completed first followed by the jump squat once the athlete feels ready to perform.

performance, it has also been shown that there is a strong association between improvements in weightlifting and vertical jump (Sheppard et al., 2009b). Further to this, Sheppard et al. (2008b) showed a moderate relationship between relative power clean performance and spike jump height providing justification for the application of this method to the preparation of volleyball athletes.

A challenge of programming strength and power development is the occurrence of plateaus in the adaptive response. This is especially evident in the development of jump height. As such, strength programming for volleyball athletes should aim to use effective training methods that can be implemented to assist with breaking through these plateaus. A method that has been widely used is complex training which involves alternating set for set between heavy resistance exercises and dynamic exercises to take advantage of the physiological phenomenon of post activation potentiation during the dynamic exercise. An example of complex training can be viewed below in Table 16.5.

All of the previously described strength training interventions are valid modalities to be used with volleyball athletes, but the S&C coach needs to make considered decisions about which interventions to implement with athletes based on their individual characteristics. As such, example programs for a developmental athlete and senior national team player are provided below in Tables 16.6 and 16.7, respectively. Due to the differences in maturity, training history and athletic

Table 16.6 Developmental volleyball athlete strength training session

Developmental athlete		Squad		Volleyball			Training phase		General preparation		Meso cycle		1

Strength training stage	Stage 3 - introduction to BB training												
Goal	Increase movement efficiency		Cycle periodization										

Session 1 focus

Global general strength development

Focus area		Exercise	Sets	Reps	Time (s)	Tempo	Load type	Load used
Activation focus 1	Calf and foot strength	Skipping	1	1	120	Dynamic		
Activation focus 2	Glute strength	Mini band lateral shuffle	2	20		Controlled	Mini Band	Blue
Stimulation focus 1	UB ballistic	MB throwdowns	2	5		Explosive		
Stimulation focus 2	LB ballistic	Altitude landing (40cm)	3	5		Controlled		

Primary lifts

	Week 1				100%	24		Week 2				100%	24		Week 3				100%	30		Week 4				100%	30	
	Planned			Actual				Planned			Actual				Planned			Actual				Planned			Actual			
	Date 7/11/16			Date				Date 14/11/16			Date				Date 21/11/16			Date				Date 28/11/16			Date			
Exercise type	3x8							3x8							3x10							3x10							
	Reps	%	Vel	Load	Reps	Vel	Load	Reps	%	Vel	Load	Reps	Vel	Load	Reps	%	Vel	Load	Reps	Vel	Load	Reps	%	Vel	Load	Reps	Vel	Load
Goblet squat	8	60%			8			8	60%			8			8	60%			8			8	60%			8		
Chin up - PG	8	80%			8			8	80%			8			10	75%			10			10	75%			10		
	8	80%			8			8	80%			8			10	75%			10			10	75%			10		
	8	80%			8			8	80%			8			10	75%			10			10	75%			10		

	LB push
Tempo	Controlled
Rest between exercises (s)	30
Super set with	Chin up - PG
Cue 1	
Cue 2	
Variations	

Exercise type	UB ver. pull	3x5				15	Reps			3x5			15	Reps			3x10			30	Reps			3x10			30	Reps		
Chin up – PG		Reps	%	Vel	Load		Load	Vel		Reps	%	Vel	Load		Load	Vel	Reps	%	Vel	Load		Load	Vel	Reps	%	Vel	Load		Load	Vel	Load
Tempo	AFAP	5	60%				5			5	60%						8	60%			8			8	60%			8			
Rest between exercises (s)	60	5	87%				5			5	87%						10	75%			10			10	75%			10			
Super set with	TRX SL squat	5	87%				5			5	87%						10	75%			10			10	75%			10			
		5	87%				5			5	87%						10	75%			10			10	75%			10			
Cue 1																															
Cue 2																															
Variations																															
Exercise type	LB pull	3x10				30	Reps			3x10			30	Reps			3x10			30	Reps			3x10			30	Reps		
SL DB RDL		Reps	%	Vel	Load		Load	Vel		Reps	%	Vel	Load		Load	Vel	Reps	%	Vel	Load		Load	Vel	Reps	%	Vel	Load		Load	Vel	Load
Tempo	AFAP	8	60%				8			8	60%						8	60%			8			8	60%			8			
Rest between exercises (s)	30	10	75%				10			10	75%						10	75%			10			10	75%			10			
Super set with	Wtd push up	10	75%				10			10	75%						10	75%			10			10	75%			10			
Cue		10	75%				10			10	75%						10	75%			10			10	75%			10			
Variations																															
Exercise type	UB hor. push	3x8				24	Reps			3x8			24	Reps			3x10			30	Reps			3x10			30	Reps		
Wtd push up		Reps	%	Vel	Load		Load	Vel		Reps	%	Vel	Load		Load	Vel	Reps	%	Vel	Load		Load	Vel	Reps	%	Vel	Load		Load	Vel	Load
Tempo	AFAP	8	60%				8			8	60%						8	60%			8			8	60%			8			
Rest between exercises (s)	60	8	80%				8			8	80%						10	75%			10			10	75%			10			
Super set with	SL DB RDL	8	80%				8			8	80%						10	75%			10			10	75%			10			
Cue		8	80%				8			8	80%						10	75%			10			10	75%			10			
Variations																															

(Continued)

Table 16.6 (Continued)

Secondary exercises	Week 1						Week 2						Week 3						Week 4					
Exercise type	Reps	%	Vel	Load	Reps	Vel	Load	Reps	%	Vel	Load	Reps	Vel	Load	Reps	%	Vel	Load	Reps	Vel	Load			
Tempo																								
Rest between exercises (s)																								
Super set with																								
Variations																								
Exercise type	Reps	%	Vel	Load	Reps	Vel	Load	Reps	%	Vel	Load	Reps	Vel	Load	Reps	%	Vel	Load	Reps	Vel	Load			
Tempo																								
Rest between exercises (s)																								
Super set with																								
Variations																								
Exercise type	Reps	%	Vel	Load	Reps	Vel	Load	Reps	%	Vel	Load	Reps	Vel	Load	Reps	%	Vel	Load	Reps	Vel	Load			
Tempo																								
Rest between exercises (s)																								
Super set with																								
Variations																								
Exercise type	Reps	%	Vel	Load	Reps	Vel	Load	Reps	%	Vel	Load	Reps	Vel	Load	Reps	%	Vel	Load	Reps	Vel	Load			
Tempo																								
Set starting every (s)																								
Super set with																								
Variations																								

Auxillary exercises

Exercise type	Exercise name	Week 1								Week 2								Week 3								Week 4							
		Sets	Reps	Time	Total	Tempo	Load Type	Load		Sets	Reps	Time	Total	Tempo	Load Type	Load		Sets	Reps	Time	Total	Tempo	Load Type	Load		Sets	Reps	Time	Total	Tempo	Load Type	Load	
Global movers core	SB crunch	3	20		60					3	22		66					3	24		72					3	26		78				
Global movers core	Hanging leg raises	3	8		24					3	10		30					3	12		36					3	12		36				
Global movers core	Back extension + twist	3	10		30					3	10		30					3	12		36					3	12		36				

'I know of no more encouraging fact than the unquestionable ability of man to elevate his life through conscious endeavour' (Henry David Thoreau).

Table 16.7 National team athlete strength training session

National team athlete	Squad			Training phase		General preparation		Meso cycle		1

Strength training stage | Stage 6 – elite maximal strength training

Goal: Increase max strength | **Cycle periodization**: 4 wk cycle, starting at 90% and increasing by 5% for the next 2 wks followed by 1 adaptation wk at 80%

Session 1 focus: Max strength development

Focus area		Exercise	Sets	Reps	Time (s)	Tempo	Load type	Load used
Activation focus 1	Calf and foot strength	Skipping	1	1	120	Dynamic		
Activation focus 2	Glute strength	Arabesque and twist	2	20		Controlled	Mini band	Blue
Stimulation focus 1	UB ballistic	Lying MB pullover	3	5		Explosive	MB	3–4kg
Stimulation focus 2	LB ballistic	Depth jump	3	5		Explosive		30, 40, 50cm

Primary lifts		Week 1					Week 2					Week 3					Week 4				
		90%					95%					100%					80%				
		Planned		Actual			Planned		Actual			Planned		Actual			Planned		Actual		
		Date		Date			Date		Date			Date		Date			Date		Date		
		7/11/16					14/11/16					21/11/16					28/11/16				
Exercise type	Olympic lift	4x2 (8,4)	12				4x2 (8,4)	12				4x2 (8,4)	12				4x2 (8,4)	12			
		Reps	%	Load	Vel		Reps	%	Load	Vel		Reps	%	Load	Vel		Reps	%	Load	Vel	
						Load					Load					Load					Load
Power clean																					
Tempo	Explosive	8	54%	55			8	57%	58			8	60%	61			8	48%	49		
Rest between sets (s)	90	4	72%	73			4	76%	78			4	80%	82			4	64%	65		
		2	86%	87			2	90%	92			2	95%	97			2	76%	78		
		2	86%	87			2	90%	92			2	95%	97			2	76%	78		
Cue 1		2	86%	87			2	90%	92			2	95%	97			2	76%	78		
Cue 2		2	86%	87			2	90%	92			2	95%	97			2	76%	78		
Variations																					

Exercise type	LB push	4x3					16					4x3					16					4x3					16					4x3					16		
Front squat		Reps	%	Vel	Load		Load	Reps	Vel	Load		Reps	%	Vel	Load		Load	Reps	Vel	Load		Reps	%	Vel	Load		Load	Reps	Vel	Load		Reps	%	Vel	Load		Load	Reps	Vel	Load
Tempo	AFAP	5	54%				69	5				5	57%				73	5				5	60%				77	5				5	48%				61	5		
Rest between sets (s)	90	4	72%				92	4				4	76%				97	4				4	80%				102	4				4	64%				82	4		
		3	84%				107	3				3	88%				113	3				3	93%				119	3				3	74%				95	3		
		3	84%				107	3				3	88%				113	3				3	93%				119	3				3	74%				95	3		
		3	84%				107	3				3	88%				113	3				3	93%				119	3				3	74%				95	3		
Cue 1		3	84%				107	3				3	88%				113	3				3	93%				119	3				3	74%				95	3		
Cue 2																																								
Variations																																								
Exercise type	UB ver. pull	3x10					30					3x10					30					3x10					30					3x10					30		
Chin up – PG		Reps	%	Vel	Load		Load	Reps	Vel	Load		Reps	%	Vel	Load		Load	Reps	Vel	Load		Reps	%	Vel	Load		Load	Reps	Vel	Load		Reps	%	Vel	Load		Load	Reps	Vel	Load
Tempo	AFAP	8	54%				15	8				8	57%				16	8				8	60%				17	8				8	48%				14	8		
Rest between exercises (s)	30	10	68%				19	10				10	71%				20	10				10	75%				21	10				10	60%				17	10		
Super set with	Overhead MB throw	10	68%				19	10				10	71%				20	10				10	75%				21	10				10	60%				17	10		
Cue		10	68%				19	10				10	71%				20	10				10	75%				21	10				10	60%				17	10		
Variations																																								
Exercise type								Reps	Vel	Load		Reps	%	Vel	Load		Load	Reps	Vel	Load		Reps	%	Vel	Load		Load	Reps	Vel	Load		Reps	%	Vel	Load		Load	Reps	Vel	Load
		Reps	%	Vel	Load		Load					Reps	%	Vel	Load		Load					Reps	%	Vel	Load		Load					Reps	%	Vel	Load		Load			
Tempo																																								
Rest between exercises (s)																																								
Super set with																																								
Cue																																								
Variations																																								

(Continued)

Table 16.7 (Continued)

Secondary exercises		Week 1						Week 2						Week 3						Week 4					
Exercise type	UB ballistic	3x5				15		3x5				15		3x5				15		3x5				15	
Overhead MB throw		Reps	%	Vel	Load	Reps	Load	Reps	%	Vel	Load	Reps	Load	Reps	%	Vel	Load	Reps	Load	Reps	%	Vel	Load	Reps	Load
Tempo	Explosive	5	54%					5	57%					5	60%					5	48%				
Rest between exercises (s)	60	5	78%					5	83%					5	87%					5	70%				
Super set with	Chin up – PG	5	78%					5	83%					5	87%					5	70%				
Variations		5	78%					5	83%					5	87%					5	70%				
Exercise type		Reps	%	Vel	Load	Reps	Load	Reps	%	Vel	Load	Reps	Load	Reps	%	Vel	Load	Reps	Load	Reps	%	Vel	Load	Reps	Load
Tempo																									
Rest between exercises (s)																									
Super set with																									
Variations																									
Exercise type		Reps	%	Vel	Load	Reps	Load	Reps	%	Vel	Load	Reps	Load	Reps	%	Vel	Load	Reps	Load	Reps	%	Vel	Load	Reps	Load
Tempo																									
Rest between exercises (s)																									
Super set with																									
Variations																									

Exercise type																																		
	Reps	%	Vel	Load		Reps	Vel	Load			Reps	%	Vel	Load		Reps	Vel	Load			Reps	%	Vel	Load		Reps	Vel	Load			Reps	%	Vel	Load
Tempo																																		
Set starting every (s)																																		
Super set with																																		
Variations																																		
Auxillary exercises			Week 1									Week 2									Week 3									Week 4					
Exercise type	Exercise name	Sets	Reps	Time	Total	Tempo	Load Type	Load		Sets	Reps	Time	Total	Tempo	Load Type	Load		Sets	Reps	Time	Total	Tempo	Load Type	Load		Sets	Reps	Time	Total	Tempo	Load Type	Load
Global movers core	BB rollout	3	8		24					3	8		24					3	10		30					3	10		30			
Global movers core	Landmines	3	8		24					3	10		30					3	12		36					3	12		36			
Global movers core	SL back extensions	3	10		30					3	10		30					3	12		36					3	12		36			

competency the content of each of these sessions is drastically different but each is appropriate for these volleyball athletes who are simply at very different stages of their athletic careers. The take home message here is that although we should program strength training with the intention of developing the capacities required for success in volleyball, it should be done within the context of the specific athlete in question.

As a final consideration, when programming the strength training for volleyball, it is vital to have a method of tracking the volume and intensity involved in each session in order to accurately determine if progressive overload is actually being achieved within the program. One method of achieving this objective is to calculate the planned and actual system mass volume load (SMVL) that was completed in each session. This figure is calculated by first summing the external load used in the movement with the body mass being shifted in order to determine the total mass of the moving system. Once the system mass has been calculated then the SMVL can be determined by finding the product of the system mass and the number of repetitions performed. This is an extremely effective method of objectively tracking the strength training load that volleyball players complete within and across sessions, cycles and phases, effectively allowing the S&C coach to make more informed decisions about future programs.

Jump training for volleyball

Jumping is an essential ability in volleyball, especially for players who play at the net (hitters and blockers). When training to improve vertical jump in volleyball, it's important to take into consideration the time of competitive year and the practice volume of jumps. If an athlete is in-season or is undergoing a high volume of jumps in practice, training to improve their jump can still be done, but the strategy taken is important. When jump volume is high or when practice participation is high, training strategies that focus on high concentric force characteristics or high eccentric strength can be a good supplement to improve vertical jump performance. Exercises such as accentuated eccentric back squats and Olympic pulling movements can enable athletes to produce high forces quickly. Additionally, these exercises can improve the mechanical strength components, which help support the high velocity nature of jumping and the high impact nature of landing from significant heights. Athletes that are not participating in a high volume of jumping in sport practice can incorporate strategies that use these same exercises, but may find benefit to using a complex system, where high strength or high force activities are paired with high velocity or reactive jumping activities such as tuck jumps, depth jump or other high intensity plyometric activity. When jump volume is high in sport practice, simply doing additional jumps (e.g. additional sets of block jumps) tends to be futile as it adds no additional novel stimulus in relation to the already high load experienced on court in practise, and is a potential injury risk.

Conditioning for volleyball

Volleyball rallies do not last long; in elite men's volleyball most rallies last 5–12 seconds on average, but rallies can last up to 45 seconds. Typically, the rest time between playing rallies can range from 10–30 seconds. From a work/rest point of view, elite men's indoor volleyball has a rest ratio range of 1:2.5–1.75:1. In addition to work/rest ratio, volleyball match length can range from 90–120 minutes. These demands result in high usage of the phosphagen and glycolytic energy systems and contributions from aerobic means to tolerate the repeated bouts and duration of a match.

When developing metabolic conditioning programs for volleyball athletes during practises, work/rest ratios can be manipulated in game play. Work durations can be extended and rest periods controlled by 'stacking' rallies of play through re-starting a rally immediately after or in specific duration after the cessation of the previous rally. This game play conditioning method has the additional benefit of skill and decision-making stress under fatigue, and is appropriately relevant for the players themselves.

In addition, complementary metabolic conditioning can be achieved through general exercises. For example, skipping, sprinting, and medicine ball circuits can be designed to stress the metabolic and strength and power demands appropriate to volleyball. However, caution should be taken on general exercise selection for this population. For example, as volleyball athletes are generally tall and heavy, extensive running (i.e. jogging) tends to be a relative chronic injury risk. Furthermore, high volumes of cycling are likely a poor choice as the muscle architecture promoted by cycling athletes is disparate from that of non-cycling activity.

Mobility

Due to the highly complex and diverse range of movements demanded by the sport of volleyball, freedom and efficiency of movement is key to achieving success at the elite level. This includes both a high degree of flexibility at isolated joints and a sufficient level of mobility in larger regions that cover multiple joints and structures. Key regions of the body requiring a high degree of flexibility include the ankle, hip and thoracic spine.

From both a performance and injury prevention perspective, the amount of dorsiflexion range at the ankle is incredibly important to the volleyball athlete. Without sufficient range of movement at this joint, extra stress will be placed on either the knees or hips of the athlete during both take-off and landing while jumping. When one considers the prevalence of patella tendinopathy and hip related lumbar spine injuries in volleyball athletes it would seem prudent to off load these joints as much as possible by achieving and maintaining an acceptable amount of dorsiflexion range at the ankle.

Hip range of motion is the next area requiring exceptional range of motion for the volleyball athlete. While the movement focus is quite specific for the ankle (i.e. dorsiflexion), the hip requires more range across many planes of movement. For efficient jump and land mechanics, flexion and extension of the hip needs to be unencumbered but for even better freedom of movement the internal and external rotational ranges of the hip are key. Rotational range in this joint not only assists with efficient landing mechanics but also allows the volleyball athlete to move freely through the wide variety of multi-directional movements demanded by the sport.

The final area of the body that needs to be prioritized during the programming of the mobility component of the program is the thoracic spine. All sports that require athletes to spend a large amount of time in an overhead position require a sufficient amount of thoracic extension range to allow freedom of movement in this area. Without this range, one of two issues may occur: the athlete will compensate for this lack of range by hinging at the thoracolumbar junction, potentially causing lumbar spine stress, or they will repeatedly put the shoulder joint into an impingement position that could manifest as an overuse injury in the shoulder joint. Furthermore, spike and jump serving requires an exceptional amount of rotational range through the thoracic spine. This kind of rotational range is required to facilitate the biomechanically optimal process of initiating movement from the proximal structures of the body, the hips and thoracic spine, and transferring this energy down the kinetic chain to the peripheral end point of the hand.

References

Agel, J., Palmieri-Smith, R. M., Dick, R., Wojtys, E. M. and Marshall, S. W. 2007. Descriptive epidemiology of collegiate women's volleyball injuries: National Collegiate Athletic Association Injury Surveillance System, 1988–1989 through 2003–2004. *Journal of Athletic Training*, 42, 295.

Bahr, M. A. and Bahr, R. 2014. Jump frequency may contribute to risk of jumper's knee: a study of inter-individual and sex differences in a total of 11 943 jumps video recorded during training and matches in young elite volleyball players. *British Journal of Sports Medicine*, bjsports-2014-093593.

Bahr, R. 2009. No injuries, but plenty of pain? On the methodology for recording overuse symptoms in sports. *British Journal of Sports Medicine*, 43, 966–972.

Bahr, R. and Bahr, I. 1997. Incidence of acute volleyball injuries: a prospective cohort study of injury mechanisms and risk factors. *Scandinavian Journal of Medicine & Science in Sports*, 7, 166–171.

Bahr, R., Lian, O. and Bahr, I. 1997. A twofold reduction in the incidence of acute ankle sprains in volleyball after the introduction of an injury prevention program: a prospective cohort study. *Scandinavian Journal of Medicine & Science in Sports*, 7, 172–177.

Bere, T., Kruczynski, J., Veintimilla, N., Hamu, Y. and Bahr, R. 2015. Injury risk is low among world-class volleyball players: 4-year data from the FIVB Injury Surveillance System. *British Journal of Sports Medicine*, bjsports-2015-094959.

Bleakley, C. M., O'Connor, S. R., Tully, M. A., Rocke, L. G., MaCauley, D. C., Bradbury, I., Keegan, S. and McDonough, S. M. 2010. Effect of accelerated rehabilitation on function after ankle sprain: randomised controlled trial. *BMJ*, 340, c1964.

Cardinale, M., Newton, R. U. and Nosaka, K. 2011. *Strength and Conditioning: Biological Principles and Practical Application*. West Sussex, UK: John Wiley & Sons.

Charlton, P. C., Kenneally-Dabrowski, C., Sheppard, J. and Spratford, W. 2016. A simple method for quantifying jump loads in volleyball athletes. *Journal of Science and Medicine in Sport*, 20(3), 241–245.

Dizon, J. M. R. and Reyes, J. J. B. 2010. A systematic review on the effectiveness of external ankle supports in the prevention of inversion ankle sprains among elite and recreational players. *Journal of Science and Medicine in Sport*, 13, 309–317.

Gageler, W. H., Wearing, S. and James, D. A. 2015. Automatic jump detection method for athlete monitoring and performance in volleyball. *International Journal of Performance Analysis in Sport*, 15, 284–296.

Jarning, J. M., Mok, K.-M., Hansen, B. H. and Bahr, R. 2015. Application of a tri-axial accelerometer to estimate jump frequency in volleyball. *Sports Biomechanics*, 14(1), 95–105.

Joyce, D. and Lewindon, D. 2016. *Sports Injury Prevention and Rehabilitation*. London, UK: Routledge.

Kettunen, J. A., Kvist, M., Alanen, E. and Kujala, U. M. 2002. Long-term prognosis for jumper's knee in male athletes a prospective follow-up study. *The American Journal of Sports Medicine*, 30, 689–692.

Lian, O. B., Engebretsen, L. and Bahr, R. 2005. Prevalence of jumper's knee among elite athletes from different sports a cross-sectional study. *The American Journal of Sports Medicine*, 33, 561–567.

McNitt-Gray, J. L. 1993. Kinetics of the lower extremities during drop landings from three heights. *Journal of Biomechanics*, 26, 1037–1046.

Reeser, J. C., Verhagen, E., Briner, W. W., Askeland, T. and Bahr, R. 2006. Strategies for the prevention of volleyball related injuries. *British Journal of Sports Medicine*, 40, 594–600.

Sheppard, J. M., Chapman, D., Gough, C., McGuigan, M. R. and Newton, R. U. 2009a. Twelve month training induced changes in elite international volleyball players. *Journal of Strength and Conditioning Research*, 23, 2096–2101.

Sheppard, J. M., Cormack, S., Taylor, K. L., McGuigan, M. R. and Newton, R. U. 2008a. Assessing the force-velocity characteristics of well trained athletes: the incremental load power profile. *Journal of Strength and Conditioning Research*, 22, 1320–1326.

Sheppard, J. M., Cronin, J. B., Gabbett, T. J., McGuigan, M. R., Etxebarria, N. and Newton, R. U. 2008b. Relative importance of strength, power, and anthropometric measures to jump performance of elite volleyball players. *Journal of Strength and Conditioning Research*, 22, 758–765.

Sheppard, J. M., Gabbett, T. and Borgeaud, R. 2008c. Training repeated effort ability in national team male volleyball players. *International Journal of Sports Physiology and Performance*, 3, 397–400.

Sheppard, J. M., Gabbett, T. and Stanganelli, L. C. 2009b. An analysis of playing positions in elite mens' volleyball: considerations for competition demands and physiological characteristics. *Journal of Strength and Conditioning Research*, 23, 1858–1866.

Sheppard, J. M., Gabbett, T., Taylor, K. L., Dorman, J., Lebedew, A. J. and Borgeaud, R. 2007. Development of a repeated-effort test for elite men's volleyball. *International Journal of Sports Physiology and Performance*, 2, 292–304.

Sheppard, J. M., McGuigan, M. R. and Newton, R. U. 2008d. The effects of depth-jumping on vertical jump performance of elite volleyball players: an examination of the transfer of increased stretch-load tolerance to spike jump performance. *Journal of Australian Strength and Conditioning*, 16, 3–10.

Tanner, R. and Gore, C. J. 2013. *Physiological Tests for Elite Athletes*. Champaign, IL: Human Kinetics.

Van Ark, M., Cook, J. L., Docking, S. I., Zwerver, J., Gaida, J. E., Van Den Akker-Scheek, I. and Rio, E. 2015. Do isometric and isotonic exercise programs reduce pain in athletes with patellar tendinopathy in-season? A randomised clinical trial. *Journal of Science and Medicine in Sport*, 19(9), 702–706.

Van Der Worp, H., Van Ark, M., Roerink, S., Pepping, G.-J., Van Den Akker-Scheek, I. and Zwerver, J. 2011. Risk factors for patellar tendinopathy: a systematic review of the literature. *British Journal of Sports Medicine*, bjsports84079.

Verhagen, E., Van Der Beek, A. J., Bouter, L., Bahr, R. and Van Mechelen, W. 2004. A one season prospective cohort study of volleyball injuries. *British Journal of Sports Medicine*, 38, 477–481.

Visnes, H. and Bahr, R. 2013. Training volume and body composition as risk factors for developing jumper's knee among young elite volleyball players. *Scandinavian Journal of Medicine & Science in Sports*, 23, 607–613.

Waldén, M., Hägglund, M. and Ekstrand, J. 2005. UEFA Champions League study: a prospective study of injuries in professional football during the 2001–2002 season. *British Journal of Sports Medicine*, 39, 542–546.

17
HANDBALL

Marco Cardinale

Introduction to the sport

Handball is an Olympic sport, part of the Olympic programme in its indoor version since the 1972 Olympic Games (Karcher and Buchheit, 2014). Handball is a fast-paced, body-contact sport, played by two competing teams of 7 players (1 player is a goalkeeper) on an indoor court (40m × 20m) over two 30 min periods. It is generally recognised that due to relatively recent changes in game rules (e.g. starting the game quickly from the centre) and improvements in the tactical use of rolling substitutions (including the most recent introduction of goalkeepers' substitution with field players), the intensity of the game is increased, with players able to perform more high intensity actions. Handball players are identified by the following positions when attacking (see Figure 17.1): goalkeepers, backcourt players (left back, right back and centre back, also sometimes defined as playmaker), wing players (left wing and right wing) and pivot (or circle runner, in some terminologies). Defensive positions depend on the defensive system applied (6:0 vs. 3:2:1 vs. 5:1 vs. 4:2 vs. 3:3).

Due to the different tasks covered in the game, handball players are characterised by different anthropometric characteristics, with wing players usually being smaller than backs, pivots and goalkeepers. Handball has been defined by many as the "ball game" version of track and field as athletes are required to run, jump and throw numerous times during a game, as well as engage in duels to gain or cover space to score or reduce scoring chances. Handball is a contact sport; therefore, body checking and blocking, as well as body contacts in various positions and in flight during shooting activities, are all part of the activities performed by handball players, which sometimes can lead to injuries. Each position has its own specificity as players are confined to specific areas of the field in both attack and defence; therefore, even if the court dimensions are 40m × 20m, once goal areas are excluded (the 6m area can in fact be entered only while in flight), it is possible to determine some marked differences between the activities of various playing positions.

Various talent identification programmes for handball have been historically targeting tall and robust players. Being tall is generally perceived as an advantage for most positions both during attacking (e.g. to play in backcourt positions) and defensive (e.g. goalkeeping and/or central defenders) phases. Body mass has also been deemed important for specific positions. A recent study from Karcher et al. (2014) conducted surveying an internet database of basic

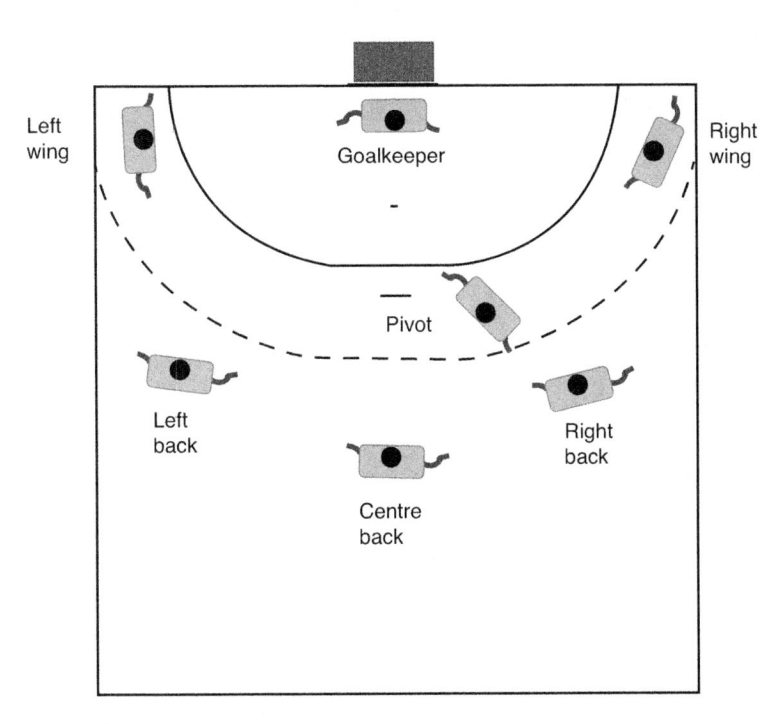

Figure 17.1 Players' positions

anthropometric data of elite handball players competing in top European Leagues, Champions League, European and World Championships, highlighted position specific differences in anthropometry as well as some differences depending on the level of competition. In this study, in fact, centre, left and right backs were slightly-to-moderately taller in the European championships, goalkeepers and right wings in Champions League, left backs in the German first league and pivots in the Spanish first league. Centre and left backs were slightly-to-moderately heavier in the European championship. Left wings were heavier in the German first league and pivots in the Spanish first league. The data distribution of the sample analysed clearly indicates that at the elite level, back players, pivots and goalkeepers are the tallest players and wingers tend to be smaller. Finally, due to the positional requirements of pivots (playing within the opposition's defence) and the nature of contacts, elite players in this position need to be heavy. The study concluded that while some goalkeepers and backs as short as 175cm may still be selected in national teams, 77% of the goalkeepers, 75% of the right backs, and 82% of the left backs were taller than 190cm. The smallest pivot in the European championship was 184cm tall; however, 93% of the other elite pivots were taller than 185cm. Taken together, the data from this study and previous observations unpublished from our group, also in junior championships, suggest that minimal body dimensions might be required, or at least may be facilitators, to reach the elite level in handball in key positions like backs and pivots. However, some exceptions can be seen in left-handed players, in particular the ones playing right backs. Anthropometry has also been shown to determine final ranking at the World Championships in 2013 (Ghobadi et al., 2013) suggesting that in men's handball, without some tall and heavy players in key positions, it becomes very difficult to succeed. In this study, European players were the tallest and heaviest, and since European teams dominate men's handball, the search for tall and agile players has become one of the main focus of most talent identification programmes in handball.

Table 17.1 Anthropometric characteristics of handball players participating in the Men's World Championships in 2013 (average values for each team, data from Ghobadi et al., 2013)

Rank	Country	Age (years)	Height (cm)	Body mass (kg)	Body mass index
1	Spain	28.19	192.88	96.88	26.02
2	Denmark	27.47	194.00	94.82	25.17
3	Croatia	25.89	194.39	96.72	25.49
4	Slovenia	26.88	191.53	94.53	25.73
5	Germany	27.00	193.44	92.19	24.62
6	France	29.44	191.00	92.69	25.35
7	Russia	28.56	192.12	96.44	26.06
8	Hungry	27.88	193.44	96.75	25.83
9	Poland	28.89	193.94	93.00	24.65
10	Serbia	26.28	191.56	94.56	25.72
11	Tunisia	24.76	190.71	90.76	24.96
12	Iceland	27.71	191.82	92.47	25.12
13	Brazil	25.62	190.19	95.12	26.28
14	Fyro Macedonia	28.82	189.53	92.65	25.76
15	Belarus	27.24	193.41	95.82	25.55
16	Egypt	24.78	184.83	90.17	26.34
17	Algeria	27.18	188.12	88.65	25.04
18	Argentina	25.89	188.56	90.00	25.40
19	Saudi Arabia	26.61	183.72	90.00	26.66
20	Qatar	26.76	185.47	87.88	25.47
21	South Korea	26.22	186.72	85.22	24.43
22	Montenegro	28.35	190.06	96.18	26.65
23	Chile	24.78	186.00	88.94	25.69
24	Australia	23.88	186.19	85.50	24.65

The wide range of body dimensions observed in modern handball for each position suggests that some players with atypical body dimensions can still make the elite level; a combination of other variables, such as technical and tactical skills and physical qualities, may provide other benefits for some of these 'atypical' players. This is particularly true for women's handball, where recent trends in successful nations show that while some tall/heavy players are parts of rosters, some of the best players in the world also in backcourt positions are not tall (e.g. Nora Mork [1.65m], Nycke Groot [1.75m], Stine Oftedal [1.68 m] and/or below team average height). Studies conducted on female handball players seem to conclude (Vila et al., 2012; Manchado et al., 2013a) that players involved in high level leagues and/or international teams are taller and have a higher fat-free mass. In particular, the authors focus on hand size and, as in men, such aspects as a bigger hand do help in controlling the ball. Also, for some key positions, larger and taller players can have an advantage, provided that technical and tactical skills are adequate to sustain the speed of movements and decision-making in elite competitions.

Strength and conditioning coaches involved in handball need to be prepared to work towards improving performance and reducing injury risk in athletes of different shapes and forms, as typical squads will have tall and small players, light and heavy players, fast and slow players. What is clear is that anthropometric characteristics of the players vary depending on the position they play, with backcourt and line players (pivot) being taller and heavier than wingers (Krüger et al., 2013; Matthys et al., 2013). Furthermore, due to the different technical and tactical requirements within each team, it is important for strength and conditioning specialists to prepare players to perform the sports specific tasks at their best, and for this reason it is necessary to have a clear understanding not only of the physiological demands of each position, but also the technical and tactical demands of each individual player within the team.

Athletic demands

Despite its popularity, a paucity of data exits to describe the games physical demands and typical physiological characteristics of elite handball players. Aerobic capacity in male handball players has been reported to be superior to 50ml•kg•min^{-1} in men (Buchheit et al., 2009a; Chaouachi et al., 2009; Rankovic et al., 2010; Sporis et al., 2010; Michalsik et al., 2012; Karcher and Buchheit, 2014) and higher than 45ml•kg•min^{-1} in women (Manchado et al., 2013a; Manchado et al., 2013a; Michalsik et al., 2014; Koga et al., 2010). Some variation of data is present in the literature because of the level of players measured as well as the differences in equipment and testing procedures. Overall it is clear that, on average, handball players present aerobic capacity values similar to other team sports athletes and while some studies report differences between elite and non-elite handball players (i.e. Granados et al., 2013; Póvoas et al., 2014a; Manchado et al., 2013a, as expected and as evidenced in other sports), it is questionable to assume that a larger aerobic capacity can improve performance sensibly. This was reiterated also in recent work from Ilic et al. (2015). Of course, improvements in such physiological aspects are important when the fitness

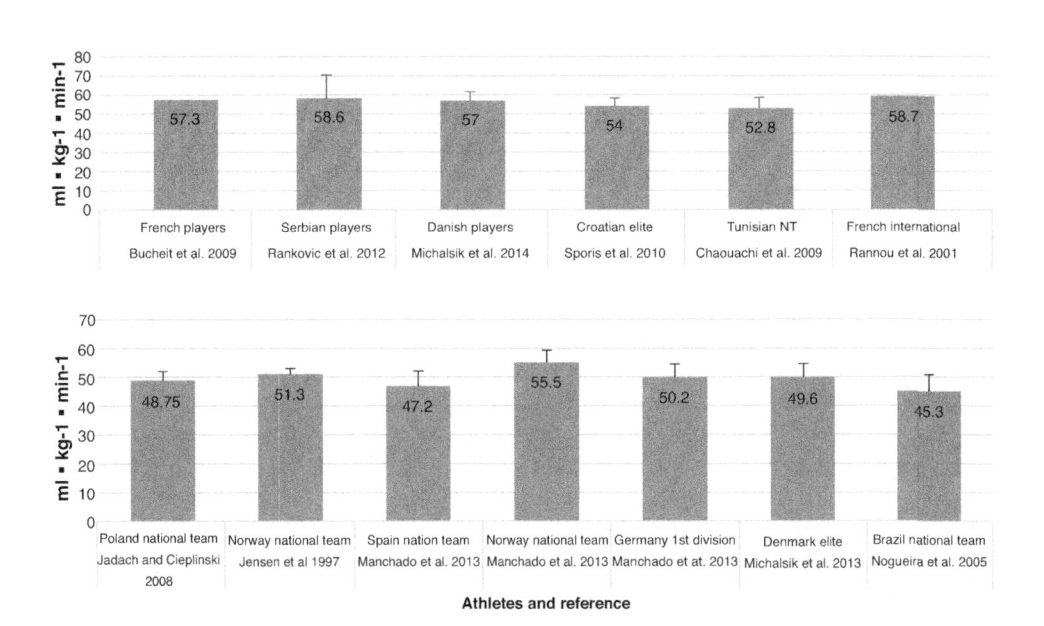

Figure 17.2 a) Aerobic capacity of male handball players, b) aerobic capacity of female handball players

level of the players is low; however, with well conditioned athletes it is likely that other aspects should be sought when planning training activities. While being aware of physiological characteristics of elite performers is important to set goals and/or define benchmarking information, it is important for strength and conditioning coaches to understand well the game demand and the positional differences in order to prescribe appropriate training programmes and support the coaching staff in developing game-specific activities able to enhance game-specific fitness.

Time-motion data from the elite men's game during the 2007 World Championships has indicated that playing time is different between positions, with wingers (37.37 ± 2.37 min) and goalkeepers (37.11 ± 3.28 min) having more court time than backcourt players (29.16 ± 1.70 min) and pivots (29.3 ± 2.70 min) (Luig et al., 2008). The total distance covered during the game also varies between positions, with larger distances covered by wing players (3710 ± 210m) as compared to backcourt (2839 ± 150m) and line player (pivot) (2786 ± 238m) positions. Recent work on elite Portuguese players has shown that players cover a mean distance of 4370 ± 702m during a game, most of which is spent performing low intensity aerobic exercise actions that is interspersed by short duration very high intensity anaerobic actions (Póvoas et al., 2012). Our work during the Qatar Handball World Championships in 2015, which was the first comprehensive study on men's handball performance conducted during a major international event, provided some recent information on how demands have evolved at the elite level in men.

A player participating in the 2015 World Championship had an average presence on court of 36:48 min:s (+ 20:27 min:s) out of the 60 min duration of games, which was lower than previously reported in handball players competing in league games at the elite level (possibly due also due to the different inclusion criteria used in that study where only players with 42 min court times were included (Michalsik et al., 2012)) but very similar to the data recorded in the World Championships in 2007 (Luig et al., 2008). Handball is a sport with rolling substitutions and therefore presence on court of players depends not only on the position they play but also on their quality within the team and the tactical tasks they need to execute while playing. While such data are indicative and can provide some information about strength and conditioning prescriptions, the role of strength and conditioning coaches should also be to collect information on the demands of players within the team they operate to make sure programs are appropriate.

The men's World Championship data showed that goalkeepers and wings spend most of the time on court, probably due to a larger use of rolling substitutions with national team players for backcourts as well as more rotations in backcourt and pivot players who are able to cover large space in defense due to their anthropometric characteristics (Karcher and Buchheit, 2014). Players competing in the men's World Championships of 2015 covered on average a total distance of 2745.8 meters, which was less than previously recorded in Danish league players (Michalsik et al., 2012), Portuguese players (Póvoas et al., 2014a) and Slovenian national team players performing a game with reduced time and fixed defensive system (Šibila et al., 2004).

The differences reported in the literature in total distance covered depend on playing style and the level of players involved as well as on the different equipment/method used. While average values are of interest to characterise the typical performance demands, a large variability in total distance covered was evident in our study and it is clear in other studies, with some players covering a distance of as much as ~6500m in a single game. For this reason, while average values are relevant for gathering a broad understanding of the general fitness requirements of handball players, it is important to acknowledge that depending on the role within a team and the style of play, there may be large individual differences in the physical demands. It is evident that players performing both attacking and defending tasks require a specific training and recovery approach due to the peculiar demands of high level international tournaments. Figure 17.4 shows typical movement

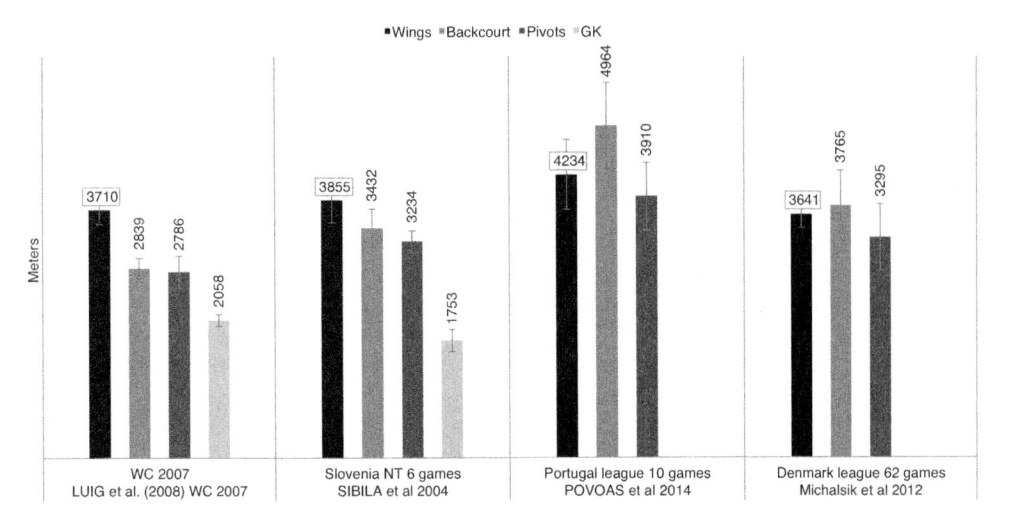

Figure 17.3 Distance covered by position in different leagues. Data presented in the literature

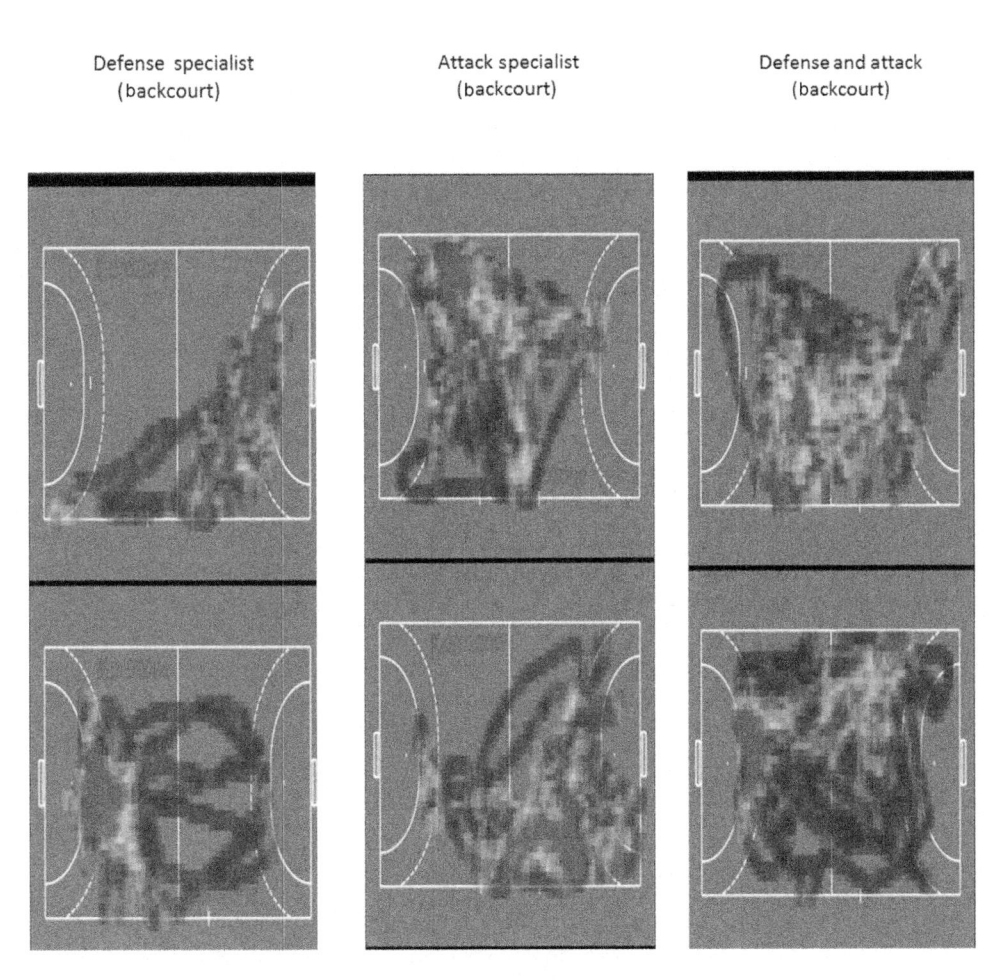

Figure 17.4 Typical movement patterns of backcourt player involved in defense, attack or both

patterns of players with attacking and defending activities, attacking only and defending only as tracked by Prozone Handball V. 1.404 using a heat map for analyses (dark indicates high density of activity).

From the heat map analysis of these 3 players, it is relatively easy to see that the amount of distance covered as well as the level of activity is remarkably different, despite all playing as a backcourt in their respective teams. Total distance covered in a game is one of the elements determining performance demands as it represents the total volume of the activity. Other characteristics are also very important to determine what happens while covering such distances. Handball players in fact are not running at constant speed. They run in different directions with and without the ball, they change direction often, they perform sidestepping movements in defence and run backwards. They jump and land. One metric of activity is also represented by the number of times a player changes activity. In our study conducted during the World Championships, the number of activity changes was higher than had been previously documented in national league players (players performed 857.2 + 445.7 activity changes in a game (Portuguese players showed less in Póvoas et al., 2014a; Póvoas et al., 2012, and Danish players showed more activity changes in Michalsik et al., 2012). Again, while differences in the quantification methods are likely to explain some of the differences observed in the different studies, handball players do change activities very often during a game. Therefore, conditioning drills should reflect this in order to match game demands.

The average running pace during the World Championships of 2015 was 78.2m•min^{-1}. This was a higher pace than reported in the Portuguese (Póvoas et al., 2012; Póvoas et al., 2014a; Póvoas et al., 2014b) and Danish league players (Michalsik et al., 2012), but lower than what reported in Slovenian national team players in experimental games (Šibila et al., 2004) and lower than the average values reported by Luig et al. (2008) in previous World Championships. Such differences are likely to be explained again by the dissimilarities in the methods used to ascertain the distance covered as well as the differences in the sample sizes between the studies. However, it is safe to state that the average running pace of handball players during a game is from 50 to 80m•min^{-1} (or 3–5km/h).

Walking, standing, and jogging represent the bulk of locomotion activities in handball players (>75% of the total distance covered) (Cardinale et al., 2016; Michalsik et al., 2012; Póvoas et al., 2012; Póvoas et al., 2014a; Póvoas et al., 2014b; Pers et al., 2002; Šibila et al., 2004; Karcher and Buchheit, 2014), indicating that high intensity activities represent a small percentage of the total distance covered and consist mainly of accelerations and decelerations in small spaces accumulating a small overall distance covered. This is true for both men and women, with female players only spending 0.8% of the total match duration performing fast running and sprinting combined (Bojsen Michalsik and Aagaard, 2015; Michalsik et al., 2014).

This is very important as the fact that only a relatively small distance is covered at what can be defined "high-intensity" activities does not mean that the physical demands in handball are low. In fact, the ability to repeat many of these high-intensity activities in crucial aspects of the game is the one of the key determinants of handball performance and training efforts should be directed towards improving this aspect. Despite this being well known in the coaching community, studies on work-to-rest ratios of high intensity actions are virtually nonexistent. A previous study reported that the average time lag between high intensity activities in handball games is 55+32s (Vaeyens et al., 2009; Vaeyens et al., 2008). Very few studies have reported similar parameters, with Povoas et al. (2012) reporting that most of the lag time between high intensity activities was larger than 90s in most instances. In our study of the men's World championships, the recovery time between activities was on average 124.3 + 143s. Variability is dictated by the pace of the game, the level of the players, the technical and tactical abilities, the tactical approach to attack and defence. For this reason, considering the paucity of data on this aspect, it is safe to assume that in general during the game there is a recovery time between activities ranging from few seconds to up to two minutes. This strongly supports the concept that specific conditioning activities cannot be based on running on a track in an athletics straight line but should include changes of directions and activities, with different intervals alternating high and low intensity movements, and with handball specific movements ideally able to condition decision-making abilities.

The dynamics of the game are such that teams can perform from 40 to 80 attacks in a game with an alternation between attack and defense phases of ~30s. The duration of attack phases ranges from very quick to relatively long (>40s). Counter-attacks are particularly important in handball despite their relatively infrequent occurrence in a game (11 + 5.8% as reported in Karcher and Buchheit, 2014) as they often create the gaps in score between teams and have a strong psychological effect if the scoring rate (or defending rate against them) is high. Such actions always involve 2–4 players and should be practiced with a lot of variety as a conditioning activity for handball players to improve their fitness and also to train decision making abilities at relatively high speed.

Recent work from Luteberget and colleagues (Luteberget and Spencer, 2015; Luteberget et al., 2017; Wik et al., 2016) introduced the use of inertial measurement units (IMUs) to quantify workloads in female players. IMUs measurements conducted in matches indicated an average of 0.7 ± 0.4 accelerations/min, 2.3 ± 0.9 decelerations/min, and 1.0 ± 0.4 changes of directions/min, providing new insights on the volume and the specificity of activity changes performed by handball players. In summary, movement patterns in handball are characterised by a variety of changes of activities and accelerations and decelerations in various directions.

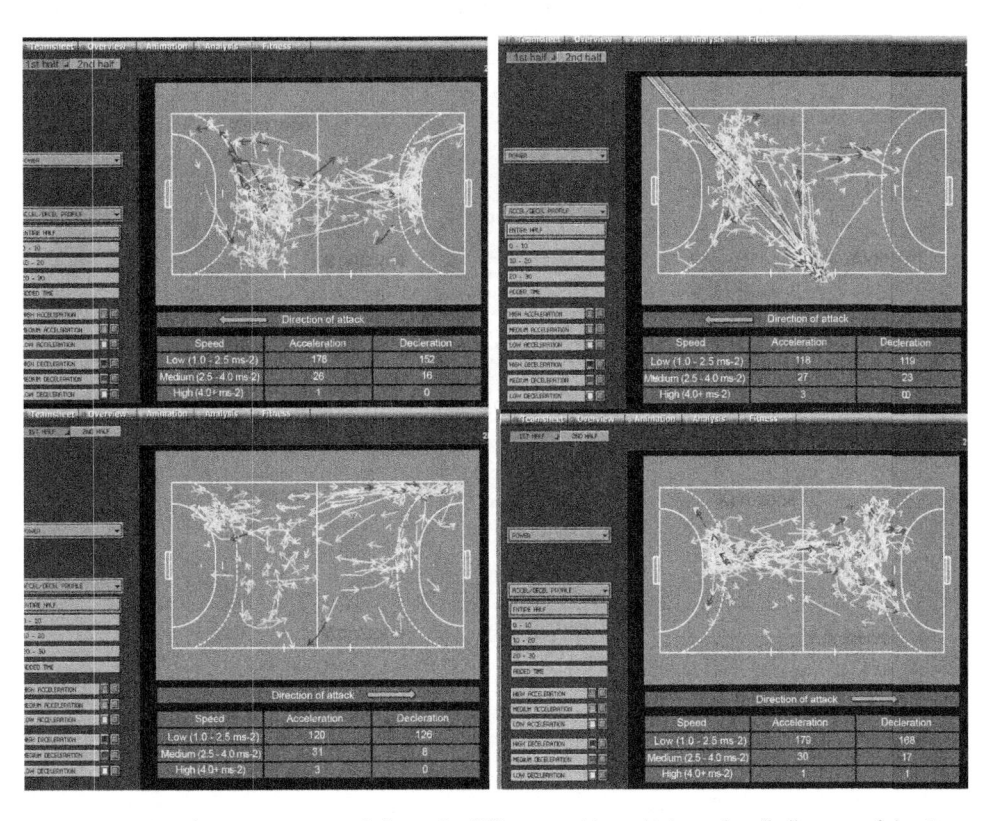

Figure 17.5 Acceleration patterns of players in different positions during a handball game of the Qatar 2015 World Championships

The cardiovascular demands of handball performance have been described in various studies over the years. Recent work during women's games of elite German and Norwegian players showed average values of heart rate during a game of 86.5 ± 4.5 % for the field players (Manchado et al., 2013b). Our study with the British women's national team in preparation for the Olympic Games showed similar values (~80% of heart rate max) with >60% of the total playing

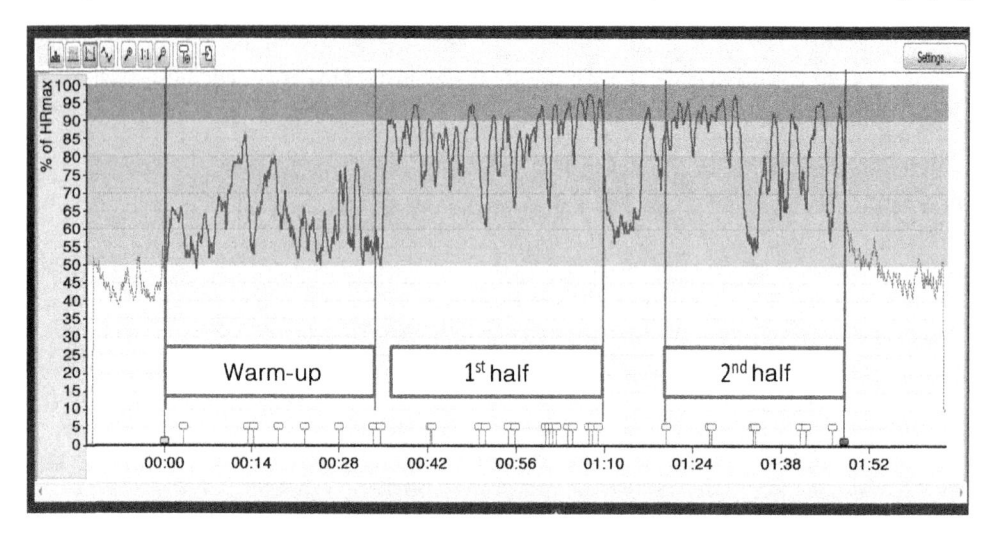

Figure 17.6 Typical heart rate pattern during a handball game

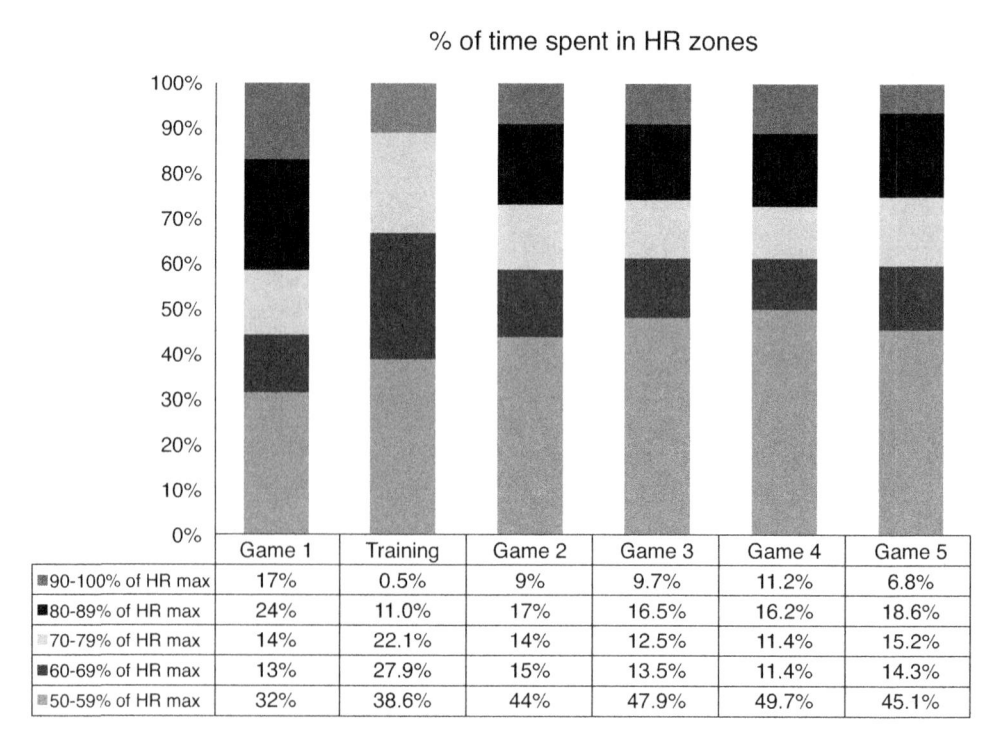

% of time spent in HR zones

	Game 1	Training	Game 2	Game 3	Game 4	Game 5
■ 90-100% of HR max	17%	0.5%	9%	9.7%	11.2%	6.8%
■ 80-89% of HR max	24%	11.0%	17%	16.5%	16.2%	18.6%
70-79% of HR max	14%	22.1%	14%	12.5%	11.4%	15.2%
■ 60-69% of HR max	13%	27.9%	15%	13.5%	11.4%	14.3%
■ 50-59% of HR max	32%	38.6%	44%	47.9%	49.7%	45.1%

Figure 17.7 Heart rate distribution (average values) in a team performing consecutive games and one training session

time spent over 80% of heart rate max (Cunniffe et al., 2015). Belk et al. (2014) reported slightly higher values in Under 19 elite Czech players. Data on male handball players is similar. Povoas et al. (2012) reported average values of 82% of max heart rate; similar values have been recorded in elite adolescent players (Chelly et al., 2011).

While quantification of workload by means of heart rate can be affected by various aspects, data continuously suggest that the cardiovascular demands of games can be high because of the fast pace, and it is important to consider that demands vary between players depending on their roles/technical and tactical tasks. Despite their well-known limitations, heart rate measurements still provide reliable and valid information about cardiovascular load during training and can be used with other measurements (such as time-motion aspects) to quantify workloads in training and in competitions and to monitor training.

Very few studies have been conducted to determine metabolic demands of handball players. So far, the data suggest that during games players rely mostly on anaerobic glycolysis, according to the few studies published on this aspect. Early work from Delamarche et al. (1987) showed blood lactate values ~7.5mmol•L^{-1} and suggested the importance of lactate tolerance training for handball players. However, in the same study, it was possible to see the differences in measured blood lactate between players with relatively similar activities showing that differences exist depending on role and tactical tasks. With rules changes, few more studies were conducted in recent years showing similar results. While average values between 1st and 2nd half of teams don't seem to really change (some studies show an increase, some a decrease), individual variability is presented in the literature. In my own experience, players have reached blood lactate values >10mmol•L^{-1}, suggesting that training activities targeted to improve lactate tolerance are important in handball players.

Previous studies have suggested that locomotor activities show a progressive decline in distance covered and pace, particularly during the last 10 minutes of a game. Previous work has evidenced a reduction in distance covered and distance covered at high speed between the 1st

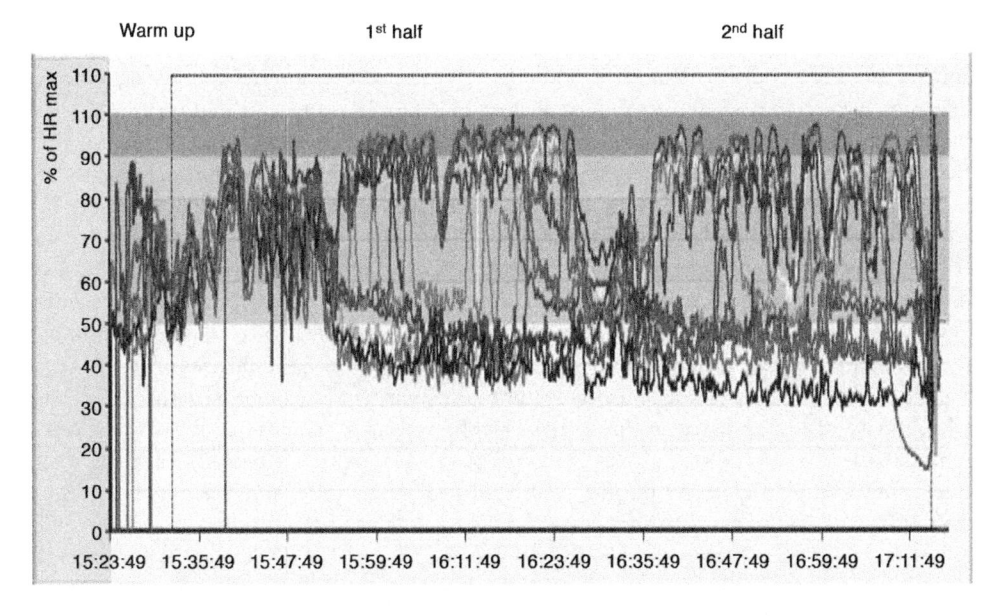

Figure 17.8 Individual variability in heart rate during games. All players taking part in the game were wearing a HR sensor

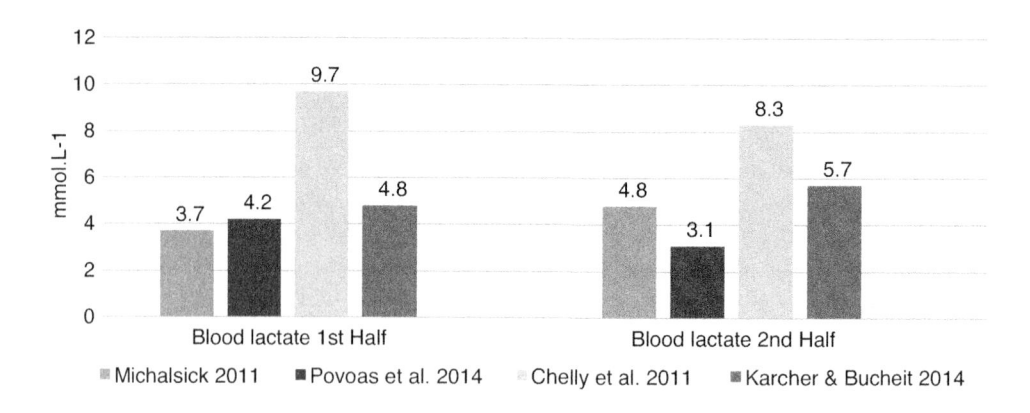

Figure 17.9 Average blood lactate values presented in various studies on handball players

and 2nd half (Michalsik et al., 2012; Póvoas et al., 2014a). Our data of the men's World Championships of 2015 showed a reduction in such activities only in the last 10 minutes of the game (but the statistical magnitude of the effect was trivial). It is possible that international level players are fitter than players involved in national or regional leagues but also that a wider use of rolling substitutions is present in international games. The difference in distance covered and speed of movement in the last part of the game have been attributed to fatigue by many authors (Ziv and Lidor, 2009; Michalsik et al., 2012; Póvoas et al., 2012; Karcher and Buchheit, 2014; Michalsik et al., 2014; Póvoas et al., 2014a; Póvoas et al., 2014b). However, it should be considered that slowing the pace of the game may be a specific strategy of the players due to the necessity to reduce the number of technical mistakes which can adversely influence the final result. During the World Championships we analysed, 47% of the games finished with 3 goals difference, with many games decided in the last few minutes. With the current amount of knowledge, it is difficult to make any definite conclusions about the cause and extent of fatigue during handball games. However, there is some documented acute reduction in neuromuscular function in male and female players after a game, albeit with studies with some limitations (Ronglan et al., 2006; Thorlund et al., 2007) as well as reduction in acceleration/deceleration activities in elite female players (Wik et al., 2016). The extent of physical impairment on decision-making abilities has not been analysed yet; however, it is fair to state that the goal of a good strength and conditioning programme should be to make sure handball players can sustain/play high-pace handball games and be able to retain decision-making abilities until the end of the game in order to increase the chances of success. From a coaching standpoint, well-planned use of rolling substitutions can definitively help in maintaining the pace of the game, reducing the chances of any physical manifestations of fatigue (as measured by volume and intensity of locomotion activities).

A paucity of studies has analysed other metabolic aspects of handball performance. Póvoas et al. (2014a) also showed that in male handball players plasma free fatty acids (FFA), glycerol, glucose, and uric acid increased during the 1st half and plasma FFA and glycerol increased further during the 2nd half, suggesting a larger reliance on fat oxidation in the 2nd half of handball games. This was observed in parallel to a decrease in sprint and jumping performance at the end of a match. Furthermore, during the matches analysed in this study, a marked decrease was observed in distance covered, with high intensity running in the 2nd half in parallel with a reduction in other quick movements/accelerations. While the data on blood lactate in various studies do seem to indicate a reliance on high glycogen utilisation in some players, such data also suggest a strong activation of lipid metabolism during game. Furthermore, a very recent study (Marin et al., 2013) showed that playing a handball game increases oxidative stress (as identified in an acute increase in TBARS and plasma antioxidant capacity in blood) and muscle damage indices (creatine kinase and lactate dehydrogenase) as well as generic inflammatory biomarkers such as IL-6 indicating that the intermittent patterns and physical contacts typical of this sport might require more than 24 hours to recover from. Playing a handball game in an indoor hall determines a degree of dehydration as evidenced in few studies analysing fluid loss during games. Hamouti et al. (2010) reported an average fluid loss of 1.1+0.3 Litres ·h^{-1} in male handball players with a marked inter-individual variability in the sweat response. A study on Portuguese male players (Póvoas et al., 2014a) reported average fluid losses of 2.1 + 0.4 L, corresponding to 2.3% of the players' body mass. In our study (Cunniffe et al., 2015) on female players, we reported average sweat rates during games of 1.02 ± 0.07 L · h^{-1}, and on 56% of occasions fluid intake matched or exceeded sweat loss. We also identified significant associations observed between player sweat rates and time spent exercising at intensities >90% HRmax and a large inter-individual variability, suggesting that a targeted approach for fluid replacement should be implemented in handball players.

At the moment, it is virtually impossible to understand the implications of long seasons on players' fitness and performance as there is no longitudinal study on handball players. However, from a strength and conditioning standpoint, knowing details about the season of your players is important. Elite players involved with clubs playing international cups and involved with national teams can play >80games per season, while national/regional level players in some nations can play <30 games. Parameters such as court time in games and training time can be a simple way to quantify and track "exposure" to handball activities and provide some information on workloads; however, other methods described in the following paragraphs can provide further information to decide on workload developments.

Tactical roles and positions and strength and conditioning specificity

Wing players have been repeatedly reported to be the fastest players on handball courts both for male (Šibila et al., 2004; Michalsik et al., 2012; Póvoas et al., 2012; Karcher and Buchheit, 2014; Póvoas et al., 2014a) and female handball players (Michalsik et al., 2014; Manchado et al., 2013b). Combined with the available data on anthropometry, wing players are smaller and faster than players occupying other positions. Their speed and agility is mostly used in fast break situations and counter attacks as well as during specific defensive tasks involving advanced/anticipatory defensive systems (e.g. 3:2:1 or 3:3, 4:2, 5:1) and/or individual marking scenarios. So, such players should be trained to maximise their speed and power expressions.

Overall, it is evident that game outcomes are mostly dominated by backcourts and pivot players (as measured during the men's World Championships). This trend is surely linked to tactical aspects of the game, which seem to be dominated and decided in the central part of the handball courts and appear confirmed by injury data. Players active in the middle of the handball court had the most injuries and pivots had the highest injury risk in previous studies (Bere et al., 2015), suggesting that players engaged in activities in the center of the court require position- and anthropometric-specific fitness and injury prevention regimes (Karcher et al., 2014). Therefore, strength and conditioning programs for backs and pivots should be directed towards the following goals: 1) increase overall robustness of players because of the contacts occurring in every position; 2) develop speed and jumping abilities; 3) develop the ability to repeat many high intensity actions; 4) focus on strength and power in players involved in heavy defensive tasks and/or attacking positions requiring many duels.

Goalkeepers' performance has been rarely studied in handball. At the elite level, they tend to be taller than other positions; however, at lower levels goalkeepers tend to have different anthropometric characteristics. Their task is to stop shots directed towards the goal and because they can use any part of the body to do it, goalkeepers tend to reach corners of the goals in extreme positions as well as condition attackers to make saves performing a variety of movements on one or both legs. Running activities are limited, and the majority of movements required are explosive-type movements to reach corners of the goal and jumps to cover goal areas in various body positions. The few studies in the literature presenting data on goalkeepers have shown that the cardiovascular demands are limited and so is their strength and endurance capacity when compared to the rest of the players. Anticipation (Rojas et al., 2012) and age/experience (Hansen et al., 2017) seem to be the main abilities discriminating elite performers; however, considering that typical throwing speed can be as fast as 25 m/s, it is clear that they have to be very fast to reach the ball to avoid a goal being scored and therefore emphasis on physical abilities needs to be put in developing fast movements in extreme ranges of motion of the lower limbs and upper limbs. While it is not the purpose of this chapter to discuss visual skills training, it is important to consider this aspect when preparing sports specific conditioning for handball goalkeepers. Considering the beneficial effects of visual skills training we have seen in goalkeepers in other sports (Wimshurst et al., 2012), it is suggested that strength and conditioning specialist work with handball coaches to develop conditioning activities also involving visual tasks to develop sports specific skills.

In the last few years, many teams have adopted the used of one or two defensive specialists in their rolling substitutions. Their main role is to enter the field of play during defensive transitions and exit the field when attacking transitions are performed and are mostly used to defend on pivots and/or try to block shots from backcourt players. Generally speaking, such players tend to be tall and heavy in order to utilise their anthropometry to cover as much space as possible in defence. For the first time, a study was conducted on the activity of these players during the world championships in Qatar 2015 (Cardinale et al., 2016), and it is evident that such players don't cover large distances compared to other players but are focused on movements characterised by quick accelerations and decelerations within short distances. Considering that these players are heavily involved in contacts with attacking players and contacts are the main

Table 17.2 Notes on specific handball positions

Position	Physical quality	Training focus	Specific notes
Goalkeeper	Strength	Explosive – Reactive – in extreme ranges of motion	Emphasis on being able to perform quick movements and be strong in hyperextension/extreme ranges. Make use of plyometrics/quick/agility drills/improve reaction time
	Speed and acceleration	Small ranges. GKs key actions consist of one-two steps movements to reach the ball	Focus on specific movements and accelerate to one-two steps maximum. Develop visual skills in parallel to acceleration/speed skills

Position	Physical quality	Training focus	Specific notes
	Game-specific endurance	Ability to repeat saves and repeated acceleration abilities	Introduce generic conditioning activities to maintain and/or improve cardiovascular capacity important to sustain training and competition workload
	Injury prevention	Develop range of motion in upper and lower limbs and the trunk. Strengthen upper lims focusing on shoulder and elbow joint to avoid elbow hyperextension when saving shots with arm extended. Focus on landing skills from jumps with one/two legs	Add exercises to teach how to fall safely. Proprioception standing on one or two legs
	Body composition/nutrition	Optimise body composition to improve power to weight ratio and facilitate quick movements	Focus on nutritional strategies to maximise attention and reaction time and minimise dehydration during games
Wing	Strength	Explosive – power focus. Improve jumping and sprinting abilities	Focus on improving acceleration/deceleration – in particular, in short spaces. Change of direction, landing and one-on one situations
	Speed and acceleration	Sprinting drills up to 30m with and without the ball. Static and dynamic starts. Completed sprinting with jumping shots or one on one situations	
	Game-specific endurance	Repeated sprint ability. Adjust work to rest ratios and distances according to attacking and defensive tasks (e.g. if forward defender in 5:1 system)	Use small sided games and/or field specific activities to improve repeated acceleration and sprint ability
	Injury prevention	Focus on preventing hamstring injuries and develop proprioception in ankle and knee joints due to frequent changes of direction/landing/pushes while in flight	Insert acitivities to learn how to fall safely as diving shots and falls are commong in wing players
	Body composition/nutrition	Maximise power to weight ratio minimising body fat	Consider in-game and post game nutritional strategies to improve recovery from repeated sprints activities
Pivot	Strength	Maximal strength and explosive power necessary for contrasts and ability to turn quickly. Hypertrophy can also be sought. Core strength important too	Consider also the use of static strength in specific positions and focus on turning movements. High incidence of back and knee injuries so strength is very important in this position

(Continued)

Table 17.2 (Continued)

Position	Physical quality	Training focus	Specific notes
	Speed and acceleration	Usually distances covered sprinting are less than 20m. Short range speed and acceleration drills (3m to 20m)	Focus on the ability to repeat accelerations and sprinting movements with a relatively short work-to-rest ratio
	Game-specific endurance	Repeated sprint ability. Adjust work to rest ratios and distances according to attacking and defensive tasks (e.g. if forward defender in 5:1 system)	Use small sided games and/or field specific activities to improve repeated acceleration and sprint ability
	Injury prevention	Core strength is key due to frequent contacts. Shoulder strength and stability also focus due to shooting in odd positions and with contact	Insert acitivities to learn how to fall safely as diving shots and falls are commong in pivots. Consider using Judo moves as an alternative training modality to develop more safe landing skills
	Body composition/ nutrition	Maximise power to weight ratio, minimising body fat and increasing muscle size	Nutritional strategies to maximise fat free mass should be sought
Backcourt	Strength	Maximal strength and explosive power necessary for contrasts and ability resist opposition in attack and defense. Hypertrophy can also be sought. Develop jumping and shooting from a distance and one-on-one abilities	Use of global exercises like squat/bench press/Olympic lifts suggested to maximise strength and power. Also use single leg strength/power activities and core strength/rotational strength
	Speed and acceleration	Usually distances covered sprinting are less than 20m. Short range speed and acceleration drills (3m to 20m). Repeated progressive acceleration as players mostly involved in breakthrough	Focus on the ability to repeat accelerations and sprinting movements with a relatively longer work to rest ratio (e.g. 20–20s).
	Game-specific endurance	Repeated sprint ability. Adjust work to rest ratios and distances according to attacking and defensive tasks (e.g. if advanced defender in 3:2:1)	Use small sided games and/or field specific activities to improve repeated acceleration and sprint ability
	Injury prevention	Core strength is key due to frequent contacts. Shoulder strength and stability also focus for fast shots from distance. One leg strength/power important for one on one situations and jump shots	Develop duel skills and landing skills mostly on one leg
	Body composition/ nutrition	Maximise power to weight ratio, minimising body fat and increasing muscle size	Nutritional strategies to maximise fat free mass should be sought. Also in-game nutritional approaches to avoid excessive dehydration and facilitate repeated sprint ability

cause of injury in handball (Bere et al., 2015), it is advisable to develop bespoke strength and conditioning activities for such positions to improve the ability to move quickly in limited spaces and focus on strength and power in order to maximise performance and reduce injury risk of defensive specialists.

Typical movements and strength requirements

If we try to simplify handball, we could state that for handball players, running/sprinting, jumping, changing direction and throwing are the key movement skills needed. As sprinting abilities and drills have been described extensively in other chapter, I have focused on jumping, throwing and change of direction in handball players.

Jump shots are the most used shooting technique by handball players (more than 70% of the shots are performed while jumping (Wagner and Müller, 2008) and are performed with a run-in, planting of the foot and take off usually on the leg opposite to the throwing arm (albeit some players at times will perform jump shots, taking off with both lower limbs and/or jumping on the leg on the same side of the shooting arm). During such movement, ground reaction forces can be larger than 3 times the player's body mass with ground contact times lower than 300 milliseconds (Laffaye et al., 2005; Lindner et al., 2012; Pori et al., 2005). This means that muscles of the lower limbs are required to produce large contractile forces in a relatively short period of time in order for the player to take off and jump. An increased jumping ability on one leg would be a big advantage for a player, as it would allow shooting from a bigger height with the possibility to avoid a block from a defender (mainly backcourt players) and would give more time in the air to wait for a goalkeeper's move or fake a shot (mainly for wings, line players and other game specific situations). Strength training should therefore be targeted to improve vertical jumping ability in handball players – in particular, with one leg take off. Also, other aspects related to injury prevention should be taken into account. In particular, due to the kinetics and kinematic characteristics of jump shots, and the large number of repetitions of such actions in training, stronger lower limbs are necessary as braking forces are large during the deceleration phase and stress on the ankle and knee joint is quite remarkable (Laffaye et al., 2005; Lindner et al., 2012) – in particular, after landing from such shots and when landing is affected by contacts with a defender from the opposite team. Jumping abilities do seem to discriminate between elite and non-elite players and therefore strength and conditioning programs should focus on this aspect for field players.

Throwing is a very important aspect as all goals are scored with throwing actions. A few studies and our own observations with national teams and club teams in Italy have in fact shown over the years that throwing speed could discriminate between elite and non-elite players (Gorostiaga et al., 2005; Granados et al., 2007). Throwing speed can be measured with a radar gun and/or with video analysis. Typical throwing speed for male handball players is 20 to 40m/s in male players and 18 to 35m/s in female players (see Figure 17.10 for some data). Therefore, maximal throwing speed can be faster than 120km/h. Despite the differences in throwing speed, it is clear that there are no gender differences in the kinematics of overarm throwing between male and female elite players (Van Den Tillaar and Cabri, 2012). Upper body strength, assessed with bench press 1RM and lifting velocity with various loads, has been shown to be predictive of throwing speed in handball players (Debanne and Laffaye, 2011; Marques et al., 2011; Cardinale Unpublished observations). For this reason, a training programme designed to improve upper body strength could use then bench press as one of the exercises not only for training purposes but also to assess the progression and the effectiveness of the programme. In my experience, 12–14 sessions of strength training, including unilateral and bilateral bench press and other exercises for

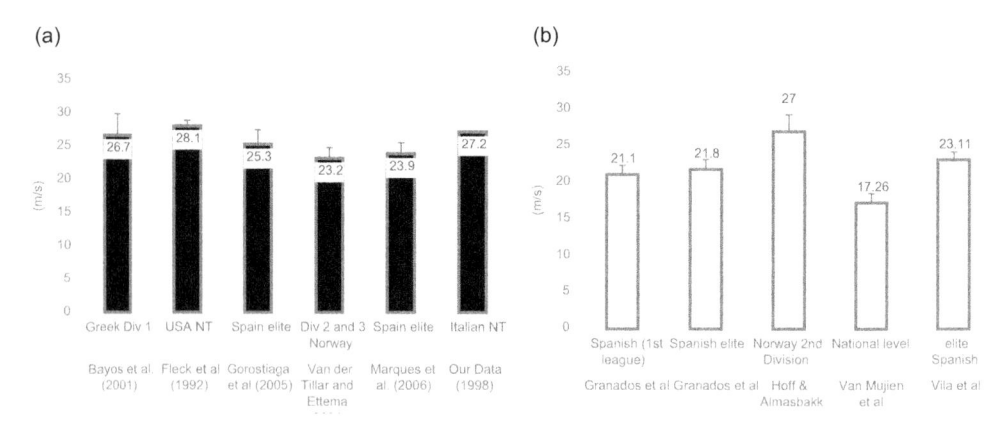

Figure 17.10 Throwing speed in a) male, b) female handball players

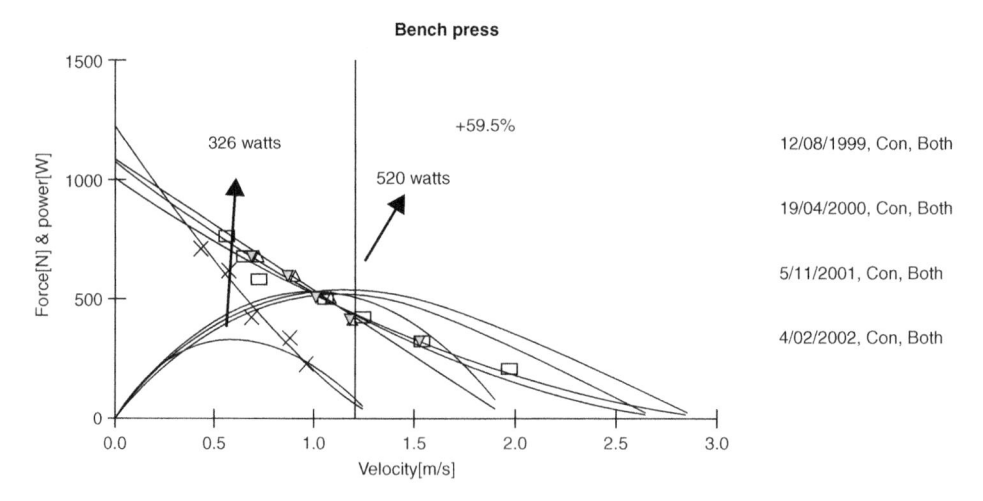

Figure 17.11 Force/velocity and power/velocity relationship measured with a bench press with 5 external loads with a linear encoder in a National Team Backcourt player during the years. Note the improvement in strength and power with targeted S&C programme

the shoulders and upper body, in pre-season in a team of the Italian elite league was successful in shifting the force/velocity and power/velocity relationships to the right and improved throwing speed (Cardinale, 2014). Furthermore, a multiannual programme focused on strength in the first year and on speed and power in the following years was effective in shifting the F/V and P/V curves to the right with large improvements in power output linked to improvements in throwing speed in a national team player (see Figure 17.11).

Changes of directions are performed routinely during handball games, in particular side-cutting manoeuvres in attacking situations to avoid the defender. Such movements are characterised by

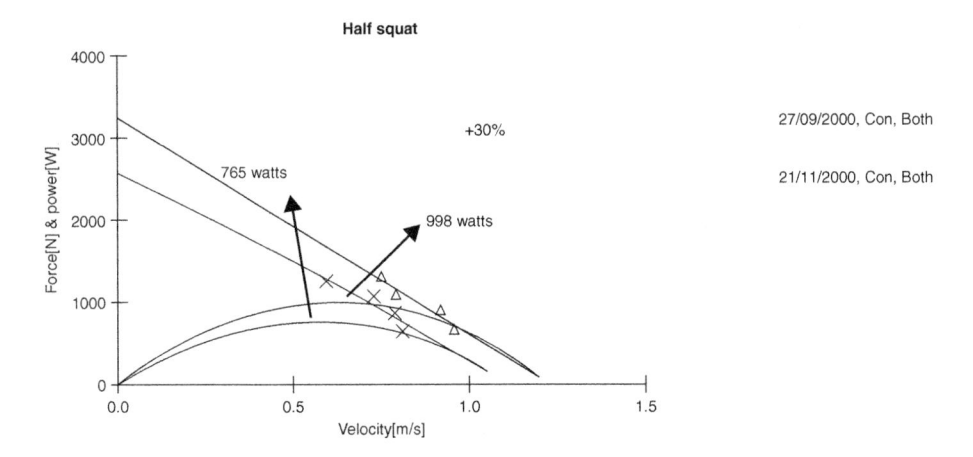

Figure 17.12 Force/velocity and power/velocity relationship measured with a half squat with 4 external loads with a linear encoder in a National Team Backcourt player over a 2 month period (12 strength sessions performed). Note the improvement in strength and power with targeted S&C programme

ground reaction forces up to 3 times the player's body mass (Bencke et al., 2000; Zebis et al., 2008; Bencke et al., 2013). In such movements, players are accelerating forward or sideward and then suddenly try to change direction to avoid a defender. High levels of strength of the lower limbs are required to decelerate and then accelerate in another direction. For this reason, strength training should be targeted to make sure handball players can decelerate safely and accelerate in various directions minimising the risks of injury. It is in fact when performing these movements that the risks of ACL injuries are very high in handball players (in particular in female players; Koga et al., 2010; Renstrom et al., 2008; Bencke et al., 2013). Strength training programmes should therefore be designed including exercises with one and two limbs, landing and deceleration drills, generic proprioceptive-type of exercise on unstable surfaces and eccentric and plyometric drills in various directions. Strength training plans designed with this approach have been effective in reducing the risks of injuries (Myklebust et al., 2003; Wedderkopp et al., 1999; Zebis et al., 2008). A good strength and conditioning programme should improve the ability of the players to perform rapid decelerations and accelerations in every possible direction with an appropriate movement pattern and control of the ankle and knee joint in order to reduce the chances of an injury.

Injury prevalence

Handball is one of the high-risk sports in terms of injury in the Olympic programme. The risk of an athlete to be injured in the London Olympics was the highest in taekwondo, football, BMX, handball, mountain bike, hockey, weightlifting, athletics and badminton (15–39% of registered athletes were affected in each sport). In the London Olympic Games, the sports with the highest rate of injuries entailing a prolonged absence from training or competition (>7 days) were taekwondo (6% of the athletes), handball (5%), BMX cycling (4%) and weightlifting (4%) (Engebretsen et al., 2013). Similar data were already reported during Beijing Games in 2008 indicating the high risk nature of playing handball at the elite level.

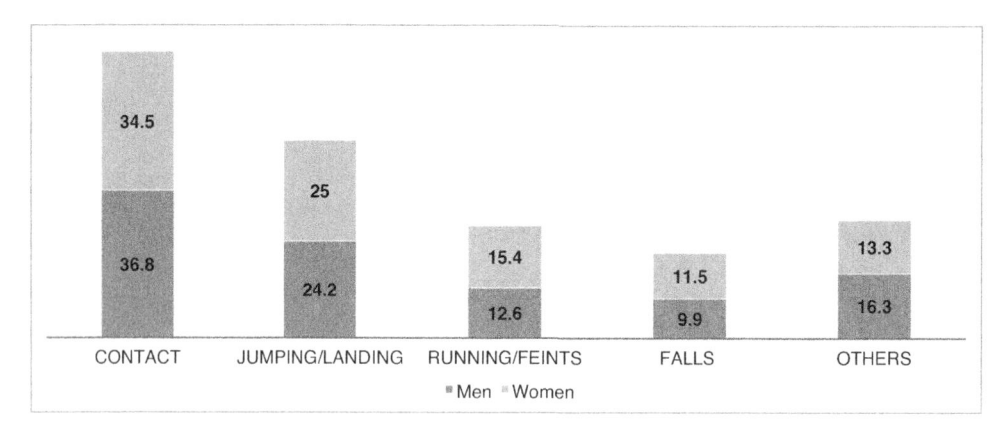

Figure 17.13 Percentage of situations leading to injury in elite handball players

(Luig & Henke, Analysis of injuries in German leagues. Data Retrieved from www.safetyinsports.eu)

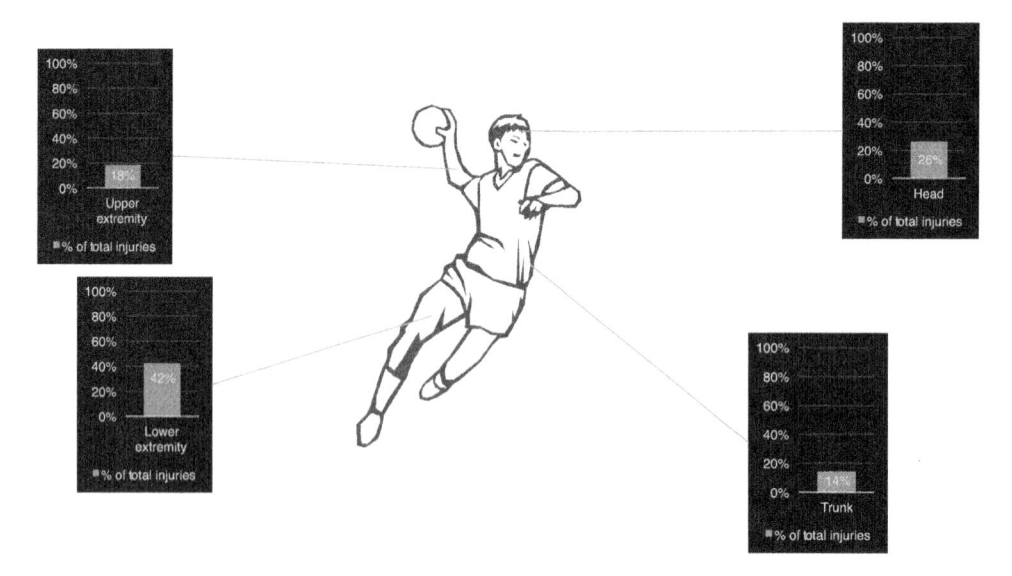

Figure 17.14 Injury sites major events (pooled data Men & Women 2001–2004)

Data from Langevoort et al., 2007

Fitness testing battery

Various tests can and have been used to assess fitness abilities of handball players. Here is a list of the most common ones with some reference data presented in the literature.

ENDURANCE CAPACITY

30–15

The 30–15IFT is a test initially developed by Dr. Martin Bucheit to assess handball players' endurance and intermittent running capacity and to develop ways to individualise training prescription. A detailed review with the history and the protocol of the test as well as reference data has been published recently and it is available online free of charge (www.cardioc.eu/wp-content/uploads/2016/12/buchheit-30-15ift-10-yrs-review-2000-2010.pdf; Buchheit, 2010). It requires the player to run 30s shuttle runs interspersed with 15s passive recovery periods. Velocity is set at 8km.h^{-1} for the first 30s run, and speed is increased by 0.5km/h every 30s stage thereafter (well-trained players can start the test at 10 or even 12km/h to save time). Players are required to run back and forth between two lines set 40m apart at a pace set by a beep. The test can be acquired online. The pre-recorded beep allows the players to adjust their running speed when they enter a 3m zone placed in the middle and at each extremity of the field. During the 15s recovery period, players walk in a forward direction towards the closest line (at either the middle or end of the running area, depending on where their previous run had stopped); this line is where they will start the next run stage from. Players are instructed to complete as many stages as possible, and the test ends when the players can no longer maintain the required running speed or when they are unable to reach a 3m zone in time with the audio signal for three consecutive times. The velocity attained during the last completed stage is defined as the player's V_{IFT}. $\dot{V}O_{2max}$ can be estimated from the V_{IFT} according to the following formula: $\dot{V}O_{2max}$30–15IFT (ml.$^{-1}$min.kg^{-1}) = 28.3−2.15 G 0.741 A − 0.0357 W + 0.0586 A ×V_{IFT} + 1.03 V_{IFT}, where G stands for gender (female = 2 ; male = 1), A for age, and W for weight.

Validity and reliability of this test has been reported extensively in the literature. Bucheit (Buchheit et al., 2009b; Buchheit, 2010) reported a typical error of measurement of 0.3km/h (95% CL, 0.26 to 0.46), which suggests that a change of about 1 stage (i.e. 0.5km/h) represents a meaningful and significant improvement.

V_{IFT} can be used to prescribe individualised training activities by identifying the most appropriate running speed for each player based on their performance on the test, and it may represent the true maximal speed a player can reach when compared to other shuttle run tests. Elite handball players have been shown to reach V_{IFT} higher than 18km/h (Buchheit, 2008; Buchheit et al., 2009b; Buchheit and Rabbani, 2014).

Shuttle run

Various tests are available, such as the University of Montreal test (also known as Leger test) (Dupont et al., 2010; Leger et al., 1988) or the Yo-Yo Intermittent Recovery 1 or 2 Test (Krustrup et al., 2003). They are multi-stage fitness tests where the players are asked to increase their running speed in stages of 1 or more minutes (according to the specific test protocol) following an audio beep. The tests are performed using a space of 20m and may be more appropriate for smaller indoor courts. A large literature exists on both tests and various studies have shown in handball that the distance covered in such assessment is linked to the distance covered during handball games (Hermassi et al., 2011; Souhail et al., 2010). The protocols are described in detail in the literature. Improvements in such tests have been reported up to 25% in elite players following 8 weeks of a targeted programme (Kvorning et al., 2017) and are similar to my findings (unpublished data) on Italian players from an A/1 team (see Figure 17.15).

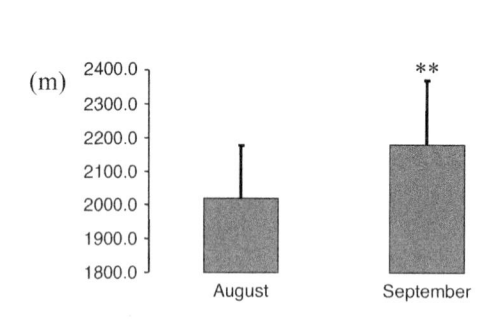

Figure 17.15 Improvement in distance covered in the Yo-Yo intermittent level 2 in handball players of the Italian first league

(n=14 ** Significant with P=0.01)

Sprint and repeated sprint

Sprint tests conducted on handball players should be used to assess acceleration and sprinting activities. As game analysis has shown that the longest sprint is likely to be less than 40 meters, the maximum distance assessed should be 20–30m. When performing sprint tests, it also helpful to record the first 5–10m times as this would provide information about the ability to accelerate. Few studies have reported some reference values in elite players and have concluded that elite performers have better sprinting abilities than non-elite (Gorostiaga et al., 2005; Granados et al., 2007). Furthermore, studies have reported improvements in sprinting abilities with strength and conditioning programmes both in male and female players (Kvorning et al., 2017; Gorostiaga et al., 2005; Granados et al., 2007; Jensen et al., 1997). Improvements up to 4% have been reported in the literature with relatively short term or season long training programmes and have been linked to improvements in strength and power.

Strength and power

Lower limb strength and power abilities can be assessed with simple tests such as the jump tests developed by Bosco (Bosco et al., 1995; Bosco et al., 1983; Bosco and Komi, 1979; Komi and Bosco, 1978). Briefly, jump tests are performed with hands on the hips and can be conducted with a contact mat and/or a force platform. The contact mat option can provide flight times and with such information it is possible to calculate the height of rise of the centre of gravity using ballistic laws. The force platform option provides more information about the time-course of the force application on the ground and can be used to determine more diagnostic parameters (e.g. asymmetries). The typical tests used are the Squat Jump (SJ), the Counter Movement Jump (CMJ), drop jumps from various heights (DJ), repeated hopping tests to determine lower limbs stiffness and reactivity, and repeated CMJs tests. Elite players have been shown to have

CMJs height higher than 40cm. Strength and conditioning programmes with various designs have been shown to improve jumping ability in handball players over the course of the season also in young athletes (Bencke et al., 2002; Cardinale, 2014; Chelly et al., 2013; Marques and González-Badillo, 2006). My early work (Wallace and Cardinale, 1997) on elite junior players also showed that a periodised well-planned strength and conditioning programme was able to improve jumping ability as measured with SJ, CMJ and repeated hopping tests.

Other assessments include the determination of the Force/Velocity and Power/Velocity relationship with the Bench Press and Half Squat Exercises. The Bench Press exercise is important as the muscles involved in such movements are the prime movers of handball throws (Grezios et al., 2006). Previous work has already identified a relationship between bench press 1RM, peak bar velocity and/or power load relationship and throwing speed in handball players (Debanne and Laffaye, 2011; Gorostiaga et al., 2005; Granados et al., 2013; Marques et al., 2011; Marques et al., 2007). As training programmes have been shown to improve throwing speed (van den Tillaar, 2004), the determination of F/V and P/V characteristics with bench press can be useful to provide individualised loads and assess the improvements and progression of athletes. In my experience, both male and female handball players can improve significantly F/V and P/V profiles in the Bench Press over the years, and improve throwing speed as a consequence (Cardinale, 2014). In order to develop appropriate testing protocols, the strength and conditioning coaches should use a Smith Machine to make sure the path of the barbell is linear (if using linear encoders to track the bar) and/or use sensors (linear encoders or accelerometers) able to take into consideration the displacement of the bar away from the vertical line. Four to five external loads of increasing magnitude should be used, asking the athlete to perform 3 trials per each external load at the maximum speed possible. It is important to assess this with concentric only and stretch shortening type movements to also assess the effects of the training programmes on the stretch shortening cycle. In my experience, bar velocities of 0.5m/s were reached with a load of ~70% of an individual's 1RM. Recent work has presented various approaches to perform such assessment and some reference data (Bosquet et al., 2010; Rahmani et al., 2017).

A similar approach can be used to establish the F/V and P/V relationships in the lower limbs using the Squat exercise. In a simplistic way, the determination of the F/V and P/V profile can be used to determine the most appropriate load for the athlete and track his/her progression according to the objective of the training plan. In general, loads in the high part of the F/V curve can improve maximal strength, and loads near the peak power can improve power output. Recent work using this approach has suggested the determination of the F-v imbalance as the difference by the athlete's actual and optimal profile to identify the optimal loading patterns with very successful outcomes (Jiménez-Reyes et al., 2016). In my experience, it was possible to use this approach regularly through the years to assess progression and improve training prescriptions in a much better way than just using 1RM measurements. Needless to say, when this method is used, it is important to always assess body mass on testing days in order to normalise F and P to the individual's body mass.

Programming

Preparing handball players for competitions requires a detailed understanding of the seasons' demands and a serious programme can only be developed when such information is available. There is in fact a large difference in what can be appropriate for teams playing national leagues and international cups (e.g. teams competing in Champions League and SEHA league while also competing in national championships and cups) with teams only competing in national and/or regional leagues. A player of international calibre and Champions League finalist can play more than 80 games in a season. Furthermore, players involved in high level competitions with clubs

Table 17.3 Typical weekly training structures

Time of day	Monday	Tuesday	Wednesday	Thursday	Friday	Saturday	Sunday
AM	Strength training	Technical focus	Strength training	Technical	Tactical focus	Travel/rest	REST
PM	Repeated acceleration ability	Specific endurance	Acceleration/sprint	Tactical focus	Tactical focus	GAME	REST
2 games in a week							
AM	Strength training	Technical focus	Low intensity Tactical or rest	REST	Tactical focus	Travel/rest	REST
PM	Repeated acceleration ability	Technical/tactical	GAME	Tactical focus	Tactical focus	GAME	REST

have to attend a number of training camps and games/official events with their national teams. For this reason, planning should take into account not only the club's activities, but also the needs for individual players involved in international competitions.

The typical weekly training structure of a team competing in a national only and national-international competitions is summarised in Table 17.3.

Most teams in Europe have a pre-season activity lasting 4–8 weeks in the summer months and begin the official matches around September-October. The seasons continue usually until May-June (Champions League finals are usually at the beginning of June). International activity tends to occur in December-January and July-August. Nowadays with the development of Beachandball many players move to play on sand during the summer months and some clubs also take part in Beachandball championships/leagues. For this reason, knowledge of the whole season is fundamental for good planning.

The process of planning the strength and conditioning activities should start with an assessment of the performance needs, followed by a comprehensive assessment of the fitness status of the players. As indicated before, testing should be used to inform and assess the status but also to provide information useful for individualised training prescription.

In the general preparation phase of pre-season, the goals should be to improve maximal strength and power, range of motion of key joints, endurance/high intensity intermittent capacity and optimise body composition. Furthermore, injury prevention strategies should be put in place to minimise the risks of injuries in-seasons. During the competition season, it is possible to maintain strength levels with one strength session per week; however, where possible two sessions per weeks are optimal to retain and/or improve power and speed in-season.

Conditioning activities in-season should be characterised by game-specific drills (Buchheit et al., 2010; Luteberget et al., 2017; Buchheit et al., 2009b), which have been shown to be effective in improving endurance and repeated sprint ability if appropriately designed and performed at high intensity by the players. The simple ways to monitor the intensity could be the combined use of heart rate monitors and inertial measurement units, as well as session RPE and Blood Lactate to be able to quantify the cardiovascular demands, the energy requirements, the movement patterns and the perceived exertion. An example of comparisons between well designed small sided games and conventional conditioning activities is provided in Figure 17.16.

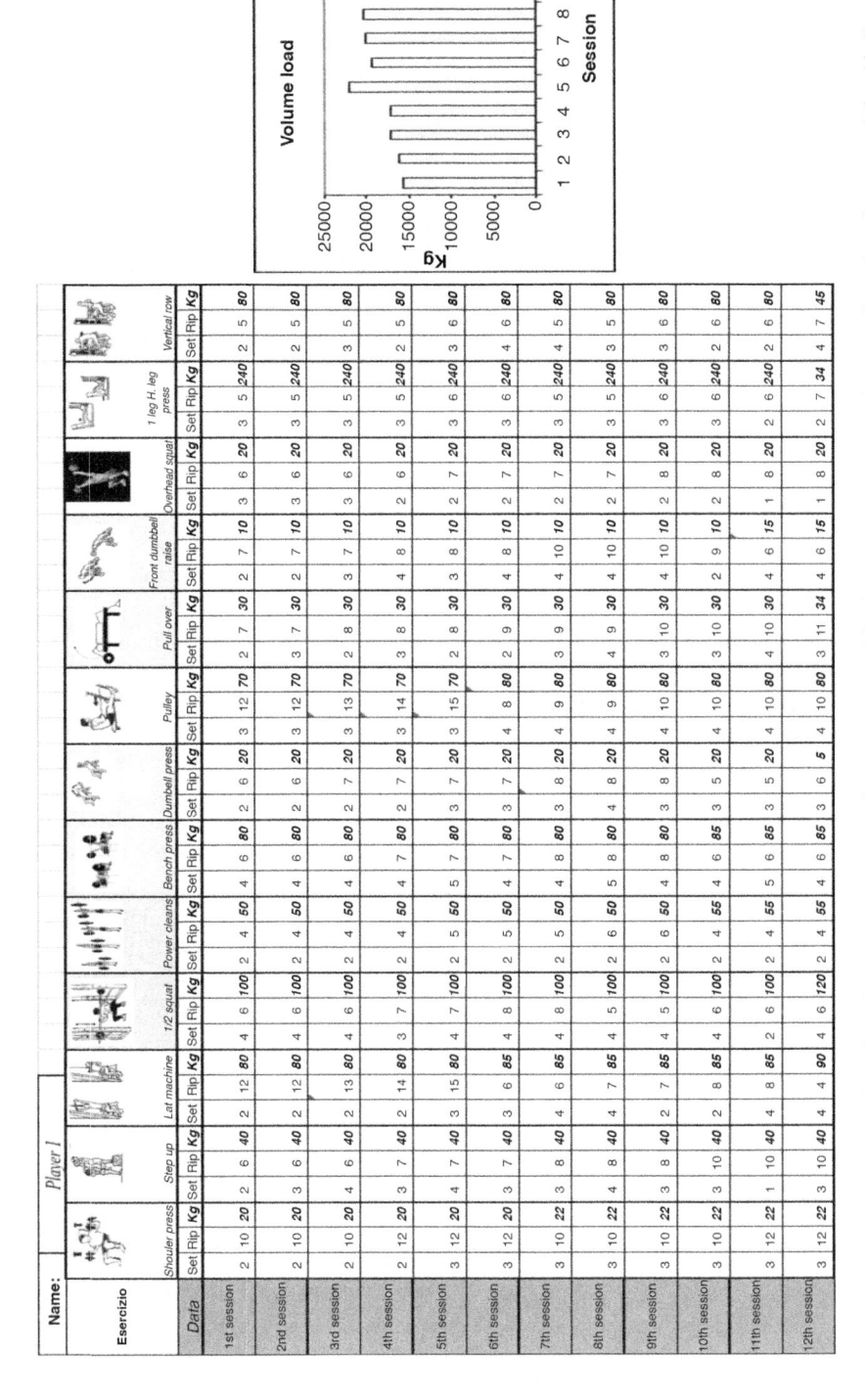

Name:		Player I																								
Esercizio		Shoulder press			Step up			Lat machine			1/2 squat			Power cleans			Bench press			Dumbell press			Pulley			Pull over			Front dumbbell raise			Overhead squat			1 leg H. leg press			Vertical row		
Data		Set	Rip	Kg	Set	Rip	Kg	Set	Rip	Kg	Set	Rip	Kg	Set	Rip	Kg	Set	Rip	Kg	Set	Rip	Kg	Set	Rip	Kg	Set	Rip	Kg	Set	Rip	Kg	Set	Rip	Kg	Set	Rip	Kg	Set	Rip	Kg
1st session	2	10	20	2	6	40	2	12	80	4	6	100	2	4	50	4	6	80	2	6	20	3	12	70	2	7	30	2	7	10	3	6	20	3	5	240	3	5	80
2nd session	2	10	20	3	6	40	2	12	80	4	6	100	2	4	50	4	6	80	2	6	20	3	12	70	2	7	30	2	7	10	3	6	20	3	5	240	2	5	80
3rd session	2	10	20	4	6	40	2	13	80	4	6	100	2	4	50	4	6	80	2	7	20	3	13	70	3	8	30	3	7	10	3	6	20	3	5	240	3	5	80
4th session	2	12	20	3	7	40	2	14	80	3	7	100	2	4	50	4	7	80	2	7	20	3	14	70	3	8	30	4	8	10	2	6	20	3	5	240	3	5	80
5th session	3	12	20	4	7	40	3	15	80	4	7	100	2	5	50	5	7	80	3	7	20	3	15	70	3	8	30	3	8	10	2	7	20	3	6	240	3	5	80
6th session	3	12	20	3	7	40	3	6	85	4	8	100	2	5	50	5	7	80	3	7	20	4	8	80	3	9	30	4	8	10	2	7	20	3	6	240	2	4	80
7th session	3	12	20	3	8	40	3	6	85	4	8	100	2	5	50	4	8	80	3	7	20	4	9	80	3	9	30	4	10	10	2	7	20	3	5	240	4	5	80
8th session	3	10	22	4	8	40	4	7	85	5	8	100	2	6	50	5	8	80	4	8	20	4	9	80	4	9	30	4	10	10	2	7	20	3	5	240	3	5	80
9th session	3	10	22	3	8	40	2	7	85	5	5	100	2	6	50	4	8	80	3	8	20	4	10	80	3	10	30	4	10	10	2	8	20	3	6	240	3	6	80
10th session	3	10	22	3	10	40	2	8	85	4	6	100	2	4	55	4	6	85	3	5	20	4	10	80	3	10	30	2	9	10	2	8	20	3	6	240	2	6	80
11th session	3	12	22	1	10	40	4	8	85	2	6	100	2	4	55	5	6	85	3	5	20	4	10	80	4	10	30	4	6	15	1	8	20	2	6	240	2	6	80
12th session	3	12	22	3	10	40	4	4	90	4	6	120	2	4	55	4	6	85	3	6	5	4	10	80	3	11	34	4	6	15	1	8	20	2	7	34	4	7	45

Figure 17.16 Typical strength and conditioning programme for pre-season and load progression. Squat and power cleans, bench press and dumbbell press, pull-over and front dumbbell always performed in complex sets. Example for one international player

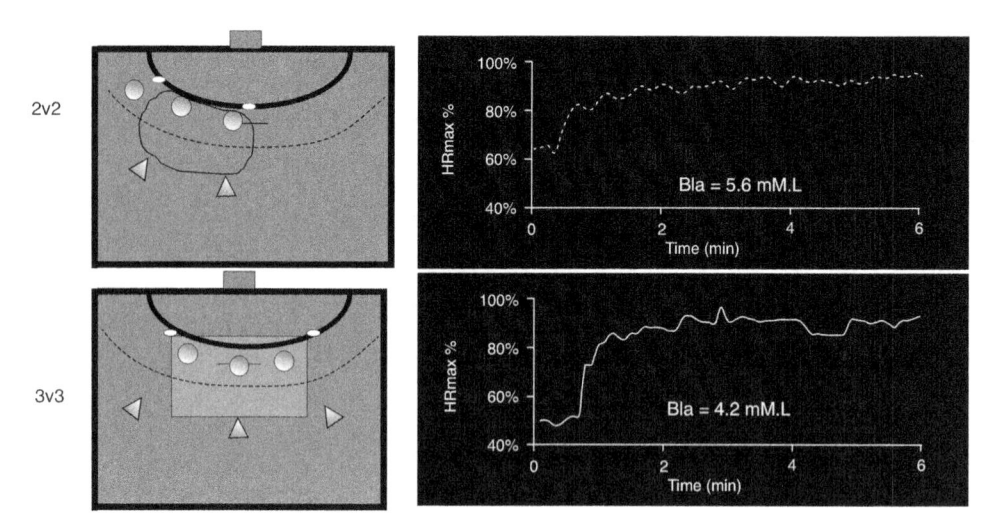

Figure 17.17 Heart rate and Blood Lactate during small sided games in handball players of a National Team.

Recovery and regeneration activities are important in handball due to the contact nature of the sport and they are fundamental when teams and athletes are involved in many games and travels. While there is a paucity of studies on the effects of various modalities on the fatigue and recovery requirements of handball games, there is indication that games cause a degree of muscle damage and oxidative stress as well as a significant energy expenditure. Furthermore, considering the intermittent nature of activities, it is likely that handball games do reduce glycogen stores in skeletal muscle. This should be taken into account when planning training post friendly or official games, and players' time on court should be considered when planning training intensities up to 48 hours following a game. Also, appropriate recovery and regeneration procedures should be put in place to speed up recovery following games.

With this in mind, it is difficult if not impossible to devise a standard periodisation approach for a handball team/player. The general preparation/pre-season phase is probably the longest time available to strength and conditioning coaches to improve physical qualities, and therefore such time should be maximised to prepare players for completion. The volume and intensities of in-season activities are dictated by the competition schedule, the travel schedule and the availability of players and should always follow the general rules of strength and conditioning programmes, making sure that progression of load is adequate to avoid sudden load spikes which would put the players at risk of injury as evidenced in similar contact sports like rugby. The main effort of strength and conditioning coaches in-season should be directed at having true individual training prescriptions for players and to optimise the on-court activities performed by the coaching staff, which is likely to be in charge of more than 80% of the total training time of the team.

Conclusion

Developing physical abilities in handball players requires a holistic approach. Research studies indicate that a training approach focused mostly on enhancing aerobic capacity to improve handball performance is possibly wrong. It is instead evident that knowledge of players' demands

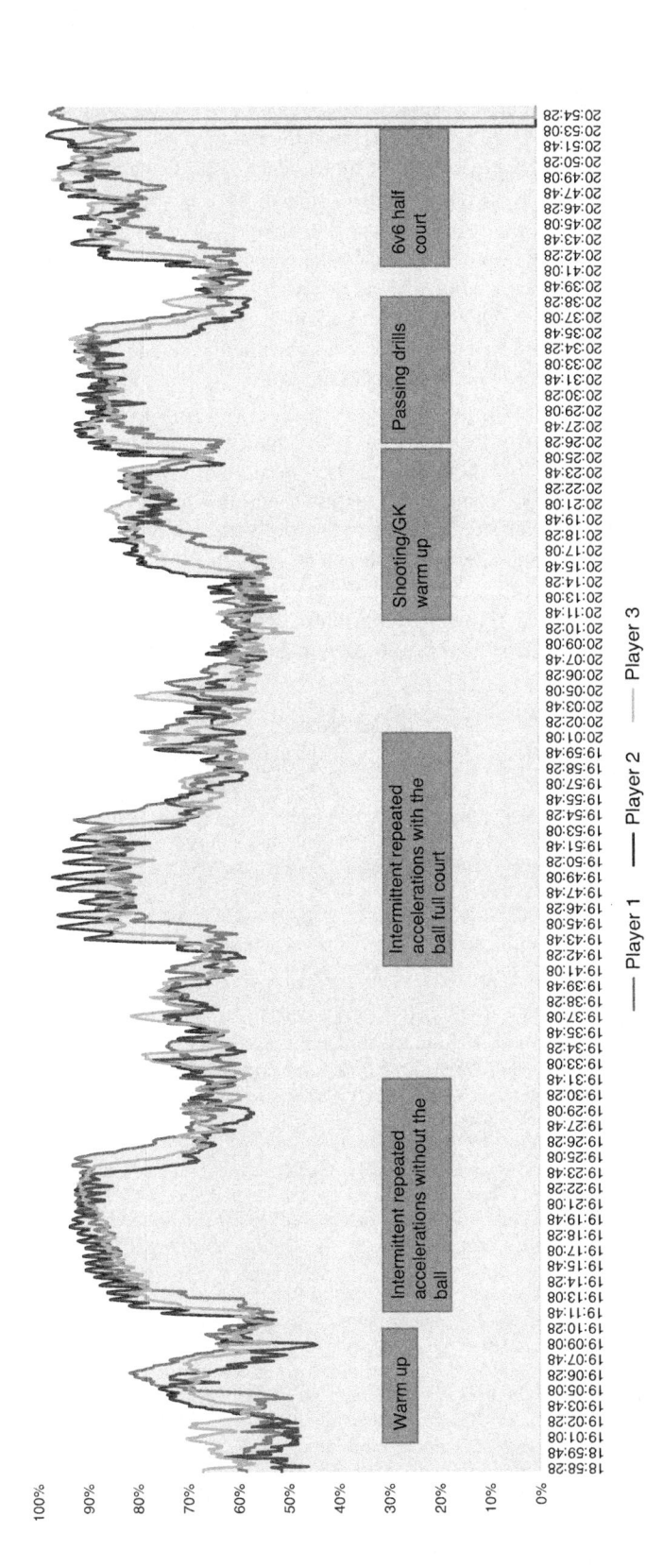

Figure 17.18 Heart rate during a typical handball training session in 3 different players

and technical and tactical requirements within a team should be the due diligence every strength and conditioning coach performs before individualising training.

Strength and conditioning activities are of fundamental importance for handball players. An effective training programme has the potential not only to improve performance but also to reduce significantly the risk of injuries. It is important to note that there are very few longitudinal studies on handball players and more needs to be done in order to understand the most effective training prescriptions for elite handball players involved in national and international competitions during very long seasons. Despite the limited information available, it is clear that strength training programmes can produce beneficial effects when performed during the sporting season, and appropriate loading patterns and variety of exercise prescription is needed due to the specific needs of the sport and the specific requirements of playing positions. Practitioners should always assess the athletes in order to identify strengths and weaknesses and monitor the effectiveness of the training prescriptions using dynamometry and assessing vertical jumping abilities and throwing speed when possible. Some of the methods indicated in this book chapter have been very useful to assess progression not only over the course of the season, but also over the years in players of international calibre. However, it should be reminded that improvements in the gym (e.g. personal bests in 1RM or in CMJ) are only significant if they have a direct translation on handball specific elements (e.g. throwing speed, jumping ability and/or reduction in injury rates) and can improve the effectiveness and the decision making of a player or a team.

References

Belka, J., Hulka, K., Safar, M., Weisser, R., and Samcova, A. (2014). Analyses of time-motion and heart rate in elite female players (U19) during competitive handball matches. *Kinesiology*, 46(1), 33–43.

Bencke, J., Curtis, D., Krogshede, C., Jensen, L. K., Bandholm, T., and Zebis, M. K. (2013). Biomechanical evaluation of the side-cutting manoeuvre associated with ACL injury in young female handball players. *Knee Surgery, Sports Traumatology, Arthroscopy: Official Journal of the ESSKA*, 21(8), 1876–81. https://doi.org/10.1007/s00167-012-2199-8

Bencke, J., Damsgaard, R., Saekmose, A., Jørgensen, P., Jørgensen, K., and Klausen, K. (2002). Anaerobic power and muscle strength characteristics of 11 years old elite and non-elite boys and girls from gymnastics, team handball, tennis and swimming. *Scandinavian Journal of Medicine & Science in Sports*, 12(3), 171–8.

Bencke, J., Naesborg, H., Simonsen, E. B., and Klausen, K. (2000). Motor pattern of the knee joint muscles during side-step cutting in European team handball. Influence on muscular co-ordination after an intervention study. *Scandinavian Journal of Medicine & Science in Sports*, 10(2), 68–77.

Bere, T., Alonso, J.-M., Wangensteen, A., Bakken, A., Eirale, C., Dijkstra, H. P., . . . Popovic, N. (2015). Injury and illness surveillance during the 24th Men's Handball World Championship 2015 in Qatar. *British Journal of Sports Medicine*, 49(17), 1151–6. https://doi.org/10.1136/bjsports-2015-094972

Bojsen Michalsik, L., and Aagaard, P. (2015). Physical demands in elite team handball: Comparisons between male and female players. *The Journal of Sports Medicine and Physical Fitness*, 55(9), 878–91.

Bosco, C., and Komi, P. V. (1979). Potentiation of the mechanical behavior of the human skeletal muscle through prestretching. *Acta Physiologica Scandinavica*, 106(4), 467–72. https://doi.org/10.1111/j.1748-1716.1979.tb06427.x

Bosco, C., Belli, A., Astrua, M., Tihanyi, J., Pozzo, R., Kellis, S., . . . Tranquilli, C. (1995). A dynamometer for evaluation of dynamic muscle work. *European Journal of Applied Physiology and Occupational Physiology*, 70(5), 379–86. https://doi.org/10.1007/BF00618487

Bosco, C., Luhtanen, P., and Komi, P. V. (1983). A simple method for measurement of mechanical power in jumping. *European Journal of Applied Physiology and Occupational Physiology*, 50(2), 273–82.

Bosquet, L., Porta-Benache, J., and Blais, J. (2010). Validity of a commercial linear encoder to estimate bench press 1 RM from the force-velocity relationship. *Journal of Sports Science & Medicine*, 9(3), 459–63.

Buchheit, M. (2008). The 30–15 intermittent fitness test: Accuracy for individualizing interval training of young intermittent sport players. *Journal of Strength and Conditioning Research*, 22(2), 365–74. https://doi.org/10.1519/JSC.0b013e3181635b2e

Buchheit, M. (2010). The 30–15 intermittent fitness test: 10 year review. *Myorobie Journal*, *1*(Top 14), 1–9.

Buchheit, M., and Rabbani, A. (2014). The 30–15 intermittent fitness test versus the yo-yo intermittent recovery test level 1: Relationship and sensitivity to training. *International Journal of Sports Physiology and Performance*, *9*(3), 522–4. https://doi.org/10.1123/IJSPP.2012-0335

Buchheit, M., Al Haddad, H., Millet, G. P., Lepretre, P. M., Newton, M., and Ahmaidi, S. (2009a). Cardiorespiratory and cardiac autonomic responses to 30–15 intermittent fitness test in team sport players. *Journal of Strength and Conditioning Research*, *23*(1), 93–100. https://doi.org/10.1519/JSC.0b013e31818b9721

Buchheit, M., Laursen, P. B., Kuhnle, J., Ruch, D., Renaud, C., and Ahmaidi, S. (2009b). Game-based training in young elite handball players. *International Journal of Sports Medicine*, *30*(4), 251–8. https://doi.org/10.1055/s-0028-1105943

Buchheit, M., Mendez-Villanueva, A., Quod, M., Quesnel, T., and Ahmaidi, S. (2010). Improving acceleration and repeated sprint ability in well-trained adolescent handball players: Speed versus sprint interval training. *International Journal of Sports Physiology and Performance*, *5*(2), 152–64.

Cardinale, M. (2014). Strength training in handball. *Aspetar Sports Medicine Journal*, *3*, 130–4.

Cardinale, M., Whiteley, R., Hosny, A. A., and Popovic, N. (2016). Activity profiles and positional differences of handball players during the World Championships in Qatar 2015. *International Journal of Sports Physiology and Performance*, 1–23. https://doi.org/10.1123/ijspp.2016-0314

Chaouachi, A., Brughelli, M., Levin, G., Boudhina, N. B. B., Cronin, J., and Chamari, K. (2009). Anthropometric, physiological and performance characteristics of elite team-handball players. *Journal of Sports Sciences*, *27*(2), 151–7. https://doi.org/10.1080/02640410802448731

Chelly, M. S., Hermassi, S., Aouadi, R., and Shephard, R. J. (2013). Effects of 8-weeks in-season plyometric training on upper and lower limb performance of elite adolescent handball players. *Journal of Strength and Conditioning Research/National Strength & Conditioning Association*, *28*(5), 1401–1410. https://doi.org/10.1519/JSC.0000000000000279

Chelly, M. S., Hermassi, S., Aouadi, R., Khalifa, R., Van den Tillaar, R., Chamari, K., and Shephard, R. J. (2011). Match analysis of elite adolescent team handball players. *Journal of Strength and Conditioning Research/National Strength & Conditioning Association*, *25*(9), 2410–7. https://doi.org/10.1519/JSC.0b013e3182030e43

Cunniffe, B., Fallan, C., Yau, A., Evans, G. H., and Cardinale, M. (2015). Assessment of physical demands and fluid balance in elite female handball players during a 6-day competitive tournament. *International Journal of Sport Nutrition and Exercise Metabolism*, *25*(1), 78–96. https://doi.org/10.1123/ijsnem.2013-0210

Debanne, T., and Laffaye, G. (2011). Predicting the throwing velocity of the ball in handball with anthropometric variables and isotonic tests. *Journal of Sports Sciences*, *29*(7), 705–13. https://doi.org/10.1080/02640414.2011.552112

Delamarche, P., Gratas, A., Beillot, J., Dassonville, J., Rochcongar, P., and Lessard, Y. (1987). Extent of lactic anaerobic metabolism in handballers. *International Journal of Sports Medicine*, *8*(1), 55–9. https://doi.org/10.1055/s-2008-1025641

Dupont, G., Defontaine, M., Bosquet, L., Blondel, N., Moalla, W., and Berthoin, S. (2010). Yo-Yo intermittent recovery test versus the Université de Montréal track test: Relation with a high-intensity intermittent exercise. *Journal of Science and Medicine in Sport*, *13*(1), 146–50. https://doi.org/10.1016/j.jsams.2008.10.007

Engebretsen, L., Soligard, T., Steffen, K., Alonso, J. M., Aubry, M., Budgett, R., . . . Renström, P. A. (2013). Sports injuries and illnesses during the London Summer Olympic Games 2012. *British Journal of Sports Medicine*, *47*(7), 407–14. https://doi.org/10.1136/bjsports-2013-092380

Ghobadi, H., Rajabi, H., Farzad, B., Bayati, M., and Jeffreys, I. (2013). Anthropometry of world-class elite handball players according to the playing position: Reports from Men's Handball World Championship 2013. *Journal of Human Kinetics*, *39*, 213–20. https://doi.org/10.2478/hukin-2013-0084

Gorostiaga, E. M., Granados, C., Ibáñez, J., and Izquierdo, M. (2005). Differences in physical fitness and throwing velocity among elite and amateur male handball players. *International Journal of Sports Medicine*, *26*(3), 225–32. https://doi.org/10.1055/s-2004-820974

Granados, C., Izquierdo, M., Ibañez, J., Bonnabau, H., and Gorostiaga, E. M. (2007). Differences in physical fitness and throwing velocity among elite and amateur female handball players. *International Journal of Sports Medicine*, *28*(10), 860–7. https://doi.org/10.1055/s-2007-964989

Granados, C., Izquierdo, M., Ibáñez, J., Ruesta, M., and Gorostiaga, E. M. (2013). Are there any differences in physical fitness and throwing velocity between national and international elite female handball players? *Journal of Strength and Conditioning Research/National Strength & Conditioning Association*, *27*(3), 723–32. https://doi.org/10.1519/JSC.0b013e31825fe955

Grezios, A. K., Gissis, I. T., Sotiropoulos, A. A., Nikolaidis, D. V, and Souglis, A. G. (2006). Muscle-contraction properties in overarm throwing movements. *Journal of Strength and Conditioning Research/National Strength & Conditioning Association*, 20(1), 117–23. https://doi.org/10.1519/R-15624.1

Hamouti, N., Coso, J. Del, Estevez, E., and Mora-Rodriguez, R. (2010). Dehydration and sodium deficit during indoor practice in elite European male team players. *European Journal of Sport Science*, 10(5), 329–36. https://doi.org/10.1080/17461391003632022

Hansen, C., Sanz-Lopez, F., and Whiteley, R. (2017). Performance analysis of male handball goalkeepers at the World Handball championship 2015. *Biology of Sport*, 34(4), 393–400.

Hermassi, S., Chelly, M. S., Tabka, Z., Shephard, R. J., and Chamari, K. (2011). Effects of 8-week in-season upper and lower limb heavy resistance training on the peak power, throwing velocity, and sprint performance of elite male handball players. *Journal of Strength and Conditioning Research/National Strength & Conditioning Association*, 25(9), 2424–33. https://doi.org/10.1519/JSC.0b013e3182030edb

Ilic, V., Ranisavljev, I., Stefanovic, D., Ivanovic, V., and Mrdakovic, V. (2015). Impact of body composition and Vo2 max on the competitive success in top-level handball players. *Collegium Antropologicum*, 39(3), 535–40.

Jensen, J., Jacobsen, S., Hetland, S., and Tveit, P. (1997). Effect of combined endurance, strength and sprint training on maximal oxygen uptake, isometric strength and sprint performance in female elite handball players during a season. *International Journal of Sports Medicine*, 18(5), 354–8. https://doi.org/10.1055/s-2007-972645

Jiménez-Reyes, P., Samozino, P., Brughelli, M., and Morin, J.-B. (2016). Effectiveness of an individualized training based on force-velocity profiling during jumping. *Frontiers in Physiology*, 7, 677. https://doi.org/10.3389/fphys.2016.00677

Karcher, C., and Buchheit, M. (2014). On-court demands of elite handball, with special reference to playing positions. *Sports Medicine*, 44(6), 797–814. https://doi.org/10.1007/s40279-014-0164-z

Karcher, C., Ahmaidi, S., and Buchheit, M. (2014). Body dimensions of elite handball players with respect to laterality, playing positions and playing standard. *Journal of Athletic Enhancement*, 3(4). https://doi.org/10.4172/2324-9080.1000160

Koga, H., Nakamae, A., Shima, Y., Iwasa, J., Myklebust, G., Engebretsen, L., . . . Krosshaug, T. (2010). Mechanisms for noncontact anterior cruciate ligament injuries: knee joint kinematics in 10 injury situations from female team handball and basketball. *The American Journal of Sports Medicine*, 38(11), 2218–25. https://doi.org/10.1177/0363546510373570

Komi, P. V, and Bosco, C. (1978). Utilization of stored elastic energy in leg extensor muscles by men and women. *Medicine and Science in Sports*, 10(4), 261–5.

Krüger, K., Pilat, C., Ueckert, K., Frech, T., and Mooren, F. C. (2013). Physical performance profile of handball players is related to playing position and playing class. *Journal of Strength and Conditioning Research/National Strength & Conditioning Association*, 28(1), 117–125. https://doi.org/10.1519/JSC.0b013e318291b713

Krustrup, P., Mohr, M., Amstrup, T., Rysgaard, T., Johansen, J., Steensberg, A., . . . Bangsbo, J. (2003). The Yo-Yo intermittent recovery test: Physiological response, reliability, and validity. *Medicine and Science in Sports and Exercise*, 35(4), 697–705. https://doi.org/10.1249/01.MSS.0000058441.94520.32

Kvorning, T., Hansen, M. R. B., and Jensen, K. (2017). Strength and conditioning training by the Danish National Handball Team before an Olympic tournament. *Journal of Strength and Conditioning Research*, 31(7), 1759–65. https://doi.org/10.1519/JSC.0000000000001927

Laffaye, G., Bardy, B. G., and Durey, A. (2005). Leg stiffness and expertise in men jumping. *Medicine & Science in Sports & Exercise*, 37(4), 536–43. https://doi.org/10.1249/01.MSS.0000158991.17211.13

Leger, L. A., Mercier, D., Gadoury, C., and Lambert, J. (1988). The multistage 20 metre shuttle run test for aerobic fitness. *Journal of Sports Sciences*, 6(2), 93–101. https://doi.org/10.1080/02640418808729800

Lindner, M., Kotschwar, a, Zsoldos, R. R., Groesel, M., and Peham, C. (2012). The jump shot – A biomechanical analysis focused on lateral ankle ligaments. *Journal of Biomechanics*, 45(1), 202–6. https://doi.org/10.1016/j.jbiomech.2011.09.012

Luig, P., Manchado Lopez, C., Pers, J., Perse, M., Kristan, M., Schander, I., . . . Platen, P. (2008). Motion characteristics according to playing positions in international men's team handball. In A. V. J. Cabri, F. Alves, D. Araújo, J. Barreiros, and J. Diniz (Ed.), *13th Annual Congress of the European College of Sports Science* (pp. 241–7). Estoril, Portugal: Faculdade de Motricidade Humana, Universidad de Lisboa.

Luteberget, L. S., and Spencer, M. (2015). High intensity events in international female team handball matches. *International Journal of Sports Physiology and Performance*, 32(4), 1002–12. https://doi.org/10.1123/ijspp.2015-0641

Luteberget, L. S., Trollerud, H. P., and Spencer, M. (2017). Physical demands of game-based training drills in women's team handball. *Journal of Sports Sciences*, 1–7. https://doi.org/10.1080/02640414.2017.1325964

Manchado, C., Pers, J., Navarro, F., Han, A., Sung, E., and Platen, P. (2013a). Time-motion analysis in women's team handball: Importance of aerobic performance. *Journal of Human Sport & Exercise*, 8(2), S376–S90. https://doi.org/10.4100/jhse.2012.82.06

Manchado, C., Tortosa-Martínez, J., Vila, H., Ferragut, C., and Platen, P. (2013b). Performance factors in women's team handball: Physical and physiological aspects – A review. *Journal of Strength and Conditioning Research/National Strength & Conditioning Association*, 27(6), 1708–19. https://doi.org/10.1519/JSC.0b013e3182891535

Marin, D. P., Bolin, A. P., Campoio, T. R., Guerra, B. A., and Otton, R. (2013). Oxidative stress and antioxidant status response of handball athletes: Implications for sport training monitoring. *International Immunopharmacology*, 17(2), 462–70. https://doi.org/10.1016/j.intimp.2013.07.009

Marques, M. C., Saavedra, F. J., Abrantes, C., and Aidar, F. J. (2011). Associations between rate of force development metrics and throwing velocity in elite team handball players: A short research report. *Journal of Human Kinetics*, 29A, 53–7. https://doi.org/10.2478/v10078-011-0059-0

Marques, M. C., van den Tilaar, R., Vescovi, J. D., and Gonzalez-Badillo, J. J. (2007). Relationship between throwing velocity, muscle power, and bar velocity during bench press in elite handball players. *International Journal of Sports Physiology and Performance*, 2(4), 414–22.

Marques, M., and González-Badillo, J. (2006). In-season resistance training and detraining in professional team handball players. *The Journal of Strength & Conditioning*, 20(3), 563–71.

Matthys, S. P. J., Fransen, J., Vaeyens, R., Lenoir, M., and Philippaerts, R. (2013). Differences in biological maturation, anthropometry and physical performance between playing positions in youth team handball. *Journal of Sports Sciences*, 31(12), 1344–52. https://doi.org/10.1080/02640414.2013.781663

Michalsik, L. B., Aagaard, P., and Madsen, K. (2012). Locomotion characteristics and match-induced impairments in physical performance in male elite team handball players. *International Journal of Sports Medicine*, 34, 590–9. https://doi.org/10.1055/s-0032-1329989

Michalsik, L. B., Madsen, K., and Aagaard, P. (2014). Match performance and physiological capacity of female elite team handball players. *International Journal of Sports Medicine*, 35(7), 595–607. https://doi.org/10.1055/s-0033-1358713

Myklebust, G., Engebretsen, L., Braekken, I. H., Skjølberg, A., Olsen, O.-E., and Bahr, R. (2003). Prevention of anterior cruciate ligament injuries in female team handball players: a prospective intervention study over three seasons. *Clinical Journal of Sport Medicine: Official Journal of the Canadian Academy of Sport Medicine*, 13(2), 71–8.

Pers, J., Bon, M., Kovacic, S., Sibila, M., and Dezman, B. (2002). Observation and analysis of large-scale human motion. *Human Movement Science*, 21(2), 295–311.

Pori, P., Bon, M., and Sibila, M. (2005). Jump shot performance in team handball: A kinematic model evaluated on the basis of expert modelling. *Kinesiology*, 37, 40–9.

Póvoas, S. C. A., Ascensão, A. A. M. R., Magalhães, J., Seabra, A. F., Krustrup, P., Soares, J. M. C., and Rebelo, A. N. C. (2014a). Physiological demands of elite team handball with special reference to playing position. *Journal of Strength and Conditioning Research*, 28(2), 430–42. https://doi.org/10.1519/JSC.0b013e3182a953b1

Póvoas, S. C. A., Seabra, A. F. T., Ascensão, A. a M. R., Magalhães, J., Soares, J. M. C., and Rebelo, A. N. C. (2014b). Physical and physiological demands of elite team handball. *International Journal of Performance Analysis in Sport*, 14(3), 1. https://doi.org/10.1519/JSC.0b013e318248

Póvoas, S. C. A., Seabra, A. F. T., Ascensão, A. A. M. R., Magalhães, J., Soares, J. M. C., and Rebelo, A. N. C. (2012). Physical and physiological demands of elite team handball. *Journal of Strength and Conditioning Research/National Strength & Conditioning Association*, 26(12), 3365–75. https://doi.org/10.1519/JSC.0b013e318248aeee

Rahmani, A., Samozino, P., Morin, J.-B., and Morel, B. (2017). A simple method for assessing upper limb force-velocity profile in bench press. *International Journal of Sports Physiology and Performance*, 1–23. https://doi.org/10.1123/ijspp.2016-0814

Rankovic, G., Mutavdzic, V., Toskic, D., Preljevic, A., Kocic, M., Nedin Rankovic, G., and Damjanovic, N. (2010). Aerobic capacity as an indicator in different kinds of sports. *Bosnian Journal of Basic Medical Sciences*, 10(1), 44–8.

Renstrom, P., Ljungqvist, a, Arendt, E., Beynnon, B., Fukubayashi, T., Garrett, W., . . . Engebretsen, L. (2008). Non-contact ACL injuries in female athletes: An International Olympic Committee current concepts statement. *British Journal of Sports Medicine*, *42*(6), 394–412. https://doi.org/10.1136/bjsm.2008.048934

Rojas, F. J., Gutiérrez-Davila, M., Ortega, M., Campos, J., and Párraga, J. (2012). Biomechanical analysis of anticipation of elite and inexperienced goalkeepers to distance shots in handball. *Journal of Human Kinetics*, *34*, 41–8. https://doi.org/10.2478/v10078-012-0062-0

Ronglan, L. T., Raastad, T., and Børgesen, A. (2006). Neuromuscular fatigue and recovery in elite female handball players. *Scandinavian Journal of Medicine and Science in Sports*, *16*(4), 267–73. https://doi.org/10.1111/j.1600-0838.2005.00474.x

Šibila, M., Vuleta, D., and Pori, P. (2004). Position-related differences in volume and intensity of large-scale cyclic movements of male players in handball. *Kinesiology*, *36*(1), 58–68.

Souhail, H., Castagna, C., Mohamed, H. Y., Younes, H., and Chamari, K. (2010). Direct validity of the Yo-Yo intermittent recovery test in young team handball players. *Journal of Strength and Conditioning Research*, *24*(2), 465–70. https://doi.org/10.1519/JSC.0b013e3181c06827

Sporis, G., Vuleta, D., and Milanović, D. (2010). Fitness profiling in handball: Physical and physiological characteristics of elite players. *Collegium Antropologicum*, *34*(3), 1009–14.

Thorlund, J. B., Michalsik, L. B., Madsen, K., and Aagaard, P. (2007). Acute fatigue-induced changes in muscle mechanical properties and neuromuscular activity in elite handball players following a handball match. *Scandinavian Journal of Medicine & Science in Sports*, *18*(4), 462–72. https://doi.org/10.1111/j.1600-0838.2007.00710.x

Vaeyens, R., Güllich, A., Warr, C. R., and Philippaerts, R. (2009). Talent identification and promotion programmes of Olympic athletes. *Journal of Sports Sciences*, *27*(13), 1367–80. https://doi.org/10.1080/02640410903110974

Vaeyens, R., Lenoir, M., Williams, A. M., and Philippaerts, R. M. (2008). Talent identification and development programmes in sport: Current models and future directions. *Sports Medicine (Auckland, N.Z.)*, *38*(9), 703–14.

Van Den Tillaar, R. (2004). Effect of different training programs on the velocity of overarm throwing: A brief review. *Journal of Strength and Conditioning Research*, *18*(2), 388–96. https://doi.org/10.1519/R-12792.1

Van Den Tillaar, R., and Cabri, J. M. H. (2012). Gender differences in the kinematics and ball velocity of overarm throwing in elite team handball players. *Journal of Sports Sciences*, *30*(8), 807–13. https://doi.org/10.1080/02640414.2012.671529

Vila, H., Manchado, C., Rodriguez, N., Abraldes, J. A., Alcaraz, P. E., and Ferragut, C. (2012). Anthropometric profile, vertical jump, and throwing velocity in elite female handball players by playing positions. *Journal of Strength and Conditioning Research/National Strength & Conditioning Association*, *26*(8), 2146–55. https://doi.org/10.1519/JSC.0b013e31823b0a46

Wagner, H., and Müller, E. (2008). The effects of differential and variable training on the quality parameters of a handball throw. *Sports Biomechanics/International Society of Biomechanics in Sports*, *7*(1), 54–71. https://doi.org/10.1080/14763140701689822

Wallace, M. Brian and Cardinale, M. (1997). Conditioning for team handball. *Strength & Conditioning Journal*, *19*(6), 7–12.

Wedderkopp, N., Kaltoft, M., Lundgaard, B., Rosendahl, M., and Froberg, K. (1999). Prevention of injuries in young female players in European team handball. A prospective intervention study. *Scandinavian Journal of Medicine & Science in Sports*, *9*(1), 41–7.

Wik, E. H., Luteberget, L. S., and Spencer, M. (2016). Activity profiles in international female team handball using PlayerLoad(TM). *International Journal of Sports Physiology and Performance*, 1–26. https://doi.org/10.1123/ijspp.2015-0732

Winshurst, Z. L., Sowden, P. T., and Cardinale, M. (2012). Visual skills and playing positions of Olympic field hockey players. *Perceptual and Motor Skills*, *114*(1), 204–16. https://doi.org/10.2466/05.22.24.PMS.114.1.204-216

Zebis, M. K., Bencke, J., Andersen, L. L., Døssing, S., Alkjaer, T., Magnusson, S. P., . . . Aagaard, P. (2008). The effects of neuromuscular training on knee joint motor control during sidecutting in female elite soccer and handball players. *Clinical Journal of Sport Medicine: Official Journal of the Canadian Academy of Sport Medicine*, *18*(4), 329–37. https://doi.org/10.1097/JSM.0b013e31817f3e35

Ziv, G., and Lidor, R. (2009). Physical characteristics, physiological attributes, and on-court performances of handball players: A review. *European Journal of Sport Science*, *9*(6), 375–86. https://doi.org/10.1080/17461390903038470

18
WHEELCHAIR RUGBY

Ed Baker

Introduction to the sport

History

Originally called "Murderball", Wheelchair Rugby is a mixed team sport for male and female quadriplegic athletes. It is a court based invasion game with elements of ice hockey, rugby and basketball, in which teams of four players compete to carry a tacky, volleyball-style ball across the opposing team's goal line. Players compete in specially constructed, manually propelled wheelchairs, designed to withstand high speed collisions. Contact between chairs is an integral aspect of the sport with tactics reflecting the need to block, hold, hit and displace opposing players.

Wheelchair Rugby was invented in 1977 in Winnipeg, Canada, by a group of quadriplegic athletes looking for an alternative to Wheelchair Basketball. Athletes with reduced arm, hand and trunk function are able to compete more equally in Wheelchair Rugby. The International Paralympic Committee (IPC) officially recognised the sport in 1994, with full medal status accorded to the sport at the 2000 Paralympic Games in Sydney, Australia. As of 2016, there are forty countries affiliated to the International Wheelchair Rugby Federation (IWRF), with twenty six competing internationally within three zones: The Americas, with six active countries; Europe, with fourteen active countries; and Asia-Oceania, with six active countries. The Paralympics and the IWRF World Championships are both quadrennial events at which the top nations compete for success.

There is a 40 second shot clock in force during the game, with 10 seconds allowed to inbound and 12 seconds allowed to advance out of the attacking team's half of the court. Coupled with the fact that different players exhibit different levels of physical impairment and thus the opportunity to create a mismatch, this temporal constraint has the effect of speeding up the game from the original version with no time limit on scoring. There is an increased reliance on passing, catching and evasive movements within the context of a specific combination of players. This presents the Strength and Conditioning Coach with a novel opportunity to support performance with the introduction of specific interventions designed to support the roles of individual players.

Participants

To obtain a classification within Wheelchair Rugby, athletes must have a disability which affects the arms and legs. Historically most players had a spinal cord injury (SCI), often to the cervical spine, resulting in full or partial paralysis of the legs and partial paralysis of the arms and hands. In recent years a wider group of disabilities has been incorporated into the sport, including athletes with cerebral palsy, muscular dystrophy, amputations and other musculo-skeletal and neurological disorders. Men and women compete on the same team in the same competitions.

The rise in the number of non-spinal cord (NSCI) injured athletes obtaining a classification within the sport has resulted in a significant change in both the technical-tactical and physical nature of the game. The prevalence of trunk muscle function in NSCI athletes coupled with greater function in the upper limbs results in players who are considerably faster, more powerful and with greater throwing range than before. As the classification system is based on function, nations fielding a player with exceptionally high function will often centre their tactics around that player being the main ball carrier. Consequently this style of play results in differing physical demands on each player within a four person line up and has implications for the optimal programming of physical training.

Classification

Table 18.1 gives an overview of the classifications within Wheelchair Rugby and the associated function that often presents with each in the context of the game. Athletes are divided into seven classifications ranging from 0.5 to 3.5. Four players on court at any one time is referred to as a "line up". This combination may not exceed a total of eight points, or 8.5 points with a female player as part of the team, to take into account the inherent discrepancy in upper body strength between males and females.

Figure 18.1 shows a visual representation of the classifications with a useful diagram of the pushing technique employed most often by a player in each class. The Strength and Conditioning Coach may observe the technique selected by the athlete to propel the sports chair and design effective programs to increase propulsive power and reduce the risk of over use injury.

Table 18.2 gives an overview of the typical impairment of upper body musculature occasioned by a spinal cord injury (SCI). Anecdotally, and at the time of writing, the most common level of cervical spine injury in the European population of Wheelchair Rugby players is at the C6 level. As shown in Table 18.2 this may mean reduced innervation to major upper body muscle groups responsible for locomotion in the sports chair such as the pectorals, latissimus and triceps. It should be noted that in the author's experience and within the literature, athletes with an insult to the spinal cord at the C6 level present with a wide array of strength, power and functional ability. Typical strength and power performances by elite players will be discussed later in this chapter. The Strength and Conditioning Coach tasked with improving the performance of an SCI athlete is advised to be open minded about the realistic outcomes of a physical training plan, to not necessarily limit their ambitions to the scope of a medical diagnosis, and to conduct a thorough investigation into the individual athlete's ability to produce force across a wide variety of upper body movements and exercises in addition to closely observing their chosen propulsive style in the sports chair.

Table 18.1 Adapted from IWRF official website

0.5 Class	
Typical role on court	Defensive/blocking, not a major ball handler.
Chair skills/function	Extensive proximal shoulder weakness, lack of triceps function. Stroke is a "pull" with bicep. Humerus internally rotated during stroke. May use back of hand/forearm for start/stop/turn.
Ball skills/function	May not catch off the body. May trap pass on lap. May bat ball using volleyball style dig. May scoop the ball from the lap with two hands.
1.0 Class	
Typical role on court	Defensive/blocking, not a major ball handler but may inbound.
Chair skills/function	Proximal shoulder/triceps weakness, but may use pull-push on wheel for propulsion. Turing skill usually evidently greater than 0.5. May still use forearm.
Ball skills/function	Weak chest pass.
1.5 Class	
Typical role on court	High value defensive/blocking player. Occasional ball handling/inbounding.
Chair skills/function	Greater shoulder strength and stability demonstrating evident advantage in movement skills over lower point players.
Ball skills/function	More distance and consistency in chest pass. Typically has a wrist/arm imbalance that may compromise catching consistency. Typically favours stronger limb.
2.0 Class	
Typical role on court	Increasing role as a ball handler.
Chair skills/function	Stronger shoulders with greater triceps function allowing more "push" than "pull" in the stroke and faster speeds.
Ball skills/function	Effective chest passing. Lack of finger flexion means vulnerable to defence when passing. Can grasp ball with wrists but does not have hand function.
2.5 Class	
Typical role on court	Ball handler and can be a fast playmaker.
Chair skills/function	Stronger shoulders should translate to higher pushing speeds. Grip function results in better start/stop/turn and holding performance. May have some trunk function to contribute to stability.
Ball skills/function	Increased finger flexion/extension – greater passing range and dribbling security. May pass and catch overhead with one hand. Often has asymmetrical upper limb function.
3.0 Class	
Typical role on court	Good ball handler and fast playmaker.
Chair skills/function	More balanced finger function therefore able to grip wheelchair rim for faster start/stop/turn. May have trunk function.
Ball skills/function	Broader palette of passing and catching with greater power and accuracy.
3.5 Class	
Typical role on court	Major ball handler and playmaker.
Chair skills/function	Has trunk function therefore able to use trunk to contribute to chair manoeuvrability.
Ball skills/function	Hand and trunk function together allows for excellent ball control/security and high strength to overcome defensive players.

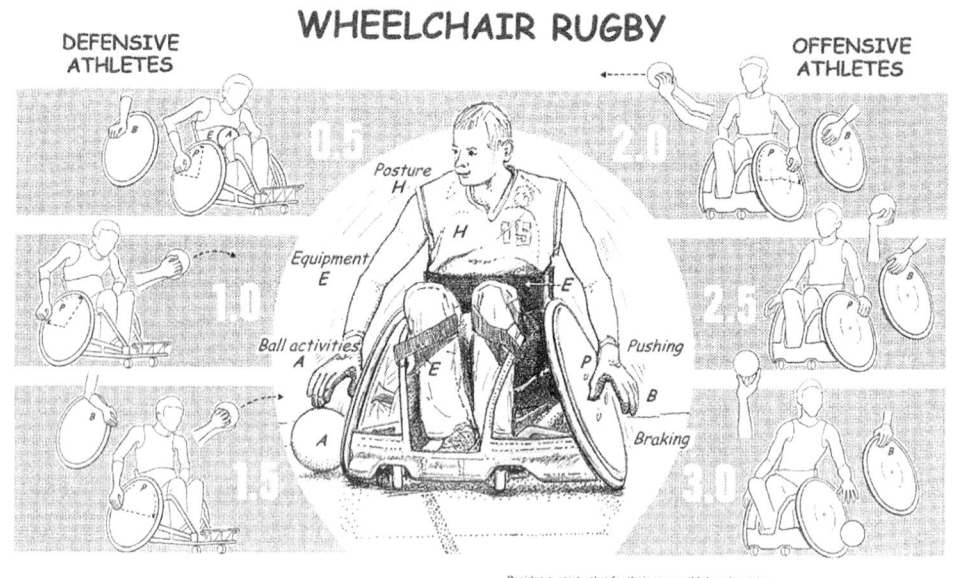

Figure 18.1 Visual representation of the Paralympic classifications

Table 18.2 Typical impairment of upper body musculature occasioned by a spinal cord injury (SCI)

	Spinal segment								
	C1	C2	C3	C4	C5	C6	C7	C8	T1
Scapula muscles		Trapezius							
			Levator scapulae						
				Rhomboids					
Thoraco-humeral muscles					Serratus anterior				
					Pectoralis major				
						Pectoralis minor			
						Latissimus dorsi			
Gleno-humeral muscles					Teres major				
					Supraspinatus				
					Infraspinatus				
						Subscapularis			
						Teres minor			
						Deltoid			
						Coracobrachialis			
Elbow flexors						Biceps			
						Brachialis			
						Brachioradialis			
Elbow extensors							Triceps		
								Anconeus	
				Voluntary control ←		∨	→ Paralysis		
Dennervation									

Athletic demands

Overview of movement demands and game intensity

Wheelchair Rugby is an intermittent sport characterised by repeated high intensity accelerations and decelerations imposed on periods of low intensity activity. External competition load requires players to cover between 3000–5000 m during the 4x8 min quarters, with an average intensity of > 90m /minute for high pointers (2.0–3.5 class) and > 75 m/minute for low pointers (0.5–1.5 class). Around 60% of the match is spent < 50% peak speed, with players performing between 35–55 high intensity activities (> 80% peak speed) over a match, which accounts for < 2% of total playing time (statistics from unpublished data from elite GB Wheelchair Rugby squad).

High intensity activities last between 2–10 seconds and 5–15 m. Successful Wheelchair Rugby performance has been associated with the number and frequency of high intensity activities. Despite the low absolute movement speeds, frequent isometric "picking" work, whereby a player physically traps an opponent's chair in a stationary position, constitutes a large amount of external load at the muscle level. In addition, high intensity decelerations provide a significant eccentric load during 242 (+/− 80) changes of direction across a game (Sporner et al., 2009).

Tables 18.3 and 18.4 provide a comparison between an elite high point player and an elite low point player in a series of international games.

Table 18.3 Player comparisons: Class 3.0 vs Class 1.5
The table below is based on a typical quarter in wheelchair rugby. This data is generated from the 2013 European's championship matches

Class		Distance	Peak speed	Relative distance	Num sprints	Avg Dur (s)	Time spent in 'rest' zone	Time spent in 'high intensity' zone
3.0 player	World best	1383	4.01	93.5	15	1.7	3:39	0:31
	Class avg	1153	3.82	78.4	9	1.9	4:19	0:21
1.5 player	World best	955	3.34	70.7	13	2.00	4:37	0:26
	Class avg	1011	3.44	69.7	11	1.7	5:01	0:23

World Best – equivalent classified player from contemporary top-4 nations
'Rest' – < 20% of peak speed
'High intensity' – > 80% of peak speed

Table 18.4 Fatigue (1st vs. 2nd half)
The table below is based on full game data, comparing two players of different class including variables from the 1st half to the 2nd half over 4 International Matches

Class		Total distance	Peak speed	Sprints	Avg dur sprints	Relative distance
3.0 player	1st half	1428	4.09	15	1.78	93
	2nd half	1360	3.93	15	1.65	93
	% decrease	5%	4%	–	7%	–
1.5 player	1st half	950	3.38	16	1.40	69.8
	2nd half	994	3.39	12	1.80	71.1
	% decrease	–	–	24%	–	–

Biomechanical features

Due to the inertial properties of a rolling chair, displacement of the athlete/chair system in the first 3–5 pushes is a key component of performance. Elite Wheelchair Rugby athletes exhibit cycle times of 0.3–0.5 seconds, with push times (hand in contact with wheel rim) of 0.09–0.2 seconds in the first 3 pushes of a maximal sprint, generating between 258 Watts (0.5 class SCI athlete) and 1083 Watts (3.0 class non SCI athlete) of Peak Power. It is clear that Rate of Force Development (RFD) is a vital component of chair speed as the time to develop maximum force is not available.

By referring to Figure 18.1 above, the reader can see that both circular and pumping methods are employed to achieve propulsion, with a higher reliance on the pumping method as speeds increase. Literature has shown a shared contribution of 50/50 between elbow flexion and extension at lower speeds, rising to 70% elbow extension at higher speeds (Miyahara et al., 1998). This, coupled with the frequency of changes in direction, also increase the eccentric load on the elbow flexors in applying a braking force to the upper limbs.

Players with a lower point classification may compensate for a lack of grip function by creating medial "squeezing" forces at the shoulder to clamp the wheel rim. However this class of player may also present as weak in shoulder/scapula adduction and therefore may present a risk of impingement and atrophy of the scapula muscles. Previous research has uncovered relationships between strength and force displayed at the rim, but not between strength and propulsion (Miyahara et al., 1998). This suggests that the technique employed by the athlete is fundamental to performance, particularly the force coupling of the elbow joint, as the most effective mechanical direction of applied force is tangential to the wheel rim.

Table 18.5 displays primary research from the Peter Harrison Centre for Disability Sport conducted with elite Wheelchair Rugby Athletes. It appears that 20 m sprint performance may underpin a number of qualities including peak game speed, speed endurance and agility. High speed propulsion of the sports chair can be viewed as a product of force applied effectively to the rim and speed of recovery. In the programming section below this theory will be explored through various suggested training interventions. The Strength and Conditioning Coach is advised to consider training methods targeted at increasing both the rate of force production as the hand couples the wheel, and the speed with which the athlete can recover the limb and

Table 18.5 Data from wheelchair rugby athletes

Lab/field	Match-play variables					
	Peak speed	Total distance	HI total distance	Num sprints	Sprint distance	Sprint duration
$\dot{V}O_{2peak}$	0.66	0.69	0.26	0.11	0.48	0.54
WERG (peak PO)	0.86	0.66	0.87	0.76	0.79	0.82
20 m sprint	0.95	0.84	0.62	0.68	0.78	0.83
Speed endurance	0.93	0.89	0.58	0.61	0.81	0.86
Agility	0.89	0.84	0.48	0.32	0.78	0.82
Box	0.83	0.83	0.39	0.53	0.72	0.73

HI total distance = Total distance covered at intensities >80% peak speed
Num sprints = Total number of sprints
Sprint distance = Total distance covered sprinting
Sprint duration = Total time spent sprinting

make greater use of elastic return in the anterior shoulder muscles to increase the economy of the stroke.

Athletes with trunk function tend to employ a more efficient stroke pattern with both a greater amount of power produced and greater economy of movement. This is due to two main factors: first the increased upper body strength available in the higher classes and second the ability to sit higher in the seat, further from the axle, and use the anterior trunk muscles to incline the torso forward and isometrically anchor the body there to provide a stable base from which to propel with the arms. Many players also use a large forward swing of the torso to aid the arms at the initiation of a sprint and provide added momentum to the acceleration. The ability of such players to lean far over the inside wheel during a turn is another example of using trunk function to reduce metabolic load on the arms and enhance movement skill, a key component that separates athletes with trunk function from those without.

Wheelchair configuration

Whilst it is beyond the scope of this chapter to provide an exhaustive exploration of how to set up the sports chair for optimal performance, it is necessary to recognise the importance of the athlete-wheelchair system and the implications of common variables within that system.

Table 18.6 gives a brief overview of some of the major considerations for the configuration of the sports chair as it relates to speed and manoeuvrability. The Strength and Conditioning Coach is advised to collaborate with the individual athlete, technical coach and the multi-disciplinary

Table 18.6 Considerations for wheelchair configuration

Area of chair setup	Possible alteration	Potential effect
Wheel camber	↑ or ↓ to change stability 18° may be considered optimal (Mason et al., 2015)	↑ camber may improve stability/turning at the expense of speed ↓ camber may improve speed at the expense of agility
Toe in/ toe out	Check alignment	As little as 2° toe-in toe-out can double the rolling resistance experienced (O'Reagan et al., 1981)
Tyre pressure	↑ or ↓ to alter friction and rolling resistance Consider the surface used for training and the balance between speed/agility	Increasing pressure from 110psi to 160psi reduced resistance by ~30% Minimises physiological demand in lab based settings (Sawatzky et al., 2004)
Spoke tightness	Ensure all spokes are tight and balanced	Wheels lose 13–21% stiffness when spoke tension is reduced, with minor impact on acceleration performance (Mason et al., 2015)
Flip tyres	Camber causes tyre to wear on inside faster than outside. Consider flipping regularly to produce even wear	Possible loss of traction with over-worn tyre
Athlete strapping	Tighten/relocate/adjust the type and amount of strapping used to fix the athlete into the chair	SCI athletes without trunk function may achieve better stability and a moderate abdominal binding effect from appropriate strapping. The placement of lower limbs may have moderate effects of centre of mass and agility performance

team to produce a holistic view of performance when considering the issue of chair configuration and performance.

Perhaps the most pertinent consideration for the Strength and Conditioning Coach is the issue of resistive forces and the mass of the combined athlete-wheelchair system. Fuss (2009) found that in absolute terms, a saving of 1 and 5 kg on a 60 kg system mass would reduce a 15 s winning time by 0.13 and 0.66 s, respectively, and a 30 s winning time by 0.63 and 2.86 s, respectively, within wheelchair racing. Concomitantly, a reduction in resistive forces occasioned by a reduction in system mass would also allow the athlete to maintain a given submaximal speed through a lower power output and therefore improve economy throughout a game or tournament. Thus, interventions that maximise fat free mass and minimise adipose tissue may be beneficial for performance.

Accommodation

An interesting empirical observation about changes to chair configuration is the potential time period taken to accommodate to such changes within an elite population. A change in camber from 18° to 16° can result in the athlete initially experiencing a reduction in 20 m speed performance but then realising significant improvements from 7–39 weeks post (Mason et al., 2013). The same athlete experienced initial improvements in 5 m time which also increased throughout 39 weeks post. This observation was not controlled for other factors such as training volume, so conclusive observations cannot be drawn. Similarly, a class 3.0 player given a new chair specifically designed to improve speed and agility, with the athlete sitting 1" higher, initially improved performance markers in testing. While performance continued to improve, 25 weeks post change the athlete developed a soft tissue malady traced to overuse of the spinal erectors, which had previously been recruited differently in the former seating position. Practitioners looking into adjustments which theoretically target performance outcomes should be mindful of potential unintended consequences and anticipate effects throughout the kinetic chain. A thorough bespoke testing battery organised around any alterations along with input from sports science and medicine staff in addition to the individual athlete is highly recommended.

Strength and power

As stated, the two key physical performance capabilities in elite Wheelchair Rugby are acceleration (displacement of the athlete/chair) during the first 3–5 pushes, and repeatability of high speed pushing over successive intermittent bouts across the course of the game, with irregular and incomplete recovery of energy substrates.

The primary physical qualities underpinning acceleration are the relative fat free mass of the athlete, the relative strength and power capacity of the upper body muscles and the technical execution of the push stroke. The primary physical qualities underpinning repeatability of high intensity pushing are the aerobic power and capacity, the specific capacity to resist fatigue due to anaerobic processes including tolerance of repeated eccentric loading of the elbow flexors, and the cross sectional area of muscle mass contributing to the pushing action.

Table 18.7 compares two athletes of the same classification (2.0 class) of similar height (6'1" and 6"2") and similar mass (63.6 and 64.3 kg) but very different body composition and includes their absolute and relative muscle mass as measured by a DEXA scan. Player 2 has an extra 9.2 kg of muscle mass and a concomitant lack of non-functional mass (fat), which is likely to be a major factor in increased speed of propulsion.

Table 18.7 Comparison of two athletes of the same classification (2.0 class)

ATHLETE	CLASS/LESION	BODY MASS	BMI	TOTAL BODY FAT %	TOTAL BODY FAT KG	TOTAL LEAN KG	% LEAN MASS	20m SPRINT TIME
PLAYER 1	2 C6 com	63.7	17.9	23.3	14.1	46.5	73.05%	6.40
PLAYER 2	2 C6/7 com	64.3	18	10.8	6.7	55.7	86.64%	5.52

SCI vs NSCI athletes

SCI athletes with an injury at the cervical level often exhibit disruption to the autonomic nervous system resulting in an abnormal response to exercise, namely a reduced maximal heart rate response (Janssen et al., 2002). An important distinction may be made between SCI players who may have a limited stroke volume as a result of this phenomenon, and players without such injury who may have a greater capacity for aerobic regeneration of energy substrates. A potentially limiting factor to performance for SCI athletes is the cross sectional area of functional muscle mass and the athletes' force potential and ability to buffer fatiguing metabolites within the muscle. Peripheral fatigue may limit force production before the cardiovascular system reaches maximum capacity (Figoni, 1993). Added to this, the absence of venous return from the lower body and the aforementioned disruption to the autonomic system and concomitant absence of catecholamine production all fundamentally constrain the optimal environment for positive cardiorespiratory and skeletal muscle adaptations. Strength and conditioning interventions for SCI athletes in Wheelchair Rugby should be targeted towards adaptations at the muscle level as a priority. Non SCI athletes often classified in the higher point range and therefore subject to a higher work rate in a game, require extensive development of systemic and peripheral systems in order to be successful.

Injury prevalence

Relatively little research is available on the incidence of injury within the elite Wheelchair Rugby population. In considering the available literature, a mixed picture emerges. The sport was ranked the fifth most injury prone among those at the London 2012 Paralympic Games (Willick et al., 2013) which supports an earlier contention that Wheelchair Rugby should be viewed as a discipline with a high risk of injury (Ferrara and Peterson, 2000).

However, in the words of Bauerfeind et al. (2015): "It can be concluded that wheelchair rugby is a discipline associated with a high incidence of minor injuries that do not require a medical intervention. The incidence rate of injuries during the analyzed period was 0.3 per athlete per training day." This study specifically examined Wheelchair Rugby athletes during a nine month training period including four tournaments. Finally Molik and Marszałek (2013) found that Paralympic athletes in general endure minor contusions that result in up to 7-day cessation of training and do not require a long-term convalescence. In considering both published literature and the author's empirical experience, a picture emerges of a sport with relatively low rates of serious time loss injuries, but rather a series of minor overuse or strain related injuries, primarily to the shoulder.

Finley and Rodgers (2004) analysed the incidence of shoulder injuries among wheelchair users (both athletes and non-athletes). They showed that involvement in sports neither increased nor decreased the risk of shoulder joint pain incidents. It may be that athletes engaged in

Wheelchair Rugby, by nature including those with more severe impairments and therefore habitual daily wheelchair users, experience chronic over use of the shoulder girdle through day to day tasks including transferring from chair to car seat as well as using the arms for all locomotive activities. This presents the Strength and Conditioning Coach with a unique opportunity to impact upon the athlete's general well-being and specific robustness, and confer meaningful benefits to their training tolerance through an increase in general strength of the upper body. As part of a multi-disciplinary team, the focus in this population can be on injury and illness prevention.

McCormack et al. (1991) profiled 90 athletes (60% competitive at National level) from a range of Wheelchair Sports and reported injuries to the upper extremities to be most common, concerning the hand 21.3% and the shoulder 16.7% of the time. More recent research has confirmed that the shoulder is the most commonly injured body part in a competitive Paralympic environment, representing 17% of injuries (Derman et al., 2016). The McCormack study also noted that blisters and abrasions accounted for 47.4% of injuries, but interestingly also mentioned that only 30.8% of all wheelchair athletes in the study sought medical assistance for their injuries.

The author considers that the multi directional nature of Wheelchair Rugby, in contrast to wheelchair racing or throwing, is an inherent advantage to the practitioner seeking to reduce the incidence of shoulder overuse injuries. The implementation of sport specific drills in confined spaces with multiple stops and turns, including the addition of reversing the chair (pushing backwards) may contribute to a more balanced development of the shoulder girdle.

Culture

Both the McCormack study and the Bauerfeind study highlight a potentially important consideration for practitioners working within elite Wheelchair Rugby and potentially other wheelchair sports. McCormack et al. reported that less than a third of participants voluntarily sought medical assistance for injuries, whilst Bauerfeind et al. examined the relationship between aggression and incidence of injury. Bauerfeind concluded that whilst there were non-significant relationships between aggression and incidence of injury, there was a trend toward offensive or higher point players demonstrating both increased aggression and a higher incidence of injury requiring medical intervention (Bauerfeind et al., 2015).

The author can confirm from empirical experience that Wheelchair Rugby is a sport which openly displays a powerful culture of competitiveness and controlled aggression, similar to able bodied contact sports such as rugby union. This is part of the appeal to both spectators and participants. It may be the case that athletes who have sustained life altering injuries and now play the sport regard "minor" knocks and aches as part and parcel of the process and may not necessarily be proactive in seeking treatment or advice relating to them. The practitioner involved with Wheelchair Rugby can be vocal and proactive in educating coaches and players about the importance of both preventative strategies and timely reporting of injuries, however minor they seem, which may in the long run contribute to fewer training hours lost.

General health of the athlete

Perhaps just as important as injuries sustained in training and competition are the various health complaints associated with the typical degree of impairment experienced by athletes in Wheelchair Rugby, particularly SCI athletes. Health conditions known to affect this population include skin abrasions, pressure sores, upper respiratory tract infections and urinary tract infections

(McKinley et al., 1999). Of most relevance to the Strength and Conditioning Coach is the issue of pressure sores, muscle tone and skin health. Athletes with advanced atrophy of the lower limb and back muscles and/or low levels of body fat may be at higher risk of developing abrasions and pressure sores where their skin meets either the chair seat or sides, or any piece of equipment onto which they have transferred for exercising. Due consideration should be given to the level of cushioning and positioning of strapping available to the athlete when performing exercises away from the sports or daily use chair. In addition, functional electrical stimulation (FES) devices may be employed as part of training and restorative work aimed at improving the health of the skin (Hamzaid and Davis, 2009); this concept will be explored more fully in the section on programming. Appropriate care taken to avoid a skin lesion may avoid the tedious process of the athlete spending six weeks lying on their front unable to train whilst the skin heals.

Fitness testing battery

Table 18.8 outlines a suggested testing battery for an elite Wheelchair Rugby team. The table is comprehensive and represents a best-case scenario. Shaded areas highlight those tests considered

Table 18.8 Suggested testing battery for an elite Wheelchair Rugby team

Test	Relationship to performance
Mass of the athlete, mass of athlete/chair system (kg)	Relative strength/power and momentum of system mass
Sum of skinfold (mm) (or DEXA scan)	Body composition
20 m sprint time (s) with split at 2.5, 5 and 10 m	Acceleration, top speed and momentum of system mass
Agility test (s)	Closed skill sports specific movement pattern with comparison of left/right turning ability
Speed endurance (m)	Sports specific anaerobic capacity, utilising an intermittent work:rest scheme
Peak power (W) on wheelchair ergometer @ rolling resistance of 100% system mass	Highly correlated (0.96) to 20 m speed
Peak velocity in bench pull @ submaximal load (m/s)	Explosive strength in sports specific movement pattern
Peak isometric bench press force @ joint angle approximating first contact with wheel (N) and/or relative peak force (N/kg)	Ability to produce force in propulsion muscles
Peak velocity in bench press @ submaximal load (m/s)	Explosive strength in sports specific movement pattern Ability
Bench press 10rm (kg) (1rm considered for high point players with trunk/hand function)	Assessment of strength endurance in upper body
Bench pull 10rm (kg) (1rm considered for high point players with trunk/hand function)	Assessment of strength endurance in upper body
(High point players with trunk muscle function only) Multi-faceted trunk muscle strength/endurance test e.g.: prone/supine/lateral hold for time (s)	Postural strength and endurance of the torso to aid in chair manoeuvrability

by the author to be most accessible to the Strength and Conditioning Coach and those which should form the core of a more limited battery of tests.

Performance models for linear speed and energy systems

Figures 18.2 and 18.3 below are derived from primary unpublished research with elite Wheelchair Rugby athletes and demonstrate a theoretical model for profiling performance qualities in Wheelchair Rugby.

Further considerations

There are several areas related to physical performance, but not strictly included in the realm of a traditional testing battery, that may of interest to the practitioner involved with Wheelchair Rugby.

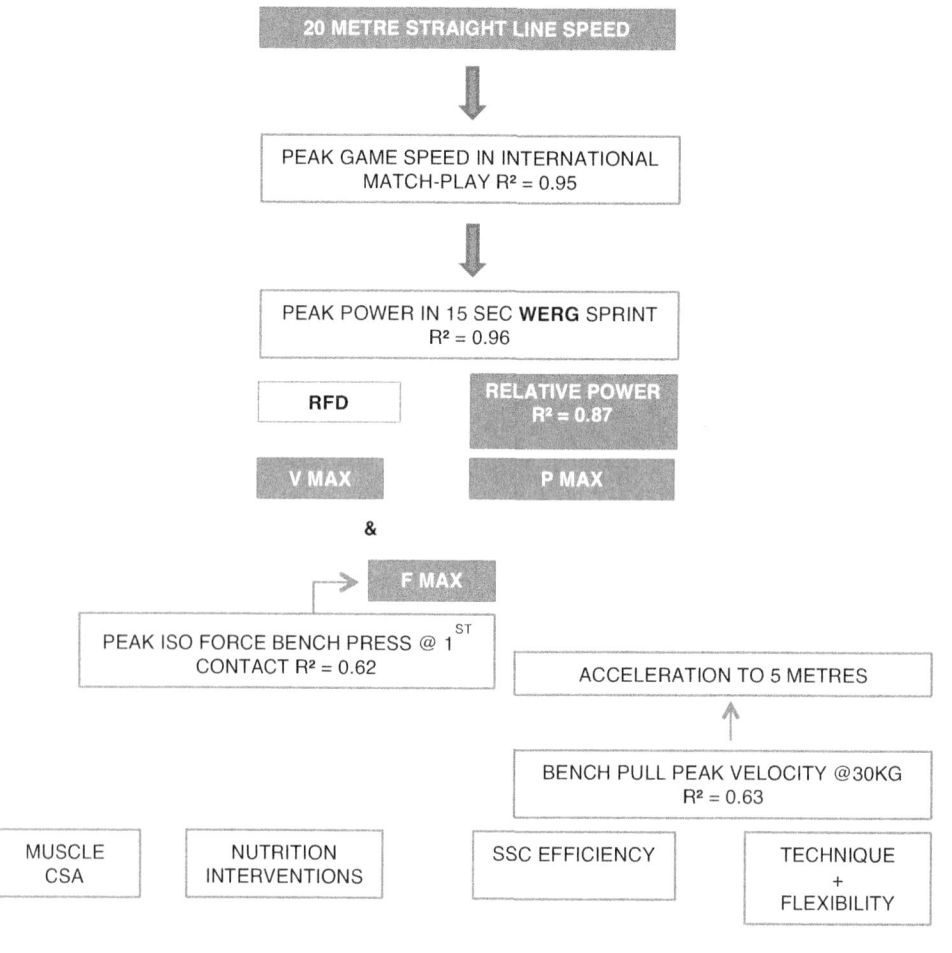

```
                    20 METRE STRAIGHT LINE SPEED
                                ↓
              PEAK GAME SPEED IN INTERNATIONAL
                    MATCH-PLAY R² = 0.95
                                ↓
              PEAK POWER IN 15 SEC WERG SPRINT
                         R² = 0.96

        RFD                        RELATIVE POWER
                                       R² = 0.87

       V MAX                          P MAX
               &
                        F MAX
                          ↑
         PEAK ISO FORCE BENCH PRESS @ 1ˢᵀ
              CONTACT R² = 0.62         ACCELERATION TO 5 METRES
                                                 ↑
                                    BENCH PULL PEAK VELOCITY @30KG
                                              R² = 0.63

   MUSCLE      NUTRITION        SSC EFFICIENCY      TECHNIQUE
    CSA       INTERVENTIONS                             +
                                                    FLEXIBILITY
```

Figure 18.2 Performance Model for linear speed

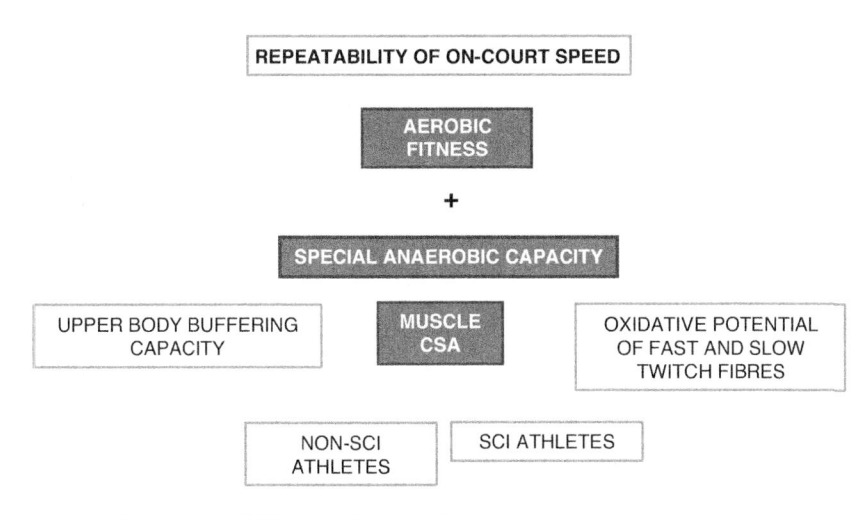

Figure 18.3 Performance Model for consideration of energy systems

Pushing technique

The issue of optimal pushing technique is potentially contentious as it is often dictated by a combination of available function (the athlete's level of impairment), anthropometry and environmental factors, such as imitation of other players. Rarely do elite athletes appear to refer to a technical model. It is worth considering that the type of pushing technique employed in linear speed exercises or exercises involving increased external resistance (such as pushing uphill) may or may not utilise kinematics comparable to the style employed in a game. The area of optimising technique in this population offers a window for improving performance.

Chair setup

As mentioned in the section on athletic demands, the configuration of the sports chair can have a profound impact on performance. Even seemingly minor changes to wheels, tyre pressures or seating posture can affect testing scores to a greater extent than the smallest worthwhile change the coach may be looking for in the results. As many variables as possible should be controlled and accounted for at each successive testing battery to avoid attributing a gain or loss in performance to the wrong means, whether it be the training programme or a change to the chair setup.

Skill acquisition

Traditionally an area reserved for the technical coach, the issue of skill acquisition has increasingly been incorporated into the sphere of influence of other practitioners (Davids et al., 2008). It should be stressed that Wheelchair Rugby, like all invasion games, is primarily a technical-tactical sport requiring, among other factors, passing and catching. Crucially, all players exhibit some impairment to the hand. Therefore the Strength and Conditioning Coach may consider working with other staff to develop and include tests for passing power, accuracy and catching competence which allow for the monitoring of player skill and learning over time.

Programming

Individuals with long term (> 20 years post injury) SCI have been shown to exhibit reduced independence, greater fatigue, weakness, shoulder pain and weight gain (Gerhart et al., 1993) due to degenerative and age related changes. This phenomenon, seen over a protracted time period, may be logically applied to wheelchair athletes over the course of an athletic career or even a training year – the absence of a continuing strength programme may leave the athlete vulnerable to a detraining effect that may impact on performance. Additionally, the presence of a classification system based upon function and the evident physical supremacy of higher point players over lower point players warrants the implementation of a thorough strength and conditioning programme designed with two concurrent goals: support the function of the athlete in day to day tasks in order to increase their ability to train, and maximise performance by targeting specific adaptations related to game play.

General programming considerations

Table 18.9 highlights major areas of interest where the programming considerations for this population differ from able bodied athletes, and the Strength and Conditioning Coach may be able to tailor their approach accordingly.

Table 18.9 Programming considerations

Medical or musculo-skeletal feature	Related to SCI? Y/N	Considerations for programming
Small amount of muscle mass available to train – limiting the achievable volume of systemic and peripheral work	Yes	Extensive focus on hypertrophy/endurance capabilities of existing muscle mass with concurrent focus on minimising body fat Appropriate temporal organisation of the annual plan to allow for specific development of this characteristic
Blood pooling in lower body – less circulating blood volume and possible ischemia in upper body muscle mass	Yes	Conduct resistance exercises out of the day chair, lying down on benches/floor surface
Low blood pressure – disrupting cognitive state and requiring rest periods and/or periods of lying the athlete down to recover	Yes	Athlete wears an abdominal binder
Disruption to sympathetic nervous system – absence of centrally controlled release of adrenaline and poor thermoregulation	Yes	
Lack of grip/hand function – inability to grasp weights or other equipment to load the upper body muscles	Yes	Use of "Active Hands" or other compensatory grip device Conduct resistance exercise in the sports chair by creating greater external friction
Loss of stability/unable to voluntarily brace – poor tolerance to unilateral loading and/or heavy external resistance due to lack of trunk/lower limb function	Yes	Extensive use of bracing/strapping to provide a more stable platform Conduct resistance exercise in the sports chair by creating greater external friction Focus on submaximal loads with extended volume

Medical or musculo-skeletal feature	Related to SCI? Y/N	Considerations for programming
Abnormal or irregular skeletal/joint structure and range of movement – problems with bilateral exercises and/or performing traditional resistance exercises in a full range of movement	N	
Inability to independently utilise exercise equipment – reliance on training partners/external assistance to perform training sessions thereby potentially impacting frequency and training density	Yes	Allow suitable time for resistance training session and include additional helpers to lift the athlete onto equipment, subject to the athlete's consent. Consider multiple daily sessions and "top up" workouts to prioritise volume over density, or the pairing of self-completed exercises with coach assisted exercise to increase density
Inability to distribute locomotion over non-exercised muscles – presence of exercise induced soreness post training may compromise both sports training and day to day living activities	Yes	Allow appropriate period of accommodation and progressive increase in loading. Closely monitor individual RPE and soreness. Introduction of supplement/nutritional interventions to obviate symptoms. Consider the daily, weekly and monthly organisation of the training plan to account for potential periods of time when muscle soreness may present.

Specific adaptations

Morphological, hypertrophy

In the needs analysis presented above, muscle cross sectional area (CSA) was identified as a contributing factor to performance. This is best achieved, as in an able bodied population, with the use of an external resistance training programme and the use of free weight and fixed machine exercises. Where possible, the use of specially adapted equipment such as a standard Paralympic Bench Press or Bench Pull station should be employed, with the athlete encouraged to exercise out of their day chair in a secure lying position to take advantage of both the relief this brings to soft tissues repeatedly held in a seated position and the extra stability, and by extension greater load bearing capacity afforded by this method.

Considering the factors detailed in Table 18.9, a high volume, low density, high frequency approach with submaximal loading is recommended. Greater use of spotting may be required where athletes perform barbell exercises, specifically to attach limbs via strapping and in the execution of a full range of motion. Lower point athletes with SCI may lack terminal elbow extension but still be able to load, for example, a bench press through the majority of the movement range.

The Strength and Conditioning Coach engaged in designing a programme for Wheelchair Rugby is advised to think creatively when implementing a hypertrophy programme and not be constrained by "normal" or commonplace repetition schemes. Table 18.10 below is an example of a typical weight training session from the hypertrophy phase of the annual plan for a SCI class 2.0 player. It should be noted that this session is likely to take over an hour,

Table 18.10 Example hypertrophy session

Exercise	Set	Rep	Example load	Notes
Warm up – dumbbell shoulder circuit				
DB side raise	3	25	2–3 kg	5–1–5 tempo
DB Arnold press	3	25	2–3 kg	5–1–5 tempo
DB bent over flye	3	25	2–3 kg	5–1–5 tempo
Developmental exercises				
Bench press from pin set 1" above chest	8	10	90% of 10RM	3 second eccentric, explosive concentric
Chin up	8	Rpe 9	BW	Coach stabilises athletes' legs and pushes chair backward
Assistance exercises				
Lying triceps extension	3	60 seconds	7kg	Can be performed with DBs, cable attachment or bar
Seated biceps curl	3	60 seconds	8kg	Perform simultaneously to avoid losing balance. Can be performed strapped to an incline bench to effect greater stretch of the elbow flexors.

possibly up to ninety minutes to complete, especially if the athlete is training in a group/squad setting. This is due to the extra time taken to transfer from wheelchair to bench, to affix limbs to bars with strapping and to carefully spot and adjust equipment throughout. It is for this reason that no mention is given for specific rest periods – if one Strength and Conditioning Coach is facilitating a session for three of four athletes then simply going between each one in between sets will preclude the observance of classical short rest periods. One to one coaching may enable the coach to make more use of this method, in addition to the selection of exercises (briefly touched on in Table 18.10) which enable the athlete to use one piece of equipment for multiple supersets without rest – for example, a dumbbell flye, press and triceps extension tri-set.

Neurological: force generation + power

Linear wheelchair speed may be considered a product of push force and cycle recovery. Training programmes oriented around increasing power production should target an increase in the amount of force applied to the wheel rim and an increase in the speed with which the athlete recovers their hand following the push phase and is able to re-apply it to the wheel (see Figure 18.4).

Resisted pushing

Unpublished data from elite British Wheelchair Rugby athletes suggests that an acute post activation potentiation phenomenon occurs when players are exposed to external resistance in the sports chair in excess of the standard friction available to the system mass. This trend is shared across impairments (SCI and non SCI) and classifications. Modest increases in the external resistance obtained via pushing sleds/prowlers and/or pushing on higher friction surfaces such as

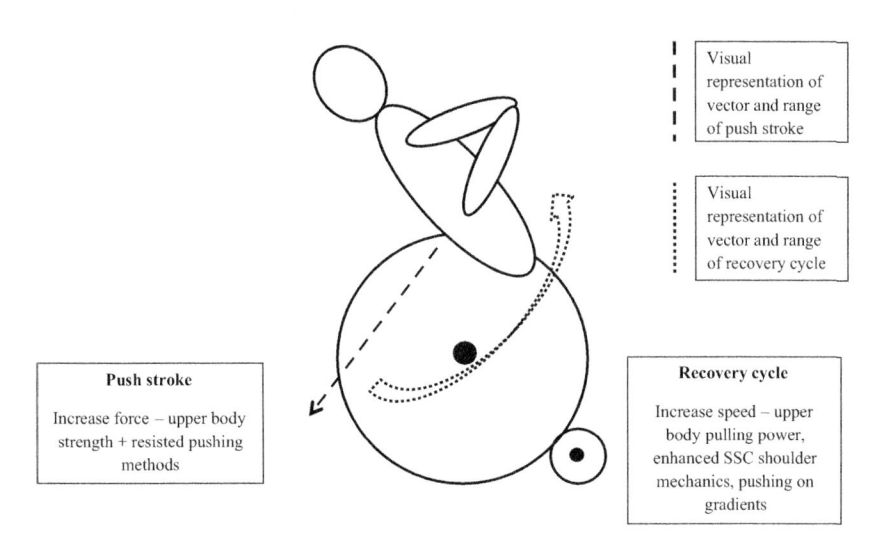

Figure 18.4 Schematic representation of these two phases of wheelchair propulsion

Push stroke

Increase force – upper body strength + resisted pushing methods

Recovery cycle

Increase speed – upper body pulling power, enhanced SSC shoulder mechanics, pushing on gradients

carpet or Mondo track may provide an appropriate stimulus for the athlete to increase power through a means that satisfies the accepted definition of dynamic correspondence (Verkoshansky, 2011). The use of resisted pushing is designed to target the "push force" component of increasing sports specific power.

Use of gradients

One disadvantage of using extensive pushing drills to target the cycle recovery element of propulsion is that the inherently low rolling resistance offered by the sports chair may encourage a "lazy" pushing style when the athlete is not constrained by the time and space of a game context. A way to avoid this and train the athlete to recover the arm quickly is to push both up and down a slope or hill. Pushing uphill encourages the athlete to quickly return the hand to the wheel rim to avoid loss of inertia due to the gradient, as well as increasing the amount of force required to displace the system mass. Pushing downhill will (if space permits) allow the athlete to achieve an over-speed effect with the upper limbs and potentially enhance the neurological efficiency of the stroke pattern. In this way the athlete can explore areas of the force-velocity curve adjacent to their current contextual location in both a "force" and "velocity" direction.

Table 18.11 shows a suggested resisted pushing session oriented toward the higher force component of wheelchair propulsion. Each variation of pushing is followed by a short series of maximal effort un-resisted sprints to enhance the training transfer of the drill to a sports specific context.

Cardio respiratory: aerobic + anaerobic endurance SCI/non SCI

Considering the information presented above concerning the varied response to exercise experienced by athletes with and without SCI, it may be appropriate to differentiate metabolic training between groups of athletes with similar impairments.

Table 18.12 summarises the main methods available to the Strength and Conditioning Coach.

Table 18.11 Suggested resisted pushing programme

Exercise	Set	Rep	Load	Rest
Sled push	3	6 × 6 seconds	External load resulting in velocity = approximately 70% of the maximum speed in un resisted pushing	30 seconds between reps, 5 minutes between sets
Un-resisted push	3	3 × 20m	Regular system mass	60 seconds between reps, 5 minutes between sets
Uphill sprint	2	8 × 10 seconds	Approximate 5 degree incline	30 seconds between reps, 5 minutes between sets
Un-resisted push	2	3 × 10m	Regular system mass	30 seconds between reps, 5 minutes between sets

Table 18.12 Major methods of metabolic conditioning for Wheelchair Rugby

Adaptation	Description/example method	Predominately suited for SCI/non SCI
Aerobic capacity	Extensive interval/continuous pushing using HR monitor	Non SCI
Aerobic power	Intensive interval pushing using HR monitor	Non SCI
Aerobic capacity/ active recovery	Swimming, using snorkel/floats for enhanced comfort and efficiency	Non SCI
Local muscular endurance/ hypertrophy of slow twitch fibres	Tempo method: slow tempo upper body resistance training utilising submaximal loads and prolonged time under tension – e.g. 60 seconds per set, 30 seconds rest between sets, 3–5 sets per exercise and 2–3 exercises per session	SCI
Lactic capacity and buffering capability	Explosive repeat method: using explosive upper body exercises such as bench pull/bench press and appropriate work:rest scheme – e.g. 15:30 seconds for 6–12 sets repeated up to 3 times. Perform 6 minutes of active rest between series	SCI
Lactic capacity and buffering capability	Prolonged high intensity intervals in sports chair, preferably on high friction surface eg Mondo track with high volume of intermittent stop/starts with emphasis on maximal effort. 90–120 seconds per rep, incomplete rest (60–120 seconds) 3–4 reps repeated up to 3 times. Perform 4 minutes of active rest between series	SCI + non SCI
Aerobic + anaerobic energy system enhancement	Short contested games with temporal/spatial constraints eg: 10 minute rolling clock with no breaks, 4v3, 2v1, scoring with multiple balls etc.	SCI + non SCI

Organisation of the training process

It is worth taking into consideration that functional impairments in this population may result in adaptations taking a longer time to manifest than in able bodied groups. This may be particularly true of significant changes to body composition, as wheelchair athletes lack the ability to undertake traditional methods of preseason conditioning, such as high volumes of intensive running. Therefore the Strength and Conditioning Coach is advised to be flexible in the temporal organisation of training blocks.

The traditional calendar for the sport in the UK reflects a competitive Spring/Summer period with the Autumn and Winter effectively an "off season". The management of cumulative workload, recovery and adaptation to training and the level of preparedness to compete are all pertinent to any elite athlete population. To the author's knowledge, no research exists into the optimal strategy for tapering and recovery in wheelchair athletes. In the author's empirical experience, SCI athletes with higher levels of physical impairment may require a longer taper than non SCI athletes in order to dissipate the accumulated fatigue of a block of concentrated loading. It is worth considering the nature of a tournament in this sport – five games in five days in a Paralympics or two games per day in a zonal competition (plus any international travel) – when designing training blocks seeking to prepare players appropriately.

Functional Electrical Stimulation (FES) and adaptive equipment

There may be complementary benefits to a strength and conditioning programme to be gained through the use of Functional Electrical Stimulation (FES) and adaptive exercise methods for a SCI population. A 2009 review by Hamzaid and Davis concluded that several positive changes manifest with the use of FES, including muscular adaptations, increased blood flow and enhanced aerobic fitness. It can be postulated that the use of FES in the lower body may increase local muscle mass and improve skin health and thereby reduce the incidence of skin lesions in a sedentary athlete. In addition, the use of special adaptive machines such as the Berkel Bike or adaptive Cross Trainer may offer a strategy to increase aerobic fitness as well as reduce fat mass.

Conclusion

Wheelchair Rugby is an exciting sport with a compelling blend of physical skill and complex technical-tactical strategy. It is played by a diverse group of people with a multitude of physical impairments who share a common bond. Many individuals within the sport show strong engagement with the concept of physical training, thereby preparing the ground well for the incoming Strength and Conditioning Coach.

Many practitioners will find working in this sport and within the wider Paralympic community to be intensely rewarding on a personal and professional level, with daily opportunities to be creative, problem solve and make measurable impacts on performance.

References

Bauerfeind, J., Koper, M., Wieczorek, J., Urbański, P. and Tasiemski, T., 2015. Sports injuries in wheelchair rugby – A pilot study. *Journal of Human Kinetics*, 48(1), pp. 123–132.

Davids, K.W., Button, C. and Bennett, S.J., 2008. *Dynamics of Skill Acquisition: A Constraints-Led Approach*. Champaign, IL: Human Kinetics.

Derman, W., Schwellnus, M. P., Jordaan, E., Runciman, P., Van de Vliet, P., Blauwet, C., . . . and Stomphorst, J., 2016. High incidence of injury at the Sochi 2014 Winter Paralympic Games: A prospective cohort study of 6564 athlete days. *Br J Sports Med*, bjsports-2016.

Ferrara, M.S. and Peterson, C.L., 2000. Injuries to athletes with disabilities: Identifying injury patterns. *Sports Medicine*, 30(2), pp. 137–143.

Figoni, S.F., 1993. Exercise responses and quadriplegia. *Medicine and Science in Sports and Exercise*, 25(4), pp. 433–441.

Finley, M.A. and Rodgers, M.M., 2004. Prevalence and identification of shoulder pathology in athletic and nonathletic wheelchair users with shoulder pain: A pilot study. *Journal of Rehabilitation Research and Development*, 41(3B), pp. 395–402.

Fuss, F.K., 2009. Influence of mass on the speed of wheelchair racing. *Sports Engineering*, 12(1), pp. 41–53.

Gerhart, K.A., Bergstrom, E., Charlifue, S.W., Menter, R.R. and Whiteneck, G.G., 1993. Long-term spinal cord injury: Functional changes over time. *Archives of Physical Medicine and Rehabilitation*, 74(10), pp. 1030–1034.

Hamzaid, N.A. and Davis, G., 2009. Health and fitness benefits of functional electrical stimulation-evoked leg exercise for spinal cord – Injured individuals: A position review. *Topics in Spinal Cord Injury Rehabilitation*, 14(4), pp. 88–121.

Janssen, T.W., Dallmeijer, A.J., Veeger, D. and van der Woude, L.H., 2002. Normative values and determinants of physical capacity in individuals with spinal cord injury. *Journal of Rehabilitation Research and Development*, 39(1), p. 29.

Mason, B.S., Lemstra, M., van der Woude, L.H., Vegter, R. and Goosey-Tolfrey, V.L., 2015. Influence of wheel configuration on wheelchair basketball performance: Wheel stiffness, tyre type and tyre orientation. *Medical Engineering & Physics*, 37(4), pp. 392–399.

Mason, B.S., van der Woude, L.H. and Goosey-Tolfrey, V.L., 2013. The ergonomics of wheelchair configuration for optimal performance in the wheelchair court sports. *Sports Medicine*, 43(1), pp. 23–38.

McCormack, D.A.R., Reid, D.C., Steadward, R.D. and Syrotuik, D.G., 1991. Injury profiles in wheelchair athletes: Results of a retrospective survey. *Clinical Journal of Sport Medicine*, 1(1), pp. 35–40.

McKinley, W.O., Jackson, A.B., Cardenas, D.D. and Michael, J., 1999. Long-term medical complications after traumatic spinal cord injury: A regional model systems analysis. *Archives of Physical Medicine and Rehabilitation*, 80(11), pp. 1402–1410.

Miyahara, M., Sleivert, G.G. and Gerrard, D.F., 1998. The relationship of strength and muscle balance to shoulder pain and impingement syndrome in elite quadriplegic wheelchair rugby players. *International Journal of Sports Medicine*, 19(03), pp. 210–214.

Molik, B. and Marszałek, J., 2013. The specificity of injuries in Paralympics sport. *Advances in Rehabilitation*, 3, pp. 39–49.

O'Reagan, J., Thacker, J., Kauzlarich, J., Mochel, E., Carmine, D. and Bryant, M., 1976. Wheelchair dynamics. *Wheelchair Mobility*, Rehabilitation Engineering Center, University of Virginia, 1981, pp. 33–41.

Sawatzky, B., Kim, W. and Denison, I., 2004. The ergonomics of different tyres and tyre pressure during wheelchair propulsion. *Ergonomics*, 47(14), pp. 1475–1483.

Sporner, M.L., Grindle, G.G., Kelleher, A., Teodorski, E.E., Cooper, R. and Cooper, R.A., 2009. Quantification of activity during wheelchair basketball and rugby at the National Veterans Wheelchair Games: A pilot study. *Prosthetics and Orthotics International*, 33(3), pp. 210–217.

Verkoshansky, Y. and Verkoshansky, N., 2011. *Special Strength Training Manual for Coaches*. Verkoshansky.com, ISBN-13:978-8890403828.

Willick, S.E., Webborn, N., Emery, C., Blauwet, C.A., Pit-Grosheide, P., Stomphorst, J. and Schwellnus, M., 2013. The epidemiology of injuries at the London 2012 Paralympic Games. *British Journal of Sports Medicine*, 47(7), pp. 426–432.

SECTION 4
Individual sports

19
MMA

Lachlan James, Brett Bartholomew, G. Gregory Haff and Vincent Kelly

Introduction to the sport

Mixed martial arts (MMA) is a combat sport with professional tiers of competition for both men and women. Recently, the sport has seen a remarkable rise in global popularity, and alongside this, professionalism. Competitors can employ a combination of both striking (e.g. punches and kicks) and grappling techniques (e.g. throws, ground fighting and submission holds) in an attempt to secure a winning outcome. Victory is achieved through a number of methods, including knockout, causing a fighter (or their corner) to indicate they are unable to continue, official's intervention, or judges' decision at the end of the scheduled time period. Professional level fights are generally allocated three or five 5 minute rounds separated by 1 minute, while amateur bouts typically employ 3 minute rounds (James et al., 2016b).

As a consequence of MMA's massive growth, there is an increasing awareness of the need for evidenced-based, yet feasible, strength and conditioning strategies to provide fighters with a competitive edge. However, the variety of techniques, multiple methods for achieving victory and the intermittent nature of the sport make it challenging for the strength and conditioning coach to identify, prioritise and develop the physiological attributes that are most important to these athletes. This makes it vital to examine the scientific evidence drawn from MMA and its athletes to properly establish the determinants of performance. Based on this information, training interventions and testing batteries can then be designed in accordance with periodisation and programming principles (Muller et al., 2000), while also considering the constraints of the training environment.

Until recently there was a lack of scholarly sports science data on MMA. However, of late a number of original research investigations have been published which provide much needed direction for strength and conditioning coaches. It is the purpose of this chapter to translate the scientific research on MMA into evidenced based programming and monitoring strategies for the practitioner working with these athletes.

Athletic demands

Characteristics of MMA

MMA is an intermittent collision sport with bout durations that may last only an instant, yet can extend to 25 minutes in some cases (James et al., 2016). The physiological demands of the high intensity intermittent activity characteristic of MMA are inherently more complicated than those of strength-power and cyclical endurance centred sports. When considered alongside the extensive array of techniques used, combined with the sports unpredictability, MMA appears to have a broad physiological and biomechanical profile.

A fundamental requirement of MMA combat is the application of force against an external resistance which is in alignment with the very definition of strength (Stone et al., 2007). High force qualities are required to manipulate the mass of an opponent, to withstand collisions, and underpin higher velocity techniques such as strikes and entry to takedowns (James et al., 2016b). Furthermore, strength contributes considerably to fatigue resistance (Paavolainen et al., 1999) and the reduction of injury risk (Lauersen et al., 2014). As MMA is a weight class sport, relative strength is of particular importance as the athlete must maximise their force producing capabilities for a given body mass.

Technical analysis into the sport has revealed that achieving victory in Ultimate Fighting Championship (UFC) bouts is largely influenced by the ability to actually land a strike or a takedown, while increasing the volume of attack attempts (which may or may not land) appears to have little influence (James et al., 2016c). Successful strikes require high velocities of execution, while many grappling techniques are driven by power expressed throughout the loading spectrum. Similarly, evasive maneuvers are underpinned by an applied impulse to rapidly and precisely shift position. As such, these can be considered vital neuromuscular functions underpinning MMA performance.

The high intensity epochs of activity within MMA reportedly occur for approximately 8 to 10s, interspersed with periods of lower intensity combat generally lasting between two to three times as long, resulting in a work to rest ratio of 1:2 to 1:4 across both regional level (Del Vecchio et al., 2011) and UFC bouts (Miarka et al., 2015). Of particular relevance to strength and conditioning coaches is the finding that 77% of fights end during these high intensity periods (Del Vecchio et al., 2011). The activity patterns of MMA occur over scheduled bout duration extending from 9 minutes at the amateur level, to professional bouts which can last up to 25 minutes (James et al., 2016b). Taken together, MMA combat requires considerable contributions from both anaerobic and aerobic pathways. However, it is important to note that the repeated explosive efforts characteristic of this sport require support from non-metabolic sources such as musculoskeletal and neuromuscular factors also (Buchheit and Laursen, 2013).

Determinants of MMA performance

Maximal strength

When comparisons were made between two groups of MMA athletes of different competition standards, it was found that higher level fighters attained a greater 1 repetition maximum (RM) relative back squat than the lower level competitors (James et al., 2016a). These differences were both statistically and practically significant, supporting the vital role lower body expressions of maximal force play in MMA performance. Interestingly, we've noted that grappling dominant MMA athletes tend to display higher strength levels than those who are striking oriented. This is echoed throughout the literature into other combat sports, where greater distinctions between higher- and lower-tier competitors in grappling disciplines have been noted when compared to striking sports (James et al., 2016b). Such findings can, in large part, be explained by the predominance of high-force actions commonplace in grappling exchanges. However, this is not to suggest that maximal lower body strength isn't important for striking performance. In fact, such qualities are predictive of punching acceleration (Loturco et al., 2014) and form the foundation for high velocity movements (Cormie et al., 2011).

Upper body strength also plays a notable role in MMA combat, although it appears not to the same extent as the lower body (James et al., 2016a). In particular, relative 1RM bench press performance distinguishes less clearly between higher- and lower-tier competitors; however, practically relevant differences are still present (James et al., 2016a). The greater need for lower body force production is unsurprising considering that most athletic actions, including those in MMA, are initiated by the lower body before being expressed distally. Such findings are consistent with what have generally been reported across other combat sports also (James et al., 2016b).

Maximal power, impulse and velocity

Higher-level MMA fighters produce greater impulse, velocity and power measures during the incremental load jump squat test when compared to their lower tier counterparts (James et al., 2016a). The notable importance of technique accuracy over alternate performance indicators reinforces the pivotal role of maximal neuromuscular expressions in MMA (James et al., 2016c). This is because, from a biomechanical perspective, what determines the outcome of a technique is the speed at which it's executed and the location on the opponent to which it is directed (Winter et al., 2016). This represents the vector quantity of velocity. Digging a little deeper, with the athlete's mass unchanged, what causes a change in velocity is an impulse. Taken together, maximal expressions of power, velocity and impulse underpin both the inherent characteristics of the decisive techniques and the physiological qualities of elite performers in the sport.

Anaerobic qualities

Because over three quarters of MMA fights end during high intensity efforts lasting only a few seconds (Del Vecchio et al., 2011), well-developed anaerobic qualities must be possessed by these athletes. This is supported by extremely high lactate accumulations induced by MMA training and competition, including levels reaching 20 mmol·L^{-1} (Amtmann et al., 2008). When assessing the short term anaerobic capability of MMA athletes, semi-professional fighters generally perform better across sprints at 5, 10 and 20m when compared to experienced amateur competitors. However, not only must the MMA athlete produce brief explosive efforts, they need to do so repeatedly. Accordingly, in tests of repeated sprint ability undertaken at a similar work to rest ratio to that of MMA, an increase in competition standard is generally associated with superior test performance amongst the athletes we have assessed.

Endurance

The scheduled duration of MMA bouts suggests that a major contributor to energy supply is aerobic metabolism, with this involvement increasing in accordance with the length of the fight (Gaitanos et al., 1993). However, because of the unpredictable duration of a bout, it is challenging to quantify the proportional demand on oxidative processes. Considerable periods near $\dot{V}O_{2max}$ have been documented in investigations into repeated sprint sequences of analogous structure to the work to rest ratio of MMA (Buchheit and Laursen, 2013). Furthermore, the highly explosive nature of the work periods in the sport likely result in even greater lengths of time operating near maximal aerobic capacity (Buchheit and Laursen, 2013). Similar to anaerobic capabilities, data from our lab has revealed that higher-tier MMA athletes generally perform slightly better on intermittent endurance tests such as the Yo-Yo Intermittent Recovery Level 2 (IR2), than those competing at a lower level of competition. However, these distinctions are somewhat less clear than those of maximal neuromuscular qualities.

Monitoring training and injury prevention in MMA

In a sport like MMA where so many components of fitness are required, it is crucial to monitor all of the training that is being performed. This is important to: 1) ensure the training dose for each individual component is appropriate, based on the strengths and weaknesses of the athlete (discussed in full detail in the section below), and 2) monitor an athlete's training adaptation (fitness) and the athlete's response to training (fatigue). Effective monitoring of training can help guide decision making on the design of future training sessions to ensure optimal performance and also help prevent injury.

When monitoring fatigue from training, it is important for practitioners to ensure the tools they use are both valid and reliable. In particular, the tests chosen need to be sensitive enough to determine a level of fatigue incurred from a training bout or block. Finally, the goal of any fatigue monitoring program is to inform decision making to make modifications to training. If a test cannot contribute to a decision to change training it should not be included in the monitoring system. Finally, the fatigue monitoring process needs to be practically simple to implement and presented in an intuitive and meaningful way for the coach to interpret and act upon. Rather than monitoring only one measure of fatigue, typical monitoring systems will comprise of a suite of tests that encompass different variables that contribute to fatigue. The following section will describe a number of these variables.

Training load

The quantification of training can examine either the *external load*, (e.g. sets and repetitions, load lifted, distance travelled and training duration) or *internal load*, the relative physiological and psychological stress imposed as a result of training (Halson, 2014). The relationship between an athlete's internal and external load may expose their level of fatigue.

External load

Traditional time-motion analysis can provide measures of external load during fight bouts and technical training sessions; however, advances in technology (accelerometers and movement pattern analysis via digital video) will allow greater accuracy of the demands of the sport in the future. This will allow the quantification of relative intensity, duration, and frequency of training components such as speed, acceleration and power outputs of movements. In the gym, external load during resistance training can be measured by calculating the volume load for individual sets and entire training sessions to provide useful information regarding the actual training stimulus (Scott et al., 2016). Finally, contact mats, force platforms or linear position transducers can measure neuromuscular function to determine the level of fatigue during a countermovement jump or squat jump test. These tests are simple to perform and require little equipment; however, practitioners should determine the validity of the measures they are monitoring. Possible variables to consider include mean power, peak velocity, peak force, jump height, flight time, contact time, and rate of force development (Taylor et al., 2012, Twist and Highton, 2013).

Internal load

The most commonly used method for measuring internal load is via heart rate (HR) monitoring, in particular prescribing the intensity of training as a percentage of maximal HR. Using maximal, resting, and average HR during exercise and training duration, sport scientists can also calculate the training impulse (TRIMP), a unit of physical effort (Morton et al., 1990). Another measure of training impulse, or internal training load, commonly used is a combination of the rating of perceived exertion of a session multiplied by session duration is referred to as the session-RPE method. The advantages of the session-RPE method is that is simple to use (only requires pen and paper), has been validated for a wide range of intensities and can be used across several training modalities including high intensity training sessions.

Recently, there has been lot of support for practitioners to use subjective measures to monitor changes in athlete well-being in response to training. This is because such measures have been shown to worsen with an acute increase in training load and improve with an acute decrease in training load (Saw et al., 2016). Perceptual responses are typically measured using questionnaires such as the profile of mood states (POMS), Daily Analysis of Life Demands (DALDA), Recovery Stress questionnaire (REST-Q) and other bespoke questionnaires that include a visual analogue scale (VAS).

Practitioners with a larger budget may consider examining biochemical markers to determine levels of fatigue. Possible markers that can be measured in blood, urine and saliva include markers of muscle damage (creatine kinase, myoglobin, troponin, urea, uric acid and ammonia; Kirwan et al., 1990; Stone et al., 1991; Stray-Gundersen et al., 1986), psychobiological stress (cortisol), anabolism (testosterone and the testosterone:cortisol ratio) and immune function (immunoglobulin-A). However, care must be taken when considering these methods as there is limited scientific support and they may be costly.

Acute:chronic

Recently the concept of monitoring training load using an acute:chronic workload ratio has been used to predict injury (Hulin et al., 2016). Acute workload is calculated as the absolute workload performed in 1 week, while chronic workload can be determined using a 4-week average acute workload or exponentially weighted moving averages. The recommendations state that sharp spikes in workload for multiple variables should be avoided, as they are associated with an increase in injury risk (Murray et al., 2016). However, in a sport like MMA when training may be periodic, with preparation emphasised in short training blocks in the lead up to bouts, including periods of limited or no monitoring, unrealistic acute:chronic ratio values will exist during the first weeks of training (Buchheit, 2016). Therefore, the session-RPE method may offer an alternative to load monitoring over measures of external load in the specific context of MMA fight preparation.

Fitness testing battery

A primary purpose of performance testing for MMA athletes is to accurately diagnose the distinct neuromuscular, anaerobic and endurance attributes identified in the needs analysis. When properly designed, it allows coaches to develop targeted training strategies (Muller et al., 2000), assess the response to training interventions and determine the preparedness of the athlete (Impellizzeri et al., 2005). Furthermore, it can be used to identify those who have the trainable qualities to be successful in the sport (Lidor et al., 2009). From a psychological perspective, it provides motivation for the athlete and educates them on the training process through objective feedback.

Physiological tests must be both valid and reliable. In an MMA performance testing context, the two questions we must ask are: "Does it measure the specific metabolic system or biomechanical function related to the sport I want to test?", and "Is this a test that distinguishes those who are successful in MMA from their less successful counterparts?" If either of these conditions are satisfied, then validity is met. However, tests must also meet a threshold of reliability. Reliability can be considered as the amount of variability in the test, and therefore its sensitivity in detecting and quantifying training and non-training induced changes in performance. For example, a coach may conceptualise a test that very closely reflects the physical and technical demands of MMA (therefore achieving validity), but has a high degree of variability in its measure. Because of this, such a testing notion has a poor sensitivity to change thereby limiting its contribution to the training process. The following tests are well documented to be highly reliable and meet one or both of the aforementioned criteria for validity. Additionally, the outlined tests are user-friendly and can be implemented in the field whilst providing data that is easily interpreted by the coach.

Maximal neuromuscular expressions

The incremental load jump squat test is an ideal method for diagnosing explosive lower body characteristics of the MMA athlete. In this test, the athlete performs maximal effort jump squats across a series of loading conditions. Often, these loads are determined as a percentage of BM (i.e. 0, 25, 50, 75, 100%), but can also be calculated from the athlete's corresponding 1RM. To reduce the time-cost of this test, conditions of 0, 50 and 100% of BM only may be performed. In addition to a barbell and plates, a linear position transducer or accelerometer are all that's needed to undertake this test. In recent years, such instrumentation has become readily accessible to coaches at all levels, with some costing as little as a few hundred dollars. The data acquired from this generates a profile of lower body explosive capabilities by providing measures such as velocity and power under a spectrum of loading conditions (Sheppard et al., 2008). By comparing these variables across loads, this test can provide valuable insight into whether an athlete is either a force or velocity dominant fighter. When considered in the context of the overall periodised plan, training interventions can then be directed to those areas that require the greatest attention. As a reference, Table 19.1 provides velocity benchmarks for MMA athletes of differing calibre.

Similar to the incremental load jump squat, the bench press throw under a series of loads provides an indication of explosive capabilities with measures derived from either inertial sensors or linear encoders. This is an excellent test; however, the need for a Smith machine may restrict it from being employed in some settings.

Table 19.1 Peak velocity benchmarks during the incremental load jump squat for MMA competitors. Instrumentation used: linear position transducer sampling at 100Hz (resolution 0.076mm, Musclelab, Ergotest Technology, Norway) (James et al., 2016a). Practitioners should be cautious when comparing velocity values across differing devices

Peak velocity $(m \cdot s^{-1})$	Professional	Semi-professional	Amateur
+0%	4.1	3.8	3.2
+25%	3.25	3.0	2.76
+50%	2.7	2.5	2.3
+75%	2.35	2.14	2.0
+100%	2.0	1.86	1.75

Table 19.2 Relative 1RM squat and bench press strength of MMA competitors across levels. Squat depth achieved was to an internal knee angle of < 85° (James et al., 2016a)

	Professional	Semi-professional	Amateur
1RM squat (kg.BM^{-1})	2.05	1.84	1.56
1RM bench press (kg.BM^{-1})	1.40	1.25	1.15

Maximal strength

The 1RM squat, bench pull and bench press is recommended to assess the maximal strength capabilities of the MMA athlete. Because maximal strength is considered the key training factor of a number of sports, these tests form the cornerstone of many testing batteries. Adding to their appeal is that normative data exist across intermittent collision sports, including MMA (James et al., 2016a). 1RM tests can also be performed as a 3RM, which allows them to be integrated into a heavy strength session as a training stimulus. Normative data based on published reports and practical experience is presented in Table 19.2.

Short term and repeated anaerobic capabilities

Actions expressed with maximal intent for only a few seconds are characteristic of pivotal moments during MMA combat (Del Vecchio et al., 2011). To assess this quality, short-duration sprint tests can be employed over distances of 10 or 20m. These tests are easy to administer, reliable and reflect the anaerobic demands of MMA. Similarly, a repeated sprint ability test is a practical option to assess longer-term anaerobic capabilities. A fitting configuration of this test consists of 12 × 20m sprints departing every 20s. When deceleration is considered it forms a work to rest ratio of 1:3, similar to that of MMA (Wadley and Le Rossignol, 1998). As such, it provides a valid measure of the MMA fighter's ability to repeatedly apply brief explosive efforts over several minutes.

Intermittent endurance

The high-intensity intermittent endurance demands of MMA are best assessed through non-continuous methods. While there are a variety of such tests available, the Yo-Yo IR2 is recommended. This test is particularly intense, resulting in higher lactate levels than common intermittent tests such as the 30–15 (Buchheit et al., 2009) and Yo-Yo IR1 (Krustrup et al., 2006), and therefore better reflects the metabolic demands of MMA. Although lower in intensity and absent of active recovery periods, a maximal aerobic speed test is also valid option and allows for training intensities to be programmed from the results.

Reporting and interpreting testing results

For testing to fully impact the training process, the results must be reported in a way that is easily interpreted by both the athlete and coaching staff. An excellent method of presenting testing data is with radar plots. These figures allow the athlete or coach to visually identify a fighter's performance across a testing battery relative to a benchmark. This benchmark may represent fellow fighters within a team, available normative data or targets set by the coach (McGuigan et al., 2013). Figure 19.1 shows the outcome of a testing battery for an MMA competitor relative to fellow athletes of the same competition level. We can see that although well developed in maximal neuromuscular expressions like lower body strength, power and short-term anaerobic efforts, she is below the standard (of other female professional competitors) for more endurance-based measures. The strength and conditioning coach can then consider prioritising the development of these deficient attributes while maintaining other qualities.

These plots can also be used to diagnose capabilities within a given set of attributes. For example, Figure 19.2 presents a strength-power profile of a semi-professional MMA athlete. If we looked at any one of these measures in isolation, while we would easily conclude that they are above the standard, such information is limited in its ability to direct strength-power programming. Alternatively, the radar plot clearly highlights that this competitor is far better developed in higher velocity

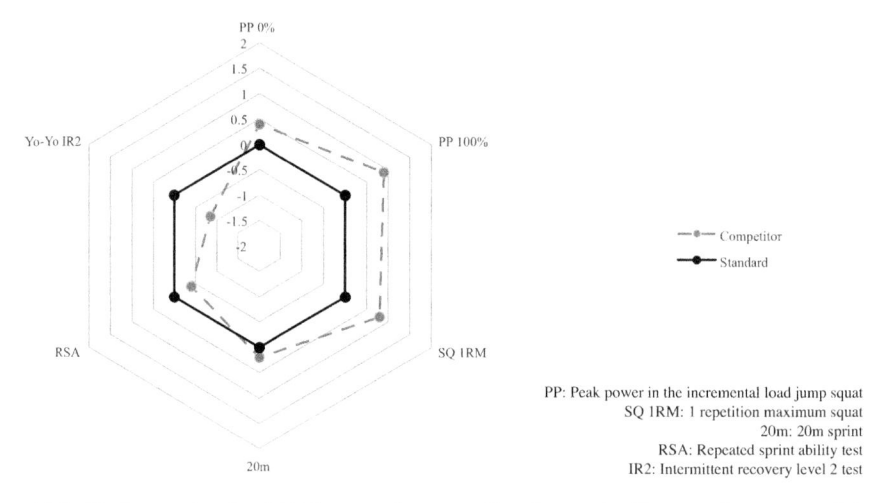

Figure 19.1 Testing results of an MMA competitor exceeding the standard in strength-power qualities, but deficient in metabolic capabilities

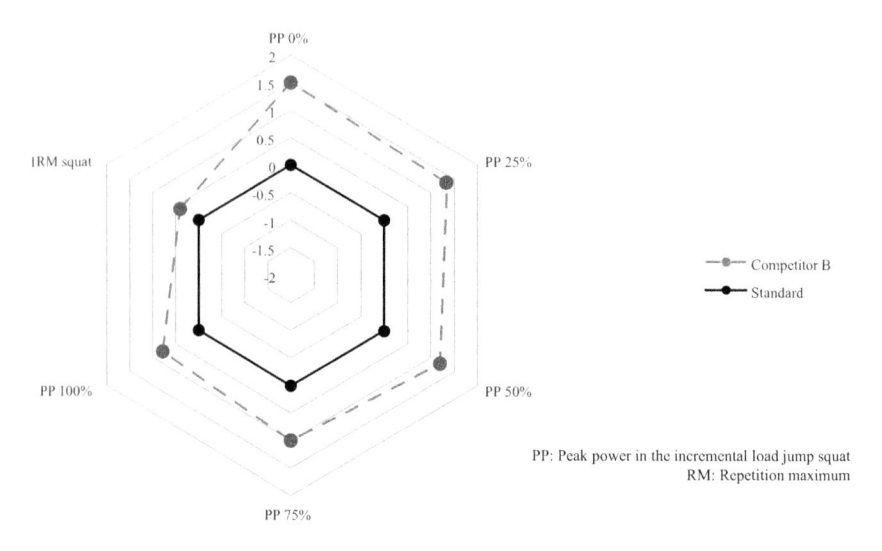

Figure 19.2 Strength-power diagnosis of an MMA competitor. Despite exceeding the standard for all tests, this plot reveals that the fighter is relatively deficient in high force conditions

actions (unloaded and low-loaded jump squats) than force dominant expressions (like the 1RM squat and heavy jump squats). To address this relative deficiency, an increased emphasis on strength training and weightlifting exercises under heavy loads (≥ 80% 1RM) might then be prescribed.

Programming

Programming overview

The inherent complexity of MMA as a sport, and the unpredictable nature of the bout require a fighter to be ready for nearly any circumstance. It is the role of the strength and conditioning coach to not only design a program that targets the required attributes, but also to ensure that they foster an environment where training modalities are managed appropriately based upon the multiple training sessions that take part throughout the day, week and particular training phase in general. The templates provided are *actual* examples that were created and used during the fight preparation for a number of elite level MMA athletes within the UFC. For the purposes of this text, certain aspects and timelines have been adapted to enhance clarity and to provide a better insight into the realities that practitioners training MMA fighters will face.

The templates

The macrocycle: a long-term performance plan

The long-term performance plan examines the phases leading up to a bout (Table 19.3). It is to be used as a general guide, illustrating how each phase will sequence together. MMA fight preparation often lends itself to being somewhat chaotic as many lead MMA coaches are not yet used to integrating their training plan with strength and conditioning tasks. This is largely a result of the amount of disciplines that need to be learned/refined as well as the number of people involved with the preparation for the bout, often spread over multiple training sites. Presenting this long-term view as it pertains to dates and general phase sequence gives the practitioner a sound reference point to build from and serves as a natural precursor to a more specific breakdown of the contents of the individual phases themselves as well as their constituent parts.

Training phase breakdown

In the *Phase Breakdown* (Tables 19.4, 19.5, 19.6 and 19.7) each specific phase is divided into clear-cut goals/directives and includes details surrounding individual training components such as the nature, frequency and focus of strength training sessions, energy system drills, mobility work, movement skills (linear and change of direction based skills) and medicine-ball, plyometric and neuromuscular control based sessions. The layout shown in the examples provided is not meant to suggest that these are all individual or separate training sessions within themselves (though they certainly could be depending on time or resource constraints) but rather to help strength and conditioning professionals think more critically about how they want to both address and advance each specific training component within the larger framework of the program. The template can be used as a blueprint to be referred to when designing not only a specific micro or mesocycle, but also each individual training session. The template will act as a powerful asset that enhances the communication between you and other members of the fight team, including the fighter themselves, leading up to the bout. If designed and utilised correctly, it should allow for more specific and scalable solutions to be added or omitted with ease, and also create the outline for the Weekly Breakdown (Table 19.8) and individual strength and energy system conditioning sessions.

Table 19.3 Macrocycle consisting of sequential phases leading up to, and following, competition. Note that phase dates & lengths are approximate. Preparatory periods will vary based on sponsorship appearances, travel, etc.

June	July	July/August	August/September
1 — Phase 1: general preparation	1 — Phase 2: specific preparation	31 — Phase 3: transition	27 — Active recovery
2	2	1	28
3	3	2	29
4	4	3	30
5	5	4	31
6	6	5	1
7	7	6	2
8	8	7	3
9	9	8	4
10	10	9	5
11	11	10	6
12	12	11	7
13	13	12	8
14	14	13	9
15	15	14	10
16	16	15	11
17	17	16	12
18	18	17	13
19	19	18 — Taper	14
20	20	19	15
21	21	20	16
22	22	21	17
23	23	22	
24	24	23	
25	25	24	
26	26	25	
27	27	**Fight night**	26
28	28	**MON**	
29	29	**TUES**	
30	30	**WED**	
	MON	**THURS**	

Table 19.4 Phase 1 – General preparation. Summary of the key training components within a fighter's program. Note the focus on the development of general movement and strength capacities across training components. The focus is to develop a non-specific foundation of overall fitness. This will lead into the subsequent intensification of training, targeting specific physical capacities in Phase 2 of the program. This template allows the strength and conditioning coach to better adapt to changing training schedule demands and last minute adjustments while still holding true to evidenced based, periodised training principles. ESD: Energy system development; RPE: Session rate of perceived exertion; SMR: Self myofascial release

Duration	Approximately 2 weeks (dependent on travel or last minute schedule changes)
Goal	Laying physiological and neuromuscular foundations through general or non-specific means of physical development.
Mobility/stability	Complete evaluations daily: Hips, shoulders, groin and ankles are main focus. Breathing techniques, SMR, and general patterning.
Plyometric	2 × per week. Low stretch load and volume: Focus on building neuromuscular control, tendon and tissue tolerance.
Medicine ball	2 × per week. Stability focus (base stance, split stance, scissor stance; wall focused).
Movement: general	Non-fight specific. General movement principles, games and skills. 3–4 × a week: 30mins or less.
Movement: linear	1–2 × per week. Focus on posture, fundamentals. Establish rhythm/coordination of movement (march, skip etc.). Light sled/harness acceleration work if desired.
Movement: multi-directional	1–2 × per week. Focus on posture, fundamentals and positioning (assist/resist lateral movement). Nothing fight specific at this time beyond the fighter's daily technical/tactical work.
Strength	4-day total push-pull split. Relative intensity should be light-moderate (refer to programming tables for percentage equivalents). Rotary and stability trunk training done daily as part of medicine ball work and normal programming.
ESD	4 × per week. 2 days at RPE: 3–5 and 2 days at RPE: 5–7. Majority should be equipment or circuit focused.

Table 19.5 Phase 2 – Specific preparation. Summary of the key training components within a fighter's program. Note the relative intensification of plyometric, strength and energy system components. Additionally, you will notice that the linear and multi-directional movement sessions, while still non-fight specific in nature, showcases an increase in sprint volume as well as an increased focus on reactive agility modalities. This template allows the strength and conditioning coach to better adapt to changing training schedule demands and last minute adjustments while still holding true to both scientifically sound programming principles and an overall organised plan.
CM: Countermovement; ESD: Energy system development; RPE: Session rate of perceived exertion; SMR: Self myofascial release

Duration	Approximately 3 weeks (dependent on travel or last minute schedule changes)
Goal	Build on previous foundation. Strengthen, condition & increase loading intensity in all components. Fighter should be prepared for rigors of fight camp.
Mobility/stability	Complete evaluations daily: Hips, shoulders, groin and ankles are main focus. Breathing techniques, SMR, and general patterning.
Plyometric tasks	2–3 × per week. With neuromuscular control established, efforts can now be maximal at a moderate volume. Introduce greater stretch loads, increased reactivity, and continuous actions. 1 and 2 leg variations are progressed in complexity.

(Continued)

Table 19.5 (Continued)

Duration	Approximately 3 weeks (dependent on travel or last minute schedule changes)
Medicine ball	2 × per week: Propulsive and stability focused: Mix throws, tosses, slams, puts etc. Partner and reactive variations added.
Movement: general	Non-fight specific. Advance general movement principles and skills. Increased focus on frontal and transverse plane. Only 2–3 days per week due to increase in technical/tactical training frequency.
Movement: linear	1–2 × per week. Build on fundamentals and increase volume of sprints via distance or repetitions.
Movement: multi-directional	1–2 × per week. Build on fundamentals. Make movements and drills more reactive. Can divide into 1–2 specific drills at end if needed or desired.
Strength	2–4 day total body maximal strength emphasis. Upper/lower splits should be prioritised if possible, but can shift to 2–3 total body sessions if time with fighter is limited.
ESD	3–4 × per week. Two days @ RPE 5–7; two days @ RPE 7–10. Observe sparring sessions if possible and adjust as needed.

Table 19.6 Phase 3 – Transition. Summary of the key training components within a fighter's program. Due to the increase in technical/tactical specificity and workload for fight specific training as the bout approaches, there is a subsequent reduced emphasis on movement skill tasks with the strength and conditioning coach. However, strategic inclusion of various multi-directional drills, shuttles or repeat sprint protocols within the energy system training on non-heavy sparring days is possible. Plyometric and medicine ball variations are at their most advanced within this phase of the program and rely heavily on maximal explosive efforts and continuous variations. Strength-power training during this phase will rely heavily on contrast modalities (alternating heavy and light explosive actions), which complement the aforementioned ballistic methods.

CM: Countermovement; ESD: Energy system development; KB: Kettlebell; RPE: Session rate of perceived exertion; SMR: Self myofascial release; S&C: Strength and conditioning

Duration	Approximately 4 weeks (dependent on travel and last minute schedule changes)
Goal	Fight preparation. Goal is to maximise neuromuscular power development and conditioning qualities within the constraints of camp and schedule.
Mobility/stability	Done daily. Based off of observation and evaluations: hips, shoulders, groin and ankles are main focus. Utilise KBs, breathing techniques, SMR, or general progressions.
Plyometric	Primarily completed on sparring days: maximal explosive efforts, emphasis on continuous jumps, lateral bounds and rotary jumps.
Medicine ball	2 × per week: reactive and partner modalities emphasised. Mix throws, tosses, slams, puts etc.
Movement: general	Minimal S&C components. Considerable time spent with technical/tactical coaches (striking, jiu-jitsu, wrestling etc.).
Movement: linear	N/A See ESD programs.
Movement: multi-directional	N/A See ESD programs.
Strength	Strength-power: contrast modalities.
ESD	3–4 × per week. Two days @ RPE 5–7 , 2 days @ RPE 7–9. Observe sparring sessions and adjust as needed.

Table 19.7 Taper. Summary of the key training components within a fighter's program. Note the rather dramatic decrease in volume amongst the plyometric, med-ball, movement skill and strength training components of the program. This reduced volume is complemented by high levels of intensity (in this context, explosiveness) for heavy strength and plyometric tasks. A primary consideration in this phase is attaining the "minimal effective dose" as the primary focus should be on the enhancement and refinement of all fight-skills leading up to the bout.
CM: Countermovement; ESD: Energy system development; KB: Kettlebell; RPE: Session rate of perceived exertion; SMR: Self myofascial release

Duration	Approximately 1 week (depending on fatigue level)
Goal	Reduction of accumulated fatigue and realisation of physiological and neuromuscular adaptations.
Mobility/ stability	Done daily. Based off of Observation and Evaluations: hips, shoulders, groin and ankles are main focus. Utilise KBs, breathing techniques, SMR, perturbations, or general progressions.
Plyo:	10–20% reduction in volume from Phase 3.
med ball:	10–20% reduction in volume from Phase 3.
movement	Minimal S&C components. Considerable time spent with technical/tactical coaches (striking, jiu-jitsu, wrestling etc.).
Linear	Low volume sprint work. 1–2 days a week for potentiation purposes. Not to exceed 30–40 meters per effort and at least 1–4 work to rest.
Multi	N/A
strength	1–3 days per week, depending on technical/tactical training schedule. Goal is to maintain intensity (combined heavy loading and high velocity actions) with any reductions coming from volume (i.e. reduced sets, reps, training sessions).
ESD	1–3 days per week low-moderate intensity (RPE of 3–5).

Table 19.8 Example weekly plan for the specific preparation period (Phase 2). ESD: Energy system development

MONDAY	TUESDAY	WEDNESDAY	THURSDAY	FRIDAY	SATURDAY	SUNDAY
Technical/ tactical: intensive	Technical tactical: extensive	Movement skills: lateral	Sparring: mod	Strength training	Heavy sparring: no formal S&C	Active recovery
Movement skills: linear	Sparring: mod	Strength training	Technical tactical: extensive	ESD: mod (adjusted if needed)	ESD: low intensity	Massage
Strength training	Recovery/ nutrition	Recovery/ nutrition	Recovery/ nutrition	Recovery/ nutrition	Recovery/ nutrition	hydrotherapy
ESD	ESD: mod (adjusted if needed)	Technical/ tactical: intensive	ESD: hard	Technical/ tactical: extensive & review		
Technical/ tactical: extensive	Recovery/ nutrition	ESD: easy (adjusted if needed)				

Weekly breakdowns

Table 19.8 provides an example of the weekly distribution of training tasks for a single phase (in this case, specific preparation). Because of the multiple factors involved, coaches should focus on prioritising the 1–2 training components that will make the most dramatic impact on performance based on the goals of the training phase and the current and future needs of the fighter. Scheduling should ensure that physical preparation allows for the athlete to have minimal acute fatigue for the sessions that provide the most return on investment.

Strength training

Tables 19.9, 19.10, 19.11 and 19.12 present strength training sessions across all phases, as well as energy system development options. To enhance clarity for the athlete, a program provides an intuitive guide to loading and intensity zones which may vary somewhat based upon the athlete's fitness level as well as their technical competency and recoverability. The layout of the template is divided into 2–4 primary sections and is labeled so that the athlete knows which exercise sequences are to be performed together.

Table 19.9 All exercises with a letter (A, B, C etc.) by their name should be completed in a circuit fashion. For example, after completing 1–2 warm-ups sets, you will do one set of A1, one set of A2, then one set of A3 before resting and repeating for the required sets. The sets you see on this template are to be actual working sets with the prescribed loads, and therefore do not include your warm-up sets. Take 15–30s rest between exercises, and 2 min rest between each lap of a circuit.
ESD: Energy system development; PB: Physioball. Maximal: 95–100% 1RM (1–2 reps); very heavy: 90–95% 1RM (2–4 reps); mod heavy: 85–90%1RM (4–6 reps); moderate: 80–85% 1RM (6–8 reps); mod light: 75–80% 1RM (8–10 reps); light: 70–75% 1RM (10–12 reps); very light: 65–70% 1RM (12–15 reps)

Phase 1, day 1, weeks 1–3

Exercise	Sets × reps	Loading per set/notes
Clean pull from the knee	Week 1: 3 × 5; week 2: 3 × 4; week 3: 3 × 3	Week 1: very light, light × 2; week 2: light, mod. light × 2; week 3: mod. light × 2, moderate
A1. Squat, eccentric: front, back, or safety (4:1:X tempo)	Week 1–3: 4 × 6	Week 1: light × 4; week 2: mod. light × 4; week 3: moderate × 4
A2. Pull-up: 3 position isometric	Week 1–3: 4 × 1–3	Week 1–3: 10 sec hold @ top, middle & bottom = 1 rep
A3. Efficiency movement	Shoulder: dowel lat. stretch × 10; torso: PB knee tuck × 15; hips: quad-hip flexor stretch × 10 ea	Choose based on needs & restrictions
B1. X-pulldown: tall kneeling	Week 1–3: 2 × 10	
B2. Lateral lunge: 2-dumbbell	Week 1–3: 2 × 8 ea	
B3. Propulsive cable lift: standing	Week 1–3: 2 × 6 ea	
B4. Side-lying kettlebell arm-bar rotation	Week 1–3: 2 × 10 ea	
ESD: air bike or treadmill	Week 1: 15 minutes Week 2: 20 minutes Week 3: 25 minutes	30 sec hard/4:30 min moderate

Phase 1, day 2, weeks 1–3

Exercise	Sets/reps	Loading
Isometric + explosive circuit: 1.) Power plate push-up hold 2.) Supine medicine ball chest pass w/ partner	Week 1–3: 1.) 2 × 30–45 sec 2.) 2 × 5	Max Hz on Power Plate or add additional load.
A1. Bench press, eccentric: 2-dumbbell or barbell (4:1:X Tempo)	Week 1–3: 4 × 6	
A2. Eccentric leg curl: PB or slides	Week 1: 8 ea; Week 2: 8 ea; Week 3: 10 ea	1-leg or 2-leg based on ability
A3. Efficiency movement	Shoulder: bent over "T" × 15; torso: band-resisted bird-dog × 10 ea; hips: band-resisted dead bug w/ breath × 10 ea	Choose based on needs & restrictions
B1. Curl to press: 2-dumbbell, half kneeling	Week 1–3: 2 × 8	
B2. Kettlebell swing	Week 1–3: 2 × 8	
B3. Stability cable push-pull	Week 1–3: 2 × 8 ea	
B4. Physioball crunches	Week 1–3: 2 × 30	
ESD: low intensity equipment work	Week 1–3: 20–40 minutes	

Phase 1, day 3, weeks 1–3

Exercise	Sets/reps	Loading
Snatch pull from the knee	Week 1: 3 × 5; week 2: 3 × 4; week 3: 3 × 3	Week 1: very light, light × 2; week 2: light, mod. light × 2; week 3: mod. light × 2, moderate
A1. Row: barbell or 2-dumbbell (2:4:x tempo)	Week 1–3: 4 × 6	Week 1: light × 4; week 2: mod. light × 4; week 3: moderate × 4
A2. Rear foot elevated split squat: eccentric, 2-dumbbell (4:1:x tempo)	Week 1–3: 4 × 6 ea	
A3. Efficiency movement	Shoulder: dowel lat stretch × 10; torso: overhead d-ball slam × 8; hips: GHF stretch × 10 ea	Choose based on needs & restrictions
B1. X-lift: tall kneeling	Week 1–3: 2 × 10	
B2. Farmer's walk to squat combo: 2-kettlebell	Week 1–3: 2 × 8	Walk 15m + 6 squats: 1 set = 4
B3. Propulsive cable chop: standing	Week 1–3: 2 × 8 ea	Record power: 35–45 psi
B4. Supine hip internal rotations stretch	Week 1–3: 2 × 8 ea	
ESD: slide-board	Week 1: 6 × (9 feet) Week 2: 7 × (9 feet) Week 3: 8 × (9 feet)	30 sec on/30 sec off

(Continued)

Table 19.9 (Continued)

Phase 1, day 4, weeks 1–3

Exercise	Sets/reps	Loading
Isometric + explosive circuit: 1.) Loaded split squat holds 2.) Cycle split jumps	Week 1–3: 1.) 2 × 30–45 sec ea 2.) 2 × 6–8 ea	
A1. Romanian deadlift, eccentric: barbell (4:1:x tempo)	Week 1–3: 4 × 6	Week 1: light × 4; week 2: mod. light × 4; week 3: moderate × 4
A2. Alternating incline dumbbell press or overhead barbell press	Week 1: 4 × 7 ea; week 2: 4 × 6 ea; week 3: 4 × 6 ea	
A3. Efficiency movement	Shoulder: bent over "T" × 15; torso: band-resisted bird-dog × 10 ea; hips: band-resisted dead bug w/ breath × 10 ea	Choose based on needs & restrictions
B1. Push-up: band staggered arm/leg	Week 1–3: 2 × 10 ea	
B2. Half Turkish get-up	Week 1–3: 2 × 3 ea	
B3. Wide stance stability "chop", rope	Week 1–3: 2 × 8 ea	
B4. Forward & reverse resisted bear crawl	Week 1–3: 2 × 20 m	
ESD: tempo-based game		

Table 19.10 All exercises with a letter (A, B, C etc.) by their name should be completed in a circuit fashion. For example, after completing 1–2 warm-ups sets, you will do one set of A1, one set of A2, then one set of A3 before resting and repeating for the required sets. The sets you see on this template are to be actual WORKING sets with challenging loads and do not include your warm-up sets. Take 15–30s rest between exercises, and 2 min rest between each lap of a circuit. ESD: Energy system development; PB: Physioball. Maximal: 95–100% 1RM (1–2 reps); very heavy: 90–95% 1RM (2–4 reps); mod heavy: 85–90%1RM (4–6 reps); moderate: 80–85% 1RM (6–8 reps); mod light: 75–80% 1RM (8–10 reps); light: 70–75% 1RM (10–12 reps); very light: 65–70% 1RM (12–15 reps)

Phase 2, day 1, weeks 4–6

Exercise	Sets/reps	Loading
Jump shrug with countermovement	Week 1: 3 × 3; week 2: 4 × 2; week 3: 4 × 1+1	Week 1: moderate × 3; week 2: mod. heavy × 4; week 3: very heavy clusters × 4
A1. Bench press: barbell or 2-dumbbell	Week 1: 3 × 5; week 2: 4 × 4; week 3: 1 × 4, 2 × 3, 2 × 2	Week 1: moderate × 3; week 2: moderate × 2, mod. heavy × 2; week 3: moderate, mod. heavy × 2, very heavy × 2
A2. Romanian deadlift: 1-leg, 2-dumbbell or barbell	Week 1: 3 × 5 ea; week 2: 4 × 5 ea; week 3: 5 × 5 ea	Week 1: moderate × 3; week 2: moderate × 4; week 3: mod. heavy × 5
B1. Inverted row: TRX + weight vest	Week 1: 3 × 8; week 2: 3 × 6; week 3: 3 × 5	
B2. Walking lunges: barbell	Week 1–3: 3 × 6 ea	

Phase 2, day 1, weeks 4–6

Exercise	Sets/reps	Loading
B3. Rotational: cable push-pull	Week 1: 3 × 8 ea; week 2: 3 × 6 ea; week 3: 3 × 5 ea	
ESD: tempo runs	Week 1–3: 1–3 sets of 8–12	50–100m distance

Phase 2, day 2, weeks 4–6

Exercise/mode	Instructions
Movement preparation	Jump rope, jog, or calisthenics × 1–2 minutes; elbow to instep × 3 ea; knee hug × 5 ea; inverted hamstring × 10 ea; lateral squat or lateral lunge × 10 ea
ESD preferred option: versaclimber	10 sec hard/50 sec off 5 sec hard/25 sec off 15 sec hard/45 sec off 10 sec hard/50 sec off 5 sec hard/25 sec off Repeat 3–6 times
ESD backup option: circuit Jump rope, jog, row, bike	Rotate 5–10 minutes through each modality
ESD compromise option: intermittent run (Woodway)	1 min @ 6 rpe 30 sec @ 3 rpe 1 min @ 7 rpe 30 sec @ 3 rpe 1 min @ 8 rpe 30 sec @ 3 rpe Repeat 2–5 times

Phase 2, day 3, weeks 4–6

Exercise	Sets/reps	Loading
Snatch grip jump shrug	Week 1: 3 × 3; week 2: 4 × 2; week 3: 4 × 1+1	Week 1: moderate × 3; week 2: mod. heavy × 4; week 3: very heavy clusters × 4
A1. Squat: front, back, or safety bar	Week 1: 3 × 5; week 2: 4 × 4; week 3: 1 × 4, 2 × 3, 2 × 2	Week 1: moderate × 3; week 2: moderate × 2, mod. heavy × 2; week 3: moderate, mod. heavy × 2, very heavy × 2
A2. Chin-up	Week 1: 3 × 5; week 2: 4 × 2+2; week 3: 5 × 1+1+1	Week 1: moderate × 3; week 2: mod. heavy clusters × 4 Week 3: very heavy clusters × 5
B1. Overhead press: 1-arm kettlebell	Week 1: 3 × 6 ea; week 2: 3 × 5 ea; week 3: 3 × 4 ea	
B2. Physioball leg curl: 1-leg	Week 1: 8 ea; week 2: 8 ea; week 3: 10 ea	
B3. Rotational medicine ball slam	Week 1: 3 × 8 ea; week 2: 3 × 6 ea; week 3: 3 × 5 ea	

(*Continued*)

Table 19.10 (Continued)

Phase 2, day 4, weeks 4–6

Exercise/mode	Instructions
Movement preparation	Jump rope, jog, or calisthenics × 1–2 minutes; elbow to instep × 3 ea; knee hug × 5 ea; inverted hamstring × 10 ea
	Lateral squat or lateral lunge × 10 ea
ESD option if sparring is cancelled: 60 yard shuttles	30-30
	5-5-10-10-15-15
	15-15-15-15
	30-30
	1–3 Sets with a 1:4 work:rest ratio
ESD preferred option: intermittent run (Woodway)	1 min @ 6 rpe
	30 sec @ 3 rpe
	1 min @ 7 rpe
	30 sec @ 3 rpe
	1 min @ 8 rpe
	30 sec @ 3 rpe
	Repeat 2–5 times
ESD backup option: circuit Jump rope, jog, row, bike	Rotate 5–10 minutes through each modality

Phase 2, day 5, weeks 4–6

Exercise	Sets/reps	Loading
Push-jerk: landmine	Week 1: 3 × 5 ea; week 2: 4 × 4 ea; week 3: 4 × 3 ea	Work up to heaviest possible load each week
A1. Romanian deadlift: 2-leg, barbell	Week 1: 3 × 5; week 2: 4 × 4; week 3: 1 × 4, 2 × 3, 2 × 2	Week 1: moderate × 3
		Week 2: moderate × 2, mod. heavy × 2
		Week 3: moderate, mod. heavy × 2, very heavy × 2
A2. Incline bench press: 2-dumbbell, alternating arm	Week 1: 3 × 5 ea; week 2: 4 × 4 ea; week 3: 5 × 3 ea	Week 1: moderate × 3; week 2: mod. heavy × 4; week 3: very heavy × 5
B1. Dumbbell row, 1-arm	Week 1–3: 3–6 ea	
B2. Lateral lunge: 2-dumbbell	Week 1: 3 × 6 ea; week 2: 3 × 5 ea; week 3: 3 × 5 ea	
B3. Plank opposites (arm/leg lift)	Week 1: 3 × 20 sec; week 2: 3 × 30 sec; week 3: 3 × 40 sec	
ESD: low intensity equipment work	20–40 minutes	

Table 19.11 All exercises with a letter (A, B, C etc.) by their name should be completed in a circuit fashion. For example, after completing 1–2 warm-ups sets, you will do one set of A1, one set of A2, then one set of A3 before resting and repeating for the required sets. The sets you see on this template are to be actual WORKING sets with challenging loads and do not include your warm-up sets. Take 30s rest between exercises, and 3 min rest between each lap of a circuit. ESD: Energy system development; PB: Physioball. Maximal: 95–100% 1RM (1–2 reps); Very heavy: 90–95% 1RM (2–4 reps); mod heavy: 85–90%1RM (4–6 reps); moderate: 80–85% 1RM (6–8 reps); mod light: 75–80% 1RM (8–10 reps); light: 70–75% 1RM (10–12 reps); very light: 65–70% 1RM (12–15 reps).

Phase 3, day 1, weeks 7–9

Exercise	Sets/Reps	Loading
Hang power clean	Week 1: 4 × 3; week 2: 4 × 3; week 3: 4 × 2	Week 1: light × 2, mod. light × 2; week 2: mod. light × 2, moderate × 2; week 3: moderate × 2, mod. heavy × 2
A1. Bench press: barbell or 2-dumbbell	Week 1: 5 × 4; week 2: 5 × 3; week 3: 5 × 2	Week 1: mod. light × 5; week 2: moderate × 5; week 3: mod. heavy × 5
A2. Push-up: plyometric	Week 1: 5 × 2; week 2: 5 × 3; week 3: 5 × 4	
B1. Split jump: alternating legs	Weeks 1–3: 2 × 5 ea	
B2. Back extension isometric hold	Week 1: 2 × 30 sec; week 2: 2 × 35 sec; week 3: 2 × 45 sec	
B3. Perpendicular throw: medicine ball	Week 1–3: 2 × 6 ea	
ESD: tempo runs	Week 1–3: 1–3 sets of 8–12	50–100 m distance

Phase 3, day 2, weeks 7–9

Exercise/mode	Instructions
Movement preparation	Jump rope, jog, or calisthenics × 1–2 minutes; elbow to instep × 3 ea; knee hug × 5 ea; inverted hamstring × 10 ea
	lateral squat or lateral lunge × 10 ea;
ESD preferred option: hill sprints	week 1: 2–3 × 8; week 2: 2–3 × 10 week 3: 2–3 × 12;
	Mark distance covered in 7–10 sec; 3 minutes rest in between sets
ESD backup option: swim (recovery tempo)	20–40 minutes @ rpe of 3–5
ESD compromise option: medicine ball circuit	Rotational slam × 8 ea
	Overhead slam × 8 ea
	1-arm rotational put × 8 ea
	Squat to throw × 8
	Chest pass to sprawl × 8 ea
	Split stance rotational throw × 8 ea
	Repeat 3–5 times
	1–2 minutes of rest between sets

(Continued)

Table 19.11 (Continued)

Phase 3, day 3, weeks 7–9

Exercise	Sets/reps	Loading
Hang power snatch	Week 1: 4 × 3; week 2: 4 × 3; week 3: 4 × 2	Week 1: light × 2, mod. light × 2; week 2: mod. light × 2, moderate × 2; week 3: moderate × 2, mod. heavy × 2
A1. Squat: front, back, or safety bar	Week 1: 5 × 4; week 2: 5 × 3; week 3: 5 × 2	Week 1: mod. Light × 5; week 2: moderate × 5; week 3: mod. Heavy × 5
A2. Unloaded jump squat	Week 1: 5 × 2; week 2: 5 × 3; week 3: 5 × 4	
B1. Incline press: 1-arm dumbbell	Week 1–3: 2 × 6 ea	
B2. Leg curl: 1-leg, PB or slides	Week 1: 2 × 10 ea; week 2: 2 × 8 ea; week 3: 2 × 8 ea	
B3. Split stance chop: medicine ball	Week 1: 2 × 8 ea; week 2: 2 × 6 ea; week 3: 2 × 6 ea	

Phase 3, day 4, weeks 7–9

Exercise/mode	Instructions
Movement preparation	Jump rope, jog, or calisthenics × 1–2 minutes; elbow to instep × 3 ea; knee hug × 5 ea; inverted hamstring × 10 ea; lateral squat or lateral lunge × 10 ea
ESD option if sparring is cancelled: sleds	Week 1: 8 reps; week 2: 10 reps; week 3: 8 reps
	Sprint 30 meters
	Rest 40 seconds
	If sprint is longer than 8–12 seconds reduce load
ESD preferred option: strongman medley	Backwards sled drag × 30 yards; farmer's carry × 30 yards; forward sled march × 30 yards; sandbag shouldering × 8 ea
	Repeat 2–5 times
ESD backup option: swim (recovery tempo)	20–40 minutes @ rpe of 3–5

Phase 3, day 5, weeks 7–9

Exercise	Sets/Reps	Loading
Push Press: 2-dumbbell or barbell	Week 1: 4 × 5; Week 2: 4 × 4; week 3: 4 × 3	Week 1: mod. light × 4; week 2: moderate × 4; week 3: mod. heavy × 4
A1. Romanian deadlift: 2-leg, barbell	Week 1: 5 × 4; week 2: 5 × 3; week 3: 5 × 2	Week 1: mod. light × 5; week 2: moderate × 5; week 3: mod. heavy × 5

Phase 3, day 5, weeks 7–9

Exercise	Sets/reps	Loading
A2. Broad jump: countermovement, bodyweight	Week 1: 5 × 2; week 2: 5 × 3; week 3: 5 × 4	
B1. Inverted row: 1-arm, TRX or rings	Week 1–3: 2 × 8	
B2. Back extension isometric hold	Week 1–3: 2 × 6 ea	
B3. Front plank w/ kettlebell pull through	Week 1: 30 sec Week 2: 35 sec Week 3: 40 sec	
ESD: tempo runs	Week 1–3: 1–3 sets of 8–12	50–100 m distance

Table 19.12 All exercises with a letter (A, B, C etc.) by their name should be completed in a circuit fashion. For example, after completing 1–2 warm-ups sets, you will do one set of A1, one set of A2, then one set of A3 before resting and repeating for the required sets. The sets you see on this template are to be actual WORKING sets with challenging loads and do not include your warm-up sets. Take 15–30s rest between exercises, and 2 min rest between each lap of a circuit. ESD: Energy system development; PB: Physioball. Maximal: 95–100% 1RM (1–2 reps); very heavy: 90–95% 1RM (2–4 reps); mod heavy: 85–90%1RM (4–6 reps); moderate: 80–85% 1RM (6–8 reps); mod light: 75–80% 1RM (8–10 reps); light: 70–75% 1RM (10–12 reps); very light: 65–70% 1RM (12–15 reps)

Phase 4, day 1, week 10

Exercise	Sets/reps	Loading
Jump shrug	Week 1: 2 × 3, 2 × 2	Week 1: mod. heavy × 4
A1. Landmine press: barbell	Week 1: 4 × 5 ea	Week 1: moderate × 2, mod. heavy × 2
A2. Deadlift, conventional	Week 1: 1 × 5, 1 × 4, 2 × 3	Week 1: mod. light × 1, moderate × 3
A3. "Stir the pot": PB	Week 1: 4 × 10 ea	

Phase 4, day 2, week 10

Exercise/mode	Instructions
Movement preparation	Jump rope, jog, or calisthenics × 1–2 minutes; elbow to instep × 3 ea; knee hug × 5 ea; inverted hamstring × 10 ea lateral squat or lateral lunge × 10 ea
ESD preferred option: station conditioning	Double-under jump rope Judo push-up Lateral bounds Bodyweight squat Sandbag slams 15 sec on/15 sec off As many rounds as possible in 5–10 minutes
ESD backup option: track or road run	20–30 minutes @ RPE of 3–5

(Continued)

Table 19.12 (Continued)

Phase 4, day 3, week 10

Exercise	Sets/reps	Loading
Depth drop to vertical medicine ball throw	Week 1: 4 × 3	Week 1: light × 2, mod. light × 3
A1. Squat: front, back, or safety bar	Week 1: 4 × 3	Week 1: moderate × 2, mod. heavy × 2
A2. Chin-up: neutral grip	Week 1: 4 × 5	Week 1: mod. heavy × 4
A3. Anti-rotation press, cable or band	Week 1: 4 × 10 ea	

Phase 4, day 4, week 10

Exercise/mode	Instructions
Movement preparation	Jump rope, jog, or calisthenics × 1–2 minutes; elbow to instep × 3 ea; knee hug × 5 ea; inverted hamstring × 10 ea Lateral squat or lateral lunge × 10 ea
ESD preferred option: swim (recovery tempo)	20–30 minutes @ rpe of 3–5

In "Phase 1", "efficiency movements" are to be performed during rest periods and target either mobility, stability or postural limitations of the athlete in order to foster enhanced movement quality and to address gross imbalances that may exist. Strength and movement quality are not only complementary; they are and should always be inextricably linked within the mind of the strength and conditioning professional. It is important to choose these movements wisely, and remember that they are a complement to the program and should never serve as the primary means of the program itself. In all things related to performance, maintain a "strength first" approach (James et al., 2014).

Compound or multi-joint exercises should be prioritised over more isolative movements due to their ability to be loaded at higher levels and because of the amount of muscle mass involved with each movement. Additionally, in order to obtain the necessary neuromuscular adaptations while mitigating the risk of producing significant hypertrophic changes (due to the weight-class nature of the sport) load lifted should be prioritised over total volume, especially during the later stages of training as the competition period/bout nears.

Another element that can never be overlooked with any athlete is that of overall movement quality. A strength and conditioning coach needs to be cognizant that the vast majority of fighters will present with a variety of maladies, asymmetries and previous injuries and need to adjust their programs accordingly. For example, in the back squat, if a fighter is unable to load him/herself due to restricted shoulder, thoracic spine, ankle or hip range of motion or injury, choosing to use a safety bar or alternative variation can protect them from exacerbating a previous injury or even potentially priming their body to incur a new one.

Energy system development

In the context of metabolic fitness, what coaches may lose sight of is that fighters need not more specificity but rather more training of energy systems that are not innately developed within technical/tactical sessions, or that are not part of their predominant fighting style. Thus, it is recommended that the strength and conditioning coach make it a priority to observe training sessions that take place outside of the weight-room so that they can accurately track the energy systems most commonly used. They can then develop a "training menu" that allows them to easily adjust any aspect of the program that they already have in place to ensure that they are not adding unnecessary stress to an energy system that is already well developed. As shown in Table 19.13, the menu options are categorised to the various energy systems targeted and also

Table 19.13 Energy system development options. *Ranges and volumes dependent on needs Above menu options are categorised to the various energy systems targeted and also their unique characteristics (multi-planar, low/high impact, etc.), highlighting the training goal. It is important to note the inclusion of the three different intensity options in the templates of the later phases provide an immediate backup plan should timeframes change or if the fighter is not recovering/progressing appropriately. Select from these options based on the needs of your athlete(s), along with the appropriate training phase and time available.
*Rest Shown for "Category B" Options is Between Sets *RPE Ranges (1–10): Rest/Easy = 0–3 Easy-Moderate = 3–5 Moderate-Hard = 5–7 Hard = 7–9 Max = 10

	What?	*Why?*	*How?*
Short task duration; high intensity	**Category A**	Sample of value provided by inclusion within the program	Programming guidelines/examples
	Sprints	CNS and anaerobic power development, enhanced tissue tolerance, budget friendly, ground based	Distance 30m reps: 8–12 sets: 2–3 rest: 30s btw reps, 2–3 minutes between sets
	Slideboard	Anaerobic power development, frontal plane oriented, hip/groin strengthening, low-impact	Protocol: 20s hard/40s rest reps: 6–10 sets 1–3 rest: 2 minutes between sets
	Versaclimber	Anaerobic power development, low-impact, coordination, short learning curve	Protocol: 10s max/50s rest reps 8–10 sets: 2–3 rest: 2–3 minutes between sets
Moderate task duration; moderate intensity	**Category B**		
	Complexes	Enhanced anaerobic capacity, increase in strength & lean mass, ground based	Protocol 3–6 compound exercises reps: 3–8 sets: 1–4 rest: 90–240s
	Medball circuits	Enhanced anaerobic & intermittent endurance capacity, multi-planar, ground based explosive movements	Protocol: 8 movements reps: 10 reps per movement sets: 1–3 rest: 1–2 minutes
	Strongman medleys	Enhanced anaerobic & intermittent endurance capacity, increase in strength & lean mass, ground based, challenging and fun	Protocol: 3–6 movements (carries, drags, sled pushes etc.) Reps: can be done for time or distance rest 90–240s

(*Continued*)

Table 19.12 (Continued)

	What?	Why?	How?
Long task duration; moderate-high intensity	**Category C**		
	Equipment based high intensity intervals	Enhanced anaerobic, intermittent endurance & aerobic capacity, low impact, easily progressed & scalable	Protocol: 30s hard/4:30s moderate reps: 1 (per set) sets: 3–6 rest: 1–3 mins between sets
	Shuttles	Enhanced anaerobic capacity, multidirectional oriented, easily progressed & scalable	Protocol: 60–300 m reps: 1 (per set) sets: 1–3 rest 1–3 mins between sets
	Station work	Enhanced anaerobic, intermittent endurance & aerobic capacity, provides both psychological and physiological variety, easily scalable	Protocol: 3–10 stations reps: can be distance, rep or time based sets: 3–10 rest: 30s btw reps, 1–3 minutes btw sets
Long task duration; low intensity	**Category D**		
	Long slow ESD	Enhanced aerobic capacity, low neuromuscular demand	Protocol 20–60 mins easy-moderate reps: 1 sets: 1 rest: n/a
	Tempo runs (50–75% peak velocity)	Enhanced anaerobic & aerobic capacity, enhanced tissue tolerance, easily progressed & scalable	Protocol: 30–100 m reps: 8–12 sets: 1–3 rest 30–90s
	Loaded walks, carries, drags or hikes	Enhanced anaerobic & aerobic capacity, increase in strength & lean mass, ground based, challenging and fun.	Protocol: circuit based or continuous reps: can be distance, rep, or time based sets: 1–5 rest: as needed

their unique characteristics (multi-planar, low/high impact, etc), highlighting the training goal. It is important to note the inclusion of the three different intensity options in the templates of the later phases provide an immediate backup plan should timeframes change or if the fighter is not recovering/progressing appropriately. Once again, flexibility is key when managing the multitude of variables outside of our control within the MMA environment.

Conclusion

The technical and physiological complexity of MMA requires particularly well informed manipulation of each stage of the training process to ensure optimal competition performance. A spectrum of neuromuscular and metabolic attributes drive performance, with maximal lower body strength and power appearing to stand out as primary physiological functions. However, the MMA fighter must be properly tested to accurately identify what capacities are in most need of attention from the strength and conditioning coach. Training interventions must then be prioritised, sequenced and integrated to minimise interference and achieve the desired adaptations in accordance with competition timelines and ecological constraints.

Acknowledgments

The authors would like to thank Ollie Richardson for his input on this book chapter.

References

Amtmann, J. A., Amtmann, K. A. and Spath, W. K. 2008. Lactate and rate of perceived exertion responses of athletes training for and competing in a mixed martial arts event. *Journal of Strength and Conditioning Research*, 22, 645–647.

Buchheit, M. 2016. Applying the acute: chronic workload ratio in elite football: worth the effort? *British Journal of Sports Medicine*, 1325–1327, bjsports-2016-097017.

Buchheit, M., Al Haddad, H., Millet, G. P., Lepretre, P. M., Newton, M. and Ahmaidi, S. 2009. Cardiorespiratory and cardiac autonomic responses to 30–15 intermittent fitness test in team sport players. *The Journal of Strength & Conditioning Research*, 23, 93–100.

Buchheit, M. and Laursen, P. B. 2013. High-intensity interval training, solutions to the programming puzzle. Part I: cardiopulmonary emphasis. *Sports Medicine*, 43, 313–338.

Cormie, P., McGuigan, M. and Newton, R. 2011. Developing maximal neuromuscular power: part 2 – training considerations for improving maximal power production. *Sports Medicine*, 41, 125–146.

Del Vecchio, F., Hirata, S. and Franchini, E. 2011. A review of time-motion analysis and combat development in mixed martial arts matches at regional level tournaments. *Perceptual and Motor Skills*, 112, 639–648.

Gaitanos, G. C., Williams, C., Boobis, L. H. and Brooks, S. 1993. Human muscle metabolism during intermittent maximal exercise. *Journal of Applied Physiology*, 75, 712–719.

Halson, S. L. 2014. Monitoring training load to understand fatigue in athletes. *Sports Medicine*, 44, S139–S147.

Hulin, B. T., Gabbett, T. J., Caputi, P., Lawson, D. W. and Sampson, J. A. 2016. Low chronic workload and the acute: chronic workload ratio are more predictive of injury than between-match recovery time: a two-season prospective cohort study in elite rugby league players. *British Journal of Sports Medicine*, bjsports-2015-095364.

Impellizzeri, F., Rampinini, E. and Marcora, S. 2005. Physiological assessment of aerobic training in soccer. *Journal of Sports Science*, 23, 583–592.

James, L. P., Beckman, E. and Kelly, V. 2014. The impact of prehabilitation training on the development of strength and power in a block periodised training plan. *Journal of Australian Strength and Conditioning*, 22, 5–16.

James, L. P., Beckman, E. M., Kelly, V. G. and Haff, G. G. 2016a. The neuromuscular qualities of higher and lower-level mixed martial arts competitors. *International Journal of Sports Physiology and Performance*, 1–27.

James, L. P., Haff, G., Kelly, V. and Beckman, E. 2016b. Towards a determination of the physiological characteristics distinguishing successful mixed martial arts athletes: a systematic review of combat sport literature. *Sports Medicine*, 46, 1525–1551.

James, L. P., Robertson, S., Haff, G. G., Beckman, E. M. and Kelly, V. G. 2016c. Identifying the performance characteristics of a winning outcome in elite mixed martial arts competition. *Journal of Science & Medicine in Sport*.

Kirwan, J. P., Costill, D. L., Houmard, J. A., Mitchell, J. B., Flynn, M. G. and Fink, W. J. 1990. Changes in selected blood measures during repeated days of intense training and carbohydrate control. *International Journal of Sports Medicine*, 11, 362–366.

Krustrup, P., Mohr, M. and Nybo, L. 2006. The Yo-Yo IR2 test: physiological response, reliability, and application to elite soccer. *Medicine & Science in Sports & Exercise*, 38, 1666–1673.

Lauersen, J. B., Bertelsen, D. M. and Andersen, L. B. 2014. The effectiveness of exercise interventions to prevent sports injuries: a systematic review and meta-analysis of randomised controlled trials. *British Journal of Sports Medicine*, 48, 871–877.

Lidor, R., Côté, J. and Hackfort, D. 2009. ISSP position stand: To test or not to test? The use of physical skill tests in talent detection and in early phases of sport development. *International Journal of Sport and Exercise Psychology*, 7, 131–146.

Loturco, I., Artioli, G. G., Kobal, R., Gil, S. and Franchini, E. 2014. Predicting punching acceleration from selected strength and power variables in elite karate athletes: A multiple regression analysis. *The Journal of Strength & Conditioning Research*, 28, 1826–1832.

McGuigan, M. R., Cormack, S. J. and Gill, N. D. 2013. Strength and power profiling of athletes: Selecting tests and how to use the information for program design. *Strength & Conditioning Journal*, 35, 7–14.

Miarka, B., Coswig, V. S., Vecchio, F. B., Brito, C. J. and Amtmann, J. 2015. Comparisons of time-motion analysis of mixed martial arts rounds by weight divisions. *International Journal of Performance Analysis in Sport*, 15, 1189–1201.

Morton, R. H., Fitzclarke, J. R. and Banister, E. W. 1990. Modeling human-performance in running. *Journal of Applied Physiology*, 69, 1171–1177.

Muller, E., Benko, U., Raschner, C. and Schwameder, H. 2000. Specific fitness training and testing in competitive sports. *Medicine & Science in Sports & Exercise*, 32, 216–220.

Murray, N. B., Gabbett, T. J., Townshend, A. D. and Blanch, P. 2016. Calculating acute: Chronic workload ratios using exponentially weighted moving averages provides a more sensitive indicator of injury likelihood than rolling averages. *British Journal of Sports Medicine*, bjsports-2016-097152.

Paavolainen, L., Häkkinen, K., Hämäläinen, I., Nummela, A. and Rusko, H. 1999. Explosive-strength training improves 5-km running time by improving running economy and muscle power. *Journal of Applied Physiology*, 86, 1527–1533.

Saw, A. E., Main, L. C. and Gastin, P. B. 2016. Monitoring the athlete training response: subjective self-reported measures trump commonly used objective measures: a systematic review. *British Journal of Sports Medicine*, 50, 281–291.

Scott, B. R., Duthie, G. M., Thornton, H. R. and Dascombe, B. J. 2016. Training monitoring for resistance exercise: theory and applications. *Sports Medicine*, 46, 687–698.

Sheppard, J., Cormack, S., Taylor, K., McGuigan, M. and Newton, R. 2008. Assessing the force-velocity characteristics of the leg extensors in well-trained athletes: the incremental load power profile. *The Journal of Strength & Conditioning Research*, 22, 1320–1326.

Stone, M. H., Keith, R., Kearney, J., Fleck, S., Wilson, G. and Triplett, N. 1991. Overtraining: a review of the signs, symptoms and possible causes. *The Journal of Strength & Conditioning Research*, 5, 35–50.

Stone, M. H., Stone, M. and Sands, W. 2007. *Principles and Practices of Resistance Training*. Windsor, Ontario: Human Kinetics.

Stray-Gundersen, J., Videman, T. and Snell, P. 1986. Changes in selected objective parameters during overtraining. *Medicine & Science in Sports & Exercise*, 18, S54.

Taylor, K., Chapman, D., Cronin, J., Newton, M. and Gill, N. 2012. Fatigue monitoring in high performance sport: a survey of current trends. *Journal of Australian Strength and Conditioning*, 20, 12–23.

Twist, C. and Highton, J. 2013. Monitoring fatigue and recovery in rugby league players. *International Journal of Sports Physiology and Performance*, 8, 467–474.

Wadley, G. and Le Rossignol, P. 1998. The relationship between repeated sprint ability and the aerobic and anaerobic energy systems. *Journal of Science and Medicine in Sport*, 1, 100–110.

Winter, E. M., Abt, G., Brookes, F. C., Challis, J. H., Fowler, N. E., Knudson, D. V., Knuttgen, H. G., Kraemer, W. J., Lane, A. M. and van Mechelen, W. 2016. Misuse of "power" and other mechanical terms in sport and exercise science research. *Journal of Strength & Conditioning Research*, 30, 292–300.

20
KARATE

James Coy, Jon Cree and Anthony Turner

Introduction

Karate is a martial art that was introduced to mainland Japan in the early 20th century. Now one of the most popular combat sports, Karate will be introduced into the Olympics for the first time at the Tokyo 2020 Games. The World Karate Federation (WKF) recognises 2 disciplines of Karate: Kata – the displaying of a sequence of movement patterns, and Kumite – actual sparring with an opponent. Within both disciplines, athletes are known as 'Karateka'. This chapter will focus on Karate Kumite, due to it being the more practiced form of Karate, which is also to be included within the next Olympics.

Within competitions, there are both Team and Individual matches – an athlete may participate in both within one competition. The team event for males consists of 5 competitors and 2 reserves, whereas the women's competition involves 3 competitors and 1 reserve. A typical competition schedule for both team and individuals involves a maximum of 5 rounds (including the final) within one day. At European and World competition level, this can increase to 6 rounds within 1 day. The final would then be usually 1–2 days later. At the point of writing, the Olympic competition schedule has not been released. Bearing the number of bouts in mind, and also the 1 day period of competition, rest periods can be as little as 5 minutes between bouts, and as much as ~ 30 minutes. Therefore appropriate recovery interventions should be employed to maximise performance.

The competition matted area for Karate Kumite spans 8 meters × 8 meters, with a 1 meter border around the edge. Referees are seated at each corner, outside of the competition area, and a fifth judge stands centered between the two competitors, maintaining a 1 m distance to enable them to have a closer view and provide directions during the bout. Bouts last 3 minutes for males, and 2 minutes for females.

Competitors must wear a white karate gi without stripes, piping or personal embroidery to prevent injury or grip-points. The jacket, when tightened around the waist with the belt, must be of a minimum length that covers the hips, but must not be more than three-quarters thigh length. Female competitors may wear a plain white T-shirt beneath the Karate jacket. Jacket ties (which are inside the jacket to prevent it opening) must be tied. Jackets without ties may not be used.

For Senior Kumite Karateka, there are 5 weight categories each for open-age males and females (see Table 20.1).

Table 20.1 Weight categories for international and Olympic Karate Kumite competitions

General & Olympic weight categories	
Male	Female
−60kg	−50kg
−67kg	−55kg
−75kg	−61kg
−84kg	−68kg
+84kg	+68kg

There are 3 primary means to scoring in Kumite, namely an 'Ippon' (3 pts), a 'Waza-Ari (2 pts), and a 'Yuko' (1 pt) – with the winner being declared based on scoring the most points during the allotted time period. The bout can also be won if a Karateka builds an 8-point difference – for example, 8–0, or 11–3. A score is awarded when a technique is performed according to the following criteria: good form, sporting attitude, vigorous application, awareness, good timing, and correct distance. An Ippon is awarded for Jodan kicks, and any scoring technique delivered on a thrown or fallen opponent. A Waza-Ari is awarded for Chudan kicks. A Yuko is awarded for a Chudan or Jodan Tsuki, and/or a Jodan or Chudan Uchi. Attacks are limited to the head, face, neck, abdomen, chest, back, and side.

This chapter will detail the movement-specific variables associated with Karate Kumite, as well as a physiological, biomechanical, and injury incidence analysis. An appropriate testing battery will be detailed, with the chapter cumulating in example programming for various levels of athletes.

Needs analysis for Karate Kumite

Time-motion characteristics

The intermittent nature of Karate is well documented. Beneke et al. (2004) observed a 2:1 activity-to-break ratio among elite Karateka (see Table 20.2). Despite Beneke et al. (2004) conceding that this intermittence owes heavily to refereeing stoppages, Chaabene et al. (2014a) reported even higher intermittence among their high-level Karateka. Their activity-to-break ratio represented 1:1.5 – a figure echoed in Chaabene et al.'s (2014b) earlier research. Unlike the latter two studies, Beneke et al.'s (2004) findings were obtained through simulated bouts, which may explain the lower intermittence. In support of this, Chaabene et al. (2014a) also obtained data from simulated bouts (not included within Table 20.2), and observed an activity-to-break ratio of 1:1 – demonstrating lower intermittence to the 1:1.5 ratio observed during their official bouts.

Regarding high intensity actions during Karate Kumite bouts, Table 20.2 demonstrates comparable findings. Individual actions were of low duration – all under 2 seconds for Chaabene et al. (2014b) and between 1 and 5s for Chaabene et al. (2014a). Iide et al. (2008) identified a total of 19.4 s (+/− 5.5 s) worth of technique combinations per 3 minute bout, with the longest enduring for 2.2 s, and the shortest for 0.2 s. It's worth noting that Koropanovski et al. (2008)

Table 20.2 Work-to-rest ratios in Karate Kumite

Author	Work (s)	Rest (s)	High intensity actions
Beneke et al. (2004)	18.6 (+/− 6)	9.6 (+/− 6)	16.3 (+/− 5.1) per bout
Chaabene et al. (2014b)	10.3 (+/− 5.0)	15.4 (+/− 5.6)	17 (+/− 7) per bout
Chaabene et al. (2014a)	10.0 (+/− 3.4)	16.2 (+/− 4.1)	14 (+/− 6) per bout

observed 89% of points during World and European Championship final matches from 2002 to 2005 as being obtained through punches – and, with VencesBrito et al. (2011) stating that the Choku-Zuki punch occurs within 0.4 s, we can begin to understand why Karate bouts are of such an intermittent nature.

It is important to note that despite the 'decisive actions' in Karate being sporadic, Karateka are continuously working at high intensities during bouts. Sterkowicz and Franchini (2009) observed that a mere 11% of 'sequences of continuous work' during European Championship bouts lasted less than 7 seconds. In fact, 80% of sequences lasted 8–50 seconds, and 9.1% lasted 51–120 seconds. In light of this, it is important to examine further which energy systems are primarily relied upon during Karate Kumite.

Physiological analysis

A 78% reliance on the aerobic energy system has been observed among elite Karateka – with just 16% reliance on the anaerobic-alactic system and 6% on the ATP-PC system (Beneke et al., 2004). In support of this data, Doria et al. (2009) produced similar findings, with their internationally ranked Kumite Karateka demonstrating a 74% dependence on the aerobic system – considerably higher than their Kata counterparts in the same study (50%). The 16% anaerobic-alactic involvement (Beneke et al., 2004) nevertheless presents a noteworthy energy contribution, and can be attributed to the intermittent high-intensity actions mentioned earlier. The regular active-recovery periods that interrupt these high-intensity actions (Karateka are continually moving even when not in engaged in contact) can therefore account for the major contribution of the aerobic system in Karate Kumite. As Tomlin and Wenger (2001) note, better aerobic fitness can also enhance recovery from high-intensity intermittent training (due to enhanced post-exercise VO^2 and blood lactate removal).

Heart rate (HR) figures recorded during Kumite bouts reinforce the argument for the inclusion of an aerobic component within Karate strength and conditioning (S&C) programmes. Chaabene et al. (2014b) observed their 14 national and international Karateka as spending 65% of their bouts over 90% of maximum HR. Imamura et al. (1996) and Chaabene et al. (2014a) submit higher figures – with mean HRs of 97% (+/− 4.2%) and 92% (of HR max) respectively. This consistently high heart rate can be attributed to the 'bouncing' movement adopted by Karateka when not engaged in high intensity actions. Other combat sports, such as boxing and Muay Thai, tend to adopt a more flat-footed stance during their periods of active-recovery. Regarding beats per minute (bpm), Imamura et al. (1996) and Iide et al. (2008) both observed mean HRs of between 160bpm (+/− 12.8) and 193bpm (+/− 8). In light of this data, strength and conditioning practitioners should consider aerobic conditioning interventions that are both intermittent and consistently demanding on HR.

Biomechanical analysis

Chaabene et al. (2014b) measured the movements of 14 elite Karateka during a national-level competition, and observed that 76% of 'techniques' were thrown with upper limbs. Of these upper limb movements, 74% were in the form of the Kizami-Zuki punch (Chaabene et al., 2014b). In line with this, Koropanovski et al. (2008) calculated that punches secured 89.09% of all points during 55 World Championship bouts – with kicks contributing just 8.36% of points. The predominance of upper limb use may therefore be attributed to their higher probability of obtaining points (compared to lower limbs). In further support of upper limb predominance, Jovanovic (1992) reported that the Kizami-Zuki takes just 110ms to perform. Having detailed the movement specific elements, the most common point scoring motions are explained in more detail.

During the execution of a Kizami-Zuki, power is primarily generated through a hip turn and arm extension (Arus, 2008). The hip turn relies heavily on the obliques – whilst the subsequent body drive principally engages the gluteus maximus, gastrocnemius, and quadriceps. The pronation of the palms during a Kizami-Zuki, ensure that the radius and ulna are mechanically firmer and less elastic (Link and Chou, 2011). VencesBrito et al. (2011) analysed the kinematic and electromyographic (EMG) patterns of another commonly used punch – the Choku-Zuki. VencesBrito et al. (2011) in turn analysed the muscular activity of the muscles involved in the arm extension of the punch – measuring the EMG of 9 upper body muscles. The biceps brachii showed greater intensity of activation than the forearm muscles (pronator teres and brachioradialis).

Although this breakdown allows for an analysis of which muscles are predominantly employed within key Karate movements, it is important for S&C practitioners to ensure that programming also includes sufficient coverage on the muscle groups used in the deceleration phase of movements. With techniques being thrown at such high speeds, both the agonist and antagonist muscles should be well conditioned, to minimise the risk of injury. Increasing antagonist muscle strength has also been suggested to increase movement speed, and accuracy of movement (Jaric et al., 1995). For example, within Karate, the hamstring muscles are employed to a greater extent than the quadriceps during the deceleration phase of a kick (Sbricolli et al., 2010). Although kicking techniques aren't used as frequently, they can prove the highest scoring techniques when executed successfully. The Mae-Geri (front kick) will therefore be analysed in more detail.

The Mae-Geri sequence requires participation of the torso, pelvis, knee, ankle, and foot (VencesBrito et al., 2014). During the hip rotation of the Mae-Geri, the foot accelerates at

Figure 20.1 Kizami–Zuki sequence

Figure 20.2 Mae-Geri sequence

approximately 108 m/s², and drops to around 78 m/s² during the lower leg movement – reaching a final velocity of approximately 19 m/s (Gianino, 2010). Research into the kinematic and EMG characteristics of the Mae-Geri is scarce (VencesBrito et al., 2014) – as is data on flexibility and the required range of movements within Karate techniques in general (Chaabene et al., 2012). The angles of the hip, knee, and ankle upon contact of a Mae-Geri have, however, been reported – and were 69° (+/– 26), 131° (+/– 8), and 98° (+/– 9) respectively (VencesBrito et al., 2014). Research on the time taken to execute the Mae-Geri is more readily available.

Males (892ms +/– 103ms) have been reported to execute the Mae-Geri faster than females (1047ms +/– 157ms); however, there was no link between speed and standing height (Sforza et al., 2002) – the fastest and the slowest males were the two shortest. Similar results were reported by Pozo et al. (2011), with their international level athletes completing the Mae-Geri faster (991ms +/– 93ms) than the national athletes (1139ms +/– 72ms). International athletes also demonstrated higher repeatability of execution time – although there was no difference in the impact force of kicks between internationals and nationals. This indicates that more emphasis should be placed on improving the speed of kicks (as opposed to force of the kick upon contact), in order for the strike to make contact before the opponent's does.

Incidence of injury

Table 20.3 presents a summary of the data collected in major studies assessing the nature of injuries within Karate.

Incidence of injury

Injury rates within Karate are generally high, with between 0.24 and 0.31 injuries per bout reported in a number of studies (Macan et al., 2001; Tuominen, 1995; Stricevic et al., 1983; McLatchie, 1976; Arriaza and Leyes, 2005; Johannsen and Noerregaard, 1988). Only two studies within Table 20.3 (Critchley et al., 1999; Macan et al., 2006) reported figures of below 0.24 injuries per bout. Furthermore, within Kujala et al.'s (1995) multi-sport injury analysis, Karate fared higher (142 injuries per 1000 person years of exposure) than all other sports investigated, including soccer (89), ice-hockey (94), and Judo (117). Despite the relatively high injury rate, Karate is nevertheless seen as a relatively safe sport, due to the minor nature of these injuries.

The majority of research has identified the head and face as the most common location for injuries in Karate Kumite (Muller-Rath et al., 2000; Stricevic et al., 1983; Critchley et al., 1999; McLatchie, 1976; Arriaza and Leyes, 2005; Macan et al., 2006). Most notably, Macan et al. (2001) and Tuominen (1995) reported that 97% and 95% of injuries recorded in their

Table 20.3 Review of literature on incidence of injury in Karate

Author	Participants	Injuries	Location of injuries	Causation of injuries
Macan et al. (2001)	Competitive Croatian pupils (10–14), Juniors (15–21), Seniors (18+)	206 in 880 bouts. Pupils – M: 17.1%/F: 20.7%, Juniors – M: 27%/F: 21.1%, Seniors – M: 26.7%/F: 21.8%	Most frequent localisation was head. 97% of injuries were 'minor'	Punches most common in all groups. Kicks more common in pupils (29%) than Seniors (11.9%)
Tuominen (1995)	647 competitors in 450 Finnish national bouts (6 competitions)	0.28 injuries per bout. 104 of 647 participants injured (16%)	95% of injuries were to the head	Most injuries from direct punch to the head
Muller-Rath et al. (2000)	392 bouts at the 1999 World Championships	142 participants suffered 168 injuries. More injuries in matches with fist padding (146/302–48%) than without (23/90–26%)	141 (84%) were bruises of the head and throat	Most injuries (152) caused by punches, with only 17 through kicks
Zetaruk et al. (2000a)	114 mixed-ability club members (mean age 27; 78% male)	87 (76%) reported injuries in past 12 months, but only 30% required time off training	No data	46.9% strains/sprains, 34% bruises, 10.9% lacerations, 8.2% fractures/dislocations
Stricevic et al. (1983)	284 participants in 309 matches, during 3 National and 3 International competitions	82 injuries by 76 athletes (27%). 1 injury every 3.7 bouts, or 0.3 injuries per bout	48 injuries to the head and face, 14 to lower extremity, and 10 to upper	65 caused by punches, 17 by kicks. 33 bruises (40%), 20 lacerations (24%)
Destombe et al. (2006)	186 participants from 3 French clubs (76% male; 43% beginners, 24.7% fairly experienced, 32.3% experienced; mean age 19.6 – ranged from 6–53 years)	48 (28.8%) had 83 injuries in past year – 63 in training, 20 in competition. Rates were similar between sexes, but increased with age	26.5% of injuries were to the head, 28.9% to upper limbs, 35% to lower limbs, and 9.6% to the torso	53% of injuries were bruises, and 19% were sprains. Sparring contributed 82.5% of injuries in training. 69.7% of bruises occurred while blocking or receiving a strike. Strikes were responsible for 87.5% of all sprains
Critchley et al. (1999)	1273 competitors in 1770 British Championship bouts (1996, 1997, and 1998)	160 injuries – 0.09 per bout, and 0.13 per competitor	57% of injuries were to the head, and 37.5% to the limbs	73 bruises/lacerations to the head, 36 to the legs, and 19 to the arms. 12 concussions – only 1 of which lost consciousness. Most facial injuries through blow to the malar region
McLatchie (1976)	295 competitive Scottish bouts	In 25% of contents there was an injury, and in 10% of contests the injury caused withdrawal. 80 participants suffered an injury. 75% of injuries occurred to those in grades below brown belt	33 injuries (41%) to the face, 25 (31%) to the trunk, and 22 (28%) to the limbs	The most common causative factor was blows to the stomach (18)

Zetaruk et al. (2000b)	68 6–16 year old club members	28% (19) sustained at least 1 injury per year – all injuries were minor	58% were bruises, 26% sprains or strains, and 16% were 'winded'
Arriaza and Leyes (2005)	2837 matches in the '96, '98, '00 World Championships	891 injuries – 0.31 injuries per bout. Incidences higher in lighter categories – 0.56 for male -60kg, and 0.42 for female -53kg	Punches caused 82.7% of injuries; kicks caused 7.3%. Bruises were the most common injury (50.3%), followed by nosebleeds (16.2%), lacerations (13.7%), concussions (3.8%), and sprains (3.5%)
Johannsen and Noerregaard (1988)	2 Danish Championships with knuckle protection ('83 and '86–290 matches), and 2 Danish Championships without knuckle protection ('84 and '85–620 matches)	With knuckle protection, 0.26 injuries were suffered per bout (by 24% of participants); without knuckle protection, 0.25 injuries were suffered per bout (by 30% of participants)	In both types of competition, head and face injuries were most common (92% of injuries with protection, and 78% without protection), followed by extremities (4% and 16%), and trunk (4% in both)
			In both types of competition, bruises were the most common injury (68% of injuries with protection, and 44% of injuries without protection), followed by lacerations (12% and 24%), nosebleeds (10% and 12%), TKOs (10% and 11%), and fractures (1.4% and 9%)
Macan et al. (2006)	The 1997 (887 matches – 287 female; 600 male) and 2002 (1604 matches – 498 female; 1106 male) Croatian Karate competition seasons	0.23 injuries per bout in 1997 (208 injuries in 887 fights), and 0.16 injuries per bout in 2002 (254 injuries in 1604 bouts). 10.28 and 9.82 injuries per 100 exposure minutes, respectively.	The injury locations were as follows (1997 data followed by 2002 data – all presented as injuries per 100 exposure minutes): head (8.05; 4.1), legs (0.54; 3.33), trunk (0.9; 1.51), arms (0.4; 0.66), and neck (0.59; 0.23)
			No data
Kujala et al. (1995)	621,691 person years of exposure in Finland between 1987 and 1991, in soccer, ice hockey, volleyball, basketball, Judo, and Karate	Injuries per 1000 person years of exposure: volleyball: 60, basketball: 88, soccer: 89, ice hockey: 94, Judo: 117, and Karate: 142	37.3% of Karate injuries to lower limbs (11% knees; 10.7% feet), 26.3% to upper limbs (9.3% fingers, 6.1% upper arm/shoulders, 6% palm/wrist), and 36.3% to other sites (10.9% head/neck, 9.7% back, and 6.4% teeth)
			No data

Table 20.4 Battery of fitness tests suitable for Karate athletes

Parameter	Test
Body fat	**Skinfold assessment**. Karateka compete in weight classes; therefore, fat levels should be regulated in order to minimise 'non-functional' mass.
Lower body power	**Countermovement jump**. A jump mat can record timing in the air, and jump height. Following familiarisation with the test, a mean score of 3 attempts should be taken.
Power	**1RM power clean**. This test evaluates an athlete's strength speed; however, it should only be included once technique is of a sufficient standard.
Upper body power	**Bench press throw**. Peak power (w) can be measured if a transducer is attached to the barbell. Optimal load of 55% of Bench press max for maximum power output during bench press throws (Baker et al., 2001).
Lower body strength	**1RM back squat**. The back squat is recognised as the primary measure for lower body strength.
Agility	**4-2-2-4 shuttle** (Turner et al., 2016). This must be completed in a karate stance (one foot leading) with the athlete always facing forwards. The athlete sprints out to the 4m line; returns 2m backwards; sprints 2m forward; returns 4m backwards to the start line. The athlete must ensure that both feet cross behind the start line after each shuttle, and some part of the lead foot must cross the 2m and 4m lines with each shuttle.
Aerobic fitness	**Karate specific aerobic test (KSAT)** (Nunan, 2006; Chaabene et al., 2012). Athletes complete a set sequence of kicks and punches on a suspended bag. The set time to complete this sequence of movements is 7 seconds. Athletes will repeat this protocol (still within 7 seconds); however, the rest times will gradually decrease with each bout – as in the multi-stage fitness test. The protocol consists of a lead straight punch, a rear leg roundhouse kick, a rear straight punch, and a lead leg roundhouse kick – repeated twice.

respective studies were to the head and face. Nevertheless, the majority of studies within Table 20.3 (of which include data on the nature of injuries) recognise bruising – minor in contrast to many sporting injuries – as the most frequent injury (Muller-Rath et al., 2000; Johannsen and Noerregaard, 1988; Zetaruk et al., 2000a; Destombe et al., 2006; Arriaza and Leyes, 2005; Stricevic et al., 1983). Strains, sprains, lacerations, and epistaxis were other commonly noted injuries.

Few studies analysed the direct contribution of punches and kicks to injuries; however, those that did (Muller-Rath et al., 2000; Stricevic et al., 1983; Arriaza and Leyes, 2005) reported between 79% and 90% of injuries as being caused by punches. This high percentage of injuries that are caused by punches corresponds with Chaabene et al.'s (2014b) observation, that 76% of 'techniques' are thrown with upper limbs. In summary, research shows that the majority of injuries suffered within Karate bouts are directly caused by opponent strikes, which limits the impact that strength and conditioning professionals can have on reducing injuries. Nevertheless, Zetaruk et al. (2000a) found that experience, training, and rank were a significant predictor of injury (risk of injury increased approximately three times with each additional year of experience). This can be attributed to the greater speed and force of techniques seen in more advanced Karateka. In order to maximise a Karateka's prospect of avoiding an opponent's strike, strength and conditioning professionals should ensure that programming includes sufficient content on power, speed, and agility – through both plyometric and loaded strength-speed exercises.

Example strength and conditioning sessions for karate

Based on the needs analysis conducted and a review of prevalent injuries, 2 appropriate strength and conditioning sessions have been outlined below (Table 20.5 and Table 20.6). The beginner and advanced sessions refer to strength and conditioning experience, not karate experience. The beginner sessions aims to get the athlete building a base of strength and power, through derivatives of the Olympic lifts and basic leg and back exercises. Exercises are performed at a low intensity, with a focus on developing technique. The advanced session assumes a sufficient base of technique, and therefore exercises are performed at a higher intensity, with lower volume. More complexes are included within the advanced session, with a focus on developing power in a lateral

Table 20.5 Beginner power and strength session

Exercise	Sets	Reps	Pointers
Clean high pull	3	3	Low load
Back squat	3	10	65%
Single-arm medicine ball throw	3	6 p/arm	Use sand-filled ball; throw against wall
Lunges/lunge jumps > lateral med ball slams	3	8 + 6	Lunge and slam the ball, then rotate 180° and repeat
Cable row	3	6 p/arm	Powerful concentric, controlled eccentric

Table 20.6 Advanced power and strength session

Exercise	Sets	Reps	Pointers
Power clean	4	2	80%
Back squat	3	6	80%
180° box jumps > Russian twist throws	3	4 + 8	Ensure both sides are worked equally
Single-arm 'scissor' landmine press > scissor lunges	3	6 + 6	See Figure 20.3
Pull ups > nordic curls	3	6 + 6	Focus on controlled eccentrics

Figure 20.3 Single-arm 'scissor' landmine press

Table 20.7 Periodisation of International English Karate athlete

Month	Jan	Feb	Mar Apr May Jun Jul	Aug	Sep Oct Nov	Dec
Phase	Specific prep		Competition	Trans	General prep	Specific
Focus	Specific strength, aerobic, & power		Power; plyometrics; strength; technique	Active Rest	Aerobic; Hypertrophy	Specific strength, aerobic, & power
Intensity	Medium		High	Low	Low/medium	Medium
Volume	Medium/high		Low	Low	High	Med/high

as well as frontal plane. As the sessions outlined below are power and strength sessions, no aerobic conditioning has been mentioned. As discussed within the needs analysis, aerobic conditioning for karate should be intermittent in nature; therefore, a tabata format would be appropriate.

Longitudinal programme design

The aim of this section is to present an example yearly schedule, and explain the role of the strength and conditioning coach within it. The programme (see Table 20.7) is from an elite level athlete; however, the principles still apply to the majority of karate athletes, due to the regular intervals of competitions during the competitive season.

The key difference between the karate programme featured in Table 20.7 and other sporting macrocycles is the structure of the competitive phase. Unlike most footballers or rugby players, Karateka are not competing weekly or bi-weekly during their competitive phases. During the competitive phases within karate there is generally 1 competition per month, which is normally contested over a weekend. An exception to this would be the World Championships, which generally last for 1 week.

The 2 sessions outlined above have been adapted from the specific preparatory phase. These can be characterised by a compound power and strength exercise (in this instance the power clean and back squat), followed by sport-specific strength and power exercises of a moderate intensity and volume. Due to the irregularity of competitions during the competitive phase, session content during this phase may not actually differ hugely from that which is featured in the specific preparatory phase – especially if 3 or so weeks out from a competition. As the competitive phase constitutes a significant part of the macrocycle (almost half a year in duration), it is important to strike the balance of not exhausting the athlete with volume while ensuring that gaps within the competition schedule are utilised appropriately and not wasted. The greatest amount of training volume will be within the general preparatory phase, where less focus will be on the specificity of the exercise and more on building an optimum base of fitness, strength, and, if required, hypertrophy.

Conclusion

Karate is a highly intermittent sport, with frequent high-intensity but low-duration actions. Even when not directly engaged in these 'actions', athletes are continuously working at a high intensity. This is reflected in research that has reported Karateka's mean heart rates to be above 90% of maximum (Imamura et al., 1996; Chaabene et al., 2014a). The regular active-recovery periods that interrupt the high-intensity actions can account for the 70%+ contribution of the aerobic system reported by Beneke et al. (2004) and Doria et al. (2009).

Within Karate, 76% of techniques are thrown with upper limbs (Chaabene et al., 2014b). This is reflected in Koropanovski et al.'s (2008) calculations – that punches secured 89.09% of all points during 55 World Championship bouts. The predominance of upper limb use may be attributed to the higher probability of punches obtaining points, and also the speed at which punches can be executed. The Kizami-Zuki punch can be completed within 110ms (Jovanovic, 1992, cited in Chaabene et al., 2014a), whereas the Mae Geri front kick has been reported to take between 721ms and 1308ms to execute (Sforza et al., 2002).

Injury rates within Karate are generally high – however due to the minor nature of these injuries, Karate is seen as a relatively safe sport. Bruises are widely reported as the most common injury (Muller-Rath et al., 2000; Johannsen and Noerregaard, 1988; Zetaruk et al., 2000a; Destombe et al., 2006; Arriaza and Leyes, 2005; Stricevic et al., 1983), with the head and face recognised as the most common location for injuries (Muller-Rath et al., 2000; Stricevic et al., 1983; Critchley et al., 1999; McLatchie, 1976; Arriaza and Leyes, 2005; Macan et al., 2006). Higher injury rates have been associated with more experienced Karateka (Zetaruk et al., 2000a), probably due to the greater speed and force of techniques seen in more advanced Karateka.

References

Arriaza, R. and Leyes, M. (2005). Injury profile in competitive karate: Prospective analysis of three consecutive world karate championships. *Knee Surgery, Sports Traumatology, Arthroscopy*, 13(7), 603–607.

Arus, E. (2008). *Sendo-ryu karate-do: The way of initiative* (2nd ed.). Santa Fe, NM: Turtle Press.

Baker, D., Nance, S. and Moore, M. (2001). The load that maximizes the average mechanical power output during explosive bench press throws in highly trained athletes. *Journal of Strength & Conditioning Research*, 15(1), 20–24.

Beneke, R., Beyer, T., Jachner, C., Erasmus, J. and Hutler, M. (2004). Energetics of karate kumite. *European Journal of Applied Physiology*, 92(4–5), 518–523.

Chaabene, H., Franchini, E., Miarka, B., Amin Selmi, M., Mkaouer, B. and Chamari, K. (2014b). Time-motion analysis: Physiological and rate of perceived exertion to karate combats: Is there a difference between winners and defeated karatekas? *International Journal of Sports Physiology and Performance*, 9, 302–308.

Chaabene, H., Hachana, Y., Franchini, E., Mkaouer, B. and Chamari, K. (2012). Physical and physiological profile of elite karate athletes. *Sports Medicine*, 42(10), 829–843.

Chaabene, H., Mkaouer, B., Franchini, E., Souissi, N., Amine Selmi, M., Nagra, Y. and Chamari, K. (2014a). Physiological responses and performance analysis difference between official and simulated karate combat conditions. *Asian Journal of Sports Medicine*, 5(1), 21–29.

Critchley, G.R., Mannion, S. and Meredith, C. (1999). Injury rates in shotokan karate. *British Journal of Sports Medicine*, 33(3), 174–177.

Destombe, C., Lejeune, L., Guillodo, Y., Roudaut, A., Jousse, S., Devauchelle, V. and Saraux, A. (2006). Incidence and nature of karate injuries. *Joint Bone Spine*, 73(2), 182–188.

Doria, C., Veicsteinas, A., Limonta, E., Maggioni, M.A., Aschieri, P., Eusebi, F., Fano, G. and Pietrangelo, T. (2009). Energetics of karate (kata and kumite techniques) in top-level athletes. *European Journal of Applied Physiology*, 107(5), 603–610.

Gianino, C. (2010). Physics of karate. Kinematics analysis of karate techniques by a digital movie camera. *Latin-American Journal of Physics Education*, 4(1), 32–34.

Iide, K., Imamura, H., Yoshimura, Y., Yamashita, A., Miyahara, K., Miyamoto, N. and Moriwaki, C. (2008). Physiological responses of simulated karate sparring matches in young men and boys. *Journal of Strength and Conditioning Research*, 22(3), 839–844.

Imamura, H., Yoshimura, Y., Uchida, K., Tanaka, A., Nishimura, S. and Nakazawa, A.T. (1996). Heart rate response and perceived exertion during twenty consecutive karate sparring matches. *Australian Journal of Science and Medicine in Sport*, 28(4), 114–115.

Jaric, S., Ropret, R., Kukolj, M. and Ilic, D.B. (1995). Role of agonist and antagonist muscle strength in performance of rapid movements. *European Journal of Applied Physiology and Occupational Physiology*, 71(5), 464–468.

Johannsen, H.V. and Noerregaard, F.O. (1988). Prevention of injury in karate. *British Journal of Sports Medicine*, 22(3), 113–115.

Jovanovic, S. (1992). *Karate 1 – Theoretic approach*. Novi Sad: Sport's world.

Koropanovski, N., Dopsaj, M. and Jovanovic, S. (2008). Characteristics of pointing actions of top male competitors in karate at world and European level. *Brazilian Journal of Biomotricity*, 2(4), 241–251.

Kujala, U.M., Taimela, S., Anitta-Poika, I., Orava, S., Tuominen, R. and Myllynen, P. (1995). Acute injuries in soccer, ice hockey, volleyball, basketball, judo, and karate: Analysis of national registry data. *The British Medical Journal*, 311(7018), 1465–1468.

Link, N. and Chou, L. (2011). *The anatomy of martial arts: An illustrated guide to the muscles used for each strike, kick, and throw* (1st ed.). CA: Ulysses Press.

Macan, J., Bundalo-Vrbanac, D. and Romic, G. (2001). The prevalence and distribution of injuries in karate (kumite). *Kinesiology*, 33(1), 137–145.

Macan, J., Bundalo-Vrbanac, D. and Romic, G. (2006). Effects of the new karate rules on the incidence and distribution of injuries. *British Journal of Sports Medicine*, 40(4), 326–330.

McLatchie, G.R. (1976). Analysis of karate injuries sustained in 295 contests. *Injury: The British Journal of Accident Surgery*, 8(2), 132–134.

Muller-Rath, R., Bolte, S., Peterson, P. and Mommsen, U. (2000). Injury profile in modern competitive karate – Analysis of 1999 WKC karate world championship games in Bochum. *Sportverletz Sportschaden*, 14(1), 20–24.

Nunan, D. (2006). Development of a sports specific aerobic capacity test for karate – A pilot study. *Journal of Sports Science & Medicine*, 5, 47–53.

Pozo, J., Bastien, G. and Dierick, F. (2011). Execution time, kinetics, and kinematics of the mae-geri kick: Comparison of national and international standard karate athletes. *Journal of Sports Sciences*, 29(14), 1553–1561.

Sbricolli, P., Camomilla, V., Di Mario, A., Quinzi, F., Figura, F. and Felici, F. (2010). Neuromuscular control adaptations in elite athletes: The case of top level Karateka. *European Journal of Applied Physiology*, 108(6), 1269–1280.

Sforza, C., Turci, M., Grassi, G.P., Shirai, Y.F., Pizzini, G. and Ferrario, V.F. (2002). Repeatability of mae-geri-keage in traditional karate: A three-dimensional analysis with black-belt Karateka. *Perceptual and Motor Skills*, 95(2), 433–444.

Sterkowicz, S. and Franchini, E. (2009). Testing motor fitness in karate. *Archives of Budo*, 5, 29–34.

Stricevic, M.V., Patel, M.R., Okazaki, T. and Swain, B.K. (1983). Karate: Historical perspective and injuries sustained in national and international tournament competitions. *The American Journal of Sports Medicine*, 11(5), 320–324.

Tomlin, D.L. and Wenger, H.A. (2001). The relationship between aerobic fitness and recovery from high intensity intermittent exercise. *Sports Medicine*, 31(1), 1–11.

Tuominen, R. (1995). Injuries in national karate competitions in Finland. *Scandinavian Journal of Medicine & Science in Sports*, 5(1), 44–48.

Turner, A.N., Bishop, C., Chavda, S., Edwards, M., Brazier, J. and Kilduff, L.P. (2016). Physical characteristics underpinning lunging and change of direction speed in fencing. *Journal of Strength and Conditioning Research*, 30(8), 2235–2241.

VencesBrito, A.M., Branco, M.A.C., Fernandes, R.M.C., Ferreira, M.A.R., Fernandes, O.J.S.M., Figueiredo, A.A.A. and Branco, G. (2014). Characterisation of kinesiological patterns of the front kick, mae-geri, in karate experts and non-karate practitioners. *Revista de Artes Marciales Asiaticas*, 9(1), 20–31.

VencesBrito, A.M., Rodrigues Ferreira, M.A., Cortes, N., Fernandes, O. and Pezarat-Correia, P. (2011). Kinematic and electromyographic analysis of a karate punch. *Journal of Electromyography and Kinesiology*, 21, 1023–1029.

Zetaruk, M.N., Violan, M.A., Zurakowski, D. and Micheli, L.J. (2000b). Karate injuries in children and adolescents. *Accident Analysis and Prevention*, 32(3), 421–425.

Zetaruk, M.N., Zurakowski, D., Violan, M.A. and Micheli, L.J. (2000a). Safety recommendations in shotokan karate. *Clinical Journal of Sports Medicine*, 10(2), 117–122.

21
TAEKWONDO

Rhys Ingram, Ailish McLaughlin and Yana Radcliffe

Introduction

Taekwondo is a martial art originating in Korea in the 1940s and 1950s having been developed from more ancient Korean martial arts that are thousands of years old. The name derives from the words Tae, "to stomp, trample" or "foot"; Kwon, "fist"; and Do, "way, discipline". As such Taekwondo translates to the "way of the foot and fist".

Taekwondo has branched off into different styles and disciplines over its history, with Kukkiwon-style, often known by the acronym of the World Taekwondo federation (WT), being the chosen style of the Olympic Games. Taekwondo was an exhibition event in the 1988 Olympic Games in Seoul, South Korea, before joining the full Olympic programme at the 2000 Olympic Games in Sydney, Australia. Taekwondo, like many other fight sports, is divided up into weight categories, with 8 weight categories in both men and women's events at most senior competitions except the Olympics, where there are only 4 for each (Table 21.1). Weigh-ins for athletes occur the day preceding their fight day, allowing the athlete approximately 12–24 hours between weigh-in and their first fight. This has implications for the fighters 'true' fight weight on the competition day and the way in which they make weight for the weigh-ins, which will be discussed later in the chapter.

During competition, WTF Taekwondo athletes can score either by kicking or punching the torso, or kicking to the head (high section). Athletes wear an electronic chest protector (hogu) that registers the power of strikes so that they can score points. The higher the weight class of the athlete, the higher the threshold is for them to register a scoring shot on the torso. Similarly the headguards have pressure sensors in them that register when a kick has been scored, with shots to the face, where the headguard doesn't cover, being scored via referee decision or video replay. The number of points that are awarded is dependent on the action performed; 1 point is awarded to punches, 2 points for straight kicks to the torso, 3 points go to athletes performing turning kicks to the torso and straight kicks to the head, and finally 4 points earned by turning kicks to the head. An athlete is able to win a fight in a number of different ways. The most common way is via a points win at the end of the full 3 rounds; if, however, the scores are equal at the end of the 3 rounds, an additional 'golden point' 1 minute round will be added that can only be won by a scoring punch or kick or by 2 Gam-Jeoms being conceded. Fights can also be won by disqualification due to the opponent conceding 10 Gam-Jeoms during a fight or by creating a gap greater than

Table 21.1 Weight categories

General weight categories		Olympic weight categories	
Male(kg)	Female(kg)	Male(kg)	Female(kg)
− 54	− 46	− 58	− 49
− 58	− 49		
− 63	− 53	− 68	− 57
− 68	− 57		
− 74	− 63	− 80	− 67
− 80	− 67		
− 87	− 73	80 +	67 +
87 +	73 +		

20 points. Deduction penalties (Gam-Jeoms) can also be scored against an athlete and are given for any foul play, such as an athlete touching the ground with any part of their body other than their foot, punching the opponent in the face or being disrespectful to the referee.

Taekwondo matches are fought over 3 rounds of 2 minutes, with a 1 minute break between each round where the athlete returns to their corner and is able to sit down with their coach. As of 2014, elite level Taekwondo is fought within a matted Octagonal ring, measuring 8 metres in diameter between each facing side, with each side measuring 3.3 metres. Athletes will usually have 5 fights in order to win a gold medal at a competition depending on the weight division and gender, although this can be as high as 7 in some larger tournaments; the Olympics typically requires 4 fights to achieve a Gold Medal. The rest time between each match on competition days varies but can typically be anywhere between 45 minutes and 3 hours.

Physical characteristics

Taekwondo is characterised by bursts of high intensity, explosive actions, interspersed by short periods of lower intensity work. During the lower intensity work the fighters aim to manage their distance from the opponent and look for scoring opportunities. The high technical and tactical demands placed on the athletes, alongside the relative importance of kicking to the high section, results in athletes spending large periods of training time at what in most sports would be deemed extreme ranges of motion. Therefore any strength and conditioning programme a Taekwondo athlete undertakes must be holistic in its approach and prepare them to perform with skill and precision at these ranges. Moreover, modern elite Taekwondo athletes are required to be close to competition fitness, year round. The Taekwondo calendar usually revolves around one major championship a year held in May/June, such as the Olympic Games, World Championships or Zonal Championships (i.e. European Championships). Leading up to this competition there are a number of smaller international competitions where athletes can score ranking points with a goal of qualifying and being selected to go by their nation. From August to December there is then the WTF Grand Prix Series: a series of three competitions where only the top ranked athletes in the world are invited to compete, culminating in a Grand Prix Final held in December. This year-round competition schedule limits the ability for an athlete to focus too heavily on general training qualities for too long, and so a performance focus must be retained throughout the year. Figure 21.1 shows what we believe the 2017 calendar will look like at the time of writing. It clearly shows the large volume of ranking competitions it is possible for an athlete to

Competition focus	World Championships (South Korea) - June 2017																									
Month	January				February				March				April				May					June				
Date week commencing	02/01/17	09/01/17	16/01/17	23/01/17	30/01/17	06/02/17	13/02/17	20/02/17	27/02/17	06/03/17	13/03/17	20/03/17	27/03/17	03/04/17	10/04/17	17/04/17	24/04/17	01/05/17	08/05/17	15/05/17	22/05/17	29/05/17	05/06/17	12/06/17	19/06/17	26/06/17
Phase	GENERAL PHASE					COMP PHASE						GENERAL				COMP PHASE										
WTF ranking comps			German Open		US Open	Euro Clubs	Luxor & Turkey	Slovenia & Fujairah	Bulgaria & Qatar	Dutch Open	Belgium Open				Fajr Open	Mexican Open	Presidents Cup		Ukraine Open	Moldova Open		Austrian Open	Luxemburg Open			World championships
Competition focus	Grand Prix season																									

Month	July					August			September					October				November					December			
Date week commencing	03/07/17	10/07/17	17/07/17	24/07/17	31/07/17	07/08/17	14/08/17	21/08/17	28/08/17	04/09/17	11/09/17	18/09/17	25/09/17	02/10/17	09/10/17	16/10/17	13/10/17	30/10/17	06/11/17	13/11/17	20/11/17	27/11/17	04/12/17	11/12/17	18/12/17	25/12/17
Phase	GENERAL PHASE					COMP PHASE																	GENERAL			
WTF ranking comps	Chuncheon Open						Ghana Open	Grand Prix	Universiade	Olympic Cat Euros	Poland & Russia	Grand Prix	Canada Open	Latvia Open	Serbian Open	Grand Prix		Greece Open	Croatia Open		Israel Open	Grand Prix Final				

Figure 21.1 The 2017 competition calendar

attend. Our programme identifies two key 'selection competitions' before the first major of the year, indicated here in dark orange, and then the Major Competitions, which account for the largest amount of ranking points, can be seen in red. We have also included an example of how we would phase the athletes' training throughout this type of calendar, with General Phase blocks of training versus Competition Phase blocks, devoted to training general physical qualities both in technical sessions and strength and conditioning (S&C), and longer blocks of performance focussed training, where fatigue is carefully managed to allow athletes to perform their best at competitions.

General Phases tend to be very short, so our ability to focus on developing significant changes in athlete's physical capacities is very limited. Instead the focus shifts to increasing the athlete's tolerance to training volume, both physically and technically, whilst reducing the amount of time the athletes spend training specific competitive scenarios such as sparring. From an S&C perspective we have more training time in the week that we can devote towards metabolic conditioning, rehabilitation or anything else that that individual might need after completing the last block of competitions.

As we move into the Competition Phase, more of the training week is devoted to technical and tactical training on the mat with only two to three focussed S&C sessions per athlete. Taekwondo sessions begin to more closely replicate the intensity found at competition, with a greater emphasis on competitive scenarios. Within the S&C sessions, again intensity comes to the fore with an increased focus on the individual 'need to have' characteristics rather than the 'nice to haves'. This may include an increase in plyometric-type activities, strength in sport specific ranges of motion, and an increase in the need for programmed recovery to allow the athlete to recover efficiently from the training so as to realise their performance potential.

Athletic demands

Needs analysis

Characteristics of competition

As previously mentioned, Taekwondo players will compete over three 2 minute rounds for between 3 and 4 fights during a medal winning performance. These rounds will see short bursts of high intensity activity (1–5 s) interspersed with longer periods of non-fighting activity. Work to rest ratios can range from 1:2 to 1:7 in different styles. During bouts they can reach near maximal heart rates and produce high blood lactate concentrations (7.0–12.2 mmol 1^{-1}) (Bridge et al., 2014). Taekwondo players predominantly utilise kicks to score on their opponents, despite also being allowed to punch to the body. At the Sydney Olympic Games, 98% of score shots were kicks (Kazemi et al., 2006) with unpublished data showing that London 2012 and Rio 2016 were perhaps weighted even more in favour of kicks.

Anthropometry

Since the rules changed to create a scoring bias towards headshots, we have seen an increased tendency towards Taekwondo players attempting to reach the lowest weight category possible, to utilise their relative height advantage (Table 21.2). As a result many of our athletes aim for extremely low body fat percentages and a predominance of muscle mass focussed on the lower limb rather than upper body, which is of relatively little use to them. Males and females should aim for a skinfold sum of 8 total of 40–60mm and 60–80mm, respectively.

Weight making strategy

Weight making strategies for Taekwondo vary greatly from athlete to athlete. Weigh-ins for all international competitions take place the day before the athlete is due to fight with no further checks on the fight day to establish how much the athlete actually weighs as they step onto the mat. Also, all fights take place on the same day, so athletes only need to achieve their weight once for each competition. This allows athletes to lose more weight than in some other fight sports where they have to maintain a certain weight for a number of days or weeks such as

Table 21.2 Height across weight category

Weight category	Average height (standard deviation) – Manchester Grand Prix, 2013(cm)	Average height (standard deviation) – Rio Olympic Games, 2016(cm)
F –49	162.0 (3.9)	167.9 (3.6)
F –57	169.1 (5.1)	170.6 (5.8)
F –67	173.1 (3.8)	176.2 (3.0)
F 67+	176.0 (4.5)	177.6 (6.1)
M –58	172.3 (6.2)	179.1 (6.7)
M –68	180.1 (4.0)	181.9 (6.2)
M –80	185.1 (4.6)	189.8 (4.9)
M 80+	189.0 (5.3)	195.1 (5.9)

Olympic Boxing. Also, in some Olympic sports, the athletes can now be reweighed on the day of the fights to ensure that they have not put on too much weight in the hours since weigh-in, indicating that they may have undergone dangerous levels of dehydration to achieve the fight weight required; this is not currently the case in Taekwondo. Historically these factors have meant that many athletes would live and train day to day at a weight significantly higher than they would look to compete at. This issue has been further exacerbated by the loss of half the possible weight categories for the Olympic Games, which results in many of the top athletes having to decide whether to try to qualify their place for the Games at a weight category either much lighter than normal or risk fighting athletes that could be appreciably heavier than them on the day. For example, a male Taekwondo athlete who normally competes in the −74kg class may live and train at 78kg or more. A 4kg weight cut for these competitions may not present much of a challenge; however, for an Olympic Games this athlete would have to consider either fighting at −80kg, which could mean competing against athletes who are at the very least 2kg heavier than them once on the fight mat – but more likely they will be heavier than this. Or they will have to attempt to reach the −68kg category, losing 10kg for the weigh-in day. This obviously poses a huge challenge, especially whilst trying to balance the need for high performance standards.

Athletes should be encouraged to stay much closer to their weight categories year round, reducing the need for any extreme and risky weight cutting strategies. Athletes should weigh-in in the morning every day and provide occasional hydration samples to help monitor their true weight. A nutritionist should take skinfold readings (sum of 8) for each athlete once per month; this enables the athlete's support team to track even small changes over time and ensure that no one is going beyond what is deemed acceptable for them to be weighing during the training cycle or as they make their approach to competition. When considering the athlete's health and wellbeing, it is not recommended that any athlete dehydrates beyond 4% of their body mass for weigh-in day.

As a result of these factors, athletes are able to focus their attention on becoming fully physically and psychologically prepared for the fight day, without the unnecessary distraction of trying to reach a challenging weight target.

Physiological demands

Due to recent rule changes within WTF-style Taekwondo, caution must be exercised when reading much of the published research on the physiological demands of the sport. Research into how some of these rule changes have affected the way in which fights are performed is currently ongoing, but a basic understanding of the demands can still be gleaned from what research has been published on the subject. Bridge et al. (2014) published a review article covering many of the physiological characteristics of Taekwondo players based off previous research. The conclusions were that 'medal-winning' Taekwondo players had a greater peak anaerobic power in their lower limb and that a moderate to high $\dot{V}O_{2max}$ were beneficial to support the demands of fighting and recovery between fights on competition days. This is supported when considering fight sports of similar round length, where research has been done into the utilisation of the energy systems during competition (Turner, 2009). Based off this data it would suggest that Taekwondo matches utilise primarily the Anaerobic Phosphagen System with moderate-low utilisation of Anaerobic Glycolysis and Aerobic Metabolism. Muscular speed and power through utilisation of both concentric muscular action and use of the stretch shortening cycle (SSC) were considered of importance, and the Taekwondo players included in the studies were able to demonstrate moderate to high maximum dynamic strength, alongside moderate muscular endurance around the hip, trunk and upper body musculature. A high degree of lower limb flexibility was found to be functionally beneficial.

From the authors' experience, it has been noted that whilst many fight styles are able to win fights, which as a result supports many different combinations of physical characteristics, some common themes prevail across our most successful athletes. Taekwondo players need a to exhibit high levels of both anaerobic and aerobic fitness, not only to cope with the demands of 6 minute competitive fight, but also of a 60–150 minute technical training session. Speed and power characteristics are of high importance both in striking speed and speed of movement, although the need for this has reduced in recent years. Special attention should be given to rotational power because of its involvement in kicking and punching. Lower limb muscular strength and endurance is of moderate importance, especially in the muscles around the hip (glutes, adductors, hamstrings, quads and hip flexors) and the calf musculature. Trunk endurance and control are of high importance to protect the spine, especially the anterior trunk due to its role in postural control when the athlete has their leg in front of the centre of gravity during kicking. Finally the role of flexibility in Taekwondo training is of high importance to allow players to kick to the high section both safely and with ease.

Injury prevalence

The fast paced, dynamic nature of Taekwondo where athletes are asked to strike each other and perform rapid changes of direction in unpredictable positions, whilst under fatigue and often at extreme ranges of motion, creates an understandably high risk of injury. The frequency with which various injuries are seen is dependent on the way in which the athlete trains during their technical sessions and their physical preparedness to cope with these loads. Due to the length of competition bouts versus training sessions that can often go well beyond 90 minutes in length, the predominance of injuries are seen in training. The nature of these injuries differs slightly depending on their aetiology.

Contact injuries can range from mild bruising due to strikes where the athlete is able to train through them, to fractures, especially to the bones in the hand or wrist from punching which depending on the severity can result in lost training days.

Non-contact injuries tend to account for greater loss of training time. Due to the range demands placed on the joints and muscles during kicking, the hip joint and surrounding soft tissue is at greatest risk. Femoroacetabular impingement (FAI) can be common, with chronic FAI symptoms putting an athlete at risk of further issues such as morphological changes i.e. cam or pincer lesions, labral issues and more. If addressed early enough with a targeted rehabilitation plan, the athlete will often lose very little training time for this issue; however, the more chronic issues can result a minimum of a month of modified training and in some cases can be career limiting. Knee and ankle injuries are the next most prevalent, with particular care taken over the ligaments found within these joints during changes of direction. Finally the lumbar spine is at risk and can often be related to problems related to weakness in the hip joint and compensations made to account for this whilst kicking with an upright posture.

Fitness testing battery

A fitness testing battery for Taekwondo has been created based upon the needs analysis of the sports demands and physical characteristics required to perform at the elite level (Table 21.3).

Table 21.3 Taekwondo fitness testing battery

Anthropometrics	• Height • Sitting height • Leg length • Body mass • Body composition (DXA/skinfolds sum of 8)
Range of motion	• Goniometric assessment of: • Hip mobility • Flexion/extension • Abduction/adduction • Internal/external rotation • Knee • Flexion/extension • Ankle • Dorsi/plantar flexion • Inversion/eversion • Spine • Lumbar – flexion/extension/lateral flexion • Thoracic rotation
Power	• Countermovement jump (CMJ) • Single leg counter movement jump (SLCMJ) • 3-hop test
Plyometric ability – stretch shortening cycle (SSC)	• Drop jump (30cm) – contact time (CT) vs flight time (FT) used for reactive strength index score (RSI)
Strength	• Back squat 1RM
Muscular endurance	• Trunk endurance • Prone hold from box • Lateral hold from box (both sides) • Double leg hold • SL hamstring bridge • SL calf raise
Metabolic conditioning	• Aerobic capacity • Treadmill VO2maxtest • Multistage fitness test • Anaerobic capacity • 30 second Wingate test

Programming

Due to the high technical and tactical demands placed upon Taekwondo players, programmes are best individualised to suit the athlete and their chosen fight style where possible. There is no 'one programme' that will work best to improve all players fighting ability. There are, however, areas with which each Taekwondo player will benefit from improving so as to optimise their training time and athletic potential. These are:

- Metabolic conditioning
- Rehabilitation/prehabilitation from injuries

- Speed & agility
- Strength & power
- Muscular endurance
- Mobility

At the elite international level the competition calendar is very congested and so finding opportunities for a long 'General' training phase where S&C can be prioritised is difficult. Instead coaches have to programme in such a way that enables the athletes to strive for improved physical adaptation between competitions whilst complementing heavy technical and tactical training regimens. Also the individual nature of the sport, combined with the need to optimise an athlete's specific technical and tactical strength, means that a traditional linear periodisation approach is not always appropriate. Instead there is a requirement to maintain several different physical characteristics concurrently throughout the year in an attempt to minimise the athlete's specific weaknesses and optimise the athlete's strengths.

Metabolic conditioning

During the General Phase, responsibility for anaerobic and aerobic capacity can be taken on by the S&C Coach and is often focussed on the athletes overall Anaerobic and Aerobic capacity. Despite the moderate $\dot{V}O_{2max}$ scores seen in Taekwondo players (Bridge et al., 2009), it is accepted that a well-developed aerobic system will help players recover from their high intensity efforts. This is of value to not only the competition days consisting of multiple high intensity efforts through a 3 round match, and across multiple matches during a day, but also to the general training week, allowing for more time spent on the mats taking part in consistent and quality technical training. The authors target a combination of long steady state Cardiac Output training or Threshold Intervals aimed at developing the player's aerobic threshold, as described in Jaimeson (2009). The central adaptations that drive an improved aerobic pathway can be well developed utilising whatever training modality that best suits the athlete.

Observation of the technical sessions has shown that they predominantly work in the anaerobic system, so we allow much of the development of this system to be trained here, especially as it is the view of the authors' that the peripheral adaptations required to optimise the anaerobic pathways will be best delivered by the sport skill, i.e. kicking.

Once we enter the Performance Phase, almost all metabolic work is done within technical sessions and led by the Taekwondo coaches to deliver specific adaptations via fatiguing technical work or conditioned sparring matches. Any additional training time given over to the S&C Coach would be focused on recovery, in order to optimise the athlete's 'on-mat' training.

Rehabilitation/prehabilitation from injuries

With athletes experiencing a high injury rate, there is a great need for effective prehabilitaion practises to be in place so as to reduce lost training time. This would specifically focus on the hips, trunk, knee and ankle structures, ensuring that they have strength in appropriate ranges of motion, as per what they will experience during their sport. Also they will need the neuromuscular control during dynamic movements to reduce the likelihood of being exposed to injurious positions.

Speed and agility

Taekwondo players of all abilities have a great need for rapid change of direction ability and mechanical efficiency in achieving optimal positons when moving in and out of offensive or defensive positions. The technical coaches take on the remit of training these characteristics, but at some points, especially with athletes with a lower training age, athletes could benefit from coaching regarding posture and force application when travelling at speed. Taekwondo differs from many running based sports in that the athlete is best served keeping their posture 'erect' or over their base of support for much of their movement patterns, apart from during evasive manoeuvres from kicks where the athlete might lean away from the opponent to reduce the likelihood of conceding a headshot. As a result a much greater emphasis when coaching speed and agility drills is focussed on application of force into the ground by the legs and appropriate footwork. Depending on the athlete you are working with, training to improve this might need to focus purely on improving lower limb strength and power characteristics; however, where these physical characteristics are present, but are not being exhibited during movement sessions, a more specific intervention may be required, for example:

1) If the athlete needs an increased awareness of their posture when moving, performing drills with a dowel or broomstick handle held across the shoulders as if the athlete is going to back squat it, and then cueing them to keep the dowel parallel to the floor throughout the execution of the drill. This accentuates any excessive or unnecessary movement to the athlete and allows them to self-correct where necessary.
2) If the athlete lacks postural control due to weakness in the trunk musculature or poor engagement of the trunk, performing the movements whilst holding an external load such as a medicine ball can serve to "feed the dysfunction" – meaning it makes it more likely that a poorly controlled torso will lose position during the drills. This gives the athlete greater kinaesthetic awareness of what's going on during the drill and hopefully enables them to correct this issue.

Many times athletes that have high general strength capacity, but lack the necessary specific force application to enable rapid changes of direction on the mat, can be improved in several ways, but most often improved cuing of the athlete will clear this up. Coaching them to "punch the ground away" or to "hit the ground like a gun is going off" can give the athlete the clarity of intent required to deliver improved agility.

Finally there is also a consistent theme of allowing an appropriate level of "chaos" into the athlete's speed and agility training. Taekwondo is a chaotic sport, where the athlete's movements are influenced by both the individual's attacking decisions and their opponent's attacking or defensive movements. Often times Taekwondo players find themselves in awkward positions after throwing a kick, whether due to it connecting and the opponent pushing their leg down, or due to it missing and the player having to control that kick's subsequent path before moving away. Evasion from these situations needs to be done as fast as possible whilst also protecting from any potential counter-attack from the opponent. As a result it is important to ensure that athletes are trained to move at speed from different start positions and whilst under different high pressure situations. It is possible to utilise many different strategies for this, including using resistance bands, heavy pads, hurdles, plyo boxes and training partners to give as many different options as possible.

Strength and power

Taekwondo players are exposed to large forces both when moving around the mat during attacking and defensive actions and also in the process of throwing kicks. Players are well served in ensuring that they have the capacity to cope with these forces, both to protect from potential injury and to optimise efficient performance of these movements. Special attention should be given to single leg strength and rotational power. In modern Taekwondo, much of the athlete's time is spent on one leg whilst travelling and during collision-type situations. Whilst performing these actions it is advantageous for the athlete to be able to remain as 'tall' as possible, not being forced to sink and flex on their stance leg. This requires strong muscles in the lower limb, relative to bodyweight, to ensure that this position can be maintained. Failure to do so results in either the athlete losing ring position or risking possible injury. Variations of lunges, split squats and single leg exercises can be used throughout a training cycle, depending on the specific areas the athletes need to develop. There is value in also combining these, depending on the athlete, with bilateral exercises such as back and front squats, sumo deadlifts and Romanian deadlifts. Due to the anthropometry of many Taekwondo athletes, however, modifying these to ensure that they can be executed safely, such as squatting to a box or lifting from a raised platform. This enables athletes with long limb lengths to reduce the injury risk to their spine.

Power can be developed using many advanced plyometric and triple extension exercises, both bilaterally and unilaterally. The Olympic lifts are of value for some athletes; however, as the competition calendar gets busier, the time available for athletes to effectively learn these and then load them to a level that they become of value is limited. As a result, time is often better spent focusing on loaded jumps, which, as the training blocks progress and an athlete gets closer to competition, use more Taekwondo specific patterns to assist in carry-over to sports performance. These specific drills can include medicine balls and resistance bands to develop the rotational power required for athletes to throw effective kicks and punches.

A moderate degree of strength/power is also required to ensure effective scoring kicks can be executed during a match. The hogu's worn by the athletes only allow a point to be scored once the kick registers above a certain threshold of pressure and the thresholds required increase in conjunction with the weight category that the athletes compete in. Registering scoring points can be aided significantly by improving the player's technique as well as ensuring that certain parts of the hogu are targeted during kicks where sensors are most prevalent; an athlete of lower relative strength will struggle to consistently score kicks. Pieter and Pieter (1995) found side kick values of 459N and 400N for males and females respectively and 634N and 543N during spinning back kicks. This also supports the need for rotational power being trained to specifically support utilisation of more forceful spinning techniques.

Muscular endurance

Despite the relatively short nature of fight rounds and matches when compared to sports such as Mixed Martial Arts (Turner, 2009), the repetitive nature of the techniques used and the way in which athletes often train during technical sessions means that athletes are well served by developing a high level of muscular endurance in key musculature. In the lower limb maximum capacity testing of both the hamstrings and the calf muscles can give an indication of the athlete's ability to cope with high kicking volumes. Athletes able to achieve high scores here should be less prone to soft tissue injuries and shin splints.

Similarly due to the postures required within the sport and compensation patterns seen in trying to achieve these positions as athletes become fatigued, a high level of anterior and lateral trunk endurance is important. Due to the long limb length of many Taekwondo fighters, anterior trunk endurance in particular is vitally important to reducing the likelihood of lower back and hip injuries. If a fighter has poor anterior trunk endurance, as they perform multiple kicks in technical sessions, it becomes increasingly difficult for the athlete to maintain an upright posture due to the leg being held in front of the centre of mass. As a result many fighters will begin to lean back more or twist their torso in order to maintain a balance point which can leave them at risk of accumulated damage over time. Throughout the year Taekwondo players should keep a strong focus on maintaining torso endurance, balanced across all planes of motion.

Mobility

With an athlete's ability to kick to the high section being the difference between winning and losing performances in modern Taekwondo, functional mobility around the hips, as well as supporting levels of strength in the outer ranges of motion that are used during the sport, is of high importance. Based on observation by the author of the mobility practises frequently utilised, martial artists appear to dedicate large periods of their training time towards static stretching in an attempt to create range even beyond those seen during real fight scenarios. Long, aggressive stretching protocols aimed at achieving spurious targets such as a full 'box-splits' are commonplace both pre and post training sessions as well as during recovery times. It is the authors' opinion, however, that a more targeted and reasoned process is better established with Taekwondo players both to optimise their training and recovery time and to reduce the unnecessary risks associated with such aggressive stretching practises. Although there is no doubt to the value this practise has in developing passive range of motion when measured in a clinical/lab setting, especially in terms of acute changes, Taekwondo players are better served with a mobility practise that encompasses long term/chronic increases in range of motion that ensure that the athlete has neuromuscular control of the limb whilst at these ranges. The value of dynamic stretching during the athlete's warm up for preparing joints and soft tissue to perform a sport has been well researched and discussed at this point; however, this also lacks merit when it comes to development of chronic changes in an athlete's mobility.

The author values the principles developed by Functional Range Conditioning®, where moderate static stretches are used in conjunction with muscular contractions or strength work at the athlete's outer ranges of motion. This aims to increase the athlete's "functional range of motion", deemed to be the range within which the athlete can actively control the chosen limb. By doing this, not only should kicks become more technical and targeted, but the athlete should also reduce their risk of injury when performing high velocity, high force movements at ranges which previously would have been outside their active range and therefore could only be controlled by passive structures such as the labrum or bone in the hip.

Training sessions

Examples of a training session for an athlete in both the General Phase and Performance Phase can be seen in Figure 21.2. A typical training week would see a Taekwondo athlete perform 3–5 S&C sessions a week during General Phase and 2–3 sessions a week during Performance Phase. As such these sessions should be considered a snapshot of what an athlete might be exposed to during a training block.

GENERAL PHASE																
	Guidelines: enter all weights lifted in the TL (training load) column			**Week commencing 09.01.17**			**Week commencing 16.01.17**			**Week commencing 23.01.17**			**Week commencing 30.01.17**			
	Intensity			**Load**			**Load**			**Load**			**Deload**			**COMPLEX'S**
	Pre-activation	**Tempo**	**Rest**	**Sets**	**Reps**	**TL**	**Sets**	**Reps**	**TL**	**Sets**	**Reps**	**TL**	**Sets**	**Reps**	**TL**	HIP COMPLEX
1	**SKIPPING**			3mins			3mins			3mins			3mins			HIP HITCHES GLUTE BRIDGE DEADBUGS X-BAND WALKS CNTRBALANCE SQTS
2	**HIP COMPLEX (SEE NOTES)**			3	10		3	10		3	10		3	10		
	Exercise	**Tempo**	**Rest**	**Sets**	**Reps**	**TL**	**Sets**	**Reps**	**TL**	**Sets**	**Reps**	**TL**	**Sets**	**Reps**	**TL**	**SHIFTING**
1	**FAST FEET / SHIFTING DRILLS**			10mins			10mins			10mins			10mins			1. SERIES OF FOOTWORK & AGILITY DRILLS. FOCUS ON QUALITY. FULL REST BETWEEN REPS.
2	**BB JUMP**			3	5	30	3	4	35	3	3	40	2	3	40	
3	**SUMO DEADLIFT**			4	6	85%	4	4	90%	4	2	95%	3	2	80%	
4a	**OFFSET R.F.E. SPLIT SQUAT**			3	8		3	8		3	8		3	6		
4b	**GLUTE HAM RAISE**			3	8		3	10		3	12		3	8		
	Extras	**Tempo**	**Rest**	**Sets**	**Reps**	**TL**	**Sets**	**Reps**	**TL**	**Sets**	**Reps**	**TL**	**Sets**	**Reps**	**TL**	
1a	**ADDUCTOR HOLD**			3	30s		3	20s		3	40s		2	30s		
1b	**PALLOF PRESS**			3	10	8	3	12	8	3	15	8	2	10	8	
1c	**SEATED KNEE RAISE**			3	10	10	3	12	10	3	15	10	2	10	10	
1d	**SA / SL PLANK**			3	10		3	12		3	15		2	10		

PERFORMANCE PHASE																
	Guidelines: enter all weights lifted in the TL (training load) column			**Week commencing 09.01.17**			**Week commencing 16.01.17**			**Week commencing 23.01.17**			**Week commencing 30.01.17**			
	Intensity			**Load**			**Load**			**Load**			**Deload**			**COMPLEX'S**
	Pre-activation	**Tempo**	**Rest**	**Sets**	**Reps**	**TL**	**Sets**	**Reps**	**TL**	**Sets**	**Reps**	**TL**	**Sets**	**Reps**	**TL**	JUMP COMPLEX
1	**SKIPPING**			3mins			3mins			3mins			3mins			SIDE HOP OVER HURDLE, HOP-HOP STICK, 90° HOP
2a	**GLUTE BRIDGE**			3	10		3	10		3	10		3	10		
2b	**WALKING LUNGE w ROTATION**			3	10		3	10		3	10		3	10		
3	**JUMP COMPLEX (SEE NOTES)**			3	5		3	5		3	5		3	5		
	Exercise	**Tempo**	**Rest**	**Sets**	**Reps**	**TL**	**Sets**	**Reps**	**TL**	**Sets**	**Reps**	**TL**	**Sets**	**Reps**	**TL**	**SHIFTING**
1	**FAST FEET / SHIFTING DRILLS**			10mins			10mins			10mins			10mins			1. SERIES OF SPORT SPECIFIC FOOTWORK & AGILITY DRILLS. FOCUS ON QUALITY. FULL REST BETWEEN REPS.
2	**HEIDEN TO MED BALL THROW**			4	3	3	4	4	3	4	5	3	3	4	3	
3	**R.F.E. SPLIT SQUAT JUMP**			4	6		4	6		4	6		3	4		
4	**STEP UP**			3	6	85%	3	6	90%	3	6	95%	3	6	80%	
5	**NORDICS**			3	6		3	6		3	6		3	6		
	Extras	**Tempo**	**Rest**	**Sets**	**Reps**	**TL**	**Sets**	**Reps**	**TL**	**Sets**	**Reps**	**TL**	**Sets**	**Reps**	**TL**	
1a	**ADDUCTOR RAISE**			3	30s		3	20s		3	40s		2	30s		
1b	**CABLE ROTATION**			3	10	8	3	12	8	3	15	8	2	10	8	
1c	**TKD STANCE DB KNEE RAISE**			3	6	7	3	8	7	3	10	7	2	6	7	
1d	**V-UP**			3	10		3	12		3	15		2	10		

Figure 21.2 Examples of a training session for an athlete in both the General Phase and Performance Phase

Conclusion

Modern elite Taekwondo is incredibly competitive and demanding for those athletes that are involved. With a minimum of 5 high scoring competitions a year and numerous other opportunities to score ranking points, the athletes need to be close to their physical peak throughout, for several years, building towards an Olympic Games. The fights themselves are becoming more and more physical as athletes become more professional in their training methods and the rules increase the requirement for those athletes to operate at the outer ranges of motion in order to score big. In the authors' experience, athletes that focus early on in their careers on quality training practises that prioritise movement competency and functional mobility, with special attention given to the hip complex, are the athletes most likely to optimise their training and competition time. Once these areas are addressed, a quality and progressive approach to strength and power development, balanced against the athlete's technical development, can strongly support the athlete's performance in competition. There is a huge amount of research needed into the sport and its recent rule changes in order to establish objective performance indicators for athletes to strive for; however, in the authors' experience the most successful and highest performing Taekwondo fighters have also been extremely competent in the S&C training environment, supporting the value of these training methods and their place in the athlete's training schedule.

References

Bridge, C.A., Ferreira da Silva Santos, J., Chaabene, H., Pieter, W. and Franchini, E. (2014), 'Physical and physiological profiles of taekwondo athletes'. *Sports Medicine*, 44, pp. 713–733.

Bridge, C.A., Jones, M.A. and Drust, B. (2009), 'Physiological responses and perceived exertion during international Taekwondo competition'. *International Journal of Sports Physiology Performance*, 4, pp. 485–493.

Jaimeson, J. (2009), *Ultimate MMA Conditioning*. Performance Sports Inc.

Kazemi, M., Waalen, J., Morgan, C. and White, A.R. (2006), 'A profile of Olympic taekwondo competitors'. *Journal of Sports Science and Medicine*, CSSI-1, pp. 114–121.

Pieter, F. and Pieter, W. (1995), 'Speed and force in selected Taekwondo techniques'. *Biology of Sport*, 12, pp. 257–266.

Turner, A. (2009), 'Strength & conditioning for Taekwondo athletes'. *Professional Strength and Conditioning*, 15, pp. 15–27.

22
BOXING

Alan Ruddock, Daniel Wilson and David Hembrough

INTRODUCTION TO THE SPORT

Similar to most weight restricted combat sports, professional boxers are required to "weigh in" and meet their contest weight 36 to 24 hours prior to competition. A (national to world championship) standard professional boxing contest usually takes place in a square "ring' 4.88 m^2 to 6.10 m^2 over 12, 3 minute rounds, with a 1 minute interval between rounds. As such a professional boxing contest can last up to 47 minutes (12 × 3 minute rounds = 36 + (11 × 1 = 11) = 47 min); however, at a minimum, lower standard contests might comprise of 4 × 2 min (total 8 min boxing). Boxers must wear a protective mouth guard; shorts and genital protection are also worn but protective head gear is not permitted. Boxing gloves are required and weigh 227 g for flyweight (52 kg) to welterweight contests (67 kg) and 283 g for heavier weight classifications. During the one minute interval between rounds, a chief "second" (trainer) is allowed in the ring to offer coaching instructions; they might also wish to provide ice, iced-towels and water but stimulants (which include carbohydrate-electrolyte beverages) are prohibited.

A professional boxing contest is overseen by a referee and typically three judges; in the majority of occasions the winner of a contest is confirmed by those individuals. The most well known, although most unlikely way to win a contest is by knockout (estimated 6% of all wins). A knockout is usually preceding by a single or successive number of high force legitimate blows that in the case of a head strike results in acute neurological trauma likely caused by large magnitudes of internal torque applied to the cerebellum and brain stem (areas of the brain involved in conduction and control of motor and sensory information) (Heilbronner et al., 2009). It may also come from a blow to another part of the body, applied with such force that the boxer falls to the ring floor and is unable to continue the contest as deemed by the referee. In the former case, one of the two ringside medical doctors must examine and monitor the boxer for signs of serious brain injury, and reference their physical and mental state to that prior to the weigh in and/or contest and the structural integrity of the brain as determined by recent magnetic resonance imagery scan.

Another way to win a contest is by technical knockout. In this instance a boxer has failed to satisfy the referee that they are in a position and condition to defend their self, or they are being outclassed by their opponent. This decision is usually made following a period of sustained high force blows and demonstration of attacking skill. If in this instance a boxer's corner feels they are being outclassed and they deem it unsafe for the bout to continue, they might "throw the towel in". In the case of a technical knockout, a medical examination is required by the ringside doctor as per a knockout decision. In both instances, it would seem that the aim of professional boxing is to induce considerable physical damage to an opponent, such that it causes acute neurological or other injury. Indeed, boxers who sustain repeated forceful blows to the head are at risk of post concussion syndrome in the days after the event or chronic traumatic encephalopathy (Heilbronner et al., 2009) in the long term.

These risks have led to several bodies issuing statements declaring that professional boxing be banned (American Medical Association, 1999 www.ama-assn.org/ama1/pub/upload/mm/443/csaa-99.pdf; Australian Medical Association, 2007 https://ama.com.au/position-statement/boxing-1997-reaffirmed-2007; World Medical Association, 2003 www.wma.net/en/30publications/10policies/b6/). Sport scientists must abide by clear ethical guidance set by their governing body or affiliation that states that the safety of an athlete is paramount. Providing scientific support to enable a boxer to inflict damage and potential neurological trauma on another human should be considered very carefully within ethical guidelines. These above concerns are alleviated slightly by routine medical assessments and in the case of well-trained athletes who are able to cope with the physical demands. However, there are specific instances, such as weight loss, dehydration and rehydration strategies that if insufficient, will place the athlete at risk of serious injury; also if within a contest a boxer is clearly being outclassed. It is reasonable to assume that in the majority of circumstances, professional boxers do not intend to cause life-threatening and long lasting injuries to their opponent.

Professional boxers compete to demonstrate superior physical, technical and tactical skills; these are paramount in the third way to win a boxing contest, by a points decision, a situation in which most professional boxing contests are decided. In major title bouts, three well experienced independent judges score each round, giving 10 points to the winner of the round and 9 points or less to loser. At the end of the contest the points are totalled and each judge declares a winner; the actual winner is the boxer who has the majority of the judge's decisions. Points are awarded using subjective criteria but are based on the boxers attacking and defensive skills, the relative importance and content of these broad categories are both judge and contest specific. In this circumstance preparation of the professional boxer is crucial to improve their chance of winning a round and the whole contest, as poor physical fitness, nutrition and mental preparation would likely limit performance capacity and place a boxer at risk of serious medical conditions. Moreover, the short period in which boxers prepare for competition (usually 8, 10 or 12 weeks) has to be optimised. This leaves little room for error and no time for malpractice. Thus, training and preparation needs to be carefully thought through, planned and delivered, with safety and wellbeing of paramount concern.

Athletic demands

Needs analysis

Davis, Benson, Pitty, Connorton and Waldock (2015) reported that elite standard amateur boxers initiate attacking or defensive actions every 1.4 seconds over a 3-minute round with 77%, 19% and 4% energy derived from aerobic, phosphocreatine and anaerobic glycolysis energy pathways, respectively, during three semi-contact 2-minute rounds (Davis, Leithäuser and Beneke, 2014). A well-developed aerobic capability is a likely possible pre-requisite for success; aerobic capacities ($\dot{V}O_{2max}$) in the range of 57.5 to 69.0 ml·kg^{-1}·min^{-1} have been reported in senior amateur boxers

(Guidetti, Musulin and Baldari, 2002; Smith, 2006) and can exceed 70 ml·kg⁻¹·min⁻¹ in elite professional boxers (unpublished observation from European champion). Smith (2006) reported that senior amateur boxers had a 21% greater $\dot{V}O_{2max}$ compared to junior-international standard boxers, suggesting aerobic capabilities of boxers might differ due to maturation and experience. Senior competitions are scheduled for 3 × 3 minutes, whereas junior bouts are limited to 3 × 2 minutes. The longer contest duration and training practices required for senior boxers might explain the differences between fighters. Blood lactate concentrations have been reported for both senior (13.5 ± 2.0 mmol·L⁻¹) and junior (14.1 ± 2.0 mmol·L⁻¹) boxers after four 2-minute rounds (Smith, 2006).

Boxers attempt to strike opponents cleanly, to gain favour with judges and disrupt an opponent's strategy. Increased force of single punches or punch combinations are also intended to cause a knockout, position an opponent for a sustained attack (leading to contest termination) or display dominance over an opponent. A punching action appears to take ~60 ms, with fist speeds around 9 m·s⁻¹ (Piorkowski, Lees and Barton, 2011; Nakano, Iino, Imura and Kojima, 2014). Peak punch forces of ~2500 N have been observed at impact (Smith, 2006); however, magnitudes might differ depending on punch type, weight classifications and skill level of the boxer (Smith, 2006; Piorkowski et al., 2011). Smith (2006) reported an accumulated punching force of 388113 ± 102020 N during simulated boxing activity, where 76 punches (single, 2- and 3-punch combinations) over 4 × 2 minute rounds were thrown. Mean punching force was ~1200 N, suggesting that reproducing forceful punches during competition is an important factor.

Depending upon the experience of a professional boxer, they might have as little as 6 weeks or as much as 16 weeks to prepare for a contest. In other cases they might not know when they are next competing and accept an offer to compete at short notice (1 to 2 weeks); these instances make the task of planning training difficult. Moreover, some professional boxers only choose to train when "on camp"; thus, they detrain in the weeks they are inactive, make poor nutritional choices and consequently increase fat mass, all of which are undesirable for training and performance.

A typical training camp lasts around 12 weeks. The first 6 weeks are usually focused around physical and mental training, whilst technical training load is increased slowly. Between 6 and 8 weeks (4 weeks before competition), technical training and open sparring becomes a priority and strength and conditioning takes a complementary role. The key to an effective strength and conditioning programme within this 6- to 8-week period is to increase physical capacity such that the boxer can cope with increased training demands of open sparring. In the remaining 6 to 8 weeks an effective strength and conditioning programme should complement technical and tactical demands of sparring. Thus establishing a good relationship and line of communication with the coaching team is essential. A professional boxer's preparation in this period relies on good quality sparring but is somewhat dependent on the sparring partners' and coaches' availability. Having the ability to adapt a training plan at short notice to take advantage of windows of trainability or limit training load is essential.

This structure is often constrained by lifestyle, financial and logistical demands in the developing professional boxer who has yet to establish a full-time income from the sport. Younger boxers often meet financial obligations by undertaking physically active jobs such manual labour and mail delivery, which needs to be taken into account when programming. As the standard of the boxer increases, these demands are limited, until the athlete can earn a full-time living from boxing. These circumstances often impose limits on the basic foundational practices required for high performance. Indeed, initial assessments of the boxers' and teams' understanding of nutritional strategies, such as hydration and fuelling for training sessions; daily, weekly and camp training structure; training history; injury awareness and common illness are elements that should be considered prior to delivery of any special interventions. Improvements in these areas can have large benefits on training quality, adaptation and therefore performance, and focusing on areas such as mobility and injury prevention can reduce the number of training hours missed due to injury and illness.

Movement dysfunctions

Boxers maintain a similar stance throughout their technical work that typically shortens the hip muscles, and they amplify this shortness with hours of running at submaximal intensities. Hip flexor tightness can cause many injuries and dysfunctions, including lower back pain, and can limit gluteal strength. Hip and trunk torque contributes to punch force; therefore, mobilising and strengthening this area can improve performance as well as reduce the likelihood of injury.

Shoulder mobility

"Hands up, chin down" is often the coaching point to a defensive guard, requiring rounding and a shrug of the shoulders. When boxers throw thousands of punches per week, the anterior shoulder musculature and trapezius muscles can become over-active. This alone can cause shoulder mobility issues for boxers. These issues are often compounded by large volumes of strength-circuit based exercises like press ups and shoulder press which are common in traditional boxing training methods. Poor shoulder mobility often creates over-active anterior deltoids and upper trapezius, causing the middle and lower trapezius to become weak, which affects the natural movement of the shoulder and arm. This can also cause shoulder impingement, rotator cuff weakness and lower back injuries.

Rotational mobility

Rotational mobility is needed to transfer force from "foot to fist" when delivering punches. However, tightness in muscles across the thoracic spine can limit rotation, causing the Quadratus Lumborum (QL) to play an overactive role during rotation, and can cause lower back pain. To make beneficial long-term changes and reduce compensatory patterns of the QL, boxers need to improve thoracic and core rotation range of movement.

Gluteal strength

Many boxers have underdeveloped gluteal strength due to time spent in their boxing stance and large endurance-type running volumes. Gluteal strength is an important contributor to forceful hip extension and rotation needed during running, jumping and more importantly, punching. The gluteal muscles have the potential to be the largest contributor to hip extension and rotation; however, many boxers have under-active gluteal musculature due to mobility and activation problems. Stronger gluteal muscles can improve a boxer's ability to engage and strengthen the core musculature, which can help protect against injuries to the lower back muscles and improve punching force.

Laboratory based fitness testing

Anthropometric profiling

As boxers compete in weight categories, characterisation of body composition is important for determining tissue contribution to body mass. Quantification of segmental lean tissue and fat mass might form the basis for nutritional interventions and strength training. For example,

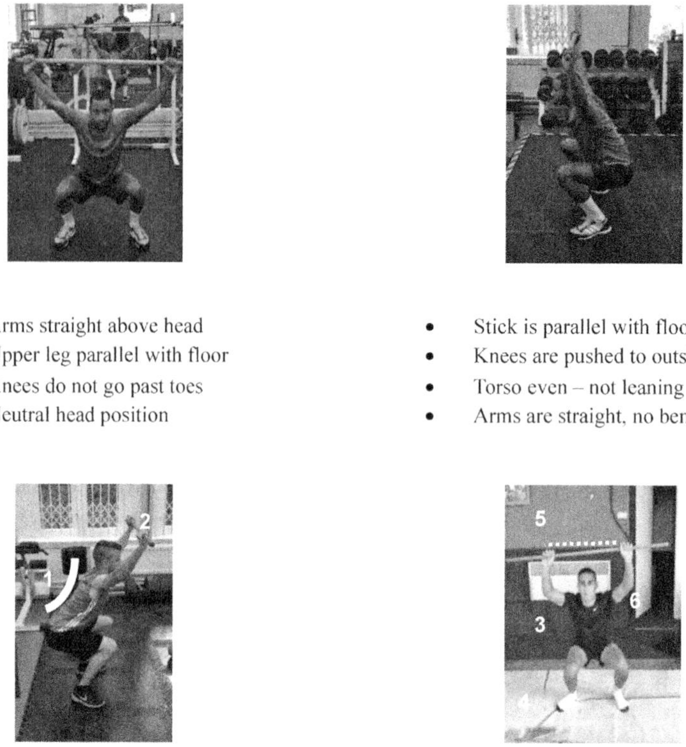

- Arms straight above head
- Upper leg parallel with floor
- Knees do not go past toes
- Neutral head position

- Stick is parallel with floor
- Knees are pushed to outside
- Torso even – not leaning to one side
- Arms are straight, no bend at elbow

Figure 22.1 Overhead squat analysis

relative lean trunk mass is an important contributor to indices of punch force. Thus, retaining and increasing lean trunk mass is important for boxing performance. Bioelectrical impedance and skin fold assessments are valid assessments of body composition and should be performed at regular intervals. Weekly assessments are recommended throughout a specific training camp (i.e. 12 week competition period) and bi-weekly assessments when boxers are not training for a specific bout. These assessments should be coupled with pre-defined weight targets set by the coaching team.

Overhead squat

This is a popular test that has been used to assess dynamic flexibility, core strength, balance and neuromuscular control. This test can identify muscular imbalances and movement dysfunction in both upper and lower extremities, making it a useful and practical test. See check points in Table 22.1 and Figure 22.1.

Single leg squat

This transitional movement assessment has been used as a reliable and valid assessment of lower extremity movement patterns. Knee valgus, hip position and trunk leans can be an indicator of joint motion, muscle activation and overall neuromuscular control. See check points in table 22.2 and figure 22.2.

Table 22.1 Basic movement analysis

Check point	Point	Compensation	Probable overactive muscles	Probable underactive muscles	Cause for concern rating and possible causes
Knee	3	Move inward (valgus)	Adductor complex Bicep femoris Tensor fascia latae (TFL) Lateral gastrocnemius Vastus lateralis	Medial hamstring Medial gastrocnemius Gluteus medius Gluteus maximus Vastus medialis oblique Anterior tibialis Posterior tibialis	This is a common issue in boxers as the stance requires an external rotation of the hip, causing TFL to be overactive. This causes underactive gluteals, meaning hip extension and rotation can become sub-optimal. This makes the adductor complex overactive in super-compensation.
	6	Move outward	Piriformis Bicep femoris Tensor fascia latae Gluteus minimus	Adductor complex Medial hamstring Gluteus maximus	Not as common as valgus due to the over activity of the adductor complex.
Lumbar pelvic hip complex	2	Excessive forward lean	Soleus Gastrocnemius Hip flexor complex Piriformis Abdominal complex	Anterior tibialis Gluteus maximus Erector spinae Intrinsic core stabilisers	Very common in boxers due to overactive muscles in the lower limbs. Hip flexor tightness is a result of hip flexion in a boxing stance and large running volumes. Gastrocnemius and soleus tightness could be a result of being on the toes for the majority of training.
	1	Low back arches	Hip flexor complex Erector spinae Latissimus dorsi	Gluteus maximus Erector spinae Intrinsic core stabilisers Hip flexor complex	Common in boxing due to the tightness of the hips and core muscles. Also, the latissimus dorsi is often overactive as plays a big role during combination punching and boxers develop these by using pull ups.
	Opposite to 1	Low back rounds	Hamstrings Adductor magnus Rectus abdominis External obliques	Gluteus maximus Hamstrings Intrinsic core stabilisers	Common due to tightness of the hamstrings as they deal with large volumes of eccentric loading during technical, sparring and fitness training.
	3	Asymmetrical weight shift	Adductor complex Tensor fascia latae Gastrocnemius Soleus Bicep femoris Gluteus medius (opposite side)	Gluteus medius Anterior tibialis Adductor complex (opposite side)	This happens in almost all boxers due to a "traditional" boxing stance requiring more weight transferred on the rear foot.

- Foot flat and pointing straight forward
- Knee aligns with second toe
- Hips remain parallel with floor
- Upper body stays in neutral position

- Hips pushed back
- Knees flex online with toes
- Spine remains in neutral position
- Controlled forward lean

Figure 22.2 Single leg squat analysis

Countermovement jump and squat jump

Jump height assessments are useful to assess lower body impulsiveness (Ruddock and Winter, 2015), which is a component of force transmission during punching (Piorkowski et al., 2011). Countermovement jump (CMJ) and squat jump (SJ) height calculated from flight time using a photocell system (Microgate, Bolzano, Italy), provide valid assessments of jump height (Glatthorn et al., 2011). Typically a boxer will jump similar heights in CMJ and SJ, which is indicative of poor eccentric utilisation in the lower body. Since high force punches are preceded by a pre-stretch in the lower body and core musculature, the ability to utilise eccentric activity is important for force transfer.

Landmine punch throw test

This test assesses the ability to produce high velocities in a movement pattern similar to a rear-hand punch. An Olympic barbell (20 kg) is inserted into a landmine attachment, which positions the bar at angles between 40–60 degrees, depending on stature. Positioned at shoulder height on the same side of the rear foot with the elbows flexed, boxers are instructed to rotate their trunk and produce maximal effort to throw the bar as fast as possible. Velocities are measured by a linear position transducer (GymAware Optical Encoder, Kinetic, Canberra, ACT). This provides the practitioner with instant feedback on the peak velocity (m/s) for each repetition. The GymAware is placed on a metal weight plate directly underneath where the participant will perform the landmine throw, and attached 15 cm from the end of the barbell (see Figure 22.3).

Figure 22.3 Landmine punch throw. Participant takes a split (boxing) stance with the bar held by the rear hand, on line with the shoulder. From a stationary position, the participant rapidly rotates to throw the bar as fast as possible. Participant must keep feet planted throughout the movement. Following five repetitions, switch stance test on opposite hand.

Boxers should complete five attempts on each arm at 20 kg, 25 kg, 30 kg, 35 kg and 40 kg. Participants should have 2 minutes rest between each incremental load. Peak velocity is plotted against load for investigation of the load-velocity profile. Peak velocity can be assessed according to normative data (Table 22.2) and linear regression can be used to estimate zero load velocity, indicative of hand speed, and zero velocity load, indicative of maximal isometric strength.

Lactate profile

This test comprises 3 min of running at 5 to 6 fixed intensities on a motorised treadmill interspersed with 1 min of recovery, during which a fingertip capillary blood lactate sample is acquired. The test can be combined with collection of expired air to enable the assessment of substrate utilisation, oxygen uptake and running economy. The trend line of running speed and blood lactate can be analysed to determine breakpoints from linearity, thus the running speed at the first and second lactate turn-points. These can be used to benchmark performance and to set heart rate training zones. Typically a 3-zone model demarked by the first and second turn-point is suitable for a boxer's training prescription (see Figure 22.4).

30:15 test treadmill test

This is a modified version of the 30:15 intermittent shuttle running test (Buchheit, 2008) as boxers find decelerating and turning at high speed difficult, which increases the risk of injury. The treadmill test follows the same speeds, running time and recovery period as the original test but does not require any change in direction. The test procedures are reported in detail elsewhere (Buchheit, 2008). Briefly athletes are required to run for 30 s at a fixed speed before a 15 s passive

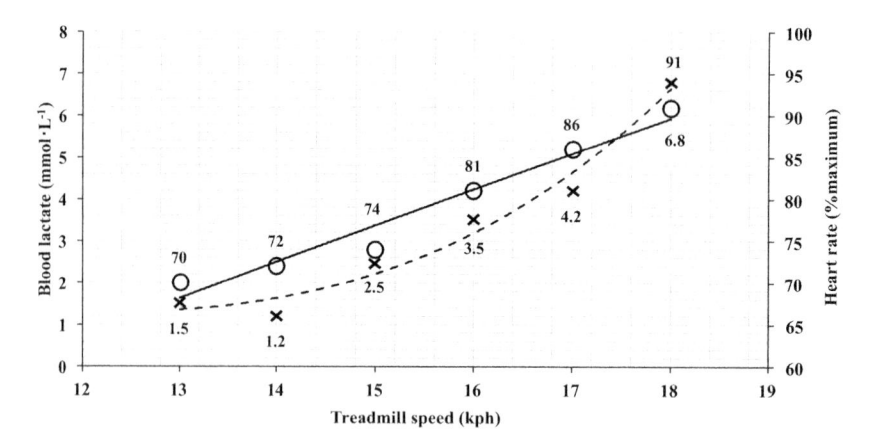

Figure 22.4 Representative data of a lactate profile obtained from a professional boxer. O = % maximum heart rate. X = blood lactate (mmol·L⁻¹). Lactate turn-point 1 = 14 kph. Lactate turn-point 2 = 17 kph.

recovery period. The test starts at a speed of 8 kph and increases by 0.5 kph each 30 s stage. The test is terminated when the athlete can no longer maintain the desired speed. The last completed stage in addition to duration (s) run at the final speed is recorded.

Field-based test alternatives 60 seconds press-up test

The ability of boxers to produce force and the rate at which force is developed is important for successful performance (Nakano et al., 2014). This press-up test is a suitable to assess muscular strength-endurance, a surrogate of maximum voluntary force production. Boxers are required to start prone with hands positioned perpendicular to the shoulder joint; elbows and knees fully extended with the trunk parallel to the floor. Elbows are flexed until the chest and thighs contact the floor. The participant returns to the start position by extending the elbows. This action is counted as one repetition; participants are encouraged to repeat as many of these actions as possible in 60 s.

Medicine ball backhand throw

This test assesses the ability of the boxers to develop force in a movement pattern similar to a rear-hand punch. A 3 kg medicine ball is positioned at shoulder height on the same side of the rear foot (e.g. right foot to the rear, medicine ball held in right hand) with the elbows flexed. Boxers are instructed to rotate their trunk and produce maximal effort to throw the ball as far as possible from a marked location on the floor. Each boxer should be instructed to rapidly rotate their body proximal to distal whilst fully extending the elbow before releasing the ball. The first point of ball to ground contact is recorded as the distance thrown (m).

Incremental shuttle tests: 30:15 intermittent running test and Yo-Yo Intermittent Recovery Test Level 1

These tests are used to assess the ability to recover from high intensity aerobic exercise, similar to the demands imposed on a boxer during competition. Both are incremental exercise tests whereby running speed is increased each minute. Methods describing the test procedures are detailed elsewhere (Bangsbo, Iaia and Krustrup, 2008; Buchheit, 2008).

Table 22.2 Reliability and assessment standards for professional boxers

Test	Reliability (CV%)	Poor			Adequate			Good			Excellent	
Countermovement jump (cm)	5.2	< 35			40–44			45–49			> 50	
Squat jump (cm)	3.2	< 30			35–39			40–44			> 50	
Landmine punch throw peak velocity (m/s)	2.5	R		L	R		L	R		L	R	L
20 kg		< 3.56		< 3.54	3.57–3.97		3.55 to 3.76	3.98–4.26		3.77–3.96	> 4.28	> 3.98
25 kg		< 3.11		< 3.0	3.11–3.51		3.01–3.3	3.52–3.65		3.31–3.48	> 3.69	> 3.5
30 kg		< 2.75		< 2.67	2.76–2.99		2.68–2.94	3.0–3.28		2.95–3.08	> 3.3	> 3.09
35 kg		< 1.92		< 1.80	1.93–2.4		1.81–2.32	2.41–2.67		2.33–2.56	> 2.68	> 2.56
40 kg		< 2.17		< 2.02	2.18–2.32		2.03–2.09	2.33–2.61		2.10–2.34	> 2.65	> 2.42
Lactate profile												
Lactate turn-point 1 (kph)		≤ 10			12			14			≥ 15	
Lactate turn-point 2 (kph)		≤ 13			15			17			≥ 18	
30:15 intermittent treadmill test (peak speed (kph))	1.5	≤ 19.5			20–21.5			22–23			≥ 23.5	
Yo-Yo IRT L1 (m)	13.7	< 1600			1600–2000			2000–2400			> 2400	
30:15 intermittent shuttle test (peak speed (kph))	1.9											
60 s press-up test (reps)	9.3	< 60			60–70			70–80			> 80	
Medicine ball back hand throw	5.8	< 9			9–11			11–13				
Dominant (m)											> 13	
Non-dominant (m)	8.2	< 8			8–10			10–12			> 12	

Programming Maximising training adaptation

Boxers are required to make weight and train for competitive performance within a relatively short time (usually 8 to 12 weeks). A well developed aerobic capacity is integral for boxing performance and is also required to support an increase in physical and technical training load (Ruddock, Wilson, Thompson, Hembrough and Winter, 2016). Thus optimising physiological stimuli for adaptations in aerobic capacity through training and amplifying cell signalling is key.

Three main sites contribute to the effectiveness of aerobic metabolism; 1) active myocytes (oxygen utilisation and cellular buffering); 2) capillary structures (oxygen extraction) and; 3) the myocardium (oxygen delivery).

Rapid changes in the oxidative phenotype of skeletal muscle mediated via beneficial adaptations in mitochondrial enzyme activity have been reported after short periods of sprint interval training (Gibala and McGee, 2008). Specifically, 30 s all-out exercise is associated with acute-upregulated activity of AMPK, CAMPK, SIRT1, p53 and p38 MAPK, important signalling cascades, associated with the transcription co-activator PGC1-α which is a key regulator of mitochondrial biogenesis thus aerobic metabolism (Liang and Ward, 2006; Gibala et al., 2009). Furthermore, short-term training studies (2 and 6 weeks) provide evidence for changes in the maximal activity of Citrate Synthase, Beta-hydroxyacid Dehydrogenase, Cytochrome C Oxidase and Pyruvate Dehydrogenase (Burgomaster et al., 2008), key enzymes involved in aerobic metabolism.

All-out high-force exercise is likely required for professional boxers with advanced training histories, particularly in the early phases of training, since these individuals might require intensive training to activate singalling pathways to a sufficient level to induce effective adaptations (Yu et al., 2003). These peripheral (skeletal muscle) adaptations and perhaps improvements in muscle architecture, mechanical force generation and neuromuscular coordination combine to improve exercise tolerance but not aerobic capacity *per se* (Weston, Taylor, Batterham and Hopkins, 2014). Nevertheless, these adaptations provide the foundation for further improvements in and complement structural adaptations required for improvements in aerobic capacity in subsequent training phases.

Central cardiovascular adaptations, (left-ventricular function, end-diastolic volume, systemic vascular resistance, muscle capillarisation) thus improvements in cardiac output and delivery of oxygen to exercising muscle seems to be improved by high-intensity interval training lasting between 4 and 10 minutes at an intensity equivalent to 90% of maximum oxygen uptake repeated 4 to 6 times (Buchheit and Laursen, 2013a, 2013b). However, although integral to improvements in aerobic capacity and performance, beneficial structural adaptations reportedly take around 8 to10 weeks, much longer than sprint interval training (SIT) (Montero, Diaz-Cañestro and Lundby, 2015). Nevertheless, these types of sessions are also important in a boxer's perception of intensity, because they challenge the athlete to exercise in a physiological state close to maximum effort, thus preparing a boxer for performance, physically and mentally.

When boxers are required to improve aerobic capacity, we recommend a 3 week SIT period, to take advantage of rapid skeletal muscle remodelling, followed by 6 to 8 weeks of HIIT, to induce central cardiovascular adaptations, and finally a 2-week taper consisting of repeated sprint training (see Table 22.3).

Table 22.3 Example conditioning programme (adapted from Ruddock et al., 2016)

Weeks before competition	Training phase	Example training session	Frequency	Intended physiological adaptations
12 to 9	Oxygen extraction and utililisation	30 s all-out maximum effort, 3 min passive recovery, 4 to 6 repetitions	2 to 4 sessions per training week	Mitochondrial biogenesis, maximal activity of oxidative and non-oxidative enzymes. Provide stimuli for recruitment of high-threshold motor units, co-ordination and rate of force development
8 to 3	Oxygen delivery	4 to 8 min at 85 to 95% maximum heart rate, 2 minute passive recovery, 4 to 6 repetitions	2 to 4 sessions per week for first 3 weeks 1 to 2 sessions per week as sparring load increases	Improve cardiovascular capacity (stroke volume, cardiac output, muscle capillarisation, and systemic vascular resistance), delivery of O_2, and enhance venous return
2 to 0	Taper	20 s all-out maximum effort, 10 s passive recovery, 4–8 repetitions, 1–2 sets, 5 min recovery between sets	1 to 2 sessions per week	Transfer adaptations to boxing specific activity profiles. Reduce accumulated fatigue. Maintain neuromuscular activity

Strength training

The force of a punch is dependent on the impulse-momentum relationship. The most obvious way to increase the momentum of the punching arm is to increase mass (from Newtonian physics) via muscular hypertrophy. However, weight classifications make hypertrophy training difficult to implement, and can be contradictory to nutritional interventions, which often induce a calorie deficit. Generating large magnitudes of force in a short space of time is the result of many integrated processes, including genetic factors, muscle fibre type composition, the ability of the nervous system to recruit motor units and the structure and ultra-structure of muscle (Andersen and Aagaard, 2006).

Furthermore, moderate to large correlations ($r = 0.60$ to 0.70) between jump height and landmine punch throw velocity, suggests boxers should concentrate on developing lower-body impulse (Ruddock and Winter, 2015). In consideration, strength training should be designed to improve peak force development, combined with low-external load jump training to improve rate of force development (McLellan, Lovell and Gass, 2011), resulting in a positive transfer to force production during punching.

Improving the strength of the hip extensors, in particular, function of the gluteal musculature, is important. These can be trained using key lifts such as squats, deadlifts, and Olympic-style lifts, where there is a focus on developing forceful hip extension (see Table 22.4). It is also important to develop force-production and transfer in the upper-body and trunk using multiple planes of movement.

Table 22.4 Progression of resistance exercise type for boxers

Exercise type	Phase 1	Phase 2	Phase 3	Phase 4
Hip hinge	DB romanian deadlift	Romanian deadlift	Sumo deadlift	Deadlift
Squat	Overhead squat	Goblet squat	Box squat	Back squat
Vertical press	Half kneeling DB Press	Kneeling DB press	Single arm DB press	DB push press
Horizontal press	Press ups	DB floor press	DB chest press	Bench press
Vertical pull	Band pull down	Banded pull up	Pull up	Weighted pull up
Horizontal pull	Suspension row	Weighted suspension row	DB row and rotate	DB prone row

For the upper body, horizontal and vertical pushing and pulling exercises are required (see TAB) to target strength development. Careful selection of load, repetition and sets is important to limit muscular hypertrophy and prevent excessive strain on movements limited by mobility particularly around the shoulder.

A double "peak" in muscle activity is evident during striking actions (McGill, Chaimberg, Frost and Fenwick, 2010). This is a stiffening of the body at impact through isometric activity and is postulated to create "effective mass" and reduce energy loss. Effective mass is best developed using pad and heavy bag training in technical training. However, physical exercises with accommodating resistance or those encouraging end range stiffening can help improve effective mass. In addition, effective cues such as "popping" of the hips and "stiffen up" at the end range can help induce isometric activity.

We have also found that the lean mass of the trunk (r 90% CI = 0.65 to 0.94) has a large correlation with medicine ball throwing distance. During rotation, a stretch of the trunk allows for a more forceful rotation through utilisation of the stretch-shortening cycle (SSC), generating torque at the shoulder joint and enhancing force transmission through the elbow musculotendinous unit. In consideration, punches require multiple angular displacements with the punch type determining segmental force contribution and a countermovement before initiation of a punch increasing the capability to produce an impulsive punch. Therefore, we recommend a selection of multi-planar exercises that challenges the mobility and stability of the trunk to help develop rotational strength and speed of the core musculature.

Movement training

Effective force transmission is derived from optimal force-coupling and length-tension relationships of active musculature; however, boxers are at risk of ineffective performance and injury because of dysfunctional movements and poor force production. This is due to repetitive movement patterns within a boxing stance and large training loads without the integration of movement and mobility training. There are various methods used to improve this, including dynamic/static stretching, proprioceptive neuromuscular facilitation (PNF) and movement training.

Shoulder and rotational mobility

The pectoralis major and anterior deltoid muscles are often overactive in boxers as their main functions are shoulder flexion and internal rotation; these actions are used during a punch. It is important to lengthen and release tension in these muscles as this can cause joint dysfunction, particularly around internal rotation of the humeral head. This can cause rotator cuff impingement, shoulder instability, bicep tendinitis and thoracic outlet syndrome. Due to the anterior muscles being overactive, posterior muscles around the shoulder joint can become inhibited. These include lower trapezius, rhomboids and rotator cuff muscles. The inhibition of these muscles can limit extension and external rotation of the shoulder with super-compensation from the lower-back muscles. Over-activity of the upper trapezius muscles can create tension in myofascial slings across the thoracic segment of the spine and can affect the ability to utilise thoracic rotation during punching actions. This results in a boxer instinctively laterally flexing the spine, causing over activity in the Quadratus Lumborum (QL), attached to L2-L5 of the spine. This is particularly common in the same side of the lead hand, due to limited rotation during the jab punch. Tightness in the QL can cause pelvic misalignment, affecting muscular activity in the lower extremities.

- *Self-myofascial release* – Massage ball over the pec, thoracic spine, latissimus dorsi
- *Static stretches/floor exercises* – Eagles, windmills, floor slides, prone TYWs, plank rows, latissimus dorsi stretch, quadruped thoracic rotation
- *Dynamic movements* – Yoga press-ups, dumbbell or suspension Y-raises, uni-lateral cable rows, half-split squat with trunk rotation, kettlebell row and rotate
- **Hip mobility and gluteal strength**

A typical boxing stance requires the athlete to externally rotate the hips and have an open stance that causes pronation of the feet. Furthermore, they are required to rapidly extend/rotate the hips during a punch; however, they do not have the strength in their hip extensors so rely on knee valgus to contribute to force development. This causes lower extremity movement impairment, with tightness in the adductor complex, psoas, iliotibial band and tensor fascia latae. Boxers need to lengthen and release tension in these areas in order to activate and strengthen the key hip extensors. Furthermore, this tension can cause misalignment of the hips – resulting in lower back pain.

- *Self-myofascial release* – IT band, gastrocnemius, soleus, hip flexors
- *Static stretches* – Kneeling hip flexor stretch, advance with rear foot elevated and trunk rotation or lateral flexion
- *Dynamic movement* – Prisoner split squat, reverse lunges, lunge and twist, spiderman and twist

Over activity of the hip flexor muscles creates pelvic misalignment and anterior tilt; this causes the gluteal muscle groups to be in a lengthened state and affects their ability to shorten and produce force. Furthermore, boxing requires good lateral movement and internal rotation of the hips. A major contributor to this is the gluteus medius muscle; however, this can be inhibited due to tightness in the adductor muscles. It should be noted that misalignment of the hips can contribute to asymmetries between left and right gluteal strength; therefore, unilateral exercises should be implemented in a boxer's training.

- *Self-myofascial release* – IT Band, TFL, piriformis
- *Floor exercises* – Banded side clams, banded glute bridges, single leg glute bridge, quadruped hip extension
- *Dynamic movement* – Walking lunges, front-foot elevated split squat, banded side-walks, ice-skaters, banded shadow-boxing

Conclusion

Successful performance in professional boxing is determined by a boxer's ability to control the contest. This is achieved by demonstrating superior offensive, defensive and ringmanship skills. A professional boxer must therefore possess a variety of technical skills supported by a wide variety of physical attributes. A large aerobic capacity is required to support physiological demands imposed by training and competition and can be developed mainly through intelligent programming of sprint and high-intensity interval training. A forceful punch is integral to contest control and is dependent on the impulse momemtum relationship. Strength training to develop hip and knee extension maximum force and rate of force development coupled with the core musculature training to improve torque through the hips and upper body should be a key focus for a professional boxer. In addition, improving range of motion and developing mobility of the shoulders and hip musculature will help improve force transmission from the foot to the fist.

References

Andersen, L. L. and Aagaard, P. (2006) 'Influence of maximal muscle strength and intrinsic muscle contractile properties on contractile rate of force development', *European Journal of Applied Physiology*, 96(1), pp. 46–52. doi:10.1007/s00421-005-0070-z.

Bangsbo, J., Iaia, F. M. and Krustrup, P. (2008) 'The Yo-Yo intermittent recovery test', *Sports Medicine*, 38(1), pp. 37–51.

Buchheit, M. (2008) 'The 30–15 intermittent fitness test: Accuracy for individualizing interval training of young intermittent sport players', *Journal of Strength & Conditioning Research*, 22(2), pp. 365–374.

Buchheit, M. and Laursen, P. B. (2013a) 'High-intensity interval training, solutions to the programming puzzle: Part I: Cardiopulmonary emphasis', *Sports Medicine (Auckland, N.Z.)*, 43(5), pp. 313–338. doi:10.1007/s40279-013-0029-x.

Buchheit, M. and Laursen, P. B. (2013b) 'High-intensity interval training, solutions to the programming puzzle: Part II: Anaerobic energy, neuromuscular load and practical applications', *Sports Medicine (Auckland, N.Z.)*, 43(5), pp. 313–338. doi:10.1007/s40279-013-0066-5.

Burgomaster, K. A., Howarth, K. R., Phillips, S. M., Rakobowchuk, M., MacDonald, M. J., McGee, S. L. and Gibala, M. J. (2008) 'Similar metabolic adaptations during exercise after low volume sprint interval and traditional endurance training in humans', *The Journal of Physiology*, 586(1), pp. 151–160. doi:10.1113/jphysiol.2007.142109.

Davis, P., Benson, P. R., Pitty, J. D., Connorton, A. J. and Waldock, R. (2015) 'The activity profile of elite male amateur boxing', *International Journal of Sports Physiology and Performance*, 10(1), pp. 53–57.

Davis, P., Leithäuser, R. and Beneke, R. (2014) 'The energetics of semicontact 3 x 2-min amateur boxing', *International Journal of Sports Physiology and Performance*, 9(2), pp. 233–239. doi:10.1123/IJSPP.2013-0006.

Gibala, M. J. and McGee, S. L. (2008) 'Metabolic adaptations to short-term high-intensity interval training', *Exercise and Sport Sciences Reviews*, 36(2), pp. 58–63. doi:10.1097/JES.0b013e318168ec1f.

Gibala, M. J., McGee, S. L., Garnham, A. P., Howlett, K. F., Snow, R. J. and Hargreaves, M. (2009) 'Brief intense interval exercise activates AMPK and p38 MAPK signaling and increases the expression of PGC-1α in human skeletal muscle', *Journal of Applied Physiology*, 106(3), pp. 929–934.

Glatthorn, J. F., Gouge, S., Nussbaumer, S., Stauffacher, S., Impellizzeri, F. M. and Maffiuletti, N. A. (2011) 'Validity and reliability of Optojump photoelectric cells for estimating vertical jump height', *Journal of Strength and Conditioning Research/National Strength & Conditioning Association*, 25(2), pp. 556–560. doi:10.1519/JSC.0b013e3181ccb18d.

Guidetti, L., Musulin, A. and Baldari, C. (2002) 'Physiological factors in middleweight boxing performance', *Journal of Sports Medicine and Physical Fitness*, 42(3), pp. 309–314.

Heilbronner, R. L., Bush, S. S., Ravdin, L. D., Barth, J. T., Iverson, G. L., Ruff, R. M., Lovell, M. R., Barr, W. B., Echemendia, R. J. and Broshek, D. K. (2009) 'Neuropsychological consequences of boxing and recommendations to improve safety: A National Academy of Neuropsychology education paper', *Archives of Clinical Neuropsychology: The Official Journal of the National Academy of Neuropsychologists*, 24(1), pp. 11–19. doi:10.1093/arclin/acp005.

Liang, H. and Ward, W. F. (2006) 'PGC-1alpha: A key regulator of energy metabolism', *Advances in Physiology Education*, 30(4), pp. 145–151. doi:10.1152/advan.00052.2006.

McGill, S. M., Chaimberg, J. D., Frost, D. M. and Fenwick, C. M. J. (2010) 'Evidence of a double peak in muscle activation to enhance strike speed and force: An example with elite mixed martial arts fighters', *Journal of Strength and Conditioning Research/National Strength & Conditioning Association*, 24(3), pp. 348–357. doi:10.1519/JSC.0b013e3181cc23d5.

McLellan, C., Lovell, D. and Gass, G. (2011) 'The role of rate of force development on vertical jump performance', *Strength and Conditioning*, 25(2), pp. 379–385.

Montero, D., Diaz-Cañestro, C. and Lundby, C. (2015) 'Endurance training and VO2max', *Medicine & Science in Sports & Exercise*, 47(10), pp. 2024–2033. doi:10.1249/MSS.0000000000000640.

Nakano, G., Iino, Y., Imura, A. and Kojima, T. (2014) 'Transfer of momentum from different arm segments to a light movable target during a straight punch thrown by expert boxers', *Journal of Sports Sciences*, 32(6), pp. 517–523. doi:10.1080/02640414.2013.843014.

Piorkowski, B. A., Lees, A. and Barton, G. J. (2011) 'Single maximal versus combination punch kinematics', *Sports Biomechanics/International Society of Biomechanics in Sports*, 10(1), pp. 1–11. doi:10.1080/14763141.2010.547590.

Ruddock, A. D., Wilson, D. C., Thompson, S. W., Hembrough, D. and Winter, E. M. (2016) 'Strength and conditioning for professional boxing: Recommendations for physical preparation', *Journal of Strength & Conditioning Research*, 38(2), pp. 81–90. doi:10.1519/SSC.0000000000000217.

Ruddock, A. D. and Winter, E. M. (August 2015) 'Jumping depends on impulse not power', *Journal of Sports Sciences*, 34(6), pp. 584–585. doi:10.1080/02640414.2015.1064157.

Smith, M. S. (2006) 'Physiological profile of senior and junior england international amateur boxers', *Journal of Sports Science & Medicine*, 5(CSSI), pp. 74–89.

Weston, M., Taylor, K. L., Batterham, A. M. and Hopkins, W. G. (Springer 2014) 'Effects of low-volume high-intensity interval training (HIT) on fitness in adults: A meta-analysis of controlled and non-controlled trials', *Sports Medicine (Auckland, N.Z.)*, 44(7), pp. 1005–1017. doi:10.1007/s40279-014-0180-z.

Yu, M., Stepto, N. K., Chibalin, A. V, Fryer, L. G. D., Carling, D., Krook, A., Hawley, J. A. and Zierath, J. R. (2003) 'Metabolic and mitogenic signal transduction in human skeletal muscle after intense cycling exercise', *The Journal of Physiology*, 546(Pt 2), pp. 327–335. doi:10.1113/jphysiol.2002.034223.

23
FENCING

Anthony Turner, Dai Fulcher, Sophie Weaver and Geoff Marshall

Introduction to the sport

Fencing is one of only a few sports that have featured at every modern Olympic Games. Fencing takes place on a 14 × 2 m strip called a 'piste', with all scoring judged electronically due to the high pace of competition. The winner is the first fencer to score 5 hits during the preliminary pool bouts or 15 hits should they reach the direct elimination bouts. During the preliminary pools, bouts last three minutes, while during elimination, each bout consists of three rounds of three minutes, with one-minute rest between rounds. In general, fencing involves a series of explosive attacks, spaced by low-intensity movements and recovery periods, predominately taxing anaerobic metabolism (Wylde, Frankie, and O'Donoghue, 2013; Guilhem, Giroux, Chollet, and Rabita, 2014). Perceptual and psychomotor skills prevail (i.e., the ability to quickly and appropriately respond to an opponent's actions), and there is a great need to repeatedly defend and attack, and often, engage in a seamless transition between the two. There are three types of weapon used in fencing; these are the foil, epee and sabre. In foil fencing, scoring is restricted to the torso, in epee the entire body may be targeted and in sabre, only hits above the waist count.

This chapter aims to identify the athletic demands of fencers so that any physical training programme developed optimally prepares athletes for competition. As an overview, this chapter will initially describe fencing according to four subsections: (1) time motion analysis, (2) physiology, (3) biomechanics, and (4) incidence of injury. An appropriate testing battery can then be subsequently addressed along with suitable training exercises. Thus the training programme that concludes this chapter will be evidence based but, of note, also based on the experiences of the authors who have acted as the sport science and medicine support team for British Fencing.

Time motion analysis

Fencing tournaments take place over an entire day (often lasting around 10 hours) and consist of around 10 bouts with a break of anywhere between 15–300 min between each bout (Roi and Bianchedi, 2008). Bouts and actual fight time consist of only 13 and 5% of actual competition time respectively, with a bout work:rest ratio (W:R) of 1:1 and 2:1 in men's and women's epee respectively, and 1:3 in men's foil (Roi and Bianchedi, 2008). On average, a foil fencer will work for 5 s while an epee fencer will work for 15 s before each rest period or interruption.

Furthermore, during each bout, a fencer may cover between 250–1000 m, attack 140 times and change direction nearly 400 times in women's epee and around 170 times in men's epee and foil.

Wylde et al. (2013) also examined TMA data during competitive bouts of elite female foilists and found a W:R of 1:1.1. They further investigated the differences between 15 hit, 5 hit and team bouts with respect to time spent engaged in low (e.g., stationary or walking), moderate (e.g., bouncing, stepping forward/backwards) and high (e.g., explosive attacking or defensive movements) intensity movements. They found that high-intensity movements accounted for 6.2 ± 2.5% of total bout time, with a mean duration of 0.7 ± 0.1 s, and a mean recovery period of 10.4 ± 3.3 s. The only 'large' difference between the bouts was found for the greater mean duration of the low-intensity movements in the 15 hit bouts (6.1 s *vs.* 4.5 s; of note this included the rest periods not available in the others). They therefore suggested that similar training plans could be used to physically prepare fencers for 15 hit, 5 hit and team bouts.

Finally, for sabre 32 men and 25 women were analysed during elimination bouts across World Cup competitions (Aquili and Tancredi, 2013). Results reveal its 'explosive' reputation is possible due to short bouts of action of ~ 2.5 s, interspersed with recovery periods of ~ 15 s, producing a W:R of ~ 1:6. On average, there are 21 lunges, 7 changes in direction and 14 attacks per bout. Total bout time rarely exceeded 9 min (including between round breaks), with only ~ 70 s of this regarded as fight time.

In summary, the W:R of each weapon differs (1:1 in epee, 1:3 in foil and 1:6 in sabre) and while epee (although much of which is submaximal) has longer fight times than foil and sabre (15, 5 and 2.5 s respectively), it appears that each weapon is still provided with sufficient recovery to work at high intensities throughout each bout. For example, within round rest periods appear to be ~ 15 s regardless of weapon, and bouts rarely last the allotted time, with only ~ 5% of a bout in foil and epee, and 70 s in sabre, actually spent 'fighting'. Perhaps the most physically demanding aspects of the bout are incurred when changing direction and attacking using a lunge (and the recovery from this), which is a frequent occurrence. Therefore, regarding programme design, it is inferred that fencing is a predominately anaerobic sport and that 'explosive' movements define performance. There is also a clear need to develop change of direction speed (CODS), lunge speed, and the ability to employ these over a possible 3 rounds of 3 min. Such conclusions advocate strength and power training (and their assessment) for the development of speed and the use of high intensity interval training (HIIT) to contend with the repeated execution of these skills.

Physiology

Until recently, only Milia et al. (2014) had looked at the physiological responses during competitive fencing. They examined 15 skilled fencers in a simulated 3 × 3 min bout while wearing a portable metabolic system. In comparison to a preliminary incremental maximum oxygen uptake ($\dot{V}O_{2max}$) test (in which they reported a low capacity of 46.3 ± 5.2 mL/min/kg), they found fencers only moderately recruited aerobic energy sources, with oxygen consumption ($\dot{V}O_2$) and heart rate (HR) remaining below the anaerobic threshold (AT). They also found that despite athletes performing below the level of AT, lactic anaerobic capacity was moderately activated to support the energy requirements of the combat rounds, with blood lactate remaining > 6 mmol/L throughout (and peaking at 6.9 mmol/L). They attributed this to the much greater use of the arms during combat compared to the incremental test used to assess AT, and the arms greater composition of fast-twitch fibers compared to the legs. Similarly, Roi and Bianchedi (2008) also reported that while the average aerobic capacity of fencers (52.9 mL/kg/min) is greater than that of the sedentary population (42.5 mL/kg/min) it is clearly lower than that of aerobic endurance based athletes.

Turner et al. (2017b) investigated intensity and fatigue in elite foil fencers across two competitions. Scores for rating of perceived exertion (RPE), blood lactate (BL) and heart rate (HR; max and > 80% max) were highest in the knockouts compared to the poules, with differences in perceptions of RPE being significantly different between the two (see Table 23.1). The high and sustained HR values, coupled with high RPE scores, further corroborate the aforementioned TMA data, that fencing (foil) is a high-intensity anaerobic sport, and for the most part, relies on alactic energy sources (i.e., phosphocreatine). That said, the spread of data (i.e., the SD) suggests that some bouts (both poules and KOs) evoke BL values of ≥ 4 mmol/L and thus derive energy from anaerobic glycolysis; again, this corroborates previous findings.

The physiological demands of a sabre competition have also been examined (Turner, Dimitriou, Marshall, Russell, Bannock, and Bishop, in press). Results reveal that across both poule and KO bouts (to which all assessed fencers progressed and one of which won the competition), fencers on average again operate under the threshold for OBLA (3.0 ± 1.2 and 3.6 ± 1.3 mmol·L^{-1} respectively), with standard deviations suggesting that it is likely that at some point during the competition (especially during KO bouts), they will operate above this. Furthermore, the intensity (RPE) of KO bouts is again greater than that of poule bouts (13.6 ± 2.6 vs. 12.1 ± 2.4 respectively). Finally, it was hypothesised that a bout statistic such as total points or rating of perceived exertion (RPE) could be used to signify a shift in energy metabolism, and thus be used to guide competition strategies aimed at facilitating recovery for subsequent bouts; surplus fatigue (or rather hydrogen ions) could accumulate and negatively affect performance, especially if bouts are only separated by short breaks. While no correlations existed during poule bouts, significant correlations ($p < 0.05$) were found in KO bouts between RPE and BL ($r = 0.63$), total points and BL ($r = 0.79$) and total points and RPE ($r = 0.85$). Figures 23.1a and 23.1b identify the former two associations, and include the OBLA deflection point and its corresponding RPE score and points total respectively.

Table 23.1 Mean (±SD) results from two competitions, separated according to poule and knockout stages

	Time (min)	RPE	BL (mmol/L)	HRave (bpm)	HRmax (bpm)	>80%HRmax
Poules	5.33 ± 2.15	5.7 ± 1.3	3.1 ± 1.4	168 ± 8	192 ± 7	68%
Knockout	15.09 ± 5.24★	8.5 ± 1.3★	3.6 ± 1.0	171 ± 5	195 ± 7	74%

Key: time = length of bout in minutes; RPE = rating of perceived exertion; BL = blood lactate; HRave = average heart rate (HR); HRmax = maximum HR; >80%HRmax = percentage of time spent above 80% of HRmax.

★ = Significantly different from pool bouts

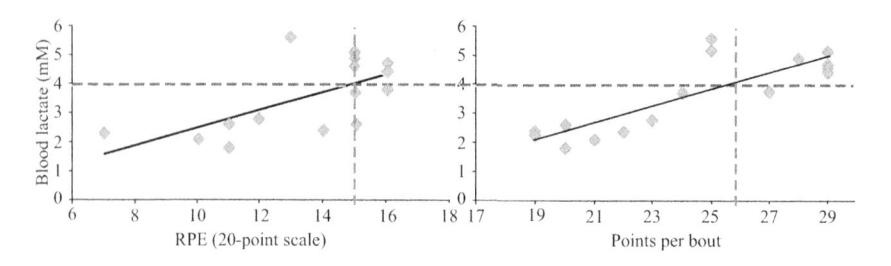

Figures 23.1a and b (left to right). Relationship between blood lactate and the rating of perceived exertion (RPE) (a) and points per bout (b). The RPE and points associated with the onset of blood lactate accumulation (i.e., 4 mmol/L) have been identified (dashed line)

The between bout timings of a fencing competition are unpredictable as is the quality of opposition, thus it is advisable to prepare athletes for the worst-case scenario; a short break followed by a maximum point bout (i.e., 29 hits) on account of an evenly contested match. In this scenario, RPE is likely to be > 8 and BL > 4 mmol/L, and given the nature of the fight, high-intensity interval training is again recommended. This type of training ensures that athletes are exposed to high concentrations of BL, building a buffering capacity and tolerance of hydrogen ions as a consequence. Noting lactate accumulation is exacerbated by poor nutrition, dehydration, and heat, fencers should also develop effective routines to address these. Fencers should be especially vigilant if they have just fenced a 26-point match or worked at an intensity they would define as 15 out of 20 (see Figure 23.1). Here an active cool-down post bout becomes essential.

Biomechanics of the lunge

By far, the lunge (Figure 23.2) is the most common form of attack, with others including those derived from in-stance counter-attacks (following a parry, for example) and the fleche. Guilhem et al. (2014) described the kinetics of the lunge, with respect to push-off and landing forces. They used a 6.6 m-long force plate system where elite female sabreurs (French national team; N = 10) performed a lunge preceded by a step. From this, displacement and velocity was calculated and compared to dynamometry strength testing of the hip and knee. The fencers' centre of mass travelled 1.49 m in 1.42 s and at a peak velocity of 2.6 m/s, generating a peak force of 496.6 N,

Figure 23.2 The lunge (right to left), commencing from the on guard position

with maximal negative (braking) power at front foot landing equaling 1446 W. Maximal velocity was significantly ($p < 0.05$) correlated to the concentric peak torque produced by the rear hip ($r = 0.60$) and knee ($r = 0.79$) extensor muscles, as well as to the front knee extensors ($r = 0.81$). Also, through EMG analysis, they showed that the activation of rear leg extensor muscles i.e., gluteus maximus, vastis lateralis and soleus, was correlated to LV ($r = 0.70, 0.59$ and 0.44 respectively). Collectively their findings illustrate that the ability to move forward and to decelerate the body mass as quickly as possible is a fundamental performance determinant of fencing, and supports the use of strength training, as previously suggested.

Turner, Bishop, Chavda, Edwards, Brazier, and Kilduff (2016a) also investigated the physical determinants of lunge performance, where fencers lunged at a target. Coupled with high-speed video analysis, this enabled the quantification of lunge distance, time, and velocity. These measures were correlated with fencer anthropometrics and athletic tests of lower body power. Height, arm-span and flexibility (the latter measured as the linear distance between the lateral malleolus of each leg during a split in the frontal plane) showed no correlation with lunge velocity. While most measures of lower-body power did, SBJ had the highest correlation ($r = 0.51$). Height, flexibility and arm span did however, correlate with lunge distance ($r = 0.45, 0.38$ and 0.37 respectively).

The lack of any correlation with lunge time across all variables may suggest that the ability to generate lower-body power cancels out the assumed shorter time expected for smaller fencers (who presumably travel a shorter distance) to hit the target. That is, enhanced lower-body power also enables smaller fencers to take up their *en guard* position further away from their opponent (i.e., at similar distances to taller fencers). Furthermore, this data appears to suggest that fencers tend to opt for standing a greater distance from the target (and staying out of range), rather than staying put and translating any enhanced power in to quicker hits. Anecdotally, coaches also tend to teach their athletes to maintain an 'out of range' distance from their opponent.

Turner et al. (2017c) subsequently sought to identify the physical characteristics used by fencers to determine their striking range. Should any be associated, and given the ability to stay out of range is important to performance, results will affect exercise selection. The research project was extended to also examine each fencer's ability to accurately estimate this, and how this differed between levels of expertise (i.e., elite *vs.* national level fencers). Fencers had to position themselves in the *en guard* position, as if they were to cut (sabre) or hit (epee or foil) the target using a lunge and then a step-lunge; the distance from the tip of the front shoe to the base of the target was then recorded. Following this, fencers were able to take practice attempts to provide a more precise position (referred to as 'actual' distance), and again distance was measured. Results revealed that elite fencers are better at estimating their lunging and step-lunge distance compared to national ranked junior fencers (−0.9 *vs.* 7.3% and 5.4 *vs.* 10.9% respectively), but surprisingly, elite fencers actual and estimated distance was significantly less (222.6 *vs.* 251.5 cm and 299.3 *vs.* 360.2 cm respectively). Also, only arm ($r = .81$) and leg-span ($r = .71$) were significantly correlated to estimated lunging distance, and this was only in elite fencers. It would be prudent to deem that the national level fencers are using excessive ranges (when lunging), as oppose to the elite fencers under performing, especially as the elites also had higher values for anthropometric and lower body power testing. Such results may again support the desire to stay out of range, with elite level fencers only closing the gap once they have developed the ability to effectively process opponent stimuli and respond quickly and accordingly. Lower body power (standing broad jump) again appeared important to estimated lunging, with associations similar to that reported by Turner et al. (2016a) and Tsolakis and Vagenas (2010) but considered non-significant here on account of sample size (although it should be acknowledged that there may be no relationship).

Currently, data again suggests the use of strength training (potentially emphasising eccentric strength given the plethora of high force landings from lunges) coupled with plyometric and ballistic type exercises to reduce ground contact times, and enhance the rate of force development respectively. Squats and deadlifts appear good exercise choices (particularly the latter) as they target the knee and hip extensors, along with bench press and seated medicine ball throws, for example, as they target upper body strength and power development respectively. With respect to these, a fencer's arm should move first in an attack to gain priority; therefore, the independent ability of the arms to rapidly thrust forward is essential. The development of reactive strength (and thus reduced ground contact times) coupled with 'deep' squats (below parallel) or split squat exercises (given the below parallel position at the end of a lunge) can help target the gluteal muscles and collectively train a fast recovery from the lunge back to on guard. Given the prolonged ground contact times (~700 ms) and flat-footed front leg drive (i.e., not involving ankle extension), and also the fact that fencers tend to move forwards in a heel-toe sequence, hip and knee extensor strength may take on added importance here (it should be noted however, that the heel-toe sequence of moving has recently been critisised, in favour of moving using the ball of the foot to generate propulsion, see Turner and Haremenberg (in press) for a review). Finally, Nordics and stiff leg deadlifts can help reduce the high incidence of hamstring strains (discussed below) and increasing adductor flexibility may enhance (or at least not limit) lunge distance.

Risk of injury

Perhaps the most insightful research project to investigate injuries in fencing was conducted by Harmer (2008), who collected data from all national events organised by the U.S. Fencing association over a 5-year period (2001–2006). In total, over 78,000 fencers (both genders) from 8–70 years of age and across all weapons were investigated. Throughout this period, all incidents that resulted in withdrawal from competition (i.e., a time-loss injury) were documented from which the incidence and characteristics of injuries were calculated. This value was determined as the rate of time-loss injuries (TLI) per 1000 hours of athlete exposures (AE), with one AE equaling one bout. There were 184 TLI in total, at a rate of 0.3/1000 AE. The TLI of foil and epee was similar and highest in sabre (0.26 vs. 0.42/1000 AE). Strains and sprains accounted for half of all injuries and contusions for 12%. The lower extremities accounted for most injuries (63%) and mostly involved the knee (20%), thigh (15%, three quarters of which were hamstring strains) and ankle (13%). Finally, above the hip, TLI of the lumbar spine (9%) and fingers (7%) predominated.

Harmer (2008) concluded that the risk of injury in fencing is very low with the chance of injury in football and basketball 50 and 31 times greater respectively. When injury does occur, it is most likely to occur at the knee; hamstring strains are the most common type of injury and male sabreurs are most at risk. Because fencers tend to use (and therefore develop) the anterior musculature more than the posterior, and one side of the body more than the other, this may leave them exposed to muscle strains in the weaker muscles (as exampled by the higher incidence of hamstring to quadriceps strains). More specifically, Guilhem et al. (2014) warn that repetitions of the lunge or maintaining the *en guard* position over prolonged periods may cause pathologies such as the adductor compartment syndrome and the compression of arteries in the iliac area due to hypertrophy of the psoas major (Cockett syndrome), or induce osteoarthritis. A difference of > 15% is generally used as a clinical marker of bilateral strength asymmetry and significant risk of injury (Impellizzeri, Rampinni, and Marcora, 2007). Strength training may be able to address this imbalance as well as increasing antagonist muscle strength. Pertinent to performance, an increase in antagonist muscle strength may increase movement speed and accuracy of movement (Jaric, Ropert, Kukolj, and Ilic, 1995). This has been hypothesised to occur due to alterations in neural firing patterns, leading to a decrease in the braking times and accuracy of the limbs in rapid ballistic movements (Jaric et al., 1995). In essence, strength balance is also needed to break the agonists succinctly in rapid limb movements and as such, increases in hamstring strength will enable faster velocities of knee extension. Of course, strength training will also enable the weaker limb (typically the back leg) to be targeted.

The data above again describes the need to develop hamstring strength and warns of the overuse injuries generated subsequent to continuous fencing in an asymmetrical stance (see Figure 23.2), which never alternates. Consequently, it would be prudent to include training that puts high landing loads through the back foot (thus training the weaker limb) and exercises such as the split jerk and split snatch (here the stance is reversed), which similarly have flat, front-foot landings, are advised. Of course, single leg jumps favouring this side would be advantageous too. When performing HIIT (as advised above) it may be advisable to not use – or at least limit the use of – fencing footwork in their orthodox stance. Instead, either their stance can be switched or use non- or reduced weight-bearing activities. While this is less sport-specific, ultimately the W:R ratios can still be used to evoke a high blood lactate response and invoke adaptions centering on the tolerance and recovery from continuous explosive exercise (discussed further in the programming section). Finally, the use of the various squat and deadlift exercise, in addition to reduced training exposure to their fencing stance, should facilitate the reduction of lower back pain.

Fitness testing battery

The testing battery of fencers contains tests that would be found in most other sports, perhaps with different rationales to govern their use. Strength measured via 1RM back squats (or isometric mid thigh pull) is important for aforementioned reasons, as is lower body power, especially via the SBJ for this population. Single leg jumps also provide a good measure of asymmetry, which is an important test given the asymmetrical nature of the sport as discussed. Plyometric ability via the reactive strength index has also become a standard test in fitness batteries, with obvious carry over to this and most other sports. Change of direction speed and repeat sprint ability tests are also common and important measures, but it is important to have some sport specificity here. These are thus described in more detail below, before the fitness battery is summarised in Table 23.3.

Change of direction speed: the 4-2-2-4

The CODS test is measured using a 4-2-2-4 m shuttle (Turner et al., 2016a) as this is considered to replicate the sport demands. For this, fencers start behind a set of timing gates set at hip height. Using fencing footwork, they travel as fast as they can up to a 4 m line, ensuring their front foot crosses the line, they then travel backwards ensuring the front foot crosses the 2 m line. Again they travel forward to the 4 m line, before moving backwards past the start line. The test should be stopped if fencers use footwork unrepresentative of proper form, if the beam is broken at the start or finish line with any part of their body other than their hips, and if the athlete fails to pass either line with their toes or lunges in order to reach a line. The test is illustrated in Figure 23.3.

Fencing

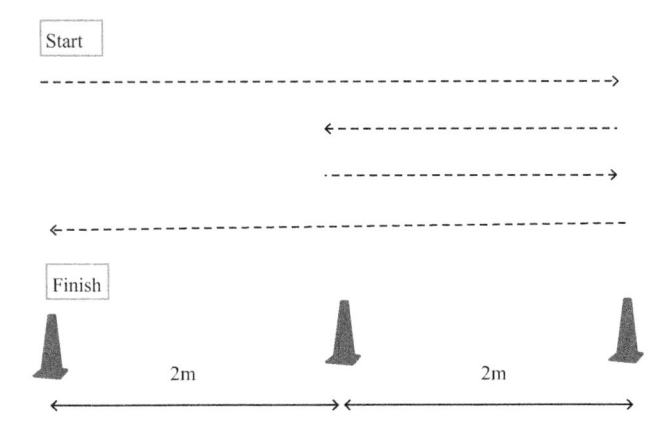

Figure 23.3 The 4-2-2-4 fencing shuttle

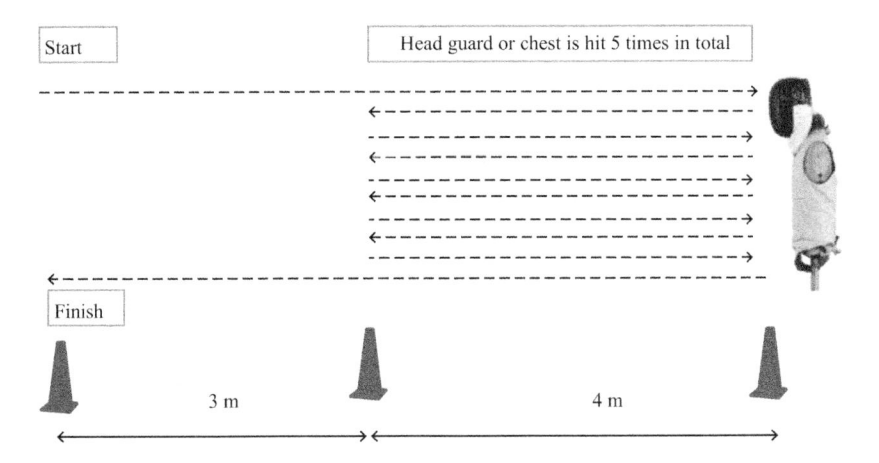

Figure 23.4 Repeat lunge ability test set-up

Repeat lunge ability

Given the repetitive demand to effectively execute lunging and changes in direction within each bout, the ability to sustain these at maximal capacity, referred to as repeat lunge ability (RLA; synonymous with repeat sprint ability as per other sports), should be considered fundamental to performance, and is a test described by Turner et al. (2016b). While the work to rest ratios vary between weapons, it is clear that as the competition progresses and fencers reach the elimination bouts, the intensity and anaerobic nature of fights increase, with lactate values rising > 4 mmol/L. The RLA test, rather than relying on each weapon's W:R, focuses on representing a worst case scenario, and is thus best described as a measure of how well a fencer can sustain sport specific anaerobic work, coping in the presence of high concentrations of H^+. To complete the test, fencers (using fencing footwork) travel 7 m towards a mannequin where they perform a lunge to hit either its chest or head guard. They then change direction, traveling backwards until their lead toe is behind a 4 m line. From here they continue to hit the mannequin a further 4 times, traveling back to the 4 m line between hits; only following the last hit (5th) do they then travel back past the start line (positioned 7 m from the mannequin). This is repeated 5 times with 10 s rest between intervals, with the score recorded as the average time across the 5 intervals (see Figure 23.4).

Table 23.2 Fencing tests along with normative data presented as means (±SD). Data was collected from fencers with the following characteristics: 18.9 ± 3.2 years of age, 174.35 ± 10.42 cm tall, 70.67 ± 7.35 kg in mass, and 8.5 ± 4.2 years fencing experience at ≥ national level.

Test	Mean	SD
Countermovement jump (cm)	40.13	7.76
Single-leg jump front foot (cm)	23.01	4.79
Single-leg jump back foot (cm)	20.57	4.78
Asymmetry (%)*	10.60	8.20
Reactive strength index**	1.65	0.44
Standing broad jump (cm)	204.17	26.22
4-2-2-4 (s)	4.65	0.41
Repeat lunge ability (s)	16.03	1.40

*Single leg jump scores were used to identify any asymmetries between legs and used the following equation: (stronger leg − weaker leg)*100/stronger leg. For most fencers, the front leg is strongest but this is not always the case. Therefore an equation that defines asymmetry values on strength rather than leg dominance is preferred.

** The RSI was calculated as flight time in milliseconds divided by ground contact time in milliseconds.

The test battery

Table 23.2 highlights the test battery typically used with fencers. While there are other tests (and of equal value), e.g., measures of strength or high-load power capability, these are the ones that can be done with minimal equipment and despite large numbers of fencers requiring testing. Table 23.2 also provides some normative data.

Programming

Before detailing the S&C program of a fencer, it is prudent to first address an obvious question: do fencers require a weapon specific approach to S&C? In short, the answer is no, but this topic is covered in detail elsewhere (Turner et al., 2017a). In essence, all fencers (epee, foil and sabre) require the ability to explosively lunge at an opponent, change direction at speed and repeat these actions numerous times throughout a bout and competition day. As such, all fencers can use the programme below.

A strength and conditioning programme for fencing should focus upon enhancing the following areas: (1) availability to train due to the high technical demand of the sport, (2) facilitating on piste movement in order to support technical output, and (3) sustaining this technical performance throughout each bout and over the competition day(s). Within these, specific areas (e.g., lunge, recovery from lunge, change of direction, repeated lunge ability) can be isolated, tested and targeted for improvement within a training block.

As is common practice within strength and conditioning, the programme must be specific to each individual and should be geared toward competition performance. Here, in line with coach and athlete feedback, physical weaknesses that may limit technical performance can be identified and become a focus for the next training cycle. The physical characteristics of the fencer will underpin this, measured through strength and power testing, for example, and movement screening, where this information can drive an holistic approach to programming in order to promote robustness, ensuring the athlete is available to train. The anthropometric characteristics of fencers often influence the style of fencing and therefore also drive programming. For example, fencers of smaller stature (and thus reduced attacking range) can compensate for this by working on the ability to generate force, especially in the horizontal direction.

The benefits of eccentric training can and should also be noted. For example, data collected among British Talent fencers identified that single leg countermovement jump height for the lead-leg correlated better with distance and velocity, and despite not being responsible for propelling the body forward whilst lunging, also produced higher jump scores than the back-leg (18.86 ± 4.65 cm *vs.* 17.1 ± 4.62 cm). It may be that this is an outcome of the high landing forces generated from the lunge, as well as the high push-off forces required to quickly recover back to the *en guard* position. These may reveal the benefits of also exposing the back-leg to higher landing/eccentric forces as part of training, as well as high concentric forces from a relatively deep squat position (thighs at least parallel to the floor). Similarly, improvements in change of direction will be met though exercises that develop lower-body power, especially with horizontal propulsion. These should also be supplemented with exercises that develop reactive (and thus eccentric) strength, such as drop jumps and hurdle jumps, perhaps the latter having a greater carry-over given the horizontal displacement. Turner and Haremenberg (in press) summarise that some of the drills used to train sprinters are ideal, given the horizontal momentum athletes are challenged to develop during them.

As aforementioned, it is advisable to prepare athletes for the worst-case scenario; a short break followed by a maximum point bout (i.e., 29 hits), with RPE > 8 and BL > 4 mmol/L. To create sufficient exposure to this intensity and metabolic environment, and given the absence of the psychological stress (and release of adrenaline, for example) associated with competition, a non-sport specific approach must be taken. This conclusion follows our unpublished data that the stimulus of fencing footwork in a training environment alone, including the use of weapon specific W:R, does not equate to the BL concentrations of competition intensity – nowhere near, in fact, and serves only to generate high levels of muscle soreness that negatively impact the following day's training. Other methods such as wattbike, rowing, and battle ropes, for example, are thus programmed to drive the exposure of competition fatigue and intensity. Any footwork that is completed with a view to conditioning the fencer is recommended to first include a pre-fatigue element via those alternate modes.

Periodised training plans

Because all international competitions (World Cup and Grand Prix – see Table 23.3. for 2013/14 Season schedule) are important, athletes should be brought to peak physical fitness for each. Our periodisation of training is dictated by the time between competitions. Where the programme aims to maintain performance (i.e., < 4 wks between competitions), an undulating approach is used (see Table 23.4), for others (≥ 4 wks between competitions) a traditional approach can be used. All types conclude with a taper week of reduced volume training, but where intensity is kept high, and maintenance programmes have an emphasis on corrective exercise. The 20-week, 5-week and 9-week programs (incorporating traditional periodisation) are identified in Table 23.5.

Table 23.3 Competition calendar for the 2013/2014 season

Start	End	Competition	Time between competitions	City	Country
24.10.13	26.10.13	World Combat Games		St. Petersburg	Russia
			20 Weeks★		
17.01.14	18.01.14	Challenge International de Paris		Paris	France
19.01.14	19.01.14	Challenge Rommel		Paris	France
			5 Weeks★		
21.02.14	22.02.14	Tournoi Ciudad de A Coruna		La Coruna	Spain
23.03.14	23.02.14	Coupe de Monde par equipes		La Coruna	Spain
			1 Week		
1.03.14	02.03.14	Fleuret de St-Peterbourg		St-Peterbourg	Russia
			2 Weeks		
15.03.14	16.03.14	Coupe Ville de Venise		Venice	Italy
			1 Week		
21.03.14	22.03.14	Lowe von Bonn		Bonn	Germany
23.03.14	23.03.14	Coupe de Monde par equips Lowe von Bonn		Bonn	Germany
			5 Weeks★		
25.04.14	26.04.14	SK Trophee Seoul		Seoul	Korea
27.04.14	27.04.14	Coupe de Monde par equipes		Seoul	Korea
			1 Week		
03.05.14	04.05.14	Prince Takamondo WC		Tokyo	Japan
			3 Weeks		
23.05.14	24.05.14	Copa Villa La Habana		La Havane	Cuba
25.05.14	25.05.14	Coupe de Monde par equipes		La Havane	Cuba
			2 Weeks		
07.06.14	14.06.14	European Championships		Strasburg	Germany
			9 Weeks★		
05.08.14	13.08.14	World Championships		Sofia	Bulgaria

★ Denotes where programming aims to improve the fencers' physical performance. Other durations denote maintenance or tapers. Of note, some fencers will not qualify/be selected for all competitions, so training durations will change.

Table 23.4 Competition phase strength and conditioning program

Undulating periodised program

Phase: competition (2–3 weeks between competition)

Session 1 (strength)	Load	Sets/reps	Session 2 (power)	Load	Sets/reps
Back squat	90% 1RM	3 × 3	Power clean	80% 1RM	5 × 2
SL RDL	80% 1RM	3 × 6	Hurdle jumps	BW	5 × 3
Bent over row	75% 1RM	3 × 8	Prowler push	BW	6 × 10 m
Cable rotations	–	3 × 10	Barbell rollouts	–	3 × 10
Watt bike	Max effort	6 × 6 s, 30 s rest			

Table 23.5 Periodisation structure for training weeks between competition

Traditional periodisation

20 week cycle		5 week cycle		9 week cycle	
Phase	Weeks	Phase	Weeks	Phase	Weeks
High volume strength	4	Strength	2	High volume strength	2
Strength	4	Power	2	Strength	3
Power	4	Taper	1	Power	3
Strength	3			Taper	1
Power	3				
Taper	2				

Conclusion

Given the repetitive demand to effectively execute lunging and changes in direction within fencing, the ability to sustain these at maximal capacity is fundamental to performance, and describes a fencer's speed and power endurance capacity. Due to the requirement to stand in an asymmetrical position, inducing potential asymmetries, strength training is necessary for both performance enhancement and injury avoidance. Strength and power lift variations, including unilateral exercise, are fundamental to support this, coupled with ballistic training and plyometric exercise, again with a focus upon unilateral jumps with emphasis on landing mechanics. Conditioning should be conversant to the differing W:R between weapon types; however, consideration of exposing athletes to 'worst case scenario' must be applied. Performing high intensity interval training is recommended, particularly involving unloaded modes of exercise (bike, row, battle ropes) in order to evoke high blood lactate response and develop adaptations surrounding tolerance and recovery from continuous explosive exercise. Finally, programming should be mindful towards exercises that favour the posterior chain, to both promote horizontal force application and address relative weakness in comparison to anterior musculature. The lack of acute (within competition) fatigue may not be surprising given the format of a fencing competition, which provides ample opportunity for recovery. In fact, and assuming consistent psychological stress and appropriate nutrition, it should be conceivable that fencers can fence at maximal intensity throughout the duration of the competition. Subsequently, and beyond strength and conditioning practices, the sport science support teams of these athletes should investigate various recovery strategies around fuel and fluid replacement (i.e., nutrition) and psychological interventions to cope with the high stress that may in turn increase intensity and fatigue. Also, post competition strategies centering on reducing muscle damage and subsequent inflammation should be investigated.

References

Aquili, A., and Tancredi, V. (2013). Performance Analysis in Sabre. *The Journal of Strength & Conditioning Research, 27* (13), 624–630.

Guilhem, G., Giroux, C. C., Chollet, D., and Rabita, G. (2014). Mechanical and Muscular Coordination Patterns During a High-Level Fencing Assault. *Medicine and Science in Sports and Exercise, 46* (2), 341–350.

Harmer, P. (2008). Incidence and Characteristics of Time-Loss Injuries in Competitive Fencing: A Prospective, 5-Year Study of National Competitions. *Clinical Journal of Sports Medicine, 18* (2), 137–142.

Impellizzeri, F., Rampinni, M. M., and Marcora, S. (2007). A Vertical Jump Force Test for Assessing Bilateral Strength Asymmetry in Athletes. *Medicine and Science in Sports and Exercise, 39* (11), 2044–2050.

Jaric, S., Ropert, R., Kukolj, M., and Ilic, D. (1995). Role of Agonist and Antagonist Muscle Strength in Rapid Movement Performance. *European Journal of Applied Physioliogy, 71*, 464–468.

Milia, R., Roberto, S., Palazzolo, G., Sanna, I., Omeri, M., Piredda, S. et al. (2014). Physiological Responses and Energy Expenditure During Competitive Fencing. *Applied Physiology, Nutrition, and Metabolism, 39* (3), 324–328.

Roi, G., and Bianchedi, D. (2008). The Science of Fencing. Implications for Performance and Injury Prevention. *Sports Medicine, 38* (6), 465–481.

Tsolakis, C., and Vagenas, G. (2010). Anthropometric, Physiological and Performance Characteristics of Elite and Sub-elite Fencers. *Journal of Human Kinetics, 23* (1), 89–95.

Turner, A., Bishop, C., Chavda, S., Edwards, M., Brazier, J., and Kilduff, L. (2016a). Physical Characteristics Underpinning Lunging and Change of Direction Speed in Fencing. *Journal of Strength and Conditioning Research, 30* (8), 2235–2241.

Turner, A., Bishop, C., Cree, J., Edwards, M., Chavda, M. et al. (2017a). Do Fencers Require a Weapon Specific Approach to Strength and Conditioning? *Journal of Strength and Conditioning Research, 31* (6), 1662–1668.

Turner, A., Dimitriou, L., Marshall, G., Russell, M., Bannock, L., and Bishop, C. (In press). Physiological Demands of Sabre Competitions in Elite Fencers. *Australian Journal of Strength and Conditioning*.

Turner, A., and Haremenberg, J. (In press). Why fencers should bounce: A new method of movement to engage the stretch-shortening cycle. *International Journal of Sport Science and Coaching*.

Turner, A., Kilduff, L., Marshall, G., Phillips, J., Noto, A., Buttigieg, C. et al. (2017b). Competition Intensity and Fatigue in Elite Fencing. *Journal of Strength and Conditioning Research, 31* (11), 3128–3136.

Turner, A., Marshall, G., Buttigieg, C., Noto, A., Phillips, J., Dimitriou, L. et al. (2016b). Physical Characteristics Underpinning Repetitive Lunging in Fencing. *Journal of Strength and Conditioning Research, 30* (11), 3134–3139.

Turner, A., Marshall, G., Noto, A., Chavda, S., Atlay, N., and Kirby, D. (2017c). Staying Out of Range: Increasing Attacking Distance in Fencing. *International Journal of Sports Physiology and Performance*.

Wylde, M., Frankie, H., and O'Donoghue. (2013). A Time-Motion Analysis of Elite Women's Foil Fencing. *International Journal of Performance Analysis in Sport, 13*, 365–376.

24
WHEELCHAIR FENCING

Alex Villiere, Michael Edwards, Baldip Sahota and Anthony Turner

Introduction to the sport

History

Wheelchair fencing (WF) is considered one of the first sport disciplines practiced by disabled people and originated in 1948 at Stoke Mandeville in a rehabilitative centre funded by Dr Ludwig Guttmann (Boguszewski and Torzewska, 2011). It was practiced by war veterans and former soldiers post World War II for rehabilitation purposes. The original rehabilitative nature of WF quickly evolved into a competitive sport. Since the first Paralympic games held in Rome in 1960, WF has been an official Paralympic sport (Chung, 2015). The sport is now governed by the International Wheelchair and Amputee Sport Federation (IWAS) and has a long European tradition; however, since the 1990s the sport has developed rapidly as teams from Asia also joined the competition.

Rules

To be entitled to participate in WF, athletes should demonstrate a permanent disability. Disabilities can include spinal cord injury (SCI), amputation, poliomyelitis, cerebral palsy (CP), multiple sclerosis, muscular dystrophy, and a variety of congenital disorders that do not fit into any traditional definition of disability (Chung, 2015). The most common impairments in the sport include athletes with CP, limb deficiency, and SCI. The rules are similar to able-bodied fencing; however, amendments have been made to accommodate the lack of movement. Similar to traditional fencing, WF includes three weapons, which are foil, epee and sabre, and wheelchair fencers compete seated on a sport-specific wheelchair (Figure 24.1); rules and regulations for the wheelchair can be found on the IWAS site (International Wheelchair & Amputee Sports Federation, 2016a). Competitions take place on a "piste" measuring 4 m × 1.5 m where the fencers' wheelchair are fixed to a metal framed platform at a 110° angle, to allow the fencers' sword arm to be directly opposed to each other. The platform also brings stability, preventing possible tipping of the wheelchair during the powerful attacks undertaken by competitors (e.g., the lunge) (Fung et al., 2013). When fencing, athletes are not permitted to rise from their chair and at least one buttock must remain in contact with the wheelchair at all times.

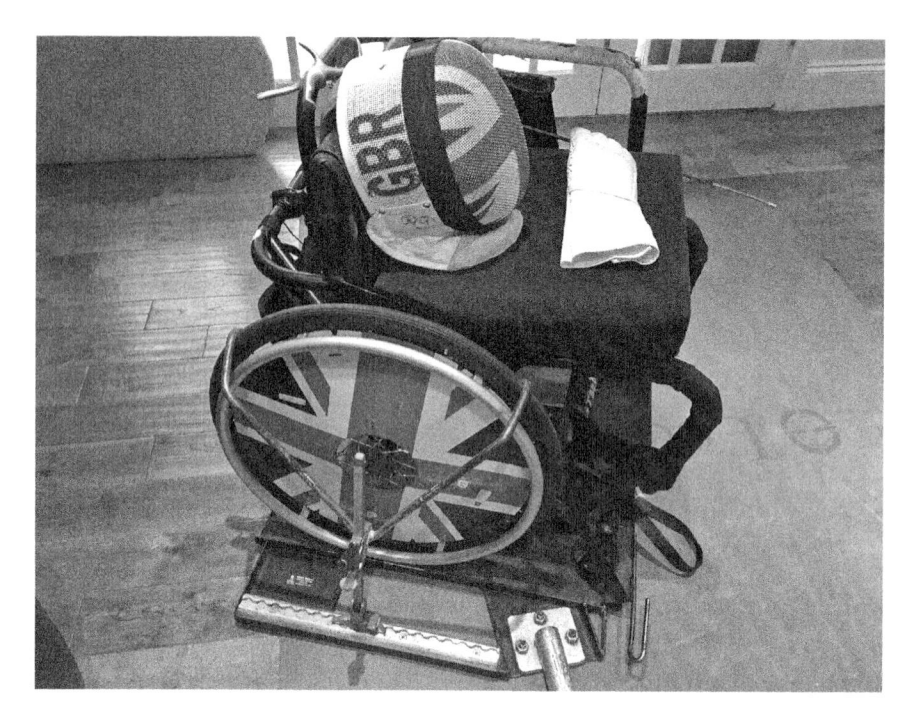

Figure 24.1 The fencing wheelchair

Prior to the start of a fencing bout, fencing distance must be determined. Distance is established by one fencer holding the weapon, flexing the elbow until the forearm is vertical and upper arm horizontal to the floor. The elbow should be directly pointing towards the other fencer. The opposite fencer then extends his/her arm until the sword reaches the inner edge of the opponent's forearm for foil, and the outer edge of the elbow for epee and sabre (International Wheelchair & Amputee Sports Federation, 2015). The fencer with the shorter reach may decide a distance lying between his and his opponent's reach.

Wheelchair fencers are required to wear the same regular clothing as able-bodied fencers, which include a protective mask, gloves and jacket. For epee, a metal-lined apron is worn below the waist to help in the cancellation of non-valid hits. Each weapon has its own scoring area, as displayed in Table 24.1. Competitors are connected electronically to a scoring box, recording hits on their opponents, which are then validated by the referee, according to the weapon's specific rules.

Table 24.1 Description of the 3 swords used in WF

Swords	Target area and weapon specificity
Foil	The target area is limited to the trunk, not including the arms or head. Hits can only be scored with the tip of the weapon.
Epee	Touches are valid from the waist up including the arms and mask. In this event, simultaneous hits can be scored; therefore, both fencers can score at the same time. Hits can only be scored with the tip of the weapon.
Sabre	Hits are valid from the waist up, including arms and mask. Touches can be scored with any part of the blade.

Competitions

The yearly competitive calendar varies on a year to year basis and includes on average 5 World Cup competitions held across the world (Table 24.2). In addition to World Cups, World Championships are held every 2 years, and Paralympics games every 4 years. Competitions include an individual event as well as a team event. During each competition, points can be earned depending on the athlete's finishing position. The points earned during these competitions contribute to the fencers overall world ranking and also dictate selection to the Paralympics Games. Official competitions are organised into two distinctive stages, the poule stage followed by the direct elimination stage (International Wheelchair & Amputee Sports Federation, 2017a).

During the poule stages, athletes are seeded based on their ranking, meaning higher ranked fencers are likely to compete against lower ranked athletes. Each fencer in the group will fence each other. The winner is the first athlete to score 5 points or with the greatest number of touches after 3 minutes. Direct elimination for foil and epee bouts are split into three 3 minute rounds interspaced with a minute break. The winner is the first athlete to reach 15 points. In sabre, bouts are split into two 3 minute rounds interspaced with a minute break, unless one of the fencers reaches 8 points prior to the end of the first round; at which point a minute break is allocated prior to the second round.

Table 24.2 2017 Wheelchair Fencing Competition calendar (International Wheelchair & Amputee Sports Federation, 2017b)

Event	Dates
World Cup Eger, Hungary	17–19 Feb
World Cup Pisa, Italy	17–19 March
World Cup Stadskanaal, Netherlands	10–14 May
World Cup Warsaw, Poland	28 June–3 July
World Championships, Rome, Italy	7–12 November

Disability classification

To promote regular and fair competitions, wheelchair fencers are classified into three different categories, A, B and C. The assessment of an athlete's disability is internationally standardised and undertaken by accredited international classifiers (International Wheelchair & Amputee Sports Federation, 2016a). Firstly, the level of disability of an athlete is determined to ensure minimum eligibility requirements are met. If so, athletes then undergo a series of tests, which includes the bench test and a variety of functional tests; these assessments further help determine an athlete's impairment levels. During the bench test (Table 24.3), five physical examinations are used to establish an athlete's muscle strength, abnormal tone, joint range of motion, level of amputation, and limb coordination (Chung, 2015). The results provide baseline medical information, impairment level, and residual motor function.

The second part of the assessment includes 6 functional tests. Examples are presented in Figure 24.2. The tests include skills that are specific to WF. Sitting balance, arm function, trunk, and lower limb muscle performance are assessed.

Following the assessment, the athlete will be assigned a category, either A, B or C. The most common impairment for category A athletes includes limb deficiency (e.g. polio or amputee) and CP. Such athletes demonstrate good sitting balance and trunk functional ability. Predominantly,

Table 24.3 Bench test card physical examination adapted from International Wheelchair & Amputee Sports Federation (2016b)

Bench test for disability sports classification						
Joint	Movement	Full range of movement	Paralysis muscle test		Range of movement dysfunction	
			Right	Left	Right	Left
Shoulder	Flexion					
Extension						
Abduction						
External rotation						
Internal rotation						
Elbow	Flexion					
Extension						
Pronation						
Supination						
Wrist	Flexion					
Extension						
Ulnar flexion						
Radial flexion						
Fingers	Flexion					
Extension						
Abduction						
Adduction						
Trunk	Flexion upper					
Flexion lower						
Extention upper						
Extension lower						
Lateral flexion						
Rotation						
Hip	Flexion					
Extension						
Abduction						
Adduction						
Knee	Flexion					
Extension						
Ankle	Plantar flexion					

category B athletes would display a SCI at thoracic level (T). Such athletes demonstrate reduced trunk functional ability and stability. Finally, category C includes athletes with high lesions at cervical level (C) ranging from T1 to C5. Fencers classified in category C have a low level of functional ability and display impaired arm function affecting gripping. Fixing the weapon to the hand of a category C fencer is common practice. Category C athletes are not included in the Paralympics games due to limited number of participants, but are merged with Category B athletes for international World Cup competitions.

Test 1
Upper extention

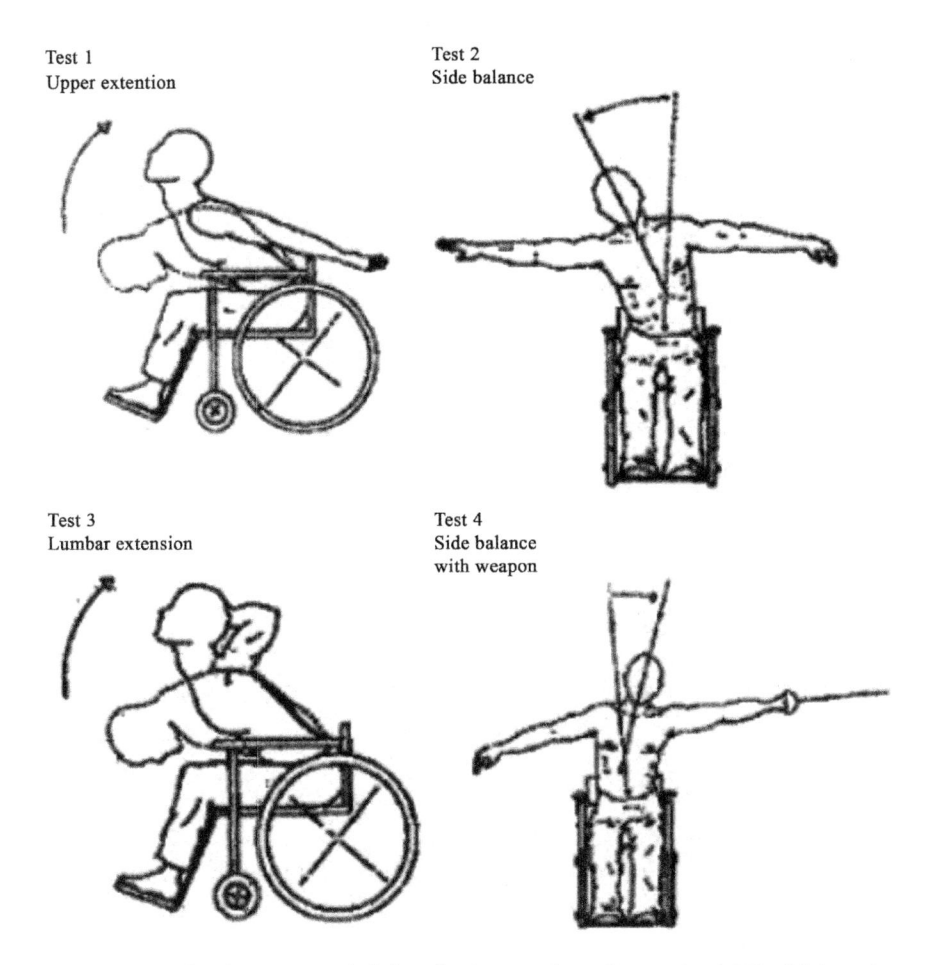

Test 2
Side balance

Test 3
Lumbar extension

Test 4
Side balance
with weapon

Figure 24.2 Example of 1–4 tests included in the functional test (International Wheelchair & Amputee Sports Federation, 2016b)

Athletic demand of wheelchair fencing

Time motion analysis of wheelchair fencing

No time motion analysis has previously been undertaken and published in WF. The information provided in this section is based on our own unpublished data, analysing 10 bouts of epee and foil (Table 24.4). WF tournaments typically take place over three consecutive days with athletes competing in their specific weapon over one day. For instance, during the 2017 Pisa World Cup, the men's individual foil category A event competition lasted approximately 4.5 hr. The winner in this event was involved in 6 poule bouts and 6 scheduled direct elimination bouts. It is not uncommon that fencers compete in two different swords (e.g. foil and epee); therefore, they may be involved in two consecutive days of competition, which can result in a significant number of bouts. Our data has revealed that the work to rest ratio (W:R) in foil is 1:17 and 1:5 for epee. On average a wheelchair foil fencer will work 1 second when compared to a wheelchair epee fencer who will work 4.7 seconds prior to periods of interruptions. The duration of effective fight time depends on the fencer's strategy, as some competitors are very aggressive and direct compared to others being more patient. As a result, athlete strategies can clearly influence indices of bout intensity and duration.

Table 24.4 Time motion characteristics of an international competition during direct elimination bouts of 10 mixed gender and category foil and epee events (unpublished data)

	Foil (n=10)	Epee (n=10)
Average total bout time (min)	12.04	6.44
Average effective fight time (min)	0.45	1.38
Average effective interruption time (min)	11.19	5.06
Average number of Interruptions (n)	43	21
Work to rest ratio (W:R)	1:17	1:5

Physiological demands of wheelchair fencing

Limited literature is available regarding the physiological demand of WF. One study has been identified and provides insights regarding physiological responses experienced by wheelchair fencers during a simulated direct elimination bout. Bernardi et al. (2010) analysed 6 national and international Italian wheelchair fencers. The study included two category A athletes, one with poliomyelitis and one with transtibial amputation, as well as four paraplegic category B athletes presenting a SCI lesion ranging from the 6th thoracic or below. Ventilatory threshold (VT) and peak oxygen uptake ($\dot{V}O_{2peak}$) was established during a laboratory incremental arm cranking exercise. Subsequently, simulations of fencing bouts were replicated and the mean and peak values obtained for heart rate were 153 ± 10 beat/min and 172 ± 14 beat/min respectively. The mean and peak VO_2 were 25.0 ± 3.60 ml/kg/min and 31.3 ± 3.90 ml/kg/min. When compared to the laboratory test, wheelchair fencers perform at 73% of $\dot{V}O_{2peak}$ during the fencing bout. In this study, blood lactate raised to 4.70 ± 1.38 mmol/L. It can be suggested that the relatively long period of interruptions observed in WF would allow athletes to metabolise the accumulated blood lactate and more precisely, deal with the accumulation of hydrogen ions (H^+). However, the level of blood lactate displayed by Bernardi et al. (2010) is above the onset of blood lactate accumulation (OBLA) established at 4mmol/L (Santos-Concejero et al., 2013). Activities above OBLA correspond to a transition from a tolerable workload to a more severe intensity, indicating WF taxes the anaerobic system.

One limitation of Bernardi et al. (2010) is that the sword utilised during the simulated bout was not mentioned. Considering the variation in W:R ratios presented in the previous paragraph, it remains unclear to what extent the anaerobic system is being taxed during each specific sword. In the authors' opinion, across all swords during preliminary poules, athletes rely more on the alactic system. During the elimination bouts (when it counts most) it can be predicted that foil and sabre athletes tax predominantly the alactic system, while the epee athletes rely more on the lactate system. Never-the-less, it is likely that at some point in a competition, all swords will produce blood lactate in excess of OBLA, and thus training intensities must match or exceed the demand of the competitive environment; training should prepare athletes for worst case scenarios. It is also important to highlight that category A athletes, due to greater trunk functional activity, have the ability to perform more powerful attacks compared to category B athletes, possibly resulting in greater contribution of the anaerobic energy system. However, Category B athletes with SCI can demonstrate reduced blood redistribution and therefore contribute to blood lactate retention and concentration. This phenomenon is further discussed in the programming section. As a result, athletes from both categories may tax the anaerobic energy system for different reasons. Contribution of the aerobic system will also inevitably occur, helping athletes to recover efficiently between bouts and consecutive days of competition.

Biomechanical features of wheelchair fencing

The lunge

In WF the lunge is the most common form of attack and a fundamental technique used to score (Chung, 2015). During a bout, the lunge is performed on numerous occasions; therefore the ability to perform this skill optimally and repetitively is crucial. During a bout, athletes are competing seated and are not permitted to rise from the chair; consequently, any footwork contribution (or contribution of the lower limb) to the lunge is prevented. As a result all spatial displacement is limited (Chung, 2015). The elimination of footwork results in athletes relying on their trunk and upper limb for all fencing tasks. The fencing wheelchairs are equipped with supporting bars on the side of the non fencing arm, which can be utilised to maintain sitting balance and assist with increasing the speed of attacks and defensive retreats (Fung et al., 2013). As the lunge is an attacking movement, the speed of its execution is essential; therefore, enhancing the rate of force development (RFD) and muscular power of recruited limbs is crucial.

The kinetics and kinematics of the lunge

Quantitative data describing the kinetics and kinematics of the lunge is limited. Chung (2015) provided an insight of the biomechanical features required during the lunge attack. Thirty elite foil fencers were recruited (15 Category A and 15 Category B), where kinematic and electromyography (EMG) analysis was undertaken. Prior to fencing, both fencers are required to hold an "on guard" position from which the lunge is initiated (Figure 24.3). In this position, the blade is raised and the athlete's shoulders are in an abducted, flexed and externally rotated position. The elbow is in a flexed position with the forearm slightly supinated, wrist extended and radial deviation. Joint angles and hand height during the "on guard" position varies from one athlete to another.

From the "on guard" position, the lunge (Figure 24.4) is initiated with shoulder abduction, slight flexion and internal rotation of the glenohumeral joint. The weapon is then advanced towards the target via elbow extension. When approaching the target, pronation of the forearm is observed with a flexed wrist and ulnar deviated to control the weapon hitting the target. Moderate to high cross correlation coefficients were observed between shoulder flexion and elbow extension ($r = 0.87–0.91$), shoulder abduction and elbow extension ($r = 0.74–0.84$) and elbow extension and forearm pronation ($r = 0.94–0.98$) (Chung, 2015). Such results would demonstrate the importance of these synergists movement in performing the lunge attack.

Figure 24.3 The "on guard" stance

Figure 24.4 The lunge attack

Kinematics and EMG differences between category A and B athletes

To replicate the competitive attacks of WF, Chung (2015) requested athletes to perform the lunge at four predetermined distances. The normalised fencing distance was established for each athlete as it occurs in competition, and was referred as 100% of their reach. To establish the other predetermined distances, 5%, 10% and 15% were added to the normalised distance (105%, 110% and 115%). Category A and B athletes, despite having differences in impairment, demonstrated similar performance, technique and muscle recruitment pattern during the lunge attack at short distances (100% and 105%). However, significant differences were observed at greater lunges distances (110% and 115%). The lunge duration was significantly increased in category B athletes when compared to category A. Peak linear horizontal and angular velocity at the shoulder and elbow joints were reduced. A 14% larger shoulder angular displacement was also observed in category B athletes. These results would indicate that at greater lunging distances, category B athletes would observe a reduction in lunging velocity and overall performance.

In addition to differences in kinematics, muscle recruitment pattern and muscle activity level also differed in category B athletes at greater lunges distances. The glenohumeral and scapulothoracic musculature including the deltoids, upper trapezius and infraspinatus shoulder musculature displayed higher activity levels in order to maintain postural stability in the absence of trunk musculature. Category B athletes also display an earlier recruitment of the biceps as it attempts to control the increased leverage of the fencing arm during the arm elevation and elbow extension when lunging. The high muscle activity of these muscles indicates their importance in executing the lunge efficiently; therefore, the program should emphasise strengthening them across all fencing categories but predominantly Category B and C athletes.

Injury prevalence

An epidemiological injury survey conducted during the London 2012 Paralympics Games concluded that WF was the 4th most injury prone sport among 22 other sport events (Willick et al., 2013). According to Chung et al. (2012), the repetitive, asymmetrical and impulsive nature of WF would expose athletes to various musculoskeletal injuries.

Cause of injuries

To date, Chung (2015) conducted the most insightful research investigating the epidemiology of injury in WF. The injury incidence rate experienced by wheelchair fencers was 3.85 per 1000 hr of exposure (3.85/1000 hr). Category B athletes appear more vulnerable with an injury rate of 4.87/1000 hr when compared to Category A athletes (2.99/1000 hr). Although WF is performed in a chair, without locomotion, both category A and B fencers display a higher risk of injury when compared to their counterpart able-bodied fencers (2.4/1000 hr). It appears that the injury risk is proportional to the degree of impairment, with athletes presenting a higher level of disability being exposed to higher injury risk. It is speculated that the increase injury rate in WF is the result of a disrupted kinetic chain (Chung, 2015). The elimination of footwork possibly disrupts the normal sequencing of the kinetic chain with such phenomenon being proportionally aggravated the more severe the impairment. This can possibly explain the compensatory strategies and reduction in lunging performance (horizontal linear velocity) observed as fencing distance increases, especially in category B fencers. The kinetic chain would be further disrupted in category B athletes due to loss of trunk activation and isolation of upper limb musculature.

Table 24.5 Nature, location and severity of injury in elite foil wheelchair fencers across category A and B athletes (per 1000h) adapted from Chung (2015)

	Category A	Category B
Nature of injury		
Tendon/ligament rupture	0	0.35
Meniscus/cartilage injury	0	0.09
Sprain	1.05	1.15
Strain	1.65	3.01
Contusion	0.3	0.27
Location of injury		
Head	0	0.09
Cervical	0.6	0.09
Thoracic	0.07	0.09
Lumbar	0.37	0.62
Trunk	0	0.09
Shoulder	0.37	1.16
Elbow & upper arm	1.2	1.59
Wrist	0.15	0.27
Hand & fingers	0.22	0.18
Severity of injury		
Minor (7 days or fewer loss)	2.69	3.8
Moderate (8–21 days loss)	0.3	0.7
Major (+21 days loss)	0	0.4

Injury profile of wheelchair fencers

According to Chung (2015), 84% of injuries in WF are considered as newly acquired across both categories as opposed to recurrent injuries. The low incidence of recurrent injury is surprising considering the repetitive and explosive nature of WF. From the authors' experience, no athlete enjoys being restrained from training or competing; therefore, they are likely to return to fencing before making a full recovery. As a result, athletes are likely to compensate and rely on uninjured body parts altering optimal biomechanics. Such alteration may promote injury to other body parts resulting in higher number of newly acquired injuries. An important role of the strength and conditioning coach is to educate athletes regarding readiness to train after sustaining an injury. The nature of injuries sustained by fencers in this study was predominantly traumatic (75.8%).

Most injuries recorded (78.8%) across category A and B were located in the upper limb with an incidence of 2.83/1000 h. Elbow strain (32.6%) and shoulder strain (15.8%) were the most commonly diagnosed. Shoulder injuries lead to longer absence from fencing and competitions. Chung (2015) reported that after experiencing a shoulder injury, 4 out of 7 category B athletes were absent from training and competition for more than 28 days. Most injuries recorded were considered minor to moderate, with athletes returning to training less than 21 days post injury (Table 24.5).

Elbows strains can possibly be explained by the rapid arm extension required to strike the opponent, leading to excessive elbow extension. Shoulder strains may be due to the repetitive and explosive nature of WF with the lunge attack requiring shoulder flexion, abduction and internal

Table 24.6 Battery of fitness tests suitable for WF

1 RM bench press:	This test evaluates the maximum strength of fencers, promoting similar proximal to distal muscle recruitment experienced when lunging. This test can be implemented by athletes with good trunk and hand function. A 10 RM alternative can be used for athletes with reduced hand function.
1 RM bench pull:	Assessment of maximum strength of the upper body posterior musculature. Maximum strength of the remaining innervated posterior musculature helps decelerate the velocity of the attacking lunge. The test can be implemented by athletes with good trunk and hand function. A 10 RM alternative can be used for lower function athletes.
Muscle balance:	The repetitive, explosive and asymmetrical nature of wheelchair fencing may lead to asymmetry in upper limbs. Asymmetry may influence bilateral force production and coordination and therefore need to be tested. Muscle balance can be tested using Isokinetics strength tests on the Biodex (e.g. right hand push vs. left hand push).
Strength ratio of opposing muscles:	Increased strength ratio of opposing muscles (e.g. push:pull or shoulder abduction:adduction) may compromise the athlete's scapular stabilisation, leading to impingement of the underlying structures (Wilbanks and Bickel, 2016). Optimal ratios are yet to be determined in this population; however, in Wilbanks and Bickel's (2016) study, ratios of 0.96 (abduction:adduction) and 1.3 (push:pull) were associated with able-bodied participants experiencing no shoulder impingement.
Lateral medicine ball throw:	Evaluate an athlete's power. The athlete is seated in the fencing chair and tosses the medicine ball laterally as for a lunge. Landing distance is recorded. This test is representative of lunging ability.
Aerobic capacity:	Aerobic capacity can be accessed using the 5 minute rowing test as discussed in the programming section. Athletes are fastened to a bench and rowing distance is recorded.
Anaerobic capacity:	Power endurance is an important part of WF therefore testing athletes' anaerobic capacity of the upper arms appears crucial. A modified 30s Wingate test using an arm crank can be utilised monitoring athletes' peak power, mean power and fatigue index. Same protocol as Kounalakis et al. (2008) can be used.
Core strength:	Core strength and endurance can be assessed monitoring athletes prone, supine and lateral holds. Time can be recorded. This test may be applicable to category A athletes unless impairment prevents it.

rotation of the fencing arm, which in turn can cause stress to the rotator cuff tendon and sub-acromial tissue. Furthermore, the arm extension in addition to the weight of the weapon can also create additional torque on the shoulder structures predisposing athletes to cuff disorders and impingement problems (Chung, 2015). To reduce the likelihood of shoulder injuries across all fencing categories, enhancing scapulothoracic and glenohumeral stability may be required. Exercise selection aiming to prevent elbow and shoulder strain are further discussed in the programming section.

Fitness testing battery

In disability sports, the heterogeneity of athlete impairments presents the practitioner with a unique challenge in the selection of appropriate and suitable fitness tests and programming (as discussed in the following paragraph). In the existing literature, no suggested testing battery is available; therefore, the tests presented are based on the authors' empirical experience working with this sporting population. Certain tests may be modified or adapted to suit an athlete's impairments. A suggested battery of fitness test is provided in Table 24.6.

Programming

General training guidelines

Despite the growing interest in Paralympics sports, the lack of research provides minimal evidence in programming for such a population. As a result, most interventions and guidelines are based on current able-bodied practices, anecdotal evidence and practitioner experience (Graham-Paulson et al., 2015). An athlete's impairment can have a large influence on trainable physical capabilities and attributes. Therefore, prior to starting an intervention, the practitioner is strongly advised to access a complete athlete's impairment profile. This information should help and guide the practitioner to understand possible physiological and neurological limitations athletes could face during training.

Impairment specific consideration

An athlete's impairment type has a large influence on possible neurological and physiological adaptations (Paulson and Goosey-Tolfrey, 2017). This section briefly introduces the possible physical limitations athletes from category A, B and C may face when undergoing specific WF preparation. For further in-depth information regarding specific impairment limitation, refer to Chapter 4.

Category A

The most common impairment in this category includes athletes with limb deficiency and CP. Athletes with limb deficiency such as amputee may remain neurologically and physiologically intact in the unaffected tissues (Paulson and Goosey-Tolfrey, 2017). As a result, similar neural and cardiovascular adaptations as able-bodied may be observed in this category. Similar training modalities as for able-bodied can then be implemented such as volume, intensity and frequency. In contrast, athletes with CP may not observe similar adaptation to training. CP athletes may demonstrate a variety of impairments, which are classified according to the anatomical site of dysfunction. The classification includes diplegia (affecting lower limb), hemiplegia (affecting one vertical half of the body) and quadriplegia (affecting four limbs). Different types of CP exist; however, spastic CP is the most frequent. Athletes with such condition display increased muscle tone and exaggerated stretch reflex preventing muscles to stretch. The excessive muscle tone of affected tissue impairs coordination, increases muscular imbalances, and reduces muscle power during voluntary contraction (Paulson and Goosey-Tolfrey, 2017). The initial stage of the program should emphasise passive stretching, which can provide an increase in range of motion and an efficient proprioceptive training. As a result, primary movement pattern and movement efficiency should be enhanced. As the athlete demonstrates enhanced movement efficiency, neuromuscular and physiological training can commence. Previous research on sedentary CP patients (diplegic and hemiplegic) has observed significant improvements in strength, aerobic capacity and anaerobic capacity after following a 6 week training program (Reid et al., 2010; Verschuren et al., 2007). Furthermore, Runciman et al. (2015) conducted a 30 s Wingate test on able-bodied participants and Paralympics level CP athletes. Similar fatigue responses between both groups were observed, suggesting that CP athletes may display near maximal physiological adaptations to training toward normal levels.

Category B and C

In these categories, athletes predominantly present a SCI impairment at either thoracic level (Category B) or cervical level (Category C). Athletes with SCI may display similar strength characteristics as able-bodied athletes when muscle innervation remains intact above the injury level. Exercise response is directly related to the level and completeness of the spinal cord lesion with proportionally slower adaptations the higher the lesion. Athletes with SCI (tetraplegic and paraplegic) previously displayed positive changes in functional performance, after following an 8 week heavy bench press training program (Turbanski and Schmidtbleicher, 2010). Athletes with SCI should not be restrained from lifting weight as intramuscular and intermuscular coordination as well as positive strength increments may occur. The exercise selection, load and volume should be athlete and impairment specific. While heavy resistance training may be suited to athletes with hand function, higher volume and submaximal loads may be more suited to athletes with high SCI (Category C). To optimise neuromuscular adaptations, the wheelchair fencer presenting SCI is advised when possible to train out of the daily chair, ideally using modified gym equipment such as a power bench (disabled bench). However, often the practitioner does not have access to modified gym equipment. This should not be seen a limiting factor as regular gym equipment such as the bench press can be used with a strapping belt in order to provide stability and thus allow for a safe working environment.

SCI athletes present impaired physiological responses to training. Athletes with SCI demonstrate reduced blood redistribution due to the lack of sympathetic vasoconstriction in the inactive tissue below the lesion level. Paraplegic athletes appear able to maintain their cardiac output by elevating both resting and sub maximal heart rate. Athletes with complete tetraplegia display further limited blood redistribution and ability to elevate cardiac output due to loss of autonomic control of vessels in the abdominal bed and cardiac tissue (Paulson and Goosey-Tolfrey, 2017). Athletes with a SCI at or above the 4th thoracic level results in the loss of sympathetic outflow to the heart, diminishing cardiac acceleration with maximum heart rate of 100–140b.min^{-1} (Paulson and Goosey-Tolfrey, 2017). As a result, maximal heart rate is primarily achieved by the withdrawal of parasympathetic tone. To enhance venous return and consequently improve vascular function in tetraplegic athletes, the use of compression socks and abdominal binders can be utilised. Compression socks may help in increasing upper limb blood flow during sub-maximal exercise performance, while abdominal binders help in reducing blood lactate accumulation and minute ventilation. It is important to highlight that athlete with high thoracic and cervical SCI exhibiting loss of autonomic function may present two distinct challenges to health and performance, namely autonomic dysreflexia and impaired thermoregulation.

Injury prevention strategies

The wheelchair fencer is prone to various musculoskeletal injuries. Shoulder injuries are the second most common injury in the sport and often responsible for long absences from fencing. The program should primarily focus on restoring optimal mobility, flexibility of muscles surrounding the shoulder joint, as well as symmetry in scapular kinematics (Mulroy et al., 2011). A combination of stretching and strengthening exercises should be implemented at the start of each training session by using various resistance elastic bands (Mulroy et al., 2011). Such exercises can also provide an effective warm up. The stretching exercises could include the anterior and posterior joint capsule stretches and surrounding musculature as well as the upper trapezius muscles (Figure 24.5). The strengthening exercises could include shoulder adduction, external rotation and scapular retraction (Figure 24.6). Exercises prescribed may vary on the basis of each

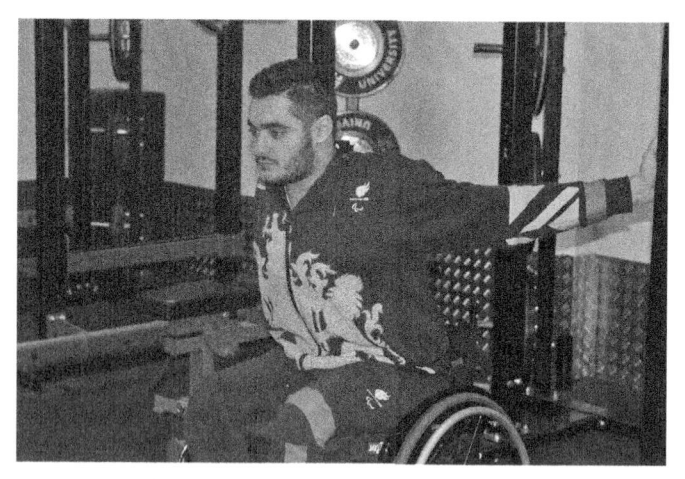

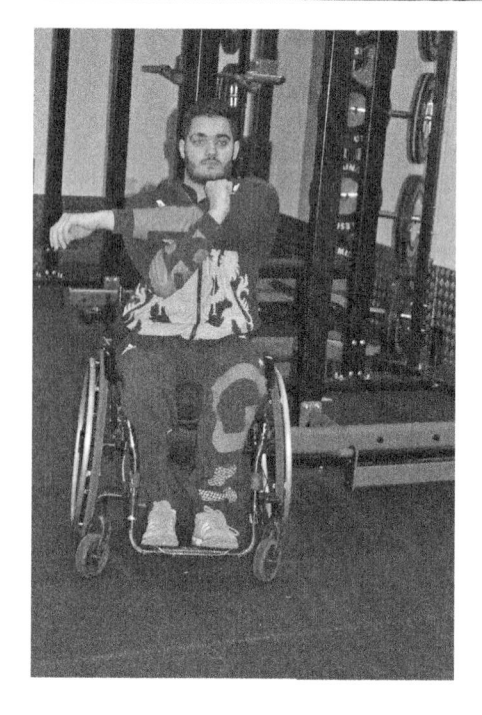

Figure 24.5 Stretching exercises for (a) anterior and (b) posterior shoulder joint structures and (c) upper trapezius muscles

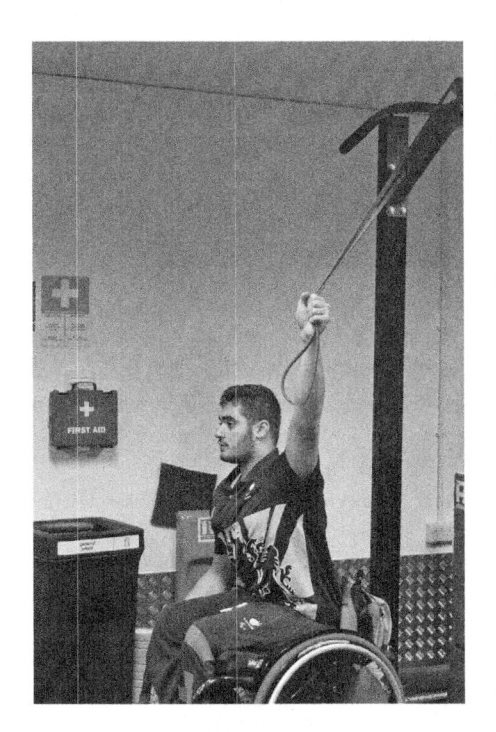

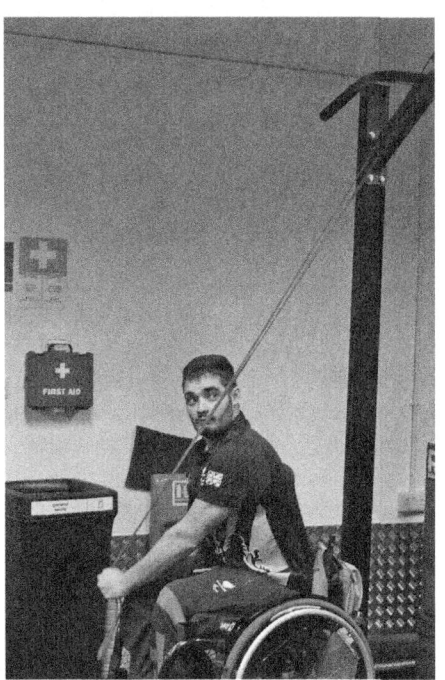

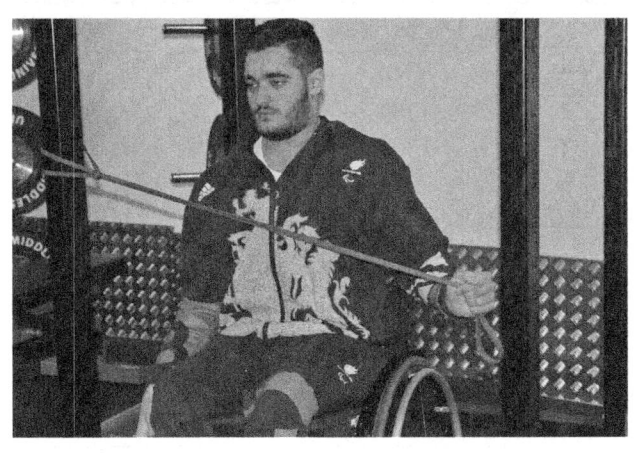

Figure 24.6 Example of injury prevention exercises with (a) shoulder adduction and (b) shoulder external rotation

athlete's needs and limitations. Full functional movement screening of the athlete, assessing range of motion, can help identify an athlete's specific needs. A full assessment can be undertaken by a qualified physiotherapist.

Strength and power development for WF performance

The initial stage of the program should address limb asymmetry which is likely to be developed by the wheelchair fencer due to the repetitive and unilateral nature of the sport. Limb asymmetry can be detrimental to performance influencing bilateral force production and coordination. The use of unilateral exercises such as dumbbell bench pull or bench press may help in regaining limb asymmetry. Furthermore, athletes with SCI require daily use of the wheelchair for ambulation purposes which is a push dominant activity. Wilbanks and Bickel (2016) observed that SCI patient with increased push to pull force ratio displayed shoulder pathology. No optimal ratio is available in the literature; however, emphasising pulling exercises at this stage of the program may help in reducing possible shoulder pathology. Pulling exercises can also enhance the robustness of the athlete's posterior shoulder muscles which display a high EMG activation when lunging and are essential for fencing performance. The biceps also exhibit high levels of activation; therefore, exercises increasing biceps eccentric strength are desired.

As lunging is a key feature to WF success, increasing its speed of execution through increased power output and rate of force development appears crucial. Lunging requires a consistent proximal to distal motor recruitment sequence of the upper limbs. This sequence when generated efficiently helps in the production of higher force and power output as well as maximising inter-muscular coordination (Chung, 2015). Strength and power exercises replicating similar sequencing need to be emphasised in the intervention (e.g. bench press or lateral medicine ball throw).

Finally, in the absence of footwork in WF, the normal sequencing of the kinetic chain is being disrupted and ultimately reducing lunging performance. It can be suggested that core strength plays an important role regarding performance and injury prevention. The practitioner is recommended to include core strengthening exercises for category A athletes. Athletes with SCI lesion conserve functional movement and strength of the remaining innervated muscles therefore any accessible core muscle should be stimulated and trained. Exercises could include short leverage crunches, prone extensions or prone, supine and lateral holds. An example of a strength endurance (Table 24.7), strength (Table 24.8) and power (Table 24.9) session for a Category B athlete is provided in the following tables.

Table 24.7 Example of a muscle endurance session

Exercise	Set	Rep	Example load	Notes
Injury prevention/warm up				
Stretch exercises	1	30s	N/A	Refer to Figure 24.5
Activation exercises	2	10	Resistance bands	Refer to Figure 24.6
Developmental exercises				
Dumbbell bench pull	4	10	70% of 1RM	3 second eccentric, explosive concentric
Dumbbell bench press	4	10	70% of 1RM	
Seated single hand cable pull down	3	10		
Assistance exercises				
Single hand triceps push down	3	10	Resistance bands	Athlete alternates from one exercise to the other

Table 24.8 Example of a strength session

Exercise	Set	Rep	Example load	Notes
Injury prevention/warm up				
Stretch exercises	1	30s	N/A	Refer to Figure 24.5
Activation exercises	2	10	Resistance bands	Refer to Figure 24.6
Developmental exercises				
Barbell bench press	5	5	85% of 1RM	Use of belt straps to bring stability
Under hand chin up	5	5	BW or assisted by resistance band	Athlete sits on a box, reaches the bar and then the box is removed
Assistance exercises				
Seated dumbbell Eccentric biceps curl	3	4	18Kg	4 second eccentric
Banded pull apart	3	10	Resistance band	

Table 24.9 Example of a power session

Exercise	Set	Rep	Example load	Notes
Injury prevention/warm up				
Stretch exercises	1	30s	N/A	Refer to Figure 24.5
Activation exercises	2	10	Resistance bands	Refer to Figure 24.6
Developmental exercises				
Barbell bench press	5	2	93% of 1RM	Use of belt straps to bring stability
Medicine ball throw	5	3	4Kg	Athlete sits in the daily chair and throws the ball laterally as if lunging. Exercise to be performed with both arms
Eccentric bench pull	5	2	110% of 1RM	The row is assisted by the S&C coaches and the athlete. A 4s eccentric on the descent
Assistance exercises				
N/A				
N/A				

Conditioning for wheelchair fencers

Wheelchair fencers are commonly involved in sparring to promote specific and optimal adaptations to competitions. In the authors' opinion, doses of sparing for conditioning purposes should be controlled and monitored as the repetitive and explosive nature of WF may expose athletes to injuries. Other modalities should be considered, therefore, and the strength and conditioning coach may need to think creatively. Exercises such as arm crank, sled drag, or modified rowing (Figure 24.7) may be implemented. As discussed in the previous sections, from an injury prevention standpoint, wheelchair fencers can benefit from strengthening the posterior musculature of the shoulder girdle. This is particularly true for athletes with SCI (Category B and C) as in addition to fencing, they require the use of their chair for daily locomotion. The excessive pushing may further contribute to shoulder impingement. Conditioning exercises promoting

Figure 24.7 Modified rowing set up

pulling motions can contribute to restore a more balanced shoulder girdle (e.g. modified rowing or reverse sled drag). An example of a conditioning session for a category B fencer is provided in Table 24.10 and inspired from the work of Baker (2011).

Table 24.10 Example of a 8 week conditioning program, including a taper

Weeks	Sessions
Week 1 low intensity	60s @ 102% of MAS; 60s rest 6 repetitions
Week 2 low intensity	60s @ 104% of MAS; 60s rest 6 repetitions
Week 3 moderate intensity	30s @ 110% of MAS; 30s rest 8 repetition
Week 4 moderate intensity	30s @ 112% of MAS; 30s rest 8 repetition
Week 5 high intensity	10s battle ropes; 20s off 12 repetitions
Week 6 high intensity	10s battle ropes; 20s off 12 repetitions
Week 7 high intensity	10s battle ropes; 20s off 10 repetitions
Week 8 high intensity	10s battle ropes; 20s off 8 repetitions

As per able-bodied fencers, wheelchair fencers may benefit from metabolic conditioning derived from High Intensity Interval Training (HIIT), which is believed to enhance both aerobic and anaerobic power. Prior to implementing such conditioning, it is recommended that maximum aerobic speed (MAS) be determined. MAS (currently) is determined by monitoring an athlete's rowing distance over 5 minutes, and is calculated by dividing distance (metres) by time (seconds) which refers to 100% MAS. For example if an athlete rows 800 meters in 300 seconds, the MAS is 2.67m/s. The initial stage of the conditioning program should include intervals of low intensity (% of MAS) and higher volume (time). As the competition approaches, the intervals should be performed at a higher intensity and a reduced volume. The degree of adaptation is likely to be proportional to the severity of the athlete's impairment.

Periodisation for WF

The periodised program in WF is dictated by the yearly competitive calendar (Table 24.2). Usually wheelchair fencers have an off-season lasting on average 2 to 3 month, varying on a yearly basis. Implementing a traditional periodisation strategy using the 3:1 loading paradigm is recommended. On an approximate 4 week cycle, specific biomotors such as muscle endurance, strength and power can be developed. During the in-season, on average, competitions occur on a 4 to 10 week basis. A traditional approach may be maintained when 8 to 10 weeks are interspaced between two competitions. A traditional approach may not be appropriate when a competition occurs within the following 4 weeks. A non traditional approach may be more favourable alternating strength and power on a session to session basis. Applying tapering strategies at the end of the off-season and pre-competitions appears beneficial for athletes to reach peak performance. In the authors' experience, the duration of the taper may vary depending on an athlete's impairment. Athletes with amputations and low SCI appear to require less time to reach peak performance when compared to athletes with high SCI. As a result athletes from category A may require a shorter taper when compared to Category B and C athletes.

Conclusion

WF is an exciting, dynamic and fast paced sport practiced exclusively seated on a specific wheelchair. The sport is performed both in teams and individually, where 3 weapons can be distinguished (foil, epee and sabre). To promote equity in competitions, a classification system has been established categorising athletes according their level of disability.

The paucity of research in WF prevents the authors from providing specific data regarding the athletic demand of the sport. However, from the authors' empirical experience, WF is expected to tax predominantly the anaerobic energy systems. Furthermore, the wheelchair fencer is required to repetitively perform high velocity lunges; therefore, an increase in RFD of the recruited muscles would appear beneficial. Differences in biomechanical features and muscle recruitment of the lunge at increased distances are observed between fencing categories. As a result, category B athletes are predisposed to a greater injury risk. A well designed strength and conditioning program accounting for an athlete's impairment can assist the wheelchair fencer to reach peak performance. The strength and conditioning coach working with such a population will require creativity to enhance specific WF physical attributes while promoting a safe working environment.

References

Baker, D., 2011. Recent trends in high-intensity aerobic training for field sports. *Professional Strength & Conditioning*, 22, pp. 3–8.

Bernardi, M., Guerra, E., Di Giacinto, B., Di Cesare, A., Castellano, V. and Bhambhani, Y., 2010. Field evaluation of paralympic athletes in selected sports: Implications for training. *Medicine & Science in Sports & Exercise*, 42(6), pp. 1200–1208.

Boguszewski, D. and Torzewska, P., 2011. Martial arts as methods of physical rehabilitation for disabled people. *Journal of Combat Sports and Martial Arts*, 2(1), pp. 1–6.

Chung, W.M., 2015. *Kinematic and electromyographic analysis of wheelchair fencing* (Doctoral dissertation, The Hong Kong Polytechnic University).

Chung, W.M., Yeung, S., Wong, A.Y.L., Lam, I.F., Tse, P.T.F., Daswani, D. and Lee, R., 2012. Musculoskeletal injuries in elite able-bodied and wheelchair foil fencers – A pilot study. *Clinical Journal of Sport Medicine*, 22(3), pp. 278–280.

Fung, Y.K., Chan, D.K.C., Caudwell, K.M. and Chow, B.C., 2013. Is the wheelchair fencing classification fair enough? A kinematic analysis among world-class wheelchair fencers. *European Journal of Adapted Physical Activity*, 6(1), pp. 17–29.

Graham-Paulson, T.S., Perret, C., Smith, B., Crosland, J. and Goosey-Tolfrey, V.L., 2015. Nutritional supplement habits of athletes with an impairment and their sources of information. *International Journal of Sport Nutrition and Exercise Metabolism*, 25(4), pp. 387–395.

International Wheelchair & Amputee Sports Federation, 2015. *IWAS wheelchair fencing. Rules for competitions: Technical rules*, accessed 1 May 2017, <www.iwasf.com/iwasf/assets/File/Fencing/Rules/1%20-%20 20161028%20IWF%20Technical%20Rules%20Oct%202015.pdf>

International Wheelchair & Amputee Sports Federation, 2016a. *IWAS wheelchair fencing. Rules for competitions: Clasification rules*, accessed 1 May 2017, <www.iwasf.com/iwasf/assets/File/Fencing/Rules/4_%20 2016_11_07%20Book%20Four%20Classification%20Rules.pdf>

International Wheelchair & Amputee Sports Federation, 2016b. *IWAS wheelchair fencing. Rules for competition: Material rules*, accessed 1 May 2017, <www.iwasf.com/iwasf/assets/File/Fencing/Rules/3%20-%20 20161101%20IWF%20Material%20Rules%20October%202016(1).pdf>

International Wheelchair & Amputee Sports Federation, 2017a. *Competitions 2017*, accessed 1 May 2017, <www.iwasf.com/iwasf/index.cfm/sports/iwas-wheelchair-fencing/competitions1/>

International Wheelchair & Amputee Sports Federation, 2017b. *IWAS wheelchair fencing. Rules for competition: Organisation rules*, accessed 1 May 2017, <www.iwasf.com/iwasf/assets/File/Fencing/Rules/2%20-%20 IWF%20Organisation%20Rules%20January%202017(2).pdf>

Kounalakis, S.N., Bayios, I.A., Koskolou, M.D. and Geladas, N.D., 2008. Anaerobic capacity of the upper arms in top-level team handball players. *International Journal of Sports Physiology and Performance*, 3(3), pp. 251–261.

Mulroy, S.J., Thompson, L., Kemp, B., Hatchett, P.P., Newsam, C.J., Lupold, D.G., Haubert, L.L., Eberly, V., Ge, T.T., Azen, S.P. and Winstein, C.J., 2011. Strengthening and Optimal Movements for Painful Shoulders (STOMPS) in chronic spinal cord injury: A randomized controlled trial/invited commentary/author response. *Physical Therapy*, 91(3), p. 305.

Paulson, T. and Goosey-Tolfrey, V., 2017. Current perspectives on profiling and enhancing wheelchair court-sport performance. *International Journal of Sports Physiology and Performance*, 2(3), pp. 275–286.

Reid, S., Hamer, P., Alderson, J. and Lloyd, D., 2010. Neuromuscular adaptations to eccentric strength training in children and adolescents with cerebral palsy. *Developmental Medicine & Child Neurology*, 52(4), pp. 358–363.

Runciman, P., Derman, W., Ferreira, S., Albertus-Kajee, Y. and Tucker, R., 2015. A descriptive comparison of sprint cycling performance and neuromuscular characteristics in able-bodied athletes and paralympic athletes with cerebral palsy. *American Journal of Physical Medicine & Rehabilitation*, 94(1), pp. 28–37.

Santos-Concejero, J., Granados, C., Bidaurrazaga-Letona, I., Zabala-Lili, J., Irazusta, J. and Gil, S.M., 2013. Onset of blood lactate accumulation as a predictor of performance in top athletes. *Retos. Nuevas Tendencias en Educación Física, Deporte y Recreación*, 23, pp. 67–69.

Turbanski, S. and Schmidtbleicher, D., 2010. Effects of heavy resistance training on strength and power in upper extremities in wheelchair athletes. *The Journal of Strength & Conditioning Research*, 24(1), pp. 8–16.

Verschuren, O., Ketelaar, M., Gorter, J.W., Helders, P.J., Uiterwaal, C.S. and Takken, T., 2007. Exercise training program in children and adolescents with cerebral palsy: A randomized controlled trial. *Archives of Pediatrics & Adolescent Medicine*, 161(11), pp. 1075–1081.

Wilbanks, S.R. and Bickel, C.S., 2016. Scapular stabilization and muscle strength in manual wheelchair users with spinal cord injury and subacromial impingement. *Topics in Spinal Cord Injury Rehabilitation*, 22(1), pp. 60–70.

Willick, S.E., Webborn, N., Emery, C., Blauwet, C.A., Pit-Grosheide, P., Stomphorst, J., Van de Vliet, P., Marques, N.A.P., Martinez-Ferrer, J.O., Jordaan, E. and Derman, W., 2013. The epidemiology of injuries at the London 2012 Paralympic Games. *British Journal of Sports Medicine*, 47(7), pp. 426–432.

25
TENNIS

Emily Fanning and Floris Pietzsch

Introduction

Tennis as a sport enjoys worldwide participation, with an estimated 75 million people playing each year (Pluim et al., 2007). It is a unique sport as it is played both indoors and outdoors, at altitude and sea level, with large temperature and environmental variations, on clay, grass, carpet and hard court surfaces. Matches have been known to last from minutes up to 11 hours and 5 minutes (Wimbledon, 2010) and across multiple days if needed (weather dependent). The tournament schedule places large travel implications, as players are expected to move countries and even across continents on a weekly basis. This requires adjustment to time zones, environmental conditions and recovery from the general fatigue of travelling itself. Due to the nature of tournaments adopting a knock out structure, a player and coach will not know how many matches will be played in any given week, requiring large flexibility in periodisation and planning. Indeed, ranking determines the level of tournament in which a player can compete; however, making the cut is dependent not only on a player's ranking but on that of others entered in that tournament during that week, and this element of unknown leads to unclear long-term tournament scheduling. Players and coaches who have previously experienced poor form may subsequently add additional tournaments onto their schedule, and therefore it is no surprise to see the top 10 players only competing in 18–22 tournaments a year, where others enter into 32 plus, which subsequently results in less recovery and training time (WTA, 2016).

There are approximately 2250 male players competing on the ATP tour, and 1300 female players on the WTA tour. Tennis is deemed an "early specialisation" sport, as many participants dedicate their time to this sport and even leave school as young as 12 years old, but the average age of the top 100 players is 26 years for men and 24 years for women. Approximately 70% of top 100 junior ranked players go on to achieve a pro ranking, but players can now expect to take 4.1 years from achieving their first senior ranking point to entering into the top 100 ranking. This is an increase from 3.4 years in 2000. Bane et al. (2014) has found similar findings within the ATP, where transition time has increased significantly between 1985 and 2010. There are some potential explanations for this duration increase, such as the introduction of the age eligibility ruling (AER) in 1995 within the WTA, which aimed to increase career longevity and decrease injury, burnout and premature retirement (Otis et al., 2006). Junior players are restricted upon how many senior tournaments they can enter during any particular year, and a new player advisory panel (PDAP) developed educational literature, workshops and advice on key identified stressors on such topics as sports science and medicine services, media training, athletic assistance and general career development (Otis et al., 2006). When evaluated over 10 years, premature retirements in female players (<21 years) reduced from 7% to under 1% of players, and median career length increased by 43% relating to 3 more playing years. It has been suggested that improvements and developments in sports science, strength and conditioning, as well as increased financial rewards have all contributed to this (Bane et al., 2014).

A growing body of evidence that suggests significant positive impacts of strength and conditioning for tennis performance (Reid and Schneiker, 2008; Fernandez-Fernandez et al., 2009; Kovacs and Ellenbecker, 2011; Roetert et al., 2009). Clearly, strength and conditioning coaches have a large array of additional considerations that are unique to tennis and that have large implications when designing and implementing training programmes. The aim for this chapter is to provide the reader with the necessary information to understand the demands of the sport, highlight key areas of injury occurrence and prevention, and also aid your programme design.

Athletic demands

Kovacs (2009) described tennis as a game of unpredictability, with point length, shot selection, court surface, strategy, match duration, environment and the opponent having the ability to significantly affect the physical and physiological requirements of matchplay. Typically matches last on average 1.5 hours (Kovacs, 2007), but they can last as long as 5 hours, of which effective playing time has been found to be 20–30% on clay courts and 10–15% on hard courts, creating exercise-to-recovery ratios of ~1:2 (Fernandez-Fernandez et al., 2008; Kovacs, 2006; Groppel and Roetert, 1992).

Average point length is 8 seconds, varying from 3–15 seconds, during which 4–15 changes of direction can be made which can equate to over a 1000 changes of direction per match (Fernandez-Fernandez et al., 2014a; Kovacs, 2009; Cooke et al., 2011). The mean is 8.7 changes of directions in each point; each of these can create a load of 1.5–2.7 times bodyweight on the knee (Kibler and Safran, 2000). The vast majority of these movements are lateral movements, 20% forwards and less than 8% backwards, requiring players to be good movers in all directions (Kovacs, 2009). The mean distance covered is 3 m, 80% within 2.5 m of the player's ready position, 10% between 2.5m-4.5 m and fewer than 5% are over 4.5 m. These distances can accumulate to 8–15 m per point and 1300–3600 m per hour dependent on a multitude of factors such as player level, opponent and court surface (Fernandez-Fernandez et al., 2008; Kovacs, 2009; Roetert and Ellenbecker, 2007). This can result in 300–500 high intensity efforts and approximately 1000 shots during a three set match (Fernandez et al., 2006; Reid and Schneiker, 2008).

Tennis research has largely reported that it is the sport specific skills that are most important, such as the ability to handle the racket and stroke skills (Smekal et al., 2001; Reid and Schneiker, 2008). Conflicting evidence exists regarding the relationship between specific physical qualities and performance, culminating in the overall conclusion that performance cannot be attributed to one component of fitness (Ulbricht et al., 2015; Roetert et al., 1996). However, as the game continues to evolve to become more dynamic, characterised by rising stroke and serve velocities, it has also been accepted that to be able to compete effectively at elite level, players require high levels of physical fitness (Fernandez-Fernandez et al., 2009; Ulbricht et al., 2015). It is also unlikely that having high levels of technical, tactical and psychological skill alone without physical fitness will allow a player to reach their full potential (Reid and Schneiker, 2008). Effective stroke production requires efficient movement and ability to repeatedly sprint and generate explosive force, amongst other factors; evidently these are physical abilities as opposed to technical skills, which facilitate the stroke being executed in the first place (Girard and Millet, 2009).

Physiology and endurance

Tennis comprises high intensity efforts interspersed with periods of variable duration and low intensity activity, inclusive of active recovery between points (10–20 s) and seated rest during changeovers and set breaks (90 s and 120 s, respectively) (Fernandez-Fernandez et al., 2009). Metabolically, tennis has been described as a moderate intensity anaerobic sport, with aerobic recovery phases, and as a result is devoid of high levels of acidosis. Mean maximum oxygen uptakes ($\dot{V}O_{2max}$) of 60–70% and mean heart rates 70–80% (HRmax) are in agreement with this summary (Reid and Schneiker, 2008; Fernandez et al., 2006; Kovacs, 2007). Metabolic analysis during matchplay has shown ATP-PC is the predominant energy supply during points, with exceptionally long rallies using anaerobic glycolysis to replenish ATP and recovery phases utilising aerobic oxidation to supply energy (Smekal et al., 2001). Fatigue has been shown to negatively affect physical components such as running speed and power production, as well as technical skills such as stroke technique, ball velocity and accuracy, and cognitive skills such as concentration and decision making (Davey et al., 2002). In a sport without fixed time limits, S&C coaches must attempt to prepare their athlete for a whole spectrum of different competitive scenarios, and this has led to the recommendation that it is more beneficial to train the anaerobic energy systems whilst maintaining sport-specific work:rest ratios, as this will allow the development of both systems.

Strength and power

Due to the reactive and unpredictable nature of the sport, the vast majority of movements are done under substantial time pressure, with the serve being the only movement which the player has complete control over. Consequently, good levels of both concentric strength and eccentric strength are required for constant acceleration and deceleration of both the upper and lower limbs. Players need to be able to quickly absorb and generate forces through various ranges of motion and positions, and subsequently effective use of the stretch-shortening cycle is essential. Development of muscle stiffness and resultant higher ground reaction forces enables players to cope with the high eccentric loads associated with decelerating at speed and increased power output corresponds to faster movement responses (Kovacs et al., 2008; Kovacs, 2009).

Similar to other sports, production of forces for tennis strokes is in a mostly proximal to distal sequence, requiring complex coordination of the kinetic chain through different planes of movement. Successful stroke performance is dependent on the summation of forces through the kinetic chain and out into the ball, which dictates racket head speed and ball velocity, two key skill performance factors (Kovacs and Ellenbecker, 2011). Underpinning these factors are strength, rate of force development and plyometric ability, in addition to synchrony of all links in the kinetic chain for optimal performance (Kovacs and Ellenbecker, 2011). Presently, it is not possible to track the transfer of mechanical energy in 3D movement, but it is generally accepted that the majority of force responsible for accelerating a racket comes from the transfer of force from the larger muscles of the legs and trunk (Roetert et al., 2009). Biomechanical analysis has identified key motions within the chain; in particular, knee flexion and extension, 3D trunk rotation and high rotational angular velocities of the upper arm play a significant role in racket head and ball velocity (Reid and Schneiker, 2008). Understanding that optimal performance with minimal injury risk comes from maximal activation of all links in the chain, without weakness, imbalance or dysfunction within any segment, should enable the S&C coach to programme effectively to the individual needs of their athlete.

Speed and agility

Needs analysis would suggest that acceleration speed, ability to change direction quickly, first step quickness and lateral movements are important determinants of tennis performance (Salonikidis and Zafeiridis, 2008). Some research has highlighted that agility may be the first factor to influence junior tennis performance; however, these are largely based on the correlation between success and pre-determined change of direction (COD) tests and not in line with the current definition of agility (Young and Farrow, 2006). In other sports, COD testing could not discriminate between higher and lesser skilled players, this potentially highlights that cognitive elements like perception and decision making time which differentiates between elite players and the levels below them, as opposed to the speed and accuracy of their movement alone; this is likely to be the case in tennis (Farrow et al., 2005). There are tests in existence assessing reactive tennis specific movement patterns in response to random light stimuli, but still a dearth of information to establish how performance in this correlates to tennis performance and subsequently if agility is in fact a key determinant of success (Cooke et al., 2011). Despite a lack of empirical evidence, it is irrefutable that given the high movements demands, the development of efficient movement patterns, speed and agility is essential, and could be the differentiating factor in the success of players of similar skill levels.

Although tennis is a sport where skill is essential, it is the multifaceted interaction between technical and physical ability that enables successful performance (Reid and Schneiker, 2008; Fernandez-Fernandez et al., 2014b).

Injury

Substantial research has been done into the epidemiology, aetiology and prevalence of injuries in tennis, and is an essential area for strength and conditioning coaches to understand to enable successful program design. Variation in the definition of injury, data collection methods and study populations makes it difficult to accurately report the prevalence and incidence across a wider population of players. However, the repetitive nature and complex biomechanical demands of the sport have been shown to result in characteristic sport-specific injury patterns and musculoskeletal adaptations (Ellenbecker et al., 2009).

Injury incidence

The average reported incidence of injury across all tennis populations is relatively low, ranging from 0.04–3.0 per 1000 hours of play and with a variance in annual frequency of 0.05–2.9 injuries per player per year (Pluim et al., 2006). This is comparable with other non-contact sports and considerably lower than in team sports.

Injury type and prevalence

The majority of documented injuries can be defined as overuse injuries, including tendinopathy, chronic muscles strains and joint instability caused by repetitive microtrauma characteristic of the sport. High training volumes are widely accepted from a young age as a key to success, and this in combination with demanding tournament schedules, puts all players, especially young elite players, at high risk of this type of injury (Pluim et al., 2015). The most regularly recorded overuse injuries are tendinous issues predominantly affecting the elbow, shoulder and knee, lower back pathology and thigh muscle strains. Macrotrauma such as sprains, fractures, dislocations, joint injury and contusions tend to occur less frequently as a consequence of a one-off event (Kibler and Safran, 2000).

Injury location

Tennis is a highly demanding, multifaceted sport and this has consequently lead to recording of injuries in all areas of the body. The most frequently injured area is the lower limb with research reporting 39–65% of injuries occurring here, followed by the upper limb at 24–46% and lastly the head/trunk region with 8–22% of all recorded injuries (Ellenbecker et al., 2009). Specifically, the ankle and thigh have been shown to have the highest frequency in the lower limb, the shoulder and elbow in the upper limb and the lower back in the head/trunk region (Kibler and Safran, 2005). Acute injuries more commonly present in the lower limb, whilst chronic injuries have been seen to be more prevalent in the upper limb and trunk (Abrams et al., 2012). Minor injuries such as blisters, abrasion and cuts to extremities are commonplace.

Lower extremity

This region is most prone to sprains and strains, and injuries occur twice as frequently as upper extremity injuries. Specifically, it is more susceptible to macrotrauma, with lateral ankle sprains and tears of the hamstring, calf, adductors and quadriceps being the most prevalent injuries in tennis (Kibler and Safran, 2005; Pluim et al., 2006).

Muscle and ligaments strains of the hip, knee or ankle may be acute or chronic in nature. Acutely, this type of injury is usually associated with rapid change of direction, acceleration and deceleration movements inherent in the sport or related to fatigue. Chronically, strains mainly occur due to insufficient rest or rehabilitation from previous injury or as a consequence of acquired muscular contractures restricting movement (Kibler and Safran, 2005; Bylak and Hutchinson, 1998).

Overuse injury of the knee joint of skeletally mature players most often manifests as patellofemoral joint pain and patellar tendinitis, and in young players this presents as Osgood-Schlatters disease (tibial tubercle apophysitis) (Bylak and Hutchinson, 1998). Overload of the lower leg and foot can present as stress fractures, shin splints, Achilles tendinitis and plantar fasciitis, particularly amongst those who play predominantly on hard courts, with the latter two conditions affecting primarily older players (Kibler and Safran, 2000).

Upper extremity

The term "tennis elbow" has been adopted in reference to lateral epicondylitis because of its high prevalence, with reported percentages of players affected ranging from 37–57% in elite and recreational players. At elite level, there is actually higher incidence of medial epicondylitis (golfer's elbow) caused by overload on the serve and forehand strokes which make up 75% of the game (Ellenbecker et al., 2009). The wrist is also prone to similar conditions primarily affecting the extensor tendons, and most susceptible to this are those who play with lots of top spin or have altered mechanics due to poor technique or ineffective use of the kinetic chain (Kibler and Safran, 2000).

The shoulder is subject to repetitive tensile loads at high velocities of 1700° per second and above, and this can bring about deleterious maladaptations. As a key component of the kinetic chain, the shoulder has to deal with the summation of force generated by the legs and trunk (Roetert et al., 2009). These forces are highest during serving, demanding high rotational velocities and extreme ranges of motion, placing stress on the shoulder complex not dissimilar to those documented in other professional throwing athletes, such as baseball pitchers. Subsequently, similar injury patterns are seen on assessment, but whereas most "throwing" athletes have the amount of throws per week monitored and limited, this is not the case for tennis players. Professional players have been documented having significantly higher volumes on serve count alone than their throwing athlete counterparts, without allowing for the additional loads created by the groundstrokes (Johnson and McHugh, 2006).

As a consequence of this one-sided overload, presentation of "tennis shoulder" is common, this term referring to an altered posture with the dominant shoulder sitting in a more depressed, internally rotated position and generally associated with one or a number of other clinical findings (Kibler and Safran, 2000) The most common of these being glenohumeral internal rotation deficit (GIRD), muscular strength imbalance between anterior and posterior muscle groups, scapular dyskinesis, joint laxity and sport acquired hypermobility (Kibler and Safran, 2000). These maladaptations, without appropriate monitoring and management, contribute to increasing the risk of rotator cuff and labral pathology and impingement (Abrams et al., 2012). As rotator cuff inflammation is one of the most prevalent injuries of the shoulder amongst all ages and levels of player, prevention of these maladaptations should be a key part of any physical program. Although largely due to overuse, in the young this injury is generally secondary to instability and in older players typically related to degeneration of the tendon or labrum (Kibler and Safran, 2000).

Trunk

Lower back pain (LBP) is one the most recurrent complaints of competitive tennis players, especially in junior populations, caused by the repeated demand for flexion, extension, lateral flexion and rotational movements of the spine. The spine also plays a pivotal role as part of the kinetic chain, functioning as a transfer link between the upper and lower limbs, capable of generating force to accelerate the arm and attenuating force to decelerate the racket after contact (Maquirriain and Ghisi, 2006). The most common cause of back pain is muscular strain, especially of the central paraspinal musculature and the quadratus lumborum, which can occur acutely, but is more often linked to chronic overuse. More serious spinal pathology, such as spondylolysis and spondylolisthesis, is often seen in elite players as consequence of overload, particularly on the serve, as has been found in other sports with repetitive extension requirements (Ellenbecker et al., 2009). The prevalence of this type of pathology may be higher than reported, as shown in a study by Alyas et al. (2007). They identified 28 out 33 asymptomatic adolescent players were found to have at least one abnormality on MRI as a result of acute or chronic stress (Alyas et al., 2007). Further research is needed, but current evidence recording 50% of elite players experiencing back pain at least once, and 30% reporting to suffer chronic back pain, with such high prevalence it is recommended that extensive preventative measures are taken to reduce risk of injury in this area (Ellenbecker et al., 2009; Abrams et al., 2012; Marks et al., 1988).

Acute muscle strain or tear of the abdominals, in particular the rectus abdominus and obliques of the non-dominant side, occurs usually with indirect trauma hitting overhead strokes and serves. The most common mechanism is during forced concentric contraction of the rectus abdominus during the throwing (acceleration) phase of the serve, whilst the spine is hyperextended, especially during a kick or topspin serve where this posture is more pronounced (Maquirriain et al., 2007). As with the lower back, conditioning programs should attempt to prepare the athlete to cope with the loads placed upon the trunk throughout multiple planes of movement and various velocities.

Gender

The majority of literature agrees that there is no statistically significant difference between gender on the rate of injury (Pluim et al., 2006). Male players show decreased flexibility in comparison to their female counterparts and it is well known that inflexibility plays a part in the pathophysiology of injury (Kibler and Chandler, 2003). Low flexibility in adolescent populations exacerbates injury risk, especially during growth, and in tennis the areas most affected by this discrepancy between bone growth and muscle length is the lower back, knee and shoulder (Kibler and Safran, 2005). The maladaptations caused by repetitive tensile overload in tennis further decrease flexibility, and this has been shown to worsen with time (Kibler and Safran, 2000).

In tennis, female players are 4–6 times more likely to sustain serious knee injuries like ACL injuries than males; this disparity is currently attributed to anatomical, hormonal and neuromuscular differences (Hewett et al., 2005) . This type of injury most commonly occurs as a non-contact incident, during sports involving a lot of cutting, pivoting and jumping movements (Hewett et al., 2005). Anatomical factors such as Q-angle are non-modifiable and control of hormonal factors influencing laxity of ligaments and tendons are outside the remit of the strength and conditioning coach. There is substantial evidence showing training to improve strength and neuromuscular control of the lower limb significantly reduces risk of ACL injury (Hewett et al., 2005). Given the high demands for change of direction, jumping and single leg landing in tennis, it is recommended coaches seek to achieve optimal biomechanics in these movements, as the recovery time for an injury like this may have a major impact on the career success and ultimately career length of a professional player.

Skill level and volume of play

At present there appears to be no link between skill level and incidence of injury, although this information may be misleading (Pluim et al., 2006). Less skilful players often have poorer technique and control of the vibration forces translated into the racket arm, as well as possibly lower level sport specific conditioning, all of which would suggest a greater predisposition to higher injury rates (Abrams et al., 2012). However, advanced playing level generally means greater volume of play, of which there is a positive correlation to increased injury rate (Abrams et al., 2012). Due to their technical proficiency, elite players are also able to produce, and are subject to, superior forces and velocities that place them under larger stresses, contributing further to injury risk (Pluim et al., 2006).

Tennis specific factors

Tennis is one of the few sports to be played on multiple surfaces, which create their own unique physical and physiological demands, as a consequence influencing injury type; however, there is limited empirical evidence in this area. Hardcourts have been found to have the highest injury rate and amount of incomplete matches, most likely due to increased speed of the ball, accelerations and torques, in comparison to clay or grass (Girard et al., 2007). Consequently, acute injuries are usually associated with the rapid accelerations and decelerations of both lower and upper limbs needed to cope with these higher velocities and forces. The reduced frictional coefficient of clay enables longer, slower rallies with a higher ball bounce, which changes both movement mechanics and contact height during groundstrokes (Fernandez-Fernandez et al., 2010). Both sliding on clay and high contact points require strength throughout wider ranges of motion in much higher volumes than on other surfaces. Given the unstable nature of clay as a surface, slipping injuries causing strains and sprains particularly of the adductors and hamstrings, are a risk for any player not conditioned for or proficient at sliding (WTA, 2016). The increased rally length demands enhanced muscular endurance to withstand fatigue and ability to generate power from positions which do not occur as frequently on other surfaces (Johnson and McHugh, 2006). Therefore, court surface, as well as other individual tennis specific factors, such as grip position, racket properties and gamestyle, should be considered when programming for an elite player.

Fitness testing battery

When undertaking any assessment, the strength and conditioning coach must always understand the importance of validity and reliability of any methods chosen. It is also important to understand the typical co-efficient of variation for each method of testing to ensure correct interpretation of data.

There are many different assessment methods to choose from, which are typically weighed up against cost, time implications, simplicity, accuracy and of course whether they are valid and reliable. Field tests are typically cheaper, easier to administer, time efficient and allow for more participants when compared to lab based assessments, but may not be as reliable or accurate. Adherence to strict protocol should minimise inter and intra administrator variability which subsequently should improve reliability. It has been suggested that field based tests are more

Table 25.1 Functional movement screening (FMS)

Tests	
Deep squat **Hurdle step** ★ **In-Line lunge** ★ **Shoulder mobility** ★ **Active straight leg raise** ★ **Trunk stability push up** **Rotatory stability** ★	The scoring of tests consists of four possibilities ranging between 0–3. Zero is given if the athlete feels any pain during any exercise. A score of one is given if unable to complete the movement pattern. Two is given if the athlete can perform the exercise but requires some form of compensatory movements to complete it. Three is given when an athlete completes the exercise without any compensation. ★ denotes which tests require scores on both sides of the body and the lowest score is used as part of an overall score. A total maximum score of 21 is possible along with an asymmetry score.

Table 25.2 Tennis functional movement screening (TFMS) (LTA, 2011)

Active shoulder elevation **Wall press up (single arm) ★** **Shoulder rotation ★** **Pectoralis minor muscle length** **Thoracic spine rotation ★** **Knee to wall ★** **Modified thomas test ★** **Hip rotation (internal and external rotation) ★** **Active knee extension ★** **Quadrant (lumbar spine clearing test) ★**	The scoring of tests consists of four possibilities ranging between 0–3. Zero is given if the athlete feels any pain during any exercise. A score of one is given is unable to complete the movement pattern. Two is given if the athlete can perform the exercise but requires some form of compensatory movements to complete it. Three is given when an athlete completes the exercise without any compensatory movement. ★ denotes which tests require scores on both sides of the body and the lowest score is used as part of an overall score. A total maximum score of 27 is possible along with an asymmetry score.

Table 25.3 Physical performance tests (LTA, 2011). Data adapted from Cooke et al. (2011) of a 15 year old player

Assessments	Example	Z-scores	
5m sprint	1.07	1.01	Age and gender specific data is used to calculate standardised scores (Z scores) which represent the distance between the raw scores compared to the population mean in units of standard deviation. This allows comparison and identification of strengths and weaknesses across each assessment (Cooke et al., 2011).
10m sprint	1.97	−0.02	
20m sprint	3.55	−1.57	
Forehand agility	2.48	0.04	
Backhand agility	2.33	0.68	
Forwards & backwards movement	3.63	−0.24	
Planned agility	7.7	0.23	
Reactive agility	8.35	1.26	
Vertical jump	40	−0.56	
Squat jump	35	−0.49	
Forehand medicine ball throw (1kg)	14.96	0.78	
Backhand medicine ball throw (1kg)	13.36	0.69	
Overhead medicine ball throw (1kg)	9.28	1.04	
Yo-yo intermittent recovery test	1680	1.00	

ecologically valid and are better suited to the demands of intermittent sports such as tennis (Fernandez-Fernandez et al., 2014b).

The Lawn Tennis Association in Britain designed a comprehensive method to evaluate their junior and professional players. Tables 25.1 and 25.2 detail the musculoskeletal screening and Tables 25.3 and 25.4 detail the fitness assessment and the physical competency assessment.

Although the application of the original Functional Movement Screening has received some widespread attention, there is still some debate over its effectiveness in identifying risks to injury, but as one of a wider array of assessments can still prove useful when evaluating athletes' injury risk (Bishop et al., 2015). The Tennis Functional Movement Assessment was designed to identify

Table 25.4 Physical competencies (LTA, 2011). To achieve in any given level the participant must satisfy strict form such as range of motion and alignment of limbs. ★denotes a deliberate "capping" of expected/desired strength level

	Level 1	Level 2	Level 3	Level 4	Level 5
Squat	1 rep	10 reps	5 reps 50%BW	5 reps125% BW	5 reps150% BW
Lunge	1 rep	10 reps	10m walking lunge 10% BW	10m walking lunge 20% BW	10m walking lunge 40% BW
Single leg Squat	1 rep	5 reps	10 reps	5 reps10% BW	10 reps10% BW
Forward Hop and hold	1 rep 50% of standing height	3 reps of 60% standing height	3 reps of 70% standing height	3 reps of 80% standing height	3 reps of 90% standing height
Lateral hop and hold	1 rep 50% of standing height	3 reps of 60% standing height	3 Reps of 70% standing height	3 reps of 80% standing height	3 reps of 90% standing height
Push up	3 reps	10 reps	30 reps male 20 reps female★	30 reps male 20 reps female★	30 reps male 20 reps female★
Pull up	1 rep supine pull	10 reps supine pull	5 reps supinated grip pull ups	5 reps wide pronated grip pull ups	5 reps wide pronated grip pull ups 30% BW

musculoskeletal imbalances that may contribute to the most common injuries and provide a means to objectively measure potential risks to injury. Like the FMS, the TFMS is judged similarly; each test can gain a score of 3 as long as there are no compensatory movements to complete any task (LTA, 2008). The USTA sports science committee have adopted a similar methodology (Fernandez-Fernandez et al., 2014b).

The physical performance tests shown in Table 25.3 are the chosen tests by the LTA to assess each key component of fitness for tennis. The planned and reactive agility tests have been designed (Cooke et al., 2011) to incorporate perception and decision making, which requires the athlete to make fast adjustments dependent upon the situation. The stimulus provided by the assessment fulfils a key criteria (Young and Farrow, 2006) differentiating agility from change of direction.

Table 25.4 details the physical competencies assessment range from level 1 to 5, which aims to demonstrate exemplar exercises and exercise progressions. The levels suggest a pathway within key exercise streams that any athlete can progress along throughout their athletic development. The key focus and aim of the physical competencies is to assess an athlete's ability to perform key exercises with a mastery level before progressing to repetitions of high quality movement and finally progressing onto added resistance (LTA, 2011). Should any athlete be developed in one exercise stream over another, then more consideration and time can be administered to correct any shortfalls.

Researchers have used physiological skill based tests to better understand the fatigue mechanisms in tennis, demonstrating that fatigue reduces performance outcomes (Davey et al., 2002;

Lyons et al., 2013; Cooke and Davey, 2008). One key finding suggests that stroke performance (stroke accuracy multiplied by ball speed) places significant additional physiological strain compared to running alone, and implies training incorporating whole body involvement may positively influence stroke performance via improved stroke efficiency.

Programming

A long term athletic development plan should be as specific as possible to a given sport, linked to the physiological, mechanical and neurological characteristics, but not at the expense of inadequate fundamentals in strength, stability and robustness, which are the cornerstones of athletic success. An understanding of training outcome for specific training prescription is vital to aid optimisation of time available (Reilly et al., 2009). As Figure 25.1 demonstrates the availability of your athlete may be very low providing minimal opportunities to achieve the required number of training sessions to generate significant adaptations of fitness. Although the WTA recommends just 23 tournaments per year, many will attempt much more (WTA, 2016). At professional level most will identify a short end of season transition period before undertaking the one and only clear off-season period. Coaches must determine where their time is best spent and adopt more long term planning, which should include developments of training programmes specifically designed to sit alongside actual competition weeks. These have typically been described as "travel programmes" (Reid and Schneiker, 2008; Jeffreys and Moody, 2016) and require a high amount of flexibility due to the uncertainty of match participation per week.

To ensure the stimulus of training does not result in a detriment in performance requires a greater need of effective load monitoring. GPS units are an increasingly popular modality, but their use in tennis has been shown to underestimate the distance covered (Duffield et al., 2010), and use within competition is problematic. Hawkeye data has made progress quantifying tennis movements (Reid et al., 2016) but lacks internal and perceptual information, not to mention that most players do not have access to such data. Many practitioners now adopt a method by multiplying the duration of the activity by the perceived exertion (RPE) as a means to quantifying "load" which has been suggested to have a dose-response relationship between training loads and illness, injury and soreness (Gomes et al., 2015; Jeffreys and Moody, 2016; Drew and Finch, 2016). However, every athlete's capability to withstand training load will vary, so care is required when interpreting load data. We know that should a tennis player be successful during a tournament week their ability to perform may be affected by on-going fatigue (Ojala and Häkkinen, 2013; Murphy et al., 2015; Gescheit et al., 2015; Murphy et al., 2014). Improving tolerance to withstand repeated matchplay will therefore increase the likelihood of success. Serena Williams' and Yulia Putintsevas' 2014 tournament calendar (Figure 25.1) illustrates two very different tournament structures, which is partially imposed and added to by choice. It is common for young enthusiastic players to extend their year to try and achieve additional world ranking points at a detriment to potential rest, recuperation and opportunity to focus upon physical preparation which consequently limits the player's potential to succeed. Periodisation in professional senior tennis is complex, but coaches working with juniors may find that a temporary fall in ranking but increased development in athletic ability may be the superior long term solution to high level performance.

The physical competencies produced by the LTA (2011) offers one method for athlete development and the author suggests development of these should be a high priority along with resolving musculoskeletal deficiencies identified via screening. Players who don't achieve level 1 physical competency may be better placed to reduce tennis time to ensure successful long term athlete development.

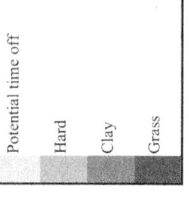

Figure 25.1 Year plans for two female players indicating two different approaches to tournament structure planning. Note how many potential training weeks are available

	Monday	Tuesday	Wednesday	Thursday	Friday	Saturday	Sunday
AM	Warm up – on court agility/ movement focused (30mins)	Warm up – injury prevention based (30-45mins)	Warm up – glute strengthening based (30mins)	Warm up – plyometric based (30mins)	Warm up – injury prevention based (30-45mins)	Warm up – plyometric based (30mins)	
AM	Tennis drilling (90-120mins)	Tennis drilling (90-120mins)	Tennis – match play (90-120mins)	Tennis drilling (90-120mins)	Tennis drilling (90-120mins)	Tennis – match play (90-120mins)	
PM	Tennis match play (points) (60-120mins)	Tennis technical/specific (60-120mins)	Recovery	Tennis match play (points) (60-120mins)	Tennis technical/specific (60-120mins)	Recovery	
PM	Strength training (60mins)	Recovery		Strength training (60mins)	Physio support		
	Recovery			Recovery	Recovery		

Figure 25.2 A typical full training week for a professional player. Training weeks can vary hugely depending upon training experience and the desired focus of the training. This represents a typical training week that aims to train all key areas of tennis performance and may shift according to a particular focus, i.e. more agility/plyometric training. Endurance training can be designed within the on court tennis "drilling" sessions where heart rate intensity can be monitored, which alleviates the need to add an additional session within a busy training week

As already mentioned, tennis requires a large amount of power, and developing strength will undoubtedly realise any subsequent power development (Reid and Schneiker, 2008). Novice athletes may still gain significant strength gains following 1–3 sets of 8–12 reps with 60–70% intensity, intermediate and advanced athletes will require multiple sets 1–8 reps with 80–100% intensity (Kraemer and Ratamess, 2004). There is a strong rationale to develop good muscular endurance, which is also important to reduce the risk of injury (Reid and Schneiker, 2008). Strength endurance may reduce the decrement of power output as the match continues. Medicine ball use enables coaches to train athletes within their natural environments through tennis specific movement patterns, incorporating the ball as a form of overload, and offers a valuable method to improving muscular endurance and can allow for technical footwork patterns to be developed (Roetert et al., 2009). These sessions can be part of a warm up session or a stand-alone session, and using work to rest ratios similar to match play demands is recommended, as previously mentioned. The coaching of technical movement patterns can fall upon the strength and conditioning coach, requiring a high degree of technical knowledge. Movement training can fall under three distinct categories; one being "technical footwork" whereby the coach helps teach correct foot placement throughout ground strokes and should include, but is not limited to, the split step, cross over step, open stance and closed

Glute

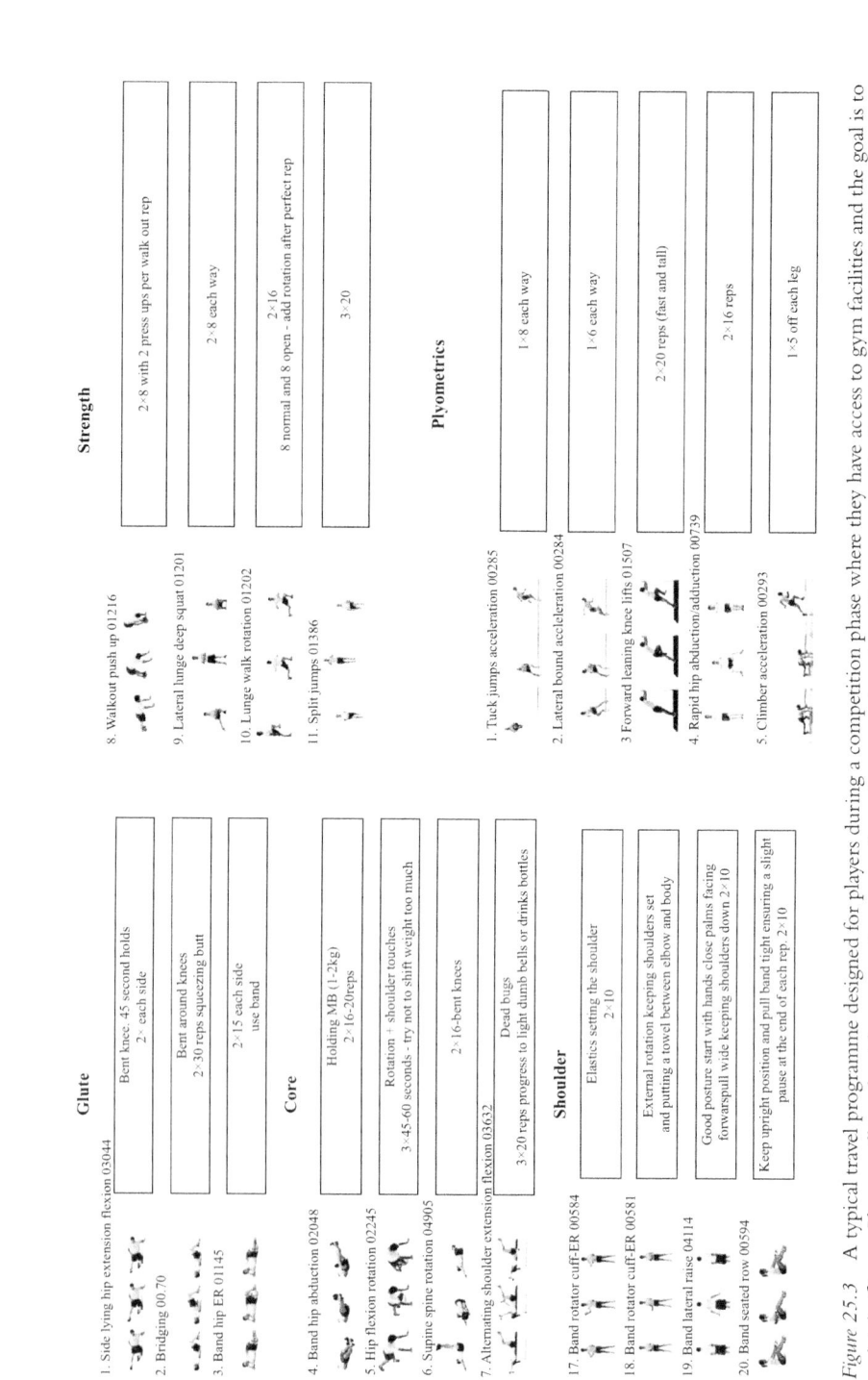

1. Side lying hip extension flexion 03044
2. Bridging 00 70
3. Band hip ER 01145
4. Band hip abduction 02048
5. Hip flexion rotation 02245
6. Supine spine rotation 04905
7. Alternating shoulder extension flexion 03632

Bent knee. 45 second holds 2 × each side	
Bent around knees 2×30 reps squeezing butt	
2×15 each side use band	

Core

Holding MB (1-2kg) 2×16-20reps	
Rotation + shoulder touches 3×45-60 seconds - try not to shift weight too much	
2×16-bent knees	
Dead bugs 3×20 reps progress to light dumb bells or drinks bottles	

Shoulder

17. Band rotator cuff-ER 00584
18. Band rotator cuff-ER 00581
19. Band lateral raise 04114
20. Band seated row 00594

Elastics setting the shoulder 2×10	
External rotation keeping shoulders set and putting a towel between elbow and body	
Good posture start with hands close palms facing forwarspull wide keeping shoulders down 2×10	
Keep upright position and pull band tight ensuring a slight pause at the end of each rep. 2×10	

Strength

8. Walkout push up 01216
9. Lateral lunge deep squat 01201
10. Lunge walk rotation 01202
11. Split jumps 01386

2×8 with 2 press ups per walk out rep	
2×8 each way	
2×16 8 normal and 8 open - add rotation after perfect rep	
3×20	

Plyometrics

1. Tuck jumps acceleration 00285
2. Lateral bound acceleration 00284
3. Forward leaning knee lifts 01507
4. Rapid hip abduction/adduction 00739
5. Climber acceleration 00293

1×8 each way	
1×6 each way	
2×20 reps (fast and tall)	
2×16 reps	
1×5 off each leg	

Figure 25.3 A typical travel programme designed for players during a competition phase where they have access to gym facilities and the goal is to maintain fitness. Players will need guidance on when to perform these exercises, depending upon match play scheduling. For instance, plyometric and strength training would not typically be advised within 3 days prior to competition

stance forehands and backhands, movement to and from wide balls, inside in and inside out forehand, volleying and the smash. Secondly movement training may be more "metabolic" in nature and aim to target the specific energy systems and using work rest ratios that resemble match play (Kovacs, 2007; Kovacs, 2004), which will differ slightly depending upon court surface (Fernandez-Fernandez et al., 2010). Thirdly, "mechanical", which aims to correct and improve poor body positioning and movement in acceleration and deceleration. It may also include the development of clay court movement which differs to hard court movement due to the nature of the surface. An example of specific court training may include the use of slide boards in the preparation for clay court tennis (Kovacs, 2009) in the gym and specific sliding with balance on the court surface.

Injury prevention exercises should look to correct any already identifiable areas of weakness or instability. As previously discussed, Kibler and Safran (2000) have identified some common maladaptations seen in tennis players. A typical programme will consider all areas and programmes are designed to incorporate specific exercises within warm ups, strength training sessions and specific injury prevention sessions to address these maladaptations.

Conclusion

Having worked within the sport for several years, we hope to pass along the importance of fully understanding the necessity of individualising the programme based on the athlete's needs and requirements in combination with their readiness to train. The programme design should be influenced by performance data, a multitude of screening methods and long term development goals. This should also include considerations surrounding the stage of development of the athlete: maturation, emotional readiness to train, training history and attitude.

The opportunities to carry out training blocks are minimal due to the nature of the tournament calendar, and all coaches will need to be able to adapt training daily. Developing good reliable and valid methods to quantify training and competition load will be paramount to ensure the correct balance of training stimulus to secure adaptation versus excessive load, resulting in a decrement of performance. The art of coaching and communicating with our athletes should not be underestimated; as coaches, we can always be improving the knowledge and skillset we apply to our programming.

References

Abrams, G. D., Renstrom, P. A. and Safran, M. R. 2012. Epidemiology of musculoskeletal injury in the tennis player. *British Journal of Sports Medicine*, 46, 492–498.

Alyas, F., Turner, M. and Connell, D. 2007. MRI findings in the lumbar spines of asymptomatic, adolescent, elite tennis players. *British Journal of Sports Medicine*, 41, 836–841.

Bane, M. K., Reid, M. and Morgan, S. 2014. Has player development in men's tennis really changed? An historical rankings perspective. *Journal of Sports Sciences*, 32, 1477–1484.

Bishop, C., Read, P., Walker, S. and Turner, A. 2015. Assessing movement using a variety of screening tests. *Professional Strength & Conditioning*, 37, 17–26.

Bylak, J. and Hutchinson, M. R. 1998. Common sports injuries in young tennis players. *Sports Medicine*, 26, 119–132.

Cooke, K. and Davey, P. 2008. Predictors of oxygen uptake and performance during tennis. *International Journal of Sports Medicine*, 29, 34–39.

Cooke, K., Quinn, A. and Sibte, N. 2011. Testing speed and agility in elite tennis players. *Strength & Conditioning Journal*, 33, 69–72.

Davey, P. R., Thorpe, R. D. and Williams, C. 2002. Fatigue decreases skilled tennis performance. *Journal of Sports Sciences*, 20, 311–318.

Drew, M. K. and Finch, C. F. 2016. The relationship between training load and injury, illness and soreness: a systematic and literature review. *Sports Medicine*, 46(6), 1–23.

Duffield, R., Reid, M., Baker, J. and Spratford, W. 2010. Accuracy and reliability of GPS devices for measurement of movement patterns in confined spaces for court-based sports. *Journal of Science and Medicine in Sport*, 13, 523–525.

Ellenbecker, T. S., Pluim, B., Vivier, S. and Sniteman, C. 2009. Common injuries in tennis players: exercises to address muscular imbalances and reduce injury risk. *Strength & Conditioning Journal*, 31, 50–58.

Farrow, D., Young, W. and Bruce, L. 2005. The development of a test of reactive agility for netball: a new methodology. *Journal of Science and Medicine in Sport*, 8, 52–60.

Fernandez, J., Mendez-Villanueva, A. and Pluim, B. 2006. Intensity of tennis match play. *British Journal of Sports Medicine*, 40, 387–391.

Fernandez-Fernandez, J., Kinner, V. and Ferrauti, A. 2010. The physiological demands of hitting and running in tennis on different surfaces. *The Journal of Strength & Conditioning Research*, 24, 3255–3264.

Fernandez-Fernandez, J., Sanz-Rivas, D., Fernandez-Garcia, B. and Mendez-Villanueva, A. 2008. Match activity and physiological load during a clay-court tennis tournament in elite female players. *Journal of Sports Sciences*, 26, 1589–1595.

Fernandez-Fernandez, J., Sanz-Rivas, D., Kovacs, M. S. and Moya, M. 2014a. In-season effect of a combined repeated sprint and explosive strength training program on elite junior tennis players. *Journal of Strength and Conditioning Research/National Strength & Conditioning Association*, 29(2), 351–357.

Fernandez-Fernandez, J., Sanz-Rivas, D. and Mendez-Villanueva, A. 2009. A review of the activity profile and physiological demands of tennis match play. *Strength & Conditioning Journal*, 31, 15–26.

Fernandez-Fernandez, J., Ulbricht, A. and Ferrauti, A. 2014b. Fitness testing of tennis players: how valuable is it? *British Journal of Sports Medicine*, 48, i22–i31.

Gescheit, D. T., Cormack, S. J., Reid, M. and Duffield, R. 2015. Consecutive days of prolonged tennis match play: performance, physical, and perceptual responses in trained players. *International Journal of Sports Physiology & Performance*, 10(7), 913–920.

Girard, O., Eicher, F., Fourchet, F., Micallef, J.-P. and Millet, G. P. 2007. Effects of the playing surface on plantar pressures and potential injuries in tennis. *British Journal of Sports Medicine*, 41, 733–738.

Girard, O. and Millet, G. P. 2009. Neuromuscular fatigue in racquet sports. *Physical Medicine and Rehabilitation Clinics of North America*, 20, 161–173.

Gomes, R., Cunha, V., Zourdos, M., Aoki, M., Moreira, A., Fernandez-Fernandez, J., Capitani, C. and Capitani, C. D. 2015. Physiological responses of young tennis players to training drills and simulated match play. *Journal of Strength and Conditioning Research/National Strength & Conditioning Association*, 30(3), 851–858.

Groppel, J. L. and Roetert, E. P. 1992. Applied physiology of tennis. *Sports Medicine*, 14, 260–268.

Hewett, T. E., Myer, G. D., Ford, K. R., Heidt, R. S., Colosimo, A. J., McLean, S. G., Van Den Bogert, A. J., Paterno, M. V. and Succop, P. 2005. Biomechanical measures of neuromuscular control and valgus loading of the knee predict anterior cruciate ligament injury risk in female athletes a prospective study. *The American Journal of Sports Medicine*, 33, 492–501.

Jeffreys, I. and Moody, J. 2016. *Strength and Conditioning for Sports Performance*. Routledge.

Johnson, C. D. and McHugh, M. P. 2006. Performance demands of professional male tennis players. *British Journal of Sports Medicine*, 40, 696–699.

Kibler, W. B. and Chandler, T. 2003. Range of motion in junior tennis players participating in an injury risk modification program. *Journal of Science and Medicine in Sport*, 6, 51–62.

Kibler, W. B. and Safran, M. R. 2000. Musculoskeletal injuries in the young tennis player. *Clinics in Sports Medicine*, 19, 781–792.

Kibler, W. B. and Safran, M. 2005. Tennis Injuries. In *Epidemiology of pediatric sports injuries* (Vol. 48, pp. 120–137). Karger Publishers.

Kovacs, M. S. 2004. Energy system-specific training for tennis. *Strength & Conditioning Journal*, 26, 10–13.

Kovacs, M. S. 2006. Applied physiology of tennis performance. *British Journal of Sports Medicine*, 40, 381–386.

Kovacs, M. S. 2007. Tennis physiology. *Sports Medicine*, 37, 189–198.

Kovacs, M. S. 2009. Movement for tennis: the importance of lateral training. *Strength & Conditioning Journal*, 31, 77–85.

Kovacs, M. S. and Ellenbecker, T. S. 2011. A performance evaluation of the tennis serve: implications for strength, speed, power, and flexibility training. *Strength & Conditioning Journal*, 33, 22–30.

Kovacs, M. S., Roetert, E. P. and Ellenbecker, T. S. 2008. Efficient deceleration: the forgotten factor in tennis-specific training. *Strength & Conditioning Journal*, 30, 58–69.

Kraemer, W. J. and Ratamess, N. A. 2004. Fundamentals of resistance training: progression and exercise prescription. *Medicine and Science in Sports and Exercise*, 36, 674–688.

Lyons, M., Al Nakeeb, Y., Hankey, J. and Nevill, A. 2013. The effect of moderate and high-intensity fatigue on groundstroke accuracy in expert and non-expert tennis players. *Journal of Sports Medicine*, 12(2), 298.

Maquirriain, J. and Ghisi, J. 2006. The incidence and distribution of stress fractures in elite tennis players. *British Journal of Sports Medicine*, 40, 454–459.

Maquirriain, J., Ghisi, J. P. and Kokalj, A. M. 2007. Rectus abdominis muscle strains in tennis players. *British Journal of Sports Medicine*, 41, 842–848.

Marks, M., Haas, S. and Wiesel, S. 1988. Low back pain in the competitive tennis player. *Clinics in Sports Medicine*, 7, 277–287.

Murphy, A. P., Duffield, R., Kellett, A., Gescheit, D. and Reid, M. 2015. The effect of predeparture training loads on posttour physical capacities in high-performance junior tennis players. *International Journal of Sports Physiology & Performance*, 10(8), 986–993.

Murphy, A., Duffield, R., Kellett, A. and Reid, M. 2014. The relationship of training load to physical capacity changes during international tours in high performance junior tennis players. *International Journal of Sports Physiology and Performance*, 10(2), 253–260.

Ojala, T. and Häkkinen, K. 2013. Effects of the tennis tournament on players' physical performance, hormonal responses, muscle damage and recovery. *Journal of Sports Science and Medicine*, 12, 240–248.

Otis, C., Crespo, M., Flygare, C., Johnston, P., Keber, A., Lloyd-Kolkin, D., Loehr, J., Martin, K., Pluim, B. and Quinn, A. 2006. The Sony Ericsson WTA Tour 10 year age eligibility and professional development review. *British Journal of Sports Medicine*, 40, 464–468.

Pluim, B. M., Loeffen, F., Clarsen, B., Bahr, R. and Verhagen, E. 2015. A one-season prospective study of injuries and illness in elite junior tennis. *Scandinavian Journal of Medicine & Science in Sports*, 26(5), 564–571.

Pluim, B. M., Staal, J. B., Marks, B. L., Miller, S. and Miley, D. 2007. Health benefits of tennis. *British Journal of Sports Medicine*, 41(11): 760–768.

Pluim, B. M., Staal, J., Windler, G. and Jayanthi, N. 2006. Tennis injuries: occurrence, aetiology, and prevention. *British Journal of Sports Medicine*, 40, 415–423.

Reid, M., Morgan, S. and Whiteside, D. 2016. Matchplay characteristics of Grand Slam tennis: implications for training and conditioning. *Journal of Sports Sciences*, 34(19), 1791–1798.

Reid, M. and Schneiker, K. 2008. Strength and conditioning in tennis: current research and practice. *Journal of Science and Medicine in Sport*, 11, 248–256.

Reilly, T., Morris, T. and Whyte, G. 2009. The specificity of training prescription and physiological assessment: a review. *Journal of Sports Sciences*, 27, 575–589.

Roetert, E. P., Brown, S. W., Piorkowskil, P. A. and Woods, R. B. 1996. Fitness comparisons among three different levels of elite tennis players. *The Journal of Strength & Conditioning Research*, 10, 139–143.

Roetert, E. P. and Ellenbecker, T. S. 2007. *Complete Conditioning for Tennis*. Champaign, IL: Human Kinetics.

Roetert, E. P., Kovacs, M., Knudson, D. and Groppel, J. L. 2009. Biomechanics of the tennis groundstrokes: implications for strength training. *Strength & Conditioning Journal*, 31, 41–49.

Salonikidis, K. and Zafeiridis, A. 2008. The effects of plyometric, tennis-drills, and combined training on reaction, lateral and linear speed, power, and strength in novice tennis players. *The Journal of Strength & Conditioning Research*, 22, 182–191.

Smekal, G., Von Duvillard, S. P., Rihacek, C., Pokan, R., Hofmann, P., Baron, R., Tschan, H. and Bachl, N. 2001. A physiological profile of tennis match play. *Medicine and Science in Sports and Exercise*, 33, 999–1005.

Ulbricht, A., Fernandez-Fernandez, J., Mendez-Villanueva, A. and Ferrauti, A. 2015. Impact of fitness characteristics on tennis performance in elite junior tennis players. *Journal of Strength and Conditioning Research/National Strength & Conditioning Association*, 30, 989–998.

Young, W. and Farrow, D. 2006. A review of agility: practical applications for strength and conditioning. *Strength & Conditioning Journal*, 28, 24–29.

Online Resources

ATP. 2016. www.atpworldtour.com <accessed June 2016>.
International Tennis Federation (ITF). 2016. www.itftennis.com <accessed June 2016>.
Lawn Tennis Association (LTA). 2008. *British Tennis: Tennis Functional Movement Screen; LTA Musculoskeletal Screening Protocol*.
Lawn Tennis Association (LTA). 2011. *Strength and Conditioning Progressions: Exercises and Tests for Ages 10–20*. London, UK: The Tennis Foundation.
WTA. 2016. www.wtatennis.com <accessed June 2016>.

26
GOLF

Paul J. Read, Justin Buckthorp, Zachariah I. Gould and Rhodri S. Lloyd

Introduction

Golf is a popular sport played at both elite and recreational levels, with previous estimates of more than 55 million participants globally (Farrally et al., 2003). Traditionally, golf has been perceived as a skill-based sport with the focus on technical improvement and psychological development. Technical factors have a profound effect on performance and it has been shown that more skilled golfers display greater club head velocity, higher ball launch angle and more rapid body-twist angular velocity (Watanabe et al., 1998). Strategies to enhance these aspects of performance have been primarily focused upon improving technology (Whittaker, 1998); however, physical conditioning is now being recognised as an essential component to provide a competitive edge and reduce injury risk (Farrally et al., 2003; Evans and Tuttle, 2015).

Recent scientific investigations have provided empirical evidence showing relationships between golf performance measures, such as club head speed (CHS) and tests of strength and power (Keogh et al., 2009, Wells et al., 2009; Read et al., 2014). Improvements in CHS are also possible for recreational and elite golfers following strength and power training interventions (Doan et al., 2006; Thompson et al., 2007; Read et al., 2013). While the sport of golf is not automatically associated with the need for high levels of physical fitness, the complexity of the golf swing, high musculoskeletal forces and repetitive nature of the practice and competitions predispose players to heightened injury risk (Hume et al., 2005). Thus, appropriate physical conditioning is a fundamental requirement for those wishing to participate in elite competition (Read et al., 2014).

This chapter will provide an evidenced based description of the biomechanical requirements, physiological demands, and injury epidemiology associated with the sport of golf. Following this, considerations and guidelines for the implementation of appropriate strength and conditioning programmes will be discussed.

Athletic demands

The first step in the design of a golf-relevant training programme is to analyse the demands of the sport and determine the physical and physiological characteristics of highly proficient performers. Understanding these characteristics will assist technical and strength and conditioning coaches, physiotherapists, and rehabilitation specialists in the design of programmes that provide effective training transfer.

Biomechanical analysis of the golf swing

The golf swing is a closed kinetic chain movement that involves all three anatomical planes and is comprised of the following sections: 1) set up, involving largely isometric actions; 2) the backswing of which its primary function is to allow the correct positioning of the club head in order to instigate an accurate and powerful downswing where agonist muscles and joint structures responsible for generating power in the downswing are pre-loaded; 3) the downswing, where the purpose is to return the club head to the ball at the correct angle with maximum angular velocity; and, finally, 4) the follow through, which is characterised largely by eccentric muscle actions (Hume et al., 2005).

Driving distance is primarily a function of angular club head velocity and the characteristics of the arm-club lever at the point of impact with the ball (Hume et al., 2005). It should be considered that the latter is largely determined by anthropometrical factors, whereas angular velocity of the club head is produced by physical factors such as ground reaction forces and transfer of

Image 26.1 Justin Rose performing a golf drive

body weight, the sequential summation of forces and utilisation of eccentric-concentric coupling (Hume et al., 2005). The role of the strength and conditioning coach will focus predominantly on increasing the production of angular club head velocity through the development of a player's ability to generate larger ground reaction forces and heightened rates of force development along the kinetic chain. Additionally, ensuring safe and efficient deceleration of force via increases in strength is of fundamental importance.

In the execution of a golf drive or approach shot, a range of involved musculature have been identified as key contributors. Specifically, the hip and knee extensors, hip abductors and adductors (Bechler, 1995), spinal extensors and abdominals (Pink et al., 1993), and shoulder internal rotators (Jobe et al., 1986). Kinetic chain sequencing is evident during the downswing, where the larger, more proximal body segments initiate the movement (right hip extensors and abductors, and the left adductor magnus in right handed golfers), followed by the trunk, shoulders, and lastly the hands and wrists (Okuda et al., 2002). This suggests a sequential order of torque generation which is required to achieve maximal club head speed (Sprigings and Neal, 2000). This has implications for the development of appropriate training programmes that should include a primary focus on the use of whole body dynamic movements to develop strength and power. Furthermore, exercise selection that is characterised by "ground up" force generation sequencing will promote a greater transfer of training effect than isolated, uni-articular approaches.

Physiology of golf performance

A commonly held misconception in golf is that there is a high requirement for aerobic fitness. Average oxygen uptake (VO_2) has been reported at 22.4 mL $\times$ min^{-1} $\times$ $^{-1}$ (Sell et al., 2008) and during a round of golf, players have been shown to function at a mean exercise intensity of just 35–41% VO_{2max} (Murase et al., 1989). Furthermore, lactate responses following the completion of 18 holes are equivalent to typical resting levels (Unverdorben et al., 2000). Cumulatively, these data indicate that golf imposes a relatively low cardio-respiratory demand; thus, it is of no surprise that reported VO_{2max} values for golfers are lower than other more demanding endurance-based sports (Wilmore and Costill, 2004). Thus, aerobic conditioning should not be viewed as the primary training focus for golf as continuous long slow duration aerobic training may also lead to reductions in strength, power and rate of force development (Elliott et al., 2007; Behm and Sale, 1993). Instead training prescription should be directed towards the development of explosive, anaerobic physical qualities to enhance a player's ability to generate high levels of force and angular velocity of the club head. In addition, developing adequate levels of flexibility, muscle balance, strength and tissue tolerance to ensure players are able to attenuate force effectively due to the high volumes, and repetitive nature of practice and competition is also recommended (Read et al., 2014).

Physical characteristics of elite golfers

The golf swing is a highly athletic movement, whereby, safe, accurate and consistent golf performance requires an individual to have the requisite mobility, stability, proprioception, neuromuscular coordination, strength, speed and power. Previous research has shown that repeated exposures to practice and competition may bring about adaptive changes in elite players compared to non-elite individuals. Specific examples include greater rotational velocities due to superior swing mechanics (Newton et al., 1996), increased gluteus maximus and medius strength (Callaway et al., 2012), heightened levels of grip strength (Crews et al., 1986) and muscle mass in the dominant arm (Dorado et al., 2002). Profiling of the physical characteristics of golfers has also reported that lower handicap players demonstrate greater static balance, hip, torso and shoulder strength and flexibility than golfers with higher handicaps (Sell et al., 2007). Additionally, moderate relationships have been reported between field-based tests of strength and power and golf club head speed in physically untrained elite golfers (Read et al., 2014). The measures with the strongest associations were a seated and standing medicine ball throw, countermovement jump height and peak power and squat jump height and peak power. These data suggest that rotational power, upper body strength and lower body strength and power are significant contributors to the development of club head speed.

Injury epidemiology

The golf swing is a complex movement that involves a series of integrated joint motions and muscle actions, where significant forces of up to eight times bodyweight can be experienced (Hosea et al., 1990). Additionally, in excess of 2000 swing repetitions are often performed by the tournament professional during practice and competition each week (Pink et al., 1993; Theriault and Lachance, 1998). Subsequently, injury risk is an inherent part of the sport, and thus, strength and conditioning coaches should be cognizant of the anatomical sites most affected, and the frequency with which the most common injuries occur.

Epidemiological data indicate that professional golfers sustain more injuries than amateurs (Gosheger et al., 2003), and the most common anatomical site of injury is the lower back, followed by the wrist and shoulders (Gosheger et al., 2003; McCarroll and Gioe, 1982). Conversely, amateur players are more likely to incur an injury to the elbow, followed by the back and shoulder (Gosheger et al., 2003; Batt, 1992). The frequency of lower back injuries has been reported to range from 23–52% of all the injuries sustained by amateur and professional golfers (McCarroll et al., 1990; McCarroll and Gioe, 1982; Finch et al., 1998; Gluck et al., 2008). This is likely due to the high magnitude of forces and ranges of motion experienced in this region due to the mechanics of the swing. For example, axial twisting alone has been established as an injury risk factor (Marras and Granata, 1995), in addition to other swing characteristics, such as downward compression, side to side bending, sliding and back to front shearing (Hosea et al., 1990). Additionally, forces imposed on the lumbar spine in the golf swing have shown a mean compression at the L4-L5 motion segment of 4400 N of force (Lim et al., 2012). To put this into perspective, that is the equivalent of over 458kg of compressive gravitational force on the lumbar spine, or over six times the body weight of subjects in the study, during the downswing. Anterior-posterior shear forces in the lumbar spine of over 1.6 times a person's body weight have also been recorded (Lim et al., 2012); thus, it is essential that golfers possess the appropriate levels of strength and motor control to withstand these forces and meet the demands of high frequency practice and competition schedules.

An alternative hypothesis for the occurrence of commonly reported golf injuries at the aforementioned anatomical sites of the lower back, shoulder and wrists is the link theory (Nadler et al., 2000). The kinetic chain functions as a unit and alterations in one or a number of regions along the chain can affect the system as a whole (Nadler et al., 2000). For example, reduced hip mobility and strength may contribute to the incidence of lower back injury (Nadler et al., 2000; Vad et al., 2004), and in the upper body, limited motion at the thoracic spine has been associated with a higher prevalence of shoulder impingement syndrome (Meurer et al., 2004; Theisen et al., 2010). Thus, practitioners should be cognizant of the integrated function of the involved joints during the golf swing (emphasising stability and mobility where appropriate) and include specific assessments and exercise prescription to target common areas of dysfunction.

> **Observations from the PGA tour**
>
> Experience on the European and PGA Tour has shown us the importance of the gluteals and torso in injury prevention and performance enhancement. They are huge 'brakes and accelerators' for the golf swing, and play a pivotal role in allowing the rest of the kinetic chain to function successfully. From both an anatomical and functional perspective this makes sense: the lumbo-pelvic-hip complex is a vital bridge connecting the upper and lower extremities and is vital in decelerating, stabilising and accelerating movement in all three planes of motion.

Adequate levels of symmetry and postural endurance of the trunk musculature should also be considered by practitioners when designing targeted interventions to reduce the risk of spinal injuries (McGill et al., 1999). Supporting this, a battery of tests designed to measure strength, flexibility and endurance in elite male youth golfers showed that asymmetry on a side bridge endurance test displayed the strongest relationship with incidences of back pain (Evans et al., 2005). Given the asymmetrical nature of the golf swing, the side bridge endurance test, which challenges the quadratus lumborum and muscles of the antero-lateral trunk wall, could be considered appropriate to detect exaggerated unilateral differences in trunk muscle endurance (McGill et al., 1999). This has implications for the identification and prevention of injury, as in instances where a left side bridge endurance test was greater than the right by 12.5 seconds, there was an increased chance of low back injury (Evans et al., 2005). However, due to the repetitive, asymmetrical nature of the golf swing, side to side differences in golfers are to be expected; thus, the achievement of symmetry may not be possible, and approaches to manage such factors are likely more realistic. Nonetheless, regular screening of muscle imbalances and postural endurance and strength is recommended. In addition, with the primary injury mechanism reported as overuse due to high volume practice and competitions (McCarroll and Gioe, 1982; McHardy et al., 2006), management of training volumes, adequate mobility, muscular stability and strength should be deemed essential in order to withstand the repetitive loading that occurs in practice and competition.

Fitness testing

Physical performance testing

Strength is a key component for golfers to ensure they can generate the sufficient muscular torques required to enhance CHS (Sprigings and Neal, 2000). Higher levels of muscle activation in the lower limbs during the downswing are displayed in lower handicap players (Marta et al., 2016), and strong relationships have been shown between lower limb strength and power and increased driving distances (Hellstrom, 2008; Wells et al., 2009) and club head speed (Read et al., 2014; Lewis et al., 2016). Specifically, these have included 1 repetition maximum (1RM) back squats (Hellstrom, 2008), squat jump height (Read et al., 2014; Lewis et al., 2016) and vertical jump peak power (Hellstrom, 2008; Wells et al., 2009), indicating that lower body strength and power are key qualities to enhance golf drive performance. The importance of upper body and rotary strength and power has also been examined with moderate relationships reported between a medicine ball chest throw, rotational power and golf CHS (Gordon et al., 2009; Read et al., 2014). However, caution should be applied when interpreting these findings, as isolated measures of trunk rotational strength have been unable to distinguish between elite and recreational players (Lindsay and Horton, 2006), highlighting the importance of the sequential torque production in the golf swing, initiated from the legs (Fujimoto-Kantani, 1995). Thus, a medicine ball rotational hip toss has been suggested as an appropriate power test and exercise for golfers, which sequentially involves force production from the leg, trunk and arm musculature, and this test has reported stronger relationships with CHS in both amateurs (Read et al., 2014) and professionals (Lewis et al., 2016). Also, although not of primary importance, testing and developing upper body power is recommended as the pectoralis major has been shown to be highly active during the downswing and will help to generate club-head speed (Marta et al., 2012).

Movement screening

In addition to strength and power testing, movement screening provides an indication of mobility, stability and coordination of body segments to help identify potential physical limitations that may impact the execution of the golf swing (Gulgin et al., 2014). Furthermore, isolated mobility testing can be performed to gain an insight into the athlete's range of motion, stability and strength at different segments along the kinetic chain. This reductionist approach may not always provide an accurate assessment of what will happen in functional movement and during the golf swing, but will provide useful information for strength and conditioning coaches in their ability to quantify deficits that ultimately affect programme design. For example, using the earlier description of the importance of 'kinetic linking', hip and thoracic spine mobility deficits may increase the risk of injury (Dickenson et al., 2016; Mun et al., 2015; Sadeghisani et al., 2015; Cole and Grimshaw, 2016).

In selecting appropriate methods to screen movement quality in golfers, practitioners should consider reliability, validity and logistical constraints. One example is the Functional Movement Screen™ (FMS) which was designed to quantify fundamental human movement, highlight asymmetries in the body and identify when there is a need to refer out to a medical professional (Cook, 2010). Research has shown the FMS can be reliably used with good interrater reliability (Smith et al., 2013; Cuchna et al., 2016; Bonazza et al., 2016), and although conflicting findings have been reported, a recent systematic review indicated that the FMS is a valid predictor of injury (Bonazza et al., 2016). More recently, golf-specific screening methods have been developed including the Titleist Performance Institute™ (TPI) Movement Screen. Like the FMS, TPI qualitatively assesses mobility, stability and coordination of body segments to help identify the player's movement needs. The TPI screen has been shown to detect physical limitations that may impact golf performance (Gulgin et al., 2014). Specifically, lower scores during a toe touch test were associated with early hip extension during the golf swing, and lower bridge scores on the right side resulted in early hip extension and a loss of swing posture. In addition, players who were unable to deep overhead squat and had lower left leg balance scores were 2–3 times more likely to display either early hip extension, loss of posture, or slide faults during the golf swing (Gulgin et al., 2014). Thus, when screening a large number of golfers, or if contact time with players is limited, it may be more appropriate to simply include the overhead squat and a measure of dynamic balance such as the star excursion or y-balance test (Plisky et al., 2006; Plisky et al., 2009). Available data have shown this test to be a valid predictor of injury and low-back pain, and can also be used to provide an indication of gluteus medius function and frontal plane stability (Ganesh et al., 2015; Coughlan et al., 2012; Steffen et al., 2013; Fullam et al., 2014; Hegedus et al., 2015). Hop performance and lateral hops are also useful measures of dynamic balance and provide an insight into frontal plane force production and control. These can be used as part of a test battery battery and during training to challenge players in multiple planes of motion.

Sport-specific performance monitoring

From a technical perspective, golf-specific technology such as Trackman™ can be used to monitor swing performance and provide feedback on how the development of athletic qualities transfers into sports performance. Key metrics from Trackman™ which practitioners should consider are:

- Club head speed (how fast the club is moving through impact)
- Ball speed (the speed of the ball coming off the face of the club after impact)
- Carry (the total distance the ball travels through the air)

It is also beneficial to utilise 3-D golf biomechanics analysis, such as Golf Biodynamics™. This technology uses electromagnetic motion tracking at different body segments to map a player's unique movement characteristics at address and throughout the golf swing. Understanding joint motion, kinematic sequencing and movement efficiency provides valuable feedback, and can be an important bridge between movement screening and physical testing, and the use of performance monitoring technology, such as Trackman™.

To more clearly describe how this approach can be used, a case study has been included. After winning the US Open in 2013, Justin Rose and Justin Buckthorp designed 'Project 300', the ability of Justin Rose to carry the ball 300 yards on demand if the hole required it. They measured Justin's Trackman™ data at the Open Championship in 2013, and results showed average club head speed with the driver of 112.1mph, ball speed of 164.5mph and a carry distance of 274.4 yards. As of May 2013, Justin was number one in total distance efficiency on the PGA Tour, so it was critical that power was not gained at the expense of accuracy. A screenshot from Trackman™ can be seen in Figure 26.1. Through engagement in a long-term

BALL SPEED	LAUNCH ANG.	SPIN RATE	LAND. ANG.	CARRY	SPIN AXIS
164.5 mph	12.0 deg	2477 rpm	42.2 deg	274.4 yds	3.4 deg
SPIN LOFT	TOTAL	CLUB SPEED	ATTACK ANG.	CLUB PATH	DYN. LOFT
14.0 deg	294.2 yds	112.1 mph	-0.5 deg	0.5 deg	13.5 deg
FACE ANG.	FACE TO PATH	SWING DIR.	SMASH FAC.	LAUNCH DIR.	
0.1 deg	-0.4 deg	0.1 deg	1.47	0.1 deg	

Figure 26.1 Justin Rose's Trackman driver data, July 2013

BALL SPEED	LAUNCH ANG.	SPIN RATE	LAND. ANG.	CARRY	SPIN LOFT
174.4 mph	12.7 deg	2114 rpm	39.4 deg	303.8 yds	10.7 deg
TOTAL	CLUB SPEED	ATTACK ANG.	CLUB PATH	DYN. LOFT	FACE ANG.
327.1 yds	118.7 mph	3.2 deg	1.5 deg	13.9 deg	0.7 deg
FACE TO PATH	SWING DIR.	SMASH FAC.	LAUNCH DIR.		
-0.8 deg	4.1 deg	1.47	0.8 deg		

Figure 26.2 Justin Rose's Trackman driver data, November 2015

periodised strength and conditioning programme, speed and power variables from Trackman™ continued to improve and the target was achieved as shown in Figure 26.2. This project was then continued and at the Dubai Championships in November 2015, average club speed was measured at 122.4mph, ball speed was up to 176.3mph and carry reached 308.5 yards. These data indicate that despite Justin being a more senior player on the PGA Tour in his mid-thirties, it was possible to both acutely enhance and maintain performance longitudinally, further demonstrating the effectiveness of integrating physical conditioning with technical skill training to aid training transfer.

Golf performance and movement screen test battery

As highlighted above, strength, lower extremity and rotatory power, mobility, and trunk strength and endurance are important characteristics for golfers to enhance performance and reduce injury risk. Having an understanding of a golfer's movement qualities, athletic capacity and technical needs is vital. The combined metrics gathered from a well-designed and carefully executed test battery will influence programme design, show a player's progression over time, and empower the golfer with tangible data they can use to improve their game.

Following the identification of the relevant physical factors that are required for successful golf performance (needs analysis), in order to link the information together, the authors propose the use of a systematic performance model to assess their athletes and subsequently develop individualised programmes (Read et al., 2016). Using this approach, each physical factor is linked to a relevant screening assessment and target exercises are then selected to improve relevant performance deficits (Read et al., 2016). It is proposed that following an appropriate training intervention, performance deficits can be minimised, with concurrent reductions in injury risk. An example performance model for golf, comprising the physical factors required for success, tests to determine the athletes level of competency and categories of exercises to enhance these qualities has been provided in Figure 26.3. Further prescriptive details in the form of a field-based test battery that could be used with minimal equipment to assess movement quality and physical performance in golfers has also been included in Table 26.1.

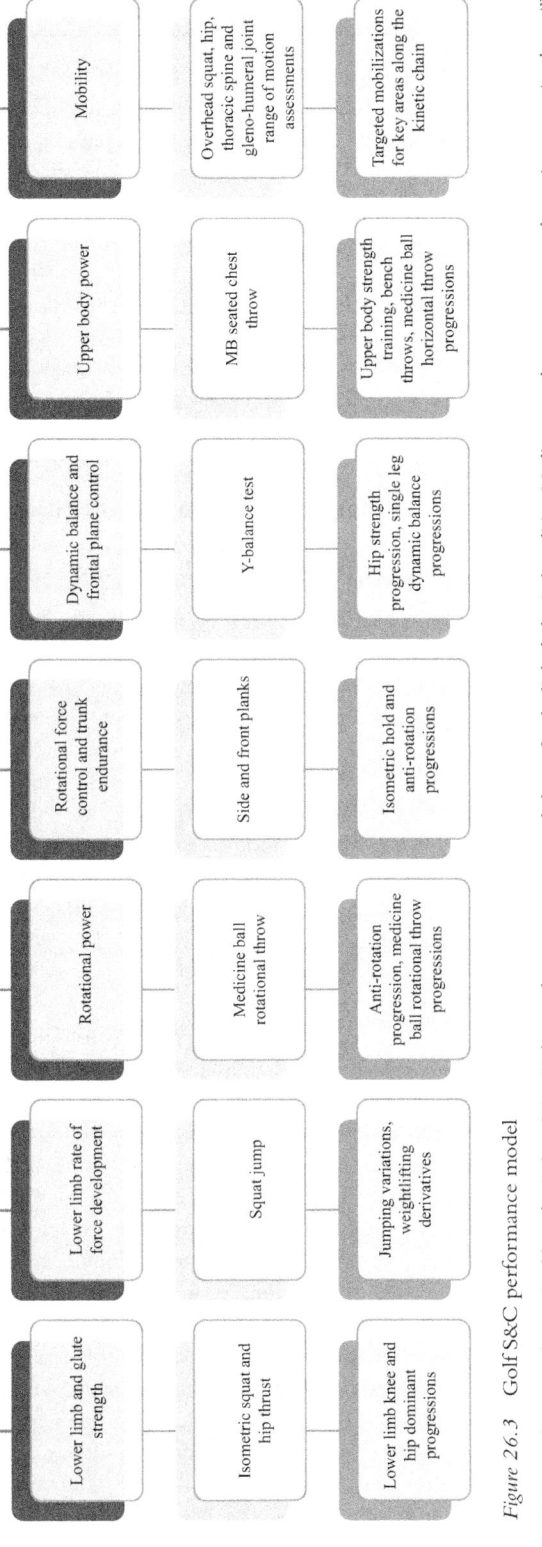

Figure 26.3 Golf S&C performance model

Dark grey boxes are the required key physical qualities. Light grey boxes are recommended tests for the linked physical qualities. Medium grey boxes are suggested exercise categories that will increase test performance and subsequently enhance the required physical quality.

Table 26.1 Suggested field-based test battery to measure physical performance in golfers

Physical characteristic	Test	Rest period
Movement screen – global mobility	Overhead squat (subjective screening of movement quality)	-
Dynamic balance and frontal plane control	Y-balance test (relative reach distance)	-
Lower limb rate of force development	Squat jump (height)	≥ 3 min
Rotational power	Standing MB rotational toss (distance)	≥ 3 min
Upper body power	Seated MB chest throw (distance)	≥ 3 min
Hip extension capacity	Bent knee single leg hip bridge repetition maximum test (1 e/s)	-
Trunk capacity	Isometric side plank maximum length hold (seconds) (1 e/s)	-

Programme design considerations

Training golfers for strength and power development

A review of strength and power training interventions in golf has shown average increases in CHS of 4.2%, leading to enhanced driving distances (Smith et al., 2011). While explosive movement is of primary importance, practitioners should be cognisant that power, a key component of the golf swing, is largely dependent on the ability to exert high levels of force; further indicating the importance of muscular strength development (Stone et al., 2003). To enhance strength and power application in the golf swing, multi-joint exercises should be included which promote effective force transfer along the kinetic chain. Training the 'core' in isolation to generate high levels of force in rotational sports may not be the optimal approach, as exercises which elicit repeated simultaneous flexion and rotations in the lumbar spine increase the chance of spinal injury (Callaghan and McGill, 2001). It has been reported that the core is never a power generator, as power is generated in the hips and transmitted through a stable trunk (McGill, 2010). Training for the enhancement of CHS should emphasise anti-motion control to reduce spinal torques (McGill, 2010), with strength and power development targeting the upper and lower limbs. Consequently, foundational movements such as hip-hinging, squatting and lunging should be included as part of the fundamental exercise prescription to provide a strong training foundation from which to develop sequential kinetic chain linking.

While foundational movements (squatting, deadlifting and lunging) should form the basis of training prescription, these exercises are performed predominantly in the sagittal plane. Thus, it is important to consider supplementing this prescription with the addition of transverse plane exercises to further enhance the transfer of training effect (Spaniol, 2012). Incorporating projectiles into the training plan (e.g. medicine balls) could therefore be considered an effective means for developing kinetic sequencing, rotational power and movement velocity (Ebben et al., 1999; Szymanski et al., 2007; Stodden et al., 2008). Such exercises are optimally performed through a closed kinetic chain sequence, allowing the initiation of force via the larger, stronger muscles of the lower body and then transferred toward the ball, allowing for maximal velocity in the target direction (Akutagawa and Kojima, 2005). Additionally, and of particular importance, medicine ball training does not involve a deceleration component, subsequently enhancing their effectiveness for the development of power through the full range of movement. However, caution should be applied by strength and conditioning coaches to avoid the 'specificity trap' and not simply overload mimicked movement patterns that occur in the sport, but focus more on developing appropriate neuromuscular adaptations that provide relevant contributions to the athletic development of golfers which can then be utilised effectively by the player's golf coach.

The importance of rate of force development

Rate of force development (RFD) may be defined as the change in force development divided by the change in time (Stone et al., 2007), or the ability to develop force within a limited timeframe. For most athletes, key sporting movements occur within 0.25–0.3s (Stone et al., 2006; Zatsiorsky, 2003); therefore, sufficient time is not available to develop peak force. In the golf swing, the time from downswing to impact is approximately 290ms for male professional players (McTeigue et al., 1994). Due to the initial forceful muscular contraction from the lower limbs and hips, shorter durations in the downswing (Marta et al., 2016) and the fact that elite players transfer more of their weight at a faster rate throughout the entire downswing phase (Okuda et al., 2002), RFD should be considered essential in enhancing club head speed. Subsequently, ballistic exercises involving rapid acceleration against a resistance in the form of the body or an object (Winchester et al., 2008) are recommended. In addition, if a player possesses the appropriate orthopaedic profile, and has established sound movement competency in a range of fundamental movements, weightlifting derivatives, due to their reported high power outputs and short execution times could also be considered for inclusion to further promote increases in RFD (Garhammer, 1993; Hori et al., 2005; Read et al., 2014).

Application of the stretch shortening cycle and the X-factor stretch

The 'X-factor' has been defined as the relative rotation of the shoulders with respect to the hips at the top of the backswing (Cheetham et al., 2001), or the maximal increase of pelvic-upper torso separation during the transition between the backswing and downswing (Cheetham et al., 2001). This action has been proposed to elicit increases in elastic energy as a result of a stretch reflex, enhancing rotational velocities in more distal limb segments (Cheetham et al., 2001). However, within the available literature, the contribution of the stretch reflex has provided ambiguous results (Hellstrom, 2009). It has been suggested that the enhanced striking distances associated with the X-factor stretch may be due to increases in force, attributable to eccentric activation of the musculature of the lower body and torso prior to the downswing (Okuda et al., 2002; Bechler et al., 1995). Also, it should be considered that performance augmentation derived from pre-stretching a muscle is reduced the greater the timeframe between the eccentric and concentric actions, with a point of diminishing returns, whereby, once the eccentric loading (stretch phase) reaches a critical threshold, the subsequent concentric contraction exhibits no further increase (Wilson et al., 1994; Turner et al., 2011). This is likely because the time frame between the eccentric contraction and the propulsive concentric contraction (i.e. the amortisation phase) is too great, with reports that the half-life of the stretch shortening cycle is 0.85 seconds, and that by 1 second the benefits have diminished by 55% (Wilson et al., 1994). With average backswing durations for elite players recorded at 0.80 seconds (McTeigue et al., 1994), this suggests slower rates of stretch occur, thus potentially negating neural influences.

In a recent study that examined relationships between strength and power tests and golf CHS, multiple regression analysis demonstrated that concentric dominant exercises, namely a squat jump and seated medicine ball throw, were the greatest predictors of club head speed in elite amateur players (Read et al., 2014). These relationships have been confirmed more recently in professional PGA golfers (Lewis et al., 2016). Based on these results, the authors suggested that the golf swing may not reflect fast stretch SSC activity (<250ms) (Read et al., 2014), which is dependent on large contributions from stretch reflex properties and elastic energy reutilisation (Bobbert et al., 1996), but rather slow stretch-shortening cycle (SSC) activity (>250ms), which takes advantage of an increased time for cross-bridge formation (Van Ingen Schenau et al., 1997). It is proposed that the back swing merely allows increases in force production through the eccentric action, providing an increase in impulse (force × time), compared with a downswing without a pre-stretch (Read et al., 2014). Therefore, increasing the magnitude and rate of initial ground reaction forces in the downswing, as developed through appropriate resistance training protocols, may be more pertinent to the production of higher club head speed values.

The importance of mobility

Joint ranges of motion in lower handicap players have been characterised by increased shoulder abduction (Doan et al., 2006; Thompson et al., 2007) and greater range of movement in right shoulder extension, external rotation, left shoulder extension, right hip extension, left hip flexion and right torso rotation (Sell et al., 2007). In the execution of the golf swing, players repeatedly achieve movements and joint angles indicative of high levels of mobility and stability, whereby adaptive changes occur in response to the specific demands of the sport (Vad et al., 2004). Sub-optimal movement mechanics may lead to a range of compensations, increasing injury risk, reducing exercise economy and creating inconsistencies in swing technique (Hume et al., 2005). Also, increasing mobility may allow a longer backswing and subsequent impulse, the net product of (force × time) enhancing swing speed. However, this has not been confirmed within the literature and requires further investigation.

It is also important to address the issue of previously held misconceptions regarding reductions in flexibility following resistance training. While few studies have examined the effects of resistance training on flexibility, available data indicate that reductions in range of motion do not occur (McCartney, 1999; Wilmore et al., 1978). Conversely, there is a body of evidence to suggest that providing weight training is performed using the full range of motion, flexibility will not be negatively affected (Beedle et al., 1991) and may even be increased (O'Sullivan et al., 2012; Beedle et al., 1991). Furthermore, increases in joint range of motion have been reported via the use of resistance training without the addition of flexibility training (Trash, 1987). However, it should be considered that the above research was not conducted with golfers and therefore caution should be applied when interpreting these findings. Furthermore, it is recommended that resistance training exercises should avoid the inclusion of protocols designed to elicit significant gains in hypertrophy and over-utilisation of isolated single joint movements, and instead focus on exercises which are multi-joint in nature and are performed through full ranges of motion to minimise the risk of unwanted losses in flexibility.

Sample training plans

To provide further details of how to structure an appropriate strength and conditioning session for a golfer, a sample training plan has been outlined in Table 26.2. A caveat here is that the programme is not based on personalised assessments; thus, certain assumptions have been made to emphasise key themes in this chapter. Also, preceding blocks of training focused towards general adaptation will be required to ensure the athlete is able to meet the demands imposed by the elicited training stress. Understanding how to regress and progress based on movement demands and manipulation of acute training variables is also essential to manage adaptation and promote career longevity.

Table 26.2 Sample strength and power development programme for a golf athlete

Focus	Exercise	Sets	Reps	Tempo	Weight	Rest
Self-myofascial release	Glutes Adductors Latissimus dorsi	1	6 6 6	Control	–	–
Active-isolated stretch	90/90 hip stretch Wide kneeling stretch w/ t-spine 3-D hip flexor	1	6 6 6	2–4s hold	–	–
Activation and movement prep	S/L Glute bridge Side plank w band clam > mini-band walks Prone plank w arm drive > t-press up BW overhead squat BW single leg deadlift Reverse lunge with medicine ball diagonal lift	1–2	5–10 es 5–10 es 5–10 es 105–10 es 5–10 es	Control	–	–
Lower body ballistics	Lateral hop & stick > progress to rebounds	2–3	5 e/s	Fast	BW	120s
Upper body ballistics	Kneeling MB chop throw > MB standing rotational throw	2–3	5 e/s	Fast	3–8 kg MB	120s
Power/RFD	1a. Jump shrug > mid-thigh hang snatch	3–5	3–5	X	40–60% 1RM	180s
Strength	2a. Trap bar deadlift	3–5	3–5	X	> 85% 1RM	180s
Strength/power	3a. Bench 1-arm row > standing cable rotary row 3b. Incline DB bench press > push press	3–5	5*5	2-0-1-0 2-0-1-0	6RM load	120s–
Trunk stability/anti-rotation	4a. Half-kneeling cable chop > standing cable chop	3–5	5 e/s	2-0-1-0	6RM load	120s

Program notes: > indicates progress to

* Perform exercises 3a and 3b as a superset resting 30s between exercises and 120s between supersets.

Perform a cool down at the end of the session to include light jogging/cycling, self-myofascial release of the foot arch, glutes and t-spine, with additional static stretches as required.

The programme begins with a mobility section, incorporating self-myofascial release, active isolated stretches and dynamic mobility drills; the latter of which is used at the end of the mobility section to raise core temperature and to provide a neuromuscular stimulus. The activation section seeks to ensure good neurological input to the gluteus maximus and medius, deep spinal stabilisers and scapula-thoracic force couples prior to loading (Sahrmann, 2002; Stevens et al., 2007). Exercises such as the reverse lunge with medicine ball diagonal lift is designed to facilitate the development of postural control, and uses a transverse plane influence via the movement of the medicine ball to teach the body how to control spinal extension and rotation, as is necessary in the golf swing.

The reactive, strength and power sections of the programme are built on foundational movement patterns including weightlifting derivatives that focus on triple extension and posterior chain recruitment and the addition of multi-planar exercises to challenge the lower body, hips, and trunk. Research suggests this three-dimensional approach is important to optimise movement (Niinimaki et al., 2016). Several progressions should also be built into the programme to allow for continued adaptation over time and avoidance of accommodation.

In the strength section, the primary movement is a deadlift to promote force production from the ground up, an effective hip hinge and activation of the posterior chain. Performing a one-arm dumbbell or low cable row in a split stance position is also useful because if it is done with a forward lean at the hip with adequate dorsiflexion, the gluteal of the leading leg is under constant eccentric load. This helps to further build postural endurance and posterior chain strength, and the contralateral one-arm row component provides a rotary line of pull that the golfer has to control. Anti-rotation exercises are also included at the end of the session as means of teaching trunk control, which will assist with effective transfer of force through the kinetic chain, reduce injury risk, and improve the ability to tolerate the high spinal loads associated with the golf swing.

Image 26.2 Single leg Romanian deadlift

Image 26.3 Cable wood chop

Image 26.4 Kettlebell swing

Image 26.5 Turkish get up

Player management

The globalisation of golf is reflected in the demands placed on many of the world's leading professional players. Tournaments are frequent and players compete in Europe, South Africa, Australia, Malaysia, the United Arab Emirates, Thailand, India, China, and the United States throughout the majority of the year. This global schedule can be very demanding on the physiology and psychology of professional tour players over the course of a season (Hawkes et al., 2013). This presents unique challenges for the strength and conditioning coach, whose role it is to proactively support a player's health and performance. If a player is travelling extensively across multiple time zones, under acute mental stress, showing impaired recovery and adding significant physiological load already through technical practice, then a high-density training programme is likely to be inappropriate. For career longevity and success, it is essential for the strength and conditioning coach to be analytical about the potential risk/reward of any programme given and the added cumulative load it places on the individual.

To provide an example of how training programmes may change at different stages of the year, a sample in-season training session has been provided (Table 26.3). This is necessary to aid in the management of players and ensure continued progression over time, reducing the risk of overtraining and/or under recovery symptoms and syndromes. Manipulation of exercise selection and various acute variables can be powerful in promoting the long-term health and performance of

Table 26.3 Sample in-season training programme

Focus	Exercise	Sets	Reps	Tempo	Weight	Rest
Self-myofascial release	Arch rolls	1	6	Control	n/a	–
	Calves		6			
	Hip complex		6			
	Latissimus dorsi					
	T-spine					
Active-isolated stretch	Hamstring band leg lowering	1	6	2–4shold	n/a	–
	90/90 hip stretch		6			
	Wide kneeling stretch		6			
	w/ t-spine		6			
	3-D hip flexor					
Activation and movement prep	Glute bridge w/ mini-band	1–2	10	Control	Light	30s
	Side plank w/ 1 arm cable row		5 es			
	Turkish get up		3–5 es			
	Goblet squat		105 es			
	Single leg deadlift		3–5 each			
	Multi-planar lunge					
Lower body ballistics	CMJ and stick – front – lateral – rotation	2–3	2 each	Explosive	BW	120s
Power/RFD	1a. KB Swing or mid-thigh clean pull	2–4	3–5	X	80–90% 1RM	180s
Strength	2a. Rack pull or trap bar deadlift	3–5	3–5	X	> 85% 1RM	180s

Program notes: Perform a cool down at the end of the session to include light jogging/cycling, self-myofascial release of the foot arch, glutes and t-spine with additional static stretches as required.

professional golfers. Depending upon the player profile and how various acute variables within the programme are manipulated on any given day, training can be used to up-regulate functional movement after travel, or develop different components of fitness needed for the game. This reinforces the key point that movement sits on a continuum, and gently adjusting factors such as tempo, load, intensity, range and plane of motion can be useful ways to elicit different outcomes, depending on the needs or goals of the athlete. For example, following a period of long-haul travel to a competition and a high volume of technical practice, the total volume should be reduced. In such occasions, the focus can be placed on recovery strategies, prehabilitation drills and movement preparation to promote efficient golf biomechanics for that day. Conversely, when players show positive recovery and have a low-volume of technical practice scheduled, greater emphasis can be placed on increased volume of work from a strength and conditioning perspective.

To manage players effectively, meticulous planning and careful monitoring is required, especially during periods of intensive competition and travel. Whilst to the knowledge of the authors no published data are available to confirm this, applied experience has shown that club head speed with the driver invariably drops by 5–10% in the 24–48 hours after strenuous strength and conditioning sessions, perhaps due to the demands placed upon the central nervous system. Thus, intensive programmes that are characterised by higher volumes of work are likely best utilised away from a tournament week. This ensures a player's club selection on course is not compromised due to changes in distances hit compared to normal. However, as the player develops their training age and level of athleticism, low volume, high intensity training may be incorporated during competition to maintain neural drive and strength. Power is strongly associated with the ability to exert high amounts of force (Stone et al., 2003), and optimal strength levels may only be maintained for two weeks (Hortobagyi et al., 1993); therefore, this approach will effectively preserve the relevant fitness components required for elite golf performance.

Summary

This chapter has examined the available literature pertaining to the biomechanical and physiological demands, injury epidemiology, and subsequent physical development strategies for testing and training to enhance golf performance. In an attempt to dispel myths surrounding various training approaches, the importance of developing strength and power generated in a 'ground up' approach using a range of resistance training modalities have been suggested as key components of a holistic training programme. In addition, the importance of mobility to optimise kinetic chain linkage and the inclusion of anti-rotation exercises to reduce injury risk and aid in spinal motion control has been promoted. For the design of effective strength and conditioning programmes for golf, it is critical to take a targeted, athlete-centred approach and be flexible in its execution. By doing so it is possible to promote career productivity as well as longevity. A systems-based approach has been suggested here to ensure the key aspects of successful performance and management of injury risk are optimised and improvements can be accurately monitored over time.

References

Akutagawa S, Kojima T. Trunk rotation torques through the hip joints during the one- and two-handed backhand tennis strokes. *J Sports Sci.* 23: 781–793, 2005.

Batt E. A survey of golf injuries in amateur golfers. *Br J Sports Med.* 26: 63–65, 1992.

Bechler JR, Jobe FW, Pink M, Perry J, Ruwe PA. Electromyographic analysis of the hip and knee during the golf swing. *Clin J Sport Med.* 5: 162–166, 1995.

Beedle B, Jessee C, Stone MH. Flexibility characteristics among athletes who weight train. *J Appl Sport Sci Res.* 5: 150–154, 1991.

Behm DG, Sale DG. Velocity specificity of resistance training. *Sports Med.* 15: 374–388, 1993.

Bobbert MF, Gerritsein KGM, Litjens MCA, Van Soest AJ. Why is countermovement jump height greater than squat jump height? *Med Sci Sports Exerc.* 28: 1402–1412, 1996.

Bonazza NA, Smuin D, Onks CA, Silvis ML, Dhawan A. Reliability, validity, and injury predictive value of the functional movement screen: a systematic review and meta-analysis. *Am J Sports Med.* 45(3): 725–732, 2016.

Callaghan JP, McGill S. Intervertebral disc herniation: studies on a porcine model exposed to highly repetitive flexion/extension motion with compressive force. *Clin Biomech.* 16: 28–37, 2001.

Callaway S, Glaws K, Mitchell M, Scerbo H, Voight M, Sells P. An analysis of peak pelvis rotation speed, gluteus maximus and medius strength in high versus low handicap golfers during the golf swing. *Int J Sports Phys Ther.* 7: 288–295, 2012.

Cheetham PJ, Martin PE, Mottram RE, St. Laurent BF. The importance of stretching the X factor in the golf downswing: the 'X-Factor stretch'. In: PR Thomas (Ed), *Optimizing Performance in Golf*. Brisbane, Australia: Australian Academic Press, 2001, pp. 192–199.

Cole MH, Grimshaw PN. The biomechanics of the modern golf swing: implications for lower back injuries. *Sports Med.* 46: 339–351, 2016.

Cook G. *Movement: Functional Movement Systems: Screening, Assessment and Corrective Strategies*. Aptos, CA: On Target Publications, 2010.

Coughlan GF, Fullam K, Delahunt E, Gissane C, Caulfied BM. A comparison between performance on selected directions of the star excursion balance test and the Y Balance Test. *J Athl Train.* 47: 366–371, 2012.

Crews DJ, Shireffs JH, Thomas G, Krahenbuhl GS, Helfrich HM. Psychological and physiological attributes associated with performance of selected players of the ladies' professional golf association tour. *Percept Motor Skills.* 63: 235–238, 1986.

Cuchna JW, Hoch MC, Hoch JM. The interrater and intrarater reliability of the functional movement screen: A systematic review with meta-analysis. *Phys Ther Sport.* 19: 57–65, 2016.

Dickenson E, Ahmed I, Fernandez M, O'Conor P, Robinson P, Campbell R, Murray A, Warner M, Hutchinson C, Hawkes R, Griffin D. Professional golfers' hips: prevalence and predictors of hip pain with clinical and MR examinations. *Br J Sports Med.* 50: 1087–1091, 2016.

Doan BK, Newton RU, Kwon Y, Kraemer WJ. Effects of physical conditioning on intercollegiate golfer performance. *J Strength Cond Res.* 20: 62–72, 2006.

Dorado C, Sanchis Moysi J, Veicente G. Bone mass, bone mineral density and muscle mass in professional golfers. In: E Thain (Ed), *Science and Golf IV: Proceedings of the World Scientific Golf Congress of Golf.* New York: Routledge, 2002, pp. 54–63.

Ebben W, Blackard D, and Jense R. Quantification of medicine ball vertical impact forces: estimating training loads. *J Strength Cond Res.* 13: 271–274, 1999.

Elliott M, Wagner P, Chiu L. Power athletes and distance training: physiological and biomechanical rationale for change. *J Sports Medicine.* 37: 47–57, 2007.

Evans K, Refshauge K, Adams R, Aliprandi L. Predictors of low back pain in young elite golfers: a preliminary study. *Phys Ther Sport.* 6: 122–130, 2005.

Evans K, Tuttle, N. Improving performance in golf: current research and implications from a clinical perspective. *Braz J Phys Ther.* 19: 381–389, 2015.

Farrally MR, Cochran AJ, Crews DJ. Golf science research at the beginning of the 21st century. *J Sports Sci.* 21: 753–765, 2003.

Finch C, Sherman C, James T. The epidemiology of golf injuries in Victoria, Australia: evidence from sports medicine clinics and emergency room department presentations. In: MR Farrally, AJ Cochran (Ed), *Science and Golf III: Proceedings of the World Scientific Congress of Golf; 1998 Jul 20–24, St Andrews.* Champaign, IL: Human Kinetics, 1998, pp. 73–82.

Fujimoto-Kantani K. *Determining the Essential Elements of Golf Swings Used By Elite Golfers.* Masters dissertation, Oregon State University, Corvallis, OR, 1995.

Fullam K, Caulfield B, Coughlan GF, Delahunt E. Kinematic analysis of selected reach directions of the Star Excursion Balance Test compared with the Y-Balance Test. *J Sport Rehabil.* 23: 27–35, 2014.

Ganesh GS, Chhabra D, Mrityunjay K. Efficacy of the star excursion balance test in detecting reach deficits in subjects with chronic low back pain. *Physiother Res Int.* 20: 9–15, 2015.

Garhammer J. A review of power output studies of Olympic and powerlifting: methodology, performance prediction, and evaluation tests. *J Strength Cond Res.* 7: 76–89, 1993.

Gluck G, Bendo J, Spivak J. The lumbar spine and low back pain in golf: a literature review of swing biomechanics and injury prevention. *Spine J.* 8: 778–788, 2008.

Gordon B, Moir G, Davis S, Witmer C, Cummings D. An investigation into the relationship of flexibility, power and strength to club head speed in male golfers. *J Strength and Cond Res.* 23: 1606–1610, 2009.

Gosheger G, Liem D, Ludwig K, Greshake, O, Winklemann, W. Injuries and overuse syndromes in golf. *Am J Sports Med.* 31: 438–443, 2003.

Gulgin HR, Schulte BC, Crawley AA. Correlation of Titleist Performance Institute (TPI) level 1 movement screens and golf swing faults. *J Strength Cond Res.* 28: 534–539, 2014.

Hawkes R, O'Connor P, Campbell D. The prevalence, variety and impact of wrist problems in elite professional golfers on the European Tour. *Br J Sports Med.* 47: 1075–1079, 2013.

Hegedus EJ, McDonough SM, Bleakley C, Baxter D, Cook CE. Clinician-friendly lower extremity physical performance tests in athletes: a systematic review of measurement properties and correlation with injury. Part 2-the tests for the hip, thigh, foot and ankle including the star excursion balance test. *Br J Sports Med.* 49: 649–656, 2015.

Hellstrom J. The relationship between physical tests, measures and club head speed in elite golfers. *Int J Sports Sci Coach.* 3: 85–92, 2008.

Hellstrom J. Competitive elite. A review of the relationships between playing results, technique and physique in golf. *Sports Med.* 39: 723–741, 2009.

Hori N, Newton RU, Nosaka K, Stone MH. Weightlifting exercises enhance athletic performance that requires high-load speed strength. *Strength Cond J.* 27: 50–55, 2005.

Hortobagyi, T, Houmard, JA, Stevenson, JR, Fraser, DD, Johns, RA, Israel, RG. The effects of detraining on power athletes. *Med Sci Sports Exerc* 25: 929–935, 1993.

Hosea TM. Biomechanical analysis of the golfers back. In: A J Cochran (Ed), *Science and Golf I. Proceedings of the World Scientific Congress of Golf: 1990, July 9–13, St Andrews.* E&FN Spon. 1990, pp. 43–48.

Hume PA, Keogh J, Reid D. The role of biomechanics in maximizing distance and accuracy of golf shots. *Sports Med.* 35: 429–449, 2005.

Jobe FW, Moynes DR, Antonelli DJ. Rotator cuff function during the golf swing. *Am J Sports Med.* 14: 388–392, 1986.

Keogh J, Marnewick M, Maluder P, Nortje J, Hume P, Bradshaw E. Are anthropometric, flexibility, muscular strength and endurance variables related to club head velocity in low and high handicap golfers? *J Strength Cond Res.* 23: 1841–1850, 2009.

Lewis, AL, Ward N, Bishop C, Maloney S, Turner AN. Determinants of club head speed in PGA professional golfers. *J Strength Cond Res.* 30: 2266–2270, 2016.

Lim YT, Chow JW, Chae WS. Lumbar spinal loads and muscle activity during a golf swing. *Sports Biomech.* 11: 197–211, 2012.

Lindsay D, Horton J. Trunk rotation strength and endurance in healthy normals and elite male golfers with and without low back pain. *Am J Sports Phys Ther.* 1: 80–89, 2006.

Marras WS, Granata KP. A biomechanical assessment and model of axial twisting in the thoracolumbar spine. *Spine J.* 20: 1440–1451, 1995.

Marta S, Silva L, Castro MA, Pezerat-Correia P, Cabri J. Electromyography variables during the golf swing: a literature review. *J Electromyogr Kinesiol.* 22: 803–813, 2012.

Marta S, Silva L, Vaz JR, Castro MA, Reinaldo G, Pezerat-Correia P. Electromyographic analysis of lower limb muscles during the golf swing performed with three different clubs. *Journal of Sports Sciences.* 34(8): 713-720, 2016.

McCarroll JR, Gioe TJ. Professional golfers and the price they pay. *Phys Sports Med.* 10: 64–70, 1982.

McCarroll JR, Rettig AC, Shelbourne KD. Injuries in the amateur golfer. *Phys Sports Med.* 18: 122–126, 1990.

McCartney, N. Acute responses to resistance training and safety. *Med Sci Sports Exerc.* 31: 31, 1999.

McGill SM. Core training: evidence translating to better performance and injury prevention. *Strength Cond J.* 32: 33–46, 2010.

McGill SM, Childs A, Liebenson C. Endurance times for low back stabilization exercises: clinical targets for testing and training from a normal database. *Arch Phys Med Rehabilitation.* 80: 941–944, 1999.

McHardy A, Pollard H, Luo K. Golf injuries: a review of the literature. *Sports Med.* 36: 171–187, 2006.

McTeigue M, Lamb SR, Mottram R. Spine and hip motion analysis during the golf swing. In A J Cochran, MR Farrally (Ed), *Science and Golf II: Proceedings of the 1994 World Scientific Congress of Golf: Jul 4–8; St Andrews.* London: E&FN Spon. 1994, pp. 50–96.

Meurer A, Grober J, Betz U, Decking J, Rompe JD. BWS-mobility in patients with an impingement syndrome compared to healthy subjects an inclinometric study. *Z Orthop Ihre Grenzgeb.* 142: 415–420, 2004.

Mun F, Suh SW, Park HJ, Choi, A. Kinematic relationship between rotation of lumbar spine and hip joints during golf swing in professional golfers. *Biomed Eng Online.* 14: 41, 2015.

Murase Y, Kamei S, Hoshikawa T. Heart rate and metabolic response to participation in golf. *J Sports Med Phys Fit.* 29: 269–272, 1989.

Nadler SF, Malanga GA, DePrince M, Stitik TP, Feinberg JH. The relationship between lower extremity injury, low back pain, and hip muscle strength in male and female collegiate athletes. *Clin J Sport Med.* 10: 89–97, 2000.

Newton RU, Kraemer WJ, Hakkinenn K, Humphries BJ, Murphy AJ. Kinematics, kinetics and muscle activation during explosive upper body movements. *J Applied Biomechanics.* 12: 31–43, 1996.

Niinimaki S, Harkonen L, Nikander R, Abe S, Knusel C, Sievanen H. The cross-sectional area of the gluteus maximus muscle varies according to habitual exercise loading: Implications for activity-related and evolutionary studies. *Homo.* 67: 125–137, 2016.

O'Sullivan K, McAuliffe S, DeBurca N. The effects of eccentric training on lower limb flexibility: a systematic review. *Br J Sports Med.* 46: 838–845, 2012.

Okuda I, Armstrong CW, Tsneuzumi H, Yoshiike H. Biomechanical analysis of professional golfer's swing: Hidemichi Tanak. In: E Thain (Ed), *Science and Golf IV: Proceedings of the World Scientific Congress of Golf.* London: Routledge, 2002, pp. 19–27.

Pink M, Perry J, Jobe F. Electromyographic analysis of the trunk in golfers. *Am J Sports Med.* 21: 385–388, 1993.

Plisky PJ, Gorman PP, Butler RJ, Kiesel KB, Underwood FB, Elkins B. The reliability of an instrumented device for measuring components of the Star Excursion Balance Test. *Am J Sports Phys Ther* 4: 92–99, 2009.

Plisky PJ, Rauh MJ, Kaminski TW, Underwood FB. Star Excursion Balance Test as a predictor of lower extremity injury in high school basketball players. *J Orthop Sports Phys Ther.* 36: 911–919, 2006.

Read PJ, Bishop, C, Brazier, J, Turner, AN. Performance modeling: A system-based approach to exercise selection. *Strength Cond J.* 38: 90–97, 2016.

Read PJ, Lloyd RS. Strength and conditioning considerations for golf. *Strength Cond J.* 36: 24–33, 2014.

Read PJ, Lloyd R, De Ste Croix M, Oliver J. Relationships between field-based measures of strength and power and golf club head speed. *J Strength Cond Res.* 27: 2708–2713, 2013.

Sadeghisani M, Manshadi FD, Kalantari KK, Rahimi A, Namnik N, Karimi MT, Oskouei AE. Correlation between hip rotation range-of-motion impairment and low back pain. A literature review. *Ortop Traumatol Rehabil.* 17: 455–462, 2015.

Sahrmann S. 2002. *Diagnosis and Treatment of Movement Impairment Syndromes*. St. Louis, MO and London: Mosby.

Sell TC, Abt JP, Lephart SM. Physical activity-related benefits of walking during golf. In: D Crews, R Lutz (Ed), *Science and Golf: V. Proceedings of the World Scientific Congress of Golf; 2008 Mar 24–28; Phoenix (AZ)*. Mesa, AZ: Energy in Motion, 2008, pp. 128–132.

Sell TC, Tsai YS, Smoliga JM, Myers JB, Lephart SM. Strength, flexibility and balance characteristics of highly proficient golfers. *J Strength Cond Res.* 21: 1166–1171, 2007.

Smith CA, Callister R, Lubans D. A systematic review of strength and conditioning programmes designed to improve fitness characteristics in golfers. *J Sports Sci.* 29: 933–943, 2011.

Smith CA, Chimera NJ, Wright NJ, Warren M. Interrater and intrarater reliability of the functional movement screen. *J Strength Cond Res.* 27: 982–987, 2013.

Spaniol F. Striking skills: developing power to turn. *Strength Cond J.* 34: 57–60, 2012.

Sprigings EJ, Neal RJ. An Insight into the importance of wrist torque in driving the golf ball. A simulation study. *J Appl Biomech.* 16: 356–366, 2000.

Steffen K, Emery CA, Romiti M, Kang J, Bizzini M, Dvorak J, Finch CF, Meeuwise WH. High adherence to a neuromuscular injury prevention programme (FIFA 11+) improves functional balance and reduces injury risk in Canadian youth female football players: a cluster randomised trial. *Br J Sports Med.* 47: 794–802, 2013.

Stevens VK, Vleeming A, Bouche KG, Mahieu NN, Vanderstraten GG, Danneels LA. Electromyographic activity of trunk and hip muscles during stabilization exercises in four-point kneeling in healthy volunteers. *Eur Spine J.* 16: 711–718, 2007.

Stodden D, Cambell B, Moyer T. Comparison of trunk kinematics in trunk training exercises and throwing. *J Strength Cond Res.* 22(1): 112–118, 2008.

Stone MH, O'Bryant, HS, McCoy, L, Coglianese, R, Lehkkuhl, M, Shilling, B. Power and maximum strength relationships during performance of dynamic and static weighted jumps. *J Strength Cond Res.* 17: 140–147, 2003.

Stone MH, Pierce KC, Sands WA, Stone ME. Weightlifting: a brief overview. *Strength Cond J.* 28: 50–66, 2006.

Stone MH, Stone M, Sands WA. *Principles and Practice of Resistance Training*. Champaign, IL: Human Kinetics, 2007, pp. 241–257.

Szymanski D, Szymanski J, Bradford T, Schade R, Pascoe D. Effect of twelve weeks of medicine ball training on high school baseball players. *J Strength Cond Res.* 21: 894–901, 2007.

Theisen C, van Wagensveld A, Timmesfeld N, Efe T, Heyse TJ, Fuchs-Winkelmann S, Schofer MD. Co-occurrence of outlet impingement syndrome of the shoulder and restricted range of motion in the thoracic spine-a prospective study with ultrasound-based motion analysis. *BMC Musculoskel Disord.* 11: 135, 2010.

Theriault G, Lachance P. Golf injuries: an overview. *Sports Med.* 26: 43–57, 1998.

Thompson CJ, Cobb KM, Blackwell J. Functional training improves club head speed and functional fitness in older golfers. *J Strength Cond Res.* 21: 131–137, 2007.

Trash K. Flexibility and strength training. *J Appl Sport Sci Res.* 4: 74–75. 1987.

Turner AN, Jeffreys I. The stretch-shortening cycle: proposed mechanisms and methods for enhancement. *Strength Cond J.* 32(4): 87–99, 2011.

Unverdorben M, Kolb M, Bauer I, Bauer U, Brune M, Vallbracht. Cardiovascular load of competitive golf in cardiac patients and normal controls. *Med Sci Sports Exerc.* 32: 1674–1678, 2000.

Vad VB, Bhat AL, Basrai D, Gebeh A, Aspergren DD, Andrews JR. Low back pain in professional golfers: The role of associated hip and low back range-of-motion deficits. *Am J Sports Med.* 32: 494–497, 2004.

Van Ingen Schenau GJ, Bobbert MF, de Haan A. Does elastic energy enhance work or efficiency in the stretch shorten cycle? *J Applied Biomech.* 13: 389–415, 1997.

Watanabe K, Kuroki S, Hokari M, Nishizawa S. Golf swing and skill. In: MR Farrally, AJ Cochran (Ed), *Science and Golf III: Proceedings of the 1998 World Scientific Congress of Golf.* Champaign, IL: Human Kinetics, 1998, pp. 29–39.

Wells GD, Elmi M, Thomas S. Physiological correlates of golf performance. *J Strength Cond Res.* 23: 741–750, 2009.

Whittaker AR. A study of the dynamics of the golf club. *Sports Engineering.* 1(2),:115–124, 1998.

Wilmore JH, Costill D. *Physiology of Sport and Exercise* (3rd edition). Champaign, IL: Human Kinetics. 2004, p. 241.

Wilmore JH, Parr RB, Girandola RN, Ward P, Vodak PA, Barstow TJ, Pipes TV, Romero GT, Leslie P. Physiological alterations consequent to circuit weight training. *Med Sci Sports Exerc.* 10: 79–84, 1978.

Wilson G, Murphy A, Pryor J. Musculotendinous stiffness: its relationship to eccentric, isometric and concentric performance. *J Applied Physiol.* 76: 2714–2719, 1994.

Winchester JB, McBride JM, Maher MA, Mikat RP, Allen BK, Kline DE, McGuigan MR. Eight weeks of ballistic exercise improves power independently of changes in strength and muscle fiber type expression. *J Strength Cond Res.* 22: 1728–1734, 2008.

Zatsiorsky VM. Biomechanics of strength and strength training. In: PV Komi (Ed), *Strength and Power in Sport* (2nd edition). Oxford, UK: Blackwell Science, 2003, pp. 114–133.

27
SPRINT RUNNING

*Jon Goodwin, Jonas Tawiah-Dodoo,
Ruth Waghorn and James Wild*

Introduction to the sport

Sprinting, as a sport skill in its own right, incorporates aspects of acceleration, maximal velocity capability, and capacity to sustain high running velocity for a defined period. The averaged accelerations of elite sprinters are in the region of 7–8ms^{-2} in the first 20m of a sprint whilst maximum velocities can reach 12.5ms^{-1}.

Sprinting is also a transferable sport skill. Being the quickest over various distances is valuable in sports like rugby and football. Acceleration ability has been highlighted (Duthie, Pyne, Marsh, and Hooper, 2006) with an ability to rapidly change pace being important to evasive play. That is not to diminish the value of high maximum velocities, with many sprints taking place from rolling starts and game breaking situations occurring above 90% of individual maximum velocity (Duthie et al., 2006). Also, higher maximum velocity potential might reduce relative effort at lower absolute speeds. The development of locomotive speed, then, in its various aspects, is a common objective for many athletes and coaches.

Athletic demands

In this section acceleration and maximum velocity sprinting will be discussed with respect to fundamental mechanics of the task, gross biomechanics and physio-mechanics, enabling the reader to understand the links between the basic requirements of the task and the trainable qualities where intervention might influence performance outcomes.

Fundamental mechanics

As with any sport skill, sprint velocity is a product of the athlete's capacity to produce and skilfully utilise force against the external environment. Simplifying the task for track athletes is the relatively closed nature of the skill, but in many other sport environments, additional constraints might be placed on the athlete which modify the optimised outcome. In its simplest form two principal constraints will need to be managed by the athlete, one being the athlete's mass and its associated inertia, and the other being gravity. Air resistance will not be extensively considered here as it is typically low.

Acceleration and maximal velocity sprinting carry with them each a principal mechanical predictor, a mechanical objective that the athlete is trying to achieve. In acceleration, this is the rapid (i.e. time dependent) accrual of horizontal impulse (Morin et al., 2015b). This impulse is directly proportional to the change in horizontal velocity and hence represents the primary objective. As acceleration progresses and velocity increases, the athlete then drifts towards a new challenge; the ability to tolerate diminishing ground contact times whilst still achieving required vertical support impulse to get back into the air for the next flight phase and retaining sufficient net positive horizontal impulse to continue to accelerate (Slawinski et al., 2017) or simply manage air resistance.

Task 1: accruing horizontal impulse

The horizontal impulse accrued is the product of the horizontal force applied (a product of the force magnitude and direction) and the ground contact period (additionally determined by the limb range utilised).

The magnitude of the average force applied to the ground

The athlete with the largest average extension force, relative to their body mass and under similar time constraints, will have the potential to accelerate at the highest rate. The 'strongest' athlete wins, if you follow a definition of strength that is the capacity to express force under specified constraints; here the constraints relate to applying force through one leg, in short time periods, with moderate contraction velocities.

The direction of the force applied to the ground

The effective direction of the force applied is a key skill. There is a fixed requirement to direct some force (more precisely some impulse) vertically to manage the downward acceleration of gravity. There is also a demand to manage rotational accelerations such that the athlete doesn't fall over. Thus, the 'strength' of the athlete determines the limit angle of forward inclination for the average force vector applied through stance. An athlete applying little force cannot direct the force forwards and stay upright. An athlete applying more force can direct their average vector further forward whilst retaining sufficient upward component to overcome gravity (Figure 27.1A). It's not quite that simple, though. The skill exhibited by the athlete will determine how close they get to reaching their limit angle (Figure 27.1B). Therefore, considering two

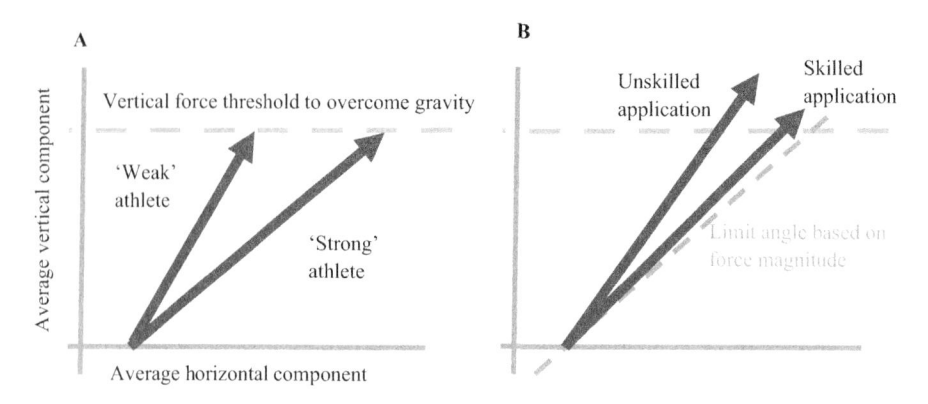

Figure 27.1 Average ground reaction force vector of two athletes during a step in the early acceleration phase

athletes that are reasonably close in the magnitude of force they can apply, a more skilled but 'weaker' athlete could quite conceivably beat a 'stronger' but less skilled athlete, as is borne out in the data of Morin, Edouard and Samozino (2011).

Time over which force is applied

It is apparent that the less skilled athlete may direct their average vector more vertically. This offers them two movement options or a combination thereof. They might utilise the faster accrual vertical impulse to shorten their contact time and increase step frequency. This defines part of the optimisation problem that the athlete and coach are trying to resolve through practice in finding the best limb orientation and range to apply force effectively. Alternately with a matched ground contact time, they will generate more vertical impulse and more upward velocity, creating a secondary problem; spending more time in the air. Longer flight times mean proportionally less time accruing horizontal impulse and would be associated with a higher vertical impulse demand on the next step to manage landing forces. Higher vertical impulses, and therein longer flight times, are negatively associated with performance in acceleration (Rabita, Dorel, Slawinski, Saez-de-Villarreal et al., 2015).

Task 2: tolerating decreasing contact times

As velocity increases, variables change for the athlete (Figure 27.2). Flight times gradually increase because, with more horizontal speed and less acceleration potential, it becomes more valuable to be airborne covering ground. Therefore, the vertical impulse demand, per step, increases until the optimal flight time is achieved (another optimisation for the athlete and coach to resolve). Additionally, the ground is passing the athlete at higher rates and ground contact time (GCT) is diminishing, both making force production more challenging. As contact time falls, the need

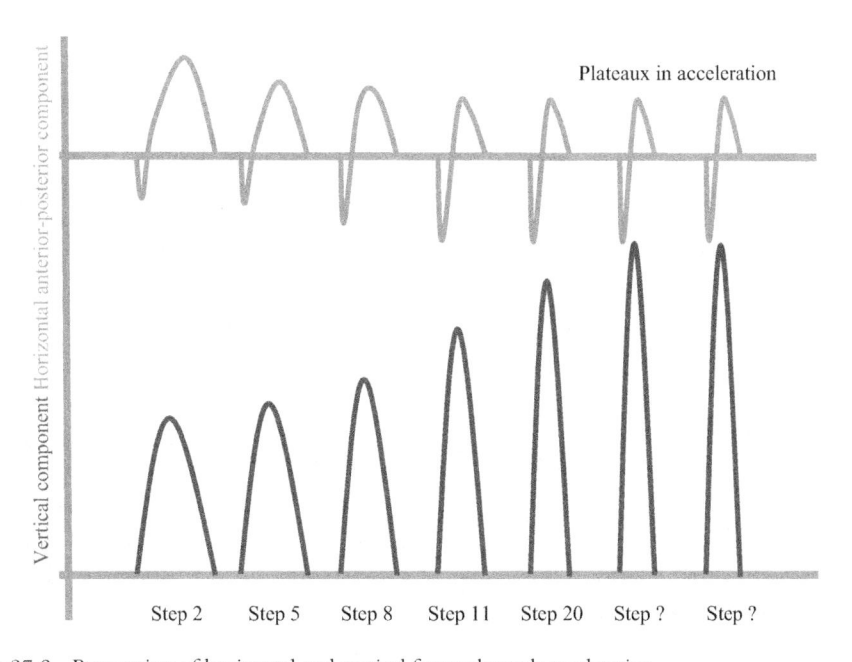

Figure 27.2 Progression of horizontal and vertical forces through acceleration

for higher average stance force increases to maintain the required impulse. The athlete reaches the point where all their leg extension capability is 'used up', predominantly meeting vertical impulse demands. Who then can travel at the highest speed? It's the athlete who can manage the effects of that diminishing contact time. The one who can quickly generate high enough forces to access the required vertical impulse and have enough 'left over' that they can do it with the average vector tipped further forward, enabling some continued acceleration or the overcoming of increasing air resistive effects.

Complexity of stance force production

Stance limb force production is influenced by a complex set of interactions incorporating the basic extension capabilities of the limb itself, elastic interactions with the muscular units, co-ordination and reflexive interaction with the contra-lateral limb, stabilisation and rotational management through the trunk and upper limbs, and aspects of skill to ensure effective patterns of co-ordinated recruitment and relaxation to enable limb recovery, ground preparation and contact. Whilst basic S&C programmes focussed on fundamental strength qualities can and often will have good benefit, there are a host of specific aspects that the S&C coach should consider impactful on whether their training might transfer effectively to performance.

Force application via the stance limb

The differing objectives and task constraints mean that the functional demands on the athlete are quite different when comparing early acceleration and maximal velocity sprinting. In the earliest steps of the sprint, extension loaded throughout range is evident through the hip, knee and ankle (Figure 27.3) and evidence suggests closer predictive value from full limb extension strength and power testing (Cunningham et al., 2013). However, at maximal velocity we see quite a different

Figure 27.3 Sprint athlete covering the initial acceleration steps

Figure 27.4 Sprint athlete during a maximal velocity running cycle

limb demand with more stiff spring-like behaviour (Figure 27.4) and a quite different inter-relation of the hip and knee function. This sets up different structural and functional qualities that will optimally serve the force production outcomes needed in these phases.

Technical components supporting optimised force production

One of the most fundamental factors to consider is the co-ordination of the athlete through technical patterns and positions. Achievement of such markers helps ensure the athlete utilises their limb potential to its fullest. Equally some technical markers will only progress as the limb extension force potential improves. Most markers are not precisely defined but rather are representative of a 'bandwidth' of potentially suitable positions and patterns based on the optimal solution for the athlete's current physical state. Table 27.1 highlights some technical checkpoints.

Mass dependence

Sprinting is not a weight category sport, but performance outcomes are just as dependent on the athlete's body mass. The demand to accrue horizontal and vertical impulse to change velocity (for horizontal acceleration or to support against gravity and return athletes to flight phases) is directly proportional to the mass of the athlete. For lighter athletes, with the same force production, equivalent velocity changes can be created with less time on the ground, and that means faster acceleration and higher maximum velocity.

Increasing cross-sectional area conveys a potential force advantage. However, several aspects associated with muscle hypertrophy mean that careful decision making is in order. Firstly, hypertrophy comes with mass, and this increases the demand for impulse to achieve matched velocity changes during stance. The gains in force from increases in mass therefore need to outstrip performance losses due to mass. Secondly, with hypertrophy can come alterations in fibre pennation and fascicle length. Training means that focus on eccentric actions and muscle operating at length would appear to offer benefits of adaptation of longer fascicles (Guex, Degache, Morisod, Sailly, and Millet, 2016), whilst concentric work would appear, in contrast, to reduce fascicle length (Timmins et al., 2016). A third factor, also potentially influenced by programming choices, is the dominant myosin isoform upregulated in the process of triggering a hypertrophy response. Whilst evidence in this area is thin on the ground, a general principle of specific adaptation to imposed demand would suggest that hypertrophy programmes focussed on high work volumes with little recovery, whilst productive for rapid hypertrophy, might not steer the hypertrophy response in a favourable direction for speed athletes.

Table 27.1 Key technical markers during sprint acceleration and maximum velocity phases

Acceleration Limb (Pistons)

Stance limb		Swing limb	
Touch down	Contact position optimised to force production profile, but approximately beneath the centre of mass. Shin parallel to trunk.	**Post toe off**	Triple joint flexion led by hip flexion. Effective switching might come with incomplete extension at toe off if impulse in late stance offers less benefit than switching to the next step.
Mid-stance	Ground contact time optimised to force profile. Contact time can fall with increases in force production.	**Top of swing**	Foot dorsiflexed, shin parallel to trunk. Flight time should be short.
Toe off	Hip, knee and ankle extension.	**Pre-contact**	Anticipatory switching action of swing leg back to ground.

Coaching points

Projection – Focus on horizontal projection of mass. Minimal vertical propulsion.

Reactivity – Stiff limb extension response.

Switching – Hip dominated extension response paired with the contra-lateral hip flexion.

Coaching points

Switching – Athlete must 'pop' thigh forwards to recover swing leg efficiently. Low foot recovery as a result of effective hip dominant switching.

Reactivity – Pretension is created prior to GC ('Strike') to maximise stiffness and reduce GCT.

Maximum Velocity

Stance limb		Swing limb	
Touch down	Front side contact distance from COM is optimised to force production capability. Should be small and reduce with improved force production and technical progression.	**Post toe-off**	Triple joint flexion led by hip flexion.
		Mid-swing	Knee cross prior to ground contact. Ankle cross over knee at mid-stance.
Mid-stance	Minimised contact time based on demand to return to flight phase. Tolerance for shorter CT improves with force production and technical progression.	**Top of swing**	Thigh blocks parallel to ground with dorsiflexed ankle. Initiation of 'whip from hip' with hip-into-knee extension from top position.
Toe-off	Minimal backside distance from knee to COM. Incomplete knee extension prior to toe off. Pattern driven by hip flexor activating in late stance to lead switching.	**Pre-contact**	Pretension is created in swing limb by whip from hip. This creates negative foot speed and preparatory limb stiffness required for force production.

Coaching points

Projection – Bouncing on a straight leg to encourage system stiffness and vertical projection.

Reactivity – Focus on force production that enables reduced contact time.

Coaching points

Switching – Hip led limb flexion from the backside, and blocking into the 'whip from hip' on the front side.

Reactivity – Focus on hitting the ground hard whilst preparing to reactively rip foot off the ground.

Contraction velocity demands

Higher levels of performance, both in acceleration and maximum velocity phases, require the achievement of high level of force production despite an increase in muscle fibre contraction rates. This is problematic since concentric contractile force reduces with velocity. Genetics play a role here. Athletes with relatively longer toes and shorter heels appear to have an advantage when it comes to sprint running performance, conveyed mostly through a reduction in the contraction velocity demands in related musculature (Lee and Piazza, 2009). Additionally, myosin isoform distribution influences the function of the system (Costill et al., 1976). However, training specificity should be considered in relation to the impact that might be had on the capacity of the muscular system to develop force at higher contraction rates in key muscles, positions or limb actions. It remains to be evidenced is whether modifiable variables (fibre pennation, tendon stiffness, muscle fascicle length etc) can be altered through training in a way that can be prescribed to enhance speed/force based performance outcomes.

Injuries

As might be expected, the lower limb is at higher risk compared to other injury cites (Edouard et al., 2011; Zemper, 2005). The greatest chance of acute and chronic injuries are hamstring strain and Achilles tendinopathy, respectively (Edouard and Alonso, 2013). A greater acute injury risk is reported in sprinting compared to less explosive athletic events (Edouard and Morel, 2010; Zemper, 2005). Whilst this is influenced by the type of activity taking place, it is also reflective of the physical qualities that fast athletes possess. Sprinters are gifted at producing high levels of force within short timeframes. Consequently, the magnitude of stressors experienced during a sprint (e.g. joint reaction forces and muscle/tendon tensile loads) are higher for these athletes compared to slower individuals. Effective athlete management through the athlete support team is essential to attenuate injury risk. Whilst there are numerous interrelated factors which influence the cause of an injury – some of which are outlined in Figure 27.5 – effective management of training load and the mechanical issues associated with the individual are two central issues.

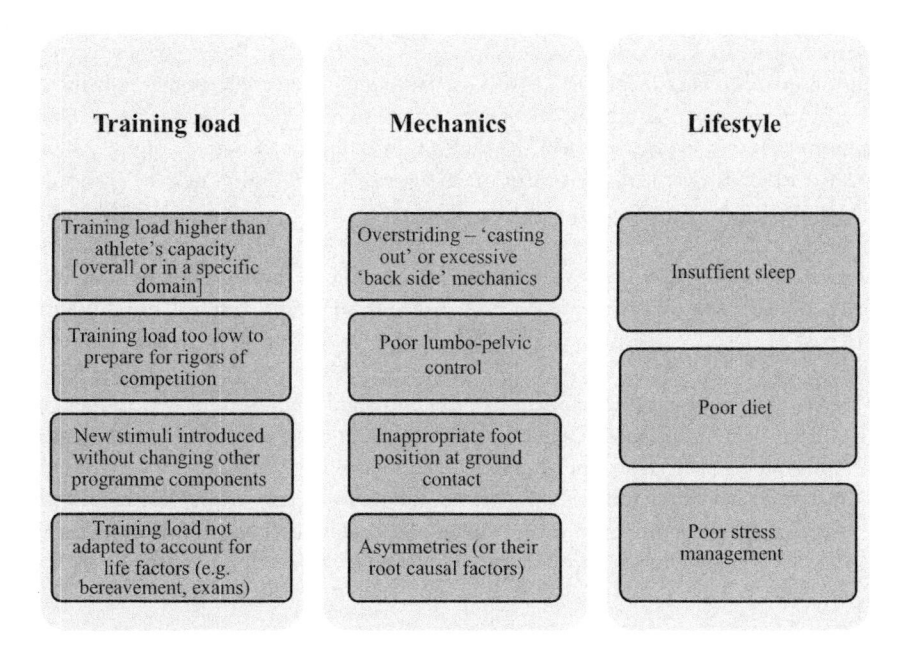

Training load	**Mechanics**	**Lifestyle**
Training load higher than athlete's capacity [overall or in a specific domain]	Overstriding – 'casting out' or excessive 'back side' mechanics	Insufficient sleep
Training load too low to prepare for rigors of competition	Poor lumbo-pelvic control	Poor diet
New stimuli introduced without changing other programme components	Inappropriate foot position at ground contact	
Training load not adapted to account for life factors (e.g. bereavement, exams)	Asymmetries (or their root causal factors)	Poor stress management

Figure 27.5 Common factors influencing injury risk

Training load

Management of training load requires understanding the athlete (what they can handle and when, their motivations etc) and effective planning and monitoring to facilitate delivery of effective training stimuli. A high training workload increases risk and without effective planning/variation the chances of injury or underperformance increase. Risks also exist with insufficient application of training stress. Monitoring the acute:chronic workload ratio of an athlete (Hulin, Gabbett, Lawson, Caputi, and Sampson, 2016) may be an appropriate strategy to ensure that sudden training spikes are not introduced and that gradual increases in training load tolerance can be built over time. New training stimuli should be phased in systematically and overall load reduced during times of increased life stress.

Mechanical issues

Coaches place a large emphasis on mechanical efficiency and technique with a view to optimise GRF production, reduce energy cost through compensatory movements, and limit inappropriate tissue loading. Due to our self-organising nature during locomotion, each athlete possesses their own movement strategy during a sprint. This is likely to be deeply embedded from progressive exposure to sprinting over time, where neural and biological structures have been shaped to deal with the event. As such, altering running mechanics which are perceived to place an athlete in a position of higher risk of injury can be a lengthy process and not without its own risk. Adjustment to sprint technique is often achievable during sprint practice relatively easily. However, it is not so straightforward for these new patterns to emerge to deliver improved competitive performance, when stress levels are high. A multi-faceted approach (e.g. strength/power, mobility, therapy, running tasks/drills and coaching/cueing) is therefore necessary to drive favourable mechanical changes over time that transfer to competition.

Primary risk factors for hamstring injury include age, previous hamstring injury and lack of eccentric strength (Gabbe, Bennell, Finch, Wajswelner, and Orchard, 2006; Opar et al., 2015; Verrall, Slavotinek, Barnes, Fon, and Spriggins, 2001). Though not evidenced to date, coaching observation that mechanical issues can influence hamstring injury risk should be considered. An excessive 'casting out' movement of the swing leg during the late-acceleration and maximum velocity phases – where the limb unfolds during the late-swing phase and the foot moves further forward of the centre of mass prior to ground contact – is thought to be a precarious leg action. Although debate exists as to where in the step cycle hamstring injuries are most likely to occur, the maximum muscle length and lengthening velocity of the hamstrings occur during the late swing phase, during which the biceps femoris also reaches its highest tensile force (Higashihara, Nagano, Ono, and Fukubayashi, 2016). It is intuitive therefore that an excessive 'casting out' action may expose an athlete to greater risk of hamstring strain.

During the early-mid stages of acceleration, more forward trunk lean relative to the angle of the shin is likely to increase muscultendinous lengths and tensile stress on the hamstrings. An increased forward trunk lean has previously been associated with increase musculotendinous lengths for all three hamstring muscles at foot strike and toe-off (Higashihara, Nagano, Takahashi, and Fukubayashi, 2015). Similar trunk and shin angles during the stance of phase of early-mid acceleration may therefore be appropriate for minimising excessive hamstring tensile load when sprinting.

Sprint running

Testing

There are numerous tests which can be used to assess an athlete's physical capabilities to help inform programming decisions. Single outcome measurements of leg strength qualities (e.g. jump height, power and load lifted) are often benchmarked against normative data, which can then be used to help drive training towards the development of apparent weaknesses or enhancement of existing strengths. Whilst this approach is valuable, single outcome measures do not provide an understanding of the strategies adopted to achieve the end results. Moreover, by comparing a test result to an 'ideal' set of standards, significant – and potentially incorrect – assumptions are made that reducing any perceived deficits will likely improve performance. Some benefit can be added by considering suitably paired test ratios and 'performance slopes' across graduated constraints, such that biases in physical qualities can be highlighted that might better help the coach understand the athlete. Whilst no test is without limitation, the following battery of assessments afford a broad understanding of the inter-related strength/power issues affecting an athlete's ability to express force optimally when sprinting.

Hip extensor profile

The hip extensor contribution to horizontal GRF production has been specifically highlighted during acceleration (Morin et al., 2015a). The hip extensors also likely play a role in optimising the horizontal force output whilst managing leg spring stiffness during high speed running. In this assessment, the athlete lies supine with their hips fixed underneath an immoveable bar or strap and pushes their heel into the force plate (Figure 27.6). The calculation of torque is made possible by multiplying the distance from the greater trochanter of the test side to the point of contact of the heel on the force plate (moment arm) by the force produced.

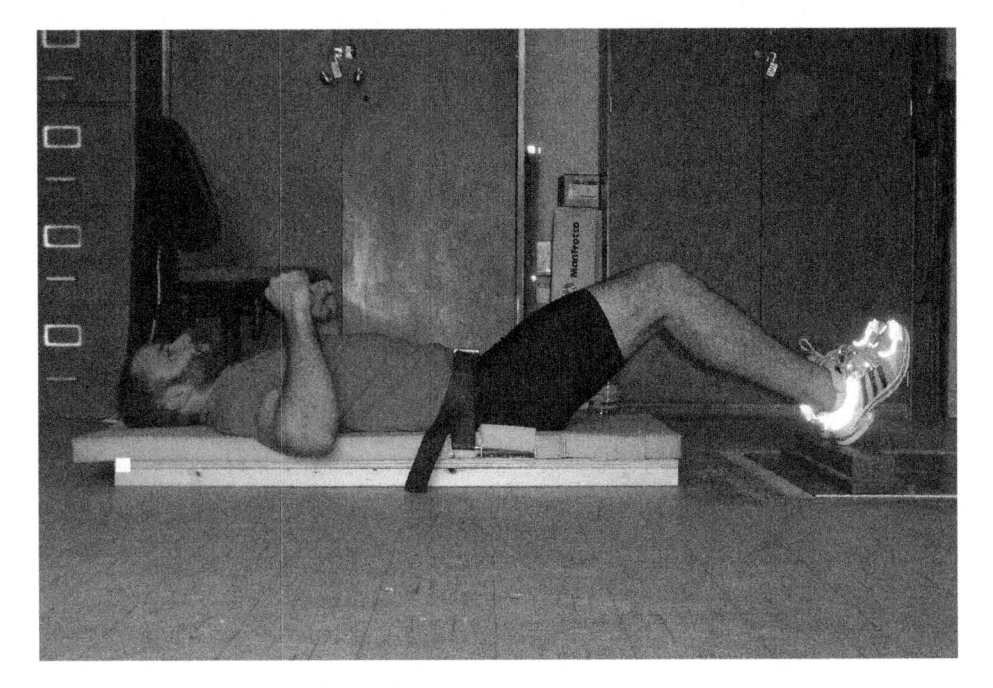

Figure 27.6 Isometric hip extension test position

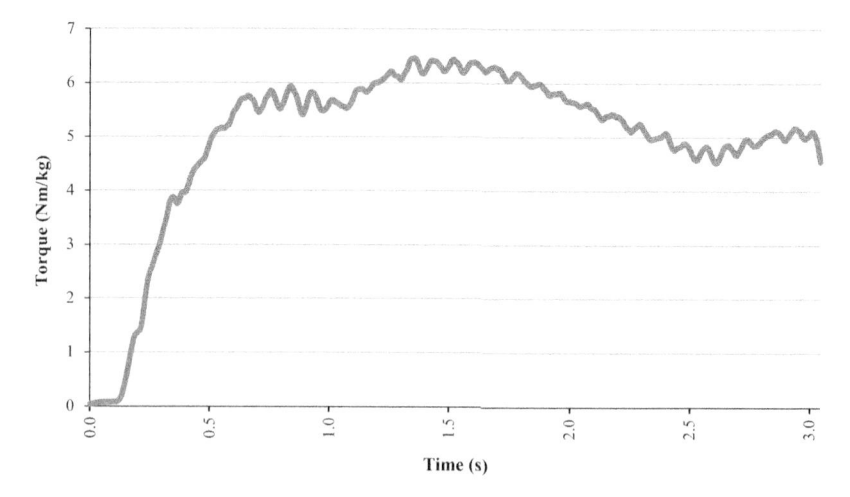

Figure 27.7 Torque-time trace during an isometric single leg hip extensor torque profile assessment for a sprint athlete. Torque has been normalised to the athlete's body mass

Unilateral comparisons can be made to identify potential imbalances, and varied magnitudes of knee flexion can be used in the assessment to emphasise the hamstring group or gluteal musculature. The former may be more related to the hip extensor qualities needed later in acceleration and during maximum velocity whereas the latter may be more relevant for the early acceleration phase of a sprint (Morin et al., 2015a). Figure 27.7 shows the torque-time trace from a unilateral hip extensor test conducted on a sprint athlete.

Reactive strength index profile

Hip extension potential is most likely to be realised when working in concert with an equally performing knee and ankle extension response. The reactive strength index (RSI) is commonly measured during a drop jump (Flanagan and Comyns, 2008), offering a 'stiffness-like'

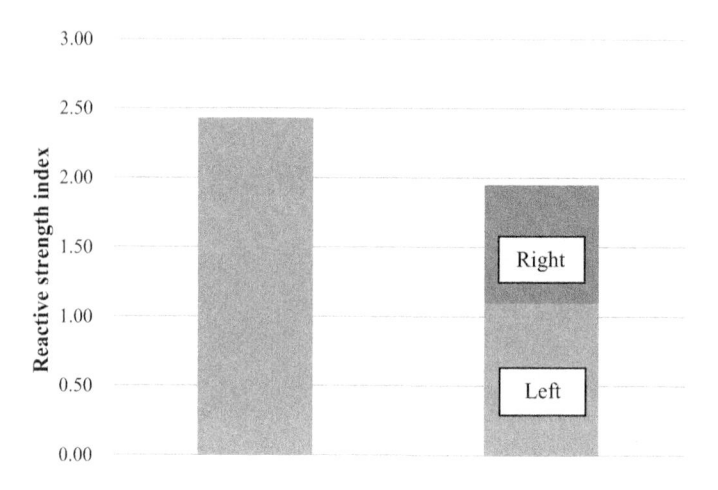

Figure 27.8 RSI profile of a male sprint athlete

measure of the leg during a fast stretch-shortening cycle (SSC), with specific emphasis on the triceps surae muscle-tendon complex. For bilateral assessment, a box height of 30–40cm is common whilst drop jumps should be performed from a box of half the height for unilateral testing. Left:Right ratio can be used to assess symmetry. Furthermore, comparing the sum of unilateral RSI scores to the bilateral performance may help to identify whether bilateral or unilateral reactive strength work may be more beneficial for the athlete at that stage in their development. For instance, a bilateral RSI which is significantly higher than the sum of unilateral RSI scores may indicate that the athlete lacks the ability to stabilise on a single limb and take advantage of the SSC, thus they could be said to have a 'steering' deficit that requires addressing. If the sum of unilateral RSI scores is significantly higher than the bilateral score, then this may signify that more general development of RSI may be appropriate. Figure 27.8 depicts the RSI profile for a sprint athlete recovering from ankle injury (right side). It is evident that there is a left to right imbalance (left side RSI = 1.20; right side RSI = 0.75) which ought to be addressed.

Squat jump force-velocity profile

The squat jump force-velocity (FV) profiling method (Samozino, Rejc, Di Prampero, Belli, and Morin, 2012; Samozino et al., 2014) provides an assessment of ballistic leg extension qualities of an individual, with greater emphasis on the knee extensors. Due to the explosive concentric

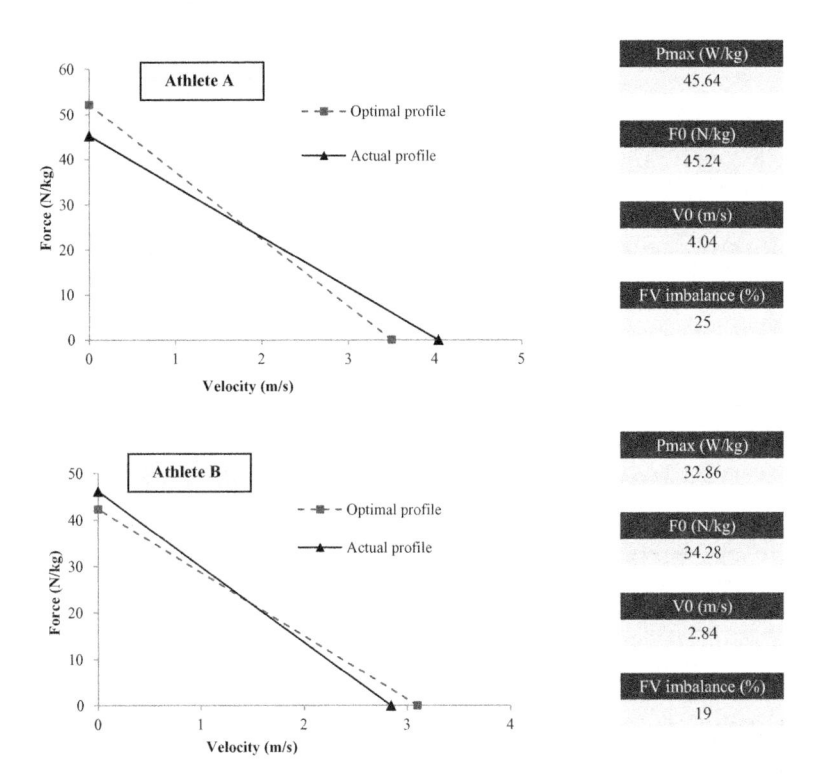

Figure 27.9 Force-velocity profile for two athletes. Athlete A and B are shown to have force and velocity deficits, respectively

nature of the squat jump, the qualities necessary to excel are relevant to those needed particularly during acceleration.

With body mass, squat jump height across a variety of different loads, extended leg length and squat jump depth, it is possible to calculate the mean force, mean centre of mass velocity and power capabilities of an athlete (Samozino, Morin, Hintzy, and Belli, 2008). Additionally, the optimal balance of force and velocity capabilities required to maximise ballistic push-off performance (i.e. jump height) at a given maximal power output can be determined (Samozino et al., 2014). These data can be used to inform programming decisions for related exercises across a FV continuum (e.g. heavy squatting – loaded squat jumps – unloaded vertical jumps – unloaded horizontal jumps – assisted jumps).

Figure 27.9 shows the FV profiles (black line) for two sprint athletes (A and B). The optimal FV profiles for each athlete to maximise push-off performance at their same maximal power (Pmax) outputs are highlighted by dotted lines. Within these profiles, adjustments have been made to the calculations to determine what the optimal profile would be when pushing off at a more horizontal angle akin to the start. Since a more horizontal push-off is less directed against gravity, there is a lower resistive effect, hence the optimal profile is more velocity oriented. F0 represents the theoretical maximum force the leg extensors can produce under zero velocity conditions (where the FV profile intercepts the vertical axis). V0 represents the theoretical maximal extension velocity of the lower limbs during a ballistic push-off (where the FV profile intercepts the horizontal axis). For full commentary on the methods and calculations used, and a full list of the variables which can be obtained, the reader is referred to the work of Samozino and colleagues (Samozino et al., 2012; Samozino et al., 2014).

Normative data

Table 27.2 shows normative data for sprint athletes which can be used for benchmarking purposes. Alongside a technical analysis of running strategy and knowledge of an athlete's injury history, these data may help identify potentially deficient aspects of function. Whilst these may be suggestive for elite level athletes, it is important for the strength and conditioning coach to establish their own set of normative values to account for any differences in testing methodologies and athletes being assessed.

Sprint force-velocity profile

From knowledge of an athlete's height, mass, and distance-time or speed-time running data (using light gates or a laser or radar device) during acceleration, we can estimate an athlete's sprint force-velocity profile (Samozino et al., 2015). This method provides an inexpensive way

Table 27.2 Strength testing diagnostics normative data for sprint athletes

	Squat jump force-velocity profiling		Single leg hip extensor torque	Drop jump reactive strength index	
	F0: maximum force at null velocity (N/kg)	Peak power (W/kg)	Peak isometric torque (Nm/kg)	Bilateral RSI (height in metres/ time in seconds)	Unilateral RSI (height in metres/ time in seconds)
Male	40–55	40–50	5–7	2.4–3.2	1.2–1.6
Female	38–46	30–35	4–6	2.0–2.8	1.0–1.3

to measure variables which affect sprint performance. Such variables include the maximal mechanical power output (Pmax, W/kg), the theoretical maximal horizontal force produced (F0, N/kg), theoretical maximal running velocity (m/s), the ratio of force application (RF, %) and the rate of decrease of RF as running velocity increases (Drf). Such analysis can support characterisation of an athlete as force or velocity dominant. It can also help differentiate levels of specific skill; for example, by comparing an athletes RFmax to high force measures like peak isometric hip extension and/or F0 during squat jump testing, or comparing Dfr to reactive strength measures.

Figure 27.10 shows the sprint force-velocity profile for two female sprinters. In the sprint effort, both athletes achieved the same time to 50m. They did so, however, with different strategies. Athlete A's superior RFmax (%) and F0 (N/kg) are reflected in their ability to change velocity at a greater rate during the early stages of acceleration leading to shorter 10, 20, 30 and 40m times. This also aligns to greater half-squat strength (Athlete A 120kg vs Athlete B 80kg). However, Athlete B better attenuates the decrease in RF as the sprint progresses, achieving a lower Drf and higher V0 (m/s), and can draw level by the 50m mark.

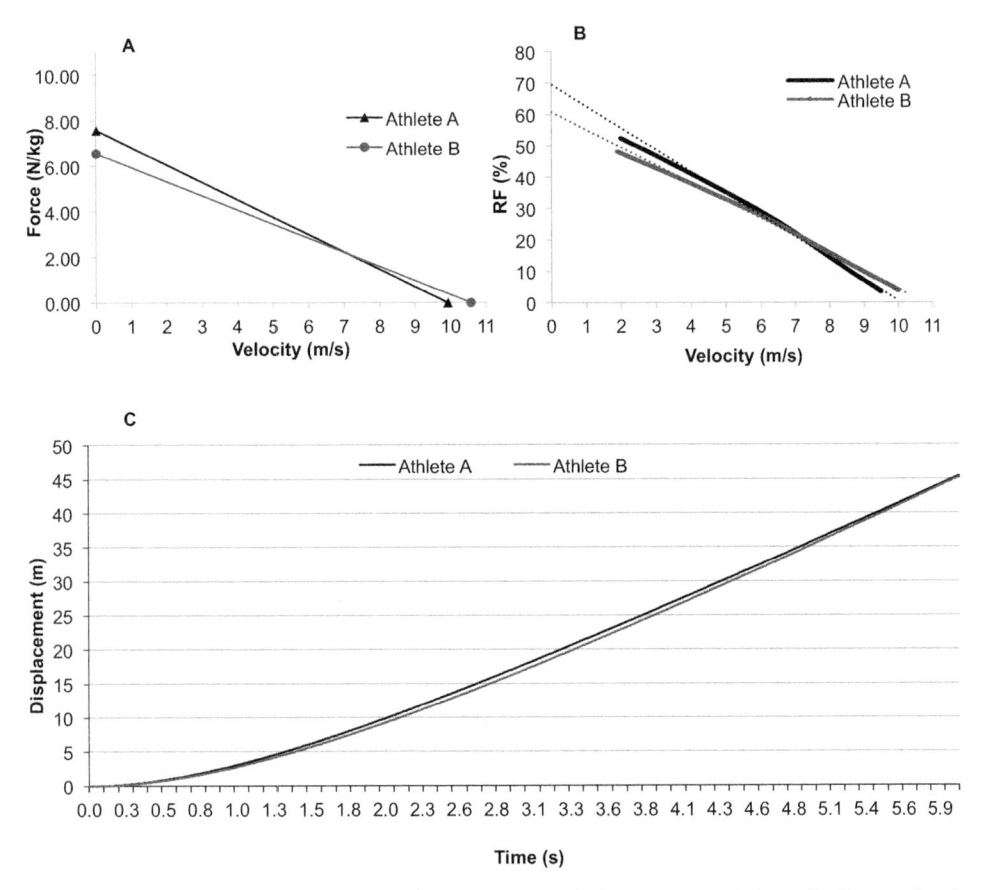

Figure 27.10 Sprint force-velocity (A), RF-velocity (B) and displacement-time (C) profiles for two female sprinters who complete a 50m sprint in exactly the same time. Despite having a lower Pmax (W/kg) Athlete B can achieve the same sprint performance likely due to more optimal balance of force and velocity at their Pmax

Programming

Training programme design for any sport requires the organisation of multiple training elements. The ability to attune physical, cognitive and skill development will be key to the success of the programme. Coaching philosophy, training theory, and evidence based knowledge are integral to this process. This section aims to cover approach to training, programme design, and some specific programming decisions catering for the sprint athlete. It isn't intended to represent a catch-all analysis but rather is a selection of current views based on the knowledge and experiences of the authors.

An approach to programme management

As a general principal of programming, there should be a clear strategy for individualisation. In the discussion that follows the basis is that the programme is managed around two strands of content. Fundamentally, and for broadly practical reasons, a core 'sprinters programme' is in operation. This sets up some of the fundamental tenets of the selected training system, periodisation structure, and basic training content. Secondly there is a derivation of more individual requirements to the programme (Figure 27.11) that will overlay and re-shape, to varying degrees, the core programme. In the discussion that follows we will cover elements of both a core programme and simple case examples of individualisation. It is also worth noting that elements covered here consolidate only training and basic performance testing. Collaboration with a physiotherapist/athletic trainer or other similar professional would deliver further insight that would facilitate individualisation of the programme.

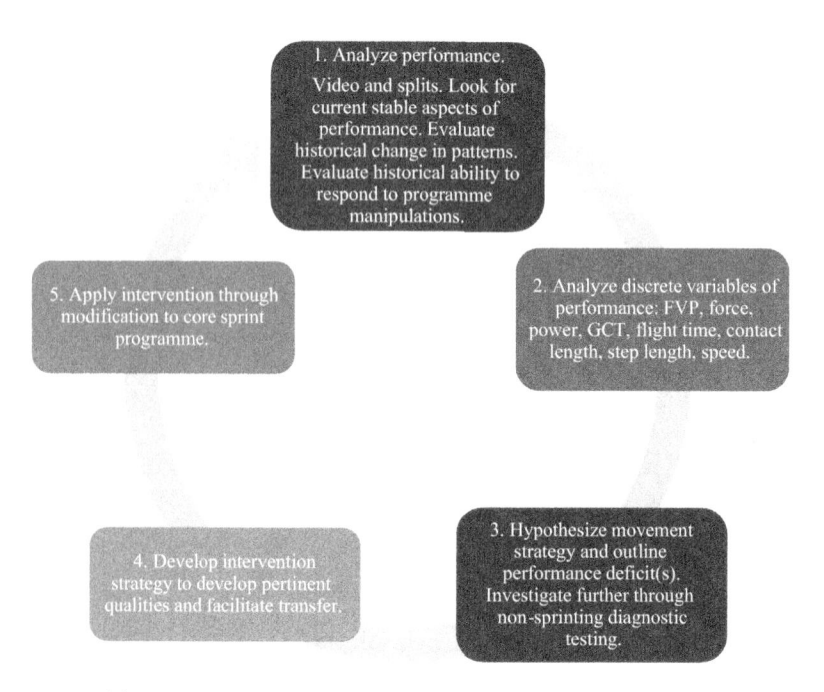

Figure 27.11 Modifying process that drives individualisation of the programme

Sprint running

Core sprinters programme

Fundamental rules of thumb for the core speed programme include:

1   Continuous work of the principal skills – acceleration and upright running abilities:

    The inclusion of skill work year-round allows for the continual interplay of physical development and technical transference necessary for skill development. A pedagogical scheme that challenges the skills and engages the athlete is essential.

2   Gradually increase density and intensity of specific work closer to competition:

    This is necessary to solidify the complex skill of sprinting and facilitate transfer of developed physical qualities from preceding phases. The competition period requires repeated execution of maximal running velocity during heats, rounds and densely packed competition schedules. The training leading to this period must be used to prepare the athlete for this.

3   *Develop required underlying physical qualities prior to exposure to high intensity work, for health and performance:*

    a   Develop hamstring robustness prior to maximal velocity running, and through maximal velocity running prior to competition stress.
    b   Develop strength, landing and jumping control prior to high level plyometric training.
    c   Develop energy systems prior to repeat speed or speed endurance blocks.

4   *Variability to support skill refinement*

    A 'dose prescription' strategy for sprint programme planning, typically focussed on volume and intensity progression, fails to fully support the refinement of motor skills over time. One goal then is to challenge the skill under varied constraints. Development of fundamental actions might be supported through slowing down or exaggerating components of a skill. Further variability permits athletes to explore their strategy in completing the task, supports acquisition of pertinent aspects of stability and adaptability in movement, and find better motor solutions over time (Ijspeert, Nakanishi, Hoffmann, Pastor, and Schaal, 2013). This supports skill development in general terms, but also specifically challenges the athlete to modify the skill over time to make better use of developing physical capacities. The use of equipment, environment, physical state or general session design can facilitate this process.

Planning the year – deconstructing our training time

Typically, competitive objectives, or competitive structure delivering appropriate developmental opportunity, drive the general structure of the year. Figure 27.12 outlines some classical shapes. However, the content of units, whilst defined as GPP/SPP/SPP2, is more fuzzy and dynamic in

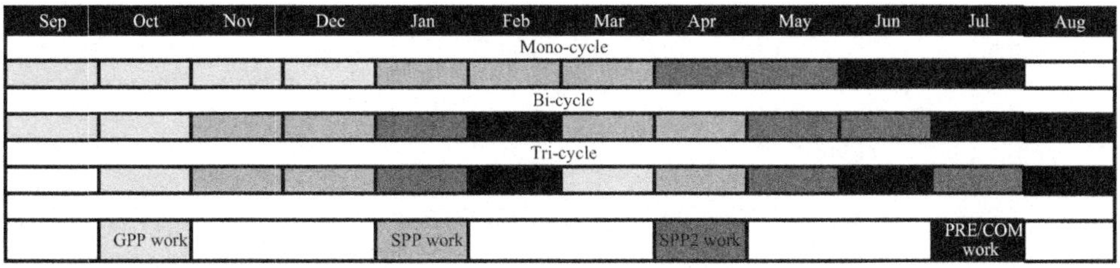

Figure 27.12 Types of macrocycle

nature than such a figure implies. Not infrequently activities that might be considered SPP/SPP2 might show up in a GPP block, and vice versa. Alternately a programme might briefly diverge from a block's signposted aim to 'check-in' or 'stress test' developing qualities. Such is the nature of individual programming and continuous skill development, and is not necessarily unique to training sprinters.

Table 27.3 Example stages of gym-based work to support running based training

	GPP	SPP	SPP 2	Pre-comp
TRACK PROGRESSIONS				
	Learn the skills – challenge the skills – stress test the skills			
Acceleration	Develop early acceleration with resisted and un-resisted runs	Intensify acceleration and extend runs to include transition	Increase acceleration volume with repeated efforts	Stress test technical model and compete in training
Speed	Develop awareness of reactive use of the leg through drills and dribbles	Introduce technical interventions for skill development and intensify with maximum velocity hurdles	Intensify maximum velocity running and build speed endurance	Stress test technical model and compete in training
Speed end	Build running conditioning – extensive tempo	Intensify running conditioning on the track – intensive tempo	Further intensify runs, and build repeat speed endurance	Stress test technical model and compete in training
GYM PROGRESSIONS				
	Prepare for fast running – transfer and support volume of fast running – enable fastest running			
Primary physical development	Develop strength. Focus on body tension, maximum strength and eccentric strength	Strength-speed, Speed-strength. Technical plyometric training – *Learn to 'stack joints'*	Intensify and individualise explosive/reactive strength	Intensify and individualise explosive/reactive strength
	Build body composition and correct weaknesses (restrictions, asymmetries, imbalances)	Develop maximal strength and balancing FVP	Maintain maximal strength	Maintain maximal strength
Secondary physical development	Develop tissue mass and quality to tolerate increased loading and higher volumes of work	Maintain body composition and tissue endurance	Maintain body composition and tissue endurance	Maintain body composition and tissue endurance
PRIMARY THEME	BUILD	GET STRONG	EXPLODE AND REACT	SHARPEN AND FRESHEN UP

Mesocycle planning and phase potentiation

Technical and physical aims are intertwined and support one another, both in parallel and consecutively over time. Preparatory cycles of training focus on developing a more foundational learning environment for running skills whereas latter cycles see increased running speeds, challenging of the skill under varied conditions, and progressively more competition specific stress testing. Strength and conditioning coaches can capitalise on periods of lower intensity running, taking the opportunity to make substantial structural development, reduce asymmetries, achieve suitable levels of mobility and build tissues to reduce future injury risk, as well as develop energy pathways to support workload maintenance. Examples of stages of 'gym work' progression to support running based training is highlighted in Table 27.3.

Microcycle and session planning – acute management of gym and track work integration

Management of multiple training stresses within a microcycle requires careful organisation to attenuate the build-up of fatigue, reduce negative interference into other sessions, promote adaptation and mitigate injury risk. Whilst the day to day planning and management of load is a marker of individualisation, some general strategies are explored here, and some specific case examples of decision making.

1   *Session order*

Strength and conditioning sessions in this period will likely be substantial as a broad set of developmental factors are prioritised. As such, a common-sense response is to place strength and conditioning work after running sessions during this period to remove an unnecessary risk of running (and trying to learn skills) under regularly high levels of fatigue.

2   *Themed days*

To increase the opportunity to recover, prioritised stresses can be focussed or centralised around 2–3 themed days across the week. This helps to reduce monotony and delivers solid blocks of 48–96 hours recovery between units of substantial stress being imposed. Other benefits might also be noted, as the signal for a particular adaptation is intensified, and some potentiation across sessions in the day might occur with appropriate management of volume-loads. An example is highlighted in Figure 27.13.

3   *Potentiation across the day*

The pattern of strength and conditioning work around running can change substantially across the year, and to good effect. Once athletes have developed work capacity and a specific tolerance for gym based loading, then it becomes progressively more available as a tool for supporting running sessions. Small volumes of explosive and/or reactive gym work can serve to improve mood, heighten arousal or even 'wake up' tired athletes prior to running training. Dependent on the athlete's capacity, further S&C content can then follow running work to ensure progression or maintenance of prioritised qualities. Examples are highlighted in Figures 27.16 and 27.19.

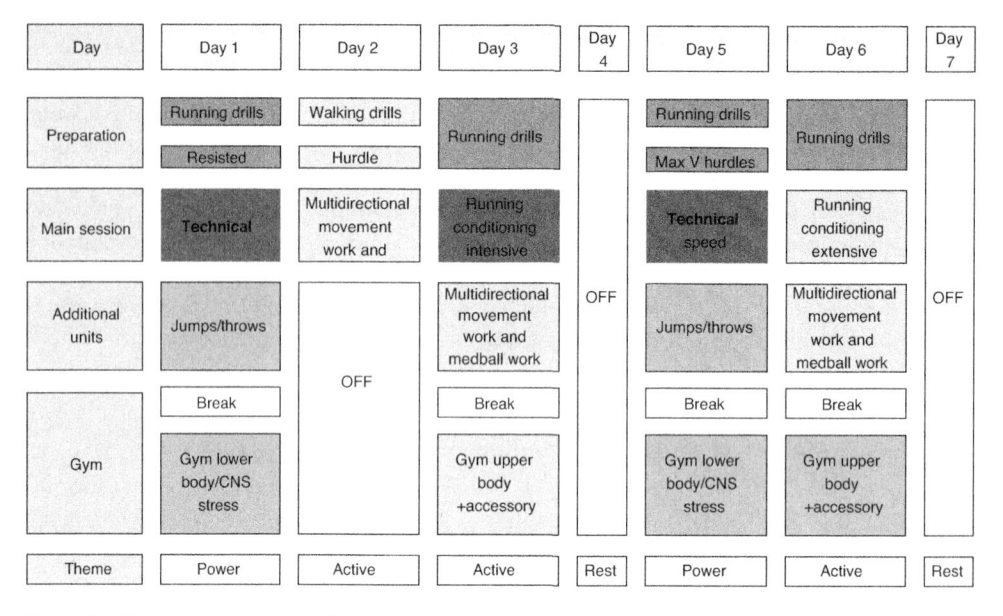

Day	Day 1	Day 2	Day 3	Day 4	Day 5	Day 6	Day 7
Preparation	Running drills / Resisted	Walking drills / Hurdle	Running drills	OFF	Running drills / Max V hurdles	Running drills	OFF
Main session	Technical	Multidirectional movement work and	Running conditioning intensive		Technical speed	Running conditioning extensive	
Additional units	Jumps/throws	OFF	Multidirectional movement work and medball work		Jumps/throws	Multidirectional movement work and medball work	
	Break		Break		Break	Break	
Gym	Gym lower body/CNS stress		Gym upper body +accessory		Gym lower body/CNS stress	Gym upper body +accessory	
Theme	Power	Active	Active	Rest	Power	Active	Rest

Figure 27.13 An example seven day GPP microcycle

4   *Protecting the hamstrings (and managing general levels of risk)*

Sensible decision making can serve to protect athletes from self-imposed risk. Take a scenario of an athlete ending a cycle of loaded acceleration training. As they de-load and complete more free acceleration runs, they are likely to hit higher than usual accelerations, and if allowed to extend runs to 40–50m might well hit unaccustomed velocities. This in itself creates risk, and if the S&C coach is also trying to progress hamstring strength and has completed a heavy dose of eccentric work within 48 hours prior, then the cumulative risk should be apparent. A decision as simple as moving a S&C dose forward by 24–48 hours, or restricting a set of acceleration runs to 30m, can mitigate risk and support longer periods of uninterrupted development. Other examples abound. Consider the inverse of the previous example with attempting to complete heavy eccentric gym work closely following maximum velocity sprinting; or the additional risk of heavy bent knee calf raises the day before an extensive grass running session; or the cessation of eccentric hamstring loading when fascicle length improvements can degrade in as little as 4 weeks (Timmins et al., 2016). Such decision making is the rule rather than the exception.

Deconstructing the sprint – tools for daily training delivery

To this point our analysis has considered temporal planning, concerned with the order of delivering training outcomes, and the time periods over which they are staggered. Consideration is also needed though of the deconstruction of the event itself to pinpoint the tools that might deliver adaptations focussed at the specific demands of a sprint run. Obviously, such analysis would also be aligned to the strengths and weaknesses of the athlete. In this section, we will consider general strategies for development of physical qualities, specific tools for facilitating technical development and transfer, and an example day of detailed training as it might be delivered to a trained athlete.

Acceleration development

1   *Development of physical qualities for acceleration*

Creating maximal horizontal projection through extension of the leg and maintenance of body orientation are important physical requirements for acceleration, and whilst they represent whole limb extension qualities, appear to be particularly dependent on the function of posterior chain. As such, limb extension with a bias towards gluteal and hamstring work tends to dominate. An example of the type of work conducted to enhance leg extension qualities for acceleration can be found in Table 27.4.

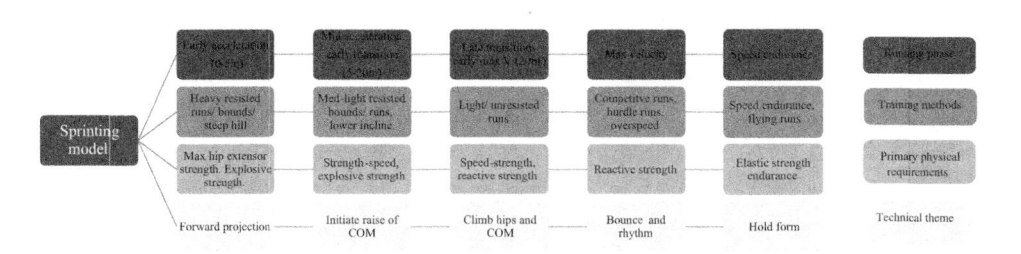

Figure 27.14 Phase specific training considerations

Table 27.4 Development of leg extension qualities for acceleration

Level of intervention	Type of work required	Example S&C content
Level 1: **Structural**	Hypertrophy/strength work	Squat, high box step up, hip thrust, RDL, trap bar deadlift, leg press, resisted walks
		Rep ranges 5–8 for barbell movements
Level 2: **General neuromuscular**	Maximal strength work, speed-strength, strength-speed, plyometric training	Jump squat, clean, 1/4 squat, CMJ, standing long jump, med-ball throws, resisted bounds, resisted runs
		Rep ranges 3–5 for barbell movements
Level 3: **Application**	Speed-strength, strength-speed, plyometric training with attention to dynamic correspondence	Hang clean, horizontal bounds, resisted runs, hill sprints
		Rep range 1–2 for barbell movements

2   *Specific tools for developing acceleration*

Resisted work: the use of pulleys, prowlers and sleds

Resisted specific training allows exploration of limit angles for body orientation and, depending on the loading point, challenges athletes in maintaining body alignment around the force vector being produced. High loads will encourage the athlete to direct forces horizontally, and have been shown to provide specific transfer to acceleration performance (Morin et al., 2016). These tools enable the movement to be slowed for teaching purposes and can support transfer with athletes being able to explore projection angles prior to unloaded acceleration runs.

Figure 27.15 Resisted sprinting

Un-resisted work: confirmation runs, rollover runs, runs from blocks, 3-point start

Un-resisted runs represent the most specific set of tools for development of acceleration ability. Confirmation runs are typically completed after constraints led work (often resisted work) to promote transfer of action/position or intensity into the real-time activity. Rollover runs, initiated from an upright position with a relaxed 'roll' forwards, encourage forward orientation and propulsion. They require less skill and force expression to begin the run, compared to block starts and so might be included for reasons relating to athlete level or exposure to training intensity. Finally accelerating from a multitude of positions can create deeper learning as the athlete learns to express the attractors of the action under different constraints.

3   *What an acceleration day may look like*

High intensity extension based activities can be used to enhance the main technical session. For the advanced athlete in this example (Figure 27.16) we have used a heavy squat to produce

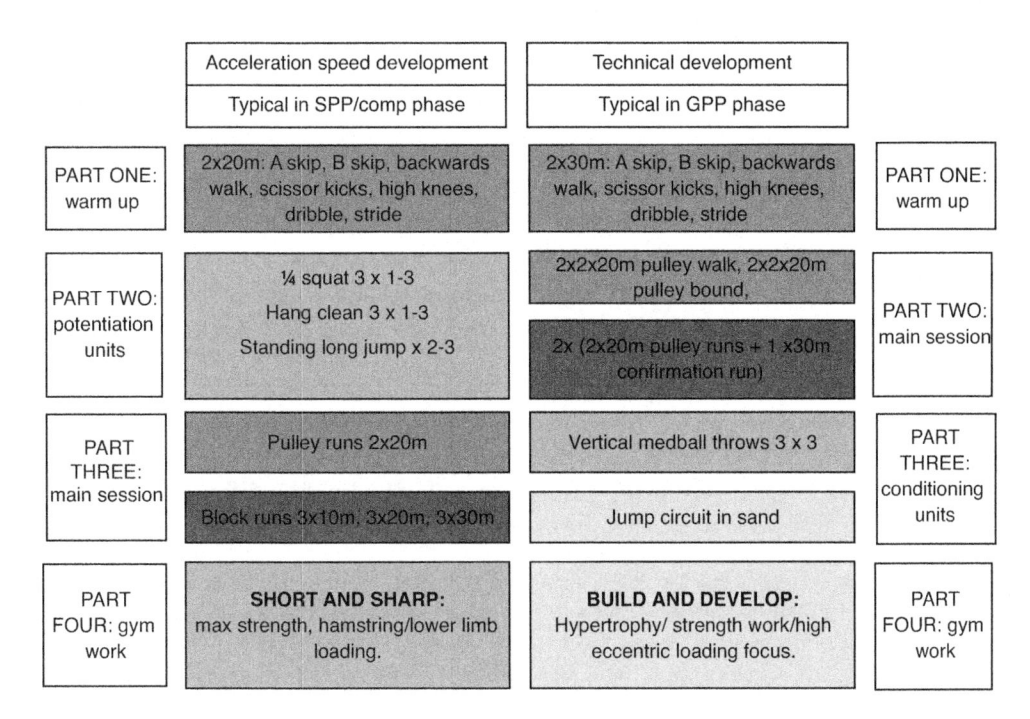

	Acceleration speed development	Technical development	
	Typical in SPP/comp phase	Typical in GPP phase	
PART ONE: warm up	2x20m: A skip, B skip, backwards walk, scissor kicks, high knees, dribble, stride	2x30m: A skip, B skip, backwards walk, scissor kicks, high knees, dribble, stride	PART ONE: warm up
PART TWO: potentiation units	¼ squat 3 x 1-3 Hang clean 3 x 1-3 Standing long jump x 2-3	2x2x20m pulley walk, 2x2x20m pulley bound, 2x (2x20m pulley runs + 1 x30m confirmation run)	PART TWO: main session
PART THREE: main session	Pulley runs 2x20m Block runs 3x10m, 3x20m, 3x30m	Vertical medball throws 3 x 3 Jump circuit in sand	PART THREE: conditioning units
PART FOUR: gym work	**SHORT AND SHARP:** max strength, hamstring/lower limb loading.	**BUILD AND DEVELOP:** Hypertrophy/ strength work/high eccentric loading focus.	PART FOUR: gym work

Figure 27.16 Example acceleration days

a high level of force, the hang clean for speed of movement under load and the standing long jump to promote horizontal projection. Volumes are low to limit fatigue, and athletes should finish the unit of work feeling optimally prepared for later parts of the session. An alternative strategy would be to use heavy, and then progressively lighter loads, in resisted runs to precede the session. For a less well conditioned athlete the bulk of their strength and conditioning work would be completed post-track. In the more developmental GPP window, volumes are higher for conditioning purposes but learning is also a focus with a wider variety of resisted actions.

Maximum velocity development

1 Development of physical qualities for maximum velocity

Physical qualities for maximum velocity running relate to the ability to absorb, produce and transmit force rapidly to deal with short ground contacts. The knee and ankle extensors, and foot, represent key structures for development due to their central role in stiffening the leg appropriately in stance. Blocking, or catching, of the leg on the front side, followed by the 'whip from the hip' and then the management of braking forces and trunk control in early stance, all make the function of the hip extensors a high priority. Finally, in the execution of an effective switching of the limbs the hip flexors are of importance to slow thigh extension in late stance and initiate rapid forward recovery. An example of the type of work to enhance physical qualities for maximum velocity is provided in Table 27.5.

Table 27.5 An example of training to enhance physical qualities for maximum velocity

Level of intervention	Type of work required	Example S&C content
Level 1: structural	Hypertrophy/strength work focussed on creation of stiff limb response.	Straight leg calf raise, bent leg calf raise
		Rep ranges 5–8, and often eccentric focus.
	Hypertrophy/strength work focussed on extensor mechanism from front side 'catch' through ground strike to mid-stance.	Hip thrust, RDL, Nordic curl, hamstring curl, hamstring bridge, good morning
		Rep ranges 5–8, and often eccentric focus
	Hypertrophy/strength work focussed on limb recovery from late stance through to mid-late swing.	Machine and banded hip flexion, hanging leg raise, straight leg raise
		Rep ranges 5–8, and often eccentric focus
Level 2: general neuromuscular	Stiff limb focus. Maximal strength work, speed-strength, strength-speed, plyometric training.	Straight leg calf raise, bent leg calf raise, 1/4 squat, heavy isometrics, pogo jumps, walking toe taps, drop jumps, double or single leg bounds
	Catch and strike focus. Maximal strength work, speed-strength, strength-speed, plyometric training. Stability challenges and band resistance can be added to semi-specific patterns.	Machine hip extension, ballistic step up, accelerated kettlebell swings, sprinter jumps, bounds
	Limb recovery focus. Maximal strength work, speed-strength, strength-speed, plyometric training. Stability challenges and band resistance can be added to semi-specific patterns.	Box step to knee drive, single leg RDL to knee drive, lumbopelvic control exercises, bounds
Level 3: application	Stiff limb focus. Jumps, plyometric training with focused dynamic correspondence.	Drills and dribbles, drills with resistance bands, bounds
	Catch and strike focus. Jumps, plyometric training with focused dynamic correspondence.	Fast foot A, skips for height, scissor bleeds
	Limb recovery focus. Jumps, plyometric training with focused dynamic correspondence.	High knee drills, drills with resistance bands, bounds

2   Specific tools for developing maximum velocity

Max velocity hurdles

Hurdles, or wickets, can be used to set up a rhythm for the run (Figure 27.17). Depending on the spacing you can preferentially explore stride length or stride frequency. Variation in the entry velocity (determined generally by the acceleration distance prior to the first hurdle) can also change the demands on the athlete with higher velocities constraining the ground contact time available.

Sprint running

Figure 27.17 Maximum velocity hurdles

Figure 27.18 Dribbles

Resisted runs

Light or moderate resisted runs can encourage the continuation of projection and force expression in upright running, likely having most direct transfer to late stage acceleration but also challenging the athlete to explore their strategies to access force from their limb extension during close to upright running.

Overspeed

Setting running velocities faster than the athlete's abilities can be achieved through the use of a towing device or downhill running. Increasing speed of the runs will reduce available ground contact time and increase stride frequency, taking the athlete into a domain of movement management they would not otherwise have access to. Care should be taken over the extent of overspeed and the competence of the athlete since excessive braking patterns, and falling, are potential risks.

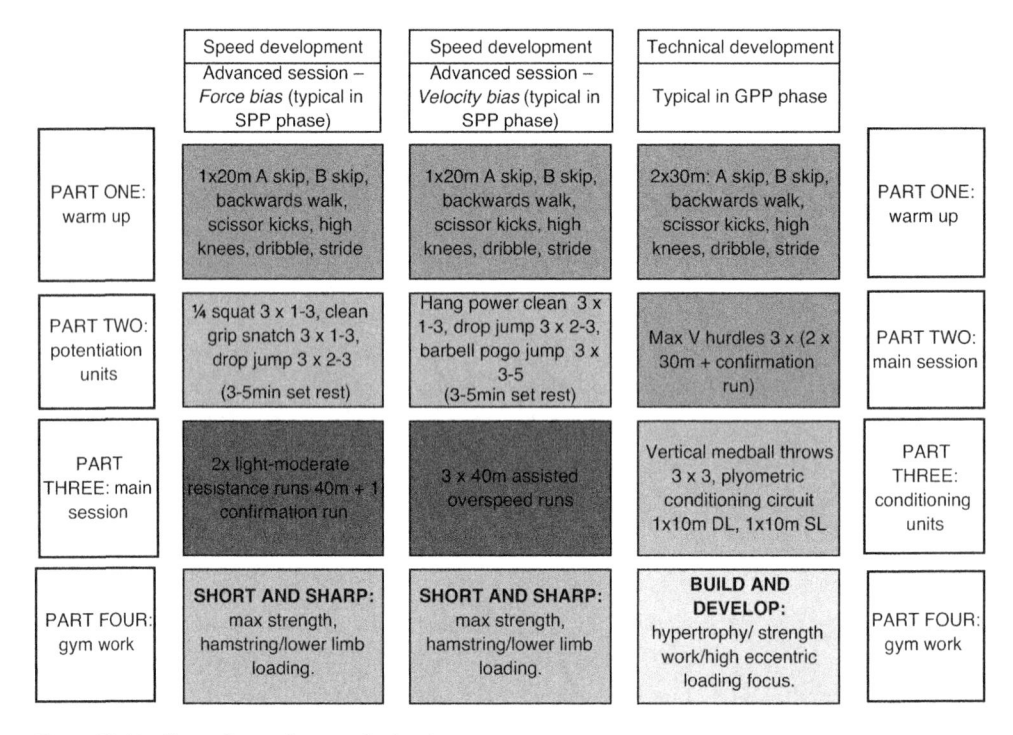

	Speed development Advanced session – *Force bias* (typical in SPP phase)	Speed development Advanced session – *Velocity bias* (typical in SPP phase)	Technical development Typical in GPP phase	
PART ONE: warm up	1x20m A skip, B skip, backwards walk, scissor kicks, high knees, dribble, stride	1x20m A skip, B skip, backwards walk, scissor kicks, high knees, dribble, stride	2x30m: A skip, B skip, backwards walk, scissor kicks, high knees, dribble, stride	PART ONE: warm up
PART TWO: potentiation units	¼ squat 3 x 1-3, clean grip snatch 3 x 1-3, drop jump 3 x 2-3 (3-5min set rest)	Hang power clean 3 x 1-3, drop jump 3 x 2-3, barbell pogo jump 3 x 3-5 (3-5min set rest)	Max V hurdles 3 x (2 x 30m + confirmation run)	PART TWO: main session
PART THREE: main session	2x light-moderate resistance runs 40m + 1 confirmation run	3 x 40m assisted overspeed runs	Vertical medball throws 3 x 3, plyometric conditioning circuit 1x10m DL, 1x10m SL	PART THREE: conditioning units
PART FOUR: gym work	SHORT AND SHARP: max strength, hamstring/lower limb loading.	SHORT AND SHARP: max strength, hamstring/lower limb loading.	BUILD AND DEVELOP: hypertrophy/ strength work/high eccentric loading focus.	PART FOUR: gym work

Figure 27.19 Example maximum velocity days

Dribbles

A dribble is, simplistically, a miniature sprint. Key technical markers mimic full sprinting but at lower velocity and with some small changes in movement amplitudes. It enables rehearsal of key technical positions and patterns and retains some essential characteristics like relative timing (arms to legs; left to right sides), pretension to set up a stiff ground contact, and early limb recovery from the back side. Compared to faster running practice, the stress imposed is low so dribbles can be useful tool where volumes of practice might be desired. Dribbles are commonly used in warm-ups for technical rehearsal on route to higher intensities, and might also be used as a component of the main session enabling overload in terms of step frequency or supporting the development of conditioning in the running cycle in preparation for upcoming volumes of faster running.

What a maximum velocity day may look like

The focus of the session is typically on producing balanced and fluid movement under high speed conditions. When very fast running is planned, the level of nervous system fatigue should be low, and the hamstrings should be well recovered. Gym activation and preparatory running should encourage readiness for elastic, reactive ground contacts on a long, extended leg lever. For example, in Figure 27.19 heavy prone isometrics for activation of the posterior chain in a long lever position, or drop jumps and pogo jumps to encourage hip and ankle coordination in stiffening the limb for rapid high force ground contact. Such work should support the athlete in coming to sprint training switched on, not fatigued. Further S&C content can continue after sprint training, with care being taken over the tolerance of the athlete, and the magnitude of dose of fast running that has been delivered.

Hamstring robustness and hip extension performance

Maximal velocity running places high loads on the hamstrings. Speed, technical efficiency and density of high speed runs will dictate hamstring exposure. Strength and conditioning should prepare the athlete for the level and timing of forces required. This likely will include general hypertrophy, and eccentric work, to deliver increases in cross sectional area and fascicle length. In addition, heavy lifts and isometrics can deliver tendon strength increases, whilst more ballistic and reactive methods can support relevant neural adaptations and retention of connective tissue elasticity.

A substantial proportion of hamstring work is completed in the early phases of the year, partly to be in advance of later speed blocks, but also because the opportunity for hamstring loading will become progressively more limited as the density of fast running increases. Hamstring loading might be included at the end of endurance or tempo running sessions, combining the conditioning stimulus and increasing the inter-session recovery window. An example of the typical work conducted is highlighted in Table 27.6.

Table 27.6 Example hamstring and hip extensor training

Level of intervention	Type of work required	Example S&C content
Level 1: structural	Hypertrophy/strength work	Hamstring curl, RDL, Nordic Rep ranges 5–8
Level 2: general neuromuscular	Maximal strength work, speed-strength, strength-speed, plyometric training	Nordic eccentric curl, Bosch variations, wall switches, Swiss ball kicks, jumps, catches – squat/lunge, Olympic style lifting
Level 3: application	Resisted runs, speed-strength, strength-speed, plyometric training with focused dynamic correspondence	Scissor runs, lunge jump switches, maximum velocity running

General robustness and control

Other discrete units of work are typically in place to support development of local work capacity and tissue conditioning, maintaining mobility, postural control, and extending the stimulus to synergistic muscle groups. Such units might be group led or individually tailored, and can be easily shifted to balance recovery and adaptation across the microcycle. Some can also be utilised as health check points with mobility, balance and control being tested. Examples of additional units are described in Table 27.7.

Case studies

In applying concepts discussed here, it is valuable to explore how data and qualitative analysis are combined in making collaborative coaching and programming decisions. In the following section we explore several case examples.

Case 1

Athlete A and B display good early acceleration profiles and reach 30m in similar times (Figure 27.20). Athlete A displays a smoother rhythm through the first 40m than Athlete B. Minimal change in speed from 40 to 60m for both athletes suggest that transition and/or upright running

Table 27.7 Example of additional general robustness and control training units

Hurdle mobility	Low level plyometric conditioning	Multiplane circuit	Medball circuit	Barefoot sand circuit
A Skip	Pogo jump style:	Lateral lunge	V sit up and throw	Star jumps
Hurdle walkovers forward	Forward	Walking plank	Lunge rotational throw	
Hurdle walkovers backward	Backward	Beast walks	Vertical medball throw	180–360 jumps
Squat under hurdles	Lateral right	Adductor drag walks	Russian twist	
Scissors over hurdles	Lateral left	5-point star excursion	Backwards throw	Speed skater
3 × 10 (1min rest)	2 × 10–15m each exercise	3 × 10 (1min rest)	Standing Rotational pass	
	Complete SL or DL as necessary		Between the legs backwards throw	Line hops
			Adductor knee toss	Dynamic step ups
			2–3 × 10 (1min rest)	Single leg butt kicks
				2–3 × 10–30s 1:1 work to rest ratio on each (1min rest)

needs development. Running characteristics vary, particularly beyond 30–40m. Athlete A shows continued reduction in ground contact time as the run progresses; however, stride length (SL) does not grow. Athlete B displays the opposite profile. Visually Athlete A remains 'bouncy' off the floor and creates vertical air time, but the lack of stride length growth implies restriction of contact length as a strategy to permit reduced GCT. Conversely, Athlete B continues to grow SL but without reduction in GCTs. Visually Athlete B's run looks flat (not showing changes in vertical hip displacement). Both athletes display 'backside mechanics'.

Athlete A interpretation

Athlete A displays good hip extensor strength in hip torque measurements and related gym lifts. Video analysis of the transition phase highlights that the athlete can 'climb the hip', delivering progressive elevation which sets up a bouncy/reactive ground contacts. Backside mechanics are manifested in lumbar extension on toe-off. Further analysis highlights poor lumbopelvic control and low hip flexor strength; qualities which are necessary to rapidly recycle the leg on toe-off. Improved limb recovery will likely support improved use of the limb 'front-side' to facilitate ground force production. Good CMJ scores and reasonable RSI suggest that the athlete can produce force quickly but may require further development when faster contraction velocities are required in the latter stage of the run. Principally intervention should be directed toward lumbopelvic control and improved use of the anterior chain to recycle the leg during swing phase, and maintenance of limb extension under high velocity conditions.

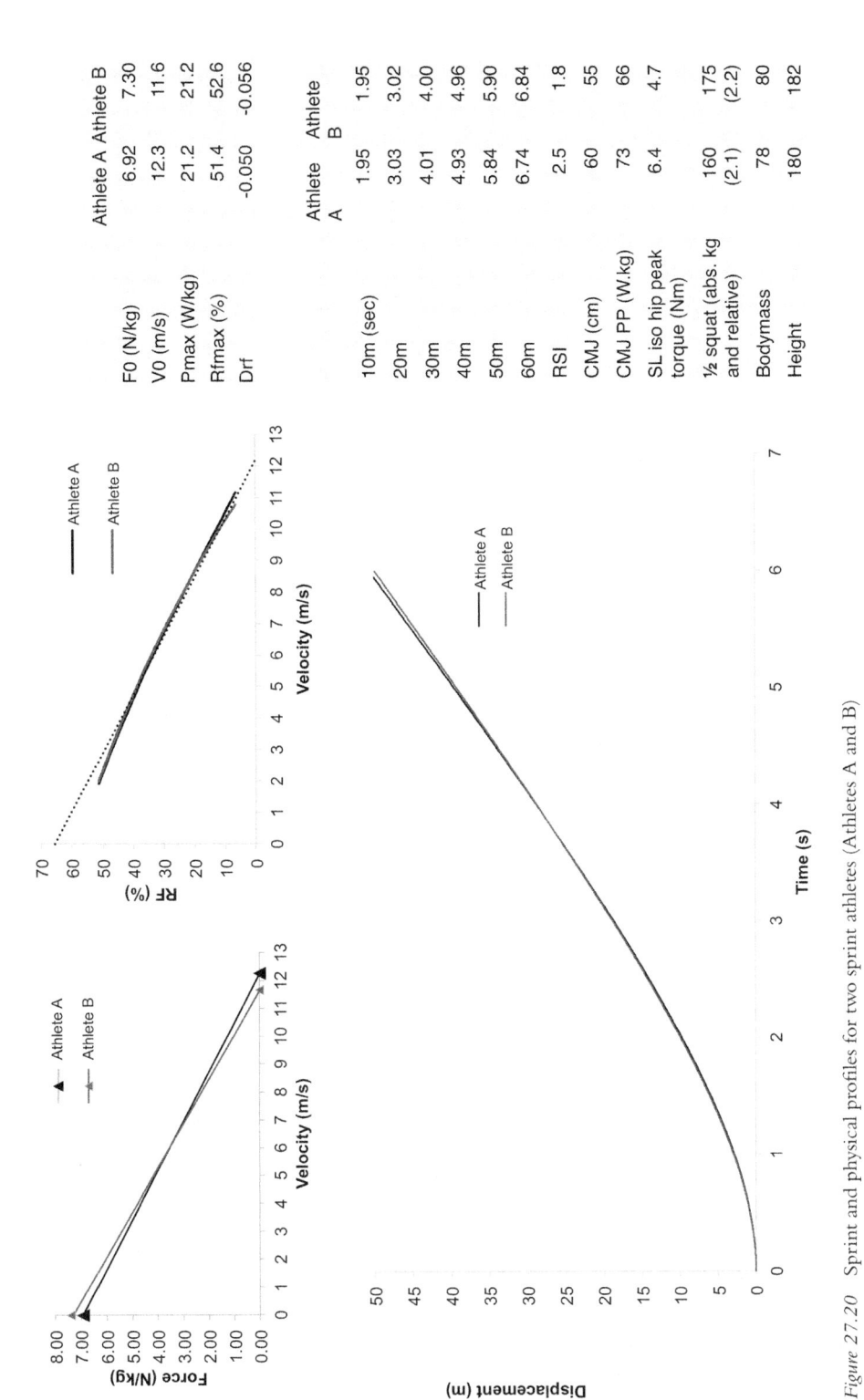

	Athlete A	Athlete B
F0 (N/kg)	6.92	7.30
V0 (m/s)	12.3	11.6
Pmax (W/kg)	21.2	21.2
Rfmax (%)	51.4	52.6
Drf	-0.050	-0.056

	Athlete A	Athlete B
10m (sec)	1.95	1.95
20m	3.03	3.02
30m	4.01	4.00
40m	4.93	4.96
50m	5.84	5.90
60m	6.74	6.84
RSI	2.5	1.8
CMJ (cm)	60	55
CMJ PP (W.kg)	73	66
SL iso hip peak torque (Nm)	6.4	4.7
½ squat (abs. kg and relative)	160 (2.1)	175 (2.2)
Bodymass	78	80
Height	180	182

Figure 27.20 Sprint and physical profiles for two sprint athletes (Athletes A and B)

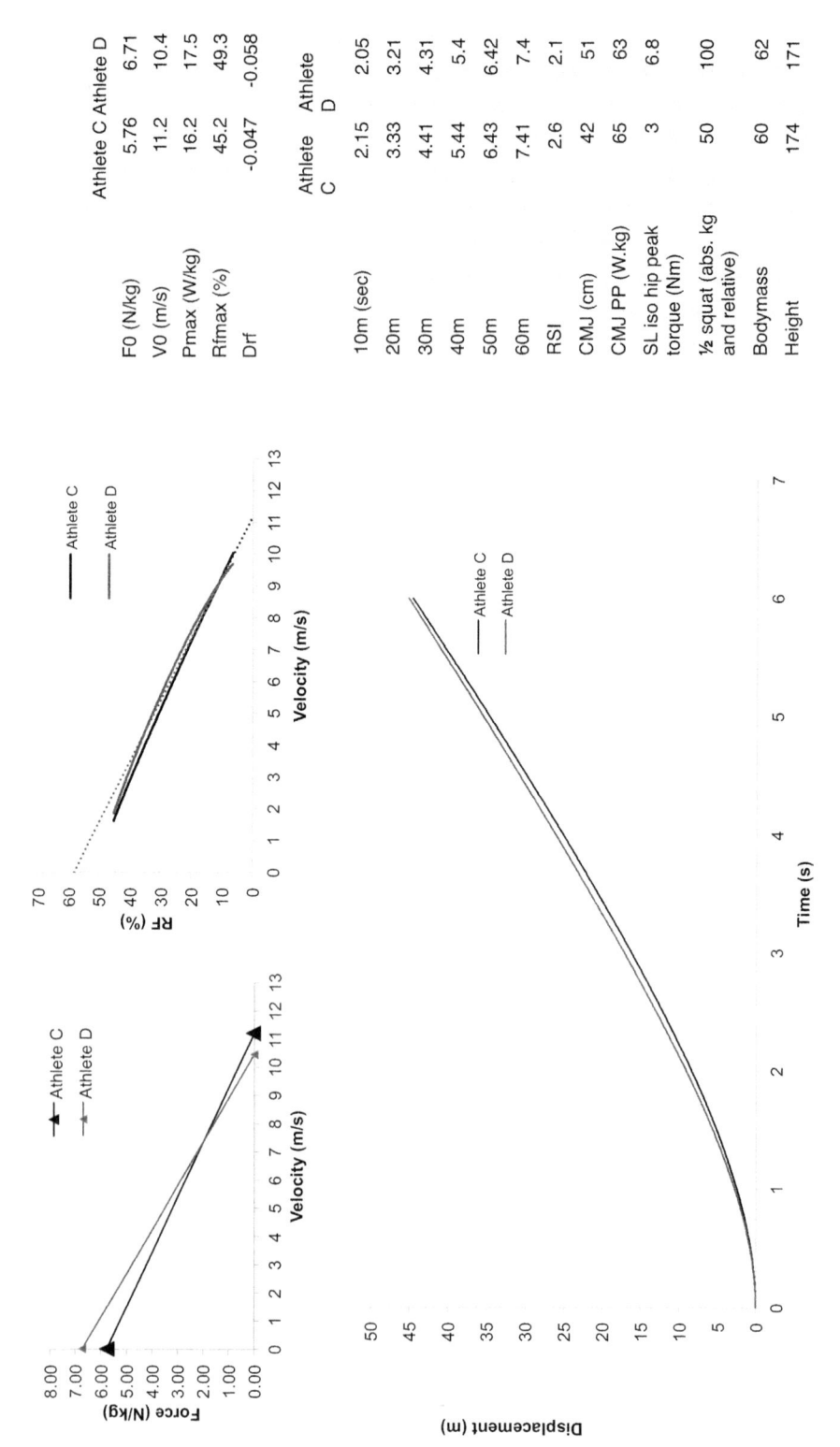

	Athlete C	Athlete D
F0 (N/kg)	5.76	6.71
V0 (m/s)	11.2	10.4
Pmax (W/kg)	16.2	17.5
Rfmax (%)	45.2	49.3
Drf	-0.047	-0.058

	Athlete C	Athlete D
10m (sec)	2.15	2.05
20m	3.33	3.21
30m	4.41	4.31
40m	5.44	5.4
50m	6.43	6.42
60m	7.41	7.4
RSI	2.6	2.1
CMJ (cm)	42	51
CMJ PP (W.kg)	65	63
SL iso hip peak torque (Nm)	3	6.8
½ squat (abs. kg and relative)	50	100
Bodymass	60	62
Height	174	171

Figure 27.21 Sprint and physical profiles for two sprint athletes (Athletes C and D)

S&C intervention objectives

- Develop hip flexor strength
  - Isolated strength training
  - Co-ordinated strength work with anterior musculature (e.g. abdominals)
  - Reactive and semi-specific work, typically using elastic resistance
- Develop lumbopelvic control
  - Progressions in level of load, dynamism and complexity
- Develop ability to produce limb extension force reactively and at high contraction rates
  - Plyometrics – drops and bounds

Athlete B interpretation

Athlete B is 'gym strong' and this corresponds to their high F0. The coach notices use of knee and back extension, preferential over the hip, during compound lifts and jumps. Hip torque measures confirm a weakness in isolated hip extension ability. Hip strength is necessary to climb during transition, and is also an essential part of 'hammering the nail' from the front side to create ground force during upright running. Furthermore, poor RSI indicates potential underperformance of the foot and ankle. These results combined with the inability to deal with decreasing GCT suggest that the athlete can produce force when there is time available but cannot produce force rapidly or from short ROM.

S&C intervention objectives

- Develop posterior chain strength – specifically glute strength
  - Hip thrust, deadlift and weightlifting derivatives from hang
- Develop ability to produce force quickly
  - Plyometrics
  - Weightlifting derivatives
- Develop ability to coordinate hip and ankle
  - Plyometrics vertical emphasis
- Specific strength and technical rehearsal of 'climbing the hips'
  - Light resisted runs to encourage climbing the hips during transition
- Ensure trunk strength, lumbopelvic control and lower limb qualities are developed in parallel

Case 2

Athletes C and D (Figure 27.21) cover 60m in similar times. Athlete C accelerates less to 10m but shows a smooth development of speed through the 60m. Athlete D accelerates to 10m rapidly but is more inconsistent in speed development from 10m. Both athletes display good upright running characteristics and split speeds, but are let down by acceleration capabilities.

Athlete C interpretation

Athlete C is a young, highly mobile athlete who has a gym training age of 1 year. Physical profiling shows the athlete to have good reactive qualities (RSI) but a general lack of strength/force expression capabilities. Analysis of drop jumps shows the athlete moves through minimal ROM and spends limited time on the ground to achieve the RSI score. This athlete is considered 'wired' by the coach, with a responsive nervous system. The combination of speed, lack of strength, and high joint mobility means the athlete can be considered high risk of injury. Intervention strategies should aim to develop strength for physical robustness and force expression, in parallel to learning how to use and direct force at speed into the technical model, specifically into the acceleration phase.

S&C intervention

- Develop lower limb strength qualities with expected changes in body composition
    - Range of primary compound lifts
- Develop whole body strength
- Pay attention to activities aligned to transfer into running
    - Use resisted runs to develop intensity and force expression into the running model

Athlete D interpretation

Athlete D displays a good physical profile (CMJ, gym strength, hip torque) and appears to use this strength in early acceleration as shown in 0–10m time. Additionally, the athlete shows a good upright running model. The biggest limitation appears to be during the acceleration/transitional phase of the run with an inconsistent acceleration profile. The coach attributes this to an ineffective transition caused by over rotation in early acceleration. This impacts rhythm and ability to climb hips during transition. Once upright rhythm is found, there is reacceleration between 40–50m. Over rotation during acceleration is often due to lack of postural strength, poor coordination and/or technique. Training observations also demonstrate asymmetrical movement patterns, and limited low body and spinal control. Athlete D appears to possess the primary physical qualities but lacks the ability to transfer into a suitably stable technical model.

S&C intervention

- Develop trunk awareness, postures and positions
    - Use a broad set of progressive movement challenges, with appropriate focus, to maximise opportunity for learning
- Investigate asymmetries and rectify where they are seen to impact performance
- Encourage smooth rising hips and COM
    - Cues during practice
    - Light pulley work through transition

Case 3

Six months post a grade II strain of the left biceps femoris, whilst pain and symptom free, Athlete E is underperforming in the acceleration phase. Analysis of step characteristics over the initial 10m from a block start revealed a 'zig-zag' pattern whereby greater than expected flight times following left foot ground contact coincided with lower than expected step velocities (Figure 27.22A). This was reflected in a stepped reduction the drive index (contact time divided by flight time) rather than a smooth progression. Strength diagnostic results and the athlete's average ten metre sprint time are shown in Table 27.8. It is evident that a sizeable difference exists between the previously injured and unaffected sides in the hip extensor torque assessment prior to the intervention detailed below.

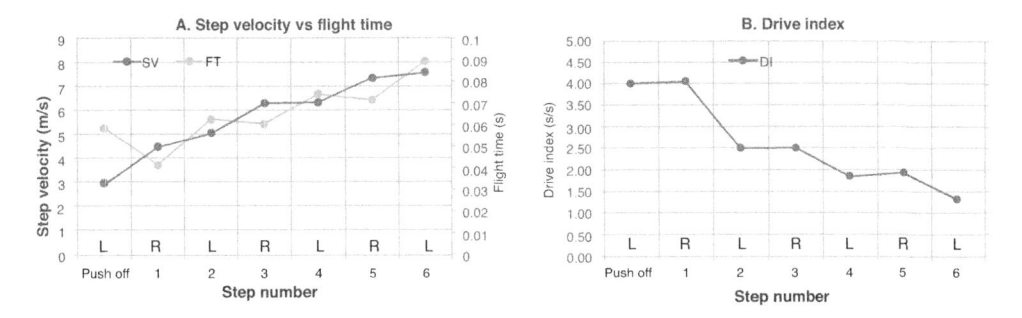

Figure 27.22 Pre-intervention step profile. (A) Mean step velocity (SV) and flight time (FT) across block exit and first six steps, pre intervention. Data were averaged over five sprint efforts on two separate occasions (ten sprints) during training (indoors). (B) Mean drive index (contact time divided by flight time) across block exit and first six steps, pre intervention

Athlete E's typical weekly training programme included three speed sessions (one acceleration session, one maximum velocity, and one speed endurance). On the same days, the athlete would perform a lifting component classically consisting of the clean, bench press, back (half) squat, glute-ham raise and some supplementary exercises. Loading variables were such that the development of explosive and maximum strength were prioritised. Hopping and bounding exercises were carried out twice per week, following acceleration or prior to speed endurance sessions.

Training intervention

The speed sessions and their typical weekly variation remained similar.

Weeks 1–6

- The barbell hip thrust exercise was carried out twice per week to provide greater focus on the gluteal musculature.
- Single leg isometric hip extension work (using the same set up as that in the hip torque assessment) was completed three times per week. The knee was in a more extended position twice within the week to emphasise the hamstrings, and more flexed once per week to emphasise the gluteal musculature. The volume of work (total reps) was the same between limbs, as was the relative intensity.
- Moderately loaded resisted sprint efforts were incorporated at the start of acceleration speed sessions to help with horizontal projection and to try facilitate transfer from strength gains in the gym.
- To offset potential risk to the athlete through increased training load the number of exposures to the back squat exercise was reduced to once per week. Hopping and bounding exercises were removed from the programme.

Weeks 6–12

- Exposure to the hip thrust was reduced to once per week.
- Single leg isometric hip extension exposure was reduced to twice per week (one hamstring and one gluteal focused).
- Bounding and hopping exercises were reinstated.
- Resisted sprinting load was reduced to light.

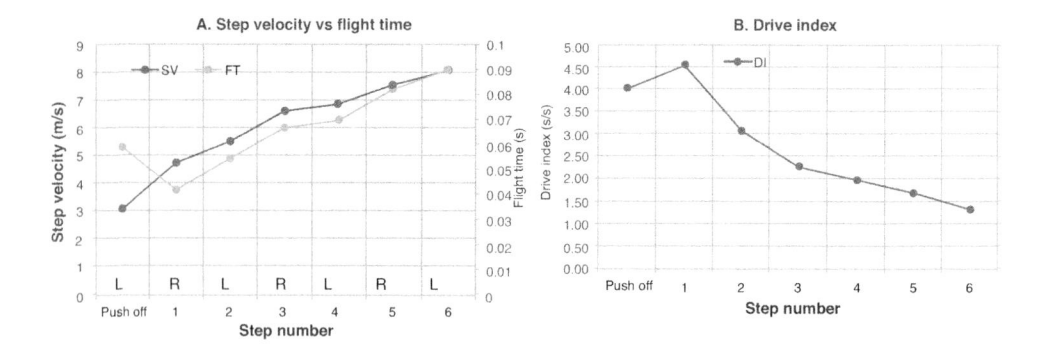

Figure 27.23 Post intervention step profile (A) Mean step velocity and flight time across block exit and first six steps. Data were averaged over four sprint efforts on two separate occasions (eight sprints) during training (indoors). (B) Mean drive index (contact time divided by flight time) across block exit and first six steps

Table 27.8 Pre and post scores from selected strength diagnostics

	Squat jump force-velocity profiling		Single leg hip extensor torque	Drop jump reactive strength index		Ten metre sprint time (s)
	F0: maximum force at null velocity (N/kg)	Peak power (W/kg)	Peak isometric torque (Nm/kg)	Bilateral RSI (height in metres/time in seconds)	Unilateral RSI (height in metres/time in seconds)	
Pre	44	47	L = 4.4; R = 6.0	2.48	L = 1.32; R = 1.27	1.76★
Post	42	46	L = 5.9; R = 6.9	2.50	L = 1.36; R = 1.31	1.69★★

★ Average across 5 sprint efforts on 2 separate occasions separate by 10 days (10 efforts in total)
★★ Average across 4 sprint efforts on 2 separate occasions separated by 1 week (8 efforts in total)

Outcomes

Changes in the athlete's profile following the 12-week intervention are shown in Figure 27.23 and Table 27.8. Such tracking of performance changes aligned to programming intervention can support coaches' understanding of their capacity to modify movement outcomes. Accruing consistent and predictable movement changes like this can help the coach to gain confidence in the causal influence of such interventions.

References

Costill, D. L., Daniels, J., Evans, W., Fink, W., Krahenbuhl, G., and Saltin, B. (1976). Skeletal muscle enzymes and fiber composition in male and female track athletes. *Journal of Applied Physiology*, 40, 149–154.
Cunningham, D. J., West, D. J., Owen, N. J., Shearer, D. A., Finn, C. V., Bracken, R. M., Crewther, B, T., Scott, P., Cook, C. J., and Kilduff, L. P. (2013). Strength and power predictors of sprinting performance in professional rugby players. *The Journal of Sports Medicine and Physical Fitness*, 53, 105–111.
Duthie, G. M., Pyne, D. B., Marsh, D. J., and Hooper, S. L. (2006). Sprint patterns in rugby union players during competition. *Journal of Strength and Conditioning Research*, 20, 208–214.
Edouard, P., and Alonso, J. (2013). Epidemiology of track and field injuries. *New Studies in Athletics*, 28, 85–92.
Edouard, P., and Morel, N. (2010). Prospective surveillance of injury in athletics. A pilot study. *Science & Sports*, 25, 272–276.

Edouard, P., Morel, N., Serra, J., Pruvost, J., Oullion, R., and Depiesse, F. (2011). Prevention of musculoskeletal injuries in track and field. Review of epidemiological data. *Science & Sports*, *26*, 307.

Flanagan, E. P., and Comyns, T. M. (2008). The use of contact time and the reactive strength index to optimize fast stretch-shortening cycle training. *Strength and Conditioning Journal*, *30*, 32–38.

Gabbe, B. J., Bennell, K. L., Finch, C. F., Wajswelner, H., and Orchard, J. W. (2006). Predictors of hamstring injury at the elite level of australian football. *Scandinavian Journal of Medicine & Science in Sports*, *16*, 7–13.

Guex, K., Degache, F., Morisod, C., Sailly, M., and Millet, G. P. (2016). Hamstring architectural and functional adaptations following long vs. short muscle length eccentric training. *Frontiers in Physiology*, *7*, 1–9.

Higashihara, A., Nagano, Y., Ono, T., and Fukubayashi, T. (2016). Relationship between the peak time of hamstring stretch and activation during sprinting. *European Journal of Sport Science*, *16*, 36–41.

Higashihara, A., Nagano, Y., Takahashi, K., and Fukubayashi, T. (2015). Effects of forward trunk lean on hamstring muscle kinematics during sprinting. *Journal of Sports Sciences*, *33*, 1366–1375.

Hulin, B. T., Gabbett, T. J., Lawson, D. W., Caputi, P., and Sampson, J. A. (2016). The acute: Chronic workload ratio predicts injury: High chronic workload may decrease injury risk in elite rugby league players. *British Journal of Sports Medicine*, *50*, 231–236.

Ijspeert, A. J., Nakanishi, J., Hoffmann, H., Pastor, P., and Schaal, S. (2013). Dynamical movement primitives: Learning attractor models for motor behaviors. *Neural Computation*, *25*, 328–373.

Lee, S. S. M., and Piazza, S. J. (2009). Built for speed: Musculoskeletal structure and sprinting ability. *Journal of Experimental Biology*, *212*, 3700–3707.

Morin, J. B., Edouard, P., and Samozino, P. (2011). Technical ability of force application as a determinant factor of sprint performance. *Medicine & Science in Sports & Exercise*, *43*(9), 1680–1688.

Morin, J., Gimenez, P., Edouard, P., Arnal, P., Jimenez-Reyes, P., Samozino, P., Brughelli, M., and Mendiguchia, J. (2015a). Sprint acceleration mechanics: The major role of hamstrings in horizontal force production. *Frontiers in Physiology*, *24*, 1–14.

Morin, J., Petrakos, G., Jimenez-Reyes, P., Brown, S. R., Samozino, P., and Cross, M. R. (2016). Very-heavy sled training for improving horizontal force output in soccer players. *International Journal of Sports Physiology and Performance*, *11*, 1–13.

Morin, J., Slawinski, J., Dorel, S., de villareal, E. S., Couturier, A., Samozino, P., Brughelli, M., and Rabita, G. (2015b). Acceleration capability in elite sprinters and ground impulse: Push more, brake less? *Journal of Biomechanics*, *48*, 3149–3154.

Opar, D., Williams, M., Timmins, R., Hickey, J., Duhig, S., and Shield, A. (2015). Eccentric hamstring strength and hamstring injury risk in australian footballers. *Medicine & Science in Sports & Exercise*, *47*, 857–865.

Rabita, G., Dorel, S., Slawinski, J., Saez-de-Villarreal, E., Couturier, A., Samozino, P., and Morin, J. B. (2015). Sprint mechanics in world-class athletes: A new insight into the limits of human locomotion. *Scandinavian Journal of Medicine & Science in Sports*, *25*, 583–594.

Samozino, P., Edouard, P., Sangnier, S., Brughelli, M., Gimenez, P., and Morin, J. B. (2014). Force-velocity profile: Imbalance determination and effect on lower limb ballistic performance. *International Journal of Sports Medicine*, *35*, 505–510.

Samozino, P., Morin, J., Hintzy, F., and Belli, A. (2008). A simple method for measuring force, velocity and power output during squat jump. *Journal of Biomechanics*, *41*, 2940–2945.

Samozino, P., Rabita, G., Dorel, S., Slawinski, J., Peyrot, N., Saez de Villarreal, E., and Morin, J. B. (2015). A simple method for measuring power, force, velocity properties, and mechanical effectiveness in sprint running. *Scandinavian Journal of Medicine & Science in Sports*, *26*, 648–658.

Samozino, P., Rejc, E., Di Prampero, P. E., Belli, A., and Morin, J. B. (2012). Optimal force-velocity profile in ballistic movements – Altius: Citius or fortius? *Medicine and Science in Sports and Exercise*, *44*, 313–322.

Slawinski, J., Termoz, N., Rabita, G., Guilhem, G., Dorel, S., Morin, J. B., and Samozino, P. (2017). How 100-m event analyses improve our understanding of world-class men's and women's sprint performance. *Scandinavian Journal of Medicine & Science in Sports*, *27*, 45–54.

Timmins, R. G., Ruddy, J. D., Presland, J., Maniar, N., Shield, A. J., Williams, M. D., and Opar, D. A. (2016). Architectural changes of the biceps femoris long head after concentric or eccentric training. *Medicine and Science in Sports and Exercise*, *48*, 499–508.

Verrall, G. M., Slavotinek, J. P., Barnes, P. G., Fon, G. T., and Spriggins, A. J. (2001). Clinical risk factors for hamstring muscle strain injury: A prospective study with correlation of injury by magnetic resonance imaging. *British Journal of Sports Medicine*, *35*, 435–439.

Zemper, E. (2005). Track and field injuries. *Medicine and Sport Science*, *48*, 138–151.

28
SPRINT CYCLING

Lynne Munroe and G. Gregory Haff

Introduction

World-standard track sprint cycling encompasses a number of events of different lengths and formats. Distinct from the track endurance events, sprint competition involves short, fixed-distance races where riders accelerate to maximal velocity from standing, rolling, or flying starts. The energetics and biomechanics of cycling have been extensively examined and reviewed in existing literature (Faria et al., 2005). However, the greater volume focuses on sub-maximal cycling where performance is delineated by efficiency and economy of movement (Faria et al., 2005). The distinct task demands of sprint cycling instead require forceful, explosive movement requiring the rider to deliver maximal mechanical power output (van Soest and Casius, 2000). Strength and conditioning work features highly in the training week of sprint cyclists, where, across the training year, athletes will seek to develop their strength capacities concurrently with on-the-bike training.

Athletic demands

In preparing riders for a variety of race conditions, the strength and conditioning professional must have an understanding of the specifics of each event. At world level, sprinters compete in rides against the clock, such as the flying 200m qualifier ride (elite times being around 10–11s) and individual 500m (women, ~34s) or 1000m (men, ~60s) time trial, as well as tactical rides against other opponents including the match sprint, where two riders challenge each other over three laps, and kierin, where six to eight riders are paced by motorbike up to the final three sprint laps. In these tactical contests the length and duration of the final all-out sprint is dependent on tactical approach. Competition day further demands fast recovery in order to sustain performance over multiple heats and rounds during the course of the event. Finally, the team sprint event uniquely highlights the varied conditioning requirements for sprint cycling. Held over two laps for women and three for men, the team members ride in-line, each taking the front for a single lap before pulling off. The event therefore requires distinct rider profiles, from the explosive, high force characteristics of a starter to the sustained speed-endurance qualities of the finisher (Craig and Norton, 2001). Given the unique demands of the various sprint disciplines, athletes may compete as an 'all-rounder' across the events or may become specialists in particular races. It is noteworthy that the wind-up and tactical laps of events additionally infers a substantial sub-maximal component to rider conditioning (Gardner et al., 2005).

Performance in sprint cycling is ultimately determined by the balance of power supply and demand (Martin et al., 2007). Power supplied is determined by the contractile properties of the contributing muscles mediated by fatigue, pedaling rate, and riding position (de Groot et al., 1994; van Soest and Casius, 2000). The distribution of energy sources for muscle contraction varies across the sprint events, with shorter distance events critically dependent on both the PCr and Glycolytic systems, while longer sprint distances involve a substantial aerobic contribution (Craig and Norton, 2001). Power demand includes overcoming air, rolling, and bearing/drive-train resistances as well as accounting for changes in kinetic and potential energy related to mass, gravity, inertia, and velocity. The impact of aerodynamics on cycling is emphatic, with the air resistance term accounting for a substantial 96% of available power when travelling at steady-state velocity on a flat surface (Martin et al., 2007). At the outset of the sprint, where velocity is low, riders adopt a standing position which increases power delivered to the bike, power surplus then affecting an increase in kinetic energy (Davidson et al., 2005). At maximal velocity, where air resistance terms dominate, riders maintain a seated and aerodynamic position. The tucked position, though compromising function of the musculature of the hip, reduces frontal area, ultimately benefiting performance (Faria et al., 2005). Critical trade-offs are, therefore, apparent in the ideal functional and anthropometric characteristics of riders. Sprint cyclists are more commonly mesomorphic, being heavier, stronger and with larger segmental girths than their endurance counterparts (McLean and Parker, 1989). However, increased cross-sectional area, while contributing to a greater capacity for force production, is alternatively detrimental through increasing aerodynamic drag (Dorel et al., 2005). Non-functional mass is similarly disadvantageous (Craig and Norton, 2001) and strength and conditioning professionals must be particularly aware of the impact of body composition on cycling performance.

The bike-rider interface ultimately governs the external mechanical power output that can be delivered. Three points of contact (feet, hands, and pelvis) provide a loci of force transfer to the system while constraining movement within fixed parameters established by bike set up and rider position. Bike geometry, rider kinematics, choice of gear, and crank length will dictate performance along the force-length-velocity relation of contributing muscles (de Groot et al., 1994). The use of fixed gears imposes a compromise between the force required to overcome inertial load and accelerate from low or zero velocity, and the leg speed required to attain peak velocity later in the sprint; a low gear will facilitate fast start times but establishes a higher, and potentially less effective, race cadence thereafter (Dorel et al., 2005). Notwithstanding a gear selection attuned to the athlete's physical attributes, performance over the course of a sprint demands function across a wide range of the power-force-velocity relationship. Elite riders will generate peak torques of over 250Nm in initiating a maximal acceleration and peak pedal rates of over 160rpm by the final stages of the sprint (Craig and Norton, 2001; Gardner et al., 2005). During acceleration, power will initially rise to a peak (around 2000–2500W in elite males and 1400–1600 in elite females), before declining towards maximum velocity and being sustained against ensuing fatigue during the velocity maintenance phase (Craig and Norton, 2001). Literature commonly ascribes optimal cadence, the pedal rate at which peak power is developed, as being between 120 and 130rpm (Martin et al., 2007). However, maximum external power output represents a compromise in the summated power-velocity relationships of contributing muscles and is therefore dependent on contractile characteristics and coordination pattern (van Soest and Casius, 2000). In fact, cadence at peak power has been acknowledged as an indirect measure of fibre-type distribution (Driss and Vandewalle, 2013). Since its value is uniquely specified, identifying the riders' optimal cadence provides valuable data to inform gear selection and is a key metric that is responsive to training adaptation (Dorel et al., 2005). Given that higher cadences are on the descending limb of the power-velocity curve, competition trends have supported a beneficial shift to bigger gearing and lower race cadences (Dorel et al., 2005). The use of higher gears is additionally supported by observations that fatigue may be influenced by the number of contractions required to complete the race distance (Tomas et al., 2010). Although a higher gear allows the rider to travel further with each pedal stroke, the increased force requirement further accentuates the need to develop strength capacity in the athlete.

Cycling power is delivered predominantly by the muscles spanning the hip, knee, and ankle, augmented by power generated by the upper body and transferred across the hip (Davidson et al., 2005). From approximately 0 to 180° of the crank cycle, triple extension of the three joints provides the primary power production for forward motion; during the recovery phase, around 180 to 360°, joint flexion predominates, returning the pedal to top dead centre as the contralateral limb extends (Driss and Vandewalle, 2013; Wozniak Timmer, 1991). Although changes in the relative contributions of muscles exist between sub-maximal and maximal cycling (Dorel et al., 2012), the coordinative patterns are largely similar; uniarticulate muscles primarily function in power production, while the biarticulate muscles more ostensibly contribute to control limb position and effective distribution of force around the crank (Driss and Vandewalle, 2013). However, while knee extension represents the greatest contribution to power development in sub-maximal conditions (Ericson, 1988), maximal cycling has been shown to be more critically dependent on hip extension power (Martin and Brown, 2009; McDaniel et al., 2014) and this should be emphasised in strength work. Additionally, where muscular work through the recovery phase is largely counteractive of limb weight in sub-maximal pedalling (Ericson, 1988), flexor action is seen to contribute significant positive work during sprinting (Driss and Vandewalle, 2013). Increased activity of the hip extensors, hip flexors, and knee flexors is observed in maximal as compared to sub-maximal cycling performance, with the knee flexors seen to play a significant role in muscle coordination and timing in order to maximise power (Dorel et al., 2012). These observations stress the need for strengthening of both the anterior and posterior kinetic chains. The ankle joint assumes a more critical role in transfer of limb segment energy to the cranks (Wozniak Timmer, 1991) and has been shown to critically limit external power delivery during conditions of fatigue (Martin and Brown, 2009). High values of torque are therefore demanded at the ankle and, in fact, isometric and eccentric contractile conditions are evident in the triceps surae complex during all-out pedalling (Driss and Vandewalle, 2013). Specific attention to the strength requirements at the ankle will therefore benefit power delivery at the pedal.

At any point in the crank cycle, force delivered normal to the crank is most effective in producing crank torque (de Groot et al., 1994). Movement control requires the rider not only to coordinate force production around the crank but to time muscle activation and relaxation appropriate to cadence. Peak force is optimally delivered between 80–110° of the crank cycle and studies of pedalling dynamics have observed retardation in the angle of peak pedal force concomitant to rising pedal rate (Samozino et al., 2007). In addition to an operational shift along the force-velocity (F-V) curve, electromyographical studies confirm that relative timing and coordination of muscle activity alters in response to increasing limb speed (Neptune et al., 1997). Electromechanical delay represents a relatively greater part of the pedal stroke at higher cadences, provoking suggestion that modified control strategies may be advancing onset timing in an attempt to maintain peak force delivery at optimal crank angles (Neptune et al., 1997). This so-called 'activation dynamics' hypothesis has been proposed as the primary muscle property limiting performance (Neptune and Kautz, 2001), and forward dynamics modelling has further inferred its importance in determining optimal cadence (van Soest and Casius, 2000). Although recent studies have disputed these findings (McGhie and Ettema, 2011), it is clear that the time available for force production is a limiting factor. The power phase of the pedal stroke may last significantly less than the time taken to develop peak force, and improving the rate of force development (RFD) and levels of force production during the early phases of the force-time curve is, therefore, paramount. To this end, improvements in excitation-relaxation kinetics and musculotendon stiffness can benefit cycling action (Driss and Vandewalle, 2013).

The interaction of bike and rider places additional demands on the physical development of sprint cyclists. Developing explosive force on a dynamic, moving platform exaggerates the need for control, balance, and internal stability. Multi-rider races also require a fast reaction time and spatial awareness. The impact of aerodynamics imposes the need to be both highly flexible and able to produce high forces in a compromised position. Athletes must, therefore, have good hip and thoracic mobility. The seated riding position involves a pronounced thoracolumbar flexion which effects recruitment of musculature and subsystems contributing to torso rigidity (Burnett et al., 2004). In contrast to the counter-rotational arm and torso action in running, handlebar grip somewhat restricts upper body movement, intensifying the demands on upper body and trunk strength in dealing with extreme torsional forces, and imposing the additional requirement for grip strength. In fact, sprint cycling technique strongly utilises a coordinated pulling action of the arm during the leg extension phase of the ipsilateral leg. At least 9% of total contribution to crank power in seated sprinting is derived from transmission across the hip (McDaniel et al., 2005), with increased cross-hip contribution being the most significant change in the biomechanics of power generation in the standing position (Davidson et al., 2005). The need to hold a fixed body position under fatigue further emphasises the importance of isometric and anti-rotational strength above the hip. While improving strength qualities of the lower limb will take precedence for sprint cycling, gym training should, additionally, include appropriate exercises to improve the strength and robustness of the trunk and upper body. Exercise selection to this end should aim to develop effective movement synergy and improve force-coupling through the kinetic chain supporting the goal intention of delivering maximal power.

Injury

Sprint cyclists have to be explosive, flexible, and able to produce and withstand high forces within a tightly constrained mechanical system. Musculoskeletal stress is, unsurprisingly, associated with the contact points, excessive flexion and extension of localised regions of the spine, and repetitive high forces through hip and knee extension (Dettori and Norvell, 2006). Given that the rider's position on the bike is central to their coordinative pattern, bike set-up is a primary extrinsic factor at the heart of overuse pain or injury (Sanner and O'Halloran, 2000). Inappropriate set-up can not only be detrimental to joint alignment but further affect range of motion and relative flexion and extension of the joints, potentially leading to excessive tissue tension or compression of joint structures (Wanich et al., 2007). However, intrinsic factors such as weakness, imbalance, and/or inflexibility through the kinetic chain will also impact riding position and pedalling mechanics, inducing inefficiencies which will be further exacerbated under fatigue (Sanner and O'Halloran, 2000). Examination of the rider's pedal stroke and position on the bike is a sensible place to start in examining causal factors in injury.

The shoe-pedal interface, or cleat, fundamentally establishes alignment of the lower limb. Inappropriate cleat positioning can lead to a number of issues associated with joint tracking (Gregor and Wheeler, 1994). While the cycling motion is predominantly in the sagittal plane, the importance of stability and alignment in the frontal and, to a lesser degree, transverse planes is crucial (Fang et al., 2015). Tightness and stiffness in muscle groups on either side of a joint can increase medial or lateral forces and contribute to poor joint alignment in the cycling motion (Sanner and O'Halloran, 2000). This will be exacerbated by underdevelopment of the balancing muscle groups.

Knee pain, particularly patella-femoral syndrome, is the most prevalent issue in cyclists and can generally be attributed to excessive loading, compressive forces, poor muscle balance, or bike fit problems (Wanich et al., 2007). Since the lower limb segments are constrained at the hip by the saddle and at the foot by the pedal, biomechanical inefficiencies and restrictions at these joints are often expressed in exaggerated lateral movement and/or poor tracking at the knee (Gregor and Wheeler, 1994). The Q-factor, or distance between the midline of each foot on the pedal, also interplays with pelvic width in establishing the position of the knee in relation to the superior and inferior joints. Knee drift in the frontal plane during pedal stroke may be equally representative of inappropriate bike fit or lack of strength and/or balance of the adductors and abductors, internal and external rotators (Sanner and O'Halloran, 2000). Excessive tension in the hamstrings and gastrocenemius-soleus complex is also contributory to injury predisposition and may be indicative of inappropriate conditioning of the posterior chain (Sanner and O'Halloran, 2000). At the hip joint, trochanteric bursitis, iliapsoas tendinitus, illiotibial band friction, and piriformis syndrome are common and may similarly be rectified by releasing muscular tension or altering saddle position (Wanich et al., 2007). Rigid cycling shoes, constraint of foot position, and poor pedalling action can further impose injury at the foot and ankle (Wanich et al., 2007). Excessive inversion/eversion or external/internal rotation of the foot will not only lead to ineffective mechanics, but can result in high stress at the Achilles tendon and joint tracking problems higher up the kinetic chain (Gregor and Wheeler, 1994).

Postural imbalances are particularly prevalent in cycling due to prolonged times in spinal flexion (Usabiaga et al., 1997). Both upper and lower cross syndrome (in particular, short-weak pectoralis major/minor and serratus anterior, and short-weak hip flexors) are commonly observed in riders. Off-bike training should therefore seek to maintain postural integrity through appropriate balance of anterior and posterior chains, thoracic strength and mobility, and maintaining appropriate length and strength of the hip flexors and extensors. Lower back pain is recurrent in cyclists and may be assumed to be related to the cycling posture (Burnett et al., 2004). Certainly, the incidence of lower back pain has been associated with the degree of lumbar flexion, with flexion strain disorders then alleviated by compensatory lumbar extension (Usabiaga et al., 1997). However, it is important to determine the underlying aetiology on an individual basis. Compromised position and mechanics of the lumbar-pelvic-hip complex, exacerbated by over-development of the knee extensors, may contribute to ineffective recruitment of the gluteal muscles and compensation by the lumbar extensors. Dysfunction or lack of sufficient co-contraction of the multifidus has also been related to incidence of lower back pain in cyclists while flexion-relaxation, where end range relaxation of the spinal erectors forces flexion torque to be supported by the spinal ligaments, has been observed in the cycling position (Burnett et al., 2004). Weak abdominal, paraspinal and pelvic stabilising muscles, and/or an ineffective stabilisation strategy, not only leads to poor movement control at the torso, but can further lead to altered pedalling mechanics and ineffective force transmission and distribution between the upper and lower extremities (Usabiaga et al., 1997). Back care, torso strength, and appropriate consideration for spinal loading patterns in cyclists are of critical importance.

Length-strength imbalances of the chest and thoracic areas, as well as at the glenohumeral joint through excessive internal rotation, can be associated with problems arising in the neck, upper trapezius, and scapulo-thoracic area (Dettori and Norvell, 2006). Again, maintaining and/or restoring balance through gym intervention will assist. In some cases, however, the origin may be inappropriate weight distribution in the upper body or an increased reliance on the contact point at the hands (Usabiaga et al., 1997). Nerve pain and tingling or numbness at the hands or other extremities may be similarly consistent with contact pressure or alternatively related to misalignment, muscle tension, or postural asymmetries (Dettori and Norvell, 2006). Strengthening of both the deep and superficial trunk and abdominal musculature will facilitate powerful leg drive without over-reliance on the contact points of the upper body to maintain support.

Although cycling is a comparatively low-impact activity, the high force demands of sprinting can affect skeletal injuries such as medial tibial stress syndrome or stress fractures (Wanich et al., 2007). Since the mechanical forces on the body are dominated by muscular rather than gravitational loading in cycling, off-bike training can take on increased importance for cyclists in maintaining skeletal health. Gym work is similarly important in the development of appropriate whole-body stiffness and stability. A holistic approach to creating and maintaining structural balance will help reduce injury predisposition while at the same time improve force coupling (Usabiaga et al., 1997).

Given the potential for high forces through the lower limb, communication with the cycling coach is essential to ensure appropriate training load to avoid injury. In particular, during heavy strength blocks, gym work may become more prevalent while on-bike work is adding load through gear selection and strength-based efforts. In all training phases, regular monitoring of the athlete's bike form and functional balance is essential. Having eliminated factors associated with bike fit and set-up, predisposition to injury can be minimised by ensuring appropriate strength and flexibility (Gregor and Wheeler, 1994). Further prehabilitation and management of causative factors may then be mediated by application of appropriate movement preparation, recovery, and tissue health regimes.

Fitness testing battery

To support the design of an effective sprint cycling specific strength and conditioning program, a strength diagnosis should be performed examining various aspects of the F-V curve (Figure 28.1). Central to this diagnosis is the use of lower body maximal strength and ballistic tests (Figure 28.2) which have strong relationships to sprint cycling performance.

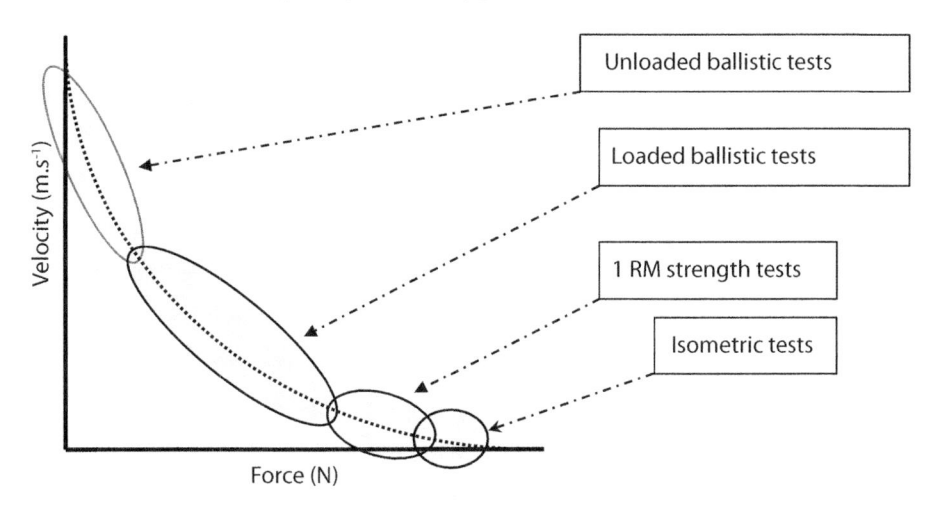

Figure 28.1 Force-velocity curve and strength diagnostic tests

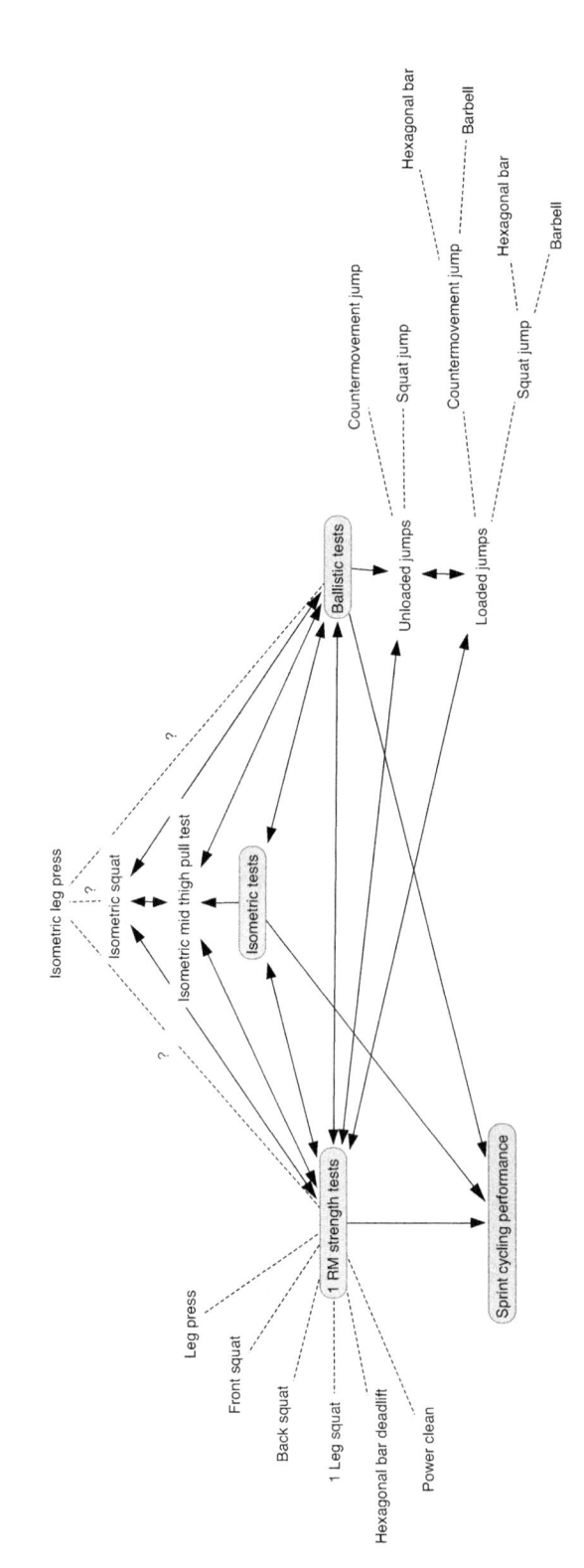

Figure 28.2 Strength diagnostic tests related to sprint cycling

Strength testing

Since power output is considered a strength-dependent behaviour (Jaric and Markovic, 2013), force generation capacity of the lower body underpins the rider's ability to accelerate the bicycle (Stone et al., 2004). Hence, maximal strength should be regularly assessed with either isometric or dynamic testing methods.

Isometric testing

Isometric testing is effective for quantifying an athlete's force-time profile (Haff et al., 2015) and can be applied to the characterisation of dynamic performance factors (Haff et al., 1997). Isometric performance capacity can be evaluated with single joint isometric muscle actions, such as the isometric leg extension, or multi-joint isometric muscle actions, such as the isometric mid-thigh pull (IMTP) (Haff et al., 2015), isometric squat (ISQT) (Nuzzo et al., 2008), or isometric leg press (ILP) (Zaras et al., 2016). Multi-joint isometric lower body tests are considered to be better assessment tools as data collected from them offer greater transferability to dynamic muscle actions and generally engage both the leg and hip extensors which are of particular importance to sprint cycling (Stone et al., 2004).

While originally designed to mirror the 2nd pull position for the assessment of weightlifters (Figure 28.3) (Haff et al., 1997), the IMTP test has been successfully applied to testing athletes from various sports and related to several sporting attributes (Haff et al., 1997; Stone et al., 2004). When performed with a standardised and systematic analysis procedure, this test has been shown to result in very reliable peak force (PF) and RFD data which can significantly inform training decisions (Haff et al., 2015).

In 2004, Stone et al. (2004) examined the relationships between IMTP force-time curve variables and accumulated sprint cycling times during a 333m sprint performed with a low (84 in.) or high gear (90 in.). Strong significant correlations ($r > 0.5$) were noted between isometric PF and sprint cycling performances regardless of gearing. Additionally, strong significant correlations were found between relative isometric PF and sprint cycling performance, while moderate correlations ($r > 0.3$) were found between the isometric peak RFD and sprint performance. More importantly the fastest sprinters exhibited higher isometric PFs (ES= 2.06; 95% CI= 0.54–3.26) and isometric peak RFD (ES= 0.72; 95% CI= −0.50–1.82). These data suggest that the IMTP test has the ability to differentiate performance capacities in sprint cyclists and has merit as part of a strength diagnostic testing battery.

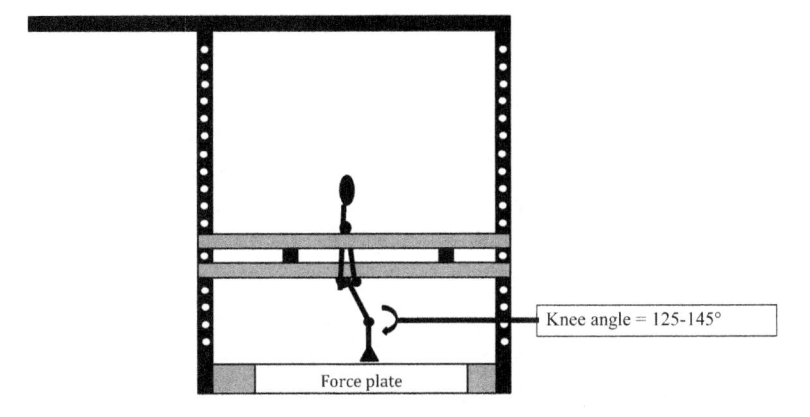

Figure 28.3 Isometric mid-thigh pull positioning schematic

The ISQT is also commonly used to investigate the force-time curve relationship to dynamic performance capacities (Nuzzo et al., 2008). This test has produced highly reliable data when knee angles of 90°, 120°, and 140° have been used with subjects experienced in the squat exercise (Nuzzo et al., 2008). While there are no known studies examining the relationship of the ISQT to sprint cycling performance, strong correlations have been found between the IMTP and the ISQT, and it is highly likely that this test would exhibit similar relationships to those seen with the IMTP (Nuzzo et al., 2008). However, it is important to acknowledge that moderate to very large effect size differences exist between the PF (g ≈ −0.51) and RFD (g = −4.17) generated with each test. More research on this test is, therefore, needed in order to fully understand its relationship to sprint cycling performance.

Given the prevalence of back issues within cyclists (Usabiaga et al., 1997), consideration should be given to spinal loading and compression in strength testing. Some concern exists over the increased risk of lower back injuries in IMPT and ISQT. Based upon the positioning of the load in the IMTP, when correctly performed, the risk of injury is marginal. Conversely, the ISQT has a greater risk of lower back injuries especially if the athlete has a history of back problems. As an alternative, the establishment of PF and RFD with the ILP performed at a knee angle of 120° and a hip angle of 140° has been seen to exhibit strong to very strong relationships with dynamic performances such as the back squat, hang power clean, and backwards overhead throw (Zaras et al., 2016). Although results have not been directly related to sprint cycling performance, this test may provide a useful alternative tool for assessing sprint cyclists' lower body force production capacity.

Regardless of methodology, essential guidelines must be adhered to in isometric force-time assessment. The isometric test itself should be conducted for a duration of ~3 seconds (McMaster et al., 2014), with ground reaction forces from force plates collected at a sampling rate >1000Hz in order to ensure reliability (Haff et al., 2015). The obtained force-time curve should then be divided into various bands to provide a more detailed picture of the athlete's force generating capacities (Haff et al., 2015). Specifically, forces at 50ms, 100ms, 150ms, 200 ms, and 250 ms and RFD between 0–50ms, 0–100ms, 0–150ms, 0–200ms, and 0–250 ms appear to give more valuable information to the strength and conditioning professional. The overall PF achieved during the test also provides key information about the athlete's maximal strength levels. Finally, independent bilateral assessment using two force plates during the IMTP, ISQT, or ILP can give limb specific force-time curve information that may help strength and conditioning professionals diagnose bilateral deficits which may be impeding or limiting performance and/or increasing the risk of lower limb injury.

Dynamic strength testing

Typically, maximal strength is assessed using repetition maximum testing (RM), with primary exercises such as the back squat, front squat, 1 leg squat, power clean, hexagonal bar deadlift, and leg press (both unilateral and bilateral test) commonly used to assess the cyclist's lower body strength development. Repetition maximum testing is completed with standardised procedures and undertaken at predetermined time points in order to re-calibrate training loads and to monitor and evaluate progress (Haff and Haff, 2012). One, three, or five RM tests may be used, depending on the exercise and training status of the athlete, with prediction equations then used to estimate other RM loads for programming (Haff and Haff, 2012). Overall there is minimal risk of injury with RM testing procedures when standardised protocols are applied and appropriate supervision by an accredited strength and conditioning professional is provided.

Alternative methods of establishing training loads and monitoring training and progress may be warranted with elite athletes. Given the demand for maximal limb speed in sprint cycling performance, tracking of movement velocity during strength work is of particular benefit. Recently, with the advent of accelerometer (Crewther et al., 2011), inertial sensor (Sato et al., 2015), and linear position transducer (Conceicao et al., 2016) technologies, it is now possible to create a force-velocity (F-V) profile from a series of dynamic lifts (e.g. squats) at percentages of 1RM or predetermined loads. Outcomes have further been used to estimate 1RM strength (Banyard et al., 2017; Conceicao et al., 2016). For example, Conceicao et al. (2016) have reported that by collecting the maximum instantaneous velocity (V_{max}) and mean propulsive velocity (MPV), training loads can be prescribed that are more specific to the cyclists current training status. While this theory is promising, recent research from Banyard et al. (2017) suggests there is significant variability in the estimated 1RM during squatting movements. Nonetheless, the F-V profile is of particular interest to sprint cyclists; indeed, on-the-bike testing will commonly assess the F-V profile across a range of pedalling cadences. However, the relationship between F-V profile assessed in dynamic lifting with that on a cycling ergometer has not been established, and more research is needed in order to determine the efficacy of using velocity based assessments in sprint cyclists.

Ballistic testing

One of the most important aspects of a strength diagnostic testing battery (Newton et al., 2011) is the use of ballistic testing methods to determine the force-time, F-V, and force-power profiles of the cyclist. In fact, quantification of impulse during ballistic movements has been shown to be a critical tool in evaluating an athlete's capacities. Assessment of these attributes typically uses combinations of loaded and unloaded countermovement vertical jumps (CMJ), with performance over a range of load conditions establishing the cyclist's high load or low load speed-strength (Newton et al., 2011).

The most common ballistic test used in a strength diagnostic battery is the unloaded CMJ (i.e. squat jump) which gives information about unloaded speed-strength capacities (Newton et al., 2011). In most instances the cyclist can handle the ground reaction forces that occur after landing from the achieved maximal height. However, the strength and conditioning professional should be aware that the predominance of concentric force conditions in the sporting movement means cyclists may have limited tolerance for high eccentric forces involved in landings. With cyclists who have lower back injuries or are at an increased risk of sustaining a lower back injury, it may be warranted to use an electronic braking system which reduces the eccentric forces undertaken during landing (McBride et al., 2002).

Due to concerns about back injury risk, strength and conditioning professionals working with sprint cyclists have explored other potential options for assessing loaded ballistic strength. For example, the use of the hexagonal bar (i.e. Trap-bar) jump squat (Turner et al., 2015) may be ideal, as the lift position is seen to reduce the peak lumbar spine moment as compared to traditional jump squat tests with a high bar position, while better approximating the unloaded CMJ position (Swinton et al., 2012). More research is needed in order to determine the optimal methodologies for using this test with track cyclists.

Unloaded and loaded concentric only squat jumps (SJ) (also known as the static jump) provide relevant information for sprint cyclists (Newton et al., 2011). The highest forces achieved during this test yield what has been termed the maximal dynamic strength (MDS) (Young et al., 1995), which has been shown to be an effective tool for predicting and differentiating levels of performance with athletes (Newton et al., 2011). Assessment of eccentric utilisation ratio (EUR) through comparison of CMJ and SJ performance may be revealing, but interpretation must be made with acknowledgement of the concentric nature of the sport. In this regard, calculation of RFD over distinct eccentric and concentric portions of the jumps may similarly provide valuable information about the cyclist's explosive strength potential (Laffaye and Wagner, 2013).

Periodisation and programming

Central to the ability to periodise the sprint cyclists' training is the annual training plan, which outlines the specific competitive goals and targets, the various periods and phases of training that will be used to guide the programming structures, and the monitoring tools and time points that will be implemented to track and make decisions around the cyclist's preparation. Conceptually, the annual plan is a global overview of the training and competitive path that the sprint cyclist will navigate for the targeted training year.

An example annual training plan is presented in Figure 28.4 and contains the basic competitive schedule as well as the strength training goals (Evans, 2016; Haff, 2016). It is important to note that the annual training plan should always be individualised based upon the sprint cyclist's training age, level of development, and specific needs established via performance and physiological testing with reference to the athlete and event demands. Sprint cyclists will include resistance training throughout the year, with the number of strength sessions in the training week being modulated based upon the specific phase of training and the models of periodisation employed.

When establishing the models of periodisation used for the development of sprint cyclists, several approaches can be employed. For example, a parallel model can be used in which multiple training factors are simultaneously developed with an equal overall focus (Figure 28.5). This approach tends to work well with youth and novice sprint cyclists, but with more advanced cyclists, compounding fatigue factors and/or lack of high enough training stress applied to any particular attribute can result in less than optimal performance adaptations.

One possible alternative approach is a sequential periodisation model (Figure 28.6) in which key training factors are sequenced in order to capitalise on delayed training effects from each targeted training factor (Haff, 2016).

In this model, key training factors are put into a sequence in order to capitalise on delayed training effects from each targeted training factor (Haff, 2016). For example, this model may commence with an aerobic or work capacity phase, a short transition phase of hypertrophy to support increase in cross-sectional areas, before progressing into general then specific strength development. The model would then peak towards competition with phases building power and finally speed.

	Month											
	March	April	May	June	July	August	September	October	November	December	January	February
Phase	Transition	Preparation						Competition				
Period	Transition	General physical preparation			Sports specific preparation			Main competition				
Competitions		No competitive events			Minor races	Minor races	Nationals champs	Europeans	World Cup #1	World Cup #2	World Cup #3	World Cup #4
Strength training goals	Recover from previous annual plan	1. ↑Muscle cross sectional area 2. ↑Work capacity 3. ↑ Fatigue resistance			1. ↑Maximal strength 2. ↑ Maximal power 3. ↑ Maximal speed of movement			1. Optimise and maintain strength and power 2. ↑Maximal speed of movement				
Specificity		Least specific			More specific			Most specific				

Note: Adapted based upon Evans (2016) and Haff (2016).

Figure 28.4 Example annual training plan for a sprint cyclist

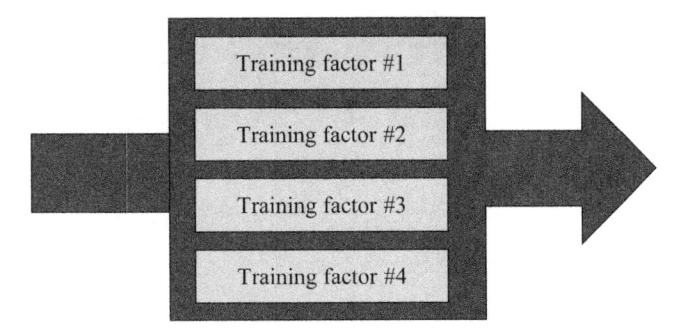

Figure 28.5 Parallel periodisation model

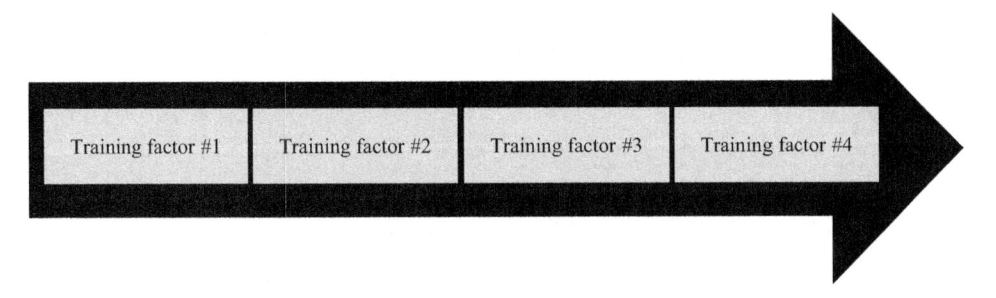

Figure 28.6 Sequential periodisation model

While this model has a number of merits, it is possible that this uni-focal sequential approach to training may be handicapped by the involution (i.e. decay of adaptation) of training factors that are not maintained during specific periods of training. Additionally, Francis (2008) has noted that this approach can result in system stiffness that may hinder speed development in sprint athletes.

An alternative approach may be a periodisation model which capitalises on the benefits of both sequential and parallel models of periodisation. First presented in 1995, Zatsiorsky's emphasis model is based upon the premise that training factors could fall into three categories 1) Stimulating, 2) Retaining (i.e. maintenance) and 3) Detraining. With this type of model the key attributes associated with sprint cycling performance can be trained to varying degrees at the same time (i.e. vertically integrated) and then sequenced over time (i.e. horizontally sequenced). Fundamentally, while some factors are being targeted as a primary emphasis other factors may receive only minimal attention in the training plan in order to maintain or slow their decay, whilst some factors are not emphasised at all (Figure 28.7). Conceptually, in this model the primary emphasis targets can echo those seen in the sequential model but be adapted to integrate several other training factors simultaneously.

For example, using the annual training plan presented in Figure 28.4, a basic emphasis model of training can be developed (Figure 28.8). After the completion of the previous annual training plan a 2–4 week transition phase will be implemented prior to initiating the preparation phase. Early in the preparation phase, the athlete will undergo a general physical preparation period (GPP) with the primary training target of regaining muscle mass (i.e. ↑Muscle Cross Sectional Area) that may have been lost during the previous competition phase (Evans, 2016). Once this has occurred the emphasis then shifts to increasing muscle mass in order to establish a foundation for subsequent training periods. Even though it is important to increase muscle mass, it is equally important to be mindful not to excessively develop upper body mass during this phase of training.

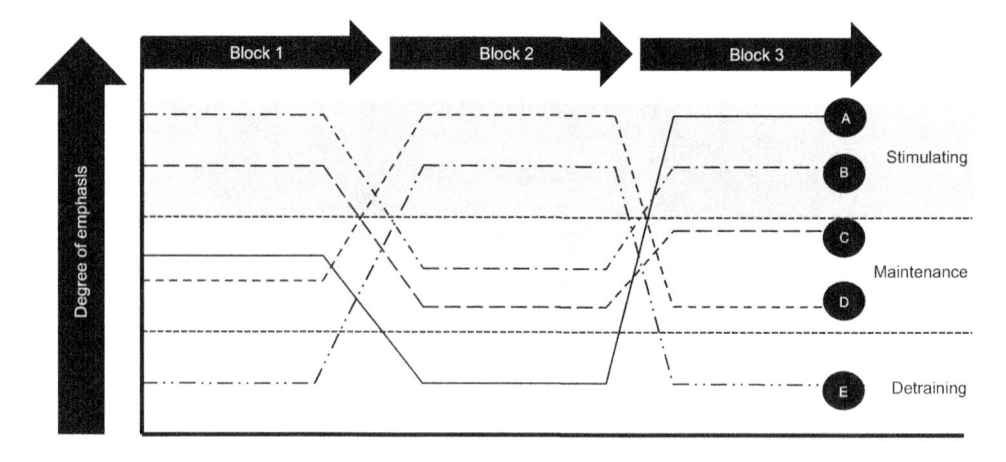

Figure 28.7 A five factor emphasis model of periodisation

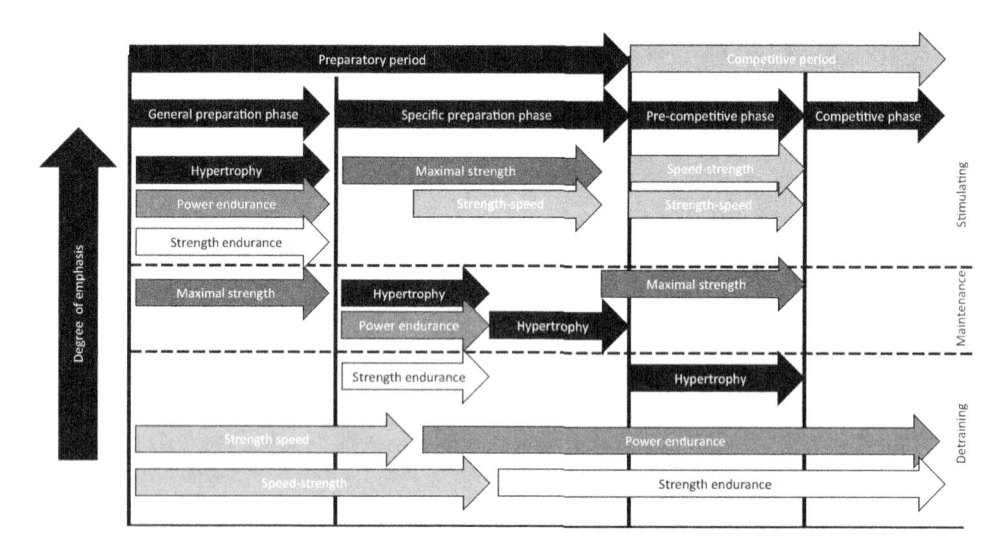

Figure 28.8 Example emphasis model for resistance training for track cycling (sprinters)

Typically, the GPP phase lasts 8–12 weeks, but will be modified depending upon the cyclist's training history and competitive schedule (Evans, 2016) or if used as a bridging phase in a long competitive season. Cyclists with a longer training history will typically have a shorter GPP period when compared to less experienced cyclists. In order to accomplish the training goals for this phase, the cyclist will typically perform 3 days per week of high volume load (i.e. high total work) strength training. An example model this period may allot 65–70% of the total completed repetitions to hypertrophy training, whilst 15–20% of the repetitions would target strength-endurance development and the remaining 10–15% would focus on power-endurance (Table 28.1).

Table 28.1 Example 4 week mesocycle for the general preparatory phase (i.e. hypertrophy focus)

Day	Exercises	Sets	Reps	Training target	Week 1 % RM	Week 2 % RM	Week 3 % RM	Week 4 % RM
1	Power clean	3	8/2	Power-endurance	80–85% 2RM	85–90% 2RM	90–95% 2RM	78–83% 2RM
	Back squat	3	8	Hypertrophy	75–80% 8RM	80–85% 8RM	85–90% 8RM	73–77% 8RM
	1-leg squat*	3	10	Hypertrophy	75–80% 10RM	80–85% 10RM	85–90% 10RM	73–77% 10RM
	Clean grip Romanian deadlift	3	10	Strength-endurance	75–80% 10RM	80–85% 10RM	85–90% 10RM	73–77% 10RM
	Pull ups	3	10	Hypertrophy	BWT	BWT +10kg	BWT +10kg	BWT
	Abdominal work	3	25	Auxiliary				
2	Trap bar jump squat	3	8/2	Power-endurance	75–80% 2RM	80–85% 2RM	85–90% 2RM	73–77% 2RM
	¼ front squat	3	8	Hypertrophy	75–80% 8RM	80–85% 8RM	85–90% 8RM	73–77% 8RM
	Incline bench press	3	10	Hypertrophy	75–80% 10RM	80–85% 10RM	85–90% 10RM	73–77% 10RM
	Prone row	3	10	Hypertrophy	75–80% 10RM	80–85% 10RM	85–90% 10RM	73–77% 10RM
	Seated good morning	3	10	Strength-endurance	70–75% 10RM	75–80% 10RM	80–85% 10RM	68–73% 10RM
	Dips	3	10	Hypertrophy	BWT	BWT + 10kg	BWT + 10kg	BWT
	Abdominal work	3	25	Auxiliary				
3	Power snatch	3	8/2	Power-endurance	70–75% 2RM	75–80% 2RM	80–85% 2RM	68–73% 2RM
	Back squat	3	8	Hypertrophy	70–75% 8RM	75–80% 8RM	80–85% 8RM	68–73% 8RM
	1-leg squat*	3	10	Hypertrophy	70–75% 10RM	75–80% 10RM	80–85% 10RM	68–73% 10RM
	Snatch grip Romanian deadlift	3	10	Strength-endurance	75–80% 10RM	80–85% 10RM	85–90% 10RM	73–77% 10RM
	Chin ups	3	10	Hypertrophy	BWT	BWT + 10kg	BWT + 10kg	BWT
	Abdominal work	3	25	Auxiliary				

Note: * For this exercise, it would be 3 sets of 10 for each leg and the back leg elevated. 6/2 = cluster sets of 6 total repetitions broken into 3 clusters of 2 separated by 20 sec recovery between clusters. Inter-set rest intervals: Power-endurance = 3 minutes, Hypertrophy = 2 minutes, Strength endurance = 2 minutes, auxiliary = 2 minutes. RM = repetition maximum. BWT = body weight.

When constructing the microcycle, it is important to vary workloads across the training week in order to combat accumulated fatigue as well as target various aspects of the load-power spectrum (Haff, 2016). There are two primary ways to reduce the volume load: 1) reduce the load lifted (↓kg) or 2) decrease the number of sets performed (↓sets). When planning lighter training days, it is also important to make sure the resistance training load reduction is complemented by the other training factors associated with the cyclist's development in order to ensure a true reduction in training load for the day. It is also important that periodically that there are unloading or recovery microcycles interspersed within the mesocycle. Typically, this would occur once every 4–6 weeks.

As the cyclist moves into the specific preparatory phase (SPP), the initial primary emphasis is centred on the development of maximal strength, with a secondary focus on the initial development of strength-speed (Figure 28.8). The early part of this phase may contain 3 sessions of strength training per week, whilst the later part of the period typically would only have 2 days per week for resistance training activities. Maximal strength will typically be developed with exercises such as heavy squatting, hex-bar deadlifting, the pulling derivatives of weightlifting (i.e. clean and snatch pulls) or pressing movements with a variety of training intensities ranging from 70–110% of 1RM (Table 28.2).

The secondary emphasis would be centred on the development of strength-speed, where strength is still targeted but some emphasis on increasing the RFD is focused on with exercises that use intensities between 30–70% of 1RM. With these exercises, it may be warranted to utilise strength-power potentiation complexes (SPPCs) and or cluster sets in order to maximise movement velocity and RFD. An example model of this period may allot 42% of the total repetitions to maximal strength targets, 32% to focus on strength-speed, and 25% to maintain hypertrophy (Table 28.3).

Table 28.2 Targeted training methods

	Strength endurance	Maximal strength	Strength-speed	Speed-strength
Target	Increasing cross-sectional area	Increasing maximal strength	Increasing maximal strength and rate of force development	Maximise rate of force development Maintain maximal strength
Repetition per sets	8–12	4–6	2–4	2–4
Number of sets	3–6	3–6	3–6	3–6
Intensities	55–75% of 1RM	80–90% of 1RM	70–90% of 1RM for weightlifting exercises 90–110% 1RM for weightlifting pulling derivatives 75–90% for non-weightlifting exercises 30–70% of 1RM for ballistic exercises	70–80% of 1RM for weightlifting exercises 70–110% 1RM for weightlifting pulling derivatives 40–60% of 1RM for weightlifting derivatives (i.e. jump shrug, hang high pull) 0–55% for ballistic exercises
Methods used	Traditional sets Standard cluster sets	Traditional sets Traditional cluster sets Ascending cluster sets	Traditional sets Undulating cluster sets Ascending cluster sets Strength-power potentiation complexes	Traditional sets Undulating cluster sets Strength-power Potentiation complexes
Technology used			Velocity of movement may be monitored with accelerometers or linear position transducers	Velocity of movement may be monitored with accelerometers or linear position transducers

Note: RM = repetition maximum

Table 28.3 Example 3 week mesocycle for the early part of a specific preparatory phase (i.e. maximal strength focus)

	Exercises	Sets	Reps	Training target	Method	Week 1 % RM	Week 2 % RM	Week 3 % RM
1	Back squat	3	6	Maximal strength	Traditional sets	80–85% 6RM	85–90% 6RM	90–95% 6RM
	Trap-bar jump squat	3	(4/2)	Strength-speed	Cluster sets	70–75% 2RM	75–80% 2RM	80–85% 2RM
	Uni-lateral leg press (each leg)	3	5	Maximal strength	Traditional sets	75–80% 5RM	80–85% 5RM	85–90% 5RM
	Prone row	3	6	Maximal strength	Traditional sets	80–85% 6RM	85–90% 6RM	90–95% 6RM
	Glute ham raise	2	8	Hypertrophy	Traditional sets	70–75% 10RM	75–80% 10RM	80–85% 10RM
	Abdominal work	3	25	Auxiliary				
2	Power clean	5	(4/2)	Strength-speed	Cluster sets	75–80% 2RM	80–85% 2RM	85–90% 2RM
	Clean grip jump shrug**	5	(4/2)	Strength-speed	Cluster sets	70–75% 2RM	75–80% 2RM	80–85% 2RM
	Trap-bar deadlift	3	6	Maximal strength	Traditional	80–85% 6RM	85–90% 6RM	90–95% 6RM
	Snatch grip Romanian deadlift	3	6	Maximal strength	Traditional	70–75% 6RM	75–80% 6RM	80–85% 6RM
	Dips	2	8	Hypertrophy	Traditional	BWT + 10kg	BWT + 15kg	BWT + 10kg
	Abdominal work	3	25	Auxiliary				
3	¼ back squat + box jump	3	5+4	Maximal strength + strength-speed	Traditional	80–85% 5RM	85–90% 5RM	90–95% 5RM
	Hang power clean	5	4	Strength-speed	Traditional	70–75% 4RM	75–80% 4RM	80–85% 4RM
	Bench press	3	6	Maximal strength	Traditional	70–75% 6RM	75–80% 6RM	80–85% 6RM
	Chin-ups	2	8	Hypertrophy	Traditional	BWT + 10kg	BWT + 15kg	BWT + 10kg
	Hyper-extensions	2	8	Hypertrophy	Traditional	BWT + 10kg	BWT + 15kg	BWT + 10kg
	Abdominal work	3	25	Auxiliary				

Note: * For this exercise, it would be 3 sets of 5 for each leg and the back leg elevated.

** For this exercise, use a load as a percentage of best power clean. 3/1 = cluster sets of 3 total repetitions broken into 1 repetitions separated by 20–30 sec recovery between reps. Inter-set rest intervals: Maximal Strength = 2–3 minutes; strength-speed = 3–4 minutes; hypertrophy = 2 minutes; Auxiliary = 2 minutes. 5+4 = 5 repetitions for the first exercise in the complex and 4 repetitions for the second exercise in the complex. RM = repetition maximum, BWT = Body weight.

Table 28.4 Example 3 week mesocycle for the pre-competitive phase (i.e. speed-strength focus)

	Exercises	Sets	Reps	Training target	Method	Week 1 % RM	Week 2 % RM	Week 3 % RM
1	Trap-bar deadlift + jump squat	3	3+3	Max strength + speed-strength	Strength power potentiation complex	70–75% 3RM + 0% RM	70–75% 3RM + 0% RM	70–75% 3RM + 0% RM
	Power clean	3	2	Strength-speed	Traditional	60–65% 2RM	65–70% 2RM	70–75% 2RM
	Jump shrug	3	3	Speed-strength	Traditional	40–45% 3RM	45–50% 3RM	50–55% 3RM
	Clean grip Romanian deadlift	3	3	Maximal strength	Traditional	70–75% 3RM	75–80% 3RM	80–85% 3RM
	Abdominal work	3	25	Auxiliary				
2	Trap-bar jump squat	3	3	Strength-speed	Traditional	55–60% 3RM	60–65% 3RM	65–70% 3RM
	Clean pull (from thigh)★★	3	3	Speed-strength	Traditional	85–90% 3RM	90–95% 3RM	95–100% 3rm
	Push press	3	3	Strength-speed	Traditional	55–60% 3RM	60–65% 3RM	65–70% 3RM

Note: ★★ For this exercise, use a load as a percentage of best power clean. 3+3 = 3 repetitions of each of the allotted exercises in the complex. Inter-set rest intervals: strength-speed = 3–4 minutes; speed-strength = 3–4 minutes; maximal strength = 2–3 minutes.

As the athlete approaches the competitive period, they will move into the pre-competitive phase where the two training targets are speed-strength and strength-speed, with maximal strength being maintained with the use of higher geared cycling activities (Evans, 2016). In this period of training there will be an increased use of SPPCs and cluster sets with ballistic exercises in order to maximise RFD and movement velocity. Typically, this period of training contains 1–2 days per week of strength training activities with the vast majority of the resistance training activities being designed to optimise RFD and movement velocity. An example model of this period may allot 53% of the total repetitions to target speed-strength, 29% to focus on strength-speed, and 18% to maintain maximal strength (Table 28.4).

The main competitive period is a highly variable period that is designed to transfer the strength gains achieved in the gym into speed on the bike (Evans, 2016). Typically, this time period uses a significantly reduced resistance training focus and as the athlete moves into competition resistance training is completely removed in order to facilitate recovery and performance optimisation (Evans, 2016). Evans (2016) suggests that removal of strength training occur between 7 and 28 days before the competition, depending upon its overall importance and the individual cyclist's ability to retain the physical qualities established by the resistance training program. The cyclist's training history will impact the ability to retain these qualities, with those with longer training histories having a significantly greater strength reserve to draw upon and transfer to cycling performance. Central to this time period is the use of on the bike strength work in which gear ratios can be modified to maintain strength levels (Evans, 2016). Additionally, depending upon the density of competitions in the main competitive period, additional mini-blocks of resistance training can be employed in order to enhance the maintenance of key physical qualities (Evans, 2016). The exact structure and placement of these training blocks will largely be dictated by the competition schedule and the importance placed upon the competitions by the cycling coaches.

Conclusions

Track cycling is a sport which requires the cyclist to apply large forces in a rapid manner in order to propel the bicycle at high velocities. The ability to effectively develop forces requires the systematic development of specific strength qualities. To effectively manage the development of these characteristics it is important to understand the sport's requirements and injury profile as well as perform appropriate fitness testing. Coupling this information with the athlete's competitive schedule allows the strength and conditioning professional to be able to appropriately periodise the training plan in order to optimise performance at key points in the competitive calendar.

References

Banyard HG, Nosaka K, and Haff GG. Reliability and validity of the load-velocity relationship to predict the 1RM back squat. *Journal of Strength and Conditioning Research* 31: 1897–1904, 2017.

Burnett AF, Cornelius MW, Dankaerts W, and O'Sullivan PB. Spinal kinematics and trunk muscle activity in cyclists: A comparison between healthy controls and non-specific chronic low back pain subjects-a pilot investigation. *Manual Therapy* 9: 211–219, 2004.

Conceicao F, Fernandes J, Lewis M, Gonzalez-Badillo JJ, and Jimenez-Reyes P. Movement velocity as a measure of exercise intensity in three lower limb exercises. *Journal of Sports Sciences* 34: 1099–1106, 2016.

Craig NP and Norton KI. Characteristics of track cycling. *Sports Medicine* 31: 457–468, 2001.

Crewther BT, Kilduff LP, Cunningham DJ, Cook C, Owen N, and Yang GZ. Validating two systems for estimating force and power. *International Journal of Sports Medicine* 32: 254–258, 2011.

Davidson CJ, Horscroft RD, McDaniel J, Tomas A, and Hunter EL. The biomechanics of standing and seating maximal cycling power. *Medicine & Science in Sports & Exercise* 37: S393, 2005.

de Groot G, Welbergen E, Clijsen L, Clarijs J, Cabri J, and Antonis J. Power, muscular work, and external forces in cycling. *Ergonomics* 37: 31–42, 1994.

Dettori NJ and Norvell DC. Non-traumatic bicycle injuries. *Sports Medicine* 36: 7–18, 2006.

Dorel S, Guilhem G, Couturier A, and Hug F. Adjustment of muscle coordination during an all-out sprint cycling task. *Medicine and Science in Sports and Exercise* 44: 2154–2164, 2012.

Dorel S, Hautier CA, Rambaud O, Rouffet D, Van Praagh E, Lacour JR, and Bourdin M. Torque and power-velocity relationships in cycling: Relevance to track sprint performance in world-class cyclists. *International Journal of Sports Medicine* 26: 739–746, 2005.

Driss T and Vandewalle H. The measurement of maximal (anaerobic) power output on a cycle ergometer: A critical review. *BioMed Research International* 2013: 589361, 2013.

Ericson MO. Mechanical muscular power output and work during ergometer cycling at different work loads and speeds. *European Journal of Applied Physiology and Occupational Physiology* 57: 382–387, 1988.

Evans M. Strength and conditioning for cycling. In: *Strength and Conditioning for Sports Performance*. I Jeffreys, J Moody, eds. Abingdon, Oxon: Routledge, 2016, pp. 642–646.

Fang Y, Fitzhugh EC, Crouter SE, Gardner JK, and Zhang S. Effects of workloads and cadences on frontal plane knee biomechanics in cycling. *Medicine and Science in Sports and Exercise* 48: 260–266, 2015.

Faria EW, Parker DL, and Faria IE. The science of cycling: Factors affecting performance – Part 2. *Sports Medicine* 35: 313–337, 2005.

Francis C. *Structure of Training for Speed*. CharlieFrancis.com, 2008.

Gardner AS, Martin DT, Barras M, Jenkins DG, and Hahn AG. Power output demands of elite track sprint cycling. *International Journal of Performance Analysis in Sport* 5: 149–154, 2005.

Gregor RJ and Wheeler JB. Biomechanical factors associated with shoe/pedal interfaces. *Sports Medicine* 17: 117–131, 1994.

Haff GG. The essentials of periodisation. In: *Strength and Conditioning for Sports Performance*. I Jeffreys, J Moody, eds. Abingdon, Oxon: Routledge, 2016, pp. 404–448.

Haff GG and Haff EE. Resistance training program design. In: *Essentials of Periodization*. MH Malek, JW Coburn, eds. Champaign, IL: Human Kinetics, 2012, pp. 359–401.

Haff GG, Ruben RP, Lider J, Twine C, and Cormie P. A comparison of methods for determining the rate of force development during isometric midthigh clean pulls. *Journal of Strength and Conditioning Research* 29: 386–395, 2015.

Haff GG, Stone MH, O'Bryant HS, Harman E, Dinan CN, Johnson R, and Han KH. Force-time dependent characteristics of dynamic and isometric muscle actions. *Journal of Strength and Conditioning Research* 11: 269–272, 1997.

Jaric S and Markovic G. Body mass maximizes power output in human jumping: A strength-independent optimum loading behavior. *European Journal of Applied Physiology* 113: 2913–2923, 2013.

Laffaye G and Wagner P. Eccentric rate of force development determines jumping performance. *Computer Methods in Biomechanics and Biomedical Engineering* 16(Suppl 1): 82–83, 2013.

Martin JC and Brown NA. Joint-specific power production and fatigue during maximal cycling. *Journal of Biomechanics* 42: 474–479, 2009.

Martin JC, Davidson CJ, and Pardyjak ER. Understanding sprint-cycling performance: The integration of muscle power, resistance, and modeling. *International Journal of Sports Physiology and Performance* 2: 5–21, 2007.

McBride JM, Triplett-McBride T, Davie A, and Newton RU. The effect of heavy- vs. light-load jump squats on the development of strength, power, and speed. *Journal of Strength and Conditioning Research* 16: 75–82, 2002.

McDaniel J, Behjani NS, Elmer SJ, Brown NA, and Martin JC. Joint-specific power-pedaling rate relationships during maximal cycling. *Journal of Applied Biomechanics* 30: 423–430, 2014.

McDaniel J, Gidley LD, Aleksandar T, Hunter EL, Grisham JD, McNeil JM, Carroll C, Thompson FT, Davidson CJ, and Horscroft RD. Joint power distribution at 60, 90, and 120 rpm during seated maximal cycling. *Medicine and Science in Sports and Exercise* 37: S123, 2005.

McGhie D and Ettema G. The effect of cadence on timing of muscle activation and mechanical output in cycling: On the activation dynamics hypothesis. *Journal of Electromyography and Kinesiology* 21: 18–24, 2011.

McLean BD and Parker AW. An anthropometric analysis of elite Australian track cyclists. *Journal of Sports Sciences* 7: 247–255, 1989.

McMaster D, Gill N, Cronin J, and McGuigan M. A brief review of strength and ballistic assessment methodologies in sport. *Sports Medicine* 44: 603–623, 2014.

Neptune RR and Kautz SA. Muscle activation and deactivation dynamics: The governing properties in fast cyclical human movement performance? *Exercise and Sport Sciences Reviews* 29: 76–80, 2001.

Neptune RR, Kautz SA, and Hull ML. The effect of pedaling rate on coordination in cycling. *Journal of Biomechanics* 30: 1051–1058, 1997.

Newton RU, Cormie P, and Cardinale M. Principles of athlete testing. In: *Strength and Conditioning: Biological and Practical Applications*. M Cardinale, RU Newton, K Nosaka, eds. Chichester, West Sussex, UK: Wiley-Blackwell, 2011, pp. 255–267.

Nuzzo JL, McBride JM, Cormie P, and McCaulley GO. Relationship between countermovement jump performance and multijoint isometric and dynamic tests of strength. *Journal of Strength and Conditioning Research* 22: 699–707, 2008.

Samozino P, Horvais N, and Hintzy F. Why does power output decrease at high pedaling rates during sprint cycling? *Medicine and Science in Sports and Exercise* 39: 680–687, 2007.

Sanner W and O'Halloran W. The biomechanics, etiology, and treatment of cycling injuries. *Journal of the American Podiatric Medical Association* 90: 354–376, 2000.

Sato K, Beckham GK, Caroll K, Bazyler CD, Sha A, and Haff GG. Validity of wireless device measuring velocity of resistance exercises. *Journal of Trainology* 4: 15–18, 2015.

Stone MH, Sands WA, Carlock J, Callan S, Dickie D, Daigle K, Cotton J, Smith SL, and Hartman M. The importance of isometric maximum strength and peak rate-of-force development in sprint cycling. *Journal of Strength and Conditioning Research* 18: 878–884, 2004.

Swinton PA, Stewart AD, Lloyd R, Agouris I, and Keogh JW. Effect of load positioning on the kinematics and kinetics of weighted vertical jumps. *Journal of Strength and Conditioning Research* 26: 906–913, 2012.

Tomas A, Ross EZ, and Martin JC. Fatigue during maximal sprint cycling: Unique role of cumulative contraction cycles. *Medicine & Science in Sports & Exercise* 42: 1364–1369, 2010.

Turner TS, Tobin DP, and Delahunt E. Optimal loading range for the development of peak power output in the hexagonal barbell jump squat. *Journal of Strength and Conditioning Research* 29: 1627–1632, 2015.

Usabiaga J, Crespo R, Iza I, Aramendi J, Terrados N, and Poza J-J. Adaptation of the lumbar spine to different positions in bicycle racing. *Spine* 22: 1965–1969, 1997.

van Soest AJ and Casius LJ. Which factors determine the optimal pedaling rate in sprint cycling? *Medicine and Science in Sports and Exercise* 32: 1927–1934, 2000.

Wanich T, Hodgkins C, Columbier JA, Muraski E, and Kennedy JG. Cycling injuries of the lower extremity. *Journal of the American Academy of Orthopaedic Surgeons* 15: 748–756, 2007.

Wozniak Timmer CA. Cycling biomechanics: A literature review. *Journal of Orthopaedic and Sports Physical Therapy* 14: 106, 1991.

Young WB, Pryor JF, and Wilson GJ. Effect of instructions on characteristics of countermovement and drop jump performance. *Journal of Strength and Conditioning Research* 9: 232–236, 1995.

Zaras ND, Stasinaki AN, Methenitis SK, Krase AA, Karampatsos GP, Georgiadis GV, Spengos KM, and Terzis GD. Rate of force development, muscle architecture, and performance in young competitive track and field throwers. *Journal of Strength and Conditioning Research* 30: 81–92, 2016.

Zatsiorsky VM. Timing in strength training. In: *Science and Practice of Strength Training*. Champaign, IL: Human Kinetics, 1995, pp. 108–135.

29
TRIATHLON

Ian Pyper, Emma Deakin and Andrew Shaw

Introduction to the sport

Triathlon originated in France in the 1920s and has become one of the fastest growing sports in the world because of its accessibility, challenging nature, and sense of achievement on completion of a 'life challenge'. It has now developed into a genuine worldwide sport with elite and challenge based events on all five continents across all of the different distances and levels of the sporting continuum. Its popularity at the elite level this was recently demonstrated in the Rio 2016 Olympic Games, where there were 31 nations from all continents represented by the 55 competing athletes in both the men's and women's races.

The sport of triathlon consists of the integration of three sports with two transition periods in a race from point A to B. Depending on the triathlon event they will either be subject to drafting or non-drafting rules. Drafting is the act of exploiting the slip stream created by riding in a group, as seen in professional cycling races; whereas non-drafting is based on an individual time trial format where an athlete is not allowed to use other competitors to aide their performance. Whether it is a drafting or non-drafting event, there are many ways that a person can complete a triathlon or be involved in a specific part of it, either at an elite level, age group championship, or as a fun/team challenge. These events include the following:

- Long course triathlon (governed by the World Triathlon Corporation)
    - 140.6 miles – Ironman: Swim 2.4 miles, Bike 112 miles, Run 26.2 miles
    - 70.3 miles – Half Ironman: Swim 1.2 miles, Bike 56 miles, Run 13.1 miles
- Short course triathlon (governed by the International Triathlon Union; www.triathlon.org)
    - Olympic distance: Swim 1.5 km, Bike 40 km, Run 10 km
    - Sprint: Swim 0.75 km, Bike 20 km, Run 5 km
    - Super sprint: Swim 0.25–0.4 km, Bike 5–20 km, Run 1.5–5 km
    - Team based relay
        - At an elite level each member of the team completes a full super sprint triathlon before handing over to their next team mate.
        - Relays are often used as part of a challenge or fun event where a different competitor completes a leg each, allowing an increased level of accessibility.

- Paratriathlon (www.triathlon.org/paratriathlon)
    - First Paralympic inclusion in Rio 2016
    - Classifications are as follows:
    - Paratriathlon HC (PTHC) – Wheelchair users
    - Paratriathlon S2 (PTS2) – Severe impairments
    - Paratriathlon S3 (PTS3) – Significant impairments
    - Paratriathlon S4 (PTS4) – Moderate impairments
    - Paratriathlon S5 (PTS5) – Mild impairments
    - Paratriathlon Visual Impaired (PTVI) – Total or partial visual impairment

The involvement of sports science in the sport has developed in a number of avenues, including training prescription (after laboratory or field based testing), training load monitoring and strength and conditioning as an injury prevention and performance enhancement intervention, using traditional gym based weight training, yoga and pilates.

Athletic demands of triathlon

Course demands

All triathlons from a sprint distance up to ultra-events are classed as endurance events. Even though the duration of effort can differ from ~1 hour to ~8 hours, the endurance nature of these events results in several key physiological and biomechanical demands that are consistent across all race distances. The following sections highlight these core physiological and biomechanical demands in triathlon, in addition to key considerations that are event specific to either Olympic distance (Short course; SC) or Ironman events (Long course; LC).

Elite triathlon races are held on temporary street courses, often being constructed based on spectator and logistical requirements within each venue. For all distances, the swim leg is completed in open water, varying between sea and fresh water, and pontoon and beach starts, depending on location. When water temperatures drop below 21.9°C, athletes are allowed to wear wet suits, which can have a positive effect on performance by increasing buoyancy and inducing less frontal resistance. The swim in SC events is characterised by an initial high intensity sprint (typically 200–400m) to the first course marker buoy, followed by a more sustained aerobic effort for the remainder of the leg. LC swims often follow a similar pattern, but both the initial high intensity effort and the remainder of the leg are performed at reduced exercise intensity.

In SC events, the bike leg is commonly comprised of short (~5km), technical 'crit' style laps, often with dead turns and short hill climbs. Consequently, athletes incur many periods of acceleration and deceleration, with the resulting metabolic demand following a stochastic profile. It is therefore advantageous for athletes to be able to produce high power outputs for both short (<1 min) and longer efforts (~60 mins). In contrast, LC bike courses comprise extended laps, with a lower technical demand. As a result, LC bike legs comprise a much more steady paced effort than those in SC events. The characteristics of the bike course are echoed in the run courses for both SC and LC events, with SC runs often including dead turns and a more technical element that increases the requirement for rapid accelerations and decelerations.

Drafting and aerodynamics

Elite level SC racing is draft legal. Drafting is the act of exploiting the slip stream created by a body in front of you, resulting in a reduction in energy expenditure at a given speed due to a reduction in drag. The greatest benefits are when travelling at high speeds or through mediums where drag is elevated (i.e. water), thus heavily influencing the swim and bike legs. During swimming, drafting directly behind (50–60cm) has been shown to notably reduce metabolic responses such as oxygen uptake and HR by ~10%; also perceived effort by up to 20% in submaximal conditions (Bassett et al., 1991). Consequently, athletes of inferior ability could maintain higher speeds for a given intensity when drafting behind competitors.

The influence of drafting becomes heightened during the bike leg of a SC triathlon. During flat riding, aerodynamic drag accounts for approximately 90% of the overall resistive forces encountered (di Prampero, 2000). Riding behind a lead rider reduces the aerodynamic drag for the following rider, and thus a reduced power output is required to maintain a given speed. Previous investigations have shown that a cyclist drafting behind a lead rider can see a decrease oxygen uptake by ~30% at speeds of 38–40 km/h (McCole et al., 1990); this is close to the race pace of male triathlon bike legs. As a result, athletes can notably reduce the metabolic demand for a given race speed when riding within a group when compared to riding solo, reducing the development of fatigue. Moreover, this provides an opportunity for weaker riders to maintain higher race speeds by situating themselves in the slip-streams of stronger riders.

In contrast, LC bike legs are non-drafting. Athletes are prohibited to be within the slip stream of the rider in front, defined as a 12 m gap by ironman guidelines, and as such becomes a solo 'time trial' effort. Athletes therefore aim to reduce the combined drag effect of their body and bike by maximising the aerodynamics of the bike position to improve performance in the absence of drafting. Typically, athletes adopt a position with a high torso angle through the use of handle bar extensions (i.e. 'tri-bars'), minimising their frontal area and thus reducing the aerodynamic drag and the subsequent metabolic cost for a given speed. However, high torso angles can be detrimental to power output and cycling efficiency (Fintelman et al., 2015), thus a balance has to be established between aerodynamics and physiological variables in order to maximise performance.

Pacing

Because the three legs are performed in series, the demands in one modality can have a direct bearing on the performance in subsequent modalities. This therefore presents the challenge of maximising race pace, whilst mitigating excessive fatigue development that would compromise performance in the subsequent legs. For SC events, as outlined above, exploitation of drafting can be critical for success. To gain the greatest advantage, athletes look to surround themselves with the strongest swimmers and cyclists in the field. In the swim leg, athletes accelerate at the start of the race to establish effective positioning behind the best swimmers in the field, with performance over the first ~200m of a swim course correlated highly with overall swim performance (Vleck et al., 2008).

Athletes in the front swim pack then have a potential to create a break in the race when entering the bike leg, establishing sufficient time over chasing riders so that their slip stream cannot be used to aid chasing riders. Consequently, the chasing pack of riders have to maintain a higher power output as a collective to close the gap to the front pack, increasing the metabolic demand and potential for fatigue. In the absence of a break from the swim leg, achieving a breakaway in SC rides are likely to occur either during the 1st km of the bike leg, or when travelling uphill due to the reduction in drafting potential when travelling at slower speeds (Vleck et al., 2008). These factors reaffirm the requirement for athletes to be capable of delivering multiple short bursts of high power outputs throughout the bike leg in order to maximise overall performance.

Of note, the critical component to determining overall success in SC triathlons is running performance. The high relative importance of the running leg in SC events is likely to be a product of the running leg being the final in the series, thus potentially the site where accumulated fatigue has the greatest bearing on performance, and the confounding influence of drafting and aerodynamics in both the swim and the bike legs. Consequently, few athletes produce medal winning performances when their run split is 10 seconds slower than the fastest run split in that particular race. when the run leg is outside 10s of the fastest run split in that given race (Ofoghi et al., 2016). However, for LC events the run leg is closely matched by the bike leg when determining overall success, likely due the non-drafting rules making the bike leg a true 'solo' effort.

Fitness testing for triathlon

Fitness testing in triathlon has historically been laboratory based with the data being used to benchmark performances and influence triathlon training prescription. However, whilst this is obviously an important area, the development of a series of tests to monitor and track potential injury risk areas as well as to track strength and conditioning development is also important; this should form part of a well-rounded physical development programme. A physical testing and monitoring battery should be tailored to inform effective decision making within the training and race environment. Central to any testing is creating a clear rationale: what is it you are testing, and how will this change practice and have impact going forward?

Performance testing

Performance tests form an important part of progression monitoring, and are used to gauge the progression of athletes in each different discipline without the requirement of racing. These assessments can be as rudimental as the performance in a 'key session' that is repeated at given intervals through the year. For SC athletes, the performances in a structured 'time trial' (TT) over various exercise durations from 3–12 minutes have been used across all three modalities, producing a curvilinear relationship between the power (cycling) or speed (swimming and running) sustained and exercise duration up to 60 mins. This curve can be used to provide insight into the aerobic and anaerobic abilities of an athlete, namely critical power/speed (where the curve 'levels off') for aerobic capability, and the ability to work above this threshold, known as the anaerobic work capacity. These assessments can be performed in the field with limited resources (i.e. requires a stop watch for swim and run assessments, and a power monitor for cycling), and as such provides a very accessible way to comprehensively monitor progression in SC athletes across the three disciplines. A more detailed overview of this concept and its applications can be found in a recent review (Jones and Vanhatalo, 2017).

Physiological testing

Given the endurance nature of triathlon, the body's ability to effectively extract, deliver and utilise oxygen is critical to success. Consequently, laboratory based assessments have focused on profiling and benchmarking an athlete's aerobic physiology and its primary determinants, namely maximum oxygen uptake ($\dot{V}O_{2max}$), the fractional utilisation of $\dot{V}O_{2max}$ (i.e. lactate threshold and lactate turnpoint), and economy/efficiency (Bassett and Howley, 2000; Joyner and Coyle, 2008). Though all these factors are primary physiological determinants of performance in triathlon, the relative importance of exercise economy/efficiency and lactate threshold increases as race distance increases, with the relative importance of $\dot{V}O_{2max}$ and lactate turn point showing the opposing trend.

Across the three modalities, submaximal physiology (i.e. lactate threshold, lactate turnpoint and economy/efficiency) is commonly assessed via graded step tests, where exercise commences at a low, 'easy' intensity and increased incrementally for the following stages. Stage durations are set so that an internal 'steady state' is established, typically requiring 3 minutes for elite athletes or $\geq$ 4 minutes for lesser trained individuals (Shaw et al., 2013), with pulmonary gas exchange and blood lactate quantified during the final 60s and at the end of each stage, respectively. Exercise stages are completed until blood lactate increases exponentially, typically identified by a rise of >2mmol.l^{-1} from the previous stage. Maximal physiology (i.e. $\dot{V}O_{2max}$) is assessed with a continuous ramp test, with exercise intensity increased at a higher rate until the onset of volitional exhaustion, with pulmonary gas exchange monitored throughout.

In addition to profiling and benchmarking, physiological testing can also provide guidance for appropriate exercise intensities to be used in training. Across all three modalities, training 'zones' are commonly prescribed based on heart rate values obtained from the submaximal assessments, anchored by the identified physiological thresholds. However, it is important to note that whilst these zones give great guidance for longer, submaximal efforts, heart rate zones do not provide good guidance for training during shorter, near maximal or supra maximal aerobic efforts. For guidance at this top end of training intensities, practitioners and coaches should look towards external indicators of intensity, using velocity in swimming and running, and power in cycling.

Strength and conditioning testing

The strength and conditioning testing is analysed as one testing battery; however, for simplicity of process and explanation the testing within this section is split into three areas. The first area to investigate is based on the traditional movement screening process to assess individual physical limitations as a way of highlighting potential injury risks and compensatory patterns. This would include ranges of movement at specific joints which are placed under repeated load during the three disciplines, assessment of any visible imbalances and the effect any previous injuries have had on the athletes' development. The information gathered in this section begins to build a picture of the athletes' movement qualities and areas for improvement, as well as providing a baseline level and 'norm' in case of any future injuries.

Due to the nature of training required to undertake the sport, muscular endurance and fatigue resistance are vital in preventing injury. Therefore a key area for assessment is the muscular capacity of key structures and the balance from anterior to posterior, and left versus right. In light of this, a measurement of calf capacity (both gastrocnemius and soleus), hamstring (bent leg and straight leg), upper body horizontal pulling and pressing, and core capacity (anterior, posterior and lateral) are all very important. There are many ways of assessing these areas as long as the tests are valid, reliable and repeatable.

If appropriate the final area is traditional strength based testing, using different repetition maximums to derive specific training loads for the athlete. The key aspect of this is whether it's appropriate physically and technically in relation their training age and stage. For example if the training age of the athlete is minimal then investing time in technical and capacity based development is a safer way of progressing their physical development. In some training centres the use of force plate and jump mat diagnostics can demonstrate a greater and more specific level of understanding about a particular athletes physical capabilities without exposing them to the potentially dangerous technical demands of a rep. maximum lift. For example tests such as an isometric mid-thigh pull (single and double leg), drop jumps/landings (single and double leg) and hamstring isometric holds (single and double leg) can give an insight into full body maximal force output, management of force and left vs right balance, and specific muscle force production capacities respectively.

Injury prevalence in triathlon

Triathlon as a sport has consistently high volumes of training; consequently, overuse injuries are the most common injury. This section will discuss some of the most common overuse injuries observed within the triathlete population.

Bone stress injuries

A stress fracture is a partial fracture (or break) of the bone. It is an overuse injury, where the bone is unable to withstand a repetitive mechanical loading/force placed on it through training. This is different from a full fracture or break of the bone caused by a sudden traumatic mechanical stress. In triathlon most bone stress injuries are in the lower limb and can be attributed to the running discipline. Commonly they occur in the metatarsals, navicular, tibia, fibula and femur.

Key risk factors

- The most common pre cursor to a stress fracture is a previous bone stress or an injury history of stress fractures.
- Poor lower limb and foot biomechanics can lead to bone stress, as often a specific area of bone is being repetitively overloaded instead of spreading the load evenly through the structures of the foot.
- Inadequate lower limb conditioning and strength relative to bodyweight are also potential risk factors. The stronger the muscles supporting the bone, the more force they can absorb and less is transferred to the bone.
- As bone stress is a management of load issue, an athlete is more prone to stress fractures if there is sudden increase or spikes in running volume or overall training volume. This is particularly a problem with athletes who are new to the sport or transferring from a predominantly non-weight bearing sport such as swimming or cycling. In addition loading changes referring to the type of load (addition of speed sessions) and running terrain can also be linked to bone stress injuries.

As this is from a strength and conditioning perspective, the key risk areas linked to that discipline are highlighted. However, there are a number of other factors that can contribute to bone stress, such as low vitamin D levels, poor energy balance, and, in females, an irregular or absent menstrual cycle.

Signs and symptoms

- Pin point pain: this may be specific to the bone itself and then radiate slightly around the point.
- Pain on mechanical loading: pain when running, standing up out of the saddle when cycling, and in some cases pushing off the wall in swimming (at other times the athlete may be completely pain free).
- The pain persists after the aggravating activity.
- An ache/pain at night.
- There may be a small area of swelling around the fracture site.
- The pain returns if only rested for a short period (i.e. 7–10 days).

Diagnosis and treatment

A GP or physiotherapist will check their history and after a number of clinical tests will be able to diagnose a potential bone stress injury. Although sometimes helpful in order to rule out other possible injuries, x-rays often won't detect a stress fracture during its early stages. To give a clearer diagnosis, a doctor can refer the patient for an imaging scan (CT or MRI) to confirm their initial diagnosis. The course of treatment is very much dependent on how early you have identified and diagnosed the injury, as well as the location of the injury. Sadly there is no quick fix to a bone injury and most will need complete off-loading and immobilising in a boot, cast/splint or crutches for up to 6 weeks to give the bone time to heal. In some more severe cases a surgical intervention may be required. A gradual return to training then needs to be specified where the bone is progressively loaded back to the normal pre-injury training level. During this time it is vital that the athlete is pain free around the injury site. The majority of athletes who suffer from a bone stress injury will return to full fitness.

Medial tibial stress syndrome

Medial tibial stress syndrome (MTSS), or more commonly referred to as shin splints, are a frequently reported problem in the athletic population – specifically endurance athletes. Shin splints can occur when the periosteum that covers the surface of the tibia bone becomes inflamed or irritated. Many people often describe it as a diffuse, dull ache along the inner border of the tibia. It's normally worse after running or weight bearing activity, and some triathletes will report feeling the same type of pain when out of the saddle on the bike. However, if the pain is ignored it can become sharp and acute, completely limiting the ability to train. Shin pain is often difficult to treat as there are so many factors that contribute to the pain, making every individual's diagnosis and treatment plan slightly different. On-going/worsening shin pain must be reviewed to rule out more serious problems, like a stress fracture or compartment syndrome.

Key risk factors

- Poor lower limb and foot biomechanics, such as inadequate control of pronation can lead to MTSS. In addition, incorrect footwear for the athlete's foot shape and running style can also act as an extrinsic change in foot biomechanics due to the loading pattern it promotes.
- Reduced muscle function around the hip and knee can overload the shin.
- Changes to the type of load (addition of speed sessions) and running terrain can also be linked to MTSS injuries.
- Poor lower limb conditioning and strength relative to bodyweight are also potential risk factors.

Signs and symptoms

- Pain in the medial aspect of the tibia – either passively or on palpation.
- Pain associated with or after impact exercise.
- Ache/throbbing at rest.

Diagnosis and treatment

A physiotherapist will be able to complete a series of clinical tests to assess the likelihood of MTSS. In order to rule out any type of bone stress, the athlete can have an MRI scan. Treatment will initially require some alteration and management of the aggravating load, whilst a strength programme is started in order to address two key areas:

- To work on the identified lower limb muscles with poor load tolerance.
- To build posterior chain strength.

In order to manage acute symptoms, the athlete can seek soft tissue therapy and joint mobilisation techniques. In addition an assessment of foot biomechanics and footwear may be required to reduce the risk of that being a cause of a re-injury in the future.

Lower limb tendinopathies

A tendinopathy, or overuse tendon injury, typically occurs in a tendon that has been overloaded. In triathlon these are common in the lower limb and frequently seen in the Achilles, flexor hallusis longus (FHL) and peroneal tendons. They commonly result in pain and a reduction in function of the tendon, leading to reduced exercise/training tolerance. Over time this leads to actual changes within the structure of the tendon and therefore it is less able to deal with repetitive loading.

Key risk factors

Intrinsic risk factors

- Previous lower limb tendinopathy
- Any other recent lower limb injuries
- Age and sex
- Strength and conditioning of the lower limb
- Biomechanics – specific to region of tendinopathy

Extrinsic risk factors

- Changes in training loads and volumes
- Alterations in training technique
- Errors in training
  - Spikes in training load
  - Alteration in training type (e.g. introduction of speed/track sessions)
  - Ground/terrain conditions

Signs and symptoms

- Pain and stiffness in the morning
- Pain, tenderness, swelling local to the affected tendon
- Crepitus in and around the tendon
- Pain on loading the tendon

Diagnosis and treatment

Tendinopathies are clinically difficult to manage, due to the variety of presentations. Most acute tendons will need some period of offload from the aggravating activity and a structured/graded rehabilitation programme to suitably strengthen the tendon to accept both a volume and intensity of training loads.

Plantar fasciitis

Plantar fasciitis is the medical term for the thickening and alteration in structure of the plantar fascia. The plantar is a thick band of flexible but tough tissue that runs under the sole of the foot connecting the heel bone to the smaller bone of the foot. The plantar fascia has two main functions:

- During walking, in the heel raise to toe off phase, the plantar fascia assists in stabilising the arch of the foot.
- It acts as a shock absorber as the foot hits and makes contact with the ground.

Key risk factors

- Poor lower limb and foot biomechanics
- Inadequate lower limb and foot strength and conditioning
- A change or alteration in footwear, wearing ill-fitting or the wrong type of shoe for your foot
- Errors/changes in training:
  - Increased volume
  - Increased speed work
  - Running fatigued
- Changes in running terrain
- Tightness in the calf and achilles complex

Signs and symptoms

The main symptom of plantar fasciitis is pain around the heel, felt when standing, walking and running. This is often worse first thing in the morning. Inflammation or injury of the plantar fascia can occur suddenly, with an acute tear or rupture, or can happen over several months as small micro tears develop in the structure, causing thickening and a decrease in its ability to absorb and transfer load.

Diagnosis and treatment

Individual athletes each have a specific combination of factors to why they have plantar fasciitis. Initially it's important to offload the fascia and stop the aggravating activity, to give the structure chance to recover – this may mean going into a cast or boot. There are lots of treatments available, stretch and strengthening programmes, as well as deep soft tissue and joint mobilisation work. Orthotics and foot supports, assessment of footwear and a gradual/progressive return to training programme are all essential, making sure that the foot is strong enough to cope with the volume and speed an athlete needs to run.

Strength and conditioning programming in triathlon

The strength and conditioning component of the overall triathlon training programme is small but very important as is demonstrated in the injury prevalence, athletic demands and fitness testing aspects of this chapter. The injury prevalence section highlights that the majority of triathlon training related issues are overuse injuries with a particular focus on the lower limbs' ability to manage load and the system's ability to function in a fatigued state. Therefore the requirement of a robust musculoskeletal system in order to withstand and manage force is important for injury prevention. Athletic demands depend on the event being undertaken by the athlete. For example, a leg in a team relay may take 20–30 mins, and a full Ironman may take 10+ hours. The key aspects that underpin these events are efficiency and economy.

Periodisation

Due to the overall volume of any triathlon training programme, there a number of competing factors for an athlete's energy and time. These therefore require careful periodisation annually but also on a week-to-week and day-to-day basis to ensure that the demands are being managed to enable an effective training programme. In general terms, during the off-season, the intensity of training reduces and the overall aerobic volume increases. Therefore in terms of strength and conditioning development, this is a key window to improve the required physical qualities to underpin training and performance. To ensure that the strength vs endurance trade-offs are as minimal as possible, it is important to have a combined periodisation plan and be aware of session timing in relation to other sports specific training sessions.

During the season there is an increased focus on specific high intensity sessions such as high speed running (such as track sessions), race specific bike sessions (including track riding/racing) and race paced swim sessions (open water race scenario practice). Therefore during the season, managing gym intensity and volume around these sessions is important in order to allow athletes to produce the efforts required in the key training sessions. It is also important to understand the outcomes and the actual physical development gained from these sessions (e.g. track running helping to develop hamstring/calf strength qualities in endurance athletes).

Evidenced based practice

In general the addition of a strength training programme to endurance sports has been widely researched. However, the linking of swim, bike and run in terms of the physical development combining the three disciplines is fairly narrow; therefore, it is best practice to analyse generic strength and conditioning research within the individual disciplines combined with endurance training principles in the first instance.

In line with the information from the previous sections, in triathlon there are specific positions, movements and physical qualities that an athlete needs to be able to inherently have or have the ability to develop over a period of time. This is split into two areas – the physical ability to achieve the desired patterns with the required forces (strength and power) and then the ability to do this efficiently to minimise the impact of fatigue on performance (Berryman et al., 2010).

In the swim it is vital to develop the ability of the athlete to reach an effective 'catch' position in order to have an efficient stroke as possible, but also to have the body position and control to manage this force. During the bike segment the ability to drive through the pedals and stabilise through the upper body and core to ensure the efficient transfer of force is key; and finally during the run, the athlete must be able to manage the ground reaction forces by utilising the stretch shortening cycle (SSC) to make the running pattern as energy efficient as possible. In addition to the direct performance areas highlighted above, there are indirect performance benefits that come with developing increased skill literacy. This is about developing generic athletic abilities in order to underpin movement patterns and the ability to transfer and learn new skills.

Looking closely at the swimming research, it mostly uses short swim efforts (50–400m freestyle) as the performance measure; therefore, the learnings are more from the speed, power and strength component. Investigations from various research groups have demonstrated positive responses from periods of high load strength training and swim performance (Aspenes et al., 2009; Girold et al., 2012; Bertoleti Junior et al. 2016). The other key area of swimming research highlights the vast amount of evidence in relation to shoulder health, symmetry and range of movement. This refers to the ability of the athlete to reach an effective 'catch' position in order to have as an efficient stroke as possible and also limiting the potential time out of the pool, allowing the athlete the consistency of training required to develop the physical capacities to improve the overall swim performance (Pink and Tibone, 2000; Weldon and Richardson, 2001; Mountjoy et al., 2010; Herrington and Horsley, 2014; Evershed et al., 2014; Matthews et al., 2017).

During the bike segment the ability to drive through the pedals and stabilise through the upper body and core to ensure the efficient transfer of force is vital. Heavy strength training has been demonstrated to lead to improved cycling performance in relation to power outputs across a large range of exercise durations (Rønnestad et al., 2015). In addition, heavy strength training also improved cycling economy and efficiency, as well as increasing time to exhaustion without changing key variables such as max oxygen uptake, cadence and bodyweight (Sunde et al., 2010). Studies have also shown that employing exercises with a similar pattern to a pedal stroke and consistent training throughout the year whilst managing load around key sessions, was also beneficial for performance (Rønnestad et al., 2015; Mujika et al., 2016).

The running research demonstrated that there are a number of associated benefits of adding consistent year round mid-to-heavy load strength training mixed with explosive efforts to endurance based athletes – these benefits include improving economy, muscle power and performance, and improvement of muscle tendon stiffness (Paavolainen et al., 1999; Millet et al., 2002; Rønnestad and Mujika, 2014; Beattie et al., 2014; Bazylar et al., 2015; Damasceno et al., 2015; Beattie et al., 2017; Booth and Orr, 2016). In addition, within endurance sports where there is high eccentric load with fast SSC demands, developing relative strength will enable the athlete to utilise the reactive strength ability more effectively – particularly eccentric strength (Beattie et al., 2017).

Programme outline

The overall outline of a triathlon strength and conditioning programme is predominantly posterior chain based lower body and lower limb training (both single and double leg), with anti-rotation and hip extension based core training and, where appropriate, the addition of mainly upper body pulling work to maintain shoulder health and posture.

A key focus area of the training programme is the lower limb and how it interacts with the ground during the running discipline; which is primarily the mode of training where the majority of injuries and injury risks are found. This includes using a variety of stimuli to train the gastrocnemius (lateral and medial aspects), soleus, tibialis anterior and tibialis posterior over a range of tempos (eccentric-concentric/eccentric only/isometric) and loading patterns across the force velocity curve. In addition, the contribution of the posterior chain to running performance is also crucial, particularly due to the anterior chain development through cycling. The key exercises utilised in this area include straight leg deadlift, hamstring bridging and good mornings to work the hamstring primarily across the hip, and a variety of hamstring curl exercises (lying hamstring curls, swiss ball/suspension trainer curls) to stress the hamstring across the distal aspects.

Double leg exercises are utilised for overall strength development and pillar strength, developing strength through a full hip range whilst controlling lumbar pelvic mechanics under load. To achieve this it is important to develop squat and deadlift patterns, including their derivatives, progressions and regressions. Squat options include bodyweight squat, kettle or dumbbell goblet squat, back squat, front squat, overhead squat; also the deadlift, including but not limited to the trap-bar deadlift, straight bar, straight leg deadlift, good morning. In some cases for safety at heavier loads, and with any athlete that is load compromised though their spine, leg press is employed as a key strength exercise and supplemented with double leg patterns through a greater range to maintain and develop lumbar pelvic mechanics.

In order to support double leg strength development, single leg exercises are also used to manage leg imbalances and aid in the transfer from gym based training to the specificity of the sport. The types of exercises programmed include split squat (rear foot elevated, front foot elevated and flat), lunge patterns (static, forward, walking, reverse), step ups, and single leg squat. The type of loading employed in these exercises is dependent on the outcome required, and range from heavy loading to overhead loading to focus on hip and trunk stability.

The key aims with upper body and core based training in triathlon are balance, posture and control. The components of the upper body programme place more emphasis on horizontal and vertical pulling exercises to help with shoulder health and mechanics such as double and single arm rowing patterns (supine row, DB rows, cable rows, suspension trainer) and lat pulldown/pull up variations. Depending on the outcome required, horizontal and vertical pressing variations are also utilised, starting with bodyweight and building to the addition of an external load. The core training component refers to the area from the athletes knees to their sternum, and should be considered around the full 360 degree view of the athlete. In general the main focus is on posterior and lateral core work which is supplemented with anterior core where appropriate. The rationale for this is that due to the nature of the sport the athletes are often over active through their anterior structures; therefore the principle aim of achieving balance with the athlete is vital in this area. The main patterns and areas are anti-rotation to manage the rotational forces they are subjected to during all three disciplines; glute and adductor strength into lower back to support posture, lumbar pelvic mechanics, and single leg strength and balance; and general core conditioning with a variety of exercises, tempos and loadings as appropriate for the individual.

Table 29.1 provides an example programme demonstrating the principles discussed.

Table 29.1 Example strength and conditioning programme

Key focus	Exercise options	Key points	Sets/reps
Double leg strength	Goblet squat	Technical development of key lift; head up, chest up, back flat, knees out, weight mid foot to heels	4 sets × 8–12 reps
Single leg strength	Box step up	Box just about knee height, minimal or no push through back foot, chest up, knee in line	5 sets × 4–6 reps
Posterior chain strength	Straight leg deadlift	Back flat, chest up, weight in the heels, move hips back	4 sets × 6–8 reps
Force absorption (as a circuit)	Hop and hold	Still within 1 sec, manage hop distance to achieve this, left to left and right to right	4 sets × 5 reps each side
	Single leg bent leg calf raises	Full range, even tempo, maintain knee angle through full movement	4 sets × 12–15 reps each side @ BW
	Skipping	Stiff ankle on contact, minimal 'sink'	4 sets × 30 secs
Core (as a circuit)	Straight leg Adductor holds	Straight line from head to feet	3 sets × (4 ×10 secs on / 5 secs off each side)
	Dumbbell plank row	Flat back, hips square, feet shoulder width apart, pull DB to chest	3 sets × 5 reps each side
	Reverse hyper	Legs together, initiate movement from hips, no swinging	3 sets × 10–12 reps

Conclusion

As is clearly documented throughout this chapter, triathlon is a multi-faceted sport with many competing demands all combining to support the athletes' ability to develop, take part and compete at any level or distance of the sport. From a strength and conditioning perspective it is a mindset shift for a practitioner, where the importance of understanding the full training programme and the impact that this will have on the S&C delivery comes to the fore; this all-encompassing understanding is vital for athlete/coach buy-in and to deliver the best service possible.

The strength and conditioning programme needs to be individualised as triathletes come from a variety of different sporting backgrounds, with many mechanical dysfunctions and imbalances. However, the broad programme principles apply to whomever the athlete is. The importance of lower limb and posterior chain strength is crucial for injury prevention but also for performance improvement. The ability to manage force and remain balanced and in control through the core to reduce energy leakages is fundamental, as is developing the work capacity and strength to allow the athlete to manage the training loads required to reach their full potential.

References

Aspenes S, Kjendlie P-L, Hoff J, Helgerud J. Combined strength and endurance training in competitive swimmers. *J Sports Sci Med*. 2009; 8(3): 357–365.

Bassett DR, Flohr J, Duey WJ, Howley ET, Pein RL. Metabolic responses to drafting during front crawl swimming. *Med Sci Sports Exerc*. 1991; 23(6): 744–747.

Bassett DR, Howley ET. Limiting factors for maximum oxygen uptake and determinants of endurance performance. *Med Sci Sports Exerc*. 2000; 32(1): 70–84.

Bazylar C, Beckahm G, Sato K. The use of the isometric squat as a measure of strength and explosiveness. *J Strength Cond Res*. 2015; 29(5): 1386–1392.

Beattie K, Carson BP, Lyons M, Rossiter A, Kenny IC. The Effect of Strength Training on Performance Indicators in Distance Runners. *J Strength Cond Res*. 2017; 31(1): 9–23.

Beattie K, Kenny IC, Lyons M, Carson BP. The effect of strength training on performance in endurance athletes. *Sport Med*. 2014; 44(6): 845–865.

Berryman N, Maurel D, Bosquet L. Effect of plyometric vs dynamic weight training on the energy cost of running. *J Strength Cond Res*. 2010; 24(7): 1818–1825.

Bertoleti Junior E, Aidar FJ, de Souza RF et al. Swimming performance evaluation in athletes submitted to different types of strength training. *J Exerc Physiol Online*. 2016; 19(6): 1–9.

Booth MA, Orr R. Effects of plyometric training on sports performance. *Strength Cond J*. 2016; 38(1): 30–37.

Damasceno MV., Lima-Silva AE, Pasqua LA et al. Effects of resistance training on neuromuscular characteristics and pacing during 10-km running time trial. *Eur J Appl Physiol*. 2015; 115(7): 1513–1522.

di Prampero PE. Cycling on Earth, in space, on the Moon. *Eur J Appl Physiol*. 2000; 82(5–6): 345–360.

Evershed J, Burkett B, Mellifont R. Musculoskeletal screening to detect asymmetry in swimming. *Phys Ther Sport*. 2014; 15(1): 33–38.

Fintelman DM, Sterling M, Hemida H, Li F-X. The effect of time trial cycling position on physiological and aerodynamic variables. *J Sports Sci*. 2015; 33(16): 1730–1737.

Girold S, Jalab C, Bernard O, Carette P, Kemoun G, Dugué B. Dry-land strength training vs. electrical stimulation in sprint swimming performance. *J Strength Cond Res*. 2012; 26(2): 497–505. doi:10.1519/JSC.0b013e318220e6e4.

Herrington L, Horsley I. Effects of latissimus dorsi length on shoulder flexion in canoeists, swimmers, rugby players, and controls. *J Sport Heal Sci*. 2014; 3(1): 60–63.

Jones AM, Vanhatalo A. The critical power concept: Applications to sports performance with a focus on intermittent high-intensity exercise. *Sport Med*. 2017; 47(s1): 65–78.

Joyner MJ, Coyle EF. Endurance exercise performance: The physiology of champions. *J Physiol*. 2008; 586(1): 35–44.

Matthews MJ, Green D, Matthews H, Swanwick E. The effects of swimming fatigue on shoulder strength, range of motion, joint control, and performance in swimmers. *Phys Ther Sport*. 2017; 23: 118–122.

McCole SD, Claney K, Conte JC, Anderson R, Hagberg JM. Energy expenditure during bicycling. *J Appl Physiol*. 1990; 68(2): 748–753.

Millet GP, Jaouen B, Borrani F, Candau R. Effects of concurrent endurance and strength training on running economy and .VO(2) kinetics. *Med Sci Sports Exerc*. 2002; 34(8): 1351–1359.

Mountjoy M, Junge A, Alonso JM et al. Sports injuries and illnesses in the 2009 FINA World Championships (Aquatics). *Br J Sports Med*. 2010; 44(7): 522–527.

Mujika I, Rønnestad BR, Martin DT. Effects of increased muscle strength and muscle mass on endurance-cycling performance. *Int J Sports Physiol Perform*. 2016; 11(April): 283–289.

Ofoghi B, Zeleznikow J, Macmahon C, Rehula J, Dwyer DB. Performance analysis and prediction in triathlon. *J Sports Sci*. 2016; 34(7): 607–612.

Paavolainen L, Hakkinen K, Hamalainen I, Nummela A, Rusko H. Explosive-strength training improves 5-km running time by improving running economy and muscle power. *J Appl Physiol*. 1999; 86(5): 1527–1533.

Pink MM, Tibone JE. The painful shoulder in the swimming athlete. *Orthop Clin North Am*. 2000; 31(2): 247–261.

Rønnestad BR, Hansen J, Hollan I, Ellefsen S. Strength training improves performance and pedaling characteristics in elite cyclists. *Scand J Med Sci Sport*. 2015; 25(1): e89–e98.

Rønnestad BR, Mujika I. Optimizing strength training for running and cycling endurance performance: A review. *Scand J Med Sci Sport*. 2014; 24(4): 603–612.

Shaw AJ, Ingham SA, Fudge BW, Folland JP. The reliability of running economy expressed as oxygen cost and energy cost in trained distance runners. *Appl Physiol Nutr Metab*. 2013; 38(12): 1268–1272.

Sunde A, Støren Ø, Bjerkaas M, Larsen MH, Hoff J, Helgerud J. Maximal strength training improves cycling economy in competitive cyclists. *J Strength Cond Res*. 2010; 24(8): 2157–2165.

Vleck VE, Bentley DJ, Millet GP, Bürgi A. Pacing during an elite Olympic distance triathlon: Comparison between male and female competitors. *J Sci Med Sport*. 2008; 11(4): 424–432.

Weldon EJ, Richardson AB. Upper extremity overuse injuries in swimming. *Clin Sports Med*. 2001; 20(3): 423–438.

30
SWIMMING

Chris Bishop

Introduction

Since the first Olympic Games, swimming performance steadily improved until a notable plateau hit the sport during the 1970s and 1980s (Wild et al., 2014). However, there has been a subsequent improvement in swimming performance at both the Olympic Games and FINA World Championships from 1994 to present day (Wild et al., 2014; Wolfrum et al., 2014). For example, average swim speeds ($m \cdot s^{-1}$) for men and women were reported as 2.21 and 1.98 respectively in 1994, and have since been recorded at 2.31 and 2.04 in 2013 (Wild et al., 2014). It has been suggested that these improvements are a result of training processes becoming more efficient in recent years, thus leading to the faster times recorded since the early 1990s (Colwin, 2002). Throughout this chapter, it will become clear just how sports science for swimming has evolved, leading to progressive improvements in the last 20 years.

The unique demands of this sport taking place in water pose many issues for swimmers such as the drag of the water (Rasulbekov et al., 1984; Cohen et al., 2014; Tor et al., 2015), which in turn may contribute towards increased turbulence (Rasulbekov et al., 1984), (unwanted side-to-side movement during the stroke) and a minimal amount of ground reaction forces (GRF) (Bishop et al., 2013). From a strength and conditioning (S&C) perspective, it is imperative that we as coaches consider the implications of these potential restrictions and they be reflected in our program design, thus minimising any detrimental effects they might have. For example, if we consider these potential problem areas, recent literature has highlighted that drag can be reduced by nearly 24% (regardless of speed) if swum at a depth of 1 metre instead of at the surface (Tor et al., 2015). This could have important effects on performance, most notably an opportunity to positively enhance velocity at the start of races when swimmers are allowed to be submerged before requiring to re-surface at the 15m mark. Similarly, with GRF only being available at the start and turn (Bishop et al., 2013; Bishop et al., 2014; Fig, 2010), dry-land training (where we have access to these forces) must aim to optimise transference to these parts of the race and be reflected in the weight room program design.

Therefore, the aim of this book chapter is to provide the S&C coach with an overview of the existing literature surrounding the athletic demands and injury considerations for swimming, and then use that information to create a proposed physical testing battery for the sport. Guidelines will also be provided in terms of some example weight room programmes that could be considered for the elite swimmer.

Athletic demands

Biomechanical demands – the start

The most notable points for the S&C coach to consider are the start and turn, of which the start has received much attention in the literature (Lyttle and Benjanuvatra, accessed January, 2013; Bingul et al., accessed November, 2015; Garcia-Hermoso et al., 2013; Takeda et al., 2012; Honda et al., 2012; Vilas-Boas et al., 2003; Nomura et al., 2010; Vantorre et al., 2010). Lyttle and Benjanuvatra (accessed January, 2013), identified the importance of a strong start as represented by it accounting for up to 30% in a 50m race. Naturally, its contribution diminishes as distance increases as signified by 15% being accounted for in a 100m race, 7.5% in 200m and 4% in the 400m events. The key areas of the start to consider are the type of start used and the time spent on the blocks or on the wall for the backstroke.

Bingul et al., (accessed November, 2015) investigated the kinematic factors associated with grab, rear-track and front-track starts (see Figure 30.1) in 10 elite male youth swimmers (mean age ± SD: 11.3 ± 2.3) from Turkey. Four variables were calculated: block time (time taken between start signal and the last point of contact off the block by the foot), flight time (time

Figure 30.1a–c   Grab, rear-track and front-track start positions in swimming

taken between the foot leaving contact with the block and the first finger to touch the water), entry time (time between the start signal and first finger to make contact with the water) and flight length (distance from the pool wall underneath the block to the point where the finger first touches the water). Results revealed no significant differences between any of the starts for all variables except flight length ($p < 0.05$), which measured a mean distance of 2.83m during the grab start compared to 2.56m during the front-track start. Although not statistically significant, the rear-track start produced faster block times (0.72 vs 0.76–0.78s) and shorter entry times (0.9 vs 0.95–1.05s) than the other two starts, whilst still managing to produce a longer flight length when compared to the front-track start. Therefore, interpreting all four variables as a collective, it would appear that the rear-track start may be favourable as it produces the fastest reaction times and the second longest dive, although this data has only been taken for 10 youth swimmers and should be interpreted with some caution.

Surprisingly, block times are not dis-similar when looking at elite adult swimmers (Garcia-Hermoso et al., 2013). In 2009, a new starting block was introduced and first used in the 2009 World Championships in Rome. The key difference was that the new Omega OSB11 start blocks have an "adjustable, slanted foot-rest" (Honda et al., 2012; Takeda et al., 2012). Garcia-Hermoso et al. (2013) analysed the relationship between block times and performance in the old and new starting blocks for elite male and female freestyle swimmers over 26 international competitions, including four Olympic Games (2000, 2004, 2008 and 2012) and six World Championships (2001, 2003, 2005, 2007, 2009 and 2011). Results can be viewed in Table 30.1.

Table 30.1 clearly demonstrates that the inclusion of the adjustable foot-rest has had a positive effect on both performance and reaction time. It has been previously suggested that faster swimmers are generally faster starters (0–15m) which is synonymous with block start performance (Thompson et al., 2000). Although block times were significantly improved in the aforementioned study with the creation and usage of the Omega OSB11 platforms, there is a "trade-off" between spending enough time on the block to produce enough force and power versus reacting quick enough to minimise the time deficit (Vantorre et al., 2010). This very

Table 30.1 A comparison of mean time/block time for male and female swimmers in the 50/100m freestyle when using old and new starting blocks (adapted from Garcia-Hermoso et al., 2013)

	Mean time in seconds (SD)		Mean block time in seconds (SD)	
	M (n = 829)	F (n = 827)	M (n = 829)	F (n = 827)
50m freestyle				
Old blocks (n = 509)	22.5 (0.41)	25.6 (0.55)	0.75 (0.64)	0.77 (0.06)
New blocks (n = 318)	22.1 (0.47)	25.1 (0.61)	0.68 (0.44)	0.71 (0.47)
100m freestyle				
Old blocks (n = 511)	49.6 (0.80)	55.6 (0.99)	0.76 (0.05)	0.79 (0.06)
New blocks (n = 318)	48.8 (0.82)	54.6 (0.94)	0.70 (0.04)	0.73 (0.05)

SD = standard deviation; M = males; F = females; all differences significant at $P < 0.001$

notion highlights the importance of how quickly a swimmer is able to produce force, namely rate of force development (RFD), a concept previously recognised in the literature (Bishop et al., 2013; Bishop et al., 2014).

To explore this concept of time on the blocks versus amount and speed of force produced further, Vilas-Boas et al. (2003), suggested that the ideal position for the centre of mass (CoM) on the blocks is not clearly understood. The older starting blocks typically encouraged a swimmer's CoM to be situated further backwards, (Nomura et al., 2010) which has been hypothesised to result in a longer time being spent on the blocks (Garcia-Hermoso et al., 2013). Therefore, if the CoM is shifted further forwards (as was seen when using the new Omega platforms), a reduced amount of time on the blocks and quicker reaction was noted. What is not fully understood is if the adjustable foot-rest automatically shifted the swimmers' CoM further forward, thus resulting in a quicker reaction time because of a more biomechanically efficient start position. To add further confusion, Garcia-Hermoso et al. (2013), also noted that female medallists tended to spend longer on the blocks in order to maximise horizontal force production ($r = -0.572, p < 0.001$) rather than aiming to get off the blocks as quickly as possible. Therefore, coaches should use the information seen in Table 30.1 as a guideline for their swimmers' targets on the blocks whilst always aiming to maximise force production simultaneously. Once again, this supports the notion of optimising RFD (discussed later in the program section).

Finally, from a practical perspective, there are a couple of notable studies that have signified the importance of strength and power for block start performance. West et al. (2011) investigated different strength and power predictors of starts in international sprint swimmers and determined correlations with 15 metre time, peak vertical and peak horizontal force (correlations can be viewed in Table 30.2).

The strong relationships seen in Table 30.2 suggest that stronger, more powerful swimmers will perform better during the start of races and will also tend to produce higher levels of vertical and horizontal force, both of which have been previously mentioned in this chapter as being highly relevant to start performance. In further support, additional research has examined different plyometric interventions and their effects on start performance (Poole and Maneval, 1987; Bishop et al., 2009). Bishop et al. (2009), noted a mean improvement in start time of 0.59 seconds after eight weeks of progressive plyometric training in addition to an increase in the distance covered from when the head came into contact with the water. Years earlier, Poole and Maneval (1987), investigated whether differing volumes of depth jump training could enhance leg power in swimmers. Forty depth jumps were programmed either two or three times a week, and although significant improvements in jump height were noted compared to the control group, there was no significant difference between the two day and three days a week intervention. The information presented in these studies highlight the requirement for both strength and power training to complement start performance in swimming.

Table 30.2 Correlations of strength and power variables with 15m time, peak vertical force (PVF) and peak horizontal force (PHF) (adapted from West et al., 2011)

Variable	Jump height (cm)	Peak power (watts)	1RM back squat (Kg)
15m time	−0.69★	−0.85★★	−0.74★★
PVF	0.78★★	0.79★★	0.62★
PHF	0.73★	0.87★★	0.71★

★ significant at $p < 0.05$; ★★ significant at $p < 0.01$

Biomechanical demands – the turn

The second aspect of the biomechanical demands for the S&C coach to consider is the turn. There is noticeably less literature concerning how the turn affects a race in comparison to the start. However, as has been previously noted (Fig, 2010; Bishop et al., 2013; Bishop et al., 2014), this is the second point in the race that can be positively enhanced by the S&C coach due to the swimmer having access to GRFs. It must be remembered that in a 50m race, there will be no turn in a 'long course' (Olympic length pool) event, and only one if the race is run over 'short course' (25m length pool).

Chow et al. (2007) analysed turning techniques of 19 elite adult swimmers with a specific focus on approach speed to the wall and push-off distance (as defined by the point at which swimmers re-surfaced) during the 100m and 400m events. Mean approach speed was notably higher in the 100m race at 1.67m/s when compared to the 400m which recorded a speed of 1.49m/s. Naturally, longer races require a certain "pacing strategy"; thus, it is unsurprising to note the differences in approach speed. The push-off distance also followed this trend of favouring the shorter race for more explosive, faster movements with the 100m portraying a distance of 5.07m in comparison to 4.71m for the 400m event. It was suggested (not confirmed) that the reduced distance in the 400m event was an energy saving strategy by the swimmers, whereby a less forceful thrust may have been utilised in an attempt to conserve energy for the longer race (Chow et al., 2007).

Potdevin et al. (2011) reported that the time spent on the wall during the turn was between 0.3–0.5s in youth swimmers and that this average length of time represented 1.5% of total race time in a 50m event. The methods in this study included a six week plyometric program ($n = 12$) consisting of horizontal, vertical and depth jump training two times a week before swimming practice. Mean countermovement jump (CMJ) height improved from 28.92cm to 32.45cm which consisted of a 12.2% increase in jump height over a six week period. Furthermore, the control group ($n = 11$) actually got worse with a mean pre-test score of 27.04cm and a mean post-test score of 25.88cm (Potdevin et al., 2011). This reduction in performance could have been down to the density of training or time of year within a specific block of training; however, the important message to draw from this study is that plyometric training had a significantly positive impact on the swimmers' lower body power, which was suggested to enhance their capacity for a more explosive turn (Potdevin et al., 2011).

It has been suggested that when swimmers perform the turn action, the movement patterns are similar to that of a CMJ (Bishop et al., 2013). It could be speculated that by incorporating vertical plyometrics such as CMJ variations and even drop jump training, this simulated pattern through training could translate to greater push-off distances, which once again, supports the idea for power training in swimming (example programs are suggested later in the chapter).

Physiological demands

Typically, the physiology of swimming is concerned with the conditioning side of the S&C coach's role and is almost certainly optimised through various strategies in the pool. It has been suggested that this may not fall entirely under the remit of the S&C coach (Bishop et al., 2014); however, optimal communication between the technical coach and S&C coach is crucial to ensure that all viewpoints are best understood.

Understanding the key energy system requirements within swimming is necessary to ensure that our conditioning strategies are appropriate for the different distances. Pyne and Sharp (2014), produced a literature review on the energy demands in competitive swimming and it was noted that the majority of events lay somewhere between 45 seconds and 15 minutes in duration, which resulted in some involvement from all the energy systems (phosphagenic, anaerobic glycolysis and aerobic) (Pyne and Sharp, 2014). Typically, the sprint events (any distance up to 200m) rely heavily on high-energy phosphates such as adenosine triphosphate and creatine phosphate, and training strategies often involve sub-maximal efforts in an attempt to create adaptations at this intensity, thus allowing swimmers to maintain speed throughout the duration of their race. However, during middle distance races (200m–800m), the contributions from these energy systems depend on the duration of the race and any pacing strategy that is being implemented at that moment (Pyne and Sharp, 2014).

Despite its efficacy, it would be even more practical for coaches to understand which strokes exhibit the highest level of energy expenditure. Holmér (1974) suggested that the energy expenditure during the breaststroke and butterfly was considerably higher than the front crawl or backstroke, due to the first two inducing substantially higher levels of drag in the water.

These results were previously supported by Capelli et al. (1998), where the authors evaluated the energy expenditure (in kilojoules/metre) of elite male swimmers across the four strokes at a velocity of $1.5 m/s^{-1}$. The highest energy expenditure was seen in the breaststroke, expending $1.87 kJ/m^{-1}$, followed by the butterfly, which reported $1.55 kJ/m^{-1}$. The backstroke and front crawl exhibited scores of 1.47 and $1.23 kJ/m^{-1}$ respectively (Capelli et al., 1998). Naturally, all strokes demonstrated higher energy expenditure as swim velocity increased. Although Holmer and Capelli concluded the same trends in energy expenditure for the different strokes, direct comparisons should be made with caution due to results being reported in different units (litres/minute^{-1} vs kilojoules/metre^{-1}) (Pyne and Sharp, 2014).

Considering the aforementioned literature on the energy systems, it is important to remember that swimmers are often required to perform over repeated heats at competitions; therefore, some understanding of how these energy contributions differ with repeated efforts would be useful. Peyrebrune et al. (2014), investigated the energy contribution of the aerobic system over single and four repeated 30-second maximal tethered efforts in eight elite swimmers. Aerobic contribution was deemed to be $33 \pm 8\%$ during the maximal 30-second effort and 25 ± 4, 47 ± 9, 49 ± 8 and $52 \pm 9\%$ throughout the four repeated trials, highlighting the importance of the aerobic system for recovery during competitions (Peyrebrune et al., 2014). Training interventions that aim to enhance the anaerobic glycolytic system will primarily aim to enhance muscle capacity and its ability to withstand high levels of lactate, which will improve the muscle's buffering capacity and the swimmer's aerobic capacity. Consequently, this may reduce the amount of pH disturbance within the muscles, once again allowing for higher intensities to be maintained over repeated efforts (Pyne and Sharp, 2014).

Injury prevalence

One of the primary purposes for any S&C coach should be to minimise training time lost due to injury, both in the weight room and the pool. Successful program design will not only aim to enhance performance but also prevent any overuse injuries from occurring (Bishop et al., 2014). In order for training programs to be most effective in this area, it is essential that we understand which areas are at the highest risk. The following section will separate the most prevalent areas at risk of injury between upper and lower body.

Upper body

The unique demands of each individual stroke likely pose different levels of stress on different joints in the kinetic chain. For example, Richardson et al. (1980) investigated the prevalence of injuries in the build up to an Olympic Games at U.S. training camps. It was reported that the shoulder was the most common injury site and that the severity of the problem increased as the standard of swimmer improved and as distance reduced; in essence, those at higher risk tended to be sprint swimmers at the highest level. Richardson's study, although dated, is supported still over thirty years later. Sein et al. (2010) looked at the relationship between the volume of swimming and reported incidence of shoulder pain in elite swimmers. Results conveyed that those swimmers who trained >15 hours per week or >35 kilometres per week had a significantly higher risk ($r = 0.34$–0.39, $p \leq 0.01$) of supraspinatus tendinopathy. Finally, Wolf et al. (2009) analysed the injury patterns of 94 NCAA division 1 swimmers at the University of Iowa during a five year period (2002–2007). It was noted that freestyle was the stroke responsible for the highest injury rate, although this stroke also included 50 out of 94 swimmers in the analysis compared to only 10 who swum breaststroke. However, when the site of injury was considered, the shoulder/upper arm was the most frequently injured site with 78 out of 94 swimmers (83%) reporting injuries and time off from training.

From a practical understanding of injury prevention, Richardson et al. (1980) noted that the freestyle was the stroke that is most prone to injury at the shoulder joint due to the high levels of rotation experienced during the stroke. However, the amount of rotation in both the backstroke and butterfly would appear to be biomechanically similar, suggesting that rotation on its own may not be the sole factor for this high injury incidence. When analysing the fastest times for each stroke at elite level (www.fina.org/discipline/swimming) it is evident that freestyle is the fastest stroke, suggesting that the force vectors experienced at the shoulder joint might be greatest during this stroke, potentially contributing to the high level of injury. It should also be noted that the author was unable to find any literature to authenticate this claim, but is merely a logical line of thinking and may provide coaches with some direction for future research regarding injury prevention.

Nonetheless, Richardson et al. (1980) did note that technique often deteriorates under fatigue as demonstrated by an "elbow drop" during the pull-through phase of the freestyle. It was suggested that strengthening the shoulder adductors would assist in maintaining postural alignment during the stroke, but additional attention should be considered for the rotator cuff group which has been reported in stabilising the shoulder joint during dynamic movement patterns (Clark et al., 2008). Further to this, compound movement patterns such as overhead press, push press and jerks will encourage swimmers to develop stability, strength and power. When all these exercises are considered collectively within the program repertoire for swimmers, the shoulder joint will be addressed in multiple planes of motion (Swanik et al., 2002), at differing velocities and under varying loads, constituting both injury prevention and performance enhancement for an area of the body at high risk for swimmers.

Lower body

From a lower body perspective, the bulk of the literature would appear to have focused on the breaststroke, most likely because of its unique demands during the kick. Grote et al. (2004) noted that the femur's peak adduction velocity can reach up to 245°/second during the breaststroke, placing high amounts of force (at high velocities) through the hip adductors. Strzala et al. (2012) reported hip internal rotation and knee extension to be 35.3° and 44°

respectively in the lateral plane for 27 adolescent (mean age: 15.7 ± 1.98) regional and national swimmers. The extreme adduction and internal rotation movements required during the breaststroke kick would indicate that hip abductor strength may play a pivotal role in offering the hip and knee some support, strength and resilience to the high velocity of adduction (Hrysomallis, 2009).

The concept of "breaststroker's knee" has also attracted some attention in swimming research (Keskinen et al., 1980; Stulberg et al., 1980; Rovere and Nichols, 1985). Studies by Keskinen et al. (1980) Stulberg et al. (1980) and Rovere and Nichols (1985), all investigated the pathology and treatment associated with this condition and concluded that the kicking action was a significant contributor to over-use movement patterns which could result in reduced hip internal rotation and even patella-femoral osteoarthritis. It was also suggested that part of the solution should be to work on technical aspects of the kick, thus optimising movement efficiency in the water. However, this undoubtedly falls under the remit of the technical coach.

In light of this evidence surrounding the risks associated with the breaststroke, a key responsibility of the S&C coach should be to optimise the strength of the hip abductors, ensure strength and flexibility are addressed in the adductor complex and maintain mobility levels in the hips through adequate internal/external rotation exercises. Therefore, an exercise such as the lateral lunge will simultaneously work on hip abductor strength and active hip adductor flexibility, offering a dual benefit to some of the high risk areas associated with the breaststroke kick (Bishop et al., 2013). Furthermore, any restrictions that may be hindering rotation levels at the hip may be addressed through specific foam rolling and stretching-based exercises (Bishop et al., 2014), provided these complement the swimmer's long-term physical development.

In conclusion, the key areas that need to be considered for injury prevention would be the shoulder joint (particularly for freestyle swimmers) and the hip adductors and knee joint (primarily for breaststroke swimmers). The repetitive nature of the sport would suggest that enhancing a swimmer's robustness, particularly in these areas, should be a key priority with strength training having been reported to be one of the most effective strategies for injury prevention (Lauersen et al., 2014). That being said, a multi-disciplinary approach to program design addressing mobility, flexibility, strength and power (discussed later) will most likely ensure all potential risks are being considered for the long-term health of elite swimmers.

Importance of strength and power

Existing literature would indicate that the requirement for strength and power (most notably for sprint swimmers) is undeniable. Gola et al. (2014) investigated the relationship between isometric strength and swimming velocity in the 25 and 50m freestyle. Flexors and extensors of the elbow, shoulder, knee and hip were examined to obtain relative torque values at each joint which were then correlated to swimming velocity. With the significance level set at $p < 0.05$, it is interesting to note that the only significant correlations that existed were with the relative sum of total torque and 25m ($r = 0.60$) and 50m time ($r = 0.57$). This would indicate that swim velocity (in the water) may be more reliant on upper body strength and power but no account has been made for the competitive advantage that can be utilised from an explosive start. To support this point further, previously discussed research from West et al. (2011) (see Table 30.2) highlights the importance of lower body strength and power in successfully achieving a good start. It may be that the lower body holds greater relevance to the start of races and the upper body once the swimmer "re-surfaces" after the start. Further research in this area from Gracanin and Gracanin

(2013) looked at the effect strength has on swim speed by testing 20 male adolescent swimmers during a "fully-tethered" 100m breaststroke swim. A dynamometer was used to measure the pulling force during the testing procedure with the strongest correlation being between absolute maximal force produced and total time ($r = 0.88$), indicating that those swimmers who can produce the strongest pull, typically tend to swim faster, again justifying the importance of upper body strength in the water. Finally, Morouco et al. (2011) looked at the associations between dry-land strength measurements (back squat, bench press and lat pulldown) and power in swimming. Ten national level swimmers (mean age: 14.9 ± 0.74 years) performed a 30 second maximal effort tethered freestyle swim whereby swim velocity was calculated. For the dry-land tests, each subjects load was gradually increased until mean concentric-only velocity fell below 0.6 m.s^{-1} for the bench press and lat pulldown and 0.9 m.s^{-1} for the back squat, although no rationale was provided as to why these methods were chosen. Once more, the only significant correlation was found between the lat pulldown and swim velocity ($r = 0.68; p \leq 0.03$), again demonstrating the importance of pulling strength in swimming.

Furthermore, due to the repetitive nature of swimming it has been previously suggested that asymmetries in strength and power may exist in swimmers (Bishop et al., 2013). Bilateral differences have been suggested to negatively affect swimming performance in two key ways – namely, reduced contribution of force and increased levels of fatigue experienced by the weaker side (Sanders, 2013; Sanders et al., 2015). Evershed et al. (2014) undertook musculo-skeletal screening on 32 national junior swimmers by assessing a symmetry index during multiple upper body movements (shoulder flexion, adduction, internal rotation and elbow flexion). Previous literature has suggested that asymmetries of <10% are an acceptable target for swimmers to aim for (Tourny-Chollet et al., 2009). Results depicted that only 5 out of 32 swimmers had a symmetry index inside that 10% cut-off point on those four upper body movements with asymmetries nearly as high as 60% in some individuals (Evershed et al., 2014). Furthermore, Barden et al. (2011) stated that any asymmetries typically become exacerbated at higher intensities; thus, these are most likely to affect sprint swimmers.

In conclusion, the evidence that swimmers are required to produce high levels of pulling force would appear to be decisive. Previously in this chapter, evidence was presented emphasising the importance of lower body strength and power for the start however, once swimmers "re-surface", it is probable that the contribution of the upper body dramatically increases. If the start can account for up to 30% in a 50m race (see biomechanical demands section), it is likely that the majority of the remaining 70% is accounted for by the upper body, with particular prominence on the "pulling muscles". Asymmetries would also appear to be apparent in many swimmers; therefore, coaches should prioritise testing procedures that aim to identify whether these differences exist and program accordingly.

Fitness testing battery

From a performance enhancement perspective, the evidence has highlighted the importance of upper and lower body strength, power and rate of force development. Injury analysis would suggest that the shoulder and the knee are the two major areas in the body that are most at risk and must also be considered in a testing battery for swimmers. The concept of asymmetries must also be addressed; hence, the inclusion of movement screening could provide the strength and conditioning professional with useful information that may help to guide program development, especially at a younger age. A proposed fitness testing battery can be seen in Table 30.3.

Table 30.3 An example fitness testing battery for swimmers

Component of fitness	Test
Lower body strength	1–3RM back squat
Upper body strength	1–3RM bench press and pull up
Lower body power	Squat jump
	Countermovement jump
	Single leg countermovement jump (right and left)
	Drop jump (30cm)
Upper body power	Kneeling medicine ball throw (10% of bodyweight)
	Single arm medicine ball throw (right and left)
Movement screening	Overhead squat single leg squat

Programming

Unlike most team sports, swimming does not have a typical in-season and off-season period, meaning that swimmers need to carefully select which events they aim to "peak" for. At the elite level, typical events that swimmers will aim to be at their physical peak will be the Olympic Games and World Championships (with these never occurring in the same year). This section will aim to identify example strength (Table 30.4) and power (Table 30.5) programmes that targets the required physical qualities to enhance swimming performance and prevent the onset of repetitive stress injuries associated with the sport.

During strength phases, it is clear that lower body strength is paramount for an effective start (West et al., 2011) therefore exercises such as back squats, deadlifts and split squats will provide the necessary strength development in the lower body to act as a foundation upon which power can be built (Haff and Nimphius, 2012). From an upper body perspective, pulling-based exercises such as pull ups and bent over rows will condition the back muscles so that pulling strength can be optimised and fatigue minimised in the water. Furthermore, it has been previously reported that pushing-based exercises such as the push press improve vertical ground reaction forces (noted as important from West et al., 2011), is a derivative lift for the jerk and focuses on enhancing rate of force development because of its capacity to occur at high velocity (Bishop et al., 2014). The use of resistance bands/chains could also be considered within the training arsenal for a swimmer. The ability to overcome the varying degree of forces from the drag of the water may provide a rationale for using these as a training aid to stimulate different levels of strength response at different points within a particular movement. Finally, supplementary exercises should aim to target enhanced scapular control and a stable knee joint (primarily for breaststrokers) which can be achieved through exercises such as cable internal/external rotations and unilateral training respectively.

As swimmers progress into power phases of training, it is still imperative that strength levels are maintained due to their potential to be detrimentally affected within a two week period (Fleck and Kraemer, 2004). Furthermore, any imbalances should have been addressed in previous blocks which will justify only 1–2 exercises when aiming to maintain strength – one for the lower body and one for pulling strength would appear to be logical based on the existing research. From a power perspective, targeting multiple points on the force-velocity curve via a "mixed methods approach" has been reported as desirable for athletic development (Haff and Nimphius, 2012). Therefore, a combination of high-load and low-load power exercises that retain the focus of

Table 30.4 Example strength program for the elite swimmer

Lifts/assistance exercises	Sets	Repetitions	Load	Rest
A1: back squat	4	5	87% 1RM	4 mins
A2: broad jumps	4	5	–	Do in rest
B1: push press	4	5	87% 1RM	4 mins
B2: DB R.F.E.S.S*	2	6 each leg	DoT**	Do in rest
C1: bent over row	4	5	87% 1RM	4 mins
C2: cable external rotation	2	10 each side	Low load	Do in rest
C3: side plank w. cable row	2	10 each side	Low load	Do in rest

* R.F.E.S.S = rear foot elevated split squat
** DoT = dependent on technique

Table 30.5 Example power program for the elite swimmer

Lifts/assistance exercises	Sets	Repetitions	Load	Rest
A1: power clean	5	3	90% 1RM	5 mins
A2: CMJ	5	3	–	Do in rest
B1: push jerks	5	3	75–80% 1RM	5 mins
B2: drop jumps	5	3	–	Do in rest
C1: trap bar deadlift	3	3	90% 1RM	3 mins
C2: wide grip pull ups	3	3–5	85–90% 1RM	3 mins

pulling power and enhancing jumping ability (for the start and turn), would support the inclusion of Olympic lifts, their derivatives and plyometrics/ballistic-based jumping exercises for optimal power development in swimmers.

Conclusion

The priorities for coaches working in swimming should be centred on three key areas. The first should aim to enhance strength and power in the lower body so that performance for the start and turn can be maximised. The second area should focus on developing high levels of pulling strength in the upper body to maximise force production throughout the stroke and to minimise fatigue at maximal intensities. Finally, the third priority should be to ensure that both the shoulders and knees are addressed within the program design (particularly in strength phases) by selecting appropriate exercises that aim to enhance the stability of the joints. The lack of "off-season" in this sport means that a concurrent method of incorporating in-pool conditioning and strength or power (dependent on time of year) may be the most practical approach to supporting a swimmer's athletic development.

References

Barden, J. M., Kell, R. T., and Dylan, K. (2011). The effect of critical speed and exercise intensity on stroke phase duration and bilateral asymmetry in 200-m front crawl swimming. *Journal of Sports Sciences*, 29: 517–526.

Bingul, B. M., Tore, O., Bulgan, C., and Aydin, M. *The kinematic analysis of the grab, rear track and front track start in swimming.* Available at: http://sportmont.ucg.ac.me. Accessed: November 18, 2015.

Bishop, C., Cree, J., Read, P., Barter, P., and Turner, A. (2014). Strength and conditioning for swimming: A practical approach. *Professional Strength and Conditioning Journal*, 33: 7–12.

Bishop, C., Cree, J., Read, P., Chavda, S., Edwards, M., and Turner, A. (2013). Strength and conditioning for sprint swimming. *Strength and Conditioning Journal*, 35: 1–6.

Bishop, D. C., Smith, R. J., Smith, M. F., and Rigby, H. E. (2009). Effect of plyometric training on swimming block start performance in adolescents. *Journal of Strength and Conditioning Research*, 23: 2137–2143.

Capelli, C., Termin, B., and Pendergast, D. R. (1998). Energetics of swimming at maximal speeds in humans. *European Journal of Applied Physiology and Occupational Physiology*, 78: 385–393.

Chow, J. W.-C., Hay, J. G., Wilson, B. D., and Imel, C. (2007). Turning techniques of elite swimmers. *Journal of Sports Sciences*, 2: 241–255.

Clark, M. A., Lucett, S. C., and Corn, R. J. (2008). *NASM essentials of personal fitness training* (3rd Edition). New York: Lippincott Williams & Wilkins, pp. 301–306.

Cohen, R. C. Z., Cleary, P. W., Harrison, S. M., Mason, B. R., and Pease, D. L. (2014). Pitching effects of buoyancy during four competitive swimming strokes. *Journal of Applied Biomechanics*, 30: 609–618.

Colwin, C. (2002). Looking back, looking ahead. In *Breakthrough swimming*. Edited by McEntire, C., Hawkins, S., and Wentworth, J. Champaign, IL: Human Kinetics, pp. 217–228.

Evershed, J., Burkett, B., and Mellifont, R. (2014). Musculoskeletal screening to detect asymmetry in swimming. *Physical Therapy in Sport*, 15: 33–38.

Fig, G. (2010). Why competitive swimmers need explosive power. *Strength and Conditioning Journal*, 32: 84–86.

Fleck, S. J., and Kraemer, W. J. (2004). *Designing resistance training programs* (3rd Edition). Champaign, IL: Human Kinetics, pp. 228, 231.

Garcia-Hermoso, A., Escalante, Y., Arellano, R., Navarro, F., Dominguez, A. M., and Saavedra, J. M. (2013). Relationship between final performance and block times with the traditional and the new starting platforms with a back plate in international swimming championship 50-M and 100-M freestyle events. *Journal of Sports Science and Medicine*, 12: 698–706.

Gola, R., Urbanik, C., Iwanska, D., and Madej, A. (2014). Relationship between muscle strength and front crawl swimming velocity. *Human Movement*, 15: 110–115.

Gracanin, I., and Gracanin, J. (2013). The effect of strength onto the speed in swimming. *Research in Kinesiology*, 41: 164–168.

Grote, K., Lincoln, T. L., and Gamble, J. G. (2004). Hip adductor injury in competitive swimmers. *American Journal of Sports Medicine*, 32: 104–108.

Haff, G. G., and Nimphius, S. (2012). Training principles for power. *Strength and Conditioning Journal*, 34: 1–17.

Holmér, I. (1974). Energy cost of arm stroke, leg kick, and the whole stroke in competitive swimming styles. *European Journal of Applied Physiology and Occupational Physiology*, 33: 105–118.

Honda, K. E., Sinclair, P. J., Mason, B. R., and Pease, D. L. (2012). The effect of starting position on elite swim start performance using an angled kick plate. In *Proceedings 30th Annual Conference of Biomechanics in Sports*. Edited by Bradshaw, J., Burnett, A., and Hume, P. A. Melbourne, pp. 72–75.

Hrysomallis, C. (2009). Hip adductors' strength, flexibility and injury risk. *Journal of Strength and Conditioning Research*, 23: 1514–1517.

Keskinen, K., Eriksson, E., and Komi, P. (1980). Breaststroke swimmer's knee: A biomechanical and arthroscopic study. *American Journal of Sports Medicine*, 8: 228–231.

Lauersen, J. B., Bertelsen, D. M., and Andersen, L. B. (2014). The effectiveness of exercise interventions to prevent sports injuries: A systematic review and meta-analysis of randomised controlled trials. *British Journal of Sports Medicine*, 48: 871–877.

Lyttle, A., and Benjanuvatra, N. *Start right? A biomechanical review of dive start performance.* Available at: www.coachesinfo.com/category/swimming/321. Accessed: January 22, 2013.

Morouco, P., Neiva, H., Gonzalez-Badillo, J. J., Garrido, N., Marinho, D. A., and Marques, M. C. (2011). Associations between dry land strength and power measurements with swimming performance in elite athletes: A pilot study. *Journal of Human Kinetics*, 29A: 105–112.

Nomura, T., Takeda, T., and Takagi, H. (2010). Influences of the back plate on competitive swimming starting motion in particular projection skill. In *Biomechanics and Medicine in Swimming XI*. Edited by Kjendlie, P., Stallman, R. K., and Cabri, J. Oslo: Norwegian School of Sport Science, pp. 137–137.

Peyrebrune, M. C., Toubekis, A. G., Lakomy, H. K., and Nevill, M. E. (2014). Estimating the energy contribution during single and repeated sprint swimming. *Scandinavian Journal of Medicine and Science in Sports*, 24: 369–376.

Poole, W. H., and Maneval, M. W. (1987). The effects of two ten-week depth jumping routines on vertical jump performance as it relates to leg power. *Journal of Swimming Research*, 3: 11–14.

Potdevin, F. J., Alberty, M. E., Chevutschi, A., Pelayo, P., and Sidney, M. C. (2011). Effects of a 6-week plyometric training program on performance in pubescent swimmers. *Journal of Strength and Conditioning Research*, 25: 80–86.

Pyne, D. B., and Sharp, R. L. (2014). Physical and energy requirements of competitive swimming events. *International Journal of Sport Nutrition and Exercise Metabolism*, 24: 351–359.

Rasulbekov, R. A., Fomin, R. A., Chulkov, V. U., and Chudovsky, V. I. (1984). Does a swimmer need explosive strength? *Strength and Conditioning Journal*, 8: 56–57.

Richardson, A. B., Jobe, F. W., and Collins, H. R. (1980). The shoulder in competitive swimming. *American Journal of Sports Medicine*, 8: 159–163.

Rovere, G. D., and Nichols, A. W. (1985). Frequency, associated factors, and treatment of breaststroker's knee in competitive swimmers. *American Journal of Sports Medicine*, 13: 99–104.

Sanders, R. H. (2013). How do asymmetries affect swimming performance? *Journal of Swimming Research*, 21(1).

Sanders, R. H., Fairweather, M. M., Alcock, A., and McCabe, C. B. (2015). An approach to identifying the effect of technique asymmetries on body alignment in swimming exemplified by a case study of a breaststroke swimmer. *Journal of Sports Science and Medicine*, 14: 304–314.

Sein, M. L., Walton, J., Linklater, J., Appleyard, R., Kirkbride, B., Kuah, D., and Murrell, G. A. C. (2010). Shoulder pain in elite swimmers: Primarily due to swim-volume-induced supraspinatus tendinopathy. *British Journal of Sports Medicine*, 44: 105–113.

Strzala, M., Krezalek, P., Kaca, M., Glab, G., Ostrowski, A., Stanula, A., and Tyka, A. (2012). Swimming speed of the breaststroke kick. *Journal of Human Kinetics*, 35: 133–139.

Stulberg, S. D., Shulman, K., Stuart, S., and Culp, P. (1980). Breaststroker's knee: Pathology, etiology and treatment. *American Journal of Sports Medicine*, 8: 164–171.

Swanik, K. A., Swanik, C. B., Lephart, S. M., and Huxel, K. (2002). The effect of functional training on the incidence of shoulder pain and strength in intercollegiate swimmers. *Journal of Sport Rehabilitation*, 11: 140–154.

Takeda, T., Takagi, H., and Tsubakimoto, S. (2012). Effect of inclination and position of new swimming starting block's back plate on track-start performance. *Sports Biomechanics*, 11: 370–381.

Thompson, K. G., Haljand, R., and MacLaren, D. P. (2000). An analysis of selected kinematic variables in national and elite male and female 100-m and 200-m breaststroke swimmers. *Journal of Sports Sciences*, 18: 421–431.

Tor, E., Pease, D. L., and Ball, K. A. (2015). How does drag affect the underwater phase of a swimming start? *Journal of Applied Biomechanics*, 31: 8–12.

Tourny-Chollet, C., Seifert, L., and Chollet, D. (2009). Effect of force symmetry on coordination in crawl. *International Journal of Sports Medicine*, 3: 182–187.

Vantorre, J., Seifert, L., Fernandes, R. J., Boas, J. P., and Chollet, D. (2010). Comparison of grab start between elite and trained swimmers. *International Journal Sports Medicine*, 31: 887–893.

Vilas-Boas, J. P., Cruz, M. J., Sousa, F., Conceiçao, F., Fernandes, R., and Carvalho, J. (2003). Biomechanical analysis of ventral swimming starts: comparison of the grab start with two track start techniques. In *Swimming science IX*. Edited by Chatard, J. C. Saint Etienne: University of Saint Etienne, pp. 249–253.

West, D. J., Owen, N. J., Cunningham, D. J., Cook, C. J., and Kilduff, L. P. (2011). Strength and power predictors of swimming starts in international sprint swimmers. *Journal of Strength and Conditioning Research*, 25: 950–955.

Wild, S., Rust, C. A., Rosemann, T., and Knechtle, B. (2014). Changes in sex difference in swimming speed in finalists at FINA World Championships and the Olympic Games from 1992 to 2013. *BMC Sports Science, Medicine and Rehabilitation*, 6: 25. doi:10.1186/2052-1847-6-25.

Wolf, B. R., Ebinger, A. E., Lawler, M. P., and Britton, C. L. (2009). Injury pattern in Division I collegiate swimming. *American Journal of Sports Medicine*, 37: 2037–2042.

Wolfrum, M., Rust, C. A., Rosemann, T., Lepers, R., and Knechtle, B. (2014). Changes in breaststroke swimming performances in national and international athletes competing between 1994 and 2011 – A comparison with freestyle swimming performances. *BMC Sports Science, Medicine and Rehabilitation*, 6: 18. doi:10.1186/2052-1847-6-18.

31
ROCK CLIMBING

Noel Carroll

Introduction to the sport

Indoor rock climbing has seen a surge in popularity over the last few decades, both as a recreational activity and as a competitive sport, and has recently been selected for inclusion at the 2020 Olympics in Tokyo. Indoor climbing is a sub-discipline of (outdoor) rock climbing, characterised by gymnastic type movements on walls fitted with artificial hand and foot holds, and is now an internationally contested event. Within the loose heading of indoor climbing, there are several distinct sub groups: (1) lead climbing, where an athlete ascends from the ground while mapping a route of their path for others to replicate; (2) seconding, where a climber follows a lead climb route, dismantling as they go; (3) top rope, which uses a rope secured via a top anchor and belayed by someone on the ground who protects the climber in the event of a fall; (4) free or solo climbing, which is where the athletes use no protection or assistance at all; and, finally, (5) bouldering, which requires climbers to negotiate routes with no harness at low heights (4–5m) in order to solve "problems".

During competitive lead climbing, climbers are scored on the height that they achieve throughout a series of rounds in which the complexity of the routes progressively increases. In Europe, the Union Internationale Des Association d'Alpinisme (UIAA) uses a scale of 1–11 to grade difficulty. In North America, the Yosemite Decimal System (YDS) is used to rank the complexity of climbs. Table 31.1 allows for comparison of the different grades by professional bodies, which should allow the reader to grade an athlete's ability and allow for comparisons when reading the literature.

To date, research investigating the most effective training programmes for the sport of climbing is limited, with this chapter highlighting the available literature. Therefore climbers tend to undertake a traditional approach when preparing for competitions. This approach involves the concept of climbing themselves fit and the use of explosive chin up type movements on specially adapted hand holds and grip type devices. This chapter aims to outline additional exercises and programming to further augment athleticism in these athletes.

Table 31.1 Comparison of classification of climbing complexity. The most common grading systems of compared with the accepted catergories of each, grouped by performance level novice, intermediate, advanced and elite

	Sport grade	British technical grade	Fontainebleau bouldering grade	Yosemite decimal grade
Novice	< 4+	4b	4	< 5.8
	5	4c	4+	5.9
Intermediate	5+	5a	5	5.10a
	6a – 6a+	5b 5c	5+	5.10b to 5.10c
	6b	5c	6a	5.10d
Advanced	6b+ – 6c+	5c/6a	6a+	5.11a to 5.11c
	7a – 7b	6a/6b	6b to 6b+	5.11d to 5.12b
	7b+ to 7c	6b/6c	6c to 6c+	5.12c to 5.12d
	7c+	6c	7a to 7a+	5.13a
Elite	8a	6c/7a	7b to 7b+	5.13b
	8a+ – 8b	6c/7a	7c to 7c+	5.13c to 5.13d
	8b+ – 8c	7a/7b	8a to 8a+	5.14a to 5.14b
	8c+	7b	8b to 8b+	5.14c
	> 9a	7b	8c to 8c+	> 5.14d

Athletic demands

On first observation, climbing is chaotic. Russell et al. (2012) defined climbing as a randomised set of movements at irregular time intervals, often characterised by periods of static inactivity, prior to phases of action. If we explore that concept further into body segments, we can start to make more sense of the patterns and movements involved.

To the casual observer, it is clear that the contribution of the upper and lower limbs are significantly different, making climbing an entirely unique sport which may account for limitations in the research. The upper limbs stabilise body position through contact forces (grip), whilst the lower limbs support the body weight through vertical force production, with the distance of the centre of gravity from the supporting wall influencing the contact force necessary for balance (Quaine and Martin 1999).

Successful movements at all wall angles must be initiated using the lower limbs and force transferred through the trunk, with anecdotal evidence suggesting that lower limb strength is an advantage to many types of moves, particularly to maintain contact on the footholds. This is a finding more recently supported and developed upon by Baláš et al. (2014) who also found more experienced climbers applied the greatest loading to the footholds. This had a significant negative correlation to VO_2 (R = −0.72) and HR (r = −0.64), suggesting that if climbers were to increase their lower limb strength, subsequent improvements in movement economy and climbing performance would be likely. Upper body strength is still fundamental, with Noé et al. (2001) demonstrating that as the incline of the surface being climbed passed 90º (vertical), there was a subsequent reduction in loading of 34% on the foot holds, and a increase in loading of approximately 47% on the hand holds. Russell et al. (2012) expands on this, showing that more experienced climbers used a style that had a more extended elbow, and greater flexion at the knee to improve efficiency, keeping their COM further from the wall to maximise torque, thus reducing muscular work which is in contrast to what may be expected. The majority of studies into forces at foot and hand holds have used only static climbing positions (i.e. a climber has 4 points of contact with a wall, and removes a hand or a foot and the subsequent reorganisation of the forces were measured). Zampagni et al. (2011) showed that expert climbers have 1.3 times greater movement of their center of mass while redistributing their body weight when compared with less experienced climbers, who tended to restrict the movement of their COM. In this way expert climbers may be allowing a more even distribution of forces across all limbs. This could be due to the better upper body strength and endurance or simply technical ability acquired through practice.

Flexibility

Traditional rock climbing training advice makes reference to the need for athletes to maintain a good level of flexibility. Of course the range of movement (ROM) at the shoulder is important among climbers; more discrete but possibly of far greater relevance are the degrees of freedom at the hip, knee and ankle. Grant et al. (1996) studied the difference between male non, recreational, and elite climbers using sit and reach, high step and a leg span test. The traditional sit and reach test showed no difference but the more climbing specific step and leg span tests (Figure 31.1) suggested a better ROM among elite levels, but not of any statistical significance. This was the first investigation towards an identification of hip ranges which found low levels of association between ability and hip flexion and abduction (Mermier et al. 2000). The unique positions adapted by climbers such as the heel hook and Egyptian knee drop, can only be obtained with high ROM, and may leave a competitor unable to complete a problem or route as they cannot

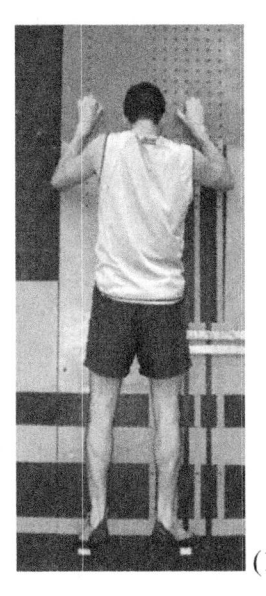

Figure 31.1 Foot-loading flexibility test Draper et al. (2009). The climber begins in an active start position (1). They raise their foot to a higher hold and transfer their mass onto that foot (2). The test was completed when the climber had loaded that now raised foot (3) and their hips above that foot. For the duration of the test the climbers hands must not lose contact with their holds. The score achieved was the measurement from the top of the start foothold to the top of the adjusted foothold and scaled to climber's height

co-ordinate the necessary limb sequence. With this information, Draper et al. (2009) designed and tested sport specific tests of climbing flexibility. They found the foot-loading flexibility test had the strongest correlation with climbing ability ($r = 0.65$, $p < 0.001$, $ICC = 0.96$).

Physiology, aerobic power and blood lactate

Until recently, physiological testing of rock climbing relied upon treadmill and cycle ergometer tests using climbers as participants. Advances in technology have allowed climbers to wear lightweight, battery powered open circuit systems whilst in situ. Russell et al. (2012) found that climbing requires 10 times more mechanical work ($18.0 + 2.2$ J.kg.m^{-1}) than walking and despite varying levels of ability and kinematic stratergies, no difference could be found in the amount of mechanical work done.

Watts et al. (2000) identified that previous studies had significant drawbacks due to the use of simulated climbing, low sample sizes and unrealistic testing protocols; thus they set about better characterising the metabolic response during a 20m ascent of a difficult (5.12b YDS) route. The elite climbers took a mean time of 2.57 min and gas collection was possible for the whole route (see Table 31.2), whereas previously reported values were only able to provide analysis of gas collection from the final 60 seconds of routes.

There is some variation in oxygen uptake during climbing, Watts et al. (2000) found a mean $\dot{V}O_{2peak}$ of 31.9ml kg min^{-1} which they suggest would be well under the (non measured) $\dot{V}O_{2max}$ for this sample population, estimated as 51–55ml kg min^{-1} (Billat et al. 1995; Watts and Drobish 1998; de Geus et al. 2006). Billat et al. (1995) found during climbing tests, climbers typically achieved 37.7% to 45.6% of their maximum $\dot{V}O_{2max}$ (measured via treadmill running).

Heart rate (HR) values are linked closely to the difficulty of climbing route (Mermier et al. 1997). The easiest route (5.6 YDS) provoked a HR of 142+19 beats·min^{-1} vs. the advanced route (5.11 YDS) at 165+11beats·min^{-1} ($p = 0.0001$). HR and VO_2 response were significantly lower among intermediate climbers vs. novices ($p < 0.05$) for the same route (Baláš et al. 2014).

The heart rates achieved in climbing are often reported as disproportionally higher for a given %$\dot{V}O_{2max}$ when compared with a dynamic form of exercise such as running or cycling. Sheel (2004) proposed this is due to the accumulation of metabolites as result of ischemia from the isometric nature of rock climbing. This is also in support of the theory that as intensity increases, heart rate becomes a weak indicator of intensity.

Increases of just $3.2 + 0.8$ mmol $\times$ L^{-1} than at pre climb were found following a 2.57 ± 0.41 min climb (difficulty 5.12b; Watts et al. 2000). Data gathered by Werner and Gebert (2000) (cited in Watts 2004) at the 2000 UIAA World Championships analysed the BLA of 46 competitors 1min post climb. Mean climbing time was 4.2mins + 1.8mins; and the mean BLA was 6.7mmol.L^{-1} +1.1 . It is likely that the difference between the two groups is both the duration

Table 31.2 Watts et al. (2000) summary of 20m sport climbing ascent ventilation (VE), oxygen uptake (VO$_2$), heart rate (HR)

	Average means	Average range	Peak means	Peak range
VE	57.03+8.31	40.08–70.9	71.85+10.54	50.7–86.5
VO$_2$ (ml min^{-1})	1660+342	1130–2240	2147+413	1380–2740
VO$_2$ (ml kg min^{-1})	24.7+4.3	16.6–32.2	31.9+5.3	20.3–42.2
HR (b min^{-1})	148+16	117–182	162+17	123–193

(2mins 57s vs. 4.2mins) and the difficulty of the climb (5.12b vs. World Championship), a concept supported by the work of Draper et al. (2010), who found an increase from 1.5+0.5 to 3.1+0.6mmol^{-1} at the intermediate Sport Grade of 6a.

De Geus et al. (2006) compared the BLA responses for climbers on routes of varying incline and direction (horizontal traverse vs. vertical ascent). The influence of an overhanging wall when compared to a vertical wall traverse saw BLA concentrations of 6.19+1.61 and 4.84+1.3 ($p <$ 0.016) respectively.

To give perspective, when compared to running or cycling, the relative increases in blood lactate (BLA) among climbers are generally lower, most likely due to the smaller muscle mass contribution of the upper limbs (relative to lower body), in particular the small finger flexors that make up the forearm (Sheel et al. 2003). A key influencer of the metabolic demands of climbing is the complexity of the climb – specifically, overhangs – which should be considered when programming.

Energy system contribution

Figure 31.2 summarises the energy system contribution for indoor rock climbing assessed over 3 difficulty gradings of 5.10 YDS, 5.11b and the most difficult 5.12b (Bertuzzi et al. 2007). Climbs were 10m in height, with a mean of 25 moves.

The data found that elite climbers predominantly use the aerobic and anaerobic alactic energy systems regardless of route difficulty, training status, or upper body strength.

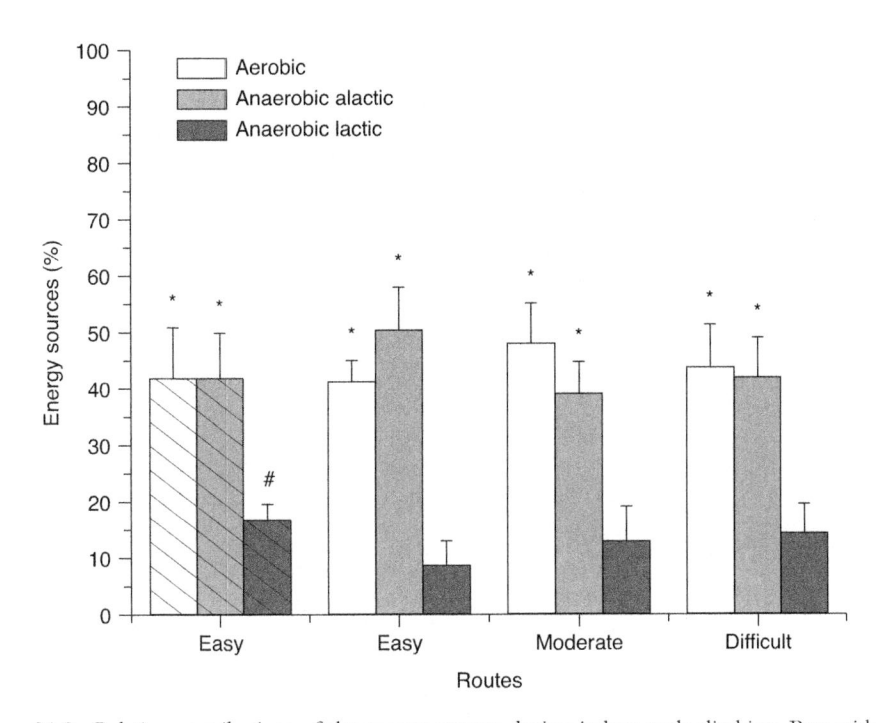

Figure 31.2 Relative contributions of the energy systems during indoor rock climbing. Bars with and without transverse stripes refer to the recreational and elite groups, respectively. Values are means ± SD. *Different from the anaerobic lactic system (P < 0.05). #Different from the anaerobic lactic system of the elite group on the easy route (P < 0.05) (Bertuzzi et al. 2007).

Motion analysis

Using 3D motion analysis, Sibella et al. (2007) demonstrated that a fluid technique using slower, less powerful movements allowing greater control of equilibrium is employed by more skillful climbers. This is supported in many climbing reference books and supported by the work of Bertuzzi et al. (2007) who propose that there may be a similar phenomenon among climbers as seen in distance runners, where among the elite levels, ability is characterised by running economy despite similar $\dot{V}O_{2max}$. Running economy (RE) is the oxygen the body consumes whilst running at a steady state, sub-maximal velocity. RE is influenced by a number of factors including, but not limited to, anthropometry, kinematics, flexibility, ground reaction forces, strength training and experience, and can be a better predictor of performance in distance running than $\dot{V}O_{2max}$ (Saunders et al. 2012; Hasegawa 2007; Helgerud et al. 2009; Ferrauti et al. 2010). A determinant of rock climbing performance could logically be the way in which elite climbers limit their energy expenditure through the use of discrete skills learnt via accumulating long hours of practice.

With these findings taken into consideration, indoor Rock Climbing is typically characterised by moderate aerobic power (as expressed by $\dot{V}O_{2max}$) and low blood lactate accumulations, and the ability to recover between repeated bouts of climbing may be of use especially during competition. It is unlikely that cardiac output would limit climbing, but maximal oxygen uptake of the upper limb musculature might, which calls into question the suitability of a traditional aerobic test and its use as conditioning protocol (Phillips et al. 2012; Watts 2004; Sheel 2004; Booth et al. 1999; Watts and Drobish 1998; Billat et al. 1995). Consequently more specific upper body tests for conditioning should be used that replicate the peripheral effects and in turn the central impact of cardio vascular stress. Although currently untested, examples include arm ergometers, battle ropes or seated rope pulls against fixed resistance.

Grip strength

Grip strength is a conflicting area among the research though the testing methodology and skill level grading of participants should be called into question. The use of a standardised "D" grip hand held dynamometer may not accurately depict the grip strength of climbers as it is lacks dynamic correspondence to technical grips as illustrated in Figure 31.3; it is more likely that the discrete techniques and skills experienced climbers employ is what makes them better climbers (Gurer and Yildiz 2015). Therefore when considering grip strength, its specificity must be noted, but there is indeed a case for a lower limit that hinders performance.

Scaling grip strength to bodyweight is more accurate when considering ability among climbers. Gajewski et al. (2009) showed that relative (pre climb) grip strength could distinguish climbers based on ability ($p < 0.001$) and also (self-reported) climbing ability. The strength to weight ratio of the finger flexors was a clear determinant of performance among elite women climbers (Wall et al. 2004; Philippe et al. 2012) and between control, intermediate, advanced and elite level climbers ($p < 0.05$, Fryer et al. 2015).

Climbers often attribute falls to no longer being able to maintain a grip due to forearm fatigue. On overhanging sections, the contribution of the legs reduces and the force generated by the upper limbs must increase placing greater strain on the smaller musculature of the forearms and the fingers (MacLeod et al. 2007). The repetitive mechanism of gripping isometrically, relaxing and re-gripping handholds also suggests that endurance of grip strength may be a limit to performance. Occlusion of blood flow occurs at 45–75% of MVC in isometric contractions, causing an increase in BLA concentration and intramuscular acidity (Barnes 1980; Loenneke et al. 2010). This has prompted tests of grip strength and endurance with a focus on BLA accumulation showing that

Figure 31.3 Variation in grip based on hand holds: a – full crimp, b – pocket, c – open crimp, d – pinch

as BLA increases, grip endurance decreases despite strength remaining similar (Watts et al. 1996). Climbers (vs. non climbers) had higher absolute grip strength ($p = .009$) despite smaller body mass, grip endurance and greater endurance, and faster re-oxygenation of the working forearm musculature ($p < .05$) (MacLeod et al. 2007; Philippe et al. 2012; Ferguson and Brown 1997).

Novel grip training devices as described in the literature that allow climbers to develop grip strength while hanging from simulated holds have elicited 21.5% finger strength and +2.5 YDS scale improvements over a 12 week training programme (Anderson and Anderson 2015). Caution should be taken as the authors highlight the low training age of the cohort and relatively ad-hoc training nature of climbing populations. This should prompt S&C coaches to consider the strategies they employ suggesting that the low training age of climbers may not suit complex training programmes. Rhythmic hand grip protocols have shown significant improvements in blood flow and strength of the forearm flexors, though the effects are short lived once training was stopped (Alomari et al. 2010).

When looking at the upper body muscular contribution to rock climbing, the effect of pre-fatiguing the digit flexors and elbow flexors was a significant reductions in the number of climbing moves that could be completed (78% and 50% of control values respectively $p < .05$). Pre-fatiguing of the shoulder adductors and lumber flexors also reduced the progress of climbers but not to a statistically significant level (Deyhle et al. 2015). This sits slightly at odds with other studies that suggest that frontal plane shoulder extension is a limit to climbers' ability (Grant et al. 1996; Mermier et al. 2000). These may be areas that the strength and conditioning coach might seek to strengthen as a result.

Shoulder rotator strength ratios are significantly different between climbers and non-climbers, with a greater eccentric internal rotational strength observed in climbers. This is most likely an adaptive mechanism due to the habitual stresses placed upon the upper limb musculature during climbing ($p < .005$ Wong and Ng 2009). These ratios may be used to guide injury prevention and "return to play" among climbing populations. As these values were obtained via isokinetic testing, it may be hard for S&C practitioners to replicate such protocols.

Injury prevalence

Improvements in training equipment and the relatively controlled environment of an indoor climbing center keeps the number of accidental injuries very low. There is some variation in the rates of injury exposure ratios as displayed in Table 31.3, which can be explained by two factors: Firstly, location, as higher rates of injury are seen outdoors vs. indoors, and, secondly, the type of climbing being performed. For example Schöffl and Winkelmann (1999) found lower rates than Schöffl and Kuepper (2006), possibly due to the latter study being conducted at the 2005 World Championships in Rock Climbing where performance is key and the authors speculate that competitors were more likely to take risks not normally taken in practice.

The finger is the most commonly injured body part among climbers, with over half of all injuries occurring at this site (Wright et al. 2001; Jones et al. 2008; Schweizer 2012; Schöffl et al. 2015; Jones et al. 2015). Previous injury to the finger increased the odds ratio to 4.0 ($p = 0.03$). When viewed as a complete athlete injury history (self reported), the number of finger injuries increased to 58% indoors with the elbow second and shoulder third (42% and 37% respectively). No relationship could be found between gender, years climbing, BMI, body weight or ability (Schweizer 2012).

Due to the mechanics of climbing, specific grips – for example the "crimp grip" with flexion at the proximal interphangeal joint (PIP) and extension of distal interphangeal joint (DIP) – combined with the high loads can lead to a highly specific injury termed closed pulley tendon rupture, with a recovery time of 4–6 months before full loading. The location with the highest likelihood of pulley injuries are D4, A2 and A4 pulley tendon sheaths on the ring or middle finger, apparently an injury not normally seen outside of climbing (Schöffl et al. 2015). Many climbers will tape their proximal phalanx to help prevent this injury. Schweizer (2012) recommends a gradual, progressive warm up of 20–30 minutes incorporating finger flexion exercises with bands and climbing 3–4 routes with 40 moves in each be used as pre/rehab. Common wrist injuries stem from falls from bouldering problems on to crash mats or, during rope climbing, falls against the wall that lead to hand or wrist injuries.

Overuse injuries at the elbow are not uncommon, specifically radial tunnel syndrome, brachialis or distal bicipital tendinitis. Though rare, coracoid impingement should not be excluded from differential diagnosis when climbers present with anterior shoulder pain (Schöffl et al. 2011;

Table 31.3 Injury risk per 1000 hours

Author	Venue	Risk	Per 1000hrs
Bowie (1988)	Outdoor	0.2–0.4% per day	37.5
Schussman et al. (1990)	Outdoors	108 over 5 years	0.6
Limb (1995)	Indoors	55 in 1.021 million visits	0.027
Schöffl and Winkelmann (1999)	Indoors	4 in 25,163 visitors 0.016%	0.079
Schöffl and Kuepper (2006)	Indoors – World Championships	4 in 1300 hours	3.1
Neuhof et al. (2011)	Indoors		0.2
Schöffl et al. (2013)	Indoors	515,337 visits over 5 years	0.02

Frostick et al. 1999; Andrews and Whiteside 1993). Strength and conditioning programmers should be wary of the postural alterations that are reportedly seen among elite level climbers due to the demands of the sport. The negative postural position of increased thoracic kyphosis, increased lumbar lordosis, and potentially shortened pectoralis muscles (Förster et al. 2009) may lead to tendon impingements (Borstad and Ludewig 2005).

Shoulder injuries, not caused by a fall, are usually the result of overload. Young climbers frequently report proximal biceps tendonitis, whereas middle-aged climbers seem to suffer more rotator cuff and AC joint issues (Schweizer 2012). Shoulder injuries account for 17.2% of all injuries seen in a recent review, with a superior labral tear from anterior to posterior (SLAP tear, 32.5%), impingement (25.5%), shoulder ligament sprain (10.8%) and dislocation combined with Bankart lesion (10.2%) the most common injuries reported (Schöffl et al. 2015).

Lower limb

The vast majority of lower limb injuries in climbers are the result of falls. There are some specific moves (e.g. Egyptian/knee drop positions and heel hook; Figure 31.4) that, because of the joint angles,

Figure 31.4 (a) Egyptian knee drop (top); (b) Heel hook (bottom)

have contributed to a rise in tendon injuries. The heel hook has been linked to proximal tendon injuries in the hamstring muscle groups (Schöffl and Lutter 2015).

The foot is a complex area when reviewing injury data. Since 2009 injury rates among the foot range from 2.2 to 6.4%, though it is not clear if those injuries were the result of impact due to falls, overuse, or ill fitting footwear (Schöffl et al. 2015; Folkl 2013). In two major reviews of injuries among rock climbers, both with sample sizes greater than 200, not one mention is made of injury to the foot (Jones et al. 2008; Wright et al. 2001). Advances in footwear have led to flexed and internally rotated forefoot, putting atypical stresses through the foot due to narrow asymmetrical toe boxes and pre-tensioned heel counters. A common theme among climbers is that a certain degree of foot pain is to be expected and tolerated with 98% of climbers wearing shoes at least a size too small, and 77% of climbers claiming to remove them between attempts to gain temporary relief (McHenry et al. 2015). It is possible that this bias is linked to the fact that there is a strong negative correlation between climbing ability and shoe size as % of foot length ($r = -0.65, p < 0.001$ McHenry et al. 2015). Hyperextension of the metatarsal phalangeal MTP and flexion of PIP and DIP can lead to callus, ingrown toenails, hallux angle valgus and sesamoiditis of the MTP joint. Climbing specific techniques such as "pointing" and "edging" may accelerate osteoarthritis (Chang et al. 2015; Schweizer 2012). Finally the foot placement known as "smearing" can lead to chronic plantar fasciitis due to the dorsiflexed position and the ball of the foot being planted against the wall (Chang et al. 2015).

Fitness testing battery

When testing athletes in any sport, the relevance of the tests and the conclusions drawn from them must relate directly to performance. Testing applies a stress to athletes and the inclusion of any test in a battery must be validated. On the basis of the previous sections, a fitness testing battery for Indoor Rock Climbing should include tests to scale finger and bent arm hang time, hip mobility via the rock over climbing move, and an expression of lower limb strength and power, and % body fat. Additions which aim to assess the efficacy of the S&C programme should be taken via ongoing strength tracking of training loads. With aerobic capacity rarely seen as a limit to climbing success, it would seem of little relevance to include a test of it.

The time to failure during bent arm hang is a popular test among climbing literature too and can differentiate between climbers (Magiera and Roczniok 2013). Baláš et al. (2012) used tests of bent arm hang time and finger hang time to create the latent variable *hand-arm strength and endurance* which they suggest accounts for 97% of the variance in the Red Point (a measure of climbing ability) in this sample size.

The lower limb contribution to rock climbing is rarely documented and the appropriateness of a 1RM squat/deadlift to climbing is likely to be of little use if the climber has a low strength and conditioning training age. If the athlete is capable, then the use of a deadlift as a measure of

Table 31.4 Performance testing for indoor rock climbing

Upper body strength	Flexibility	Screening	Lower body	Climbing ability
Finger hang (s)	Rock over	Single leg squat	Squat jump (cm)	YDS level
Bent arm hang (s)		Shoulder IR:ER ROM	Countermovement jump (cm)	
		Body fat %	Deadlift 1RM (kg)	

lower body strength should be included. Brent et al. (2009) took a highly specific rock climbing move the "rock-over" and found it could accurately discern between climbers of different abilities ($r = 0.67, p < 0.0005$). The rock-over requires a high degree of flexibility and strength to allow a climber to place one foot on a higher hold, transfer their body mass onto that leg, and extend the leg to move vertically up the wall. Elite climbers will apply more lower limb force to the footholds than their non elite counterparts which suggests a sparing effect for the upper body (Zampagni et al. 2010).

Programming

Climbers' training to date is often ad-hoc, trial and error, and adapted from other sports (Anderson and Anderson 2015; Brent et al. 2009). Typical training volumes are 7.5+5, 10.1+3.6, 13+4 hrs per week (Mermier et al. 2000; Magiera and Roczniok 2013; de Geus et al. 2006). Consequently the (S&C) training age is low and programmes in the initial stages must reflect this. Traditional periodisation seems the most appropriate with rep ranges that avoid hypertrophy. The postural imbalances of climbing should be addressed with the addition of upper body pressing and overuse injuries around the elbow and fingers must be taken into account.

Pulling movements are included, but the volume is kept low with the aim of prefatiguing the grip on total body programme 1 with DB walking lunge into fat grip bench pull. Zercher squats, while uncomfortable on the elbows, are included as they encourage a deeper bottom position while reducing stress at the shoulder and elbows, and reinforce the need to keep the torso upright, encourage bicep contraction and upper back strength gains.

Table 31.5 Sample strength programmes

	Total body 1	Sets	Reps
A1	Single arm dumb bell snatch	3	3e/s
B1	Zercher squat	4	6
C1	Dumb bell walking lunge	3	8
C2	Fat grip bench pull	3	6
C3	Hollow body holds	3	30s
	Total body 2	Sets	Reps
A1	Medicine ball vertical toss	3	3e/s
B1	Hang clean	4	6
C1	Push press	3	8
C2	Single leg RDL	3	6
C3	Half kneeling wood chop	3	10e/s
	Lower body strength	Sets	Reps
A1	Step up	3	4e/s
B1	Trap bar deadlift	4	6
C1	Barbell hip thrust	3	6
C2	Back extension w over head band pull	3	8–12
C3	Plate pinch farmers walk	3	Max distance

These programmes lean towards a lower body strength improvement that, based on the current literature, seems to be a key factor in improving performance but is perhaps being overlooked. Olympic lifts, aiming to enhance full body power development, can only be implemented when sufficient base strength and technique have been developed.

Sample corrective programme

The focus of this programme is on improving thoracic spine, shoulder and hip mobility and strength. These sessions could precede gym sessions or climbing sessions as a pre-activation if preferred.

Sample conditioning programmes

With the aerobic and anaerobic alactic energy systems contribution being the most to the sport of indoor climbing, below are two sample sessions designed to develop the anaerobic alactic system with the aim to improve the aerobic system via repeated climbing sessions. Of course should climbers lack very basic fitness, this would need to be addressed.

Exercise selection should vary greatly, but the closer the athlete moves to competition, the more specific the choice of conditioning method to the sport. Variety will have good effects, but stick to one exercise per session. Suggested exercises could include sprints, boxing, Watt Bike, ski

Table 31.6 Sample corrective exercise programmes

	Upper body bias correctives	*Sets*	*Reps*
SMR	Thoracic spine – wrist flexors	n/a	1 min per site
	Pec minor – triceps		
	Latisumus dorsi		
Mobility	Dowel thoracic rotations	1	12 e/s
Mobility	Band shoulder dislocates	1	10
Activation	Scapular wall slides	2	10
Activation	Mini band serratus wall slides	2	12
	Lower body bias correctives	Sets	Reps
SMR	Quadriceps – adductors	n/a	1 min per site
	TFL – ITB		
Mobility	Spider man lunges	1	8 e/s
Mobility	Lateral lunge	2	8 e/s
Activation	Cook band single leg RDL	2	6 e/s
Activation	Mini band glute walk series	2	12 e/s

Table 31.7 Sample conditioning programmes

	Work	*Rest*	*Reps*	*Sets*	*Rest between sets*
Alactic power	10s	3 mins	6	2	12 mins
Alactic tolerance	15s	60s	10	2	10 mins

erg, battle ropes; the key to development is all out effort. Active recovery between sets is encouraged to maximise results.

Conclusion

The chaotic nature of climbing and the rich tradition seen within the sport has meant that for some time there has been little to no formalised strength and conditioning preparation of athletes. In recent years the increases in research into the physiological and muscular demands of the sport have started to provide the practitioner with insights into the underlying needs of the sport. Supplementary training away from the wall should aim to promote postural symmetry, increase flexibility around the pelvic girdle, improve lower limb strength and improving upper body strength whilst maintaining a balanced programme given the predominantly pulling bias of the sport. Of interest would be the use of integrated conditioning either by pre-fatiguing the forearm musculature, or by manipulating climbing conditions such as complexity, overhang work and work to rest ratios.

References

Alomari, M.A., Mekary, R.A. and Welsch, M.A., 2010. Rapid vascular modifications to localized rhythmic handgrip training and detraining: Vascular conditioning and deconditioning. *European Journal of Applied Physiology*, 109(5), pp. 803–809.

Anderson, M. and Anderson, M., 2015. A novel tool and training methodology for improving finger strength in rock climbers. *Procedia Engineering*, 112, pp. 491–496.

Andrews, J.R. and Whiteside, J.A., 1993. Common elbow problems in the athlete. *The Journal of Orthopaedic and Sports Physical Therapy*, 17(6), pp. 289–295.

Baláš, J. et al., 2012. Hand – Arm strength and endurance as predictors of climbing performance. *European Journal of Sport Science*, 12(1), pp. 16–25.

Baláš, J. et al., 2014. The effect of climbing ability and slope inclination on vertical foot loading using a novel force sensor instrumentation system. *Journal of Human Kinetics*, 44(1), pp. 75–81.

Barnes, W.S., 1980. The relationship between maximum isometric strength and intramuscular circulatory occlusion. *Ergonomics*, 23(4), pp. 351–357.

Bertuzzi, R.C. de M. et al., 2007. Energy system contributions in indoor rock climbing. *European Journal of Applied Physiology*, 101(3), pp. 293–300.

Billat, V. et al., 1995. Energy specificity of rock climbing and aerobic capacity in competitive sport rock climbers. *Journal of Sports Medicine and Physical Fitness*, 35(1), pp. 20–24.

Booth, J. et al., 1999. Energy cost of sport rock climbing in elite performers. *British Journal of Sports Medicine*, 33(1), pp. 14–18.

Borstad, J.D. and Ludewig, P.M., 2005. The effect of long versus short pectoralis minor resting length on scapular kinematics in healthy individuals. *The Journal of Orthopaedic and Sports Physical Therapy*, 35(4), pp. 227–238.

Bowie, W.S., Hunt, T.K. and Allen, Jr, H.A., 1988. Rock-climbing injuries in Yosemite National Park. *Western Journal of Medicine*, 149(2), p. 172.

Brent, S. et al., 2009. Development of a performance assessment tool for rock climbers. *European Journal of Sport Science*, 9(3), pp. 159–167.

Chang, C.Y., Torriani, M. and Huang, A.J., 2015. Rock climbing injuries: Acute and chronic repetitive trauma. *Current Problems in Diagnostic Radiology*, 45(3), pp. 205–214.

de Geus, B., O'Driscoll, S.V. and Meeusen, R., 2006. Influence of climbing style on physiological responses during indoor rock climbing on routes with the same difficulty. *European Journal of Applied Physiology*, 98(5), pp. 489–496.

Deyhle, M.R. et al., 2015. Relative importance of four muscle groups for indoor rock climbing performance. *Journal of Strength and Conditioning Research*, 29(7), pp. 2006–2014.

Draper, N. et al., 2009. Flexibility assessment and the role of flexibility as a determinant of performance in rock climbing. *International Journal of Performance Analysis in Sport*, 9(1), pp. 41–42.

Draper, N. et al., 2010. Physiological and psychological responses to lead and top rope climbing for intermediate rock climbers. *European Journal of Sport Science*, 10(1), pp. 13–20.

Ferguson, R.A. and Brown, M.D., 1997. Arterial blood pressure and forearm vascular conductance responses to sustained and rhythmic isometric exercise and arterial occlusion in trained rock climbers and untrained sedentary subjects. *European Journal of Applied Physiology and Occupational Physiology*, 76(2), pp. 174–180.

Ferrauti, A., Bergermann, M. and Fernandez-Fernandez, J., 2010. Effects of a concurrent strength and endurance training on running performance and running economy in recreational marathon runners. *The Journal of Strength & Conditioning Research*, 24(10), pp. 2770–2778.

Folkl, A.K., 2013. Characterizing the consequences of chronic climbing-related injury in sport climbers and boulderers. *Wilderness and Environmental Medicine*, 24(2), pp. 153–158.

Förster, R. et al., 2009. Climber's back – Form and mobility of the thoracolumbar spine leading to postural adaptations in male high ability rock climbers. *International Journal of Sports Medicine*, 30(1), pp. 53–59.

Frostick, S.P., Mohammad, M. and Ritchie, D.A., 1999. Sport injuries of the elbow. *British Journal of Sports Medicine*, 33(5), pp. 301–311.

Fryer, S. et al., 2015. Oxygen recovery kinetics in the forearm flexors of multiple ability groups of rock climbers. *The Journal of Strength & Conditioning Research*, 29(6), pp. 1633–1639.

Gajewski, J. et al., 2009. Changes in handgrip force and blood lactate as response to simulated climbing competition. *Biology of Sport*, 26(1), pp. 13–21.

Grant, S. et al., 1996. Anthropometric, strength, endurance and flexibility characteristics of elite and recreational climbers. *Journal of Sports Sciences*, 14(4), pp. 301–309.

Gurer, B. and Yildiz, M., 2015. Investigation of sport rock climbers' handgrip strength. *Biology of Exercise*, 11(2), pp. 55–71.

Hasegawa, H., 2007. Foot strike patterns of runners at the 15-km point during an elite-level half marathon. *The Journal of Strength & Conditioning Research*, 21(3), pp. 888–893.

Helgerud, J., Støren, O. and Hoff, J., 2009. Are there differences in running economy at different velocities for well-trained distance runners? *European Journal of Applied Physiology*, 108(6), pp. 1099–1105.

Jones, G., Asghar, A. and Llewellyn, D.J., 2008. The epidemiology of rock-climbing injuries. *British Journal of Sports Medicine*, 42(9), pp. 773–778.

Jones, G., Llewellyn, D. and Johnson, M.I., 2015. Previous injury as a risk factor for reinjury in rock climbing: A secondary analysis of data from a retrospective cross-sectional cohort survey of active rock climbers. *BMJ Open Sport & Exercise Medicine*, 1(1), pp. 1–6.

Limb, D., 1995. Injuries on British climbing walls. *British Journal of Sports Medicine*, 29(3), pp. 168–170.

Loenneke, J.P., Wilson, G.J. and Wilson, J.M., 2010. A mechanistic approach to blood flow occlusion. *International Journal of Sports Medicine*, 31(1), pp. 1–4.

MacLeod, D. et al., 2007. Physiological determinants of climbing-specific finger endurance and sport rock climbing performance. *Journal of Sports Sciences*, 25(12), pp. 1433–1443.

Magiera, A. and Roczniok, R., 2013. The climbing preferences of advanced rock climbers. *Human Movement*, 14(3), pp. 254–264.

McHenry, R.D. et al., 2015. Footwear in rock climbing: Current practice. *Foot*, 25(3), pp. 152–158.

Mermier, C.M. et al., 1997. Energy expenditure and physiological responses during indoor rock climbing. *British Journal of Sports Medicine*, 31, pp. 224–228.

Mermier, C.M. et al., 2000. Physiological and anthropometric determinants of sport climbing performance. *British Journal of Sports Medicine*, 34(5), p. 359–365; discussion 366.

Neuhof, A. et al., 2011. Injury risk evaluation in sport climbing. *International Journal of Sports Medicine*, 32(10), pp. 794–800.

Noé, F., Quaine, F. and Martin, L., 2001. Influence of steep gradient supporting walls in rock climbing: Biomechanical analysis. *Gait and Posture*, 13(2), pp. 86–94.

Philippe, M. et al., 2012. Climbing-specific finger flexor performance and forearm muscle oxygenation in elite male and female sport climbers. *European Journal of Applied Physiology*, 112(8), pp. 2839–2847.

Phillips, K.C., Sassaman, J.M. and Smoliga, J.M., 2012. Optimizing rock climbing performance through sport-specific strength and conditioning. *Strength & Conditioning Journal*, 34(3), pp. 1–18.

Quaine, F. and Martin, L., 1999. A biomechanical study of equilibrium in sport rock climbing. *Gait & Posture*, 10(3), pp. 233–239.

Russell, S.D., Zirker, C.A. and Blemker, S.S., 2012. Computer models offer new insights into the mechanics of rock climbing. *Sports Technology*, 5(December), pp. 120–131.

Saunders, P.U. et al., 2012. Factors affecting running economy in trained distance runners. *Sports Medicine*, 34(7), pp. 465–485.

Schöffl, V.R. et al., 2015. Injury trends in rock climbers: Evaluation of a case series of 911 injuries between 2009 and 2012. *Wilderness and Environmental Medicine*, 26(1), pp. 62–67.

Schöffl, V.R., Hoffmann, G. and Küpper, T., 2013. Acute injury risk and severity in indoor climbing – A prospective analysis of 515,337 indoor climbing wall visits in 5 years. *Wilderness and Environmental Medicine*, 24(3), pp. 187–194.

Schöffl, V.R. and Kuepper, T., 2006. Injuries at the 2005 World Championships in Rock Climbing. *Wilderness & Environmental Medicine*, 17(3), pp. 187–190.

Schöffl, V.R. and Lutter, C., 2015. The 'Heel Hook' – A climbing-specific technique to injure the leg. *Wilderness & Environmental Medicine*, 27, pp. 294–301.

Schöffl, V.R., Schneider, H. and Küpper, T., 2011. Coracoid impingement syndrome due to intensive rock climbing training. *Wilderness and Environmental Medicine*, 22(2), pp. 126–129.

Schöffl, V.R. and Winkelmann, H.P., 1999. Accident statistics at 'indoor climbing walls'. *Sportverletz Sportschaden*, 13(1), pp. 14–16.

Schussman, L.C. et al., 1990. The epidemiology of mountaineering and rock climbing accidents. *Journal of Wilderness Medicine*, 1(4), pp. 235–248.

Schweizer, A., 2012. Sport climbing from a medical point of view. *Swiss Medical Weekly*, 142(October), pp. 1–9.

Sheel, A.W., 2004. Physiology of sport rock climbing. *British Journal of Sports Medicine*, 38(3), pp. 355–359.

Sheel, A.W. et al., 2003. Physiological responses to indoor rock-climbing and their relationship to maximal cycle ergometry. *Medicine & Science in Sports & Exercise*, 35(7), pp. 1225–1231.

Sibella, F. et al., 2007. 3D analysis of the body center of mass in rock climbing. *Human Movement Science*, 26(6), pp. 841–852.

Wall, C.B. et al., 2004. Prediction of indoor climbing performance in women rock climbers. *Journal of Strength and Conditioning Research/National Strength & Conditioning Association*, 18(1), pp. 77–83.

Watts, P.B., 2004. Physiology of difficult rock climbing. *European Journal of Applied Physiology*, 91(4), pp. 361–372.

Watts, P.B. et al., 2000. Metabolic response during sport rock climbing and the effects of active versus passive recovery. *International Journal of Sports Medicine*, 21(3), pp. 185–190.

Watts, P.B. and Drobish, K., 1998. Physiological responses to simulated rock climbing at different angles – Lactate. *Medicine & Science in Sports & Exercise*, 30(7), pp. 1118–1122.

Watts, P., Newbury, V. and Sulentic, J., 1996. Acute changes in handgrip strength, endurance, and blood lactate with sustained sport rock climbing. *The Journal of Sports Medicine and Physical Fitness*, 36(4), pp. 255–260.

Werner, I. and Gebert, W., 2000. Blood lactate responses to competitive climbing. *The science of climbing and mountaineering*.

Wong, E.K.L. and Ng, G.Y.F., 2009. Strength profiles of shoulder rotators in healthy sport climbers and nonclimbers. *Journal of Athletic Training*, 44(5), pp. 527–530.

Wright, D.M., Royle, T.J. and Marshall, T., 2001. Indoor rock climbing: Who gets injured? *British Journal of Sports Medicine*, 35(3), pp. 181–185.

Zampagni, M.L. et al., 2010. Idiosyncratic control of the center of mass in expert climbers. *Scandinavian Journal of Medicine and Science in Sports*, 21(5), pp. 688–699.

Zampagni, M.L., Brigadoi, S., Schena, F., Tosi, P. and Ivanenko, Y. P., 2011. Idiosyncratic control of the center of mass in expert climbers. *Scandinavian Journal of Medicine & Science in Sports*, 21(5), pp. 688–699.

32
ALPINE SKIING

Pete McKnight

Introduction to the sport

Alpine skiing is practiced by millions of participants worldwide, and was first introduced to the Winter Olympics in 1936. It is currently the 28th largest sport via participation. The sport of Alpine skiing is governed by the Fédération Internationale de Ski (FIS). There are four main disciplines, Slalom (SL), Giant Slalom (GS), Super Giant Slalom (SG) and Downhill (DH), which are divided into technical events (SL and GS) and speed events (SG and DH). In these different disciplines, there are varying speeds and levels of technical difficulty. Furthermore, there are two additional events: Combined (C), which involves 2 runs of SL and one run of DH, and Super Combined (SC), which involves one run of SL and one run of SG or DH.

At the highest level, there is the FIS World Cup circuit, which generally has nine races per event, per season, most of which are contested in Europe; however, there are some races in Canada and the USA. Below this level, there is the European Cup, the North American Cup (NORAM), or South American Cup races. In addition, there is the held once every two years Alpine Ski World Championships, the last one being held in St. Moritz, Switzerland, in 2017, and the Winter Olympic Games every 4 years, the last one being Sochi, Russia, in 2014.

This chapter aims to provide the reader with a well-rounded introduction to the multiple factors and variables associated with working in Alpine Ski Racing. It will outline the physiological demands of the sport and common injuries, as well as how to effectively test, programme, and organise training.

Athletic demands

To understand the athletic demands of Alpine Skiing, a thorough needs analysis must be carried out. This involves aspects such as the biomechanics of skiing, as it is a very technical sport; metabolic demands; and the organisation of training (number of ski runs performed, length of runs, and rest between each run).

The four disciplines

The fastest time ever recorded in an alpine ski race was 100.6mph (161.9kph) by Johan Clarey, the French World Cup skier in 2013 in the downhill. The downhill follows a slightly different

Table 32.1 The differences and unique attributes of each event

	Slalom (SL)	Giant slalom (GS)	Super giant slalom (SG)	Downhill (DH)
Length of run (s)	60–90	60–90	60–90	60–210
Average speeds (kmh^{-1})	35–70 (20–45 mph)	40–80 (25–50 mph)	88–105 (55–65 mph)	Up to160 (100 mph)
Number of runs	Combined time of two runs	Combined time of two runs	One	One
Space between gates (m)	4–13	18–25	25–40	25–40
Vertical drop (m)	140–220	250–450	350–650	450–1100
Level of technical difficulty	Most technical event	Less technical than slalom	More technical than downhill	Least technical event
Other important factors	The short distance between gates requires the athletes to go at slower speeds in a more upright position	Like slalom, there is typically 2–4 hours between the start of the first run and the start of the second run	Wider gate separation allows and requires the athletes to utilise the tuck position at times during the race, enabling the skiers to reach up to 113kph (70 mph)	The athletes spend a large proportion of the race in the tuck position, transitioning between gates which are "speed controlling" gates to keep the skiers under control as they descend the mountain

format with one to three training runs on days leading up to the race, with an allotted hour course inspection each day. The other disciplines allow a 45-minute course inspection on the day of the race.

Skiing is a highly technical sport where ski racers typically start skiing at the age of 5 or 6 years old, start training around 6–8 years old, and generally compete at the highest level between the ages of 17 and 30 years old. Alpine skiing is not a sport that requires early *specialisation* to compete at the highest level, but it does require an early *start* to develop the necessary skills. At young ages, athletes compete and train in all four disciplines, but generally specialise into either technical or speed events as they get older. At the elite level, very few skiers compete in all four events.

Biomechanics of skiing

EMG analysis of muscles at the hip and knee show the highest activity in the turning phase of skiing, where centripetal forces are highest. Forces of 1–2.5g in turns are typical, with up to 3g in slalom turns. Force is applied through the forefoot, to take advantage of the steering nature of the ski. Additionally, high EMG activity has been shown in the rectus abdominis muscles, showing that the truck musculature plays a key component in ski racing.

The speed of contractions, seen in the angular knee velocities are relatively slow (Kibele and Behm, 2009). In SL it is typically 69 ± 11 °s^{-1}, with 34 ± 2 °s^{-1} in GS, and 17 °s^{-1} in SG. Running by contrast has angular velocities of around 300 °s^{-1} with 600–700 °s^{-1} being seen in sprinting. The percentages of maximal voluntary contractions (MVC) are relatively high, with SL showing 74 ± 33% and GS 73 ± 21% (Kibele and Behm, 2009; Stark et al., 1987). Maximum forces exceeding 100% MVC have been recorded (Karlsson et al., 1989) and are due to the magnitude of eccentric contractions.

Hip and knee flexion is more extreme in GS and SG, but equally knee flexion regularly goes below 80 degrees in Slalom and Downhill. Eccentric contractions are slow; however, fast powerful foot adjustments are necessary, warranting the need for reactive and agility type work. This ability to be able to feel and adjust/react to snow conditions becomes increasingly important as the piste deteriorates throughout the race, impacting the racers who set off later down the order.

There are a few biomechanical positions that are required for the technical execution of the skills in skiing, that would not be encouraged in traditional training in the gym. Valgus knee angles, for example, are a necessity when initiating the turns in skiing. Another example is the need for a frequently flexed lumbar spine, the degree to which will vary depending on the athlete and their style of skiing. These may not be ideal from a physical training viewpoint for the transfer of forces through the body, but are a necessary component of the sport. Whilst skiing may seem bilateral in that there are almost always two skis touching the snow, the distribution of forces is far from equal during a turn. In fact, the majority of force, if not all, needs to be applied through the outside ski (exterior limb).

Physical demands of alpine skiing

Due to the technical and physical nature of the sport, skiing requires a multitude of capabilities including anaerobic and aerobic endurance, muscle strength, flexibility, balance, agility, co-ordination, control and concentration. This blend of metabolic, muscular and neuromuscular demands means that a well-rounded, holistic approach to athletic preparation must be taken.

There is limited research on the physiological requirements of competing in any of the specific events; however, when we consider their duration and technical requirements, they are all likely to have different metabolic demands. All disciplines are high intensity, short duration with the greatest contributions coming from the lactate/glycolytic system, with the ATP-PCr and aerobic systems also playing significant roles. The discipline with the longest duration is the downhill, lasting between 60 and 210 secs, meaning that well developed glycolytic pathways are essential. Saibene et al. (1985) calculated the contribution of the different energy systems to be 46.4% oxidative, 28.3% ATP-PCr, and 25.3% lactate in alping ski racing.

Skiers can reach up to 97% of their maximum heart (Andersen and Montgomery, 1988; Johnson, 1995) showing the anaerobic demands of the event. This is also backed by a study showing the Austrian world cup skiers reporting lactate levels of 12–15mmol/L (Andersen and Montgomery, 1988; Berg and Eiken, 1999; Hame et al., 2002; Johnson, 1995), suggesting that lactate (or rather H$^+$) tolerance training is vital. During alpine ski racing and training, the prolonged muscle contractions cause vascular profusion deficits which is due to > 50% MCV, and vibration loads. As a result, there is a large oxygen deficit and a subsequent build-up of lactate in the muscles. This highlights the importance of lactate threshold and lactate tolerance work. Lactate threshold training may not improve $\dot{V}O_{2max}$ directly, but will increase the percentage of $\dot{V}O_{2max}$ that the ski racer can effectively operate at. This supports the findings that average $\dot{V}O_{2max}$ values of male elite skiers are not particularly high (56.9 mLKg^{-1}min^{-1}) (Hame et al., 2002), with a slightly higher average of 60.2 mLKg^{-1}min^{-1} found amongst the French Europa Cup Men's Team in 2013.

Neumayr et al. (2003) studied three groups of the Austrian National Team over a three-year period. There was a significant correlation between aerobic power and ranking in the sport. This suggests that although skiing requires a large anaerobic contribution, the athletes are also well-trained aerobically. This could either be to enhance recovery in training, or as a base on which to build further anaerobic adaptations. Furthermore, it could be that they possess evidence of well-developed aerobic systems as a by-product of skiing and living in a high altitude environment, as opposed to the fact that they have intentionally trained their aerobic system.

When compared with many other sports, the actions in ski racing are relatively slow. The unweighting phase between turns, which is the shortest phase of the turn or carve, is about 150 ms in SL (Kroell et al., 2005) and approximately 250 ms in GS (Raschner et al., 1999). Although slow eccentric actions dominate in ski racing (Berg and Eiken, 1999; Berg et al., 1995), explosive jumping power has also been related to skiing performance. This could be due to the need for quick changes and adjustments of foot placements when finding the best line to take or avoiding holes in the snow.

Bacharach and Duvillard (Bacharach and Duvillard, 1995) reported that SL skiers had greater maximal power outputs in a 30s Wingate test, but were unable to sustain these, whereas DH racers had lower maximal powers and were able to sustain power outputs longer, as reflected in a 90s Wingate test. This concurs with the stereotypes for technical and speed racers. DH racers also have to sustain more isometric contractions throughout the race (Seifert et al., 2009), due to sitting in the tucked position.

Demands of racing and training

Aerobic capacity is important in skiing for two main reasons. Firstly, it is important that the athletes are aerobically fit enough for racing and, secondly, that they are fit enough for training. Generally, unlike many other sports, training is often more demanding than racing, as more volume is done in training due to the difficulty of setting up a training session. That means that athletes will have a physical buffer in fitness. In downhill, however, long training runs may not be available due to the availability of the piste, making racing physically more demanding than training for a one-off run.

Days are typically long, and skiers could be up at 5:30 am, and on the snow from 7am or 8am, with races finishing around 2pm or 3pm. Generally, the skiers start their day with 30 minutes of free-skiing, followed by one to four warm-up runs. The athletes then inspect the course, and begin the training runs that will often be set to mirror the course. Practice session runs can last between 1 and 10 minutes with a total of four to fourteen runs, meaning training volume can be large. The logistics of getting back up the slope provides the rest interval for the athletes, with chairlifts usually taking between 5–15 minutes, allowing for full regeneration of ATP stores. All of this is at altitudes of up to 3900m with extreme weather conditions of sun, snow, fog, and blizzards all possible. In addition, the athletes often carry a spare pair of race skis and a kit bag with them, adding to the physical stress.

Injury prevalence

ACL injuries

Injury is a big part of Alpine Skiing. Anterior cruciate ligament (ACL) injuries are the most prominent injury with many ski racers suffering an ACL injury, and some suffering two or more ACL injuries during their career. In total ACL injuries make up 10–20% of all skiing injuries (Bacharach and Duvillard, 1995).

There are a number of different mechanisms which contribute to ACL injuries, namely, knee extension, full dynamic flexion with anterior draw of the tibia and/or internal or external rotation (Berg et al., 1995), and crashes (often into the side netting).

Interestingly, athletes who went 3 years without ACL injury showed peak hamstring torque at deeper angles of flexion (de Ruiter et al., 2007), suggesting that strength throughout the full range of motion of knee flexion is a key component to conditioning when considering injury prevention or reduction.

Shoulder injuries

The second most common injuries are shoulder injuries, which make up 4–11% of all injuries and 22–41% of upper body injuries (Emeterio and Gonzalez-Badillo, 2011). The injuries are caused upon impact with either the snow or the gate. The most common shoulder injuries include rotator cuff contusion, anterior glenohumeral dislocation where the ball fully separates from the socket, glenohumeral subluxation where the ball and socket are not fully separated, acromioclavicular separation, and clavicle fractures. These injuries predominantly occur as a result of falling with an outstretched arm.

Other injuries

There is a high prevalence of Non-Specific Lower Back Pain in Alpine skiers. This is due to many factors including shortened and/or tight psoas muscles, excessive time spent in hip and lumbar flexion, transfer of forces through the spine in atypical postures, accumulation of tension in the glutes, and large training volumes.

Muscle contusions, or bruises, are second only to sprains as a leading cause of sports injuries. In skiing, they are common at the knee, shoulder, and thumb, and can be caused by a multitude of reasons, including contact with the gates or snow.

Other considerations

Athletes should be screened for risk factors and indicators related to ACL injuries. This can be done through force plate analysis. Landing screens that look at landing mechanics and force absorption differences between the limbs are important in determining risk factors and can inform areas of focus in training. Multiple factors contribute to the risk of ACL injury, including high velocity collisions, changing snow conditions, or the athlete taking a poor line. Finally, the volume of training that skiers undertake contributes to increased injury risk due to factors such as overuse injuries, greater exposure to risk, fatigue related injuries like a lapse in concentration, and injury to muscles that are not fully recovered.

Fitness testing

Since ski racing requires a multitude of physical capabilities, each one of must be tested to determine pre- and post- training intervention measures in each area, so that the level of improvement can be determined. These are general tests of strength, agility, or endurance, for example, which can be seen as indicators of general athleticism. In addition to these, there are some 'ski specific' tests that can be performed; however, due to the highly technical nature of skiing, it is very difficult to draw correlations between 'dry land' testing results, and ski performance on the snow. Hence athletes should be tested in all areas of physical abilities that are deemed important for ski racing performance.

Ski racing has become more 'athletic' in the last decade due to shorter, more responsive skis. Quicker turns at higher speeds require skiers to be more agile and simply better athletes. Ski racing technique is constantly evolving, with the FIS making changes to rules. More force is required by the skier to bend the skis in the turn, and the athlete must be more active in the transition between turns. Clearly this increases the importance of strength, anaerobic power, and anaerobic capacity.

As ski racers start training regularly from the age of 6, and have been skiing regularly from the age of 3 or 4, it is imperative that coaches have test batteries which will determine the development of the athlete. Alongside this, a long-term athlete development programme based around movement skills and physical competencies will best prepare the skiers for their careers.

Fitness testing in general cannot be objectively measured on snow because training runs on snow cannot be standardised, making the tests non-repeatable. Monitoring of physical qualities and athlete's responses to skiing can be done by taking lactate values at the end of a run, for example; however, repeatable testing, as such, cannot be done.

General rules for testing

Simulating ski racing in a laboratory is impossible, but tests should simulate the physical demands of racing. Testing should be comprised predominantly of 'general tests', testing the general physical qualities of 'athleticism' that have an impact or relate to the sport, not testing the specific ability to ski. Tests should be sensitive enough to detect adaptations in training, easily repeatable, reliable, and validated. There should not be too many tests to avoid disrupting the athlete. It can also be helpful to use well-known tests where norms exist, so that data can be compared between athletes.

Table 32.2 Recommended battery of physical tests

Physical capacity	Recommended test	Comments
Strength	Squat 3RM, bench press 1RM, bench pull 1RM	Should encompass key exercises that measure overall body strength. Generally, a leg exercise and an upper body pull and push exercise provide the strength and conditioning coach with a good idea of the athlete's strength. Other examples would be a dead lift, leg press, and/or a unilateral leg test, for the leg exercise, and a weighted pull-up for the upper body exercises.
Power	CMJ	US Ski and Snowboard Association (USSA) rankings of skiers correlated with highest vertical jump heights and the average of 5 vertical jumps (Von Duvillard and Knowles, 1997).
Speed	40m sprint (with timing gates at 10m, 20m, and 40m)	This allows the strength and conditioning coach to understand the physical capacities of the skier such as their ability to accelerate, or produce maximum speed, which, although not directly related to skiing, can help to understand their underlying physiology better.
Agility	Harres test or t-test	It has been suggested that athletes who rank higher in slalom score better in agility tests, despite the fact that change of direction is very different on skis from that on land.
Aerobic endurance	$\dot{V}O_{2max}$	In cases where laboratory facilities to test $\dot{V}O_{2max}$ are not available, alternatives like the Bleep test, Yo Yo test, or a maximum aerobic speed (MAS) calculation via a 1.5Km run or 5-minute effort are possible.

(Continued)

Table 32.2 (Continued)

Physical capacity	Recommended test	Comments
Anaerobic endurance	90s box jump test (40cm box)	GS rankings in Canadian elite racers correlated with a 90s Wingate peak power (Viola et al., 1999). The loaded repeated jump test (LRJT) is another reliable test for measuring anaerobic power and capacity (Patterson et al., 2014). The athlete performs 60 countermovement jumps over a period of 2.5min with a barbell equivalent to 40% of bodyweight.
Trunk strength	Shirado-Ito abdominal hold, Sorensen prone hold test, lateral holds	A normal ratio of trunk flexors/extensors is considered to be between 0.7 to 0.8.
Balance	Wobble board test (Kibele and Behm, 2009)	Balance, rhythm, kinaesthetic sense and other coordination type abilities are physical attributes vital to ski racing; however, they can be difficult to test. Finding appropriate tests for these is a challenge and one of the areas that needs more research moving forwards.
Body composition	Skinfolds and bodyweight	Bodyweight can play a role in helping skiers to go faster; hence there is a tendency for skiers in speed events to be heavier.

In addition to tests of general athleticism, the test battery should include some 'ski-specific' tests (with respect to body position), where the duration or intensity, or types of muscle contractions are as close as possible to the ski race. This tests the individual under more familiar conditions. It could be that some individuals score less well on the pure tests of general athleticism, but score well on a ski-specific test, which requires a *combination* of physical qualities interacting with each other simultaneously. The downside of specific tests is that if the athlete improves in the test, it is sometimes difficult to determine which physical quality has improved, and which one still needs work, as the combination has improved. This illustrates further the need for tests of pure physical qualities where there are less variables involved.

Programming

There are plenty of challenges when planning training for Alpine ski racers, including deciding how best to organise training all the elements that are required. One of the positive aspects of this sport is that there is a long off-season, which with appropriate planning and periodisation, can be used to train the broad spectrum of elements that contribute to the performance of the athlete. The planning of training should be based around the physical requirements of skiing and the individual needs of the athlete.

Conditioning for skiing

Alpine ski racing demands a multitude of technical skills underpinned by excellent physical abilities. There is currently, however, relatively little published scientific data regarding the conditioning characteristics of a successful alpine ski racer. Neumayr et al. (2003), using data from Austrian world cup athletes during the period of 1997 to 2000, concluded that aerobic capacity is of paramount importance (Neumayr et al., 2003). Bosco (1997) maintained after testing Italian ski racers that anaerobic endurance was most important in determining performance potential and advised against high volume aerobic training (Patterson et al., 2009). Older literature indicates aerobic as well as anaerobic power as important factors for athletes in skiing racing (Turnbull et al., 2009). Strength also plays a significant role here, with maximal strength being shown as the greatest influence in reducing injuries across all sports.

Experts generally agree that alpine ski racers must possess very high leg strength and power. Several EMG measurements demonstrated the importance of eccentric muscle action during racing situations (Raschner and Patterson, 2009). Biomechanical analysis of the ski turns, shows that the body must overcome 3–4 times bodyweight during eccentric contractions. Frick et al. (1997) in their analysis of slalom turns, assumed that muscle actions use a slow type of stretch-shortening cycle. More recently, Austrian strength training programs focus on increasing maximal core strength and co-ordination/proprioception in all age groups. The possible rationale for this is supported by research by Leeturn et al. (2004) that suggested decreased core stability has contributed to lower extremity injuries (e.g. ACL ruptures in ski racing) (Leeturn et al., 2004). Kibler et al. (2006) also stated that core function (for body stabilisation and force generation) is a pivotal component in athletic activities (Kibler et al., 2006).

This highlights existing and somewhat contrasting opinions in current research, which can be attributed to the complexity of alpine ski racing and the difficulty in quantifying the physiological demands of the sport. Even though the physical demands have not been thoroughly quantified, by looking at what has been reported in the literature, it is safe to say that multiple facets of aerobic and anaerobic endurance, high levels of leg strength, trunk strength and stability, utilisation of the stretch-shortening cycle, proprioception and balance, all play a role in alpine skiing.

There are several extraneous variables that suggest that there is no single specific physiological parameter that can predict results in high level alpine ski racing. These include:

- Changing environmental factors (wind, visibility, temperature, altitude)
- Snow quality and temperature (proportion of ice, whether the piste has been injected or not); how soft the snow is impacts how active and responsive the skiers need to be on their skis
- Ski wax used
- Time of day
- Bib number (this determines how cut up the course is)

Any planning of training must first start with a clear overview of the year. Table 32.3 shows a typical yearly outline for a European based elite ski racer. The majority of the physical training

Table 32.3 A typical year outline

May Jun Jul Aug	Sep	Oct	Nov Dec Jan Feb Mar	Apr
Physical training	**Skiing**	**Rest**	**Competition season**	**Rest**
16–17 weeks	Southern	1 week		
Skiing + physical	hemisphere	**Physical**		
1 week per month	(e.g. Chile,	1 week		
(On a glacier or in	Argentina,	**Skiing**		
snow dome)	New Zealand)	2 weeks		

for adaptations occurs during the summer period from May to August, where the athletes will be doing a minimum amount of skiing, perhaps one week per month, and the focus is primarily on physical gains. Even during weeks where ski training does happen, this is usually limited to the morning, and physical training would still happen in the afternoon. There is some debate around the periodisation of strength and endurance in alpine skiing, the difficulty being how best to train both capacities concurrently, so that the athlete can develop the mixture of qualities they need.

Strength training

Strength training promotes an increase in the force generating capability of a muscle or group of muscles. Leg strength has been identified as one of the important physical capacities for alpine skiers to possess. Renowned sports physiologist Steven Plisk describes how elite downhill skiers have exceptional strength in the extensors of the foot, leg, thigh, and trunk (Andersen and Montgomery, 1988; Plisk, 1988). Strength work would typically be built up of multiple sets of 1–5RM.

Strength work should focus primarily on legs; however, upper body strength is often developed as a by-product of training. In addition, some upper body muscular development is important to protect the bodies skeletal system when falling. In particular, developing musculature of the shoulders could help minimise shoulder injuries from crashing and falling.

Typical exercises useful for a ski athlete:

- Squat, front squat, overhead squat. single-leg variations of squats
- Lunges, step-ups
- Olympic lifts and their variations, jerks & overhead presses
- Dead lifts (modified heights, grips, bars), RDLs
- Nordic hamstring curls
- Leg press (special situations). For high loading when biomechanical or other reasons prevent loading the squat. Injured athletes can also use it when they are in a compromised situation. Very experienced athletes looking for a high stimulus or overloading the system (i.e. want to increase load on legs without strengthening the trunk)
- Pushing vs. pulling exercises (horizontal vs. vertical) e.g. weighted pull ups, bench press, shoulder press

Hamstring strength work is a vital part of a ski racer's programme and plays a big role in protecting the knee against injury. ACL injuries are so commonplace that hamstring strength should be a focus of every skier's programme. The off-season period should be used to gain structural adaptation and max strength. Nordic hamstring curls are an effective way of working the hamstring hard eccentrically and, eventually, concentrically, too. During the season, direct hamstring work should be minimised due to the high volume of skiing. There could be an increased injury risk by training in a fatigued state, preventing the hamstring from playing its protective role.

General conditioning

In addition to the strength focused work, more general strength and conditioning is also necessary, where repetitions would be in the 6–12 range for more traditional exercises and in the 20–40 rep range for trunk training and rehab type exercises.

The trunk gets worked in strength training when exercises are done in the right way with good form. In these cases, the trunk works mostly isometrically. However, additional trunk work may be necessary for working rotation, flexion, or in a diagonal pattern, and in more complex, integrated movements. The warning here would be to be mindful of the pitfalls of too much isolated trunk work. These include shortening the psoas, which gets shortened in skiing anyway due to flexed hip position, and lower back pain.

Some exercises that can be beneficial for trunk strengthening are:

- Crunching (including lateral)
- Rotation, anti-rotation
- Medicine ball throws and catches
- Elastics/bands
- TRX exercises
- Leg lifts – straight/bent leg
- Plank and side plank variations, dead bugs
- Roll-out progressions

As part of general conditioning, mobility and flexibility work should be an integral part of pre-exercise warm-up, where joints are mobilised; and post exercise cool-down where stretching for improved range of motion and recovery becomes important. There should be both static and dynamic aspects to this training.

Disassociation of hips and shoulders is important from a technical point of view in skiing, and so some drills and exercises are often used when off the skis to develop this awareness and ability. An example exercise of this is the skier dead lift/woodchop with variations.

Weak areas and asymmetries should also be addressed as part of the general conditioning exercises. This often involves ironing out unilateral differences in leg strength and power, especially in skiers who have experienced ACL injuries in the past. It can also include further eccentric work, hamstring conditioning, shoulder conditioning, and hypertrophy.

Aerobic/anaerobic

Energy system training is an important aspect of training for ski racing. All work or activity requires energy and, simply put, two main pathways that can be adapted with training: the aerobic energy system and the anaerobic energy system.

The contribution of each of these pathways of energy supply is influenced predominantly by the intensity and duration of the activity. Both systems are always working, and as the intensity of the exercise increases there is an increasing contribution from the anaerobic system. The advantages of a well-developed aerobic system extend beyond racing, and can help skiers to cope with demands of training at altitude, recovery from training, and travel. Training with a heart-rate monitor enables the athlete and coach to know what zone of training the athlete is in, and therefore which system is predominantly being trained.

There are many modalities of training that can be used for metabolic training which include:

- Cycling – mountain bike, road bike, time trial
- XC-skiing, ski machine
- Mountain walking
- Running, sprinting
- Swimming
- Rowing

There should be periodisation of energy system development, peripheral to central adaptations. Polarising the training is one effective way of doing this.

Speed/power

Speed training promotes an improvement in the velocity capabilities of a muscle or group of muscles. Power training promotes and increases the force and velocity capabilities of a muscle or group of muscles. A high level of both speed and power are needed in ski racing, to execute quick changes in the placement of the skis and apply force quickly into the snow or ice.

Reactivity, or the neuromuscular system's ability to react and activate quickly also plays a part. This demand for quick, explosive, reactive movements on snow is important for adapting to changing conditions on the piste and can help prevent crashing or injury. This quality can be developed through various types of jumping, plyometrics and sprinting. When training these qualities, it is as much about the stimulus, or the intention of execution (for maximum recruitment), as it is about needing to jump high or sprint fast. It is about developing the right neuromuscular pathways for higher levels of recruitment.

Key exercises for this development include:

- Box jumps
- Drop jumps
- Hurdle jumps
- Bunny hops/ankling drills
- Mini hurdles
- Skater jumps
- Sprinting

Speed training should never include a lactic (anaerobic) element. Maximum velocity of movement is required to improve maximal speed. Therefore, speed training must involve FULL recovery (3 to 10 minutes) between bouts of work, and fatigue should be avoided; otherwise, it is not speed training, but is lactic, anaerobic training.

Agility/coordination

Agility and coordination training is part of developing the qualities needed for fast lateral movements and change of direction of the feet. These skills are specific to the sensation of being on snow; however, from a purely physical point of view, they can be learned on land. This type of training should not be a big part of the skiers programme, as very little stimulus is gained; however, control and coordination of your body are vital in ski racing, and so some off-snow drills can help. These skills are often fast gained and can be used as part of a session to activate the body for other activities. Exercises can involve a change of rhythm, change of speed, and varying complexity. Complexity can be increased through progressing and mixing the drills, and adding external cues which could be audio or visual. A large part of ski racing involves reacting and adjusting to a visual stimulus.

Agility drills involve a change of direction. The purpose of agility training is to teach the body to move efficiently and to improve coordination. This then allows the athlete to cope better with unknown situations like falling. Being able to fall well, and roll under control, can be the difference between a serious injury and a slight bruise. Gymnastics can also be used to help develop some of these qualities, as a key area of coordination is spacial awareness, which can be developed through rolling and tumbling type activities. Some of the basic agility skills that can be learned include cutting, weaving, crawling and lateral movements like a simple gorilla band walk or something more complex like a lateral duck walk with a medicine ball overhead.

Proprioception and balance

The integration of proprioception and balance training is important to the ski training programme (Raschner and Patterson, 2009), and should not replace other important work like strength and metabolic conditioning, but should complement training. This can be done on both land and on skis.

This type of work helps develop motor patterning, specifically the co-contraction of hamstrings and quadriceps in deep flexion positions. This co-contraction of hamstring counters the anterior displacement of the tibia, thus protecting the knee. In skiing, a lot of the time is spent on one ski, and often on the edge of it, so balance plays an important role. Progressions using unstable objects like agility cushions, Swiss balls, balance discs, mini trampolines, Bosu balls, and slacklines, for example, can be beneficial. A creative coach can make up fun games and challenges using this type of equipment. Blind-folding the athlete or getting them to perform exercises with their eyes closed can further challenge the individual. It is important that basic competency training is done first, before getting onto complex balance and proprioception work, so that the athlete develops good movement first as part of their progression down the physical development pathway.

Thinking outside the box

Other modes of training can be used to challenge the athlete further in the development of essential qualities and to make the programme more interesting.

The skiing action itself can be broken down into drills and exercises that are performed on skis, on different types of snow, or with varying distance between gates. This is a change from just skiing a standard course and can challenge the body and mind to react and adapt to changing conditions and tasks.

Activities like roller blading or ice skating can help with rhythm, and the technical placement of hips and knees when the athlete is unable to get to snow. They can also be used to train endurance and require similar levels of balance and coordination, and they incorporate a lot of lateral movement. Powder skiing can be used as a form of cross-training to develop local muscle development in the quadriceps, cardiovascular endurance, or balance and coordination. Additionally, ski touring can be a complementary way of developing endurance and adapting to altitude in the off-season.

Downhill mountain biking, or activities in a skate-park like roller blading, skateboarding, or BMX riding can help the athlete with the psychological side of engaging with speed and fear. Hypoxic and hyperoxic training can also add value if used in the right way within the right parameters.

Creative ways of training on the road

When traveling, the athlete needs to find a way of maintaining their levels of fitness, and in some cases, getting a training stimulus to improve some areas, if they are away for a particularly long time. The season is relatively long, from the end of October to the end of March, or beginning of April, so creative ways of training on the road are sometimes necessary. Staying in hotels in ski resorts can present the challenge of access to adequate gym facilities.

Table 32.4 A typical off-season training week for an elite level alpine ski racer

	Monday	Tuesday	Wednesday	Thursday	Friday	Saturday	Sunday
Morning	Strength, plyometrics	Anaerobic intervals on bike	Strength	Anaerobic intervals on bike (hypoxia)	Strength, plyometrics,	Bike aerobic	REST
Afternoon	Agility, coordination	Proprioception General conditioning	Speed and plyometrics	Proprioception General conditioning	Agility, coordination	Roller blading in skate park	
Evening	Stretching, massage, self-management strategies						

Traveling overland, however, makes it possible to take weights for strength training, a static bike for intervals or recovery, and other small pieces of conditioning equipment like hurdles, a Swiss ball, or a TRX, for example. If these pieces of equipment or a gym are not available, then bounding on the flat or on steps, and sprinting can be a good stimulus for maintaining strength, speed and the stretch-shortening cycle. Locations like carparks (preferably indoors) and even hotel corridors are often used by the best skiers in the world as their make-shift gym.

Organisation of training

Training so many different physical capacities to such a high level can provide the challenge of fitting it all in. Considerations should be taken around frequency of the training stimulus, the intensity of the stimulus, the duration of the session, all which are part of the organisation of the training day, week, and overall periodisation/plan.

Order of training

When choosing exercises and methods of training, it is important to perform the training in the right order. The exercises done first (after a thorough warm-up) should be ones that are the most demanding neurologically, i.e. strength, power, and speed exercises. Then exercises or training that is more metabolically demanding should be done next/last. If this is not the case, the athlete will be too fatigued to train with the right level of intensity, thus not achieving the desired outcome for the session.

Conclusion

There are many challenges when working with alpine ski racers. Obvious challenges which lie within the sport come from travel related issues like managing sleep, minimising jet-lag, training with compromised facilities, and accessing good nutrition. Challenges related to the environment include performing in the cold, in bad weather, or at altitude.

There is a culture of trying to mimic the sport and its movements when on land. Breaking down the ski training into smaller parts of skill development, instead of always practicing the whole ski run, would be beneficial. This way the athlete has the chance to isolate skills and improve them in a closed environment, and not just when skiing a run, when there are too many variables to consider. This would perhaps help prevent the desire to try to mimic the ski action and develop on land what can only be developed on skis.

Clearly the advice given here will be much more effective if the athlete has already developed physical literacy over a long-term approach to physical education. One of the key mistakes with conditioning for skiers is that there is often a misguided focus on early specialisation. A better understanding of long-term athlete development within the sport would help create more all-round athletes with well-ingrained physical competencies.

More studies are needed to determine what physical qualities significantly impact the outcome of ski races, or what physical qualities are most prominent in ski champions. This could help towards a clearer emphasis on what qualities make the biggest difference once an athlete has developed all areas of general athleticism and conditioning.

There is generally a poor culture of recording and quantifying training. More monitoring of internal and external loads is needed, to find what makes a meaningful change, and to track the athlete's well-being over the season. Smartphone applications, daily self-evaluation questionnaires, GPS, load cells in ski boots, and other such technology can help with moving this forwards.

Skiing has a very traditional culture, and it is recommended that a strength and conditioning coach seeks to understand that culture first, before trying to influence big changes based on their beliefs of best practice in high performance sport. Some of the cultural practices that are carried out are merely tradition; however, some are there for a good reason, and a clear rationale for certain practices can be justified.

Psychology is an area of development within alpine ski racing. This chapter does not cover the necessity of promoting positive mental and psychosocial strategies within a properly designed programme, which is fundamental to a speed based sport.

References

Andersen, RE and Montgomery, DL. Physiology of Alpine skiing. *Sports Med* 6(1): 210–221, 1988.

Bacharach, DW and Duvillard, SP. Intermediate and long-term anaerobic performance of elite Alpine skiers. *Med Sci Sports Exerc* 27: 305–309, 1995.

Berg, HE and Eiken, O. Muscle control in elite alpine skiing. *Med Sci Sports Exerc* 31: 1065–1067, 1999.

Berg, HE, Eiken, O and Tesch, PA. Involvement of eccentric muscle actions in giant slalom racing. *Med Sci Sports Exerc* 27: 1666–1670, 1995.

Bosco, C. Evaluation and planning of conditioning training for alpine skiers. In: *Proceedings of the 1st International Congress on Skiing and Science*. E Muller, H Schwameder, E Kornexl, and C Raschner, eds. London: E & Fn Spon, 1997, pp. 229–250.

de Ruiter, CJ, Goudsmit, JF, Van Tricht, JA and de Haan, A. The isometric torque at which knee-extensor muscle reoxygenation stops. *Med Sci Sports Exerc* 39(9): 443–453, 2007.

Emeterio, CA and Gonzalez-Badillo, JJ. The physical and anthropometric profiles of adolescent alpine skiers and their relationship with sporting rank. *J Strength Cond Res* 24(10): 1007–1012, 2011.

Frick, U, Schmidtbleicher, D, Raschner, C and Müller, E. *Types of muscle action of leg and hip extensor muscles in slalom*. NA, 1997.

Hame, SL, Oakes, DA and Markolf, KL. Injury to the anterior cruciate ligament during alpine skiing: A biomechanical analysis of tibial torque and knee flexion angle. *Am J Sports Med* 30(16): 537–540, 2002.

Johnson, SC. Anterior cruciate ligament injury in elite alpine competitors. *Med Sci Sports Exerc* 27(20): 323–327, 1995.

Karlsson, E et al. *The Physiology of Alpine Skiing*. Park City, UT: US Coaches Association, 1989.

Kibele, A and Behm, D. Seven weeks of instability and traditional resistance training effects on strength, balance and functional performance. *J Strength Cond Res* 23(9): 2443–2450, 2009.

Kibler, WB, Press, J and Sciascia, A. The role of core stability in athletic function. *Sports Med* 36(3): 189–198, 2006.

Kroell, J, Schiefermueller, C, Birklbauer, J and Mueller, E. Inlineskating as a dry land modality for slalom racers – Electromyographic and dynamic similarities and differences. In: *Science and Skiing III*. E Mueller, D Bacharach, R Klika, S Lindinger, and H Schwameder, eds. Oxford, UK: Meyer and Meyer Sport Ltd, 2005, pp. 76–86.

Leeturn, DT, Ireland, ML, Willson, JD, Ballantyne, BT and Davis, IM. Core stability measures as risk factors for lower extremity injury in athletes. *Med Sci Sports Exerc* 36(6): 926–934, 2004.

Neumayr, G, Hoertnagl, H, Pfister, R, Koller, A, Eibl, G and Raas, E. Physical and physiological factors associated with success in professional alpine skiing. *Int J Sports Med* 24(35): 571–575, 2003.

Patterson, C, Raschner, C and Platzer, HP. Power variables and bilateral force differences during unloaded and loaded squat jumps in high performance alpine ski racers. *J Strength Cond Res* 23: 779–787, 2009.

Patterson, C, Raschner, C and Platzer, H-P. The 2.5-minute loaded repeated jump test: Evaluating anaerobic capacity in alpine ski racers with loaded countermovement jumps. *J Strength Cond Res* 28(9): 2611–2620, 2014.

Plisk, S. SKIING: Physiological training for competitive alpine skiing. *Strength & Conditioning Journal* 10(1): 30–33, 1988.

Raschner, C, Koesters, A, Mueller, E, Schwameder, H, Zallinger, G and Niessen, G. Dynamische und kinematische Technikanalyse im Riesenslalom bei Weltklasserennla üfern. *Spektrum der Sportwissenschaften* 11(Suppl): 57–64, 1999.

Raschner, C and Patterson, C. Hans-Peter Platzer Institute of Sport Science, University of Innsbruck, Austria longitudinal fitness testing – Supervision of training in young alpine ski racers cumulative muscle fatigue during recreational alpine skiing. *J Strength Cond Res* 23: 698–704, 2009.

Saibene, F, Cortili, G, Gavazzi, P and Magistri, P. Energy sources in alpine skiing (giant slalom). *Eur J Appl Physiol Occup Physiol* 53(39): 312–316, 1985.

Seifert, J, Kroll, J and Muller, E. The relationship of heart rate and lactate to cumulative muscle fatigue during recreational alpine skiing. *J Strength Cond Res* 23: 698–704, 2009.

Stark, RM, Reed, AT and Wenger, HA. Power curve characteristics of elite slalom and downhill skiers performing a modified 90 s Wingate test. *Can J Sport Sci* 12: 24, 1987.

Turnbull, JR, Kilding, AE and Keogh, JW. Physiology of alpine skiing. *Scand J Med Sci Sports* 19(49): 146–155, 2009.

Viola, S et al. Anterior cruciate ligament injury incidence among male and female professional alpine skiers. *Am J Sports Med* 27: 792–795, 1999.

Von Duvillard, SP and Knowles, W. Relationship of anaerobic performance tests to competitive alpine skiing events. In: *Science and Skiing*. E. Mueller, H. Schwameder, E. Kornexl, and C. Raschner, eds. London and New York: E & FN Spon, Chapman and Hall Publishers, 1997, pp. 297–308.

33
FREESTYLE SNOWSPORT

John Noonan

Introduction

Freestyle snowsport has emerged as one of the fastest growing Winter Olympic sports in the past decade, with a record number of 5 freestyle events featuring at the 2014 Winter Olympic Games in Sochi, Russia: Slopestyle (SS) and Halfpipe (HP) ski and snowboard, Mogul Skiing, Aerial Skiing and Ski and Snowboard Cross (SBX). Progressive aerial events, like SS and Big Air, have encountered the largest growth in professional sport participation and an increased total number of professional competitions and media attention in the past few years. More countries have produced athletes capable of competing on the international scene than ever before. As such, national performance programmes have rapidly expanded in size and resource, with more teams working to create freestyle-specific training facilities and performance services to produce more talent capable of performing on the world stage. Several national teams have already begun to invest in more conventional high performance support services, including sport science and strength and conditioning to investigate where applied science can support and impact upon freestyle performance. Although to date, no countries/teams have published data from freestyle athletes in training or competition, leaving a void in empirical evidence of the sports key physical demands. Of concern currently, is the high prevalence of sports injuries impacting elite male and female freestyle athletes. Greater awareness of the training and competition activity loading would greatly increase understanding and ability to offer evidence-based injury prevention/performance solutions.

Using current available evidence and practical experience gained by the author in the field, this chapter will provide the reader with knowledge of demands, challenges faced with freestyle athletes and applied strength and conditioning recommendations.

Athletic demands

Slopestyle event characteristics

Slopestyle ski and snowboard competitions are characterised by explosive, ground and aerial free-flowing, acrobatic manoeuvres, including terrain features, rail slides and aerial boosting 'kickers' (Jumps). A World Cup course comprises 6–8 features over 3 sections, interspersed with short,

Figure 33.1 The Sochi Winter Olympics 2014 Slopestyle course, consisting of the rails section (3 initial features), and the jumps section (3 progressively larger kickers toward the bottom of the course)

Photo: Jenny Bletcher.

flat transitions allowing set-up time between tricks (see Figure 33.1). Athletes compete individually in qualifying rounds through to finals comprising of 2/3 separate runs. Like gymnastics, freestyle athletes compete to gain points awarded to riders/skiers that utilise challenging features in a sequential and creative manner. Athletes endeavour to produce a well-balanced run, incorporating qualities established by the International Ski Federation, and include variety, combinations, execution, difficulty and amplitude, each contributing to overall impression. Deductions are made for missed features, mistakes, stops and falls/crashes. High scoring runs require athletes to ride/ski the most technical course line, utilising a range of novel and progressive tricks including 'board grabs'. Athletes capable of achieving podium spots at competitions like 'Dew Tour' at Breckenridge, Colorado, and 'X-Games', held in Aspen, need to produce the most advanced and progressive range of tricks within the field. For example, versions of the 'Triple Cork 1620', and the 'Backside 1080' (see Figure 33.2) (spinning backside 1080 degrees about their axis) have become increasingly common for athletes placed in the top 5 of competition within the last 3 years.

Biomechanical demands

To date, advancements in microtechnology have enabled scientists to measure aspects of aerial manoeuvres, global movement kinematics and joint load kinetics during snowboard jumps. For example, total air-time and average degree of rotation values where investigated in elite HP athletes in training and during staged competition (Harding and James, 2010).

Most injury-based reviews examining body load and limb mechanics have assessed demands of the ankle joint complex during snowboard carving, to understand the incidence of reported ankle ligamentous and fracture injuries in recreational snowboarders. Delorme et al. (2005)

Figure 33.2 'Backside 1080' trick; rotating backside 1080 degrees on a large kicker, Stubai, Austria. Athlete: Jamie Nicholls, GB Park & Pipe

Photo: Jenny Bletcher.

assessed ankle motion of 4 recreationally experienced snowboarders during carved turns on a snow-based terrain. They showed that ankles are asymmetrically rotated during toe-side and heel-side snowboard turns, where the front ankle (lead leg) is everted, and the back ankle is inverted. This is caused by rotation of the upper body toward the nose of the snowboard, allowing riders to have more control of the back leg during turns.

Krüger and Edelmann-Nusser (2009) completed an assessment of the ankle joint complex using 1 recreationally experienced snowboarder during a single 'test run' in a prepared snow park, in Austria. Authors found during snowboard landings the rear leg of the rider was exposed to 3020 Newton (N) force in a short loading time of 0.1 seconds, whilst in 25 degrees dorsiflexion and 8 degrees external-rotation. Similar load values have been reported by McAlpine and Kersting (2009) during snowboard landings, who showed that vertical external loads of 3521 and 2496N were sustained to 2 subjects during landing impacts on a snowboard. These findings indicate that both the load tolerance and available range of movement of the ankle joint may be important considerations when determining the likelihood of joint or ligamentous injuries sustained from snowboard jump landings (Bladin et al., 2004).

While the aforementioned studies provide insights for snowboard carving and a single jump, no available research has investigated activity demands of professional freestyle snowsport athletes. A paper by Turnbull et al. (2011) provided an in-depth discussion about the kinetics and kinematics of landings in the HP. In summary, they noted a positive correlation between the height of each trick and the resulting kinetic energy (mass × velocity) which riders experience on landing. Riders will, however, land on a sloped surface, which reduces the normal landing forces compared to a flat landing surface (Determan et al., 2010). Generally speaking, the magnitude of impact forces experienced are dependent on; the amount of absorption done by the legs, how compact the snow is, gradient of the landing slope and rider fall line, and also horizontal velocity of the rider prior to impact. An optimal landing will occur high on the eccentric wall and involve high degrees of muscle stiffness to maximise the transfer of gravitational potential energy to kinetic energy of the rider. Frederick et al. (2006) reported that loads of 4–5 times body weight are experienced on landings from a skateboard Ollie with a jump height of less than 0.5m. While a sloped snow-covered landing may be less impacting than a flat one, it's worth noting riders and skiers will experience very large ground reaction forces (GRFs) from aerial manoeuvres performed at least 5 metres distance from landing. Anecdotally, athletes who are physically unprepared to tolerate landing impacts suffer joint compressive injuries from landings of a high amplitude. No information is currently available that explains the nature or range of forces involved during landings from freestyle aerial manoeuvres.

Commonly, much of what is currently known about freestyle snowsport has been derived from research in Alpine Skiing and other aerial based sports such as Gymnastics. In Alpine Skiing, studies have shown that the predominant muscle forces are eccentric in nature (Berg et al., 1995). It is well known that quadricep and hamstring muscle groups have particular importance during the landing phase of a jump; differing activation loads have been reported to affect the external abduction moments at the knee (Lloyd and Buchanan, 2001) where high GRFs on landing are thought to contribute to anterior cruciate ligament (ACL) injury.

Physiological demands

Literature investigating physiological demands of freestyle training and competition remains limited and largely undiscovered. Only studies measuring training activity of elite HP riders (athletes) has been studied to date (Kipp, 1998; Turnbull et al., 2011). Where information concerning SS ski/snowboard is unavailable, literature relating to SBX, HP and Alpine Skiing events could be used to inform sport scientist and athletic trainers supporting athletes and coaches. A typical HP feature includes repeated short-term high force concentric (jumping) and eccentric (landing) muscular contractions up to ~30 seconds in duration (Harding and James, 2010) which is similar to time taken to ride/ski courses in SS. An investigation by Kipp (1998) remains the only study to collect physiological markers from elite athletes during a HP snowboard training session. Other studies have presented information from snowsport athletes testing sport-related activities exclusively in the laboratory in an effort to draw comparisons between muscular and cardiovascular performance tests with performance in competition (Platzer et al., 2009; Raschner et al., 2013). Although, a direct relationship between physical performance tests and competition performance has proven largely unsuccessful to date.

While there is no reported information of heart rate (HR) responses in freestyle competition, one study reported HR activity during a one-hour HP training session, showing peak elevations up to 92% of snowboarder's age predicted maximum, averaging 140 beats per minute (bpm) for three elite riders (Kipp, 1998). Generally, snow-based sport training sessions last in the region of 3–5 hours, with 10–20 laps of the park done. Caution should therefore be taken when interpreting this information alone. Reported blood lactate values of 2.9mmol L^{-1} in this study, sampled at the end of every third training run during a 60-minute session suggested this HP training session was predominantly anaerobic in nature (Kipp, 1998). In the training environment athletes are expected to complete extended periods of hiking between runs, sometimes climbing steep alpine terrain, which requires significant aerobic fitness to sustain this activity for extended periods (Kipp, 1998; Żebrowska et al., 2012; Turnbull, 2013).

The duty cycle between jumps in a single SS or HP run are brief, with 6–8 total features (jumps) performed with full recovery (<15 minutes) between runs. Athletes may be expected to repeat this activity across a 2–3 hour competition window depending on progress in each contest.

Each contest includes 1–2 practice days, 1 qualification day, and a finals day. With travel to each competition event bookending practice and competition, fatigue is likely to impair athlete recovery and performance (Turnbull, 2013).

Snow training often takes place at high altitude environments (<3000m above sea level) at venues like Breckenridge, Colorado, USA, where the reduced oxygen availability up-regulates glycolytic rates. This in turn reduces glycogen stores and strains the anaerobic system from supplying energy for high force dependent activities, like jump landings (Turnbull et al., 2009; Seifert et al., 2009). With this in mind, it should be considered that enhanced anaerobic and aerobic capacities, supporting fast twitch type II fibres, may reduce peripheral limitations placed on the leg muscles to prevent a decrease in performance of repeated jump landing tasks. It is currently unknown if concentrated snow-based training cycles provide sufficient conditioning stimulus for elite athletes competing in World Cup competitions.

Despite the lack of attention paid to physiological investigations to date, future investigations that examine athlete activity in training are essential to understand sport demands. This information is of great significance to coaches when designing physical training programs, to prepare athletes optimally for the demands of training and competition (Turnbull, 2013).

Injury prevalence

Despite a lack of knowledge around the physical demands of freestyle snowsport on male and female athletes, evidence reporting the type and frequency of sports injuries is readily available. Several epidemiological studies point out a greater number of injuries are sustained by riders than freeskiers (Torjussen, 2006; Flørenes et al., 2010; Flørenes et al., 2012). In addition, evidence shows a consistently high prevalence of knee injuries above all other injured sites, across all freestyle disciplines. Knee and in particular ACL injuries account for 38% of all reported injuries in elite freestyle athletes (Flørenes et al., 2010). Injuries sustained to the head/face (concussion) injuries rank second highest, followed by chest/rib and shoulder injuries as the most frequently injured body parts amongst freestyle athletes (FIS, 2016). The frequency of total injuries sustained in training and competition are reportedly higher than Alpine Skiing (4.0 every 1000 days) with 4.1–6.3 injuries occurring every 1000 days on average (Flørenes et al., 2012).

The frequency of head injuries from falls and crashes are reported to be similar across Alpine Skiing and freestyle disciplines, with findings ranging from 10–14% across groups (Steenstrup et al., 2014). Currently it is unknown if the aerial requirements of freestyle pose greater risk to these athletes over Alpine Skiers, although the higher volume of training conducted on aerial features in terrain parks is undoubtedly an important risk factor to consider. Athletes reportedly miss around 4 weeks of total time after sustaining a head injury, with female athletes reportedly at 1.5 times greater risk of sustaining head injuries than males (Steenstrup et al., 2014). The most common injury mechanism associated with head trauma results from an over/under-rotation in aerial jumping, causing the "backslap episode" where the upper back and head make direct contact with the ground. Direct and rotational acceleration impacts have been recorded during backslaps ranging between 29 to 92g. There have been 2 fatal head injuries in International Ski Federation World Cup competition in recent years; traumatic head injuries are an ongoing concern for the freestyle community.

Seemingly, most injuries associated with freestyle athletes are sustained from jump landings, or falls/crashes following failed jumps/tricks. In freestyle skiers especially, one of the primary concerns for knee injuries during landings is the boot-induced anterior draw mechanism caused by the ski boot when landing in deep knee flexed positions (Flørenes et al., 2012). Freestyle skiers appear to "hang" on the back of their ski boots during deep landings, which inadvertently decreases hamstring activity and increases anterior shear forces acting on the knee and the ACL (Turnbull et al., 2011). Similarly, the knee-flexed riding postures adopted by skiers and riders increases loading and activation of the anterior chain musculature, such as the quadricep groups. Inevitably, this creates an anterior muscle dominance over posterior structures around the knees, and thus a mechanical imbalance and potential for increased shear force loading. Moreover, the snowboard stance requires the tibia to internally rotate and load into hip adducted riding postures, in take-off and landing actions which increases knee joint torque and ACL loading (Determan et al., 2010). While this is a biomechanically inefficient position for absorbing high GRF on landing, the importance of good ankle, hip and thoracic spine mobility is essential for the body to achieve key positions, and withstand forces produced during jumping and landings. For this reason, the fundamentals of efficient movement variability, active full range of movement and strength throughout the kinetic chain is crucial for the body to tolerate a summation of muscular, gravity and inertial forces acting in multiple planes during freestyle movements.

Fitness testing battery

In view of the documented athletic demands, a comprehensive battery of assessments should be employed to identify an athlete's physical strengths and weaknesses, and how this compares with the physical requirements of the sport. Principally, assessments should carry strong scientific rigour to denote reliable and strong objective outcomes. The type and application of physical assessments should also consider the cultural and behavioural values held by the action sport population, for best impact and athlete/coach compliance. Therefore, tests used should be simple by design, reliable, provide actionable outcomes, and where possible, be reproducible at various locations to suit the travelling demands on the athlete. A testing battery should be applied roughly 3–4 times throughout the year to aid training prescription for developmental periods, and performance status prior to and following competitive periods of the season.

Based on the complex physical requirements of athletes competing in the sport, the following is an outline of the key considerations and a list of recommended assessments to assess elite freestyle athletes.

Movement competency

Performance in freestyle snowsport requires athletes to produce a range of dynamic actions at various speeds, heights, surfaces, relative to the task (skill) and sensory information about the environment. For example, the biomechanical demands of a jumping and landing task demands that athletes generate force propulsion and absorption through a range of joint angles and velocities at the ankle, knee, hip and spine, across three-dimensional planes of movement. The successful completion of this task requires athletes to perform a complex set of body positions with finite motor control, and the ability to change aspects of the skill in relation to sensory feedback during the task. Clearly, athletes should possess a state of high movement variability to combat the plethora of skill demands in the sport (Hamill et al., 2012). For this reason, an athletic 'movement competency assessment' should be utilised to identify an athlete's movement profile and overall literacy, including jumping and landing capacity. This will indicate potential movement restrictions and/or dysfunctions, which may result in unwanted movements affecting performance, and cause potential injury risks. The following are examples of movement assessments used in practice:

- Athletic Competency Assessment [modified version] (McKeown et al., 2014): Assessment of Overhead Squat, Single Legged Squat, Double Lunge, Push Ups, Chin Ups. Movements

are assessed against a movement quality criteria and given a score of either 1, 2 or 3. Scores of each movement are summed to indicate overall movement competency.
- Cross-Over Hop for Distance: Comparison of force absorption and force production, and limb symmetry in three dimensional joint planes, to indicate risk of knee injuries (Clark et al., 2002).
- Medial Triple Hop for Distance: Comparison of force absorption and force production in the frontal plane, assessing limb symmetry and risk of hip pathology (Kivlan et al., 2013).

Strength and power capacity

How much muscular strength freestyle athletes require to execute the primary actions of jumping and landing is currently unknown. Research conducted in other aerial/gravity based sports like skate boarding, gymnastics and surfing advocate that an adequate level of muscular strength is required to perform explosive jumps and endure high GRFs from landings (Determan et al., 2010; McNitt-Gray et al., 2001; Secomb et al., 2016). As riders/skiers frequently land from great heights, these athletes need to produce very high magnitudes of muscle voluntary contraction (MVC) very rapidly to dissipate GRFs upon landing (Turnbull et al., 2011). The complexity of these motor skills is even more challenging, considering the variance of joint torques and soft tissue loading from landing in uncommon and unstable body positions; from corked and inverted tricks, for example. Methods to assess sport-specific jumping demands are yet to be addressed in the scientific research. Assessing the primary qualities of absolute maximal strength, eccentric strength, and rate of force development in practice is useful to understand an athlete's physical readiness to perform the primary sports demands. Assessing lower-limb strength and power in bilateral and unilateral actions should be carried out to identify physical capacities in double and single legged riding/ skiing postures.

Assessing upper extremity strength is vital for success in many sports. In freestyle, the upper body has an integral role in assisting jump take-off, also force attenuation in landings as part of the kinetic chain along with lower limb and spine structures. In addition, muscular strength of the shoulder and back is important to protect against the risk of shoulder dislocations noted in the sport from crashes/falls (McCall and Safran, 2009). For these reasons, upper-body testing should be part of a comprehensive assessment.

Strength profile:

- 3RM Squat (Trap Bar Squat or Back Squat): Maximum load achieved over × 3 repetitions maximum, to assess bilateral lower-limb absolute hip and knee flexor strength. A full squat depth is preferential but should be based on the individual's anatomical capability.
- 3RM Single Legged Leg Press: Maximum load achieved over × 3 repetitions maximum, to assess maximum unilateral leg strength in an isokinetic action.
- 3RM Nordbord Eccentric Hamstring Lower: Measuring eccentric knee extensor strength, absolute hamstring strength, and strength asymmetry over × 3 repetitions. Peak and mean force measures are reviewed to understand absolute and global muscle force.
- Narrow Grip Chin-Ups (endurance test): Maximum number of repetitions achieved at bodyweight through a 'complete' chin up range to assess back, shoulder and arm strength-endurance. The test is discontinued when the athlete cannot complete a chin up with proper control and over a full range of movement. If an athlete can perform >10 reps at bodyweight then a Weighted 3RM Chin Up test should be used.

Power profile:

- Counter Movement Jump (CMJ): Using Force Platform (FP) equipment, athletes perform ×5 isolated CMJs without arm swing, to a fixed squat depth. Values of mean and peak vertical jump power are analysed to indicate stretch-shortening cycle ability. CMJ performance has previously been related to jump height performance in the sport (Platzer et al., 2009).
- Drop-and-Stick Landing Test: Athletes drop from a 0.5m box height and aim to stick the landing with control (Tran et al., 2015). Values of time to stabilisation (TTS) and relative peak landing force (rPLF) are assessed to measure eccentric jump landing capacity, with comparisons between limbs to understand symmetry differences.

Aerobic/anaerobic capacity

Assessing the physical fitness capacities of freestyle riders and skiers should provide information relating to two key areas: 1) The athlete's absolute capacity to endure long training sessions lasting 2–5 hours over repetitive training days. 2) The ability to perform intense training and competition runs lasting on average 30–60s demanding brief, intermittent, explosive actions primarily of the lower-limb structures. A study by Platzer et al. (2009) showed that maximal aerobic power using a bicycle ergometry test could be recruited as a good indicator of physical capacity in SBX and HP athletes. A well-developed aerobic system is important to recover between anaerobic bouts and sustain anaerobic power activity. The short durations seen in competition performance (<30 seconds) indicate that adenosine tri-phosphate phosphocreatine activity is dominant during contest runs, which has been identified previously in U.S. HP athletes (Kipp, 1998). Assessing mean and peak anaerobic power is important to understand capacities related to competition performance. Tests which enable this include:

- Maximal Aerobic Capacity Test: Using a cycle ergometer, perform an incremental cycling test usually lasting 8–12 minutes or until volitional exhaustion is achieved. Measures of oxygen, heart rate and lactate are ideally used to identify mean and peak values denoting to maximal aerobic capacity.
- Anaerobic Power, 30 second Wingate Test: Using a Wattbike, athletes perform a 3-minute warm up at airbrake level 4, speed 70 rpm. Then immediately perform an all-out 30 second effort at airbrake level 4, to assess relative mean and peak power ability.

Programming

Considering the multi-faceted physical demands of freestyle snowsport, a periodised training plan should be implemented that maximises athletic availability for skills training development, and on snow training time. Secondly, such a plan should strategically augment physical capacities, and enable realisation of peak performance at the desired stages of the season and periods of the quadrennial Olympic cycle. Where possible, the training plan should also be designed in collaboration with the technical coach to ensure training objectives support the coach's requirements and meet wider performance expectations.

To provide athletes with a comprehensive and well-designed training programme, a range of information should be considered, relating to the following: chronological and biological athlete age, injury history, performance in physical testing, specific strengths and weaknesses highlighted by the athlete/coach, and the athlete's performance goals throughout the season/programme.

The latter should not be overlooked when working with highly independent and free-spirited freestyle athletes. Often, on-snow training and decisions made around contests are self-directed by the athlete and not the coach. This enables athletes to remain highly creative in the process of trick learning and progression, which is critical given the need for creativity in performance, alongside the threats facing athletes who literally risk their lives for the sport, based on their own decisions. Creating options within the strength and conditioning programme allows athletes to remain autonomous throughout the training process, and has been shown to be highly effective in maintaining adherence, motivation and athlete wellbeing (Deci and Ryan, 2008). Performance specialists should aim to provide athletes with well-structured and organised programmes drawn from sound scientific principles. However, a successful program is not determined by its design, rather our ability to make athletes the experts at self-directing the training process, based on biological and psychosocial 'feedback'. Providing athletes with a fluid framework empowers them to 'steer' the programme and feel connected with effective training solutions befitting the wider performance culture.

The purpose of the snowsport strength and conditioning programme is to maximise lower-body strength, with a focus on slow-eccentric strength, and high-velocity rate of force development for jump power and landing robustness. Also, development of aerobic and anaerobic metabolism should be cycled methodically at various stages of the season. The macrocycle can be broken into 5 mesocycles: 1) active recovery, 2) off-season hypertrophy and strength, 3) preseason strength and multi-skills training, 4) preseason strength and power, with skills training continued, and 5) in-season maintenance and peaking. While this presents a blocked model approach by design, it is important to note that each physical component is trained concurrently in each phase, with the hierarchy of each component modulated by its value at each stage. Mesocycles can be seen in Table 33.1, where programme examples are illustrated across the year from preparatory months (July-November) and competition months (December-May), with restitution generally for 1 month in June.

Strength training

The development of athletic lower-limb absolute strength to increase force absorption capability for landings, and force production on take-off should form the cornerstone of the strength training programme. Developing lower-limb strength with bilateral and unilateral lifts (see Table 33.2) in multiple planes is essential to prepare athletes for the rigours of the sport, and develop a broad movement vocabulary. Further, increasing knee flexor/extensor eccentric strength throughout the season could serve as a protective effect against high volume, repetitive joint loading of the knees and lower-back sustained throughout the competition period, which are associated with pathology and/ or injuries (FIS, 2016). Janssen et al. (2012) demonstrated that increased trunk flexion occurs during loaded landing conditions, causing greater trunk inertia. This suggests trunk strength has an integral role to play in deceleration of the trunk, where inefficient control of the spine may impact lower limb peak joint moments, resulting in a loss of control and/or momentum on landing.

Upper-limb strength should also be developed to support the global movement actions during 'pumping' (generating momentum) take-off and landing actions. As mentioned previously, developing upper-limb strength at the shoulder girdle is important to protect against shoulder injuries from falls and crashes. The training programme should factor in developmental time addressing upper-body strength through a variety of options as outlined in Table 33.2.

Table 33.1 Example weekly mesocycles

	Monday	Tuesday	Wednesday	Thursday	Friday	Saturday	Sunday
#1 active recovery July (4 weeks)							
	Movement & stability circuit	Fun activities: surfing, ball games, etc.	Rest	Stability/ strength-endurance circuit x8 exercises	Rest	Fun activities: mountain biking, hiking, skating	Rest
#2 off-season strength and multi-skills August-September (6 weeks)							
AM	Skate boarding skills practice 60mins	Strength (heavy) lower-limb	Regeneration: yoga, foam rolling	Skate boarding skills practice 60mins	Strength (heavy) lower-limb	Off	Off
PM	Lactate threshold conditioning and jumping	Strength (light) upper-limb/ core	Off	Lactate threshold conditioning and jumping	Strength light upper-limb/core	Off	Off
#3 pre-season strength and skills training September-October (6 weeks)							
AM	Skate boarding skills practice 90mins	Regeneration: yoga, foam rolling	Gymnastics/ free running skills practice 60mins	Strength (heavy) lower-limb	Strength light upper-limb/core	Regeneration: yoga, foam rolling	Off
PM	Strength (heavy) lower-limb	Off	Strength-endurance circuit x8 ex's	Off	Indoor snowdome skills practice <2 hours	Off	Off
#4 pre-season maintenance and power November (4 weeks)							
AM	On-snow skills practice (park) 4 hours	On-snow skills practice (jumps) 2–4 hours	On-snow skills practice 4 hours	On-snow skills practice (park) 4 hours	On-snow skills practice (jumps) 2–4 hours	On-snow skills practice (park) 4 hours	Off
PM	Gymnastics session 60mins	Strength/power lower-limb	Regeneration: yoga	Gymnastics session 60mins	Strength lower/ upper-limb	Off	Off
#5 in-season maintenance and peaking December-May (2–3/4 week undulating cycles)							
AM	Off-travel	On-snow skills practice 4 hours	On-snow skills practice 4 hours	On-snow skills practice 4 hours/qualifiers day 1	On-snow skills practice 4 hours/finals day	Rest/gym recovery	Off
PM	Regeneration session; foam roll, mobility, pool/cycle, stretch	Rest – mobility and yoga	Strength maintenance OR climbing, skating, gymnastics	Strength maintenance OR climbing, skating, gymnastics/ Rest	Rest – mobility and yoga	Off	Off/ travel

Table 33.2 Example strength and power sessions

Strength lower-limb	Special strength/stability	Power
Light volume: 2–4 sets × 12–20 reps	*Stability:* (volume: 2–3 sets × 8–12 reps)	Volume: 2–3 sets × 2–5 reps
Moderate volume: 2–6 sets × 8–10 reps	3D clock face SL squat – all points	
Heavy volume: 4–6 sets × 1–5 reps	SL alt. reverse hamstring Plank – 3 sec ISO	
	KB Turkish get-up	
Back squat/front squat/ Trap bar squat	*Eccentric:* (volume: 2–4 sets × 5 sec × 3–5 reps)	Loaded CMJ @ 30–50% 1RM
Loaded split squat: Barbell bulgarian	Double legged (DL) leg press	Box jumps
Goblet lateral squat/lunge	Single legged (SL) leg press	12" box drop jumps to high box
Slideboard leg curl/ Nordic hamstring curl		Single legged hurdle hop re-bound to box jump (linear/lateral)
	Loaded landings: (volume: 2–3 sets × 2–5 reps)	Single legged rotational hop & stick with knee drive
Dead bug variations (–/+ load)	Double leg/single leg drop squats	
Split-stance cable chop/lift variations	18" box DL/SL landings (w/w-out rotation)	Med. ball rotational wall throws
	18" box landings dumbbell loaded	Drop squat + reactive cable pallof press

SL: single leg, alt: alternate, ISO: isometric, KB: kettlebell, CMJs: counter movement jump

Power training

Developing athletes' skill acquisition, kinaesthetic awareness and motor learning for performance in aerial tasks is important, and features heavily in skill acquisition training. Interestingly, the landing portion of the jump receives less attention from coaches in skill development than the take-off. Many athletes, therefore, fail to intuitively develop sound landing efficacy techniques and develop chronic ankle, knee, hip and lower-back impact associated pathologies from improper landing technique. Where specific teaching of landing techniques is absent from the skills training programme, strength and conditioning coaches should bridge the gap and begin priming deceleration skills during the off-season with positional strength work, utilising a range of isometrics strength exercises in conjunction with low intensity depth jump landings to commence skill teaching. There should then be an increase in the magnitude and velocity of loading performed, with loaded jump landings including altitude jumps with/without rotations to develop sport-specific qualities in preparation for high volume on-snow skills training (see Table 33.2). Developing athletic ability to achieve high joint stiffness across large joint flexion positions is critical to achieve dissipation of forces and produce effective shock attenuation, reducing joint loading in landings (Turnbull et al., 2011).

Sport-specific skills

On-snow skills training is the primary choice of training whenever possible. Where this option is unavailable, coaches should place high importance on exposing athletes to a menu of kinesthetically rich, skill-based activities to increase motor learning and skills transfer (Turnbull et al., 2011). Directing training towards options like Gymnastics, Skateboarding and Free-running activities in 'dry-land training' enables athletes to train aspects of aerial jumps at high volume in low-risk training environments, like the trampoline. Additional skills-training is vital to accelerate trick learning in controlled conditions, to later transfer skill progressions in the snow park. It is fair to say that a range of mixed training methods exist among elite teams, with many freestyle athletes opting preferentially for combinations of off-snow skill-based training.

Conditioning

Physiological adaptations resulting from training such as anaerobic power and aerobic capacity are not the primary objectives of snow training, yet it is likely that cardiovascular changes occur following high volumes of on/off-snow skills training as a by-product (Turnbull et al., 2011). Given the high volume of skills training completed throughout much of the preparatory and competition cycles, athletes tend to possess a reasonably well-developed aerobic system. Early in the preparatory phase, athletes should spend sufficient time developing their aerobic capacity, increasing muscle endurance alongside the ability to handle high volumes of training later in the season. Later, in the pre-season phase, athletes should develop their anaerobic capacity through intensive specific skills training and/or isolated conditioning to increase glycolytic activity in fast-twitch tissues, and the ability to perform explosive and sustained high-intensity muscle contractions (Żebrowska et al., 2012).

Conclusion

Working with elite freestyle athletes presents strength and conditioning coaches and performance practitioners with a range of challenges which have been outlined in this chapter. The most noteworthy challenges affecting athletes appear to exist in travel fatigue, training in the cold, physical training fatigue, a frequently changing training 'base', and disturbed sleep and nutritional behaviours. Due to the fact that freestyle snowsport is a relatively new discipline, programme resources and the number of performance staff working with each team has steadily risen in the past decade. Most teams now have access to a full-time strength and conditioning coach/athletic trainer, in addition to a once seldom recruited physiotherapist. Furthermore, there has been an explosion in interest of microtechnology within the sport, where numerous devices are being developed to measure biomechanical and physical demands of the sport. Until further literary evidence regarding the physical profile of athletes becomes available, strength and conditioning coaches and sport scientists should make every effort to connect with technical coaches and medical staff to increase understanding and to identify performance threats and issues facing this population.

It is hoped that this chapter will provide strength and conditioning coaches and practitioners alike with insights and knowledge pertaining to the modern physical needs of freestyle snowsport athletes. It should be stressed that the importance of establishing a set of simple, performance based questions developed from an understanding of traditional sports in order to inform reasoning and guide practice should not be overlooked, alongside developing a series of ecological solutions to performance problems based on observations, with creativity and simplicity held firmly at the centre of our thought process. Within this chapter, recommendations from alternative sports, alongside the author's experience within the field, have been used to address gaps in the literature and direct the reader to a clearer understanding of the current challenges, knowledge and training opportunities for the practitioner within freestyle snowsport.

References

Berg, H. E., Eiken, O. and Tesch, P. A. 1995. Involvement of eccentric muscle actions in giant slalom racing. *Medicine & Science in Sports & Exercise*, 27, 1666–1670.

Bladin, C., McCrory, P. and Pogorzelski, A. 2004. Snowboarding injuries current trends and future directions. *Sports Medicine*, 34, 133–138.

Clark, C., Gumbrell, C. J., Rana, S., Traole, C. M. and Morrissey, M. C. 2002. Intratester relaibilty and measurement error of the adapted crossover hop for distance. *Physical Therapy in Sport*, 3, 143–151.

Deci, E. L. and Ryan, R. M. 2008. Self-determination theory: A macrotherapy of human motivation, development, and health. *Canadian Psychology*, 49, 182–185.

Delorme, S., Tavoularis, S. and Lamontagne, M. 2005. Kinematics of the ankle joint complex in snowboarding. *Journal of Applied Biomechanics*, 21(4), 394–403.

Determan, J. J., Frederick, E. C., Cox, J. S. and Nevitt, M. N. 2010. High impact forces in skateboarding landings affected by landing outcome. *Footwear Science*, 2, 159–170.

FIS. 2016. *FIS Injury Surveillance System 2006–2016*. Oslo Sports Trauma Research Center. www.fis-ski.com/mm/Document/documentlibrary/Medical/08/57/62/FIS_ISS_report_2015-16_Neutral.pdf.

Flørenes, T. W., Heir, S., Nordsletten, L. and Bahr, R. 2010. Injuries among World Cup freestyle skiers. *British Journal of Sports Medicine*, 44, 803–808.

Flørenes, T. W., Nordsletten, L., Heir, S. and Bahr, R. 2012. Injuries among World Cup ski and snowboard athletes. *Scandinavian Journal of Medicine & Science in Sports*, 22, 58–66.

Frederick, E. C., Determan, J. J., Whittlesey, S. N. and Hamill, J. 2006. Kinetics of skateboarding: Kinetics of the Ollie. *Journal of Applied Biomechanics*, 22, 33–40.

Hamill, J., Palmer, C. and Van Emmerik, R. E. A. 2012. Coordinative variability and overuse injury. *Sports Medicine, Arthroscopy, Rehabilitation, Therapy & Technology*, 4, 45.

Harding, J. W. and James, D. A. 2010. Analysis of snowboarding performance at the Burton Open Australian Half-Pipe Championships. *International Journal of Performance Analysis in Sport*, 10, 66–81.

Janssen, I., Sheppard, J. M., Dingley, A. A., Chapman, D. W. and Spratford, W. 2012. Lower extremity kinematics and kinetics when landing from unloaded and loaded jumps. *Faculty of Science, Medicine and Health*, 28, 687–693.

Kipp, R. W. 1998. Physiological analysis and training for snowboard's Halfpipe Event. *Strength and Conditioning Journal*, 20(4), 8–12.

Kivlan, B. R., Carcia, C. R., Clemente, F. R., Phelps, A. L. and Martin, R. L. 2013. Reliability and validity of functional performance tests in dancers with hip dysfunction. *The International Journal of Sports Physical Therapy*, 8, 360–369.

Krüger, A. and Edelmann-Nusser, J. 2009. Biomechanical analysis in freestyle snowboarding: Application of a full-body inertial measurement system and a bilateral insole measurement system. *Sports Technology*, 2, 17–23.

Lloyd, D. G. and Buchanan, T. S. 2001. Strategies of muscular support of varus and valgus isometric loads at the human knee. *Journal of Biomechanics*, 34, 1257–1267.

McAlpine, P. and Kersting, U. 2009. Development of a field testing protocol for the biomechanical analysis of a snowboard jump landings – A pilot study. *Sports Technology*, 2, 17–23.

McCall, D. and Safran, M. R. 2009. Injuries about the shoulder in skiing and snowboarding. *British Journal of Sports Medicine*, 43, 987–992.

McKeown, I., Taylor-Mckeown, K., Woods, C. and Ball, N. 2014. Athletic ability assessment: A movement assessment protocol for athletes. *The International Journal of Sports Physical Therapy*, 9, 862–873.

Mcnitt-Gray, J. L., Hester, D. M. E., Mathiyakom, W. and Munkasy, B. A. 2001. Mechanical demand and multijoint control during ladning depend on orientation of the body segments relative to the reaction force. *Journal of Biomechanics*, 34, 1471–1482.

Platzer, H., Raschner, C., Patterson, C. and Lembert, S. 2009. Comparison of physical characteristics and performance among elite snowboarders. *Journal of Strength and Conditioning Research*, 23, 1427–1432.

Raschner, C., Müller, L., Patterson, C., Platzer, H. P., Ebenbichler, C., Luchner, R., Lembert, S. and Hildebrandt, C. 2013. Current performance testing trends in junior and elite Austrian alpine ski, snowboard and ski cross racers. *Sport Orthopadie Traumatologie*, 29(3), 193–202.

Secomb, J. L., Nimphius, S., Farley, O. R., Lundgren, L., Tran, T. T. and Sheppard, J. M. 2016. Lower-body muscle structure and jump performance of stronger and weaker surfing athletes. *International Journal Sports Physiology Performance*, 11, 652–657.

Seifert, J., Kroll, J. and Muller, E. 2009. The relationship of heart rate and lactate to cumulative muscle fatigue during recreational alpine skiing. *Journal of Strength and Conditioning Research*, 23, 698–704.

Steenstrup, S. E., Bere, T. and Bahr, R. 2014. Head injuries among FIS World Cup alpine and freestyle skiers and snowboarders: A 7-year cohort study. *British Journal of Sports Medicine*, 48, 41–45.

Torjussen, J. 2006. Injuries among elite snowboarders (FIS Snowboard World Cup). *British Journal of Sports Medicine*, 40, 230–234.

Tran, T. T., Lundgren, L., Secomb, J., Farley, O. R., Haff, G. G., Newton, R. U., Nimphius, S. and Sheppard, J. M. 2015. Development and evaluation of a drop-and-stick method to assess landing skills in various levels of competitive surfers. *International Journal of Sports Physiology and Performance*, 10, 396–400.

Turnbull, J. 2013. *Monitoring training-induced fatigue in snowboard and freeski halfpipe athletes*. Master of Sports Science, Auckland University.

Turnbull, J., Keogh, J. W. L. and Andrew, E. K. 2011. Strength and conditioning considerations for elite snowboard halfpipe. *The Open Sports Science Medical Journal*, 5, 1–11.

Turnbull, J. R., Kilding, A. E. and Keogh, J. W. L. 2009. Physiology of alpine skiing. *Scandinavian Journal of Medicine & Science in Sports*, 19, 146–155.

Żebrowska, A., Żyła, D., Kania, D. and Langfort, J. 2012. Anaerobic and aerobic performance of elite female and male snowboarders. *Journal of Human Kinetics*, 34(1), 81-88.

34
BODYBUILDING

Paul Comfort

Needs analysis for bodybuilding and physique competitions

Introduction to the sport(s)

The specific requirements for bodybuilding and physique competitions are relatively simple: symmetrical and proportional increases in muscle mass, which are the primary focus in the off season, with the primary focus on decreasing body fat while maintaining muscle mass prior to competition. The exact requirements of each competition should be considered at all stages of training, as different governing bodies and competition categories (e.g. female bodybuilding, bikini and figure classes) have different judging guidelines and in some instances criteria for the competitors' weight and height (e.g. classic bodybuilding) are clearly defined. Bodybuilding generally requires individuals to maximise muscle mass and minimise body fat, whereas physique competitors can be marked down by judges for being too muscular or too lean. Judging criteria also varies between governing bodies and therefore should be considered during competition preparation.

Physical demands of the sport

Unlike many other sports where the athletic demands should be the primary focus, aesthetics must be prioritised here as success in these types of competitions is judged purely on aesthetics. Therefore the primary focus away from competitions should be the development of muscle mass, while maintaining symmetry between limbs and areas of the body, without an excessive gain in body fat. Pre competition the focus should change to the maintenance of muscle mass while reducing body fat, to the level desired by the specific competition and the relevant governing body/level of competition.

The other aspect of preparation and athlete development which should not be overlooked is posing. As competitions are judged on aesthetics it is essential that athletes are competent and confident in all poses to ensure that they display their physique in the best possible way. The posing routines can be quite fatiguing, especially as athletes are generally energy depleted and dehydrated at the time of competition and therefore adequate preparation of individual poses and the athletes' specific posing routine are essential.

In terms of monitoring progress of such athletes it is advised that body mass, skin fold thickness (sum of skin folds, or used to calculate body fat percentage) and circumference measurements should be monitored and recorded periodically (see section titled 'Fitness testing battery').

Injury prevalence

In a recent review of injuries in 'weight-training sports', bodybuilding was reported to have the lowest level of injuries compared to weightlifting, powerlifting, strongman, Highland Games and CrossFit (Keogh and Winwood, 2016). The most common sites of injury in bodybuilders have been reported to include the spine, shoulder and knees (Siewe et al., 2014). More specifically diagnosed spinal injuries or reported sites of pain are the cervical, thoracic and lumbar spine, including disc herniation and sciatica (Siewe et al., 2014). Reported shoulder injuries include inflammation, rotator cuff lesions and impingement, while knee injuries include patella disorders and meniscus injury (Siewe et al., 2014). Musculo-tendinous injuries are also commonly reported, with injuries to the bicep tendon, triceps tendon and pectorals notable for such athletes (Lavallee and Balam, 2010).

Many of the injuries are potentially preventable with the use of good technique during training, especially in relation to injuries relating to the spine, which may be avoidable with maintenance of correct spinal posture, which reduces loading on the vertebrae and inter-vertebral discs. For example, during squat and deadlift variations, maintenance of a neutral spine and the avoidance spinal flexion is essential. Moreover, periodically varying exercises for each body part may further reduce the risk of chronic and repetitive strain injuries.

Fitness testing battery

As athletic performance (e.g. strength, jump, sprint performance) is not essential for bodybuilders and physique/figure athletes, the testing required is relatively simple. The focus for monitoring changes related to training and for goal setting should include body mass, skin fold thickness (sum of skin folds, or used to calculate body fat percentage) and circumference measurements (always taken in the same place with the athlete in a consistent posture). While it is not essential, if the individual is interested in monitoring their strength or muscular endurance levels they could perform repetition maximum (RM) testing for specific compound exercises (e.g. squat, deadlift, pull-ups, bent-over row, bench press, shoulder press). Such RM testing can be used not only to monitor progress but also to determine training loads for subsequent training phases.

Procedures should be standardised for all testing protocols, including time of day, previous activity and dietary intake. For strength testing, standardising activity levels ensures that there is no difference in residual fatigue, while standardising dietary intake should decrease the impact of hydration status or stimulation from substances such as caffeine. Time of day has also been shown to notably impact strength levels and therefore must be standardised. For assessment of body composition hydration levels, time of day and activity levels (as a results of changes in hydration status), may impact not only body weight, but also body composition assessments.

Strength testing

If strength testing is performed, strict technique and a full/appropriate range of motion is essential, not only to minimise the risk of injury, but also to ensure accurate and reliable testing results. Results of several studies have shown a high reliability of 1RM testing protocols, even in youth

Table 34.1 Example of repetition maximum testing range after specific training phases

Previous phase (repetitions)	Repetition maximum	Subsequent phase (sets/repetitions/load)
Hypertrophy (8–12)	6 RM	Strength (3 × 5 @ 6 RM)
Strength (4–6)	3 RM	Max' strength (5 × 2 @ 3 RM)
Max' strength (2–3)	1 RM*or 10 RM	Hypertrophy (3 × 10 @ 70% 1 RM) or (3 × 10 @ 10 RM)

*A 1 RM test is not essential and a 10 RM alternative could easily be used, especially for individuals who are less experienced in training with near maximal loads, or those that have had musculotendinous injuries

(Faigenbaum et al., 2012) and inexperienced collegiate athletes (Comfort and McMahon, 2015), with an increased reliability with increased training experience (Benton et al., 2013). However, if the athlete has any concern regarding injury risk with maximal testing, the use of submaximal loads to assess strength has also been shown to be reliable, although the reliability is not as high as for maximal loads (Brzycki, 1993; Julio et al., 2012).

Towards the end of each training phase, testing using RM loads within repetition ranges slightly lower than those used within the training phase can be implemented and therefore inform the loads to be used during the subsequent phase (Table 34.1).

Body composition testing

Numerous methods of assessing body composition are available, including dual X-Ray absorptiometry (DEXA), hydrostatic weighing, Bod-Pod, bioelectrical impedance analysis (BIA) and skin fold measurements. Unfortunately many of these methods (DEXA, hydrostatic weighing, Bod-Pod) are not easily accessible to many individuals.

Bioelectrical impedance analysis is relatively cheap and easy to use; however, the biggest source of error tends to be the level of hydration of the athlete. As hydration can substantially impact the resultant percentage body fat, BIA may not be a valid assessment of body composition in athletes (Saunders et al., 1998).

Assessing body fat percentage using skin fold measures appears relatively simple; however, there are numerous sites which can be used, ranging from the sum of three sites up to as many as eight sites, with numerous equations available to calculate body fat percentage. A study by Espana Romero et al. (2009) compared 17 different equations to calculate body fat from the sum of 8 sites, noting differences between each approach, with the equation of Durnin and Womersley (1973, 1974) resulting in the closest body fat percentage compared to DEXA. It is therefore suggested that these equations be used to calculate body fat percentage, or that the sum of skin folds alone is used to monitor changes, although the author acknowledges that athletes like to know a percentage rather than the sum of the skin folds. For monitoring an individuals' progress, as long as the methods are standardised between testing sessions (including sites and tester) the results should be comparable.

Programming

Programming for bodybuilders and physique competitors should be divided into two primary areas of focus: ***increasing lean mass*** while minimising increases in body fat (General and Specific Preparation), and ***decreasing body fat*** while maintaining lean mass (Competition Preparation).

Increasing lean mass

Exercise induced mechanisms suggested to stimulate muscle hypertrophy are metabolic stress, mechanical tension, mechano-transduction, muscle damage, localised and systemic hormone production, cellular oedema (swelling), and the production of reactive oxygen species (ROS) (Cooper, 1994; Pope et al., 2013; Pearson and Hussain, 2015). It is worth noting that metabolic stress, mechanical tension, mechano-transduction and muscle damage are likely the most prominent mechanisms during 'normal' hypertrophy training.

Training Considerations: There are numerous variables which should be considered when developing a resistance training programme: exercise selection, intensity, volume (sets × repetitions × load), training frequency, exercise selection. In addition there are alternative methods of training, e.g. blood flow restriction (also known as occlusion training), that can also be used.

Exercise selection

For most sports, where the purpose of training is to maximise lower body force and power output, the selection of resistance training exercises needs to consider transference to performance in sporting tasks. However, in the case of bodybuilding and physique competitions the selection of exercises should be based on which muscles require focussed hypertrophy to ensure a balanced and symmetrical physique.

Appropriate exercise selection and variation in exercises to ensure optimal development of each muscle group is of utmost importance, as researchers have demonstrated differential adaptation in individual muscles within a muscle group. For example Narici et al. (1996) reported that the vastus lateralis did not demonstrate any increase in cross sectional area after 6 months of knee extension training, whereas the other three quadriceps muscles exhibited a hypertrophic response. More recently researchers reported similar increases between quadriceps muscles, excluding the rectus femoris, after 8 weeks of heavy parallel-depth squat training, whereas different hypertrophic responses were observed through jump training (Earp et al., 2015). Moreover, the researchers observed differential hypertrophic responses at the proximal and distal ends of the muscles which they attributed to the range of motion used and the utilisation of the stretch shortening cycle during the jump training. It is therefore recommended that a full range of motion is utilised in all exercises, where possible, and that each muscle is trained not just in its inner range (e.g. standing bicep curls), but across the outer ranges too (e.g. concentration curls, incline curls). It is worth noting that this does not mean that a large variety of exercises is essential within a single training programme, which can result in excessively long training sessions. The solution is to vary exercises across training sessions within a training week to ensure appropriate development of each muscle group, which also adds to the variety and reduces boredom.

Training intensity and volume

Training intensity is usually reported as a percentage of one repetition maximum (1RM), although this does not mean that 1RM needs to be assessed for each exercise; although such testing can be beneficial for the primary compound (multi-joint) exercises. The percentage 1RM directly corresponds to the number of repetitions that can be performed, due to the inverse relationship between load and repetitions. This permits 1 RM to be predicted from submaximal repetition maximum attempts (e.g. 5 RM) (Morales and Sobonya, 1996); therefore, if the prescribed repetition range increases the corresponding load needs to decrease to permit the completion of the desired number of repetitions. It is worth noting that this relation has been shown to alter between strength and endurance training athletes (Richens and Cleather, 2014). One simple solution to this potential problem is to determine the repetition maximum for individual exercises with the first sessions of a new training cycle. For example, after performing warm up sets for a particular exercise, perform an appropriate repetition maximum test for that exercise; therefore, during a hypertrophy mesocycle (8–12 reps, 3–4 sets, 65–75% 1 RM), perform a 10 RM test to establish the working weight for that particular exercise (see also this chapter's section on strength training and Table 34.1). A 10 RM load should initially permit 3–4 sets of 8 repetitions to be performed; once 8 repetitions can be performed across all sets, the individual should start attempting to complete 9 repetitions per set, and so on.

One other consideration regarding the interaction between sets, repetitions and intensity is the rest period required between sets, with short rest periods (<90 seconds) commonly recommended between sets when focussing on hypertrophy, and longer rest periods (3–5 minutes) when focussing on strength development. However, a recent review noted that self selected rest periods, which may be <3 minutes, are adequate for strength training and that longer rest periods for hypertrophy training are not detrimental (Henselmans and Schoenfeld, 2014). It should be noted, however, that longer rest periods will increase the total training duration, which may not be feasible for some individuals, and that excessively short rest periods may result in fewer repetitions performed during the subsequent set and therefore a decrease in total volume performed.

When comparing the effects of high load (3 sets of 8–12 repetitions) vs. low load (3 sets of 25–35 repetitions) training performed to momentary muscle failure, Schoenfeld et al. (2015b) reported that similar changes in muscle hypertrophy were observed between groups. However, increases in quadriceps thickness were noticeably greater in the high load group, who also demonstrated a greater increase in maximum strength. It is worth noting that the high load group still used sets, repetitions and intensities (3 sets of 8–12 repetitions at 60–75% 1RM) that are usually associated with hypertrophy training and not the ranges associated with strength training (3–6 sets of 1–6 repetitions at 85–95% 1RM). In a previous study where volume was matched and a higher intensity used, 7 sets of 3RM vs. 3 sets of 10RM also resulted in similar increases in muscle mass, although the heaviest loads resulted in the greatest increase in maximal strength (Schoenfeld et al., 2014). Therefore, appropriate periodisation of training, including mesocycles of strength training, where the volume load remains high, should be advantageous.

Volume is usually monitored by multiplying the load by the number of repetitions performed per set and the number of sets performed (Volume load = Load × Sets × Reps), although it is suggested that load should be system load (barbell load, plus body mass) where appropriate (McBride et al., 2009). For example, an athlete also lifts their mass during squats and pull-ups, and therefore body mass should be included; however, body mass should be excluded during exercises such as the bench press and isolation exercises where the athlete's body mass is not lifted.

Due to the inverse relationship between load and repetitions, it is important to monitor volume load as changes in intensity directly affect the volume load performed during a training session. As intensity increases, the disproportionate decrease in repetitions results in decrease in volume, even with an increase in the number of sets performed (Table 34.2).

Training volume appears to be one of the key factors in the stimulation of increased muscle protein synthesis (MPS) and hypertrophy, although the intensity still needs to be sufficient to provide a sufficient mechanical and/or metabolic stimulus. In a study where volume was matched

Table 34.2 Example of the effect of intensity on volume load

	Body mass (kg)	Intensity (% 1RM)	System mass (kg)	Sets	Repetitions	Volume (kg)
Hypertrophy	100	70	240	3	10	7,200
Strength	100	85	270	3	5	4,050
Max' strength	100	90	280	5	3	4,200
Power	100	~55★	210	5	3	3,150

Based on a 100 kg athlete with a 1RM back squat of 200 kg
★ Optimal load to elicit power during the back squat (Cormie et al., 2007)

to permit comparisons of MPS in response to exercise intensity intensities of 20–40% 1RM had little effect on MPS, whereas 60–90% 1RM resulted in noticeable increases in MPS (Kumar et al., 2009). No differences in MPS were observed between intensities of 60, 75 and 90% 1RM. It is worth noting, however, that acute changes in MPS are not correlated with muscle hypertrophy in untrained young men (Mitchell et al., 2014), although this may be attributable to the fact that early adaptations to resistance training are predominantly neurological (Folland and Williams, 2007).

Some individuals recommend increasing volume by changing the tempo of the repetitions performed, by intentionally reducing the speed of movement. A recent review, however, concluded that there are a lack of studies substantiating the use of super slow repetitions (>10 seconds per repetition) at low loads (<60% 1RM) (Schoenfeld et al., 2015a).

Training frequency

When comparing the format and frequency of training, Schoenfeld et al. (2015c) reported that increased frequency (3 × week), via completion of whole body training sessions, as opposed to reduced frequency (2 × week), via the use of a split routine (session 1 upper body, session 2 lower body, session 3 whole body), resulted in greater increases in muscle mass. Both groups demonstrated associated increases in muscle strength, with no differences in improvements in strength between groups. Similarly, a recent review of literature concluded that two training sessions per body part, per week, is superior to one session per week, but that the additional benefits of three sessions per week requires further study (Schoenfeld et al., 2016).

Blood flow restriction

Occlusion training or blood-flow restriction training requires restriction of venous blood flow, with minimal to no restriction of arterial inflow to the target muscles, usually achieved through the use of an elastic tourniquet (Shinohara et al., 1998) or elastic wraps (Wilson et al., 2013) (in a clinical/research setting a pressurised cuff is usually used). When venous blood flow is restricted during exercise, metabolic stress is substantially increased due to the reduced ability for the removal of metabolic bi-products (i.e. lactic acid) which also results in localised swelling, both of which have been reported to stimulate hypertrophy (Pope et al., 2013; Pearson and Hussain, 2015). Due to this metabolic stress slow twitch muscle fibres begin to fatigue, even at light loads (<50% 1RM), resulting in the recruitment of higher threshold motor units and therefore intermediate and fast twitch muscle fibres, even in light of the low external load (Pope et al., 2013; Pearson and Hussain, 2015).

One of the simplest protocols to follow has been reported by Wilson and colleagues (Wilson et al., 2013), where elastic wraps are tightened around the proximal portion of the arms or legs to a perceived discomfort level of 7 out of 10. Individuals then perform a set of 30 repetitions, followed by three sets of 15 repetitions, with a 30 second rest between each set using a load of approximately 30% 1RM; once completed the wraps are removed. In terms of lower body exercises, for most people the load required is body mass, with no external load, for example a 100 kg person with a 200 kg 1RM back squat actually lifts 300 kg during their 1RM (body mass + barbell mass); therefore, 30% of the load lifted is body mass.

Dietary considerations for increasing lean mass

Macronutrient intake

Resistance training enhances cellular sensitivity to amino acids for 24–48 hours (Cuthbertson et al., 2004; Cuthbertson et al., 2006; Burd et al., 2011), thereby enhancing the transportation of amino acids to skeletal muscle cells, enhancing muscle protein synthesis. The addition of 15 g whey protein immediately pre and post workout demonstrated greater increases in muscle mass over a 21 week period compared to both the placebo and control groups (Hulmi et al., 2009). However, the appropriate balance of resistance training (frequency, intensity, volume, type) and protein ingestion (frequency, source, quantity) is essential to optimise this interaction between exercise and nutrient intake.

The recommendations for daily protein consumption for individuals regularly performing resistance training ranges from 1.4–2.3 $g.kg.d^{-1}$ (Campbell et al., 2007; Churchward-Venne et al., 2013), although much of the information in the popular press suggests a higher intake. A recent study comparing the effects of a normal protein intake (2.3 ± 0.6 $g.kg.d^{-1}$) to a high protein intake (3.4 ± 0.6 $g.kg.d^{-1}$), during an 8 week period of standardised resistance training, reported greater improvements in body composition in the high protein group, which was attributed to a decrease in body fat (Antonio et al., 2015). However, there were no significant increases in lean body mass in each group and no differences in changes in lean mass between groups. Similarly, a previous study comparing normal protein intake (1.8 ± 0.4 $g.kg.d^{-1}$) to an even higher protein intake (4.4 ± 0.8 $g.kg.d^{-1}$), in resistance trained men, found no differences in improvements in lean body mass between groups, although interestingly the higher energy intake in the high protein group did not result in any increases in body fat (Antonio et al., 2014). Therefore, very high protein intakes do not appear be advantageous in terms of increases in muscle mass.

Recommendations for post training protein intake usually suggest 20–25 g of high quality protein, ideal from a rapidly absorbable source which is rich in leucine (e.g. whey protein) (Murphy et al., 2015). However, a very recent study observed a meaningful increase in protein synthesis when 40 g of whey protein was consumed post training compared to 20 g protein (MacNaughton et al., 2016).

Supplementation

As the term suggests, such sources of nutrients should be used to 'supplement' the consumption of high quality food and not as a replacement. Clearly the ingestion of nutrients in a liquid form, as many supplements are consumed, has some advantages, but also results in some disadvantages in terms of ease of consumption, taste, rapid vs. prolonged absorption of nutrient. Rapid absorption of nutrients is likely to be advantageous immediately post training; however, prolonged release is likely advantageous prior to sleep.

The majority of studies investigating the effects of whey protein and/or essential amino-acid supplementation combined with resistance training on muscle hypertrophy demonstrate that the addition of supplemental protein results in increases in hypertrophy and therefore muscle cross-sectional area (Hulmi et al., 2010).

Decreasing body fat

One of the key aspects of reducing body fat levels is creating a moderate energy deficit (~500 kcal.day^{-1}) (Murphy et al., 2015), and therefore the interaction between energy expended (in both training and daily activities) and energy consumed (from both food and fluid) is essential. If insufficient energy is available for metabolic processes and physical activity, the body will have to use its own reserves: glycogen, fats and proteins. There has to be an appropriate balance between depletion of glycogen and utilisation of stored fats (adipose tissue) as the athlete still needs to be able to maintain the intensity of training, especially resistance training, to prevent/minimise any losses in lean muscle mass via the catabolism of proteins as an energy source.

Training considerations

The volume and intensity of resistance training sessions should be maintained, where possible, to minimise the loss of lean muscle mass. Once the athlete becomes glycogen depleted it is likely that the number of repetitions at a given load will reduce, especially across multiple sets.

More importantly during this phase of training the total volume of aerobic training should increase to facilitate an increase in energy expenditure, further increasing the energy deficit. Both low intensity prolonged aerobic exercise and high intensity interval training have been reported to be effective at increasing energy expenditure and reducing body fat levels; however, to date no research has conclusively demonstrated which mode is most beneficial. To some extent this will depend on the athletes preferred type of activity, level of motivation and the time that they have available to train.

Aerobic training

As mentioned above, resistance training should not vary noticeably; however, a much greater emphasis should be placed on aerobic exercise to ensure that an appropriate energy deficit is created to facilitate a reduction in body fat. To achieve this, the volume of aerobic exercise should be progressively increased. The debate is how to achieve this increase in volume, with two opposing viewpoints being the use of either low intensity prolonged aerobic exercise and high intensity interval training.

Low intensity (<70% MHR) prolonged (>45 minutes) aerobic exercise is thought to be beneficial as such intensities result in a greater percentage of fats used as a fuel source. However, it must be noted that due to the intensity of the activity the rate of fat oxidation is relative low, as is total energy expenditure, resulting in the need to perform such activities for a prolonged duration.

High intensity interval training consists of numerous bouts of high intensity (>90% MHR), short duration (10 seconds to 4 minutes) bouts of activity, interspersed with lower intensity (<70% MHR) rest periods lasting 10 s to 3 minutes. As the duration of the high intensity interval increases the intensity decreases, with the shortest duration being maximal intensity efforts; similarly, as the duration of the high intensity bout increases so does the rest period, which is essential to permit adequate recovery for the athlete to complete the subsequent high intensity bout.

The findings of numerous studies appears to suggest that high intensity intermittent exercise is superior than steady state exercise when training to decrease body fat levels (Boutcher, 2011; Shiraev and Barclay, 2012). In addition, such training may be more convenient when trying to schedule training around normal life.

Dietary considerations

As already mentioned it is essential that an energy deficit is achieved; however, this should not be at the expense of protein intake which should be maintained between 1.8–2.7 g.kg.d^{-1} (Murphy et al., 2015), with the reduction in energy coming from carbohydrates and fats.

It is important to note that even though resistance exercise results in an increase in muscle protein synthesis, if performed while in a fasted state it is actually catabolic, but this can be overcome when adequate amino acids are available (Brook et al., 2015), demonstrating the importance of the consumption of high quality sources of protein. Additionally, resistance training enhances cellular sensitivity to amino acids for 24–48 hours (Cuthbertson et al., 2004; Cuthbertson et al., 2006; Burd et al., 2011), thereby enhancing the transportation of amino acids to skeletal muscle cells enhancing muscle protein synthesis.

High protein intakes (~2.3 g.kg.d^{-1}) have been shown to have a beneficial effect on maintenance of lean mass during energy restricted diets compared to lower protein intakes (~1.0 g.kg.d^{-1}), although this did not affect fat loss (Mettler et al., 2010; Churchward-Venne et al., 2013; Longland et al., 2016). Post training, 20–25 g of high quality protein should be ingested; ideal protein sources should be rapidly absorbable and rich in leucine (e.g. whey protein) (Murphy et al., 2015). During each meal 0.25–0.30 g.kg^{-1} should be consumed, ensuring that all essential amino acids are available (Murphy et al., 2015), either from animal sources or appropriately combining non-animal sources.

Periodisation

Periodisation of training should focus on hypertrophy for the majority of the individual's training; however, interspersing this with periods of strength training may result in beneficial adaptations during the subsequent hypertrophy phases as the individual would be able to use higher loads (Figure 34.1). More specific examples of programmes can be found in Tables 34.1–34.4 (these are examples of how variables and exercises can be manipulated and are not prescriptive).

Tables 34.3 and 34.4 illustrate progressions of example lower body training sessions from hypertrophy to strength, with the aim of the strength sessions to set the foundations for the subsequent hypertrophy session where increased loads will be possible.

Tables 34.5 and 34.6 illustrate the progressions of example upper body training sessions from hypertrophy to strength, with the aim of the strength sessions to not only increase strength but also enhance the hypertrophic adaptations following a similar protocol to that described by Schoenfeld et al. (2014).

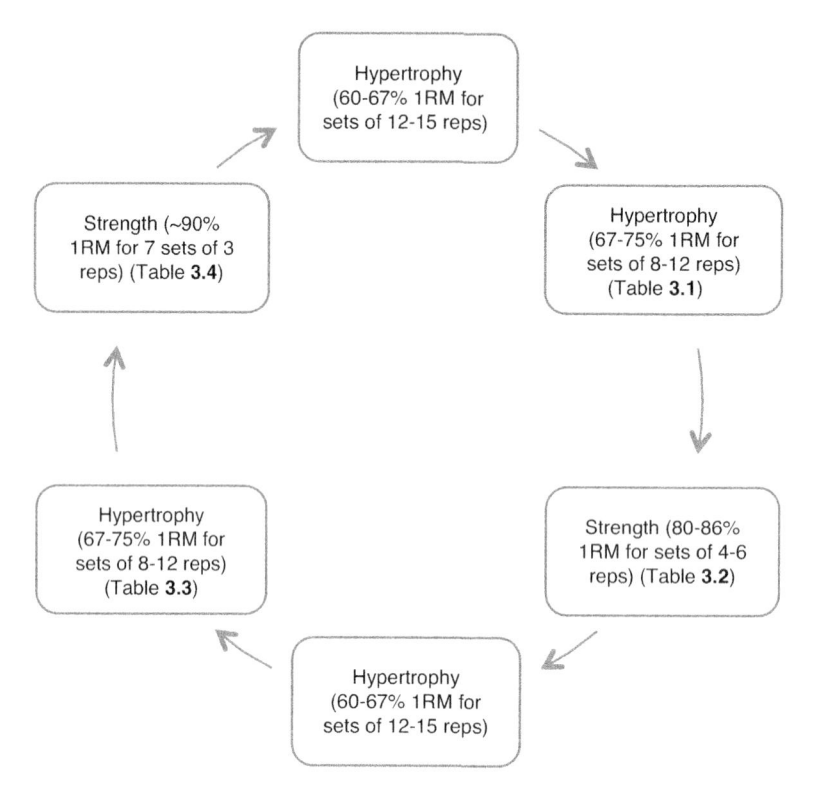

```
        ┌─────────────────┐
        │   Hypertrophy   │
        │  (60-67% 1RM for│
        │ sets of 12-15 reps)│
        └─────────────────┘
       ↗                    ↘
┌─────────────────┐      ┌─────────────────┐
│ Strength (~90%  │      │   Hypertrophy   │
│ 1RM for 7 sets of 3│   │  (67-75% 1RM for│
│ reps) (Table 3.4)│     │ sets of 8-12 reps)│
└─────────────────┘      │   (Table 3.1)   │
                         └─────────────────┘
        ↑                         ↓
┌─────────────────┐      ┌─────────────────┐
│   Hypertrophy   │      │ Strength (80-86%│
│  (67-75% 1RM for│      │ 1RM for sets of 4-6│
│ sets of 8-12 reps)│    │ reps) (Table 3.2)│
│   (Table 3.3)   │      └─────────────────┘
└─────────────────┘
       ↖             ┌─────────────────┐  ↙
                     │   Hypertrophy   │
                     │  (60-67% 1RM for│
                     │ sets of 12-15 reps)│
                     └─────────────────┘
```

Figure 34.1 Schematic example of periodised approach

Table 34.3 Example lower body hypertrophy training programme

	Muscle groups	Exercise	Week 1	Week 2	Week 3	Week 4
			Sets × repetitions (% 1-RM)			
Day 1	Quads & glutes	Squat variation e.g. front squat	3 × 12 (~65%)	3 × 13 (~65%)	3 × 14 (~65%)	3 × 15 (~65%)
	Quads & glutes	Lunge variation e.g. reverse	3 × 12 (~65%)	3 × 13 (~65%)	3 × 14 (~65%)	3 × 15 (~65%)
	Hamstrings	RDL	3 × 12 (~65%)	3 × 13 (~65%)	3 × 14 (~65%)	3 × 15 (~65%)
	Calves	Standing calf raise	3 × 12 (~65%)	4 × 12 (~65%)	5 × 12 (~65%)	6 × 12 (~65%)
Notes	Hamstring focus on hip extension and calf focus on the gastrocnemius, during Day 1. Overload during compound exercises achieved through progressive increase in repetition (and load if possible), while volume increased during isolation exercises via increased number of sets					
Day 2	Quads & glutes	Squat variation e.g. back squat	3 × 12 (~65%)	3 × 13 (~65%)	3 × 14 (~65%)	3 × 15 (~65%)
	Quads	Leg extensions	3 × 12 (~65%)	3 × 13 (~65%)	3 × 14 (~65%)	3 × 15 (~65%)
	Hamstrings	Leg curls e.g. standing	3 × 12 (~65%)	4 × 12 (~65%)	5 × 12 (~65%)	6 × 12 (~65%)
	Calves	Seated calf raise	3 × 12 (~65%)	4 × 12 (~65%)	5 × 12 (~65%)	6 × 12 (~65%)
Notes	Hamstring focus on knee flexion and calf focus on the soleus, during Day 2. Overload during compound exercises achieved through progressive increase in repetition (and load if possible), while volume increased during isolation exercises via increased number of sets					

Table 34.4 Example lower body strength training programme

	Muscle groups	Exercise	Week 1 Sets × reps (% 1-RM)	Week 2 Sets × reps (% 1-RM)	Week 3 Sets × reps (% 1-RM)	Week 4 Sets × reps (% 1-RM)
Day 1	Quads & glutes	Squat variation e.g. front squat	3 × 5 (80%)	3 × 5 (82%)	3 × 5 (84%)	3 × 5 (86%)
	Quads & glutes	Lunge variation e.g. forward	3 × 5 (80%)	3 × 5 (82%)	3 × 5 (84%)	3 × 5 (86%)
	Hamstrings	RDL	3 × 5 (80%)	3 × 5 (82%)	3 × 5 (84%)	3 × 5 (86%)
	Calves	Standing calf raise	3 × 5 (80%)	3 × 5 (82%)	3 × 5 (84%)	3 × 5 (86%)
Notes	Hamstring focus on hip extension and calf focus on the gastrocnemius, during Day 1. Overload achieved through progressive increase in load					
Day 2	Quads & glutes	Squat variation e.g. back squat	3 × 5 (80%)	3 × 5 (82%)	3 × 5 (84%)	3 × 5 (86%)
	Quads & glutes	Leg press	3 × 5 (80%)	3 × 5 (82%)	3 × 5 (84%)	3 × 5 (86%)
	Hamstrings	Leg curls e.g. seated	3 × 5 (80%)	3 × 5 (82%)	3 × 5 (84%)	3 × 5 (86%)
	Calves	Seated calf raise	3 × 5 (80%)	3 × 5 (82%)	3 × 5 (84%)	3 × 5 (86%)
Notes	Hamstring focus on hip extension and calf focus on the soleus, during Day 2. Overload achieved through progressive increase in load					

Table 34.5 Example upper body hypertrophy training programme

	Muscle group	Exercise	Week 1	Week 2	Week 3	Week 4
			Sets × repetitions (% 1-RM)			
Day 1	Lats	Pull-down variation e.g. wide grip	3 × 12 (~65%)	3 × 13 (~65%)	3 × 14 (~65%)	3 × 15 (~65%)
Superset	Chest	Bench press variation e.g. flat	3 × 12 (~65%)	3 × 13 (~65%)	3 × 14 (~65%)	3 × 15 (~65%)
	Lats	Row variation e.g. bent-over	3 × 12 (~65%)	3 × 13 (~65%)	3 × 14 (~65%)	3 × 15 (~65%)
Superset	Deltoids	Cable lateral raises	3 × 12 (~65%)	3 × 13 (~65%)	3 × 14 (~65%)	3 × 15 (~65%)
	Deltoids	Shoulder press variation e.g. dumbell	3 × 12 (~65%)	3 × 13 (~65%)	3 × 14 (~65%)	3 × 15 (~65%)
Superset	Triceps	Tricep extensions	3 × 12 (~65%)	4 × 12 (~65%)	5 × 12 (~65%)	6 × 12 (~65%)
	Biceps	Incline curls	3 × 12 (~65%)	4 × 12 (~65%)	5 × 12 (~65%)	6 × 12 (~65%)
Notes	Overload during compound exercises achieved through progressive increase in repetition (and load if possible), while volume increased during isolation exercises via increased number of sets					

(*Continued*)

Table 34.5 (Continued)

		Muscle group	Exercise	Week 1	Week 2	Week 3	Week 4
				Sets × repetitions (% 1-RM)			
Day 2		Lats	Pull-down variation e.g. close grip	3 × 12 (~65%)	3 × 13 (~65%)	3 × 14 (~65%)	3 × 15 (~65%)
	Superset	Chest	Bench press variation e.g. dumbbell	3 × 12 (~65%)	3 × 13 (~65%)	3 × 14 (~65%)	3 × 15 (~65%)
		Lats	Row variation e.g. dumbbell	3 × 12 (~65%)	3 × 13 (~65%)	3 × 14 (~65%)	3 × 15 (~65%)
	Superset	Deltoids	Cable upright row	3 × 12 (~65%)	3 × 13 (~65%)	3 × 14 (~65%)	3 × 15 (~65%)
		Deltoids	Shoulder press Variation e.g. barbell	3 × 12 (~65%)	3 × 13 (~65%)	3 × 14 (~65%)	3 × 15 (~65%)
	Superset	Triceps	Tricep pushdowns	3 × 12 (~65%)	4 × 12 (~65%)	5 × 12 (~65%)	6 × 12 (~65%)
		Biceps	Concentration curls	3 × 12 (~65%)	4 × 12 (~65%)	5 × 12 (~65%)	6 × 12 (~65%)
Notes	Overload during compound exercises achieved through progressive increase in repetition (and load if possible), while volume increased during isolation exercises via increased number of sets

Table 34.6 Example upper body strength training programme

	Muscle group	Exercise	Week 1	Week 2	Week 3	Week 4
			Sets × repetitions (% 1-RM)			
Day 1	Lats	Pullup variation e.g. wide grip	5 × 3 (90%)	7 × 3 (90%)	7 × 3 (90%)	7 × 3 (90%)
	Chest	Bench press variation e.g. flat	5 × 3 (90%)	7 × 3 (90%)	7 × 3 (90%)	7 × 3 (90%)
	Deltoids	Shoulder press variation e.g. dumbbell	5 × 3 (90%)	7 × 3 (90%)	7 × 3 (90%)	7 × 3 (90%)
	Triceps	Tricep extensions	5 × 3 (90%)	7 × 3 (90%)	7 × 3 (90%)	7 × 3 (90%)
	Biceps	Incline curls	5 × 3 (90%)	7 × 3 (90%)	7 × 3 (90%)	7 × 3 (90%)
Notes	Overload progressively increased by increasing the number of sets from 5 to 7 across the first 3 sessions. If all repetitions across all 7 sets can be performed the load should be increased slightly for the next session
Day 2	Chest	Bench press variation e.g. dumbbell	6 × 3 (90%)	7 × 3 (90%)	7 × 3 (90%)	7 × 3 (90%)
	Lats	Row variation e.g. bent over	6 × 3 (90%)	7 × 3 (90%)	7 × 3 (90%)	7 × 3 (90%)
	Deltoids	Shoulder press variation e.g. barbell	6 × 3 (90%)	7 × 3 (90%)	7 × 3 (90%)	7 × 3 (90%)
	Triceps	Tricep pushdowns	6 × 3 (90%)	7 × 3 (90%)	7 × 3 (90%)	7 × 3 (90%)
	Biceps	Concentration curls	6 × 3 (90%)	7 × 3 (90%)	7 × 3 (90%)	7 × 3 (90%)
Notes	The total number of exercises is reduced due to the strength focus and the high number of total sets, to ensure that the programme is achievable within a realistic duration

Conclusion

Appropriate periodisation of training and dietary intake should be planned and appropriately revised, based on regular monitoring of the individual's current training status. As such periodic monitoring (every 4–6 weeks) of the athlete's weight, skin folds and circumferences should be undertaken to monitor progress and inform subsequent phases of training. In general, a high protein intake (1.8–2.3 g.kg.d^{-1}) should be maintained, with manipulation of fat and carbohydrate intake to used to increase or decrease total energy intake, in line with training goals and the monitoring of body fat levels.

References

Antonio, J., Ellerbroek, A., Silver, T., Orris, S., Scheiner, M., Gonzalez, A. and Peacock, C.A. (2015). A High Protein Diet (3.4 G/Kg/D) Combined with a Heavy Resistance Training Program Improves Body Composition in Healthy Trained Men and Women – A Follow-up Investigation. *Journal of the International Society of Sports Nutrition*, 12(1), 39.

Antonio, J., Peacock, C.A., Ellerbroek, A., Fromhoff, B. and Silver, T. (2014). The Effects of Consuming a High Protein Diet (4.4 G/Kg/D) on Body Composition in Resistance-Trained Individuals. *Journal of the International Society of Sports Nutrition*, 11(1), 19.

Benton, M.J., Raab, S. and Waggener, G.T. (2013). Effect of Training Status on Reliability of One Repetition Maximum Testing in Women. *Journal of Strength and Conditioning Research*, 27(7), 1885–1890.

Boutcher, S.H. (2011). High-Intensity Intermittent Exercise and Fat Loss. *Journal of Obesity*, 2011(868305).

Brook, M.S., Wilkinson, D.J., Smith, K. and Atherton, P.J. (2015). The Metabolic and Temporal Basis of Muscle Hypertrophy in Response to Resistance Exercise. *European Journal of Sport Science*, 16(6), 1–12.

Brzycki, M. (1993). Predicting a One-Rep Max From Reps to Failure. *Journal of Physical Education and Recreation*, 64, 88–90.

Burd, N.A., West, D.W.D., Moore, D.R., Atherton, P.J., Staples, A.W., Prior, T., Tang, J.E., Rennie, M.J., Baker, S.K. and Phillips, S.M. (2011). Enhanced Amino Acid Sensitivity of Myofibrillar Protein Synthesis Persists for up to 24 H After Resistance Exercise in Young Men. *The Journal of Nutrition*, 141(4), 568–573.

Campbell, B., Kreider, R.B., Ziegenfuss, T., La Bounty, P., Roberts, M., Burke, D., Landis, J., Lopez, H. and Antonio, J. (2007). International Society of Sports Nutrition Position Stand: Protein and Exercise. *Journal of the International Society of Sports Nutrition*, 4(1), 6.

Churchward-Venne, T.A., Murphy, C.H., Longland, T.M. and Phillips, S.M. (2013). Role of Protein and Amino Acids in Promoting Lean Mass Accretion With Resistance Exercise and Attenuating Lean Mass Loss During Energy Deficit in Humans. *Amino Acids*, 45(2), 231–240.

Comfort, P. and McMahon, J.J. (2015). Reliability of Maximal Back Squat and Power Clean Performances in Inexperienced Athletes. *The Journal of Strength & Conditioning Research*, 29(11), 3089–3096.

Cooper, D.M. (1994). Evidence for and Mechanisms of Exercise Modulation of Growth-an Overview. *Medicine & Science in Sports & Exercise*, 26(6), 733–740.

Cormie, P., McCaulley, G.O., Triplett, N.T. and McBride, J.M. (2007). Optimal Loading for Maximal Power Output During Lower-Body Resistance Exercises. *Medicine & Science in Sports & Exercise*, 39(2), 340–349.

Cuthbertson, D.J., Babraj, J., Smith, K., Wilkes, E., Fedele, M.J., Esser, K. and Rennie, M. (2006). Anabolic Signaling and Protein Synthesis in Human Skeletal Muscle After Dynamic Shortening or Lengthening Exercise. *American Journal of Physiology – Endocrinology and Metabolism*, 290(4), E731–E738.

Cuthbertson, D.J., Smith, K., Babraj, J., Leese, G., Waddell, T., Atherton, P., Wackerhage, H., Taylor, P.M. and Rennie, M.J. (2004). Anabolic Signaling Deficits Underlie Amino Acid Resistance of Wasting, Aging Muscle. *The FASEB Journal*, 19(3), 422–424.

Durnin, J.V. and Womersley, J. (1973). Total Body Fat, Calculated From Body Density, and Its Relationship to Skinfold Thickness in 571 People Aged 12–72 Years. *Proceedings of the Nutrition Society*, 32(1), 45A.

Durnin, J.V. and Womersley, J. (1974). Body Fat Assessed From Total Body Density and Its Estimation From Skinfold Thickness: Measurements on 481 Men and Women Aged From 16 to 72 Years. *British Journal of Nutrition*, 32(1), 77–97.

Earp, J.E., Newton, R.U., Cormie, P. and Blazevich, A.J. (2015). Inhomogeneous Quadriceps Femoris Hypertrophy in Response to Strength and Power Training. *Medicine & Science in Sports & Exercise*, 47(11), 2389–2397.

Espana Romero, V., Ruiz, J.R., Ortega, F.B., Artero, E.G., Vicente-Rodriguez, G., Moreno, L.A., Castillo, M.J. and Gutierrez, A. (2009). Body Fat Measurement in Elite Sport Climbers: Comparison of Skinfold Thickness Equations With Dual Energy X-Ray Absorptiometry. *Journal of Sports Sciences*, 27(5), 469–477.

Faigenbaum, A.D., McFarland, J.E., Herman, R.E., Naclerio, F., Ratamess, N.A., Kang, J. and Myer, G.D. (2012). Reliability of the One-Repetition-Maximum Power Clean Test in Adolescent Athletes. *Journal of Strength and Conditioning Research*, 26(2), 432–437.

Folland, J.P. and Williams, A.G. (2007). The Adaptations to Strength Training: Morphological and Neurological Contributions to Increased Strength. *Sports Medicine*, 37(2), 145–168.

Henselmans, M. and Schoenfeld, B.J. (2014). The Effect of Inter-Set Rest Intervals on Resistance Exercise-Induced Muscle Hypertrophy. *Sports Medicine*, 44(12), 1635–1643.

Hulmi, J.J., Kovanen, V., Selanne, H., Kraemer, W.J., Hakkinen, K. and Mero, A.A. (2009). Acute and Long-Term Effects of Resistance Exercise With or Without Protein Ingestion on Muscle Hypertrophy and Gene Expression. *Amino Acids*, 37(2), 297–308.

Hulmi, J.J., Lockwood, C.M. and Stout, J.R. (2010). Effect of Protein/Essential Amino Acids and Resistance Training on Skeletal Muscle Hypertrophy: A Case for Whey Protein. *Nutrition & Metabolism*, 7(1), 51.

Julio, U.F., Panissa, V.L.G. and Franchini, E. (2012). Prediction of One Repetition Maximum From the Maximum Number of Repetitions With Submaximal Loads in Recreationally Strength-Trained Men. *Science & Sports*, 27(6), e69–e76.

Keogh, J.W.L. and Winwood, P.W. (2016). The Epidemiology of Injuries Across the Weight-Training Sports. *Sports Medicine*, 47(3), 479–501.

Kumar, V., Selby, A., Rankin, D., Patel, R., Atherton, P., Hildebrandt, W., Williams, J., Smith, K., Seynnes, O., Hiscock, N. and Rennie, M.J. (2009). Age-Related Differences in the Dose – Response Relationship of Muscle Protein Synthesis to Resistance Exercise in Young and Old Men. *The Journal of Physiology*, 587(1), 211–217.

Lavallee, M.E. and Balam, T. (2010). An Overview of Strength Training Injuries: Acute and Chronic. *Current Sports Medicine Reports*, 9(5), 307–313.

Longland, T.M., Oikawa, S.Y., Mitchell, C.J., Devries, M.C. and Phillips, S.M. (2016). Higher Compared With Lower Dietary Protein During an Energy Deficit Combined With Intense Exercise Promotes Greater Lean Mass Gain and Fat Mass Loss: A Randomized Trial. *American Journal of Clinical Nutrition*, 103(3), 738–746.

MacNaughton, L.S., Wardle, S.L., Witard, O.C., McGlory, C., Hamilton, D.L., Jeromson, S., Lawrence, C.E., Wallis, G.A. and Tipton, K.D.C.e. (2016). The Response of Muscle Protein Synthesis Following Whole-Body Resistance Exercise Is Greater Following 40 g Than 20 g of Ingested Whey Protein. *Physiological Reports*, 4(15), n/a–n/a.

McBride, J.M., McCaulley, G.O., Cormie, P., Nuzzo, J.L., Cavill, M.J. and Triplett, N.T. (2009). Comparison of Methods to Quantify Volume During Resistance Exercise. *The Journal of Strength & Conditioning Research*, 23(1), 106–110. doi:10.1519/JSC.0b013e31818efdfe.

Mettler, S., Mitchell, N. and Tipton, K.D. (2010). Increased Protein Intake Reduces Lean Body Mass Loss During Weight Loss in Athletes. *Medicine & Science in Sports & Exercise*, 42(2), 326–337.

Mitchell, C.J., Churchward-Venne, T.A., Parise, G., Bellamy, L., Baker, S.K., Smith, K., Atherton, P.J. and Phillips, S.M. (2014). Acute Post-Exercise Myofibrillar Protein Synthesis Is Not Correlated With Resistance Training-Induced Muscle Hypertrophy in Young Men. *PLoS ONE*, 9(2), e89431.

Morales, J. and Sobonya, S. (1996). Use of Submaximal Repetition Tests for Predicting 1-Rm Strength in Class Athletes. *The Journal of Strength & Conditioning Research*, 10(3), 186–189.

Murphy, C.H., Hector, A.J. and Phillips, S.M. (2015). Considerations for Protein Intake in Managing Weight Loss in Athletes. *European Journal of Sport Science*, 15(1), 21–28.

Narici, M.V., Hoppeler, H., Kayser, B., Landoni, L., Claassen, H., Gavardi, C., Conti, M. and Cerretelli, P. (1996). Human Quadriceps Cross-Sectional Area, Torque and Neural Activation During 6 Months Strength Training. *Acta Physiologica Scandinavica*, 157(2), 175–186.

Pearson, S.J. and Hussain, S.R. (2015). A Review on the Mechanisms of Blood-Flow Restriction Resistance Training-Induced Muscle Hypertrophy. *Sports Medicine*, 45(2), 187–200.

Pope, Z.K., Willardson, J.M. and Schoenfeld, B.J. (2013). Exercise and Blood Flow Restriction. *Journal of Strength and Conditioning Research*, 27(10), 2914–2926.

Richens, B. and Cleather, D.J. (2014). The Relationship Between the Number of Repetitions Performed at Given Intensities Is Different in Endurance and Strength Trained Athletes. *Biology of Sport*, 31(2), 157–161.

Saunders, M.J., Blevins, J.E. and Broeder, C.E. (1998). Effects of Hydration Changes on Bioelectrical Impedance in Endurance Trained Individuals. *Medicine & Science in Sports & Exercise*, 30(6), 885–892.

Schoenfeld, B.J., Ogborn, D.I. and Krieger, J.W. (2015a). Effect of Repetition Duration During Resistance Training on Muscle Hypertrophy: A Systematic Review and Meta-Analysis. *Sports Medicine*, 45(4), 577–585.

Schoenfeld, B.J., Ogborn, D.I. and Krieger, J.W. (2016). Effects of Resistance Training Frequency on Measures of Muscle Hypertrophy: A Systematic Review and Meta-Analysis. *Sports Medicine*, 46(11), 1689–1697.

Schoenfeld, B.J., Peterson, M.D., Ogborn, D., Contreras, B. and Sonmez, G.T. (2015b). Effects of Low- Vs. High-Load Resistance Training on Muscle Strength and Hypertrophy in Well-Trained Men. *The Journal of Strength & Conditioning Research*, 29(10), 2954–2963.

Schoenfeld, B.J., Ratamess, N.A., Peterson, M.D., Contreras, B., Sonmez, G.T. and Alvar, B.A. (2014). Effects of Different Volume-Equated Resistance Training Loading Strategies on Muscular Adaptations in Well-Trained Men. *The Journal of Strength & Conditioning Research*, 28(10), 2909–2918.

Schoenfeld, B.J., Ratamess, N.A., Peterson, M.D., Contreras, B. and Tiryaki-Sonmez, G. (2015c). Influence of Resistance Training Frequency on Muscular Adaptations in Well-Trained Men. *The Journal of Strength & Conditioning Research*, 29(7), 1821–1829. Shinohara, M., Kouzaki, M., Yoshihisa, T. and Fukunaga, T. (1998). Efficacy of Tourniquet Ischemia for Strength Training With Low Resistance. *European Journal of Applied Physiology and Occupational Physiology*, 77(1–2), 189–191.

Shiraev, T. and Barclay, G. (2012). Evidence Based Exercise – Clinical Benefits of High Intensity Interval Training. *Australian Family Physician*, 41(12), 960–962.

Siewe, J., Marx, G., Knoll, P., Eysel, P., Zarghooni, K., Graf, M., Herren, C., Sobottke, R. and Michael, J. (2014). Injuries and Overuse Syndromes in Competitive and Elite Bodybuilding. *International Journal of Sports Medicine*, 35(11), 943–948.

Wilson, J.M., Lowery, R.P., Joy, J.M., Loenneke, J.P. and Naimo, M.A. (2013). Practical Blood Flow Restriction Training Increases Acute Determinants of Hypertrophy Without Increasing Indices of Muscle Damage. *The Journal of Strength & Conditioning Research*, 27(11), 3068–3075.

35
POWERLIFTING

Sean Maloney

Introduction to the sport

General overview

The sport of powerlifting is an athletic event in which competitors attempt to lift the maximum possible weight in three different barbell lifts. The three lifts performed are the squat, bench press and deadlift. Competitors may participate in two types of competition depending on whether or not supportive equipment is worn. These are referred to as either 'equipped' (with supportive equipment) or 'classic' (without) competitions. Classic competitions may also be referred to as 'raw' or 'unequipped'. The use of supportive equipment infers different demands on the powerlifter as technique is altered substantially in order to achieve maximal benefits from the equipment. Such discussion is complex and beyond the scope of this chapter. This chapter will focus solely on the sport of 'classic' powerlifting.

Powerlifting is not an Olympic sport, although is recognised by the International World Games Association (IWGA) and contested in the World Games alongside other non-Olympic sports such as Squash and Lacrosse. Whilst a number of worldwide powerlifting federations exist, the International Powerlifting Federation (IPF) is recognised by SportAccord and the IWGA as the international governing body for the sport of powerlifting. There are a number of small but important discrepancies in regulations employed by different powerlifting federations; weight classification, permissible equipment and even performance of the three lifts will commonly differ. This chapter will consider the rules and regulations of the IPF as of 2016 (IPF, 2016).

Rules and regulations

In competition, athletes are grouped by sex and body weight. Since 2011, the IPF has used the age and weight categories shown in Table 35.1. Competitors are required to weigh-in on the day of competition. The weighing-in period commences two hours before the scheduled start time and lasts for a duration of ninety minutes. Each lifter must meet the requirements of their chosen weight class (i.e. they cannot be heavier or lighter).

Each competitor is permitted three attempts on each of the squat, bench press and deadlift. The successful outcome of each lift is judged by three referees. For a lift to be deemed successful,

Table 35.1 Current age and weight categories in the IPF

Age classes	Weight classes	
	Male	Female
Open (14 and upwards)	Up to 53kg	Up to 43kg
Sub-junior (14–18)	(sub-junior and	(sub-junior and
Junior (19–23)	junior only)	junior only)
Masters 1 (40–49)	59kg	47kg
Masters 2 (50–59)	66kg	52kg
Masters 3 (60–69)	74kg	57kg
Masters 4 (70	83kg	63kg
and upwards)	93kg	72kg
	105kg	84kg
	120kg	84kg+
	120kg+	

Table 35.2 Example structure of a two-flight powerlifting meet

	Session 1 (morning)	Session 2 (afternoon)
Includes:	All female classes, males up to 74kg (inclusive)	All male classes above 83kg (inclusive)
Weigh-in:	08:00–09:30	12:00–13:30
Lifting commences:	10:00	14:00
Flight one:	All female lifters	Males up to 93kg (inclusive)
Flight two:	Males up to 74kg (inclusive)	All remaining male lifters

the lift must receive the approval of at least two of the three referees. Referees may fail a lift not only if it cannot be completed by the lifter, but also if any technical infringement is deemed to have occurred. Some of the most common infringements are alluded to the following Competition Lifts section.

The lifter's heaviest successful attempt on each lift counts toward a cumulative competition total. Should a lifter fail to make a successful attempt in any of the three lifts, they are disqualified from the competition and are not awarded a total. Within each weight class, the lifter with the highest total wins. In certain international competitions, separate medals may also be awarded for performance within each of the three individual lifts. If two or more lifters achieve the same total within a given class, the lighter lifter ranks above the heavier lifter. Comparisons of lifters across different weight classes can be made using handicapping system such as the Wilks coefficient. In the Wilks scoring system, each lifter is given a coefficient number based upon their sex and body mass which is then multiplied by the load lifted.

Competition lifts

Squat

During the squat the barbell is worn across the shoulders/upper back of the lifter. Upon receiving the 'squat' command from the centre referee, the lifter must flex the hips and knees, descending until the top surface of the leg is lower than the knee. The lifter then extends the hips and knees back to an upright position, finishing with the hips and knees fully extended. When the referee gives the 'rack' command the barbell is racked and the attempt is completed.

Bench press

In the bench press, the lifters must lower the barbell to the chest/upper abdominals upon receiving the 'start' command from the centre referee. The barbell must be paused motionless on the chest until the referee gives the 'press' command; the duration of the pause is subject to the referee's interpretation. Following completion of the press, the lifter must wait until receiving the 'rack' command from referee before re-racking the barbell and completing the attempt.

Deadlift

The deadlift requires the lifter to raise the barbell from the floor to full extension of the hips and knees. Lifters are permitted to slide the bar up the thighs (often using magnesium silicate (talcum powder) to reduce friction) but must not use the thighs to support the bar or re-bend the knees to assist with the lockout of the lift. The centre referee will then give the 'down' command to the lifter to complete the lift.

The powerlifting meet

Although lifters will perform only nine competition lifts, a powerlifting meet takes place over a duration of several hours. Competitions will commonly group lifters into both sessions and flights based upon the class entered. An example structure of a two-flight powerlifting meet, such as would be anticipated at a regional level, is shown in Table 35.2.

With this format, flight one will complete their three squat attempts before flight two completes their three squat attempts. Flight one will then complete their three bench attempts before flight two completes their three bench attempts. Finally, flight one completes their three deadlift attempts before flight two completes their three deadlift attempts. This will then be repeated in the afternoon for lifters in session two.

General athletic demands

Physiology

Activity profile

The recovery between competitors' three attempts on a given lift is dependent on the number of competitors within the flight. As a rule of thumb, competitors typically allow one minute per lifter in the flight to estimate when they will be required to lift. A duration of 10–15 minutes would typically be expected between lifts, considerably greater than 3–5 minutes that would commonly be recommended in one repetition maximum (1RM) testing procedures.

As the powerlifting meet takes place over a number of hours, the competitor will spend a large percentage of the meet in what could be referred to as a state of rest. The duration between weigh-in, lift-off and between competitors' lifts (i.e. from squat to bench press and bench press to deadlift) will vary from competition to competition, depending on the number of lifters and number of flights. Competitors will use these periods to prepare for the next lift. The IPF stipulate a minimum of 20 minutes between the last lifter in one lift and the first lifter in the next lift during single flight competitions. It is therefore unlikely that competitors will have less than 30 minutes between lifts. During two-flight competitions, a period of 45–75 minutes is perhaps more typical.

The time-window in-between lifts can be seen in both positive and negative regard. On the positive side, this time-window should facilitate physiological recovery and allow the lifter time to engage in nutritional practices. On the negative side, the time between lifts is likely to result in the reduction of core/muscle temperature and neural excitation. Effectively, this requires the lifter to warm-up three times and thereby increases the total amount of work performed by the lifter. Typically, a warm-up duration of 20–40 minutes for each lift would be expected although this will vary greatly between competitors and the individual lifts.

Energy systems

The competition lifts last a matter of seconds and are therefore reliant on intra-muscular ATP and ATP-PC stores. For this reason, metabolic fatigue is unlikely to influence powerlifting performance. Given that competitors will only perform sets of multiple repetitions at a low relative effort during the warm-up, the replenishment of energy stores during powerlifting competition is not of critical importance beyond the general sustenance required across several hours of competition.

Muscle temperature

Changes in muscle temperature will have a profound effect on the contractile properties. It is therefore important that the warm-up for each lift effectively elevates muscle temperature. In addition, the periods between attempts and lifts must also be considered. Strategies such as passive heat maintenance (i.e. layering with sweat tops and pants) may be employed in an attempt to maintain muscle temperature during periods of inactivity and partially offset reductions in performance.

Endocrinology

During an international powerlifting competition, La Panse et al. (2012) reported elevations in cortisol and dehydroepiandrosterone (DHEA) from weigh-in to post-competition in both males and females, and testosterone was elevated in males. La Panse et al. (2012) also observed a correlation between post-competition cortisol levels and Wilks score in female lifters ($R = 0.65$; $P < 0.05$). Short bursts of intense activity can elicit rapid elevations in hormones such as testosterone, adrenaline, cortisol and growth hormone. Such changes may contribute to enhanced strength and power performance and may be a desired response to the warm-up. Indeed, Cook et al. (2012) have reported that elite competitors within an array of sports exhibit greater baseline concentrations of testosterone and cortisol than their non-elite counterparts.

Psychology

Powerlifting is recognised to require high arousal states in order to maximise performance. The potential of psychological strategies to enhance maximal strength performance is well established and therefore an important factor for the powerlifter to consider. The goal of such 'psyching-up' practices is to increase physical and mental activation, together with focusing attention, and these are employed more commonly as the perception of required effort is increased. For example, the use of ammonia inhalants (designed to irritate the respiratory tract and 'stimulate' the lifter) is greater prior to third attempts (Pritchard et al., 2014). Also, these strategies are likely to be employed more prior to the deadlift, where the load cannot be 'felt' prior to lifting (Pritchard et al., 2014). Whilst the use of ammonia inhalants is not banned by the IPF (IPF, 2016), it is important to note that their safety or efficacy has not been evaluated empirically.

During competition, dealing with emotional stress (i.e. anxiety) is ranked as the highest concern amongst powerlifters (Ljdokova et al., 2014a). Judge et al. (2016) reported that anxiety scores were negatively correlated to collegiate powerlifting performance, highlighting the importance of adopting strategies to deal with the stressors of competition. Powerlifters rank receiving assistance from their coach as the most important factor in dealing with competition stress, followed then by mental attitude (Ljdokova et al., 2014b). Indeed, it is how stress is appraised which may determine its effect on performance. Lifters able to reappraise competition stress as 'excitement' or 'challenge' are likely to be successful.

Biomechanics

Force requirements

Lifters have one minute to begin each attempt from the time they are called to the platform. However, there is no limit on the time that may be taken to perform the lift. For this reason, rate of force development should not strictly be a limiting factor within powerlifting. The development of maximal muscle tension is likely to take 0.6–0.8 seconds (Zatsiorsky, 2003) with competition lifts typically lasting 2–5 seconds (McGuigan and Wilson, 1996; Escamilla et al., 2000; Miletello et al., 2009).

Muscle mass and architecture

Whilst the relationship between muscle cross-sectional area and force production capacity is not linear, increased muscle mass is likely to be advantageous. Strong relationships between muscle mass and powerlifting performance have been reported in a number of studies (Brechue and Abe, 2002; Keogh et al., 2009; Akagi et al., 2014; Lovera and Keogh, 2015). For example, performance of the three power lifts was strongly correlated with fat free mass ($R = 0.86$ to $0.95, P \leq 0.001$) by Brechue and Abe (2002). Lovera and Keogh (2015) also demonstrated that winners across a broad range of weight classes had more muscle mass (+2.7%, $P = 0.03$) than less successful counterparts. The ability of the muscle to produce force also depends on the architecture of the muscle; longer fascicle lengths and increased pennation angles are advantageous to force production and noted adaptations to resistance training. Indeed, Brechue and Abe (2002) note correlations between muscle fascicle length and performance in the three power lifts ($R = 0.45$–$0.56; P \leq 0.05$).

Anthropometry

Given the association between muscle mass and performance, it is not surprising that powerlifters are typically characterised by high levels of mesomorphy and large limb girths (Keogh et al., 2007; Keogh et al., 2009). Compared to the average population, powerlifters are typically shorter in stature and subsequently have shorter limbs (Keogh et al., 2007); this is likely to be advantageous to performance by reducing range of motion and joint moment arms. Although Keogh et al. (2009) reported that successful powerlifters carried greater muscle mass than non-successful counterparts, no difference in estimated body fat percentage (circa 15%) was observed.

Mechanical work

The goal in powerlifting is to lift the greatest possible load whilst meeting the required regulations for the performance of each lift. As such, lifters should seek to complete attempts in the most efficient way possible. Two important objectives for the powerlifter are common to each of the three lifts:

- Minimise the range of motion
- Minimise the moment arms of the prime movers

These factors will be discussed in regards to each lift later in this chapter. As well as being influenced by height and limb length, moment arms may also be reduced as a consequence of hypertrophy.

Spinal loading

The spinal column is subject to substantial forces during the squat and deadlift, these will be discussed in greater detail in the following section. Effective bracing and breathing techniques are therefore required to minimise the risk of injury. Indeed, powerlifters have demonstrated larger and stronger diaphragm musculature (Brown et al., 2013). The use of a powerlifting belt up to 13 mm in diameter and 40 mm in width is permitted in classic powerlifting. In combination with the Valsalva manoeuvre, the use of a lifting belt has been purported to increase intra-abdominal pressure, reduce spinal loading, reduce the extension moment created by the back extensors and generate an extension moment within the belt itself (Kingma et al., 2006).

The sticking point

Kompf and Arandjelović (2016) define the sticking point as portion of the lift where failure will occur. Explanations of the sticking point (also termed the sticking region) are multi-factorial. The sticking point could be consequential of a position where specific musculature is biomechanically disadvantaged for the production of force and/or a position where the contribution of passive elements is diminished (Kompf and Arandjelović, 2016). It has been proposed that completion of a successful lift appears to be determined by the attainment of a minimum velocity threshold that is lift specific (Jovanović and Flanagan, 2014). Whilst rate of force development may not appear to be a limiting performance factor in a direct sense, it may carry an indirect effect to performance. If a given force output can be generated quicker, the barbell will carry greater velocity earlier in the lift. This may contribute to achieving a greater minimum velocity during the lift and successful navigation through the sticking region.

Lift-specific demands

Squat

The primary joint actions that take place during the squat involve extension of the hip and knee. The prime movers are therefore the muscles comprising the gluteals and quadriceps. The lifter must also have adequate flexibility to squat to required competition depth. The most common restriction prohibiting this depth is inadequate dorsiflexion. Lifting in shoes with an elevated heel, such as Olympic weightlifting shoes, will typically allow an athlete to achieve greater squat depth and also maintain a more upright torso.

Powerlifting squats are typically characterised by a low-bar position. Low-bar squats bring the barbell closer to the lifter's centre of mass, reducing the vertical moment arm and lowering the centre of mass of the lifter-barbell system (Glassbrook et al., 2017). For this reason, low bar squats commonly facilitate heavier loads. Low-bar squats also induce greater hip flexion and forward lean than high bar squats. This reduces the horizontal moment arm of the knee and increases the horizontal moment arm of the hip. The low-bar squat is therefore purported to increase torques acting at the hip and lower back whilst reducing torque at the knee.

Hip extension torque provides the greatest contribution during the squat relative to the knee and ankle (Flanagan et al., 2015). Powerlifting squats are also more commonly performed with a wider stance in comparison to traditional weightlifting squats, further increasing the hip extension moment (Swinton et al., 2012). However, analyses of successful versus unsuccessful lifts demonstrated that squat performance may be limited by force production of the knee extensors or the hip extensors (Flanagan et al., 2015). Whether the knee or the hip is identified as the 'weakest link' will direct the programming and cueing required for an individual. This highlights the importance for the coach and lifter to identify specific technical factors which may indicate the likely limitations.

Given the position of the barbell on the back of the lifter, the spinal column is subject to substantial loading. For example, Cappozzo et al. (1985) found L3-L4 compressive loads of up to 10×bodyweight when half squatting up to 1.6×bodyweight. It is commonly recognised that squat technique should ensure a rigid, neutral spine which resists any planar motion. However, the ability of the spinal column to maintain a neutral lordotic curve is challenged with increasing load and increasing depth. McKean et al. (2010) reported lumbo-sacral flexion of approximately 12° in females and 25° in males squatting with a 50% bodyweight load. Vigotsky et al. (2015) demonstrated a similar degree of flexion (22–27°) in males performing the good morning exercise up to 90% 1RM. It is perhaps best, therefore, to consider neutral spine as a range as opposed to a position; full lumbar flexion is documented to be in the range of 60° (Norkin and White, 2009). However, it is important to emphasise positions of lumbar flexion beyond the neutral range are associated with a greatly elevated risk of injury (McGill, 2007).

Bench press

Simple one-dimensional analyses of the bench press demonstrate that the primary joint actions are horizontal adduction of the shoulder joint and extension of the elbow. The prime movers during the bench press are therefore the pectoralis major and triceps brachii, with the anterior deltoid acting as an important synergist. However, the bench press is associated with extension and flexion of shoulder, an action further emphasising the importance of the anterior deltoids.

The range of motion required to complete the lift can be reduced by four main factors:

- Arching the back
- Retracting the shoulders
- Widening the grip
- Hypertrophy of the chest and upper back

Wagner et al. (1992) reported that greater loads were lifted using a grip width equivalent to 165% or 200% of bi-acromial width in comparison to narrower or wider grips. Gomo and Van Den Tillar (2016) demonstrated similar, a competition width grip (self-selected by each lifter) eliciting greater 1RM values than narrower grips. Whilst a wider grip width will reduce the required range of motion, grip width will also influence the strategy required to complete the lift. Narrower grips reduce the angles of elbow extension and shoulder abduction at the chest (Gomo and Van Den Tillar, 2016) and increase activity of the triceps (Lehman, 2005). Conversely, wider grips will increase the angles of elbow extension and shoulder abduction (Gomo and Van Den Tillar, 2016) and increase activity of pectoralis major (Lehman, 2005). Grip width is also likely to change where the sticking point will occur, a narrower grip resulting the sticking point occurring further from the chest (Gomo and Van Den Tillar, 2016).

Experienced lifters have been reported to adopt a different bar path in comparison to novice lifters, pressing the bar slightly backwards towards the head (McLaughlin and Madsen, 1984). This will work to reduce the distance the bar has to travel. Activation of the lower body during the bench press in experienced powerlifters is evidenced by increased activation of the vastus lateralis (Kristiansen et al., 2015). By creating extension moments in the lower body and pushing it in the vertical direction, stiffness and stability of the trunk is increased (Kristiansen et al., 2015). Also, specific patterns of muscular activation have been shown to be more variable among experienced powerlifters versus controls (Kristiansen et al., 2015). This is indicative of powerlifters adopting a more individualised and specific pressing technique versus novice lifters.

Deadlift

As with the squat, the primary joint actions during the deadlift are extension of the knee and hip. However, there is minimal correspondence or carryover between the two lifts. During deadlifting the largest moment is commonly observed at the hip (Brown and Abani, 1985; Cholewicki et al., 1991; Escamilla et al., 2000; Escamilla et al., 2001). However, Swinton et al. (2011) has reported a greater moments at the lower back. Moments at the knee are widely demonstrated to be lower than at the hip (Brown and Abani, 1985; Cholewicki et al., 1991; Escamilla et al., 2000; Escamilla et al., 2001; Swinton et al., 2011), highlighting why the deadlift is recognised as a hip and back dominant exercise.

Substantial demands are place upon the spine during deadlifting. Cholewicki et al. (1991) reported compressive forces acting on L4/L5 of 6,000–7,000 N for national level female powerlifters and 10,000–17,000 N for their male counterparts (Cholewicki et al., 1991). Granhed et al. (1987) reported compressive L3 loads of between 18,800 and 36,400 N in international level powerlifters. The maintenance of a neutral lordotic curve is challenged with increasing load, a likely consequence of the inability of the erector spinae to counteract the increasing hip moment (Gracovetsky and Farfan, 1986). Any reduction of lordosis in the lumbar spine or excessive kyphosis of the thoracic spine (i.e. rounding of the back) as the deadlift breaks the floor draws the ligaments and surrounding fascia into tension, allowing them to assist the external moment (Gracovetsky and Farfan, 1986). As well as generating tension within the passive components surrounding the spine, rounding the thoracic and/or lumbar regions of the spine brings the barbell close to the body in the sagittal plane, reducing the moment arm of the hip and lower back. Also, this posture opens the knee and hip angles placing these joints in a more advantageous position. The downside of adopting a kyphotic position off the floor is that by the knees and hips will have fully extended before the lift is completed. To lockout the lift the back then has to be unfurled, placing great demands upon the erector spinae. As discussed previously, notable deviation from neutral spine should not be seen as desirable as this is associated with an increased likelihood of injury. Lifters should be encouraged to maintain a neutral spine throughout the full lift.

The powerlifting deadlift is recognised as a slow, grinding lift. Lift durations of 1.5–2.5 seconds have been reported by a number of authors (Brown and Abani, 1985; McGuigan and Wilson, 1996; Escamilla et al., 2001). However, durations of 3.6–4.1 seconds have been reported in higher level lifters (Cholewicki et al., 1991; Escamilla et al., 2000). Given the slow velocity of the movement and absence of an eccentric countermovement during the lift, maximal force production is integral to deadlift performance. Rate of force development is also less important to the deadlift than to the squat or bench press given the speed of the movement.

There are two main styles of deadlifting: conventional and sumo. The conventional deadlift is characterised by a narrow stance and grasping the barbell with hands outside the legs. Conversely, the sumo deadlift is characterised by a wide stance and grasping the bar with the hands inside the legs. Potential benefits of the sumo deadlift include:

- Reduction in the vertical displacement necessary to lockout the lift; reductions of 10–25% have been noted (Escamilla et al., 2000; Escamilla et al., 2001).
- It brings the hips closer to the bar in the sagittal plane, potentially reducing the moment arm and joint moment at the hip. However, 3D analyses by Escamilla et al. (2000) reported that this difference was not significant.
- It facilitates a more upright torso, reducing the demands placed upon the back; Cholewicki et al. (1991) reported reductions in L4/L5 joint moment (-10%) and in L4/L5 shear force (-8%) at lift-off.

Potential benefits of the conventional deadlift include:

- It reduces the knee extension demands.
- It opens the angle of knee and hip at the floor, placing these joints in a mechanically advantageous position.

It is important to highlight that no one style of deadlift is inherently better than the other. Whilst it is generally considered that lifters with longer arms relative to their torso are better suited to conventional deadlifting and those with shorter arms make better sumo lifters, world class performances may be seen using both techniques. The powerlifter should seek to determine which style works best for them at any given point in time.

Injury prevalence

Injury incidence

Approximately 43% of 245 competitive and elite powerlifters surveyed by Siewe et al. (2011) noted the occurrence of injury problems during routine training and a total of 0.3 injuries per lifter per year were reported., Keogh et al. (2006) had previously reported a higher incidence of 1.2 ($\pm$ 1.1) injuries per lifter per year among national and international lifters, comparable to the 1.4 injuries per lifter per year observed by Brown and Kimball (1983) in teenage powerlifters. When evaluating injuries sustained per hours of training, the lowest incidence has been reported by Siewe et al. (2011) with 1 injury per 1,000 hours. Haykowsky et al. (1999) noted a similar 1.1 incidence in visually impaired powerlifters. Raske and Norlin (2002) reported 2.7 injuries per 1,000 hours for elite Swedish lifters; the same lifters were questioned in 1995 and 2000 with the incidence of injury unchanged. Brown and Kimball (1983) and Quinney et al. (1997) report 3.0 and 3.7 injuries per 1,000 hours respectively. The greatest incidence has been reported by Keogh et al. (2006) at 4.4 ($\pm$ 4.8) injuries per 1,000 hours.

Modulating factors

Goertzen et al. (1989) reported a higher incidence of injury among males versus females; 2.1 and 1.3 injuries per lifter per year respectively. Keogh et al. (2006) reported no difference between males and females when expressed as injuries per year (1.2 vs. 1.1); however, a larger number of injuries per 1,000 hours of lifting was reported in males (4.7) than in females (3.1). Siewe et al. (2011) noted a significantly greater number of hand/wrist injuries in female lifters, but no differences for any other body part.

Competitive level and age may also influence injury incidence. Keogh et al. (2006) reported that national competitors had a greater rate of injury than international competitors (5.8 versus 3.6 per 1,000 hours, respectively). Injuries of the upper extremities are more common in older lifters (Siewe et al., 2011) and increase with age. Raske and Norlin (2002) reported that the incidence of shoulder injury was greater in elite lifters sampled in 2000 (26%) than when they were sampled in 1995 (21%). The incidence of injury for other body parts was not changed.

Injury location and severity

Injuries have been most commonly reported at the shoulder (36% of all injuries) and lower back (24%), followed then by the elbow (12%) and knee (9%) (Keogh et al., 2006). These trends were also observed by Raske and Norlin (2002) and Siewe et al. (2011). 78% of injuries were classified as mild (39%) or moderate (39%) in severity, necessitating a change in the training (modification or abstinence from a lift) for a period of one or more weeks (Keogh et al., 2006). 22% were classified as major, necessitating a complete cessation of training for a period of at least one week.

Aetiology of injury

Shoulder

The overdevelopment of movements (i.e. bench press) and musculature (i.e. pectorals, latissimus dorsi) associated with internal rotation may contribute to a strength imbalance between the internal and external rotators. Strengthening the musculature of the posterior shoulder and upper back is therefore an important part of the powerlifting programme. The lifts themselves are also associated with provocative positions, which may contribute to overuse injury or acerbate existing problems. The abducted and externally rotated position of the shoulder during the back squat has been shown to contribute to anterior instability and hyperlaxity of the joint (Kolber et al., 2013). In addition, the nature of the bench press means that the scapula is unable to glide across the rib cage and likely to cause anterior translation of the humeral head.

Lower back

The substantial loadings placed upon the spinal column during the squat and deadlift have already been discussed. Positions of lumbar flexion beyond the neutral range are associated with a greatly elevated risk of injury and lifters should therefore attempt to maintain a position as close as possible to a neutral lordotic curve. The programme should ensure that lifters are not compromising technique through the prescriptions of appropriate exercises and loadings. The teaching of appropriate bracing techniques and the inclusion of accessory work for the musculature of the trunk are also important parts of the powerlifting programme.

Fitness testing battery

Physical testing batteries are not commonplace within powerlifting as coaches/lifters will programme based upon performance in a previous competition and their anticipated or required performance in an upcoming competition. In the case of the former, this is likely to include both quantitative data (i.e. load successfully or not successfully lifted) and qualitative data (i.e. perceived reasons for failure and locations of sticking points).

When constructing the performance profile of the powerlifters, there are several metrics that warrant assessment and monitoring given their association with performance.

Anthropometrics

Body mass is a critical metric to monitor as participation in competition depends on making the required weight class. As with all weight-categorised sports, competitors are likely to seek a performance advantage by competing at the very top of their weight class. In order to maximise the amount of functional mass (i.e. muscle mass) and minimise the amount of non-functional mass (i.e. body fat) at the point of competition it is also important to monitor body composition.

Powerlifters will commonly train at a body mass above their chosen class, often 5–10% above the upper limit, and then look to reduce body mass in the lead up to competition. In the medium- to long-term (4–12 weeks out), strategies to reduce body mass will typically focus on the reduction of body fat. In the short-term (i.e. competition week), strategies such as carbohydrate restriction and low residue diets may then be employed. Finally, acute losses of 1–2% body mass are commonly be sought through water manipulation strategies (i.e. partial dehydration and/or water loading) in the 8–72 hours preceding the weigh-in.

Strength

Performance in powerlifting relies almost entirely on a single bio-motor quality – maximal strength. Whilst this may suggest a requirement for regular 1RM testing, it must be considered that this is assessed directly during competition and typically an unnecessary practice. Given the specificity of powerlifting training to the sport itself, lifters will be able to estimate 1RM performance based upon training loads and perceived exertion with a high level of accuracy.

Estimation of 1RM using sub-maximal loadings and measures of barbell velocity offer a potential monitoring tool for the powerlifter. For example, if a lifter is able to increase their velocity at a pre-determined absolute loading (i.e. 100 kg) it is likely that their strength has improved. However, it is important to state that a high correlation with 1RM is not synonymous with a high agreement with 1RM and acknowledge that the ability to grind-out slow, heavy lifts is a skill within itself.

Programming

The specific nature of powerlifting may appear to make programming an easy concept, although it is perhaps the specificity of the sport that provides the biggest challenge. The powerlifting programme will typically have four goals:

1. Improve technique in the competition lifts (skill)
2. Increase maximal force production (strength)
3. Increase muscle mass (hypertrophy)
4. Increase rate of force development (power)

Improving skill and increasing strength will always be the overarching theme across the programme and prioritised as such. The relative emphasis placed upon hypertrophy and power will vary between individuals. For example, a lifter at the top of their weight class may not prioritise hypertrophy training.

Periodisation

The purpose of periodisation is to manage the training stimulus in order to maximise the desired neuromuscular adaptions and avoid excessive accumulation of fatigue. This allows the coach or lifter to schedule when specific qualities can be developed and when fatigue will need to be minimised around competition. It is therefore unsurprising that 97% of British powerlifters reported periodising their training (Swinton et al., 2009). Powerlifters will commonly target one or two key competitions each year (i.e. national and/or international championships) for which they will look to peak. To qualify for these events lifters will typically be required to participate in regional competitions and achieve qualifying totals or placings. Depending on the performance level of the lifter, these preliminary competitions will require differing levels of consideration and emphasis within the training plan.

Macrocycle

Given the competition calendar, the sport of powerlifting is well suited to the linear progression of intensity on a macrocycle level. Detailed discussion of specific periodisation models is beyond the scope of this chapter, instead the ultimate goals of the programme should be considered. Skill and strength should be greatest at the point of competition whilst fatigue should be minimised. For example, Pritchard et al. (2015b) reported that total training volume of elite powerlifters from New Zealand peaked just over 5 weeks from competition and training intensity peaked about 2 weeks before.

Linear approaches also consider the progression from more general, less specific training into more sport-specific training. Models will typically refer to two phases: the preparatory phase and the competitive phase (Bompa and Carrera, 2005). During the preparatory phases of the macrocycle, lifters may choose to employ different exercise variations or use lighter loads by means of recovery. This is also likely to be the time where hypertrophy training may carry greater importance within the macrocycle.

Tapering

Tapering is a practice which involves the temporary reduction of training load in an effort to increase the state of preparedness of an athlete. Pritchard et al. (2015b) noted that powerlifters began tapering 2–3 weeks out from competition. During the taper, training volume was reduced by about 60% while intensity was either maintained or slightly reduced. This appears to fall in-line with evidence-based recommendations from Pritchard et al. (2015a) for maximising strength performance. The improved recovery associated with the taper may be linked to muscle recovery, greater neural activation and an enhanced hormonal environment (Pritchard et al., 2015a).

Microcycle

Whilst the macrocycle and mesocycles typically consider a linear approach, the powerlifter's microcycle will more commonly adopt a non-linear approach. Training volume and intensity are typically varied within the microcycle, a concept termed daily undulating periodisation (DUP).

Literature examining the long term effectiveness of DUP against linear periodisation is lacking; however, greater short-term improvements in strength have been observed using a DUP protocol in trained individuals (Rhea et al., 2002; Prestes et al., 2009). Zourdos et al. (2016) compared two DUP configurations in 18 collegiate powerlifters (average Wilks: 328) over six weeks. A configuration of hypertrophy, power, strength led to greater improvements in 1RM (effect sizes: 0.48–0.74) for all three lifts versus a more traditional configuration of hypertrophy, strength, power. This is a likely consequence the former facilitating the accumulation of a greater volume of work.

Training session

The exercises undertaken within the session may typically be referred to as:

- Main exercises

The one or two most important exercises within the session. These lifts will be either the competition lifts or a variation thereof. Their prescription will fall in line with the objectives of the mesocycle or the specific day within the DUP configuration.

- Assistance lifts

These one or two lifts within the session have the objective of addressing a particular weakness within a lift or to accumulate a greater total training volume to augment strength or hypertrophy. The objective of the assistance lifts may deviate slightly from the mesocycle or DUP objectives. For example, dumbbell bench press performed for hypertrophy within a strength-focussed block.

- Accessory exercises

These exercises are performed to target areas of the body that may not be well developed by the main and assistance lifts. Common areas will include the musculature of the posterior shoulder/upper back, glutes/hamstrings and abdominals. Accessory lifts are not typically determined by the macrocycle phase and are performed for multiple sets of high repetitions.

Training

Types of training

Zatsiorsky and Kraemer (2006) outline three main types of strength training:

- Maximal effort method
- Repeated effort method
- Dynamic effort method

Given the nature of powerlifting, the maximal effort method demonstrates the greatest specificity to performance. Repeated effort training may be used to target strength and hypertrophic gains. The dynamic effort method is employed to improve rate of force development and may also be referred to as 'speed work' or compensatory acceleration training.

Specificity

The expression of force within any given exercise is a skill. For that reason, training with the competitive power lifts at heavy loads is undoubtedly an integral aspect of the training programme for the powerlifter. The maximum effort method is considered superior for improving both intra- and inter-muscular co-ordination and will deliver the greatest improvements in strength (Zatsiorsky and Kraemer, 2006).

One of the primary differences between Eastern- and Western-style programmes is the frequency and specificity of the competition lifts performed. For example, Russian programmes tend to favour performance of the competition lifts 2–3 times per week. Conversely, Western programmes tend to perform more variations of the lifts (i.e. box squats and board presses) and train movement patterns 1–2 times per week. It is rationalised that regular performance of lifts teaches the body to perform them more efficiently, and therefore maximise performance at a given level of strength (i.e. gross capacity for maximal force production).

Where lifters have identified that a specific lift requires greater emphasis within their training, they may choose to undertake a short programme designed to focus on that lift. For example, initial case study documentations suggest that daily max training in the squat may prove an efficacious strategy in trained lifters. Following an initial drop in 1RM during the first three days of training, Zourdos et al. (2015) reported increases in 1RM squat of 5.8%, 9.5% and 10.8% for three lifters squatting to a daily 1RM for 37 days. Such strategies warrant empirical consideration by the literature as the reasons for these improvements and long-term effectiveness is not well understood.

Variation

The powerlifting programme requires a finely tuned balance between specificity and variety. The sole use of heavy competitive lifts provides a specific stimulus that will ultimately restrict the range of potential adaptations, increase the monotony of training and may increase the risk of symptoms associated with overtraining. Moreover, heavy competition lifts such as the wide-grip bench press and low-bar squat are often associated with discomfort and pain. During the preparatory phases of the macrocycle, lifters may choose to employ different exercise variations or use lighter loads for these reasons.

When used effectively, variation provides the powerlifter with the opportunity to target a specific adaptation, minimise the risk of accommodation and also work around minor injuries. Variation may be achieved by completely removing a lift or by using a different lift with a transferrable adaptation – for example, good mornings instead of squats or overhead press instead of bench press. Subtler variation may be achieved by modifying some of the following:

- The position of load (i.e. high bar, front rack, Zercher)
- The type of implement (i.e. safety squat bar, trap bar, kettlebell)
- The nature of resistance (i.e. regular weight, chains, bands)
- The magnitude of the load (i.e. heavy, moderate, light)
- The tempo of the lift (i.e. pause, slow eccentric, explosive)

The squat and bench press are commonly modified by incorporating a pause between the eccentric and concentric phases, or by removing the eccentric phase of the movement (i.e. squats from pins). This minimises the contribution of stretch-shorting cycle and therefore emphases the initial rate of force development. Another advantage of this type of modification is that it allows the lifter extra time to focus on technical points in weaker positions of the movement where errors are most likely to occur.

Exercise execution

82% of powerlifters reported performing explosive training with submaximal loads (Swinton et al., 2009), characteristics of the dynamic effort method. Performing movements with lighter loads not only allows the lifter to focus on improving rate of force development and barbell velocity, but provides a means of variation within the programme. Modelling simulations devised by Arandjelović (2011) suggest that focusing on improving the initial rate of force development at the start of the lift may also prove the most effective way to overcome the sticking point. Accumulating the greatest possible momentum of the barbell prior to the sticking point will increase the likelihood of a successful lift. Moreover, this strategy is likely to benefit performance in athletes with sticking points at any point in the lift.

Specialised techniques

The use of specialised techniques is commonplace within powerlifting programmes. The goal of each technique is to adapt the competition lift in a certain manner with the ultimate objective of targeting a specific adaptation. Specialised techniques are commonly used for short durations (i.e. 1–2 mesocycles) to provide the neuromuscular system with a novel stimulus. As such, it is perhaps best to consider these modalities as an adjunct to the powerlifting programme for more advanced lifters.

ACCOMMODATING RESISTANCE

The three powerlifts exhibit ascending strength curves (i.e. the lift is weakest at the bottom of the lift and strongest at the top of the lift). The premise behind accommodating resistance is to provide progressively increasing resistance during the concentric portion of the lift to more closely match the ascending strength curve. This is typically achieved through the addition of elastic bands or chains to the barbell. Swinton et al. (2009) reported that 39% of lifters regularly used bands in training and 57% incorporated chains, the majority noting their use in the bench press. Programmes incorporating accommodating resistance for 7–12 weeks have been shown to increase 1RM beyond traditional resistance training (Soria-Gila et al., 2015), longer durations are yet to be well explored.

PARTIAL RANGE OF MOTION TRAINING

Powerlifters often employ partial range of motion training with supramaximal loads to accustom themselves to heavy weights (Swinton et al., 2009). Examples of partial range of motion training may include half squats, board presses for the bench press or block pulls for the deadlift. As with accommodating resistance, partial training allows the lifter to overload the terminal range of motion. These exercises are will typically replace some of the volume of their respective competition lift but not replace them entirely. When used in this manner, partial training has been shown to confer small benefits in 1RM performance versus full range of motion training only (Bazyler et al., 2014).

Conclusion

The goal of powerlifting is simple, to post the heaviest possible total across three barbell lifts. Whist force requirements are important, powerlifters must first seek to maximise technical proficiency within each lift. Given the duration of each lift, maximal force production (i.e. strength) is a critical determinant of performance. Each lift is associated with a sticking point where failure will occur. As the sticking point is commonly associated with a decrease in barbell velocity, improving rate of force development and barbell velocity prior to the sticking point is likely to be beneficial to maximum attempts. The amount of muscle mass carried by a lifter is strongly associated with powerlifting performance. As increased muscle mass should increase the capacity for force production, hypertrophy may be a goal of the powerlifting programme. The most commonly injured areas of the body in powerlifting are the shoulder and lower back. In addition to emphasising the maintenance of technique at heavy loads, the programme should consider the inclusion of exercises to mitigate the risk of injury. There are common features to all successful powerlifting programmes, such as progressive overload and the management of fatigue. However, there are no absolutes. The 'best' programme at any given time will depend on the individual lifter, the coach that delivers it and the environment in which they train.

References

Akagi R, Tohdoh Y, Hirayama K, Kobayashi Y. Relationship of pectoralis major muscle size with bench press and bench throw performances. *Journal of Strength and Conditioning Research*. 2014: **28**: 1778–1782.

Arandjelović O. Optimal effort investment for overcoming the weakest point: New insights from a computational model of neuromuscular adaptation. *European Journal of Applied Physiology*. 2011: **111**: 1175–1123.

Bazyler CD, Sato K, Wassinger CA, Lamont HS, Stone MH. The efficacy of incorporating partial squats in maximal strength training. *Journal of Strength and Conditioning Research*. 2014: **28**: 3024–3032.

Bompa TO, Carrera MC. *Periodization Training for Sports*. 2nd ed. Champaign, IL: Human Kinetics, 2005.

Brechue WF, Abe T. The role of FFM accumulation and skeletal muscle architecture in powerlifting performance. *European Journal of Applied Physiology*. 2002: **86**: 327–336.

Brown EW, Abani K. Kinematics and kinetics of the dead lift in adolescent power lifters. *Medicine and Science in Sport and Exercise*. 1985: **17**: 554–566.

Brown EW, Kimball RG. Medical history associated with adolescent powerlifting. *Pediatrics*. 1983: **72**: 636–644.

Brown PI, Venables HK, Liu H, de-Witt JT, Brown MR, Faghy MA. Ventilatory muscle strength, diaphragm thickness and pulmonary function in world-class powerlifters. *European Journal of Applied Physiology*. 2013: **113**: 2849–2855.

Cappozzo A, Felici F, Figura F, Gazzani F. Lumbar spine loading during half-squat exercises. *Medicine & Science in Sport & Exercise*. 1985: **17**: 613–620.

Cholewicki J, McGill SM, Norman RW. Lumbar spine loads during the lifting of extremely heavy weights. *Medicine and Science in Sport and Exercise*. 1991: **23**: 1179–1186.

Cook CJ, Crewther BT, Smith AA. Comparison of baseline free testosterone and cortisol concentrations between elite and non-elite female athletes. *American Journal of Human Biology*. 2012: **24**: 856–858.

Escamilla RF, Francisco AC, Fleisig GS, Barrentine SW, Welch CM, Kayes AV, Speer KP, Andrews JR. A three-dimensional biomechanical analysis of sumo and conventional style deadlifts. *Medicine & Science in Sport & Exercise*. 2000: **32**: 1265–1275.

Escamilla RF, Lowry TM, Osbahr DC, Speer KP. Biomechanical analysis of the deadlift during the 1999 Special Olympics World Games. *Medicine & Science in Sport & Exercise*. 2001: **33**: 1345–1353.

Flanagan SP, Kulik JB, Salem GJ. The limiting joint during a failed squat: A biomechanics case series. *Journal of Strength and Conditioning Research*. 2015: **29**: 3134–3142.

Glassbrook DJ, Brown SR, Helms ER, Duncan JS, Storey AG. The high-bar and low-bar back squats: A biomechanical analysis. *Journal of Strength and Conditioning Research*. 2017.

Goertzen M, Schöppe K, Lange G, Schulitz K-P. Medical history associated with body-building and powerlifting. *Sportverletz Sportschaden*. 1989: **3**: 32–36.

Gomo O, Van Den Tillar R. The effects of grip width on sticking region in bench press. *Journal of Sports Sciences*. 2016: **34**: 232–238.

Gracovetsky S, Farfan H. The optimum spine. *Spine*. 1986: **11**: 543–573.

Granhed H, Jonson R, Hansson T. The loads on the lumbar spine during extreme weight lifting. *Spine*. 1987: **12**: 146–149.

Haykowsky MJ, Warburton DER, Quinney HA. Pain and injury associated with powerlifting training in visually impaired athletes. *Journal of Visual Impairment & Blindness*. 1999: **93**: 236–241.

IPF. *Technical Rules Book 2016*. 2016.

Jovanović M, Flanagan EP. Researched applications of velocity based strength training. *Journal of Australian Strength and Conditioning*. 2014: **22**: 58–69.

Judge LW, Urbina L, Hoover DL, Craig B, Judge LM, Leitzelar B, Pearson D, Holtzclaw K, Bellar DM. The impact of competitive trait anxiety on collegiate powerlifting performance. *Journal of Strength and Conditioning Research*. 2016.

Keogh JWL, Hume PA, Pearson SN. Retrospective injury epidemiology of one hundred one competitive Oceania power lifters: The effects of age, body mass, competitive standard, and gender. *Journal of Strength and Conditioning Research*. 2006: **20**: 672–681.

Keogh JWL, Hume PA, Pearson SN, Mellow PJ. Anthropometric dimensions of male powerlifters of varying body mass. *Journal of Sports Sciences*. 2007: **25**: 1365–1376.

Keogh JWL, Hume PA, Pearson SN, Mellow PJ. Can absolute and proportional anthropometric characteristics distinguish stronger and weaker powerlifters? *Journal of Strength and Conditioning Research*. 2009: **23**: 2256–2265.

Kingma I, Faber GS, Suwarganda EK, Bruijnen TB, Peters RJ, van Dieën JH. Effect of a stiff lifting belt on spine compression during lifting. *Spine*. 2006: **31**: E833–E839.

Kolber MJ, Corrao M, Hanney WJ. Characteristics of anterior shoulder instability and hyperlaxity in the weight-training population. *Journal of Strength and Conditioning Research*. 2013: **27**: 1333–1339.

Kompf J, Arandjelović O. Understanding and overcoming the sticking point in resistance exercise. *Sports Medicine*. 2016: **46**: 751–762.

Kristiansen M, Madeleine P, Hansen EA, Samani A. Inter-subject variability of muscle synergies during bench press in power lifters and untrained individuals. *Scandinavian Journal of Medicine and Science in Sports*. 2015: **25**: 89–97.

La Panse B, Labsy Z, Baillot A, Vibarel-Rebot N, Parage G, Albrings D, Lasne F, Collomp K. Changes in steroid hormones during an international powerlifting competition. *Steriods*. 2012: **77**: 1339–1344.

Lehman GJ. The influence of grip width and forearm pronation/supination on upper-body myoelectric activity during the bench press. *Journal of Strength and Conditioning Research*. 2005: **19**: 587–591.

Ljdokova GM, Razzhivin OA, Volkova KR. Confounding factors in sport activities of powerlifters. *Life Science Journal*. 2014a: **11**: 410–413.

Ljdokova GM, Razzhivin OA, Volkova KR. Powerlifters' ways to overcome confounding factors at competitions. *Life Science Journal*. 2014b: **11**: 477–480.

Lovera M, Keogh J. Anthropometric profile of powerlifters: Differences as a function of bodyweight class and competitive success. *Journal of Sports Medicine and Physical Fitness*. 2015: **55**: 478–487.

McGill SM. *Low Back Disorders: Evidence-Based Prevention and Rehabilitation*. 2nd ed. Champaign, IL: Human Kinetics, 2007.

McGuigan MRM, Wilson BD. Biomechanical analysis of the deadlift. *Journal of Strength and Conditioning Research*. 1996: **10**: 250–255.

McKean MR, Dunn PK, Burkett BJ. The lumbar and sacrum movement pattern during the back squat exercise. *Journal of Strength and Conditioning Research*. 2010: **24**: 2731–2741.

McLaughlin TM, Madsen NH. Bench press techniques of elite heavyweight powerlifters. *National Strength & Conditioning Association Journal*. 1984: **6**: 44–65.

Miletello WM, Beam JR, Cooper ZC. A biomechanical analysis of the squat between competitive collegiate, competitive high school, and novice powerlifters. *Journal of Strength and Conditioning Research*. 2009: **23**: 1611–1617.

Norkin CC, White DJ. *Measurement of Joint Motion: A Guide to Goniometry*. Philadelphia, PA: FA Davis, 2009.

Prestes J, Frollini AB, De Lima C, Donatto FF, Foschini D, de Marqueti RC, Figueira Jr A, Fleck SJ. Comparison between linear and daily undulating periodized resistance training to increase strength. *Journal of Strength and Conditioning Research*. 2009: **23**: 2437–2442.

Pritchard HJ, Keogh J, Barnes M, McGuigan M. Effects and mechanisms of tapering in maximizing muscular strength. *Strength & Conditioning Journal*. 2015a: **37**: 72–83.

Pritchard HJ, Stannard SR, Barnes MJ. Ammonia inhalant & stimulant use among powerlifters: Results from an international survey. *Journal of Australian Strength and Conditioning*. 2014: **22**: 52–54.

Pritchard HJ, Tod DA, Barnes MJ, Keogh JW, McGuigan MR. Tapering practices of New Zealand's elite raw powerlifters. *Journal of Strength and Conditioning Research*. 2015b: **30**(7): 1796–1804.

Quinney HA, Warburton DER, Webster A, Calvert R, Haykowsky M. Powerlifting injuries associated with elite powerlifting training. *Canadian Journal of Applied Physiology*. 1997: **20**: 49.

Raske A, Norlin R. Injury incidence and prevalence among elite weight and power lifters. *American Journal of Sports Medicine*. 2002: **30**: 248–256.

Rhea MR, Ball SD, Phillips WT, Burkett LN. A comparison of linear and daily undulating periodized programs with equated volume and intensity for strength. *Journal of Strength and Conditioning Research*. 2002: **16**: 250–255.

Siewe J, Rudat J, Röllinghoff M, Schlegel UJ, Eysel P, Michael JW. Injuries and overuse syndromes in powerlifting. *International Journal of Sports Medicine*. 2011: **32**: 703–711.

Soria-Gila MA, Chirosa IJ, Bautista IJ, Baena S, Chirosa LJ. Effects of variable resistance training on maximal strength: A meta analysis. *Journal of Strength and Conditioning Research*. 2015: **29**: 3260–3270.

Swinton PA, Lloyd R, Agouris I, Stewart A. Contemporary training practices in elite British powerlifters: Survey results from an international competition. *Journal of Strength and Conditioning Research*. 2009: **23**: 380–384.

Swinton PA, Lloyd R, Keogh JWL, Agouris I, Stewart AD. A biomechanical comparison of the traditional squat, powerlifting squat, and box squat. *Journal of Strength and Conditioning Research*. 2012: **26**: 1805–1816.

Swinton PA, Stewart A, Agouris I, Keogh JWL, Lloyd R. A biomechanical analysis of straight and hexagonal barbell deadlifts using submaximal loads. *Journal of Strength and Conditioning Research*. 2011: **25**: 2000–2009.

Vigotsky AD, Harper EN, Ryan DR, Contreras B. The effects of load on good morning kinematics and EMG activity. *PeerJ*. 2015: **2**: 1–15.

Wagner LL, Evans SA, Weir JP, Housh TJ, Johnson GO. The effect of grip width on bench press performance. *International Journal of Sport Biomechanics*. 1992: **8**: 1–10.

Zatsiorsky VM. Biomechanics of strength and strength training. In: Komi PV, ed. *Strength and Power in Sport*. 2nd ed. Oxford: Blackwell Science, 2003: 439–487.

Zatsiorsky VM, Kraemer WJ. *Science and Practice of Strength Training*. 2nd ed. Champaign, IL: Human Kinetics, 2006.

Zourdos MC, Dolan C, Quiles JM, Klemp A, Blanco R, Krahwinkel AJ, Goldsmith JA, Jo E, Loenneke JP, Whitehurst M. Efficacy of daily one-repetition maximum squat training in well-trained lifters: Three case studies. *Medicine & Science in Sport & Exercise*. 2015: **47**: 940.

Zourdos MC, Jo E, Khamoui AV, Lee S-R, Park B-S, Ormsbee MJ, Panton LB, Contreras RJ, Kim J-S. Modified daily undulating periodization model produces greater performance than a traditional configuration in powerlifters. *Journal of Strength and Conditioning Research*. 2016: **30**: 784–791.

36
WEIGHTLIFTING

Shyam Chavda and Greg Everett

Introduction

Weightlifting is a sport consisting of 2 lifts: the snatch (Figure 36.1) and the clean and jerk (C&J) (Figure 36.2 and Figure 36.3, respectively). The athlete has 3 attempts to post at least 1 successful lift on each discipline, with the snatch preceding the C&J. If an athlete misses all attempts in either discipline, they are disqualified from the competition, with the exception of World championships, where athletes can medal in the snatch, the C&J and total. The success of a lift is determined by three officials looking for any technical infringements as outlined in the International Weightlifting Federation (IWF) technical and competition rules and regulations (TCRRs) (Ajan, 2017, pp. 8–10). Some of the most common infringements, which can also be prevalent in novice training, include stopping the upward movements of the bar during the pull, touching the platform with any part of the body other than the feet and finishing overhead with an arm press out.

Competitions are split into male and female groups, with further sub divisions into weight classes (Table 36.1). The outcome of a competition is defined by the highest weight lifted in the group. Should two individuals achieve the same lift (for individual medals), or same total, the lifter who achieved it first would be the successor. For a more detailed description of the classification process, the authors suggest referring to the IWF's TCRR resource, available on the IWF website.

Although not a deciding factor of success, the Sinclair total can also be reported at competitions, allowing lifters to see what their total would be if they were in the heaviest weight class. This enables us to fairly compare lighter lifters to the heavier lifters and means the "best lifter" title can be awarded to the person who achieved the highest Sinclair total. To do this the Sinclair equation is utilised (Equation 1), where each bodyweight has an assigned coefficient based on most recent world records (Canadian Weightlifting Federation, 2015).

(a) Set position

(b) End of first pull

(c) Power position

(d) End of second pull

Figure 36.1 Snatch phases

(e) Peak bar height

(f) Catch

(g) Recovery

Figure 36.1 (Continued)

(a) Set position

(b) End of first pull

(c) Power position

(d) Second pull

Figure 36.2 Clean phases

(e) Peak bar height

(f) Catch

(g) Recovery

Figure 36.2 (Continued)

(a) Set

(b) Dip

(c) Drive and split

(d) Catch

Figure 36.3 Split jerk phases

(e) Recovery

Figure 36.3 (Continued)

Table 36.1 Senior and junior weight class categories for males and females

Male	Female
56kg (≤ 56.00kg)	48kg (≤ 48.00kg)
62kg (56.01–62.00kg)	53kg (48.01–53.00kg)
69kg (62.01–69.00kg)	58kg (53.01–58.00kg)
77kg (69.01–77.00kg)	63kg (58.01–63.00kg)
85kg (77.01–85.00kg)	69kg (63.01–69.00kg)
94kg (85.01–94.00kg)	75kg (69.01–75.00kg)
105kg (94.01–105.00kg)	90kg (75.01–90.00kg)
+105kg (≥ 105.01kg)	+90kg (≥ 90.01kg)

Equation 1 – The Sinclair coefficient (S.C.)

$$S.C. = \begin{cases} 10^{AX^2} & (x \leq b) \\ 1 & (x > b) \end{cases}$$

Where $X = \log_{10}\left(\dfrac{x}{b}\right)$

X = athlete bodyweight (kg)

	Men	Women
A	0.751945030	0.783497476
b	175.508 kg	153.655 kg

Technical proficiency in weightlifting can help optimise the lifter's chance of success, but given that the aim is to lift the most weight as possible, several performance associated characteristics, such as strength and power, also impact the ability to perform (Stone et al., 2006). The unique aspect of weightlifting is that a development of technique, strength and power can be developed concurrently. It will therefore be the aim of chapter to provide sound scientific evidence that can help support the development of success in weightlifting.

Athletic demands

The snatch and C&J both require high levels of skill and power (Gourgoulis et al., 2000). The kinetics and kinematics of weightlifting have therefore been extensively studied (Kipp and Harris, 2015; Harbili and Alptekin, 2014; Akkus, 2012; Gourgoulis et al., 2009; Rossi et al., 2007; Bartonietz, 1996), with the most common biomechanical variables measured being barbell and joint kinematics and kinetics. From Figures 36.1 and 36.2 it is evident that two commonalities exists between the snatch and the clean: bar path and key positions, with subtle differences of bar placement during the power position (Figures 36.1 and 36.2c) due to grip width. It is important that the reader understands how the barbell and joints interact with one another as to enable them to appropriately recognise any technical issues or weaknesses in the lifts. Due to the similarities between the two lifts, we have looked at the snatch and clean concurrently, with the jerk independently.

Bar kinematics and kinetics

The shared sequences from the snatch and the clean elicit similar bar trajectories that display a shallow "S" type curve (Figure 36.4). Optimising bar path is a characteristic often considered as prudent in enhancing the chance of success (Stone et al., 1998). Results presented by Stone et al. (1998) stated that the most successful snatches displayed rearward displacement of the bar from the set to the catch. For both lifts this displacement initially starts from the set-position to the 1st pull (Figures 36.1 and 36.2, a to b), and continues to do so until the lifter is in the power position (Figures 36.1 and 36.2c), and ready to start the 2nd pull. This rearward movement enables the lifter to shift the bars centre of mass closer to their own, thus enabling better transfer of mechanical power from the body to the bar through sequential, intersegmental movements (Funato et al., 1996). Once extension of the ankle, knee and hip is achieved during the 2nd pull (Figure 36.1 and 36.2d), the bar will display a small loop due to the contact on the hip or mid-thigh, for the snatch and clean respectively. The loop is defined as the horizontal displacement from the bar's most forward position during the 2nd pull to the catch (Stone et al., 1998). Should the bar loop "excessively" this would adversely affect the lift and increase the likelihood of failure, with the lifter catching too far forward on their feet or jumping forward to realign their centre of mass under the bar. Information pertaining to success on the snatch has shown that when the loop exceeded 20 cm, there was a 100% failure rate, with the authors suggesting that minimising the loop to approximately 11cm would increase the chance of success (Stone et al., 1998). This can be measured through video analysis software freely available online, providing a lateral view of the lifter is taken, thus allowing the coach to accurately measure bar path.

Figure 36.4a and b Typical shallow "S" bar trajectory displayed in the snatch and the clean

Optimising bar path will inherently assist in increasing the bar's vertical velocity, with previous literature reporting that a steady bar velocity between the end of the 1st pull and the start of the 2nd pull allows for the key positions to be met (Bartonietz, 1996). Although technically undesirable, there is a commonality that velocity of the barbell during the transition phase (between the first pull and power position) slightly decreases, due to the knees moving forward under the bar. Too much of a decrease would mean the lifter is required to overcome the barbell's velocity deficit, and to re-accelerate the bar, potentially becoming deleterious to the lift (Bartonietz, 1996; Gourgoulis *et al.*, 2000). This therefore means the bar may not travel to the optimum vertical height in order to allow the lifter sufficient time to drop under the bar in preparation for the catch (Hoover *et al.*, 2006). Literature attaining information on peak vertical displacement of the bar during the snatch equates to approximately 70% of the lifter's height, with lower values (approximately 60%) experienced during the clean (Campos *et al.*, 2006; Haff *et al.*, 2003). This insinuates that a threshold of vertical bar displacement may exist and the ability of the lifter to drop under the bar is of great importance. This is evident in highly skilled weightlifters who achieve a relatively lower barbell height during the catch phase and a faster drop during the turnover (Figures 36.1 and 36.2e) (Gourgoulis *et al.*, 2002). This suggests that as loads get heavier, vertical displacement of the bar will be limited, thus requiring the lifter to drop under at a faster rate, as previously reported (Hoover *et al.*, 2006).

Understanding mechanical energy, work and power production during the 1st and 2nd pull is of great importance (Table 36.2), as this can help inform programming and has been associated with totals achieved by lifters (Funato *et al.*, 1996). The mechanical work output of the 1st pull has been shown to be greater than that of the 2nd pull (Akkus, 2012; Gourgoulis *et al.*, 2002), but displays relatively lower power outputs (Hoover *et al.*, 2006; Gourgoulis *et al.*, 2002). This suggests that the 1st pull during both lifts may be a more strength oriented movement and that other physiological mechanisms such as the stretch shortening cycle contribute to the higher

Table 36.2 Key biomechanical terminology

Term	Definition	Equation (unit)	Example
Work	Work (J) results when force (N) acts upon the barbell to cause displacement.	Work = force × displacement (joules) $W = Fd$ (J)	High forces are generated to displace the bar during the 1st pull, thus more work is performed to overcome the barbell's inertia.
Power	This is the rate at which work (J) is done, thus is a time based quantity.	Power = work/time (watts) $P = W/t$ (W)	The 1st pull is a slow movement thus producing less power, whereas the 2nd pull is performed explosively at a faster rate thus producing more power.
Mechanical energy	Energy acquired by the barbell as a result of the lifters work.	Mechanical energy = kinetic energy + potential energy (joules) $M.E = \frac{1}{2}mv^2 + mgh$ Where m is mass, v is velocity, g is gravity and h is height.	If low amounts of work is conducted during the 1st pull and the bar is not drawn back, there will be an increase in mechanical energy during the 2nd pull, thus potentially being deleterious to the lift.

power outputs observed in the 2nd pull. Comparatively the snatch and the clean present differing mechanical barbell power outputs, with absolute wattages of 1,847.62 ± 336.06 and up to 3,691 during the 2nd pull of the snatch and clean respectively (Akkus, 2012; Garhammer, 1991). Variances in both bar trajectories and power output exist between load (Harbili and Alptekin, 2014; Hadi et al., 2012; Comfort et al., 2012), gender (Gourgoulis et al., 2002; Garhammer, 1991) and weight class (Isaka et al., 1996). It is therefore recommended that individual variances are likely to be apparent, and that optimising barbell trajectory based on the aforementioned will require adaptations to body position, in order to meet the key phases, and increase chance of consistency and success. Therefore understanding how the joints interact with one another may help give insight to coaches and lifters alike to be able to adapt coaching methods and programming to each individual lifter as no two lifters are the same.

Joint kinematics and kinetics

The movement of the bar is manipulated by the body's ability to leverage itself and get into the most favourable position to develop power; therefore, understanding joint kinematics and kinetics can help facilitate the technical and physical training of weightlifters. Primary joints such as the ankle, knee and hip tend to be the most researched joints within weightlifting, based on their ability to harmoniously develop high ground reaction forces, and power outputs (Kipp et al., 2012; Gourgoulis et al., 2002; Baumann et al., 1988; Enoka, 1979). This synchronisation helps the lifter overcome the system mass (sum of barbell mass and body mass) experienced during the lift, as well as optimise barbell trajectory. During the set position, knee, hip and torso angles of 47 and 80°, 34 and 41°, and 118 and 135° have been reported, respectively, for 2 athletes differing in body dimensions (Figure 36.5) (Lippmann and Klaiber, 1986). The extent at which these angles form the set position will differ between lifters, depending on anthropometric variables

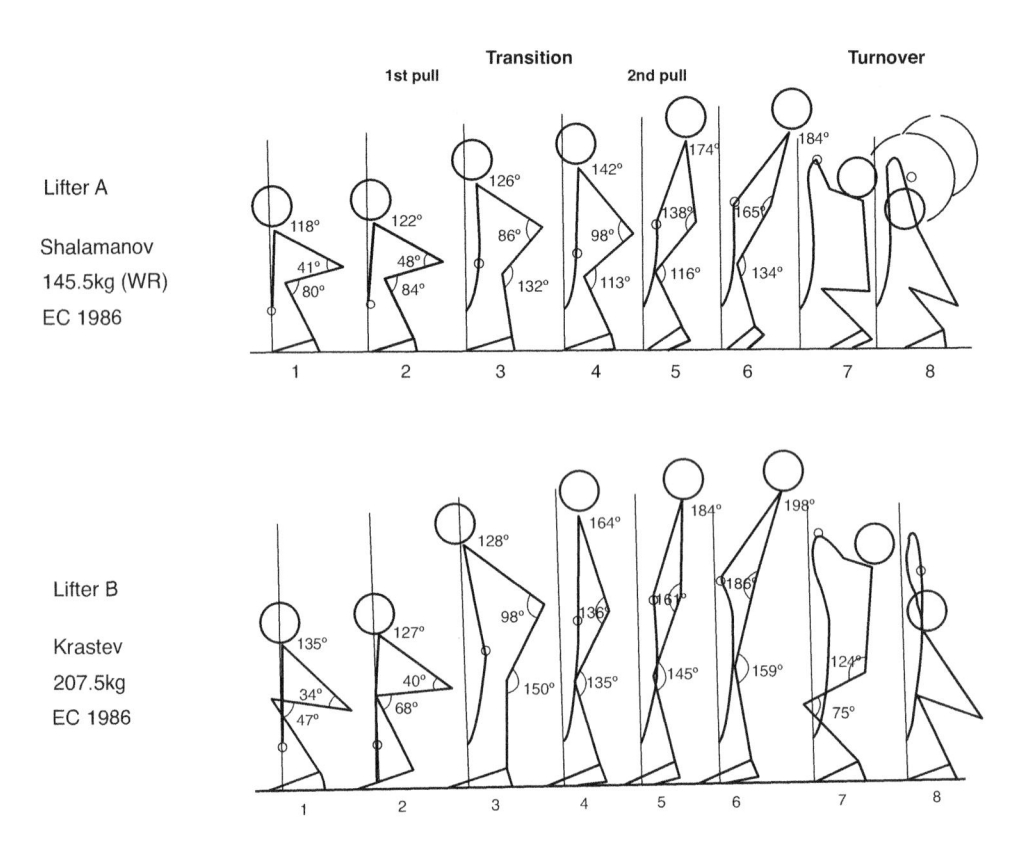

Figure 36.5 Variation between taller (Lifter A) and shorter (Lifter B) lifter set up. Adapted from unpublished research of Lippmann and Klaiber (1986), presented in Bartonietz (1996)

and flexibility. Generally speaking, it has been suggested that from a lateral view, a lifter should display hips higher than the knees, the torso in an upright position, with the shoulders slightly over the bar (DeWeese et al., 2012).

The 1st pull is initiated when the lifter raises the barbell off the ground, back, and towards the knee (Figures 36.1 and 36.2b). This movement is typically controlled in nature, taking the longest duration with maximum knee angles reported to be 139 ± 4.19° for male and 129 ± 11° for female elite lifters (Gourgoulis et al., 2002). From a technical standpoint, extending the knees, keeping the chest up and delaying the rise of the hips help contribute to maintain a constant torso angle relative to the set (DeWeese et al., 2012). If hip extension is too rapid in the 1st pull, barbell trajectory will be ineffective (Bartonietz, 1996). To support this, research from Kipp et al. (2012) found that greater loads were associated ($r = 0.766$–0.870) with a steady trunk position and less hip extension during the 1st pull. Due to the bi-articular function of the hamstrings across the knee and hip, knee extension and reduced hip extension would allow adequate tension in the hamstrings, imperative for maximal power production in the 2nd pull (Everett, 2009, p. 67). As the knees move through the transition phase, the lifter is now in a power position (Figures 36.1 and 36.2c) and ready to start the 2nd pull. Research measuring clean pulls from the power position present angles at the knee and hip of 141 ± 10° and 124 ± 11°, respectively (Kawamori et al., 2006), with ground reaction forces displaying the highest force and power outputs relative to the other phases, showing their importance within the lift. It becomes evident that the 1st and

2nd pulls play pivotal roles in enhancing a lifter's success, and furthermore lends themselves to enhancement through programming for both strength and power.

The jerk

Little literature has been conducted on the jerk alone, but its importance is imperative, as the lifter must jerk what they have cleaned for it to be a successful lift. There are two styles of the jerk: the squat and, more commonly, the split. Regardless of which one a lifter uses, the dip (Figure 36.3a) and drive (Figure 36.3b) add an upward momentum to the bar to allow the athlete enough time to drop under and catch. It is typically conceived that this jerk motion is similar to that of a countermovement jump; however, literature from Cleather *et al.* (2013) found that joint moments were not significantly correlated to jump height and that the jerk is primarily knee dominant, whereas jumping is more reliant on knee and hip moments. Nevertheless, the high peak powers observed during a jerk (Garhammer, 1980), suggest that there is a utilisation of a stretch reflex, similar to that of a loaded jump. During the catch phase of the jerk (Figure 36.3d) the lifter can experience up to 3.4 ± 1.2 BW$^{.s-1}$ on the lead leg (Lake *et al.*, 2006). Upon observation, this leg should finish at approximately 113° with the back knee bent at 130° to enable stabilisation. The feet may move out and away from each other slightly, with the front foot slightly turned in to increase the base of support (Figure 36.6).

Physiology of weightlifting

There is limited research on the acute physiological responses of competitive weightlifting, due to its brevity. Based off the execution times for the lifts, and with weightlifters exhibiting large percentages of type IIA muscle fibers (Fry *et al.*, 2003), it can be assumed that the ATP-PCr system is the primary energy system in use. While fiber type composition can be heavily influenced by genetics, non-genetic factors associated with weightlifting training, such as neural and endocrine adaptations, may influence the morphology of fiber composition. Although difficult to measure directly, neural factors have previously been associated with performance features of

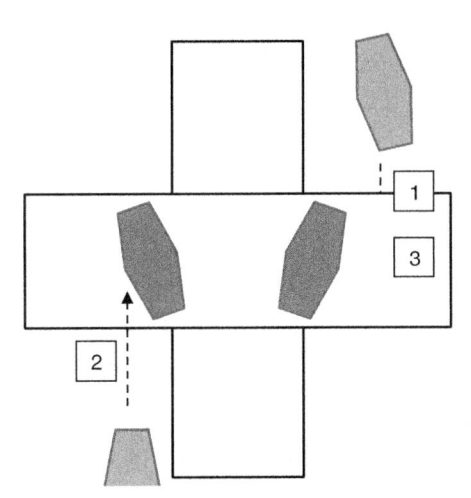

Figure 36.6 Foot position for the jerk. Blue displays the set and red displays the catch. The arrows depicted represent the recovery steps for each foot

elite weightlifters (Häkkinen et al., 1986), with high load squat jumps and countermovement jumps correlating well with weightlifting performance ($r = 0.76$–0.79), potentially due to the stretch shortening rates experienced during the lifts themselves. Neural adaptations have also been associated with increases in strength with a minimal increase in fat-free muscle mass over a 1 year training period (Fry et al., 1994), lending us to think that weightlifting training can increase neural factors such as rate coding and motor unit recruitment.

Endocrine responses to weightlifting programs have shown acute alteration in the testosterone: cortisol ratio (T:C), with significant increases in maximal force (PF) and peak rate of force development (PRFD), with strong correlations ($r = -0.83$, $r^2 = 0.69$) found between T:C and volume load (Haff et al., 2008). This suggests that manipulating load correctly would help elevate the lifter's force producing capabilities based on their hormonal status. More long term research looking at endocrine adaptations purported that testosterone levels are augmented after a period of one year of weightlifting training with exposure to one week of overreaching. This suggests that over time, the lifter builds a physiological tolerance to overreaching and has a more optimal hormonal state (Fry et al., 1994), proving important when considering program design. The biomechanical and physiological requirements of weightlifting suggest that weightlifters require good anaerobic power, and the ability to generate maximum force and power. They need to be able to express these characteristics during both the snatch and C&J, while executing key technical positions to further optimise their chance of success.

Injury prevalence

The loads experienced in weightlifting can far surpass an individual's bodyweight. Current world records show athletes achieving two and a half times bodyweight for the snatch and over three times bodyweight for the C&J. One would think such feats of strength displayed in a competition would evoke high levels of injury, but relative to other sports weightlifting has shown only a 0.0013 injury rate per 100 hours of training in teenagers (Hamill, 1994). A published source from the IWF, courtesy of Doerr (2012), looked at injury occurrence during European and international events, from 2007 to 2012. His findings illustrate that during this period only 3.2% of 1,414 athletes experienced injuries at European competitions, with a marginally higher occurrence of 3.4% of 1,582 athletes at international events. Further research during competitive periods conducted by Junge et al. (2009) reported that during the 2008 Olympic games, weightlifting showed one of the highest injury rates amongst all sports, with 89.7% of injuries reported during competition, and only 10.3% in training. The reader should approach these latter findings with caution as only the training conducted in the championship period was accounted for; therefore, it will not be a good representation of the athlete's typical training. Furthermore, the study was governed on response rate of 75.1% from national Olympic committee physicians. Although Junge's research provides a good insight to injury prevalence in elite weightlifting, it does not give us the details required to understand where these injuries occur. Fortunately, the published data from Doerr presented the site spread of injuries in European weightlifting competitions from 2007–2012, as illustrated in Table 36.3.

To better understand the onset of injuries in weightlifting and to help inform programming and regeneration strategies, we might classify them into acute and chronic types. Acute injuries by nature tend to be related to muscle and connective tissue strains and sprains (Stone et al., 1994). These types of injuries may not stop the athlete from competing, but could result in a brief respite from lifting, depending on the severity (Lavallee and Balam, 2010). Chronic injuries are typically insidious, and are often a result of overuse or repetitive strain, thus giving us better insight as to vulnerability of specific sites. Let us consider the results displayed in Table 36.3, where it is

Table 36.3 Injury sites and total number of injuries during the periods of 2007–2012 from the European weightlifting championships (EWC) (adapted from Doerr, 2012)

Anatomical region	Female	Male	Total
Head	1		1
C-spine	1		1
Hand & finger			
Elbow	5	7	12
Shoulder	1	3	4
Back	2	4	6
Belly	1		1
Hip		2	2
Thigh		12	12
Knee		3	3
Lower limb		3	3
Foot			
TOTAL	**11**	**34**	**45**

apparent that the main site of injury is the elbow. Although not stated as to the type of injury that occurred, one could assume it to be an acute, musculoskeletal injury in which dislocations and tendon ruptures are common, usually as a result from loss of control of the weight during vulnerable positions (Lavallee and Balam, 2010). This is somewhat supported by Junge et al.'s (2009) results indicating that 5 incidences of injuries in weightlifting at the 2008 Olympic games were dislocations and ruptures. From a technical standpoint the elbows are used to aggressively lock the bar out over head in both the snatch and the jerk. Typically, the elbow is thought to be at greater risk during the snatch than the C&J (Lavallee and Balam, 2010) due to the wider grip and faster rotations around the shoulder. However, the loads experienced in the jerk could have also contributed to the high injury prevalence in the elbow. Alternatively, the risk of injury at the elbow could also be due to anatomical predispositions such as hypermobility, in which case an increase in technical skill would be advantageous as to allow the body to naturally adapt to the load and bar kinematics relative to one's anatomical make up.

Given that weightlifters spend more time training than competing, it is important to address injury prevalence during training. It is in agreement across the literature that weightlifters often experience overuse injuries (Lavallee and Balam, 2010; Junge et al., 2009; Hedrick and Wada, 2008; Calhoon and Fry, 1999). This in turn can cause both acute and chronic injuries, potentially leading to missed training days. A comprehensive study by Calhoon and Fry (1999) on national US weightlifters, documented injury reports over a 6 year period that 64.2 % of athletes had reported training related injuries, with the lower back accounting for 23.1% of cases, followed by the knee (19.1%) and shoulder (17.7%). Of importance, the most common injuries were strains, tendinitis and sprains, making up 44.8%, 24.2% and 13 % of injury types, respectively, with strains being the most common in the lower back and shoulder, and tendinitis most common in the knees. With over 50% of injuries being acute in nature, 87.3–95.3% of the primary injury sites returned to training in less than a day. This provides valuable information to coaches and reinforces that overuse injuries prevalent in weightlifting can be relatively minor in nature.

When considering the types and sites of injuries it becomes evident that general conditioning work in vulnerable areas would provide a useful means of pre-habilitation, as well as enhancing performance. With the back being the highest reported injury site it is important to understand that the spinal column itself is not strong enough to bear compression forces from lifting heavy weights (Norris, 2008, p. 34). Compression forces are somewhat unavoidable, as a primary method of developing leg strength in weightlifting is through back squats, with elite lifters regularly squatting over three times bodyweight. The high torques generated during weightlifting training must be distributed to the connective tissues and muscles surrounding the spine; thus, if these muscles are not sufficiently trained, the likelihood and severity of injury can be high (Norris, 2008, p. 34). It is therefore advised that additional strengthening of the torso, specifically the back extensors such as the erector spinae, would prove advantageous to lifters to cope with the torques experienced during training and competition, as well as serve a functional purpose of better transmitting force from the floor to the barbell. Second to this the chronic injury experienced at the knee is likely due to the constant deep squat patterns associated with weightlifting, thus providing additional anterior shearing forces on the tibio-femoral joint (Gullett *et al.*, 2008). Although this is somewhat unavoidable, we suggest that the volumes of squats and full lifts are monitored and are appropriately loaded, with particular attention to the clean as unpublished data from Stone 1980–1983 suggested that the more frequently cleans are performed at 90% or above, the more training days missed (Stone *et al.*, 1994).

Sufficient conditioning for the upper extremities such as the shoulder and elbow will help assist in stabilising the bar overhead during the snatch and jerk. The complexity and freedom of movement at the shoulder makes it vulnerable; thus, it is warranted to spend time working on general shoulder health, including strength, mobility and stability, which can generally be achieved through correct lifting technique and traditional assistance exercises discussed later on in this chapter. It is evident from the literature that weightlifting carries a risk of injury. It is repetitive in nature and constantly stresses the body with high loads, and it is therefore suggested that weightlifting movements are performed with good technique, under supervision of an accredited coach. Secondly, the programme should be appropriately structured, with the inclusion of pre-habilitative or assistance exercises with volumes and loads monitored, thus lessening the likelihood of overuse injuries.

Fitness testing battery

It goes without saying that the ability and progress of a weightlifter can simply be judged on the weight they achieve during the snatch and C&J. It is therefore not uncommon practice to have lifters go to 1RM during the end of a training phase, with some countries advocating daily maxes as to dictate the loads used for training (Illiou, 1993 and Ganev, 2003, cited in Garhammer and Takano, 2003, p. 512). Non-direct measures of the lifts have also been conducted, utilising isometric and dynamic pulls as well as various jump tests. The variables extrapolated from these include peak force (N), peak RFD ($N.s^{-1}$) and power output (W) and have been shown to have moderate to strong relationships ($r = 0.47–0.83$) with the snatch, clean and competition total (Haff *et al.*, 2005; Häkkinen *et al.*, 1986). This provides us with good justification to utilise these tests, but the practicality may be limited due to the requirements of expensive equipment.

More field based tests have been reported in weightlifting, primarily in talent identification. Research from Fry *et al.* (2006) established that body mass, vertical jump, relative fat, grip strength and torso angle during an overhead squat classified 84.35% of national juniors competitors as either elite or non-elite. This proves useful as we know power is a desirable characteristic for a weightlifter, and that lean muscle mass would contribute to its production. Therefore, utilising jumps could help determine whether an increase in power has been achieved during a training phase.

Another method of better informing program design is utilising percentage variances between lifts. Although some variations may exist between lifters it has been long suggested that the snatch and the C&J should be within a certain percentage of one another, or of other key lifts, as outlined in Table 36.4. This, however, should only be used as a guideline, and any divergence of these numbers is not indicative of problems (Everett, 2009, p. 239).

To conclude we have presented both lab and field based (Table 36.5) testing batteries to assess qualities associated to weightlifting. However, it is important for the reader to understand that these tests can only help better understand the requirements of training and may not represent a direct increase in the snatch or C&J.

Table 36.4 Suggested percentage ranges lifts should fall within of one another. Adapted from Everett (2009, p. 239)

Primary lift	Of lift	Percentage
Snatch	Clean and jerk	80–85%
Power snatch	Snatch	80–85%
Power clean	Clean	80–85%
Front squat	Back squat	85–90%

Table 36.5 Field and lab based performance testing battery for weightlifting

	Characteristic	Test	Equipment	Variable
Field tests	Strength	Snatch	Barbell	Absolute load (Kg)
		Clean	Weight plates	Predicted 1RM based on barbell velocity profile.
		Back squat	Tape measure, iPhone + powerlift application	
		Front squat		
		Deadlift		
	Power	Counter movement jump with arm swing (Sargent jump)	Chalk to wall	Absolute height (cm)
		Force velocity profiling	iPhone + myjump application	Jump height, predicted peak force, predicted peak power, optimal force-velocity profile.
Lab tests	Strength	Clean grip Isometric mid-thigh pull at an angle of 141 ± 10° at the knee and 124 ± 11° at the hip. Alternatively angles can be established from the power position during an actual lift.★ ★Freeze frame required.	Isometric rig Cold steel bar Force plate Laptop Goniometer Video camera (optional)★	Peak force (N) PRFD (N)
	Power	Counter movement jump.	Force plate	Jump height (cm) Peak force (N) Impulse (N.s) Peak Power (W)

Programming

The purpose of program design is to deliberately manipulate training variables to provide adequate stress to the body as to elicit a desired outcome (Everett, 2009, p. 231). Before discussing the process of programming some key definitions must be understood as outlined in Table 36.6. Three primary principles need to be considered when designing a weightlifting program: specificity of exercise, overload and variability (Garhammer and Takano, 2003). Specificity refers to lifts which replicate or are similar to that of the competitive lifts as outlined in Table 36.7. Overload relates to an increase in stress to the body through elevating intensity and/or volume. Finally, variability relates to the composition of training load to avoid maladaptation (Garhammer and Takano, 2003). The organisation of training will largely affect the desired outcome, and it is therefore prudent the reader understands the concepts of structuring a training programme.

Table 36.6 Key terminology and definitions for programming

Term	Definition
Macro cycle	Typically refers to the complete training cycle that can span over a year or between major competitions.
Mesocycle	Relates to a phase of training, lasting between 4–6 weeks or more.
Microcycle	The smallest phase of training generally referring to one week.
Intensity	This relates to the difficulty of the exercise and generally refers to a percentage of your one repetition maximum (1RM).
Volume	This is the culmination of repetitions performed in a session, micro- , meso- or macro-cycle.
Volume load	This refers to the work or tonnage lifted during a session, micro- , meso- or macro-cycle. This is typically calculated by multiplying the volume by the absolute intensity (total reps × total load lifted)

Table 36.7 Weightlifting specific exercises

Snatch	Clean	Jerk	General assistance exercises
Over head squat	Front squat	Over head press	Back squat
Snatch balance	Clean from power position★#	Push press	Deadlift
Snatch from power position★#	Hang clean★#	Jerk balance	Good morning
Hang snatch★#	Halted clean 1st pull	Behind neck jerk	Romanian deadlift (RDL)
Halted snatch 1st pull	Clean pull		Bent over row
Snatch pull	Power clean		Glute hamstring raise (GHR)
Power snatch			Back extensions

★Refers to power snatch or power clean variations of the full catch.
#Refers to snatch or clean variations from the block.

Structuring a training cycle

In weightlifting the primary stressor with which we're concerned is intensity. The long term increase in average intensity is progressive overload. All training creates local and systemic fatigue along with increased performance potential through responsive adaptation. This adaptation will not be immediate and will only be measurable after the associated fatigue of the training in question has abated. In order to achieve positive adaptation at specific time points, periodic manipulation of volume, intensity and exercise selection must be planned. This is known as periodisation. Typically, one would start designing a macrocycle with specific competitions in mind to peak for. Over the course of a macrocycle, on average, volume will decrease and exercise specificity and intensity will increase. A macrocycle will begin with one or more preparatory mesocycles in which strength and/or hypertrophy is emphasised utilising lifts such as squats, pulls and presses (Programme 1). The competition lifts and their variants are employed with relatively low frequency (1–2 exercises per session) and intensity (60–70% 1RM), and higher repetitions per set (4–6). The final mesocycle will be a competition phase (typically the final 4–6 weeks) in which the competition lifts are emphasised, with higher frequency (2–4 exercises per session) and intensity (80%+), and lower repetitions per set (1–3). At this point strength work is minimised (1–2 exercises per session) and largely used to maintain existing strength rather than develop it (Programme 2). The models of periodisation utilised during preparatory and competition cycles can vary depending on the desired outcome.

Program 36.1 Preparatory cycle example

	Exercise	Week 1	Week 2	Week 3	Week 4
Session 1	Power jerk	4×4 60%	4×4 65%	5×3 70%	3×4 60%
	Push press	4×6 50%	4×5 53%	5×5 56%	3×6 50%
	Back squat	4×10 70%	4×8 75%	5×6 80%	3×10 70%
Session 2	Snatch	4×4 65%	5×4 70%	6×3 75%	3×4 65%
	Snatch pull	4×4 70%	4×4 75%	4×3 70%	3×4 70%
	Halted snatch deadlift	3×6 75%	4×4 80%	3×3 75%	3×6 75%
Session 3	Behind neck jerk	4×4 65%	4×4 68%	5×3 72%	3×4 65%
	Snatch push press + overhead squat (3+3)	4×6 65%	4×6 70%	5×6 73%	3×6 65%
	front squat	4×4 75%	4×4 78%	5×4 80%	3×4 75%
Session 4	Clean	4×4 70%	4×4 73%	5×4 77%	3×4 70%
	Halted clean deadlift	4×6 75%	4×4 80%	3×3 83%	3×6 75%
	Romanian deadlift	3×6 80%	3×6 80%	3×6 80%	3×6 80%
Session 5	Snatch	4×1 > 90%	5×1 > 90%	5×1 > 90%	2×1 > 90%
	Clean and jerk	4×1 > 90%	4×1 > 90%	4×1 > 90%	2×1 > 90%
	Back squat	3×6 77%	4×4 80%	4×4 82%	3×6 77%
	Overhead press	3×8 50%	4×8 53%	4×8 53%	3×8 50%
Weekly average volume/ Weekly average intensity		**294 / 71%**	**283 / 74%**	**279 / 76%**	**238 / 71%**

Macrocycle volume and average intensity distribution (total reps/average intensity)

Squat; 264 / 77%
Pull; 184 / 75%
Competitive (Snatch + C&J); 160 /83%
Accessory; 485 / 64%

Program 36.2 Competitive cycle example

	Exercise	Week 1	Week 2	Week 3	Week 4
Session 1	Snatch	5×2 80%	5×2 80%	5×2 80%	3×2 80%
	Clean and jerk	4×1 80%	4×1 80%	4×1 80%	3×1 80%
	Snatch pull	4×3 90%	4×3 95%	4×2 100%	3×3 90%
	Front squat	4×3 80%	4×3 80%	4×3 80%	4×3 80%
Session 2	Power snatch	4×3 65%	4×3 68%	4×2 70%	3×3 65%
	Power clean + power jerk	4×3 65%	4×3 68%	4×2 70%	3×3 65%
	Clean pull	5×2 100%	5×2 100%	5×2 100%	3×2 100%
Session 3	Snatch	5×1 > 90%	5×1 > 90%	5×1 > 90%	5×1 > 90%
	Clean and jerk	4×1 > 90%	4×1 > 90%	4×1 > 90%	4×1 > 90%
	Snatch pull	4×3 100%	4×3 105%	4×2 110%	4×3 100%
	Back squat	4×4 80%	5×3 82%	5×2 85%	4×4 80%
Session 4	Hang snatch	3×3 65%	3×3 68%	3×3 68%	3×3 65%
	Hang power clean	3×3 65%	3×3 68%	3×3 68%	3×3 65%
	Jerk off rack	5×1 80%	5×1 80%	5×1 80%	5×1 80%
Session 5	Snatch	5×2 80%	4×2 83%	5×1 86%	3×2 80%
	Clean and jerk	4×1 80%	4×1 83%	5×1 86%	3×1 80%
	Hang clean pull	4×2 110%	4×2 110%	4×3 110%	3×2 110%
	Front squat	6×2 80%	6×2 82%	6×2 85%	3×3 80%
Weekly average volume/ Weekly average intensity		**146 / 82%**	**163 / 84%**	**144 / 86**	**138 / 82**

Macrocycle volume and average intensity distribution (total reps/average intensity)

Squat: 150 / 81%
Pull: 155 / 102%
Competitive (Snatch + C&J): 306 /78% *the slightly lower intensity is due to light power days.
Accessory: 0

The idea of the preparatory phase is to allow the lifter to build a physiological tolerance to the high volume loads associated with the more advanced phases and would therefore utilise basic and intermediate periodisation models. The basic model would entail the sole development of a single biomotor during a mesocycle. The volume load will be uniform in nature with an inverse relationship between volume and intensity as a new mesocycle is started (Graph 36.1). An intermediate model would display summations during each mesocycle with a linear increase in volume load for three weeks followed by an unload week during the fourth as to allow for recovery (Graph 36.2). Each week could have a different biomotor focus, thus allowing for greater variability in training. This is useful for those who present a smaller window of adaptation, thus requiring the additional variability. The loading schematics from basic and intermediate periodisation can be useful when looking to develop work capacity in the legs, for example, so they are able to tolerate higher volume loads later experienced in their lifting career. Typically, as the training year advances the type of model used could also be advanced. The advanced model (also termed conjugate model) advocates accumulation blocks and restitution blocks, where a specific biomotor is overloaded for 2–3 weeks and is followed by a lower load, equal length mesocycle of a secondary biomotor (e.g. strength accumulation phase followed by a power restitution phase). This model of periodisation promotes purposeful

Weightlifting

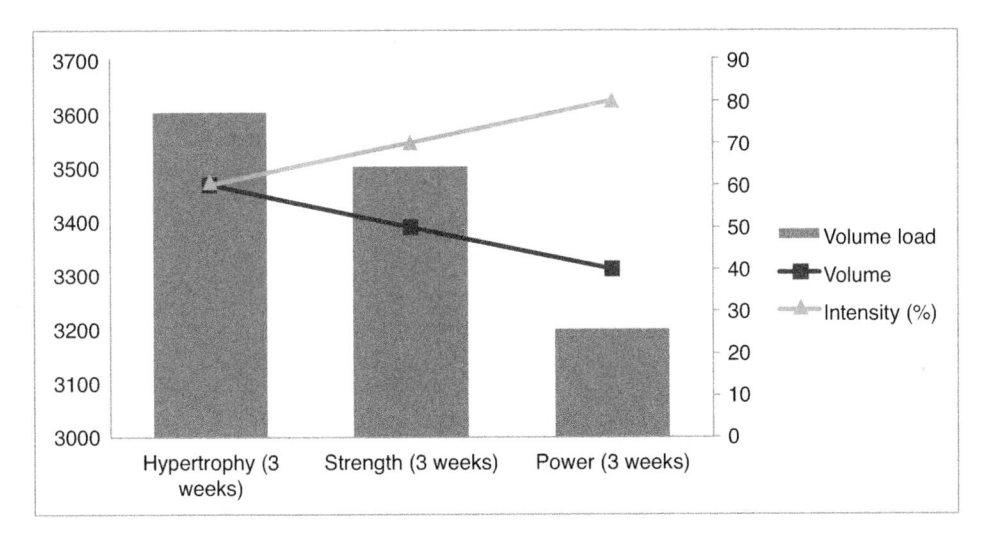

Graph 36.1 Basic periodisation model

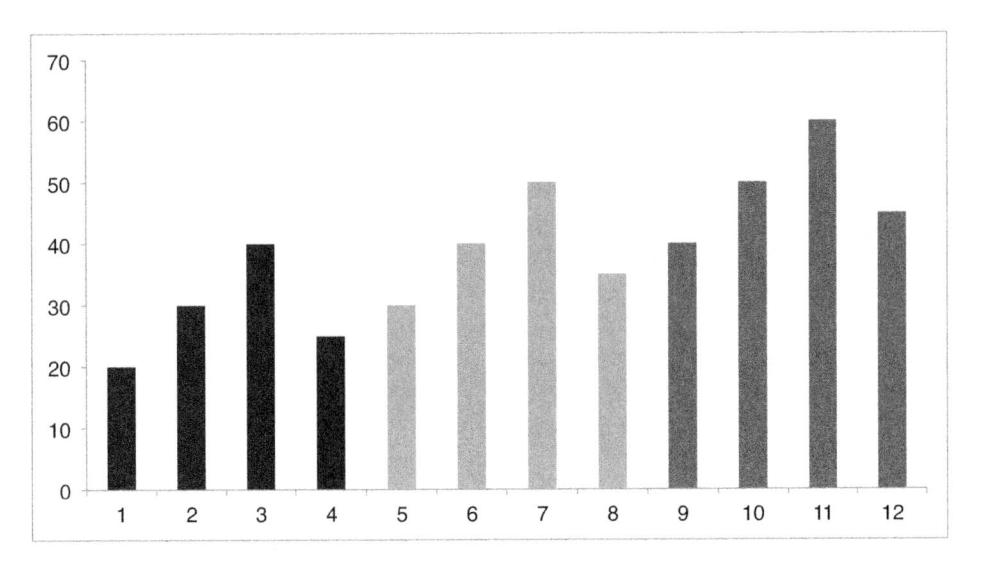

Graph 36.2 Intermediate summated periodisation model

overreaching a phenomena in which significant fatigue and a concurrent decrease in performance is experienced (Turner, 2011). It is during the restitution block in which the pervious biomotor will super compensate as a virtue of a delayed training effect. This can be achieved by manipulating the frequency of training during each block. This model may prove useful when approaching a competition; however, to apply these interventions requires high levels of skilful loading and monitoring, as to avoid overtraining.

It is worth mentioning that non-traditional methods of periodisation such as daily undulating periodisation (DUP) can also be utilised for weightlifters. Here the volume and intensity is manipulated daily, thus focusing on a different biomotor. This method of periodisation is extremely adaptive and is possibly more suited for the amateur weightlifter that may not be able to train to such a rigid schedule which the traditional models require. This method, however, has been shown to not be as effective as the traditional method when looking to increase strength (Haff et al., 2012). The strong correlation that exists between volume load and T:C suggests that manipulating volume load correctly may elevate the lifter's force generating capabilities (Haff et al., 2008). Secondly volume loads experienced during purposeful overreaching may help to develop a physiological tolerance over time as found after 1 year's weightlifting training (Fry et al., 1994).

Mesocycles to elicit the desired performance effect, such as strength and power, will typically culminate with a tapering period. The taper refers to a reduction in volume load in the build up to a competition, with the primary objective to dissipate accumulated fatigue from the previous mesocycle (Turner, 2011). There are multiple methods of tapering: linear, a small decrease in volume loads every session; step, a large decrease in volume load on the first day of the taper, with maintenance of that volume load until competition; exponential, where volume load is decreases at a proportional rate to its current value; and a 2 phase taper, a classical reduction in volume load with a moderate increase closely coming up to competition (Turner, 2011). Information from a meta-analysis (Bosquet et al., 2007) revealed that the optimal taper is a two week exponential taper, with a decrease in volume of between 41–60%, whilst maintaining intensity and frequency. This, however, may not fit all athletes, and the accumulated fatigue from the previous mesocycle must be considered as this may largely dictate the reduction in volume load and the period and type of taper utilised. That is to say, the greater the accumulated fatigue the greater the taper.

Developing strength and power

Neurological adaptation is the primary manner in which weightlifters improve strength and power over the long term, and the reason why a lifter can continue to gain strength over a long period of time without gaining weight or increasing in size. Training works to improve motor unit recruitment, rate coding, synchronisation, golgi tendon organ inhibition, and intermuscular coordination to allow the weightlifter to produce the greatest amount of force and power with a given mass of muscle. Given the high importance of the 1st pull, 2nd pull and a fast drop under speed, it is pertinent that exercise selection and intensity look to improve these variables through kinematic and kinetic similarities to the full lifts, with the addition of utilising exercises that best improve general strength and power.

The intensities of weightlifting specific exercises will vary depending on the model used; however, the volume distribution of the exercises will be dependent on the phase of training (Graphs 36.3a and 36.3b). The development of leg strength for weightlifting is pivotal, with strong correlations found between 1RM squat and snatch and clean (r = 0.94 and 0.95, respectively) (Stone et al., 2005). This provides us with a strong rationale to spend time in the preparatory phase developing leg strength with maintenance in the competitive phase, and a shift to front squats to elicit specific adaptation transferable to the clean. This transfer of leg strength should also help develop the back extensors and stabilisers as both back and front squats have shown to have muscles activities of over 40% relative to maximal voluntary contraction in the erector spinae (Gullet et al., 2008), potentially reducing the risk of back injury. Coupled with specific 1st and 2nd pull drills (Halted 1st pull and pulls), this should enhance one's ability to optimise bar path during this phase and perform greater work, since traditional pulls can be performed at loads 10–40% greater than that of the lifter's maximum competitive lifts (Garhammer and Takano, 2003). That said, a review by Suchomel et al. (2017) reviewed

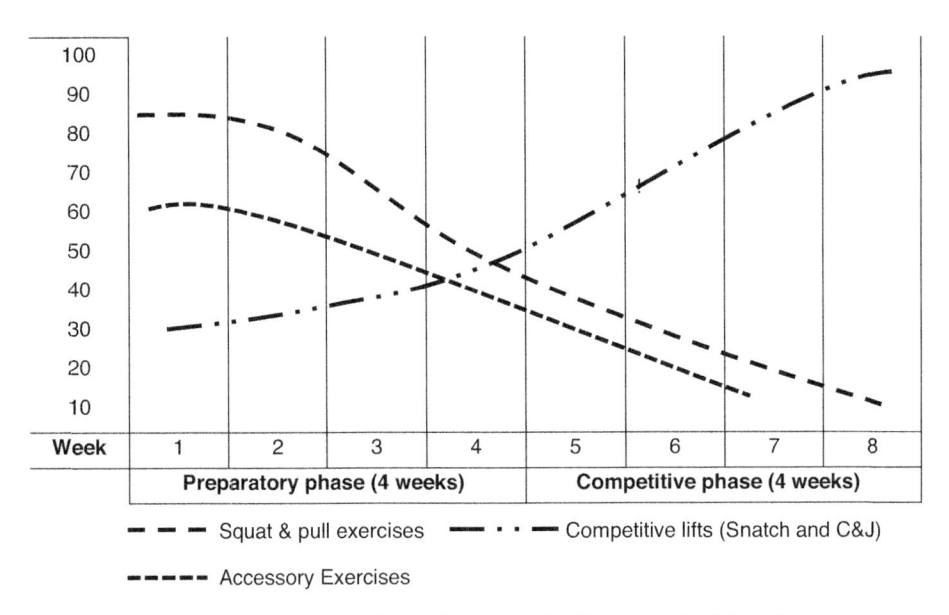

Graph 36.3a The volume distribution of strength (squat and pull), competitive lifts and accessory exercises over the preparatory and competitive phase

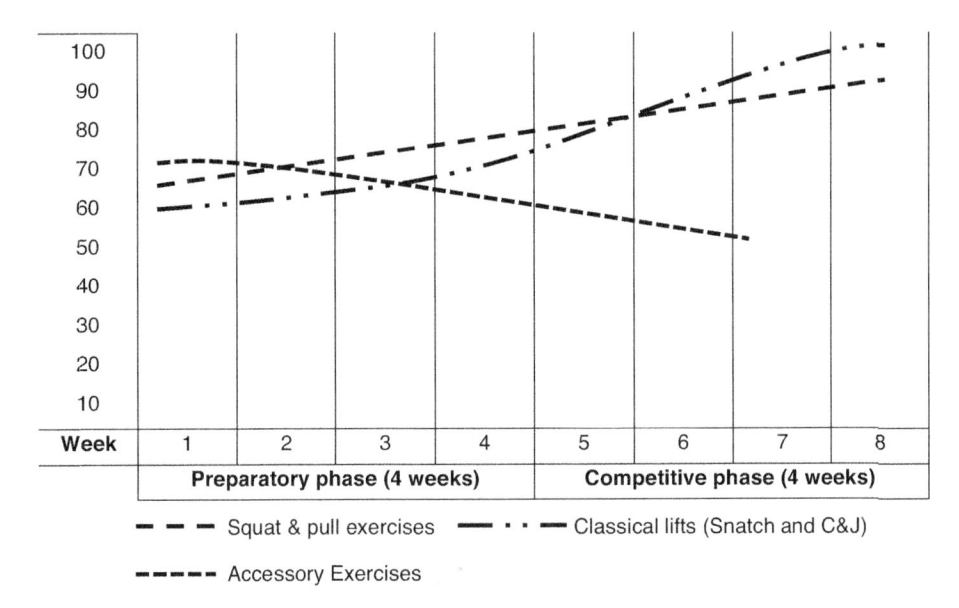

Graph 36.3b The intensity of strength (squat and pull), competitive lifts and accessory exercises over the preparatory and competitive phase

weightlifting derivatives relative to barbell velocity, finding that the exercises prescribed can vary in load to meet the specific demands of the training phase, thus enhancing different aspects of the force-velocity curve.

Developing vertical velocity on the bar and catch speed is related to the power we can produce during the 2nd pull as well as how quickly one can drop in the catch position. In order to develop these qualities, an emphasis on derivatives from the hang position or power position variants may be advantageous at loads of 70–85% (Garhammer and Takano, 2003). Alternatively, Comfort et al. (2012) had found that peak power during mid-thigh clean pulls was developed at 40% with peak force developed at 140% of clean 1RM, so potentially overloading this power position at both ends of the force curve may help an individual become stronger and faster during the 2nd pull. During the competitive phase it is recommended that lifters spend more time on the full lifts, as to be able to utilise the developed strengths and skills in the previous phase. A study conducted by González-Badillo et al. (2006), concluded that moderate volumes (91 reps) of high relative intensity (90%) on competition lifts and squats, over 10 weeks, produced greater weightlifting performance enhancement compared to low (44 reps) and high volumes (182 reps) of high relative intensity.

To conclude, the organisation of training should consider the primary objective of each mesocycle approaching the competition. We suggest that working backward from a competition date may help better organise the allocations of specific mesocycles. Developing a lifter's weakness, both physical and technical, and maintaining their strengths will be determined by the exercise selection and intensity that is prescribed. Typically loads of 70–90% over the course of the preparatory and competitive phase are most beneficial, with occasional supramaximal loads for partial movements, such as pulls. This overload with additional variability during each mesocycle should elicit the greatest enhancement in weightlifting performance.

Conclusion

The sport of weightlifting requires high amounts of muscular power, strength and skill. It is evident that the most successful weightlifters are able to display a rearward movement of the bar during the 1st pull, creating a steady bar velocity which increases exponentially during the 2nd pull. This allows the lifter to keep the bar close to the body and transfer mechanical energy to the bar, thus contributing to greater vertical bar displacement, allowing the lifter sufficient time to drop under and receive the bar in the catch. The primary contributing factors to these preferred bar kinetics and kinematics stem from greater work being carried out during the 1st pull with a decrement evident during the 2nd pull; however, power production is far greater during the 2nd pull as a result of an increase in hip, knee and ankle angular displacement, furthered by a contribution of the stretch reflex.

Weightlifting has shown high levels of injury rates when compared to other Olympic sports, particularly in the elbow, but this may be due to individuals attempting higher loads than usual with more at stake. Injury rates in training are typically experienced in the lower back; they tend to be acute in nature and result in a loss of less than one day of training. Commonly strains are the most experienced type of injury, and are typically down to over use, thus showing the importance of organising rest days and variability into the program. In terms of programming we must consider the exercise selection, volume and intensity prescribed at different periods, namely the preparatory and competitive phase. Typically, greater assistance and strength work will be performed during the preparatory phase with a greater emphasis on squatting and pulling strength, whereas the competitive phase would focus on maintaining these strength qualities and transferring them to the competitive lifts, ready for competition.

With weightlifting being multifactorial in nature, one can enhance the chance of success by understanding the key technical aspects of the lifts and the exercises associated with their development. We therefore suggest that adaptations should be made in one's physical condition and capabilities, as the ability to perform the competitive lifts with appropriate competency will ensure the greatest chance of success in the future.

References

Ajan, T. (2017). *IWF technical and competition rules and regulations* [Online]. Hungary: The International Weightlifting Federation. Available at: www.iwf.net/downloads/?category=23 [Accessed: 03 March 2017].

Akkus, H. (2012). Kinematic analysis of the snatch lift with elite female weightlifters during the 2010 world weightlifting championship. *Journal of Strength and Conditioning Research*, 26(4), 897–905.

Bartonietz, K.E. (1996). Biomechanics of the snatch: Toward a higher training efficiency. *Strength and Conditioning*, 18(3), 24–31.

Baumann, W., Gross, V., Quade, K., Galbierz, P., and Schwirtz, A. (1988). The snatch technique of world class weightlifters at the 1985 world championships. *International Journal of Sport Biomechanics*, 4, 68–89.

Bosquet, L., Montpetit, J., Arvisais, D., and Mujika, I. (2007). Effects of tapering on performance: A meta-analysis. *Medicine and Science in Sports and Exercise*, 39(8), 1358–1365.

Calhoon, G., and Fry, A.C. (1999). Injury rates and profiles of elite competitive weightlifters. *Journal of Athletic Training*, 34(3), 232–238.

Campos, J., Cuesta, A., and Pablos, C. (2006). Kinematical analysis of the snatch in elite male junior weightlifters of different weight categories. *Journal of Strength and Conditioning Research*, 20(4), 843–850.

Canadian Weightlifting Federation. (2015). *The Sinclair coefficients for the Olympiad January 1, 2013 to December 31 2016 for men's and women's Olympic weightlifting* [Online]. Canada: Alberta weightlifting association. Available at: www.iwf.net/downloads/?category=68 [Accessed: 01 April 2016].

Cleather, D.J., Goodwin, J.E., and Bull, M.J. (2013). Intersegmental moment analysis characterizes the partial correspondence of jumping and jerking. *Journal of Strength and Conditioning Research*, 27(1), 89–100.

Comfort, P., Udall, R., and Jones, P.A. (2012). The effect of loading on kinematic and kinetic variables during the midthigh clean pull. *Journal of Strength and Conditioning Research*, 26(5), 1208–1214.

DeWeese, B.H., Serrano, A.J., Scruggs, S.K., and Sams, M.L. (2012). The clean pull and snatch pull: Proper technique for weightlifting movement derivatives. *Strength and Conditioning Journal*, 34(6), 82–86.

Doerr, D. (2012). In-Competition injury monitoring. *IOC medical and scientific department*. Lausanne, CHE.

Enoka, R.M. (1979). The pull in olympic weightlifting. *Medicine and Science in Sports*, 11(2), 131–137.

Everett, G. (2009). *Olympic weightlifting: A complete guide for athletes and coaches*. 2nd ed. Sunnyvale: Catalyst Athletics.

Fry, A.C., Ciroslan, D., Fry, M.D., LeRoux, C.D., Schilling, B.K., and Chiu, L.Z.F. (2006). Anthorpometric and performance variables discriminating elite American junior men weightlifters. *Journal of Strength and Conditioning Research*, 20(4), 861–866.

Fry, A.C., Kraemer, W.J., Stone, M.H., Warren, B.J., Fleck, S.J., Kearney, J.T., and Gordon, S.E. (1994). Endocrine responses to overreaching before and after 1 year of weightlifting. *Canadian Journal of Applied Physiology*, 19(4), 400–410.

Fry, A.C., Schilling, B.K., Staron, R.S., Hagerman, F.C., Hikida, R.S., and Thrush, J.T. (2003). Muscle fiber characteristic and performance correlates of male Olympic-style weightlifters. *Journal of Strength and Conditioning Research*, 17(4), 746–754.

Funato, K., Matsuo, A., and Fukunaga, T. (1996). Specific movement power related to athletic performance in weightlifting. *Journal of Applied Biomechanics*, 12(1), 44–57.

Garhammer, J. (1980). Power production by Olympic weightlifters. *Medicine and Science in Sports and Exercise*, 12(1), 54–60.

Garhammer, J. (1991). A comparison between elite male and female weightlifters in competition. *International Journal of Sport Biomechanics*, 7, 3–11.

Garhammer, J., and Takano, B. (2003). Training for weightlifting. In: Komi, P.V. ed. *Strength and power for sports*. Oxford: Blackwell Science Ltd, pp. 502–517.

González-Badillo, J.J., Izquierdo, M., and Gorostiaga, E.M. (2006). Moderate volume of high relative training intensity produces greater strength gains compared with low and high volumes in competitive weightlifters. *Journal of Strength and Conditioning Research*, 20(1), 73–81.

Gourgoulis, V., Aggelousis, N., Garas, A., and Mavromatis, G. (2009). Unsuccessful Vs. successful lifts: A kinematic approach. *Journal of Strength and Conditioning Research*, 23(2), 486–494.

Gourgoulis, V., Aggelousis, N., Mavromatis, G., and Garas, A. (2000). Three-dimensional kinematic analysis of the snatch of elite Greek weightlifters. *Journal of Sports Sciences*, 18(8), 643–652.

Gourgoulis, V., Aggeloussis, N., Antoniou, P., Christoforidis, C., Mavromatis, G., and Garas, A. (2002). Comparative 3-Dimensional kinematic analysis of the snatch technique in elite male and female Greek weightlifters. *Journal of Strength and Conditioning Research*, 16(3), 359–366.

Gullet, J.C., Tillman, M.D., Gutierrez, G.M., and Chow, J.W. (2008). A biomechanical comparison of back and front squats in healthy trained individuals. *Journal of Strength and Conditioning Research*, 23(1), 284–292.

Hadi, G., Akkius, H., and Harbili, E. (2012). Three-dimensional kinematic analysis of the snatch technique for lifting different barbell weights. *Journal of Strength and Conditioning Research*, 26(6), 1568–1576.

Haff, G.G., Carlock, J.M., Hartman, M.J., Lon Kilgore, J., Kawamori, N., Jackson, J.R., Morris, R.T., Sands, W.A., and Stone, M.H. (2005). Force-time curve characteristics of dynamic and isometric muscle actions of elite women olympic weightlifters. *Journal Strength and Conditioning Research*, 19(4), 741–748.

Haff, G.G., Jackson, J.R., Kawamori, N., Carlock, J.M., Hartman, M.J., Kilgore, J.L., Morris, R.T., Ramsey, M.W., Sands, W.A., and Stone, M.H. (2008). Force-time curve chracteristics and hormonal alterations during an eleven week training period in elite women weightlifters. *Journal of Strength and Conditioning Research*, 22(2), 433–446.

Haff, G.G., Ramsey, M., McBride, J., and Triplett, T. (2012). Strength gains: Block versus daily undulating periodization weight training among track and field athletes. *International Journal of Sports Physiology and Performance*, 7, 161–169.

Haff, G.G., Whitley, A., McCoy, L.B., O'Bryant, H.S., Kilgore, J.L., Haff, E.E., Pierce, K., and Stone, M.H. (2003). Effects of different set configuration on barbell velocity and displacement during a clean pull. *Journal of Strength and Conditioning Research*, 17(1), 95–103.

Häkkinen, K., Komi, P.V., and Kauhanen, H. (1986). Electromyogrpahcis and force production characteristics of leg extensor muscles of elite weightlifters during isometric, concentric, and various stretch shortening cycle exercises. *International Journal of Sports Medicine*, 7, 144–151.

Hamill, B. (1994). Relative safety of weightlifting and weight training. *Journal of Strength and Conditioning Research*, 8(1), 53–57.

Harbili, E., and Alptekin, A. (2014). Comparative kinematic analysis of the snatch lifts in elite male adolescent weightlifters. *Journal of Sport Science and Medicine*, 13, 417–422.

Hedrick, A., and Wada, H. (2008). Weightlifting movements: Do the benefits outweigh the risks? *Strength and Conditioning Journal*, 30(6), 26–35.

Hoover, D.L., Carlson, K.M., Christensen, B.K., and Zebas, C.J. (2006). Biomechanical analysis of women weightlifters during the snatch. *Journal of Strength and Conditioning Research*, 20(3), 627–633.

Isaka, T., Okada, J., and Funato, K. (1996). Kinematic analysis of the barbell during the snatch movement of elite Asaian weightlifters. *Journal of Applied Biomechanics*, 12, 508–516.

Junge, A., Engebretsen, L., Mountjoy, M., Alonso, J.M., Renström, P., Aubry, M., and Dvorak, J. (2009). Sports injuries during the sumer Olympic games 2008. *The American Journal of Sports Medicine*, 37(11), 2165–2172.

Kawamori, N., Rossi, S.J., Justice, B.D., Haff, E.E., Pistilli, E.E., O'Bryant, H.S., Stone, M.H., and Haff, G.G. (2006). Peak force and rate of force development during isometric and dynamic midthigh clean pulls performed at various loads. *Journal of Strength and Conditioning Research*, 20(3), 483–491.

Kipp, K., and Harris, C. (2015). Patterns of barbell acceleration during the snatch in weightlifting competition. *Journal of Sport Sciences*, 33(14), 1467–1471.

Kipp, K., Redden, J., Sabick, M.B., and Harris, C. (2012). Weightlifting performance is related to kinematic and kinetic patterns of the hip and knee joints. *Journal of Strength and Conditioning Research*, 26(7), 1838–1844.

Lake, J., Lauder, M., and Dyson, R. (2006). Exploring the biomechanical characteristics of the weightlifting jerk. *XXIV ISBS Symposium*. Salzburg, Austria.

Lavallee, M.E., and Balam, T. (2010). An overview of strength training injuries: Acute and chronic. *Current Sports Medicine Reports*, 9(5), 307–313.

Lippmann, J., and Klaiber, V. (1986). *Analysis of the sporting technique in weightlifting, European championships 1986 in Karl-Marx Stadt*. Unpublished Research.

Norris, C.M. (2008). *Back stability: Integrating science and therapy*, 2nd ed. Champaign, IL: Human Kinetics.

Rossi, S.J., Buford, T.W., Smith, D.B., Kennel, R., Haff, E.E., and Haff, G.G. (2007). Bilateral comparison of barbell kinetics and kinematics during a weightlifting competition. *International Journal of Sports Physiology and Performance*, 2, 150–158.

Stone, M.H., Fry, A.C., Ritchie, M., Stoesell-Ross, L., and Marsit, J.L. (1994). Injury potential and safety aspects of weightlifting movements. *Strength and Conditioning*, 16(3), 15–21.

Stone, M.H., O'Bryant, H.S., Williams, F.E., and Johnson, R.L. (1998). Analysis of bar paths during the snatch in elite male weightlifters. *Strength and Conditioning*, 20(4), 30–38.

Stone, M.H., Pierce, K.C., Sands, W.A., and Stone, M.E. (2006). Weightlifting: A brief overview. *Strength and Conditioning Journal*, 28(1), 50–66.

Stone, M.H., Sands, W.A., Pierce, K.C., Carlock, J., Caridnale, M., and Newton, R.U. (2005). Relationship of maximum strength to weightlifting performance. *Medicine in Sport and Exercises Science*, 37(6), 1037–1043.

Suchomel, T. J., Comfort, P., and Lake, J. P. (2017). Enhancing the force–velocity profile of athletes using weightlifting derivatives. *Strength & Conditioning Journal*, 39(1), 10–20.

Turner, A.N. (2011). The science and practice of periodization: A brief review. *Strength and Conditioning Journal*, 33(1), 34–46.

INDEX

Page numbers in italic indicate a figure or image and page numbers in bold indicate a table or graph.

Abe, T. 616
AB *see* able-bodied athletes
able-bodied athletes (AB) 38, 40, 41, 43, 45, 413, 414, 421, 424, **423**, 424, 431
Achilles tendon 145, 437, 479, 510, 533, 534
ACL injury *see* anterior cruciate ligament
aerobic metabolism 68, 158, **249**, 335, 375, 394, 400, 591
Agel, J. **159**, **160**, 182, 183
Alpine skiing 568–581; ACL injuries 571; aerobic/anaerobic 577–578; agility/coordination 578–579; athletic demands 568–571; biomechanical considerations 569–571, 575, 576; conditioning 574–577. **575**; demands of racing and training 571; differences of each event **569**; fitness testing 572–574, **573**; four disciplines 568–569, **569**; hypertrophy 477; injury prevalence 571–572; Olympic Games 568, 576; other injuries 572; oxygen consumption 570, **573**; physical demands 570–571; programming 574–580; proprinception and balance 579; shoulder injuries 572; strength training 576; thinking outside the box 579; training off-season **580**; training on the road 579–580; training order 580; training organisation 580
Alyas, F. 438
American football 102–122; accommodation methods 118–119; agility 121–122; biomechanical considerations 103; cluster methods 118; current impact of athletic performance 107–109, **108**; difference between drafted and non-drafted players **105**; game analysis 104; general methods 116–119; hypertrophy 117, 118; injury rates **159**; lower body strength 107, 109, 110, 114, 116, 117; maximal power development 117–118; maximal strength development 116–117; playing requirements 103–107; plyometrics 119–120; positional analysis 103, **105**; program design considerations **115**, 115–116; specific methods 119–122; sprinting 120–121; strength and speed quality analysis 104–107, **106**; training residuals 114–115; transfer of training 109–114, **111**, **112**
amputation 43, 44, 312, 413, 415, 418, 431
anaemia 14, 15
anaerobic alactic 259, 361, 557, *557*, 564
anaerobic glycolysis 157, 158, 259, 289, 375, 385, 402, 435, 545
anaerobic lactic 259, *557*
anterior cruciate ligament (ACL) injury **89**, 127, **127**, 183, 190, 234, 297; Alpine skiing 571–572, 576, 577; female athletes 15–17, 19, 235, 439; free style snowport 586, 587, 588
anthropometry: Australian football 128; boxing 387; disabled athletes 38, 40; female athletes 8; fencing 404, 409; golf 452; handball 280, 281, **282**, 283, 284, 291, 292; netball 234; powerlifting 616, 622; rock climbing 558; rowing 224, *225*; rugby union **77**; soccer 58, 69; sprint cycling 507; Taekwondo 374, **377**, 380; wheelchair rugby 323; weightlifting 639
Arnadjelović, O. 617, 626
Arnason, A. 55
Arriaza, R. **365**
athlete exposures 159, 182, 183, 405

Australian football 126–141; anthropometry 128; athletic demands 126–127; bench press throw *134*; cable row *140*; conditioning programming 132; dumbbell press *138*; fitness testing 128; hypertrophy **130**; injury prevalence **127**, 127–128; injury prevention 135–137; in-season programming 131–132; medicine ball *135*; pallof press and lift *139*; periodization 129–130; power step up *136*; preseason programming **130**, 130–131; programming 128–129; running performance 135; 7-day break between games **131**; special exercises 134; strength/power 134; strength programming 132–133; trunk integration 138; warm ups 138–140; water skier *137*; youth development 140–141
Australian Institute of Sport Repeat Effort Test 266
autonomic dysreflexia 42, 47, 425

Babault, N. 114
Bach, B. **159**
Bacharach, D. W. 571
Bahr, R. 56
Baker, D. 113–114, 430
Barden, J. M. 548
basketball 15, 24, 41, 45, 178–191, 311, 365, 405; athletic demands 179–182; blood lactate 181; court interval training principles 189; fatigue 181; fitness assessment 183–187, **185–186**; functional movement screening (FMS) 184; heart rate response 180–181; hydration 190; hypertrophy 187; injury prevalence 182–183; intercollegiate 183; junior **185**; oxygen consumption 181, **185**; periodisation 187; physical competency assessment 184–187; playing time proportion of different intensities 179–180; plyometric training 190; programming 188; tactical strategy and implication on athletic demands 182; training prescription and exercise selection 188–190; training programme design 187–190, **190**; wheelchair 41–42, 311; *see also* International Basketball Federation; National Basketball Association
Battaglini, C. L. 105
Bauerfeind, J. 319, 320
Behringer, M. 31
Ben Abdelkrim, N. 178, 179, 180, 181, 182, **185**, 188
Beneke, R. 360, **361**, 368
Benson, P. R. 385
Bernardi, M. 418
Bernardin, M. 114
Bianchedi, D. 401
Bingul, B. M. 541
biological maturation 24

biomechanical considerations 4; Alpine skiing 570, 575, 576; American football 103; amputated athletes 43–44; cricket 194, 195–197, 198; disabled athletes 43; female athletes 16–18; field hockey 145; free style snowport 584–586, 588, 594; golf 451, 452–453, 468; ice hockey 162; karate 360, 362–363; MMA 334, 338; powerlifting 617; soccer 58, 59; sprint cycling 510; swimming 541–544, 546; tennis 435, 436; triathlon 527; volleyball 277; weightlifting 637, **639**, 642; wheelchair fencing 419–421, 431; wheelchair rugby 316–317, **317**; young athletes 25
Bishop, C. 404
Bishop, D. 241, 543
Bishop, P. A. 104
blood lactate: basketball 179, 181, 182; boxing 386, 391, **392**; disabled athletes 43; fencing 401, 402, **402**, 406, 411; free style snowport 586; handball 289, **290**, 290–291, 302, 304; ice hockey 158; karate 361; limb deficiency 43–44; rock climbing 557, 558; rugby sevens 86; soccer 52; taekwondo 374; triathlon 530; wheelchair fencing 418, 425
BMD 8, 10–11, *11*, 13, 221
bodybuilding 597–609; aerobic training 604–605; blood flow restriction 602–603; body composition testing 599; decreasing body fat 604–605; dietary considerations for decreasing body fat 605; dietary considerations for increasing lean mass 603–604; exercise selection 600; fitness testing battery 598–599, **599**; hypertrophy **599**, 600, 601, 602, **602**, 604, 605, **606**, **607–608**; increasing lean mass 600; injury prevalence 598; lower body building **607**; macronutrient intake 603; muscle protein synthesis 601–602, 603, 605; periodisation 605–608, *606*; physical demands 597; programming 599–608; strength training 598–599, **607**, **608**; supplementation 603–604; training for decreasing body fat 604; training frequency 602; training intensity and volume 600–602, **602**
bone mineral: accrual 10–11; density (BMD) 8, 10–11, *11*, 13, 221
Bosco, C. 300, 574–575
Bowie, **560**
boxing 384–398; anthropometric profiling 387–388; athletic demands 385–387; conditioning programme **395**; countermovement jump and squat jump 390; gluteal strength 387; hypertrophy **395**, 396; laboratory based fitness testing 387–390; lactate profile 391; landmine punch throw test 390–391, *391*; medicine ball backhand throw 392; movement analysis **389**; movement dysfunctions 387; movement training 396; needs analysis 385–387; Olympic

Index

Games 375; overhead squat analysis *388*; oxygen consumption 385, 386; reliability and assessment standards 393; resistance exercises **396**; rotational mobility 387; shoulder mobility 387; shuttle tests 392; single leg squat 388, *390*; 60 seconds press-up test 392; shoulder and rotational mobility 396–397; strength training 395–396; 30:15 test treadmill test 391–392; training adaptation 394–395
Bradley, P. S. 51, 52, 53, 54
Brainard, I. 160
Brazier, J. 404
Brechue, W. F. 616
Brent, S. 563
Bridge, C. A. 375
Brown, E. W. 620
Buckthorp, J. 457
Burkett, L. N. 105

Capelli, C. 545
Cappozzo, A. 618
Castagna, C. 182, **185**,
cerebral palsy (CP) 38, 40, 44–45, 259, 312, 413, 415, 424
Chaabene, H. 360, 361, **361**, 362, 366
Chad, K. E. **234**
Chatard, J. C. 114
Chavda, S. 404
Cholewicki, J. 619, 630
Chow, J. W. 544
Chung, W. M. 419, 421, 422, **422**
Clarey, J. 568
Collins, D. 230
Comfort, P. 652
Cometti, G. 114
Comfort, P. 652
Commonwealth Games 233
Conchola, E. G. 107
Connorton, A. J. 385
Cook, C. J. 615
Cook, G. 184
Cormack, D. A. R. 320
Cormack, S. J. 128
Cormie, P. 111, 113
CP *see* cerebral palsy
cricket 194–214; batter trunk conditioning **211**; biomechanical considerations 194, 195–197, 198; bowler alternative exercises **206**; bowler strength/power program **203**; bowler trunk conditioning **207**; fitness testing battery **199**, 199–201, **200**; injury prevalence **197**, 197–199, **198**; international 194; lower body strength 214; periodization **202**; player alternative exercises **212**; programming 201–214, *204–205*, *208*, *209*, *210*, *211*, *213*, *214*; *see also* English Cricket Board; International Cricket Council
Critchley, G. R. **364**

Cronin, J. 114
Cumps, E. 183
Cuppett, M. M. 105

Davidson, A. **234**
Davis, A. 109
Davis, G. 329
Davis, P. 385
de Geus, B. 557
dehydration 43, 191, 291, **293**, **294**, 375, 385, 403, 622
Deitch, J. R. 182
Delextrat, A. 179
Delorme, S. 594–595
Destombe, C. 364
de Villarreal, E. S. 110, 119, 120
Di Mascio, M. 52
disabled athletes 38–47; active hands *42*, **324**; anthropometry 38, 40; biomechanical considerations 43; elite performance preparation *40*; hypertrophy 45; impairment specific considerations 40–45; limb deficiency 40, 43–44, 413, 415, 424; oxygen consumption 45; practical applications 46–47; spinal cord injury (SCI) 40–43; sport-specific considerations 45–46; stump care 43; wheelchair innovations *39*; *see also* cerebral palsy; Lewis, Andy
Ditroilo, M. 118
Doria, C. 361, 368
Draper, N. *555*, 556, 557
Dubai Championship 458
Duvillard, S. P. 571

ECB *see* English Cricket Board
Edelmann-Nusser, J. 585
Edouard, P. 475
Edwards, M. 404
electromyography (EMG) 362, 363, 404, 419, 428, 508, 569, 575
EMG *see* electromyography
English Cricket Board (ECB) 195, 199
English Premier League 51, 52, **52**, **53**, 54, 60
Eto, D. 119
Evans, M. 522
Evershed, J. 548

fat mass 7, 8, 30, 41, 58, **77**, 329, 386, 387
Faude, O. 52
Federation International De Volley-Ball 259
female athletes 7–19; anterior cruciate ligament (ACL) injury 15–16; anthropometry 8; biomechanical considerations with injury 16–18; bone mineral accrual 10–11; contemporary considerations for health 12; health and well-being 10–15; hypertrophy 9; injury considerations 15–18; injury risk factor *18*; iron status 14–15; menorrhagia 12, 14, **14**,

19; menstrual cycle 10, 11, *11*, 12–13, 14, 19, 531; menstrual cycle irregularities 13–14; muscle mass 8; power training 9; resistance training 10; strength development 8; strength training 8–9; trainability 9; triad *11*, 11–12, *12*
femoroacetabular impingement 376
fencing 400–411; anthropometry 404, 409; biomechanics of lunge *403*, 403–405; blood lactate *402*; British Talen 409; CODS test 406; competition calendar **410**; fitness testing battery 406; hypertrophy 405; lunge ability; *407*, 407–408; mean results from competitions *402*; Olympic Games 400; oxygen consumption 401; periodised training plans 409–411, **411**; physiology 401–403; programme goals and exercise selection 408–409; programming 408–410; risk of injury 405–406; test battery 408; time motion analysis 400–401; *see also* wheelchair fencing
field hockey 143–155; athletic demands and fitness testing battery 143–145, **145**; biomechanical considerations 145; competition countdown *153*; injury prevalence 145–146, **159**; patterns **144**; programming 146–154; tournament durability 152; tournament preparation 152–155; training **151**, **152**, *154*, *155*; warm up **146–151**
FINA World Championships
Finley, M. A. 319
Flik, K. **159**, **160**
FMS *see* functional movement skill; functional movement screening
Football League Championship 60
Foster, D. 198
Fox, A. **234**
free style snowport 583–595; aerobic/anaerobic capacity 590; athletic demands 583–587; backside 1080' trick *585*; biomechanical considerations 584–586, 588, 594; conditioning 594; hypertrophy 591; fitness testing battery 588–590; injury prevalence 587–588; lower body strength 591; mesocycles **592**; movement competency 588–589; Olympic Games 583, *584*, 590; physiological demands 586–587; programming 590–594; slopestyle event characteristics 583–584; sport-specific skills 594; strength and power 589–593, **592**, **593**
Fry, A. C. 104, 643, 644
functional movement skills (FMS) 24, 25, 41
functional movement screening (FMS) 184, **199**, 428, **440**, 441, **441**, 456
fundamental movement skills 18, 24, 26, *26*

Gajewski, J. 558
Galitski, H. M. 107, **108**
Garcia-Hermoso, A. 542, 543
Garstecki, M. A. 105

Gasston, V. **234**
Gebert, 556
general preparation phase (GPP) 32, 79, 302, 487, **487**, **488**, *490*, 493, *493*, *496*, 517, 518
Gill, N. 114
Glass, R. G. 107
glenohumeral joint 419, 421, 423, 438, 510, 572
goalies 172, **173–174**, **175**
Gola, R. 547
golf 451–468; anthropometry 452; athletic demands 451–454; biomechanical considerations 451, 452–453, 468; cable wood chop *465*; field-based test battery **460**; fitness testing 455–460; hypertrophy 462; injury epidemiology 454–455; in-season training **467**; kettlebell swing *465*; lower body strength 454, 455; mobility 462; movement screening 456–457; observations from PGA tour 455; oxygen consumption 453; performance and movement screen test battery 458–460; physical characteristics 453–454; physical performance testing 455–456; physiology of performance 453; player management 466–468; programme design considerations 460–462; rate of force development 461; S&C performance model 459; single leg Romanian deadlift *464*; sport-specific performance monitoring 457–458; strength and power development 460–461, **463**; stretch shortening cycle and X-factor stretch 461–462; training plans 462–466; Turkish get up *466*
Gomo, O. 618
Gonzaláz-Badillo, J. J. 652
GPP *see* general preparation phase
Granhed, H. 619
Grant, S. 555
Grote, K. 546
ground reaction forces (GRFs) 16, 17, 91, 106, 188, 196, 235, 295, 297, 435, 452, 453, 462, *474*, 480, 514, 515, 535, 540, 544, 558, 586, 588, 589, 639, 640; horizontal 481–482; vertical 196, 234, 235, 549
Guilhem, G. 403, 405
Gulgin, H. 184
Guttmann, L. 413
GymAware 189, 390

Haff, G. G. 110, 120
hamstring 56, 235, 255, 362, 376, 380, 482, 491, 496, 503, 579, 586, 640; bridge **238**, **377**, **494**, 536; capacity test **92**; complex 220; deficient 236; exercises **349**, **350**, **351**, **352**, **353**, **354**, **467**, *493*, *494*, *496*, 497, 577, **606**, 624; functional hamstring: quadriceps (H:Q) 16–17; injuries 127, 128, 137, 145, 198, 261, **293**, 437, 440, 480, 510, 530, 562; isometric bridge 62, **98**; medial **389**; muscle strain 89, **89**; Nordic curl 128, 137, **253**, 576, **593**; protecting 490; recruitment 16;

resistance training 16; robustness 497; strains **127**, 145, 405, 479; strengthening 18, *62*, **92**, 128, 137, 406, 487, 490, 535, 589, **593**, **606**, **607**; torque 572

handball 280–306; acceleration patterns *287*; aerobic capacity *283*; anthropometric characteristics **282**; athletic demands 283–297; blood lactate values *290*, *304*; endurance capacity 299–301; fitness testing battery 298; Force/Velocity and Power/Velocity relationship *296*, *297*; heart rate *288*, *289*, *304*; hypertrophy **293**, **294**; injury prevalence 297–298, *298*; leagues 281; Leger test 299; movement patterns of backcourt player *285*; movements and strength requirements 295–297; Olympic Games 280, 288, 294, 297; oxygen consumption 299; players' positions *281*, *285*, *292*–*294*; programming 301–304, **302**, *303*; SEHA league 301; shuttle run 299–301; sprint and repeated spring 300; strength and power 300–301; tactical roles and positions and strength and conditioning specificity 291–295; 30-15 299; Yo-Yo intermittent level 2 300; *see also* Qatar Handball World Championships

Harley, R. A. **185**
Harmer, P. 405
Harvey, E. J. **159**
heavy menstrual bleeding (HMB) 12, 14, **14**
heterogeneity 40, 422
high intensity interval training (HIIT) 61, 63, 66, 69, 302, **328**, 334, 339, **356**, 361, 394, 398, 401, 403, 406, 411, 431, 604, 605
HIIT *see* high intensity interval training
HMB *see* heavy menstrual bleeding
Hoffman, J. R. 107, **108**, 109, 110, 178
Holmér, I. 545
Hong, Y. 55, 56
horizontal ground reaction forces 481
Hulin, B. T. 198
hydration 190, 191, 375, 386, 598, 599
hypertrophy: Alpine skiing 577; American football 117, 118; Aussie rules football **130**; basketball 187; bodybuilding **599**, 600, 601, 602, **602**, 604, 605, **606**, **607**; boxing 395, 396; disabled athletes 45; female athletes 9; fencing 405; free style snowport 591; golf 462; handball **293**, **294**; karate 368, **368**; powerlifting 617, 618, 622–623, 624, 627; rock climbing 563; rowing 219, **227**, 229–230, *230*; rugby union 79; sprint cycling 516, 518, *518*, **519**, 520, **521**; sprint running 477, **491**, **493**, *493*, **496**, **497**, *497*; weightlifting 647, **649**; Wheelchair rugby 324, 325–326, **326**, **328**
hypohydration 191

ice hockey 157–175, 311, 363, **365**; agility/change of direction 170–172; athletic demands 157–159; biomechanical considerations 162; difference between in-season and off-season energy systems development 172–175; difference between in-season and off-season warm-ups 166–175; energy **172**; fitness testing battery 160–162, **161**; goalies 172, **173–174**, **175**; injury prevalence **159**, 159–160, **160**; in-season training 164; lower body strength 160, 161, **161**, 162, 175; maximal oxygen uptake of players **158**; movement training 170; off-season ESD plan **173**; off-season training 164; oxygen consumption **158**, 161, **172**; power pairings 167; primary lifts and accessory lifts 169; programming 162–164, **163**; SAQ coaching points **171**; skating simulations 169; speed 169–170; warm ups 164–166, **165**, **166**, 166–175, **167**, **168**

Iide, K. 360
Imamura, H. 361
impaired thermoregulation 42, 425
inspiratory muscle training 41
International Basketball Federation 178
International Cricket Council 194
International Football Association 51
International Ice Hockey Federation 157
International Paralympic Committee 311
International Powerlifting Federation (IPF) 612, **613**, 614, 616
International Wheelchair and Amputee Sport Federation 415
International Wheelchair Rugby Federation (IWRF) 311, 313
International Weightlifting Federation (IWF) 630, 642
International World Games Association 612
IPF *see* International Powerlifting Federation
iron deficiency 14, 15
iron status 12, 14–15, 19
isometric mid thigh pull (IMTP) 59, 91, **91**, 162, **264**, 406, 513, *513*, 514, 530, **645**
Issurin, V. B. 114
IWF *see* International Weightlifting Federation
IWRF *see* International Wheelchair Rugby Federation

Jacobson, B. H. 107, **108**, 109, 110
Jiménez-Reyes, P. 117
Johanssen, H. V. **365**
Judge, L. W. 616
Junge, A. 642, 643

Kang, J. 107
karate 359–369; battery of fitness tests **366**; biomechanical considerations 360, *362*, 362–363, *363*; hypertrophy 368, **368**; injury incidence 363, **364–365**; longitudinal programme design 368; lower body strength

366; needs analysis for karate kumite 360–366; Olympic Games 359, **360**, 367; physiological analysis 361; strength and conditioning **367**, 367–368, **368**; time motion characteristics 360–361; weight categories 360; work-to-rest ratios **361**; World Karate Federation 359, 361
Karcher, C. 280, *290*,
Kawamori, N. 120
Keogh, J. W. L. 616, 620, 621
Keskinen, K. 547
Kilduff, L. 404
Kimball, R. G. 620
Kompf, J. 617
Kraemer, W. J. 104, 109, 119, 624
Krosshaug, T. 17, 56
Krüger, A. 585
Kuepper, T. 560, **560**
Kujala, U. M. 363, **365**

Lago-Peñas, C. 54
La Liga 52
La Panse, B. 615
Latin, R. W. 105, **108**
Lawn Tennis Association (LTA) 187, 441, 442, 443
leg dominance 17, *18*, **408**
Leger test 299
Lewis, Andy *44*
Leyes, M. **365**
ligament dominance 16, *18*
Limb, D. **560**
limb deficiency 43–44, 413, 415, 424
Lloyd, R. S. 28
Loughran, B. 233, **234**
Lovera, M. 616
lower back 198, 220, 397, 406, 437, 438, 439, 454, 510, 593, 618, 619, 621, 627, 652; injuries 261, 381, 387, 454, 514, 515, 621; pain 146, 387, 397, 406, 438, 510, 572, 577, 643
lower body strength: American football 107, 109, 110, 114, 116, 117; bodybuilding **607**; cricket 214; female athletes 8–9; free style snowport 591; golf 454, 455; ice hockey 160, 161, **161**, 162, 175; karate **366**; MMA 334, 340, 356; rock climbing 563, **563**, 564; rugby union 76; sprint cycling 514; swimming 547, 548, 549, **549**
lower limb tendinopathies 533–534; diagnosis and treatment 533–534; key risk factors 533; signs and symptoms 533
LTA *see* Lawn Tennis Association
LTAD 141

Macan, J. 363, **364**, 365
Marín, P. J. 117
Marshall, S. 118
Martinez, A. 179
McColloch, P. **159**

McCormack, D. A. R. 320
McGee, K. J. 105
McGuigan, M. R. 111, 114
McInnes, S. E. 178, 179, 181
McKay, C. **159**, **160**
McKean, M. R. 618
McLatchie, G. R. **364**
McMaster, D. T. **77**, 114, 116, 117
McNeely, E. 221
medial tibial stress syndrome 511, 532–533; diagnosis and treatment 532–533; key risk factors 532; signs and symptoms 532
Meeuwisse, W. H. **159**, 183
menorrhagia 12, 14, **14**, 19
menstrual cycle 10, 11, *11*, 12–14, 19, 531
Mihalik, J. P. 105
Milia, R. 401
Mina, M. A. 120
mixed martial arts (MMA) 333–356, 380; acute workload 337; anaerobic qualities 335, 339; athletic demands 333–335; biomechanical considerations 334, 338; characteristics 333–334; determinants 334–335; endurance 335; endurance, intermittent 339–341, *340*; energy system development 355, **355**; external load 336; fitness testing battery 337–338; internal load 336–337; intermittent endurance 339–341; lower body strength 334, 340, 356; macrocycle 341, **342**; maximal neuromuscular expressions **338**, 338–339, **339**; maximal power, impulse and velocity 335; maximal strength 334–335, 339; oxygen consumption 335; programming 341; strength training **346–354**; templates 341–356; training and injury prevention 336–337; training load 336; training phase breakdown 341–345, **343–345**; Ultimate Fighting Championship 334, 341; weekly breakdowns 346
MMA *see* mixed martial arts
Morin, J. B. 475
Morouco, P. 548
movement competency 25, 66, 68, 190, 382, 461, 588–589
Muller-Rath, R. **364**
Murderball *see* Wheelchair Rugby
muscle cross-sectional area 9, 27, 187, 604, 616
muscle hypertrophy: Alpine skiing 577; American football 117, 118; Aussie rules football **130**; basketball 187; bodybuilding **599**, 600, 601, 602, **602**, 604, 605, *606*, **607**; boxing 395, 396; disabled athletes 45; female athletes 9; fencing 405; free style snowport 591; golf 462; handball **293**, **294**; karate 368, **368**; powerlifting 617, 618, 622–623, 624, 627; rock climbing 563; rowing 219, **227**, 229–230, *230*; rugby union 79; sprint cycling 516, 518, *518*, **519**, 520, **521**; sprint running 477, **491**, 493, **493**, **496**, 497, **497**;

weightlifting 647, **649**; Wheelchair Rugby **324**, 325–326, **326**, **328**
Myatt, C. 158

National Basketball Association (NBA) 178, 184, 187
National Football League (NFL) 102, 104; Combine 105, **105**, 106, 120
NBA *see* National Basketball Association
NCAA 104, **158**, **159**, 183, 184, **185**, 190, 546
netball 233–257; acute performance question 250–253, **253**; aerobic power 249, **249–250**; athlete profile 245–246; athletic demands 233–234; Austrian National Team 570; change of directions 246–248, *247*, **248**; context/coordination 256; fitness testing battery 236–242, **238**, *238*, 239, *241*; fitness testing battery 236–242: fitness testing battery: stage one: information gathering 237; fitness testing battery: stage two: testing and interpreting 237–239; fitness testing battery: stage three: creating individual performance frameworks 239; fitness testing battery: stage four: decision making 240–242; hip conditioning 254–257, **257**; injury prevalence 234–236; oxygen consumption 241, 249; programming 242–246, *243*, **244**; research on distance **234**; space 254–255; specific injury risk factors 253–257, **254**; time 256–257
Neuhof, A. **560**
Neumayr, G. 570, 574
Newton, R. U. 111
NFL *see* National Football League
Nielsen, A. B. 56
Noakes, T. D. 54
Noerregaard, F. O. 365
non-spinal cord injured (NSCI) athletes 312, 319
Norlin, R. 620, 621
NSCI athletes *see* non-spinal cord injured (NSCI) athletes

Oakland Raiders 109
O'Donoghue, P. G. 233, **234**,
oligomenorrhea 13, 14
Olympic Games 45, 72, 152, 153, 154, 221; Alpine skiing 568, 576; barbells **25**, *62*, *66*, 390; Bavaria 568; bodyweight *222*; boxing 375; fencing 400; free style snowport 583, *584*, 590; lifts 43, 79, 80, 98, 117, 119, 134, 188, 189, 294, 380, 395, **497**, 550, 564, 576; handball 280, 288, 294, 297; karate 359, **360**, 367; London 297; medals 33; powerlifting 612; Rio 218, **374**, 526; rock climbing 553, 564; rowing 230; Seoul 371; Sochi 568, 583, *584*; sprint running **497**; St. Moritz 568; swimming 540, 542, 544, 546, 549, 550; Sydney 371, 374; Taekwondo 371, 372, **372**, *373*, 374, 375, 380, 382; Tokyo 259, 359, 553;
triathlon 526, 527; volleyball 259, **272**, 276; weightlifting 9, 642, 643, 652; weightlifting shoes 618
Opar, D. A. 128
oral contraceptives **12**, 13
Otago, L. 234
oxygen consumption (VO2): Alpine skiing 570, **573**; basketball 181, **185**; boxing 385, 386; disabled athletes 45; fencing 401; golf 453; handball 299; ice hockey 158, 161, **172**; MMA 335; netball 241, 249; rock climbing 554, 556, **556**, 558; Taekwondo 375, **377**, 378; tennis 435; triathlon 529, 530; wheelchair fencing 418; Wheelchair rugby **316**

Paralympic Games 3, 38, 44, 311, *314*, 319, 320, 325, 329, 413, 415, 416, 421, 424; first 527
peak height velocity 8, 28, 29
Petersen, C. 195, 196
Peterson, L. 56
PGA Tour 455, 457, 458
Pitty, J. D. 385
plantar fasciitis 437, 534, 562; diagnosis and treatment 534; key risk factors 534
Poliquin, C. 117, 118
Potdevin, F. J. 544
Pousson, M. 114
powerlifting 612–627; activity profile 614–615; aetiology of injury 621; anthropometry 616, 622; bench press 618–619; energy systems 615; athletic demands 614–617; bench press 614; biomechanical considerations 616–617; competition lifts 613–614; deadlift 614, 619–620; endocrinology 615; fitness testing battery 621–622; force requirements 616; hypertrophy 617, 618, 622–623, 624, 627; injury incidence 620–621; injury location and severity 621; injury prevalence 620–621; International Powerlifting Federation (IPF) 612, **613**, 614, 616; International World Games Association 612; lift-specific demands 617–620; lower back 621; mechanical work 617; macrocycle 623; microcycle 623–624; muscle mass and architecture 616; muscle temperature 615; Olympic Games 612; periodisation 623–624; physiology 614–615; programming 622–623; psychology 615–616; rules and regulations 612–613, 613; shoulder 621; spinal loading 617; squat 613–614, 617–618; sticking point 617; strength 622; tapering 623; training 624–626; training: accommodating resistance 626; training: exercise execution 626; training: partial range of motion training 626; training: specialised techniques 626; training: specificity 625; training: types 624; training: variation 625; Wilks scoring system 613, 615, 624

Pritchard, H. J. 623
puberty 8, 16, 17, 26

Qatar Handball World Championships 284, 292
quadriceps 56, 58, 235, 261, 362, 437, **564**, 579, 586, 588, 600, 601, 617; dominance 16, *18*, 236; haematoma **89**; strains **127**, 405
Quinney, H. A. 620

Raske, A. 620, 621
Ratamess, N. A. 107
Read, P. J. 18
rehydration 385
repeated sprint ability 60, 74, 75, **145**, 161, **293**, **294**, 302, 335, 339
reproduction 12
Reyes, A. 110
Rhea, M. R. 104, 117
Rhodes, J. 46
Richardson, A. B. 546
Richardson, O. 356
Robinson, S. 23
rock climbing 553–565, **556**; athletic demands 554–556; complexity **554**; energy system contribution 557, *557*; fitness testing battery **562**, 562–563; flexibility *555*, 555–556; grip strength 558–560, *559*; hypertrophy 563; injury prevalence **560**, 560–561; lower body strength 563, **563**, 564; lower limb *561*, 561–562; motion analysis 558; Olympic Games 553, 564; oxygen consumption 554, 556, **556**, 558; physiology, aerobic power and blood lactate 556–557; programming **563**, 563–564; sample conditioning programmes **564**, 564–565; sample corrective programme 564, **564**
Rodgers, M. M. 319
Roi, G. 401
Rose, J. *452*, 457, *457*, *458*
Rovere, G. D. 547
rowing 218–232; athletic demands 218–219; fitness test battery 221; heavy strength training 221–223, **222**; hypertrophy 219, **227**, 229–230, *230*; injury prevalence 219–221; monitoring 224; Olympic Games 230; power assessment **223**, 223–224; programming 224–229, **226**, **227**, *228*, *229*; training experience consideration 230; training plan for high performance rower *225*
rugby sevens 72, 73–74, 75, 76, 84–100, **85**, **87**, *88*; epidemiology 88–90, **89**, **90**; metabolic qualities/fitness **99**, 99–100; "physical assessments" vs. "fitness testing" 90–93, **91**, **92**; physical demands 84–85; programming 93–100, **96**; speed and agility 96; strength and power **97**, 97–99, **98**; tapering 100; work and rest 86–88
rugby union 72–81, 85, 88, 100, 114, 126, 127, 320; athletic demands 72–75; fitness testing 76–78, **77**; frequency 78; hypertrophy 79; injury prevalence 75–76; in season 80–81; lower body strength 76; match characteristics and physical qualities of rugby sevens players 73–74, **74**; match characteristics of 15-a-side rugby match play 72–73, **73**; off season 78–79; physical qualities on rugby match play and injury 74–75; practicality 78; pre-season 79–80; programming 78–81; reliability 78; sensitivity 78; specificity 76
Rumpf, M. C. 29, 110, 111, **112**, 121
Runciman, P. 45, 424
Rushton, A. 220
Russell, M. 402
Russell, S. D. 554, 556

Samozino, P. 475, 484
Scanlan, A. 179, 180
Schick, D. **159**
Schöffl, V. R. 560, **560**,
Schussman, L. C. **560**
SCI *see* spinal cord injury
Scott, D. J. 118
Sein, M. L. 436
Seitz, L. B. 110, 111, 120
self-myofascial release 63, **165**, 166, 397, 463, **463**, 467
sex-related differences 7, 8–9
Sheppard, J. M. 121, 266, 267
Shields, E. W. 105
Sierer, S. P. 105
Siewe, J. 620, 621
Simenz, C. J. 184, 187
Simpson, C. A. 234
Sindall, P. 45
small-sided games 30, 63, 80, 81, 179, 189, 249, **293**, **294**, 302, *304*
Snyder, A. 158
soccer 51–69; age variations 53–54; agility 59; anatomical location, nature, and severity 56; anthropometry 58; biomechanical considerations 57, 59; closed season training 66–68; conditioning 63–68, *67*, *68*; distances in speed zones **52**, *53*; endurance 60; fatigue implications 54; fitness testing 57–60; gender variations 54, **54**; injury prevalence 55–56; match demands 51–52; positional variations **52**, 52–53; power 58–59; practice structure and physical outcomes **63**; preseason training 61–63; programming 60–61; risk factors 56–57; situational and tactical factors 54–55; speed 60; standard of competition 53; strength 59, *62*; training *64*, **65**
Soriano, M. A. 117
specific preparation phase (SPP) 32, 79–80, 487, *487*, **488**, *493*, *496*, 520, 522
Spencer, S. 220; *Spinal-Exercise Prescription in Sport* 224

Index

spinal cord injury (SCI) 40–43, 46, 312, **314**, 316, **317**, 320, *323*, 324, **324–325**, 326, 327, **328**, 329, 413, 416, 418, 425, 428, 429, 431; vs NSCI athletes 319
SportAccord 612
SPP *see* specific preparation phase
sprint cycling 506–523; athletic demands 506–509; ballistic testing 515; biomechanical considerations 510; dynamic strength testing 514–515; fitness testing battery 511–512; hypertrophy 516, 518, *518*, **519**, 520, **521**; injury 509–511; isometric testing *513*, 513–514; lower body strength 514; periodisation and programming *516*, 516–523, *517*, *518*, **519**, **520**, **521**, **522**; strength testing *512*, 513–515
sprint running 473–504; acceleration *475*, *476*, **478**, 490, 492–493, *493*; athletic demands 473; case studies 497–504, *499*, *500*, 504, **504**; contact times 475–476; contraction velocity demands 479; core sprinters programme 487; deconstructing sprint 490; dribbles *495*, 496; force application via stance limb 476–477; force-velocity 483–484, *483*, 484–485, *485*; fundamental mechanics 473–504; ground reaction force vector *474*; hamstring robustness and hip extension performance 497, **497**; hip extension 481–482, *481*; horizontal impulse 474–475; hypertrophy 477, **491**, *493*, **493**, **496**, 497, **497**; injuries 479, *479*; macrocycle 487; mass dependence 477; maximum velocity 493–494, **494**, *496*, 496; max velocity hurdles 494, *495*; mechanical issues 480; mesocycle planning and phase potentiation 489; microcycle and session planning 489–490, *490*; normative data 484; Olympic Games 497; optimizes force production 477; outcomes 504; overspeed 495; pre-intervention step profile *503*; programming 486; progression of horizontal and vertical forces through acceleration *475*; resisted 491, *492*; resisted runs 495; robustness and control 497, **498**; squat jump force-velocity 483–484; stance force production 476; strength 482–483, **484**; testing 481; torque *482*; training 480, *491*; training time 487–488, **488**; un-resisted work 492–493; velocity running cycle *477*
Steele, J. R. 234, **234**,
Stewart, P. F. 59
Stodden, D. F. 107, **108**
Stricevic, M. V. **364**
Strzala, M. 546
Stulberg, S. D. 547
swimming 540–550; athletic demands 541–545; biomechanical considerations 541–544, 546; fitness testing battery 548, **549**; injury prevalence 545–547; lower body strength 546–547, 548, 549, **549**; mean time/block time **542**; Olympic Games 540, 542, 544, 546, 549, 550; physiological demands 544–545; programming 549–550, **550**; start position *541*; strength and power **543**, 547–548; upper body 546; *see also* FINA World Championships
Swinton, P. A. 619626

Taekwondo 371–383; athletic demands 374–376; anthropometry 374; competition calendar 373; competition characteristics 374; fitness testing battery 376–377, **377**; height across weight category **374**; injury prevalence 376; mobility 381; muscular endurance 380–381; Olympic Games 371, 372, **372**, *373*, 374, 375, 380, 382; oxygen consumption 375, **377**, 378; physical characteristics 372–373; physiological demands 375–376; programming 377–378; rehabilitation/prehabilitation from injuries 378; speed and agility 379; strength and power 380; training sessions 381–382, *382*; weight categories **372**; weight making strategy 374–375; World Taekwondo Federation (WTF) 371, 372, 375
Taylor, J. 188
tennis 433–447; athletic demands 434–436; biomechanical considerations 435, 436; Dubai Championship 458; fitness testing battery 440–443; functioned movement screening **440**; gender 439; injury 436–440; injury incidence 436; injury location 437; injury type and prevalence 436–437; lower extremity 437–438; oxygen consumption 435; physical competencies **442**; physical performance tests **441**; physiology and endurance 435; programming 443–447, *444*, *445*, *446*; skill level and volume of play 439; specific factors 440; speed and agility 436; strength and power 435–436; tennis functional movement screening 441, **441**, 442; trunk 438–439; WTA 433, 443; *see also* Lawn Tennis Association; PGA Tour; Titleist Performance Institute; US Open
Thibaudeau, C. 118
Thigpen, L. K. 190
Thompson, B. J. 107
Thompson, P.: *Training for the Complete Rower* 224
time-loss injuries 235, 261, 405
Titleist Performance Institute 456
Tomasini, N. T. 105
Tomlin, D. L. 361
Trackman *457*, 457–458, *458*
training impulse 158, 337
Tran, T. T. 110
Trewartha, G. **234**
triad, female athlete *11*, 11–12, *12*, 13
triathlon 526–538; athletic demands 527–529; biomechanical considerations 527; bone stress injuries 531–532; course demands 527; drafting

and aerodynamics 527–528; evidenced based practice 535–536; fitness testing 529–530; injury prevalence 531; lower limb tendinopathies 533–534; medial tibial stress syndrome 532–533; Olympic Games 526, 527; oxygen consumption 529, 530; pacing 528–529; performance testing 529; periodisation 535; physiological testing 529–530; plantar fasciitis 534; programme outline 536–537; strength and conditioning 530, 534–537, **537**; World Triathlon Corporation 526
trigger hypothesis 30
TRIMP 158, 337
trunk dominance 16, 17, *18*
Tsolakis, C. 404
Tuominen, R. **159**, 363, **364**
Turnbull, J. 585
Turner, A. 402, 404, 407
Tyler, T. 160, 255

UEAFA Champions League 53
UFC *see* Ultimate Fighting Championship
UIAA *see* Union Internationale Des Association d'Alpinisme
Ultimate Fighting Championship 334, 341
Union Internationale Des Association d'Alpinisme (UIAA) 553, 556
US Open *373*, 457

Vagenas, G. 404
Van Den Tillaar, R. 618
vertical ground reaction forces (VGRFs) 196, 234, 235, 549
VGRFs *see* vertical ground reaction forces
Vilas-Boas, J. P. 543
volleyball 259–277; athletic demands 259–260; biomechanical considerations 277; conditioning 276–277; conditioning assessment 265–266; fitness testing battery 262–266; injury prevalence 260–262; injury prevention 261–262; injury rehabilitation 262; injury risk factors 261; jump training 276; medical assessment 262; mobility 277; mobility and competence test **263**, 263–264; Olympic Games 259, **272**, 276; programming 266–276; strength and power 266–276, **267**, **268–271**, **272–275**; strength and speed-strength assessment 264, 264–265; vertical jumping assessment 265, **265**; *see also* Australian Institute of Sport Repeat Effort Test; Federation International De Volley-Ball

Wagner, L. L. 618
Waldock, R. 385
Wallace, B. J. 119
Watts, P. B. 556, **556**
weightlifting 630–652; athletic demands 637–642; bar kinematics and kinetics 637–639, *638*; biomechanical considerations 637, **639**, 642; clean phases *633–634*; fitness testing battery 644–645, **645**; height variations *640*; hypertrophy 647, **649**; International Weightlifting Federation (IWF) 630, 642; injury prevalence 642–644, **643**; jerk 641, *641*; joint kinematics and kinetics 639–644; Olympic Games 9, 642, 643, 652; periodisation **649**; physiology 641–642; programming 646–652, **646**, **647**, **648**; snatch phases *631–622*; split jerk phases 635–636; strength and power 650–652, **651**; training 646–650
Wenger, H. A. 361
Werner, 556
West, C. 41
West, D. J. 543, 547
wheelchair basketball 41, 311
wheelchair fencing 413–431, *414*, **415**; bench test card **416**; biomechanical considerations 419–421, 431; cause of injuries 421; competitions 415; conditioning 429–431, **430**; disability classification 415–418; fitness testing battery 423–424, **423**; functional test *417*; history 413; impairment specific consideration 424–425; injury prevalence 421–423, **422**; injury prevention strategies 425–428, *427*; injury profile 422–423; kinematics 419–421; lunge attack *420*; modified rowing set up *430*; muscle endurance **428**; "on guard" stance *420*; oxygen consumption 418; periodisation 431; physiological demands 418–419; programming 424–431; rules 413–415; strength and power 428, **429**; stretching exercises *426*; swords **414**; time motion characteristics 417; training guidelines 424
wheelchair innovations *39*
Wheelchair Rugby 311–329; accommodation 318; athletic demands 315–329; biomechanical considerations **316**, 316–317, **317**; British 326; cardio respiratory 327–328; chair setup 323; classification 312, **313**, *314*; culture 320; fatigue **315**; fitness testing battery **321**, 321–322; force generation and power 326; functional electrical stimulation 329; general health of athlete 320–321; gradients 327; history 311; hypertrophy **324**, 325–326, **326**, **328**; injury prevalence 319–320; metabolic conditioning **328**; movement demands and game intensity 315, **315**; Murderball 311; muscle hypertrophy 325–326, **326**; neurology 326; oxygen consumption 316; participants 312; Performance Model for linear speed and energy systems 322, *322*, *323*; player comparisons **315**; programming 324, **324–325**; pushing technique 323; resisted pushing 326–327, **328**; SCI vs NSCI athletes 319; skill acquisition 323; specific adaptations 325–327; strength and power 318, **319**; training process 328–329; upper body musculature occasioned by spinal cord injury

314; wheelchair configuration **317,** 317–318; wheelchair propulsion *327; see also* International Wheelchair and Amputee Sport Federation; International Wheelchair Rugby Federation
Wilks scoring system 613, 615, 624
Williams, R. **234**
Williams, S. 443, *444*
Winkelmann, H. P. 560, **560**
Wolf, A.: *Training for the Complete Rower* 224
Wolf, B. R. 546
Wong, P. 56
World Cup 72, 88, 233, 401, 415, **415,** 416, 417, *516,* 583, 587; Austrian 570, 574; FIS 568; French 568; Ski Federation 587
World Karate Federation 359
World Rugby 72, 88
World Series 84, **85, 87,** 88, 100
World Taekwondo Federation (WTF) 371, 372, **373,** 375
WTA 433, 443
WTF *see* World Taekwondo Federation
Wylde, M. 401

Yde, J. 56
young athletes 23–33; biomechanical considerations 25; determinants of endurance 30; determinants of movement skills 24–25; determinants of speed 28–29; determinants of strength and power 27; endurance development 30–31, **31;** growth and maturation 23–24; movement skill competency 24–27, **25,** *26;* programming for athletic development 31–33; speed development 28–29; strength and power development 27–28; systemic progression of force production *32;* trainability of endurance 30–31; trainability of movement skills 25–27; trainability of speed 29; trainability of strength and power 27–28
Youth Physical Development 141

Zampagni, M. L. 555,
Zatsiorsky, V. M. 109, 517, 624
Zetaruk, M. N. **364, 365,** 366
Zourdos, M. C. 624, 625

Printed in Great Britain
by Amazon